GREAT BRITAIN
The Lion at Home

GREAT BRITAIN
The Lion at Home

A Documentary History
of Domestic Policy
1689-1973

EDITOR
Joel H. Wiener
CITY COLLEGE OF NEW YORK

VOLUME
I

New York
CHELSEA HOUSE PUBLISHERS
in association with R. R. BOWKER COMPANY
New York and London
1974

For Paul, Deborah and Jane

PROJECT EDITOR: Jeanette Morrison
MANAGING EDITOR: Roberta Morgan
ASSISTANT EDITORS: Amy Resnick, Kathryn Hammell
EDITORIAL CONSULTANT: Leon Friedman

Published by Chelsea House Publishers in association
with R. R. Bowker Company (a Xerox Education Company)
Copyright © 1974 by Chelsea House Publishers
(A Division of Chelsea House Educational Communications, Inc.
70 West 40th Street, New York, N.Y. 10018)
All Rights Reserved
PRINTED AND BOUND IN THE UNITED STATES OF AMERICA
LIBRARY OF CONGRESS CATALOGING IN PUBLICATION DATA
Wiener, Joel H   comp.
Great Britain: the lion at home.
Includes bibliographical references.
1. Great Britain—History—18th century—Sources.
2. Great Britain—History—19th century—Sources.
3. Great Britain—History—20th century—Sources.
I. Title.   DA470.W48   942   74-7447
ISBN 0-8352-0776-5

Preface

This collection of documents is intended to illustrate the great internal themes of modern British history—constitutional, political, economic, and social—and to provide the necessary tools with which they can be studied. It makes available for the first time a great deal of the primary source material covering the crucial events in domestic British history from the constitutional aftermath of the Glorious Revolution at the end of the seventeenth century to the industrial and educational controversies of the early 1970s. It complements my previously published volumes, *Great Britain: Foreign Policy and the Span of Empire,* 4 vols. (Chelsea House/McGraw-Hill, 1972)—a documentary narrative of imperial, diplomatic, and Irish problems during the same time span. Hopefully these sets, in combination, will provide students, teachers, researchers, and general readers with the most comprehensive documentary analysis of modern British history in print.

My aim has been to encapsulate contemporary responses to a wide range of developing problems and issues. The fabric of historical movement is an intricate one and, in my judgment, its texture can be perceived fully only through a multiplicity of lenses. To this end I have followed several specific criteria in compiling and arranging the documents. There has been no "updating" of documents and contemporary calendar usage has been uniformly followed. Textual emendations have been eschewed and the documents reprinted in an unabridged format wherever possible. Although large numbers of well-known texts are included, they are supplemented by many obscure source materials which cast a considerable illumination upon events.

The documents are arranged according to chronology and subject. There are five broad chronological sections and each of these units is further divided by theme. The five sections are preceded by general introductions which are primarily interpretive although they also supply a narrative framework. The headnotes which precede individual and groups of documents are more directly aimed at providing a linked background.

The process of choosing subjects and documents was not always easy. Ireland, for example, is excluded from these volumes since it was covered fully in *Great Britain: Foreign Policy and the Span of Empire*. Every work of history is, in the final analysis, deeply personal in its origin. An "objective" documentary compilation of this nature is structurally no different; it is the result of probings as elliptical and indirect as they are measured, precise, and deliberate. I offer *The Lion at Home* in this spirit—as a consciously personal amalgam but one which, I hope, will possess considerable value for all those interested in the endlessly fascinating web of realism and myth that makes up the history of modern Britain.

My debts are considerable. I have benefited at first hand and by indirection from the knowledge of many friends and scholars. I want to express particular gratitude to two persons: Ms. Jeanette Morrison, for her intellectual rigor and editorial efficiency; and my wife, Suzanne, for her willingness to share her wise counsel with me and to partake equally in the frustrations and exhilarations of authorship.

Joel H. Wiener

London, England
January 1974

Contents

VOLUME I

Lords and Commons

Foundations of Economic Expansion

Jacobite Threat

The Church and Dissent

Social Policy and Administration

A NATION TRANSFORMED
1760-1830

First Industrial Revolution

George III and the Constitution

Beginning of the Reform Movement

Financial Policy of William Pitt

Policy of Repression

Spread of Literacy

Revival of Radicalism

Factories and Poor Relief

Administrative and Legal Reforms

Government and the Economy

Claims of Catholics and Dissenters

VICTORIAN BRITAIN AT ITS APOGEE
1830-1870

Crisis Over Parliamentary Reform

Working-Class Activism

VOLUME II

Education in a Changing Society

Poverty and the State

Central and Local Government

Mid-Victorian Political Life

Further Extension of the Franchise

Weakening of the Church of England

Treatment of Non-Anglicans

Growth of Professionalism

VOLUME III

THE DISSOLUTION OF THE VICTORIAN CONSENSUS 1870-1914

Military Reforms

Victorian Administrative State

Extension of Democracy

Victorian Liberalism and Its Critics

Impact of Religion

Legal and Property Rights

Challenge of Labor

Trade Unions and the Law

Prewar Social Reform

Conflict between Lords and Commons

THE LION IN DECLINE
1914-1973

VOLUME IV

Postwar Reforms

Politics of Democracy

World Depression

Abdication of Edward VIII

Policy of Nationalization

Creating a Welfare State

Economic Decline

Decades of Constructive Achievement

Unresolved Questions

A Century of Transition
1689-1760

A Century of Transition
1689-1760

In the eighteenth century the pace of change in English society flowed deceptively beneath the surface of events. The constitutional and political conflicts of previous decades were resolved and a range of personal rights secured. A new royal line was placed on the throne—the stolid and bumptious Hanoverians—and all attempts to unseat it were beaten back. Although the great experiment of industrialization was not yet under way, the foundations for economic expansion were laid. And in tandem with these changes, the contours of a massive world empire were shaped.

Between the accession of William and Mary (1689) and that of George III (1760), a delicate constitutional balance was struck. The Revolution settlement of 1689-1720 established the rights of the subject against royal and parliamentary interference. The Bill of Rights (1689), the Toleration Act (1689), the end of the licensing power over the press (1695), and the Trial of Treason Act (1696) guaranteed constitutional protections to the individual that are among the most important ever sanctioned by Parliament. Likewise, the settlement ensured the supremacy of Parliament over monarch and, within the legislature, of Commons over Lords. In the realms of membership and financial initiative, the Commons increasingly asserted its supremacy, as can be seen in the *Ashby* v. *White* case and in the renewal of the annual mutiny acts. William and Mary, Anne, and the Hanoverian kings who followed them to the throne were constricted within a permanent framework of law and precedent.

It must be emphasized, however, that the pace of change was uneven, a matter of nuance. Monarchical and aristocratic powers were gradually peeled away by the creation of an executive structure formed around a first, or prime, minister and a Cabinet composed of leading members of Parliament. Whigs and Tories, linked together by a corpus of heterogeneous and mostly prerevolutionary political attitudes, jostled for party advantage. The monarchy suffered a proportionate eclipse.

Some of the more significant and lasting eighteenth-century constitutional developments, such as the lapsing of the royal veto power, last used in 1707 by Queen Anne, are impossible to document. Others fall into "grey" areas; for example, the maturation of the practice of ministerial responsibility, whereby the Cabinet's relationship to Parliament rather than to the monarch became predominant. By the 1750s the politicians Robert Walpole and Henry Pelham had seemingly established important precedents in this and related constitutional matters. But contemporaries remained ignorant of these developments, and historians have stressed their tentative nature. Given such a situation, it is not surprising that George III was able to reopen many of these constitutional questions in 1760.

During the eighteenth century the keynote of constitutional change was moderation. The nation turned away from the convulsions and flashpoints of the immediate past and rested content with a policy of greater rationalization of government. By the Act of Union (1707) relations with Scotland were normalized, and financial dealings between crown and Parliament were made more efficient through the mechanism of a Civil List Act (1698).

Nevertheless, Jacobitism (i.e., the desired return of the Stuart line) remained a problem. The Act of Settlement (1701) exacerbated royalist tensions by providing for the transfer of the line of descent after Anne's death to a collateral Protestant connection. By inflicting these further indignities upon the Stuarts, it made the uprisings known as the Fifteen and the Forty Five, as well as related acts of conspiracy and rebellion, inevitable. Military force had to be used to suppress these outbreaks. Yet by the time of George III (specifically, with the defeat of Charles Stuart in 1745-46) the Jacobite threat had been substantively dealt with; it never reemerged in an overt form.

The fortunes of the Church of England in the eighteenth century were linked to these constitutional developments. Compelled to come to grips with active forms of Dissent, the Church maneuvered adroitly through the extremes of intolerance and rationality. It exuded a pragmatic tolerance. At the same time, however, it sought to dilute the liberalizing effects of the Toleration Act (1689) by resort to such extreme legislative sanctions as the Occasional Conformity measures. Methodism—the enthusiastic new form of Dissent animated by the oratorical talents of the Wesleys and John Whitefield—provided *the* new challenge to the Church of England. Because it failed to contain this growing sect within its own institutional structure, the Church suffered many setbacks in the struggle for domination of the minds of the new poor, those disgorged by industrialization and the shift of economic power to the north of England.

Although realistic guidelines for toleration were set up by 1760, the direct confrontation between Nonconformity and Anglicanism was not resolved for another century. Not surprisingly, rationalist religious thought flourished within the framework of Anglicanism, while outside its purview Nonconformity made similar adjustments, as with the growing influence of Unitarianism. Parsons continued to exercise virtually undiminished social power in their localities and to prop up the most traditional forms of the system. But relationships of authority and subordination—under assault since the preceding century—could not be wholly repaired. Catholics remained largely outside the pale. Denied the fruits of constitutional monarchy, they continued to be objects of discrimination, penally and socially, and occasionally were victims of outright violence. Nevertheless, they were increasingly recognized as a permanent fixture, a minority which could no longer be facilely equated with lack of patriotism and allegiance to foreign enemies.

The period between 1689 and 1760 was decisive in the economic history of Britain. Although the pace of economic change did not speed up appreciably until the late eighteenth century, the crucial underpinnings that gave stability to the whole system were laid during these years. Finances were set on a durable base by such measures as the formation of the Bank of England in 1694 and the later establishment of a sinking fund. Even the South Sea crisis of 1720-21, which unleashed speculative and inflationary forces, did not distort the pace of advance since the incident educated public opinion on financial matters and led to the passage of several Bubble Acts. Moreover, the South Sea Bubble incident, by tarnishing the reputations of his colleagues, ensured that Robert Walpole as first minister would work to sustain Britain's credit and international standing. Since her later economic transformation was tied to her diplomacy, the relative success of British foreign policy during this period guaranteed fruitful trading patterns and expanding markets and productivity.

One seemingly important restraining influence on Britain's economy during this period was mercantilism. Mercantilist policies, aiming at a measure of autarchic self-sufficiency, were encouraged between 1689 and 1760. In theory at least, colonial ties were strengthened and protectionism reenforced. Nevertheless, some movement toward free trade—essential to the unhindered flow of capital resources upon which future expansion hinged—can be discerned in the government's continuing and deliberate failure to enforce the navigation acts and in Walpole's abortive efforts to rationalize the excise structure. His excise proposals of 1733 were a proffered sop to the ruling classes, their immediate objective being the relief of burdens on landed property, but this in itself was a recognition of the nation's changed economic fabric. Commercial activity on an imposing scale was now an established social fact.

Virtually all of the elements of economic change included in the concept of industrial revolution appeared in rudimentary forms between 1689 and 1760. The Royal Society of Arts, the Lunar Society of Birmingham, and similar associations gave a considerable fillip to the development and popularization of science and mechanics. Agrarian improvements were stimulated by the pioneering propaganda efforts of Jethro Tull and others, by technical innovations in the use of fertilizers and crop rotation, and by land enclosure, a process which started on a small scale in the sixteenth century and accelerated during this period owing to the shift from sheep raising to arable farming. Even the textile and silk industries, which remained wedded to the domestic form of production, showed signs of change. Economic relationships became more impersonal, and a new obsession with size—in apprenticeship and works patterns and in the scale of productivity—signalled things to come.

Notwithstanding these dynamic elements in the economic sphere, this was a placid society that had not undergone significant external change for hundreds of years. Insofar as the texture of everyday life is concerned, these were quiet decades in a century of stability. For the most part, social patterns did not exhibit great alterations. This remained a world founded upon commitments to a common culture and to a common past, and time-honored pecking orders still held sway. Aristocracy, landed gentry, and Churchmen dominated the sources of power, framed social policy, and made administrative decisions.

The ever-widening gap between economic and political power within a social structure that encouraged the accumulation of personal commercial wealth but failed to distribute commensurate political rewards eventually produced major social readjustments; these, however, were a century away. The poor, who faced the prospect of uncertain relief at the end of lives abbreviated unnecessarily by deprivation, indulged in food riots and other forms of antisocial behavior. Yet these were traditional expressions of discontent, and before 1760 they could still be contained by a society in which, for most people, the human universe was still bounded by the parish.

The historian, with hindsight, can see that Britain in 1760 was a nation ready to unleash her energies on the stage of world history. Having resolved long-standing constitutional conflicts, she began to respond to the first stirrings of incalculable economic growth. For all the portents of the future, however, she was as yet a country more recognizable for what she had been than for what she was to become.

REVOLUTION SETTLEMENT

Bill of Rights, 1689

1 W. & M., c. 2   *Statutes at Large*, IX, 67-73.

This statute reaffirmed the illegality of many Stuart acts and defined the rights and liberties of the subject.

Whereas the lords spiritual and temporal, and commons, assembled at Westminster, lawfully, fully, and freely representing all the estates of the people of this realm, did upon the thirteenth day of February, in the year of our Lord one thousand six hundred eighty eight, present unto their Majesties, then called and known by the names and stile of William and Mary, prince and princess of Orange, being present in their proper persons, a certain declaration in writing, made by the said lords and commons, in the words following; viz.

Whereas the late King James the Second, by the assistance of divers evil counsellors, judges, and ministers employed by him, did endeavour to subvert and extirpate the protestant religion, and the laws and liberties of this kingdom.

1. By assuming and exercising a power of dispensing with and suspending of laws, and the execution of laws, without consent of parliament.
2. By committing and prosecuting divers worthy prelates, for humbly petitioning to be excused from concurring to the said assumed power.
3. By issuing and causing to be executed a commission under the great seal for erecting a court called, The court of commissioners for ecclesiastical causes.
4. By levying money for and to the use of the crown, by pretence of prerogative, for other time, and in other manner, than the same was granted by parliament.
5. By raising and keeping a standing army within this kingdom in time of peace, without consent of parliament, and quartering soldiers contrary to law.
6. By causing several good subjects, being protestants, to be disarmed, at the same time when papists were both armed and employed, contrary to law.
7. By violating the freedom of election of members to serve in parliament.
8. By prosecutions in the court of King's bench, for matters and causes cognizable only in parliament; and by divers other arbitrary and illegal courses.

9. And whereas of late years, partial, corrupt, and unqualified persons have been returned and served on juries in trials, and particularly divers jurors in trials for high treason, which were not freeholders.
10. And excessive bail hath been required of persons committed in criminal cases, to elude the benefit of the laws made for the liberty of the subjects.
11. And excessive fines have been imposed; and illegal and cruel punishments inflicted.
12. And several grants and promises made of fines and forfeitures, before any conviction or judgment against the persons, upon whom the same were to be levied.

All which are utterly and directly contrary to the known laws and statutes, and freedom of this realm.

And whereas the said late King James the Second having abdicated the government, and the throne being thereby vacant, his highness the prince of Orange (whom it hath pleased Almighty God to make the glorious instrument of delivering this kingdom from popery and arbitrary power) did (by the advice of the lords spiritual and temporal, and divers principal persons of the commons) cause letters to be written to the lords spiritual and temporal, being protestants; and other letters to the several counties, cities, universities, boroughs, and cinque-ports, for the choosing of such persons to represent them, as were of right to be sent to parliament, to meet and sit at Westminster upon the two and twentieth day of January, in this year one thousand six hundred eighty and eight, in order to such an establishment, as that their religion, laws, and liberties might not again be in danger of being subverted: upon which letters, elections have been accordingly made,

And thereupon the said lords spiritual and temporal, and commons, pursuant to their respective letters and elections, being now assembled in a full and free representative of this nation, taking into their most serious consideration the best means for attaining the ends aforesaid; do in the first place (as their ancestors in like case have usually done) for the vindicating and asserting their ancient rights and liberties, declare;

1. That the pretended power of suspending of laws, or the execution of laws, by regal authority, without consent of parliament, is illegal.
2. That the pretended power of dispensing with laws, or the execution of laws, by regal authority, as it hath been assumed and exercised of late, is illegal.
3. That the commission for erecting the late court of commissioners for ecclesiastical causes, and all other commissions and courts of like nature are illegal and pernicious.
4. That levying money for or to the use of the crown, by pretence of prerogative, without grant of parliament, for longer time, or in other manner than the same is or shall be granted, is illegal.
5. That it is the right of the subjects to petition the King, and all committments and prosecutions for such petitioning are illegal.
6. That the raising or keeping a standing army within the kingdom in time of peace, unless it be with consent of parliament, is against law.

7. That the subjects which are protestants, may have arms for their defence suitable to their conditions, and as allowed by law.
8. That election of members of parliament ought to be free.
9. That the freedom of speech, and debates or proceedings in parliament, ought not to be impeached or questioned in any court or place out of parliament.
10. That excessive bail ought not to be required, nor excessive fines imposed; nor cruel and unusual punishments inflicted.
11. That jurors ought to be duly impanelled and returned, and jurors which pass upon men in trials for high treason ought to be freeholders.
12. That all grants and promises of fines and forfeitures of particular persons before conviction, are illegal and void.
13. And that for redress of all grievances, and for the amending, strengthening, and preserving of the laws, parliaments ought to be held frequently.

And they do claim, demand, and insist upon all and singular the premisses, as their undoubted rights and liberties; and that no declarations, judgments, doings or proceedings, to the prejudice of the people in any of the said premisses, ought in any wise to be drawn hereafter into consequence or example.

To which demand of their rights they are particularly encouraged by the declaration of his highness the prince of Orange, as being the only means for obtaining a full redress and remedy therein.

Having therefore an entire confidence, That his said highness the prince of Orange will perfect the deliverance so far advanced by him, and will still preserve them from the violation of their rights, which they have here asserted, and from all other attempts upon their religion, rights, and liberties.

II. The said lords spiritual and temporal, and commons, assembled at Westminster, do resolve, That William and Mary prince and princess of Orange be, and be declared, King and Queen of England, France and Ireland, and the dominions thereunto belonging, to hold the crown and royal dignity of the said kingdoms and dominions to them the said prince and princess during their lives, and the life of the survivor of them; and that the sole and full exercise of the regal power be only in, and executed by the said prince of Orange, in the names of the said prince and princess, during their joint lives; and after their deceases, the said crown and royal dignity of the said kingdoms and dominions to be to the heirs of the body of the said princess; and for default of such issue to the princess Anne of Denmark, and the heirs of her body; and for default of such issue to the heirs of the body of the said prince of Orange. And the lords spiritual and temporal, and commons, do pray the said prince and princess to accept the same accordingly.

III. And that the oaths hereafter mentioned be taken by all persons of whom the oaths of allegiance and supremacy might be required by law, instead of them; and that the said oaths of allegiance and supremacy be abrogated.

I A. B. do sincerely promise and swear, That I will be faithful, and bear true allegiance, to their Majesties King William and Queen Mary: So help me God.

I A. B. do swear, That I do from my heart abhor, detest, and abjure as impious and heretical, that damnable doctrine and position, That princes excommunicated or deprived by the pope, or any authority of the see of Rome, may be deposed or murdered by their subjects, or any other whatsoever. And I do declare, That no foreign prince, person, prelate, state, or potentate hath, or ought to have any jurisdiction, power, superiority, pre-eminence, or authority ecclesiastical or spiritual, within this realm: So help me God.

IV. Upon which their said Majesties did accept the crown and royal dignity of the kingdoms of England, France, and Ireland, and the dominions thereunto belonging, according to the resolution and desire of the said lords and commons contained in the said declaration.

V. And thereupon their Majesties were pleased, That the said lords spiritual and temporal, and commons, being the two houses of parliament, should continue to sit, and with their Majesties royal concurrence make effectual provision for the settlement of the religion, laws and liberties of this kingdom, so that the same for the future might not be in danger again of being subverted; to which the said lords spiritual and temporal, and commons, did agree and proceed to act accordingly.

VI. Now in pursuance of the premisses, the said lords spiritual and temporal, and commons, in parliament assembled, for the ratifying, confirming and establishing the said declaration, and the articles, clauses, matters, and things therein contained, by the force of a law made in due form by authority of parliament, do pray that it may be declared and enacted, That all and singular the rights and liberties asserted and claimed in the said declaration, are the true, ancient, and indubitable rights and liberties of the people of this kingdom, and so shall be esteemed, allowed, adjudged, deemed, and taken to be, and that all and every the particulars aforesaid shall be firmly and strictly holden and observed, as they are expressed in the said declaration; and all officers and ministers whatsoever shall serve their Majesties and their successors according to the same in all times to come.

VII. And the said lords spiritual and temporal, and commons, seriously considering how it hath pleased Almighty God, in his marvellous providence, and merciful goodness to this nation, to provide and preserve their said Majesties royal persons most happily to reign over us upon the throne of their ancestors, for which they render unto him from the bottom of their hearts their humblest thanks and praises, do truly, firmly, assuredly, and in the sincerity of their hearts think, and do hereby recognize, acknowledge and declare, That King James the Second having abdicated the government, and their Majesties having accepted the crown and royal dignity as aforesaid, their said Majesties did become, were, are, and of right ought to be, by the laws of this realm, our sovereign liege lord and lady, King and Queen of England, France, and Ireland, and the dominions thereunto belonging, in and to whose princely persons the royal state, crown, and dignity of the said realms, with all honours, stiles, titles, regalities, prerogatives, powers, jurisdictions and authorities to the same belonging and appertaining, are most fully, rightfully, and intirely invested and incorporated, united and annexed.

VIII. And for preventing all questions and divisions in this realm, by reason of any pretended titles to the crown, and for preserving a certainty in the succession thereof, in and upon which the unity, peace, tranquillity, and safety of this nation doth, under God, wholly consist and depend, The said lords spiritual and temporal, and commons, do beseech their Majesties that it may be enacted, established and declared, That the crown and regal government of the said kingdoms and dominions, with all and singular the premisses thereunto belonging and appertaining, shall be and continue to their said Majesties, and the survivor of them, during their lives, and the life of the survivor of them: And that the intire, perfect, and full exercise of the regal power and government be only in, and executed by his Majesty, in the names of both their Majesties during their joint lives; and after their deceases the said crown and premisses shall be and remain to the heirs of the body of her Majesty; and for default of such issue, to her royal highness the princess Anne of Denmark, and the heirs of her body; and for default of such issue, to the heirs of the body of his said Majesty; And thereunto the said lords spiritual and temporal, and commons, do, in the name of all the people aforesaid, most humbly and faithfully submit themselves, their heirs and posterities for ever; and do faithfully promise, That they will stand to, maintain, and defend their said Majesties, and also the limitation and succession of the crown herein specified and contained, to the utmost of their powers, with their lives and estates, against all persons whatsoever, that shall attempt any thing to the contrary.

IX. And whereas it hath been found by experience, that it is inconsistent with the safety and welfare of this protestant kingdom, to be governed by a popish prince, or by any King or Queen marrying a papist; the said lords spiritual and temporal, and commons, do further pray that it may be enacted, That all and every person and persons that is, are or shall be reconciled to, or shall hold communion with, the see or church of Rome, or shall profess the popish religion, or shall marry a papist, shall be excluded, and be for ever incapable to inherit, possess, or enjoy the crown and government of this realm, and Ireland, and the dominions thereunto belonging, or any part of the same, or to have, use, or exercise any regal power, authority, or jurisdiction within the same; and in all and every such case or cases the people of these realms shall be, and are hereby absolved of their allegiance; and the said crown and government shall from time to time descend to, and be enjoyed by such person or persons, being protestants, as should have inherited and enjoyed the same, in case the said person or persons so reconciled, holding communion, or professing, or marrying as aforesaid, were naturally dead.

X. And that every King and Queen of this realm, who at any time hereafter shall come to and succeed in the imperial crown of this kingdom, shall on the first day of the meeting of the first parliament, next after his or her coming to the crown, sitting in his or her throne in the house of peers, in the presence of the lords and commons therein assembled, or at his or her coronation, before such person or persons who shall administer the coronation oath to him or her, at the time of his or her taking the said oath (which shall first happen) make, subscribe, and audibly repeat the declaration mentioned in the statute made in the thirtieth year of the reign of King Charles the Second, intituled, *An act for the more effectual preserving the*

King's person and government, by disabling papists from sitting in either house of parliament. But if it shall happen, that such King or Queen, upon his or her succession to the crown of this realm, shall be under the age of twelve years, then every such King or Queen shall make, subscribe, and audibly repeat the said declaration at his or her coronation, or the first day of the meeting of the first parliament as aforesaid, which shall first happen after such King or Queen shall have attained the said age of twelve years.

XI. All which their Majesties are contented and pleased shall be declared, enacted, and established by authority of this present parliament, and shall stand, remain, and be the law of this realm for ever; and the same are by their said Majesties, by and with the advice and consent of the lords spiritual and temporal, and commons, in parliament assembled, and by the authority of the same, declared, enacted, and established accordingly.

XII. And be it further declared and enacted by the authority aforesaid, That from and after this present session of parliament, no dispensation by *non obstante* of or to any statute, or any part thereof, shall be allowed, but that the same shall be held void and of no effect, except a dispensation be allowed of in such statute, and except in such cases as shall be specially provided for by one or more bill or bills to be passed during this present session of parliament.

XIII. Provided that no charter, or grant, or pardon, granted before the three and twentieth day of October, in the year of our Lord one thousand six hundred eighty nine shall be any ways impeached or invalidated by this act, but that the same shall be and remain of the same force and effect in law, and no other than as if this act had never been made.

Mutiny Act, 1689

1 W. & M., c. 5   *Statutes of the Realm,* VI, 55-56.

This act provided for the de facto legalization of a standing army. The need to renew it annually ensured the summoning of Parliament into session at least once per year.

Whereas the raising or keeping a Standing Army within this Kingdome in time of Peace unlesse it be with Consent of Parlyament is against Law And whereas it is judged necessary by Their Majestyes and this present Parliament That dureing this time of Danger severall of the Forces which are now on foote should be continued and others raised for the Safety of the Kingdome for the Common Defence of the Protestant Religion and for the reduceing of Ireland

And whereas noe Man may be forejudged of Life or Limbe or subjected to any kinde of punishment by Martiall Law or in any other manner than by the Judgement of his Peeres and according to the knowne and Established Laws of this Realme Yet neverthelesse it being requisite for retaineing such Forces as are or shall be raised dureing this Exigence of Affaires in their Duty an exact Discipline be observed And that Soldiers who shall Mutiny or stirr up Sedition or shall desert Their Majestyes Service be brought to a more Exemplary and speedy Punishment then the usuall Forms of Law will allow

Be it therefore Enacted by the King and Queenes most Excellent Majestyes by and with the Advice and Consent of the Lords Spirituall and Temporall and Commons in this present Parlyament Assembled and by Authorities of the same That from and after the Twelfth day of Aprill in the Yeare of our Lord One thousand six hundred eighty nine every Person being in Their Majestyes Service in the Army and being Mustered and in Pay as an Officer or Soldier who shall at any time before the Tenth Day of November in the Yeare of our Lord One thousand six hundred eighty nine Excite Cause or Joyne in any Mutiny or Sedition in the Army or shall desert Their Majestyes Service in the Army shall suffer Death or such other Punishment as by a Court-Martiall shall be Inflicted

And it is hereby further Enacted and Declared That Their Majestyes or the Generall of Their Army for the time being may by vertue of this Act have full Power and Authority to grant Commissions to any Lieftenants Generall or other Officers not under the Degree of Collonells from time to time to Call and Assemble Court Martialls for Punishing such Offences as aforesaid

And it is hereby further Enacted and Declared That noe Court Martiall which shall have power to inflict any punishment by vertue of this Act for the Offences aforesaid shall consist of fewer than thirteene whereof none to be under the degree of Captaines.

Provided alwayes That noe Field Officer be Tryed by other then Field Officers And that such Court Martiall shall have Power and Authoritie to administer an Oath to any Witnesse in order to the Examination or Tryall of the Offences aforesaid

Provided alwayes that nothing in this Act contained shall extend or be construed to Exempt any Officer or Soldier whatsoever from the Ordinary Processe of Law

Provided alwayes That this Act or any thing therein contained shall not extend or be any wayes construed to extend to or concerne any the Militia Forces of this Kingdome

Provided alsoe that this Act shall continue and be in Force until the said Tenth day of November in the said Yeare of our Lord One thousand six hundred eighty nine and noe longer

Provided alwayes and bee it enacted That in all Tryalls of Offenders by Courts Martiall to be held by vertue of this Act where the Offence may be punished by death every Officer present at such Tryall before any Proceeding be had thereupon shall take an Oath upon the Evangelists before the Court (and the Judge Advocate or his Deputy shall and are hereby respectively Authorized to Administer the same) in these words That is to say

You shall well and truely Try and Determine according to your Evidence the Matter now before you betweene Our Soveraigne Lord and

Lady the King and Queens Majestyes and the Prisoner to be Tryed. Soe helpe you God.

And noe Sentence of Death shall be given against any Offender in such Case by any Court Martiall unlesse nine of Thirteene Officers present shall concurr therein And if there be a greater number of Officers present then the Judgement shall passe by the concurrence of the greater part of them soe Sworne and not otherwise and noe Proceedings Tryall or Sentence of Death shall be had or given against any Offender but betweene the houres of Eight in the Morning and One in the Afternoone.

Act establishing the Coronation Oath, 1689

1 W. & M., c. 6   *Statutes at Large*, IX, 3-5.

The wording of the Coronation Oath reaffirmed the supremacy of law as established in the Revolution settlement.

Whereas by the law and ancient usage of this realm, the Kings and Queens thereof have taken a solemn oath upon the evangelists at their respective coronations, to maintain the statutes, laws, and customs of the said realm, and all the people and inhabitants thereof, in their spiritual and civil rights and properties: but forasmuch as the oath itself on such occasion administred, hath heretofore been framed in doubtful words and expressions, with relation to ancient laws and constitutions at this time unknown: to the end therefore that one uniform oath may be in all times to come taken by the Kings and Queens of this realm, and to them respectively administred at the times of their and every of their coronation: may it please your Majesties that it may be enacted:

II.   And be it enacted by the King's and Queen's most excellent majesties, by and with the advice and consent of the lords spiritual and temporal, and the commons, in this present parliament assembled, and by the authority of the same, That the oath herein mentioned, and hereafter expressed, shall and may be administred to their most excellent majesties King William and Queen Mary (whom God long preserve) at the time of their coronation, in the presence of all persons that shall be then and there present at the solemnizing thereof, by the archbishop of Canterbury, or the archbishop of York, or either of them, or any other bishop of this realm, whom the King's majesty shall thereunto appoint, and who shall be hereby thereunto respectively authorized; which oath followeth, and shall be administred in this manner; that is to say,

III.   The archbishop or bishop shall say, *Will you solemnly promise and swear to govern the people of this kingdom of* England, *and the dominions thereto belonging, according to the statutes in parliament agreed on, and the laws and customs of the same?*

The King and Queen shall say, *I solemnly promise so to do.*

Archbishop or bishop. *Will you to your power cause law and justice in mercy to be executed in all your judgements?*

King and Queen. *I will.*

Archbishop or bishop. *Will you to the utmost of your power maintain the laws of God, the true profession of the gospel and the protestant reformed religion established by law? and will you preserve unto the bishops and clergy of this realm, and to the churches committed to their charge, all such rights and privileges as by law do or shall appertain unto them, or any of them?*

King and Queen. *All this I promise to do.*

After this, the King and Queen laying his and her hand upon the holy gospels, shall say,

King and Queen. *The things which I have here before promised, I will perform and keep: So help me God.*

Then the King and Queen shall kiss the book.

IV. And be it further enacted, That the said oath shall be in like manner administred to every King or Queen, who shall succeed to the imperial crown of this realm, at their respective coronations, by one of the archbishops or bishops of this realm of England, for the time being, to be thereunto appointed by such King or Queen respectively, and in the presence of all persons that shall be attending, assisting, or otherwise present at such their respective coronations; any law, statute, or usage to the contrary notwithstanding.

Toleration Act, 1689

1 W. & M., c. 18   *Statutes at Large,* IX, 19-25.

This landmark act established a significant measure of toleration for Protestant Nonconformists by exempting them from the provisions of several penal statutes.

Forasmuch as some ease to scrupulous consciences in the exercise of religion may be an effectual means to unite their Majesties protestant subjects in interest and affection:

II. Be it enacted by the King's and Queen's most excellent majesties, by and with the advice and consent of the lords spiritual and temporal, and the commons, in this present parliament assembled and by the authority of the same, That neither the statute made in the three and twentieth year of the reign of the late Queen Elizabeth, intituled, *An act to retain the Queen's majesty's subjects in their due obedience;* nor the statute made in the twenty ninth year of the said Queen, intituled, *An act for the more speedy and due execution of certain branches of the statute made in the three and twentieth year of the Queen's majesty's reign, viz.* the aforesaid act; nor that branch or clause of a statute made in the first year of the reign of the said Queen, intituled, *An act for the uniformity of common prayer and service in the church, and administration of the sacraments;* whereby all persons, having no lawful or reasonable excuse to be absent, are required to resort to their parish church or chapel, or some usual place where the common prayer shall be used, upon pain of punishment by the censures of the church, and also upon pain that every person so offending shall forfeit for every such offence twelve pence; nor the statute made in the third year of the reign of the late King James the First, intituled, *An act for the better discovering and repressing popish recusants;* nor that other statute made in the same year, intituled, *An act to prevent and avoid dangers which may grow by popish recusants;* nor any other law or statute of this realm made against papists or popish recusants, except the statute made in the five and twentieth year of King Charles the Second, intituled, *An act for preventing dangers which may happen from popish recusants;* and except also the statute made in the thirtieth year of the said King Charles the Second, intituled, *An act for the more effectual preserving the King's person and government, by disabling papists from sitting in either house of parliament*; shall be construed to extend to any person or persons dissenting from the church of England, that shall take the oaths mentioned in a statute made this present parliament, intituled, *An act for removing and preventing all questions and disputes concerning the assembling and sitting of this present parliament;* and shall make and subscribe the declaration mentioned in a statute made in the thirtieth year of the reign of King Charles the Second, intituled, *An act to prevent papists from sitting in either house of parliament;* which oaths and declaration the justices of peace at the general sessions of the peace, to be held for the county or place where such person shall live, are hereby required to tender and administer to such persons as shall offer themselves to take, make, and subscribe the same, and thereof to keep a register: and likewise none of the persons aforesaid shall give or pay, as any fee or reward, to any officer or officers belonging to the court aforesaid, above the sum of six pence, nor that more than once, for his or their entry of his taking the said oaths, and making and subscribing the said declaration; nor above the further sum of six pence for any certificate of the same, to be made out and signed by the officer or officers of the said court.

III. And be it further enacted be the authority aforesaid, That all and every person and persons, already convicted or prosecuted in order to conviction of recusancy, by indictment, information, action of debt, or otherwise, grounded upon the aforesaid statutes, or any of them, that shall take the said oaths mentioned in the said statute made this present parliament, and make and subscribe the declaration aforesaid, in the court of exchequer, or assizes, or general or quarter sessions to be held for the country where such person lives, and to be thence respectively certified into the exchequer, shall be thenceforth exempted and discharged from all the penalities, seizures, forfeitures, judgments, and executions, incurred by force of any of the aforesaid statutes, without any composition, fee, or further charge whatsoever.

IV. And be it further enacted by the authority aforesaid, That all and every person and persons that shall, as aforesaid, take the said oaths, and made and subscribe the declaration aforesaid, shall not be liable to any pains, penalties, or forfeitures, mentioned in an act made in the five and thirtieth year of the reign of the late Queen Elizabeth, intituled, *An act to retain the Queen's majesty's subjects in their due obedience;* nor in an act made in the two and twentieth year of the reign of the late King Charles the Second, intituled, *An act to prevent and suppress seditious conventicles;* nor shall any of the said persons be prosecuted in any ecclesiastical court, for or by reason of their non-conforming to the church of England.

V. Provided always, and be it enacted by the authority aforesaid, That if any assembly of persons dissenting from the church of England shall be had in any place for religious worship with the doors locked, barred, or bolted, during any time of such meeting together, all and every person or persons, that shall come to and be at such meeting, shall not receive any benefit from this law, but be liable to all the pains and penalties of all the aforesaid laws recited in this act, for such their meeting, notwithstanding his taking the oaths and his making and subscribing the declaration aforesaid.

VI. Provided always, That nothing herein contained shall be construed to exempt any of the persons aforesaid from paying of tythes or other parochial duties, or any other duties to the church or minister, nor from any prosecution in any ecclesiastical court or elsewhere, for the same.

VII. And be it further enacted by the authority aforesaid, That if any person dissenting from the church of England, as aforesaid, shall hereafter be chosen or otherwise appointed to bear the office of high-constable, or petit-constable, church-warden or overseer of the poor, or any other parochial or ward office, and such person shall scruple to take upon him any of the said offices in regard of the oaths, or any other matter or thing required by the law to be taken or done in respect of such office, every such person shall and may execute such office or employment by a sufficient deputy, by him to be provided, that shall comply with the laws on this behalf. Provided always, the said deputy be allowed and approved by such person or persons, in such manner as such officer or officers respectively should by law have been allowed and approved.

VIII. And be it further enacted by the authority aforesaid, That no person dissenting from the church of England in holy orders, or pretended holy orders, or pretending to holy orders, nor any preacher or teacher of any congregation of dissenting protestants, that shall make and subscribe the declaration aforesaid, and take the said oaths at the general or quarter sessions of the peace to be held for the county, town, parts, or division where such person lives, which court is hereby impowered to administer the same, and shall also declare his approbation of and subscribe the articles of religion mentioned in the statute made in the thirteenth year of the reign of the late Queen Elizabeth, except the thirty-fourth, thirty-fifth, and thirty-sixth, and these words of the twentieth article, viz. [the church hath power to decree rites or ceremonies, and authority in controversies of faith, and yet] shall be liable to any of the pains or penalties mentioned in an act made in the seventeenth year of the reign of King Charles the Second, intituled, *An act for restraining nonconformists from inhabiting in corporations;* nor the penalties mentioned in the aforesaid act made in the two and twentieth year of his said late Majesty's reign, for or by reason of such persons preaching at any meeting for the exercise of religion;

nor to the penalty of one hundred pounds mentioned in an act made in the thirteenth and fourteenth of King Charles the Second, intituled, *An act for the uniformity of publick prayers, and administration of sacraments, and other rites and ceremonies: and for establishing the form of making, ordaining, and consecrating of bishops, priests, and deacons in the church of England,* for officiating in any congregation for the exercise of religion permitted and allowed by this act.

IX. Provided always, That the making and subscribing the said declaration, and the taking the said oaths, and making the declaration of approbation and subscription to the said articles, in manner as aforesaid, by every respective person or persons herein before-mentioned, at such general or quarter sessions of the peace as aforesaid, shall be then and there entred of record in the said court, for which six-pence shall be paid to the clerk of the peace, and no more: provided that such person shall not at any time preach in any place, but with the doors not locked, barred, or bolted, as aforesaid.

X. And whereas some dissenting protestants scruple the baptizing of infants; be it enacted by the authority aforesaid, That every person in pretended holy orders, or pretending to holy orders, or preacher, or teacher, that shall subscribe the aforesaid articles of religion, except before excepted, and also except part of the seven and twentieth article touching infant baptism, and shall take the said oaths, and make and subscribe the declaration aforesaid, in manner aforesaid, every such person shall enjoy all the privileges, benefits, and advantages, which any other dissenting minister, as aforesaid, might have or enjoy by virtue of this act.

XI. And be it further enacted by the authority aforesaid, That every teacher or preacher in holy orders, or pretended holy orders, that is a minister, preacher, or teacher of a congregation, that shall take the oaths herein required, and make and subscribe the declaration aforesaid, and also subscribe such of the aforesaid articles of the church of England, as are required by this act in manner aforesaid, shall be thenceforth exempted from serving upon any jury, or from being chosen or appointed to bear the office of churchwarden, overseer of the poor, or any other parochial or ward office or other office in any hundred of any shire, city, town, parish, division, or wapentake.

XII. And be it further enacted by the authority aforesaid, That every justice of the peace may at any time hereafter require any person, that goes to any meeting for exercise of religion, to make and subscribe the declaration aforesaid, and also to take the said oaths or declaration of fidelity herein after mentioned, in case such person scruples the taking of an oath, and upon refusal thereof, such justice of the peace is hereby required to commit such person to prison without bail or mainprize, and to certify the name of such person to the next general or quarter-sessions of the peace to be held for that county, city, town, part or division, where such person then resides; and if such person so committed shall upon a second tender at the general or quarter-sessions refuse to make and subscribe the declaration aforesaid, such person refusing shall be then and there recorded, and he shall be taken thenceforth to all intents and purposes for a popish recusant convict, and suffer accordingly, and incur all the penalties and forfeitures of all the aforesaid laws.

XIII. And whereas there are certain other persons, dissenters from the church of England, who scruple the taking of any oath; be it enacted by the authority aforesaid, That every such person shall make and subscribe the aforesaid declaration, and also this declaration of fidelity following, viz.

I A. B. do sincerely promise and solemnly declare before God and the world, that I will be true and faithful to King William and Queen Mary; and I do solemnly profess and declare, that I do from my heart abhor, detest, and renounce, as impious and heretical, that damnable doctrine and position, That princes excommunicated or deprived by the pope, or any authority of the see of Rome, may be deposed or murthered by their subjects, or any other whatsoever. And I do declare, that no foreign prince, person, prelate, state, or potentate, hath or ought to have, any power, jurisdiction, superiority, pre-eminence, or authority ecclesiastical or spiritual within this realm.

And shall subscribe a profession of their christian belief in these words:

I A. B. profess faith in God the father, and in Jesus Christ his eternal son, the true God, and in the holy spirit, one God blessed for evermore, and do acknowledge the holy scriptures of the Old and New Testament to be given by divine inspiration.

Which declarations and subscription shall be made and entred of record at the general quarter-sessions of the peace for the county, city, or place where every such person shall then reside. And every such person that shall make and subscribe the two declarations and profession aforesaid, being thereunto required, shall be exempted from all the pains and penalties of all and every the aforementioned statutes made against popish recusants, or protestant nonconformists, and also from the penalties of an act made in the fifth year of the reign of the late Queen Elizabeth, intituled, *An act for the assurance of the Queen's royal power over all estates and subjects within her dominions,* for or by reason of such persons not taking or refusing to take the oath mentioned in the said act; and also from the penalties of an act made in the thirteenth and fourteenth years of the reign of King Charles the Second, intituled, *An act for preventing mischiefs that may arise by certain persons called Quakers, refusing to take lawful oaths;* and enjoy all other the benefits, privileges, and advantages under the like limitations, provisoes, and conditions, which any other dissenters shall or ought to enjoy by virtue of this act.

XIV. Provided always, and be it enacted by the authority aforesaid, That in case any person shall refuse to take the said oaths, when tendred to them, which every justice of the peace is hereby impowered to do, such person shall not be admitted to make and subscribe the two declarations aforesaid, though required thereunto either before any justice of the peace, or at the general or quarter-sessions, before or after any conviction of popish recusancy, as aforesaid, unless such person can, within thirty one days after such tender of the declarations to him, produce two sufficient protestant witnesses, to testify upon oath, that they believe him to be a protestant dissenter, or a certificate under the hands of four protestants, who are conformable to the church of England, or have taken the oaths and subscribed the declaration above mentioned, and shall also produce a certificate under the hands and seals of six or more sufficient men of the congregation to which he belongs, owning him for one of them.

XV. Provided also, and be it enacted by the authority aforesaid, That until such certificate, under the hands of six of his congregation, as aforesaid, be produced, and two protestant witnesses come to attest his being a protestant dissenter, or a certificate under the hands of four protestants, as aforesaid, be produced, the justice of the peace shall and hereby is required to take a recognizance with two sureties in the penal sum of fifty pounds, to be levied of his goods and chattels, lands, and tenements, to the use of the King's and Queen's majesties, their heirs and successors, for his producing the same; and if he cannot give such security, to commit him to prison, there to remain until he has produced such certificates, or two witnesses, as aforesaid.

XVI. Provided always, and it is the true intent and meaning of this act, That all the laws made and provided for the frequenting of divine service on the Lord's day commonly called Sunday, shall be still in force, and executed against all persons that offend against the said laws, except such persons come to some congregation or assembly of religious worship, allowed or permitted by this act.

XVII. Provided always, and be it further enacted by the authority aforesaid, That neither this act, nor any clause, article, or thing herein contained, shall extend or be construed to extend to give any ease, benefit or advantage to any papist or popish recusant whatsoever, or any person that shall deny in his preaching or writing the doctrine of the blessed Trinity, as it is declared in the aforesaid articles of religion.

XVIII. Provided always, and be it enacted by the authority aforesaid, That if any person or persons, at any time or times after the tenth day of June, do and shall willingly and of purpose, maliciously or contemptuously come into any cathedral or parish church, chapel, or other congregation permitted by this act, and disquiet or disturb the same, or misuse any preacher or teacher, such person or persons, upon proof thereof before any justice of peace, by two or more sufficient witnesses, shall find two sureties to be bound by recognizance in the penal sum of fifty pounds, and in default of such sureties shall be committed to prison, there to remain till the next general or quarter sessions; and upon conviction of the said offence at the said general or quarter sessions, shall suffer the pain and penalty of twenty pounds, to the use of the King's and Queen's majesties, their heirs and successors.

XIX. Provided always, That no congregation or assembly for religious worship shall be permitted or allowed by this act, until the place of such meeting shall be certified to the bishop of the diocese, or to the archdeacon of that archdeaconry, or to the justices of the peace at the general or quarter sessions of the peace for the county, city, or place in which such meeting shall be held, and registred in the said bishop's or archdeacon's court respectively, or recorded at the said general or quarter sessions; the register or clerk of the peace whereof respectively is hereby required to register the same, and to give certificate thereof to such person as shall demand the same, for which there shall be no greater fee nor reward taken, than the sum of six pence.

Triennial Act, 1694

6 W. & M., c. 2   *Statutes at Large*, IX, 331-32.

This act provided for the election of a new Parliament at least once every three years.

Whereas by the ancient laws, and statutes of this kingdom, frequent parliaments ought to be held; and whereas frequent and new parliaments tend very much to the happy union and good agreement of the King and people; we your Majesties most loyal and obedient subjects, the lords spiritual and temporal, and commons, in this present parliament assembled, do most humbly beseech your most excellent Majesties, that it may be declared and enacted in this present parliament; and it is hereby declared and enacted by the King's and Queen's most excellent majesties, by and with the advice and consent of the lords spiritual and temporal, and commons, in this present parliament assembled, and by the authority of the same, That from henceforth a parliament shall be holden once in three years at the least.

II. And be it further enacted by the authority aforesaid, That within three years at the farthest, from and after the dissolution of this present parliament, and so from time to time for ever hereafter, within three years at the farthest, from and after the determination of every other parliament, legal writs under the great seal shall be issued by directions of your Majesties, your heirs and successors, for calling, assembling and holding another new parliament.

III. And be it further enacted by the authority aforesaid, That from henceforth no parliament whatsoever, that shall at any time hereafter be called, assembled or held, shall have any continuance longer than for three years only at the farthest, to be accounted from the day on which by the writs of summons the said parliament shall be appointed to meet.

IV. And be it further enacted by the authority aforesaid, That this present parliament shall cease and determine on the first day of November, which shall be in the year of our Lord one thousand six hundred ninety six, unless their Majesties shall think fit to dissolve it sooner.

Commons resolutions opposing the re-enactment of the Printing Act of 1662 with its licensing regulations, 18 April 1695

Journals of the House of Lords, XV, 545-46.

These resolutions effectively terminated censorship of the press.

And the *Earl of Bridgewater* reported, That the Commons have agreed to all the Amendments made by their Lordships, except the Clause (A), to be added at the End of the Bill for reviving the Printing Act; to which they disagree, and give the Reasons following; (videlicet,)

The Commons cannot agree to the Clause marked (A):

1. Because it revives and re-enacts a Law which in no Wise answered the End for which it was made; the Title and Preamble of that Act being, *to prevent printing seditious and treasonable Books, Pamphlets, and Papers:* But there is no Penalty appointed for Offenders therein, they being left to be punished at Common Law (as they may be) without that Act; whereas there are great and grievous Penalties imposed by that Act, for Matters wherein neither Church nor State is any Ways concerned.

2. Because that Act gives a Property in Books to such Persons as such Books are or shall be granted to by Letters Patents; whether the Crown had, or shall have, any Right to grant the same or not, at the Time of such Grant.

3. Because that Act prohibits printing any Thing before Entry thereof in the Register of the Company of Stationers (except Proclamations, Acts of Parliament, and such Books as shall be appointed under the Sign Manual, or under the Hand of a Principal Secretary of State); whereby both Houses of Parliament are disabled to order any Thing to be printed; and the said Company are empowered to hinder the printing all innocent and useful Books; and have an Opportunity to enter a Title to themselves, and their Friends, for what belongs to, and is the Labour and Right of, others.

4. Because that Act prohibits any Books to be imported (without special License) into any Port in England (except London); by which Means the whole Foreign Trade of Books is restrained to London, unless the Lord Archbishop of Canterbury or the Lord Bishop of London shall, in Interruption of their more important Affairs in governing the Church, bestow their Time *gratis* in looking over Catalogues of Books, and granting Licenses; whereas the Commons think the other Ports of the Kingdom have as good Right as London to trade in Books, as well as other Merchandize.

5. Because that Act leaves it in the Power, either of the Company of Stationers, or of the Archbishop of Canterbury and Bishop of London, to hinder any Books from being imported, even into the Port of London; for if One or more of the Company of Stationers will not come to the Custom-house, or that those Reverend Bishops shall not appoint any learned Man to go thither, and be present at the opening and viewing Books imported, the Custom-house Officer is obliged to detain them.

6. Because that Act appoints no Time wherein the Archbishop, or Bishop of London, shall appoint a learned Man, or that One or more of the Company of Stationers shall go to the Custom-house, to view imported Books; so that they or either of them may delay it till the Importer may be undone, by having so great a Part of his Stock lie dead; or the Books, if wet, may rot and perish.

7. Because that Act prohibits any Custom-house Officer, under the Penalty of losing his Office, to open any Packet wherein are Books, until some or One of the Company of Stationers, and such learned Man as shall be so appointed, are present; which is impracticable, since he cannot know there are Books till he has opened the Packet.

8. Because that Act confirms all Patents of Books granted, and to be granted; whereby the sole printing of all or most of the Classic Authors are, and have been for many Years past, together with a great Number of the best Books, and of most general Use, monopolized by the Company of Stationers; and prohibits the importing any such Books from beyond Sea, whereby the Scholars in this Kingdom are forced, not only to buy them at the extravagant Price they demand, but must be content with their ill and incorrect Editions, and cannot have the more correct Copies which are published Abroad, nor the useful Notes of Foreigners or other learned Men upon them.

9. Because that Act prohibits any Thing to be printed till licensed; and yet does not direct what shall be taken by the Licenser for such License; by Colour whereof, great Oppression may be, and has been, practised.

10. Because that Act restrains Men bred up in the Trade of Printing and Founding of Letters from exercising their Trade, even in an innocent and inoffensive Way (though they are Freemen of the Company of Stationers), either as Masters or Journeymen; the Number of Workmen in each of these Trades being limited by that Act.

11. Because that Act compels Master Printers to take Journeymen into their Service, though they have no Work or Employment for them.

12. Because that Act restrains all Men who are not licensed by the Bishop from selling innocent and inoffensive Books, though never so useful, in any Part of England, except Freemen of the Company of Stationers, who may sell without such License; so that neither Church nor State is taken Care of thereby, but the People compelled to buy their Freedom of Trade in all Parts of England from the Company of Stationers in London.

13. Because that Act prohibits any one, not only to print Books whereof another has entered a Claim of Property in the Register of the Company of Stationers, but to bind, stitch, or put them to Sale, and that under a great Pecuniary Penalty; though it is impossible for a Bookbinder, Stitcher, or Seller, to know whether the Book brought to him were printed by the Proprietor or another.

14. Because that Act prohibits Smiths to make any Iron-work for any Printing Press, without giving Notice to the Company of Stationers, under the Penalty of Five Pounds; whereas he may not know to what Use the Iron bespoke of him, and forged by him, may be put.

15. Because that Act prohibits printing and importing, not only heretical, seditious, and schismatical Books, but all offensive Books, and doth not determine what shall be adjudged offensive Books; so that, without Doubt, if the late King James had continued in the Throne till this Time, Books against Popery would not have been deemed offensive Books.

16. Because that Act subjects all Mens Houses, as well Peers as Commoners, to be searched at any Time, either by Day or Night, by a Warrant under the Sign Manual, or under the Hand of One of the Secretaries of State, directed to any Messenger, if such Messenger shall upon probable Reason suspect that there are any unlicensed Books there; and the Houses of all Persons free of the Company of Stationers are subject to the like Search, on a Warrant from the Master and Wardens of the said Company, or any One of them.
17. Because the Penalties for Offences against that Act are excessive; it being in the Power of the Judges or Justices of the Peace to inflict what Punishment they please, not extending to Life or Member.
18. Lastly, There is a Proviso in that Act for John Streater, that he may print what he pleases, as if the Act had never been made; when the Commons see no Cause to distinguish him from all the rest of the Subjects of England.

After Debate, The Question was put, "Whether this House will agree with the Commons, in leaving out the Clause (A)?"

It was Resolved in the Affirmative.

Trial of Treason Act, 1696

7 & 8 W. 3, c. 3   *Statutes at Large*, IX, 389.

This act regulated treason trials and determined that two witnesses were necessary to prove the offence.

Whereas nothing is more just and reasonable than that persons prosecuted for high treason and misprision of treason, whereby the liberties, lives, honour, estates, blood and posterity of the subjects may be lost and destroyed, should be justly and equally tried, and that persons accused as offenders therein should not be debarred of all just and equal means for defence of their innocencies in such cases; in order thereunto, and for the better regulation of trials of persons prosecuted for high treason and misprison of such treason; be it enacted by the King's most excellent Majesty, by and with the advice and and consent of the lords spiritual and temporal, and the commons, in this present parliament assembled, and by the authority of the same, That from and after the five and twentieth day of March in the year of our Lord one thousand six hundred ninety-six all and every person and persons whatsoever, that shall be accused and indicted for high treason, whereby any corruption of blood may or shall be made to any such offender or offenders or to any the heir or heirs of any such offender or offenders, or for misprision of such treason, shall have a true copy of the whole indictment, but not the names of the witnesses, delivered unto them, or any of them, five days at the least before he or they shall be tried for the same, whereby to enable them, and any of them respectively, to advise with counsel thereupon, to plead and make their defence, his or their attorney or attorneys, agent or agents, or any of them, requiring the same, and paying the officer his reasonable fees for writing thereof, not exceeding five shillings for the copy of every such indictment; and that every such person so accused and indicted, arraigned or tried for any such treason, as aforesaid, or for misprision of such treason, from and after the said time shall be received and admitted to make his and their full defence, by counsel learned in the law, and to make any proof that he or they can produce by lawful witness or witnesses, who shall then be upon oath, for his and their just defence in that behalf; and in case any person or persons so accused or indicted shall desire counsel, the court before whom such person or persons shall be tried, or some judge of that court, shall and is hereby authorised and required immediately, upon his or their request, to assign to such person and persons such and so many counsel, not exceeding two as the person or persons shall desire, to whom such counsel shall have free access at all reasonable hours; any law or usage to the contrary notwithstanding.

II. And be it further enacted, That from and after the said five and twentieth day of March in the year of our Lord one thousand six hundred ninety-six, no person or persons whatsoever shall be indicted, tried or attainted, of high treason, whereby any corruption of blood may or shall be made to any such offender or offenders or to any the heir or heirs of any such offender or offenders, or of misprision of such treason, but by and upon the oaths and testimony of two lawful witnesses, either both of them to the same overt act, or one of them to one, and another of them to another overt act of the same treason; unless the party indicted, and arraigned, or tried, shall willingly, without violence, in open court, confess the same, or shall stand mute, or refuse to plead, or in cases of high treason shall peremptorily challenge above the number of thirty five of the jury; any law, statute, or usage, to the contrary notwithstanding.

III. Provided always, That any person or persons, being indicted, as aforesaid, for any of the treasons, or misprisions of the treasons aforesaid, may be outlawed, and thereby attainted of or for any of the said offences of treason, or misprision of treason; and in cases of the high treasons aforesaid, where-by the law, after such outlawry, the party outlawed may come in, and be tried, he shall, upon such trial, have the benefit of this act.

IV. And be it further enacted and declared by the authority aforesaid, That if two or more distinct treasons of divers heads or kinds shall be alleged in one bill of indictment, one witness produced to prove one of the said treasons, and another witness produced to prove another of the said treasons, shall not be deemed or taken to be two witnesses to the same treason, within the meaning of this act.

V. And to the intent that the terror and dread of such criminal accusations may in some reasonable time be removed, be it further enacted by the authority aforesaid, That from and after the said five and twentieth day of March in the year of our Lord one thousand six hundred ninety-six, no person or persons whatsoever shall be indicted, tried or prosecuted, for any such treason as aforesaid, or for misprision of such treason, that shall be committed or done within the kingdom of England, dominion of Wales, or town of Berwick upon Tweed, after the said five and twentieth day of March in the year of our Lord one thousand six hundred ninety-six, unless the same indictment be found by a grand jury within three years next after the treason or offence done and committed; and that no person or persons shall be prosecuted for any such treason, or misprision of such treason, committed or done, or to be committed or done, within the kingdom of England, dominion of Wales, or town of Berwick upon Tweed, before the said five and twentieth day of March, unless he or they shall be indicted thereof within three years after the said five and twentieth day of March.

VI.   Always provided and excepted, That if any person or persons whatsoever shall be guilty of designing, endeavouring, or attempting, any assassination on the body of the King, by poison or otherwise, such person or persons may be prosecuted at any time, notwithstanding the aforesaid limitation.

VII.   And that all and every person and persons who shall be accused, indicted, or tried, for such treason as aforesaid, or for misprision of such treason, after the said five and twentieth day of March in the year of our Lord one thousand six hundred ninety-six, shall have copies of the panel of the jurors who are to try them, duly returned by the sheriff, and delivered unto them and every of them so accused and indicted respectively, two days at the least before he or they shall be tried for the same; and that all persons so accused and indicted for any such treason as aforesaid, shall have the like process of the court where they shall be tried, to compel their witnesses to appear for them at any such trial or trials, as is usually granted to compel witnesses to appear against them.

VIII.   And be it further enacted, That no evidence shall be admitted or given of any overt act that is not expressly laid in the indictment against any person or persons whatsoever.

IX.   Provided also, and be it enacted by the authority aforesaid, That no indictment for any of the offences aforesaid, nor any process or return thereupon, shall be quashed on the motion of the prisoner, or his counsel, for mis-writing, mis-spelling, false or improper Latin, unless exception concerning the same be taken and made in the respective court where such trial shall be, by the prisoner or his counsel assigned, before any evidence given in open court upon such indictment; nor shall any such mis-writing, mis-spelling, false or improper Latin, after conviction on such indictment, be any cause to stay or arrest judgment thereupon: but nevertheless any judgment given upon such indictment, shall and may be liable to be reversed upon a writ of error, in the same manner, and no other, than as if this act had not been made.

X.   And whereas by the good laws of this kingdom in cases of trials of commoners for their lives, a jury of twelve freeholders must all agree in one opinion before they can bring a verdict, either for acquittal or condemnation of the prisoner:

XI.   And whereas upon the trials of peers or peeresses, a major vote is sufficient, either to acquit or condemn; be it further enacted by the authority aforesaid, That upon the trial of any peer or peeress, either for treason or misprision, all the peers who have a right to sit and vote in parliament shall be duly summoned, twenty days at least before every such trial, to appear at every such trial; and that every peer, so summoned and appearing at such trial, shall vote in the trial of such peer or peeress so to be tried, every such peer first taking the oaths mentioned in an act of parliament made in the first year of the reign of King William and Queen Mary, entituled, *An Act for abrogating the oaths of supremacy and allegiance and appointing other oaths,* and also every such peer subscribing and audibly repeating the declaration mentioned in *An Act for the more effectual preserving the king's person and government by disabling papists from sitting in either House of Parliament,* and made in the thirtieth year of the reign of the late King Charles the Second.

XII. Provided always, That neither this act, nor any thing therein contained, shall any ways extend to, or be construed to extend to any impeachment or other proceedings in parliament, in any kind whatsoever.

XIII. Provided always, That neither this act, nor any thing therein contained, shall any ways extend to any indictment of high treason, nor to any proceedings thereupon, for counterfeiting his Majesty's coin, his great seal, or privy seal, his sign manual, or privy signet.

Civil List Act, 1698

9 Will. 3, c. 23   *Statutes of the Realm,* VII, 382-85.

This act provided a fixed parliamentary grant to the king for the support of his household. By fusing personal and governmental expenses it strengthened the system of political patronage. The Civil List was not abolished until 1831.

Whereas Your Majesties most dutiful and loyal Subjects the Commons of England in Parliament assembled being deeply sensible of the greate Blessings which by the Goodnesse of Almighty God Wee and all other the Subjects of Your Majesties Realmes and Dominions in the free Exercise of the true Christian Religion (the most valuable Benefitt which can be bestowed upon any Nation or People) as also in our Liberties and Properties do [fully] enjoy under Your Majesties most auspicious Government and being desirous to make a gratefull Acknowledgement of Your Majesties unparalleld Grace and Favour to us Your Commons and particularly for the greate and succesfull Undertakings and Atchivements whereby Your Majesty hath been the happy Instrument of securing the aforesaid Blessings to us and our Posterities have therefore freely & unanimously resolved to increase Your Majesties Revenue dureing Your Majesties Reign (which God long continue) and do give and grant unto Your most Excellent Majesty the further Rates Duties and Sums of Money herein after mentioned and do humbly beseech Your Majesty That it may be enacted and be it enacted by the Kings most Excellent Majesty by and with the Advice and Consent of the Lords Spiritual & Temporal and of the Commons in this present Parliament assembled and by Authority of the same That over and above all Subsidies of Tunnage and Poundage and over and above all additional Duties Impositions and other Duties whatsoever by any other Act or Acts of Parliament or otherwise howsoever already due or payable or which ought to be paid to His Majesty for or upon any Wines Goods or Merchandizes whatsoever imported or to be imported there shall be raised levied collected paid and satisfied unto His Majesty one other Subsidy called Tunnage for and upon all Wines which from and after the last Day of January which shall be in the Yeare of our Lord One thousand six hundred ninety nine att any time or times dureing His Majesties Life shall be imported or brought into the Kingdome of England Dominion of Wales or Towne of Berwick upon Tweed (that is to say)

Of every Tun of Wine of the Growth of France or of any the Dominions of the French King or Crowne of France that shall come into the Port of London and the Members thereof by way of Merchandize by His Majesties natural borne Subjects the Sum of Foure Pounds and Ten Shillings of current English Money and so after that Rate & by Strangers and Aliens Six Pounds of the like Money And of every Tun of the like Wine which shall be brought into all and every the other Ports and Places of this Kingdome and the Dominions thereof by way of Merchandize by His Majesties natural borne Subjects the Sum of Three Pounds and by Aliens Foure Pounds Ten Shillings.

And of every Butt or Pipe of Muscadells Malmseys Cutes Tents Alicants Bastards Sacks Canaries Malaga's Madera's and other Wines whatsoever commonly called Sweet Wines of the Growth of the Levant Spaine Portugal or any of them or any the Islands or Dominions to them or any of them belonging or elsewhere that shall come or be brought into the Port of London by His Majesties natural borne Subjects the Sum of Forty five Shillings of Current English Money and so after that Rate And by Strangers and Aliens Three Pounds of like Money And of every Butt and Pipe of the like Wine which shall come or be brought into all & every or any the other Ports and Places of this Kingdome and Dominions thereof by way of Merchandize by His Majesties [natural] borne Subjects the Sum of Thirty Shillings and by Strangers Forty five Shillings.

And of every Awme of Rhenish Wine or Wine of the Growth of Germany that shall be brought into this Realme and the Dominions thereof by His Majesties natural borne Subjects the Sum of Twenty Shillings of Current English Money and by Strangers and Aliens Twenty five Shillings And that such Wines that shall be landed in any the Out-Ports and afterwards brought to the Port of London by Certificate shall pay so much more Subsidy by this Act as they paid short of the Duty due in the Port of London Which several Rates for Wines are the same which are expressed in a certaine Book of Rates which was signed by Sir Harbottle Grimstone Baronett formerly Speaker of the House of Commons and which is referred to by an Act of Parliament made in the Twelfth Years of the Reigne of King Charles the Second intituled A Subsidy granted to the King of Tunnage and Poundage and other Sums of Money payable upon Merchandizes exported and imported And one further Subsidy called Poundage (that is to say) of all manner of Goods and Merchandizes of every Merchant natural borne Subjects Denizen and Alien to be imported or brought into this Realm or any His Majesties Dominions to the same belonging at any time or times after the said last Day of January One thousand six hundred ninety nine dureing His Majesties Life by way of Merchandize of the Value of every Twenty Shillings of the same Goods and Merchandizes according to the severall and perticular Rates and Values of the same

Goods and Merchandizes as the same are particularly and respectively rated and valued in the aforesaid Book of Rates Twelve Pence and soe after that Rate And if there shall happen to be brought into this Realm any Goods liable to the Payment of Subsidy by this Act granted which are not particularly rated in the said Book of Rates that in every such Case every Customer or Collector for the time being shall levy the Subsidy by this Act granted according to the Value and Price of such Goods to be affirmed upon the Oath of the Merchant in the Presence of the Customer Collector Comptrollor and Surveyor or any Two of them except and foreprized out of this Grant of Subsidy of Poundage all Wines before limitted to pay Subsidy of Tunnage and all manner of Fish English taken and broght by English Bottoms into this Realm and all manner of Fresh Fish and Beastiall that shall come into this Realm and all other Goods and Merchandizes which in the said Book of Rates are mentioned to be Custom-free and except and foreprized out of this Grant of Subsidy of Poundage all Goods and Merchandizes which are commonly used in dying.

Provided alwaies and it is hereby further enacted That all Drugs chargable by this Act which shall be imported directly from the Place of their Growth in English built Shipping shall be rated to pay by this Act One third part of what is charged thereupon in the said Book of Rates and noe more And that all Spicery except Pepper which shall be imported directly from the Place of its Growth in English built Shipping shall be rated to pay by this Act One third part of what is charged in the said Book of Rates and noe more And [that] this Act shall not extend to charge Linen imported with the additionall Duty of One Moiety of the Rate mentioned in the said Book of Rates And that all Foreign Wrought Silks exported within One Year from the Importation shall have Two thirds of the Rate hereby charged repaid at the Custom-house And this Act shall not extend to charge wrought Silks imported with the Additionall Duty of One Moiety mentioned in the said Book of Rates or to charge Tobacco of the English Plantation with the additionall Duty of One Peny per Pound over and above the Subsidy mentioned in the said Book of Rates or to charge Wines of the Growth of France Germany Portugall or Madera with the additional Duty of Three Pounds per Tun or any other Wines with the additional Duty of Four Pounds per Tun mentioned in the said former Acts or Book of Rates And that for all Tobacco of the English Plantations which shall be imported and exported again within One Year after such Importation the further Subsidy of One Peny per Pound hereby granted shall be repaid at the Custom-house.

And be it further enacted by the Authority aforesaid That out of the several Subsidies of Tunnage and Poundage by this Act granted there shall be such and the like Allowances and Abatements in all Cases as are or were prescribed in the like Cases by the said former Act or by the said Book of Rates or the Rules thereunto annexed and to be made and allowed under the same Restrictions and in the same manner and form as are therin expressed.

And be it further enacted by the Authority aforesaid That the said severall Subsidies of Tunnage and Poundage hereby granted shall be raised levyed and collected by the respective Officers of His Majesties Customs for the time being under the Management and Direction of the Commissioners of the Customs for the time being and shall be brought and paid or answered into the Receipt of His Majesties Exchequer for the purposes in this Act mentioned (such additionall Charge as shall be necessary for the Management of this Revenue only excepted) and that all and every the Clauses Powers Directions Penalties Forfeitures Matters and Things whatsoever contained in the said former Act of Tunnage and Poundage or in the said Book of Rates or the Rules thereunto annexed or in any other Laws or Statutes whatsoever now in Force for raiseing levying securing collecting answering or paying the Subsidy of Tunnage and Poundage thereby granted shall be applied practised and put in Execution for the raiseing levying securing collecting answering and paying the Subsidy of Tunnage and Poundage by this Act granted as fully and effectually to all intents and purposes as if all and every the said Clauses Powers Directions Penalties Forfeitures Matters and Things were particularly repeated and again enacted in the Body of this present Act.

Provided always and be it enacted That the whole further Subsidy laid by this Act upon all Sugars that shall be imported from the English Plantations in America shall and may be drawn and paid back at the Exportation thereof Any thing in this Act contained to the contrary notwithstanding.

And whereas great Quantities of Brown and Muscavado Sugars have formerly been refined here in England and afterwards exported to Foreign Markets whereby a great Number of People have been imployed and a Manufacture carryed on very profitable to this Kingdom which Trade of refining Sugars for Exportation will be lost unless a Drawback be allowed when such Sugars are exported after they are refined here sutable to the Draw back allowed on the Exportation of Brown and Muscavado Sugars by reason Foreign Nations will be thereby enabled to refine them cheaper abroad than they can be done here at home Be it therefore enacted by the Authority aforesaid That for every Hundred Weight of Sugar refined in England (and so in proportion for a greater or lesser quantity) exported out of this Kingdom after the said last day of January which [shall] be in the Year of our Lord One thousand six hundred ninety nine during the Continuance of this Act there shall be [re]paid at the Custom-house to the Exporter within One Month after Demand thereof the Sum of Three Shillings Oath being first made by the Refiner That the said Sugar so exported was produced from Brown and Muscavado Sugar charged by this Act and that as he verily believes the same was imported from His Majesties Plantations in America and that as he verily believes the Duty of the said Brown and Muscavado Sugar was duly paid at the time of the Importation thereof and that the same was duly exported His Majesties Searcher also certifying the Shipping thereof and all other Requisites duly performed according to the Book of Rates.

And be it enacted by the Authority aforesaid That for the further Subsidy hereby granted upon Tobacco of the English Plantations in American the Merchant Importer shall have Three Months time from the Importation to pay the same giving Security for the Payment thereof accordingly And in case of paying the same sooner than the said Three Months the said Merchant Importer shall be allowed a Discount after the Rate of Ten Pounds per Centum p Ann for prompt Payment Any thing herein contained to the contrary notwithstanding.

Provided always That Ginger of the English Plantations in the West-Indies which by the said Book of Rates is valued at Sixteen Pence a Pound shall pay for the said former Subsidy One Shilling for every Hundred Weight and for the Subsidy by this Act One Shilling for every Hundred Weight and after that Proportion for a greater or lesser Quantity and no more Any thing in this Act or the said former Act to the contrary notwithstanding.

And whereas great Quantities of Cut-Whale-bone fit for Use are frequently imported in Short-Lengths and small Parcells by means whereof not only His Majesty is defrauded of the Duties laid thereupon but the Merchants importing and the Manufacturers imployed in cutting of Fin Whale-bone are greatly prejudiced and discouraged Be it therefore declared and enacted by the Authority aforesaid That if any Person or Persons Natives or Foreigners Bodies Politick or Corporate shall import or bring into this Kingdom of England Dominion of Wales or Town of Berwick upon Tweed any Cut Whale-bone (other then in Fins only) he she or they shall forfeit the Goods and Double the Value of the Cut Whalebone so imported One Moiety thereof to His Majesty His Heirs and Succesors and one other Moiety to him or them that shall seize or sue for the same in any of His Majesties Courts of Record wherein no Essoign Protection or Wager of Lawe shall be allowed nor any more then one Imparlance Any thing in this Act or any former Law to the contrary in any wise notwithstanding.

Provided always and it is hereby enacted and declared by the Authority aforesaid That in all Cases where any the Foreign Goods or Merchandizes by this Act charged with the Subsidy of Tunnage or Poundage hereby granted (other than and except Foreign Wrought Silk Tobacco Sugars and refined Sugars touching which other Provisions are hereby made) shall at any time or times be again exported by any Merchant English within Twelve Calendary Months or Stranger within Nine Calendary Months after the Importation thereof and that due Proof be first made by Certificate from the proper Officers of the due Entry and Payment of the Subsidy hereby granted of any such Goods Wines or Merchandies inward together with the Oath of the Merchant importing and exporting the same affiring the truth thereof and that all other Requisites shall be performed which are by Law required to be performed in Cases where the half Subsidy is repaid by the said former Act the whole Subsidy by this Act granted and which shall have been actually paid for such Goods Wines or Merchandizes shall without any Delay or Reward be repaid unto such Merchant or Merchants who do export the same within One Month after Demand thereof or the Security for the said Subsidy by the Act charged shall be vacated as to soe much as shall be so exported And that as to the said Foreign Wrought Silks Tobacco Sugars and refined Sugars no Repayment or Draw back of or for the Subsidy by this Act shall be made or allowed for the same unless they respectively be again exported within the times hereby lymitted for other Goods And that the like due Proof be made and other Requisites performed for the said Silks Tobacco Sugar and refined Sugar as are hereby directed in the like Case for other Goods or Merchandizes exported And that upon such Exportation of Foreign Wrought Silks and such due Proof made and other Requisites performed for the same not only the Two thirds of the Subsidies by this Act directed to be repaid for such Silks as aforesaid but also the remaining One third of the same Subsidy shall be entirely repaid at the Custome-house Any thing herein contained to the contrary notwithstanding.

And whereas it is intended that the yearly Sum of Seven hundred thousand Pounds shall be supplied to His Majestie for the Service of His Houshold and Family and for other His necessary Expences and Occasions out of the Hereditary Rates and Duties of Excise upon Beer Ale and other Liquors which were granted to the Crown in the Twelfth Year of the Reign of King Charles the Second and out of the Rates and Duties of Excise of Beer Ale and other Liquors payable for the Term of His Majesties Life by an Act of Parliament made and passed in the Second Year of the Reign of His Majesty and the late Queen of blessed Memory after all the Talleys charged upon the Weekly Sum of Six thousand Pounds issuing out of the said severall Rates and Duties of Excise pursuant to an Act of [Parliant] passed in the Seventh Year of His Majesties Reign in that behalf and still remaining unsatisfyed (with the Interest thereof) shall be fully paid off and cleared And out of the Revenue of the Generall Letter Office or Post Office or the Office of the Postmaster Generall after all the Talleys charged upon the Weekly Sum of Six hundred Pounds issuing out of that Revenue pursuant to the said Act of Parliament of the Seventh Year of His Majesties Reign and still remaining unsatisfyed and all the Interest thereof shall be fully paid and disharged And out of the small Branches of His Majesties Revenues herein after mentioned and expressed that is to say The First Fruits and Tenths of the Clergy The Fines for Writts of Covenant and Writts of Entry payable in the Alienation Office The Post Fines The Revenue of the Wine Licences The Moneys arising by Sheriffs Proffers and Compositions in the Exchequer and by the Seizures of uncustomed and prohibited Goods The Revenue of the Dutchy of Cornwall and any other Revenue arising by the Rents of Lands in England or Wales or for Fine of Leases of the same or any of them and the Duty of Four and an half per Cent in Specie arising in Barbadoes and the Leeward Islands in America And out of the Moneys which from and after the Commencement of this Act shall arise by the further Subsidies and Duties hereby granted Be it therefore further enacted and it is hereby enacted and provided by the Authority aforesaid That if the said great and small Branches and Revenues herein before mentioned and out of which the said yearly Sum of Seven hundred thousand Pounds is intended to be supplied as aforesaid and every or any of them shall produce in clear Money more than the yearly Sum of Seven hundred thousand Pounds to be reckoned from the Five and twentieth Day of December which shall be in the Year of our Lord One thousand six hundred ninety nine that then the Overplus of such Produce (being more than the said yearly Sum of Seven hundred thousand Pounds) shall not be issued disposed made use of or applied to any Use or Purpose or upon any pretext whatsoever without the Authority of Parliament And that all Grants and Dispositions whatsoever hereafter to be made of such Overplus or any part thereof from time to time without [the] Authority of Parliament shall be utterly void and of none Effect And the Grantees or other Persons to whom such Grants or Dispositions or any of them shall be made of such Overplus or any part thereof shall be adjudged uncapable in Law to take hold keep detain or enjoy the same Any Law Custom or Usage to the contrary notwithstanding.

Act of Settlement, 1701

12 Will. 3, c. 2   *Statutes at Large*, X, 357-60.

This important act transferred succession of the crown to the Hanoverian line and placed further restrictions on the monarch.

Whereas in the first year of the reign of your Majesty, and of our late most gracious sovereign lady Queen Mary (of blessed memory) an act of parliament was made, intituled, *An act for declaring the rights and liberties of the subject, and for settling the succession of the crown,* wherein it was (amongst other things) enacted, established, and declared, That the crown and regal government of the kingdoms of England, France, and Ireland, and the dominions thereunto belonging, should be and continue to your Majesty and the said late Queen, during the joint lives of your Majesty and the said Queen, and to the survivor: and that after the decease of your Majesty and of the said Queen, the said crown and regal government should be and remain to the heirs of the body of the said late Queen; and for default of such issue, to her royal highness the princess Anne of Denmark, and the heirs of her body: and for default of such issue, to the heirs of the body of your Majesty. And it was thereby further enacted, That all and every person and persons that then were, or afterwards should be reconciled to, or should hold communion with the see or church of Rome, or should profess the popish religion, or marry a papist, should be excluded, and are by that act made for ever uncapable to inherit, possess, or enjoy the crown and government of this realm, and Ireland, and the dominions thereunto belonging, or any part of the same, or to have, use, or exercise any regal power, authority, or jurisdiction within the same: and in all and every such case and cases the people of these realms shall be and are thereby absolved of their allegiance: and that the said crown and government shall from time to time descend to and be enjoyed by such person or persons, being protestants, as should have inherited and enjoyed the same, in case the said person or persons, so reconciled, holding communion, professing or marrying, as aforesaid, were naturally dead. After the making of which statute, and the settlement therein contained, your Majesty's good subjects, who were restored to the full and free possession and enjoyment of their religion, rights and liberties, by the providence of God giving success to your Majesty's just undertakings and unwearied endeavours for that purpose, had no greater temporal felicity to hope or wish for, than to see a royal progeny descending from your Majesty, to whom (under God) they owe their tranquillity, and whose ancestors have for many years been principal assertors of the reformed religion and the liberties of Europe, and from our said most gracious sovereign Lady, whose memory will always be precious to the subjects of these realms: and it having since pleased Almight God to take away our said sovereign Lady, and also the most hopeful prince William duke of Gloucester (the only surviving issue of her royal highness the princess Anne of Denmark) to the unspeakable grief and sorrow of your Majesty and your said good subjects, who under such losses being sensibly put in mind, that it standeth wholly in the pleasure of Almighty God to prolong the lives of your Majesty and of her royal Highness, and to grant to your Majesty, or to her royal Highness, such issue as may be inheritable to the crown and regal government aforesaid, by the respective limitations in the said recited act contained, do constantly implore the divine mercy for those blessings: and your Majesty's said subjects having daily experience of your royal care and concern for the present and future welfare of these kingdoms, and particularly recommending from your throne a further provision to be made for the succession of the crown in the protestant line, for the happiness of the nation, and the security of our religion; and it being absolutely necessary for the safety, peace, and quiet of this realm, to obviate all doubts and contentions in the same, by reason of any pretended title to the crown, and to maintain a certainty in the succession thereof, to which your subjects may safely have recourse for their protection, in case the limitations in the said recited act should determine: therefore for a further provision of the succession of the crown in the protestant line, we your Majesty's most dutiful and loyal subjects, the lords spiritual and temporal, and commons, in this present parliament assembled, do beseech your Majesty that it may be enacted and declared, and be it enacted and declared by the King's most excellent majesty, by and with the advice and consent of the lords spiritual and temporal, and commons, in this present parliament assembled, and by the authority of the same, That the most excellent princess Sophia, electress and dutchess dowager of Hanover, daughter of the most excellent princess Elizabeth, late Queen of Bohemia, daughter of our late sovereign lord King James the First, of happy memory, be and is hereby declared to be the next in succession, in the protestant line, to the imperial crown and dignity of the said realms of England, France, and Ireland, with the dominions and territories thereunto belonging, after his Majesty, and the princess Anne of Denmark, and in default of issue of the said princess Anne, and of his Majesty respectively: and that from and after the deceases of his said Majesty, our now sovereign lord, and of her royal highness the princess Anne of Denmark, and for default of issue of the said princess Anne, and of his Majesty respectively, the crown and regal government of the said kingdoms of England, France, and Ireland, and of the dominions thereunto belonging, with the royal state and dignity of the said realms, and all honours, stiles, titles, regalities, prerogatives, powers, jurisdictions and authorities, to the same belonging and appertaining, shall be, remain, and continue to the said most excellent princess Sophia, and the heirs of her body, being protestants: and thereunto the said lords spiritual and temporal, and commons, shall and will, in the name of all the people of this realm, most humbly and faithfully submit themselves, their heirs and posterities; and do faithfully promise, That after the deceases of his Majesty, and her royal highness, and the failure of the heirs of their respective bodies, to stand to, maintain, and defend the said princess Sophia, and the heirs of her body, being protestants, according to the limitation and succession of the crown in this act specified and contained, to the utmost of their powers, with their lives and estates, against all persons whatsoever that shall attempt any thing to the contrary.

II.   Provided always, and it is hereby enacted, That all and every person and persons, who shall or may take or inherit the said crown, by virtue of the limitation of this present act, and is, are or shall be reconciled to, or shall hold communion with, the see or church of Rome, or shall profess the popish religion, or shall marry a papist, shall be subject to such incapacities, as in such case or cases are by the said recited act provided, enacted, and established; and that every King and Queen of this realm, who shall come to and succeed in the imperial crown of this kingdom, by virtue of this act, shall have the coronation oath administred to him, her or them, at their respective coronations, according to the act of parliament made in the first year of the reign of his Majesty, and the said late Queen Mary, intituled, *An act for establishing the coronation oath,* and shall make, subscribe, and repeat the declaration in the act first above recited mentioned or referred to, in the manner and form thereby prescribed.

III. And whereas it is requisite and necessary that some further provision be made for securing our religion, laws and liberties, from and after the death of his Majesty and the princess Anne of Denmark, and in default of issue of the body of the said princess, and of his Majesty respectively; be it enacted by the King's most excellent majesty, by and with the advice and consent of the lords spiritual and temporal, and commons, in parliament assembled, and by the authority of the same,

That whosoever shall hereafter come to the possession of this crown, shall join in communion with the church of England, as by law established.

That in case the crown and imperial dignity of this realm shall hereafter come to any person, not being a native of this kingdom of England, this nation be not obliged to engage in any war for the defence of any dominions or territories which do not belong to the crown of England, without the consent of parliament.

That no person who shall hereafter come to the possession of this crown, shall go out of the dominions of England, Scotland, or Ireland, without consent of parliament.

That from and after the time that the further limitation by this act shall take effect, all matters and things relating to the well governing of this kingdom, which are properly cognizable in the privy council by the laws and customs of this realm, shall be translated there, and all resolutions taken thereupon shall be signed by such of the privy counsel as shall advise and consent to the same.

That after the said limitation shall take effect as aforesaid, no person born out of the kingdoms of England, Scotland, or Ireland, or the dominions thereunto belonging (although he be naturalized or made a denizen, except such as are born of English parents) shall be capable to be of the privy council, or a member of either house of parliament, or to enjoy any office or place of trust, either civil or military, or to have any grant of lands, tenements or hereditaments from the crown, to himself or to any other or others in trust for him.

That no person who has an office or place of profit under the King, or receives a pension from the crown, shall be capable of serving as a member of the house of commons.

That after the said limitation shall take effect as aforesaid, judges commissions be made *quamdiu se bene gesserint,* and their salaries ascertained and established; but upon the address of both houses of parliament it may be lawful to remove them.

That no pardon under the great seal of England be pleadable to an impeachment by the commons in parliament.

IV. And whereas the laws of England are the birth-right of the people thereof, and all the Kings and Queens, who shall ascend the throne of this realm, ought to administer the government of the same according to the said laws, and all their officers and ministers ought to serve them respectively according to the same: the said lords spiritual and temporal, and commons, do therefore further humbly pray, That all the laws and statutes of this realm for securing the established religion, and the rights and liberties of the people thereof, and all other laws and statutes of the same now in force, may be ratified and confirmed, and the same are by his Majesty, by and with the advice and consent of the said lords spiritual and temporal, and commons, and by authority of the same, ratified and confirmed accordingly.

Act of Union, 1707

6 Anne, c. 11   *Statutes at Large*, XI, 196-201, 205-13.

This act provided for the union of the kingdoms of England and Scotland.

Most gracious Sovereign,

Whereas articles of union were agreed on, the twenty second day of July, in the fifth year of your Majesty's reign, by the commissioners nominated on behalf of the kingdom of England, under your Majesty's great seal of England, bearing date at Westminster the tenth day of April then last past, in pursuance of an act of parliament made in England, in the third year of your Majesty's reign, and the commissioners nominated on the behalf of the kingdom of Scotland, under your Majesty's great seal of Scotland, bearing date the twenty seventh day of February, in the fourth year of your Majesty's reign, in pursuance of the fourth act of the third session of the present parliament of Scotland, to treat of and concerning an union of the said kingdoms: and whereas an act hath passed in the parliament of Scotland at Edinburgh, the sixteenth day of January, in the fifth year of your Majesty's reign, wherein 'tis mentioned, That the estates of parliament considering the said articles of union of the two kingdoms, had agreed to and approved of the said articles of union, with some additions and explanations, and that your Majesty, with advice and consent of the estates of parliament, for establishing the protestant religion and presbyterian church government within the kingdom of Scotland, had passed in the same session of parliament an act, intituled, *An act for securing of the protestant religion and presbyterian church government,* which by the tenor thereof was appointed to be inserted in any act ratifying the treaty, and expresly declared to be a fundamental and essential condition of the said treaty or union in all times coming: the tenor of which articles, as ratified and approved of, with additions and explanations by the said act of parliament of Scotland, follows:

Article I

That the two kingdoms of England and Scotland shall upon the first day of May, which shall be in the year one thousand seven hundred and seven, and for ever after, be united into one kingdom by the name of Great Britain; and that the ensigns armorial of the said united kingdom be such as her Majesty shall appoint, and the crosses of St. George and St. Andrew be conjoined in such manner as her Majesty shall think fit, and used in all flags, banners, standards, and ensigns, both at sea and land.

Article II

That the succession of the monarchy to the united kingdom of Great Britain, and of the dominions thereto belonging, after her most sacred Majesty, and in default of issue of her Majesty, be, remain, and continue to the most excellent princess Sophia, electoress and dutchess dowager of Hanover, and the heirs of her body being protestants, upon whom the crown of England is settled by an act of parliament made in England in the twelfth year of the reign of his late Majesty King William the Third, intituled, *An act for the further limitation of the crown, and better securing the rights and liberties of the subject:* and that all papists, and persons marrying papists, shall be excluded from, and for ever incapable to inherit, possess, or enjoy the imperial crown of Great Britain, and the dominions thereunto belonging, or any part thereof; and in every such case, the crown and government shall from time to time descend to, and be enjoyed by such person, being a protestant, as should have inherited and enjoyed the same, in case such papist, or person marrying a papist, was naturally dead, according to the provision for the descent of the crown of England, made by another act of parliament in England in the first year of the reign of their late majesties King William and Queen Mary, intituled, *An act declaring the rights and liberties of the subject, and settling the succession of the crown.*

Article III

That the united kingdom of Great Britain be represented by one and the same parliament, to be stiled the Parliament of Great Britain.

Article IV

That all the subjects of the united kingdom of Great Britain shall, from and after the union, have full freedom and intercourse of trade and navigation to and from any port or place within the said united kingdom, and the dominions and plantations thereunto belonging; and that there be a communication of all other rights, privileges, and advantages, which do or may belong to the subjects of either kingdom; except where it is otherwise expresly agreed in these articles.

Article V

That all ships or vessels belonging to her Majesty's subjects of Scotland, at the time of ratifying the treaty of union of the two kingdoms in the parliament of Scotland, though foreign built, be deemed, and pass as ships of the built of Great Britain; the owner, or where there are more owners, one or more of the owners, within twelve months after the first of May next, making oath, That at the time of ratifying the treaty of union in the parliament of Scotland, the same did, in whole or in part, belong to him or them, or to some other subject or subjects in Scotland, to be particularly named, with the place of their respective abodes; and that the same doth then, at the time of the said deposition, wholly belong to him or them; and that no foreigner, directly or indirectly, hath any share, part, or interest therein; which oath shall be made before the chief officer or officers of the customs, in the port next to the abode of the said owner or owners; and the said officer or officers shall be impowered to administer the said oath; and the oath being so administred shall be attested by the officer or officers, who administred the same; and being registred by the said officer or officers, shall be delivered to the master of the ship for security of her navigation; and a duplicate thereof shall be transmitted by the said officer or officers, to the chief officer or officers of the customs in the port of Edinburgh, to be there entred in a register, and from thence to be sent to the port of London, to be there entred in the general register of all trading ships belonging to Great Britain.

Article VI

That all parts of the united kingdom for ever, from and after the union, shall have the same allowances, encouragements, and drawbacks, and be under the same prohibitions, restrictions, and regulations of trade, and liable to the same customs and duties on import and export; and that the allowances, encouragements, and drawbacks, prohibitions, restrictions, and regulations of trade, and the customs and duties on import and export, settled in England when the union commences, shall, from and after the union, take place, throughout the whole united kingdom; excepting and reserving the duties upon export and import of such particular commodities, from which any persons, the subjects of either kingdom, are specially liberated and exempted by their private rights, which after the union, are to remain safe and entire to them in all respects, as before the same. And that from and after the union, no Scots cattle carried into England, shall be liable to any other duties, either on the publick or private accounts, than those duties to which the cattle of England are or shall be liable within the said kingdom. And seeing by the laws of England, there are rewards granted upon the exportation of certain kinds of grain, wherein oats grinded or ungrinded are not expressed; that from and after the union, when oats shall be sold at fifteen shillings sterling per quarter, or under, there shall be paid two shillings and six pence sterling for every quarter of the oatmeal exported in the terms of the law, whereby and so long as rewards are granted for exportation of other grains, and that the bear of Scotland have the same rewards as barley: and in respect the importation of victuals into Scotland, from any place beyond sea, would prove a discouragement to tillage, therefore that the prohibition as now in force by the law of Scotland, against importation of victuals from Ireland, or any other place beyond sea into Scotland, do, after the union, remain in the same force as now it is, until more proper and effectual ways be provided by the parliament of Great Britain, for discouraging the importation of the said victuals from beyond sea.

Article VII

That all parts of the united kingdom be for ever, from and after the union, liable to the same excises upon all exciseable liquors, excepting only that the thirty four gallons English barrel of beer or ale, amounting to twelve gallons Scots present measure, sold in Scotland by the brewer at nine shilling six pence sterling, excluding all duties, and retailed, including duties and the retailers profit, at two pence the Scots pint, or eighth part of the Scots gallon, be not after the union liable, on account of the present excise upon exciseable liquors in England, to any higher imposition than two shillings sterling upon the aforesaid thirty four gallons, English barrel, being twelve gallons the present Scots measure: and that the excise settled in England on all other liquors, when the union commences, take place throughout the whole united kingdom.

Article VIII

That from and after the union, all foreign salt which shall be imported into Scotland, shall be charged at the importation there, with the same duties as the like salt is now charged with being imported into England, and to be levied and secured in the same manner: but in regard the duties of great quantities of foreign salt imported may be very heavy upon the merchants importers, that therefore all foreign salt imported into Scotland, shall be cellared and locked up under the custody of the merchant importers, and the officers employed for levying the duties upon salt, and that the merchant may have what quantity thereof his occasion may require, not under a wey or forty bushels at a time, giving security for the duty of what quantity he receives, payable in six months. But Scotland shall, for the space of seven years from the said union, be exempted from paying in Scotland, for salt made there, the duty or excise now payable for salt made in England; but from the expiration of the said seven years, shall be subject and liable to the same duties for salt made in Scotland as shall be then payable for salt made in England, to be levied and secured in the same manner, and with proportionable drawbacks and allowances as in England, with this exception. That Scotland shall, after the said seven years, remain exempted from the duty of two shilling four pence a bushel on home salt, imposed by an act made in England in the ninth and tenth of King William the Third of England; and if the parliament of Great Britain shall, at or before the expiring of the said seven years, substitute any other fund in place of the said two shillings four pence of excise on the bushel of home salt, Scotland shall, after the said seven years, bear a proportion of the said fund, and have an equivalent in the terms of this treaty; and that during the said seven years, they shall be paid in England, for all salt made in Scotland, and imported from thence into England, the same duties upon the importation, as shall be payable for salt made in England, to be levied and secured in the same manner as the duties on foreign salt are to be levied and secured in England; and that after the said seven years, as long as the said duty of two shillings four pence a bushel upon salt is continued in England, the said two shillings and four pence a bushel shall be payable for all salt made in Scotland, and imported into England, to be levied and secured in the same manner; and that during the continuance of the duty of two shillings four pence a bushel upon salt made in England, no salt whatsoever be brought from Scotland to England by land in any manner, under the penalty of forfeiting the salt, and the cattle and carriages made use of in bringing the same, and paying twenty shillings for every bushel of such salt, and proportionably for a greater or lesser quantity, for which the carrier as well as the owner shall be liable, jointly and severally, and the persons bringing or carrying the same to be imprisoned by any one justice of the peace, by the space of six months without bail, and until the penalty be paid. And for establishing an equality in trade, that the flesh exported from Scotland to England, and put on board in Scotland to be exported to parts beyond the seas, and provisions for ships in Scotland, and for foreign voyages, may be salted with Scots salt, paying the same duty for what salt is so employed as the like quantity of such salt pays in England, and under the same penalties, forfeitures, and provisions for preventing of frauds as are mentioned in the laws of England; and that from and after the union, the laws and acts of parliament in Scotland, for pining, curing, and packing of herrings, white fish and salmon for exportation with foreign salt only, without any mixture of British or Irish salt, and for preventing of frauds in curing and packing of fish, be continued in force in Scotland, subject to such alterations as shall be made by the parliament of Great Britain; and that all fish exported from Scotland to parts beyond the seas, which shall be cured with foreign salt only, and without mixture of British or Irish salt, shall have the same eases, premiums, and drawbacks, as are or shall be allowed to such persons as export the like fish from England; and that for encouragement of the herring fishing, there shall be allowed and paid to the subjects, inhabitants of Great Britain, during the present allowances for other fish, ten shillings five pence sterling for every barrel of white herrings which shall be exported from Scotland; and that there shall be allowed five shilling sterling for every barrel of beef or pork salted with foreign salt, without mixture of British or Irish salt, and exported for sale from Scotland to parts beyond sea, alterable by the parliament of Great Britain; and if any matters of fraud relating to the said duties on salt shall hereafter appear, which are not sufficiently provided against by this article, the same shall be subject to such further provisions as shall be thought fit by the parliament of Great Britain.

Article IX

That whensoever the sum of one million nine hundred ninety seven thousand seven hundred and sixty three pounds, eight shillings, and four pence halfpenny, shall be enacted by the parliament of Great Britain to be raised in that part of the united kingdom now called England, on land and other things usually charged in acts of parliament there, for granting an aid to the crown by a land tax; that part of the united kingdom now called Scotland, shall be charged by the same act, with a further sum of forty eight thousand pounds, free of all charges, as the quota of Scotland, to such tax, and so proportionably for any greater or lesser sum raised in England by any tax on land, and other things usually charged together with the land; and that such quota for Scotland, in the cases aforesaid, be raised and collected in the same manner as the cess now is in Scotland; but subject to such regulations in the manner of collecting, as shall be made by the parliament of Great Britain. . . .

Article XVI

That from and after the union, the coin shall be of the same standard and value throughout the united kingdom, as now in England, and a mint shall be continued in Scotland, under the same rules as the mint in England, and the present officers of the mint continued, subject to such regulations and alterations as her Majesty, her heirs or successors, or the parliament of Great Britain shall think fit.

Article XVII

That from and after the union, the same weights and measures shall be used throughout the united kingdom, as are now established in England, and standards of weights and measures shall be kept by those burghs in Scotland, to whom the keeping the standards of weights and measures, now in use there, does of special right belong: all which standards shall be sent down to such respective burghs, from the standards kept in the Exchequer at Westminster, subject nevertheless to such regulations as the parliament of Great Britain shall think fit.

Article XVIII

That the laws concerning regulation of trade, customs, and such excises to which Scotland is, by virtue of this treaty, to be liable, be the same in Scotland, from and after the union, as in England; and that all other laws in use within the kingdom of Scotland, do after the union, and notwithstanding thereof, remain in the same force as before, (except such as are contrary to, or inconsistent with this treaty) but alterable by the parliament of Great Britain; with this difference betwixt the laws concerning publick right, policy, and civil government, and those which concern private right, that the laws which concern publick right, policy, and civil government, may be made the same throughout the whole united kingdom; but that no alteration be made in laws which concern private right, except for evident utility of the subjects within Scotland. . . .

Article XXII

That by virtue of this treaty, of the peers of Scotland, at the time of the union, sixteen shall be the number to sit and vote in the house of lords, and forty five the number of the representatives of Scotland in the house of commons of the parliament of Great Britain; and that when her Majesty, her heirs or successors, shall declare her or their pleasure for holding the first or any subsequent parliament of Great Britain, until the parliament of Great Britain shall make further provisions therein, a writ do issue under the great seal of the united kingdom, directed to the privy council of Scotland, commanding them to cause sixteen peers, who are to sit in the house of lords, to be summoned to parliament, and forty five members to be elected to sit in the house of commons of the parliament of Great Britain, according to the agreement of this treaty, in such manner as by an act of this present session of the parliament of Scotland is or shall be settled; which act is hereby declared to be as valid as if it were a part of, and ingrossed in this treaty. And that the names of the persons so summoned and elected shall be returned by the privy council of Scotland into the court from whence the said writ did issue. And that if her Majesty, on or before the first day of May next, on which day the union is to take place, shall declare under the great seal of England, That it is expedient that the lords of parliament of England, and commons of the present parliament of England, should be the members of the respective houses of the first parliament of Great Britain, for and on the part of England, then the said lords of parliament of England, and commons of the present parliament of England, shall be the members of the respective houses of the first parliament of Great Britain, for and on the part of England: and her Majesty may by her royal proclamation, under the great seal of Great Britain, appoint the said first parliament of Great Britain to meet at such time and place as her Majesty shall think fit; which time shall not be less than fifty days after the date of such proclamation; and the time and place of the meeting of such parliament being so appointed, a writ shall be immediately issued under the great seal of Great Britain, directed to the privy council of Scotland, for the summoning the sixteen peers, and for electing forty five members, by whom Scotland is to be represented in the parliament of Great Britain. And the lords of parliament of England, and the sixteen peers of Scotland, such sixteen peers being summoned and returned in the manner agreed in this treaty, and the members of the house of commons of the said parliament of England, and the forty five members for Scotland, such forty five members being elected and returned in the manner agreed in this treaty, shall assemble and meet respectively, in the respective houses of the parliament of Great Britain, at such time and place as shall be so appointed by her Majesty, and shall be the two houses of the first parliament of Great Britain; and that parliament may continue for such time only, as the present parliament of England might have continued if the union of the two kingdoms had not been made, unless sooner dissolved by her Majesty. And that every one of the lords of parliament of Great Britain, and every member of the house of commons of the parliament of Great Britain, in the first and all succeeding parliaments of Great Britain, until the parliament of Great Britain shall otherwise direct, shall take the respective oaths appointed to be taken instead of the oaths of allegiance and supremacy, by an act of parliament made in England in the first year of the reign of the late King William and Queen Mary, intituled, *An act for the abrogating of the oaths of supremacy and allegiance, and appointing other oaths,* and make, subscribe, and audibly repeat the declaration mentioned in an act of parliament made in England in the thirtieth year of the reign of King Charles the Second, intituled, *An act for the more effectual preserving the King's person and government, by disabling papists from sitting in either house of parliament;* and shall take and subscribe the oath mentioned in an act of parliament made in England, in the first year of her Majesty's reign, intituled, *An act to declare the alterations in the oath appointed to be taken by the act,* intituled, *An act for the further security of his Majesty's person, and the succession of the crown in the protestant line, and for extinguishing the hopes of the pretended prince of Wales, and all other pretenders, and their open and secret abettors, and for declaring the association to be determined;* at such time, and in such manner as the members of both houses of parliament of England are by the said respective acts directed to take, make, and subscribe the same, upon the penalties and disabilities in the said respective acts contained. And it is declared and agreed, That these words, *This realm, The crown of this realm,* and *The Queen of this realm,* mentioned in the oaths and declaration contained in the aforesaid acts, which were intended to signify the crown and realm of England, shall be understood of the crown and realm of Great Britain, and that in that sense the said oaths and declaration be taken and subscribed by the members of both houses of the parliament of Great Britain.

Article XXIII

That the aforesaid sixteen peers of Scotland mentioned in the last preceding article, to sit in the house of lords of the parliament of Great Britain, shall have all privileges of parliament, which the peers of England now have, and which they, or any peers of Great Britain shall have after the union, and particularly the right of sitting upon the trials of peers: and in case of the trial of any peer, in time of adjournment, or prorogation of parliament, the said sixteen peers shall be summoned in the same manner, and have the same powers and privileges at such trial, as any other peers of Great Britain. And that in case any trials of peers shall hereafter happen, where there is no parliament in being, the sixteen peers of Scotland, who sat in the last preceding parliament, shall be summoned in the same manner, and have the same powers and privileges at such trials, as any other peers of Great Britain; and that all peers of Scotland, and their successors to their honours and dignities, shall from and after the union, be peers of Great Britain, and have rank and precedency next and immediately after the peers of the like orders and degrees in England at the time of the union, and before all peers of Great Britain of the like orders and degrees, who may be created after the union, and shall be tried as peers of Great Britain, and shall enjoy all privileges of peers, as fully as the peers of England do now, or as they, or any other peers of Great Britain may hereafter enjoy the same, except the right and privilege of sitting in the house of lords, and the privileges depending thereon, and particularly the right of sitting upon the trials of peers.

Article XXIV

That from and after the union, there be one great seal for the united kingdom of Great Britain, which shall be different from the great seal now used in either kingdom: and that the quartering the arms, and the rank and precedency of the lyon king of arms of the kingdom of Scotland, as may best suit the union, be left to her Majesty: and that in the mean time, the great seal of England be used as the great seal of the united kingdom, and that the great seal of the united kingdom be used for sealing writs to elect and summon the parliament of Great Britain, and for sealing all treaties with foreign princes and states, and all publick acts, instruments and orders of state, which concern the whole united kingdom, and in all other matters relating to England, as the great seal of England is now used: and that a seal in Scotland after the union be always kept and made use of in all things relating to private rights or grants, which have usually passed the great seal of Scotland, and which only concern offices, grants, commissions, and private rights within that kingdom; and that until such seal shall be appointed by her Majesty, the present great seal of Scotland shall be used for such purposes: and that the privy seal, signet, casset, signet of the justiciary court, quarter seal, and seals of courts now used in Scotland be continued; but that the said seals be altered and adapted to the state of the union, as her Majesty shall think fit; and the said seals, and all of them, and the keepers of them, shall be subject to such regulations as the parliament of Great Britain shall hereafter make. And that the crown, scepter, and sword of state, the records of parliament, and all other records, rolls and registers whatsoever, both publick and private, general and particular, and warrants thereof, continue to be kept as they are within that part of the united kingdom now called Scotland; and that they shall so remain in all time coming, notwithstanding the union.

Article XXV

That all laws and statutes in either kingdom, so far as they are contrary to, or inconsistent with the terms of these articles, or any of them, shall, from and after the union, cease and become void, and shall be so declared to be, by the respective parliaments of the said kingdoms.

As by the said articles of union, ratified and approved by the said act of parliament of Scotland, relation being thereunto had, may appear. And the tenor of the aforesaid act for securing the protestant religion and presbyterian church government within the kingdom of Scotland, is as follows:

II. Our sovereign Lady, and the estates of parliament, considering that by the late act of parliament, for a treaty with England for an union of both kingdoms, it is provided, That the commissioners for that treaty should not treat of or concerning any alteration of the worship, discipline, and government of the church of this kingdom as now by law established: which treaty being now reported to the parliament, and it being reasonable and necessary that the true protestant religion, as presently professed within this kingdom, with the worship, discipline, and government of this church, should be effectually and unalterably secured: therefore her Majesty, with advice and consent of the said estates of parliament, doth hereby establish and confirm the said true protestant religion, and the worship, discipline, and government of this church, to continue without any alteration to the people of this land in all succeeding generations; and more especially her Majesty, with advice and consent aforesaid, ratifies, approves, and for ever confirms the fifth act of the first parliament of King William and Queen Mary, intituled, *Act ratifying the confession of faith, and settling presbyterian church government;* with all other acts of parliament relating thereto, in prosecution of the declaration of the estates of this kingdom, containing the claim of right, bearing date the eleventh of April, one thousand six hundred and eighty nine: and her Majesty, with advice and consent aforesaid, expresly provides and declares, That the foresaid true protestant religion, contained in the above mentioned confession of faith, with the form and purity of worship presently in use within this church, and its presbyterian church government and discipline (that is to say) the government of the church by kirk sessions, presbyteries, provincial synods, and general assemblies, all established by the foresaid acts of parliament, pursuant to the claim of right, shall remain and continue unalterable, and that the said presbyterian government shall be the only government of the church within the kingdom of Scotland.

III. And further, for the greater security of the foresaid protestant religion, and of the worship, discipline, and government of this church, as above established, her Majesty, with advice and consent aforesaid, statutes and ordains, That the universities and colleges of Saint Andrews, Glasgow, Aberdeen, and Edinburgh, as now established by law, shall continue within this kingdom for ever; and that in all time coming, no professors, principals, regents, masters, or others, bearing office in any university, college, or school within this kingdom, be capable to be admitted, or allowed to continue in the exercise of their said functions, but such as shall own and acknowledge the civil government in manner prescribed or to be prescribed by the acts of parliament; as also, that before, or at their admissions, they do and shall acknowledge and profess, and shall subscribe to the foresaid confession of faith, as the confession of their faith, and that they will practise and conform themselves to the worship presently in use in this church, and submit themselves to the government and discipline thereof, and never endeavour directly or indirectly the prejudice or subversion of the same, and that before the respective presbyteries of their bounds, by whatsoever gift, presentation or provision they may be thereto provided.

IV. And further, her Majesty, with advice aforesaid, expresly declares, and statutes, That none of the subjects of this kingdom shall be liable to, but all and every one of them for ever free of any oath, test or subscription within this kingdom, contrary to, or inconsistent with the foresaid true protestant religion, and presbyterian church government, worship, and discipline, as above established; and that the same within the bounds of this church and kingdom, shall never be imposed upon, or required of them, in any sort. And lastly, That after the decease of her present Majesty, (whom God long preserve) the sovereign succeeding to her in the royal government of the kingdom of Great Britain, shall in all time coming at his or her accession to the crown, swear and subscribe, that they shall inviolably maintain and preserve the foresaid settlement of the true protestant religion, with the government, worship, discipline, right, and privileges of this church, as above established by the laws of this kingdom in prosecution of the claim of right.

V. And it is hereby statute and ordained, That this act of parliament, with the establishment therein contained, shall be held and observed in all time coming, as a fundamental and essential condition of any treaty or union to be concluded betwixt the two kingdoms, without any alteration thereof, or derogation thereto in any sort for ever: as also, That this act of parliament, and settlement therein contained, shall be insert and repeated in any act of parliament that shall pass for agreeing and concluding the foresaid treaty or union betwixt the two kingdoms; and that the same shall be therein expresly declared to be a fundamental and essential condition of the said treaty or union in all time coming: which articles of union, and act immediately above-written, her Majesty, with advice and consent aforesaid, statutes, enacts, and ordains to be and continue, in all time coming, the sure and perpetual foundation of a compleat and entire union of the two kingdoms of Scotland and England, under the express condition and provision, that this approbation and ratification of the foresaid articles and act shall be no ways binding on this kingdom, until the said articles and act be ratified, approved, and confirmed by her Majesty, with and by the authority of the parliament of England, as they are now agreed to, approved and confirmed by her Majesty, with and by the authority of the parliament of Scotland; declaring nevertheless, that the parliament of England may provide for the security of the church of England as they think expedient, to take place within the bounds of the said kingdom of England, and not derogating from the security above provided for establishing of the church of Scotland within the bounds of this kingdom; as also the said parliament of England may extend the additions and other provisions contained in the articles of union, as above insert, in favours of the subjects of Scotland, to and in favours of the subjects of England; which shall not suspend or derogate from the force and effect of this present ratification, but shall be understood as herein included, without the necessity of any new ratification in parliament of Scotland.

VI. And lastly, her Majesty enacts and declares, That all laws and statutes in this kingdom, so far as they are contrary to, or inconsistent with, the terms of these articles, as above-mentioned, shall from and after the union cease and become void. . . .

Articles of impeachment by the House of Commons against Dr. Henry Sacheverell, and his reply, 10 January 1709

Compleat History of the Whole Proceedings of the Parliament of Great Britain, against Dr. Henry Sacheverell (London: J. Baker, 1710), 11-24.

Impeached for preaching sermons critical of the Revolution of 1688, Sacheverell (1674?-1724) was subsequently convicted by the House of Lords and his sermons were publicly burnt.

Whereas his late Majesty King William the Third, then Prince of Orange, did, with an armed Force, undertake a Glorious Enterprize, for delivering this Kingdom from Popery, and arbitrary Power; and divers Subjects of this Realm, well affected to their Country, joined with, and assisted his late Majesty in the said Enterprize: And it having pleased Almighty God to Crown the same with Success, the late happy Revolution did take Effect, and was established. And whereas the said Glorious Enterprise is approved by several Acts of Parliament, and amongst others by an Act made in the first Year of the Reign of King William and Queen Mary, entitled, *An Act declaring the Rights and Liberties of the Subject, and settling the Succession of the Crown;* and also by another Act made in the same Year, entitled, *An Act for preventing vexatious Suits, against such as acted, in Order to the bringing in their Majesties, or for their Service;* and also by another Act in the same Year, entitled, *An Act for appropriating certain Duties for paying the States-General of the united Provinces their Charges for his Majesty's Expedition into this Kingdom, and for other Uses:* And the Actings of the said well-affected Subjects, in Aid and Pursuance of the said Enterprize, are also declared to have been Necessary, and that the same ought to be Justified. And whereas the happy and blessed Consequences of the said Revolution, are the Enjoyment of the Right of God's true Religion established among us, and of the Laws and Liberties of the Kingdom, the uniting her Majesty's Protestant Subjects in Interest and Affection, by a Legal Indulgence, or Toleration, granted to Dissenters; the Preservation of her Majesty's Sacred Person; the many and continual Benefits arising from her Majesty's wife and glorious Administration, and the Prospect of Happiness for future Ages, by the Settlement of the Succession of the Crown in the Protestant Line, and the Union of the two Kingdoms. And whereas the Lords Spiritual and Temporal, and Commons in Parliament assembled, did, by their Address of the 17th of December, 1705, lay before her Majesty the following Vote, or Resolution, viz. That the Church of England, as by Law established, which was rescued from the extreamest Danger by King William the Third, of glorious Memory, is now, by God's Blessing, under the happy Reign of her Majesty, in a most safe and flourishing Condition; and that whoever goes about to suggest and insinuate, that the Church is in Danger under her

Majesty's Administration, is an Enemy to the Queen, the Church, and the Kingdom. And by their said Address, did humbly beseech her Majesty to take effectual Measures for making the said Vote or Resolution publick; and also for the punishing Authors and Spreaders of such seditious and scandalous Reports. And on the 20th Day of the same December, her Majesty was pleased to issue her Royal Proclamation accordingly: Yet nevertheless the said Henry Sacheverell preached a Sermon at the Assizes held at Darby, August the 15th, in the Year of our Lord 1709, and afterwards published the same in Print, with a Dedication thereof. And the said Henry Sacheverell also preached a Sermon at the Cathedral Church of St. Paul, before the Lord Mayor, Aldermen, and Citizens of London, on the 5th of November last, being the Anniversary from the Gun-powder-Treason, and for beginning the late happy Revolution by giving his late Majesty a safe Arrival here, and for compleating the same, by making all Opposition fall before him, 'till he became our King and Governor, which said Sermon, he the said Henry Sacheverell afterwards likewise published in Print, with a Dedication thereof to Sir Samuel Gerrard, Baronet, Lord Mayor of the City of London: And with a wicked, malicious, and seditious Intention to undermine and subvert her Majesty's Government, and the Protestant Succession, as by Law established; to defame her Majesty's Administration; to asperse the Memory of his late Majesty; to traduce and condemn the late happy Revolution; to contradict and arrain the Resolution of both Houses of Parliament; to create Jealousies and Divisions amongst her Majesty's Subjects, and to incite them to Sedition and Rebellion.

Article I

He, the said Henry Sacheverell, in his said Sermon preached at St. Paul's doth suggest and maintain, That the necessary Means used to bring about the said happy Revolution, were odious and unjustifiable; that his late Majesty in his Declaration, disclaimed the least Imputation of Resistance; and that to impute Resistance to the said Revolution, is to cast black odious Colors upon his late Majesty and the said Revolution.

Article II

He, the said Henry Sacheverell, in his Sermon preached at St. Paul's doth suggest and maintain, That the aforesaid Toleration, granted by the Law, is unreasonable, and the Allowance of it unwarrantable; and asserts, That he is a False Brother with Relation to God's Religion, or the Church, who defends Toleration and Liberty of Conscience; That Queen Elizabeth was deluded by Arch-bishop Grindall, whom he scurrilously calls a false Son of the Church, and a perfidious Prelate to the Toleration of the Genevian Discipline; and that it is the Duty of superior Pastors to thunder out their Ecclesiastical Anathema's against Persons entitled to the Benefit of the said Toleration, and insolently dares, or defies any Power on Earth to reverse such Sentences.

Article III

He, the said Henry Sacheverell, in his Sermon preached at St. Paul's doth falsely and seditiously suggest and assert, That the Church of England is in a Condition of great Peril and Adversity under her Majesty's Administration; and in order to arraign and blacken the said Vote, or Resolution of both Houses of Parliament, approved by her Majesty aforesaid; he, in Opposition thereto, doth suggest the Church to be in Danger; and as a Parallel; mentions a Vote; That the Person of King Charles was Voted to be out of Danger at the same time that his Murderers were conspiring his Death; hereby wickedly and maliciously insinuating, That the Members of both Houses, who passed the said Vote, were then conspiring the Ruin of the Church.

Article IV

He, the said Henry Sacheverell, in his Sermons and Books, doth falsely and maliciously suggest, That her Majesty's Administration, both in Ecclesiastical and Civil Affairs, tends to the Destruction of the Constitution, and that there are Men of Characters and Stations in Church and State, who are False Brethren; and do themselves, weaken, undermine, and betray; and do encourage, and put it into the Power of others, who are professed Enemies, to over-turn and destroy the Constitution and Establishment, and chargeth Her Majesty, and those in Authority under Her, both in Church and State, with a general Male-Administration; and, as a publick Incendiary, he persuades Her Majesty's Subjects to keep up a Distinction of Factions and Parties; instills groundless Jealousies, foments destructive Divisions among them, and excites and stirs them up to Arms and Violence; and that his said malicious and seditious Suggestions may make the stronger Impressions upon the Minds of her Majesty's Subjects. He, the said Henry Sacheverell, doth wickedly wrest and pervert divers Texts and Passages of holy Scripture.

All which Crimes and Misdemeanors the Commons are ready to prove, not only by the general scope of the said Sermons or Books, but likewise by several Clauses and Sentences, and Expressions in the said Sermons or Books contained; and that the said Henry Sacheverell, by preaching the Sermons, and publishing the Books aforesaid, did abuse his holy Function, and hath most grievously offended against the Peace of her Majesty, her Crown and Dignity, the Rights and Liberties of the Subject, the Laws and Statutes of this Kingdom, and the Prosperity and good Government of the same. And the said Commons, by Protestation, saving themselves the Liberty of exhibiting at any time hereafter, any other Articles or Impeachment against the said Henry Sacheverell, and also of replying to his Answer, or any of them; and of offering Proofs of all the Premises, or any of them, and of any other Article or Impeachment, that shall be exhibited by them, as the Case, according to Courts of Parliament shall require, do pray, that the said Henry Sacheverell may be put to answer to all and every the Premises: And that such Proceedings, Examination, Tryal, Judgment, and exemplary Punishment may be thereupon had and executed, as is agreeable to Law and Justice.

On the 13th the Serjeant at Arms acquainted the House, that, in pursuance of their Order of the 15th of December last, he did, yesterday, deliver Dr. Henry Sacheverell to the Deputy of the Gentleman-Usher of the Black-Rod; and had taken a Discharge for him.

Dr. Sacheverell having petitioned the Lords to be Bailed, their Lordships ordered a Committee to enquire into the Validity of his Bail, allowed him Council, and a Copy of the Articles.

The next Day, January 14th, Dr. Sacheverell was ordered to give in his Answer to the Articles next Wednesday. The Lords accepted of Dr. Lancaster, Vice-Chancellor of Oxon, and Dr. Bowes, for his Bail. And accordingly, he was Bailed, himself in a Recognizance of 6000*l.* and his Sureties each in three Thousand Pounds.

Serjeant Prat, Sir Simon Harcourt, Mr. Raymond, and Mr. Phipps, were allowed, by the Lords, to be Council for Dr. Sacheverell: And Mr. Huggins to be his Solicitor.

On the 16th of January Dr. Sacheverell, upon his Petition, had farther Time given him, to put in his Answer.

On the 25th of the same Month, he attended the House of Lords, and delivered in his Answer to the Articles of Impeachment against him, which was read, as follows.

DR. HENRY SACHEVERELL'S ANSWER TO
THE ARTICLES EXHIBITED AGAINST
HIM BY THE COMMONS, IN
MAINTENANCE OF THEIR IMPEACHMENT
FOR HIGH CRIMES AND MISDEMEANORS

The said Hen. Sacheverell, saving to himself all the Advantages of Exception to the said Articles for the Generality, Uncertainty, and Insufficiency thereof, and of not being prejudiced by any Words, or Want of Form in this his Answer, admits, That he preached a Sermon at the Assizes held for the County of Derby, on the 15th Day of August, 1709, at the Request of George Sacheverell, Esq; High-Sheriff of the said County; and another at the Cathedral of St. Paul, at the Desire of the Lord-Mayor of London, Sir Samuel Gerrard, and before the said Lord-Mayor, Aldermen, and Citizens on the 5th of November last; and that he caused the said Sermons to be printed: But denies that he preached, or caused those Sermons to be printed or published, with any such wicked, malicious, or seditious Intent, as in the Preamble to the said Articles is affirmed. The Sermon preached at Derby having been by him printed at the Request of the Gentlemen of the Grand-Jury of that County, and Dedicated it to them as an Acknowledgment for the Honour he received by their publick Approbation of it. And the said Lord-Mayor approved of the Sermon preached at St. Pauls, was at his Request printed with a Dedication to him.

And for Answer to the said Articles Henry Sacheverell humbly said.

Answer to the First Article

To the first Part of the first Article, the said Henry Sacheverell, denies that in his Sermon preached at St. Pauls, He does suggest and maintain, that the necessary Means used to bring about the Revolution, were odious, and unjustifiable. Nor does he in any part of that Sermon, affirm any Thing concerning the Means to bring about the Revolution. He is so far from reflecting on his late Majesty, or the Revolution, that he there endeavours to clear both from the Aspersions of their Enemies.

As to that Part of the said Article, whereby the said Henry Sacheverell is charged, with Suggesting and Maintaining that his late Majesty in his Declaration, disclaimed the least Imputation of Resistance; he does acknowledge himself to have made such Suggestion, and declares he did it in Vindication of his Majesty. The Resistance he represents the late King to have disclaimed, being such as tended to the Conquest of this Realm, as appears by his said Majesty's Declaration referred to, and verbatim set forth at the Bottom of the page, where his Majesty's disclaiming that Imputation is mentioned.

Whether the said Henry Sacheverell was mistaken or not, in expressing himself as if the late King disclaimed any Imputation of Resistance, when he, the said Henry Sacheverell, meant thereby a Design of Conquest, he humbly conceives such a Suggestion, by him designed for the Honour of the late King, cannot reasonably be construed as a Rebellion on his said Majesty, or any Crime, or Misdemeanor.

Farther, to justify what the said Henry Sacheverell said, as to his late Majesty's having disclaimed Resistance, he humbly observes that the following Passages are in his late Majesty's Declaration; *We have thought fit to go over to England, and to carry over with us a Force sufficient, by the Blessing of God, to defend our selves from the Violence of evil Counsellors.—We think fit to declare, that this our Expedition is intended for no other Design, but to have a Free and Lawful Parliament assembled.*

As to the last Charge in the said Article, the said Henry Sacheverell denies, that he doth in his said Sermon suggest and maintain, that to impute Resistance to the said Revolution, is to cast black and odious Colours upon his late Majesty, and the said Revolution; the Persons whom he describes, as reflecting on his late Majesty, and the Revolution, are not those who impute Resistance to the late Revolution, of whom he affirms Nothing, But those new Preachers and new Politicians, who teach, in Contradiction to the Gospel, and the Laws, that the People have the Power vested in them, the Fountain and Original of it, to cancel their Allegiance at their Pleasure, and to call their Sovereign to Account for High-Treason against his Subjects, nay, and to dethrone and murder him for a Criminal, as they did the Royal Martyr by a judiciary Sentence; who are Maintainers of Antimonarchical Schemes, and of such damnable Positions as are, by the Laws of Church and State, condemned for Rebellion and High-Treason; and who urge the Revolution in Defence of such Principles: Unless then those who impute Resistance to the Revolution, be the same with those new Preachers and new Politicians above specifyed, the said Henry Sacheverell affirms Nothing concerning them.

The said Henry Sacheverell does not find that he has given any Pretence to the first Article exhibited against him, in his Sermon preached at St. Pauls, but his bare asserting the Illegality of resisting the Supream Power upon any Pretence whatsoever; for which Assertion he humbly conceives he has the Authority of the Church of England, which, in divers Passages of her Homilies, too numerous to be here specifyed, but by him ready to be produced, teaches this Doctrine, as founded, on the Word of God, particularly in the second Part of the Sermon of Obedience in the Book of Homilies, set forth in the Time of King Edward VI, where are these Words? Here good People, let us all mark diligently: It is not lawful for Inferiors and Subjects in any Case to resist and stand against the Superior Powers, for St. Paul's Words be plain, that whosoever withstandeth, shall get to themselves Damnation; for whosoever withstandeth, withstandeth the Ordinance of God.

The said Book of Homilies, is affirmed in one of the 39 Articles to contain good and wholsome Doctrine, and is ordered to be read in Churches, by the Ministers, to the People. And in farther Maintenance of the said Doctrine contained in the Book of Homilies and their Authority, the said Henry Sacheverell saith, That by an Act of Parliament made in the 13th Year of the Reign of Queen Elizabeth, entituled, *An Act for the Ministers of the Church to be of sound Doctrine,* 'Tis enacted, That no Person should thereafter be admitted to any Benefice with Cure, except he should first have subscribed the said Articles, in the Presence of the Ordinary, and publickly read the same in the Parish-Church of that Benefice, with Declaration of his unfeigned Assent to the same. And that by an Act made in the 5th Year of Her Present Majesty's Reign, entituled, *An Act for securing the Church of England, as by Law established,* it was enacted, That the said Act made in the 13th Year of Q. Elizabeth, should remain and be in full Force for ever; and be inserted in express Terms in any Act which should be made, for ratifying the Union of the two Kingdoms of England and Scotland, and therein declared to be an Essential and Fundamental Part thereof. And the same was accordingly done in an Act for Union of the two Kingdoms.

And the said Henry Sacheverell does further insist that the aforesaid Assertion is warranted by the Common-Law of England, and several Acts of parliament still in Force.

He does farther aver the illegality of Resistance on any Pretence whatsoever to be the Doctrine of the Church of England, and the general Opinion of our most Orthodox Divines, from the Time of the Reformation to this Day; it has been taught by that University, whereof he has been a Member above 30 Years, and often preached and printed, with publick Approbation of each House of Parliament, and maintained by the Reverend Fathers of our Church, Dead and Living, in Terms of greater Force than any used by the said Henry Sacheverell.

Another Motive to him to preach on the 5th of November, against the Doctrine of Resistance, was because then the Church commemorates our Deliverance from the Attempts of Rebellious Papists, the Doctrine of Resisting supreme Powers, being originally theirs, and therefore he conceives the Rubrick of the Office appointed for that Day by the late Q. Mary, directs, that after the Creed, if there be no Sermon, one of the six Homilies against Rebellion shall be read.

The said Henry Sacheverell therefore hopes, That whilst the Church of England flourishes under Her Majesty, whilst Popish Tenets are condemned, and the Laws of the Kingdom continue in their Vigour, a Dutiful Son of the Church shall not be condemned for Asserting the Doctrine of Non-Resistance, but if it should be declared erroneous, and he suffer for asserting it, he trusts God will enable him to shew his steady Belief of it, by a meek Resignation to whatever shall befall him on that Account.

Answer to the Second Article

To that Part of the second Article which charges the said Henry Sacheverell with suggesting and maintaining, That the Toleration granted by Law is unreasonable, and the Allowance of it unwarrantable; he saith, That upon the strictest Enquiry he has not been able to find, that a Toleration has been granted by Law; but admits, that an Act passed in the first Year of K. William and Q. Mary, entituled, *An Act for exempting their Majesty's Protestant Subjects Dissenting from the Church of England from the Penalties of certain Laws.* Which Exemption the said Henry Sacheverell does not any where suggest to be unreasonable, or unwarrantable; but hoped he had prevented any such Misapprehension, by the following Words in his Sermon at St. Pauls: "I would not be here misunderstood, as if I intended to cast the least invidious Reflection upon that Indulgence, which the Government has condescended to give them, which I am sure all those who wish well to our Church are ready to grant to Consciences truly scrupulous: Let them enjoy it in the full Limits the Law has prescribed."

If any other Expressions in the Sermon seem to carry a dubious Sense towards Toleration, he hopes they will be interpreted agreeably to his avowed Approbation of that Law.

To such Part of the second Article as charges the said Henry Sacheverell with asserting, That he is a False Brother, with Relation to God, Religion, or the Church, who defends Toleration and Liberty of Conscience: He saith, That having so plainly declared himself, in Favour of the Exemption granted by Law, he cannot be thought to reflect on the Defenders of that legal Indulgence, which he himself approves, when he blames those who, upon all Occasions, defend Toleration and Liberty of Conscience: He does indeed suggest it to be one Part of the Character of a False Brother, upon all Occasions to defend Toleration and Liberty of Conscience; and, to excuse the Separation, lay the Fault upon the true Sons of the Church, for carrying Matters too high. Which universal Defence of Toleration, and Excuse of Separation, with the laying the Fault of it on the True Sons of the Church, are by him joyntly mentioned in the same Clause, and Branch of the Character. So that he reflects not on all who defend Toleration, much less the Exemption granted by Law to Dissenters, but on those who are for universal Toleration, and lay the Fault of Separation on the True Sons of the Church; whom he did and still does conceive to be blameable, and if Members of the Church to be False Brethren.

As to that Part of the second Article which charges the said Henry Sacheverell with asserting, That Q. Elizabeth was deluded by Archbishop Grindal, to the

Toleration of the Genevian Discipline; he saith, he humbly conceives he has good Authority for it from the Histories of those Times; but whether he has, or not, he apprehends such Assertion to be no Proof of his Suggesting, That the Exemption of Dissenters from certain Laws, granted by an Act in the first Year of K. William, and Q. Mary, is unreasonable or unwarrantable. For he thinks the Difference very great between a Toleration of the Genevian Discipline, and an Exemption of Protestant Dissenters from certain Laws; which Exemption he wisheth under the same Limitations to all Her Majesty's Protestant Subjects.

As to such Part of the second Article, which charges the said Henry Sacheverell, with scurrilously calling the said Archbishop Grindal, a False Son of the Church, and a perfidious Prelate; he hopes any harsh Expressions concerning that Prelate, may be excused, because that Archbishop permitting Innovations in the Church, incurred the Displeasure of Q. Elizabeth, was by her Order Suspended, and so continued to his Death. However, the said Henry Sacheverell presumes, that no Words spoken of a Prelate that has been dead above 120 Years, will amount to an High Crime and Misdemeanor.

To that part of the second Article, which charges the said Henry Sacheverell with maintaining, That it is the Duty of superior Pastors to thunder out their Ecclesiastical Anathema's against Persons entituled to the Benefit of the said Toleration; he saith, He doth not Suggest any such Duty in Pastors, as mentioned in the said Charge; but if the Expressions unapplyed to any, must be determined to any one Sort of Persons, he humbly conceives that Connection in his Discourse will determine them, to those Schismatical and Factious Persons, who take Permission for Power, and advance Toleration immediately into an Establishment; such Schismatical, Factious Persons, he apprehends are not entituled to the Act of Exemption, designed only for the Ease of scrupulous Consciences.

As to the last part of the second Article, which charges the said Henry Sacheverell with insolently daring and defying any Power on Earth to reverse such sentences; he saith, The Sentence he dares any Power on Earth to Reverse is only such as is Ratifyed in Heaven, which he still affirms, and conceives would be Blasphemy in any one to deny. And does further believe, some Sentences pronounced by the Pastors of the Church are Ratifyed in Heaven; and that some Persons exempted from Punishment by the Laws of the Land, may be lyable by the Laws of Christ; and that Schism from a Church imposing no Sinful Terms of Communion, is a Sin, exposing the Persons guilty of it to the Censures of the Church.

Answer to the Third Article

As to so much of the third Article as charges the said Henry Sacheverell, That he does falsly and seditiously suggest, the Church of England is in great Peril and Adversity under her Majesty's Administration, etc. He denies that he has so suggested, or asserted; but does acknowledge, That in his Sermon he suggested, That when National Sins are ripened to a full Maturity, to call down Vengeance from Providence, etc. all the Members of such a Church, or Kingdom, are in Danger in such deplorable Circumstances. Which Suggestion of Danger arising from Vice and Infidelity, he presumes is not opposite to the Vote of the two Houses, or Seditious, but agreeable to what is declared in an Act of the 9th and 10th of the late King William III for the more effectual suppressing of Blasphemy and Prophaness, wherein it is affirmed, That many Persons had, of late Years, openly Avowed and Published many Blasphemous and Impious Opinions, contrary to the Doctrines and Principles of the Christian Religion, greatly tending to the Dishonour of Almighty God, which might prove destructive to the Peace and Welfare of this Kingdom. And he conceives, that since passing that Act, those detestable Crimes have greatly increased. And he apprehends the said Suggestions of Dangers arising from Vice and Infidelity, to be no way more Seditious, than the like Suggestions frequently used before each House of Parliament in the Prayers of the Church, Authorized by her Majesty, wherein we beseech God, that no Sedition may disturb this State, nor Schism distract this Church; and that he would give us Grace seriously to lay to Heart the great Dangers we are in by our unhappy Divisions.

As to so much of the third Article, whereby it is charged, That the said Henry Sacheverell, as a Parallel mentions a Vote, That the Person of K. Charles the first was voted to be out of Danger, at the same Time that his Murderers were conspiring his Death; thereby wickedly and maliciously insinuating, that the Members of both Houses, who passed the said Vote, were then conspiring the Ruin of the Church. He answers, That he draws no Parallel between those two Votes, the latter of which he no where mentions in his Sermon. But had he suggested any such Parallel, which he did not, it would not have insinuated that the Members of both Houses who passed the late Vote, were conspiring the Ruin of the Church; but only that as some innocent Persons voted the King to be out of Danger, whilst others were conspiring his Murders; so when the two Houses voted the Church to be out of Danger, some others might be conspiring its Ruin, and others drawing down God's Vengeance by their Vice and Infidelity.

As the Vote of both Houses, made four Years ago, only concerned those who did insinuate the Churches being in Danger under Her Majesty's Administration; so he presumes it cannot affect those who suggest the Christian Faith to be in Danger by those Atheistical, and irreligious Principles daily propagated from the Press. So that he thinks he might with Truth affirm in his Sermon at Derby, That there never were such outragious Blasphemies against God, etc. of which Assertion he is ready to bring undeniable and ample Proofs.

Answer to the Fourth Article

The fourth Article contains several Charges of a very high and criminal Nature, of which the said Henry Sacheverell knows his Heart to be entirely innocent; and with Comfort observes, that in the other Articles he is said to have maintained and asserted, as well as suggested the Matter charged upon him, but in this fourth he is only accused of Suggesting and Insinuating.

To that Part of the fourth Article, whereby it is charged, That the said Henry Sacheverell, in his said Sermons and Books, doth falsly and maliciously suggest, that Her Majesty's Administration, both in Ecclesiastical and Civil Affairs, tends to the Destruction of the Constitution, he answers, That he has not, in either of his Books or Sermons, made any mention of her Majesty's Administration, or of her Ministers; but is so far from suggesting, that it leads to the Destruction of the Constitution, that amongst the Blessings owing to our Deliverance, annually Commemorated on the Fifth of November, he reckons this to be one, That her Majesty sits on the Throne, and prays to God to preserve her, etc. And in his Dedication of his said Sermon preached at St. Pauls, solemnly declares, as he did before in his Discourse, That his only Aim and Intention was earnestly to contend for the Safety, Rights, and Establishment of her Majesty, together with those of the Church.

To that Part of the fourth Article, whereby it is charged, That the said Henry Sacheverell does suggest, That there are Men of Characters and Stations in the Church, who are False Brethren; he saith, That the False Brethren, as described by him in his Sermon, are either those who propagate false Doctrines, or who give up the Discipline and Worship of the Church, or who are for a Neutrality in Religion, or who wish well to the Church of England, and are ready to Sacrifice their Persons and Estates in her Vindication, but not show their Zeal in the Communion of the Church, as well as for it, in obeying her Precepts as well as defending her Rights. These being the Sorts of False Brethren by him enumerated, if he should have suggested, that there are Men of Characters and Stations in the Church, Words not restrained to the highest Characters and Stations, to whom that Denomination in some Sense does belong, he hopes that suggestion would not be deemed False, Malicious, or highly Criminal.

Whereas in this fourth Article it is charged, That the said Henry Sacheverell does suggest, That there are Men of Characters and Stations in the Church and State, who do themselves weaken, undermine and betray, and do encourage, and put into the power of others who are professed Enemies, to overturn and destroy the Constitution and Government; he denies the suggesting any such Things of Men of Characters and Stations in Church or State, those not being mentioned where he speaks of such as weaken, undermine, betray, etc. as above in the Charge; and where they are mentioned twelve Pages afterwards, he speaks nothing of weakening, and undermining, betraying, etc. or above, and therefore hopes he shall not be answerable for a supposed Reflection, depending upon a Conjunction of Passages so remote from one another. The Weakeners, Underminers, and Betrayers, to whom he refers, will, upon Examination, appear to be one of these three Sorts of Persons; either, First such as by their Writings endeavour to subvert the Foundations of our Church and State; or, Secondly, such whether Writers or others who are for a Latitudinarian Heterogeneous mixture of all Persons of what Faith soever, uniting only in Protestancy, etc. or Thirdly, Those Occasional Conformists, who have so far eluded the Corporation, and Test Acts by their abominable Hypocrisie, as to have undermined and endangered the Government, by filling it (as far as they could) with its professed Enemies, that is, with themselves. Of these and their Encouragers he confesses he has suggested that, in his Opinion, they weaken, undermine, and betray the Constitution; but has no where suggested, that they are Men of Characters and Stations in the Church or State.

As to the Part of the fourth Article that accuses the said Henry Sacheverell, of charging Her Majesty, and those in Authority under Her, both in Church and State, with a general Male-Administration; he says, He abhors the Thoughts of such a Charge against her Majesty; nor does he ever tax those in Authority with any Male-Administration, a Word he has never used, nor any other by which the Thing may be implyed. And he is so far from making any undutiful Reflections on her Majesty, or her Administration, that in several Writings he has published, and particularly one in Defence of her Title to the Crown, and Justification of her entering into a War with France, he has expressed himself with the most Hearty and Loyal Zeal for her Majesty's Person, Government, and Administration.

To the Charge, That the said Henry Sacheverell, as a publick Incendiary persuades her Majesty's Subjects to keep up a Distinction of Factions and Parties; he says he is so far from it, that in his said Sermon, he invites the Separalists to renounce their Schism, and come sincerely into the Church, etc.

To the accusation in the same Article, That the said Henry Sacheverell instils groundless Jealousies, and foments destructive Divisions among her Majesty's Subjects; he says, That in his said Sermon, he, on the contrary, Rebukes and Condemns those, who, by false Insinuations, imbroil the Publick.

To what is farther urged, That the said Henry Sacheverell excites and stirs up her Majesty's Subjects to Arms and Violence, he answers, God forbid he should be guilty to so heinous a Crime; who asserts the Utter illegality of Resistance to the Supreme Power; which assertion he conceives to be the chief, or only Ground of the Charge exhibited against him in the first Article.

For Confutation of this Charge, he offers one Passage out of his Sermon preached at Derby, in these Words; "We may be Partakers of other Mens Sins, if we do not, to the utmost of our Power, endeavour to obstruct, or prevent their Commission, when they manifestly endanger the Good of the Publick, etc." And he hopes, That what he has said in the Dedication of the same Sermon, "That there are not wanting some to preach the Truth, and others to support it, at the expence of their Lives and Fortunes," will not be construed, as exciting her Majesty's Subjects to Sedition, and Rebellion, since that Truth is by him opposed to the Attempts of those who betray the Principles and Interests of our Church and Constitution.

In the Sermon preached at St. Pauls, he excites Christians to put on the whole Armour of God, as wrestling, not only against Flesh and Blood, but against Principalities, against Powers, against the Rulers of the Darkness of this World, against Spiritual Wickedness in high Places. But the same St. Paul has taught him, That the Arms of Resistance taken up by Subjects against the higher Powers, are none of that Spiritual Armour; and the Principalities and Powers he speaks of, being plainly distinguished from Flesh and Blood, cannot, he thinks, be understood of Earthly Rulers.

As to the last part of this fourth Article, charging the said Henry Sacheverell with wickedly wresting and perverting divers Texts and Passages of Holy Scripture for imprinting his malicious Suggestions; he says, He had no Malicious Suggestions to imprint, and therefore no occasion to wrest the Scriptures. It is hard with the Ministers of the Gospel, if the Texts they cite shall be construed in the most criminal Sense, when they use them to excite Virtue, or reprove Mens Transgressions.

As to all other Matters in the said Articles contained, and nowhere Answered unto, the said Henry Sacheverell says, he is not Guilty of them, or any of them, in Manner and Form as they are Charged on him in and by the said Articles; and humbly submits himself to your Lordships Judgments.

LORDS AND COMMONS

Ashby v. White: Judgment by Chief Justice Holt of the Court of Queen's Bench, 1704

English Reports, XC, 1188-89.

Sir John Holt (1642-1710), the chief justice, supported Matthew Ashby's contention that he had been unfairly deprived of the right to vote in a parliamentary election at Aylesbury. This judgment was upheld by the Lords but rejected in a series of resolutions by the Commons. At stake was the relationship between common law and parliamentary privilege.

In action upon the case against the constables of Ailesbury, the plaintiff declared, that such a day the late King's writ issued and was delivered to the Sheriff of B. for election of members of Parliament in his country; whereupon the said sheriff made out his precept or warrant to the defendants, being constables of A. to chuse two burgesses for that borough, which precept was delivered to the said constables; and that, in pursuance thereof, the burgesses were duly assembled, etc. and the plaintiff, being then duly qualified to vote for the election of two burgesses, offered to give his voice for Sir. T. L. and S. M. Esq; to be burgesses of Parliament for the said borough; but the defendants knowing the premises, with malice, etc. obstructed him from voting, and refused and would not receive his vote, nor allow it; and that two burgesses were chose, without allowing or receiving his voice: a verdict was found for the plaintiff; and upon motion in arrest of judgment, three Judges held, that this action would not lie, 'till the Parliament had decided, whether the plaintiff had a right to vote as an elector.

Holt C. J. The case is truly stated, and the only question is, whether or not, if a burgess of a borough, that has an undoubted right to give his vote for the chusing a burgess of Parliament for that borough, is refused giving his vote, has any remedy in the King's Courts for this wrong against the wrong-doer? All my brothers agree, that he has no remedy; but I differ from them, for I think the action well maintainable, that the plaintiff had a right to vote, and that in consequence thereof the law gives him a remedy, if he is obstructed; and this action is the proper remedy. By the common law of England, every commoner hath a right not be subjected to laws, made without their consent; and because it cannot be given by every individual man in person, by reason of number and confusion, therefore that power is lodged in their representatives, elected by them for that purpose, who are either knights, citizens or burgesses: and the grievance here is, that the party not being allowed his vote, is not represented. The election of knights of shires is by freeholders; and a freeholder has a right to vote by reason of his freehold, and it is a real right; and the value of his freehold was not material till the Statute of H. 7, which requires it should be 40s. a-year, for before that every freeholder, though of never so small a value, had a right to vote at these elections. In boroughs, some of which are by prescription, they have a right of voting ratione burgagii, and ratione tenurae; and this like the case of a freeholder before mentioned is a real right, annexed to the tenure in burgage: and in cities and corporations, it is a personal inheritance, and vested in the whole corporation, but to be used and exercised by the particular members; and such a privilege cannot be granted but to a corporation. This is a noble franchise and right, which entitles the subject in a share of the Government and Legislature. And here the plaintiff having this right, it is apparent that the officer did exclude him from the enjoyment of it, wherein none will say he has done well, but wrong to the plaintiff; and it is not at all material whether the candidate, that he would have voted for, were chosen, or likely to be, for the plaintiff's right is the same, and being hindered of that, he has injury done him, for which he ought to have remedy. It is a vain thing to imagine, there should be right without a remedy; for want of right and want of remedy are convertibles: if a statute gives a right, the common law will give remedy to maintain it; and where-ever there is injury, it imports a damage: and there can be no petition in this case to the Parliament, nor can they judge of this injury, or give damages to the plaintiff. Although this matter relates to the Parliament, yet it is an injury precedaneous to the Parliament; and where Parliamentary matters come before us, as incident to a cause of action concerning the property of the subject, which we in duty must determine, though the incident matter be Parliamentary, we must not be deterred, but are bound by our oaths to determine it. The law consists not in particular instances, but in the reason that rules them; and if where a man is injured in one sort of right he has a good action, why shall he not have it in another? And though the House of Commons have right to decide elections, yet they cannot judge of the charter originally, but secondarily in the determination of the election; and therefore where an election does not come in debate, as it doth not in this case, they have nothing to do: and we are to exert and vindicate the Queen's jurisdiction, and not to be frighted because it may come in question in Parliament; and I know nothing to hinder us from judging of matters depending on charter or prescription: he concluded for the plaintiff.

Here judgment being given for the defendant, contrary to the opinion of the Chief Justice; on a writ of error afterwards brought in the House of Lords, the judgment was reversed by a great majority of the Lords, who concurred with Holt C. J.

Parliamentary Qualification Act, 1710

9 Anne, c. 5   *Statutes of the Realm*, IX, 365-66.

This act established property qualifications for members of the House of Commons. Such qualifications were not removed until 1858.

For the better preserving the Constitution and Freedom of Parliament Be it enacted and declared by the Queen's most Excellent Majesty by and with the Advice and Consent of the Lords Spiritual and Temporal and Commons in this present Parliament assembled and by the Authority of the same That from and after the Determination of this present Parliament no Person shall be capable to sit or vote as a Member of the House of Commons for any County City Borough or Cinque-Port within that Part of Great Britain called England the Dominion of Wales and Town of Berwick upon Tweed who shall not have an Estate Freehold or Copyhold for his own Life or for some greater Estate either in Law or Equity to and for his own Use and Benefit of or in Lands Tenements or Hereditaments over and above what will satisfie and clear all Incumbrances that may affect the same lying or being within that Part of Great Britain called England the Dominion of Wales and Town of Berwick upon Tweed of the respective annual Value hereafter limited videlicet the annual Value of Six hundred Pounds above Reprizes for every Knight of a Shire and the annual Value of Three hundred Pounds above Reprizes for every Citizen Burgess or Baron of the Cinque-Ports and that if any Person who shall be elected or returned to serve in any Parliament as a Knight of a Shire or as a Citizen Burgess or Baron of the Cinque-Ports shall not at the Time of such Election and Return be seised of or entitled to such an Estate in Lands Tenements or Hereditaments as for such Knight or for such Citizen Burgess or Baron respectively is herein before required or limited such Election and Return shall be void

Provided always That nothing in this Act contained shall extend to make the eldest Son or Heir Apparent of any Peer or Lord of Parliament or of any Person qualified by this Act to serve as Knight of a Shire uncapable of being elected and returned and sitting and voting as a Member of the House of Commons in any Parliament

Provided always That nothing in this Act contained shall extend or be construed to extend to either of the Universities in that Part of Great Britain called England but that they and each of them may elect and return Members to represent them in Parliament as heretofore they have done Any thing herein contained to the contrary notwithstanding

Provided always and it is hereby enacted by the Authority aforesaid That every Person (except as aforesaid) who from and after the Determination of this present Parliament shall appear as a Candidate or shall by himself or any others be proposed to be elected to serve as a Member of the House of Commons for any County City Borough or Cinque Port in England Wales or Berwick upon Tweed shall and he is hereby enjoyned and required upon reasonable Request to him to be made (at the Time of such Election or before the Day to be prefixed in the Writ of Summons for the Meeting of the Parliament) by any other Person who shall stand Candidate at such Election or by any Two or more Persons having Right to vote at such Election take a Corporal Oath in the Form or to the Effect following

I, A. B. do swear That I truly and bona fide have such an Estate in Law or Equity to and for my own Use and Benefit of or in Lands Tenements or Hereditaments (over and above what will satisfie and clear all Incumbrances that may affect the same) of the annual Value of Six hundred Pounds above Reprizes as doth qualify me to be elected and returned to serve as a Member for the County of   according to the Tenour and true Meaning of the Act of Parliament in that Behalf and that my said Lands Tenements or Hereditaments are lying or being within the Parish Township [or Precinct of   or in the several Parishes Townships] or Precincts of   in the County of   or in the several Counties of   (as the Case may be)

And in case such Candidate or Person is to serve for any City Borough or Cinque-Port then the said Oath shall relate only to the said Value of Three hundred Pounds per Annum and be taken to the same Effect (mutatis mutandis) as is hereby prescribed for the Oath of a Person to serve as a Member for such County as aforesaid

And it is hereby enacted That the respective Oaths aforesaid shall and may be administered by the Sheriff of Undersheriff for any such County as aforesaid or by the Mayor Bailiff or other Officer or Officers for any City Borough or Port to whom it shall appertain to take the Poll or make the Return at such Election for the same County Borough or Port respectively or by any Two or more Justices of the Peace within England Wales and Berwick upon Tweed And the said Sheriff Mayor Bailiff or other Officers and the said Justices of the Peace respectively who shall administer the said Oaths are hereby required to certify the taking thereof into Her Majesties High Court of Chancery or the Queens Bench within Three Months after the taking the same under the Penalty of forfeiting the Sum of One hundred Pounds to wit One Moiety thereof to the Queen and the other Moiety thereof to such Person or Persons as will sue for the same to be recovered with full Costs of Suit by Action of Debt Bill Plaint or Information in any of Her Majesties Courts of Record at Westminster and if any of the said Candidates or Persons proposed to be elected as aforesaid shall wilfully refuse upon reasonable Request to be made at the Time of the Election or at any Time before the Day upon which such Parliament by the Writ of Summons is to meet to take the Oath hereby required then the Election and Return of such Candidate or Person shall be void

And it is hereby enacted That no Fee or Reward shall be taken for administering any such Oath or making receiving or filing the Certificate thereof except One Shilling for administring the Oath and Two Shillings for [making the Certificate and Two Shillings for] receiving and filing the same under the Penalty of Twenty Pounds to be forfeited by the Offender and to be recovered and divided as aforesaid.

Report of the Commissioners for examining the duke of Marlborough's accounts, 21 December 1711

Parliamentary History, VI, 1049-56.

Accused of mismanagement and bribery, John Churchill, first duke of Marlborough (1650-1722), was dismissed by Queen Anne from all his offices. In 1714, on the accession of George I, he returned to his military post.

Your Commissioners humbly represent, That though they have used their utmost application in taking and examining the Public Accounts, yet they are unprepared to offer any perfect state of the particular branches of the Revenue to the House: but will endeavour to lay before you, after the recess, a general Account of the Receipts and Issues of her majesty's exchequer for the current year 1711; which they hope, is all will, for the present, be expected from them: as well in regard of the shortness of the time they have been engaged in this work, as of the great variety and extent of it: they beg leave also to observe, that many of the accounts are not yet completely brought before them; particularly those of the Army, which are very large and voluminous.

But in the course of their Examinations relating to the Affairs of the Army, they have already discovered some Practices, which they conceive highly detrimental to the public, and such as they are obliged to report to you. In obedience therefore to your order, of Tuesday the 11th instant, your commissioners here present a State of several Facts; which with their circumstances and proofs, they humbly offer to the wisdom and justice of the House.

Your commissioners having ground to believe, that there had been some Mismanagements in making the contracts for the use of the Army, summoned, and examined, Sir Solomon De Medina, the Contractor for the Bread, and Bread-Waggons, in the Low-countries, who, after expressing much uneasiness on the apprehensions he had of being thought an informer and of accusing a great man, did depose:

That for the years 1707, 1708, 1709, 1710, and 1711, he has been solely, or in partnership, concerned in the contracts for supplying bread, and bread-waggons, to the forces in the Low countries, in the queen of Great Britain's pay; and that he gave to the duke of Marlborough, for his own use, on each contract, the several sums following; part of which was paid at the beginning, and part at the end, of each respective contract, in bills or notes delivered by the deponent into the duke's own hands; viz. for the year 1707, 66,600 guilders; for the year 1708, 62,625 guilders; for the year 1709, 69,578 guilders and 15 stivers; for the year 1710, 66,810 guilders 19 stivers and 8 pennings: Total, 265,614 guilders 14 stivers and 8 pennings: for the year 1711, 21,000 guilders; which sum is, in part of a like sum with those above-mentioned, intended to be paid at the end of the contract for this year: That he was obliged to allow yearly, during the time of his being contractor, 12 or 14 waggons, gratis, to the duke of Marlborough: That during the time of his being contractor, as aforesaid, he gave on sealing each contract, a gratuity of 500 gold ducats to Mr. Cardonnell, Secretary to the duke of Marlborough: That for the money he received of Mr. Sweet, deputy paymaster at Amsterdam, he was obliged to pay 1*l*. per cent: that the former contractor, Machado, did the same; and that he acquainted the duke of Marlborough with this deduction of 1*l*. per cent.

He further deposed, That it appeared by the accounts of Antonio Alvarez Machado, who had been a contractor before him, and had supplied the bread, and bread-waggons, to the forces in English pay, for the years 1702, 1703, 1704, 1705, and 1706, That he, the said Machado, had paid as large yearly sums to the duke of Marlborough, during the time of his being contractor, as this deponent has since done.

From whence it appears, that the duke of Marlborough has received, on account of the bread, and bread-waggon contracts, from sir Solomon de Medina (admitting the sum already paid, and what is intended to be paid, for this present year 1711, to be the same with that of the preceding year, 1710,) 332,425 guilders and 14 stivers. From Antonio Alvarez Machado, during the five years he was contractor, the like sums, which together make 664,851 guilders 8 stivers, and computed at 10 guilders 10 stivers to the pound sterling, amount to 63,410*l*. 3*s*. 7*d*.

Some time after this Evidence was given by sir Solomon de Medina, your commissioners received a letter from the duke of Marlborough by the hands of James Craggs, esq. wherein the duke desires your commissioners, that when they make their Report they would lay some facts before the parliament in a true light, and this justice they think they cannot better do than in his grace's own words.

Hague, Nov. 10, 1711

Gentlemen;

Having been informed upon my arrival here yesterday, that sir Solomon Medina had acquainted you with my having received several sums of money from him, that it may make the less impression upon you, I would lose no time in letting you know, that this is no more than what has always been allowed as a perquisite to the general or commander in chief of the army in the Low-countries, both before the Revolution and since; and I do assure you, at the same time, that whatever sums I have received on that account, have constantly been applied for the service of the public, in keeping secret correspondence, and getting intelligence of the enemies motions and designs; and it has fallen so short, that I take leave to acquaint you with another article that has been applied to the same use, and which arises from her majesty's warrant whereof the inclosed is a copy, though this does not properly relate to the public accounts, being a free-gift from the foreign troops. You will have observed, by the several establishments, that, before the late king's death, when the parliament voted 40,000 men for the quota of England in the Low-countries, 21,612 were to be foreigners, and the rest English; for the last they gave 10,000*l*. a year for intelligence, and other contingencies, without account; but his majesty being sensible, by the experience of the last war, that this sum would not any way answer that service, and being unwilling to apply for any more to the parliament, he was pleased to order, that the foreign troops should contribute 2½ per cent towards it; and I being then his ambassador and commander in chief abroad, he directed me to propose it to them, with an assurance that they should have no other stoppage made from their pay; this they readily agreed to, and her majesty was afterwards pleased to confirm it by her warrant, upon my acquainting her with the use it was intended for; and it has accordingly been applied from time to time for intelligence and secret service, with such success, that, next to the blessing of God on the bravery of out troops, we may, in a great measure, attribute most of the advantages of the war in this country to the timely and good advices procured with the help of this money. And now, gentlemen, as I have laid the whole matter very fairly before you, and that I hope you will allow, I have served my queen and country with that zeal and faithfulness which becomes an honest man, the favour I am to entreat of you, is, that, when you make your report to the parliament, you will lay this part before them in its true light, so as that they may see this necessary and important part of the war has been provided for and carried on without any other expence to the public than the 10,000l. a year; and I flatter myself, that, when the accounts of the army in Flanders come under your consideration, you will be sensible the service on this side has been carried on with all the economy and good husbandry that was possible.

I am, Gentlemen, etc.

Marlborough

[Enclosure]

Anne R.

Right trusty, and right well-beloved cousin and counsellor, we greet you well. Whereas, pursuant to the direction you have received in that behalf, you have agreed with the persons authorised to treat with you for the taking into our service a certain number of foreign troops, to act in conjunction with the forces of our allies, that there be reserved 2½ per cent. out of all moneys payable to, and for the said troops, as well for their pay and entertainment, as on any other account, towards defraying such extraordinary, contingent expences relating to them, as cannot otherwise be provided for. Now, we do hereby approve and confirm all such agreements as you have, or may hereafter make, for reserving the said 2½ per cent. accordingly; and do likewise hereby authorise and direct the paymaster general of our forces for the time being, or his deputy, to make the said deduction of 2½ per cent. pursuant thereunto, out of all moneys he shall be directed to issue, for the use of the foreign troops in our pay, and thereupon to pay over the same from time to time according to such warrants, and in such proportions as you shall direct; for which this shall be to you, and to all others whom it may concern, a sufficient warrant and direction.

Given at our court at St. James's, this 6th day of July, 1702, and in the first year of our reign.

By her Majesty's Command,

C. Hedges

To our right trusty, and right well-beloved Cousin and Counsellor, John, Earl of Marlborough, our Ambassador Extraordinary, and Plenipotentiary to the States General of the United-Provinces, and Captain-General of our Land-Forces.

Your Commissioners having thought themselves obliged to recite this letter and warrant at large, humbly conceive it will be expected that they should make some observations upon them; as to what therefore relates to the evidence of sir Solomon de Medina, his grace has been pleased to admit it in general, but with this distinction, that he claims the sums received, as perquisites to the general in the Low-countries.

On which your Commissioners observe, that so far as they have hitherto been capable of informing themselves in the constitution of the army, the great sums, which appear to have been annually paid to the duke, on account of these contracts, can never be esteemed legal or warrantable perquisites.

For they do not find, by the strictest enquiry they can make, that any other English general in the Low-countries, or elsewhere, ever claimed, or received such perquisites; but if any instance should be produced, they humbly apprehend it will be no justification of it, because the public or the troops must necessarily suffer in proportion to every such perquisite; and how agreeable this practice is to that economy and good husbandry with which the service in Flanders is said to be carried on, remains yet to be explained. By the assurance his grace is pleased to give, that this money has been constantly employed for the service of the public, it must be either allowed, that he relinquishes his right to this pretended perquisite, or that he has been wanting to himself in concealing so great an instance of his own generosity to the public.

The great caution and secrecy with which this money was constantly received, gives reason to suspect that it was not thought a justifiable perquisite, for Mr. Cardonnell the duke's secretary, and auditor of the bread-account, has declared on oath, that he never knew or heard of any such perquisite, until the late rumour of sir Solomon de Medina's evidence before your Commissioners. By the contracts for bread, and bread-waggons, the general appears to be the sole check on the contractors; he is to take care that the terms of the contractors are duly performed; he is to judge of all deductions to be made from, and allowance to the contractors; and whether, in such circumstances, he can receive any gratuity, or perquisite from the contractors, without a breach of his trust, your Commissioners presume not to determine. The general may with equal reason claim a perquisite for every other contract relating to the army, as for these of the bread, and bread-waggons; but his grace being silent as to this, your Commissioners ought to suppose he has not received any such allowance, unless they shall understand otherwise when they come to examine into those contracts, which hitherto they have not been able to do, by reason the contractors are foreigners, and constantly reside in Holland.

As to what his grace is pleased to say in the second part of his letter, concerning the deduction of the 2½ per cent. from the foreign troops in her majesty's pay, your Commissioners can only offer such remarks as occur to them, on comparing what is urged in the duke's letter, with the tenor of the warrant, and with the method of accounting for other payments to the army. Your Commissioners in the first place take leave to observe, that this warrant has been kept dormant for 9 years, and the deduction concealed so long from the knowledge of the parliament; for which, in their humble apprehension, his grace has not assigned sufficient reasons.

He is pleased to say, that this 2½ per cent. is a free gift from the foreign troops, and that it does not belong to the Public Accounts. But the first of these assertions seems inconsistent, not only with the words of the warrant, which supposes and expresses an agreement, but with that part of his grace's letter which takes notice, that he being ambassador and general, stipulated for this very stoppage by the late king's order. Your Commissioners therefore must be of opinion, that a deduction so made is public money, and ought to be accounted for in the same manner as other public money is.

His grace is further pleased to observe, that the 10,000*l.* granted yearly for the contingencies of the army, is without account, and for the use of the British forces only; whereas this money was at first intended by parliament, as your Commissioners with great submission apprehend, for the service of the 40,000 men, without distinction. And they find it is so far from having always been thought exempt from account, that in a privy seal dated the 5th day of March, 1706, for passing Mr. Fox's accounts, there is a clause to release and discharge the duke of Marlborough, his heirs, executors, and administrators, from a sum of 7,499*l.* 19*s.* 10*d.* part of this money, which supposes his grace would otherwise have been accountable for it. But your Commissioners do not here meet with any mention of this deduction of 2½ per cent. and must therefore presume, the reason why it has never been brought to an account, is what his grace is pleased to suggest, that he never considered it as public money.

Your Commissioners must submit it to the House, whether the warrant produced to justify this deduction be legal, and duly countersigned; or whether admitting it to be so, either the stoppage, or the payment of it has been regularly made. The warrant directs, that it should be stopt in the hands of the paymaster or his deputy, and issued thence by the duke's order only: But this method does not appear by the paymaster's accounts to have been at all pursued, so far otherwise, that the payments to the foreign troops are always made compleat, and their receipts always taken in full without any notice of this deduction. When any part of the above-mentioned 10,000*l.* contingent-money is drawn out of the paymasters' hands for any secret service, the general's warrant, and the secretary's receipts, are the paymaster's vouchers: But Mr. Cardonnell, as he declares on oath, never gave any receipt for any part of this 2½ per cent. nor did Mr. Bridges, as he also declares on oath, ever see any warrant for that purpose, or knew any thing, as paymaster-general, of this deduction.—If Mr. Sweet at Amsterdam, has taken upon himself to transact the disposition of this 2½ per cent. with the duke of Marlborough, your commissioners are humbly of opinion that he ought to have transmitted constant accounts of it to Mr. Bridges, whose agent he only is, and not to have negociated so large sums of public money in so clandestine a manner.—By the Warrant this deduction is reserved for the defraying extraordinary contingent expenses of the troops, from whom it is stopped: And if the whole has been employed in secret correspondence and intelligence, there must have been some neglect of the other services for which it was originally designed; and such a disposition being in no sort authorised by the warrant, is a misapplication of it. Besides, your commissioners apprehend, that the article for secret service, to which this deduction is pretended to have been applied, was always included in the 10,000*l.* above-mentioned for the contingencies of the army; and, if so, the whole remains to be accounted for; which, on a computation made from the whole sum of 11,294,659*l.* 4*s.* 1½*d.* paid per Britain to, and for all the foreign forces since the 13th Dec. 1701, (according to the Returns of the auditor and paymaster) amounts to 282,366*l.* 9*s.* 7*d.*—On a computation made from the sum of 7,107,873*l.* 18*s.* 11½*d.* paid to and for the foreign forces since the time aforesaid, (exclusive of Italy, Spain, and Portugal) amounts to 177,695*l.* 17*s.* 0¼*d.*

Your Commissioners humbly lay before you some facts relating to the Forage-contracts, (for the troops in North Britain) made by Robert Walpole, esq. late secretary of war, pursuant to a power given him by Sidney earl of Godolphin then Lord High Treasurer of Great-Britain.

By the rate allowed in these contracts, it appearing that her majesty had been put to an extraordinary expence above the pay of the soldiers, your commissioners thought it their duty to enquire, whether, in this part of the service, sufficient care had been taken to procure the most advantageous terms for the public; and being informed that John Montgomery, esq. was concerned in these contracts, they examined him, and he declared upon oath, that col. George Douglas, and himself, were assumed partners with sir Samuel Macklellan, and Mr. John Campbell, in the contract made by Mr. Walpole to provide forage from the middle of May, 1709, to May, 1710, for all the troops in North Britain at 3*d.* an horse for green, and 9*d.* for dry forage, each 24 hours.

That the said colonel George Douglas, and he the said Mr. Montgomery, were also assumed partners with Mr. John Campbell in a subsequent contract, commencing in May, 1710, and ending in May, 1711, made likewise by Mr. Walpole, and at the same rates with the former.

That the first of these contracts was made by Mr. Walpole in London with sir Samuel Macklellan, who before he went into Scotland told the said Montgomery, that Mr. Walpole, in making the contract, reserved a share for a friend of his, who was to have the benefit of a fifth part, if not redeemed by the contractors with a sum of money; and sir Samuel soon after, on his death-bed, at Edinburgh, declared the same: Whereupon, colonel Douglas, and Mr. John Campbell, directed him, the said Mr. Montgomery, to pay 500 guineas to the said Mr. Walpole: And accordingly he delivered into Mr. Walpole's own hands a note for that sum, payable to Mr. Walpole, or order; And the said Montgomery, afterwards, paid the sum of 500 guineas to one Mr. Man, Mr. Walpole's agent; who gave him up the note, with the receipt on the back of it signed by Mr. Walpole. That the second contract was made by Mr. Walpole, with Mr. John Campbell; who, thereupon, directed the said

Montgomery to give a note for 500 guineas or pounds, he could not remember which, to Mr. Walpole, which he accordingly did; and made it payable to Mr. Walpole, or order; and delivered it into his own hands. This second note was left with the said Mr. Man; of which the said Mr. Montgomery hath paid about 400*l.*

He further declared upon oath, That 200 guineas were given by the contractors to sir David Dalrymple, in consideration, That his son-in-law, sir Alexander Murray, was proposed, but not admitted, to be a partner in the first contract: That the earl of Leven, commander in chief of her majesty's forces in North Britain, had 100 guineas each year, from the contractors, for regulating the quarters of the troops: That 100*l.* a year were paid to Mr. Merrill, deputy to Mr. How, for receiving the queen's bounty-money, and keeping an account of it between the queen and her officers: That the said Mr. Montgomery gave a note for 50*l.* to Mr. Taylor, chief clerk to Mr. Walpole; which is not yet paid.

Your Commissioners cannot exactly state the loss the public has sustained by these contracts; but find, That if the forage had been furnished in 1709, at the rates settled by the contract for the present year, there had been saved to the government more than 9,500*l.* which is near a fourth part of the whole charge.

They do not apprehend, That this difference has arisen, altogether, from the scarcity of forage in the two last years: for captain William Preston, of col. Kerr's regiment, hath declared before them, on oath, That he agreed with the contractors to furnish green forage for his own troops, in those years, at 2½*d.* an horse, for 24 hours, which cost the government 3½*d.* with an addition only of 7*l.* each year, for providing extraordinary forage for the officers horses belonging to that troop; and that the contractors assured him, they had made the same agreement with other officers. How far these practices have been injurious to the public, is humbly submitted to the consideration of the House.

(Signed) Geo. Lockhart, Hen. Bertie, S. Wilmington, Fra. Annesley, Tho. Lister, Will. Shippen, H. Campion

Letter from the duke of Marlborough to Queen Anne protesting his dismissal from office, 1 January 1712

Parliamentary History, VI, 1058-59.

Madam;

I am very sensible of the honour your majesty does me, in dismissing me from your service by a letter of your own hand; though I find by it, that my enemies have been able to prevail with your majesty to do it, in the manner that is most injurious to me. And, if their malice and and inveteracy against me had not been more powerful with them, that the consideration of your majesty's honour and justice, they would not have influenced you to impute the occasion of my dismission to a false and malicious insinuation, contrived by themselves, and made public when there was no opportunity for me to give in my answer; which, they must needs be conscious, would fully detect the falshood and malice of their aspersions, and not leave them that handle for bringing your majesty to such extremities against me. But I am much more concerned at an expression in your majesty's letter, which seems to complain of the treatment you had met with. I know not how to understand that word, nor what construction to make of it. I know I have always endeavoured to serve your majesty faithfully and zealously through a great many undeserved mortifications. But if your majesty does intend by that expression, to find fault with not my coming to the cabinet council, I am very free to acknowledge, that my duty to your majesty and my country would not give me leave to join in the counsel of a man, who in my opinion puts your majesty upon all manner of extremities. And it is not my opinion only, but the opinion of all mankind, that the friendship of France must needs be destructive to your majesty, there being in that court a root of enmity irreconcileable to your majesty's government, and the religion of these kingdoms. I wish your majesty may never find the want of so faithful a servant, as I have always endeavoured to approve myself to you.

> I am with the greatest duty and
> submission, Madam, your majesty's
> most dutiful, and obedient subject,
> *Marlborough*

Septennial Act, 1716

1 Geo. 1, c. 38   *Statutes at Large*, XIII, 282.

This act provided for the election of a Parliament at least once every seven years. The duration of Parliament was reduced to five years in 1911.

Whereas in and by act of parliament made in the sixth year of the reign of their late Majesties King William and Queen Mary (of ever blessed memory) intituled, *An act for the frequent meeting and calling of parliaments:* it was, among other things enacted, That from thenceforth no parliament whatsoever, that should at any time then after be called, assembled or held, should have any continuance longer than for three years only at the farthest, to be accounted from the day on which by the writ of summons the said parliament should be appointed to meet: and whereas it has been found by experience, that the said clause hath proved very grievous and burthensome, by occasioning much greater and more continued expences in order to elections of members to serve in parliament, and more violent and lasting heats and animosities among the subjects of this realm, than were ever known before the said clause was enacted; and the said provision, if it should continue, may probably at this juncture, when a restless and popish faction are designing and endeavouring to renew the rebellion within this kingdom, and an invasion from abroad, be destructive to the peace and security of the government: be it enacted by the King's most excellent majesty, by and with the advice and consent of the lords spiritual and temporal, and commons, in parliament assembled, and by the authority of the same, That this present parliament, and all parliaments that shall at any time hereafter be called, assembled or held, shall and may respectively have continuance for seven years, and no longer, to be accounted from the day on which by the writ of summons this present parliament hath been, or any future parliament shall be, appointed to meet, unless this present, or any such parliament hereafter to be summoned, shall be sooner dissolved by his Majesty, his heirs or successors.

Lords debate on the Peerage Bill, February-April 1719

Parliamentary History, VII, 589-94.

The aim of this measure was to restrict the creation of new peers. It passed in the Lords but was defeated in the House of Commons.

[28 February]

The Duke of Somerset rose, and represented, that the number of Peers being, of late years, very much increased, especially since the Union of the two kingdoms, it seemed absolutely necessary to fix the same, both to preserve the dignity of Peerage, and to prevent the inconveniencies that may attend the creation of a great number of Peers to serve a present purpose, of which they had a remarkable instance in the late reign, he therefore moved for the bringing in a Bill to settle and limit the Peerage, in such a manner, "That the number of English Peers should not be enlarged beyond six above the present number, which upon failure of male issue might be supplied by new creations: That instead of the Sixteen elective peers in Scotland, 25 be made hereditary on the part of that kingdom, whose number, upon failure of heirs male, should be supplied by some other Scotch peers.

The Duke of Argyle seconded this motion; which was also backed by the earls of Sunderland and Carlisle; but the last of these added, That this was a matter of so great importance, that it became the wisdom of that august assembly maturely to consider of it, before they came to any Resolution; and thereupon his lordship moved, "That a day may be appointed, for the House to be in a Committee, to take into consideration the present State of the Peerage of Great Britain."

The Earl of Oxford excepted against the duke of Somerset's proposal, and among other things, said, That as it tended to take away the brightest gem from the crown, it was matter of wonder to see it supported by those, who, by the great employments they enjoyed, seemed under the strictest obligation to take care of the royal prerogative; that therefore there must be a secret meaning in this motion; that for his own part, though he expected nothing from the crown, yet he would never give his vote for lopping off so valuable a branch of the prerogative, because this would put it out of the power of the crown to reward merit and virtuous actions. To this

The Earl of Sunderland answered, That though the number of peers were limited, yet the crown would still be the fountain of honour, and preserve its prerogative of creating new Peers, upon the extinction of old titles, for want of male issue, which happened frequently; and that those extinctions would give the prince on the throne sufficient opportunities to bestow honours upon commoners of distinguished merit and abilities. His lordship concluded with backing the earl of Carlisle's motion, and no member opposing it, the debate was adjourned accordingly, till the second of March; for which day the Lords were summoned.

[2 March]

The King's Message relating to the Peerage
Earl Stanhope delivered to the House the following Message from the King.

G. R.

His majesty being informed, that the House of Peers have under consideration the state of the Peerage of Great Britain, is graciously pleased to acquaint this House, that he has so much at heart the settling the Peerage of the whole kingdom, upon such a foundation, as may secure the freedom and constitution of parliament in all future ages, that he is willing his prerogative stand not in the way of so great and necessary a work.

Further Debate in the Lords on the State of the Peerage
Then a motion being made for an Address of Thanks for the said Message,

The Earl of Nottingham excepted against it, saying, It was unusual for the king to take notice of any thing depending in parliament, before the same was laid before his majesty in a parliamentary way.

The Duke of Buckingham over-ruled this objection, and said, It could not be supposed, that the king alone should be ignorant of what every body else knew; and that since his majesty was pleased, for the good of his subjects, to suffer his prerogative to be restrained, they ought readily to accept, and thankfully to acknowledge so great and so gracious a condescension.

Hereupon it was agreed, without dividing, to present an Address of Thanks to his majesty; but some words have passed between the earls of Sunderland and Oxford about this extraordinary Message, the House thought fit to interpose, and require from them, that the whole affair should go no farther, and the intended debate was adjourned to the next.

[3 March]

The Lords, in a committee of the whole House, of which the earl of Clarendon was chairman, took into consideration the present State of the Peerage of Great Britain.

The Earl of Sunderland ran over the several changes that have happened in the Peerage since the reign of queen Elizabeth to this time; urging the necessity of limiting the number of peers, and demonstrated the advantage of the scheme proposed by the duke of Somerset.

Earl Cowper endeavoured to shew, that what was intended to be done, with relation to the Scots peerage, was a manifest violation of the Treaty of Union, and the highest piece of injustice; for it was no less than to deprive persons of their right without being heard, and without any pretence of forfeiture upon their part, urging, That the Scots peers, who should be excluded from the number of the twenty five hereditary, would be in a worse condition than any other subjects, since they would neither be electing nor elected, neither representing nor represented, which could not fail of raising dangerous discontents amongst them; that, besides, it would be a breach of trust in those who represented the Scots peerage, wholly to divest their principals of a power, with which they had entrusted them only for a few years; and therefore his lordship was of opinion, that the Scots peers ought to have been consulted, before any steps were made in so nice and so important an affair.

These objections were replied to by the earls of Sunderland and Stanhope, Cholmondeley and Poulet, the dukes of Buckingham and Newcastle, the bishop of Gloucester, and some other English lords, who were supported by several Scots peers, particularly the dukes of Roxburgh and Montrose, the marquis of Annandale, and the earl of Ilay. In the first place, it was alledged, That the settling the peerage in the manner proposed, was rather a benefit than a disadvantage to the Scots peerage, whose representatives were thereby increased by nine, and all made hereditary; and as for those peers who for the present would be excluded, they would afterwards have a chance to come in, upon failure of any of the twenty five: That this regulation could not be looked upon as a violation of the Union, two things only being made unalterable fundamentals of that contract, viz. religion, and the proportion of public taxes: to prove which, several Articles of the Act of Union were read: and that the consulting of the Scots peers in this affair, would be altogether improper and unparliamentary, and attended with great inconveniencies.

The Earl of Ilay, in particular, represented, That the bringing in a number of peers into that House by election, was certainly derogatory to the dignity of that august assembly, and of the highest tribunal in the united kingdom; and therefore he had long before wished to see this defect in the Union rectified, and the Scots peers freed from that ignominious mark of distinction, which made them be looked upon as dependent on the court and ministry, and not at liberty to vote, like the other members, for the good and interest of their country.

The Earl of Nottingham and the lord Townshend declared, That they were not against limiting the peerage, but only against the doing it in a manner, which, in their opinion, was unjust, and might be attended with dangerous consequences.

Resolutions of the Lords in relation to the Peerage

But after a debate that lasted till near seven of the clock in the evening, by a majority of 83 votes against 30, their lordships came to the following Resolutions, viz.

1. That in lieu of the 16 elective peers, to sit in this House on the part of Scotland, 25 peers to be declared by his majesty, shall have hereditary seats in parliament, and be the peers on the part of the peerage of Scotland.

2. That such 25 peers shall be declared by his majesty, before the next session of parliament.

3. That 9 of the said 25 shall be appointed by his majesty to have immediate right to such hereditary seats in parliament, subject to the qualifications requisite by the laws now in being.

4. That none of the remaining 16 so to be declared by his majesty, or their heirs, shall become sitting peers of the parliament of Great Britain, until after the determination of this present parliament, except such are of the number of the 16 peers now sitting in parliament on the part of Scotland, and their heirs.

5. That if any of the 25 peers so to be declared by his majesty, and their heirs shall fail, some one or other of the peers of Scotland shall be appointed by his majesty, his heirs and successors, to succeed to every such peer so failing; and every peer so appointed shall be one of the peers on the part of the peerage of Scotland; in the parliament of Great Britain, and so, *toties quoties*, as often as such failure shall happen.

6. That the hereditary right of sitting in parliament, which shall accrue to the 25 peers of Scotland, to be declared by his majesty, shall be so limited as not to descend to females.

7. That the number of peers of Great Britain, on the part of England, shall not be enlarged, without precedent right, beyond six above what they are at present; but as any of the said present peers, or such six new peers, in case they be created, shall fail, their numbers may be supplied by new creations of commoners of Great Britain, born within the kingdom of Great Britain or Ireland, or any of the dominions thereunto belonging, or born of British parents, and so, *toties quoties*, as often as such failure shall happen.

8. That no person be at any time created by writ, nor any peerage granted by patent, for any longer estate than for the grantee, and the heirs made of his body.

9. That there be not any restraint upon the crown, from creating any of the princes of the blood, peers of Great Britain, with right to sit in parliament.

10. That whenever those Lords now sitting in parliament, whose sons have been called by writ, shall die; then it shall be lawful for his majesty, his heirs and successors, to create a peer to supply the number so lessened.

11. That every creation of a peer hereafter to be made, contrary to these Resolutions, shall be null and void to all intents and purposes.

[5-14 March]

The Peerage Bill brought in

The Earl of Clarendon reported these Resolutions to the House, which being agreed to, the Judges were ordered to bring in a Bill thereupon; which they did accordingly on the 14th, when the said Bill was read the first, and ordered to be read a second time.

[16-18 March]

The Peerage Bill dropped

The Lords having read this Bill the second time, three Scotch lords petitioned to be heard by their counsel against the said Bill; but it being represented by some English peers, that the Lords being sole judges of what relates to the Peerage, they could not allow their rights and privileges to be questioned and canvassed by lawyers; and having to that purpose cited a precedent, viz the case of the late duke Hamilton, when he claimed a seat in that house as duke of Brandon, the said petition of the three Scotch Lords was rejected without dividing.

March 18, the Lords, in a grand committee, took the said bill again into consideration, but adjourned it to the 20th.

[2-28 April]

It being moved in the House of Lords to receive the report from the committee of the whole House upon the Bill for settling the Peerage of Great Britain, the same was put off to the 6th, when the Amendments made to the said Bill were agreed to, and the Bill ordered to be engrossed. But on the 14th, the day appointed for the third reading, lord Stanhope observed, That this Bill had made a great noise, and raised strange apprehensions; and since the design of it had been so misrepresented, and so misunderstood, that it was like to meet with great opposition in the other House, he thought it advisable to let that matter lie still, till a more proper opportunity: And thereupon the third reading of the said Bill was put off to the 28th of that month: by which Resolution the said Bill was dropped for the present session.

First attempt to provide a monthly summary of parliamentary events, May 1731

Gentleman's Magazine, May 1731, 210-14.

His Majesty's most gracious Speech to
both Houses of Parliament,
on Friday May. 7

My Lords and Gentlemen, It is a great Pleasure to me, that at the close of this Session of Parliament, I am able to acquaint you, that the hope I had conceived and given you, of seeing very suddenly a happy period put to the troubles and disorders, which had been so long apprehended, are now by the Treaty signed at Vienna, answered and accomplished.

A project of a Convention betwixt the Emperor and the Maritime Powers, for accommodating the Differences and Disputes that were subsisting, having been formed, the Treaty is concluded and signed by Me and the Emperor, and is now under the Consideration of the States General; the Forms of that Government not admitting a previous Concert in a Negotiation of that nature. And, as this Treaty principally regards the Execution of the Treaty of Seville, it is likewise communicated to the Courts of France and Spain, as Parites to the Treaty of Seville: And I have just received Advice, that the Ratifications between me and the Emperor are exchanged.

The Conditions and Engagements, which I have entered into upon this Occasion, are agreeable to that necessary Concern, which this Nation must always have for the Security and Preservation of the Balance of Power in Europe; and as the uncertain and violent State of Affairs, to which Europe was reduced, and the Mischiefs of an immediate general War, which began to be thought unavoidable, are now removed: This happy Turn duly improved, with a just regard to our former alliances, which it shall be my Care to preserve, gives us a favourable Prospect of seeing the publick Tranquillity re-established.

Gentlemen of the House of Commons.

I return you my Thanks for the effectual Supplies, which you have granted me for the Service of the present Year, and for the proper Disposition you have made of the publick Funds, towards lessening and discharging the national Debt; the remarkable Dispatch and Unanimity which you have shewn at this critical Conjuncture, has added very much to the Credit and Weight of your Proceedings; and you shall find as great a Readiness on my part to ease the Burthens of my People, as soon as the Circumstance and Situation of Affairs will admit of it, as you have shewn to raise the Supplies necessary for the Service of the Publick.

My Lords and Gentlemen, I hope at your Return into the Country, you will find all Attempts to raise a Spirit of Discontent among my People, by unjust

Clamours and Misrepresentations, vain and ineffectual. All malicious Insinuations to the prejudice of my Measures must surely vanish, when it shall appear, that my first and principal Care has been for the Interest and Honour of this Kingdom: Let it be your Endeavour to remove all groundless Jealousies and Apprehensions, that the Satisfaction of the Nation may be as general, as it is my earnest Desire that their Happiness may be; let all my People, let all Orders of Men enjoy quietly and unenvied, the Rights, Privileges, and Indulgencies, which by Law they are intitled to; let no Innovations disturb any part of my Subjects in the Possession of their legal Property; let all that are zealous in the Support of Me and my Government, partake in common the Benefits of the present happy Establishment; and let your Good-will to one another be as extensive as my Protection, which all my good and faithful Subjects have a Right to, and may equally depend upon.

At the same time his Majesty gave the Royal Assent to the following Acts of Parliament.

Acts passed 1731

An Act for raising 1,200,000*l.* by Annuities and a Lottery.

That all Proceedings in Courts of Justice in England, and in the Court of Exchequer in Scotland, shall be in English.

For continuing the Duties for encouraging the coinage of Money.

To prevent Frauds in the Excise, with respect to Starch, Coffee, Tea and Chocolate.

For importing from America Goods not enumerated in any Act of Parl.

For encouraging the making of British Sail-cloth.

To prevent the inhancing the price of Coals in the River Thames, by keeping turn in delivering of Coals there.

For obviating a Doubt concerning Letters sent by the Peny-Post to places out of the Cities of London and Westminster, and Borough of Southwark.

For the more effectual punishing stealers of Lead, Iron Bars, or any fence belonging to the Houses.

For granting an allowance upon the exportation of British Gun-powder.

For more effectual preventing frauds in tenants.

For rebuilding the Church of Gravesend, as one of the 50.

To explain and amend a Clause in an Act for making more effectual several Acts relating to Watermen, etc.

To explain a Clause in an Act of 7th of Q. Anne, for naturalizing foreign Protestants.

To prevent the stealing of Linnen, etc. from places used for whitening, etc.

To enable Ideots and Lunaticks to make Conveyances, etc.

For continuing the Hop-market in the City of Worcester, etc.

For repairing the Pier of Newhaven in Sussex.

For repairing the Pier of Illfordcomb in Devonshire.

The Oxford, Bristol, Preston, and Fulham Road Acts.

And to about 26 private Acts.

An Abstract of the Speaker's
Speech on presenting the Bills

Your Majesty has perfected the great work (of Peace) of which all your Subjects will share the benefit, and may you long enjoy the Fruits of it, in the quiet Affections, and gratitude of your People; may you have leasure to do what your Majesty desires, in adorning your Country with those things so desirable; no doubt, Sir, several of them have been under Consideration of your faithful Commons. May you ever find your Parliament ready to effect those great Ends, so that you may be remarkable for the Blessings of Society, for the Honour of Government, and Liberty of the People; and may your faithful Commons always attend the Throne with that Duty with which they now beg leave to present to your Majesty these Bills.

Of the Bankrupts Bill

Among other Reasons offered for dropping the Bankrupts Bill, one was, That the Privileges of the Peers was in the greatest danger, since a Power was given to the Commissioners, to summons and examine all Persons whatsoever; and if they refuse to give their Oath, they are liable to be imprisoned, by Order of the said Commissioners; and that supposing a Peer be imprisoned, the Judges could not relieve him, insomuch as they could not dispense with the Law.

Of the Act relating to Starch

Enacts, 1. That from the after June 24, 1731, if any maker of Hair-powder, Perfumer, Peruke-maker, Barber, shall mix any Powder of Alabaster, Plaister of Paris, Taik, Chalk, Whiting, Lime, or other Materials (Rice first made into Starch, and sweet Scents only excepted) with Starch, or Powder of Starch to be used for Hair-powder; or shall use, sell, or offer to sell Powder so mixed. shall forfeit the sum of 20*l*.

2. That all dealers in Hair-powder having in their Possession any of the Materials hereby prohibited, shall forfeit the said materials and 10*l*.

3. And shall enter their Place of Abode and Workhouses at the next chief Office of Excise, on the Penalty of 20*l*.

Substance of the Act for Naturalizing, etc.

It declares natural born Subjects to all Intents and Purposes, such Children as are or shall be born out of Ligeance of the Crown of Great-Britain, whose Fathers were natural born Subjects, and not at the time of the birth of their Children, in the Service of any foreign Prince at Enmity with us, or attainted of High Treason, or Outlawed; and in case their Fathers were under such Attainder, etc. if the Child hath come into Great-Britain or Ireland, and between Nov. 16, 1708, and March 25,

1731, resided there 2 Years, professing the Protestant Religion, or hath been in possession, or taken the Rents and Profits of any Lands, Tenements, etc. one whole Year, or hath conveyed or settled Lands, etc. and any Person claims Title thereto, and hath been in Possession thereof for the space of six Months, between the 16th Day of Nov. 1708, and the 25th of March 1731, every such Child shall be deemed and taken to be a natural born Subject of the Crown of England.

Of the Act for Englishing the Law

This Act commences at Lady-day 1733, and contains in Substance, That Writs and Proceedings in any Court of Justice in England, and in the Court of Exchequer in Scotland, shall not only be in the English Language, but shall be written in such a legible Hand as Acts of Parliament are engrossed in, not Court Hand; and the Lines and Words as close as the said Acts usually are, and in Words at length.

For every Offence against this Act, the Transgressor is to forfeit 50*l.* to the Prosecutor.

This enacted also, That Mistranslation, Variation in Form by reason of Translation, Mispelling, or Mistake of Clerkship, in Pleadings or Proceedings begun before the 25th of March 1733, being part in Latin and part in English, shall be no Error, nor make void any Proceedings by reason thereof, but that they may at any time be amended, whether in Paper, or on Record, or otherwise, before or after Judgment, on payment of reasonable Cost only. But nothing in this Act is to extend to certifying beyond the Seas, any Case or Proceedings in the Court of Admiralty, in which cases the Commissions and Proceedings may be certified in Latin as formerly.

Finally, 'Tis enacted, That all Statutes for amending the Delays arising from any Jeofails shall extend to all Forms and Proceedings in the Courts of Justice, (except in criminal Cases) where the Proceedings are in English, and that every Error which might be remedied by any Statute of Jeofails, if the Proceedings had been in Latin, shall be, when the Terms are in English, remedyed by the Statutes now in force for the amendment of any Jeofails.

The Debates relating to the Bill were to this effect, viz. Those who were against it apprehended that great Difficulties would arise in translating the Laws out of Latin into English, and might multiply Law suits, in regard to the Interpretation of English Words. And a certain Lord, and great Lawyer, said, That if the Bill passed, the Laws ought also to be translated into Welch, since many in Wales did not understand English, To which the Duke of Argyle replyed, That the Meaning of the Law had been long understood by the Interpreters (Judges) thereof, and would surely be so when translated: That our Prayers were in our native Tongue, that they might be intelligible; and why should not the Laws, wherein our Lives and Properties were concerned, be so for the same Reason? and added, that he was glad to hear that the said Lord had nothing else to say against the Bill than a Joke. Other Lords instanced, That in the Reign of Edward III an Act of Parliament passed for having the Laws in English, and not in French (as they were then) for the ease of the People. After which a Debate arose about Law Proceedings being wrote in a plain legible Hand, and not in Court Hand, wherein the Earl of Isla said, That in Scotland they were come to that pass, that the Sheriffs knew nothing of the Contents of the Writs they executed; and therefore moved, that the Proceedings in the Exchequer in Scotland, which were in the English manner, might be also wrote in a plain legible Hand, which was agreed to; as likewise that Records be wrote in the same Hand as Acts of Parliament are engrossed; and that the Time allowed the Lord Chancellor and Judges for translating the Law into English, be till the Year 1733.

Of the Irish Wooll Bill

On the second reading of the Bill in the House of Lords for preventing the Running of Wooll and Yarn from England and Ireland to foreign Parts, and for taking off the Duties on the importation of Wool, Yarn, etc. Those who spoke against it, alledged, that the Importation of Yarn, would be a great Prejudice to our laborious poor; particularly the Spinners, and that it seemed calculated for the service of Ireland only. Those who were for the Bill observed, That formerly 300000 Stone of Wool were imported yearly from Ireland, and then our Manufactures were at the height, and most, or all foreign Markets were supplyed by us, and which we may again do, if we can have the manufacturing of their Wool and Yarn here as formerly. 'Twas likewise remarked, that some Years ago, when Barbadoes permitted the importation of Sugars from the French, and other Colonies, that Island was the Channel thro' which all Sugars were conveyed; but they no sooner prohibited that Importation, than the foreign Colonies found other Markets for it. And it was the same with regard to Irish Wool and Yarn. At last it was referred to the Commissioners of Trade and Plantations, to draw up a Scheme to be laid before the Parliament the next Sessions.

Commons debate on a motion for the removal of Sir Robert Walpole as first lord of the treasury, 13 February 1741

Parliamentary History, XI, 1318-35, 1367-70, 1379-87.

Sir Robert Walpole (1676-1745; KG, 1725; first earl of Orford, 1742) was the leading, or prime, minister (holding the portfolio of first lord of the treasury) and chancellor of the exchequer from 1715 to 1717 and again from 1721 to January 1742, when he was forced to resign. The debate which follows focusses upon the increasing powers of the first minister and illuminates the political issues of the day. The motion was defeated, 209-106.

Mr. Sandys: Such, Sir, has been the conduct of Sir Robert Walpole, with regard to foreign affairs: he has deserted our allies, aggrandised our enemies, betrayed our commerce, and endangered our colonies; and yet this is the least criminal part of his ministry. For what is the loss of allies to the alienation of the people from the government, or the diminution of trade to the destruction of our liberties?

That the people are universally discontented, I am under no obligation of endeavouring to prove, while an army is supported only to restrain them from rebellion: for no other reason has been given by the annual advocates for a military establishment. Those indeed, who urge the danger of the Pretender's attempts, may perhaps make use of other words, but their meaning, if any meaning can be allowed them, is apparently the same, for the Pretender can never obtain this throne but by the concurrence of the majority, and that concurrence can only arise from their disapprobation of the present government.

But to what cause, Sir, can be imputed a discontent so general, and a detestation so vehement, to what can we ascribe a desire of an apparent evil, an affection to a prince of a different religion, of a religion which privileges perfidy, and sanctifies persecution? How can it be imagined that men should form a wish to be subject to a monarch educated among their enemies, in countries governed by arbitrary power, and who must consequently be infatuated with every wild opinion of the unlimited extent of royal prerogatives, and believe himself entitled to trample upon law, to subvert privilege, and to plunder property?

How miserable must be the condition of that people, whom an army is necessary to restrain from a choice like this! what calamities, what oppression must they feel, who can fly to such remedies for relief! Were we governed like reasonable beings, that man only ought to be condemned as disaffected to his majesty, who should dare to charge the people with disaffection: for surely no man can more openly or more virulently libel the government, than those who declare that the nation would change it for subjection to the Pretender.

That there is any such desire among the people, Sir, I am far from affirming or believing, for they are too well instructed in the tendency of the religion which the Pretender professes, to desire to see it the religion of their king, and too well acquainted with their own rights, to think that when they cannot deliver themselves from misery, the Pretender will be able to deliver them.

The representations which have been made of their impatience, every man knows to be true; every man sees their misery, and hears their complaints and their menaces; but their menaces must be feared before their complaints are regarded by those whose hearts corruption has hardened, and whose sensibility is extinguished by the luxuries of a court.

To dissipate their own fears they have established an army in opposition to the fundamental laws of the kingdom, and defend their concurrence in this establishment by alleging the discontent of the people; that discontent which only their measures have produced, and which nothing can more increase or confirm than a Standing Army.

By an army, Sir, distinct from the rest of the community, subjected to particular laws, commanded with absolute authority, and quartered in the country, to fatten in idleness, and insult those by whom they are supported, the anger of the nation must be continually enflamed, though the effects of it may for a short time be prevented; and what fatal consequences may be produced by hourly aggravations of distress and new incentives to sedition, any man may venture to foretell from a common acquaintance with the conduct of mankind, and a very slight knowledge of the history of former ages.

It may reasonably be expected, that the people will not always groan under their burdens in submission; that after having enquired why they were imposed, and from what necessity it arises that they are every day increased, they will at length resolve to shake them off, and resume into their own hands that authority which they have intrusted to their governors, that they will resolve to become judges of their own interest, and regulate those measures, of which they must support the expence, and in which nothing but their advantage ought to be regarded.

When this important period shall arrive, when justice shall call out for the corrupters of their country, the deserters of their allies, and the enemies of commerce; when liberty shall publish the crimes of those by whom she has been long ridiculed and oppressed; when the cries of the exasperated people shall be too loud to be repressed, and vengeance shall impend over those heads which have so long been lifted up with confidence, against truth and virtue, then will be the time in which the army must become the refuge of those who have so long supported it.

Then will the corrupter and his associates, the lacqueys of his train, and the slaves of his levee, then will those who have sold their country for opportunities of debauchery, and wasted the rewards of perfidy in the pleasures of the stews of the court, implore the protection of their military friends, and request them to repay those benefits which they have formerly received. What is, then, to be expected, but that either they will be given up to punishment by those whom they have pampered at the expence of the public to secure them from it, which is most ardently to be hoped? or that the people will have recourse to arms in assertion of their demands, and that the nation will be laid waste with all the devastations of a civil war? that at length either Britons will be for ever deprived of their liberty, that all our rights will be extinct and our constitution at an end? or that victory will declare on the side of justice, that the arms of the people will be successful, and that the courtiers and their protectors will perish together?

Such, Sir, are the prospects which the continuance of a Standing Army sets before our eyes, a species of oppression unknown to any former age, and which must end either in the ruin of the nation, or the destruction of those who have introduced it for their own advantage.

The defenders of this hateful establishment, first calumniate the nation, and then punish those crimes which they have falsely charged upon it; they affirm that those are enemies to the king who censure the minister, and raise and maintain those forces for the defence of the government which they can use only for their own.

The murmurs of the people, Sir, however incessant, or their menaces however loud, are no proofs of disaffection to his majesty, nor arise from any persuasion that another is entitled to his throne. The people indeed desire a change, not from a restless lust of novelty, and much less from a surfeit of happiness, as some have affirmed who grew rich by taxes and imposts, and who have learned the art of regarding no interest but their own, and of charging all those with counterfeited distress, who complain of miseries not felt by themselves. The people, Sir, desire a change from a just impatience of intolerable burthens, and a wise foresight of approaching miseries, they desire a change not of their sovereign, but of his minister, and desire it so ardently, that it will not be safe longer to deny them the satisfaction of discovering, that their cries are not entirely disregarded, and that the interest of a single man is not put in the balance against the happiness of the whole community.

It may be asked, why their resentment is directed against this person, why they have singled him out from the crowd with which he is surrounded, as the open and declared enemy of his country, why they look upon him as the principal author of all their miseries, why they should imagine that the public prosperity can never be restored, till his counsels shall be no longer heard, and his authority no longer regarded?

To these demands it will readily be answered, Sir, that they consider him as the source of their misery, because they see him the source of wealth and power; that wealth which has been drained from them by exactions, only to be lavished on those who betray them; and that power which is of no other use in the hands to which it is committed but to add oppression to oppression, to arm the laws against them, and subject them to the will of the court.

They select him from those that encompass him, by the same tokens that distinguish an idol from its worshippers; they see all that surround him cringing to his superior power, and making humble offerings of their consciences, their votes, their liberties, and their posterity.

What are the measures, Sir, by which he has drawn the universal hatred upon him, neither he nor his dependants can be ignorant; he has exasperated the nation by destroying its alliances, diminishing its commerce, and obstructing its arms, and drawn yet a severer resentment upon him by projecting the ruin of its liberties.

It is well known, Sir, that to enjoy liberty, is to be governed by laws not arbitrarily imposed, but enacted by the consent of those whose obedience is required to them, and it is equally evident, that the people can only consent by the voices of their deputies, that therefore they can only be free by the possession of a free choice of their representatives, and that so far as they are constrained in those elections, their liberties are taken away. For of what importance is it, whether I am obliged to accept every proclamation for a law, or am compelled by menaces of prosecutions, and the terrors of oppression, to chuse a representative, who, without enquiring into my opinion, will vote at the direction of the reigning party, will regard no advantage but his own, and will raise his fortune by the sale of his constituents? Where is the difference, whether my property is taken away by open violence, or given up by a man whom I was constrained to trust, in whose integrity I have no confidence, and of whose abilities I have had no experience?

This foundation of all our privileges, this basis of our constitution, Sir, which our ancestors imagined they had fixed too deep to be over-turned, and spread too wide to be shaken, it has been the hourly labour of the minister to weaken by imperceptible degrees. No expedient has been forgotten that might diffuse corruption, and promote dependence; fear and hope have been equally employed;

those who could not be terrified have been caressed, and those whose understanding enabled them to discover the tendency of false caresses, have been harrassed with menaces and hardships.

Not only the great employments of the kingdom, but every petty post, Sir, has been divided upon various pretences, under various denominations. Thus those offices which formerly secured a single vote, because they were usually conferred upon men of spirit and integrity, have now been made sufficient to influence boroughs, by being distributed among wretches who have neither understanding to know their duty, nor resolution to perform it, and who, therefore, sell their honesty and their freedom at a very low rate.

For the same purpose, Sir, penal laws have been multiplied, which may be relaxed or enforced at the pleasure of the minister, who, having in his own hands the nomination of all the officers employed in the execution of them, can exasperate or moderate them at pleasure; can direct them where to be vigilant against the appearance of transgression, and where to connive at real violation; when to slumber over the most notorious frauds, and when to magnify suspicions, and harrass the innocent.

This method, Sir, of propagating his power, has indeed been sufficiently successful; he has reduced many of the boroughs of the kingdom under absolute dominion, and can now sit in his closet, and nominate a great part of those men who yet assume the stile of the representatives of the people.

The vigilance with which he has extended his regard to the whole subordination of the government, and the care with which he has chosen the lowest officers, are indeed proofs of a very active mind, and an extensive comprehension, which it had been happy if he had endeavoured to apply to better purposes.

But, Sir, his most masterly attempt for the establishment of universal slavery, on which he laid out all his interest, and all his subtilty, in which he laboured with incessant application, and defended with the most tenacious obstinacy, was the scheme of extending the laws of excise. By this he would have put a stop to all farther opposition of ministerial power; by this he would have secured himself from the future trouble of corrupting and seducing individuals; he would have crushed the constitution at once, and as the tyrant of old wished to destroy mankind at a blow, our minister, not less heroically wicked, endeavoured by one fatal vote to oppress liberty for ever.

This, Sir, was indeed a compendious method of oppression, by which he would have diffused his spies and his agents over the nation, by which he would have forced his way into houses, learned the private affairs of families, and be enabled to govern every man in his own dwelling; he would have received every day the homage of the nation in the persons of the excisemen, his representatives, whom he had deputed to exact obedience to his will, and to deliver up his enemies to punishment.

To expatiate upon the nature of the excise laws, Sir, and to show how much they infringe our most important privileges, would be to explain what every man has long known, and what the whole nation declared in the numberless Petitions by which this House was every day solicited while that dreadful question was depending, to have regard to the rights with which it was intrusted, and to preserve the people of England from becoming slaves to the drudges of corruption, from being plundered by the caterpillars of power, and insulted by the slaves of the slaves of the minister.

With how little compassion their terrors were regarded, Sir, and with how much contempt their remonstrances and arguments were heard by those whom a long dependence on the minister had hardened equally against reason and compassion, who had been taught by the example of their lord, to insult that misery which they had themselves occasioned, and to ridicule those arguments which they could not answer, is still remembered with resentment proportioned to the crime; nor can it be wondered that the people hold that man in abhorrence, who has openly professed to despise, and no less openly endeavoured to enslave them, who has attacked their privileges, and punished those who refused to resign them.

For to the opposition which the merchants of this kingdom raised against the project of extending the excise laws, it is reasonable to impute that settled hatred which the minister has conceived against them, which he seldom fails to express, however indecently, and which he exerts upon all opportunities without regard to policy or justice. Every motive, every principle has given way to the favourite design of harrassing the merchants, whom he considers as the most inflexible enemies of his claims, as situated most remote from his influence, and as the last whom he shall be able to sink into that implicit submission which he has been long accustomed to require.

To his scheme of subjecting this stubborn body of men, no less than to his alliance with the house of Bourbon, is perhaps to be ascribed his connivance at the Spanish depredations; from which, though it is not likely that his influence in foreign courts would have enabled him to prevent them, he might at least have secured many of our ships by convoys. But how little such favours were to be expected from him in time of peace, may be discovered from his unwillingness to grant them protection in open war, from his care to conceal their losses, and his attempts to vindicate those to whose treachery or negligence they may justly be deputed.

And that no method of ruining his country may remain unattempted, that he may at least be secure in his designs against the public, he has found means of introducing dependance into parliament, and of depriving the people of all hope of justice or relief, by influencing that assembly to which in all former ages they have appealed; and which has seldom failed to redress their grievances, to drag from behind the throne the oppressors of the nation, and to stop up the sources of the public treasure, till these men have been punished who were found to have promoted wicked measures, and to have favoured any other interest than that of Great Britain.

To what can it be imputed, Sir, that the people have now for many years in vain solicited their representatives for enquiries into the conduct of public offices, that they have annually laid before them their miseries and their fears, without any other effect than the new mortification of seeing themselves neglected by those to whom they have entrusted the care of the commonwealth? What cause can be alleged for the conduct of late parliaments so different from that of their predecessors? Why do they now meet only to tax the people, and to flatter the court, to offer addresses, and to vote supplies? Why is there no regard paid to the remonstrances of our constituents, or why have so many years elapsed without one example of justice?

It surely will not be urged on this occasion, that this age is uncorrupt beyond the example of former times; since the open wickedness of the present generation has been often represented in this House in terms of the strongest detestation, by the vindicators of the ministry; and as it is not to be supposed that virtue is encreased by temptations to wickedness, or that those posts which have always been imagined dangerous to integrity, have now so much changed their nature, that they are become preservatives from corruption; as it is not to be conceived that they who dissipate their private fortunes in riot and luxury, have been always upright dispensers of the public treasure, the nation cannot but be excited to enquire, why parliament has been content to grant money without any solicitude how it was employed?

This alteration, Sir, of which the consequences are equally obvious and dreadful, can be imputed to no other cause than the endeavours which have been used by the minister to fill this House with dependants on the court, by scattering lucrative employments amongst them, which are to be held by no other tenure, than that of an implicit submission to his will, and a resignation of all private opinions to his unerring dictates.

When I see in this House, Sir, so great a number of men whose determination I know before the question is proposed, I am in doubt whether the motion which I am about to make will not be an useless effort, an unavailing appeal to a court whose sentence is already past, yet as the public miseries are too great to be any longer borne without some endeavours to redress them; as in my opinion no redress can be obtained but by depriving the minister of the power which he has so long and so openly abused, as the obstacles which are most likely to hinder the success of this attempt are every day multiplied, as corruption is continually advanced, and virtue hourly more contemned, I take this opportunity of moving, while yet the right of offering any motion against the minister remains, "That an humble Address be presented to his majesty, that he will be graciously pleased to remove the right honourable sir Robert Walpole, knight of the most noble order of the garter, first commissioner for executing the office of treasurer of the exchequer, chancellor and under-treasurer of the exchequer, and one of his majesty's most honourable privy-council, from his majesty's presence and counsels for ever."

Lord Limerick: Sir; as I have been for some time a constant opponent of the measures by which the motion now offered has been produced, I suppose it will create no surprize, either in the vindicators or adversaries of the gentleman to whom it relates, that I stand up to second it. To add any thing to the representation which you have already heard of the miseries of the nation, will be equally difficult and unnecessary. It is known to all, that we are oppressed with taxes, and involved in war, that the war has been hitherto unsuccessful and ignominious, that our fleets have been manned by violence, and detained in our harbours upon false pretences, that our trade has been at once diminished by impresses, and betrayed by the denial of convoys.

If it were necessary, Sir, to give any other proof of the difficulties and distresses to which we are reduced, let it be remembered, how lately the right hon. gentleman himself declared, in the midst of our deliberations upon the ravages and insults of Spain, that we were not able to engage in a war, that we were without a single ally to support us, and that our own strength was not sufficient. Either this account of our condition was true or false. If it was true, what can be said in defence of the person who has destroyed those ties that conjoined our interest with that of the powers on the continent; who has broken the union which nature seemed to have formed, and which religion had confirmed; who has conducted our affairs with so much ignorance or perfidy, that he has disgusted one party without gratifying the other; who has drawn equally upon the nation the hatred of France and her enemies, and whom neither the house of Bourbon nor of Austria can be expected to favour?

How this could have been effected, Sir, it would not be easy for any man but our minister to discover; nor would even his absurd policy, and perverse subtilty, have been sufficient, had he not aided his own abilities by French counsels, and concurred with the inveterate and implacable enemies of Great Britain, to involve his country in distress.

If his account of the condition of the nation was false, this falshood alone is a sufficient motive to the proposition which has been offered; for surely that man ought to be removed from his majesty's counsels for ever, who, when his country was harrassed by the attacks of a contemptible enemy, when its commerce was every day obstructed, and its honour impaired, was so far from encouraging his fellow-subjects to the assertion of their rights, the revenge of their losses, and the reparation of their honour, that he endeavoured to sink them into cowardice, to depress them with false comparisons of the strength of their enemies with their own, and whose counsels have no other tendency than to encourage new insults, and prepare the people for submissive slavery.

Such counsels, Sir, must proceed, in my opinion, from other motives than regard to public felicity, and since nothing is more evident than that no man, who prefers any interest to that of Great Britain, ought to be intrusted with power or admitted to confidence, I declare, that in my opinion, the motion now made is necessary and just.

Mr. Wortley: Sir; before the propriety of this motion becomes the subject of our debates, I think it necessary to propose, that the order of the House be strictly observed, which is well known to require, that every member against whom an accusation is brought, should retire out of this assembly, while his conduct is examined.

This procedure, which is established by immemorial custom, and confirmed by innumerable precedents, is founded likewise upon right reason; for as any member of this assembly may be said to be here tried by his associates, by men with whom he has at least concurred in public affairs, and with whom he has probably been more intimately conversant, it is proper to free our debates from those prejudices, which cannot but be raised by the presence of a man, who has been long regarded with friendship or esteem by those who are now become his judges: to banish that tenderness which may be produced by the sight of a companion or an acquaintance perplexed and disturbed; and perhaps sometimes to suppress that awe which may be raised in part of this assembly by a powerful offender, whose looks may upbraid some with the benefits which they have formerly received from him, and whose eyes may dart menaces upon those who are dependent on his favour.

It is evident that to preserve impartiality in our enquiries, and integrity in our decisions, all private regards must be laid aside; and that therefore objects which may impress or enforce them, ought to be carefully removed; and as the presence of the person accused may exasperate or intimidate his adversaries, or encourage his friends, or awe his followers, I move, That, while this question is debated, sir Robert Walpole be ordered to withdraw.

Mr. Gybbon: Sir; this motion is so agreeable to the strictest maxims of justice, the most prudent methods of trial, and the standing practice of this House, that I cannot but second it as necessarily previous to the principal question.

The practice of this House is only to be proved by precedents, which are indeed sufficiently numerous; but because to recite all the instances which might be found in our journals, would unnecessarily retard the business of this day, I shall select only some of later date, which may shew beyond controversy, that our immediate predecessors did not deviate in this respect from the custom of ancient parliaments, and that this method of procedure was found too useful to be laid aside.

In the reign of king James the 2nd, when Mr. Coke was censured for the use of expressions disrespectful to the king, while the House was deliberating upon his offence, he was ordered to withdraw.

When in the following reign, among other captains of the navy, capt. Churchill, a member of this House, was accused of taking money from the merchants whose ships he was appointed to convoy, he was first heard in his place, and then withdrew; so far as it appears, without waiting for an order which he knew the practice of the House would regularly produce.

When in the examination of Francis Rainsford, the committee for receiving the public accounts, having reported that lord Faulkland had withdrawn a Letter which had been written by him, a debate arose upon the nature of the offence, and the punishment which it might be proper to inflict. Lord Faulkland having spoken in his own vindication, withdrew, and afterwards being called in and heard a second time, withdrew again. And another dispute arising on a succeeding day concerning 2,000*l.* irregularly received by lord Faulkland from the king, he again withdrew, after having made his defence.

In the same reign, Mr. Manley being charged with indecent expressions used by him in the debate upon the proceeding against sir John Fenwick; when the debate began, he was required to withdraw.

More instances, Sir, might easily be collected, if more were necessary; but as these are sufficient to shew what has been the practice of this House, and as that practice may be justified by reason, I hope we shall be careful not to depart from it on this occasion.

Mr. Bromley: Sir; I am very far from being convinced either by the arguments or precedents which have been produced, that the right hon. gentleman, to whom this motion relates, ought to be required to withdraw.

All the persons mentioned in the precedents which have been alleged, and all those that have been forbidden to be present at the debates relating to themselves, have been charged with some known crime, and are to be considered as standing for their trial. But the question in the present case, is not whether the right hon. gentleman has been guilty of the actions imputed to him, or the author of any particular counsels, but whether those actions are in themselves criminal, or those counsels really pernicious. He is not charged with any word or act which the laws of his country have determined to deserve punishment; but with conduct which his enemies propose first to prove criminal, and then to punish by a new method of prosecution.

In the instances, Sir, which have been mentioned to support this motion, the offenders have been allowed to hear their accusation, and to make their defence in their places; nor can I discover how any man's conduct is impartially examined, where he is not allowed to speak in his own defence; or how any man can defend himself, who is not permitted to hear the charge against him.

Mr. Howe: Sir; these precedents are in my opinion so far from proving what is intended by them, that they seem to me not to have any relation to the present question, of which I have not yet been able to discover how it differs from the common enquiries that are made in this House.

Whenever we enquire into the expediency of past measures, our disquisitions cannot but affect those by whom they were conducted or advised; yet they are not therefore required to withdraw during our deliberations, but are expected to justify their counsels, to explain their motives, and excuse their miscarriages.

The charge, Sir, against the right hon. gentleman, is only a political enquiry into the conduct of the ministry for many years; nor has it been urged in such a manner as to relate particularly to him. There is, therefore, no reason for requiring him to withdraw, which will not equally shew that all those should retire at the same time, who have concurred in the measures disapproved by the gentleman that made the motion; who may then safely promise himself victory, when all those from whom he expects opposition shall be banished from the House.

Mr. Ereskine: Sir; I am not surprized to find that on this occasion the friends of the minister have recourse to their usual arts of sophistry; and that they endeavour to protect his person by the same fallacies with which they have always vindicated his measures; that they labour to perplex our enquiries by an artful confusion of distinct questions, and that they are desirous to exclude light when it will only discover what it is their interest to conceal.

In their first fallacy, Sir, they have not indeed been very successful. Whether their anxiety for the event of the day has disconcerted their sophisms, or whether their cause will in reality admit of no better defence, their present plea is such as men celebrated for the acuteness of their penetration, and the readiness of their invention, might have been expected not to have alledged in a debate of so much importance to the nation, and, what has always more sensibly affected them, to themselves. Having had warning of the storm that was hanging over them, they should have provided themselves with some shelter against it that might not be easily thrown down; and not have thought it sufficient to assert, what they can never hope to prove, that there is no distinction to be made between this and any other political enquiry.

There is the same difference, Sir, between this and other political enquiries, as between national and personal transactions, between consultations and trials. The question in other debates relates equally to every man in the House; this affects one man of this assembly in a particular manner: and surely it will not be again asserted that it is an enquiry of the same nature, whether a member shall be expelled this House, or whether peace shall be concluded with Spain.

That this question will incidentally produce political debates, may reasonably be expected, because the errors or crimes charged upon this gentleman are chiefly political; and when the principal question is personal, that man to whom it relates ought to be withdrawn while it is debated.

Colonel Bladen: Sir; I know not upon what arguments it is so positively asserted, that this is a question of a peculiar nature, and that it ought to be distinguished from other political disquisitions; and I hope the zeal of the opponents of the ministry, however ardent, will not prompt them to require, that what is not proved should be admitted.

I have always hitherto imagined, that those debates which are properly political in the interest of the public, are objects of enquiry; and as I know only two motives that can give occasion to the present motion, regard to public happiness, and the gratification of private resentment, I have been candid enough to believe, that it was made with no other view than the advantage of the nation.

Of this, Sir, indeed I was persuaded, by the observations with which the motion was introduced; for to what other purpose were all the disappointments, misfortunes and errors, whether real or pretended, of near twenty years so laboriously enumerated? For what end are we informed of the long continued insolence of the Spaniards, of our destructive alliances with the French, of the decline of our commerce, and the weakness of our arms? Why else are the losses of our merchants so pathetically exaggerated, and why are we told once more of the load of our taxes, and the discontent of the people?

If it be not imagined, Sir, that our compliance with the motion will remedy these calamities; and that the removal of one gentleman from his majesty's counsels, will revive our trade, and invigorate our forces; awe our enemies, and animate our allies; this long, this elegant declamation, has been nothing more than an effusion of ostentatious eloquence, without any intention of informing us; it has been only an overflow of malice, a torrent of invectives.

But if, as we ought to imagine, those by whom this motion is made and defended, are persuaded, that the counsels of one man have sunk the nation into disgrace, and that by depriving him of his influence, they shall restore the public honour and felicity, the debate, like all others, is an enquiry whether the measures which they propose will produce the consequences expected from them.

In the precedents cited to support the second motion, Sir, there is not the least appearance of a parallel with the present case. They were persons who had either committed an offence in the presence of the assembly by which they were to be judged, and against whom it was therefore unnecessary to produce evidence; or men convicted of offences by legal testimonies, and whose punishment was therefore the only subject of deliberation.

Nothing is more reasonable, Sir, than that in these circumstances the offender should withdraw; for to what purpose should he continue in the House? The only reason he has a seat, the reason for which every other man has a seat, in this assembly, is the right of examining, deliberating and voting: and this right has undoubtedly ceased; since it would be absurd to consult any man with regard to censures which are to be inflicted upon himself, or to suffer him to vote in his own cause.

But, Sir, with regard to the right hon. gentleman mentioned in the present motion, the first enquiry must be, whether any of the measures objected to him are in themselves criminal; an enquiry at which he has the same right to be present with any other member, and may claim more justly a right to speak in the vindication of, as he is supposed to have been principally the author of them, and consequently to be more than others acquainted with the motives which influenced him in his advice.

If it should appear, Sir, which can hardly be hoped even by those who have been long accustomed to deceive themselves with sanguine expectations, and whom a perpetual train of defeats hath not awakened from their dream of success, that these measures have been really pernicious, and that the authors of them deserve punishment; must not those authors be discovered? Will not any particular person be at liberty to deny the guilt imputed to him, and may he not claim the common right of a British subject to stand face to face against his accuser?

That this may be justly demanded by him, Sir, appears even from those precedents which have been produced to prove that he ought to withdraw; for all the offenders were allowed to vindicate themselves in their places: and if it be allowed that the right hon. gentleman against whom the motion is directed, may hear his accusation, and offer his defence, I doubt not but his innocence will be evidently shewn, and that therefore there will be no room for deliberating on his punishment.

Mr. Gybbon: Sir; if it be only required that the gentleman to whom this motion relates should hear his accusation, that privilege has been already enjoyed. He has already been accused of almost every crime which ministerial power could enable him to commit; he has been charged with destroying the security of those alliances which it is the invariable interest of this nation to preserve; with contributing to the exaltation of that house, which has never formed any designs but for the destruction of the common liberties of mankind, and for the attainment of universal empire; with neglecting the protection of our commerce, and betraying our merchants to plunder, and our seamen to slavery; with concealing and palliating the insolence of our enemies, and the violation of our rights; and with obstructing the operations of the war by treacherous delays, and hindering its success by denying our commanders the liberty of action.

The accusations, Sir, with regard to his domestic conduct are still more atrocious. He is taxed as an enemy to our privileges, and a violator of our constitution; as the projector of a military establishment by which the most pernicious measures may be defended; and as the corruptor of that assembly to which the rights of the people are intrusted. He has been openly charged with betraying his country, and with attempting to enslave it; and, after this, is it demanded that he may hear his accusation?

What other crimes those who know him best expect to hear alleged against him, I am not able to conceive; but by their demands they give us reason to imagine that they are yet afraid of some heavier charge, and that to have supported the public enemies, or to have formed a plan of general slavery, is not the highest instance of his guilt.

But whatever crimes, Sir, his favourites may have had opportunities of remarking, as their fidelity is too well known to afford any hopes that they will discover them, we should proceed to consider the facts already mentioned; he may therefore now produce what he may have to urge in his own defence; after which it is allowed by all, that he ought to withdraw.

Mr. Pulteney: Sir; in all debates it ought to be our first care, that we do not suffer ourselves to be diverted from the principal question by considerations of small importance; and that we do not in the preliminaries of our disquisitions weary that attention, and squander those moments which should be reserved for higher purposes, in the pursuit of obscure enquiries, and the explication of intricate reasonings.

Whether it is not required by the rules of strict justice, that the gentleman should retire, I cannot suddenly determine; but since we ought not, in the prosecution of an oppressor, to make use of those arts which we are endeavouring to prevent; and since to insist with much vehemence on his absence may be imagined to betray some diffidence of our cause, or fear of his abilities; I think it may very properly be left in his own choice to stay or retire on this occasion. . . .

Mr. Henry Pelham: Sir; it is not without uncommon astonishment, that I hear the motion now under our consideration defended and applauded by gentlemen, whose zeal for equity and regard to the laws of their country, I never had before any reason to suspect, however I might differ from them in my opinion of the public measures, or in my affection or esteem for particular persons.

It is well known that one of the principal advantages of our constitution, that happy constitution that is so much reverenced and praised, and of which the least violation has been represented as an enormous and inexpiable crime, consists in the established methods of proceeding in criminal trials, by which every man is secured from being overborn by violence and clamour, or sacrificed to resentment or suspicion, by which the criminal is intitled to hear the testimonies which are produced against him, and expose any falshood by unexpected interrogatories, and by which he may claim to be held innocent upon his own assertion till his guilt shall appear from sufficient evidence.

Nothing is more certain, Sir, than that this practice, which the wisdom of our remotest ancestors established, and which the care and vigilance of our intermediate progenitors has been principally employed in preserving and confirming, has been the strongest bulwark of our other privileges, and the barrier which has a thousand times hindered the prerogative from breaking in with a torrent of violence upon our properties, and sinking us in servitude and misery for ever. Yet is this bulwark now to be thrown down and this barrier to be irreparably broken, that way may be made for vengeance to rush upon one man, to whom no greater crime is imputed than that he has exalted the regal power, and propagated the influence of the court.

I have been too long acquainted with mankind, and have had too much experience both of my own weakness and that of others, to think that hypocrisy may be always with justice imputed to those whose conduct is inconsistent with their declarations. I know that the wisest men do not always make choice of means adapted to their end, and that they often disappoint their own designs by those measures, which they think most necessary for their accomplishment. I do not therefore assert, nor indeed do I suspect, that those who have offered and defended this motion, are in reality enemies to liberty; but can affirm with confidence, that their zeal has blinded their prudence, and that the methods by which they propose to secure our constitution, can have no tendency but to weaken and destroy it.

It has often been urged in this House against measures not improper at the time in which they were proposed, that they would establish a precedent which might hereafter be made use of for the introduction of the same practices without the same necessity, and it has been long received as a maxim among the wisest and most considerate men of all parties, that it is more eligible to neglect the acquisition of a present advantage, or the removal of a temporary inconvenience, than to give the enemies of our liberties any opportunity of employing our own determinations against us, and oppressing us by methods which we ourselves invented or approved.

This caution, if we think it reasonable and just, if we acknowledge ourselves indebted to it for the enjoyment of property, and the felicity of independence, we ought surely to imitate, and nothing is more evident than that we cannot without departing from it admit this motion: for if this new method of prosecution be established, it will not be possible for any man to execute a public office with tranquillity or safety, since innocence and guilt will be equally in danger.

The only advantage which innocence can have over corruption, consists not in exemption from suspicion, which is often raised by envy and propagated by ignorance, and to which therefore, men eminent for their virtue are perhaps most exposed. The advantage of innocence arises from security that this suspicion can never ripen into conviction, that it can never be confirmed by evidence, and therefore must at last languish into nothing, that it is only an *Ignis Fatuus*, which may lead those who follow it into danger, but has in itself no power to consume or injure. The innocent man proceeds in his measures with steadiness and intrepidity, because he knows that he shall at last baffle those enemies which are only exasperated by his success: since the utmost effort of their malice can only call him to a trial, and a trial can have no other effect than to justify his conduct and exalt his reputation.

But who does not see that the proposal now before us, must for ever deprive integrity of the only confidence that can support it against the opposition of wickedness and censure of folly? Who does not discover that suspicion is now substituted in the place of evidence, and that punishment is to be inflicted without a trial? Who does not see that innocence is levelled with guilt, and that no man can hereafter be safe, but by complying with the passions of the people, and gratifying the majority, at whatever hazard of the public, or with whatever disapprobation of his own conscience?

In considering this motion, I therefore lay aside all regard to the character of the right hon. person, to whom it immediately relates, nor do I think it necessary to declare that opinion which long observation of his conduct has enabled me to form. The question is not, Whether he is an upright or corrupt minister; because it does not judicially appear that he is engaged in the transaction of affairs. It is now to be debated, whether to be suspected and to be criminal shall be henceforward equally dangerous; whether we are to judge in consequence of allegations and proofs, or of outcries and declamations, and whether it be not necessary that every innocent man should have, in a country that boasts of freedom, the means of refuting accusation?

Of a prosecution which bears any resemblance to that which is now attempted, very few precedents have been furnished by whole centuries of contests and disturbances: the utmost rage of faction has generally endeavoured to preserve at least the appearance of equity and the forms of law, and the most ardent eagerness of pursuit has hitherto shrunk back from precipices like this.

The case with which the motion, if it should succeed, will be generally mentioned by our posterity, is that of lord Clarendon in the reign of Charles 2, which the presence of a right hon. member, one of his descendants, recalls to my memory. The arts by which this great minister was exposed to the hatred of the people, the subtle malice with which his most innocent actions were misrepresented, and by which his casual failings were exaggerated into crimes, the confidence with which those transactions were imputed to him which he opposed, or in which he never concurred, and the fallacious reasonings by which every miscarriage or misfortune were imputed to his counsels, are now never mentioned but with detestation. It is now universally acknowledged, that we owe to the moderation of that noble person who was censured as the projector of servitude, the continuance of our liberty, and that he only restrained the prerogative within its just bounds, who was prosecuted as the inexorable enemy of the people.

This man, after having superintended the public affairs with abilities, diligence and integrity scarcely equalled in any nation by the most celebrated patriots, was at last driven by the storms of faction to seek for security on a foreign coast, and condemned to spend the remnant of his life in compassionating that people whom it was no longer in his power to assist, and whom the madness of their leaders hurried into measures of which perhaps the ill consequences are yet felt.

Such was at time the fate of integrity, and such is always to be feared, when the nation is inflamed by the calumnies of faction, when the public counsels are intangled with the secret interests of popular orators, and private men assume the province of judging for the parliament.

Nothing, Sir, appears to me more necessary to the happiness of mankind, than that rewards and punishments should be equitably distributed, and in order to their distribution, it is requisite that every man's merits and crimes should be made public by an impartial trial; to this impartiality the motion now offered is in my opinion directly opposite, and therefore I hope it will be generally rejected. . . .

Mr. Pulteney rose and said: Sir; I rise up, I confess, sooner than I intended, because as the request made, for whatever reason, by the right hon. gentleman, that he may hear the whole of his accusation before he offers his defence, has not been opposed, I perceive it is expected by the House, that every gentleman present, who has declared himself an enemy to the late destructive measures, and has any thing to urge against their author, should produce it, that the whole charge appearing, it may be answered at once, and nothing remain but to put the question.

That the charge will be answered by the right hon. gentleman, I can make no doubt, because he has never wanted an answer to any arguments that have been alleged against the most incredible of his assertions, or the most pernicious of his measures; but that it will be confuted by him, whatever my natural candour may incline me to wish, I confess, I do not expect: because he never yet was able to overthrow the arguments of those who opposed him, and time has been very far from adding to the facility of a vindication.

If we may guess at the nature of the defence which he will offer, from that which has already been advanced by his advocates and adherents, we may reasonably conclude that it will produce no remarkable effects upon this assembly, nor persuade any man of his innocence who has not already determined to acquit him. The gentlemen who have hitherto attempted to justify him, have only insisted on the insufficiency of the proof, and instead of vindicating the measures which have given occasion to the motion, have implicitly denied that he was the author of them, by enquiring upon what evidence he is accused.

That those, Sir, whose employments have long doomed them to the drudgery of low fallacies and sophistical evasions, who have been hired from year to year to darken truth and embarrass reason, and who having vowed fidelity to their master are insensible of any other merit, than that of inviolable adherence to his interest, and account it a laudable instance of steadiness and resolution to repeat his assertions however notoriously false, and follow his opinions however absurd, should have recourse to subterfuges like this, is no subject of astonishment, this is not the first time that they have put a stop to justice by the meanest artifices, and sheltered guilt by the most open and shameless protection.

But that such a vindication should be sufficient to suspend the judgment of gentlemen of integrity and public spirit, that it should operate upon members untainted with avarice or ambition, and procure him advocates without the assistance of a commission, a pension, or a place, I cannot reflect without amazement, nor can conceive what induces those who condemn the measures, to require any farther discovery of the author, or to call for any other evidence than their own memory and observation.

In the trial, Sir, of common criminals, witnesses are required, because the crime is commonly denied, and the judge can attain a knowledge of the question no otherwise than by evidence; but how, Sir, can any parallel be drawn between the case of a minister and a common criminal? If we compare their conduct indeed, we shall find them equally charged with invading the property to which they had no right, we shall find them equally endeavouring to escape from justice, and perhaps when they are at last reduced to make a stand, with equal insolence, setting their accusers at defiance, insisting on their innocence with equal effrontery, and calling out with equal vehemence for proof of that guilt which is already evident. But whatever similitude may appear in their behaviour, the other circumstances of their trial must be very different. The felon stands before a judge unacquainted with his character, and a stranger to his person, whom he may therefore soften by pathetic protestations, or deceive by artful evasions, and false testimonies. But the criminal is now in the midst of an assembly in which his conduct has been year to year examined, and in every examination discovered to be wrong, to the greatest number of which his insolence, his profusion and his power have been long the subjects of observation, and to whom the means are well known by which they are supported, supported in opposition to the universal voice of the people, and in open contempt of justice and of policy.

Yet when the day arrives in which the question is to be discussed, whether the cries of the nation shall at last be heard, whether the king shall be informed of the miseries of his subjects, whether the pride of corruption shall be repressed and rapacity withheld from plunder, it is enquired, what is the evidence against the man whom we are called upon to censure? Or how is it proved by external testimonies, that he is the author of evil counsels? or that the miseries which oppress, and the dangers which threaten us are to be imputed to him and to him only?

If we reflect that the difference between this assembly and common courts consists principally in this, that we are to consider facts of which we know the original, the progress, and the event, and are therefore only to decide a question which we understand in its full extent, and that other judges are to examine the circumstances of crimes, and the characters of persons which they never heard of before, it will easily be understood, why, though the inferior courts of justice require evidence, we may reasonably and justly proceed without it.

This difficulty, Sir, which I persuade myself is raised by a scrupulous regard to equity, may perhaps be removed by asking, whether if a criminal were to stand before judges who had been witnesses of his crimes, and who could refer him to no other judicature, it would be necessary for them to acquit him for want of proof? This question I suppose is already determined by every man's reason, and this is the case of the present motion.

But since more proof is required, I shall endeavour to produce it, and though I have no witnesses to summon to this bar, I have such circumstantial evidence to offer, as would not fail to convict a housebreaker, a pick-pocket, or a murderer and which I hope will not lose its force when it is employed against crimes of greater enormity.

That this person has long enjoyed all that power and influence with which the prime viziers of arbitrary monarchs are invested, and exerted them with the same licentiousness; that he has distributed at pleasure the favours of his master; that he has transferred authority by his nod, scattered riches and honours by caprice, and made it his amusement to exalt and depress without regard to any other motives than his own inclination, is apparent from multitudes who without merit or birth are now rioting in affluence, and imitating the luxury, the insolence, and wantonness of their patron; who are now the underagents of pillage and oppression, who are betraying their country in foreign courts, or projecting in our own the means of enslaving it.

Nor is his power to degrade, less discovered by those who have fallen victims to that pride which they could not persuade themselves to worship, and been devoured by that rapacity which they would not feed, and who have been deprived of employments which only they knew how to execute, for want of sufficient reverence for the abilities of the minister, of implicit submission to his will, and unbounded confidence in his integrity.

That he has been long the sole disposer of places of profit, appears from those which he has accumulated upon his own family, of whom I believe, no gentleman will stand up and affirm, that they have any other claim than their relation to him, which can entitle them to receive so large a part of the public treasure; yet among these is a revenue squandered by which a sovereign might be supported; by these is the nation beggared, and insulted for murmuring at beggary.

Surely, Sir, no other proof than this will be required against him; for it was never yet pleaded that discovering a man with stolen goods upon him, was not a sufficient reason for apprehending him as a robber.

That he has the distribution of places in his hands, appears from the manner in which they are bestowed, and that he is master of the national treasure is no less evident from his profusion; profusion to which no fund but the exchequer can be sufficient, and of which the income of his estate and the known salaries of his visible employments are not equal to the tenth part. His conduct has indeed in this respect been such, that he seems to have thought his triumph not complete, unless he showed how little he regarded detection, and how much he despised the resentment of the nation.

For this reason, Sir, he has pleased himself with enriching palaces, and extending parks, planting gardens in places to which the very earth was to be transported in carriages, and contriving cascades and fountains where water was only to be obtained by aqueducts and machines, and imitating the extravagance of oriental monarchs at the expence of a free people whom he at once impoverished and betrayed.

Some of the sources of his wealth are indeed easily traced, the bank contract especially has been publicly exposed. Nor are his negociations with regard to the army-debentures less criminal, by which how much, and how reproachfully he was enriched ought for ever to be remembered.

As many of the younger members may be reasonably supposed unacquainted with the nature of this affair, I shall endeavour to explain it.

The debts of the army, having been for a long time unpaid, were considered as desperate, and consequently valued at a very low rate; this opinion our minister, who has frequently boasted of his concern for national credit, suffered to prevail, however detrimental to the public service, till at length, when they were reduced almost to nothing, he thought it a proper time to circulate among his dependents an intimation that they would be discharged by the parliament, and that therefore great advantage might arise from purchasing them.

The character of his followers is too well known to raise any doubt of their ready compliance with a proposal of this kind; they, who had been always eager after the scent of lucre, rushed at once upon the prey when it lay before them, bought up the debentures before those that sold them knew how much their value was increased, and were in a few months repaid by the government with immense profit.

I suppose I need not prove that he was himself a sharer in this corrupt traffic, for it is well known that he was never inclined to overlook any opportunities of gain, nor ever regarded the interest of his followers but as subsequent to his own.

In his disposal of the favours of the crown, it is not to be imagined that he has passed over himself; many favours are visible, and it may be reasonably imagined that he has received others which are less public, since he only is the fountain of merit, and no man can have any desert but what arises from his relation to him, or his dependence on him.

I cannot therefore but conclude, that he has enjoyed this power till it is time to take it away, and divide it among others who may use it with more justice and moderation; that it is time to call him or thrust him down from the summit of authority, and try whether the nation does not afford men who will be less intoxicated with elevation, and be content with their proper provinces. Having said this, I need not add, that I shall vote for the motion.

Sir Robert Walpole: Sir; having now heard the charge against me, with all the aggravation which suspicion has been able to form, and eloquence to inforce; after the most fruitful inventions have combined to multiply crimes against me, and the most artful rhetoric has been employed to blacken them, I stand up to offer to the House a plain unstudied defence, nor do I solicit any other favour than I shall appear to deserve, or wish to be protected in this storm of accusation by any other shelter than that of innocence.

The gentlemen who have already spoken in my favour have indeed freed me from the necessity of wearying the House with a long defence, since their knowledge and abilities are so great that I can hope to add nothing to their arguments, and their zeal or their friendship so ardent, that I shall speak with less warmth in my own cause.

Nor is this, Sir, the only reason for which it is superfluous to dwell long upon my own vindication; for I have not only the assistance of my friends, but the concurrence of the parliament to alleviate my task, since all the public transactions have been approved by the legislature, which are now charged upon me as instances of ignorance, negligence, or treachery. Upon the modesty or justice of such accusations, it is not my business to remark. The vindication of their own honour is properly the business of the parliament. But I cannot forbear to observe how far backwards the charge has been extended, and how many facts have been mentioned, which are forgotten by all who do not propose to gratify some passion, or promote some private interest by remembering them, and which may be therefore misrepresented without fear, since the true state of these affairs are so little known, and so difficult to be explained.

In such cases the approbation of the parliament, given at a time when the questions to which it related had been lately discussed, when they were yet the subjects of conversation, and were examined with all the acrimony of malice, and the sagacity of interest; that approbation which a complete knowledge and exact enquiry produced, will surely outweigh a subsequent censure offered by private men at the distance of many years, and after a long train of disappointments which may be supposed at least to have vitiated their temper, if it has not perverted their conduct.

But lest it should be thought that an appeal to former parliaments proceeded from diffidence in the judgment of this, those to whom my conduct has appeared not to deserve the censure proposed, have recollected the arguments which prevailed at those times over discontent, ambition and resentment, and of which I do not doubt but that they will now produce the same conviction.

The gentlemen by whom the motion has been supported, have indeed failed in the most essential part of their accusation. They have not yet attempted to prove that I am the author of those measures which they have so clamourously condemned, but surely they cannot be ignorant that till they have proved the criminal, their declamations upon the crime are empty sounds, that they are arrows shot without a mark, which lose their force in the air, or fall down upon those who discharged them.

It has indeed, Sir, been prudent not to attempt what they are not able to accomplish, for I defy them to shew that in any of these transactions I was engaged otherwise than as one among many, as a member of the council in which they were determined on, or of the parliament by which they were approved.

Of the exorbitant power with which I am invested, of the influence which I extend to all parts of the nation, of the tyranny with which I oppress those that oppose, and the liberality with which my followers are rewarded, no instance has been produced, as indeed no effects have been felt. But having first conferred upon me a kind of mock dignity, and stiled me the prime minister, they carry on the fiction which has once heated their imaginations, and impute to me an unpardonable abuse of that chimerical authority, which only they have thought it necessary to bestow.

If their dream has really produced in them the terrors which they express, if they are really persuaded that the army is annually established by my authority, that I have the sole disposal of posts and honours, and that I employ this power only to the destruction of liberty and the diminution of commerce, compassion would direct us to awaken them from so painful a delusion, to force their eyes open, and stimulate them to a clear view of their own condition and that of the public, to shew them that the prerogative has made no incroachments, that every supply is granted by the parliament, and every question debated with the utmost freedom, as before the fatal period in which they were seized with this political delirium, that has so long harrassed them with the loss of trade, the approach of slavery, the power of the crown, and the influence of the minister.

But I am indeed, Sir, far from believing that they feel in themselves those emotions which they endeavour to communicate to others, I cannot but think so highly of their sagacity as to conclude that even in their own opinion, they are complaining of grievances which they do not suffer, and promoting rather their own interest than that of the nation.

Whatever, Sir, is their intention, the House will undoubtedly require, that their assertions should be confuted; I shall therefore proceed to some transactions of a more private kind, in which it may be suspected that I was personally engaged.

Among these, Sir, I do not number the affairs of the debentures, with which the gentleman who spoke last has so warmly upbraided me. I have indeed long expected that the fury of the opponents of the government, every day encreased by new defeats, would at last hurry them into some wild measures, or ridiculous assertions, by which their reputation among the people, that reputation which they have with so much labour established, would be totally destroyed.

The day which I have long expected is at last arrived, they must henceforward no longer expect to be reverenced as the great dispensers of political truth, as the guardians of virtue, or the supporters of justice, but must be content to be levelled with those whom they have so long affected to despise, with courtiers, placemen, and adherents to the government; for which of all these, however dependent or corrupt, has attempted to ruin the reputation of another by charging him with a transaction in which he had no part? The debentures of the army were settled before I was advanced to any of the offices which I now enjoy, nor had I any other concern in them, than that of promoting and regulating the payment of them; and yet I am charged in this assembly, with enriching myself by an illegal traffick on this occasion.

The apparent falshood of this charge will, Sir, I hope, dispose the House to hear more favourably my defence against the rest, since it may be easily imagined that they who advance falshood will aggravate truth.

With regard to the employments which have been granted to my family, I know not whether any man can accuse me of doing what he would not have done in the same circumstances; nor do I believe that the most abstemious of my accusers, had he been able to obtain the same interest, would not have employed it to the same end. It will not surely be expected that I should obstruct his majesty's favours when offered to my family, and I hope their advancement cannot be imputed to me as a crime, unless it shall appear that I procured them by false representations of their virtue or abilities.

As to myself, I know not how I have given occasion to any charge of rapacity or avarice, or why I should be suspected of making exorbitant demands upon his majesty's liberality, since, except the places which I am known to possess, I have obtained no grant from the crown, or fewer at least than perhaps any man who has been supposed to have enjoyed the confidence of his sovereign. All that has been given me is a little house at a small distance from this city, worth about seven hundred pounds, which I obtained that I might enjoy the quiet of retirement, without remitting my attendance on my office.

The little ornament upon my shoulder I had indeed forgot, but this surely cannot be mentioned as a proof of avarice; nor though it may be looked on with envy or indignation in another place, can it be supposed to raise any resentment in this House, where many must be pleased to see those honours which their ancestors have worn restored again to the Commons.

Having now, Sir, with due submission offered my defence, I shall wait the decision of the House, without any other solicitude than for the honour of their counsels, which cannot but be impaired if passion should precipitate, or interest pervert them. For my part, that innocence which has supported me against the clamour of opposition, will establish my happiness in obscurity, nor shall I lose by the censure which is now threatened any other pleasure than that of serving my country.

FOUNDATIONS OF ECONOMIC EXPANSION

Act imposing customs duties on East India goods and manufactures, wrought silks, and other merchandise, 1690

2 W. & M., c. 4   *Statutes at Large*, IX, 87-95.

Most gracious Sovereigns,

The commons assembled in parliament, for a further supply of your Majesties present occasions, in the necessary defence of your realms, the perfect reducing of Ireland, and the effectual prosecution of the war against France, have given and granted, and hereby give and grant unto your Majesties the additional and other rates, impositions, duties, and charges upon the several sorts of goods and merchandize to be imported into this your Majesties kingdom, herein after expressed, during such time, and in such manner and form, as herein after followeth: and do humbly pray your Majesties that it may be enacted;

II. And be it enacted by the King's and Queen's most excellent majesties, by and with the advice and consent of the lords spiritual and temporal, and commons, in this present parliament assembled, and by the authority of the same, That there shall be answered and paid to their Majesties and their successors, for the several goods and merchandizes hereafter mentioned, over and above all impositions, duties and charges already imposed and payable upon and for the same, the further rates and duties following, viz.

III. For all callicoes, and all other Indian linen, and for all wrought silks, and other manufactures of India and China (except indigo) imported after the five and twentieth day of December, one thousand six hundred and ninety, and before the tenth day of November, one thousand six hundred and ninety five, twenty pounds for every hundred pounds value thereof.

IV. For all wrought silks imported within the time aforesaid, from any other place, ten pounds for every hundred pounds value thereof.

V. For all raw silks imported within the time aforesaid, from China or from the East Indies, five pounds for every hundred pounds value thereof.

VI. For all linen imported within the time aforesaid, from any parts from whence the same may be by law imported (other than linen cloth of the manufacture of the Spanish Netherlands, or of the United Provinces, not exceeding an English ell and half quarter in breadth) one moiety over and above what is already imposed upon the same in the book of rates.

VII. And for all linen cloth of the manufacture of the Spanish Netherlands, or of the United Provinces, of the breadth of two ells or upwards, and under three ells,

102

as much more as what the same is charged with in the book of rates, and of the breadth of three ells or upwards, treble as much as what the same is charged with in the book of rates.

VIII. And for all deal timber, or other timber, boards, wainscot, pipe staves, box wood, and other wood imported within the time aforesaid from any part of Europe (except Ireland) ten pounds for every hundred pound value thereof, above what is charged thereupon in the book of rates.

IX. For every ton of hempseed oil, rape oil, and other seed oil, imported after the five and twentieth day of December, one thousand six hundred and ninety, and before the tenth day of November, one thousand six hundred and ninety five, eight pounds; and so in proportion for any greater or lesser quantity of the respective goods and merchandize before mentioned.

X. For every hundred weight of hops, containing one hundred and twelve pounds, imported from foreign parts after the said five and twentieth day of December, one thousand six hundred and ninety, and before the tenth day of November, one thousand six hundred and ninety five, twenty shillings, over and above what the same are charged with in the book of rates; and so in proportion for any greater or lesser quantity.

XI. For every hundred weight of pepper, containing one hundred and twelve pounds, imported after the said five and twentieth day of December, and before the said tenth day of November, one thousand six hundred and ninety five, twenty eight shillings, over and above what the same is charged with in the book of rates; and so in proportion for any greater or lesser quantity; one third part of the said duty charged upon pepper to be paid down, and bond to be given for payment of the residue at the end of twelve months, or else to discount after the rate of ten pounds per centum, on paying down the whole duty.

XII. For every hundred pound value of grocery wares and druggs (other than pepper and liquorice, which are hereby particularly charged; and also except currants, sugar, tobacco, mace, cinnamon, nutmegs, and cloves) imported after the said five and twentieth day of December, one thousand six hundred and ninety, and before the tenth day of November, one thousand six hundred and ninety five, ten pounds.

XIII. And for every hundred pound value of currants imported within the time aforesaid, five pounds, over and above what the same are respectively charged with in the book of rates; and so in proportion for any greater or lesser quantity.

XIV. For every ton of iron wrought or unwrought, or cast (except bushel iron) imported from any foreign parts after the five and twentieth day of December, one thousand six hundred and ninety, and before the tenth day of November, one thousand six hundred and ninety five, in any other ship or vessel than such as are English built, and whereof the master and three fourths of the mariners at the least are English, thirty three shillings.

XV. And for every ton of such iron which shall be imported in such English built ship or vessel so navigated, three and twenty shillings, over and above what the same is charged with in the book of rates; and so in proportion for any greater or lesser quantity.

XVI. And for all sorts of foreign iron wire (except card wire, and all sorts of iron wire smaller than the sorts commonly called or known by the names of fine fine and super fine, and all wool cards, or any other wares made of iron wire) to be imported between the five and twentieth day of December, one thousand six hundred and ninety, and the tenth day of November, one thousand six hundred and ninety five, there shall be paid for every hundred weight, containing one hundred and twelve pounds, two and twenty shillings and six pence, and also the duty mentioned in the book of rates, to be paid by the importer, and so in proportion for any greater or lesser quantity; which sorts of iron wire (except as aforesaid) it shall and may be lawful for any person or persons whatsoever to import within the time aforesaid, and no longer; any law, statute, or usage to the contrary notwithstanding.

XVII. And for all sorts of steel wire imported within the time aforesaid, the sum of fourteen shillings for every hundred weight, containing as aforesaid, over and above the duty charged in the book of rates; and so in proportion for any greater or lesser quantity.

XVIII. And for every iron pot, and iron kettle, imported within the time aforesaid, one shilling and three pence, over and above what is charged in the book of rates.

XIX. For every small back for chimnies, imported within the time aforesaid, one shilling and two pence, over and above what is charged in the book of rates.

XX. For every large back for chimnies, imported within the time aforesaid, two shillings and four pence, over and above what is charged in the book of rates.

XXI. For every hundred weight of iron slit or hammered into rods, commonly known by the name of rod iron, containing one hundred and twelve pounds, imported within the time aforesaid, five shillings, over and above what is charged in the book of rates; and so in proportion for a greater or lesser quantity.

XXII. For every hundred weight of frying pans, containing as aforesaid, imported within the time aforesaid, four shillings, over and above what is charged in the book of rates; and so in proportion for any greater or lesser quantity.

XXIII. For every hundred weight of steel, containing one hundred and twelve pounds, imported within the time aforesaid, five shilling and six pence, over and above what is charged in the book of rates; and so in proportion for any greater or lesser quantity.

XXIV. For every hundred weight of anvils wrought, containing one hundred and twelve pounds, imported within the time aforesaid, nine shillings and three pence, over and above what is charged in the book or rates; and so in proportion for any greater or lesser quantity.

XXV. For every hundred of single white or black plates imported within the time aforesaid, four shillings and four pence, over and above what is charged in the book of rates; and so in proportion for any greater or lesser quantity.

XXVI. For every hundred of double white or black plates, imported within the time aforesaid, eight shillings and eight pence, over and above what is charged in the book of rates; and so in proportion for any greater or lesser quantity.

XXVII. For every harness plate, or iron double, imported within the time aforesaid, one shilling and four pence, over and above what is charged in the book of rates.

XXVIII. For every hundred weight of iron drawn or hammered, less than three quarters of an inch square, and all other iron ware manufactured, containing one hundred and twelve pounds, imported within the time aforesaid, five shillings, over and above what is charged in the book of rates.

XXIX. Provided, That no manufactured iron or iron ware, which by this act is charged to pay by the piece or hundred weight, shall be liable to pay the duty of thirty three shillings, or twenty three shillings by the ton, imposed by this act.

XXX. And for every hundred weight of brass, latten, or copper wire, containing one hundred and twelve pounds, imported within the time aforesaid, fifteen shillings, over and above what is charged in the book of rates; and so in proportion for any greater or lesser quantity.

XXXI. For every last of hemp seed, cole seed, and rape seed, imported after the said five and twentieth day of December, one thousand six hundred and ninety, and before the tenth day of November, one thousand six hundred and ninety five, four pounds, above what the same is charged with in the book of rates.

XXXII. For all yarn of flax or hemp, other than cable yarn, imported after the said five and twentieth day of December, one thousand six hundred and ninety, and before the tenth day of November, one thousand six hundred and ninety five, an additional duty of as much as what is now charged thereupon in the book of rates.

XXXIII. For every hundred weight of cable yarn, containing one hundred and twelve pounds, imported within the time aforesaid, five shillings; and so in proportion for any greater or lesser quantity of the said seeds or yarn.

XXXIV. For all drinking glasses and other glass, and all manufactures of glass (except Rhenish and Muscovia window glass) imported within the time aforesaid, three shillings for every twenty shillings value thereof, above what the same is charged with in the book of rates.

XXXV. For every hundred weight of molosses, containing one hundred and twelve pounds, imported within the time aforesaid, from any other place than the English plantations in America, eight shillings, over and above what the same is charged with in the book of rates.

XXXVI. For every hundred weight of tallow, containing one hundred and twelve pounds, imported within the time aforesaid, five shillings; and so in proportion for any greater or lesser quantity.

XXXVII. For every hundred weight of tallow candles imported within the time aforesaid, and containing one hundred and twelve pounds, ten shillings; and so in proportion for any greater or lesser quantity.

XXXVIII. For every pound of bever wool cut and combed, imported within the time aforesaid (except wool combed in Russia, and imported from thence in English ships) fifteen shillings.

XXXIX. For every barrel of pot ashes, containing two hundred weight neat, imported within the time aforesaid, eight shillings, above what the same is charged with in the book of rates; and so proportionably for any greater or lesser quantity.

XL. For every hundred weight of cordage ready wrought, containing one hundred and twelve pounds, imported within the time aforesaid, five shillings, over and above what the same is charged with in the book of rates; and so in proportion for any greater or lesser quantity.

XLI. For every ton of olive oil imported within the time aforesaid, four pounds, above what the same is charged with in the book of rates; and so in proportion for any greater or lesser quantity.

XLII. For all paper imported within the time aforesaid, the several duties following, over and above what the same are respectively charged with in the book of rates (that is to say) for every ream of royal paper two shillings; for every ream of blue paper, demy paper, and painted paper, one shilling and six pence; for every bundle of brown paper two pence; and for all other paper so imported, as much more as what the same is now charged with in the book of rates.

XLIII. For every hundred weight of liquorice, containing one hundred and twelve pounds, imported within the time aforesaid, eighteen shillings and eight pence, above what the same is charged with in the book of rates; and so proportionably for any greater or lesser quantity.

XLIV. And for every such hundred weight of liquorice powder imported within the time aforesaid, one pound, seventeen shillings, and four pence.

XLV. And for every pound weight of juice of liquorice imported within the time aforesaid, one shilling, and so proportionably for any greater or lesser quantity.

XLVI. For every hundred weight of barilla or saphora, containing one hundred and twelve pounds, imported within the time aforesaid, two shillings and six pence above what the same is charged with in the book of rates; and so in proportion for any greater or lesser quantity.

XLVII. For every hundred weight of sope imported within the time aforesaid, containing one hundred and twelve pounds, ten shillings, over and above what is charged in the book of rates; and so in proportion for any greater or lesser quantity.

XLVIII. For all earthen ware, not mentioned in the book of rates, imported within the time aforesaid, two shillings and six pence for every twenty shillings value thereof.

XLIX. For every hundred weight of starch, containing one hundred and twelve pounds, imported within the time aforesaid, twenty shillings, above what the same is charged with in the book of rates; and so in proportion for any greater or lesser quantity.

L. For every hundred weight of allom, containing one hundred and twelve pounds, imported within the time aforesaid, two shillings and six pence, above what the same is charged with in the book of rates; and so in proportion for any greater or lesser quantity.

LI. For every hundred weight of brimstone, containing one hundred and twelve pounds, imported within the time aforesaid, four shillings and eight pence, above what the same is charged with in the book of rates; and so in proportion for any greater or lesser quantity.

LII. For every hundred weight of tin, imported within the time aforesaid, containing one hundred and twelve pounds, thirty shillings, over and above what the same is charged in the book of rates; and so in proportion for any greater or lesser quantity.

LIII. Provided always, and be it enacted, That where any duties upon goods and merchandize herein before granted, are to be levied according to the value of the same, where such goods or merchandizes are particularly rated in the book of rates, the value shall be understood and taken according to such rate; and where they are not particularly rated, the value shall be taken by and according to the oath of the importer, and not otherwise; the duties imposed by this act not to be reckoned into the value of the same.

LIV. And be it further enacted by the authority aforesaid, That for all additional duties hereby imposed upon the aforementioned goods and merchandize to be imported as aforesaid, the importer, giving security at the custom-house, shall have time, not exceeding twelve months (where the same is not otherwise hereby limited) for the payment of the same, from the importation, to be paid by four equal and quarterly payments; or in case such importer shall pay ready money, he shall have after the rate of ten pounds per cent. for a year of the said duty abated to him or her; and if the goods and merchandize to be imported as aforesaid, for which the additional duty is paid or secured at the importation thereof, be again exported within twelve months after the importation, then the aforesaid duties shall be wholly repaid, or the security vacated, as to what shall be so exported.

LV. Provided nevertheless, and be it enacted by the authority aforesaid, That the new or additional duties, imposed by this act, shall not extend to affect such foreign stores as have been sold to the use of their Majesties navy, by contract with the navy board, or commissioners of the victualling, before the fifteenth day of November, one thousand six hundred and ninety, so as a certificate be given from the commissioners of the navy or victualling, that such foreign stores have been so contracted for by them for their Majesties service as aforesaid, and so as the importer of the same do make oath before the commissioners appointed to manage the customs (which oath they are hereby impowered to administer) of the truth of the said contract, and that he will deliver the said goods into their Majesties stores, pursuant to the contract so certified by the commissioners of the navy or victualling.

LVI. And be it enacted, That the several impositions and duties above mentioned shall be raised, levied, collected, and paid unto their Majesties and their successors, during the times afore mentioned, in the same manner and form, with such advantages, and by such rules, means and ways, and under such penalties and forfeitures, as are mentioned and expressed in one act of parliament made in the twelfth year of the reign of King Charles the Second, intituled, *A subsidy granted to the King of tunnage and poundage, and other sums of money payable upon merchandize exported and imported,* and the rules and orders thereunto annexed; which said act, and every article, rule, and clause therein contained, shall stand and be in force for the purposes aforesaid, during the continuance of this act.

LVII. Provided always, and it is hereby enacted, That it shall and may be lawful to and for any person and persons to advance and lend unto their Majesties, upon the security of this act, any sum or sums of money, and to have and receive for the forbearance thereof any sum not exceeding eight pounds, by the hundred for one whole year, and no more, directly or indirectly.

LVIII. And to the end that all monies, which shall be lent unto their Majesties upon the credit of this act, may be well and sufficiently secured out of the monies arising and payable by this act; be it further enacted by the authority aforesaid, That there shall be provided and kept in their Majesties exchequer (that is to say) in the office of the auditor of the receipts, one book or register, in which all monies that shall be paid into the exchequer by virtue of this act, shall be entred and registred apart and distinct from all other monies paid or payable to their Majesties upon any other branch of their Majesties revenue, or upon any other account whatsoever; and that all and every person and persons, who shall lend any money to their Majesties upon the credit of this act, and pay the same into the receipt of the exchequer, shall immediately have a talley of loan struck for the same, and an order for his repayment, bearing the same date with his talley; in which order shall be also contained a warrant for payment of interest for forbearance after the rate so to be allowed for the same, so as such interest do not exceed the rate of eight pounds per cent. per ann. for his consideration, to be paid every three months, until repayment of his principal; and that all orders for repayment of money shall be registred in course, according to the date of the talley respectively, without preference of one before another; and that all and every person and persons shall be paid in course, according as their orders shall stand entred in the said register book, so as that the person, native or foreigner, his executors, administrators, and assigns, who shall have his order or orders first entred in the said book of register, shall be taken and accounted as the first person to be paid upon the monies to come in by virtue of this act; and he or they who shall have his or their order or orders next entred, shall be taken and accounted to be the second person to be paid, and so successively, and in course; and that the monies to come in by this act shall be in the same order liable to the satisfaction of the said respective parties, their executors, administrators, or assigns successively, without preference of one before another, and not otherwise, and not to be divertible to any other use, intent, or purpose whatsoever; and that no fee, reward, or gratuity, directly or indirectly, be demanded or taken of any of their Majesties subjects for providing or making of any such book, registers, entries, view or search in or for payment of money lent, or the interest, as aforesaid, by any of their Majesties officer or officers, their clerks, or deputies, on pain of payment of treble damages to the party grieved by the party offending, with costs of suit, or if the officer himself take or demand any such fee or reward, then to lose his place also. And if any undue preference of one before another shall be made, either in point of registry or payment, contrary to the true meaning of this act, by any such officer or officers, then the party offending shall be liable by action of debt, or on the case, to pay the value of the debt, damages, and costs, to the party grieved, and shall be forejudged from his place or office; and if such preference be unduly made by any his deputy or clerk, without direction or privity of his master, then such deputy or clerk only shall be liable to such action, debt, damages, and costs, and shall be for ever after uncapable of his place or office; and in case the auditor shall not direct the order, or the clerk of the pells record, or the teller make payment, according to each person's due place and order, as afore directed, then he or they shall be judged to forfeit, and their respective deputies and clerks herein offending, to be liable to such action, debt, damages, and costs, in such manner as aforesaid. All which said penalties, forfeitures, damages, and costs, to be incurred by any of the officers of the exchequer, or any their deputies or clerks, shall and may be recovered by action of debt, bill, plaint, or information, in any of their Majesties courts of record at

Westminster, wherein no essoin, protection, privilege, wager of law, injunction, or order of restraint, shall be in any wise granted or allowed.

LIX. Provided always, and be it hereby declared, That if it happen that several tallies of loan, or orders for payment as aforesaid, bear date, or be brought the same day to the auditor of the receipt to be registred, then it shall be interpreted no undue preference which of those he enters first, so he enters them all the same day.

LX. Provided also, That it shall not be interpreted any undue preference to incur any penalty in point of payment, if the auditor direct, and the clerk of the pells record, and the teller do pay subsequent orders of persons that come and demand their money, and bring their orders, before other persons that did not come to demand their money, and bring their orders in their course, so as there be so much money reserved as will satisfy precedent orders, which shall not be otherwise disposed, but kept for them; interest upon loan being to cease from the time the money is so reserved and kept in bank for them.

LXI. And be it further enacted by the authority aforesaid, That every person or persons to whom any monies shall be due by virtue of this act, after order entred in the book of register aforesaid for payment thereof, his executors, administrators, or assigns by indorsement of his order, may assign and transfer his right, title, interest, and benefit of such order, or any part thereof, to any other; which being notified in the office of the auditor of receipt aforesaid, and an entry or memorial thereof also made in the book of register aforesaid for orders (which the officers shall, upon request, without fee or charge accordingly make) shall entitle such assignee, his executors, administrators, and assigns, to the benefit thereof, and payment thereon; and such assignee may in like manner assign again, and so *toties quoties;* and afterwards it shall not be in the power of such person or persons, who have or hath made such assignments, to make void, release, or discharge the same, or any the monies thereby due, or any part thereof.

Act founding the National Debt, 1693

5 W. & M., c. 5   *Statutes at Large,* IX, 239-43.

This act launched an annuity scheme for those advancing sums of money to the government. It marked the first assumption of responsibility by Parliament for repayment of the public debt.

Whereas by an act of this present parliament, intituled, *An act for granting to their Majesties certain rates and duties of excise, for securing certain recompences and advantages in the said act mentioned, to such persons as shall voluntarily advance the sum of ten hundred thousand pounds towards carrying on the war against France,* it was enacted, That it should be lawful for any persons, natives or foreigners, to contribute towards the advancing the sum of ten hundred thousand pounds for the purposes therein mentioned, by paying into their Majesties receipt of Exchequer such sum or sums of money, at such times, and upon such terms respectively, as in the said act are particularly mentioned and expressed: and whereas the several sums paid in upon the said act by the several contributors did and do in the whole amount but to the sums of eight hundred eighty one thousand four hundred ninety three pounds fourteen shillings and two pence: We your Majesties most loyal and dutiful subjects, the commons in parliament assembled, being sensible of the great and necessary expences, in which your Majesties are engaged for carrying on the present war against the French king, and being desirous to supply the same in such manner as may be least grievous to your Majesties subjects, do beseech your Majesties that it may be enacted:

II. And be it enacted by the King's and Queen's most excellent majesties, by and with the advice and consent of the lords spiritual and temporal, and commons, in this present parliament assembled, and by the authority of the same, That it shall and may be lawful for any persons, natives or foreigners, to contribute towards the advancing the sum of one hundred and eighteen thousand five hundred and six pounds five shillings and ten pence, to make up the whole sum of ten hundred thousand pounds by the said recited act intended to be advanced, by paying into the receipt of their Majesties Exchequer, at any time before the first day of May, one thousand six hundred ninety four, any sum or sums of money, not exceeding in the whole the sum of one hundred and eighteen thousand five hundred and six pounds five shillings and ten pence, upon the terms following; (that is to say,) That every such person, out of the rates and duties of excise granted by the said recited act, shall have and receive, for every sum of one hundred pounds by them respectively advanced and paid, a yearly annuity, rent, or payment of fourteen pounds of lawful English money, and proportionably for a greater sum, for and during the life of such person so advancing or paying the same, or during any other life to be nominated by the person advancing or paying any such sum as aforesaid, the same to be nominated within six days after payment of such sum; which yearly annuities, rents, or payments, shall commence from the four and twentieth day of June next ensuing, and shall be paid and payable at the four most usual feasts of the year, that is to say, the annunciation of the blessed virgin Mary, the nativity of Saint John Baptist, the feast of Saint Michael the archangel, and the feast of the birth of our Lord Christ, by even and equal portions; and every person, on payment of any such sum or sums as aforesaid, shall immediately have one or more tally or tallies, importing the receipt of the consideration money, and orders for the payment of the said annuities, bearing the same date with the tally; the said tallies to be levied, and the said orders to be signed, in the same manner as in the said recited act is mentioned touching tallies and orders to be given to the contributors for annuities upon the said act, and the said orders not to be determinable, revocable, or countermandable, as touching the forementioned orders in the said recited act is enacted; which said orders shall be assignable and transferable in such and the same manner, as is mentioned in the said recited act, touching orders given to the contributors in the said act mentioned; and all the rates and duties by the said recited act granted, over and besides so much as shall bear proportion, at the rates in the said act mentioned, to the whole sum of eight hundred eighty one thousand four hundred ninety three pounds fourteen shillings and two pence, already advanced by the contributors upon the said recited act, are and shall be appropriated and applied, and are hereby appropriated, to and for the payment of the said annuities, yearly rents, or sums, after the rate of fourteen pounds per centum per annum, for every hundred pounds to be advanced as aforesaid, according to the true intent and meaning of this act, and shall not be diverted or divertible to any other use, intent, or purpose whatsoever, under the like penalties, forfeitures, and disabilities, in respect to all and every the officers and other persons in the said recited act mentioned, as are in the said act appointed and enacted, in case of diverting or misapplying any part of the monies which ought to be paid to the contributors upon the said act; and the said officers are hereby required to keep books and registers, and make entries of the names of all persons who shall advance any monies before the said first day of May as aforesaid, and of the several sums so advanced, and the times of paying in the same respectively, and the names of such persons for whose lives the several annuities or yearly payments are to be payable, without fee or reward, in such manner as in the said recited act is mentioned; to which books all persons concerned shall have access, as in the said act also is directed; all which the said officers are to do and perform, under the like penalties and forfeitures, and disabilities, as in the said recited act are mentioned: and every person, who shall advance and pay any such sum as aforesaid, before the first day of May as aforesaid, shall receive out of the money granted by the said recited act, for all money so advanced by him and paid, from the respective days of payment unto the four and twentieth day of June as aforesaid, interest at the rate of ten pounds per centum per annum.

III. And be it further enacted, That any monies payable to any person or persons, upon or by virtue of this act, shall not be charged or chargeable with any rates, duties, or impositions whatsoever: and in case there shall be any surplus or remainder of the monies arising by the said rates and duties of excise, at the end of any year during the term of ninety nine years granted therein by the said former act, after making all the payments which by this, or the said former act, are appointed to be paid or satisfied within the same year, or reserving money for the same, such surplus or remainder shall be to the use of their Majesties, their heirs and successors.

IV. And to make the payment of the annuities more easy to the several contributors upon this and the before recited act, both upon the terms of survivorship, and the annuity of fourteen pounds per centum; be it enacted, That every contributor upon this or the former act, his or her executors, administrators, or assigns, upon their demanding any half yearly or quarterly payment of his, her, or their respective shares of either of the said funds (unless the nominee appear in person at the said receipt) shall produce a certificate of the life of his, her, or their respective nominee, signed by the minister and churchwardens of the parish where such nominee shall be then living, as by the said recited act is appointed, or otherwise it shall and may be lawful to and for every contributor, his or her executors, administrators or assigns, at his, her or their election, to make oath of the truth of his, her or their respective nominee's life, upon the day when the said payments shall become due, before any one or more justices of the peace of the respective county, riding, city, town, or place wherein such person at the time of making the said oath shall reside (which oath he or they are hereby impowered to administer) and the said justice or justices shall make a certificate thereof, for which oath and certificate no fee or reward shall be required; and the said certificates shall be filed in the said office of receipt of the Exchequer: and if any person shall be guilty of a false oath, or forging any certificate, touching the premises, and be thereof lawfully convicted, he shall incur the pains and penalties to be inflicted upon persons who commit wilful perjury or forgery: and in case any nominee shall at the time of such demand be resident in Scotland, or beyond the seas, and any one or more of the barons of the Exchequer for the time being shall certify, that upon proof to him or them made (which proof he and they is and are hereby authorized and required to take in a summary way) it doth seem probable to him or them, that the said nominee is living (which certificate is to be given, and examination made, without fee or charge) the said certificate, being filed as aforesaid, shall be a sufficient warrant for making the said quarterly payment to the respective contributors or advancers, their executors, administrators or assigns: and if any person or persons shall receive one or more quarterly payments upon his, her or their annuity or annuities, for any time beyond the death of his, her or their nominee, when the same ought to cease, such person or persons shall forfeit treble the value of the monies so by him, her or them received; the one half thereof to their Majesties, their heirs and successors, and the other half to him or them that will sue for the same, by action, suit, bill, or information, in which no essoin, protection, privilege, or wage of law, or more than one imparlance shall be allowed.

V. And whereas several persons, who did contribute, advance, or pay several of the sums of money which have been contributed, advanced, or paid upon the said recited act, for shares, dividends, annuities, or other benefits in the said act mentioned respectively, as well upon the benefit of survivorship, as upon the yearly annuities of fourteen pounds per centum, did not name to the auditor of the receipt, or clerk of the pells in the receipt of the Exchequer, by or within the respective times by the said act appointed, the respective lives, during which such dividends, shares, annuities, or other benefits respectively were to continue; it is hereby further enacted and provided by the authority aforesaid, that if such persons, or any of them, shall at any time or times before the first day of March next, nominate to the auditor of the receipt, or the clerk of the pells in the said Exchequer, the respective lives (their own or others) during which such dividends, shares, annuities, or other benefits, should continue respectively, that then and in every such case his, her or their nominees shall be entred in the books kept in the said receipt for the nominees; and every such contributor or contributors, his, her and their executors, administrators and assigns respectively, shall have, receive and enjoy, and be intituled to have, receive and enjoy, such and the like dividends, shares, annuities and other benefits, for and in respect of the monies so contributed, advanced or paid, as he, she or they might, should or ought to have had, received or enjoyed, in case the respective lives for the same had been named within the respective times by the said act prescribed; any thing in this or the said former act contained to the contrary notwithstanding.

VI. Provided also, and be it further enacted, that the surplus or remainder of the monies arising by the said rates and duties, appointed by the said act to be to the use of their Majesties, their heirs and successors, shall not be charged or chargeable with any gift, grant or pension whatsoever; and that all and every grant and grants of any such pensions shall be and is hereby declared to be utterly void; and all and every person and persons to whom such grants are or shall be passed, shall be and are hereby made accountants unto their Majesties, their heirs and successors, and shall pay back all sums of money received by pretence of such grants, and the court of Exchequer is hereby required to issue out process accordingly.

Act establishing the Bank of England, 1694

5 & 6 W. & M., c. 20   *Statutes at Large*, IX, 291-97.

XVIII. And be it further enacted by the authority aforesaid, That for the better raising and paying into the receipt of the Exchequer the sum of twelve hundred thousand pounds, part of the sum of fifteen hundred thousand pounds, the yearly sum of one hundred and forty thousand pounds, arising by and out of the duties and impositions granted by this act, shall be kept separate and apart in the said receipt of Exchequer, to be paid over from time to time unto such person and persons, and in such manner, proportion, and form, as is herein after directed.

XIX. And be it further enacted by the authority aforesaid, That it shall and may be lawful to and for their Majesties, by commission under the great seal of England, to authorize and appoint any number of persons to take and receive all such voluntary subscriptions as shall be made on or before the first day of August, which shall be in the year of our Lord one thousand six hundred ninety four, by any person or persons, natives or foreigners, bodies politick or corporate, for and towards the raising and paying into the receipt of Exchequer the said sum of twelve hundred thousand pounds, part of the sum of fifteen hundred thousand pounds, and that the yearly sum of one hundred thousand pounds, part of the said yearly sum of one hundred and forty thousand pounds, arising by and out of the said duties and impositions before mentioned, shall be applied, issued, and directed, and is hereby appropriated, to the use and advantage of such person and persons, bodies politick and corporate, as shall make such voluntary subscriptions and payments, their heirs, successors, or assigns in the proportion hereafter mentioned (that is to say) that each weekly or other payment arising by and out of the duties and impositions granted by this act, shall, by the auditor of the receipt of Exchequer, from time to time, as the same shall be paid in, be separated and divided into five seventh parts and two seventh parts, which is according to the proportion of the said yearly sum of one hundred thousand pounds, to the said yearly sum of one hundred and forty thousand pounds, which five seventh parts, of the said several payments arising by and out of the duties and impositions granted by this act, and so set apart, is and are hereby intended and appropriated for and towards the payment and satisfaction of the said yearly sum of one hundred thousand pounds, and shall from time to time be issued and paid, as the same shall come into the said receipt of Exchequer, to the uses and advantages of such subscribers and contributors, their heirs, successors, or assigns, as shall subscribe and contribute for and towards the raising and paying into the receipt of Exchequer the said sum of twelve hundred thousand pounds, part of the said sum of fifteen hundred thousand pounds.

XX.   And be it further enacted, That it shall and may be lawful to and for their Majesties, by letters patents under the great seal of England, to limit, direct, and appoint, how and in what manner and proportions, and under what rules and directions, the said sum of twelve hundred thousand pounds, part of the said sum of fifteen hundred thousand pounds, and the said yearly sum of one hundred thousand pounds, part of the said yearly sum of one hundred and forty thousand pounds, and every or any part or proportion thereof, may be assignable or transferrable, assigned or transferred, to such person or persons only, as shall freely and voluntarily accept of the same, and not otherwise; and to incorporate all and every such subscribers and contributors, their heirs, successors, or assigns, to be one body corporate, and politick, by the name of *the governor and company of the bank of England,* and, by the same name of *the governor and company of the bank of England,* to have perpetual succession, and a common seal, and that they and their successors, by the name aforesaid, shall be able and capable in law to have, purchase, receive, possess, enjoy, and retain to them and their successors, lands, rents, tenements, and hereditaments, of what kind, nature, or quality soever; and also to sell, grant, demise, aliene, or dispose of the same, and by the same name to sue and implead, and be sued and impleaded, answer and be answered, in courts of record, or any other place whatsoever, and to do and execute all and singular other matters and things by the name aforesaid, that to them shall or may appertain to do; subject nevertheless to the proviso and condition of redemption herein after mentioned.

XXI.   Provided always, and it is hereby further enacted, That in case the whole sum of twelve hundred thousand pounds, part of the said sum of fifteen hundred thousand pounds, shall not be advanced and paid into the receipt of Exchequer before the first day of January, which shall be in the year of our Lord one thousand six hundred ninety four, that then the subscribers and contributors for and towards the raising and paying of the said sum of twelve hundred thousand pounds, part of the said sum of fifteen hundred thousand pounds, their heirs, successors and assigns, shall only have and receive so much, and such part and proportion to the said sum and sums so respectively paid and advanced, as shall be after the rate of eight pounds per centum per annum; and that at any time upon twelve months notice, after the first day of August, which shall be in the year of our Lord one thousand seven hundred and five, upon repayment by parliament, of the said sum of twelve hundred thousand pounds, part of the said sum of fifteen hundred thousand pounds, or such part thereof as shall be paid and advanced as aforesaid, unto the respective subscribers and contributors of the said sum of twelve hundred thousand pounds, part of the said sum of fifteen hundred thousand pounds, or such part thereof as shall be paid and advanced, their heirs, successors, or assigns, and of all the arrears of the said yearly payments of one hundred thousand pounds, part of the said yearly payments of one hundred and forty thousand pounds, or such proportionable part thereof according to the sum which shall be paid and advanced as aforesaid, then and from thenceforward the said yearly payments, and every of them, of one hundred thousand pounds, part of the said yearly payments of one hundred and forty thousand pounds, or such proportionable part as aforesaid, and every part thereof, and the said corporation, shall absolutely cease and determine; any thing herein contained in any wise to the contrary notwithstanding.

XXII. And for the better and more speedy payment of the said yearly sum of one hundred thousand pounds, part of the said yearly sum of one hundred and forty thousand pounds, in the proportions herein before mentioned and appointed, the commissioners of their Majesties treasury, and the under treasurer of the Exchequer now being, and the lord high treasurer, and under treasurer, or commissioners of the treasury for the time being, are hereby strictly enjoined and required by virtue of this act, and without any further or other warrant to be sued for, had or obtained from their Majesties, their heirs or successors, to direct their warrants yearly for the payment of the said yearly sums of one hundred thousand pounds, to the contributors of the said sum of twelve hundred thousand pounds, in the manner and proportions as is herein before directed and appointed; and the auditor of the receipt of Exchequer, and all other officers of the Exchequer now and for the time being, are hereby directed and enjoined to issue the said monies so set apart for the uses before mentioned, from time to time, without any fee or reward, in the manner and proportions before mentioned, and under the like penalties, forfeitures, and disabilities, as are hereafter inflicted upon any officer for diverting any money appropriated or applied by this act.

XXIII. Provided always, and be it further enacted by the authority aforesaid, That no person or persons, bodies politick or corporate, shall by themselves, or any other person or persons in trust for him or them, subscribe or cause to be subscribed, for and towards the raising and paying the said sum of twelve hundred thousand pounds, any sum or sums of money, exceeding the sum of twenty thousand pounds; and that every such subscriber shall, at the time of such subscription, pay or cause to be paid unto the commissioners who shall be authorized and appointed for taking and receiving subscriptions as aforesaid, one full fourth part of his, her, or their respective subscriptions, and in default of such payments as aforesaid, every such subscription shall be utterly void and null: and that the residue of the said subscriptions shall be paid into the receipt of their Majesties Exchequer, as their Majesties shall direct, before the said first day of January next; and in default of such payments, that then the fourth part, first paid as aforesaid, shall be forfeited to and for the benefit of their Majesties, their heirs and successors.

XXIV. Provided also, and be it enacted, That it shall not be lawful to or for any person or persons, natives or foreigners, bodies corporate or politick, at any time or times before the first day of July next ensuing, to subscribe in his, her, or their own name or names, or in any other name or names in trust for him, her, or them, for and towards the raising and paying into the receipt of the Exchequer, the said sum of twelve hundred thousand pounds, part of the said sum of fifteen hundred thousand pounds, any sum or sums, exceeding in the whole the sum of ten thousand pounds; anything in this act contained to the contrary in any wise notwithstanding.

XXV. Provided always, and be it declared and enacted to be the true intent and meaning of this act, That in case the whole sum of twelve hundred thousand pounds, or a moiety thereof, be not subscribed on or before the first day of August, one thousand six hundred ninety four as aforesaid, that then the powers and authorities in this act for erecting a corporation as aforesaid shall cease and determine; any thing herein contained to the contrary notwithstanding. And in such case so much of the said yearly sum of one hundred thousand pounds as shall belong to the said subscribers, according to the meaning of this act, shall be transferrable, and may be from time to time transferred by the respective persons so subscribing, advancing and paying any part of the said twelve hundred thousand pounds into the Exchequer, or their respective heirs, successors or assigns, to any person or persons whatsoever, by any writing or writings under the hand and seal of the person or persons transferring the same, attested by two or more credible witnesses, and entred within twenty days after the sealing thereof, in a book or books to be for that purpose kept in the said Exchequer by their Majesties remembrancer for the time being (for the entring whereof nothing shall be paid) which entries the said remembrancer is from time to time upon request directed to make; and such part of the said yearly sum of one hundred thousand pounds, as shall by this act be due to the said subscribers, shall not at any time or times hereafter be made use of, or be a fund or security for, or liable or applied to raise, pay or secure any more, further or other sum or sums of money whatsoever, save only such money as shall in pursuance of, and according to the intent of this act, be advanced and paid into their Majesties Exchequer within the time by this act limited for the same.

XXVI. And it is hereby enacted by the authority aforesaid, that the said corporation so to be made, shall not borrow or give security by bill, bond, covenant or agreement under their common seal for any more, further or other sum or sums of money, exceeding in the whole the sum of twelve hundred thousand pounds, so that they shall not owe at any one time more than the said sum, unless it be by act of parliament upon funds agreed in parliament; and in such case only such further sums as shall be so directed and allowed to be borrowed by parliament, and for such time only, until they shall be repaid such further sums as they shall borrow by such authority: and if any more, or further or other sum or sums of money shall be borrowed, taken up, lent, or advanced, under their common seal, or for payment of which any bond, bill, covenant or agreement, or other writing shall be made, sealed or given, under the common seal of the said corporation so to be made; then and in such case all and every person and persons who shall be a member or members of the said corporation, his and their respective heirs, executors, and administrators, shall in his and their respective private and personal capacities be chargeable with, and liable in proportion to their several shares or subscriptions to the repayment of such monies which shall be so borrowed, taken up or lent, with interest for the same, in such manner as if such security had been a security for payment of so much money, and interest for the same, sealed by such respective member or members of the said corporation, and delivered by him or them as their respective acts and deeds, in proportion to their several shares or subscriptions as aforesaid; and that in every such case an action of debt shall and may be brought, commenced, prosecuted and maintained in any of their Majesties courts of record at Westminster, by the respective creditor or creditors, to whom any such security under the common seal of the said corporation shall be made, or his or their respective executors or administrators, against all and every, or any one or more of the persons who shall be members of the said corporation, or any of their respective heirs, executors or administrators, in proportion to their respective shares or subscriptions as aforesaid, and therein recover and have judgment for him or them, in such and the like manner, as if such security were respectively sealed by the respective person or persons who shall be so sued, or his or their respective ancestor, or testator, or intestate, and by him and them executed and delivered, as his or their respective acts and deeds; any condition, covenant, or agreement, to be made to the contrary thereof in any wise notwithstanding: and if any condition, covenant, or agreement shall be made to the contrary, the same shall be, and is hereby declared to be void; any thing herein contained, or any law or usage to the contrary notwithstanding; and in such action or actions so to be brought, no privilege, protection, essoin, or wager of law, nor any more than one imparlance shall be allowed.

XXVII. And to the intent that their Majesties subjects may not be oppressed by the said corporation, by their monopolizing or ingrossing any sort of goods, wares or merchandizes, be it further declared and enacted by the authority aforesaid, That the said corporation to be made and created by this act, shall not at any time, during the continuance thereof, deal or trade, or permit or suffer any person or persons whatsoever either in trust or for the benefit of the same, to deal or trade with any of the stock, monies or effects of or any ways belonging to the said corporation, in the buying or selling of any goods, wares, or merchandizes whatsoever; and every person or persons, who shall so deal or trade, or by whose order or directions such dealing or trading shall be made, prosecuted, or managed, shall forfeit for every such dealing or trading, and every such order and directions, treble the value of the goods and merchandize so traded for, to such person or persons who shall sue for the same by action of debt, bill, plaint, or information, in any of their Majesties courts of record at Westminster, wherein no essoin, protection, nor other privilege whatsoever, nor any injunction, order of restraint, nor wager of law shall be allowed, nor any more than one imparlance.

XXVIII. Provided, That nothing herein contained shall any ways be construed to hinder the said corporation from dealing in bills of exchange, or in buying or selling bullion, gold, or silver, or in selling any goods, wares, or merchandize whatsoever, which shall really and bona fide be left or deposited with the said corporation for money lent and advanced therein, and which shall not be redeemed at the time agreed on, or within three months after, or from selling such goods as shall or may be the produce of lands purchased by the said corporation.

XXIX. Provided always, and be it enacted by the authority aforesaid, That all and every bill or bills obligatory and of credit under the seal of the said corporation made or given to any person or persons, shall and may, by indorsement thereon under the hand of such person or persons, be assignable and assigned to any person or persons who shall voluntarily accept the same, and so by such assignee, *toties quoties,* by indorsement thereupon; and that such assignment and assignments, so to be made, shall absolutely vest and transfer the right and property in and unto such bills or bills obligatory and of credit, and the monies due upon the same; and that the assignee or assignees shall and may sue for, and maintain an action thereupon in his own name.

XXX. Provided always, and it is hereby further enacted, That if the governor, deputy governor, the directors, managers, assistants, or other members of the said corporation so to be established, shall upon the account of the said corporation, at any time or times purchase any lands or revenues belonging to the crown, or advance or lend to their Majesties, their heirs or successors, any sum or sums of money, by way of loan or anticipation, on any part or parts, branch or branches, fund or funds of the revenues now granted or belonging, or hereafter to be granted or belonging to their Majesties, their heirs or successors, other than such fund or funds, part or parts, branch or branches of the said revenues only, on which a credit of loan is or shall be granted by parliament; that then the said governor, deputy governor, directors, managers, or assistants, or other members of the said corporation, who shall consent, agree to, or approve of, the advancing or lending to their Majesties, their heirs or successors, such sum or sums of money as aforesaid, and each and every of them so agreeing, consenting, or approving, and being thereof lawfully convicted, shall for every such offence forfeit treble the value of every such sum or sums of money so lent, whereof one fifth part shall be to the informer, to be recovered in any of their Majesties courts of record at Westminster, by action of debt, bill, plaint, or information, wherein no protection, wager of law, essoin, privilege of parliament, or other privilege shall be allowed, nor any more than one imparlance; and the residue to be disposed of towards publick uses, as shall be directed by parliament, and not otherwise. . . .

Natural and Political Observations by **Gregory King, a contemporary tract providing invaluable information about the state of the economy, 1696**

Natural and Political Observations and Conclusions upon the State and Condition of England, 1696 (reprinted with George Chalmers, *Estimate of the Comparative Strength of Great Britain,* 1804), 39-40, 47-49, 52-53, 61-63.

III.—The several Distinctions of the People, as to Males and Females, Married and Unmarried, Children, Servants, and Sojourners

That the 5 millions and a half of souls, in England, including the transitory people, and vagrants, appear, by the assessments on marriages, births, and burials, to bear the following proportions, in relation to males, and females; viz.

	Males Females	Males	Females	Both
In London and the Bills of Mortality	10 to 13	230,000	300,000	530,000
In the other Cities and Market Towns	8 to 9	410,000	460,000	870,000
In the Villages and Hamlets	100 to 99	2,060,000	2,040,000	4,100,000
	27 to 28	2,700,000	2,800,000	5,500,000

That, as to other distinctions, they appear, by the said assessments, to bear these proportions:—

		People	Males	Females
Husbands and Wives, at above	34½ per Cent.	1,900,000	950,000	950,000
Widowers, at above	1½ per Cent.	90,000	90,000	
Widows, at almost	4½ per Cent.	240,000		240,000
Children, at above	45 per Cent.	2,500,000	1,300,000	1,200,000
Servants, at almost	10½ per Cent.	560,000	260,000	300,000
Sojourners and single Persons	4 per Cent.	210,000	100,000	110,000
	100	5,500,000	2,700,000	2,800,000

And, that the different proportions, in each of the said articles, between London, the great towns, and the villages, may the better appear, we have exhibited the following scheme:—

	London and Bills of Mortality		The other Cities and great Towns		The Villages and Hamlets	
Husbands and Wives	37 per Ct.	196,100	36 per Ct.	313,200	34 per Ct.	1,394,000
Widowers	2 per Ct.	10,600	2 per Ct.	17,400	1½ per Ct.	61,500
Widows	7 per Ct.	37,100	6 per Ct.	52,200	4½ per Ct.	184,500
Children	33 per Ct.	174,900	40 per Ct.	348,000	47 per Ct.	1,927,000
Servants	13 per Ct.	68,900	11 per Ct.	95,700	10 per Ct.	410,000
Sojourners, etc.	8 per Ct.	42,400	5 per Ct.	43,500	3 per Ct.	123,000
	100	530,000	100	870,000	100	4,100,000

IV.—The several Ages of the People

That the Yearly Births of the Kingdom being 190,000 Souls;

	In all	Males	Females
Those under 1 year old are	170,000	90,000	80,000
Those under 5 years old are	820,000	415,000	405,000
Those under 10 years old are	1,520,000	764,000	756,000
Those under 16 years old are	2,240,000	1,122,000	1,118,000
Those above 16 years old are	3,260,000	1,578,000	1,682,000
Those above 21 years old are	2,700,000	1,300,000	1,400,000
Those above 25 years old are	2,400,000	1,150,000	1,250,000
Those above 60 years old are	600,000	270,000	330,000

So that the number of communicants is, in all - - - - - - - - - 3,260,000 souls

And the number of fighting men, between 16 and 60, is - - - - - - - 1,310,000

That the batchelors - - - - - - - - - - - - - - are about 28 per cent. of the whole

    Whereof those under 25 years - - - - - - - - - - - - - - - are 25½ per cent.

    And those above 25 years - - - - - - - - - - - - - - - - - - are 2½ per cent.

That the maidens - - - - - - - - - - - - - - are about 28½ per cent. of the whole

    Whereof those under 25 years - - - - - - - - - - - - - - - are 26½ per cent.

    And those above 25 years - are 2 per cent.

That the males and females, in the kingdom in general, are aged, one with another, 27½ years.

That in the kingdom in general, there is near as many people living under 20 years of age, as there is above 20. Whereof one half of the males is under 19 years, and one half of the females is under 21 years.

At a Medium

That the Husbands are aged	 43	Years apeice, which, at	17¼	per Cent. makes ...	742
The Wives	 40	Years apeice	17¼	....	690
The Widowers	 56	Years apeice	1½	....	84
The Widows	 60	Years apeice	4½	....	270
The Children	 12	Years apeice	45	....	540
The Servants	 27	Years apeice	10½	....	284
The Sojourners	 35	Years apeice	4	....	140
At a Medium	27½			100 Persons	2750

* * *

VI.—The Annual Income, and Expence, of the Nation, as it stood Anno 1688

That the yearly Income of the Nation, Anno 1688, was	£43,500,000 Sterling
That the yearly expence of the nation was	41,700,000
That then the yearly increase of wealth was	1,800,000
That the yearly Rent of the lands was about	10,000,000
Of the burgage, or houseing, about	2,000,000
Of all other hereditaments, about	1,000,000
In all	13,000,000
That the yearly Produce of trade, arts, and labours, was about	30,500,000
In all	43,500,000
That the number of inhabited houses being about	1,300,000
the number of families about	1,360,000
and the number of people about	5,500,000

The People answer to 4¼ per house, and 4 per family.

That the Yearly Estates, or Income, of the several families, answer,

In common, to about	£32. 0. 0. per Family
And about	7. 18. 0. per Head
That the yearly expence of the nation is about	7. 11. 4. per Head
And the yearly increase about	0. 6. 8. per Head

That the whole value of the kingdom, in general, is about	£650,000,000 Sterling
Viz. The 13 millions of yearly rents, at about 18 years purchase	234,000,000 Sterling
The 30 millions and a half per annum, by trade, arts, labours, etc. at near 11 years purchase, (which, being the value of the 5 millions and a half of people, at £60 per head) comes to	330,000,000
The stock of the kingdom, in money, plate, jewels, and household goods, about	28,000,000
The stock of the kingdom, in shipping, forts, ammunition, stores, foreign or home goods, wares, and provisions for trade abroad, or consumption at home, and all instruments and materials relating thereto	33,000,000
The live stock of the kingdom, in cattle, beasts, fowl, etc.	25,000,000
In all	£650,000,000 Sterling

Number of Families	Ranks, Degrees, Titles, and Qualifications	Heads per Family	Number of Persons
160 — —	Temporal Lords -------------------------	40	6,400
26 — —	Spiritual Lords -------------------------	20	520
800 — —	Baronets ------------------------------	16	12,800
600 — —	Knights -------------------------------	13	7,800
3,000 — —	Esquires ------------------------------	10	30,000
12,000 — —	Gentlemen -----------------------------	8	96,000
5,000 — —	Persons in Offices ---------------------	8	40,000
5,000 — —	Persons in Offices ---------------------	6	30,000
2,000 — —	Merchants and Traders by Sea ----------	8	16,000
8,000 — —	Merchants and Traders by Land ---------	6	48,000
10,000 — —	Persons in the Law ---------------------	7	70,000
2,000 — —	Clergymen -----------------------------	6	12,000
8,000 — —	Clergymen -----------------------------	5	40,000
40,000 — —	Freeholders ----------------------------	7	280,000
140,000 — —	Freeholders ----------------------------	5	700,000
150,000 — —	Farmers -------------------------------	5	750,000
16,000 — —	Persons in Sciences and Liberal Arts -----	5	80,000
40,000 — —	Shop-keepers and Tradesmen ------------	4½	180,000
60,000 — —	Artizans and Handicrafts ---------------	4	240,000
5,000 — —	Naval Officers -------------------------	4	20,000
4,000 — —	Military Officers -----------------------	4	16,000
511,586 Families	-------------------------------------	5¼	2,675,520
50,000 — —	Common Seamen ------------------------	3	150,000
364,000 — —	Labouring People and Out Servants --------	3½	1,275,000
400,000 — —	Cottagers and Paupers ------------------	3¼	1,300,000
35,000 — —	Common Soldiers -----------------------	2	70,000
849,000 Families	-------------------------------------	3¼	2,795,000
- - - - - - - - - - - -	Vagrants ------------------------------	—	30,000
849,000 — —	-------------------------------------	3¼	2,825,000

So the General Account is

511,586 Families	Increasing the Wealth of the Kingdom ----------	5¼	2,675,520
849,000 Families	Decreasing the Wealth of the Kingdom --------	3¼	2,825,000
1,360,586 Families	Nett Totals --------	1 1/20	5,500,520

FAMILIES of England; calculated for the Year 1688

Yearly Income per Family	Total of the Estates or Income	Yearly Income per Head	Expence per Head	Increase per Head	Total Increase per Annum
£ s	£	£	£ s d	£ s d	£
2,800 —	448,000	70 —	60 — —	10 — —	64,000
1,300 —	33,800	65 —	55 — —	10 — —	5,200
880 —	704,000	55 —	51 — —	4 — —	51,000
650 —	390,000	50 —	46 — —	4 — —	31,200
450 —	1,200,000	45 —	42 — —	3 — —	90,000
280	2,880,000	35 —	32 10 —	2 10 —	240,000
240 —	1,200,000	30 —	27 — —	3 — —	120,000
120	600,000	20 —	18	2 — —	60,000
400 —	800,000	50 —	40 — —	10 — —	160,000
200 —	1,600,000	33 —	28 — —	5 — —	240,000
140 —	1,400,000	20 —	17 — —	3 — —	210,000
60 —	120,000	10 —	9 — —	1 — —	12,000
45 —	360,000	9 —	8 — —	1 — —	40,000
84 —	3,360,000	12 —	11 — —	1 — —	280,000
50 —	7,000,000	10 —	9 10 —	— 10 —	350,000
44 —	6,600,000	8 15	8 10 —	— 5 —	187,000
60 —	960,000	12 —	11 10 —	1 10 —	40,000
45 —	1,800,000	10 —	9 10 —	— 10 —	90,000
40 —	2,400,000	10 —	9 10 —	— 10 —	120,000
80 —	400,000	20 —	18 — —	2 — —	40,000
60 —	240,000	15 —	14 — —	1	16,000
6/ —	34,495,800	12 18	12 — ·	— 18 —	2,447,100
					Decrease
20 —	1,000,000	7 —	7 10 —	— 10 —	75,000
15 —	5,460,000	4 10	4 12 —	— 2 —	127,500
6 10	2,000,000	2 —	2 5 —	— 5 —	325,000
14 —	490,000	7 —	7 10 —	— 10 —	35,000
10 10	8,950,000	3 5	3 9 —	— 4 —	562,000
— —	60,000	2 —	3 — —	1 — —	60,000
10 10	9,010,000	3 3	3 7 6	— 4 6	622,000
67 —	34,495,800	12 18	12 — —	— 18 —	2,447,000
10 10	9,010,000	3 3	3 7 6	— 4 6	622,000
32 —	43,505,800	7 18	7 11 3	— 6 9	1,825,100

VII.—The several sorts of Land in England, with the Value, and Product thereof

England and Wales contain 39 Millions of Acres; viz.

	Acres	Value per Acre	Rent
Arable land	11,000,000 at 5s.	10d. per acre	£3,200,000
Pasture and meadow	10,000,000 at 9s.	per acre	4,500,000
Woods and coppices	3,000,000 at 5s.	per acre	750,000
Forests, parks, and commons	3,000,000 at 3s.	6d. per acre	550,000
Heaths, moors, mountains, and barren lands	10,000,000 at 1s.	per acre	500,000
Houses, and homesteads, gardens, and orchards, churches, and churchyards	1,000,000 { The land / The buildings		450,000 / 2,000,000
Rivers, lakes, meres, and ponds	500,000 at 2s.	per acre	50,000
Roads, ways, and waste lands	500,000 at	per acre	
In all	39,000,000 at 6s.	2d. per acre	12,000,000

	True Yearly Value	Value as rated to the 4s. Tax	Produce of the 4s. Tax
So the yearly rents, or value of the land is	10 millions	6,500,000	1,300,000
The houses and buildings	2 millions	1,500,000	300,000
All other hereditaments	1 million	500,000	100,000
Personal estates, etc.	1 million	550,000	100,000
In all	14 millions	9,050,000	1,800,000

So that, whereas the tax of 4s. per pound produces but - - - - -   £1,800,000

It should produce (if duly assessed) -   2,800,000

The Produce of the Arable Land, I thus estimate:

	Of Bushels	Per Bushel	Value
Wheat - - - - - - - - - - -	12 Millions,	at 3s. 6d. - - - - - - - - - - -	£2,100,000
Rye - - - - - - - - - - - - -	8 Millions,	at 2s. 6d. - - - - - - - - - -	1,000,000
Barley - - - - - - - - - - -	25 Millions,	at 2s. - - - - - - - - - - - - -	2,500,000
Oats - - - - - - - - - - - -	16 Millions,	at 1s. 6d. - - - - - - - - - -	1,200,000
Peas - - - - - - - - - - - -	7 Millions,	at 2s. 6d. - - - - - - - - - -	875,000
Beans - - - - - - - - - - -	4 Millions,	at 2s. 6d. - - - - - - - - - -	500,000
Vetches, etc. - - - - - - -	1 Million,	at 2s. - - - - - - - - - - - - -	100,000
	73 Millions,	at 2s. 3d. - - - - - - - - - -	8,275,000

This is the only nett Produce exclusive of the Seed Corn, which in some Sorts of Grain, being nearly a 4th of the Produce in others, a 5th, may in general be reckoned, about 17 Millions of Bushels more, which make the whole Produce to be 90 Millions of Bushels, which at 2s. 3d. per Bushel in common are full 10 Millions Sterling.

These 73 millions of bushels of grain are the product of 10 of the 11 millions of acres of arable land; the other million of acres producing hemp, flax, woad, saffron, dying weeds, etc.; the value of the product whereof is about 1 million sterling. So that the rent of the corn land being under £3,000,000 per annum, and the nett produce thereof above 8 millions, the produce is near treble to the rent.

Now the Rents or Yearly Value of the pasture and meadow, woods, coppices, forests, parks, commons, heaths, and moors, mountains and barren land, being - - - £6,250,000 sterling.

The produce can scarce make above two rents, or 12 millions; there being little charge either in cultivating the land, or gathering the product thereof, comparatively to what there is in the arable land.

This produce is principally in and by cattle, hay, timber, and firewood.

The produce by cattle, in butter, cheese, and milk, is about -----------	£ 2,500,000
The value of the wool yearly shorn is about -----------------------	2,000,000
The value of the horses yearly bred is about ----------------------	250,000
The value of the flesh yearly spent as food is about -------------------	3,350,000
The value of the tallow and hides of the cattle -----------------------	600,000
The value of hay yearly consumed by horses about -------------------	1,300,000
The hay yearly consumed by other cattle --------------------------	1,000,000
The timber yearly felled for building and such uses -------------------	500,000
The wood yearly spent in firing and petty uses ---------------------	500,000
So the produce (including one million sterling in hay spent by cattle) is in all -------------------------------------	12,000,000

*   *   *

X.—The State of the Nation, Anno 1695

That the present income of the nation is a million less
  than it was anno 1688, and is now but about - - -   42½ millions sterling
That the yearly expence is about 40½ millions, and the
  taxes 5 millions—In all - - - - - - - - - - - - - - - - - -   45½ millions sterling
That the kingdom does now yearly decrease - - - - -   3   millions sterling

That if the war were to continue to anno 1698 inclusive:
That the yearly income will in probability be but -   38½ millions sterling
        The expence - - - - - - - 38½ millions⎱ In all   42½ millions sterling
          Taxes - - - - - - - - - 4 millions⎰
The yearly decrease -   4   millions sterling

According to the following Scheme:

Anno	Annual Income of the Nation	Annual Expence of the Nation	Ordinary Revenue of the Crown	Extraordinary Taxes actually raised	Annual Expence in all		Increase or Decrease of the Nation
1688	43,500	41,700	2,000,000		41,700,000	Incr.	1,800,000
1689	43,600	41,500	1,800,000	3,000,000	44,500,000	Decr.	900,000
1690	43,700	41,500	1,800,000	4,000,000	45,500,000	Decr.	1,800,000
1691	43,800	41,400	1,700,000	4,000,000	45,400,000	Decr.	1,600,000
1692	43,800	41,200	1,700,000	4,000,000	45,200,000	Decr.	1,400,000
1693	43,600	41,000	1,600,000	4,000,000	45,000,000	Decr.	1,400,000
1694	43,100	40,800	1,600,000	5,000,000	45,800,000	Decr.	2,700,000
1695	42,500	40,500	1,500,000	5,000,000	45,500,000	Decr.	3,000,000
1696	41,600	40,100	1,500,000	4,500,000	44,600,000	Decr.	3,000,000
1697	40,200	39,300	1,400,000	4,500,000	43,800,000	Decr.	3,600,000
1698	38,500	38,500	1,400,000	4,000,000	42,500,000	Decr.	4,000,000

    Hence we may infer,
That in 7 years, from 1688 to 1695 inclusive, the taxes
  have amounted to, effectually - - - - - - - - - - - - - -   29   millions sterling
But, that the kingdom is scarce actually decreased -   13   millions
So that, by industry, and frugality, there have been
  saved full -   16   millions
That, by the year 1698, inclusive, the taxes will, in 10
  years, have amounted to, in all probability,
  effectually -   42   millions
And the kingdom will be actually decreased - - - - -   23½ millions

    That, after the year 1695, the taxes actually raised will fall short every year,
more and more, to that degree, that the war cannot well be sustained beyond the
year 1698 upon the foot it now stands, unless—
    1. The yearly income of the nation can be increased:
    2. Or the yearly expence diminished:

3. Or a foreign or home credit be obtained or established:

4. Or the confederacy be enlarged:

5. Or the state of the war altered:

6. Or a general excise, in effect, introduced:

Now, whereas, by the foregoing scheme, the wealth of the kingdom seems to be actually decreased almost 13 millions sterling, between 1688 and 1695, inclusive; and will probably decrease by 1698, inclusive, above 10 millions and a half more— In all about 23 millions and a half in ten years:—The said decrease seems to be thus chargeable:

	The Stock of the Kingdom 1688	Decrease by the Year 1695	Remaining Stock, Anno 1695	Decrease by the Year 1698	Remaining Stock, Anno 1698
Coined Silver	8,500,000	4,000,000	4,500,000	1,500,000	3,000,000
Coined Gold	3,000,000	— —	3,000,000	1,500,000	1,500,000
Uncoined Silver and Gold	500,000	400,000	100,000	100,000	
Wrought Plate, Rings, etc	4,000,000	1,600,000	2,400,000	1,200,000	1,200,000
Jewels	1,500,000	500,000	1,000,000	200,000	800,000
Furniture, Apparel, etc.	10,500,000	2,500,000	8,000,000	1,500,000	6,500,000
	28,000,000	9,000,000	19,000,000	6,000,000	13,000,000
Stock for Trade, Consumption, etc.	33,000,000	3,000,000	30,000,000	3,500,000	26,500,000
The Live Stock in Cattle, etc.	25,000,000	1,000,000	24,000,000	1,000,000	23,000,000
	86,000,000	13,000,000	73,000,000	10,500,000	62,500,000

Hence it follows, that if the stock of the nation, which was 86 millions sterling anno 1688; viz. about double to the yearly income and expence, shall be decreased to 62 millions and a half by anno 1698; the war cannot well be sustained longer than that year, for these reasons:—

1. For that the money of the kingdom will then be but 4½ millions; viz. but one-tenth of the annual expence, less than which cannot circulate the whole;

2. That the wrought plate will be little above a million, consequently, nothing to be spared further from that article;

3. That 7 millions in jewels, household stuff, furniture, apparel, etc. is the least quantity we can imagine that article reduceable unto, the bedding of the kingdom amounting to one half of that sum;

4. That, if the stock of the kingdom, in shipping, forts, and castles, and in naval and military stores, and appointments, and for foreign trade and home consumption, and all the branches of that article, be reduced from 33 to 26 millions; if it should be further lessened the nation cannot be secure, trade cannot be carried on, nor a sufficient stock of provisions left to supply us in time of difficulty;

5. That if the live stock of the nation, which will then be diminished a 12th part, should be further diminished, it may occasion an excessive rise of the price of wool, leather, flesh, butter, and cheese, not much short of a famine, unless the number of people decrease proportionably; the effect whereof will be equally pernicious.

Act banning imported Persian, Chinese, and Indian calicoes, 1700

11 & 12 Will. 3, c. 10   *Statutes at Large*, X, 328-31.

In line with prevailing economic theory, the objectives of this act were to conserve specie and to develop national self-sufficiency.

Whereas it is most evident, that the continuance of the trade to the East Indies, in the same manner and proportions as it hath been for two years last past, must inevitably be to the great detriment of this kingdom, by exhausting the treasure thereof, and melting down the coin, and taking away the labour of the people, whereby very many of the manufacturers of this nation are become excessively burdensome and chargeable to their respective parishes, and others are thereby compelled to seek for employment in foreign parts: for remedy whereof be it enacted by the King's most excellent majesty, by and with the advice and consent of the lords spiritual and temporal, and commons, in this present parliament assembled, and by the authority of the same, That from and after the twenty ninth day of September, one thousand seven hundred and one, all wrought silks, bengalls, and stuffs mixed with silk or herba, of the manufacture of Persia, China, or East India, and all calicoes, painted, dyed, printed, or stained there, which are or shall be imported into this kingdom, shall not be worn, or otherwise used within this kingdom of England, dominion of Wales, or town of Berwick upon Tweed, but under such limitations as are herein after mentioned and expressed.

II. And for the better effecting the same, be it enacted by the authority aforesaid, That from and after the said twenty ninth day of September, one thousand seven hundred and one, all such wrought silks, bengalls, and stuffs mixed with silk or herba, of the manufacture of Persia, China, or East India, as aforesaid, and all calicoes, painted, dyed, printed, or stained there, which are or shall be imported into this kingdom of England, dominion of Wales, or town of Berwick upon Tweed, shall, after entry thereof, be forthwith carried and put into such warehouse or warehouses, as shall be for that purpose approved of by the commissioners of his Majesty's customs for the time being, so as none of them shall be taken or carried out thence upon any account whatsoever, other than in order for exportation, and not until sufficient security be first given to the King's majesty, his heirs and successors (which the said commissioners are hereby required and impowered to take) that the same and every part thereof shall be exported, and not landed again in any part of this kingdom of England, dominion of Wales, and town of Berwick upon Tweed; which said securities shall be discharged without any fee or reward, upon certificate returned under the common seal of the chief magistrate in any place or places beyond the seas, or under the hands and seals of two known English merchants upon the place, that such goods were there landed, or upon proof by credible persons that such goods were taken by enemies, or perished in the seas; the examination and proof thereof being left to the judgment of the said commissioners; and all such of the aforesaid goods, whether the same shall be mixed, sewed, or made up together for sale, with any other goods or materials, or otherwise, which shall be found in any house, shop, or warehouse, or other place whatsoever (other than in such warehouses as shall be approved of by the said commissioners, as aforesaid) shall be forfeited, and subject and liable to be searched for, and seized, in like manner as prohibited and uncustomed goods are, by an act (intituled, *An act for preventing frauds, and regulating abuses in his Majesty's customs*) made in the fourteenth year of the reign of our late sovereign lord King Charles the Second; and all such goods so forfeited, as aforesaid, shall, upon seizure thereof, be carried to the next custom house, and after condemnation shall be sold to the best advantage for exportation, at publick sale by candle; the buyer and buyers giving security for the exportation thereof, in manner as aforesaid; and one third part of the monies to be raised by such sale shall be paid to the King's majesty, his heirs and successors, and the other two third parts thereof to him, her, or them that shall seize or prosecute for the same; and over and above the loss of the said goods, the person or persons in whose custody, knowing thereof, the same shall be found or seized, or that shall sell or dispose thereof to any person or persons whatsoever, shall forfeit and lose the sum of two hundred pounds, one third part thereof to the King's majesty, his heirs and successors, and the other two third parts thereof to such person or persons that shall sue for the same, to be recovered by action of debt, bill, plaint, suit, or information, in any of his Majesty's courts of record at Westminster, wherein no essoin, protection, or wager of law, shall be allowed, or any more than one imparlance.

III. And for preventing all clandestine importing or bringing into this kingdom of England, dominion of Wales, or town of Berwick upon Tweed, any of the aforesaid goods hereby prohibited, or intended to be prohibited, from being worn or used in England; be it further enacted by the authority aforesaid, That if any person or persons, or bodies corporate, from and after the said twenty ninth day of September, one thousand seven hundred hundred and one, shall import or bring into any port of or in this kingdom of England, dominion of Wales, or town of Berwick upon Tweed, other than the port of London, any of the aforesaid prohibited goods, or into the port of London, and shall not make due entries of such goods so imported, or brought in, the same shall be, and is hereby adjudged, deemed, accounted, and taken to be clandestine running thereof, and such person or persons, or bodies corporate so offending therein, and their abettors, shall not only forfeit and lose the said goods so clandestinely run, as aforesaid, but also the sum of five hundred pounds, to be recovered and divided in such manner as aforesaid.

IV. And be it further enacted, That if any question or doubt shall arise where the said goods were manufactured, the proof shall lie upon the owner or owners thereof, and not upon the prosecutor; any law, usage, or custom to the contrary notwithstanding.

V. And be it further enacted by the authority aforesaid, That if any action, bill, plaint, suit, or information, shall be commenced, or prosecuted against any person or persons, for any seizure, or other thing to be made or done, in pursuance or in execution of any thing before in this act contained, such person or persons, so sued in any court whatsoever, may plead the general issue, and give this act and the special matter in evidence, for their excuse or justification; and if the plaintiff or plaintiffs, or prosecutor or prosecutors, shall become nonsuit, or forbear prosecution, or suffer discontinuance, or if a verdict pass against him, her, or them, in any such action, bill, plaint, suit, or information, as aforesaid, the defendant or defendants shall have treble costs, for which they shall have the like remedy, as in any case where costs by law are given to the defendant.

VI.   And for preventing clandestinely carrying out of the said warehouses any of the said goods hereby prohibited, and by this act intended for exportation, as aforesaid; be it further enacted by the authority aforesaid, That the warehouse-keeper or warehouse-keepers shall keep one or more book or books, wherein he or they shall fairly enter or write down an exact, particular, and true account of all and every chest, bale, and number of pieces therein contained, of such of the aforesaid goods only, which shall be brought into, and carried out of, his or their said warehouse or warehouses, and the days and times when the same shall be so brought in and carried out; and shall every six months in the year transmit in writing an exact account thereof, upon oath, to the said commissioners, together with an exact account how much shall be remaining in his or their said warehouse or warehouses respectively; and the said commissioners are hereby impowered and injoined, within one month after the same shall be transmitted to them, as aforesaid, to appoint one or more persons or persons to inspect the said book or books, warehouse or warehouses, and examine the said accounts, and to lay a true account of the same before the parliament, within the first week of every sessions thereof; and if upon examination it shall appear, that any of the aforesaid goods were carried out, unless for exportation, or before sufficient security given for their exportation, as aforesaid, that then the warehouse-keeper or warehouse-keepers, so offending therein, shall not only forfeit and lose the value of the said goods so carried out, as aforesaid, and be for ever disabled from any publick employment for the future, but shall also forfeit the sum of five hundred pounds for every such offence, to be recovered and divided in manner as aforesaid.

VII.   Provided always, and it is hereby enacted, That this act shall not extend to any silks, bengals, stuffs mixed with silk or herba, or painted, dyed, printed, or stained calicoes manufactured in Persia, China, or East-India, which shall have been made up and used in any sort of apparel or furniture, before the said twenty ninth of September, one thousand seven hundred and one.

VIII.   Provided always, and be it further enacted, That it shall and may be lawful to and for the proprietor or proprietors of the said goods so lodged in any warehouse or warehouses, as aforesaid, to affix one lock to every such warehouse or warehouses, the key of which shall remain in the custody of the said proprietor or proprietors; and that he or they may view, sort, or deliver the said goods, in order for exportation, as aforesaid, in the presence of the said warehouse-keeper or warehouse-keepers, who is and are hereby obliged, at seasonable times, to give attendance for that purpose.

IX.   Provided also, that be it enacted by the authority aforesaid, That every person or persons, or bodies corporate, who shall, on or before the said twenty ninth day of September, one thousand seven hundred and one, import into this kingdom, dominion of Wales, or town of Berwick upon Tweed, any of the commodities aforesaid, and shall, within the space of three years from such importation, export the same again, shall be allowed and paid the several duties payable upon the exportation thereof, as fully as if the same had been exported within twelve months after the importation thereof.

X. And be it further enacted by the authority aforesaid, That from and after the said twenty ninth day of September which shall be in the year of our Lord, one thousand seven hundred and one, there shall be no customs or duties whatsoever paid or secured to be paid for any of the said goods or commodities, which shall be imported at any time from and after the said twenty ninth day of September, one thousand seven hundred and one, other than and except the half subsidy, which is to remain by law after the goods are exported; but that all other customs and duties, now chargeable upon or payable for the said goods, shall from that time cease and determine.

Act for enlarging the capital stock of the Bank of England, 1708

7 Anne, c. 7   *Statutes at Large*, XI, 445-52.

May it please your most excellent Majesty, whereas by or in pursuance of an act of parliament made in the fifth year of the reign of their late majesties King William and Queen Mary, of glorious memory, intituled, *An act for granting to their Majesties several rates and duties upon tonnage of ships and vessels, and upon beer, ale, and other liquors, for securing certain recompences and advantages in the said act mentioned, to such persons as shall voluntarily advance the sum of fifteen hundred thousand pounds, towards carrying on the war against France,* the corporation or body politick of the governor and company of the bank of England was erected and established with such capacities, powers, privileges, benefits, and advantages, and subject to such restrictions, and in such manner and form as are therein mentioned; and in pursuance of the same act the sum of one million two hundred thousand pounds was advanced and lent to their said late Majesties, for which there is now payable to the said governor and company, and their successors, the yearly sum of one hundred thousand pounds out of certain rates and duties of excise, which were thereby granted to their said late Majesties, their heirs and successors; in which act it was provided, That at any time upon twelve months notice, after the first day of August, in the year of our Lord one thousand seven hundred and five, upon repayment by parliament of the said sum of one million two hundred thousand pounds, and of all the arrears of the said yearly sum of one hundred thousand pounds, then the said one hundred thousand pounds per annum, and the said corporation, should absolutely cease and determine: and whereas by another act made in the eighth year of the reign of his said late majesty King William the Third, intituled, *An act for making good the deficiencies of several funds therein mentioned, and for enlarging the capital stock of the bank of England, and for raising the publick credit,* the said corporation was enlarged and established with divers other powers, privileges, benefits, and advantages, and subject to such other restrictions and rules as are therein particularly expressed; in which act last-mentioned it was provided and enacted, That at any time upon twelve months notice, after the first day of August, which should be in the year of our Lord one thousand seven hundred and ten, and not before, and upon repayment by parliament of the said sum of one million two hundred thousand pounds, and of all arrears of the said one hundred thousand pounds per annum, and also upon payment of all the principal and interest monies which should be owing to the said governor and company of the bank of England, upon all such tallies, Exchequer orders, or parliamentary funds, which the said governor and company should have remaining in their hands, or be entitled to at the time of such notice to be given, as aforesaid, then, and in such case, and not till then, the said one hundred thousand pounds per annum, and also the said corporation, should cease and determine: and whereas by an act made in the fifth year of your Majesty's reign (intituled, *An act for continuing the duties upon houses, to secure a yearly fund for circulating Exchequer bills, whereby a sum not exceeding fifteen hundred thousand pounds is intended to be raised for carrying on the war, and other her Majesty's occasions*) several duties upon houses therein mentioned or referred unto, are continued from the last day of July, one thousand seven hundred and ten, and from thenceforth made payable to your Majesty, your heirs and successors for ever, for the purposes in that act expressed, subject to the proviso or condition of redemption therein contained; and the duties so continued, together with such remainder and arrears of house money, as are therein mentioned, are thereby charged with the yearly fund, after the rate of four pounds ten shillings per centum per annum, to be paid to the said governor and company of the bank of England, for circulating all such Exchequer bills as should be issued by or in pursuance of that act; and by the same act a power was given for making forth Exchequer bills for any sum not exceeding fifteen hundred thousand pounds for your Majesty's supply; and it was thereby enacted, that like bills should be made out quarterly for so much as should be computed to be due and owing upon and for the said allowance of four pounds ten shillings per centum per annum, until the feast of St. Michael the archangel, one thousand seven hundred and ten inclusively, in the manner therein mentioned; and it was thereby enacted, that the said governor and company, after the said Exchequer bills, or any of them, should be issued upon that act, as aforesaid, should, from time to time, exchange all such Exchequer bills as they should be required to exchange by any person or persons whatsoever for ready money; and that the said governor and company, and their successors, should continue and remain a corporation until all the said Exchequer bills should be redeemed and cancelled in the manner in that act mentioned; and in the same act there is contained a proviso, that at any time, upon one year's notice and payment of the principal money to be due on the said Exchequer bills, and of so much as should be due for the said allowance, after the rate of four pounds ten shillings per centum per annum, for circulating the said Exchequer bills, then, and not till then, the said Exchequer bills should be cancelled and discharged, and the said allowance after the rate of four pounds ten shillings per centum per annum, should cease and determine; and so much of the said duties on houses as should have been applied for the payment of the said four pounds ten shillings per centum per annum, in case the same had continued, shall from thenceforth be understood to be redeemed by parliament, and should not be issued, paid, or applied to any use or purpose whatsoever but by authority of parliament; and it is also thereby enacted, that the said governor and company might call in from their respective members proportionably, any sums of money as they should think necessary for the said circulation; and that until all the Exchequer bills by that act directed to be issued, should be paid off, discharged, and cancelled, no more or other bills of the like nature should be made out and issued at the receipt of her Majesty's Exchequer, either with or without the authority of parliament, unless with the consent of the said governor and company; and that nothing in that act contained should hinder the redemption of the said original fund of one hundred thousand pounds per annum, or of any other funds granted or to be granted by parliament, upon which the said governor and company had or should have lent any monies, and which were redeemable by parliament, but that the same might be redeemed from the said governor and company, according to former acts for that purpose, without redeeming the said four pounds ten shillings per centum per annum, nevertheless, without determining or dissolving the corporation of the said governor and company, until the said four pounds ten shillings per centum per annum, should be redeemed from them; as by the said several acts, relation being thereunto respectively had, more at large may appear: and whereas the said governor and company, for the better enabling themselves to supply the public exigencies, did lately consent to admit new subscriptions for doubling their then present stock of two millions two hundred and one thousand one hundred seventy one pounds ten shillings, at the rate of one hundred and fifteen pounds to be paid for every one hundred pounds subscribed, and upon a commission granted by your Majesty, under the great seal of Great Britain, bearing date the sixteenth day of February, in the seventh year of your reign, to Sir Thomas Abney, and others directed, grounded upon an address of the commons of Great Britain in parliament assembled, several persons have subscribed several sums, amounting to two million two hundred and one thousand one hundred seventy one pounds ten shillings for doubling the said stock, as aforesaid, and have paid down to the said governor and company, at or before their respective subscriptions, one fifth part of the sums by them respectively subscribed, and are to pay the remaining four fifth parts thereof, together with fifteen pounds per centum more (being in all one hundred and fifteen pounds for every one hundred pounds subscribed) in manner hereafter mentioned; all which subscriptions are contained in books of vellum or parchment for that purpose, attested by three or more of the said commissioners, and now remaining in the custody of the governor and company of the bank of England, whereof there are two duplicates made in vellum or parchment, attested by seven or more of the said commissioners, and one of the said duplicates is delivered into the office of the auditor of the receipt, and the other of them into the office of the clerk of the pells in your Majesty's Exchequer, there to remain for ever: now for the better pursuing the ends and intent of the said subscribers in making such subscriptions and payment, as aforesaid, it is hereby enacted, at the humble suit of the said governor and company of the bank of England, and be it enacted by the Queen's most excellent majesty, by and with the advice and consent of the lords spiritual and temporal, and commons, in this present parliament assembled, and by authority of the same, That the several sums subscribed or written in the said books, amounting to the said sum of two millions two hundred and one thousand one hundred seventy one pounds ten shillings, shall be added and united, and be judged and deemed to be added and united to the stock of the said governor and company, which before such addition consisted of the like sum of two millions two hundred and one thousand one hundred seventy one pounds ten shillings, as aforesaid, so that the capital stock of the said governor and company so increased, shall be and amount, and be deemed to amount in the whole to the sum of four millions four hundred and two thousand three hundred forty three pounds; and that all and every the person and persons, natives and foreigners, who have subscribed or written any sum or sums of money, or for whom any sum or sums of money have been subscribed or written in the said books of subscription, for or towards the making up the said sum of two millions two hundred and one thousand one hundred seventy one pounds ten shillings, therein compleatly subscribed, and who have paid to the said governor and company one fifth part of each subscribed sum, as aforesaid, and the executors, administrators, and assigns of such person and persons respectively, shall be, and be deemed and reputed to be members of, united to, and incorporated with the said governor and company of the bank of England, and shall at all times, together with the other members of the said corporation and body politick, and their successors respectively, be, and be adjudged, construed, reputed, accepted, and taken to be one body politick and corporate, by the name of *The governor and company of the bank of England*.

II. And it is hereby enacted by the authority aforesaid, That the capital stock of the said governor and company, now amounting, as aforesaid, to four millions four hundred and two thousand three hundred forty three pounds, shall be assignable and transferrable in the same manner as the original capital stock of the said governor and company was assignable and transferrable before the making of this act.

III. And whereas the said governor and company of the bank of England so enlarged or constituted, being the better enabled by such new subscriptions and payments thereupon, as aforesaid, to serve the publick, are willing to advance and lend to her Majesty a further sum on the said yearly fund of one hundred thousand pounds, upon such terms, conditions, and advantages as are hereafter in this act expressed in relation thereunto, and are willing to accept an annuity after the rate of six pounds per centum per annum, out of the said duties on houses, for all the said Exchequer bills that have been made out, or are to be made out, in pursuance of the last recited act, and to deliver up the said bills as fast as they can get them into their custody, to be cancelled, upon such terms, conditions, and advangages as are also hereafter in this act expressed, in relation to such annuity to be settled, and such bills to be cancelled, as aforesaid; and are also willing to undertake a circulation, (in the manner and form herein after mentioned) of two millions five hundred thousand pounds in other Exchequer bills to be issued for the use of the war, and other your Majesty's occasions, upon such terms, conditions, and advantages as are likewise hereafter in this act expressed in relation thereunto; and are likewise willing upon the like terms, conditions, and advantages to undertake the circulation of such Exchequer bills as shall be made out quarterly as well to discharge the allowance of three pounds per centum per annum which shall be due to the said governor and company for circulating the Exchequer bills to be issued, in pursuance of this act, from the time such bills shall begin to be issued, as also to discharge, or raise money to discharge the interest of two pence per diem for every one hundred pounds to be born upon the said bills, until the funds, which by this act are settled and intended to discharge the said allowances for circulation and interest, shall take effect, and be sufficient for those purposes: now we your Majesty's most dutiful and loyal subjects the commons of Great Britain in parliament assembled, being desirous, not only to raise the necessary supplies with as much ease to your Majesty's subjects as is possible, for the carrying on and finishing the present war with success, but also to use such ways and means in the doing thereof, as that your Majesty may have the better and more speedy effect of the said supplies, do most humbly beseech your Majesty that it may be enacted; and be it enacted by the authority aforesaid, That the said governor and company of the bank of England so enlarged or constituted, as aforesaid, and their successors, shall advance and pay into the receipt of her Majesty's Exchequer, for her Majesty's use, the full sum of four hundred thousand pounds, or so much thereof as shall remain after deduction of such discount as is hereafter in this act allowed to be made out of the same, such payment to be made by such proportions, and at such times, as are herein after appointed for payment thereof; that is to say, one third part thereof on or before the tenth day of May, one thousand seven hundred and nine, one other third part thereof on or before the eight and twentieth day of June, one thousand seven hundred and nine, and the residue thereof on or before the five and twentieth day of August, one thousand seven hundred and nine

IV. Provided always, and it is hereby declared and enacted by the authority aforesaid, That out of the said sum of four hundred thousand pounds, the said governor and company shall have and receive back, or shall and may retain and keep to their own use, by way of discount, so much as the rate of six pounds per centum per annum, for each sum of money which shall be actually advanced and paid for or upon account of the said sum of four hundred thousand pounds, shall amount unto, from the day of the actual payment thereof, until the first day of August, one thousand seven hundred and eleven: and in case the said governor and company of the bank of England shall make failure in any of the said payments, so by this act appointed to be made into her Majesty's Exchequer, as aforesaid, at or before the respective days or times before limited in that behalf, the money whereof such failure in payment shall be made, shall and may be recovered to her Majesty's use, by action of debt, or upon the case, bill, suit, or information, in any of her Majesty's courts of record at Westminster, wherein no essoin, protection, privilege, or wager of law shall be allowed, or any more than one imparlance; in which action, bill, suit, or information, it shall be lawful to declare, That the said governor and company of the bank of England, are indebted to her Majesty the monies of which they shall have made default in payment, according to the form of this statute, and have not paid the same, which shall be sufficient; and in or upon such action, bill, suit, or information, there shall be further recovered to her Majesty's use, against the said governor and company of the bank of England, damages after the rate of twelve pounds per centum, for the monies so unpaid contrary to this act, besides full costs of suit; and the said governor and company of the bank of England, and their successors, and their said stock and funds, shall be and are hereby made subject and liable thereunto.

V. And for the encouragement of the said governor and company of the bank of England, to advance and pay the said sum of four hundred thousand pounds, with such discount out of the same, as aforesaid, and to perform the other services in this act mentioned, and to the end the said governor and company, and their successors, may have a competent recompence and consideration for so doing, it is hereby declared and enacted by the authority aforesaid, That the said several and respective provisoes or conditions contained in the said recited act of the fifth year of the reign of their said late majesties King William and Queen Mary, and in the said act of the eighth year of the reign of his said late majesty King William, and each of them, for determining the said fund of one hundred thousand pounds per annum, and the said corporation of the governor and company of the bank of England, upon the respective notices and payments in the same respective acts mentioned, shall be, and are hereby repealed and made void; and that the said governor and company of the bank of England, so enlarged as aforesaid, and their successors, for ever, shall remain, continue, and be one body corporate and politick, by the name aforesaid, and shall for ever have, receive, and enjoy the said entire yearly fund of one hundred thousand pounds out of the said rates and duties of excise, together with a perpetual succession, and all abilities, capacities, powers, authorities, franchises, exemptions, privileges, profits, and advantages whatsoever whereunto the governor and company of the bank of England are, or before the making of this act, were entitled by the said act of the fifth year of the reign of their said late majesties King William and Queen Mary, and by the said act of the eighth year of the reign of his said late majesty King William, or either of them, or by any other act or acts of parliament, grants, or charters whatsoever now in force; all which are by this act ratified and confirmed to the said governor and company so enlarged, and their successors (the said allowance after the rate of four pounds ten shillings per centum per annum, for circulating of Exchequer bills, and the powers only concerning such circulation, given by the said act of the fifth year of her now Majesty's reign, excepted) freed and discharged of and from the said provisoes and conditions of redemption hereby repealed, or intended to be repealed, as aforesaid, and all other provisoes, powers, acts, matters, and things whatsoever heretofore had, made, done, or committed, for the redeeming, determining, or making void the said corporation or yearly fund of one hundred thousand pounds, and the said abilities, capacities, powers, authorities, franchises, exemptions, privileges, profits, and advantages, or any of them; subject nevertheless to such restrictions, rules, and directions, and also to such other agreements, matters, and things, as in the said acts and charters, or any of them now in force, are contained or prescribed; and also subject to the power and condition of redemption hereafter in this act contained in this behalf. . . .

Act placing duties upon paper, pamphlets, and advertisements, 1711

10 Anne, c. 18   *Statutes of the Realm*, IX, pt. 2, 595, 601, 603-04, 617-21.

This was the first of several financial restrictions on the press which came to be known as the "taxes on knowledge." They were not repealed completely until 1861.

Most gracious Sovereign Wee Your Majesties most dutifull and loyall Subjects the Comons of Great Britain in Parliament assembled finding it absolutely necessary to raise large Supplies of Money to carry on the present War until Your Majesty shall be enabled to establish a good and lasting Peace and for defraying Your Majesties other extraordinary Expences have for those Ends and Purposes given and granted and doe by this Act give and grant to Your Majesty the severall and respective Rates and Duties

For and upon all Sope made in Great Britain or imported into the same and

For and upon all Paper made in Great Britain or imported into the same and

For and upon all chequered and striped Linens to be imported into Great Britain and

For and upon certain Silks Callicoes Linens and Stuffs printed painted stained or dyed as are herein after menconed and

For and upon [such] stampt Vellum [and] Parchment and Paper and other Things as are hereafter in this Act more particularly described for and during such Term and Terms of Years and in such Manner and Forme as are herein after expressed . . .

And be it enacted by the Authority aforesaid That there shall be raised levyed collected and paid unto and for the Use of Her Majesty Her Heires and Successors for and upon all Paper of what Kind soever and all Pastboards Mildboards and Scaleboards and all Books Prints and Maps which at any Time or Times within or during the Terme of Thirty two Years to be reckoned from the Foure and tweentieth Day of June One thousand seven hundred and twelve shall be imported or brought into the Kingdome of Great Britain (over and above all other Customes Subsidies and Duties imposed upon or payable for the same) the severall and respective Rates and Duties herein after expressed (that is to say) . . .

And it is hereby enacted That there shall be answered and paid to Her Majestie Her Heires and Successors for and upon all Books Prints and Mapps printed or wrought off in any Parts beyond the Seas which at any Time or Times within or during the Terme last menconed shall be imported or brought bound or unbound into Great Britain (over and above the present Duties thereupon) a Duty after the Rate of Thirty Pounds for every One hundred Pounds of the true and reall Vallue of the same and after that Rate for greater or lesser Quantities which said Duties for and upon the said severall Sorts of Paper and the said Pastboards Mildboards and

Scaleboards and the said Books Prints and Maps to be imported as aforesaid shall be paid by the respective Importers thereof from time to time

And it is hereby declared That the Values of such of the said Paper and of the [said] Bookes Prints and Maps as are to pay the said Duties ad valorem shall in all Cases be taken to be soe much as such imported Kinds are really Worth to be sold at the Port of Importation without any Abatement for the Duties thereupon [charged] by this or any former Acts and that the respective Customer Collector Comptroller or other Person or Persons Officer or Officers of the Customes for the Time being shall receive and levy the same Duties soe payable ad valorem upon the Oath of the Merchant or Importer accordingly And such Oath shall and may be administred and all other Matters done for ascertaining the said Duties of such Paper and of such Books Prints and Mapps soe payable ad valorem in the same Manner and Forme as are lawfully used and practised for ascertaineing any Duties payable ad valorem upon any other Commodities imported

And be it further enacted by the Authority aforesaid That the severall Rates and Duties by this Act sett or imposed upon all or any of the said Sorts of Paper and upon all or any the said Pastboards Mildboards and Scaleboards and the said Bookes Prints and Mapps to be imported or brought into Great Britaine shall from time to time be satisfied and paid in Ready Money upon the Entry or Entries made and before the Landing thereof And that in case any of the said imported Paper or any the said Pastboards Mildboards and Scaleboards Bookes Prints or Maps shall be landed or put on Shore out of any Shipp or Vessell before due Entry be made thereof at the Custome-house in the Port or Place where the same shall be imported and before the said Duties by this Act charged or chargeable thereupon shall be duely paid or without a Warrant for the landing or delivering the same first signed by the Commissioners Collectors or other proper Officer or Officers of the Customes respectively that all such Paper and all the said Pastboards Mildboards and Scaleboards Books Prints and Maps as shall be soe landed or put on Shore or taken out of any Shipp or Vessell contrary to the true Meaning hereof or the Value of the same shall be forfeited and shall and may be seized and recovered of the Importer or Proprietor thereof to witt One Moiety of the same to the Use of Her Majesty Her Heirs and Successors and the other Moiety of the same to the Use of such Person or Persons as will seize informe or sue for the same or the Value thereof in any Her Majesties Courts of Record at Westminster for any such Offences committed in England Wales or Berwick upon Tweed or in Her Majesties Court of Session Court of Justiciary or Court of Exchequer in Scotland for any such Offences committed in Scotland by Action Bill Suit or Information wherein noe Essoign Protection or Wager of Law shall be allowed

And be it further enacted by the Authority aforesaid That the said Duties upon the said imported Paper and Boards and upon the said imported Bookes Prints[&] Maps during the Continuance thereof shall be ascertained secured raised levied recovered and answered for the Uses and Purposes in this Act expressed by such Rules Waies Means and Methods and under such Penalties and Forfeitures and in such Manner and Forme as the present Duties upon such Paper Boards or such Bookes Prints or Mapps respectively or any of them are by any Law or Statute now in force to be ascertained secured raised levied recovered and answered during the Continuance thereof respectively

And be it enacted and declared by the Authority aforesaid That such of the Duties imposed by this Act upon the said Paper and Boards and upon the said Bookes Prints and Mapps as shall arise in England Wales and the Towne of Berwick upon Tweed shall be under the Management of the Commissioners and Officers of the Customs in England for the Time being and such of the Duties imposed by this Act upon imported Paper and Boards or such Books Prints or Maps as aforesaid as shall arise in Scotland shall be under the Management of the Commissioners and Officers of the Customes in Scotland for the Time being and that the respective Receivers Generall of the Customes in England and Scotland for the Time being shall from time to time pay or cause to be paid all the Monies that they respectively shall receive of the said Duties for the said Paper and Boards and for such Books Prints and Maps imported as aforesaid (the necessary Charges of raiseing and accounting for the same excepted) into the Receipt of Her Majesties Exchequer in England distinctly and apart from all other Branches of the publick Revenues for the Purposes in this Act expressed and under the like Penalties [Forfeitures] and Disabilities as are to be inflicted by this Act for diverting or misapplying any Money by this Act appropriated or appointed for any the Purposes herein after menconed

And be it further enacted by the Authority aforesaid That there shall be raised levied collected and paid to and for the Use of Her Majesty Her Heires and Successors for and upon all Paper of what Kind soever and upon all Pastboards Mildboards and Scaleboards which shall at any Time or Times within or during the Terme of Thirty two Years to be reckoned from the Foure and twentieth Day of June One thousand seven hundred and twelve be made in Great Britain the severall and respective Duties herein after menconed (that is to say) . . .

And be it enacted by the Authority aforesaid That there shall be raised levied collected and paid to and for the Use of Her Majesty Her Heirs and Successors for and upon all Books and Papers commonly called Pamphletts and for and upon all News Papers [or Papers] containing publick News Intelligence or Occurrences which shall at Time or Times within or during the Terme last menconed be printed in Great Britain to be dispersed and made public and for and upon such Advertisements as are herein after menconed the respective Duties following that is to say

For every such Pamphlet or Paper contained in Halfe a Sheet or any lesser Piece of Paper soe printed the Sume of One Halfe peny Sterling

For every such Pamphlet or Paper (being larger than Halfe a Sheet [and] not exceeding One whole Sheet) soe printed a Duty after the Rate of One Peny Sterling for every printed Coppy thereof

And for every such Pamphlet or Paper being larger than One whole Sheet and not exceeding Six Sheets in Octavo or in a lesser Page or not exceeding Twelve

Sheets in Quarto or Twenty Sheets in Folio soe printed a Duty after the Rate of Two Shillings Sterling for every Sheet of any Kind of Paper which shall be contained in One printed Coppy thereof

And for every Advertisement to be contained in the London Gazette or any other printed Paper such Paper being dispersed or made public Weekly or oftner the Sume of Twelve Pence Sterling

Provided always That this Act shall not extend to charge any Acts of Parliament Proclamacon Order of Councill Forms of Prayer and Thanksgiveing or any Acts of State which shall be ordered by Her Majesty Her Heires or Successors to be printed or the printed Votes or other Matters which are or shall be ordered to be printed by either House of Parliament with any of the said Duties on Pamphlets or News Papers or to charge any Bookes commonly used in any the Schools of Great Britain or any Books containing only Matters of Devotion or Piety with the said Duties on Pamphlets or to charge any single Advertisement printed by it selfe or the dayly Accounts or Bills of Goods imported and exported or the Weekly Bills of Mortality (soe as such Accounts or Bills doe contain noe other Matters than what have been usually comprized therein) with any the Duties aforesaid Any thing herein contained to the contrary notwithstanding

And be it further enacted by the Authority aforesaid [aforesaid] That for the better and more effectuall levying collecting and paying unto Her Majesty Her Heirs and Successors the said severall Dutyes hereby granted and made payable for or in respect of the said severall and respective Matters and Things to be engrossed written or printed as aforesaid the same shall be under the Government Care and Management of the Commissioners for the Time being appointed to manage the Duties payable to Her Majesty Heirs and Successors and charged on Stampt Vellom Parchment and Paper whoe or the major Part of them are hereby required and impowered to imploy the necessary Officers under them for that Purpose and to cause all such further new Stamps to be provided to denote the Duties last menconed as shall be requisite and to do all other Things necessary to be by them done for the putting this Act in due Execution with relation to those Duties

And it is hereby further enacted by the Authority aforesaid That all Vellom Parchment and Parchment and Paper upon which any of the last menconed severall and respective Matters and Things shall from and after the said First Day of August One thousand seven hundred and twelve be respectively engrossed written or printed (the Paper to be used in printing the said Pamphlets exceeding One Sheet as aforesaid onely excepted) shall before such engrossing writing or printing be brought to the Head Office for stamping or marking of Vellom Parchment and Paper and the same Commissioners by themselves or by their Officers imployed under them shall and they are hereby impowered and required forthwith upon Demand to them made by any Person or Persons from time to time to stamp or marke as this Act directs any Quantities or Parcells of Vellom Parchment or Paper he or they paying to the Receiver Generall of the Stamp Duties for the Time being or to his Deputy or Clerk for the Use of Her Majesty Her Heires and Successors the respective Duties payable for the same by this Act without any other Fee or Reward and without Delay which Stamp or Mark to be put thereupon in pursuance of this Act shall be a sufficient Discharge for the severall and respective Duties hereby payable for the said Vellom Parchment and Paper which shall be soe stamped or marked

And be it further enacted by the Authority aforesaid That if any Person or Persons or Corporation shall from and after the said First Day of August One thousand seaven hundred and twelve within or during the Terms last menconed write engross or print or cause to be written engrossed or printed or signe any of the last menconed severall and respective Matters and Things or sell utter or expose to Sale any such Pamphlet or News Paper as aforesaid (the said Pamphletts exceeding One Sheet as aforesaid onely excepted) before the Vellum Parchment or Paper whereupon the same shall be respectively engrossed written or printed shall appear to have been soe duly stamped or marked as aforesaid that then every such Person or Corporacon soe offending in any of the Particulars before menconed shall for every such Offence forfeit the Sum of Ten Pounds together with full Costs of Suit and every Steward or other Officer or his Deputy offending herein and being convicted of any such Offence shall (over and besides the Forfeiture or Penalty aforesaid) forfeit and loose his Office and Imployment and be incapable to hold the same and that if any of the said severall and respective Matters and Things soe to be engrossed or written as aforesaid shall during the Term last menconed be written or engrossed contrary to the true Intent and Meaning hereof upon Vellom Parchment or Paper not appearing to have been duly stamped or marked according to Law that then and in every such Case there shall be due answered and paid to Her Majesty Her Heirs and Successors (over and above the Duties hereby payable for every such Matter and Thing respectively the Sume of Five Pounds and that noe such Matter or Thing shall be available in Law or Equity or be given in Evidence or admitted in any Court unless as well the said Duties hereby charged as the said Sume of Five Pounds shall be first paid to the Use of Her Majesty Her Heirs or Successors and a Receipt produced for the same under the Hand of the Receiver General for the Time being of the Stamp Duties or of his Deputy or Clerk and untill the Vellom Parchment or Paper on which such Matter or Thing is soe written or ingrossed shall be marked or stamped according to the Tenor and true Meaning hereof and the said Receiver Generall and his Deputy or Clerk are hereby enjoyned and required upon Payment or Tender of the said Duty payable by virtue hereof and of the said Sume of Five Pounds to give) Receipt for such Money and the other proper Officers are thereupon required to mark or stamp such Matter or Thing with the proper Marke or Stamp requisite in that Behalfe

And be it further enacted by the Authority aforesaid That every Commissioner and Officer whoe shall act in or about the managing or collecting the Duties last menconed and hereby granted shall before he shall act in or about the same take the Oath following (that is to say)

I A. B. do swear That I will faithfully execute the Trust reposed in me pursuant to the Act of Parliament whereby certain Duties are charged

upon Surrenders of and Admittances [to] Copyhold Lands or Tenements
and other the Matters and Things thereby directed to be stamped as is
therein menconed without Fraud or Concealment and shall from time to
time true Account make of my Doings therein and deliver the same to such
Person or Persons as Her Majesty Her Heirs and Successors shall appoint
to receive such Account and shall take noe Fee or Reward or Profit for the
Execution or Performance of the said Trust or the Businesse relating
thereto from any Person or Persons other than such as shall be allowed by
Her Majesty Her Heirs and Successors or some other Person or Persons
by Her or Them to that Purpose authorized

Which Oath shall and may be administred by any Two or more of the
Commissioners last menconed or any Justice of the Peace

And be it further enacted by the Authority aforesaid That the said
Commissioners for manageing the said Duties on stampt Vellom Parchment and
Paper and all other Officers whoe shall be employed in or about the collecting or
managing of the Duties last menconed and hereby granted shall in and for the better
Execution of their said Offices and Trusts observe and performe such Rules
Methods and Orders as they respectively shall from time to time receive from the
Lord High Treasurer of Great Britain now being or from the Lord High Treasurer
of Great Britain or Three or more of the Commissioners of the Treasury for the
Time being and that noe Fee or Reward shall be demanded or taken by any Her
Majesties Officers relating to the said Stamp Duties from any of Her Majesties
Subjects for any Matter or Thing to be done in pursuance of this Act and in case any
Officer intrusted or to be intrusted in the Execution of this Act in relation to the said
Stamp Duties shall refuse or neglect to performe any Matter or Thing by this Act
required to be done [and] performed by him whereby any of Her Majesties Subjects
shall or may sustain any Damage whatsoever such Officer soe offending shall be
liable by any Action to be founded on this Statute to answer to the Party grieved all
such Damages with Treble Costs of Suit

And it is hereby further enacted by the Authority aforesaid That the Duties by
this Act granted on stampt Vellom Parchment and Paper and the said Duties upon
News Papers and Pamphlets shall be all paid from time to time into the Hands of the
Receiver Generall for the Time being of the said Duties on stampt Vellom
Parchment and Paper whoe shall keepe a seperate and distinct Account thereof and
pay from time to time all the Monies arising thereby (the necessary Charges of
raising paying and accounting for the same excepted) into the Receipt of the
Exchequer of Her Majesty Her Heirs and Successors for the Purposes in this Act
expressed

Provided always and it is hereby enacted That as often as Her Majesty Her
Heirs or Successors shall thinke fitt to alter or renew the said Marks or Stamps to be
provided and used for Vellom Parchment or Paper in pursuance of this Act or any
of them it shall be lawfull for all Persons whoe shall at that Time have in their

Custody or Possession any Vellom Parchment or Paper marked with the Stamp or Stamps which shall be soe altered or renewed and upon which none of the Matters and Things hereby charged shall be engrossed written or printed at any Time within the Space of Sixty Days after such Intention of renewing or altering shall be published by Proclamation to bring or send such Vellom Parchment or Paper to the Commissioners last menconed at the said Head-Office or to such Officers as shall be appointed in that Behalfe and the same Commissioners and Officers respectively are hereby required to deliver or cause to be delivered to the severall Persons whoe shall soe bring and deliver any Quantity of Vellom Parchment and Paper the like Quantity of Vellom Parchment and Paper and as good in Quantity stampt with such new Stamps without demanding or taking directly or indirectly for the same any Sume of Money or Consideracon whatsoever under the Penalty of forfeiting for every such Offence One hundred Pounds to be sued for recovered and divided in such Manner as the other Penalties in this Act relating to the said Duties hereby charged on Vellom Parchment and Paper are directed to be sued for recovered and divided and in case any Person shall neglect or refuse within the Time aforesaid to bring or cause to be brought and delivered to such Commissioners or Officers as aforesaid any such Vellom Parchment or Paper the same is hereby declared to be of noe other Effect or Use than if itt had never been stamped and that all Matters or Things charged with the Duties last menconed and hereby granted which shall after that Time be engrossed or written thereon shall be of noe other Effect than if they had been engrossed or written on Vellom Parchment or Paper not marked or stamped at all and all Persons whoe shall engrosse write or print any the Matters or Things hereby charged on such Vellom Parchment or Paper after the said Time shall forfeit and sufferr as herein before is enacted for Persons writing engrossing or printing on Vellom Parchment or Paper not marked or stamped

Provided alwayes and be it further enacted That as often as Her Majesty Her Heires or Successors shall thinke fitt to alter the said Stamps or any of them that the [Proclation] which is hereby intended to be made for the giveing all Persons due Notice thereof shall within Thirty Days after the Date thereof be sent to the Mayor Chief Magistrate or other Head Officer of every City Corporation Borough and Market-Towne throughout Her Majesties Kingdom of Great Britain which Officers respectively shall cause the same to be published to the Inhabitants of such City Corporacon Borough or Towne either on the next Market-Day or next Sunday in the Church immediately after the Time of Divine Service upon pain of forfeiting the Sume of Two hundred Pounds

And for the better collecting and securing the Duties hereby charged on such Pamphlets containing more than One Sheet of Paper as aforesaid Be it further enacted by the Authority aforesaid That one printed Coppy of every such Pamphlet which from and after the said First Day of August One thousand seven hundred and twelve and during the said Terme of Thirty and two Years from thence next ensuing shall be printed or published within the Cities of London or Westminster or within the Limitts of the Weekly Bills of Mortality shall within the Space of Six Days after the printing thereof be brought to the said Head-Office for [making] or stamping of

Vellom Parchment and Paper and the Title thereof with the Number of Sheets contained therein and the Duty hereby charged thereon shall be registred or entered in a Book to be there kept for that Purpose which Duty shall be thereupon paid to the said Receiver Generall of the Stamp-Duties or his Deputy or Clerk whoe shall thereupon forthwith give a Receipt for the same on such printed Coppy or the same shall be stamped to denote the Payment of the Duty hereby charged on such Pamphlet and that One printed Coppy of every such Pamphlet as last menconed which during the same Terme shall be printed or published in any Part of Great Britain not being within the Limitts last before menconed shall within the Space of Fourteene Days after the printing thereof be brought to some Head-Collector of the said Stamp Duties whoe is hereby required forthwith to enter the Title thereof with the Number of Sheets contained therein and the Duty hereby charged thereon in a Booke to be by him kept for that Purpose which Duty shall be thereupon paid to such Collector whoe shall thereupon give a Receipt for the same on such printed Coppy

And be it further enacted by the Authority aforesaid That if any such Pamphlet containing more than One Sheet of Paper as aforesaid shall during the last menconed Terme of Two and thirty Years be printed or published and the Duty hereby charged thereon shall not be duly paid and the Title thereof registred and One Coppy thereof stamped where required soe to be within the respective Times herein before for those severall Purposes limitted that [then] the Author Printed & Publisher of and all other Persons concerned in or about the printing or publishing of such Pamphlet shall lose all Property therein and in every Copy thereof although the Title thereto were registred in the Booke of the Stationers in London according to the late Act of Parliament in that Behalfe soe as any Person (notwithstanding the said Act) may freely print and publish the same paying the Duty payable in respect thereof by virtue of this Act without being lyable to any Accon Prosecution or Penalty for soe doing Any thing in the said Act of Parliament for vesting the Copies of printed Bookes in the Authors or Purchasers of such Coppyes or in any By-Law contained or any Custome or other thing to the contrary notwithstanding And the Printer and Publisher of such Pamphlet and every other Person concerned in the printing or publishing thereof shall in such Case forfeit the Sume of Twenty Pounds with full Costs of Suit

And it is hereby further enacted by the Authority [aforesaid] That during the same Terme of Two and thirty Years noe Person whatsoever shall sell or expose to Sale any such Pamphlet without the true respective Name or Names and Place or Places of Abode or some knowne Person or Persons by or for whome the same was really and truly printed or published written or printed thereupon pain that every Person offending herein shall for every such Offence forfeit the Sume of Twenty Pounds with full Costs of Suit

And in regard of the incertainty how many Coppies of the said printed News Papers or Pamphletts to be contained in One Sheet or in a less Piece of Paper may be sold and to the Intent the Duties hereby granted thereupon may not be lessened by printing a less Number than may be sold out of a fear of a Losse thereby in printing more such Coppies than will be sold It is hereby provided and enacted That the Commissioners for managing the [said] Stamp Duties or the major Part of them or such Head Officers as they shall appoint in this Behalfe shall and may cancell or cause to be cancelled all the Stamps upon such Copies of any Impression of such News Paper or Pamphlett as last menconed as shall really and truly remain unsold in the Hands of the Person or Persons by or for whome the same shall be printed or published and upon Oath or Oaths made before the same Commissioners or the major Part of them or such Head Officer (who are hereby impowered to administer the same and to examine into all Circumstances relating to the selling or disposing of the printed Coppies of such News Paper or Pamphlet) to the Satisfaccon of such Commissioners or Head Officer that all such Coppies soe cancelled shall be really and truly remaining unsold in the Hands of the Person or Persons by or for whome the same [are] printed or published and that none of them shall have been fraudulently returned or rebought after the same shall have been sold or disposed of shall and may cause the like Number of other Sheets Halfe Sheets or less Pieces of Paper to be stamped with the same respective Stamps (gratis and without paying any Duties for the same) for the Person or Persons whoe paid the Duties for such Stamps as shall be on such Copies soe remayning unsold Any thing herein contained to the contrary notwithstanding And the same Commissioners or the major Part of them are hereby impowered to make such Rules and Orders for regulating the Methods and limiting the Times for such cancelling and Allowances as aforesaid with respect to such severall and respective News Papers or Pamphlets as last menconed as they shall upon Experiance and Consideracon of the severall Circumstances find necessary or convenient for the effectuall securing the Duties on such News Papers and Pamphlets and doing Justice to the Persons concerned in the printing and publishing thereof . . .

And be it further enacted by the Authority aforesaid That all pecuniary Penalties hereby imposed relating to the Duties on stampt Vellom Parchment and Paper or upon Cards Dice Pamphlets or Advertisements (except such touching which other Provisions or Directions are made or given in this Act) shall be divided and distributed to witt One Moiety thereof to Her Majesty Her Heirs and Successors and the other Moiety thereof with full Costs of Suit to such Person or Persons as shall informe and sue for the same in any of Her Majesties Courts at Westminster for Offences committed in England Wales or Berwick upon Tweed and in Her Majesties Court of Session Court of Justiciary or Court of Exchequer in Scotland by Action of Debt Bill Plaint or Information wherein no Essoign Protection Privilege or Wager of Law or more than One Imparlance shall be allowed

Provided always and it is hereby enacted by the Authority aforesaid That it shall and may be lawfully to and for Two or more Justices of the Peace to hear and determine any Offence against this Act in or by the printing selling uttering or exposeing to Sale within the Limitts of the Commission by which such Justices of the Peace are or shall be impowered to act any Pamphlet or Pamphlets News Paper or News Papers not marked or stamped as this Act directs which said Justices of the Peace are hereby authorized and required upon any Information exhibited or Complaint made in that Behalfe within Three Months after [any] such Offence committed to sumon the Party accused and alsoe the Wittnesses on either Side and upon the Appearance or Contempt of the Party accused in not appearing (upon Proof of Notice given) to proceed to the Examinacon of the Witness or Witnesses upon Oath (which Oath they are hereby impowered to administer) and to give Judgement or Sentence accordingly and where the Party accused shall be convicted of such Offence either by the View of the said Justices or either of them or upon such Information as aforesaid to award and issue Warrants for the levying any pecuniary Penalty or Penalties soe adjudged on the Goods of the Offender and to cause Sale to be made thereof in case they shall not be redeemed with [in] Six Dayes rendring to the Party the Overplus if any and where Goods of such Offender cannot be found to commit such Offender to Prison there to remaine until such pecuniary Penalty shall be paid and satisfied and if any Party shall finde himselfe or herselfe aggrieved or remain unsatisfied in the Judgment of the said Justices then he she or they shall and may by virtue of this Act complaine or appeal to the Justices of the Peace at the next Quarter Sessions for the County Riding Shire or Place wherein such Offence shall be committed whoe are hereby impowered to summons and examine Witnesses upon Oath and finally to hear and determine the same and in case of Conviction to issue Warrants for levying or compelling by such Means as aforesaid the Payment of the said Penalties . . .

Defense by Robert Walpole of his Sinking Fund proposal, 1717

Sir Robert Walpole, *Some Considerations Concerning the Publick Funds, the Publick Revenues, and the Annual Supplies, Granted by Parliament: Occasioned by a late Pamphlet, intitled, an Essay into the Conduct of our Domestic Affairs, from the Year 1721, to Christmas 1733* (London: J. Roberts, 1735), 8-31.

The purpose of the fund, which was introduced before Walpole came into office, was to consolidate the debt and facilitate its repayment. In spite of its controversial nature, it simplified the financial system.

The first Article that I shall proceed upon, shall be what concerns the *Sinking Fund.*

That the *Sinking Fund* was originally intended, projected, formed, and appropriated to the Discharge of National Debts, incurred before *December* 1716, as far as the Declaration of the Legislature in one Parliament, can bind all future Parliaments, was never doubted, but is equally contended for on all Sides; that that Appropriation should be preserved, and that the Application of the *Sinking Fund* should, in general, go to the Discharge of the old National Debt, is just and prudent; and that it ought not to be diverted to any other Use, but when publick Utility, and the Interest of the Nation, requires it, has never been disputed; but that it may sometimes, and occasionally be made use of, by Authority of Parliament, when the Exigency of the Publick makes it necessary, is, what I think, is most evident.

To clear this Point it must be considered, whether the Nation, as a Body politick, having a Right to the *Sinking Fund,* towards discharging their Incumbrances, have, by their declaratory Appropriations, so far tied themselves down, by Authority of Parliament, that the Obligation cannot be dispensed with, or suspended for a Time, for the Benefit of the Nation, by the same Authority of Parliament; and whether the Creditors of the Publick, and the Proprietors of the National Debts, have such an Interest in the *Sinking Fund,* and such a Right to receive the Produce of the *Sinking Fund,* in Discharge of their principal Debt, as make it a Breach of publick Faith, to apply the *Sinking Fund* to any other Use, or Purpose, how necessary and expedient soever. And I do admit, if the Appropriation of the *Sinking Fund* towards discharging the national Debt, be any Part of the Contract betwixt the Publick, and the Creditors of the Publick; if either upon the original Loans made by the Proprietors to the Publick, or if upon any subsequent Alterations since made in the Funds by Consent of the Proprietors, this was made a Condition, as an Inducement to the publick Creditors, to accept the Changes and Alterations, that have been made in the publick Funds; I say, I do admit, if that be true, that the making any other Use of the *Sinking Fund,* without the Consent of the Proprietors, would be a Breach of publick Credit, and ought never to be thought of, or attempted; and its having been done, would be a just Complaint of the Creditors of the Publick; but until they complain, not a reasonable Cause of Clamour, if what has been done, has been for the Benefit and Advantage of the Publick.

I have read over the several Pages in this Libel, that concern this particular Question, with great Attention, to see if I could possibly follow the Author in his own Method; but I must be excused, if I say, I found it impossible: His Manner of treating the Argument is so imperfect and uncorrect, and so unlike the Performance of a Man of Business, that to follow him, would lead me into the like Confusion, and not tend at all to clear up this important Question, which is all I aim at. I will not say, there is not one Paragraph upon this Point, that does not show, that the Question is either misunderstood, or misrepresented by the Author, I will not say it, altho' he is pleased to assert, that the contrary Notions are absurd, *inconsistent with common Sense, and common honesty, and lately propagated to serve a particular Turn.* I do agree with him, that the common Use of the Words, *Sinking Fund, has made the true Meaning of them a Mystery to many Readers,* and let me say, to some Writers: I do likewise agree, *that Gentlemen have talked very wildly upon this Subject, in Places where they ought to be a little better informed* (which as an Attender in the Gallery, I have frequently heard) and that *it is necessary to make the Nature of the Sinking Fund a little more intelligible to every Reader:* How far it was necessary to be better understood by this Author, I believe will appear, by truly stating the Question.

The first Mention that ever was made in Parliament of *A Sinking Fund* to be established for discharging the *National Debt,* was in the Session of Parliament *Anno* 1716.

To obviate an Objection, which I am sensible will be made by some, tho' not at all to the present Purpose, I do admit there had been *Sinking Funds* before this Time; as in the Case of Exchequer Bills; where, in most of the Funds that were granted for circulating and exchanging them, there was a Surplus, of the Fund itself, estimated and computed to be sufficient, to cancel and discharge annually some Part of the Exchequer Bills, and in the *Aggregate Fund Act* of the First of the late King, there was a Sum of 270,999 *l*. 7 *s*. 0 *d.* directed to be paid annually, towards lessening and discharging the Exchequer Bills, the Charge of circulating and exchanging of which, was by that Act provided for. It has been likewise asserted, that in all the Short Annuities, granted for 32 Years, or the like, the Principal being to be sunk and lost at the End of the Term granted, this was to be looked upon as a *Sinking Fund* attending those particular publick Debts. Be it, or be it not so, this does not at all affect my Assertion, that a *Sinking Fund* made and established with regard to *the National Debt* in general, was first projected and formed in the Year 1716, and till that Time unthought of, unheard of.

The National Debt, by Means of long and expensive Wars, carried on, in Support of the Revolution, and in Consequence in the Defence of the Religion, Laws, and Liberties of *Great Britain*; and which, I believe, no Man will confess that he thinks were dearly purchased, was become very large and burthensome; but the Circumstances of Time, high Credit, and low Price of Money, led those, whose particular Province and Business it was, to consider of proper Means to make Use of that favourable Opportunity, that the Publick might share in the common Advantage of the flourishing State of publick Credit.

It was then contended, that it was very just and reasonable, that the Publick should have the same Liberty, that every private Man has, to pay off his Debts when he is able; or to reduce the high Interest, which Necessity had subjected him to, as soon as he could borrow the Money elsewhere at more easy Rates; unless his Creditors would consent to accept of the common Rate of Interest upon good Security.

I must here, to avoid Tediousness and Obscurity, take the Liberty to deal in Generals, without entring into any Subdivisions, or minute Distinctions, and lay it down, that the *National Debt* was then considered under two Heads, *Redeemable* and *Irredeemable Debts*: The *Redeemables*, the Publick had a Right and Power to redeem, and pay off whenever they were able; which was to be done, either by providing Money for such Proprietors of *Redeemable Debts*, as insisted upon Money; or by the Publick offering, and the Proprietors accepting in lieu of ready Money, new Terms and Conditions, in Discharge of all former Conditions; and this Change and Variation at the Choice and Option of the Proprietors, instead of ready Money, which was offered and provided, must be as much looked upon, as an actual Discharge or Redemption of the first Debt, as if it had been paid off in ready Money.

As for the *Irredeemables*, nothing could be done with them, without the absolute Consent of the Proprietors; and the only Method therefore to treat with them, was to offer them such Conditions, as they should think it their Interest to accept.

Upon these Principles, in a Committee of the whole House, to consider of the State of the Nation, in relation *to the National Debt*, several Resolutions were taken; which, upon a Report of the 23d of *March*, 1716, were agreed to by the House; and a Bill or Bills were ordered to be brought in upon the several Resolutions. A Bill was accordingly presented on the 10th of *April* following.

But a Change of Hands in the Administration happening at that Time, made the new Officers of the Revenue think some Alteration in the Measures likewise necessary; but they were forced to build upon the same Foundation; and if it was material to my present Purpose, I could demonstrate, that every Variation was to the manifest Detriment of the Publick.

But I will dwell no longer upon this, and only request, that every body who has a Desire to go to the Bottom of this Question, will give himself the Trouble to read the Votes of Parliament of the 23d of *March*, 1716, and of the 6th of *June* following, 1717, and there he will find among the first Resolutions;

> Resolved, *That all Savings that shall arise upon any of the present Funds by the proposed Redemptions or Reductions, be reserved and applied, after all Deficiencies that may happen upon any of the said Funds are made good, towards discharging and reducing the National Debt:*

Which I affirm to be the first Resolution that was ever taken in Parliament, in order to raise or establish *a Sinking Fund* towards discharging *the National Debt.*

This was omitted in the second Resolutions, but was supplied, on the 28th of *June* following, by an Instruction, to the Committee, upon the Bill, that was brought in upon the last Resolutions.

I take Notice of this here, not as a conclusive Argument, but as an Observation that helps to confirm what will be fully proved, *that the applying the Sinking Fund to the Discharge of the National Debt, was no Condition, either expressed or understood, between the Publick, and the Creditors of the Publick.* In Confirmation of this, I have heard the honourable Person, who had the original Conduct and Management of this Affair, affirm, That no Mention was ever made of any such Condition, in all the previous Transactions and Considerations, had upon this Affair; and it cannot be doubted, but many Conferences and Considerations were had upon this extensive Question, among the monied Men, and Money Corporations, in order to bring the Scheme to Maturity, before it should be laid before the Parliament.

And as the Foundation of this Work was built upon paying off or satisfying the publick Creditors, we see in both Cases, a Provision made for borrowing Money, to answer such Demands as should be made, in Case any had been made: And in the last Resolutions, *the Bank of England*, and *the South-Sea Company* are obliged to advance, the one 2,500,000 *l.* the other 2,000,000 *l.* to carry on this great Work; and the then subsisting Funds, in Part or in the Whole, of both those Companies, were either to be redeemed or the Interest to be reduced.

Is it then to be supposed, that these Resolutions were taken in Parliament, without the previous Consent and Concurrence of these great monied Bodies? And is it to be supposed, that when they consented to an actual Reduction of their Funds, from 6 to 5 *per Cent. per Annum*, if it had been a Condition to apply and appropriate this Saving towards discharging their Principal, this Condition would not have been expressed? We see this was not done in the Resolutions taken upon the 6th of *June* 1717; and I believe there is no Man living, who will say he remembers at that Time, that this was insisted upon, as a Condition, in Behalf of the publick Creditors.

That it was always insisted upon on Behalf of the Publick, as it was designed for the Benefit of the Publick, is most certain; and this explains, how it came to be added by War or Instruction to the Bill. The House of Commons, who had before resolved it upon the first Scheme, took Care to supply this Defect or Omission in the second Scheme; and therefore gave this Instruction, which there is no Pretence to say, was a conditional Provision, in Favour, or Behalf of the Creditors.

These Things premised, I will proceed to consider this Question, as it appears to me upon the several Acts of Parliament relating thereto; and I will speak in the Words of Acts of Parliament, a Language unknown, or unused by our Author, but the only Authority that I shall rely upon.

Pursuant to the last-mentioned Resolutions, three Bills were brought into the House, and all passed into Laws, in the third Year of the Reign of the Late King, *viz.*

An Act for redeeming the Duties and Revenues which were settled to pay off Principal and Interest on the Orders made forth on four Lottery Acts passed in the 9th and 10th Years of her late Majesty's Reign; and for redeeming certain Annuities payable on Orders out of the Hereditary Excise, according to a former Act in that Behalf; and for establishing a general yearly Fund, not only for the future Payment of Annuities at several Rates, to be payable and transferrable at the Bank of *England*, and redeemable by Parliament; but also to raise Monies for such Proprietors of the said Orders, as shall chuse to be paid their Principal and Arrears of Interest in Ready Money; and for making good such other Deficiencies and Payments, as in this Act are mentioned, and for taking off the Duties on Linseed imported, and *British* Linnen exported.

An Act for redeeming several Funds of the *Governor and Company of the Bank of* England, pursuant to former Provisoes of Redemption, and for securing to them several new Funds and Allowances redeemable by Parliament, and for obliging them to advance further Sums not exceeding 2,500,000 *l.* at 5 *l. per Cent. per Annum*, as shall be found necessary to be employ'd in lessening the National Debts and Incumbrances, and for continuing certain Provisions formerly made for the Expences of his Majesty's Civil Government, and for Payment of Annuities formerly purchased at the Rate of 5 *l. per Cent.* and for other Purposes in this Act mention'd.

An Act for redeeming the yearly Fund of *the South-Sea Company*, (being after the Rate of 6 *l. per Cent. per Annum*) and settling on the said Company a yearly Fund, after the Rate of 5 *l. per Cent. per Annum*, redeemable by Parliament; and to raise for an Annuity or Annuities at 5 *l. per Cent. per Annum*, any Sum not exceeding two Millions, to be employ'd in lessening the National Debts and Incumbrances, and for making the said new yearly Fund and Annuities to be hereafter redeemable in the Time and Manner thereby prescribed.

Which three Acts are commonly known and called the *General Fund Act*; The *Bank Act* of the 3d of *George* the First; and the *South-Sea Act* of the 3d of *George* the First; by which Names, I shall call them as I have Occasion to mention them in the present Debate.

In the First of these Acts is to be found the Clause that establishes the Sinking Fund, where it is enacted in the Words following,

> *That all the Monies to arise from Time to Time, as well of or for the said Excess or Overplus by Virtue of the said Act made for redeeming the Funds of the Governour and Company of the Bank of* England; *and of or for the said Excess or Surplus, by Virtue of the said Act made for redeeming the Funds of the said Governor and Company of Merchants of* Great Britain *trading to the* South Seas *and other Parts of* America, *and for encouraging the Fishery; as also of und for the said Excess or Surplus of the said Duties and Revenues by this Act appropriated as aforesaid, and the said Overplus Monies of the said general yearly Fund by this Act established or intended to be established as aforesaid, shall be appropriated, reserved and employed to and for the discharging the Principal and Interest of such National Debts and Incumbrances as were incurred before the 25th Day of* December 1716, *and are declared to be National Debts, and are provided for by Act of Parliament, in such Manner and Form as shall be directed or appointed by any future Act or Acts of Parliament to be discharged therewith or out of the same, and to and for none other Use, Intent or Purpose whatsoever.*

This Clause then constitutes the *Sinking Fund.* Here is to be found, of what it consists, and to what Uses it is appropriated; and it is to be observed, that there is not to be found in this Clause, nor in any Part of this Act, nor in either of the other two Acts, whose Surplusses are here taken in, to make and constitute Part of the *Sinking Fund,* any Mention, Preamble, Recital or Insinuation whatsoever, of any Desire Request, or Condition, on Behalf of the Proprietors, whose redeemable Debts were by these Acts redeemed, that the Surplusses arising from the Saving and Reduction of their former Interests, should be appropriated to this Purpose, and this Purpose only.

Let us now examine these Acts of Parliament, and in the first Place *the General Fund Act,* which will, in the Main, clear the whole Dispute, unless in the two other Acts any material Alteration or Deviation can be found, that at all affects this Question.

The *famous South-Sea Act* of the 6th of the late King, which is so emphatically and unintelligibly called, *The Great Charter of National Faith between the Public and their Creditors,* shall be afterwards considered, as far as it concerns this Dispute.

The *General Fund Act* then recites the several Acts of Parliament for establishing the four Lotteries, the Terms of Years for which those Revenues were granted, and states and estimates the annual Produce of the several Funds, at certain Sums, which, together with the Annuity charged for the Bankers Debt, and another small Sum amounting to about 27,300*l. per Annum*, amounted together to 724,849*l*. 6 *s*. 10*d*. 1/5. which is the *General Fund*, the Deficiency whereof is to be made good annually out of the first Aids granted by Parliament.

This Act recites,

That whereas since the making the several Acts therein recited, the common Rate of Interest for Money is very much lessened, so that it is become just and reasonable for the Publick to have and enjoy the Benefit of redeeming the several Duties and Revenues charged and chargeable as before recited.

And whereas the Proprietors of the said Lottery Orders, or several of them, *are or may be willing or desirous* to accept, *in lieu and discharge thereof*, an Annuity or Annuities after the Rate of 5 *l. per Cent. per Annum*, redeemable by Parliament.

And several of the Proprietors are or may be *willing or desirous* to have their Principal and Interest due thereon, paid and satisfied to them in ready Money.

And several Persons or Corporations are or may be *willing or desirous* to advance ready Money for the Purposes aforesaid; so as for their Money so to be advanced, they may have such Annuities as are therein expressed, until Redemption by Parliament.

Now to the End that a good, sure and sufficient Security may be settled and established for the due, constant and regular Payment of all such Annuities as shall be payable by this Act; all the Duties and the Revenues aforesaid, shall continue and be paid and payable to his Majesty, *etc. for ever*.

With a Proviso, that the Revenues by this Act continued and made perpetual, shall be subject to Redemption.

Proprietors, who are willing, and desirous to accept the 5 *l. per Cent.* redeemable Annuities, *in lieu and discharge of their Lottery Orders,* shall declare and signify such *their Desire or Option*, by subscribing, *etc.*

And such as are *willing and desirous* to receive their Principal and Interest in ready Money, shall likewise declare and signify their *Desire or Option* in Writing.

And that this Provision of ready Money might not be thought Imaginary or Chimerical, *The Bank*, by the Act afore-mentioned, of the same Session, were obliged to furnish 2,500,000 *l*. and the *South Sea* Company 2,000,000 for this Purpose, or as much as should be called for; the Companies to have annuities of 5 *l. per Cent.* for the Money advanced to be charged upon the Funds redeemed.

And if it had been necessary, the Government was authorized to raise such further Sums as should be wanting, by taking in Subscriptions for Annuities at 5 *l. per Cent. per Annum*.

But it so happened, that not one Farthing was ever demanded in ready Money, except very small principal Sums, amounting in the Whole but to 471 *l*. 4 *s*. but all the other Proprietors of the Lottery Orders, without any other Exception, subscribed their Orders at the Bank, and accepted Bank Annuities, payable and transferrable at the Bank, at *their own Desire and Option*, declared and signified by subscribing, *in lieu and discharge of their former Debts, and in Preference to ready Money.*

I desire now to know, what Pretence there is to say, that these Creditors of the Publick, (and their Debts amounting to 9,533,195 *l*. 10 *s*. 5 *d*. ¾ is no inconsiderable Part of the National Debt) have any right to receive *the Produce of the Sinking Fund* in discharge of their Principal, or where the least Shadow of such a Condition is to be found in this new Contract or Bargain with the Publick? Their old Debt was discharged, for they accepted the Bank Annuities *in lieu and discharge of their Lottery Orders:* This Subscription to the Bank was in the Nature of a new Loan; and no Conditions can be supposed to be annexed to it, but what are expressed in the Act of Parliament.

That the Hopes or Prospect of receiving their Principal out of the Produce of the *Sinking Fund*, was no Motive or Inducement to their subscribing, is manifest, for they might have been paid their Principal in ready Money, and they rejected it; but in plain Terms, their Debt was at that Time charged upon a temporary Fund, great Part of which was worn out, and the Remainder yearly growing nearer to an Expiration, when the Interest was to cease, and the Principal to be sunk, and lost; they therefore wisely chose an Annuity of 5 *l. per Cent.* in Perpetuity, until redeemed, and then to receive their Principal again, rather than to receive a larger Income for a certain Time, and at last to lose their Principal; and, I believe, there is not one Proprietor of a Lottery Order now living, who subscribed it into the Bank Annuities, who will say, that he looked upon the Right of receiving his Principal out of *the Produce of the Sinking Fund*, as a valuable Consideration, or as a Condition of his becoming a Creditor to the Publick, in this new Form and Shape.

There is one Thing so very weak and inconsiderate, that I would not think it worth the Notice, if it did not properly come in here, where it is said, *In order to give the Creditors this Satisfaction, the several Acts of Parliament on which their Debts are founded, are recited in the* South Sea *Act, and made Perpetual, to render their Repayment more certain.* I will not criticise upon Acts of Parliament being made Perpetual; I cannot comprehend how this can be applied to the Claim made of receiving the Principal out of *the Produce of the Sinking Fund:* the Repayment indeed is in one Sense made more certain, because the Interest is not to cease till the Principal is repaid; but if the Government thinks fit to continue the Annuity to all Eternity, the Perpetuity no ways secures the Repayment of the Principal, at least not out of *the Sinking Fund:* But it must suffice to say, upon the several Funds being made Perpetual, that it was with no other Intent or Purpose than in the Words of the Act of Parliament, *To the End that a good, sure and sufficient Security may be settled and established for the due, constant and regular Payment of all such Annuities as shall be payable by this Act.* Where is there a Word said for Repayment of the Principal?

Having more than sufficiently proved, that the Proprietors of the publick Debts, interested in that Part of the National Debt, which is the Subject of the *General Fund Act*, have no Right to receive the *Produce of the Sinking Fund*, as a Condition of the new Contract, or as any Part of the Consideration, upon the new Agreement which they made with the Publick, by virtue of, or in pursuance of that

Act: I shall proceed now to inquire whether any Thing contained in the other two Acts of the same Session, I mean the Bank Act and *South Sea* Act of the 3d of the late King, which passed at the same Time, and are to be deemed Part of the Scheme for establishing the *Sinking Fund*, and more properly ought to have been made Parts of one and the same Act, gives this Right to the Proprietors of those Funds.

And this Consideration is very material upon this Question, for as the Consent of these two great Bodies was necessarily and actually taken upon this great Change and Variation of their Properties, it must be admitted, that in their corporate Capacity, they had well considered every Part of the Proposition, before they gave their Consent to it in Parliament, and had insisted upon and stipulated with the Officers of the Revenue, with whom this Affair must be supposed to have been transacted and settled, the saving and preserving all their former Rights, Privileges and Advantages, with such new Concessions as are found to be expressly granted to them in these Acts. And it is not at all probable, if this Right of receiving their Principal out of the *Sinking Fund* in due Proportions, had been then looked upon as a valuable Consideration, but that in Regard to the Interest of their Proprietors, and in common Justice, an express Provision would have been insisted upon, and made, not only for receiving the Produce of the *Sinking Fund* from Time to Time, as it should arise in Discharge of their Principal, but that a Course of Payment would have been expressly established, to prevent all undue Preference in favour of either Company; as is always done when any publick Funds and Revenues are appropriated to different Uses.

But it has so happened, that this supposed Right or Claim of being paid off with any Preference, or in Course, and in Proportion with other publick Creditors, was not only not mentioned, and not thought of at that Time; but ever since, when by subsequent Alterations in the publick Funds, these two Companies have, by virtue of the Power of Redemption preserved to the Publick, been liable to receive the Produce of the *Sinking Fund*, as it hath been applied to this Purpose, the only Contest between them has been, who should not be paid; and the Exercise of the Power of Redemption in the Publick has hitherto been looked upon rather as a Hardship than as a Favour: So little have these great Bodies hitherto looked upon the being made liable and subject to Redemption, and a Right to be redeemed, to be one and the same Thing.

But not to inlarge any further upon Arguments, and Reasonings, let us now consider what is the Sense and Purport of the Acts of Parliament, and first what concerns the Bank: The Bank at that Time, as Proprietors of redeemable Debts, were intitled to an Annuity of 106,501 *l*. 13 *s*. 5 *d*. *per Annum*, in lieu of Exchequer Bills formerly cancelled, amounting to 1,775,027 *l*. 17 *s*. 10 *d*. ½. And the Exchequer Bills standing out on the 22d of *March* 1716, made forth by the several Acts of the 7th, 8th, and 12th, of Queen *Anne*, are stated at 4,561,025 *l*. over and above the Charge of Circulation, which was then due to the Bank. The Bank, by virtue of their Contracts for circulating and exchanging these Bills for ready Money, were intitled to 3 *l. per Cent. per Annum,* for all these Bills; and the Bills carried an Interest of 2 *d. per Cent. per Diem*, to the Bearer, which is 3 *l. per Cent. per Annum* more; and the Bank having generally been the Bearers, or Holders of all, or the greatest Part of the Exchequer Bills standing out, may be looked upon as intitled likewise to that, or far the greatest Part of that 3 *l. per Cent. per Annum*; which together make 6 *l. per Cent. per Annum* on the whole Sum of 4,561,025 *l.* of Exchequer Bills; and it must be remembered, that over and above the Charge of Circulation and Interest of the Bills, there was granted to the Bank, upon the memorable Change of the Ministry, at the latter End of the late Queen's Reign, (an usual Effect of the Advancement of *mock Patriots* and *clamorous Reformers*) the Sums of 45,000 *l.* and 8,000 *l. per Annum*, making together 53,000 *l. per Annum*, which the Bank at this Time enjoyed, and which make together 7 *l.* 4 *s.* 0*d.* ¾ *per Cent. per Annum* upon all the Exchequer Bills. The Annuity payable to the Bank for the cancelled Exchequer Bills, together with the whole Charge to the Publick for circulating the Exchequer Bills then standing out, will be found to amount to above 435,000 *l. per Annum*. In these Circumstances, what says the Act of Parliament,

> *The Governor and Company of the Bank of England, in Regard the common Rate of Interest for Money, is very much lessened under your Majesty's most auspicious Reign,* and their several Funds, before-mentioned, are redeemable at such Times, and in such Manner, as aforesaid, *are willing and content to accept* one Annuity of 88751 *l.* 7 *s.* 10 ½, being after the Rate of 5 *l. per Cent. per Annum* on the said principal Sum of 1,775,027 *l.* 17 *s.* 10.½, in lieu of their present Annuity or Sum of 106501 *l.* 13 *s.* 5 *d. per Annum*.

And not to be too tedious with particular Recitals, the Act goes on and declares, *the Bank willing and contented,* to discharge, and deliver up to be cancelled, as many Exchequer Bills, as amount to *Two Millions,* and to accept of an Annuity of 100,000 *l. per Annum*, being after the Rate of 5 *l. per Cent. per Annum,* redeemable by Parliament after one Year's Notice, to circulate the remaining Exchequer Bills at 3 *l. per Cent. per Annum,* with an Interest of 1 *d. per Cent. per Diem,* the former Allowances to be continued to *Christmas* 1717, and from and after *Christmas* 1717, the Bank to have for circulating the 2,561,025 *l.* remaining Exchequer Bills, an Annuity of 76,830 *l.* 15 *s.* 0 *d.* at the Rate of 3 *l. per Cent. per Annum,* until redeemed, over and above the 1 *d. per Cent. per Diem* for Interest.

The Bank then is *enjoyned and required* to advance and pay into the Exchequer, any Sum not exceeding 2,500,000 *l.* towards discharging and lessening the National Debts and Incumbrances, if wanted and required; and to have an Annuity of 5 *l. per Cent.* for as much as they shall advance, redeemable by Parliament.

This being the Case, the Bank, which was in Possession of Receipts, out of the Exchequer, amounting to 435063 *l.* 16 *s.* 0 *d.* ½ *per Annum*, accept voluntarily of three Annuities upon the three different Heads, amounting to about 304,531 *l.* 1 *s.* 3 *d.* ¾ *per Annum*, whereby the Saving to the Publick appears to be 130,532 *l.* 14 *s.* 8 *d.* ¾ *per Annum,* which Saving, it was presumed, would make a Surplus or Excess upon the appropriated Funds. How then is this Surplus or Excess disposed of by this Act? It is expresly declared and enacted, *That the Excess or Surplus which at any Time shall or may be produced by the several Rates, Duties, Revenues, and Incomes thereby appropriated, shall attend the Disposition of Parliament, and be applied according to Act or Acts of Parliament in that Behalf, and not otherwise.*

From whence I make this plain and just Inference, (there being no apparent Reason, why distinct Acts of Parliament were passed for what concerned the *Bank* and the *South-Sea* Company upon this Redemption and Reduction of their Interests, but that the particular Interest of each Corporation might have a distinct and separate Consideration, and that thereby express Provision might be made for all Privileges, Advantages, Conditions, and Considerations, that were to be saved, continued, or granted to them,) that it is impossible to imagine, if it had been the Design or View of the Bank, to secure to themselves, as a valuable Condition, a Right to receive their Proportion out of these Savings and Surplusses, in Discharge of their principal Debt, that it would not have been inserted in this very Act; which being left and reserved for the General Fund Act, when the Sinking Fund was to be established, and which regarded the general Benefit of the Nation, more than the particular Interest of any particular Class of the publick Creditors, seems to me a manifest Declaration, that these Surplusses and Excesses were not to be considered any longer as any Part of the Property, which the Creditors of the Publick had in their appropriated Funds, (the Interests and Annuities reserved to them being first made good to them, before the Surplusses are computed and set apart) but that they were to be deemed a new created Property, which the Publick had, by the flourishing State of publick Credit, recovered to themselves in those Funds, saved and redeemed, *with Justice, Honour, and Equity,* and with the Consent of the Proprietors, *to ease the present Burthen of National Debts and Incumbrances, and in due Time the heavy Taxes lying upon this Kingdom.*

I do foresee a Construction upon this last Quotation, which it may be conceived may possibly be turned upon me; but as I think, if the Cavil is made, it is but a Cavil, immaterial, and inconclusive upon the main Argument, I shall omit taking any further Notice of it at present.

I have spent the longer Time in considering this Bank Act of the 3*d* of the late King, that it may serve in a great Measure, equally as an Explanation of the *South-Sea Act* of the same Year, which is the next Business that I undertook.

To avoid unnecessary Repetitions, it will be sufficient to say, that the Capital Stock, of the *South-Sea* Company, was at that Time *Ten Millions,* for which they received an Interest or *Annuity* at the Rate of 6 *l. per Cent. per Annum,* amounting to 600,000 *l. per Annum,* and likewise 8000 *l. per Annum* for Management. In the same Words, as in the former Act relating to the Bank, the Governour and Company of Merchants of *Great Britain* trading to the *South-Seas,* etc. declare, *that in Regard the common Rate of Interest for Money is very much lessened under your Majesty's most auspicious* Reign, etc. they are *willing and contented* to accept an Annuity of 500,000 *l.* in Lieu of the 600,000 *l.* with 8000 *l. per Annum* for Charges of Management; And it is further enacted, by and with the Consent of the Company, *that they shall be enjoined and required to advance and pay into the Exchequer, any Sum not exceeding two Millions, to be applied towards discharging the Principal and Interest due on the Four Lottery Funds of the 9th and 10th of Queen* Anne, *if wanted and required*; the Company to have an Annuity for as much as they shall advance, at the Rate of 5 *l. per Cent. per Annum,* redeemable by Parliament.

The Surplus and Excess of the *South-Sea* Funds, after the Reduction of their Interest, are directed likewise by this Act, to attend the Disposition of Parliament, *to be applied according to Act or Acts of Parliament in that behalf, and not otherwise.*

And, as has been before observed, the Surplusses or Excesses arising from the three several Acts of the 3*d* of the late King, are, by the *General Fund Act* erected into, and made the *Sinking Fund*, for discharging of National Debts, incurred before *December* 1716.

The Substance and Purport of this Act being thus stated, all the Inferences that were justly drawn from the Observations upon the preceeding Act, will equally hold in this; to which I may add one further Observation; These two great Companies, being obliged by the respective Acts of Parliament to furnish respectively 2,500,000 *l.* and 2,000,000*l.* towards rendring the Redemption of the Four Lottery Funds practicable, for which they were to receive Annuities at the Rate of 5 *l. per Cent. per Annum*, which was to become a new National Redeemable Debt; and as their Merit to the Publick had been great, because without their undertaking to advance such very large Sums, the Scheme of redeeming the Four Lottery Funds might have been defeated, and in Consequence, the Saving from that Redemption had been lost; I desire to know, if the receiving the *Produce of the* Sinking Fund, founded upon these several Reductions of Interest and Redemptions, had been at that Time looked upon as a valuable Right or Privilege, whether it had been possible for the Companies not to have insisted upon an express Provision for that Purpose, or for the Publick in Justice and Equity, to have refused to them the Benefit of what they so largely contributed to the bringing about.

Let me observe here, what, in the common Notion of Business of this Kind, one would think it was impossible that it should be necessary to observe, which is, that some People who write and talk upon this Subject, do not seem to make a Distinction between the Power of Redemption reserved to the Publick, and a Right to Redemption in the publick Creditors; which are so far from being the same Thing, that they are almost direct Opposites; and it is most certain, that the Power of Redemption is always inserted in Favour of the Publick, and may be to the Prejudice or Loss of the Creditors, as it may happen to be put in Execution.

All the Annuities that were settled in the Year 1716, by Virtue of the three last-mentioned Acts, were *Perpetuities* granted at the Rate of 5 *l. per Cent. per Annum* upon a Principal of about 25,869,247 *l.* 18 *s.* 4 *d.* ¼, the Amount of the National Debt at that Time redeemed or reduced: But these Annuities were made subject to Redemption; For whose Benefit, or to what Purpose? For the Sake of the Publick only; that, as it was thought prudent at that Time, not to attempt the Reduction of Interest lower than 5*l. per Cent.* if the State of the publick Credit, and the lower Rate of Interest should afterwards make it reasonable to make a further Reduction to 4*l. per Cent*, it might be in the Power of the Publick to take the Advantage of such a favourable Time and Circumstances; which happened afterwards, and the Interest paid now upon the National Debt in general, is known to be at the Rate of 4*l. per Cent.* Let it be remembred, that all the publick Funds of 4 *l. per Cent.* have been sold at above *Par*, and that at the same Time the publick Creditors were obliged to receive Part of their Principal. Let it be remembered, that it was lately apprehended, that the Interest of Money was falling down to 3 *l. per Cent*; which, if it had been thought prudent or expedient, might possibly have been effected; Who then would have advanced this Doctrine of a Right to receive their Principal, carrying 4 *l. per Cent.* to be laid out again at 3 *l. per Cent.*? But the Publick then would have had a Right to pay, what the Creditors of the Publick would have been glad to have been excused receiving. . . .

Act prohibiting the use and wear of calicoes, 1720

7 Geo. 1, c. 7   *Statutes at Large*, XIV, 318-21.

This measure, the aim of which was to encourage domestic woolen and silk manufactures, was liberalized substantially in 1736.

Whereas it is most evident, That the wearing and using of printed, painted, stained and dyed callicoes in apparel, household stuff, furniture, and otherwise, does manifestly tend to the great detriment of the woollen and silk manufactures of this kingdom, and to the excessive increase of the poor, and if not effectually prevented, may be the utter ruin and destruction of the said manufactures, and of many thousands of your Majesty's subjects and their families, whose livelihoods do intirely depend thereupon: for remedy thereof, may it please your most excellent Majesty, That it may be enacted, and be it enacted by the King's most excellent majesty, by and with the advice and consent of the lords spiritual and temporal and commons, in this present parliament assembled, and by the authority of the same, That from and after the twenty fifth day of December which shall be in the year of our Lord one thousand seven hundred and twenty two, it shall not be lawful for any person or persons whatsoever to use or wear in Great Britain, in any garment or apparel whatsoever, any printed, painted, stained or dyed callico, under the penalty of forfeiting to the informer the sum of five pounds of lawful money of Great Britain for every such offence, being lawfully convicted thereof by the oath or oaths of one or more credible witness or witnesses before any one or more justice or justices of the peace; which justice or justices is and are hereby respectively authorized and strictly enjoined and required, upon any complaint or information upon oath exhibited or brought of any such offence committed, contrary to this act, within six days after commitment thereof, to summon the party accused, and upon his or her appearance or contempt to proceed to examination of the matter of fact, and upon due proof made thereof, either by voluntary confession of the party, or by the oath or oaths of one or more credible witness or witnesses (which oath or oaths the said justice or justices is and are hereby respectively impowered and required to administer) to hear and determine the same, and upon such conviction to cause the said penalty, by warrant under his or their hand and seal, or hands and seals respectively, to be levied by distress and sale of the offender's goods and chattels, rendring to the party the overplus (the charge of such distress and sale being first deducted;) nevertheless it shall be lawful for any party aggrieved to appeal to the justices of the peace at the next general quarter-sessions to be holden for the county, city, riding or place where the said offence or offences shall have been committed, giving six days notice at the least of such appeal to the prosecutor or prosecutors; which justices at such general quarter-sessions are hereby authorized and impowered to hear and determine the same, and their judgment therein shall be final.

II. And be it further enacted by the authority aforesaid, That if any mercer, draper, upholder, or any other person or persons or corporation whatsoever, shall at any time or times after the said twenty fifth day of December one thousand seven hundred and twenty two, sell, utter or expose to sale any printed, painted, stained or dyed callico, or any bed, chair, cushion, window-curtin or other household stuff or furniture whatsoever, made up of or mixed with any printed, painted, stained or dyed callico, unless for exportation thereof, and unless the same shall be cleared outwards accordingly, as is usual in case of sale for exportation, every such person or corporation so offending shall for every offence, being lawfully convicted thereof, forfeit and pay the sum of twenty pounds of lawful money of Great Britain, to be recovered as is herein after directed; and every steward or other officer of such corporation, or his deputy, offending herein, and being lawfully convicted of such offence, shall, over and besides the forfeiture or penalty aforesaid, forfeit and lose his office and employment and be incapable to hold the same.

III. And be it further enacted by the authority aforesaid, That from and after the said twenty fifth day of December one thousand seven hundred and twenty two, it shall not be lawful for any person or persons to use or wear in Great Britain, in or about any bed, chair, cushion, window-curtain or any other sort of household stuff or furniture, any printed, painted, stained or dyed callico (except as herein after is excepted) under the penalty of forfeiting (being thereof lawfully convicted) the sum of twenty pounds of lawful money of Great Britain, to be recovered as herein after is directed.

IV. And be it further enacted by the authority aforesaid, That one moiety of all pecuniary penalties and forfeitures imposed by this act, where the same shall exceed five pounds, shall be to the informer or prosecutor, and the other moiety to the poor of the parish or place where the offence shall be committed; and such penalties as are not herein directed to be otherwise recovered, shall be recovered by action of debt, bill, plaint or information in any of his Majesty's courts of record at Westminster, for offences committed in England, Wales or Berwick upon Tweed, or in his Majesty's court of session, court of justiciary, or court of exchequer in Scotland, for offences committed in that part of Great Britain, together with full costs of suit, by any person or persons who shall sue for the same within six calendar months next after the offence committed; and that in any such action or suit no essoin, protection, privilege or wager of law shall be allowed, nor any more than one imparlance.

V. And be it enacted by the authority aforesaid, That if it shall appear, that any person convicted of any offence against this act shall be sheltered or protected, or doth or shall reside or inhabit in any pretended privilege place whatsoever, every such offender shall and may be taken from thence by warrant under the hand and seal of any of his Majesty's justices of the court of King's bench, common pleas or barons of the exchequer, in England, Wales or Berwick upon Tweed, or by warrant under the hand and seal of any of the lords of session, judges of the court of justiciary or barons of the exchequer, in Scotland; and shall be by any such justice, lord of session, judge or baron committed to the common gaol of the county or place where the offence was committed, there to remain without bail or mainprize, till payment and satisfaction of all penalties and forfeitures imposed by this act, with full costs.

VI.   Provided always, and it is hereby further enacted by the authority aforesaid, That this act, or any thing therein contained, shall not extend or be construed to extend in any wise to any callicoes which have already been, or which before the said twenty fifth day of December one thousand seven hundred and twenty two shall be made up or used in any bed, chair, cushion, window-curtain or other sort of household stuff or furniture: provided the same be continued to be worn and used in such household stuff or furniture, and not otherwise.

VII.   Provided also, That nothing in this act contained shall extend or be construed to extend to repeal, make void or alter any law now in force for prohibiting callicoes printed, painted, dyed or stained in foreign parts, or for prohibiting any other goods or manufactures whatsoever.

VIII.   Provided also, and be it enacted and declared by the authority aforesaid, That all persons and bodies corporate who shall, on or before the said twenty fifth day of December one thousand seven hundred and twenty two, export any callicoes, shall be entitled to and have such and the same allowances and advantages upon the exportation thereof, as fully as if the same had been exported within twelve months after the importation thereof; any law, usage or custom to the contrary notwithstanding.

IX.   And be it further enacted by the authority aforesaid, That if any person or persons shall be sued or prosecuted for any thing done or to be done, in pursuance of this act, such person or persons may plead the general issue, and give this act and the special matter in evidence; and if the plaintiff or plaintiffs, prosecutor or prosecutors, shall become nonsuit, or forbear prosecution, or suffer discontinuance; or if a verdict pass against him, her or them, the defendant or defendants shall have treble costs, and shall have the like remedy for the same, as in any case where costs are by law given to defendants.

X.   And be it further enacted by the authority aforesaid, That the prohibition of callicoes intended by this act, and the penalties thereby inflicted for wearing or using printed, painted, stained or dyed callico in apparel, household stuff or furniture, after the twenty fifth day of December one thousand seven hundred and twenty two, contrary to this act, shall respectively extend to prohibit, and shall be levied and recovered for wearing or using in apparel, household stuff or furniture, after the said twenty fifth day of December one thousand seven hundred and twenty two, any stuff made of cotton or mixt therewith, which shall be printed or painted with any colour or colours, or any callico chequered or striped, or any callico stitched or flowered in foreign parts with any colour or colours, or with coloured flowers made there (muslins, neckcloths and sustains excepted) in such manner as the penalties inflicted by this act for wearing or using printed, painted, stained or dyed callico in apparel, household stuff or furniture after the said twenty fifth day of December one thousand seven hundred and twenty two, contrary to this act, are to be levied or recovered; but under such limitations, and with such liberties, privileges and advantages are are mentioned and expressed in this act, or in any other act or acts of parliament now in force relating thereto or relating to printed, painted, stained or dyed callicoes.

XI. Provided, That nothing in this act contained shall extend or be construed to extend to such callicoes as shall be dyed all blue.

SOUTH SEA BUBBLE INCIDENT

First Report of the Committee of Secrecy investigating the South Sea Company, 16 February 1721

Parliamentary History, VII, 711-26, 731-39.

The South Sea Company was established in 1711. Its intricate financial dealings brought about its collapse in 1720 and produced a political crisis owing to the involvement of many leading politicians.

The Committee of Secrecy appointed to enquire into all Proceedings relating to the execution of the Act passed last session of parliament, intitled, *an Act for enabling the South Sea Company to increase their present capital stock and fund,* etc. have endeavoured, with continued application to discharge the trust reposed in them. At the entrance into their enquiry they observed the matters referred to them were of great variety and extent. Many persons were entrusted with different parts in the execution of this law, and under the colour thereof acted in an unwarrantable manner, in disposing of the properties of many thousands of persons, amounting to many millions of money.

In the progress of their enquiry your Committee found it attended with many difficulties.

In some of the Books produced before them, false and fictitious entries were made; in others, entries with blanks; in others, entries with razures and alterations; and in others, leaves were torn out. They found farther, that some books had been destroyed, and others taken away or secreted; nevertheless, your Committee are enabled to lay some matters of importance before the House for their present consideration.

The first matter that offered itself to the consideration of your Committee was a scene of iniquity and corruption, the discovery of which your Committee conceived to be of the highest importance to the honour of parliaments, and the security of his majesty's government.

Your Committee observed, in the account laid before the House by the court of directors of the South Sea Company, pursuant to your order the 12th day of December, that the Company were therein supposed to have received the sum of 1,259,325*l*. upon account of stock sold to the amount of 574,500*l*. stock: whereupon your Committee ordered the Company's cash-book to be laid before them, and upon inspection thereof, they found (at fol. 120 and 121) the several entries of stock, as sold for the Company, annexed at the end of this report, No. 1. the total of which entries amount to the said sums of 574,500*l*. in stock; and of 1,259,325*l*. in cash; but it is very observable, that from the article of the 4th of February, 1719, unto that of the 12th of April, 1720, both inclusive, there is no mention made of the name of any person whatsoever to whom the stock is supposed to be sold.

The whole accounts comprehended in these two pages of the cash-book, and entered in this concealed manner, appear, nevertheless, to have been stated and balanced by the Company's committee of treasury, without expressing the day when such accounts were stated, and are subscribed by sir John Fellows, then sub-governor, Mr. Charles Joye, then deputy-governor, sir Lambert Blackwell, sir Robert Chaplin, sir Theodore Janssen, Mr. Jacob Sawbridge, and Stephen Child, then directors all of them of the said Committee, and Sir Robert Chaplin, sir Theodore Janssen, and Mr. Sawbridge, at that time members of this House.

Your Committee, upon this occasion, take the liberty to remind the House of a remarkable period in the last session of parliament; that upon the 2nd of February, 1719, the House agreed to the report of the Committee of the whole House, appointed to consider of that part of his majesty's speech which related to the public debts, that the proposals made by the South Sea Company should be accepted, and ordered a bill to be brought in pursuant to the said resolution, which bill having passed this House, and afterwards the House of Peers, had the royal assent upon Thursday the 7th of April, 1720.

Your Committee, surprized to see so large an account of stock disposed of by the Company, before the passing the bill to enable the Company to increase their capital stock and fund, and before any subscription or redemption could be made, whereby their capital stock was increased, proceeded to examine carefully into that transaction.

And upon examination of the late sub and deputy-governors, and the late directors of the South Sea Company, Mr. Robert Knight, then cashier, Mr. Robert Surman, the deputy-cashier, Mr. John Grigsby, then accountant, Mr. Charles Lockyer, then 2nd accountant, and Mr. Matthew Weymondsold, broker, it manifestly appeared to your Committee, that the Company at that time was not possessed of such a quantity of stock, whereof they could then make an actual sale and transfer; the Company having at that time, in their own right, only a small quantity of stock, not exceeding 25,000*l*. or 30,000*l*. at the most. And upon the inspection of the transfer books of that time, as well as upon examination of the before-mentioned persons, your Committee cannot find any transfers made by the Company, of any part of that great quantity of stock, at the times specified in the cash-book, (excepting to the duke of Portland, the lord Delawar, and the honourable John West, esq.; who sold their annuities to the Company) and no account of any transfers of such stock has as yet been given into this House, although by your order of the 17th of December last it was expressly required.

Upon farther examination of the persons before-mentioned, your Committee discovered that this supposed sale of stock was colourably entered in the book for the benefit of persons, whose names were designed to be concealed, with intention to make an interest in favour of the Company, and to facilitate the acceptance of the South Sea Proposals, and the passing the bill, which were at that time depending in parliament. And to that end, the late sub and deputy-governors, sir John Blunt, Mr. Gibbon, Mr. Chester, and Mr. Holditch, late directors, who had the care of soliciting the passing the bill, together with Mr. Knight, the cashier, had the power of disposing of this stock.

And the general method by which this practice was carried on, was thus:

This stock was set down, as sold at several days and at several prices, from 150l. per cent. to 325l. per cent. and was from those times to be esteemed as taken in, or holden by the Company, for the benefit of the pretended purchasers, although no mutual agreement was then made for the delivery, or acceptance of the stock, at any certain time, and although no money was paid down, nor any deposit, or other security, given to the Company for payment, by the supposed purchasers: so that if the price of stock had fallen, as might be expected, if the scheme had miscarried, no loss could have been sustained by them; but if the price of stock should advance (as it actually did by the success of the scheme) the difference by the advance price was to be made good to the pretended purchasers· and accordingly the account of such stock was made up, and adjusted with Mr. Knight, and the money arising by the difference of the price, between the times of such taking in, or holding of the stock, and the making such adjustments, was paid, or allowed, out of the company's cash, to the pretended purchasers; but no entries of such adjustments, or of names of the persons with whom the said were made, appear to your Committee in any of the books of the Company.

Sir *Theodore Janssen* affirmed, that when the said account in the cash-book was laid by Mr. Knight before their Committee of treasury, to be passed and signed, an objection being made that blanks were left for the buyers of this stock, the late sub-governor, and Mr. Knight, said, there were reasons for passing the account in that manner, and that the stock was disposed of to persons whose names were not proper to be known to a great many, but at a fit time a perfect account thereof should be made up, and that if the bill did pass the stock would be well sold.

Mr. *Robert Surman* declared, that about the 3d of April, 1720, Mr. Knight the cashier, shewed him that account of stock sold in the cash-book (fol. 120, and 121) and told the examinant, that there was a Committee appointed to look into the state of the cash that night, and that he, Mr. Knight, having thereby charged himself with the value of so large a quantity of stock sold, would appear to have a great sum of money in his hands, which he really had not, and therefore said, he would write off a supposed sum of 800,000l. as lent by the Company to sundry persons upon 400,000l. stock, and Mr. Knight did then accordingly enter the same with his own hand, (fol. 120) of the said cash-book, in the following words,

1720. April 3. By loan to sundries on security of 400,000*l*. South-Sea Stock, at an interest of 5*l*. per cent. per annum. 800,000*l*.

That Mr. *Robert Surman* farther declared, he did not know that any part of the said money was really lent, but the entry was made to that effect by Mr. Knight, with an intention to answer, in part, the account of stock sold: he believed also that the entry in the same book was written by Mr. Knight, as follows, (fol. 121.)

April 14. By account of loan on South-Sea Stock, lent to sundries on security of 100,000*l*. stock at 250, at an interest of 5 per cent. per annum, 250,000*l*.

As to the greatest part, if not the whole of that sum, it was entered with the same view; and the examinant at that time took it, that this stock entered as sold in the cash-book, was not paid for, and for that reason Mr. Knight entered these sums of 800,000*l*. and 250,000*l*. as actually disbursed, to help to make a balance upon the account, as it now stands in the cash-book.

That the examinant observing the said entry of stock sold, Mr. Knight told him, that it was a transaction of a private nature, and that a great part of it was disposed of to persons of distinction.

Mr. *Astell*, one of the late directors, likewise declared, that he believed the said article of loan of 800,000*l*. on 400,000*l*. stock was entered as a blind to answer the account of receipts on the other side of the cash-book, for that he could not find any minute thereof in the other books of the company.

Mr. *Stephen Child* said, that he took the articles of stock bought and sold in the cash-book, to be fictitious, and to be entered in that manner merely to make a balance.

Whilst your committee had this matter under examination, viz. upon the 27th day of January last, the court of directors (pursuant to your order of the 17th of December preceding, requiring a particular account of this stock sold, and by whom, and to whom transferred) laid before this House a book containing an account of stock sold, as they received it from their committee of treasury, without mentioning that any part of such stock was actually transferred.

And your committee examining into that account, sir John Blunt (from whom your committee received the first material informations) the late sub and deputy-governors, Mr. Gibbon, Mr. Astell, Mr. Chester, late directors, and Mr. Robert Surman, informed them, that they believed, and that it was generally so understood among the directors, that the said account laid before this House, is not a true account; and that there are many fictitious names therein, as the names of several brokers and others, which are made use of to cover the names of other persons, who had the real benefit of such stock, and who nevertheless are not mentioned in that account, but that the names of persons of distinction or condition therein contained are real.

Mr. *Astell* declared, that pressing Mr. Knight upon the repeated orders of the directors to make up the account of this stock, Mr. Knight answered, that he could not comply with these orders, without giving up forty or fifty of the Company's best friends.

Mr. *Robert Surman* gave your committee a farther explanation of the framing this account as follows.

That since the order of the House requiring this account, he assisted Mr. Knight in preparing a draught thereof, and by Mr. Knight's direction, he wrote down several names, which Mr. Knight read to him out of a book with a green cover, wherein Mr. Knight had kept an account of this stock entered in the cash-book of the Company, and also of subscriptions, but believed Mr. Knight did not give him all the true names, because Mr. Knight sometimes turned over a leaf or two without giving him a name, although there were in those leaves names of persons with whom an account was there entered. And Mr. Surman farther said, that he remembered, that in the same book, at the head of a large account, wherein the debtor side came near to the bottom of the page, he saw, the name of John Aislabie, esq. late chancellor of the exchequer, but Mr. Knight turned over that leaf, and did not give him that name to insert in the account.

That at the head of another account, in the same book, he saw the name of James Craggs, esq.

That at the head of another account in that book, he saw the name of Charles Stanhope, esq.

All which were accounts of stock and subscriptions, but Mr. Knight left out all these names in this account; and after it was thus drawn out from the green book, and from some letters which Mr. Knight then delivered to this examinant, the sums not coming right, Mr. Knight made several alterations in the names and prices, and inserted other names and prices to frame the account in the manner it now appears.

Mr. *Francis Hawes*, one of the late directors, likewise declared, that about the time of making the last Midsummer dividend, Mr. Knight informed him, that he (Mr. Knight) held stock for John Aislabie, esq, and that he had an account of stock depending with Mr. Aislabie, and the examinant believed that such stock had been taken in some time before, and that Mr. Knight held such stock with the Company's money.

And the examinant added, that he believed the reason of entering the 574,500*l.* stock sold, in the cash-book, was to give persons an opportunity of having stock at low prices, and that great part of the stock sold, was disposed of for the forwarding the bill.

Your committee proceeding to examine sir John Blunt, concerning the disposal of the fictitious South-Sea Stock before-mentioned, he acquainted them, that the latter end of February, or the beginning of March last, Mr. Knight told him, and (as he remembered) the late deputy-governor, Mr. Gibbon, and Mr. Chester, that Mr. Craggs the post-master desired to have 80,000*l.* stock bought, or taken in at the current price, viz. 50,000*l.* for the earl of Sunderland, or his friends, and the remaining 30,000*l.* for Mr. Craggs, or his friends: that this request was complied with, and 80,000*l.* of the company's stock was directed to be applied accordingly, which the examinant takes to be part of the sum of 113,000*l.* entered into the company's cash-book as sold on the 27th day of February 1719, at 175*l.* per cent. That no money appears to have been paid for the above-mentioned 80,000*l.* But sir John Blunt said, that some time in March Mr. Knight shewed him a note for the 50,000*l.* stock, signed Sunderland, which Mr. Knight said was the earl of

Sunderland's hand, and the examinant believed it to be so, having seen his lordship's hand to treasury-warrants and orders. The note, to the best of his remembrance, was to the effect following. That whereas Mr. Knight had bought several parcels of South-Sea Stock for the earl of Sunderland, the particulars of which were therein specified, amounting in the whole to 500,000*l.* stock, at several prices, the money payable for which amounts to more than 80,000*l.* his lordship promised to pay the said money, with interest, at a certain time therein mentioned: that since the beginning of this session of parliament, the examinant and Mr. Knight discoursing about the company's fictitious stock, and particularly concerning the earl of Sunderland's part of it, the examinant asked how he would conceal that? Mr. Knight replied, he would go through thick and thin rather than discover it. That the examinant does not know of any money paid, or note, or other security, given by Mr. Craggs for the 30,000*l.* residue of the 80,000*l.* stock.

Mr. *Edward Gibbon,* another of the late directors, said, that Mr. Knight told him, that some time in February, 1719, he was to supply and furnish the earl of Sunderland, with 50,000*l.* stock, at between 170 and 180*l.* per cent. which was the price of stock at that time.

Mr. *Joye,* late deputy-governor, declared, that Mr. Knight, about ten or eleven months since, told him, that 100,000*l.* stock must be reserved for Mr. Craggs of the Post-office, in trust for others; whereupon the examinant asking, What! for my lord Sunderland; he replied, not for himself, but his friends. Mr. Joye said farther, that Mr. Knight told him since the inquiry began, that the sum promised to Mr. Craggs was but 30,000*l.*

The before-named *James Craggs,* esq. being examined, said, that he never did apply to Mr. Knight, or any other person whatsoever, to have any of the Company's stock, or to have any stock taken in for him by the Company.

Mr. *Richard Holditch,* another of the late directors, said, that he was told by Mr. Knight, That 50,000*l.* of the company's stock, said to be sold, was held for a noble lord in a high station. That he apprehended and believed that by the lord in a high station, Mr. Knight meant the earl of Sunderland; but Mr. Knight being since asked about it, said, that it did not go that way, but it went another way, or words to that effect.

Your Committee in the course of sir *John Blunt's* examination asked him, whether he knew of any more of the Company's stock disposed of, in order to facilitate the passing the bill? He answered, that he believed the duchess of Kendal, her two nieces, and the countess of Platen, were the persons for whose benefit 36,000*l.* stock was entered in the Company's cash-book, as sold on the 4th of February, 1719.

That some time after the 4th day of February, 1719, and while the said scheme, or bill, was depending in the House, Mr. Secretary Craggs, in Westminster-hall, spoke to him, and to the late sub and deputy-governors, and to Mr. Chester, on the behalf of the persons above-named, and said, he really thought it was for the interest of the Company to engage persons of their rank to be concerned in it, or words to that effect; whereupon it was agreed, that they should have 36,000*l.* of the Company's stock at the price mentioned, which was 150 per cent. although the market price, as he believed, was then somewhat bigger: That he took it for granted the agreement was since made good.

That Mr. Knight had the management of this affair, and used to keep an account of the stock thus disposed of in a book of his own; but he then apprehended the duchess of Kendal, and the countess of Platen, did not either of them know that the other was to have any stock.

Sir *John Fellows,* late sub-governor, on his examination said, that whilst the proposals from the South-Sea Company, or the Bill in the House of Commons was depending, Mr. Knight told him, that Mr. Secretary Craggs proposed, that 12,000*l.* of the company's stock should be disposed of to the duchess of Kendal, 12,000*l.* to the countess of Platen, and 12,000*l.* to the duchess's two nieces. The examinant agreed they should have the stock, paying the market-price, which was then above 150 per cent. But Mr. Knight telling the examinant, that he thought they were entitled to the stock from the first application made for it, at which time the price was about 150 per cent.; this examinant consented that they should have it at that price. He added farther, that Mr. Secretary Craggs did at his office recommend the above-mentioned proposal, and said that it would be for the service of the company to have such persons proprietors. He said likewise, that the same proposal was at another time made to him and others by Mr. Secretary Craggs in Westminster-hall. That the examinant and the deputy-governor waited on the duchess of Kendal, and acquainted her with the proposals, and that Mr. Knight should have orders to follow her directions, and desired her good offices on the Company's behalf; that the duchess received them civilly, and thanked them for it. The examinant said also, That a letter was wrote by Mr. Knight to the countess of Platen, signed by the examinant, and the deputy-governor, to acquaint her with the said proposal, and that she wrote an answer, signifying her acceptance, but that he had lost the letter.

Mr. *Edward Gibbon,* another of the said directors, being examined, declared, That whilst the South-Sea bill was depending in the House, he was at a conversation in Westminster-hall, at which were present Mr. Secretary Craggs, the sub and deputy-governors, and Mr. Chester, where Mr. Secretary proposed, that about 30,000*l.* stock should be disposed of to certain ladies, whose having stock would be of service to the Company, or to that effect, which was consented to; and he believed they were foreigners, but did not know their names.

Mr. *Joye,* the late deputy-governor, informed the Committee that some time before the above-mentioned conversation in Westminster-hall, Mr. Knight told him, Mr. Secretary Craggs had mentioned to him, that it would be adviseable to have some great ladies concerned in the Company's stock, and that they should have it at 150 per cent. That soon after sir John Fellows, Mr. Knight, and himself, being at Mr. Secretary Cragg's office, the same proposal was again renewed by the secretary, and was consented to by sir John Fellows, Mr. Knight, and himself; he did not exactly remember the proportions in which the stock was to be provided, but on the best recollection he could make, he thought the duchess of Kendal was to have 10,000*l.* stock, and the countess of Platen the like sum, and the duchess's nieces 5,000*l.* each.

Mr. *Joye* said also, That there was a conversation with Mr. Secretary Craggs in Westminster-hall, concerning the afore-mentioned proposal; That he could not recollect what then passed, but remembered that soon after sir John Fellows and himself were introduced to the duchess of Kendal, by Mr. Secretary Craggs, who interpreted between them; that they acquainted her with the offer, and that directions would be given to Mr. Knight, to transfer the stock on payment of the money; that the duchess seemed well pleased with the offer, thanked them, and wished them good success.

He farther said, that talking with Mr. Knight, since this inquiry began, he said, that neither the duchess of Kendal, nor her nieces, had any stock transferred to them, but that the countess of Platen had; to which Mr. Joye replied, that he did not believe him.

Mr. *Robert Chester*, one of the late directors, being examined likewise about the said conversation in Westminster-hall, concurred, in substance, with what sir John Fellows has before declared.

Sir *John Blunt* said likewise, that after this examination on Friday the 27th of January last, Mr. Joye came to his lodgings, and asked him touching what had passed in his examination before your committee. That sir John Blunt told him, he had said nothing of the ministry: What! says Mr. Joye, nor of the ladies neither? To which sir John replied, that he had not.

That on Saturday the 28th of January last, soon after sir John Blunt had been again examined by your committee at the South-Sea house, Mr. Joye came to him, and asked him what had passed; that sir John told him he was under an obligation of secrecy; that he loved him very well, and that the best way was to tell the whole truth: What, says Mr. Joye, of the ladies, and all? Yes (says sir John) the examination is very strict, and nothing but the truth will do.

Mr. *Joye* being examined by your committee to the above-mentioned conversation between him and sir John Blunt, did admit that the substance of it was true.

Mr. *Holditch* also informed your Committee that Mr. Knight told him, that 20,000*l.* of the Company's stock, said to be sold, was for a certain person, who had deserved well; and that some other person, or persons of distinction at court (or words to that effect) were to have 40 or 50,000*l.* of the Company's stock reserved for them.

Sir *John Blunt* being again examined, informed your committee, that Mr. Knight had the chief management of the disposal of the Company's stock; and, that whilst the South-Sea bill was depending in the House of Commons, Mr. Knight acquainted him, that Mr. Charles Stanhope, one of the secretaries of the treasury, desired to have 10,000*l.* stock bought, or taken in, for him, at the market-price, which was then about 250*l.* per cent, but the said Mr. Stanhope did not absolutely agree to have the stock at that time; but the same day, or the day following, Mr. Knight shewed sir John Blunt a letter, signed Charles Stanhope, where he desired to have the said 10,000*l.* stock bought, or taken in, for him, and sir John Blunt consented that he should have it accordingly.

That on the strictest enquiry your Committee cannot discover, that the said Mr. Stanhope ever paid, or gave any security to pay, for the said stock, or that any actual transfer was made to him of it.

Mr. *Richard Holditch* being again examined, said, he understood by Mr. Knight, that 10 or 12,000*l.* of the Company's stock, said to be sold, was held for Mr. Charles Stanhope of the treasury.

That Mr. Knight told him, that the said Mr. Stanhope was undetermined in the morning, when he first mentioned it, whether he would have it or no, but in the evening agreed to have it.

Your Committee find upon inspection of the account of cash kept by the South-Sea Company with the Bank of England, that by notes drawn upon the Bank by the cashier of the South-Sea Company the sums following, amounting to 51,736*l.* 13*s.* were paid to Charles Stanhope, esq. one of the secretaries of the treasury, out of the cash of the South-Sea Company, at the days following, viz. May the 7th, 5,662*l.* 13*s.* May the 12th, 600*l.* June the 18th, 40,609*l.* September the 10th, 4,865*l.*

Upon the examination of Jacob Sawbridge, esq. late one of the directors, and of the Committee of treasury of the South-Sea Company, and also a copartner with Elias Turner and company, with whom part of the cash of the South-Sea Company had been usually kept, till within three or four months past, and upon perusal of their books, your Committee discovered a disposition of 50,000*l.* of the Company's stock, (as it was then called) unto the said Turner, Sawbridge, and sir George Caswall, which sum now appears in the account of stock sold, laid before this House, viz.

March 21, Turner, Caswall, and Company, (50,000*l.* 250) 120,000*l.*

Ditto. 10,000*l.* (270) 27,000*l.*

The particular of which affair, so far as it relates to the said 50,000*l.* your committee do now lay before the House; and for the better information of the House, they have annexed in the Appendix to their Report, No. II. exact transcripts of their several articles and accounts contained in the several books of Turner and company, unto which their Report has reference.

Sir *Jacob Sawbridge* being examined, as to his passing and signing the account of stock sold, entered in the cash-book of the South-Sea Company, without the names of the persons to whom it was sold; and also the disposition thereof, acknowledged that he allowed and signed the said account, and made no objection thereto, Mr. Knight saying, that the account was right; but the examinant said he could not tell to whom that stock was sold, Mr. Knight not giving the committee of treasury any particulars thereof; but at length Mr. Sawbridge owned that he had 50,000*l.* part of the 68,000*l.* stock mentioned in the cash-book to be sold the 21st day of March 1719, at 250*l.* per cent. and said that when the charter of Turner and company was ordered to be laid before the committee, appointed the last session of parliament, to enquire into and examine the several subscriptions for fishery, and other projects, the said Turner and company were obliged to sell 50,000*l.* South-Sea stock more than they had, (which he called 'selling the bear') and hearing that the South-Sea Company were selling stock, he bought (as he said) this 50,000*l.* stock of the Company, but admitted that he did not pay down any money for it, and that there was no agreement in writing relating thereunto, but if the price of stock had fallen, he said he must have stood to the loss of it; that this stock was not then delivered to him, but was delivered to him, or his order, by Mr. Robert Surman, upon the 11th of June 1720, at which time he paid the money for it, amounting to 125,000*l.* that the price of stock was then advanced to 750*l.* per cent. so that at the market-price this 50,000*l.* stock comes to 375,000*l.* and that he entered in his book

125,000*l.* paid to the South-Sea Company, and entered 250,000*l.* as paid to his own cash, but did not receive any money.

That he directed this account of stock to be entered in a fictitious name, that their servants might not know it to be the proper stock of Turner and company, and carried it to the account of stock in their books, where it is blended with the rest of the stock.

But Sir *John Fellows* said, that he did not know of any particular parcel of stock holden for Turner and company, till lately; and said he did not remember the disposal of the 50,000*l.* stock, to them; that Mr. Knight used to transact with them, and he (the examinant) believed, the Company did not intend to give them the benefit of so much stock.

Your committee proceeding to inspect the books of Turner and company, and to examine Daniel Watkins, one of their clerks, and also Mr. Jacob Sawbridge, do find, that upon the 11th of June, 1720, this 50,000*l.* stock and the improved value thereof, amounting to 375,000*l.* was regularly placed to the account of Charles Stanhope, esq. in the several stock ledger books of Turner and company, mentioned in the Appendix, under the following letters viz. in the stock ledger book, letter A, fol. 99, and in the stock ledger, letter B, fol. 7, and 62. The entry in the ledger, letter A, is in these words on the debtor side.

1720, June 11,
To cash for 22,000*l.* South-Sea stock to Robert Knight and
    Robert Surman's order   £202,230
To Do. 28,000*l.* Do. to J. Stokes's account   172,770
                                             £375,000

And this account was upon the same 11th of June 1720, regularly entered in their book, called the general or clearing-book, letter C. fol. 110, and was placed to Charles Stanhope, esq. accordingly.

Daniel Watkins declared, that he at first wrote those several entries in the said book, in the name of Charles Stanhope, esq. by the direction of sir George Caswall, one of the copartners with Turner and Sawbridge, or from some other account, and believed, that he had seen the said Charles Stanhope, esq. at the office of Turner and company, once or oftener, in or about the months of May or June last, coming there to receive money, that he was then told Mr. Stanhope's name by some clerk in the office, and upon his examination described Mr. Stanhope to be a tall thin man, of a black or brown complexion, according to his remembrance.

The said accounts mentioning 28,000*l.* stock, part of the said 50,000*l.* to be adjusted with Joseph Stokes at 172,770*l.* your Committee sent for the said Joseph Stokes, and for Joseph Stanborough his partner, who acted for Turner and company, in the selling of stock, who being examined, and producing their account book, and comparing it with an account in the said ledger of Turner and company, letter D, fol. 36, kept with the said Joseph Stokes, for the produce of this 28,000*l.* stock, at 172,770*l.* John [*sic*] Stanborough said, that he transacted this affair for Mr. Sawbridge, and that the said 28,000*l.* South Sea stock, was sold, or disposed of by him or Joseph Stokes, upon the 10th of June, 1720, or a day or two before, together with another sum of 1,000*l.* South-Sea stock, at several prices, amounting in the whole to 180,280*l.* which sum he actually paid and answered to Jacob Sawbridge, esq. upon the 10th or 11th of June, 1720, who caused the said stock to be transferred accordingly; thereupon your Committee proceeded to enquire into the time and manner of payment for this stock unto Mr. Charles Stanhope, and inspecting the several other books of Turner and company, mentioned in the appendix, called the note book, the cash note book, the drawing ledger, and the cash note ledger, wherein the account of all notes issued and paid by Turner and company are duly entered, it appeared by the note book, letter F, fol. 100, and by the cash note ledger, letter A, fol. 289, and 299, that upon the 11th of June, 1720, one cash note of the said Turner and company was regularly made out for 202,230*l.* payable to the said Mr. Charles Stanhope, and another cash note of Turner and company was also regularly made out the same day for 47,770*l.* payable to Mr. Charles Stanhope, which last note in the note book, letter F, fol. 100, is entered, Robert Surman; both which notes were regularly entered, paid, and satisfied, unto Mr. Charles Stanhope, by Turner and company, upon the 12th of December, 1720, in the note book of Turner and company, letter G, fol. 70, and their cash note ledger, letter H, fol. 77, and by another book of Turner and company, called the drawing cash ledger, letter I, fol. 758, it appears, that upon the said 11th day of June, 1720, when the said notes were issued, the sum of 47,770*l.* being the contents of one of the said notes, was charged to the account of Mr. Robert Surman, deputy cashier of the South Sea Company, as paid that day out of the cash kept by Turner and company, unto the order of the said Robert Surman; Robert Surman being examined thereunto, upon inspection of cash-draughts kept by Turner and company, in his name, wherein it appears, that he is charged with the aforesaid sum of 47,770*l.* paid by Turner and company, the 11th of June, 1720, out of the cash kept with them, by Mr. Knight, as cashier of the South-Sea Company, and for which Surman was accountable to Knight, did verily believe, that the said sum, accordingly paid by them, by order of Mr. Knight was given to the examinant out of the said cash, and was no part of the examinant's proper cash.

Your Committee in this place observe, that the two sums of 202,230*l.* and 47,770*l.* amount to 250,000*l.* which being added to the 125,000*l.* the supposed price of the said 50,000*l.* stock, amounts to the whole sum charged in the said stock ledger, viz. 375,000*l.* as the produce of the said stock upon the 11th of June, 1720, and deducting out of the 375,000*l.* the sum of 125,000*l.* for the prime cost of the said stock, there remains a clear difference of 250,000*l.* accruing to the person for whose benefit the 50,000*l.* stock was charged, as sold in the Company's cash book, which is the exact amount of the said two cash notes, made payable to Charles Stanhope, esq. and accordingly entered, paid, and satisfied unto him, the 12th of December, 1720.

In confirmation of which payment, it appears to your Committee by the drawing cash-ledger, letter K, now kept by Turner, Caswall, and Sawbridge, in the new co-partnership with Mr. Henry Blunt, son of sir John Blunt, and Mr. Robinson Knight, nephew of Mr. Robert Knight, which commenced the 25th of June, 1720, fol. 512 and 570, in an account kept between Turner, Caswall and Sawbridge, and the new co-partners, that the said 250,000*l.* was entered paid in discharge of the two notes upon the 12th of December, 1720, and placed to the account of money disbursed upon the separate account of Turner, Caswall and Sawbridge, out of their separate cash actually paid into the hands of the new co-partners, upon the 25th of June, 1720, amounting in real cash unto the sum of 1,166,875*l.* 4*s.* 1*d.* out of which the 250,000*l.* are accordingly set off in discharge of the new co-partners.

Your Committee examined John Mount and John Maddy, cashier to Turner and company, as well before as since the new co-partnership, Richard Fenton their book-keeper, and also Jacob Sawbridge, jun. son of Jacob Sawbridge, esq. the said Robinson Knight and Henry Blunt, who, before the 25th of June, 1720, were assistants in the office of Turner and company, relating to the several books and entries, and to the transactions therein contained; and John Mount, John Maddy, and Richard Fenton declared, that they verily believed, that all the said accounts and entries of receipts and payments, and of issuing and paying notes, were true; and that the respective sums mentioned therein to have been received and paid, were really received and paid; and that the notes therein mentioned to have been issued, and paid, were actually issued and paid according to the import of the several entries; and that those two notes for 202,230*l.* and 47,770*l.* were actually issued, payable to Mr. Charles Stanhope, upon the 11th of June, 1720, in the usual and regular manner; the note for the 202,230*l.* being entered and filled up by the said Henry Blunt, and the other note for 47,770*l.* being entered and filled up by Jacob Sawbridge, jun. by the direction of Jacob Sawbridge, sen. esq. and both the said notes, signed by Robinson Knight, then entrusted by Turner and company to sign notes for them, as Jacob Sawbridge, jun. Robinson Knight, and Henry Blunt did acknowledge; and that Turner and company, did thereby become chargeable with the payment of the money mentioned in the two notes, which were actually paid and satisfied upon the 12th of December, 1720, according to the entries thereof, made in the same books out of the cash, amounting to 1,166,875*l.* 4*s.* 1*d.* really paid and answered by Turner, Caswall and Sawbridge, into the new co-partnership, which Henry Blunt and Robinson Knight, the new co-partners, did likewise confess, and that the two notes being then discharged, were delivered up to Turner and company.

The Committee observing, that in the stock-ledger, book (A) and (B), the name as it now stands at the head of accounts there, and also in the accounts in the said book-ledger, letter (B) fol. 7, is 'Stangape,' although in the alphabets or indexes of the said books, referring to the true folios, the name still remains 'Stanhope,' and also that in the said general or clearing book, the name now appearing in the account of the said 50,000*l.* stock, is 'Stangape,' and that the said books had been razed, and the letters altered; did examine Jacob Sawbridge, esq. and Daniel Watkins, one of the clerks of Turner and company, upon the fact. Mr. Sawbridge acknowledged that the name at first entered in the said books was 'Stanhope,' and said it was entered in a fictitious name, that their servants might not know of it; that he gave directions to Daniel Watkins, about two months past, to make the several razures and alterations in the sir-name, and to turn it into 'Stangape,' but owned, that his name referred to the name 'Stanhope,' mentioned in the alphabets and in the other books, and that it meant the same person. . . .

Here your committee must observe, that in the account of stock sold, laid before this House, they found the names of several members of this House and of the House of Peers, not concerned in the administration, or in the management of the public revenue, whose cases your committee could not particularly examine, but must wait for the consideration and direction of the House, in what manner each examination shall proceed. In the mean time, your committee think it proper to acquaint the House, with divers practices made use of to raise the nominal value of South-Sea stock, to that extravagant rate to which it was afterwards advanced, above the real and intrinsic value thereof.

Your committee find, that by computation made by direction of your committee it appears, that the directors of the South-Sea Company, might have raised the whole sum stipulated for the public, with a profit of near one million and an half for the benefit of the proprietors of the old stock, without setting their stock to sale at any higher price than 150l. per cent.

That after the said directors had taken in the first money-subscription at 300l. per cent. and the second money-subscription at 400l. per cent. and the first subscription of the long and short annuities at 375l. per cent. the value of 100l. South-Sea stock was but 120l. or thereabouts, supposing the whole money of the said first and second subscriptions (amounting to 12,750,000l.) had been all paid in.

That the said court of directors did afterwards proceed to take in a third and fourth money-subscription at the rate of 1,000l. per cent. and a second subscription of the long and short annuities, and a subscription of the redeemable debts at the rate of 800l. per cent. after which the value of 100l. South-Sea stock was but 332l. or thereabouts, supposing the whole money of the said four money-subscriptions (amounting to 68,750,000l.) had been all paid in.

That if all the remaining public debts had been taken in, and all the remaining stocks of the Company sold, on the terms which the said directors pretended to expect, 100l. South-Sea stock would have been worth but 547l. or thereabouts, supposing the money of the said four subscriptions, and the money for the remaining stock, (which together would have amounted to 205,039,401l.) had been all paid in.

That on the 30th day of August last, the court of directors of the South-Sea Company came to a resolution (which on the 8th day of September last was confirmed by a general court) to declare a dividend of 30l. per cent. to be made at Christmas, 1720, and of not less than 50l. per cent. per ann. for not less than 12 years to come from that time.

That soon after this Resolution, (viz. at a general court held the 20th day of September last) the sub-governor acquainted the general court, that the affairs of the court, in relation to the price of their stock, and subscriptions, had taken an unexpected turn, and thereupon proposed their giving a power to the court of directors to relieve the last subscribers of the public debts, and the proprietors of the two last money-subscriptions, which was accordingly granted; and at a court of directors held the 29th day of September last, it was resolved, that the said subscribers should have the same terms with the Bank, viz. that their subscriptions should be reduced from 1,000l. and 800l. per cent. to 400l. and that they should also have the benefit of the Midsummer dividend of 10*l.* per cent. which was accordingly confirmed by a general court held the 30th day of the same month; upon which your committee observe that it appears to them very extraordinary that the directors on the 8th day of September (when the said high dividend was declared in a general court) should have had no foresight of the turn which so soon after (viz. on the 20th day of the same month) happened in their affairs.

That on the said 8th day of September, the sub-governor acquainted the general court, that their directors had been unanimous in all their proceedings, which among other things, includes the before-mentioned several subscriptions by them taken in, except the first; and upon the examination of the directors it doth not appear to your committee that any one of them protested against, or declared any public dissent from any of the said proceedings: and it appears that all of them took their shares and proportions of the subscriptions, which were allotted for the respective directors to dispose of.

And your committee have been informed by sir Theodore Janssen, that there was a meeting at the house of sir John Fellows, betwixt sixteen of the court of directors, Mr. Secretary Craggs, and Mr. Aislabie, at which time it was proposed, that a subscription should be taken in at 300*l.* per cent. which was approved of by Mr. Secretary Craggs, and Mr. Aislabie; and that, when the said company broke up, it was agreed, that every person should use their best endeavours to promote it; which is also confirmed by the information of sir Lambert Blackwell.

And at a court of directors, held the 13th day of April last, it was resolved, to take in a subscription for two millions, at the rate of 300*l.* per cent. but the same was afterwards increased, without any previous resolution to that purpose, to 2,250,000*l.* and your committee observe that the imaginary value of the said subscriptions rose very fast; and that those who had the benefit of the said additional subscription, if they sold, and disposed of the same, made very great gains thereby.

That at a court of directors held the 28th day of April last, it was resolved to take in a second money-subscription, at the rate of 400*l.* per cent. for 1,000,000*l.* but by the accounts delivered into this House, it appears, that the said subscription was for 1,500,000*l.* yet it does not appear that there was any previous Resolution of the court of directors for the addition of 500,000*l.* nor was the said addition declared till the 8th of September last, at which time the sub-governor acquainted the general court therewith; upon which your committee cannot but observe the great distance of time between the taking in of the second subscription at 1,000,000*l.* and the 8th of September, when the same was reported to the general court at 1,500,000*l.* during which interval the imaginary value of that subscription was excessively increased, whereby the persons who had the same, had the advantage of that extraordinary rise.

That at a court of directors, held the 15th day of June last, it was resolved to take in a third money-subscription at the rate of 1,000*l.* per cent. one tenth part whereof was to be paid down at the time of subscription; and at a court of directors held the 23d day of the same month, the sub-governor acquainted the court, that the said third money-subscription was completed, without mentioning to what sum:

but at the before-mentioned general court, held the 8th day of September last, he declared the same to be for five millions; and Mr. Knight, late cashier of the South Sea Company, by an article dated the 20th day of June last, in the cash-book, fol. 125, charges the said sum of five millions as received; which account was passed, and allowed by the Company's committee of treasury, on, or some time after, the 4th day of August last; and yet in the account of the third money-subscription delivered into this House, it is stated at 4,400,000*l*. only, the remaining sum of 600,000*l*. being entered on the credit side of the said cash-book on the 19th of December, 1720, as a supposed deficiency of the payment on this subscription; although it appears to your committee upon the evidence of Mr. Lockyer and others, that not only the whole sum of five millions, but even a considerable exceeding thereon was paid in; that a great deal of money was repaid back to reduce the subscription to five millions; and that they had money enough paid in for near eight millions.

That at a court of directors, held the 12th day of August last, it was resolved to take in a fourth money-subscription for one million, at the rate of 1,000*l*. per cent. And at a court of directors, held the 25th of the same month, it was declared, that upon casting up the books, it was found the said fourth money-subscription, instead of one million, was increased to 1,250,000*l*. which was occasioned by taking the said subscription in several books; and at the before-mentioned general court, held the 8th day of September last, the sub-governor declared the fourth money-subscription was compleated to 1,250,000*l*. and Mr. Knight the cashier hath, in an article dated the 30th day of August last, and entered in the cash-book, fol. 128, given the Company credit for the first payment, made on the 4th subscription, viz. for 2,500,000*l*. which account was passed, and allowed by the committee of treasury, on the 4th day of October last; and yet in the account of the said fourth money-subscription delivered into this House, it is stated at 1,200,000*l*. only: That upon the examination of Mr. Knight, and several of the directors, in relation to the deficiency of the said third and fourth money-subscriptions, their answers were very unsatisfactory: And your committee cannot but observe, that as by the before-mentioned additions to the first two money-subscriptions, some persons made great gains, whilst the price of the said subscriptions continued high, so when the price of the subscriptions fell, many other persons were favoured, by having their subscriptions withdrawn, which was the cause of the deficiency.

That on the second money-subscription each director was allowed for himself and friends, 26,000*l*. and that the remainder of the million at first resolved to be taken in, was at the disposal of the sub and deputy-governors; but for whose benefit the additional subscription of 500,000*l*. was intended, your committee have not yet been able to discover.

That on the third money-subscription each director was allowed 54,000*l*. for himself and friends, and that several large lists of the names of persons were sent to the sub-governor, to be admitted into the said third subscription; viz. by the earl of Sunderland, first lord commissioner of the treasury, a list amounting to 167,000*l*. By John Aislabie, esq. late chancellor of the exchequer, another of the lords of the treasury, a list amounting to 75,300*l*. By James Craggs, esq. one of his majesty's principal secretaries of state, two lists, amounting to 695,000*l*. and by Charles

Stanhope, esq. one of the secretaries of the treasury, a list amounting to 49,700*l.* which four last mentioned lists amount to 987,000*l.*

That upon examination, it appears, that other lists have been given in, as well on the third as on the second subscription; but the same being lost or mislaid, as your committee have been informed, they are thereby disabled at present, from making any report thereon.

They find 25,000*l.* of the second subscription hath been given unto John Aislabie, esq. about eight or ten days after the opening of that subscription, at which time the subscriptions were at an advanced price, of about 40*l.* per cent. and soon after rose vastly higher.

That it doth not appear to your committee that any of the persons, who had the honour to serve his majesty in the treasury, or any other part of the administration, used any endeavours to prevent the directors of the South-Sea Company from taking in subscriptions at the aforesaid extravagant prices; but, on the contrary, it doth appear, that some of them, by the lists they gave in aforesaid, did not only encourage and promote the said subscriptions, but did greatly enlarge the same.

Your committee observing that sir John Fellows, late sub-governor of the South-Sea Company, did at a general court of the said Company, held the 21st day of April, 1720, acquaint that court, that the design of the government's million of Exchequer bills to be lent to the Company, by virtue of the late act of parliament for issuing Exchequer bills, to be circulated at or near the Exchequer, was to enable the Company to lend money upon their stock; and finding that by order of the court of directors of the said Company the same had been so lent out, your committee proceeded to enquire into this affair.

And on examination of Mr. Robert Knight, late cashier of the said Company, he declared, that he did not remember that any application was made by the directors to have those bills issued; but that the first discourse of this matter was by John Aislabie, esq. then chancellor of the exchequer, a week before the proposals of the South-Sea Company were offered to this House; that Mr. Aislabie said, it would be more acceptable to have those bills circulated at the Exchequer, than to send them to the Bank or elsewhere, and that the company might afford to circulate them for nothing, they being to be lent to the Company to enable them to execute their scheme. That the examinant believed, the intention of lending the said bills upon stock, had been communicated to Mr. Aislabie, (and that he the examinant) on his attending at the treasury to solicit the issuing of these bills, did mention that design, and never heard that the treasury disapproved of it.

That sir *John Blunt* declared, it would be better to employ those bills in the lending upon stock, than in paying off the redeemables, which would take up more time.

Hereupon your committee examining sir John Fellows, he said, that he and others of the directors treated with Mr. Aislabie and others at the treasury, about the issuing the said Exchequer bills; but that it was first proposed to Mr. Aislabie, and the examinant believed, it was at first mentioned by sir John Blunt, in a committee of the directors, and that it was the general opinion of the directors.

Your committee examining sir John Blunt upon this transaction, he declared, that he spoke to Mr. Aislabie to hasten the issuing of the said bills; and that himself, or some other of the directors acquainted Mr. Aislabie, as he believes at the treasury, with the Company's design to lend them upon stock; that it did not, at first, arise from the directors, but that it was intimated to them before, or very soon after the Company's proposals were laid before the House, by some of the treasury, and on recollection, the examinant said it was by Mr. Aislabie, to enable the Company to carry on their scheme, and thereby to raise the price of their stock, the borrowers being enabled to buy stock.

That by the book of loans delivered into this House, it appears that the sum of 9,039,936*l*. 11*s*. was lent to several persons on the security of 2,563,117*l*. 17*s*. 5*d*. stock: and that the farther sum of 2,219,089*l*. was lent on the security of 773,600*l*. subscription-receipts; the money so lent, and still remaining due, amounting in the whole to the sum of 11,259,025*l*. 11*s*.

That by several resolutions of the court of directors of the 21st of April, the 20th of May, and the 9th of June last, for three several loans, it appears, that the sum resolved by them to be lent on stock from the 21st of April, to the 21st of May, was limited to 500,000*l*. in the whole, and that not more than 5,000*l*. should be lent to any one person, and such loan to be only at the rate of 250*l*. on 100*l*. stock; that from the 20th of May to the 9th of June, the rule of lending was at the rate of 300*l*. on 100*l*. stock, and that not more than 3,000*l*. should be lent to any one person; and from the 9th of June, the rule of lending was at 400*l*. on 100*l*. stock, and that not more than 4,000*l*. should be lent to any one person.

That on examination of the book of loans, it appears, that on the first loan, the rules of lending were greatly exceeded, viz. That there was lent in the whole 943,631*l*. more than the sum of 500,000*l*. to which the said loan was confined. That the excess above 250*l*. on 100*l*. stock, amounts to 316,740*l*. and the excess above 5,000*l*. to one person, amounts in the whole to 779,231*l*. That on the second loan the excess above the rate of 300*l*. on 100*l*. stock amounts to 30,750*l*. and the excess above 3,000*l*. to one person, amounts in the whole to 169,025*l*. And that on the third loan, the excess above 400*l*. on 100*l*. stock amounts to 59,413*l*. and the excess above the rate of 4,000*l*. to one person, amounts in the whole, to 1,447,677*l*. For the particulars of all which, your committee refer to the book marked No. 4, in which the same are distinctly expressed, and the resolutions of the general court, and court of directors, in relation to loans, are transcribed.

That your committee do not find any resolution, either of a general court, or a court of directors, for lending money on subscription-receipts; but by the examinations which they have taken, it appears that Mr. Knight, the late cashier of the South-Sea Company, and his under cashier and clerks, by his directions, did lend money on the subscription-receipts, by verbal orders from the directors of the said company, and under colour of an order of a general court, made the 21st of April 1720, to empower the court of directors from time to time, as they shall see for the interest of the company, to lend any sum or sums of the company's money, on the company's present, and to be increased, capital stock; and to do all such matters and things, as they should judge most for the good of the company.

But your committee find, that by the second by-law of the said company, relating to the keeping the cash of the company, it was ordained, that the cash of the corporation should from time to time be kept under three several locks, with different wards, the keys of which to be kept, one by the cashier, and the other two by such of the governor, sub-governor, deputy-governor, or directors, as the said court should from time to time appoint, except such sum or sums as the court of directors should think necessary to let remain in the custody of the cashier; and no money relating to the trade or affairs of the said company should be disposed of, without an order of the said court of directors; and that the interest and all other advantages, arising and growing upon the cash of the said company, should be brought to the account of the said company. However, it appears that the said loans on subscriptions were generally known, and never objected against, by any of the directors in a general court, or in any court of directors.

That on the said loans on stock, the stock was transferred to persons for that purpose nominated, in the same manner as if the same had been absolutely sold, without any defeazance on the part of the company, or of the persons to whom the stock was transferred, for retransferring the same, on repayment of the money, nor was any covenant or other security taken, for repayment from the borrowers, except the stock so transferred; nor doth there appear any distinction between the said transfers on loans, and the other transfers, which were made of stock absolutely purchased, on account of the company; upon which your committee observe, that it was in the power of the persons to whom the said pawned stock was transferred, to dispose thereof at any time, as they thought fit, when the price of stock was high, and to replace the same when it fell.

And your Committee do find, that on the 19th day on October last, the said Mr. Knight, to whom the said pawned stock was transferred, did, pursuant to an order of the Court of Directors, transfer stock to the amount of 2,141,867*l*. 17*s*. 5*d*. to sir Harcourt Masters, col. Hugh Raymond, Edward Gibbon, and John Gore, trustees, for that purpose, nominated by the Court of Directors, in whose names the same now remains; but the sum is 421,250*l*. short of the aforesaid sum of 2,563,117*l*. 17*s*. 5*d*. which is mentioned in the said book of loans, to have been pledged for the security of the repayment of the aforesaid sum of 9,039,936*l*. 11*s*. from which it is evident, that the said sum of 421,250*l*. of the stock mortgaged or pawned on loans, as aforesaid, has been sold, or otherwise disposed of, by the trustees, or agents of the South-Sea Company; and till replaced, cannot be re-transferred to those, by whom the same was pawned or mortgaged: Upon which your Committee observe, how easy it was for the trustees of the company to have sold the said stock when it was at high prices, and to have replaced the same again when it fell; for on examination it appears, that there was no distinct and separate account kept of the said mortgaged and pawned stock, nor was the same any ways distinguished from the other stock of those persons, to whom it was at first transferred.

That as to the said sum of 2,219,087*l*. lent on 773,600*l*. subscription receipts, it appears by the aforesaid book of loans, that the general rule of lending was at the rate of 300*l*. on 100 subscription receipts; but excluding from the said loans on subscriptions the two great loans, the one to the million-bank, and the other to Turner and company, the loans, to the other borrowers, will at an average come out above 300 per cent. It appears that on the first subscription receipts, at the time of the said lending, there was paid in only from 90*l.* to 120*l.* per cent. and on the second subscription receipts generally 40*l.* and on some few 80*l.* per cent. but how much more there hath been paid in since, or whether all the said subscription receipts, on which money was lent, be now remaining in the custody of any person for the security of the company, your Committee cannot at present discover; the receipts not having been as yet produced to them.

That it appears that Turner and company were employed by the directors, to lend out 500,000*l.* on subscription receipts, and that they accordingly lent 150,000*l.* on such receipts, after the rate of 190*l.* per cent, on the first subscription, and 40*l.* per cent. on the second. But such rates being by the said directors thought too low, the said Turner and company were ordered to proceed no farther in disposing of the remaining part of the said 500,000*l.* and were told at the same time, that by lending at such low rates on subscriptions, they were ruining the stock. And it also appears, that Mr. Knight did issue a considerable sum to be disposed of by brokers, for the refusal of South-Sea stock at certain times, at very high prices; and likewise, that on the declension of the price of the stock, large sums were issued to purchase stock on account of the company, at very high prices; and part of the stock then bought, appears to have belonged to some of the directors of the said company: and although your Committee are not yet prepared to set this matter in a full light, they cannot but observe, that the said directors, in all their proceedings in the execution of their scheme, appear to have had chiefly in view the raising and supporting the imaginary value of the stock, at an extravagant and high price, for the benefit of themselves, and those who were in the secret with them.

That as to the aforesaid loans on subscription receipts, it appears, there were no defeazances executed by those with whom the receipts were deposited, for a re-delivery of the same, on repayment of the money, nor any security given by the borrowers, besides the receipts by them so delivered, nor doth any thing else appear to distinguish the receipts so pledged, from such receipts as were, or might have been, absolutely sold to the company; for all the said receipts were made out in one name, viz. Joseph Safford, and by his indorsement the bearer became intitled to the property thereof; upon which your Committee observe, the security of the company, as to the money lent on the said subscription receipts, is more precarious than the loans on stock; for by the transfer book it might appear by whom such stock was transferred; but it hath not yet appeared to your Committee that any books have been kept, or entries made, of the names of the persons to whom such loans have been made on subscription receipts: and your Committee do farther observe, that it was in the power of the persons, with whom such subscription receipts were deposited, to sell the same at high prices, and to replace them again when the price fell. And upon the whole it doth appear to your Committee that the said loans on stock and on subscriptions have been managed with the utmost negligence, with respect to the interest of the company, and were contrived for the raising and keeping up the price of stock at an extravagant height.

Before your Committee conclude this report, they think it proper to observe, that it has appeared to them throughout their examination, that Mr. Knight, cashier of the South-Sea Company, was principally concerned in their most secret transactions. And your Committee have been informed by sir Theodore Janssen, soon after Mr. Knight's withdrawing himself, that upon his pressing Mr. Knight, two or three days before he went away, to make a discovery of whatsoever he knew relating to the whole proceedings; Mr. Knight answered, that if he should disclose all he knew, it would open such a scene as the world would be surprized at.

Your Committee having made this progress in their enquiry, have thought themselves obliged to lay this report before the House; and will proceed in their farther examination of the matters referred to them, with the utmost diligence.

Bubble Act, 1721

7 Geo. 1, c. 2   *Statutes at Large*, XIV, 360-67.

This act sought to restore public credit after the collapse of the South Sea Company. It forbade joint stock organizations except through private Acts of Parliament.

Whereas in and by an act of parliament of the sixth year of his Majesty's reign, intituled, *An act for enabling the South-Sea company to increase their present capital stock and fund, by redeeming such publick debts and incumbrances as are therein mentioned; and for raising money to be applied for lessening several of the publick debts and incumbrances; and for calling in the present exchequer-bills remaining uncancelled; and for making forth new bills in lieu thereof, to be circulated and exchanged upon demand at or near the exchequer,* it was enacted, That the said company should pay into the receipt of his Majesty's exchequer the sum of four millions one hundred fifty six thousand three hundred and six pounds four shillings and eleven pence, by such proportions, and at such times, as were thereby appointed for the payment thereof; and such further sums to be computed after the rate of four years and an half's purchase, and such further sums to be computed after the rate of one year's purchase, as are therein mentioned, by quarterly payments, at such feast-days as were thereby limited for payment of the same; and in and by an act of parliament of the seventh year of his Majesty's reign, intituled, *An act to enable the South-Sea company to ingraft part of their capital stock and fund into the stock and fund of the Bank of England, and another part thereof into the stock and fund of the East-India company; and for giving further time for payments to be made by the said South-Sea company, to the use of the publick,* it is provided, declared and enacted, That the said company shall pay, and be obliged, by force and virtue of that act, to pay into the receipt of his Majesty's exchequer the said sum of four millions one hundred fifty six thousand three hundred and six pounds four shillings and eleven pence, and the said several sums after the rate of four years and an half's purchase, and one year's purchase; and that the same shall be payable by such proportions, and at or by such respective days or times of payment, as are therein limited and appointed, and herein after mentioned for the payment thereof, and not otherwise; that is to say, one full and equal fourth part of the respective sums so payable, shall be paid on or before the feast of the annunciation of the blessed Virgin Mary, which shall be in the year of our Lord one thousand seven hundred and twenty two; one other full and equal fourth part thereof, on or before the feast of the nativity of Saint John Baptist, which shall be in the year of our Lord one thousand seven hundred and twenty two; one other full and equal fourth part thereof, on or before the feast of Saint Michael the archangel, which shall be in the year of our Lord one thousand seven hundred and twenty two; and the remaining full and equal fourth part of the said respective sums so payable, on or before the feast of the birth of our Lord Christ, which shall be in the said year of our Lord one thousand seven hundred and twenty two; and that the said South-Sea company, and their stock and funds, (except as therein is excepted) are and shall be subject and liable to the payment of the said several sums at or before the said respective days and times by the last mentioned act appointed for the payment thereof, without any deduction, defalcation or abatement whatsoever: and it is thereby further enacted, That in case default shall be made by the said South-Sea company in the payment of all or any part or parcel, parts or parcels, of the said several sums of four millions one hundred fifty six thousand three hundred and six pounds four shillings and eleven pence, and of the said sums to be paid after the rate of four years and an half's purchase, and one year's purchase, or any of them, at the respective days or times by that act limited for the payment thereof, then the commissioners of the treasury, or any three or more of them, or the high treasurer for the time being, or the officers of the exchequer for the time being, shall, and they respectively are thereby authorized, injoined and required, to cause the money, whereof such default in payment shall be made, with interest for the same, after the rate of five pounds per centum per annum, (to be computed as is therein mentioned) to be stopt out of the monies which, weekly or otherwise, shall be payable to the said company at the exchequer, for or upon their annuities or yearly funds (except as therein is excepted) and to cause the principal and interest so stopt, to be applied as is therein after directed in that behalf; as by the said several acts of parliament, relation being thereunto respectively had, may more fully appear: and whereas by the many frauds, abuses, and breaches of trust, which were committed by the late sub-governor, deputy-governor, and directors of the said company, and others in confederacy with them, or some of them, the said company has suffered an immense loss and damage, and the publick credit (as well as the credit of the said company) hath been extremely reduced and disordered, contrary to the purport and true meaning of the act of parliament first above in part recited, whereby the said company is become unable to comply with all the payments required to be made by the act of parliament last in part before recited; and if their capital stock, and the annuities and yearly funds payable in respect thereof, should continue subject and liable to all the said payments, and to such stoppages as are directed by the said act last mentioned, the credit of the said company would be utterly impaired, and the sufferings of the members would be extremely increased: and whereas in regard to the inability of the said company, under the bad circumstances to which the same is reduced, and to the intent that the said company may be obliged and better enabled to give some further relief (as this act directs) to the several proprietors and persons concerned in interest in or with the said company, in order to the ascertaining and settling their respective properties and interests, and the re-establishing of the publick credit, and thereby quieting the minds of his Majesty's subjects, it is thought meet, that the said sum of four millions one hundred fifty six thousand three hundred and six pounds four shillings and eleven pence, and the said several and respective sums, which were intended to be computed after the said respective rates of four years and an half's purchase, and one year's purchase, be remitted and discharged, so as from and after the feast of the nativity of Saint John Baptist, which shall be in the year of our Lord one thousand seven hundred and twenty two, the sum of two millions sterling, part of the capital stock which shall then belong to the said company, be reduced and annihilated, and so as a proportionable part of their annuities or yearly funds, in respect of the said two millions, do from that time cease and determine for the benefit of the publick; be it therefore enacted by the King's most excellent majesty, by and with the advice and consent of the lords spiritual and temporal and commons, in this present parliament assembled, and by the authority of the same, That the said sum of four millions one hundred fifty six thousand three hundred and six pounds four shillings and eleven pence, and the said several and respective sums, which were intended to be computed and paid after the said several and respective rates of four years and an half's purchase, and one year's purchase, and all actions, suits, executions, demands, stoppages, detentions, and other remedies for recovering or obtaining the same, or any part thereof, are and shall, by force and virtue of this present act, be and be deemed and adjudged to be remised, released, and for ever discharged.

II.   Provided always nevertheless, and it is hereby enacted, That from and after the said feast of the nativity of Saint John Baptist, which shall be in the year of our Lord one thousand seven hundred and twenty two, the full sum of two millions of pounds sterling, part of the capital stock which shall then belong to the said company, shall by force and virtue of this act, be and be deemed and adjudged to be reduced, sunk and annihilated for ever; and that a proportional part of their annuities or yearly funds, payable at the exchequer in respect of two millions, shall, by force and virtue of this act, from and after the said feast of the nativity of Saint John Baptist, which shall be in the year of our Lord one thousand seven hundred and twenty two; be no longer payable, but shall from thenceforth for ever cease and determine for the benefit of the publick; any thing in the said recited acts, or either of them, or any other law, statute or provision whatsoever, to the contrary in any wise notwithstanding.

III.   And whereas several persons or corporations, who were intitled to several redeemable debts and annuities, payable at the receipt of the exchequer, or by the cashier of the bank of England, or otherwise, and who were enabled to subscribe the same into the capital stock of the said South-Sea company, did subscribe, or cause or procure to be subscribed, many of the said redeemable debts and annuities; and the proprietors of such of the said redeemable debts and annuities as were payable at the receipt of the exchequer, or at particular pay-offices at or near the exchequer, did deliver in their respective orders, tallies, tickets or other securities, for payments of such debts or annuities to persons for that purpose appointed; and the accounts of the proprietors of such of the said redeemable debts and annuities as were payable by the said cashier of the bank of England, were debited in the books of the bank; and an additional capital stock was, upon books or duplicates signed and attested by three or more of the directors or managers in that behalf appointed, created or settled by the commissioners of his Majesty's treasury for the time being, to be allowed to the said company for or in respect of the said redeemable debts and annuities; which said redeemable debts and annuities were subscribed, or pretended to be subscribed, at several high rates or prices in stock, exceeding the rate or price of four hundred per centum; and a general court of the said company, on or about the thirtieth day of September one thousand seven hundred and twenty, towards relieving those proprietors, did agree that the same redeemable debts and annuities, should be taken in at par, being one hundred pounds for each one hundred pounds principal money of those redeemable debts and annuities; and that the proprietors of the same should be entitled to the interest due thereon, until the twenty ninth day of September one thousand seven hundred and twenty, and be paid for the principal sums in the stock of the said company, at the rate of four hundred per centum, with an addition of ten per centum in stock for a dividend at Midsummer one thousand seven hundred and twenty: and whereas the said company, or their late court of directors, did exhibit, or cause to be exhibited, books for taking subscriptions of money for purchasing stock of the said company, commonly called the four money subscriptions; whereupon several persons or corporations did advance, or cause to be advanced, monies amounting to a large sum; and the general court of the said company, on or about the ninth day of March one thousand seven hundred and twenty, did resolve that no more money than what had been then actually paid on the said four money subscriptions, should be demanded or insisted on, and that stock should be given for the money actually paid by the respective proprietors in the said first money subscriptions, at three hundred per centum, with the dividend of Midsummer one thousand seven hundred and twenty, of ten per centum in stock; and that stock should be given for the money actually paid by the respective proprietors in the said second money subscription, at four hundred per centum, with the like dividend; and a general court of the said company, on or about the eighteenth day of the said month of March one thousand seven hundred and twenty, did resolve that stock should be given for the monies paid on the said third and fourth money subscriptions at the rate of four hundred per centum, with the like dividend of ten per centum in stock: now in order to put an end to all disputes between the said company and the proprietors of the said redeemable debts and annuities subscribed into the said company, and between the proprietors of the said money subscriptions; and for the further relief, as well of the proprietors of the said redeemable debts and annuities, as also of the proprietors of the said second, third and fourth money subscriptions, who now have or (pursuant to the said resolutions of the said general court) may have stock allowed them at the said rate of four hundred per centum, with the dividend of Midsummer one thousand seven hundred and twenty, in stock as aforesaid; be it further enacted by the authority aforesaid, That the said corporation, called the South-Sea company, shall, and the same is hereby enjoined and required to allow and make an addition after the rate of thirty three pounds, six shillings and eight pence, in stock, upon every one hundred pounds stock already allowed or allowable, as aforesaid, to the respective proprietors of the said redeemable debts and annuities, and to the respective proprietors of the said second, third and fourth money subscriptions; which said addition of thirty three pounds six shillings and eight pence, in stock to the said proprietors of redeemable debts and annuities, together with the stock already allowed them at the rate of four hundred per centum, with the dividend at Midsummer one thousand seven hundred and twenty, in stock as aforesaid, shall be in full discharge and satisfaction of their respective debts and annuities which were redeemable, and were subscribed or intended to be subscribed, as aforesaid, and for which the securities were delivered up, or for which the books at the office of the bank were debited, and for which an additional stock was created by the commissioners of the treasury as aforesaid; and the said addition of thirty three pounds six shillings and eight pence, in stock, to the proprietors of the monies which were actually paid upon the said second, third and fourth money subscriptions respectively, together with the stock already allowed or allowable to them at the rate of four hundred per centum, with the dividend at Midsummer one thousand seven hundred and twenty, in stock as aforesaid, shall be in full discharge and satisfaction of the monies which were actually paid upon the second, third and fourth money subscriptions respectively, notwithstanding any defect or error, or supposed defect or error, in taking in the said subscriptions of the said redeemable debts and annuities, and the said money subscriptions, or any of them, or any misnomer, misspelling or omission of entry of money paid for the said money subscriptions in any wise, and notwithstanding any doubt or question touching or concerning the validity of the subscriptions of the said redeemable debts and annuities in any wise; and that no more money shall be demanded or insisted on by the said company (other than what was actually paid as aforesaid) on the said four money subscriptions, or any of them.

IV. And whereas on or about the twenty third day of June one thousand seven hundred and twenty, several irredeemable annuities (part of them payable for several long terms of years, others payable for the remainder of a term of thirty two years, commonly called the nine per cents, and others of them payable for the remainder of another term of thirty two years, commonly called the lottery-annuities of one thousand seven hundred and ten) were subscribed into the capital stock of the said company, for several rates or prices, which the same company did resolve to give the proprietors, to wit, for the said long terms at thirty two years purchase, and the said shorter terms seventeen years purchase; which rates or prices were satisfied partly with money, and partly with stock at the rate of three hundred seventy five pounds per centum: and whereas on or about the fifteenth day of October one thousand seven hundred and twenty, several other irredeemable annuities, part of them payable for several long terms of years, others payable for the remainder of the said several terms of thirty two years, were subscribed into the capital stock of the said company; which subscriptions so made on or about the said fifteenth day of October one thousand seven hundred and twenty, are commonly called the second subscriptions of the irredeemable annuities; and by a resolution of the said general court, the annuities of the said second subscription were likewise to be paid for at several rates or prices, viz. The long terms at thirty two years purchase, and the said shorter terms at seventeen years purchase, all in stock at four hundred per centum, with the addition of the Midsummer dividend of ten per centum in stock thereon (except such odd sums as did not amount to one pound in stock, which were to be paid in money;) now for a further relief to be given to the proprietors of the said irredeemable annuities in the second subscription, by an addition of stock valued at one hundred and fifty per centum, be it further enacted by the authority aforesaid, That the said company shall make, or cause to be made, an addition at that rate in stock to the proprietors last mentioned, over and above the stock allowed or allowable to them by the said resolution of the general court; which addition shall be made in the respective proportions herein after mentioned; that is to say, On every annuity of one hundred pounds per annum, which was subscribed for the remainder of ninety nine years comprehended in the said second subscription, two hundred and three pounds, six shillings and eight pence stock, and so in proportion for every greater or lesser annuity which was subscribed for the remainder of ninety nine years; on every annuity of ninety eight pounds per annum, which was subscribed for the remainder of ninety six or eighty nine years, commonly called fourteen per centums, comprehended in the said second subscription, one hundred seventy eight pounds, five shillings and four pence stock, and so in proportion for every greater or lesser sum of such annuities; on every ninety pounds per annum, which was subscribed for the remainder of thirty two years, commonly called the nine per centums, comprehended in the said second subscription, seventy three pounds nine shillings and four pence stock, and so in proportion for every greater or lesser sum of such annuities; on every annuity of one hundred pounds per annum, which was subscribed for the remainder of thirty two years, commonly called benefits of the lottery one thousand seven hundred and ten, comprehended in the said second subscription, sixty five pounds, sixteen shillings and eight pence stock, and so in proportion for every greater or lesser sum of such annuities; and on every ninety eight pounds per annum, subscribed for the remainder of thirty two years, commonly called blank pay-tickets of the said lottery, one thousand seven hundred and ten, comprehended in the said subscription, one hundred twenty six pounds fourteen shillings and eight pence stock, and so in proportion for any greater or lesser sum of such annuities; and that all dividends due, or to become due, from and after the feast of the nativity of our Lord Christ one thousand seven hundred and twenty, shall be payable upon the said several additions of stock as aforesaid.

V. And be it further enacted by the authority aforesaid, That all the increased capital stock which was gained by the said company, by taking in publick debts and incumbrances which were intended to be taken in by the said act of the sixth year of his Majesty's reign, and which, after the distribution of such parts thereof as are intended, pursuant to any the former clauses in this act, to be distributed, shall remain undisposed, shall be divided to and among all the proprietors of the whole capital stock of the said company, in proportion to their several and respective interests therein; and that credit be given for the same respectively in the books of the said company.

VI. And be it further enacted by the authority aforesaid, That such persons (brokers, or such persons as have acted as brokers for brokeridge, excepted) as at any time or times since the five and twentieth day of March in the year of our Lord one thousand seven hundred and twenty, have borrowed money from the said

South-Sea company upon any share or shares in the stock of the said company, actually transferred and pledged (at the time of borrowing, or within twenty one days after) to or for the use of the said company, or the respective heirs, executors or administrators of such persons, who shall pay to the cashier of the said company for the time being, to and for the use of the said company, at their publick office in London, so much money as a rate of ten per centum, to be computed upon the respective sums so borrowed, shall amount unto; to wit, one moiety thereof on or before the five and twentieth of December one thousand seven hundred and twenty one, and the other moiety thereof on or before the five and twentieth day of June one thousand seven hundred and twenty two; shall (upon such payment made, or being lawfully tendred and refused, and not otherwise) by force and virtue of this present act, be discharged of, from and against all further demands of the said company, in law or equity, of, for , or in respect of the monies so borrowed upon stock; and that all the stock so transferred and pledged, for which such payment shall be made, or lawfully tendred and refused, together with the dividends and profits belonging or to belong to such stock respectively, shall be, and is, and are, by virtue hereof, absolutely vested in the said company, for the use and benefit thereof. . . .

The New Horse-Houghing Husbandry by **Jethro Tull, 1731**

The New Horse-Houghing Husbandry; or, an Essay on the Principles of Tillage and Vegetation (London: privately printed, 1731), 133-48.

Agriculturist Jethro Tull (1674-1741), the inventor of the machine drill for sowing seed (around 1701), was a Berkshire farmer. In this famous tract he set out the advantages of a scientific or "improving" agriculture.

In order to make a Comparison between the Houghing Husbandry, and the Old Way, there are four Things; whereof the Differences ought to be very well considered.

    I. The Expence of a Crop.
    II. The Goodness of a Crop.
    III. The Certainty of a Crop.
    IV. The Condition in which the Land is left after a Crop.

The Profit or Loss arising from Land, is not to be computed, only, from the Value of the Crop it produces; but from its Value, after all Expences of Seed, Tillage, etc. are deducted.

Thus when an Acre brings a Crop worth four Pounds, and the Expences thereof amount to five Pounds, the Owner's Loss is one Pound; and when an Acre brings a Crop which yields thirty Shillings, and the Expence amount to no more than ten Shillings, the Owner receives one Pound clear Profit from this Acre's very small Crop, as the other loses one Pound by his greater Crop.

The usual Expences of an Acre of Wheat, sown in the Old Husbandry, in the Country where I live, is, in some Places, for two Bushels and a half of Seed; in other Places four Bushels and a half, the least of these Quantities at three Shillings per Bushel, being the present Price, is Seven Shillings and Six-pence. For three Ploughings, Harrowing, and Sowing, sixteen Shillings; but if ploughed four times, which is better, one Pound. For thirty Load of Dung, to a Statute Acre, is two Pounds five Shillings. For Carriage of the Dung, according to the Distance, from two Shillings to Six-pence the Load; one Shilling being the Price most common, is one Pound ten Shillings. The Price for Weeding is very uncertain; it has sometimes cost twelve Shillings, sometimes two Shillings per Acre.

	l.	s.	d.
In Seed and Tillage, nothing can be abated of	01	03	06
For the Weeding, one Year with another, is more than	00	02	00
For the Rent of the Year's Fallow	00	10	00
For the Dung; 'tis in some Places a little cheaper, neither do they always lay on quite so much; therefore abating 15 s. in that Article, we may well set Dung and Carriage at	02	10	00
Reaping commonly 5 s. sometimes	00	04	06
Loss	04	10	00

Folding of Land with Sheep is reckoned abundantly cheaper than Cart-Dung; but this is to be questioned, because much Land must lie still for keeping a Flock (unless there be Downs) and for their whole Year's Keeping, with both Grass and Hay, there are but three Months of the twelve wherein the Field is of any considerable Value, this makes the Price of their Manure quadruple to what it would be, if equally good all the Year, like Cart-Dung: And Folding Sheep yield little Profit, besides their Dung, because the Wool of a Flock, except it be a large one, will scarce pay the Shepherd and the Shearers. But there is another Thing yet, which more inhances the Price of Sheep Dung, and that is the dunging the Land with their Bodies, when they all die of the Rot, which happens too frequently in many Places; and then the whole Crop of Corn must go to purchase another Flock, which may have the same Fate the ensuing Year, if the Summer prove wet: And so may the Farmer be served for several more successive Years, unless he should break, and another take his Place, or that dry Summers come in Time to prevent it. To avoid this Misfortune he would be glad to purchase Cart-Dung at the highest Price, for supplying the Place of his Fold; but 'tis only near Cities and great Towns, that a sufficient Quantity can be procured.

But, supposing the Price of Dunging to be only two Pounds ten Shillings, and the general Expence of an Acre of Wheat, when sown, at three Shillings per Bushel, to be four Pounds ten Shillings, with the Year's Rent of the Fallow.

The Expences of planting an Acre of Wheat in the Houghing Husbandry, is three Pecks of Seed, at three Shillings per Bushel, is two Shillings and Three-pence.

The whole Tillage, if done by Horses, would be eight Shillings; because our two Ploughing and six Houghings, are equal to two Stirrings, the common Price whereof is four Shillings each; but this we diminish half, when done by Oxen kept on St. Foin, in this manner, viz. Land, worth thirty Shillings Rent, drilled with St. Foin, will well maintain an Ox an Year, and sometimes Hay will be left to pay for the Making; we cannot therefore allow more than one Shilling a Week for his Work, because his Keeping comes but to Seven-pence a Week round the Year.

In plain Ploughing, six Foot contains eight Furrows; but we plough a Six-Foot Ridge at four Furrows, because in this there are two Furrows covered in the Middle of it, and one on each Side of it lies open. Now, what we call one Houghing, is only two Furrows of this Ridge, which is equal to a fourth Part of one plain Ploughing; so that the Houghing of four Acres requires an equal Number of Furrows with one Acre, that is ploughed plain, and equal time to do it in (except that the Land that is kept in Houghing, works much easier than that which is not).

All the Tillage we ever bestow upon a Crop of Wheat that follows a houghed Crop, is equal to eight Houghings, two of which may require four Oxen each, one of them three Oxen, and the other five Houghings two Oxen each. However, allow three Oxen to each single Houghing, taking them all one with another, which is three Oxen more than it comes to in the whole.

Begin at five in the Morning; and in about six Hours you may hough three Acres, being equal in Furrows to three Rood, i.e. three Quarters of an Acre. Then turn the Oxen to Grass, and after resting, eating, and drinking two Hours and a half, with another Set of Oxen begin Houghing again; and by, or before half an Hour after Seven at Night, another like Quantity may be houghed. These are the Hours the Statute has appointed all Labourers to work, during the Summer Half-year.

To hough these six Acres a Day, each Set of Oxen draw the Plough only eight Miles and a Quarter, which they may very well do in five Hours; and then the Holder and Driver will be at their Work of Ploughing ten Hours, and will have four Hours and a half to rest, etc.

The Expence then of Houghing six Acres in a Day, in this manner, may be accounted; at one Shilling the Man that holds the Plough, Six-pence the boy that drives the Plough, one Shilling for the six Oxen, and Six-pence for keeping the Tackle in Repair. The whole Sum for Houghing these six Acres is three Shillings, being Six-pence per Acre.

They who follow the Old Husbandry cannot keep Oxen for cheap, because they can do nothing without the Fold, and Store-Sheep will spoil the St. Foin. They may almost as well keep Foxes and Geese together, as Store-Sheep and good St. Foin. Besides, the sowed St. Foin cost ten times as much the Planting as drilled St. Foin does, and must be frequently manured, or else it will soon decay; especially upon all Sorts of chalky Land, whereon 'tis most commonly sown.

The Expence of Drilling cannot be much, for as we can Hough six Acres a Day, at two Furrows on each Six-Foot Ridge, so may we drill twenty-four Acres a Day, with a Drill that plants two of those Ridges at once; and this we may reckon a Penny Half-penny an Acre.

I had five Acres of Wheat weeded this Year for Six-pence, being the second Crop: And the greatest Part of my drilled Wheat wants no Weeding at all; every successive Crop being still more free from Weeds than the preceding Crop; therefore I will set it all together at Six-pence an Acre for Weeding.

For a Boy to follow the Hough-Plough, to uncover the young Wheat, when any Clods or Earth happen to fall on it, for which Trouble there is seldom occasion above once to a Crop, Two-pence an Acre. One Penny is too much for Brine and Lime for an Acre.

Reaping this Wheat is not worth above half as much as the Reaping of a sown Crop of equal Value; because the Drilled standing upon about a sixth Part of the Ground, a Reaper may cut almost as much of the Row at one Stroke, as he could at six, if the same stood dispersed all over the Ground, as the Sowed does. And because he who reaps sowed Wheat, must reap the Weeds along with the Wheat; but the Drilled has no Weeds; and besides, there goes a greater Quantity of Straw, and more Sheaves, to a Bushel of the sowed, than of the drilled. And since some hundred Acres of drilled Wheat has been reaped at two Shillings and Six-pence per Acre, I will count that to be the Price.

The whole Expence of an Acre of Drilled Wheat

	l.	s.	d.
For Seed	00	02	03
For Tillage	00	04	00
For Drilling	00	00	06
For Weeding	00	00	06
For Uncovering	00	00	02
For Brine and Lime	00	00	01
For Reaping	00	02	06
Total	00	10	00
The Expence of an Acre of Sowed Wheat is	04	00	00
To which must be added, for the Year's Rent of the Fallow	00	10	00
Total	04	10	00

If I have reckoned the Expence of the Drilled at the lowest Price, to bring it to an even Sum, I have also abated in the other more than the whole Expence of the Drilled amounts unto.

And thus the Expence of a drilled Crop of Wheat is but the ninth Part of the Expence of a Crop sown in the common Manner.

'Tis also some Advantage, that less Stock is required where no Store-Sheep are used.

II. Of the different Goodness of a Crop

The Goodness of a Crop consists in the Quality of it, as well as the Quantity; and Wheat being the most useful Grain, a Crop of this is better than a Crop of any other Corn, and the houghed Wheat has larger Ears (and a fuller Body) than sowed Wheat. We can have more of it, because the same Land will produce it every Year, and even Land which, by the Old Husbandry, would not be made to bear Wheat at all: So that in many Places, the New Husbandry can raise Ten Acres of Wheat for One that the Old can do; because where Land is poor, they sow but a Tenth Part of it with Wheat.

We do not pretend, that we have always greater Crops, or so great as some sown Crops are, especially if those mentioned by Mr. Houghton, be not mistaken.

The greatest Produce I ever had from a single Yard in Length of a double Row, was Eighteen Ounces; the Partitions of this being Six Inches, and the Interval Thirty Inches, was, by Computation, Ten Quarters (or Forty Bushels) to an Acre.

I had also Twenty Ounces to a like Yard of a Third successive Crop of Wheat; but this being a treble Row, and the Partitions and Interval being wider, and supposed to be in all Six Foot (though not quite so much) was computed to Six Quarters to an Acre. And if these Rows had been better ordered than they were, and the Earth more pulverized, more Stalks would have Tillered out, and more Ears would have attained their full Size, and have equaled the best, which must have made a much greater Crop than either of these were.

But to compare the different Profit, we may proceed thus: The Rent and Expence of a drilled Acre being one Pound, and of a sowed Acre five Pounds; One Quarter of Corn produced by the Drilled, bears an equal Proportion in Profit to the one Pound, as Five Quarters produced by the other do to the five Pounds. As suppose it be of Wheat, at two Shillings and Six-pence a Bushel, there is neither Gain nor Loss in the one nor the other Acre, though the former yield but One Quarter, and the other, Five; but if the drilled Acre yield Two Quarters, and the sowed Acre Four Quarters at the same Price, the drilled brings the Farmer one Pound clear Profit, and the sown, by its Four Quarters, brings the other one Pound Loss. Likewise, Suppose the Drilling Farmer to have his five Pounds laid out on Five Acres of Wheat, and the other to have his five Pounds laid out on One dunged Acre, then let the Wheat they produce be at what Price it will, if the Five Acres have an equal Crop to the One Acre, then the Gain or Loss must be equal. But when Wheat is Cheap, as we say it is, when Sold at Two and Six-pence a Bushel, then if the Virgilian has Five Quarters on his acre, he must sell it all to pay his Rent and Expence; but the other having Five Quarters on each of his Five Acres, the Crop of One of them will pay the Rent and Expence of all his Five Acres, and he may keep the remaining Twenty Quarters, till he can sell tham at five Shillings a Bushel, which amounts to forty Pounds, wherewith he may be able to buy four of his five Acres at twenty Years Purchase, out of one Year's Crop, whilst the Virgilian Farmer must be content to have only his Labour for his Travel; or if he pretends to keep his Wheat till he sells it at five Shillings a Bushel, he commonly runs in Debt to his Neighbours, and in Arrear of his Rent; and if the Markets do not rise in time, or if his Crops fail in the Interim, his Landlord seizes on his Stock, and then he knows not how it may be sold, Actions are brought against him, the Bailiffs and Attornies pull him to Pieces; and then our Virgilian Farmer is broke.

III. The Certainty of a Crop

The Certainty of a Crop is much to be regarded, it being better to be secure of a moderate Crop, than to have but a mere Hazard of a great one. The Virgilian is often deceived in his Expectation, when his Crop at coming into Ear, is very big, as well as when 'tis in Danger of being too little. Our Houghing Farmer is much less liable to the Hazard of either of those Extreams; for when his Wheat is big, 'tis not apt to lodge or fall down, which Accident is usually the utter Ruin of the other, he is free from the Causes which make the Virgilian Crop too little.

A very effectual Means to prevent the failing of a Crop of Wheat, is to plough the pulverized Earth for Seed early, and when 'tis dry. The early Season also is more likely to be dry than the latter Season is. The Virgilian is commonly late in his Sowing; because he can't Fallow his Ground early, for fear of killing the Couch, and other Grass that maintains his folding Sheep, which are so necessary to his Husbandry; And when 'tis sowed late, it must not be sowed dry, for then the Winter might kill the young Wheat. Neither can he at that time plough dry, and sow wet, because he commonly sows under Furrow; that is, sows the Seed first, and ploughs it in as fast as 'tis sown. If he sows early (as he may if he will) in light Land, he must now sow dry, for fear the Poppies and other Weeds should grow and devour his Crop; and if his Land be strong, let it be sown early, wet or dry (tho' wet is worst) 'tis apt to grow so stale and hard by the Spring, that his Crop is in danger of Starving, unless the Land be very rich, or much dunged, and then the Winter and Spring proving kind, it may not be in less danger of being so big as to fall down and be spoiled. Another thing is, that though he had no other Impediment against ploughing dry, and sowing wet, 'tis seldom that he has time to do it in; for he must plough all his Ground, which is eight Furrows in six Foot, and whilst it is wet, must lie still with his Plough. When he sows under Furrow, he fears to plough deep, lest he bury too much of his Seed, and if he ploughs shallow, his Crop loses the Benefit of deep Ploughing, which is very great. When he sows upon Furrow (that is after 'tis ploughed) he must harrow the Ground level to cover the Seed, and that exposes the Wheat the more to the cold Winds, and suffers the Snow to be blown off it, and the Water to lie longer on it; all which are great Injuries to it.

Our Houghing Husbandry is different in all of the forementioned Particulars.

1. We can plough the two Furrows whereon the next Crop is to stand, either before the present Crop is reaped, or immediately after 'tis off.

2. We have no use of the Fold; because our Ground has annually a Crop growing on it, and it must lie still a Year, if we would fold it, and that Crop would be lost; and all the Good the Fold could do to the Land, would be only to help to pulverize it for one single Crop; its Benefit not lasting to the second Year. And so we should be certain of losing one Crop for the very uncertain Hopes of procuring one the ensuing Year by the Fold; when 'tis manifest by the adjoining Crops, that we can have a much better Crop every Year, without a Fold or any other Manure.

3. We can plough dry, and drill wet, without any manner of Inconvenience.

4. He fears the Weeds will grow and destroy his Crop: We hope they will grow, to the end we may destroy them.

5. We do not fear to plant our Wheat early (so that we plough dry) because we can help the Hardness or Staleness of the Land by Houghing.

6. The two Furrows of every Ridge whereon the Rows are to be drilled, we plough dry; and if the Weather prove wet before these are all finished, we can plough the other two Furrows up to them, until it be dry enough to

return to our Ploughing the first two Furrows, and after finishing them, let the Weather be wet or dry, we can plough the last two Furrows. We can plough our two Furrows in the fourth part of the Time they can plough their eight, which they must plough dry all of them, in every six Foot; for they can't plough dry, when 'tis wet, as we can.

7. We never plant our Seed under Furrow, but place it just at the Depth, which we judge most proper, and that is pretty shallow, about two Inches deep, and then there is no danger of burying it.

8. We not only plough a deep Furrow, but also plough to the Depth of two Furrows; that is, we Trench-plough where the Land will allow it; and we have the greatest Convenience imaginable for doing this, because there are two of our four Furrows always lying open; and two ploughed Furrows (that is one ploughed under another) are as much more advantageous for the nourishing a Crop, as two Bushels of Oats are better than one for nourishing a Horse. Or if the Staple of the Land be too thin or shallow, we can help it by raising the Ridges prepared for the Rows the higher above the Level.

9. We also raise a high Ridge in the Middle of each Interval above the Wheat before Winter, to protect it from the cold Winds, and to prevent the Snow from being driven away by them. And the Furrows or Trenches, from whence the Earth of these Ridges is taken, serve to drain off the Water from the Wheat, so that it being dryer, it must be warmer than the harrowed Wheat, which has neither Furrows to keep it dry, nor Ridges to shelter it, as every Row of ours has on both Sides of it.

IV. The Condition in which the Land
is left after a Crop

The different Condition the Land is left in after a Crop, by the one and the other Husbandry, is not less considerable than the different Profit of the Crop.

A piece of eleven Acres of a poor thin chalky Hill, was sown with Barley in the common Manner, after a houghed Crop of Wheat, and produced full five Quarters and a half to each Acre (reckoning the Tythe) which was much more than any Land in all the Neighbourhood yielded the same Year; tho' some of it be so rich, as that one Acre is worth three Acres of this Land: And no Man living can remember that ever this produced above half such a Crop before, even when the best of the common Management has been bestowed upon it.

A Field that is a sort of a Heath Ground, used to bring such poor Crops of Corn, that heretofore the Parson carryed away a whole Crop of Oats from it, believing it had been only his Tythe. The last Management that ever they did or could bestow upon it, was to let it rest two or three Years, and then fallow and dung it, and sow it with Wheat, next to that with Barley and Clover, and then let it rest again; but I cannot hear of any Crop that ever it produced by this or any other of their Methods; 'twas still reckoned so poor, that nobody cared to rent it. They said Dung and Labour were thrown away upon it; then immediately after two Crops of black Oats had been taken off it, the last of which was scarce worth the Mowing, the Clover always looked yellow, and so does the Grass that grows all round the Field.

Three houghed Crops were taken from it, and then being sown with Barley, it brought a very good Crop, much better than ever it was known to yield before; and then a good Crop of houghed Wheat succeeded the Barley, being drilled upon one plain Ploughing, immediately after the Barley was taken off; and then it was again sown with Barley, and upon the Wheat Stubble; and that also was better than the Barley used to be after a dunged Crop of Wheat.

Now, all the Farmers of the Neighbourhood affirm, that it is impossible but that this must be very rich Ground, because they have seen it produce six Crops in six Years, without Dung or Fallows, and never a one of them fail. But, alas! this different Reputation they give to the Land, does not at all belong to it, but to the different Sorts of Husbandry; for the Nature of it cannot be altered but by that, the Crops being all carried off it, and nothing added to supply the Substance those Crops taken from it, except (what Mr. Evelyn calls) the Celestial Influences, and that these are received by the Earth, in Proportion to the Degrees of its Pulveration.

A field was Drilled with Barley after a houghed Crop, and another adjoining to it on the same Side of the same poor Hill, and exactly the same Sort of Land, was drilled with Barley also, Part of it after the sown Crop, the same Day with the other; there was only this Difference in the Soil, that the former of these had no manner of Compost on it for many Years before, and the latter was dunged the Year before, yet its Crop is not near so good as that which followed the houghed Crop; though the latter had twice the Ploughing that the former had before Drilling, and the same Houghings afterwards, viz. Each was houghed three times.

A field of about seventeen Acres was Summer fallowed, and drilled with Wheat, and with the Houghing, brought a very good Crop (except Part of it, which being eaten by trespassing Sheep in the Winter, was somewhat blighted); the Michaelmas after that was taken off, the same Field was drilled again with Wheat, upon the Stubble of the former, and houghed but twice in all: This second Crop was a good one, scarce any in the Neighbourhood better. A Piece of Wheat adjoining to it, on the very same Sort of Land (except that this latter was always reckoned better, being thicker in Mould above the Chalk) sown at the same time on dunged Fallows, and the Ground always dunged once in three Years, yet this Crop failed so much, as to be judged, by some Farmers, not to exceed the Tythe of the other: That the houghed Field has received no Dung or Manure for many Years past, it lying out of Reach for carrying of Cart-Dung, and no Fold being kept on my Farm: But I cannot say, I think, there was quite so much Odds betwixt this second undunged houghed Crop and the sown; yet this is certain, that the former is a good, and the latter a very bad Crop.

I could give many more Instances of the same Kind, where houghed Crops and sown Crops have succeeded better after houghed Crops than after sown Crops, and never yet have seen the contrary; and therefore am convinced, that the Houghing (if it be duly performed, enriches the Soil more than Dung and Fallows, and leaves the Land in a much better Condition for a succeeding Crop; the Reason I take to be very obvious. The artificial Pasture of Plants is made and increased by Pulveration only; and nothing else there is in our Power to enrich our Ground, but to pulverize it, and keep it from being exhausted by Vegetables. (Superinductions of Earth are an Addition of more Ground, or changing it, and is more properly Purchasing than Cultivating.)

This one Year's Tillage, which is but two Ploughings before Seed-time, commonly makes but little Dust, and that which it does make, has but a short time to lie exposed for Impregnation; and after the Wheat is sown, the Land lies unmoved for near twelve Months, all the while gradually losing its Pasture, by subsiding, and by being continually exhausted in feeding a treble Stock of Wheat Plants, and a Stock of Weeds, which are sometimes a greater Stock. This put the Virgilians upon a Necessity of using of Dung, which is, at least, but a poor Succedaneum of the Hough; for it depends chiefly on the Weather, and other Accidents, whether it may prove sufficient by Fermentation to pulverize in the Spring, or no: And, 'tis a Question whether it will equal two additional Houghings, or but one; though, as I have computed it, one Dunging costs the Price of one hundred Houghings.

'Tis possible, perhaps, to pulverize the Ground with a Pen, and they seem to act almost as oddly, when, at such a vast Expence, instead of a Hough, they make Use of a T——, to help them in their Pulveration.

When they have done all they can, the Pasture, they raise, is generally too little for the Stock that is to be maintained upon it, and much the greatest Part of the Wheat Plants are starved; for from twenty Gallons of Seed they sow on an Acre, they receive commonly no more than twenty Bushels of Wheat in their Crop, which is but an Increase of eight Grains for one: Now, considering how many Grains there are in one good Ear, and how many Ears on one Plant, we find, that there is not one Plant in ten that lives till Harvest, even when there has not been Frost in the Winter sufficient to kill any of them; or if we count the Number of Plants that come up on a certain Measure of Ground, and count them again in the Spring, and likewise at Harvest, we shall be satisfied, that most, or all of the Plants that are missing, could die by no other Accident than want of Nourishment.

They are obliged to sow this great Quantity of Seed, to the End that the Wheat, by the great Number of Plants, may be the better able to contend with the Weeds; and yet, too often at Harvest, we see a great Crop of Weeds, and very little Wheat among them. Therefore, this Pasture being insufficient to maintain the present Crop, without starving the greatest Part of its Plants, is likely to be less able to maintain a subsequent Crop, than that Pasture which is not so much exhausted.

When their Crop of Wheat is much less than ours, their Vacancies (if computed all together) may be greater than those of our Partitions and Intervals; theirs, by being irregular, serve chiefly for the Protection of Weeds; for they cannot be ploughed out, without destroying the Corn, any more than Cannons Firing at a Breach, whereon both Sides are contending, can kill Enemies, and not Friends.

Their Plants stand on the Ground in a confused Manner, like a Rabble; ours like a disciplined Army; we make the most of our Ground; for we can, if we please, cleanse the Partitions with a Hand-Hough; and for the rest, if the Soil be deep enough to be drilled on the Level, in treble Rows, the Partitions at six Inches, the Intervals five Foot; five Parts in six of the whole Field may be pulverized every Year, and at proper times all round the Year.

The Partitions being one sixth Part for the Crop to stand on, and to be nourished by the Winter, one other sixth Part being well pulverized, may be sufficient to nourish it from thence till Harvest; the Remainder, being two Thirds of the whole, may be kept unexhausted, the one Third for one Year, and the other Third of it two Years, all kept open for the Reception of the Benefits descending from above, during so long a time; whilst the sowed Land is shut against them, every Summer, except the little time in which it is fallowed, once in three Years, and a little, perhaps, whilst they plough it for the Barley in the Winter, which is a Season seldom proper for pulverizing the Ground.

Their Land must have been exhausted as well by those supernumerary Plants of Wheat, while they lived, as by those that remain for the Crop, and by the Weeds. Our Land must be much less exhausted, when it has never above one third Part of the Wheat-Plants to nourish that they have, and generally no Weeds; so that our houghed Land having much more Vegetable Pasture made, and continually renewed, to so much a less Stock of Plants, must needs be left, by every Crop, in a much better Condition than theirs is left in by any one of their sown Crops, although our Crops of Corn at Harvest be better than theirs.

They object against us, saying, That sometimes the Houghing makes Wheat too strong and gross, whereby it becomes the more liable to the Blacks (or Blight of Insects), but this is the Fault of the Hougher, for he may chuse whether he will make it too strong, because he may apply his Houghings at proper times only, and apportion the Nourishment to the Number and Bulk of his Plants. However, by this Objection they allow, that the Hough can give Nourishment enough, and therefore they cannot maintain that there is a Necessity of Dung in the Houghing Husbandry; and that, if our Crops of Wheat should happen to suffer by being too strong, our Loss will be less than theirs, when that is too strong, since it will cost them nine times our Expence to make it so.

A second Objection is, that as Houghing makes poor Land become rich enough to bear good Crops of Wheat for several Years successively, the same must needs make very good Land become too rich for Wheat. I answer, That if possibly it should so happen, there are two Remedies to be used in such a Case; the one is to plant it with Beans, or some other Vegetables, which cannot be over-nourished, as Turnips, Carrots, Cabbages, and such like, which are excellent Food for fatting of Cattle; or else they may make Use of the other infallible Remedy, when that rich Land, by producing Crops every Year in the Houghing-Husbandry, is grown too vigorous and resty, they may soon take down its Mettle, by Sowing it a few Years in their Old Husbandry, which will fill it again with a new Stock of Weeds, that will suck it out of Heart, and exhaust more of its Vigour, then the Dung, that helps to produce them, can restore.

There is a third Objection, and that is, that the Benefit of some Ground is lost where the Hough-Plough turns at each End of the Lands; but this cannot be much, if any, Damage; because, about two square Perch to a Statute Acre, is sufficient for this Purpose, and that, at the Rate of ten Shillings Rent, comes to but Three-pence, though this varies, according as the Piece is longer or shorter; and supposing the most to be eight Perch, that is but Six-pence per Acre; and that is not lost neither, for whether it be of natural or artificial Grass, the Hough-Plough in turning on it, will scratch it, and leave some Earth on it, which will enrich it so much, that it may be worth its Rent to Baiting of Horses or Oxen upon it. And besides, these Ends are commonly near Quick-Hedges or Trees, which do so exhaust it, that when no Cattle come there to manure it, 'tis not worth the Labour of Ploughing it.

WALPOLE'S EXCISE SCHEME

Walpole sought to extend the excise duty to tobacco and wine, and ultimately to eliminate the land tax. Opposition to his proposals was intense, and they were subsequently withdrawn from the Commons.

Speech by Sir Robert Walpole, first lord of the treasury and chancellor of the exchequer, House of Commons, 12 March 1733

Parliamentary History, VIII, 1268-81.

As I had the honour to move that the House should resolve itself into this Committee, I think it incumbent on me to open to you, what was then intended to be proposed as the subject of your consideration. This Committee is appointed for the better security of the duties and revenues already charged and payable upon tobacco. This can be done in no way so proper and effectual, as by preventing the commission of those frauds by which the revenue has already sustained such great injuries. As the proposed improvement is to be made by an alteration in the method of collecting and managing the duties already imposed, without any addition, or subjecting to the same duties any articles not already chargeable, I might have avoided stating this project to a Committee of the whole House; but I have deserted the old road, and proposed a supply not immediately necessary for the current service of the year, that I might leave a greater freedom of consideration, by taking away every appearance of pressing necessity. I shall therefore only observe, that some previous provision must be made for the future application of the increased sum which, should the plan I am about to propose to be adopted, will be received into the exchequer.

The contest, in the present instance, is between the unfair trader, on one side; the fair trader, the planter, and the public, on the other; but to the public must be referred my most forcible appeal, as they, in truth, bear the whole weight of the injury: for though the fraudulent factor seems to make the planter, retailer, and consumer equally his prey, yet the landed interest ultimately suffers the whole effect of the fraud, by making good what the subject pays, and the government does not receive.

In such a cause, I might reasonably expect the approbation of the fair trader, and the assistance of parliament; for assuredly, if in these times any cause can possibly be considered exempt from the operations of party, it is the cause now before the Committee. But, Sir, I am not to learn, that whoever attempts to remedy frauds, attempts a thing very disagreeable to all those who have been guilty of them, or who expect to derive future benefits from them. I know that these men, who are considerable in their numbers, and clamorous in their exertions, have found abettors in another quarter, in persons much worse than themselves; in men who are fond of improving every opportunity of stirring up the people to mutiny and sedition. But as the scheme I have to propose, will not only be a great improvement to the revenue, an improvement of two or three hundred thousand pounds by the year, but also great benefit to the fair trader, I shall not be deterred, either by calumny or clamour, from doing my duty as a member of this House, and bringing forward a measure, which my own conscience justifies me in saying, will be attended with the most important advantages to the revenues and commerce of my country.

> Justum et tenacem propositi virum,
> Non civium ardor prava jubentium,
> Mente quatit solida.

Amongst the many slanders to which the report of this project has exposed me, I cannot avoid mentioning one, which has been circulated with an assiduity proportioned to its want of truth, that I was about to propose *a general excise*. In all plans for the benefit of government, two essential points must be considered, justice and practicability: many things are just which would not be practicable; but such a scheme would be neither one or the other. Various are the faults of ministers, various their fates: few have had the crimes of all; none till now found that the imputation of crime to him, became a merit in others. Yet if I were to propose to you such a scheme, popular opinion would run exactly in that channel. It would be a crime in me to propose, a crime in you to accept; and the only chance left to the House of retaining the favour of the people, would be the unqualified rejection of the project. But *I do most unequivocally assert, that no such scheme ever entered my head, or, for what I know, into the head of any man I am acquainted with.* Yet though I do not wish to do wrong, I shall always retain a proper share of courage and self-confidence to do what I judge right, and in the measures I am about to propose, shall rest my claim to support and approbation on the candid, the judicious, and the truly patriotic.

My thoughts have been confined solely to the revenue arising from the duties on wine and tobacco: and it was the frequent advices I had of the shameful frauds committed in these two branches, and the complaints of the merchants themselves, that induced me to turn my attention to discover a remedy for this growing evil. I am persuaded, that what I am about to propose, will, if granted, be an effectual remedy. But if gentlemen will be prevailed on by industry, artifice and clamour, to indulge the suggestions of party prejudice, they and their posterity must pay dear for it, by the grievous entail of a heavy land tax, which they will have sanctioned by their pusillanimity, in not daring to brave the outrages of the fraudulent and self-interested. For myself, I shall only say, I have so little partiality for this scheme, except what a real and constitutional love of the public inspires, that if I fail in this proposal, it will be the last attempt of the kind I shall ever make, and I believe, a minister will not soon be found hardy enough to brave, on the behalf of the people, and without the slightest motive of interest, the worst effects of popular delusion and popular injustice.

I shall for the present, confine myself entirely to the tobacco trade, and to the frauds practised in that branch of the revenue. If there is one subject of taxation more obvious than another, more immediately within the direct aim of fiscal imposition than another, it is such an article of luxury as depends for its use on custom or caprice, and is by no means essential to the support of real comfort of human life. If there is a subject of taxation where it is more immediately the province of the legislature to suppress fraud, and strictly to insist on the payment of every impost, it must be that where the wrong is felt by every class of persons, and none are benefited, except the most dishonest and profligate part of the community. Both these descriptions apply to the subject before us. For though the use of tobacco is perhaps less sanctioned by natural reason than any other luxury, yet so great is the predilection for it, in its various forms, that from the palace to the hovel there is no exemption from the duty; and surely it must be considered an intolerable grievance, that by the frauds which are daily committed, the very poorest of the peasantry are obliged to pay this duty twice: once in the enhanced price of the article; for though the fraudulent trader contrives to save to himself the amount of the tax imposed by parliament, yet he does not sell it cheaper to the public; and a second time, in the tax that is necessarily substituted to make good the deficiency which has been by these means occasioned. Did it ever happen till now, that when an abuse of this kind was to be remedied, endeavours were used to make the attempt unpopular?

In discussing this subject, it will be necessary first to advert to the condition of our planters of tobacco in America. If they are to be believed, they are reduced to the utmost extremity, even almost to a state of despair, by the many frauds that have been committed in that trade, and by the ill usage they have sustained from their factors and correspondents in England, who from being their servants, are become their tyrants. These unfortunate people have sent home many representations of the bad state of their affairs; they have lately deputed a gentleman with a remonstrance, setting forth their grievances, and praying for some speedy relief: this they may obtain by means of the scheme I intend now to propose; but I believe it is from that alone they can expect any relief.

The next thing to be considered is, the state of the tobacco trade with respect to the fair trader. The man who deals honourably with the public, as well as individuals, the man who honestly pays all his duties, finds himself forestalled in almost every market within the island, by the smuggler and fraudulent dealer. As to our foreign trade in tobacco, those who have no regard to honour, to religion, or to the welfare of the country, but are every day contriving ways and means for cheating the public by perjuries and false entries, are the greatest gainers; and it will always be so, unless we can contrive some method of putting it out of their power to carry on such frauds for the future.

We ought to consider the great loss sustained by the public, by means of the frauds committed in the tobacco trade, and the addition that must certainly be made to the revenue, if those frauds can be prevented in future. By this addition, parliament will acquire the means of exercising one of its most enviable privileges, that of diminishing the burthens of the country, the power of doing which will thus be presented to them in various forms. If it should be the prevailing opinion, that the discharge of the national debt should be accelerated, this increase offers an abundant resource. If the idea should prevail, that those taxes ought to be alleviated which fall heaviest on our manufacturers and the labouring poor, as soap and candles, this increase will replace the difference. Or if it should be judged that more immediate attention ought to be paid to the current service, the fund may be reserved for that use: and it is manifestly unjust and impolitic, that the national debt should be continued, and the payment postponed; or that the heavy duties on our manufactures should remain, which are justly paid, and without fraud; or that ways and means for the current service should be annually imposed, if the present revenues will answer all or any of these purposes. This, I am convinced, will be the effect of the scheme I am to propose, and whoever views it in its proper light, must see the planters, the fair traders, and the public, ranged on one side in support of it; and none but the unfair traders and tobacco factors on the other.

I am aware that the evidence to be adduced in proof of the existence of the frauds I am about to enumerate, is not such as would be sufficient to induce a court of justice to pronounce the guilt of those to whom they may be imputed. But as I do not undertake the task of inculpation, if I make out such a case to the Committee, as will enable them to decide on the existence of the crime, they will not hesitate to apply the remedy. They will consider the deficiency of strict legal proof, as a motive for their interference, rather than their forbearance; more particularly when they reflect, that if persons are with difficulty induced to give testimony in such a case as this, where the good of the country only is to be pursued, without injury to any one, they will be still less easily brought forward to give such information as will tend to the ruin of others. In this case it is hardly too much to say, that gentlemen should learn from the example of those interested, how to conduct themselves: they have, with an alacrity and unblushing eagerness which proves, which confesses their guilt, hastily inferred the most violent intentions in the friends of government; they have assumed facts, and inferred intentions, without the smallest data on which to found their presumptions. I ask no more than this: if I succeed in making it appear that gross frauds are daily practised, and the revenue injured in a most daring and profligate manner; that the proposed remedy, should it appear adequate and applicable, may be resorted to, without subjecting me to the necessity of procuring that which is, in fact, unattainable, such precise proof as would satisfy the administrators of the laws in the disposal of property, or deciding on guilt. Such evidence, and such facts as I have been able to collect, it is my duty to lay before you; and it is your duty to support me, unless my plan appears totally void of reason and justice.

The minister then proceeded to give such preliminary statements and calculations, as were necessary to render his plans intelligible, to make the abuses obvious, and to demonstrate the propriety and necessity of reform. From these statements it appeared, that the existing duties on tobacco amounted to sixpence and one-third of a penny on every pound. The discounts, allowances, and drawbacks, were a total drawback on re-exportation; ten per cent. on prompt payment; and fifteen per cent. on bonded duties. The gross produce of the tax, at a medium, 754,131*l*. 4*s*. 7*d*. the net produce only 161,000*l*.

Having made these statements with the utmost exactness and perspicuity, he proceeded:

I shall now point out as clearly as I can, and as amply as my knowledge will enable me, the principal frauds and most glaring instances of dishonesty, which occasion this amazing disproportion. And first I shall mention one, which seems alone capable of diverting from its proper channel the amount of any tax. I mean that of using light weights inwards, and heavy weights outwards, of paying by the first, and taking the drawback by the last, and charging the planter, and taking commission by the whole. This evil is farther enhanced by negligence; for it is customary to weigh a few hogsheads only, and if they answer, the whole pass according to the numbers in the cocket.

A particular instance of this fraud came lately to our knowledge by mere accident; one Mitford, who had been a considerable tobacco merchant in the city, happened to fail, at a time when he owed a large sum of money on bond to the crown. An extent was immediately issued against him, and government obtained possession of all his books, by which the fraud was discovered. For it appeared, as may be seen by one of his books, which I have in my hand, that upon the column where the false quantities which had been entered at the importation were marked, he had, by a collusion with the officer, got a slip of paper so artfully pasted down, that it could not be discovered, and upon this slip of paper were written the real quantities which were entered, because he was obliged to produce the same book when that tobacco was entered for exportation. But upon exportation, the tobacco was entered and weighed according to the quantities marked on this slip of paper, by which he secured a drawback, or his bonds returned, to near double the value of what he had actually paid duty for upon importation. Yet this Mitford was as honest a man, and as fair a trader, as any in the city of London. I desire not to be misunderstood; I mean, that before he failed, before these frauds came to be discovered, he was always reckoned as honest a man, and as fair a trader, as any in the city of London, or in any other part of the nation.

After enumerating several other instances where government had been defrauded of a full third of the duties imposed, and legally payable, he came to Peele's case, which is singular from its enormity. "In September 1732, this Peele entered in the James and Mary, from Maryland, 310 hogsheads of tobacco, for which he paid the duty in ready money. In October following, he sold 200 hogsheads to one Mr. Hyam, for exportation, and they were immediately exported. It appears on these 200 hogsheads, that the duties paid at importation, according to the weights in the land-waiters books, were short of the real weights by 13,292 pounds. The certificates sworn to for Mr. Peele to obtain debentures, were to discharge bonds given on a former entry of Virginia tobacco, imported in November 1731. The indorsement on the cocket made by Mr. Peele, in order to receive the debentures, exceeded the real weights actually shipped by 8,288 pounds, so that the total of the pounds weight gained by this fraud, amounts to 21,580.

The next fraud to which I shall direct your attention, is that of receiving the drawback on tobacco for exportation, and relanding it. The effects of this practice are too obvious to require elucidation, and it has been carried to such an extent, that a great number of ships were employed at Guernsey, Jersey, and the Isle of Man, in receiving and relanding such tobacco. Nor was the evil confined to these ports; a very intelligent gentleman, Mr. Howel, who resided many years in Flanders, has frequently observed several quantities of tobacco imported into Ostend and Dunkirk, and there repacked in bales of one hundred pounds each, and put on board vessels which waited there to reland it in England or Ireland. About twelve months ago, nine British vessels were employed in taking cargoes for this purpose at Dunkirk.

The third fraud to which I shall direct the attention of the committee, is that of receiving the whole drawback for a commodity of almost no value, namely, the stalks of the tobacco, which it is usual, after the leaf has been stripped off, to press flat and cut, and by mixing this offal with sand and dust, impose on the revenue officers, and obtain the same drawback as for an equal weight of the entire plant. This miserable stuff, when the fraudulent purpose has once been answered, is either thrown into the sea, or relanded and sold at three farthings a pound, with an allowance of 1,010 pounds of weight in five hogsheads.

The fourth fraud I shall advert to, is one of very great consequence, known by the name of *socking*, which is a cant term for pilfering and stealing tobacco from ships in the river. This iniquitous practice, which was discovered in 1728 and 1729, was chiefly carried on by watermen, lightermen, tide-waiters, and city porters, called gangs-men: the commodity so pilfered was deposited in houses from London Bridge to Woolwich, and afterwards sold, frequently to eminent merchants. Five hundred examinations have been taken on the subject, from which it appears, that, in the space of one year, fifty tons were socked on board ships and on the quays. Sixteen tons were seized, but that quantity was reckoned an inconsiderable part of the whole. In consequence of these informations, 150 officers were dismissed, nine were convicted, of whom six are ordered for transportation, three to be whipt: these prosecutions were all carried on at the expence of government; and it is not a little remarkable, when we recollect the professions of patriotism, virtue, and disinterestedness, which are now so copiously poured forth, that not a single merchant, though the facts were so notorious and shameful, assisted the state, either by information or pecuniary exertion, to suppress the fraud, or bring the delinquents to punishment.

The last grievance I shall mention, cannot so properly be denominated a fraud, as an abuse arising from the nature of the duties paid, and the manner of paying them; I mean the advantage afforded to the merchant of trading with the public money, or making government pay more than they receive. Bonds are given for eighteen months, three years are allowed for the exportation of the article, and new importations discharge old bonds. The losses which result to government from the failure of the obligors in these bonds, is immense; besides the ungracious task to which it subjects them of suing the sureties, who had no interest in the contract. The rich trader has another advantage; he avoids giving bonds, by paying the amount of his duties in ready money, for which he is allowed a discount of ten per cent. Now it is very common, and not out of the line of fair trade, for a merchant to pay this duty, receive the discount, and by immediately entering the same commodity for exportation, gain an advantage (I will not say defraud the revenue) of ten per cent. without loss, risque, or expenditure.

The frauds which I have here enumerated are, I apprehend, sufficiently proved to satisfy the Committee of their existence, and their enormity is obvious enough to demand active interference. The only remedy I can devise, is that of altering the manner of collecting the duties. Frauds become practicable by having but one check at importation, and one at exportation; if there is but one sentinel at a garrison, and he sleeps, or is corrupted, the castle is taken; but if there are more than one, it is in vain to corrupt the first, without extending the same influence to those who remain; and when difficulties are so multiplied, the project becomes hazardous and uncertain, and is abandoned.

If the grievance then is admitted, it only remains to mention the remedy, and to consider whether it is effectual, or whether it is worse than the disease.

The laws of the customs are manifestly insufficient to prevent the frauds which already exist; I therefore propose to add the laws of excise: and by means of both, it is probable, I may say certain, that all such frauds will be prevented in future.

I have already stated to the committee, that the several imposts on tobacco amount to sixpence and one third of a penny per pound, all of which must be paid down in ready money upon importation, with the allowance of ten per cent. upon prompt payment; or there must be bonds given, with sufficient sureties, for payment, which is often a great loss to the public, and always a great inconvenience to the merchant importer. Whereas, by what I shall propose, the whole duty will amount to no more than fourpence three farthings per pound, and will not be paid till the tobacco is sold for home consumption; so that if the merchant exports his tobacco, he will be quite free from all payment of duty, or giving security: he will have nothing to do but re-load his tobacco for exportation, without being at the trouble of attending to have his bonds cancelled, or taking out debentures for the drawbacks; all which, I conceive, must be a great ease to the fair trader; and to every such trader the prevention of frauds must be a great advantage, because it will put all the tobacco traders in Britain on the same footing, which is but just and equitable, and what ought, if possible, to be accomplished.

Now, in order to make this ease effectual to the fair trader, and to contribute to his advantage, by preventing, as much as possible, all frauds for the future, I propose, as I have said, to join the laws of excise to those of the customs, and to leave the one penny, or rather three farthings per pound, called the farther subsidy, to be still charged at the custom house, upon the importation of tobacco, which three farthings shall be payable to his Majesty's civil list as heretofore; and I propose for the future that all tobacco, after being weighed at the custom-house, and charged with the said three farthings per pound, shall be lodged in a warehouse or warehouses, to be appointed by the commissioners of excise for that purpose, of which warehouse the merchant importer shall have one lock and key, and the warehouse-keeper to be appointed by the said commissioners shall have another, that the tobacco may lie safe in that warehouse, till the merchant finds a market for it, either for exportation or home consumption; if his market be for exportation, he may apply to his warehouse-keeper, and take out as much for that purpose as he has occasion for, which, when weighed at the custom-house, shall be discharged of the three farthings per pound with which it was charged upon importation, so that the merchant may then export it without any farther trouble. But if his market be for home consumption, he shall pay the three farthings charged upon it at the custom-house upon importation, and then, upon calling his warehouse-keeper, he may deliver it to the buyer, on paying an inland duty of fourpence per pound, to the proper officer appointed to receive the same.

And whereas all penalties and forfeitures to become due by the laws now in being, for regulating the collection of the duties on tobacco, or at least all that part of them which is not given to informers, now belong to the crown. I now propose that all such penalties and forfeitures, in so far as they formerly belonged to the crown, shall for the future belong to the public, and be applicable to the same uses to which the said duties shall be made applicable by parliament; and for that purpose I have the King's commands to acquaint the House, that he, out of his great regard for the public good, with pleasure consents that they shall be so applied; which is a condescension in his Majesty, that I hope every gentleman in this House is fully sensible of, and will freely acknowledge.

Having thus explained my scheme to the Committee, I shall briefly touch on the advantages to be derived from, and anticipate some of the objections which may probably be made to it.

First then, turning duties upon importation into duties on consumption, is manifestly a great benefit to the merchant importer. The paying down of duties, or bonding, are heavy burthens. The payment of duties requires a treble stock to what would else be requisite in trade; and the asking securities, besides numerous other inconveniences, subjects the merchant to the necessity of returning the favour. It hardly requires to be mentioned, that it is a very great accommodation to be obliged to provide for the payment of one penny only, instead of sixpence and one third of a penny.

The next benefit is the great abatement on the whole duty. The inland duty being fourpence per pound, and the remaining subsidy three farthings, gives an abatement of 10 per cent. and of 15 per cent. upon the whole: whereas, the 25 per cent. is at present given only on the money paid down, which is not a fifth of the whole, and but 15 per cent. allowed on the four fifths which is bonded. Thus a duty of five pence farthing is paid on four fifths of the tobacco, and fourpence three farthings on the other fifth; while by the plan I propose, no more than fourpence three farthings will be paid on the whole. It is easy to calculate how great the advantage must be to the planter and fair trader from this arrangement, which demands so small an advance, exempts them from all the inconveniences of finding sureties, and requires no payment of any consequence, till the moment when a purchaser presents himself to refund the cost.

If it should be objected against this project, that it makes the tobacco trade a ready money business, which it cannot bear; I answer, that it may be so or not, as the parties themselves may chuse to arraign it; for if the merchant gives the consumer credit, as he now does, for the duties as well as the commodity, the objection ceases to have any weight.

The great advantage to the public will be this, that no duty being paid on tobacco designed for exportation, an immediate stop will be put to the fraud on drawbacks, and to most of the disgraceful efforts of dishonesty, which I have previously enumerated. This fact does not require to be verified by an experiment; it is sufficiently proved by the success and facility which attend the collection of the malt duty.

I come now to the main point, and which alone can admit of debate; the grand objection of making the dealers in tobacco subject to the laws of excise. I am aware, that on this subject I have arguments or rather assertions to encounter, which are of great import in sound, though of very little in sense. Those who deal in these general declamations stigmatize the scheme in the most unqualified manner, as tending to reduce those subjected to it to a state of slavery. This is an assertion, the fallacy of which can only be determined by comparison. There are already ten or twelve articles of consumption subjected to the excise laws; the revenue derived from them amounts to about 3,200,000*l.* per annum, which is appropriated to particular purposes. A great number of persons are, of course, involved in the operation of these laws: yet, till the present moment, when so inconsiderable an addition is proposed, not a word has been uttered about the dreadful hardships to be apprehended from them. These clamours of interested and disaffected persons are best answered by the contented taciturnity of those in whose behalf their arguments, if of any force, ought to operate. Are the brewers and maltsters slaves, or do they reckon themselves so? Are they not as free in elections, to elect or be elected, as any others? Or let any gentleman present say, if he ever met with any opposition from, or by means of an exciseman?

I quit this general topic to advert to more particular and specific objections: The chief of them are, houses liable to be searched; the being subject to the determination of commissioners without appeal, who are necessarily creatures of the crown; the number of excise officers, the injury the subject will sustain in being tried without a jury; and the particular interest of the crown in this alteration.

To all these objections one general observation will apply; that if for these reasons this scheme is to be relinquished, the whole system of excise laws ought to be abandoned. But I shall examine them one by one. I begin with the last, the most cruel and unjust, because it tends to set up an improper distinction, and draw a strong line of opposition between the interests of the crown and the interests of the people; that is to say, between the estate and particular property of the crown, and the estate and particular property of the public: this naturally leads to a general consideration of the public revenues.

The revenues may be computed at 6,700,000*l.* per annum. The public has of this, as its particular interest and property, about 5,900,000*l.* per annum, namely, the appropriated funds and annual supplies. The proportion remaining to the crown, 800,000*l.*, is not an eighth part of the whole. And here, in order to obviate a general misrepresentation, it is necessary to state, that the civil list revenues, in five years, from Midsummer 1727 to Midsummer 1732, have fallen short of the sum they are supposed to produce by upwards of 26,000*l.* a year on the average. Happy indeed would be the state of the country, if the appropriated duties would answer all the proper engagements, and leave a surplus sufficient for the current service! But if that great object is not attainable, it is surely well worth the attention of parliament to provide for a moiety, or even a fourth part of the current service. The appropriated duties were funds for paying the interest of the national debt. These had been deficiencies in several, but now a supply is made; a sinking fund for gradually discharging the principal. A million per annum has for several years been applied, and that, by the public creditors, is now thought more than sufficient.

If under the present management, the duties produce much less than ought to be paid to the public, has the public a right to make the most of their own revenues, or are they alone excluded from doing themselves justice? To object against the improvement of the king's part, is to say, that the public had better be defrauded of seven parts in eight, than that justice should be done to the crown in the eighth. If manifest frauds were discovered in a branch belonging entirely to the civil list, the post office for example, would you rather sanction the wrong than do justice to the crown? Why then this unreasonable jealousy in the present instance? I call the jealousy unreasonable, because in this proposition all possible care has been taken to avoid the imputation of being designed for the benefit of the crown. The penny which goes to the civil list is left to be paid at the Custom house. All increase from the inland duty is not to go to the crown, but to the public. All fines, forfeitures, and penalties arising from the inland duties, are renounced by the crown, and appropriated to the public. In a word, the crown will have no interest in the inland duty, but as trustee for the public.

This fact, duly considered, answers the great objection to the determination of commissioners. For granting, for a moment, that commissioners are to be supposed corrupt, venal, and creatures of the crown, what influence can their regard for the crown have on them, to induce them to oppress the people, when the crown has no interest in their determination? But though this answer might reasonably be deemed satisfactory and sufficient, yet to obviate even speculative objections, a remedy is supplied for this supposed grievance, by investing three of the twelve judges with a power of determining, in a summary way, all appeals brought before them within the bills of mortality; and in the country, the same power is to be vested in one of the judges of the assize going the next circuit. This renders it impossible that the interest of the subject can be sacrificed to undue influence on the one hand, or the revenue to private solicitation, personal friendship or regard on the other. While such a tribunal presents itself, no offender would chuse to be carried into Westminster-hall, rather than have his cause judged in a summary way. The benefit of a trial by jury would not induce a man to encounter the tedious, vexatious, and expensive proceedings in a court of law, more burthensome than the penalties and forfeitures in dispute, as far as my own observation enables me to judge on the present system, where the commissioners have, in most cases, a power to determine themselves, or to bring informations, I have found that most people, against whom informations have been laid, have been desirous that their causes should be determined by commissioners; but I never yet heard of one who was willing to take his cause out of the hands of the commissioners to have it tried in Westminster-hall. One reason which contributes to render the exercise of power by the commissioners more popular is, that they possess the privilege of mitigation, which is not entrusted to the judges, who are merely administrators of the law according to the letter.

The next objection is the increase of revenue officers, which fear, interest, and affectation have magnified into a standing army. This standing army, allowing the proposed addition to extend to tobacco and wine, will not according to the estimate of the commissioners, exceed one hundred and twenty-six persons; that number, in addition to those already employed, will do all the duty. In this computation, warehouse-keepers are of course not included, their number must be uncertain, for the satisfaction and accommodation of the merchants: Few houses, however, out of London, will be subject to the Excise laws which are not so already.

The only remaining objection is, the power of officers to enter and search houses. This objection could not possibly have any weight, without the aid of gross misconception, or misrepresentation. All warehouses, cellars, shops, and rooms used for keeping, manufacturing, or selling tobacco, are to be entered at the inland office. These are to be always liable to the inspection of the officer, and it is to be made penal to keep or conceal tobacco in any room or place not entered. But no other part of the house is liable to be searched without a warrant and a constable, which warrant is not to be granted without any affidavit of the cause of suspicion. The practice of the customs is now stronger; they can enter with a writ of assistance without any affidavit. But why all this solicitude in the behalf of fraud? If the powers given by either, or both the systems of revenue law are not sufficient (as I am informed they are not in the case of tea,) it is an argument to add more checks, but no argument against the application of this.

The regulation in these two commodities, can affect neither trade, the poor, or the manufacturer. The poor are not all concerned in the question of tobacco, as the retailer now sells all tobacco at the rate of duty paid. The manufacturer is concerned as little, for the same reason, and neither one or the other drinks any wine. The landed interest cannot be affected by it in consequence of an advanced charge on the poor and the manufacturer. The whole clamour then is in favour of the retailer or tradesman, and even he cannot suffer, unless guilty of frauds. This is the scheme which has been represented in so dreadful and terrible a light; this is the monster, the many headed monster, which was to devour the people, and commit such ravages over the whole nation. How justly it has been represented in such a light, I shall leave to this Committee and to the world without doors to judge. I have said, and will repeat it, that whatever apprehensions and terrors people may have been brought under from a false and malicious representation of what they neither did, or could know or understand, I am fully persuaded, that when they have duly considered the Scheme I have now the honour to open to you, they will view it in another light; and that if it has the good fortune to meet the approbation of parliament, and comes to take effect, the people will soon feel the happy consequences of it; and when they experience these good effects, they will no longer look on those persons as their friends, who have so grossly imposed on their understandings.

I look upon it as a most innocent scheme; it can be hurtful to none but smugglers and unfair traders. I am certain it will be of great benefit to the revenue, and will tend to make London a free port, and by consequence, the market of the world. If I had thought otherwise of it, I would never have ventured to propose it in this place.

Therefore I shall now beg leave to move that it may be resolved, That it is the Opinion of this Committee, that the Subsidy and additional Duty upon Tobacco of the British Plantations, granted by an act of the 12th of King Charles II. and the Impost thereon, granted by an Act of the first of King James II. and also the one third Subsidy thereon, granted by an Act of the 2d of Queen Anne, amounting in the whole to 5-1/3d. per Pound, for several terms of years in the said respective acts mentioned, and which have since been continued and made perpetual, subject to Redemption by Parliament, shall from and after the 24th day of June 1733, cease and determine.

Speech by Sir John Bernard opposing Walpole's excise proposals, House of Commons, 12 March 1733

Parliamentary History, VIII, 1291-95.

I find that the honourable gentleman who opened this scheme to the Committee, (sir R. Walpole,) and the learned gentleman who spoke since (sir Philip Yorke) make great complaints of some people's having grossly and maliciously misrepresented their scheme, before those malicious persons knew what is was. For my part, I happen to be of a very different way of thinking; for though I am far from thinking that the scheme, as now opened to us, is the very same with what it was when first formed; yet, even as it is now opened, it is such a scheme, in my opinion, as cannot even by malice itself, be represented to be worse than it really is.

Now that I know it; now that I see what it is, it appears to me to be a scheme that will be attended with all those bad consequences, that ever were apprehended from it before it was known; and I plainly foresee, that it will produce none of those good effects, which gentlemen have been pleased to entertain us with the hopes of: They have, indeed, gilded the pill a little, but the composition within is still the same; and if the people of England be obliged to swallow it, they will find it as bitter a pill as ever was swallowed by them since they were a people.

The learned gentleman was pleased to say that he was of opinion, that the opposition to this wicked scheme, for so I must call it, proceeded from other motives than gentlemen are willing to own. I do not know what motives he can mean: But I am persuaded, that those gentleman who propose this scheme, have some secret views, which it would neither be convenient or safe for them to own in this place; for as to any reasons or views, which may be openly avowed for the proposing of this scheme, I know of none, but that of preventing the frauds that may be committed in that branch of the revenue now under our consideration: and that it will not answer that purpose, has been made plainly appear by my worthy brother near me (Mr. Perry); but granting that this scheme should answer such a purpose, if the laws now in being, duly executed, are sufficient to answer that purpose, what necessity is there for applying this new, this desperate remedy, a remedy which is certainly much worse than the disease? But before I proceed any farther, I shall desire that the Commissioners of the customs, who are attending at the door, may be called in.

[The commissioners were accordingly called in, and being asked by sir John Barnard, What they thought the value of the frauds committed in the tobacco trade might amount to one year with another? Their answer was, That they had never made any computation: but one of them said, that by a computation he had made only to satisfy his own private curiosity, he believed the frauds come to their knowledge, might amount to 30 or 40,000l. per annum, one year with another. Then sir John Barnard asked them whether it was their opinion, that if the officers of the customs performed their duty diligently and faithfully, it would not effectually prevent all, or most of the frauds that could be committed in the tobacco trade? To which they answered, that it was their opinion it would. Then he asked them farther, whether it was their opinion, that if the commissioners of the customs had the same power over their officers, as the commissioners of the excise have over theirs, it would not contribute a great deal towards making them more faithful in the discharge of their duty than they now are? To this their answer was, that they believed it would. After this, the commissioners being withdrawn, sir John Barnard proceeded thus:]

Sir; I now leave it to every gentleman in this House to consider, what real pretence can be formed for introducing such a dangerous scheme, as what has been proposed to us; the only pretence I have yet heard made use of is, the preventing of frauds, by which, say they, the fair trader will be encouraged, and the revenue encreased: but now you see, that is the opinion, even of the commissioners of the customs, that, by a due execution of the laws now in being, all or most of those frauds may be effectually prevented: and I am sure, if they can be prevented by the laws in being, the preventing of them by that method will contribute much more to the increase of the public revenue, and to the encouragement of the fair trader, than the preventing of them by means of the dangerous scheme now proposed to us. I now leave it to the whole world to judge, who are they that have secret motives which they are not willing to own; which they dare not own; Whether it be those who are the proposers and promoters of this scheme, or those who are the opposers of it?

The learned gentleman seemed to be surprised how our constitution, or the liberties of our country came to be brought into the present debate: he said, 'he thought they had no manner of concern in the present question.' I am sorry to differ from a gentleman who, by his profession, ought, who certainly does understand the nature of our constitution, as well as any man in England; but I am of opinion, that the constitution of our government, and the liberty of the subject, was never more nearly or more immediately concerned in any question, than they are in the present; they are both so deeply concerned, that their preservation or their total overthrow depends entirely upon the success of the scheme now under our consideration: If the scheme succeeds, they must tumble of course; if the scheme is defeated, they may be preserved: I hope they will be preserved till time shall be no more. But I must say, that the learned gentleman, and every gentleman who appears as an advocate for the scheme now proposed to us, is much in the right to keep, if they can, the constitution and the liberties of their country out of the debate; it is from thence that the principal arguments are to be formed against their scheme; it is from thence that such arguments may be formed against it, as must appear unanswerable to every man who has a regard for either.

The gentleman tells us, "That there are but 120, or 150 excise officers, besides warehouse-keepers, to be added by the scheme now before us;" and this additional number they seem to make a ridicule of; but considering the swarms of tax-gatherers we have already established, this small number, as they call it, is no trivial matter; and I would be glad to know from those gentlemen, what they call warehouse-keepers, and what number of them may be necessary? I hope they will allow, that a warehouse-keeper appointed by the treasury, and paid by the treasury, is an officer of the revenue, as much as any other officer whatsoever; and if the number that there must be of these be added to the other, I believe we may find that the number of revenue officers to be added by this scheme must be very considerable.

As for the new method of appeal proposed, I can see no advantage that it will be of to any unfortunate man that may have occasion for it: in all cases, the charge and trouble of attending must be very great, and the event very precarious; but in most cases, where poor retailers may have occasion to be concerned, the charge and trouble of attendance must be greater than the subject can bear, so that all such people must succumb; they must submit to the determination of the commissioners of the excise, and can expect no other redress, but what they meet with from the mercy of those commissioners. The judges of Westminster Hall are, it is true, for life, but they are all named by the crown; I shall say nothing of the present judges, who so worthily fill the several benches of Westminster Hall; but if they should die, and if the crown should be resolved to use that power, which the Parliament had put into their hands, in order to oppress the subject, they will always find Judges fit for their purpose: judges are but men, they are subject to the same frailties that other men are, and the crown has always plenty of baits wherewithal to tempt them. A judge may be made a lord chief justice, a lord chief justice may be made a lord chancellor, and every one may have a son, a brother, or a cousin to be provided for; and the crown has many other ways, by which they may win over a judge to administer justice according to the directions he shall receive from court; more especially when he is to administer justice in a summary way, and without the usual forms of proceeding in courts of law equity. For by this new method of appeal, and which has been so much bragged of, care has been taken that the subject shall not be restored to his ancient birthright: No, this I find is most carefully avoided, and yet I think it must be allowed, that it is the inherent right of every Englishman to be tried by his peers; I am not so much acquainted with law, as to give an account of the several cases in which this method of trial has been set aside, or the reasons for so doing; but I will venture to say, that wherever that method has been set aside, whether the same was done by the wisdom of the nation or otherwise, such an alteration was an innovation, and was a dangerous encroachment upon the original charter of our constitution.

As to the pretended partiality of juries, so much complained of by the learned gentleman, it is of no weight with me; I cannot see how that honourable gentleman, or any gentleman, can pretend to know what reasons a jury may have for giving their verdict: no gentleman has a right to be believed upon his single say-so, against a verdict given by twelve honest men upon oath. If there have been so many verdicts given against the crown, as that learned gentleman seems to insinuate, it is to me a strong proof that prosecutions have been set on foot against the subject, upon the evidence of witnesses, whose credibility or veracity have not been very much to be depended on; which is so far from being an argument for altering the method of trial by jury, that it is a very strong argument for the continuance of that method in all time to come. But as it is now very late, and as I shall probably have another opportunity of giving my sentiments more fully upon the affair now before us, I shall trouble you no farther at present, but only to declare, that now, after hearing this scheme opened to us, I dislike it as much as ever I did any representation of it that ever I heard of, and therefore shall give my negative to the question proposed.

Act easing restrictions on the wearing of printed and dyed calicoes, 1736

9 Geo. 3, c. 4   *Statutes at Large*, XVII, 1-3.

Whereas by an act passed in the seventh year of the reign of his late majesty King George the First, intituled, *An act to preserve and encourage the woollen and silk manufactures of this kingdom, and for more effectual employing the poor, by prohibiting the use and wear of all printed, painted, stained, or dyed callicoes, in apparel, houshold stuff, furniture, or otherwise, after the twenty fifth day of December, one thousand seven hundred and twenty two* (except as is therein excepted) it is enacted, That the prohibition of callicoes intended by the said act, and the penalties thereby inflicted, for wearing or using printed, painted, stained, or dyed callicoes, in apparel, houshold stuff, or furniture, after the twenty fifth day of December, one thousand seven hundred and twenty two, contrary to the said act, should respectively extend to prohibit, and should be levied and recovered for, wearing or using in apparel, houshold stuff, or furniture, after the said twenty fifth day of December, one thousand seven hundred and twenty two, any stuff made with cotton, or mixed therewith, which should be printed or painted with any colour or colours, or any callicoe chequered or striped, or any callicoe stitched or flowered in foreign parts with any colour or colours, or with coloured flowers made there (muslins, neckcloths, and fustians excepted) in such manner as the penalties inflicted by the said act, for wearing or using printed, painted, stained, or dyed callicoes, in apparel, houshold stuff, or furniture, after the said twenty fifth day of December, one thousand seven hundred and twenty two, contrary to the said act, are to be levied or recovered, but under such limitations, and with such liberties, privileges, and advantages, as are mentioned and expressed in the said act, or in any other act or acts of parliament then in force relating thereto, or relating to printed, painted, stained, or dyed callicoes: and whereas great quantities of stuffs made of linen yarn and cotton wooll have for several years past been manufactured, and have been printed and painted, within this kingdom of Great Britain, and the said manufactures so printed or painted are a branch of the ancient fustian manufacture of this kingdom, and have been and are now used and worn in apparel and furniture: and whereas some doubts have lately arisen, whether the use and wearing of the said stuffs, when the same are so printed or painted, be prohibited by the said recited act, whereby the said manufacture is discouraged, and may be utterly lost, and great numbers of his Majesty's subjects and their families, whose livelihoods intirely depend thereupon, may be ruined, and the poor greatly increased, if not timely prevented: for remedy whereof be it enacted by the King's most excellent Majesty, by and with the advice and consent of the lords spiritual and temporal, and commons, in this present parliament assembled, and by the authority of the same, That nothing in the said recited act shall extend or be construed to prohibit the wearing or using in apparel, houshold stuff, furniture, or otherwise, any sort of stuff made of linen yarn and cotton wooll manufactured and printed or painted with any colour or colours within the kingdom of Great Britain, provided that the warp thereof be intirely linen yarn; and that no person shall incur, or be deemed, or adjudged, or taken to incur, any penalty or forfeiture whatsoever for wearing or using such manufacture so printed or painted, as aforesaid; any thing in the said act to the contrary thereof in any wise notwithstanding.

II. And be it further enacted by the authority aforesaid, That none of the penalties in the said former act, which may have been incurred for the wearing or using any sort of stuff made of linen yarn and cotton wooll manufactured and printed or painted within this kingdom, as aforesaid, shall be recovered, or levied, unless some prosecution for the same hath been already commenced, and judgment already obtained thereupon; any thing in the said former act contained to the contrary in any wise notwithstanding.

Plan of the Society for the Encouragement of Arts, Manufactures and Commerce, 19 February 1755

The Plan of the Society for the Encouragement of Arts, Manufactures and Commerce (London, 1755), 4-page pamphlet.

The society subsequently became the Royal Society of Arts.

Whereas the Riches, Honour, Strength and Prosperity of a Nation depend in a great Measure on the Knowledge and Improvement of useful Arts, Manufactures, etc. several of the Nobility and Gentry of this Kingdom, being fully sensible that due Encouragements and Rewards are greatly conducive to excite a Spirit of Emulation and Industry, have resolved to form themselves into a Society, by the Name of *The Society for the Encouragement of Arts, Manufactures and Commerce,* by bestowing Premiums for such Productions, Inventions, or Improvements, as shall lend to the employing of the Poor, and the Increase of Trade.

And as all Communities must be established under certain Regulations, it is thought necessary for the orderly Dispatch of Business in this Society, that there be one President, four Vice-Presidents, a Treasurer, and a Secretary; to be elected by Ballot, on the first Wednesday in March annually.

And whereas the Right Honourable Jacob Lord Viscount Folkestone, being unanimously requested, has been pleased to accept the Office of President; the Right Honourable Robert Lord Romney, being also unanimously requested, has been pleased to accept the Office of Vice-President; the Rev. Dr. Stephen Hales, Charles Whitworth, and James Theobald, Esqrs. have unanimously been elected Vice-Presidents; John Goodchild, Esq., Treasurer; and Mr. William Shipley, Secretary: Each of them to continue in his respective Office until the first Wednesday in March, 1756, when a new Election of Officers shall be made: any seven or more of the subscribing Members shall, for the Time to come, elect Persons into this Society by Ballot, who have been regularly proposed, by giving in their Names in writing at a preceding Meeting.

There shall be four General Meetings of this Society in every Year, within the Bills of Mortality, *viz*. On the Second Wednesday in December, the Third Wednesday in January, the First Wednesday in March, (which is the Day of the Election of Officers) and the First Wednesday in April; and also as many other Meetings as the President, a Vice-President; or five or more of the said Society shall appoint. And at the General Meetings, (but not at any other Meetings) if seven Members at the least are present (whereof the President or a Vice-President always to be one) they shall have full Power to make Rules and Orders for the good Government of the said Society: to be valid and take Place, provided the same be confirmed at some succeeding General Meeting, where seven at least of the Members shall be present, the President or a Vice-President being one: And the same Method shall be observed in the altering or repealing any Rules or Orders that have been so made and confirmed.

And at all general and other Meetings, if the President be absent, the Vice-President then present, first named in the List of Vice-Presidents, shall be Chairman of the said Meeting; and in the Case the President and all the Vice-Presidents shall be absent, any Five or more shall appoint one of the Members then present to preside for that Time.

And whereas the Intent and Purpose of this Society is to encourage Ingenuity and Industry, by bestowing of Premiums on the most Deserving the Expense of which must be defrayed by the voluntary Contributions of its Members; no Person shall be deemed a Member until he shall have paid Two Guineas (or such larger Sum as he thinks proper) for the first Year. And every Person shall continue to pay Two Guineas (or what more he pleases to) annually, so long as he shall be willing to continue a Member of this Society. But whoever shall at once pay down Twenty Guineas (or more) in lieu of all Contributions, shall be a Member during his Life. And as the Good the Society can do, will be in Proportion to the Rewards it is able to bestow, all occasional Benefactions or Donations from any Person or Persons whatever, will be thankfully received by the Society: And fair Accounts in Writing shall be kept of all Receipts, Payments, and other Transactions of the said Society, and of its Officers and Agents, to be viewed and inspected by any Subscriber or Benefactor, upon Occasion: For the Examination, auditing and subscribing of which accounts, a Committee shall be appointed, annually, on the Third Wednesday in January; which Committee shall make their Report to the General

Meeting on the First Wednesday in March: and that before they proceed to the Election of their Officers.

And as the proposing proper Subjects for Encouragement, and the Distribution of Rewards with the strictest Impartiality and Justice, are what this Society most earnestly wishes and desires: and in order to effect the same, it seems absolutely necessary, to consult with such Person or Persons as are best able to judge of, or discover the Truth or Value of any Matter or Thing offered or proposed to this Society: It shall therefore be allowable for any Member thereof, with Leave of the Society, to introduce, at the general, or other Meetings, any such Person or Persons as he shall think capable of giving some useful Information, Assistance, or Advice.

Foreigners, or Persons that do not usually reside in Great Britain, may be elected, by Ballot, to be corresponding Members of this Society, without being subject to Contributions: And if they happen to come to London, shall be admitted to the Meetings of the Society, but shall have no Right to vote, unless they become Contributors.

If Differences of Opinion should arise concerning Matters or Things brought before this Society, a Ballot, if demanded, shall in all such Cases determine the Resolution of the said Society: and if the Votes be equal, the President, or Vice-President, or presiding Member, shall give the casting Vote.

And if the President shall happen to die or resign, in such case a new President shall be elected, at the next General Meeting of the Society, by a Majority of the Members then present, provided their Number be not less than seven, whereof a Vice-President shall be one: And until such President shall be so elected, the first Vice-President in Nomination, present at any Meeting, shall preside. And if any Vice-President shall die or resign, seven or more of the Members of this Society, (the President or a surviving Vice-President being one) shall in like Manner elect a new Vice-President.

Finally, In all Matters this Society shall be directed and governed by such Rules and Orders, as, from Time to Time, shall for that Purpose be made, confirmed, and established.

JACOBITE THREAT

Speech by the lord high steward upon the conviction of six lords for participating in the Stuart rebellion, House of Lords, 22 February 1716

Journal of the House of Lords, XX, 286-88.

The abortive Stuart uprising of 1715 reflected continuing discontent with the Hanoverian succession, notably in Scotland. The Stuart claim to the throne posed a serious threat to the crown until the suppression of the more dangerous rebellion of 1745.

And the Articles of Impeachment, exhibited by the House of Commons, against the Six Lords who have pleaded guilty, and the Earl of Wintoun, were read; as likewise the Answers and Pleas of the said Six Lords.

Then the Lord High Steward acquainted them, "That, when they should find Occasion to say any Thing, they must address themselves to the Lords in general; and likewise all other Persons must do the same." And then further acquainted the said Lords, "That they stood impeached by the House of Commons of High Treason, which was contained in the Articles now read; to which they had all pleaded guilty:" And asked them severally, "If they had any Thing to offer, why Judgement should not pass against them, according to Law?"

To which they all severally (after making the like Requests as they did at the Time they put in their Pleas) answered, "They had nothing to offer in Arrest of Judgement."

Then, Proclamation being again made for keeping Silence;

The Lord High Steward spake as follows: James Earl of Derwentwater, William Lord Widdrington, William Earl of Nithisdale, Robert Earl of Carnwath, William Viscount Kenmure, William Lord Nairn;

You stand impeached, by the Commons of Great Britain in Parliament assembled, of High Treason, in traiterously imagining and compassing the Death of His Most Sacred Majesty; and in conspiring, for that End, to levy a bloody and destructive War against His Majesty, in order to depose and murder Him; and in levying War accordingly, and proclaiming a Pretender to His Crown to be King of these Realms.

Which Impeachment, though One of your Lordships, in the Introduction to his Plea, supposes to be out of the ordinary and common Course of the Law and

214

Justice, is yet as much a Course of proceeding according to the Common Law as any other whatsoever.

If you had been indicted, the Indictment must have been removed, and brought before the House of Lords (the Parliament sitting); in that Case you had ('tis true) been accused only by the Grand Jury of One County: In the present, the whole Body of the Commons of Great Britain, by their Representatives, are your Accusers.

And this Circumstance is very observable (to exclude all possible Supposition of Hardship as to the Method of proceeding against you), that, however all great Assemblies amongst us are apt to differ on other Points, you were impeached by the unanimous Opinion of the House of Commons (not One Contradicting.)

They found themselves, it seems, so much concerned in the Preservation of His most truly Sacred Majesty and the Protestant Succession (the very Life and Soul of these Kingdoms), that they could not omit the First Opportunity of taking their proper Part, in order to so signal and necessary an Act of His Majesty's Justice.

And thus the whole Body Politic of this free Kingdom has in a Manner rose up in its own Defence, for the Punishment of those Crimes, which, it was rightly apprehended, had a direct Tendency to the everlasting Dissolution of it.

To this Impeachment, you have severally pleaded and acknowledged yourselves guilty of the High Treason therein contained.

Your Pleas are accompanied with some Variety of Matter, to mitigate your Offences, and to obtain Mercy.

Part of which, as some of the Circumstances said to have attended your Surrender (seeming to be offered rather as Arguments only for Mercy, than any Thing in Mitigation of your preceding Guilt), is not proper for me to take Notice of.

But as to the other Part, which is meant to extenuate the Crimes of which you are convicted, it is fit I should take this Occasion to make some Observations to your Lordships upon it; to the End that the Judgement to be given against you may clearly appear to be just and righteous, as well as legal; and that you may not remain under any fatal Error in respect of a greater Judicature, by reflecting with less Horror and Remorse on the Guilt you have contracted than it really deserves.

It is alledged by some of your Lordships, "That you engaged in this Rebellion without previous Concert or Deliberation, and without suitable Preparations of Men, Horses, and Arms."

If this should be supposed true, on some of your Lordships averring it; I desire you to consider, that, as it exempts you from the Circumstance of contriving this Treason, so it very much aggravates your Guilt in that Part you have undoubtedly borne in the Execution of it.

For it shews, that your Inclinations to rebel were so well known (which could only be from a continued Series of your Words and Actions), that the Contrivers of that horrid Design depended upon you, and therein judged rightly: That your Zeal to engage in this Treason was so strong, as to carry you into it on the least Warning, and the very First Invitation: That you would not excuse yourselves by Want of Preparation, as you might have done; and that, rather than not have a Share in the Rebellion, you would plunge yourselves into it almost naked, and unprovided for such an Enterprize: In short, that your Men, Horses, and Arms, were not so well prepared, as they might and would have been on longer Warning; but your Minds were.

It is alledged, also, as an Extenuation of your Crime, "That no cruel or harsh Action (I suppose is meant no Rapine or Plunder, or worse) has been committed by you."

This may in Part only be true: But then your Lordships will at the same Time consider, that the laying waste a Tract of Land bears but a little Proportion, in Point of Guilt, compared with that Crime of which you stand convicted; an open Attempt to destroy the best of Kings, to ruin the whole Fabric, and raze the very Foundations of a Government the best suited of any in the World to perfect the Happiness and support the Dignity of human Nature: The former Offence causes but a Mischief that is soon recovered, and is usually pretty much confined; the latter, had it succeeded, must have brought a lasting and universal Destruction on the whole Kingdom.

Besides, much of this was owing to Accident: Your March was so hasty, partly to avoid the King's Troops, and partly from a vain Hope to stir up Insurrections in all the Counties you passed through, that you had not Time to spread Devastations, without deviating from your main and, as I have observed, much worse Design.

Farther, it is very surprizing, that any concerned in this Rebellion should lay their engaging in it on the Government's doing a necessary and usual Act, in like Cases, for its Preservation; the giving Orders to confine such as were most likely to join in that Treason: 'Tis hard to believe that any one should rebel, merely to avoid being restrained from rebelling; or that a gentle Confinement would not much better have suited a crazy State of Health, than the Fatigues and Inconveniencies of such long and hasty Marches in the Depth of Winter.

Your Lordships rising in Arms therefore has much more justified the Prudence and Fitness of those Orders, than those Orders will in any Wise serve to mitigate your Treason: Alas! happy had it been for all your Lordships, had you fallen under so indulgent a Restraint.

When your Lordships shall in good Earnest apply yourselves to think impartially on your Case; surely you will not yourselves believe that it is possible, in the Nature of the Thing, to be engaged, and continue so long engaged, in such a difficult and laborious Enterprize, through Rashness, Surprize, or Inadvertency; or that, had the Attack at Preston been less sudden (and consequently the Rebels better prepared to receive it), your Lordships had been reduced the sooner, and with less, if not without any, Bloodshed.

No, my Lords, these and such like are artful Colourings, proceeding from Minds filled with Expectation of continuing in this World; and not from such as are preparing for their Defence before a Tribunal, where the Thoughts of the Heart, and the true Springs and Causes of Actions, must be laid open.

And now, my Lords, having thus removed some false Colours you have used; to assist you yet farther in that necessary Work of thinking on your great Offence as you ought, I proceed to touch upon several Circumstances, that seem greatly to aggravate your Crime, and which will deserve your most serious Consideration.

The Divine Virtues ('tis one of your Lordships own Epithets), which all the World, as well as your Lordships, acknowledge to be in His Majesty, and which you now lay Claim to, ought certainly to have withheld your Hands from endeavouring to depose, to destroy, to murder, that most Excellent Prince; so the Impeachment speaks, and so the Law construes your Actions; and this is not only true in the Notion of Law, but almost always so in Deed and Reality. It is a trite, but very true Remark, that there are but few Hours between Kings being reduced under the Power of Pretenders to their Crown and their Graves: Had you succeeded, His Majesty's Case would, I fear, have hardly been an Exception to that general Rule; since it is highly improbable that Flight should have saved any of that illustrious and valiant Family.

It is a farther Aggravation of your Crime, that His Majesty, whom your Lordships would have dethroned, affected not the Crown by Force, or by the Arts of Ambition; but succeeded peaceably and legally to it; and, on the Decease of Her late Majesty without Issue, became undoubtedly the next in Course of Descent, capable of succeeding to the Crown, by the Law and Constitution of this Kingdom, as it stood declared some Years before the Crown was expressly limited to the House of Hanover: This Right was acknowledged, and the Descent of the Crown limited or confirmed accordingly, by the whole Legislature in Two successive Reigns; and more than once in the latter, which your Lordships Accomplices are very far from allowing would byass the Nation to that Side.

How could it then enter into the Heart of Men to think, that private Persons might with a good Conscience endeavour to subvert such a Settlement, by running to tumultuary Arms, and by intoxicating the Dregs of the People with contradictory Opinions and groundless Slanders; or that God's Providence would ever prosper such wicked, such ruinous, Attempts?

Especially if in the next Place it be considered, that the most fertile Inventions on the Side of the Rebellion have not been able to assign the least Shadow of a Grievance as the Cause of it: To such poor Shifts have they been reduced on this Head, that, for Want of better Colours, it has been objected, in a solemn Manner, by your Lordships Associates, to His Majesty's Government, "That His People do not enjoy the Fruits of Peace, as our Neighbours have done, since the last War:" Thus they first rob us of our Peace, and then upbraid us that we have it not. It is a monstrous Rebellion, that can find no Fault with the Government it invades, but what is the Effect of the Rebellion itself.

Your Lordships will likewise do well to consider what an additional Burthen your Treason has made necessary on the People of this Kingdom, who wanted, and were about to enjoy, some Respite: To this End, it is well known, that all new or Increase of Taxes were the last Year carefully avoided; and His Majesty was contented to have no more Forces than were just sufficient to attend His Person, and shut the Gates of a few Garrisons.

But what His Majesty thus did for the Ease and Quiet of His People, you most ungratefully turned to His Disadvantage, by taking Encouragement from thence, to endanger His and His Kingdom's Safety, and to bring Oppression on your Fellow-subjects.

Your Lordships observe, I avoid expatiating on the Miseries of a Civil War, a very large and copious Subject: I shall but barely suggest to you on that Head, that whatever those Calamities may happen to be in the present Case, all who are at any

Time, or in any Place, Partakers in the Rebellion (especially Persons of Figure and Distinction), are in some Degree responsible for them; and therefore your Lordships must not hold yourselves quite clear from the Guilt of those Barbarities which have been lately committed by such as are engaged in the same Treason with you, and not yet perfectly reduced, in burning the Habitations of their Countrymen, and thereby exposing many Thousands to Cold and Hunger in this rigorous Season.

I must be so just to such of your Lordships as profess the Religion of the Church of Rome, that you had One Temptation, and that a great one, to engage you in this Treason, which the others had not; in that it was evident, Success on your Part must for ever have established Popery in this Kingdom, and that probably you could never have again so fair an Opportunity.

But then, good God! how must those Protestants be covered with Confusion, who entered into the same Measures without so much as capitulating for their Religion (that ever I could find from any Examination I have seen or heard); or so much as requiring, much less obtaining, a frail Promise, that it should be preserved, or even tolerated.

It is my Duty to exhort your Lordships, thus to think of the Aggravations, as well as the Mitigations (if there be any), of your Offences. And if I could have the least Hopes, that the Prejudices of Habit and Education would not be too strong for the most earnest and charitable Entreaties, I would beg you not to rely any longer on those Directors of your Consciences, by whole Conduct you have very probably been led into this miserable Condition; but that your Lordships would be assisted by some of those pious and learned Divines of the Church of England, who have constantly bore that infallible Mark of sincere Christians, universal Charity.

And now, my Lords, nothing remains, but that I pronounce upon you (and sorry I am that it falls to my Lot to do it) that terrible Sentence of the Law, which must be the same that is usually given against the meanest Offender in the like Kind.

The most ignominious and painful Parts of it are usually remitted, by the Grace of the Crown, to Persons of your Quality: But the Law, in this Case, being deaf to all Distinctions of Persons, requires I should pronounce, and accordingly it is adjudged by this Court,

That you, James Earl of Derwentwater, William Lord Widdrington, William Earl of Nithisdale, Robert Earl of Carnwath, William Viscount Kenmure, and William Lord Nairn, and every of you, return to the Prison of The Tower, from whence you came; from thence you must be drawn to the Place of Execution; when you come there, you must be hanged by the Neck, but not till you be dead, for you must be cut down alive; then your Bowels must be taken out, and burnt before your Faces; then your Heads must be severed from your Bodies, and your Bodies divided each into Four Quarters; and these must be at the King's Disposal.

And God Almighty be merciful to your Souls!

Then the Lord High Steward declaring, "That there was nothing more to be done by Virtue of the present Commission;"

He stood up uncovered, and broke the Staff, and declared it dissolved.

Then the House was adjourned to the House above; and the Lords and others returned in the same Order they went down.

And the House being resumed;

The following Order was made:

Ordered, That the Thanks of this House be, and are hereby, given to the Lord High Steward, for the Speech made by him this Day in Westminster Hall, at the Time he pronounced the Judgement of this House upon the Six Lords who had pleaded guilty to the Impeachment of High Treason exhibited by the House of Commons against them: And further, that the Lord High Chancellor do cause the said Speech to be forthwith printed and published; as also that the whole Proceedings on the said Impeachment be printed and published; and that the said Speech made by the Lord High Steward be entered in the Journal of this House.

Lords debate on a Bill of Pains and Penalties against Francis Atterbury, bishop of Rochester, on charges of leading a Jacobite conspiracy, 13 May 1723

Parliamentary History, VIII, 332-47.

The bill passed, 83-43, and Bishop Atterbury (1662-1732) was banished from the country.

The Lord Bathurst, who took notice of the ungracious distinctions that were fixed on the members from those who happened to have the majority: that for his part, as he had nothing in view but truth and justice, the good of his country, the honour of that House, and the discharge of his own conscience, he would freely speak his thoughts, notwithstanding all discouragements: that he would not complain of the sinister arts that had been used of late to render some persons obnoxious, and under pretence of their being so, to open their letters about their minutest domestic affairs; for these small grievances he could easily bear; but when he saw things go so far, as to condemn a person of the highest dignity in the church, in such an unprecedented manner, and without any legal evidence, he thought it his duty to oppose a proceeding so unjust and unwarrantable in itself, and so dangerous and dismal in its consequences. To this purpose, he begged leave to tell their lordships a story he had from several officers of undoubted credit, that served in Flanders in the late war. "A Frenchman, it seems, had invented a machine, which would not only kill more men at once, than any yet in use, but also disable for ever any man that should be wounded by it. Big with the hopes of a great reward, he applied to one of the ministers, who laid his project before the late French king; but that monarch, considering that so destructive an engine might soon be turned against his own men, did not think proper to encourage it, whereupon the inventer came over into England, and offered his service to some of our generals, who likewise rejected the proposal with indignation." The use and application of this story, added his lordship, is very obvious: for if this way of proceeding be admitted, it will certainly prove a very dangerout engine: no man's life, liberty, or property will be safe; and if those, who were in the administration some years ago, and who had as great a share in the affections of the people, as any that came after them, had made use of such a political machine, some of those noble persons, who now appear so zealous promoters of this bill, would not be in a capacity to serve his Majesty at this time. His lordship added, that if such extraordinary proceedings went on, he saw nothing remaining for him, and others to do, but retire to their country houses, and there, if possible, quietly enjoy their estates, within their own families, since the least correspondence, the least intercepted letter, might be made criminal. To this purpose his lordship quoted a passage out of cardinal de Retz's Memoirs, relating to that wicked politician, cardinal Mazarin, who boasted, "That if he had but two lines of any man's writing, with a few circumstances attested by witnesses, he could cut off his head when he pleased." His lordship also shrewdly animadverted on the majority of the venerable bench, towards which turning himself, he said, He could hardly account for the inveterate hatred and malice, some persons bore the learned and ingenious bishop of Rochester, unless it was that they were intoxicated with the infatuation of some of the wild Indians, who fondly believe they inherit not only the spoils, but even the abilities of any great enemy they kill.

The Lord Strafford spoke on the same side, as did also

Lord Trevor, who urged, That if men were in this unprecedented manner, proceeded against without legal proof, in a short time men would be tried, as they were liked by ministers: that for his own part, he believed he stood but indifferently in the opinion and liking of some persons, and therefore he had reason to think himself the more in danger, because at present they wanted the protection of the law, [meaning the Suspension of the Habeas Corpus Act] and as in a short time, they were like to be so unhappy as to be deprived of his Majesty's personal protection, and were still liable to be confined upon suspicion, which he took to be no more than will and pleasure; they were consequently at the will and pleasure of the ministers: That, however, no apprehension of what he might suffer should deter him from doing what he thought his duty: that, consonant to that principle, he had all along, and still opposed these extraordinary proceedings, which tended to lodge an exorbitant power in their fellow-subjects: That if he were to lose his liberty, he had rather give it up to one single tyrant, than to many: for a tyrant, if a man of common understanding, would, for his own sake, be tender of the lives of his subjects; whereas many tyrants would endeavour to destroy one another, to get one another's employments.

The Earl of Finlater endeavoured to shew, That the evidence that had been produced before them, being sufficient to convince any reasonable man, that there had been a detestable Conspiracy; and that the bishop of Rochester had a great share in it, was likewise sufficient to justify this extraordinary proceeding against him, especially since they inflicted on him so light a punishment, considering the heinousness of his crime.

The Duke of Argyle pursued the same argument; run through and confuted the most essential parts of the Bishop's defence; and, with vehemence, aggravated his offence, by which he had debased his holy function and character, and acted contrary to the solemn and repeated oaths he had taken.

The Lord Gower spoke against the Bill.

Lord Lechmere, who had all along expressed his dislike of these extraordinary proceedings, declaring it as his opinion, that there was sufficient evidence to support the charge. He was answered by

Lord Cowper, who spoke as follows:
My Lords, This debate has been already carried to that length, and is by all agreed to be of such importance, that I am sure your lordships will permit me to enter into it without any apology

I am, my lords, against this bill, not only because I think nothing has been offered sufficient for the support of it, but because I think the honour and dignity of the crown, the dignity and authority of this House, and the credit and reputation of the House of Commons, concerned in the event of it. My lords, The proceedings of that House have been, in this case, very remarkable and uncommon: They voted the bishop guilty of high-treason the very first thing they did; and it was reasonable to expect, that the consequence of that vote would have been an order for an impeachment in parliament, or a prosecution in the ordinary course of law. But, my lords, we see they have taken another method, and that without weighing what the consequences might be. They have taken a method, whereby they have made themselves both judges and accusers. They could not, as judges, decently proceed against the bishop, without hearing him, and therefore they gave him a day for that purpose, and thereby they discovered the dilemma into which they had run themselves. They found themselves obliged to hear him, and yet they could not acquit him, because they had already prejudged him. It is not therefore to be wondered that they have passed this bill; though, I believe, they would be very well pleased your lordships should reject it, that the knowledge of their having taken so wrong a step, might the sooner be forgotten.

My Lords, A great deal has been said, and surely too much cannot be said, to shew that this bill is an infringement upon the authority of this House. It becomes your lordships to support your dignity, and to shew a suitable resentment, when the least of your privileges is invaded. Your lordships, upon this occasion, would do well to follow the example even of this very House of Commons: How contemptuously did they throw out a bill lately sent them, because they thought it looked like a money bill? And will your lordships suffer them to share your authority, to become judges equal with yourselves, when there is no necessity for it? In this case, it is manifest, there can be no necessity, because the bishop is amenable to justice: He has been confined several months; he is not strictly guarded; and, no doubt, the zeal of the governor will prevent his running away. But, my lords, if it could be supposed that this bill did not affect your lordships' authority; yet if it affects the honour of the crown, I am sure, it will raise a becoming indignation in us all against it. This bill, if your lordships pass it, will put his Majesty under the unavoidable necessity of refusing the royal assent to it, or of condemning one of his subjects, a lord of parliament, and a bishop of that church of which his Majesty is guardian and protector, in a case at least doubtful; and that without hearing one word either of the charge, or of the defence. My lords, It hath been often said, (I wish it were said without grounds) that we have a disaffected party amongst us. I am persuaded, it is far from the intention of any lord here, to advise his Majesty to do any thing that might possibly increase that disaffection: But whether the passing of such a bill against a bishop of the church of England, unheard, may not give a handle to the clamorous, to raise an odium against his Majesty's administration, is submitted to your lordships. His Majesty's great clemency and mercy are known to all the world; and he has been in nothing more conspicuous, than in the exercise of those royal virtues: supposing, then, your lordships should pass this Bill, how can you ever hope for the royal assent to it? These objections, that concern the king, appear to me unanswerable, not only with regard to this bill, but to all bills of attainder in general. I think they ought never to be allowed, but when the offender flies from justice, or is in open rebellion; and then, perhaps, the notoriety of the fact may be some excuse for the extraordinariness of the proceeding.

My Lords, I expected to have heard from that reverend bench many arguments of another king against this bill, which are properly within their sphere, and which I am sure they are perfect masters of. The old champions of our church used to argue very learnedly, "That to make or to degrade bishops was not the business of the state; that there is a spiritual relation between a bishop and his flock, derived from the church, with which the state has nothing to do:" But this bill deprives the bishop of that spiritual relation, without the concurrence of the church. The parliament alone does it; and it must be owned, that if the parliament can do it, they can as well make a new one in his room; and a clause for that purpose, added to this bill, would as effectually do the one as the other. What the thoughts of our reverend prelates are upon these points, does not yet fully appear; something of their conduct intimates, as if our old divines were mistaken: But, be that as it will, as the judgment of our prelates will carry great weight, and as the reasons for such their judgment must needs be convincing, I do not doubt but they will give your lordships full satisfaction before this debate comes to a period. In the mean time, I speak my concern, that if acts of parliament are made to interfere with church-affairs: if bishops are to be put in or turned out at pleasure; and all this to be done without the concurrence of the church, the world abroad may, though unjustly, look upon our church as a creature only of the state, and treat our bishops, as if they were no more than state officers. I hope, however, from the courage, zeal, and conduct of our present reverend prelates, whatsoever becomes of this bill, that they will be able to wipe off any such scandal: They certainly have the honour, the dignity, and authority of our church always at heart; and every thing tending to her interest, they will most zealously promote. But whether the passing of this bill promote her interest, or be of any service to her, they best know: For my part, I cannot even guess at any advantage she possibly can receive by it, unless it be this, That it will make the bishoprick of Rochester, and the deanry of Westminster, to become vacant.

My Lords, This bill carried in the frame of it an invincible objection to it; for the preamble and the enacting part, the crime and the punishment, bear no proportion to each other. The preamble contains a charge of high-treason against the bishop; and, pray, my lords, why should he not be punished accordingly? Is it because he is a bishop of the church of England, or a lord of parliament, or in high favour with the king or his ministers? I have not heard that the bishop hath been at court of late; but be it either of these, it would be so far from being a reason for mitigating his punishment, that it ought, if possible, to increase it. My Lords, Our laws have wisely taught us to have a just abhorrence of high-treason, and have ordained for it the severest punishment that English clemency will admit of, and shall be, who has been voted the principal contriver and director of this most horrid and detestable treason, escape with a punishment less than his crimes deserve, and that too in full parliament? Methinks, if it were necessary that the legislature should interpose in this case, the heinousness of the offence should fire their resentment; and instead of abating the punishment, should put them upon heightening it with all the circumstances of severity that their wisdom could contrive. As in the case of the late South-Sea directors: No one will say, but that they might have been punished as cheats, without the help of an act of parliament; but as the punishment ordained by our laws for such offences came not up to the aggravating circumstances of their guilt, a law was made to punish them on purpose; and they were justly stripped of their estates, who had before so notoriously cheated, bubbled, and beggared the whole nation. What reason, then, can be given why the bishop should not be punished, at least equal with others, in cases of high-treason? Why truly, the want of legal evidence is the only reason pretended: A reason! in my apprehension, so very mean and trifling, that it ought not to have been heard in the supreme judicature of a nation, without the severest censure, and such as would well become your lordships to treat with the utmost indignation and contempt.

For, my Lords, is it come to this at last, that after so much grimace, so much noise and stir, after committing the bishop for high-treason, after voting him a traitor, and treating him as such, must at length come out, that there is no legal evidence against him! To palliate the matter a little, a distinction is endeavoured to be made between legal evidence and real evidence, or between such evidence as our law requires, and such as in natural justice and equity ought to be admitted. But, my Lords, this is a distinction entirely without a difference: for what is evidence of a fact before any judicature whatsoever, but such testimony as the nature of the case requires, to induce a moral certainty of the truth of the thing testified: The greater or less consequence the case is of, the more or less proof is required to induce such certainty. Thus, in ordinary matters, barely to prove a hand-writing is held sufficient evidence; because, in such cases, it is not to be supposed the hand-writing should be counterfeited: In other cases, seeing the party write, is necessary to be proved; and still as the weight of the case increases, stronger proof is required. Ever since the reversal of the attainder of colonel Algernon Sidney, the proving of treason by the proving of hand-writing, hath been, with great justice, condemned; and, why, I pray? But because there can be no hand-writing but what will admit of a counterfeit; and nothing that is capable of being counterfeited, carries with it such a degree of certainty, as is necessary where a man's life and fortune is concerned. My

Lords, legal evidence is nothing else but such real and certain proof, as ought, in natural justice and equity, to be received; and therefore the oath of one credible witness, being certain and sufficient to induce a belief of the thing he swears, is legal evidence; and yet so tender is our law, so great a degree of certainty doth it require, that, as it now stands, two positive witnesses are required to convict a man of high-treason. This, however, hath been preposterously enough urged, to shew a difference between legal and real evidence: and sir John Fenwick's Case hath been cited for the same purpose. But this, with submission, shews no difference at all; for will any one say, that one credible witness is not legal evidence? Can any court in the kingdom, upon a trial of high-treason, refuse to hear such evidence? And is not such evidence sufficient too in all cases, where some positive law, for the greater certainty, doth not require more?

One of the learned gentlemen at the bar, (Mr. Waerg,) I suppose out of pure zeal for this bill, and not with a design to misguide his audience, did soundly affirm before your lordships, that no evidence, strictly speaking, was legal, but what was mathematical. I am confident, that gentleman would not have given this as his opinion under his hand at his chamber, because he knows it is directly contrary to truth: He knows very well that no offender, that puts himself upon his trial, can be convicted, but upon the oath of one or more witnesses: he dares not deny but that such conviction is founded upon legal evidence, strictly so speaking; and no one will pretend to say, that any evidence of witnesses can be called mathematical. But the gentleman goes on, and says, That the evidence for this bill is legal, in the general sense of the word: On the contrary, I beg leave to affirm, That it is not legal in any sense whatsoever. No act of Parliament hath made it legal, nor can it, in natural justice and equity, be called so, for want of sufficient certainty; and, indeed, it hath been admitted throughout this debate, and even by the counsel who spoke first for this bill, that it is not supported by legal evidence. But this gentleman was pleased to go still farther, for he affirmed before your lordships, That depositions taken in writing, were not evidence in any court of law. My Lords, it is pity that in so fine a speech there should be so much false doctrine: It is very true, that the law doth require the best evidence that the nature of the case will admit of; and therefore will not suffer the depositions of a witness in writing to be read, where such witness can be examined viva voce: But that gentleman could not but know, that where such living witness is not to be had, his depositions in writing are never refused, not any other evidence that, in natural justice and equity, can tend to discover the truth of the fact in question with certainty.

My Lords, The wisdom and goodness of our law appear in nothing more remarkably, than in the perspicuity, certainty, and clearness of the evidence it requires to fix a crime upon any man, whereby his life, his liberty, or his property may be concerned: Herein we glory and pride ourselves, and are justly the envy of all our neighbour nations. Our law, in such cases, requires evidence so clear and convincing, that every by-stander, the instant he hears it, must be fully satisfied of the truth of it; It admits of no surmises, inuendo's, forced consequences, or harsh constructions, nor any thing else to be offered as evidence, but what is real and substantial, according to the rules of natural justice and equity.

These are the rules the judges go by, nor have they any other in determining what is, or what is not to be admitted as evidence before them; and therefore to say, that the law refuses such evidence as is real, and ought, in natural justice and equity, to be admitted, is to cast an imputation upon the law, which is not only unjust, but entirely groundless. My Lords, I think sufficient hath been said to shew the mistake of those noble lords who have endeavoured to distinguish between legal and real evidence. The distinctions that have been made, and the instances that have been produced, shew only what legal evidence is sufficient for conviction, and what not; and if that were the question now before your lordships, it would deserve another consideration.

The present question is, Whether any evidence at all has been offered to your lordships to fix treason upon the bishop of Rochester; and for my part, my Lords, I am clearly of opinion, that you have had no such evidence: It is on all hands agreed, that no legal evidence of treason has been offered against him; and, I hope, I have sufficiently satisfied your lordships, that if it be not legal evidence, it is not real evidence, or such, as in natural justice and equity, ought to be admitted, and consequently no evidence at all. My Lords, the counsel for the bill have not attempted to prove positively against the bishop any one single criminal act: The circumstances that they have offered are in my opinion, so far from affecting him, that they carry in them no appearance of guilt in him whatsoever. If indeed there had been any one positive witness against him, your lordships, perhaps, (as was done in sir John Fenwick's Case) might, with some appearance of reason, have admitted circumstances in support of such witness, rather than a man of the bishop's rank and character should go unpunished; and, indeed, I think, no man's cunning ought to be a protection for his villainy; and I hope, and do not doubt, but all traitors will, one time or other, meet with their just rewards. But, my lords, in the case before you, the whole charge is built upon circumstances, and these are said to be supported by other circumstances; but all of them are so remote, so general, and, I may say, so inoffensive, that they might suit any lord here as well as the bishop; for there is not one single circumstance of them all, such as in its nature would be admitted as evidence of any crime against any man in any court in the kingdom.

To come, my Lords, to particulars, the treason charged upon the bishop is, That he dictated to Kelly the three letters, dated the 20th of April, 1722, signed, Jones, Illington, and 1378. And in maintainance of this charge, it is said, that those three letters were the same hand-writing with another letter produced before your lordships, and dated the 20th of August following: That from the 20th of April to the 20th of August, letters were continually sent abroad in the same hand-writing; that these letters contained a treasonable correspondence; that they are the hand-writing of Kelly; that Kelly had been with the bishop two or three times within these two or three years past; that there are circumstances in the case of Jones in this correspondence, that suit with the case of Illington, and circumstances in the case of both that suit with the bishop. These are the facts that are the main foundation upon which the bishop's heavy charge is built; and surely it well behoves your lordships to consider seriously how they are proved, and in what manner, and with what degree of certainty they affect him.

The three letters taken simply carry no treason in them; they have not yet been decyphered into treason, and were it not for a name in the direction of one of them, which is said to be a cant name of the Pretender's, they probably might have passed as harmless undesigning letters; will your lordships therefore suppose that the writer directed his letter to the Pretender by the cant name of Jackson, when yet it does not appear that he ever knew the Pretender had such a cant name? Ought we not rather to suppose in favour of innocence, that the letter was not intended for the Pretender, but for one whose real name it bears? These cant names, and the art of the decypherers have been the means made use of to make this correspondence treasonable; but will it not be thought hard that a man must be conjured into treason by a magic art that none of us understand, and by a parcel of names that the wisest of us are not yet able to discover whether they were designed for cant names or for real ones? To make the matter clearer, the clerks of the post-office are called, and they prove that the several letters, produced before your lordships, are true copies of original letters, sent abroad as directed; which originals, according to the best of their judgment and belief, are the same hand-writing with the letter of the 20th of August abovementioned. This judgment and belief of theirs is founded, without comparing any two of these originals together, or without pretending to say whose hand-writing they are, or to whom they belong. My Lords, I have already observed, that the proving of a hand-writing is, at best, but evidence too precarious and uncertain, to make good a charge of so weighty a nature as this in judgment before you; but I cannot help taking notice, that the proof of these letters, so as to make them treasonable, is still more precarious, more uncertain and slippery, than any thing of the kind I ever met with. The usual way to prove a hand-writing, so as to fix a charge upon the writer, is, for the witness to swear that he hath frequently seen the party write, or that he hath corresponded with him, and received several letters from him, and therefore is very well acquainted with his usual character and way of writing: and then the writing itself is produced, the witness swears to it, and the import of it is discovered by every by-stander. But here these post-office clerks are forced to call in aid, a messenger and a servant, to fix the hand-writing of the letters they produce; the letters themselves are unintelligible, and therefore the assistance of the decypherers and some cant names must be added, before they can wire-draw treason out of them. My Lords, these decypherers refuse to give your lordships any reason for the construction they have made; they shelter themselves by saying, that to give you a reason, would be to discover their art; happy art, indeed, that shall enable the artist to swear a man into high-treason, and yet it shall not be in the power of the accused person to disprove him. I do not find that these gentlemen pretend to act by unerring rules; they themselves own they may be mistaken, and therefore until your lordships are let farther into their secret, you will judicially look upon the art of decyphering to be no more than the art of guessing, and esteem him that guesses best to be the best decypherer.

The messenger and servant that have been called to finish the doubtful evidence of this hand-writing, and to fix it upon Kelly, are far from giving your lordships such an account of it, as can induce you to believe they are sufficiently acquainted with it; they do not pretend to say, that they have been frequently accustomed to see or observe him write, or that they ever received any letters from him, or ever were privy to any of his correspondences; these things, one would have thought, might easily have been proved against a man of Kelly's great dealing and acquaintance, in as full and clear a manner as the nature of the thing would admit of. Your lordships then are pleased to observe, that the evidence offered to prove this hand-writing, so as to make it criminal, consists of three distinct branches, supported by three different sets of witnesses; and that each of these three several sets have given a very lame, doubtful and obscure evidence; but if their evidence had been ever so full and positive, yet I must beg leave to insist, that it is such as is in its nature dubious and uncertain, and therefore in a case of this consequence ought not to be relied on. This will appear still the plainer from the different opinions observable among the different witnesses, insomuch that I may well venture to say your lordships are as yet at a loss by whom these letters were wrote; but if you will have any regard to numbers, and to the nature and circumstances of the testimony given by those numbers, the evidence is much stronger, and more clear and convincing, that they were not wrote by Kelly, than that they were; and if they were not wrote by him, it will become your lordships to consider carefully what you are a-doing; for then the foundation of this bill will be sapped, and of course the whole fabric must fall to the ground.

But, my lords, supposing these letters were really the hand-writing of Kelly, that they were of that treasonable signification that the decypherers contend for, and that the names mentioned in them did not belong to real persons, but were cant names to denote the Pretender and his agents; I say, my Lords, supposing all this true of Kelly, how will it affect the bishop? Might not Kelly write these letters, and carry on this correspondence without the bishop's direction? Must the bishop answer for Kelly's crimes, because Kelly happens to be a non-juror? or because he was employed to buy gloves and stockings for the bishop, must your lordships therefore infer that he was employed to write treason for him? Suppose Kelly had actually lived in the bishop's family as his secretary, have we not seen, not many years since, even a Jesuit a bishop's domestic without offence? Give me leave, my Lords, to carry this point a little farther: Has any thing been offered to induce your lordships to believe that Kelly saw the bishop, or heard from him for several months before this correspondence began? Has any one word been said, or hint given, either from cant names or decyphered letters, or any otherwise howsoever, tending to that purpose? Nay, my Lords, have you not had as much evidence as the nature of the thing is capable of, that the bishop could not dictate, nor Kelly write those letters, at any time near the time of their date? And if they were dictated by the bishop, it must be about that time, because the circumstances mentioned in the letter would not suit him at any other time. And here, my Lords, it is proper to observe, that the managers for the bill, when they were to apply the circumstances of Jones and Illington in the letters to the bishop's case, they built the whole of their arguments upon the date of those letters; but when they saw that the bishop had fully proved that it was impossible he could dictate them at that time, why then truly they vary their charge, and say, that it was not his dictating the letters at that time, but his dictating the letters of that date that they contended for; and they tax the bishop with a partial and fallacious defence, for applying it to the time, and not to the fact. But, I think, with great submission, that the bishop has made a very just defence. I think he could not have made a better; and under the disadvantage of proving a negative, I think it was almost impossible he should have made one so good. For your lordships well remember, he was charged as the author of the letters signed Jones and Illington, because he was under the circumstances of Jones and Illington at the time of the date of those letters: But the bishop hath fully proved, that he could not be the author of them at that time; and if he were not at that time, he could not be so at any other time; for take away the date of those letters, and the relation between Jones and Illington, and the bishop, you must of course take away likewise. But then as your lordships are yet at a loss when, or by whom, these letters were either dictated or wrote, shall the tallying of a few circumstances in them with the bishop's case, supposing them to be wrote about the time of their date, make him guilty of high-treason; especially when his counsel have shewed us, from the letters themselves, as many instances wherein they differed? Must Mrs. Jones and the bishop's lady signify the same person, because they died about the same time? Or must Mrs. Jones and Mrs. Illington signify the same person, because by a letter wrote, no one knows by whom, or when, mention is made of the death of one Mrs. Jones, and another letter condoles the death of one Mrs. Illington? Or is the bishop guilty of high-treason, because he is supposed to be meant by Jones and Illington; when yet, through the whole correspondence, there is no treason committed either by Jones or Illington? But admitting that all the circumstances that have been produced against the bishop, hit him so exactly, that it is morally impossible they could mean any body else; yet still, my Lords, what has the bishop to do with it? Might he not be thus described, and thus spoke of, and yet know nothing at all of the matter? And if he is thus to suffer for what another man may have said of him, I am sure he is the first, and I hope he will be the last that ever will be distinguished in so extraordinary a manner. The sum then of all the circumstances that have been offered as evidence against the bishop, amounts to this; here have been a parcel of cant names produced and made use of against him, which, for ought appears, he never heard of. Here have been letters produced, and read against him, wrote in cyphers, and of a hand-writing not pretended to be the bishop's, and of which your lordships have as yet had no manner of certainty. A construction hath been put upon these letters, which, in several circumstances, hit the bishop, and, in several other, miss him; but amongst all these circumstances, there is not the least hint of any word said, or act done by him, relating to this conspiracy, from first to last; nor doth it appear, that he was ever privy to it, or so much as heard of it, till it was known to all the world. And yet, my lords, these, and such as these, are the circumstances whereby the bishop is to be guessed into high-treason; but I hope your lordships will be very cautious how you make precedents of such wretched guesswork. The celebrated letter of Dubois, now before you, is a notable proof of the necessity of such caution; for we see the grand promoters of this bill cannot agree in their construction, or they have at least changed their opinions about that famous letter.

The uncertainty of this way of guessing, puts me in mind of some remarkable circumstances relating to the renowned Mr. Neynoe, which I had like to have forgotten, and which, though they seem to be under the misfortune of being slighted here, do yet, in the Report of the committee of the House of Commons, make a very considerable figure. Those circumstances of Neynoe in that Report, appear to be not only the foundation of the charge against Kelly and the bishop, but even the foundation of the plot itself; and the art and management with which they are there dressed up, do well deserve your lordships' attention. It seems, my Lords, this worthy man had been examined four several times; his examinations were taken in writing, and contained an historical account of the carrying on of this conspiracy. The learned committee, at the same time that they would represent him as a vile and infamous fellow, and would be thought to look upon his examinations as insufficient, do yet open their scene with this very account, and build entirely upon it. But would any one believe that Neynoe was never sworn to, or so much as signed any one of these examinations? Can any body think that he was not required to do one or both? Does not every body know, that they would otherwise be of no use? May we not therefore reasonably suppose, that he refused to do either the one or the other? And can any reason be given for such refusal, but that they were not true?

My Lords, The committee were well aware, that great objections would be made to this kind of evidence, and therefore they have added to it some circumstantial hearsays, which they call the corroborating and concurrent proofs of Neynoe's testimony. But pray, my Lords, what are these corroborating and concurrent proofs? Why, they are of this kind, one man heard another man say, that a third man was concerned in this conspiracy. Behold then the sum of the argument, Neynoe's examination is admitted of itself to signify nothing; the same likewise cannot be denied of Pancier's hearsay: But however both these nothings make up something to prove the plot, because they are the corroborating and concurrent proofs of each other. And thus the learned committee have so contrived it, that they have made these examinations of Neynoe to be of more use, and to serve their purpose better, than if Neynoe himself had been now living, and produced before your lordships; and therefore it looks as if it were prophetically known, that the man intended to hurl himself out of the world with a winding sheet. But however that be, it is matter of surprize, that these examinations, which the committee treated so respectfully, should now by the counsel be so slighted, that they have scarce mentioned them, but as if they were ashamed of them; and yet they are as good evidence as any that have been offered in favour of the bill now before your lordships.

But, my Lords, in the course of this debate, it hath been warmly urged, that though there be not legal evidence against the bishop, yet that all the circumstances that have been offered against him are sufficient to convince any man in his private judgment that the bishop is guilty. Nay, it hath been said, that these circumstances put together, are stronger and more convincing, than any positive evidence whatsoever; and therefore that no one can doubt of the bishop's guilt, though some, out of compassion or good nature, might be induced to vote in his favour. How strong and convincing, or rather how impertinent and trifling these circumstances are, I have already observed to your lordships; and I must say, it was not without a good deal of concern, that I heard that urged as the result of judgment, which could have no other foundation than in opinion only. But, my Lords, this is not the first instance wherein I have observed judgment and opinion to be confounded and mistaken the one for the other, and that too in a very gross and dangerous manner. My Lords, men's opinions, generally speaking, are nothing else but their fancies or imaginations, and are usually grounded upon personal pique, or party prejudice. These are weak and slender foundations, and have nothing to do, and I hope in England never will have any thing to do, where a man's life, his liberty, or his property is concerned. But, my Lords, a man forms his judgment according to the evidence that is offered him, that alone is his rule; and as the perspicuity or uncertainty of that appears, justice requires a determination accordingly. The compliment therefore upon the noble lords that have appeared against this bill (if it was intended as a compliment) carries a very severe sting in the tail of it, as it supposes those noble lords to be possibly capable of giving an unjust judgment. My Lords, the earl of Strafford lost his head for accumulative treason. A great many facts were laid to his charge, and though it was agreed on all hands, that not one of them singly amounted to treason, yet it was insisted on that all of them put together shewed an intention in him to subvert the government, and therefore that he was a traitor. The torrent of those times taught men to argue, that though the charge against the earl did not contain legal treason, yet it was morally impossible that he could commit the crimes contained in that charge, and not intend the destruction of the state; that the facts by him done, shewed him more a traitor than any positive act of treason could do; and that if men were satisfied in their private opinions that the earl was, in the main, guilty of treason, he ought to suffer accordingly. My Lords, this was the reasoning of those days; a reasoning which I hope your lordships will neither imitate nor encourage, because it was the foundation of those proceedings against that great earl, which were soon after in full Parliament so justly branded; and if future Parliaments should not be able to discover any difference between the inconveniencies arising from accumulative evidence and accumulative treason, may they not with great justice censure us by condemning the one equally with the other? That which was then called accumulative treason, was afterwards adjudged to be no treason, and I hope your lordships will yet adjudge this accumulative evidence to be no evidence. I am sure you will not punish a man in the severest manner, until you have had some reason given you, why you should punish him at all. You will not first believe a man a criminal without proof, and then admit a criminal construction to be forced upon every innocent action, only to support such belief. You will not adjudge a man guilty of the highest crime against the law, when his prosecutors themselves own, they cannot make good any one branch of their charge according to law.

The bishop's case must be owned to be very hard, and the evidence against him very weak, when his own letter to his son, and the letter to Dubois, are put to the torture to help out the charge against him. As for the letter to Dubois, it is amazing to consider that such pains should be taken from a similitude of a broken impression on wax with a whole one, and a similitude of two little E's, to fix it upon the bishop; which, when fixed, can serve no purpose at all against him; for that letter hath neither date, subscription, cypher, nor cant name in it; and for ought appears may have been wrote before the man was born whom they would mean by Johnson, therein named. Nothing treasonable is pretended to be guessed out of it, nor, for ought appears, was it ever seen by any one besides the writer; and yet because it is there said that the writer wrote something (no one knows what, or when, or to whom) in the hand of one Mr. Johnson, your lordships are persuaded to infer, in opposition to the positive evidence of all the bishop's family, that Kelly was an intimate of the bishop's, and employed to write his treasons. The use that is made of the bishop's letter taken from his servant, is still more extraordinary. I have indeed too often observed doubtful actions, by the help of bold innuendoes, construed criminally; but to give that in evidence which was neither said nor done, to innuendo silence itself into high-treason, is entirely new, and the learned counsel deserve the glory of the discovery. But the bishop's case will still appear the harder, when it is considered, that such stress hath been laid upon such remote and distant circumstances in favour of this Bill, and at the same time your lordships were not pleased to receive on the bishop's behalf legal evidence, real evidence, and such as in natural justice and equity ought to have been admitted.

The bill that hath lately passed both Houses against Kelly, doth not hinder him from being still a witness, for it hath not yet had the royal assent, and perhaps never may; but if it had, there is, as I apprehend, nothing in that bill, that will take away his testimony in any court in the kingdom. But be that as it will, I must beg leave to insist that he is at present a good witness, and as every body is satisfied that it was in his power to clear up this whole affair, who knows what the awe of an oath might have extorted from him? He appears to be a man under the influence of conscience, for his refusing the oaths to the government, and thereby suffering his subsistence to be taken from him, is a manifest proof of it. If therefore your lordships had permitted Kelly to be produced when the bishop called for him, something probably might have been discovered to have ascertained either the bishop's guilt or his innocence. But as his case now stands, the evidence of his guilt appears very dark, and for ought I can observe, is like to continue so.

My Lords; I have now done: and if upon this occasion, I have tired your patience, or discovered a warmth unbecoming me, your lordships will impute it to the concern I am under, lest, if this Bill should pass, it should become a dangerous precedent for after ages. My zeal, as an Englishman, for the good of my country, obliges me to set my face against oppression in every shape; and wherever I think I meet with it (it matters not whether one man or five hundred be the oppressors) I shall be sure to oppose it with all my might: For vain will be the boast of the excellency of our constitution; in vain shall we talk of our liberty and property secured to us by laws, if a precedent shall be established to strip us of both, where both law and evidence are confessedly wanting.

My Lords; Upon the whole matter, I take this Bill to be derogatory to the dignity of the Parliament in general, to the dignity of this House in particular: I take the Pains and Penalties in it to be much greater, or much less than the bishop deserves; I take every individual branch of the charge against him to be unsupported by any evidence whatsoever. I think there are no grounds for any private opinion of the bishop's guilt, but what arises from private prejudice only; I think private prejudice has nothing to do with judicial proceedings, I am therefore for throwing out this Bill.

Manifesto by Prince Charles Stuart, Paris, 16 May 1745

A full Collection of all the Proclamations and Orders Published by the Authority of Charles Prince of Wales, Regent of Scotland, England, France and Ireland, and Dominions thereunto belonging, Since His Arrival in Edinburgh the 17th Day of September, till the 15th of October, 1745 (n.p., 1745), pt. 1, 8-13.

Prince Charles Edward Stuart (1720-88), known as the Young Pretender or Bonnie Prince Charlie, was the grandson of James II and elder son of James Stuart ("James III"), the Old Pretender. After leading an unsuccessful French invasion of England in 1744, he landed in the Hebrides in 1745 and raised his father's standard in Scotland. The rebellion ended the following year when Charles was defeated by the duke of Cumberland at Culloden Moor; he escaped to Brittany several months later, but was expelled from France in 1748.

Charles P. R.

By Virtue and Authority of the above Commission of Regency, granted unto us by the King our Royal Father; we are now come to execute his Majesty's Will and Pleasure, by setting up his Royal Standard, and asserting his undoubted Right to the Throne of his Ancestors.

We do therefore, in his Majesty's Name, and pursuant to the Tenor of his several Declarations, hereby grant a free, full, and general Pardon for all Treasons, Rebellions, and Offences whatsoever, committed at any Time before the Publication hereof, against our Royal Grandfather, his present Majesty, and ourselves. To the Benefit of this Pardon, we shall deem justly entitled all such of his Majesty's Subjects, as shall testify their Willingness to accept of it, either by joining our Forces with all convenient Diligence, by setting up his Royal Standard in other Places, by repairing for our Service to any Place where it shall be so set up; or, at least, by openly renouncing all pretended Allegiance to the Usurper, and all Obedience to his Orders; or to those of any Person or Persons commissioned, or employed by him, or acting avowedly for him.

As for those who shall appear more signally zealous for the Recovery of his Majesty's just Rights, and the Prosperity of their Country, We shall take effectual Care to have them rewarded according to their respective Degrees and Merits: And we particularly promise as aforesaid, a full, free, and general Pardon to all Officers, Soldiers, and Sailors, now engaged in the Service of the Usurper; provided, That upon the Publication hereof, and before they engage in any Fight or Battle against his Majesty's Forces, they quit the said unjust and unwarrantable Service, and return to their Duty, since they cannot but be sensible, that no Engagements, entred into with a foreign Usurper, can dispense with the Allegiance they owe to their natural Sovereign. And as a further Encouragement to them to comply with their Duty, and our Commands; we promise to every such Officer the same, or a higher Post in our Service than that which at present he enjoys, with full Payment of whatever Arrears may be due to him at the Time of his declaring for us; and to every Soldier, Trooper, and Dragoon, who shall join us, as well as to every Seaman and Mariner of the Fleet, who shall declare for, and serve us, all their Arrears, and a whole Year's Pay to be given to each of them as a Gratuity, as soon as ever the Kingdoms shall be in a State of Tranquillity.

We do hereby further promise and declare, in his Majesty's Name, and by Virtue of the above said Commission; That as soon as ever that happy State is obtained, he will, by and with the Advice of a free Parliament, wherein no Corruption, nor undue Influence whatsoever shall be used to byass the Votes of the Electors, or Elected; settle, confirm, and secure all the Rights, Ecclesiastical and Civil, of each of his respective Kingdoms; his Majesty being fully resolved to maintain the Church of England, as by Law established, and likewise the Protestant Churches of Scotland and Ireland, conformable to the Laws of each respective Kingdom; together with a Toleration to all Protestant Dissenters; he being utterly averse to all Persecution and Oppression whatsoever, particularly on Account of Conscience and Religion. And we ourselves being perfectly convinced of the Reasonableness and Equity of the same Principles; do, in consequence hereof, further promise and declare, That all his Majesty's Subjects, shall be by him and us maintained in the full Enjoyment and Possession of all their Rights, Privileges, and Immunities, and especially of all Churches, Universities, Colleges and Schools, conformable to the Laws of the Land, which shall ever be the unalterable Rule of his Majesty's Government, and our own Actions.

And, That this our Undertaking may be accompanied with as little present Inconveniency as possible to the King's Subjects; we do hereby authorise and require all Civil Officers and Magistrates now in Place and Office, to continue, till further Orders, to execute their respective Employments in our Name, and by our Authority, as far as may be requisite for the Maintenance of common Justice, Order and Quiet. Willing and requiring them, at the same Time, to give strict Obedience to such Orders and Directions, as may, from Time to Time, be issued out by us, or those who shall be vested with any Share of our Authority and Power.

We also command and require all Officers of the Revenue, Customs and Excise, all Tax-gatherers, of what Denomination soever; and all others who may have any Part of the Publick Money in their Hands, to deliver it immediately to some principal Commander authorised by us, and take his Receipt for the same, which shall be to them a sufficient Discharge; and in case of Refusal, we authorise and charge all such our Commanders, to exact the same for our Use, and to be accountable for it to us, or our Officers for that Purpose appointed.

And having thus sincerely, and in the Presence of Almighty God, declared the true Sentiments and Intentions of the King our Royal Father, as well as our own, in this Expedition, we do hereby require and Command all his loving Subjects to be assisting to us in the Recovery of his just Rights, and of their own Liberties: And that all such, from the Age of Sixteen to Sixty, do forthwith repair to his Majesty's Royal Standard, or join themselves to such as shall first appear in their respective Shires for his Service: And also, to seize the Horses and Arms of all suspected Persons, and all Ammunition, Forage, and whatever else may be necessary for the Use of our Forces.

Lastly, We do hereby require all Mayors, Sheriffs, and other Magistrates, of what Denomination soever, their respective Deputies, and all others to whom it may belong, to publish this our Declaration at the Market Crosses of their respective Cities, Towns and Boroughs, and there to proclaim his Majesty, under the Penalty of being proceeded against according to Law, for the Neglect of so necessary and important a Duty: For as we have hereby graciously and sincerely offered a free and general Pardon for all that is past; so we, at the same Time, seriously warn all his Majesty's Subjects, That we shall leave to the Rigour of the Law all those who shall from henceforth oppose us, or wilfully and deliberately do or concur in any Act or Acts Civil or Military, to the Lett or Detriment of us, our Cause or Title, or to the Destruction, Prejudice, or Annoyance of those, who shall, according to their Duty and our Intentions thus publickly signified, declare and act for us.

Given at Paris, the 16th May, 1745.

C. P. R.

Declaration by Prince Charles Stuart, Scotland, 10 October 1745

A full Collection of all the Proclamations and Orders Published by the Authority of Charles Princes of Wales, Regent of Scotland, England, France and Ireland, and Dominions thereunto belonging, Since His Arrival in Edinburgh the 17th Day of September, till the 15th of October, 1745 (n.p., 1745), pt. 1, 27-33.

Charles, Prince of Wales, etc. Regent of the Kingdoms of England, Scotland, France and Ireland, and the Dominions thereunto belonging: Unto all his Majesty's Subjects, of what Degree soever, greeting.

Charles P. R.

As soon as we, conducted by the Providence of God, arrived in Scotland, and were joined by a Handful of our Royal Father's faithful Subjects, our first Care was, to make publick his most gracious Declaration; and in consequence of the large Powers by him vested in us, in Quality of Regent, we also emitted our own Manifesto, explaining and enlarging the Promises formerly made, according as we came to be better acquainted with the Inclinations of the People of Scotland. Now that it has pleased God so far to smile on our Undertaking, as to make us Master of the ancient Kingdom of Scotland, we judged it proper, in this publick Manner, to make manifest what ought to fill the Hearts of all his Majesty's Subjects, of what Nation or Province soever, with Comfort and Satisfaction.

We therefore hereby, in his Majesty's Name, declare, That his sole Intention is to re-instate all his Subjects in the full Enjoyment of their Religion, Laws, and Liberties; and that our present Attempt is not undertaken, in order to enslave a free People, but to redress and remove the Encroachments made upon them; not to impose upon any a Religion which they dislike, but to secure them all in the

Enjoyment of those which are respectively at present established among them, either in England, Scotland or Ireland; and if it shall be deemed proper that any further Security be given to the established Church or Clergy, we hereby promise, in his Name, That he shall pass any Law that his Parliament shall judge necessary for that Purpose.

In Consequence of the Rectitude of our Royal Father's Intentions, we must further declare his Sentiments with Regard to the National Debt: That it has been contracted under an unlawful Government, no Body can disown, no more than that it is now a most heavy Load upon the Nation; yet, in regard that it is for the greatest Part due to those very Subjects whom he promises to protect, cherish and defend, he is resolved to take the Advice of his Parliament concerning it, in which he thinks he acts the Part of a just Prince, who makes the Good of his People the sole Rule of his Actions.

Furthermore, we here in his Name declare, That the same Rule laid down for the Funds, shall be followed with respect to every Law or Act of Parliment since the Revolution; and, in so far as, in a free and legal Parliament, they shall be approved, he will confirm them. With respect to the pretended Union of the two Nations, the King cannot possibly ratify it, since he has had repeated Remonstrances against it from each Kingdom; and since it is incontestable, that the principal Point then in View, was the Exclusion of the Royal Family from their undoubted Right to the Crown, for which Purpose the grossest Corruptions were openly used to bring it about: But whatever may be hereafter devised for the joint Benefit of both Nations, the King will most readily comply with the Request of his Parliaments to establish.

And now that we have, in His Majesty's Name, given you the most ample Security for your Religion, Properties and Laws, that the Power of a British Sovereign can grant; we hereby for ourselves, as Heir apparent to the Crown, ratify and confirm the same in our own Name, before Almighty God, upon the Faith of a Christian, and the Honour of a Prince.

Let me now expostulate this weighty Matter with you, my Father's Subjects, and let me not omit this first publick Opportunity of awakening your Understandings, and of dispelling that Cloud, which the assiduous Pens of ill designing Men have all along, but chiefly now, been endeavouring to cast on the Truth. Do not the Pulpits and Congregations of the Clergy, as well as your weekly Papers, ring with the dreadful Threats of Popery, Slavery, Tyranny and arbitrary Power, which are now ready to be imposed upon you, by the formidable Powers of France and Spain? Is not my Royal Father represented as a Blood-thirsty Tyrant, breathing out nothing but Destruction to all those who will not immediately embrace an odious Religion? Or, have I myself been better used? But listen only to the naked Truth.

I, with my own Money, hired a small Vessel, ill provided with Money, Arms or Friends; I arrived in Scotland, attended by seven Persons; I publish the King my Father's Declaration, and proclaim his Title, with Pardon in one Hand, and in the other Liberty of Conscience, and the most solemn Promises to grant whatever a free Parliament shall propose for the Happiness of a People. I have, I confess, the greatest Reason to adore the Goodness of Almighty God, who has, in so remarkable a Manner, protected me and my small Army through the many Dangers to which we were at first exposed, and who has led me in the Way to Victory, and to the Capital of this ancient Kingdom, amidst the Acclamations of the King my Father's Subjects: Why then is so much Pains taken to spirit up the Minds of the People against this my Undertaking?

The Reason is obvious, it is, lest the real Sense of the Nation's present Sufferings should blot out the Remembrance of past Misfortunes, and of the Outcries formerly raised against the Royal Family. Whatever Miscarriages might have given Occasion to them, they have been more than atoned for since; and the Nation has now an Opportunity of being secured against the like for the Future.

That Our Family has suffered Exile during these Fifty seven Years, every Body knows. Has the Nation, during that Period of Time, been the more happy and flourishing for it? Have you found Reason to love and cherish your Governors, as the Fathers of the People of Great Britain and Ireland? Has a Family, upon whom a Faction unlawfully bestowed the Diadem of a rightful Prince, retained a due Sense of so great a Trust and Favour? Have you found more Humanity and Condescension in those who were not born to a Crown, than in my Royal Fore-fathers? Have their Ears been open to the Cries of the People? Have they, or do they consider only the Interest of these Nations? Have you reaped any other Benefit from them, than an immense Load of Debts? If I am answered in the Affirmative, Why has their Government been so often railed at in all your publick Assemblies? Why has the Nation been so long crying out in vain for Redress against the Abuse of Parliaments, upon Account of their long Duration, the Multitude of Place-men, which occasions their Venality, the Introduction of penal Laws, and in general, against the miserable Situation of the Kingdom at Home and Abroad? All these, and many more Inconveniencies must now be removed, unless the People of Great Britain be already so far corrupted, that they will not accept of Freedom when offered to them; seeing the King, on his Restoration, will refuse nothing that a free Parliament can ask, for the Security of the Religion, Laws and Liberty of his People.

The Fears of the Nation from the Powers of France and Spain, appear still more vain and groundless: My Expedition was undertaken unsupported by either: but indeed, when I see a foreign Force brought by my Enemies against me, and when I hear of Dutch, Danes, Hessians, and Swiss, the Elector of Hanover's Allies, being called over to protect his Government against the King's Subjects, is it not high Time for the King my Father, to accept also of the Assistance of those who are able, and who have engaged to support him? But will the World, or any one Man of Sense in it, infer from thence, that he inclines to be a tributary Prince, rather than an independent Monarch? Who has the better Chance to be independent on Foreign Powers? He, who with the Aid of his own Subjects, can wrest the Government out of the Hands of an Intruder: Or he, who cannot without Assistance from abroad, support his Government, tho' established by all the Civil Power, and secured by a strong Military Force, against the undisciplined Part of those he has ruled over for so many Years? Let him, if he pleases, try the Experiment, let him send off his foreign Hirelings, and put the whole upon the Issue of a Battle; I will trust only to the King my Father's Subjects, who were or shall be engaged in mine and their Country's Cause: But, notwithstanding all the Opposition he can make, I still trust in the Justice of my Cause, the Valour of my Troops, and the Assistance of the Almighty, to bring my Enterprize to a glorious Issue.

It is now Time to conclude, and I shall do it with this Reflection. Civil Wars are ever attended with Rancour and ill Will, which Party-rage never fails to produce in the Minds of those, whom different Interests, Principles or Views set in Opposition to one another; I therefore earnestly require it of my Friends to give as little Loose as possible to such Passions; this will prove the most effectual Means to prevent the same in the Enemies of our Royal Cause. And this my Declaration will vindicate to all Posterity the Nobleness of my Undertaking, and the Generosity of my Intentions.

Given at our Palace of Holy-rood-house the tenth Day of October, One thousand seven hundred and forty five.

By His Highness's Command.

C. P. R.
J. Mureay

THE CHURCH AND DISSENT

Act establishing Queen Anne's Bounty, 1703

2 & 3 Anne, c. 11   *Statutes at Large*, IV, 151-52.

This act distributed the revenues of the first fruits and tenths of the Church of England to poorer Anglican clergymen for their maintenance.

Whereas at a Parliment holden in the six and twentieth Year of the Reign of King Henry the Eighth, the First Fruits, Revenues and Profits for one Year, upon every Nomination or Appointment to any Dignity, Benefice, Office or Promotion Spiritual, within this Realm, or elsewhere within the said King's Dominions, and also a perpetual yearly Rent or Pension, amounting to the Value of the tenth Part of all the Revenues and Profits belonging to any Dignity, Benefice, or Promotion Spiritual whatsoever, within any Diocese of this Realm, or in Wales, were granted to the said King Henry, the Eighth, his Heirs and Successors; and divers other Statutes have since been made touching the First Fruits and annual Tenths of the Clergy, and the ordering thereof: And whereas a sufficient settled Provision for the Clergy, in many Parts of this Realm, hath never yet been made, by reason whereof divers mean and stipendiary Preachers are in many Places entertained to serve the Cures, and officiate there; who depending for their necessary Maintenance upon the Good-will and Liking of their Hearers, have been, and are thereby under Temptation of too much complying and suiting their Doctrines and Teaching to the Humours rather than the Good of their Hearers, which hath been a great Occasion of Faction and Schism, and Contempt of the Ministry: And forasmuch as your Majesty, taking into your princely and serious Consideration the mean and insufficient Maintenance belonging to the Clergy in divers Parts of this your Kingdom, has been most graciously pleased, out of your most religious and tender Concern for the Church of England (whereof your Majesty is the only supream Head on Earth) and for the poor Clergy thereof, not only to remit the Arrears of your Tenths due from your poor Clergy, but also to declare unto your most dutiful and loyal Commons your royal Pleasure and pious Desire, that the whole Revenue arising from the First Fruits and Tenths of the Clergy might be settled for a perpetual Augmentation of the Maintenance of the said Clergy, in Places where the same is not already sufficiently provided for: We your Majesty's most dutiful and loyal subjects, the Commons of England, in Parliament assembled, to the End that your Majesty's most gracious Intentions may be made effectual, and that the Church may receive so great and lasting an Advantage from your Majesty's parting with so great a Branch of your Revenue, towards the better Provision for the Clergy not sufficiently provided for; and to the Intent your Majesty's singular Zeal for the Support of the Clergy, and the Honour, Interest, and future Security of the Church, as by Law established, may be perpetuated to all Ages, do most humbly beseech your Majesty that it may be enacted; and be it enacted by the Queen's most Excellent Majesty, by and with the Advice and Consent of the Lords Spiritual and Temporal and Commons, in this present Parliament assembled, and by the Authority of the same, That it shall and may be lawful for the Queen's most Excellent Majesty, by her Letters Patents under the Great Seal of England, to incorporate such Persons as her Majesty shall therein nominate or appoint, to be one Body Politick and Corporate, to have a common Seal, and perpetual Succession; and also at her Majesty's Will and Pleasure, by the same, or any other Letters Patents, to grant, limit, or settle, to or upon the said Corporation, and their Successors for ever, all the Revenue of First Fruits, and yearly perpetual Tenths of all Dignities, Offices, Benefices, and Promotions Spiritual whatsoever, to be applied and disposed of, to and for the Augmentation of the Maintenance of such Parsons, Vicars, Curates, and Ministers, officiating in any Church or Chapel within the Kingdom of England, Dominion of Wales, and Town of Berwick upon Tweed, where the Liturgy and Rites of the Church of England, as now by Law established, are or shall be used and observed, with such lawful Powers, Authorities, Directions, Limitations and Appointments, and under such Rules and Restrictions, and in such Manner and Form, as shall be therein expressed; the Statute made in the first Year of her said Majesty's Reign, intituled, *An Act for the better Support of her Majesty's Houshold, and of the Honour and Dignity of the Crown* or any other Law to the contrary in any wise notwithstanding.

II.   Provided always, and it is hereby declared, That all and every the Statutes and Provisions, touching or concerning the ordering, levying, and true answering and Payment, or Qualification of the said First Fruits and Tenths, or touching the Charge, Discharge, or Alteration of them, or any of them, or any Matter or Thing relating thereunto, which were in Force at the Time of making this Act, shall be, remain and continue in their full Force and Effect, and be observed and put in due Execution according to the Tenors and Purports of the same, and every of them, for such Intents and Purposes nevertheless, as shall be contained or directed in or by the said Letters Patents.

III.   Provided also, That this Act, or any thing therein contained, shall not extend to avoid, or any way to impeach or affect any Grant, Exchange, Alienation, or Incumbrance, at any Time heretofore made, of or upon the said Revenues of First Fruits and Tenths, or any Part thereof; but that the same shall, during the Continuance of such Grant, Exchange, Alienation, or Incumbrance respectively, be and remain of and in such Force and Virtue, and no other, to all Intents and Purposes, as if this Act had not been made.

IV.   And for the Encouragement of such well-disposed Persons as shall, by her Majesty's Royal Example, be moved to continue to so pious and charitable a Purpose, and that such their Charity may be rightly applied; Be it enacted by the Authority aforesaid, That all and every Person and Persons, having in his or their own Right any Estate or Interest in Possession, Reversion, or Contingency, of or in any Lands, Tenements or Hereditaments, or any Property of or in any Goods or

Chattels, shall have full Power, Licence and Authority, at his, her and their Will and Pleasure, by Deed inrolled, in such Manner, and within such Time, as is directed by the Statute made in the twenty-seventh Year of the Reign of King Henry the Eighth, for Inrolment of Bargains and Sales, or by his, her, or their last Will or Testament in writing, duly executed according to Law, to give and grant to, and vest in the said Corporation, and their Successors, all such his, her or their Estate, Interest or Property in such Lands, Tenements and Hereditaments, Goods and Chattels, or any Part or Parts thereof, for and towards the Augmentation of the Maintenance of such Ministers as aforesaid, officiating in such Churches or Chapel, where the Liturgy and Rites of the said Church are or shall be so used or observed as aforesaid, and having no settled competent Provision belonging to the same, and to be for that Purpose applied according to the Will of the said Benefactor, in and by such Deed inrolled, or by such Will or Testament executed as aforesaid, expressed: And in Default of such Direction, Limitation or Appointment, in such Manner as by her Majesty's Letters Patents shall be directed or appointed as aforesaid. And such Corporation, and their Successors, shall have full Capacity and Ability to purchase, receive, take, hold and enjoy, for the Purposes aforesaid, as well from such Persons as shall be so charitably disposed to give the same, as from all other Persons as shall be willing to sell or aliene to the said Corporation any Manors, Lands, Tenements, Goods or Chattels, without any Licence or Writ of *Ad quod Damnum;* the Statute of Mortmain, or any other Statute or Law to the contrary notwithstanding.

V.   Provided always, That this Act or any thing therein contained shall not extend to enable any Person or Persons, being within Age, or of *Non sane* Memory, or Women Covert, without their Husbands, to make any such Gift, Grant or Alienation; any thing in this Act contained to the contrary in any wise notwithstanding.

VI.   And whereas four Bonds for four half yearly Payments of the First Fruits, as the same are rated, and also a fifth Bond for a further Value or Payment, in respect of the same First Fruits, have been required and taken from the Clergy, to their great and unnecessary Burden and Grievance: For Remedy thereof be it enacted and declared by the Authority aforesaid, That from and after the twenty-fifth Day of March in the Year of our Lord one thousand seven hundred and four, one Bond only shall in such Case be given or required for the four Payments of the said First Fruits: Which said First Fruits, as well as the Tenths payable by the Clergy, shall hereafter be answered and paid by them according to such Rates and Proportions only as the same have heretofore been usually rated and paid: And no such fifth Bond already given shall, from and after the said twenty-fifth Day of March in the Year one thousand seven hundred and four, be sued or recovered.

Occasional Conformity Act, 1711

10 Anne, c. 6   *Statutes of the Realm*, IX, pt. 2, 551-53.

This act strengthened penalties on Nonconformists by prohibiting officeholders from only "occasionally conforming" to the rites of the Church of England. It was repealed in 1719.

Whereas an Act was made in the Thirteenth Year of the Reign of [the late] King Charles the Second intituled An Act for the well governing and regulating of Corporations and another Act was made in the Five and twentieth Year of the Reign of the said late King Charles the Second intituled An Act for the preventing Dangers which may happen from Popish Recusants both which Acts were made for the Security of the Church of England as by Law established Now for the better securing the said Church and quieting the Minds of Her Majesties Protestant Subjects dissenting from the Church of England and rendring them secure in the Exercise of their religious Worship as also for the further strengthning the Provision already made for the Security of the Succession to the Crown in the House of Hanover Be it enacted by the Queens most Excellent Majesty by and with the Advice and Consent of the Lords Spiritual and Temporal and Commons in Parliament assembled and by the Authority of the same That if any Person or Persons after the Five and twentieth Day of March which shall be in the Year of our Lord One thousand seven hundred and twelve either Peers or Commoners who have or shall have any Office or Offices Civil or Military or receive any Pay Salary Fee or Wages by reason of any Patent or Grant from or under Her Majesty or any of Her Majesties Predecessors or of Her Heirs or Successors or shall have any Command or Place of Trust from or under Her Majesty Her Heirs or Successors or from any of Her Majesties Predecessors or by Her or Their Authority or by Authority derived from Her or Them within that Part of Great Britain called England the Dominion of Wales or Town of Berwick upon Tweed or in the Navy or in the several Islands of Jersey or Guernsey or shall be admitted into any Service or Employment in the Household or Family of Her Majesty Her Heirs or Successors or if any Mayor Alderman Recorded Bayliff Town Clerk Common Council Man or other Person bearing any Office of Magistracy or Place or Trust or other Imployment relating to or concerning the Government of any the respective Cities Corporations Boroughs Cinque-Ports and their Members or other Port Towns within that Part of Great Britain called England the Dominion of Wales Town of Berwick or either of the Isles aforesaid who by the said recited Acts or either of them were or are obliged to receive the Sacrament of the Lords Supper according to the Rites and Usage of the Church of England as aforesaid shall at any Time after their Admission into their respective Offices or Employments or after having such Patent or Grant Command or Place of Trust as aforesaid during his or their Continuance in such Office or Offices Employment or Employments or having such Patent or

Grant Command or Place of Trust or any Profit or Advantage from the same knowingly or willingly resort to or be present at any Conventicle Assembly or Meeting within England Wales Berwick upon Tweed or the Isles aforesaid for the Exercise of Religion in other Manner than according to the Liturgy and Practice of the Church of England in any Place within that Part of Great Britain called England Dominion of Wales and Town of Berwick upon Tweed or the Isles aforesaid at which Conventicle Assembly or Meeting there shall be Ten Persons or more assembled together over and besides those of the same Houshold if it be in any House where there is a Family inhabiting or if it be in an House or Place where there is no Family inhabiting then where any such Ten Persons are so assembled as aforesaid or shall knowingly and willingly be present at any such Meeting in such House or Place as aforesaid although the Liturgy be there used where Her Majesty (whom God long preserve) and the Princess Sophia or such others as shall from time to time be lawfully appointed to be prayed for shall not there be prayed for in express Words according to the Liturgy of the Church of England except where such particular Offices of the Liturgy are used wherein there are no express Directions to pray for Her Majesty and the Royal Family [shall forfeit Forty Pounds to be recovered by him or them that shall sue for the same by any Action of Debt Bill Plaint or Information in any of Her Majesties Courts at Westminster wherein no Essoign Protection or Wager of Law shall be allowed or any more than One Imparlance

And be it further enacted That every Person convicted in any Action to be brought as aforesaid or] upon any Information Presentment or Indictment in any of Her Majesties Courts at Westminster or at the Assizes shall be disabled from thenceforth to hold such Office or Offices Employment or Employments or to receive any Profit or Advantage by reason of them or of any Grant as aforesaid and shall be adjudged incapable to bear any Office or Employment whatsoever within that Part of Great Britain called England the Dominion of Wales or the Town of Berwick upon Tweed or the Isles of Jersey or Guernsey.

Provided always and be it further enacted by the Authority aforesaid That if any Person or Persons who shall have been convicted as aforesaid and thereby made incapable to hold any Office or Employment or to receive any Profit or Advantage by reason of them or of any Grant as aforesaid shall after such Conviction conform to the Church of England for the Space of One Year without having been present at any Conventicle Assembly or Meeting as aforesaid and receive the Sacrament of the Lords Supper according to the Rites and Usage of the Church of England at least Three Times in the Year every such Person or Persons shall be capable of the Grant of any the Offices or Employments aforesaid

Provided also and be it further enacted That every such Person so convicted and afterwards conforming in Manner as aforesaid shall at the next Term after his Admission into any such Office or Employment make Oath in Writing in some one of Her Majesties Courts at Westminster in publick and open Court or at the next Quarter Sessions for that County or Place where he shall reside between the House of Nine and Twelve in the Forenoon that he hath conformed to the Church of England for the Space of One Year before such his Admission without having been present at any Conventicle Assembly or Meeting as aforesaid and that he hath received the Sacrament of the Lords Supper at least Three Times in the Year which Oath shall be there enrolled and kept upon Record

Provided That no Person shall suffer any Punishment for any Offence committed against this Act unless Oath be made of such Offence before some Judge or Justice of the Peace (who is hereby impowered and required to take the said Oath) within Ten Days after the said Offence committed and unless the said Offender be prosecuted for the same within Three Months after the said Offence committed nor shall any Person be convicted for any such Offence unless upon the Oaths of Two credible Witnesses at the least.

Provided always That this Act or any thing therein contained or any Offence against the same shall not extend or be judged to take away or make void any Office of Inheritance nevertheless so as such Person having or enjoying any such Office of Inheritance do or shall substitute and appoint his sufficient Deputy (which such Officer is hereby impowered from time to time to make or change any former Law or Usage to the contrary notwithstanding) to exercise the said Office until such Time as the Person having such Office shall conform as aforesaid

And it is hereby further enacted and declared by the Authority aforesaid That the Toleration granted to Protestant Dissenters by the Act made in the First Year of the Reign of King William and Queen Mary intituled An Act for exempting Their Majesties Protestant Subjects dissenting from the Church of England from the Penalties of certain Laws shall be and is hereby ratified and confirmed and that the same Act shall at all Times be inviolably observed for the exempting of such Protestant Dissenters as are thereby intended from the Pains and Penalties therein mentioned

And for the rendring the said last mentioned Act more effectual according to the true Intent and Meaning thereof Be it further enacted and declared by the Authority aforesaid That if any Person dissenting from the Church of England (not in Holy Orders or pretended Holy Orders or pretending to Holy Orders nor any Preacher or Teacher of any Congregation) who should have been entitled to the Benefit of the said last mentioned Act if such Person had duly taken made and subscribed the Oaths and Declaration or otherwise qualified him or herself as required by the said Act and now is or shall be prosecuted upon or by virtue of any of the penal Statutes from which Protestant Dissenters are exempted by the said Act shall at any Time during such Prosecution take make and subscribe the said Oaths and Declaration or being of the People called Quakers shall make and subscribe the aforesaid Declaration and also the Declaration of Fidelity and subscribe the Profession of their Christian Belief according to the said Act or before any Two of Her Majesties Justices of the Peace (who are hereby required to take and return the same to the next Quarter Sessions of the Peace to be there recorded) such Person shall be and is hereby entitled to the Benefit of the said Act as fully and effectually as if such Person had duly qualified himself within the Time prescribed by the said Act and shall be thenceforth exempted and discharged from all the Penalties and Forfeitures incurred by force of any the aforesaid penal Statutes

And whereas it is or may be doubted whether a Preacher or Teacher of any Congregation of dissenting Protestants duly in all respects qualified according to the said Act be allowed by virtue of the said Act to officiate in any Congregation in any County other than that in which he so qualified himself altho in a Congregation or Place of Meeting duly certified and registred as is required by the said Act Be it declared and enacted by the Authority aforesaid That any such Preacher or Teacher so duly qualified according to the said Act shall be and is hereby allowed to officiate in any Congregation although the same be not in the County wherein he was so qualified provided that the said Congregation or Place of Meeting hath been before such officiating duly certified and registred or recorded according to the said Act And such Preacher or Teacher shall if required produce a Certificate of his having so qualified himself under the Hand of the Clerk of the Peace for the County or Place where he so qualified himself which Certificate such Clerk of the Peace is hereby required to make and shall also before any Justice of the Peace of such County or Place where he shall so officiate make and subscribe such Declaration and take such Oaths as are mentioned in the said Act if thereunto required

And be it further enacted by the Authority aforesaid That on or before the Fifteenth Day of June next all Advocates Writers to the Signet Notaries Publick and other Members of the College of Justice within that Part of Her Majesties Kingdom of Great Britain called Scotland shall be and are hereby obliged to take and subscribe the Oath appointed by the Act of the Sixth Year of Her Majesties Reign intituled An Act for the better Security of Her Majesties Person and Government before the Lords of Session of the aforesaid Part of Her Majesties Kingdom except such of the said Persons who have already taken the same And if any of the Persons aforesaid do or shall neglect or refuse to take and subscribe the said Oath as aforesaid such Person shall be ipso facto adjudged incapable and disabled in Law to have enjoy or exercise in any Manner his said Employment or Practice

And be it further enacted by the Authority aforesaid That in all Time coming no Person or Persons shall be admitted to the Employment of Advocate Writer to the Signet Notary Publick or any Office belonging to the said College of Justice until he or they have taken and subscribed the aforesaid Oath in Manner as is above directed.

Schism Act, 1713

13 Anne, c. 7   *Statutes of the Realm,* IX, pt. 2, 915-17.

This act placed additional restrictions upon Nonconformists in the sphere of education. It was repealed in 1719.

Whereas by an Act of Parliament made in the Thirteenth and Fourteenth Years of His late Majesty King Charles the Second intituled An Act for the Uniformity of Publick Prayers and Administration of Sacraments and other Rites and Ceremonies and for establishing the Form of making ordaining and consecrating Bishops Priests and Deacons in the Church of England it is amongst other things enacted That every Schoolmaster keeping any Publick or Private School and every Person instructing or teaching any Youth in any House or Private Family as a Tutor or Schoolmaster should subscribe before his or their respective Archbishop Bishop or Ordinary of the Diocese a Declaration or Acknowledgment in which amongst other things was contained as follows viz I A. B. do declare That I will conform to the Liturgy of the Church of England as it is now by Law established and if any Schoolmaster or other Person instructing or teaching Youth in any Private House or Family as a Tutor or Schoolmaster should instruct or teach any Youth as a Tutor or Schoolmaster before Licence obtained from his respective Archbishop Bishop or Ordinary of the Diocese according to the Laws and Statutes of this Realm for which he should pay Twelve Pence only and before such Subscription and Acknowledgment made as aforesaid then every such Schoolmaster and other instructing and teaching as aforesaid should for the First Offence suffer Three Months Imprisonment without Bail or Mainprize and for every Second and other such Offence should suffer Three Months Imprisonment without Bail or Mainprize and also forfeit to His Majesty the Sum of Five Pounds And whereas notwithstanding the said Act sundry Papists and other Persons dissenting from the Church of England have taken upon them to instruct and teach Youth as Tutors or Schoolmasters and have for such Purpose openly set up Schools and Seminaries whereby if due and speedy Remedy be not had great Danger might ensue to this Church and State For the making of the said recited Act more effectual and preventing the Danger aforesaid Be it enacted by the Queens most Excellent Majesty by and with the Advice and Consent of the Lords Spiritual and Temporal and Commons in this present Parliament assembled and by the Authority of the same That every Person or Persons who shall from and after the First Day of August next ensuing keep any publick or private School or Seminary or teach and instruct any Youth as Tutor or Schoolmaster within that Part of Great Britain called England the Dominion of Wales or Town of Berwick upon Tweed before such Person or Persons shall have subscribed so much of the said Declaration and Acknowledgment as is before recited and shall have had and obtained a Licence from the respective Archbishop Bishop or Ordinary of the Place under his Seal of Office (for which the Party shall pay One Shilling and no more over and above the Duties payable to Her Majesty for the same) and shall be thereof lawfully convicte upon an Information [Presentment] or Indictment in any of Her Majesties Courts of Record at Westminster or at the Assizes or before Justices of Oyer and Terminer shall and may [be] committed to the Common Gaol of such County Riding City or Town Corporate as aforesaid there to remain without Bail or Mainprize for the Space of Three Months to commence from the Time that such Person or Persons shall be received into the said Gaol

Provided always and be it hereby enacted That no Licence shall be granted by any Archbishop Bishop or Ordinary unless the Person or Persons who shall sue for the same shall produce a Certificate of his or their having received the Sacrament according to the Usage of the Church of England in some Parish Church within the Space of One Year next before the Grant of such Lycence under the Hand of the Minister and One of the Church-wardens of the said Parish nor until such Person or Persons shall have taken and subscribed the Oaths of Allegiance and Supremacy and Abjuration as appointed by Law [and shall have made and subscribed the Declaration against Transubstantiation contained in the Act made in the Twenty fifth Year of the Reign of King Charles the Second intituled An Act for preventing Dangers which may happen from Popish Recusants] before the said Archbishop Bishop or Ordinary [which said Oaths and Declarations the said Archbishop Bishop or Ordinary] are hereby impowered and required to administer and [receive and] such Archbishops Bishops and Ordinaries are required to file such Certificates and keep an exact Register of the same and of the taking and subscribing such Oaths and Declarations

And be it further enacted by the Authority aforesaid That any Person who shall have obtained a Lycence and subscribed the Declarations and taken and subscribed the Oaths as above appointed and shall at any Time after during the Time of his or their keeping any publick or private School or Seminary or instructing any Youth as Tutor or Schoolmaster knowingly or willingly resort to or be present at any Conventicle Assembly or Meeting within England Wales or Town of Berwick upon Tweed for the Exercise of Religion in any other Manner than according to the Liturgy and Practice of the Church of England or shall knowingly and willingly be present at any Meeting or Assembly for the Exercise of Religion although the Liturgy be there used where Her Majesty (whom God long preserve) and the Elector of Brunswick or such others as shall from time to time be lawfully appointed to be prayed for shall not there be prayed for in express words according to the Liturgy of the Church of England except where such particular Offices of the Liturgy are used wherein there are no express Directions to pray for Her Majesty and the Royal Family shall be liable to the Penalties in this Act and shall from thenceforth be incapable of keeping any publick or private School or Seminary or instructing any Youth as Tutor or Schoolmaster

And be it further enacted by the Authority aforesaid That if any Person lycensed as aforesaid shall teach any other Catechism than the Catechism set forth in the Book of Common Prayer the License of such Person shall from thenceforth be void and such Person shall be liable to the Penalties of this Act

And be it further enacted by the Authority aforesaid That it shall and may be lawful to and for the Bishop of the Diocese or other proper Ordinary to cite any Person or Persons whatsoever keeping School or Seminary or teaching without Licence as aforesaid and to proceed against and punish such Person or Persons by Ecclesiastical Censure subject to such Appeals as in Cases of ordinary Jurisdiction this Act or any other Law to the contrary notwithstanding

Provided always That no Person offending against this Act shall be punished Twice for the same Offence

[Provided also That where any Person shall be prosecuted without Fraud or Covin in any of the Courts aforesaid for any Offence contrary to this Act the same Person shall not be afterwards prosecuted for the same Offence in any of the said Courts whilst such former Prosecution shall be pending and carried on without any wilful Delay and in case of any such after Prosecution the Person so doubly prosecuted may alledge plead or shew forth in his Defence against the same such former Prosecution pending or Judgment or Sentence thereupon given the said Pleader first making Oath before the Judge or Judges of the Court where such after-

Prosecution shall be pending and which said Oath he or they are hereby impowered and required to administer that the said prior Prosecution was not commenced or carried on by his Means or with his Consent or Procurement or by any Fraud or Collusion of any other Person to his Knowledge or Belief]

Provided always That this Act or any thing therein contained shall not extend or be construed to extend to any Tutor teaching or instructing Youth in any College or Hall within either of the Universities of [that Part of Great Britain called England nor to any Tutor who shall be employed by any Nobleman or Noblewoman to teach his or her own Children Grand Children or Great Grand Children only in his or her Family provided such Tutor so teaching in any Nobleman or Noblewomans Family do in every respect qualify himself according to this Act except only in that of taking a Licence from the Bishop]

Provided also That the Penalties in this Act shall not extend to any Foreigner or Alien of the Foreign reformed Churches allowed or to be allowed by the Queens Majesty Her Heirs or Successors in England for instructing or teaching any Child or Children of any such Foreigner or Alien only as a Tutor or Schoolmaster

Provided always and be it further enacted by the Authority aforesaid That if any Person who shall have been convicted as aforesaid and thereby made incapable to teach or instruct any Youth as aforesaid shall after such Conviction conform to the Church of England for the Space of One Year without having been present at any Conventicle Assembly or Meeting as aforesaid and receive the Sacrament of the Lords Supper according to the Rites and Usage of the Church of England at least Three Times in that Year every such Person or Persons shall be again capable of having and using a License to teach School or to instruct Youth as a Tutor or Schoolmaster he or they also performing all that is made requisite thereunto by this Act

Provided also and be it further enacted That every such Person so convicted and afterwards conforming in Manner as aforesaid shall at the next Term after his being admitted to or taking upon him to teach or instruct Youth as aforesaid make Oath in Writing in some one of Her Majesties Courts at Westminster in publick and open Court or at the next Quarter Sessions for that County or Place where he shall reside between the Hours of Nine and Twelve in the Forenoon that he hath conformed to the Church of England for the Space of One Year before such his Admission without having been present at any Conventicle Assembly or Meeting as aforesaid and that he hath received the Sacrament of the Lords Supper at least Three Times in the Year which Oath shall be there enrolled and kept upon Record

Provided always That this Act shall not extend or be construed to extend to any Person who as a Tutor or Schoolmaster shall instruct Youth in Reading Writing Arithmetick or any Part of Mathematical Learning only so far as such Mathematical Learning relates to Navigation or any mechanical Art only and so as such Reading Writing Arithmetick or Mathematical Learning shall be taught in the English Tongue only

And whereas by an Act of Parliament made in Ireland in the Seventeenth and Eighteenth Years of His said late Majesty King Charles the Second intituled An Act for the Uniformity of publick Prayers and Administration of [the] Sacraments and other Rites and Ceremonies and for establishing the Form of making ordaining and consecrating of Bishops Priests and Deacons in the Church of Ireland it is enacted concerning Schoolmasters and other Persons instructing Youth in private Families in Ireland as in and by the above recited Act is enacted concerning Schoolmasters and others instructing youth in private Families in that Part of Great Britain called England And whereas it is reasonable that where the Law is the same the Remedy and Means for enforcing the Execution of the Law should be the same Be it therefore enacted by the Authority aforesaid That all and every the Remedies Provisions and Clauses in and by this Act given made and enacted shall extend and be deemed construed and adjudged to extend to Ireland in as full and effectual Manner as if Ireland had been expresly named and mentioned in all and every the Clauses in this Act

Standing orders of the Society for Promoting Christian Knowledge, 1717

The Standing Orders and Resolutions of the Society for Promoting Christian Knowledge (London: Joseph Downing, 1717), 15-page pamphlet.

The SPCK was founded by the Church of England in 1699. It engaged, often successfully, in educational and related activities and established the popular Saturday Magazine *in 1832.*

Orders Relating to the Society in General

I. That this Society be called by the Name of *The Society for Promoting Christian Knowledge*, and that they meet Weekly on every Thursday, at Five of the Clock in the Evening precisely.

II. That no Business be begun till the Devotions agreed upon by the Society are performed; and if the Day of Meeting happens to be on a Holy-Day, the Collect for the Day shall be added to the Prayers, which the Secretary is to put the Society in mind of.

III. That the Chair be filled Monthly by a Rotation of Members, that shall be present the last Thursday of every Month, according to their Seniority in the Society, excepting in that Month when the Society shall have their general Anniversary Meeting to Dine together; and that this Order be read when a Choice of Chairman is to be made.

IV. That the Chairman shall attend at each Meeting in the Month he is to serve; but in Case of his Absence, he may depute any Resident Member in his Room; and that it be the Chairman's Part to preserve Order, prevent Heats, and to take Care that no one interrupts another in Speaking.

V. That no Business shall be begun before Five a Clock; nor then, unless the Chairman and Four more of the Resident Members be present.

VI. That in the Want of a sufficient Number of Members to make a Quorum any two Residing Members, with the Secretary, may peruse the Letters sent to the Society, and direct the Abstracting of them.

VII. That three Residing Members do make a Quorum, to do Business at the Committee.

VIII. That at every Meeting of the Society, the Minutes taken the preceding Meeting shall be read twice over; then the Abstracts of Letters of the said Day; after which, all new Motions and Reports shall be made, and Letters read.

IX. That before any Person be admitted a Residing Member, the Person who proposes him shall assure the Society of his having taken the Oaths, and that he is well affected to His Majesty King George and His Government, and to the Church of England as by Law Established; That such Proposal be made at two several Meetings, and then, if it be thought fit to procede, (except in the Case after-mentioned,) two of the Residing Members shall be desired to enquire, Whether the Person proposed be of a sober and religious Life and Conversation, and of an humble and charitable Disposition? After whose Report, the Society shall proceed to choose or refuse such Person: And the Members directed to make such Enquiry, are to make their Report either by Word or Writing, at the next Meeting: And that this Order be read, when such Enquiry is directed. But when any Bishop of the Church of England is proposed as aforesaid, he may be chose a Member, without any such Enquiry.

X. That the Choice of Resident Members be made by Balloting; as also the Determination of such Questions as the Society shall not otherwise decide; which Balloting shall be made by the Resident Members only; and for preventing the Messenger from presenting the Box to any other, this Order shall be read upon every Occasion of Balloting; and when the Numbers in Balloting are equal, it be in the Power of the Chairman to determine the Matter.

XI. That every Person chosen a Residing Member, do, at his Admission, or if not in Town, upon Notice of his Election, pay or cause to be paid down a voluntary Sum to the Treasurer for the Time being; and do also subscribe or cause to be subscribed, a Yearly Sum, to be paid Quarterly, for carrying on the Designs of the Society: But the Corresponding Members may attend the Meetings of the Society without being obliged to make such Subscriptions, in regard to the Charge they are supposed to be at, in promoting the same Designs in or about the respective Places of their Abode.

XII. That no Member do withdraw his Subscription from this Society, without a previous Notice of three Months.

XIII. That no Person be taken Notice of on the Minutes as a Resident Member, till he has paid down and subscribed by himself, or Proxy, as mentioned Order XI.

XIV. That the Secretary, once a Quarter, lay before the Society, a List of such have been chosen for Resident Members; to the End, that those that have not attended and subscribed, may be called upon by the Persons that proposed them.

XV. That every Person proposed for a Corresponding Member, shall stand proposed a Week before he be admitted; and that no one, except a Foreigner, be chosen a Corresponding Member, before the Society is certifyed of his Willingness to correspond with them; and that such Choice be declared in the Minutes.

XVI. That if any Corresponding Members shall omit to correspond with the Society, by Letter or otherwise, for twelve Months, the Secretary shall give Notice of such Omission to the Society.

XVII. That this Society will always decline the Intermeddling with such Matters as are Foreign to their Design of Promoting Christian Knowledge.

XVIII. That no Order proposed for a Standing Order, shall be esteemed such, till three Months after its being proposed; and that a Copy of all such Orders be laid before the Chairman every first Thursday in the Month.

XIX. That none of the Standing Orders be repealed, suspended, or altered, till such Repeal, Suspension, or Alteration, has been proposed at two successive Meetings, and not determined till a third Meeting, when there shall be at least Nine Members present; and that the same Rule be observed for revoking or altering any Thing that has been settled by Balloting.

XX. That it be recommended to every Member, to pray to Almighty God for a Blessing on the Consultations and Endeavours of the Society.

XXI. That when any Member of the Society is indisposed, and desires the Prayers of the Society, that the Collect or Collects used in the Office for Visiting the Sick, be added to the Collects used by the Society.

XXII. That the Orders of this Society be read the first Thursday after every Quarter Day, before any new Motion is made; and that the Secretary do put the Chairman in mind thereof.

Orders Relating to the Treasurer

I. That a distinct Account be kept of all Gifts made to the Society.

II. That the Accounts of this Society be Audited every Year, within a Month after Christmas: and that an Account of all Arrears be, upon the Report of such Audit, laid before the Society; and that such Members as shall be found in Arrear above Eight Quarters, be put in mind thereof by the Secretary.

III. That no Sum exceeding Forty Shillings be disposed of, without considering the State of the Society's Cash.

IV. That the Treasurer do, after every Quarter Day, send to all the Resident Members, one of a Sort of all new Books and Papers admitted by the Society the preceding Quarter.

Orders Relating to the Secretary

I. That the Secretary do make an Abstract of all Letters sent to and from the Society, and enter the same in a Book to be kept for that Purpose; And also enter into another Book, Copies of all General Letters sent by the Society, and such others as the Society shall Direct.

II.   That all Letters be directed to the Secretary, to be left at the Reverend Mr. Shute's, and brought to the Society by Messenger.

III.   That the Secretary do, at the Beginning of each Quarter, lay before the Society an Abstract of the most material Transactions of the preceding Quarter.

IV.   That there be an Index of Names and Things contained in the Abstract of Letters, and in the Minutes.

V.   That the Secretary do enter the Accounts of the Society into the Great-Book, immediately after every Audit.

VI.   That the Account of Charity-Schools be, for the future, ready to be sent to the Press at Whitsuntide, without waiting for further Account from the Correspondents.

VII.   That a Copy of all the Standing Orders of the Society, be laid before the Chairman at every Meeting of the Society.

VIII.   That a List be made Yearly of all the Corresponding Members to whom Packets are sent, and that the same be laid before the Society within a Month after all the Packets are sent away.

IX.   That Copies of such Things as are especially directed to be preserved among the Society's Papers, be henceforth entered into a Book for that Purpose.

X.   That the Secretary lay before the Society, at every Meeting, an Account of such Business as remains undetermined.

Orders Relating to the Choice of Books

I.   That no Manuscript be printed, nor any Printed Book or Paper bought, in order to be dispersed by the Society, but such shall have been first approved in manner following; that is to say, When any Manuscript or Printed Book, etc. shall be recommended to the Society, such Manuscript, or Printed Book, etc. shall be referred to the Committee, to consider, Whether a Book on such a Subject be wanting, or may be useful to the Design of the Society; and if they are of Opinion, such a Book may be useful, it shall be referred to the Perusal of Four Resident Members, to be severally named at Four several Meetings, who are to report their Opinions thereof to the Society as soon as may be; after which, if it be thought fit to proceed, it shall be determined by Balloting, whether such Manuscript shall be printed, or such Book bought, in order to be dispersed.

II.   That the Time for such Determination concerning a Printed Book, etc. shall be the last Thursday in the Month, wherein the last Report touching the same is made; and if a Manuscript, it shall be the last Thursday in the following Month, after the last Report concerning such Manuscript is made: And in the mean time, Copies of such Printed Book, etc. and such Manuscript, shall lie on the Table for the Perusal of any of the Members if they please. . . .

IV.   That any Paper drawn up by the Committee, and afterwards read and approved of by the Society, may be Printed, and dispersed as the Society shall think fit, without being examined in the Manner aforesaid.

V.   That the Sermon preached at the Anniversary Meeting of the Children educated in the Charity-Schools, with the Account of the said Schools; The Sermon at the Anniversary Meeting of *The Society for Propagating the Gospel in Foreign Parts;* and The Anniversary Sermon before *The Societies for Reformation of Manners,* may be printed and dispersed, without such Perusal and Examination as aforesaid.

VI. That if any Book, approved of in Manner aforesaid, shall be altered, or receive any Additions, such Book shall not be printed or dispersed, till such Alterations, or Additions, shall have been referred to the Committee, and afterwards approved by the Society.

Orders Relating to the Packets

I. That a Packet of the Society's Books and Papers be sent to each Resident Member at his Admission.

II. That but one occasional Parcel be sent to each of the Correspondents in one Year; and that the same be forwarded as soon as the Yearly Account of Charity-Schools, and the Sermon, be printed, without staying for any other Book.

III. That no Book or Paper be at any Time put into the Society's Packet, but by their Orders; excepting such Books or Papers relating to the Protestant Mission to the East-Indies, as the Malabar Committee shall appoint.

Sermon by Benjamin Hoadly, bishop of Bangor, attacking the theory of a divinely ordained Church of England, 31 March 1717

Benjamin Hoadly, bishop of Bangor, *The Nature of the Kingdom, or Church, of Christ: A Sermon Preached before the King, at the Royal Chapel at St. James's, on Sunday, March 31, 1717* (London: James Knapton, 1717), 10-31.

This important and bitterly disputed sermon, which touched off the Bangorian controversy, weakened the High Church faction in the Anglican church. Hoadly (1676-1761) was later bishop of Hereford, Salisbury, and Winchester, successively.

It is with this View, that I have chosen those Words, in which our Lord himself declared the Nature of his own Kingdom. This Kingdom of Christ, is the same with the Church of Christ. And the Notion of the Church of Christ, which, at first, was only the Number, small or great, of Those who believed Him to be the Messiah; or of Those who subjected themselves to Him, as their King, in the Affair of Religion; having since that Time been so diversified by the various Alterations it hath undergone, that it is almost impossible so much as to number up the many inconsistent Images that have come, by daily Additions, to be united together in it: nothing, I think, can be more useful, than to consider the same thing, under some other Image, which hath not been so much used; nor consequently so much defaced.

And since the Image of His Kingdom, is That under which our Lord himself chose to represent it: We may be sure that, if we sincerely examine our Notion of his Church, by what He saith of his Kingdom, that it is not of this World, we shall exclude out of it, every thing that he would have excluded; and then, what remains will be true, pure, and uncorrupted. And what I have to say, in order to this, will be comprehended under Two General Heads.

I. As the Church of Christ is the Kingdom of Christ, He himself is King: and in this; it is implied, that He is himself the sole Law-giver to his Subjects, and himself the sole Judge of their Behaviour, in the Affairs of Conscience and Eternal Salvation. And in this Sense therefore, His Kingdom is not of this World; that He hath, in those Points, left behind Him, no visible, humane Authority; no Vicegerents, who can be said properly to supply his Place; no Interpreters, upon whom his Subjects are absolutely to depend; no Judges over the Consciences or Religion of his People. For if this were so, that any such absolute Vicegerent Authority, either for the making new Laws, or interpreting Old Ones, or judging his Subjects, in Religious Matters, were lodged in any Men upon Earth; the Consequence would be, that what still retains the Name of the Church of Christ, would not be the Kingdom of Christ, but the Kingdom of those Men, vested with such Authority. For, whoever hath such an Authority of making Laws, is so far a King: and whoever can add new Laws to those of Christ, equally obligatory, is as truly as King, as Christ himself is: Nay, whoever hath an absolute Authority to interpret any written, or spoken Laws; it is He, who is truly the Law-giver, to all Intents and Purposes; and not the Person who first wrote, or spoke them.

In humane Society, the Interpretation of Laws may, of necessity, be lodged, in some Cases, in the Hands of Those who were not originally the Legislators. But this is not absolute; nor of bad Consequence to Society: because the Legislators can resume the Interpretation into their own Hands, as they are Witnesses to what passes in the World, and as They can, and will, sensibly interpose in all those Cases, in which their Interposition becomes necessary. And therefore, They are still properly the Legislators. But it is otherwise in Religion, or the Kingdom of Christ. He himself never interposeth, since his first Promulgation of his Law, either to convey Infallibility to Such as pretend to handle it over again; or to assert the true Interpretation of it, amidst the various and contradictory Opinions of Men about it. If He did certainly thus interpose, He himself would still be the Legislator. But, as He doth not; if such an absolute Authority be once lodged with Men, under the Notion of Interpreters, They then become the Legislators, and not Christ; and They rule in their own Kingdom, and not in His.

It is the same thing, as to Rewards and Punishments, to carry forward the great End of his Kingdom. If any Men upon Earth have a Right to add to the Sanctions of his Laws; that is, to increase the Number, or alter the Nature, of the Rewards and Punishments of his Subjects, in Matters of Conscience, or Salvation: They are so far Kings in his stead; and Reign in their own Kingdom, and not in His. So it is, whenever They erect Tribunals, and exercise a Judgment over the Consciences of Men; and assume to Themselves the Determination of such Points, as cannot be determined, but by One who knows the Hearts; or, when They make any of their own Declarations, or Decisions, to concern and affect the State of Christ's Subjects, with regard to the Favour of God: this is so far, the taking Christ's Kingdom out of His Hands, and placing it in their own.

Nor is this matter at all made better by their declaring Themselves to be Vicegerents, or Law-makers, or Judges, under Christ, in order to carry on the Ends of his Kingdom. For it comes to this at last, since it doth not seem fit to Christ himself to interpose so as to prevent or remedy all their mistakes and contradictions, that, if They have this power of interpreting, or adding, Laws, and judging Men, in such a sense, that Christians shall be indispensably and absolutely obliged to obey those Laws, and to submit to those Decisions; I say, if They have this power lodged with them, then the Kingdom, in which They rule, is not the Kingdom of Christ, but of Themselves; He doth not rule in it, but They: And, whether They happen to agree with Him, or to differ from Him, as long as They are the Law-givers, and Judges, without any Interposition from Christ, either to guide or correct their Decisions, They are Kings of this Kingdom; and not Christ Jesus.

If therefore, the Church of Christ be the Kingdom of Christ; it is essential to it, That Christ himself be the Sole Law-giver, and Sole Judge of his Subjects, in all points relating to the favour or displeasure of Almighty God; and that All His Subjects, in what Station soever They may be, are equally Subjects to Him; and that No One of them, any more than Another, hath Authority, either to make New Laws for Christ's Subjects; or to impose a sense upon the Old Ones, which is the same thing; or to Judge, Censure, or Punish, the Servants of Another Master, in matters relating purely to Conscience, or Salvation. If any Person hath any other Notion, either thro' a long Use of Words with Inconsistent Meanings, or thro' a negligence of Thought; let Him but ask Himself, whether the Church of Christ be the Kingdom of Christ, or not: And, if it be, whether this Notion of it doth not absolutely exclude All other Legislators and Judges, in matters relating to Conscience, or the favour of God; or, whether it can be His Kingdom, if any Mortal Men have such a Power of Legislation and Judgment, in it. This Enquiry will bring Us back to the first, which is the only True, Account of the Church of Christ, or the Kingdom of Christ, in the mouth of a Christian: That it is the Number of Men, whether Small or Great, whether Dispersed or united, who truly and sincerely are Subjects to Jesus Christ alone, as their Law-giver and Judge, in matters relating to the Favour of God, and their Eternal Salvation.

II. The next principal point is, that, if the Church be the Kingdom of Christ; and this Kingdom be not of this World: this must appear from the Nature and End of the Laws of Christ; and of those Rewards and Punishments, which are the Sanctions of his Laws. Now his Laws are Declarations, relating to the Favour of God in another State after this. They are Declarations of those Conditions to be performed, in this World, on our part, without which God will not make us Happy in that to come. And they are almost All general Appeals to the Will of that God; to his Nature, known by the Common Reason of Mankind; and to the imitation of that Nature, which must be our Perfection. The Keeping his Commandments is declared the Way of Life; and the doing his Will, the Entrance into the Kingdom of Heaven. The being Subjects of Christ, is to this very End, that We may the better and more effectually perform the Will of God. The Laws of this Kingdom, therefore, as Christ left them, have nothing of this World in their view; no Tendency, either to the Exaltation of Some, in worldly pomp and dignity; or to their absolute Dominion, over the Faith and Religious conduct of Others of his Subjects; or to the erecting of any sort of Temporal Kingdom, under the Covert and Name of a Spiritual one.

The Sanctions of Christ's Law are Rewards and Punishments. But of what sort? Not the Rewards of this World; not the Offices, or Glories, of this State; not the pains of Prisons, Banishments, Fines, or any lesser and more Moderate Penalties; nay, not the much lesser Negative Discouragements that belong to Humane Society. He was far from thinking that These could be the Instruments of such a Perswasion, as He thought acceptable to God. But, as the Great End of his Kingdom, was to guide Men to Happiness, after the short Images of it were over here below; so, He took his Motives from that place, where His Kingdom first began, and where it was at last to end; from those Rewards and Punishments in a future State, which had no relation to this World: And, to shew that his Kingdom was not of this World, all the Sanctions which He thought fit to give to His Laws, were not of this World at all.

St. Paul understood this so well, that He gives an Account of His own Conduct, and that of Others in the same Station, in these words, *Knowing the terrors of the Lord, we perswade men:* whereas, in too many Christian Countries, since his days, if Some, who profess to succeed Him, were to give an Account of their own Conduct, it must be in a quite contrary strain; *Knowing the terrors of this World, and having them in our power, We do, not perswade men, but force their outward Profession against their inward Perswasion.*

Now, wherever this is practised, whether in a great degree, or a small, in that place there is so far a Change, from a Kingdom which is not of this world, to a Kingdom which is of this world. As soon as ever you hear of any of the Engines of this world, whether of the greater, or the lesser sort, you must immediately think that then, and so far, the Kingdom of this world takes place. For, if the very Essence of God's worship be Spirit and Truth; If Religion be Virtue and Charity, under the Belief of a Supreme Governour and Judge; if True Real Faith cannot be the effect of Force; and, if there can be no Reward where there is no Willing Choice: then, in all, or any of these Cases, to apply Force or Flattery, Worldly pleasure or pain; is to act contrary to the Interests of True Religion, as it is plainly opposite to the Maxims upon which Christ founded his Kingdom; who chose the Motives which are not of this world, to support a Kingdom which is not of this world. And indeed, it is too visible to be hid, that wherever the Rewards and Punishments are changed, from future to present, from the World to come, to the World now in possession; there, the Kingdom founded by our Saviour is, in the Nature of it, so far changed, that it is become in such a degree, what He professed, His Kingdom was not: that is, of this world; of the same sort, with other Common Earthly Kingdoms, in which the Rewards are, Worldly Honours, Posts, Offices, Pomp, Attendance, Dominion; and the Punishments are, Prisons, Fines, Banishments, Gallies and Racks; or something Less, of the same sort.

If these can be the true supports of a Kingdom which is not of this World; then Sincerity, and Hypocrisy; Religion, and No Religion; Force, and Perswasion; A Willing Choice, and a Terrified Heart; are become the same things: Truth and

Falshood stand in need of the same methods, to propagate and support them; and our Saviour himself was little acquainted with the Right way of increasing the Number of such Subjects, as He wished for. If He had but at first enlightened the Powers of this World, as He did St. Paul; and employed the Sword which They bore, and the Favours They had in their hands, to bring Subjects into his Kingdom; this had been an Expeditious and an effectual way, according to the Conduct of some of his professed Followers, to have had a Glorious and Extensive Kingdom, or Church. But this was not his Design; unless it could be compassed in quite a different way.

And therefore, when You see Our Lord, in his methods, so far removed from Those of Many of his Disciples; when You read Nothing, in his Doctrine about his own Kingdom, of taking in the Concerns of this World, and mixing them with those of Eternity; no Commands that the Frowns and Discouragements of this present State should in any Case attend upon Conscience and Religion; No Rules against the Enquiry of All His Subjects into his Original Message from Heaven; no Orders for the kind and charitable force of Penalties, or Capital Punishments, to make Men think and chuse aright; no Calling upon the secular Arm, whenever the Magistrate should become Christian, to inforce his Doctrines, or to back his Spiritual Authority; but, on the contrary, as plain a Declaration as a few Words can make, that His Kingdom is not of this World: I say, when You see this, from the whole Tenor of the *Gospel*, so vastly opposite to Many who take his Name into their Mouths, the Question with you ought to be, Whether He did not know the Nature of his own Kingdom, or Church, better than Any since his Time? whether you can suppose, He left any such matters to be decided against Himself, and his own Express professions; and, whether if an Angel from Heaven should give you any Account of his Kingdom, contrary to what He himself hath done, it can be of any Weight, or Authority, with Christians.

I have now made some such observations, drawn from the Church being the Kingdom of Christ, and not of any Men in that Kingdom; from the Nature of his Laws, and from those Rewards and Punishments, which are the Sanctions of those Laws; as lead us naturally into the true Notion of the Church, or Kingdom, of Christ, by excluding out of it every thing inconsistent with His being King, Lawgiver and Judge; as well as with the Nature of His Laws, and of His promises and Threatnings. I will only make Two or Three Observations, grounded upon this: And so conclude. And

1. From what hath been said it is very plain, in general, that the Grossest Mistakes in Judgment, about the Nature of Christ's Kingdom, or Church, have arisen from hence, that Men have argued from Other visible Societies, and Other Visible Kingdoms of this World, to what ought to be Visible, and Sensible, in His Kingdom: Constantly leaving out of their Notion, the most Essential Part of it, that Christ is King in his own Kingdom; forgetting this King himself, because He is not now seen by mortal Eyes; and Substituting Others in his Place, as Law-givers and Judges, in the same Points, in which He must either Alone, or not at all, be Lawgiver and Judge; not contented with such a Kingdom as He established, and desires to reign in; but urging and contending, that His Kingdom must be like Other Kingdoms. Whereas He hath positively warned them against any such Arguings, by

assuring Them that this Kingdom is His Kingdom, and that it is not of this World; and therefore that No one of His Subjects is Law-giver and Judge over Others of them, in matters relating to Salvation, but He alone; and that We must not Frame our Ideas from the Kingdoms of this World, of what ought to be, in a visible and sensible manner, in His Kingdom.

2. From what hath been said it appears that the Kingdom of Christ, which is the Church of Christ, is the Number of Persons who are Sincerely, and Willingly, Subjects to Him, as Law-giver and Judge in all matters truly relating to Conscience, or Eternal Salvation. And the more close and immediate this Regard to Him is, the more certainly and the more evidently true it is, that They are of his Kingdom. This may appear fully to their own Satisfaction, if They have recourse to Him himself, in the *Gospel*; if They think it a sufficient Authority that He hath declared the Conditions of their Salvation, and that No Man upon Earth hath any Authority to declare any other, or to add one tittle to them; if They resolve to perform what They see, He laith a stress upon; and if They trust no mortal, with the absolute direction of their Consciences, the pardon of their Sins, or the determining of their Interest in God's favour; but wait for their Judge, who alone can bring to light the hidden things of darkness.

If They feel themselves disposed and resolved to receive the Words of Eternal Life from Himself; to take their Faith from what He himself once delivered, who knew better than All the rest of the World what He required of his own Subjects; to direct their Worship by his Rule, and their whole practice by the General Law which He laid down: If They feel themselves in this disposition, They may be very certain that They are truly his Subjects, and Members of his Kingdom. Nor need They envy the Happiness of Others, who may think it a much more evident Mark of their belonging to the Kingdom of Christ, that They have other Law-givers, and Judges, in Christ's Religion, besides Jesus Christ; that They have recourse not to his own Words, but the Words of Others who profess to interpret them; that They are ready to Submit to this Interpretation, let it be what it will; that They have set up to Themselves the Idol of an unintelligible Authority, both in Belief, and Worship, and Practice; in Words, under Jesus Christ, but in deed and in truth over Him; as it removes the minds of his Subjects from Himself, to Weak, and passionate Men; and as it claims the same Rule and Power in his Kingdom, which He himself alone can have, But,

3. This will be Another observation, that it evidently destroys the Rule and Authority of Jesus Christ, as King, to set up any Other Authority in His Kingdom, to which His Subjects are indispensably and absolutely obliged to Submit their Consciences, or their Conduct, in what is properly called Religion. There are some Professed Christians, who contend openly for such an Authority, as indispensably obliges All around Them to Unity of Profession; that is, to Profess even what They do not, what They cannot, believe to be true. This sounds so grossly, that Others, who think They act a glorious part in opposing such an Enormity, are very willing, for their own sakes, to retain such an Authority as shall oblige Men, whatever They themselves think, though not to profess what They do not believe, yet, to forbear the profession and publication of what They do believe, let them believe it of never so great Importance.

But these Pretensions are founded upon the mistaken Notion of the Peace, as well as Authority, of the Kingdom, that is the Church, of Christ. Which of them is the most insupportable to an honest and a Christian mind, I am not able to say: because They both equally found the Authority of the Church of Christ, upon the ruines of Sincerity and Common Honesty; and mistake Stupidity and Sleep, for Peace; because They would both equally have prevented All Reformation where it hath been, and will for ever prevent it where it is not already; and, in a word, because both equally devest Jesus Christ of his Empire in his own Kingdom; set the obedience of his Subjects loose from Himself; and teach them to prostitute their Consciences at the feet of Others, who have no right in such a manner to trample upon them.

The Peace of Christ's Kingdom is a manly and Reasonable Peace; built upon Charity, and Love, and mutual forbearance, and receiving one another, as God receives us. As for any other Peace; founded upon a Submission of our Honesty, as well as our Understandings; it is falsely so called. It is not the Peace of the Kingdom of Christ; but the Lethargy of it: and a Sleep unto Death, when his Subjects shall throw off their relation to Him; fix their subjection to Others; and even in Cases, where They have a right to see, and where They think They see, his Will otherwise, shall shut their Eyes and go blindfold at the Command of Others; because those Others are not pleased with their Enquiries into the Will of their great Lord and Judge.

To conclude, The Church of Christ is the Kingdom of Christ. He is King in his own Kingdom. He is Sole Law-giver to his Subjects, and Sole Judge, in matters relating to Salvation. His Laws and Sanctions are plainly fixed: and relate to the Favour of God; and not at all to the Rewards, or Penalties, of this World. All his Subjects are equally his Subjects; and, as such, equally without Authority to alter, to add to, or to interpret, his Laws so, as to claim the absolute Submission of Others to such Interpretation. And All are His Subjects, and in his Kingdom, who are ruled and governed by Him. Their Faith was once delivered by Him. The Conditions of their Happiness were once laid down by Him. The Nature of God's Worship was once declared by Him. And it is easy to judge, whether of the Two is most becoming a Subject of the Kingdom of Christ, that is, a Member of his Church; to seek all these particulars in those plain and short Declarations of their King and Law-giver himself: or to hunt after Them thro' the infinite contradictions, the numberless perplexities, the endless disputes, of Weak Men, in several Ages, till the Enquirer himself is lost in the Labyrinth, and perhaps sits down in Despair, or Infidelity. If Christ be our King; let us shew our selves Subjects to Him alone, in the great affair of Conscience and Eternal Salvation: and, without fear of Man's judgment, live and act as becomes Those who wait for the appearance of an All-knowing and Impartial Judge; even that King, whose Kingdom is not of this World.

Minutes of the First Methodist Conference, held at London, 25-29 June 1744

Minutes of the Methodist Conferences, from the first, held in London, by the late Rev. John Wesley, A.M., in the Year 1744 (London: Methodist Conference Office, 1812), 1, 3-21.

At this conference the theological framework of Methodism was defined and the basis was laid for much of its organizational success.

Monday, June 25, 1744

The following persons met at the Foundry, John Wesley, Charles Wesley; John Hodges, Rector of Wenvo; Henry Piers, Vicar of Bexley; Samuel Taylor, Vicar of Quinton; and John Meriton.

It is desired, That all things be considered as in the immediate presence of God.

That we may meet with a single eye, and as little children, who have every thing to learn:

That every point which is proposed, may be examined to the foundation:

That every person may speak freely whatever is in his heart:

And, That every question which may arise, should be thoroughly debated and settled.

Q. Need we be fearful of doing this? What are we afraid of? Of overturning our first principles?

A. If they are false, the sooner they are overturned, the better. If they are true, they will bear the strictest examination. Let us all pray for a willingness to receive light, to know of every doctrine, whether it be of God.

Q. How may the time of this Conference be made more eminently a time of watching unto prayer?

A. 1. While we are conversing, let us have an especial care, to set God always before us.

2. In the intermediate hours, let us visit none but the sick, and spend all the time that remains, in retirement.

3. Let us then give ourselves to prayer for one another, and for a blessing upon this our labour.

Q. How far does each of us agree, to submit to the judgment of the Majority?

A. In speculative things, each can only submit so far as his judgment shall be convinced:

In every practical point, each will submit so far as he can without wounding his conscience.

Q. Can a Christian submit any farther than this, to any man, or number of men upon earth?

A. It is undeniable, he cannot; either to council, bishop, or convocation. And this is that grand principle of private judgment, on which all the Reformers proceeded. "Every man must judge for himself; because every man must give an account for himself to God."

After some time spent in prayer, the design of our Meeting was proposed, namely, to consider,

1. What to teach.
2. How to teach. And,
3. What to do? i.e. How to regulate our doctrine, discipline, and practice.

We began with considering the doctrine of justification: the questions relating to which, with the substance of the answers given thereto, were as follows:

Q. 1. What is it to be justified?

A. To be pardoned, and received into God's favour, into such a state, that if we continue therein, we shall be finally saved.

Q. 2. Is faith the condition of justification?

A. Yes; for every one who believeth not is condemned; and every one who believes, is justified.

Q. 3. But must not repentance, and works meet for repentance, go before this faith?

A. Without doubt: if by repentance you mean conviction of sin; and by works meet for repentance, obeying God as far as we can, forgiving our brother, leaving off evil, doing good, and using his ordinances according to the power we have received.

Q. 4. What is faith?

A. Faith in general is, a divine, supernatural elenchos of things not seen; i.e. of past, future, or spiritual things. It is a spiritual sight of God, and the things of God.

First, a sinner is convinced by the Holy Ghost, "Christ, loved me, and gave himself for me."—This is that faith by which he is justified or pardoned, the moment he receives it. Immediately the same Spirit bears witness, "Thou art pardoned: thou hast redemption in his blood." And this is saving faith, whereby the love of God is shed abroad in his heart.

Q. 5. Have all Christians this faith? May not a man be justified, and how know it?

A. That all true Christians have such a faith, as implies an assurance of God's love, appears from Rom. viii. 15. Eph. iv. 32. 2 Cor. xiii. 5. Heb. viii. 10. 1 John iv. 10 v. 19. And that no man can be justified and not know it, appears farther from the nature of the thing. For faith after repentance, is ease after pain, rest after toil, light after darkness. It appears also from the immediate, as well as distant fruits thereof.

Q. 6. But may not a man go to heaven without it?

A. It does not appear from holy writ, that a man who hears the gospel, can: (Mark xvi. 16.) whatever a heathen may do, Rom. ii. 14.

Q. 7. What are the immediate fruits of justifying faith?

A. Peace, joy, love, power over all outward sin, and power to keep down inward sin.

Q. 8. Does any one believe, who has not the witness in himself, or any longer than he sees, loves, obeys God?

A. We apprehend not; *seeing God* being the very essence of faith; love and obedience the inseparable properties of it.

Q. 9. What sins are consistent with justifying faith?

A. No *wilful sin.* If a believer *wilfully sins,* he casts away his faith. Neither is it possible he should have *justifying faith* again, without previously *repenting.*

Q. 10. *Must* every believer come into a state of doubt, or fear, or darkness? Will he do so, unless by ignorance or unfaithfulness? Does God otherwise withdraw himself?

A. It is certain, a believer *need* never again come into condemnation. It seems, he need not come into a state of doubt, or fear, or darkness: and that (ordinarily at least) he *will* not, unless by ignorance or unfaithfulness. Yet it is true, that the first joy does seldom last long; that it is commonly followed by doubts and fears; and that God frequently permits great heaviness, before any large manifestation of himself.

Q. 11. Are works necessary to the continuance of faith?

A. Without doubt; for a man may forfeit the free gift of God, either by sins of omission or commission.

Q. 12. Can faith be lost, but for want of works?

A. It cannot but through disobedience.

Q. 13. How is faith *made perfect by works?*

A. The more we exert our faith, the more it is increased. To him that hath shall be given.

Q. 14. St. Paul says, Abraham was *not justified by works.* St. James, He was *justified by works.* Do they not contradict each other?

A. No: 1. Because they do not speak of the same justification. St. Paul speaks of that justification, which was when Abraham was seventy-five years old, above twenty years before Isaac was born. St. James of that justification which was when he offered up Isaac on the altar.

2dly. Because they do not speak of the same works. St. Paul speaking of works that precede faith; St. James, of works that spring from it.

Q. 15. In what sense is Adam's sin imputed to all mankind?

A. In Adam all die, i.e. 1. Our bodies then became mortal. 2. Our souls died, i.e. were disunited from God. And hence, 3. We are all born with a sinful, devilish nature; By reason whereof, 4. We are children of wrath, liable to death eternal, Rom. v. 18. Eph. ii. 3.

Q. 16. In what sense is the righteousness of Christ imputed to all mankind, or to believers?

A. We do not find it expressly affirmed in Scripture, that God imputes the righteousness of Christ to any. Although we do find, that faith is imputed to us for righteousness.

That text, "As by one man's disobedience all men were made sinners; so by the obedience of one, all were made righteous," we conceive means, by the merits of Christ, all men are cleared from the guilt of Adam's actual sin.

We conceive farther, that through the obedience and death of Christ, 1. The bodies of all men become immortal after the resurrection. 2. Their souls receive a capacity of spiritual life. And, 3. An actual spark or seed thereof. 4. All believers become children of grace, reconciled to God; and, 5. made partakers of the Divine nature.

Q. 17. Have we not, then, unawares leaned too much towards Calvinism?

A. We are afraid we have.

Q. 18. Have we not also leaned towards Antinomianism?

A. We are afraid we have.

Q. 19. What is Antinomianism?

A. The doctrine which makes void the law through faith.

Q. 20. What are the main pillars hereof?

A. 1. That Christ abolished the moral law.

2. That therefore Christians are not obliged to observe it.

3. That one branch of Christian liberty, is liberty from obeying the commandments of God.

4. That it is bondage, to do a thing because it is commanded; or forbear it, because it is forbidden.

5. That a believer is not *obliged* to use the ordinances of God, or to do good works.

6. That a preacher ought not to exhort to good works. Not unbelievers, because it is hurtful; not believers, because it is needless.

Q. 21. What was the occasion of St. Paul's writing his Epistle to the Galatians?

A. The coming of certain men amongst the Galatians, who taught, "Except ye be circumcised, and keep the law of Moses, ye cannot be saved."

Q. 22. What is his main design therein?

A. To prove, 1. That no man can be justified or saved by the works of the law, either moral or ritual. 2. That every believer is justified by faith in Christ, without the works of the law.

Q. 23. What does he mean, by "the works of the law?" Gal. ii. 16, etc.

A. All works which do not spring from faith in Christ.

Q. 24. What, by being "under the law?" Gal. iii. 23.

A. Under the Mosaic Dispensation.

Q. 25. What Law has Christ abolished?

A. The ritual law of Moses.

Q. 26. What is meant by *liberty*? Gal. v. 1.

A. Liberty, 1. From the law. 2. From sin.

On Tuesday Morning, June 26, was considered,

The doctrine of sanctification. With regard to which, the questions asked, and the substance of the answers given, were as follows:

Q. 1. What is it to be sanctified?

A. To be renewed in the image of God, in righteousness and true holiness.

Q. 2. Is faith the condition, or the instrument of sanctification?

A. It is both the condition and instrument of it. When we begin to believe, then sanctification begins. And as faith increases, holiness increases, till we are created anew.

Q. 3. What is implied in being *a perfect Christian*?

A. The loving the Lord our God with all our heart, and with all our mind, and soul, and strength, Deut. vi. 5. xxx. 6. Ezek, xxxvi. 25-29.

Q. 4. Does this imply, that all inward sin is taken away?

A. Without doubt: or how could he be said to be saved "from all his uncleannesses?" Ezek. xxxvi. 29.

Q. 5. Can we know one who is thus saved? What is a reasonable proof of it?

A. We cannot, without the miraculous discernment of spirits, be infallibly certain of those who are thus saved. But we apprehend, these would be the best proofs which the nature of the thing admits. 1. If we had sufficient evidence of their unblamable behaviour, at least from the time of their justification 2. If they give a distinct account of the time and manner wherein they were saved from sin, and of the circumstances thereof, with such sound speech as could not be reproved. And,

3. If, upon a strict inquiry from time to time, for two or three years following, it appeared that all their tempers, and words, and actions, were holy and unreprovable.

Q. 6. How should we treat those who think they have attained this?

A. Exhort them to forget the things that are behind, and to watch and pray always, that God may search the ground of their hearts.

Wednesday, June 27

We began to consider points of discipline: with regard to which, the questions asked, and the substance of the answers given, were as follows:

Q. 1. What is the Church of England?

A. According to the 20th Article, the visible Church of England is, The congregation of English *believers*, in which the *pure Word* of God is preached, and the Sacraments *duly* administered.

(But the word *Church* is sometimes taken in a looser sense, for "a congregation professing to believe." So it is taken in the 26th Article, and in the 1st, 2d, and 3d chapters of the Revelation.)

Q. 2. What is a member of the Church of England?

A. A believer, hearing the *pure word* of God preached, and partaking of the Sacraments duly administered, in that Church.

Q. 3. What is it to be zealous for the Church?

A. To be earnestly desirous of its welfare and increase: Of its welfare, by the confirmation of its present members, in faith, hearing, and communicating; and of its increase, by the addition of new members.

Q. 4. How are we to defend the doctrine of the Church?

A. Both by our preaching and living.

Q. 5. How should we behave at a false, or railing sermon?

A. If it only contain personal reflections, we may quietly suffer it: if it blaspheme the work and Spirit of God, it may be better to go out of the church. In either case, if opportunity serve, it would be well to speak or write to the minister.

Q. 6. How far is it our duty to obey the bishops?

A. In all things indifferent. And on this ground of obeying them, we should observe the Canons, so far as we can with a safe conscience.

Q. 7. Do we separate from the Church?

A. We conceive not. We hold communion therewith, for conscience' sake, by constantly attending both the word preached, and the sacraments administered therein.

Q. 8. What then do they mean who say, "You separate from the Church?"

A. We cannot certainly tell. Perhaps they have no determinate meaning; unless, by the Church, they mean *themselves*: i.e. that part of the clergy who accuse us of preaching false doctrine. And it is sure we do herein separate from them, by maintaining that which they deny.

Q. 9. But do you not weaken the Church?

A. Do not they who ask this, by *the Church*, mean *themselves*? We do not purposely weaken any man's hands. But accidentally we may, thus far: they who come to know the truth by us, will esteem such as deny it less than they did before.

But the Church, in the proper sense, the congregation of English believers, we do not weaken at all.

Q. 10. Do you not entail a schism on the Church? i.e. Is it not probable, that your hearers, after your death, will be scattered into all sects and parties? Or that they will form themselves into a distinct sect?

A. 1. We are persuaded the body of our hearers will, even after our death, remain in the Church, unless they be thrust out.

2. We believe notwithstanding, either that they will be thrust out, or that they will leaven the whole Church.

3. We do, and will do, all we can, to prevent those consequences, which are supposed likely to happen after our death.

4. But we cannot, with a good conscience, neglect the present opportunity of saving souls while we live, for fear of consequences which may possibly or probably happen, after we are dead.

Thursday, June 28

Q. What may we reasonably believe to be God's design, in raising up the Preachers, called *Methodists*?

A. To reform the nation, more particularly the Church; to spread scriptural holiness over the land.

Q. Is it advisable, only to preach in as many places as we can, without forming any Societies?

A. By no means. We have made the trial in various places; and that for a considerable time. And all the seed has fallen as by the way-side. There is scarce any fruit of it remaining.

Q. But what particular inconveniences do you observe, where Societies are not formed?

A. These among many others: 1. The Preacher cannot give proper instructions and exhortations to them that are convinced of sin. 2. They cannot watch over one another in love. Nor, 3. Can the believers bear one another's burdens, and build up each other in faith and holiness.

Q. Where should we endeavour to preach most?

A. 1. Where we (clergymen) can preach in a church. 2. Where there is the greatest number of quiet and willing hearers. 3. Where there is most fruit.

Q. Is field-preaching then unlawful?

A. We conceive not. We do not know that it is contrary to any law, either of God or man.

A. Have we not used it too sparingly?

A. It seems we have: 1. Because our call is, To save that which is lost. Now we cannot expect such to seek *us*: therefore we should go and seek *them*. 2. Because we are particularly called, by going into the highways and hedges (which none else will) to compel them to come in. 3. Because that reason against it is not good, "The house will hold all that come." The house may hold all that come to the house, but not all that *would come* to the field.

The greatest hinderances to this, you are to expect from the rich, or cowardly, or lazy Methodists. But regard them not, neither Stewards, Leaders, nor people. Whenever the weather will permit, go out in God's Name, into the most public places, and call all to "repent, and believe the Gospel." Every Assistant at least, in every circuit, should endeavour to preach abroad every Sunday. Especially in the old Societies, lest they settle upon their lees.

Q. Ought we not diligently to observe, in what places God is pleased, at any time, to pour out his Spirit more abundantly?

A. We ought, and at that time to send more labourers than usual into that part of the harvest.

Q. What is a sufficient call to a new place?

A. 1. An invitation from a serious man, fearing God, who has a house to receive us. 2. A probability of doing more good by going thither, than by staying longer where we are.

Q. How often shall we permit strangers to be present, at the meeting of the Society?

A. Let every other meeting of the Society, in every place, be strictly private; no one stranger being admitted, on any account or pretence whatsoever. On the other nights we may admit them with caution; but not the same persons above twice or thrice. In order to this, see that all in every place, shew their tickets before they come in. If the Stewards and Leaders are not exact and impartial herein, employ others which have more resolution.

Q. May a relapser into gross sin, confessing his fault, be readmitted into the Soceity?

A. Not as a member, till after three months; but he may be permitted to stay as a stranger.

Q. How may the Leaders of classes be made more useful?

A. 1. Let each of them be diligently examined, concerning his method of meeting a class.

2. Let us recommend to all, the following directions.

1. Let each Leader carefully inquire, How every soul in his class prospers? Not only, How each person observes the outward rules, but how he grows in the knowledge and love of God.

2. Let the Leaders converse with all the Preachers, as frequently and as freely as possible.

3. Let every Leader come into the room on Tuesday, as soon as the service is ended, and then sit down, and commune with God in his heart till the Preacher comes in.

4. Let no Leader go out till the Preacher goes.

5. Let none speak there, but the Preacher or the Steward, unless in answer to a question.

6. Let every Leader bring a note of every sick person in his class.

7. Let every Leader send the same note to the visiter of the sick weekly.

Q. Can any thing further be done, to make the meetings of the classes lively and profitable?

A. 1. Let the Leaders frequently meet each other's classes.

2. Let us observe, which Leaders are most blest to those under their care. And let these meet in other classes as often as possible, and see what hinders their growth in grace.

Q. How can we farther assist these under your care?

A. 1. By examining them more closely, at the general meeting of the classes.

2. By then meeting those who are in bands, every morning before the rest: and examining them both as to their inward state, and their observance of the rules.

3. By meeting the married men and married women apart, the first Wednesday and Sunday after every visitation. The single men and single women apart, on the second Wednesday and Sunday.

4. By examining and instructing them at their own houses, at times set apart for that purpose.

This has never been effectually done yet; though Thomas Walsh took some steps therein. Who will take up that cross? It will be of great use to others, and a blessing to his own soul.

Do all you *can* herein, if not all you *would*. Inquire in each house, Have you family prayer? Do you read the Scripture in your family? Have you a fixed time for private prayer? Examine each as to his growth in grace, and discharge of relative duties.

Q. How shall we prevent improper persons from insinuating themselves into the Society?

A. 1. Give tickets to none, till they are recommended by a Leader, with whom they have met three months on trial.

2. Give notes to none but those who are recommended by a Leader, with whom they have met three or four times.

3. Give them the rules the first time they meet.

Q. How can we add a proper solemnity to the admission of new members?

A. 1. In all large towns, admit new members into the bands, only at the quarterly love-feasts following the visitation. 2. Read the names of the men to be admitted, to the men bands; of the women to the women bands, the week before. 3.

Admit into the Society, only on the Sunday, following the quarterly visitation. 4. Read the names of those to be admitted, on the Sunday evening before. 5. Then also let the names of those be read, who are excluded from the Society.

Q. Should we insist every where on the band rules? Particularly that relating to ruffles?

A. By all means. This is no time to give any encouragement to superfluity of apparel. Therefore, give no band-tickets to any in England or Ireland, till they *have left them* off.

In order to this, 1. Read in every Society the "Thoughts concerning Dress." 2. In visiting the classes, be very mild, but very strict. 3. Allow no exempt case, not even of a married woman, better one suffer than many.

To encourage meeting in band, 1. In every large Society, have a love-feast quarterly, for the bands only. 2. Never fail to meet them apart from the Society, once a week. 3. Exhort all believers to embrace the advantage. 4. Give a band-ticket to none, till they have met a quarter on trial.

Q. Might not the children in every place, be formed into a little Society?

A. Let the Preachers try, by meeting them together, and giving them suitable exhortations.

At each meeting, we may first set them a lesson in the Instructions or Tokens for Children. 2. Hear them repeat it. 3. Explain it to them in an easy, familiar manner. 4. Often ask, "What have I been saying?" And strive to fasten it on their hearts.

Q. Do we observe any evil which has lately prevailed among our Societies?

A. Many of our members have lately married with unbelievers, even with such as were wholly unawakened; and this has been attended with fatal consequences. Few of these have gained the unbelieving wife or husband. Generally they have themselves either had a heavy cross for life, or entirely fallen back into the world.

Q. What can be done to put a stop to this?

A 1. Let every Preacher take occasion publickly to enforce the Apostle's caution, "Be ye not unequally yoked with unbelievers."

2. Let it be openly declared in every place, That he who acts contrary to this, will be expelled the Society.

3. When any such is expelled, let an exhortation be subjoined, dissuading others from following that bad example.

4. And let all be exhorted, to take no step in so weighty a matter, without first advising with the most serious of his brethren.

Q. Ought any woman to marry without the consent of her parents?

A. In general, she ought not: yet there may be an exception. For if, 1. A woman be under a necessity of marrying. If, 2. Her parents absolutely refuse to let her marry any Christian; then she may: nay, ought to marry without their consent. Yet even then, a Methodist Preacher ought not to marry her.

Q. Do not Sabbath-breaking, dram-drinking, evil-speaking, unprofitable conversation, lightness, gaiety or expensiveness of apparel, and contracting debts without sufficient care to discharge them, still prevail in several places? What method can we take to remove these evils?

A. 1. Let us preach expressly and strongly, on each of these heads. 2. Read the sermon on Evil-Speaking, in every Society. 3. Let the Leaders closely examine, and exhort every person to put away the accursed thing. 4. Let the Preacher warn the Society in every place, that none who is hereafter guilty, can remain with us. 5. In order to give them clearer views of the evil of these things, let every Preacher recommend to every Society, and that frequently and earnestly, the reading the books we have published, preferably to any other. And when any new book is sent to any place, let him speak of it in the public congregation. 6. Extirpate smuggling, buying or selling uncustomed goods, out of every Society; particularly in Cornwall, and in all seaport towns. Let no person remain with us, who will not totally abstain from every kind and degree of it. 7. Extirpate bribery, receiving any thing, directly or indirectly, for voting in any election. Shew no respect of persons herein, expel all who touch the accursed thing. Let this be particularly observed at Grimsby and St. Ives.

Friday, June 29

Q. What is the office of a Christian minister?

A. To watch over souls, as he that must give an account.

Q. What does St. James mean, by "respect of persons?"

A. The regarding one person more than another, on account of some outward circumstances, particularly riches.

Q. Have we not fallen into this, 1. By spending more of our time with the rich than with the poor? 2. By not speaking so plain and home to them? And, 3. By suffering them to be present at the love-feasts?

A. These are palpable instances of respect of persons. We will endeavour to avoid them for the time to come.

Q. Would it not be well for every Preacher in town to visit the sick constantly?

A. No time could be employed more profitably, either for them or us.

Q. How may we be most useful herein?

A. 1. Examine carefully what state the sick is in. 2. Instruct, reprove, or exhort accordingly.

Q. How shall we be more easy of access?

A. Speak to any that desire it, every day after preaching, morning and evening.

Q. Is it expedient for us to converse more with the clergy?

A. When any of them desire it.

Q. With our chief opposers and persecutors?

A. It may do good, 1. When they make any overtures towards it. 2. When any of them will converse with us in private.

Q. National sins call aloud for national judgments. What can we do to prevent them?

A. The first week in every month (at least) speak expressly on this head, and insist on the necessity of a general repentance, to prevent a general visitation.

Q. Should we talk of persecution before it comes?

A. To talk or think before, of any particular persecution, only weakens our hands. And how long the general persecution may be deferred, God only knows.

Q. In what view may we and our helpers be considered?

A. Perhaps as extraordinary messengers, designed by God, to provoke others to jealousy.

Q. What is the office of an helper?

A. In the absence of a minister, to feed and guide the flock. In particular,

1. To expound every morning and evening.

2. To meet the United Society, the Bands, the Select Society, and the Penitents every week.

3. To receive on trial for the Society and Bands, and to put the disorderly back on trial.

4. To meet the Leaders of the Bands and Classes weekly, and the Stewards, and to overlook their accounts.

Let every preacher be particularly exact in the morning preaching, and meeting the Leaders.

Q. What are the rules of a Helper?

A. 1. Be diligent. Never be unemployed a moment. Never be triflingly employed. Never while away time: neither spend any more time at any place than is strictly necessary.

2. Be serious. Let your motto be, Holiness to the Lord.—Avoid all lightness, jesting, and foolish talking.

3. Converse sparingly and cautiously with women: particularly with young women in private.

4. Take no step toward marriage, without first acquainting us with your design.

5. Believe evil of no one: unless you see it done, take heed how you credit it. Put the best construction on every thing. You know the judge is always supposed to be on the prisoner's side.

6. Speak evil of no one, else *your* word especially would eat as doth a canker. Keep your thoughts within your own breast, till you come to the person concerned.

7. Tell every one what you think wrong in him, and that plainly, and as soon as may be, else it will fester in your heart. Make all haste to cast the fire out of your bosom.

8. Do not affect the gentleman. You have no more to do with this character, than with that of a dancing-master. A preacher of the Gospel, is the servant of all.

9. Be ashamed of nothing but sin: not of fetching wood, (if time permit,) or of drawing water; not of cleaning your own shoes, or your neighbours'.

10. Be punctual. Do every thing exactly at the time. And, in general, do not *mend* our rules, but keep them; not for wrath, but for conscience' sake.

11. You have nothing to do, but to save souls. Therefore spend and be spent in this work. And go always, not only to those who want you, but to those who want you most.

12. Act in all things, not according to your own will, but as a son in the Gospel. As such, it is your part to employ your time, in the manner which we direct: partly in

preaching, and visiting the flock from house to house; partly in reading, meditation, and prayer. Above all, if you labour with us in our Lord's vineyard, it is needful you should do *that part* of the work which we advise, at *those* times and places, which we judge most for his glory.

Q. What general method of employing our time would you advise us to?

A. We advise you, 1. As often as possible, to rise at four. 2. From four to five in the morning, and from five to six in the evening, to meditate, pray, and read; partly the Scriptures, with the *Notes* on the New Testament; partly *Kempis*, and the Instructions for Children; and partly, the closely practical parts of the Christian Library. 3. From six in the morning till twelve, (allowing an hour for breakfast,) to read in order, with much prayer, Bishop Pearson on the Creed, Mr. Boehms and Nalson's Sermons, the remaining parts of the Christian Library, our other Tracts and Poems, Paradise Lost, and Professor Frank's works.

Q. How may we be more useful in conversation?

A. 1. Fix the end of each conversation before you begin. 2. Watch and pray during the time. 3. Spend two or three minutes every hour in earnest prayer. 4. Strictly observe the morning and evening hour of retirement. 5. Rarely spend above an hour at a time in conversing with any one. 6. Earnestly recommend the five o'clock hour to all.

Q. Do we sufficiently watch over our helpers?

A. We might consider those that are with us as our pupils: Into whose behaviour and studies, we should therefore make a particular inquiry every day.

Should we not frequently ask each, Do you walk closely with God? Have you now fellowship with the Father and the Son? At what hour do you rise? Do you punctually observe the morning and evening hour of retirement? Do you spend the day in the manner which we advise? Do you read the books we advise, and no other? Do you fast as often as your health will permit? Do you converse seriously, usefully, and closely? Do you pray before, and have you a determinate end in every conversation?

To be more particular:

Do you use all the means of grace yourself, and enforce the use of them on all persons?

They are either instituted or prudential.

I. The instituted are,

1. Prayer; private, family, public: consisting of deprecation, petition, intercession, thanksgiving.

Do you use each of these constantly (at set times) and fervently?

Do you use private prayer every morning and evening? If you are your own master, at five in the evening, and the hour before or after morning preaching?

Do you forecast, wherever you are, how to secure these hours?

Do you avow it every where?

Are you resolute herein?

Do you call your family together at five?

Do you ask every where, 1. Have *you* family prayer? 2. Do you retire at five o'clock?

II. Searching the Scripture, by

1. Reading: *constantly*, some part of every day, and at all vacant hours; *regularly*, all the New Testament, (at least,) and the Lessons for Children in order; *carefully*, with the Notes, *seriously, deliberately,* with much prayer preceding, accompanying, and following: *fruitfully*, immediately practising what you learn there?

What other books do you read? Is it wise to read any, till you have read our Tracts, and the Christain Library?

Do you give the morning to reading, writing, and prayer?

2. Meditating: At set times? How? By Bishop Hall's, or Mr. Baxter's rule? How long?

3. Hearing: constantly? Every morning?

Humbly? Uncritically, devoutly?

Carefully? With prayer before, at, after?

Fruitfully? Immediately putting in practice?

Have you a New Testament always in your pocket?

(See that the Notes are in every Society. Explain them to the congregation.)

III. The Lord's Supper. Do you use this?

At every opportunity? With due preparation? i.e. with solemn prayer? With careful self-examination? With deep repentance suited thereto? With earnest and deliberate self-devotion?

Do you, in communicating, discern the Lord's body?

Do you afterward retire, not formally, but in earnest?

IV. Fasting: God led us to this at Oxford. And he led all of you to it, when you first set out.

How often do you fast now? Every Friday? In what degree?

I purpose generally to eat only vegetables on Friday, and take only toast and water in the morning.

V. Christian Conference.

Are we convinced, how important, and how difficult it is, to order our conversation aright?

Is it always *in grace*? Seasoned with salt? Meet to minister grace to the hearers?

Do we not converse too long at a time? Is not an hour at a time commonly enough?

Would it not be well, to plan our conversation before-hand? To pray before and after it?

II. Prudential means, we may use either as common Christians, as Methodists, as Preachers, or as Assistants.

1. As common Christians. What particular rules have *you*, for avoiding evil, doing good? Growing in grace? What arts of holy living?

2. As Methodists. Do you never miss any meeting of the Society? Neither your Class or Band?

3. As Preachers. Do you meet every Society weekly? Also the Leaders? And Bands, if any?

Do you visit the sick; and the well? Instructing masters and parents? And in all relative duties?

4. As Assistants. Do you fill up and regulate the Bands wherever you come? Diligently inquire into the state of the books, and do all you can to propagate them? Keep watch-nights once a month? And love-feasts? With one twice a year, for all the Society?

Do you visit every Society once a quarter, and regulate all things therein?

Do you take a regular catalogue of your Societies, at least one a year?

Do you write me an account of all the defects of the common Preachers, which you cannot yourself cure?

These means may be used without fruit. But there are some means which cannot. Namely, watching, denying ourselves, taking up our cross, exercise of the Presence of God.

1. Do we steadily watch against the world, the devil, ourselves? The besetting sin?

2. Do you deny yourselves every useless pleasure of sense? Imagination? Honour? Are you temperate in all things? To take one instance, in food? Do you use only that *kind*, and that *degree*, which is best both for the body and soul? Do you see the necessity of this?

Do you eat no flesh suppers? No late suppers? These naturally tend to destroy bodily health.

Do you eat only three meals a day? If four, are you not an excellent pattern to the flock?

Do you take no more food than is necessary at each meal? You may know if you do, by a load at your stomach: by drowsiness, or heaviness: and, in a while, by weak or bad nerves.

Do you use only that *kind*, and that *degree* of drink, which is best both for your body and soul?

Do you drink water? Why not? Did you ever? Why did you leave it off? If not for health, when will you begin again? Today?

How often do you drink wine or ale? Every day? Do you *want* or *waste* it?

3. Wherein do you *take up your cross* daily? Do you cheerfully *bear your cross*, (whatever is grievous to nature,) as a gift of God, and labour to profit thereby?

4. Do you endeavour to set God always before you? To see his eye continually fixed upon you? Never can you use these means, but a blessing will ensue. And the more you use them, the more will you grow in grace, and in the knowledge of our Lord Jesus Christ.

Q. What can be done, in order to a closer union of our Helpers with each other?

A. 1. Let them be deeply convinced of the want there is of it at present, and the absolute necessity of it.

2. Let them pray for an earnest desire of union.

3. Let them speak freely to each other.

4. When they meet, let them never part without prayer.

5. Let them beware, how they despise each other's gifts.

6. Let them never speak slightingly of each other in any kind.

7. Let them defend one another's character in every thing, to the utmost of their power. And,

8. Let them labour, in honour each to prefer the other before himself.

Q. How shall we avoid popularity? We mean such esteem or love from the people, as is not for the glory of God?

A. 1. Earnestly pray for a piercing sense of the danger there is, and the sinfulness of it.

2. Take care how you ingratiate yourself with any people, by slackness of discipline.

3. Or by any method which another Preacher cannot follow.

4. Warn the people among whom you are most, of esteeming or loving you too much.

5. Converse sparingly with those who are particularly fond of you.

Q. How often should our Helpers preach?

A. Not more than twice a day, unless on a Sunday, or some extraordinary occasion.

Q. Which is the best general method of preaching?

A. 1. To invite. 2. To convince. 3. To offer Christ. 4. To build up. And to do this in some measure in every sermon.

Q. Are there any smaller advices relating to preaching, which might be of use to us?

A. Perhaps these: 1. Be sure to begin and end, precisely at the time appointed.

2. Endeavour to be serious, weighty, and solemn, in your whole deportment before the congregation.

3. Always suit your subject to the audience.

4. Choose the plainest texts you can.

5. Take care not to ramble from your text, but keep close to it, and make out from it what you take in hand.

6. Beware of allegorizing or spiritualizing too much.

7. Take care of any thing awkward or affected, either in your phrase, gesture, or pronunciation.

8. Tell each other, if you observe any thing of this kind.

9. Sing no hymns of your own composing.

10. Without a pressing reason, do not pray above eight or ten minutes (at most) without intermission.

11. It would be well for every young Preacher, frequently to exhort, without taking any text. And for every one, young or old, frequently to read and enlarge upon a portion of the Notes.

Q. What sermons do we find, by experience, to be attended with the greatest blessing?

A. 1. Such as are most close, convincing, searching. 2. Such as have most of Christ. 3. Such as urge the heinousness of men's living in contempt or ignorance of him.

Q. But have not some of us been led off from practical preaching, by (what was called) *preaching* Christ?

A. Indeed we have. The most effectual way of preaching Christ, is to preach him in all his offices, and to declare his Law as well as his Gospel, both to believers and unbelievers.

Q. Do we now all preach strongly and closely, concerning both inward and outward holiness?

A. It would be well, if we were more frequently and more largely to insist upon it in all its branches.

Q. Do we insist enough upon practical religion in general? And in particular, on relative duties? Using the means of grace? Private prayer? Self-denial? Fasting? Seriousness?

A. It seems most of us have been wanting here. Let us take care to supply this defect for the future.

Q. How shall we be assured, that no Preacher will ever disappoint a congregation?

A. Ask every one, 1. Do you see the great sin, and fatal consequences of it? 2. Will you break a limb, rather than wilfully break your word herein? 3. If you do, can you blame us, for not employing you any more?

Q. How shall we guard against formality in public worship; particularly in singing?

A. 1. By preaching frequently on that head. 2. By taking care to speak only what we feel. 3. By choosing such hymns as are proper for the congregation; generally hymns of prayer or praise, rather than descriptive of particular states. 4. By not singing too much at once; seldom more than five or six verses. 5. By suiting the tune to the nature of the hymn. 6. By often stopping short and asking the people, "Now! do you know what you said last? Did you speak no more than you felt? Did you sing it as unto the Lord; with the spirit and with the understanding also?"

Q. What can be done to make the people sing true?

A. 1. Learn to sing true yourselves. 2. Recommend the tunes every where. 3. If a preacher cannot sing himself, let him choose two or three persons in every place, to pitch the tune for him.

Q. What is it best to take just after preaching?

A. Lemonade; candied orange peel, or a little soft, warm ale. But egg and wine is downright poison. And so are late suppers.

"A Plain Account of the People called Methodists, in a Letter to the Reverend Mr. Perronet, Vicar of Shoreham, in Kent" by John Wesley, 1748

The Works of John Wesley (Grand Rapids, Mich.: Zondervan Publishing House, n.d.), VIII, 248-68.

In the document which follows, the origins and objectives of the Methodist movement are described by its famous founder, John Wesley (1703-91).

1. Some time since, you desired an account of the whole economy of the people commonly called *Methodists*. And you received a true, (as far as it went,) but

not a full, account. To supply what I think was wanting in that, I send you this account, that you may know, not only their practice on every head, but likewise the reasons whereon it is grounded, the occasion of every step they have taken, and the advantages reaped thereby.

2. But I must premise, that as they had not the least expectation, at first, of any thing like what has since followed, so they had no previous design or plan at all; but every thing arose just as the occasion offered. They saw or felt some impending or pressing evil, or some good end necessary to be pursued. And many times they fell unawares on the very thing which secured the good, or removed the evil. At other times, they consulted on the most probable means, following only common sense and Scripture: Though they generally found, in looking back, something in Christian antiquity likewise, very nearly parallel thereto.

I. 1. About ten years ago, my brother and I were desired to preach in many parts of London. We had no view therein, but, so far as we were able, (and we knew God could work by whomsoever it pleased him,) to convince those who would hear what true Christianity was, and to persuade them to embrace it.

2. The points we chiefly insisted upon were four: First, that orthodoxy, or right opinions, is, at best, but a very slender part of religion, if it can be allowed to be any part of it at all; that neither does religion consist in negatives, in bare harmlessness of any kind; nor merely in externals, in doing good, or using the means of grace in works of piety (so called) or of charity; that it is nothing short of, or different from, "the mind that was in Christ;" the image of God stamped upon the heart; inward righteousness, attended with the peace of God; and "joy in the Holy Ghost." Secondly, that the only way under heaven to this religion is, to "repent and believe the gospel;" or, (as the Apostle words it,) "repentance towards God, and faith in our Lord Jesus Christ." Thirdly, that by this faith, "he that worketh not, but believeth on him that justifieth the ungodly, is justified freely by his grace, through the redemption which is in Jesus Christ." And, Lastly, that "being justified by faith," we taste of the heaven to which we are going; we are holy and happy; we tread down sin and fear, and "sit in heavenly places with Christ Jesus."

3. Many of those who heard this began to cry out that we brought "strange things to their ears;" that this was doctrine which they never heard before, or at least never regarded. They "searched the Scriptures, whether these things were so," and acknowledged "the truth as it is in Jesus." Their hearts also were influenced as well as their understandings, and they determined to follow "Jesus Christ, and him crucified."

4. Immediately they were surrounded with difficulties;—all the world rose up against them; neighbours, strangers, acquaintance, relations, friends, began to cry out amain, "Be not righteous overmuch; why shouldest thou destroy thyself?" Let not "much religion make thee mad."

5. One, and another, and another came to us, asking what they should do, being distressed on every side; as every one strove to weaken, and none to strengthen, their hands in God. We advised them, "Strengthen you one another. Talk together as often as you can. And pray earnestly with and for one another, that you may 'endure to the end, and be saved.' " Against this advice we presumed there could be no objection; as being grounded on the plainest reason, and on so many

scriptures both of the Old Testament and New, that it would be tedious to recite them.

6. They said, "But we want you likewise to take with us often, to direct and quicken us in our way, to give us the advices which you well know we need, and to pray with us, as well as for us." I asked, Which of you desire this? Let me know your names and places of abode. They did so. But I soon found they were too many for me to talk with severally so often as they wanted it. So I told them, "If you will all of you come together every Thursday, in the evening, I will gladly spend some time with you in prayer, and give you the best advice I can."

7. Thus arose, without any previous design on either side, what was afterwards called *a Society*; a very innocent name, and very common in London, for any number of people associating themselves together. The thing proposed in their associating themselves together was obvious to every one. They wanted to "flee from the wrath to come," and to assist each other in so doing. They therefore united themselves "in order to pray together, to receive the word of exhortation, and to watch over one another in love, that they might help each other to work out their salvation."

8. There is one only condition previously required in those who desire admission into this society,—"a desire to flee from the wrath to come, to be saved from their sins."

They now likewise agreed, that as many of them as had an opportunity would meet together every Friday, and spend the dinner hour in crying to God, both for each other, and for all mankind.

9. It quickly appeared, that their thus uniting together answered the end proposed therein. In a few months, the far greater part of those who had begun to "fear God, and work righteousness," but were not united together, grew faint in their minds, and fell back into what they were before. Meanwhile the far greater part of those who were thus united together continued "striving to enter in at the strait gate," and to "lay hold on eternal life."

10. Upon reflection, I could not but observe, This is the very thing which was from the beginning of Christianity. In the earliest times, those whom God had sent forth "preached the gospel to every creature." And the . . . , "the body of hearers," were mostly either Jews or Heathens. But as soon as any of these were so convinced of the truth, as to forsake sin and seek the gospel salvation, they immediately joined them together, took an account of their names, advised them to watch over each other, and met these . . . , "catechumens," (as they were then called,) apart from the great congregation, that they might instruct, rebuke, exhort, and pray with them, and for them, according to their several necessities.

11. But it was not long before an objection was made to this, which had not once entered into my thought:—"Is not this making a schism? Is not the joining these people together, gathering Churches out of Churches?"

It was easily answered, If you mean only gathering people out of buildings called churches, it is. But if you mean, dividing Christians from Christians, and so destroying Christian fellowship, it is not. For, (1.) These were not Christians before they were thus joined. Most of them were barefaced Heathens. (2.) Neither are they Christians, from whom you suppose them to be divided. You will not look me in the face and say they are. What! drunken Christians! cursing and swearing Christians! lying Christians! cheating Christians! If these are Christians at all, they are devil Christians, as the poor Malabarians term them. (3.) Neither are they divided any more than they were before, even from these wretched devil Christians. They are as ready as ever to assist them, and to perform every office of real kindness towards them. (4.) If it be said, "But there are some true Christians in the parish, and you destroy the Christian fellowship between these and them;" I answer, That which never existed, cannot be destroyed. But the fellowship you speak of never existed. Therefore it cannot be destroyed. Which of those true Christians had any such fellowship with these? Who watched over them in love? Who marked their growth in grace? Who advised and exhorted them from time to time? Who prayed with them and for them, as they had need? This, and this alone, is Christian fellowship: But, alas! where is it to be found? Look east or west, north or south; name what parish you please: Is this Christian fellowship there? Rather, are not the bulk of the parishioners a mere rope of sand? What Christian connexion is there between them? What intercourse in spiritual things? What watching over each other's souls? What bearing of one another burdens? What a mere jest is it then, to talk so gravely of destroying what never was! The real truth is just the reverse os this: We introduce Christian fellowship where it was utterly destroyed. And the fruits of it have been peace, joy, love, and zeal for every good word and work.

II. 1. But as much as we endeavoured to watch over each other, we soon found some who did not live the gospel. I do not know that any hypocrites were crept in; for indeed there was no temptation: But several grew cold, and gave way to the sins which had long easily beset them. We quickly perceived there were many ill consequences of suffering these to remain among us. It was dangerous to others; inasmuch as all sin is of an infectious nature. It brought such a scandal on their brethren as exposed them to what was not properly the reproach of Christ. It laid a stumbling block in the way of others, and caused the truth to be evil spoken of.

2. We groaned under these inconveniences long, before a remedy could be found. The people were scattered so wide in all parts of the town, from Wapping to Westminster, that I could not easily see what the behaviour of each person in his own neighbourhood was: So that several disorderly walkers did much hurt before I was apprized of it.

3. At length, while we were thinking of quite another thing, we struck upon a method for which we have cause to bless God ever since. I was talking with several of the society in Bristol concerning the means of paying the debts there, when one stood up and said, "Let every member of the society give a penny a week till all are paid." Another answered, "But many of them are poor, and cannot afford to do it." "Then," said he, "put eleven of the poorest with me; and if they can give anything, well: I will call on them weekly; and if they can give nothing, I will give for them as well as for myself. And each of you call on eleven of your neighbours weekly; receive what they give, and make up what is wanting." It was done. In a while, some of these informed me, they found such and such an one did not live as he ought. It struck me immediately, "This is the thing; the very thing we have wanted so long." I called together all the Leaders of the classes, (so we used to term them and their companies,) and desired, that each would make a particular inquiry into the

behaviour of those whom he saw weekly. They did so. Many disorderly walkers were detected. Some turned from the evil of their ways. Some were put away from us. Many saw it with fear, and rejoiced unto God with reverence.

4. As soon as possible, the same method was used in London and all other places. Evil men were detected, and reproved. They were borne with for a season. If they forsook their sins, we received them gladly; if they obstinately persisted therein, it was openly declared that they were not of us. The rest mourned and prayed for them, and yet rejoiced, that, as far as in us lay, the scandal was rolled away from the society.

5. It is the business of a Leader, (1.) To see each person in his class, once a week at the least, in order to inquire how their souls prosper; to advise, reprove, comfort, or exhort, as occasion may require; to receive what they are willing to give, toward the relief of the poor.

(2.) To meet the Minister and the Stewards of the society, in order to inform the Minister of any that are sick, or of any that are disorderly and will not be reproved; to pay to the Stewards what they have received of their several classes in the week preceeding.

6. At first they visited each person at his own house; but this was soon found not so expedient. And that on many accounts: (1.) It took up more time than most of the Leaders had to spare. (2.) Many persons lived with masters, mistresses, or relations, who would not suffer them to be thus visited. (3.) At the houses of those who were not so averse, they often had no opportunity of speaking to them but in company. And this did not at all answer the end proposed,—of exhorting, comforting, or reproving. (4.) It frequently happened that one affirmed what another denied. And this could not be cleared up without seeing them together. (5.) Little misunderstandings and quarrels of various kinds frequently arose among relations or neighbours; effectually to remove which, it was needful to see them all face to face. Upon all these considerations it was agreed, that those of each class should meet alltogether. And by this means, a more full inquiry was made into the behaviour of every person. Those who could not be visited at home, or no otherwise than in company, had the same advantage with others. Advice or reproof was given as need required, quarrels made up, misunderstandings removed: And after an hour or two spent in this labour of love, they concluded with prayer and thanksgiving.

7. It can scarce be conceived what advantages have been reaped from this little prudential regulation. Many now happily experienced that Christian fellowship of which they had not so much as an idea before. They began to "bear one another's burdens," and naturally to "care for each other." As they had daily a more intimate acquaintance with, so they had a more endeared affection for, each other. And "speaking the truth in love, they grew up into Him in all things, who is the Head, even Christ; from whom the whole body, fitly joined together, and compacted by that which every joint supplied, according to the effectual working in the measure of every part, increased unto the edifying itself in love."

8. But notwithstanding all these advantages, many were at first extremely averse to meeting thus. Some, viewing it in a wrong point of light, not as a privilege, (indeed an invaluable one,) but rather a restraint, disliked it on that account,

because they did not love to be restrained in anything. Some were ashamed to speak before company. Others honestly said, "I do not know why; but I do not like it."

9. Some objected, "There were no such meetings when I came into the society first: And why should there now? I do not understand these things, and this changing one thing after another continually." It was easily answered: It is pity but they had been at first. But we knew not then either the need or the benefit of them. Why we use them, you will readily understand, if you read over the rules of the society. That with regard to these little prudential helps we are continually changing one thing after another, is not a weakness or fault, as you imagine, but a peculiar advantage which we enjoy. By this means we declare them all to be merely prudential, not essential, not of divine institution. We prevent, so far as in us lies, their growing formal or dead. We are always open to instruction; willing to be wiser every day than we were before, and to change whatever we can change for the better.

10. Another objection was, "There is no scripture for this, for classes and I know not what." I answer, (1.) There is no scripture against it. You cannot show one text that forbids them. (2.) There is much scripture for it, even all those texts which enjoin the substance of those various duties whereof this is only an indifferent circumstance, to be determined by reason and experience. (3.) You seem not to have observed, that the Scripture, in most points, gives only general rules; and leaves the particular circumstances to be adjusted by the common sense of mankind. The Scripture, for instance, gives that general rule, "Let all things be done decently and in order." But common sense is to determine, on particular occasions, what order and decency require. So, in another instance, the Scripture lays it down as a general, standing direction: "Whether ye eat or drink, or whatever ye do, do all to the glory of God." But it is common prudence which is to make the application of this, in a thousand particular cases.

11. "But these," said another, "are all man's inventions." This is but the same objection in another form. And the same answer will suffice for any reasonable person. These are man's inventions. And what then? That is, they are methods which men have found, by reason and common sense, for the more effectually applying several Scripture rules, couched in general terms, to particular occasions.

12. They spoke far more plausibly than these, who said, "The thing is well enough in itself. But the Leaders are insufficient for the work: They have neither gifts nor graces for such an employment." I answer, (1.) Yet such Leaders as they are, it is plain God has blessed their labour. (2.) If any of these is remarkably wanting in gifts or grace, he is soon taken notice of and removed. (3.) If you know any such, tell it to me, not to others, and I will endeavour to exchange him for a better. (4.) It may be hoped they will all be better than they are, both by experience and observation, and by the advices given them by the Minister every Tuesday night, and the prayers (then in particular) offered up for them.

III. 1. About this time, I was informed that several persons in Kingswood frequently met together at the school; and, when they could spare the time, spent the greater part of the night in prayer, and praise, and thanksgiving. Some advised me to put an end to this; but, upon weighing the thing thoroughly, and comparing it with the practice of the ancient Christains, I could see no cause to forbid it. Rather, I believed it might be made of more general use. So I sent them word, I designed to watch with them on the Friday nearest the full moon, that we might have light thither and back again. I gave public notice of this the Sunday before, and, withal, that I intended to preach; desiring they, and they only, would meet me there, who could do it without prejudice to their business or families. On Friday abundance of people came. I began preaching between eight and nine; and we continued till a little beyond the noon of night, singing, praying, and praising God.

2.   This we have continued to do once a month ever since, in Bristol, London, and Newcastle, as well as Kingswood; and exceeding great are the blessings we have found therein: It has generally been an extremely solemn season; when the word of God sunk deep into the heart, even of those who till then knew him not. If it be said, "This was only owing to the novelty of the thing, (the circumstance which still draws such multitudes together at those seasons,) or perhaps to the awful silence of the night:" I am not careful to answer in this matter. Be it so: However, the impression then made on many souls has never since been effaced. Now, allowing that God did make use either of the novelty or any other indifferent circumstance, in order to bring sinners to repentance, yet they are brought. And herein let us rejoice together.

3.   Nay, may I not put the case farther yet? If I can probably conjecture, that, either by the novelty of this ancient custom, or by any other indifferent circumstance, it is in my power to "save a soul from death, and hide a multitude of sins," am I clear before God if I do it not, if I do not snatch that brand out of the burning?

IV.   1.   As the society increased, I found it required still greater care to separate the precious from the vile. In order to this, I determined, at least once in three months, to talk with every member myself, and to inquire at their own mouths, as well as of their Leaders and neighbours, whether they grew in grace and in the knowledge of our Lord Jesus Christ. At these seasons I likewise particularly inquire whether there be any misunderstanding or difference among them; that every hinderance of peace and brotherly love may be taken out of the way.

2.   To each of those of whose seriousness and good conversation I found no reason to doubt, I gave a testimony under my own hand, by writing their name on a ticket prepared for that purpose; every ticket implying as strong a recommendation of the person to whom it was given as if I had wrote at length, "I believe the bearer hereof to be one that fears God and works righteousness."

3.   Those who bore these tickets, (these . . . or *tesseroe*, as the ancients termed them, being of just the same force with the . . . , *commendatory letters* mentioned by the Apostle,) wherever they came, were acknowledged by their brethren, and received with all cheerfulness. These were likewise of use in other respects. By these it was easily distinguished, when the society were to meet apart, who were members of it, and who not. These also supplied us with a quiet and inoffensive method of removing any disorderly member. He has no new ticket at the quarterly visitation; (for so often the tickets are changed;) and hereby it is immediately known that he is no longer of the community.

V.   The thing which I was greatly afraid of all this time, and which I resolved to use every possible method of preventing, was, a narrowness of spirit, a party zeal, a being straitened in our own bowels; that miserable bigotry which makes many so unready to believe that there is any work of God but among themselves. I thought it might be a help against this, frequently to read, to all who were willing to hear, the accounts I received from time to time of the work which God is carrying on in the earth, both in our own and other countries, not among us alone, but among those of various opinions and denominations. For this I allotted one evening in every month; and I find no cause to repent my labour. It is generally a time of strong consolation to those who love God, and all mankind for his sake; as well as of breaking down the partition-walls which either the craft of the devil or the folly of men has built up; and of encouraging every child of God to say, (O when shall it once be!) "Whosoever doeth the will of my Father which is in heaven, the same is my brother, and sister, and mother."

VI. 1. By the blessing of God upon their endeavours to help one another, many found the pearl of great price. Being justified by faith, they had "peace with God, through our Lord Jesus Christ." These felt a more tender affection than before, to those who were partakers of like precious faith; and hence arose such a confidence in each other, that they poured out their souls into each other's bosom. Indeed they had great need so to do; for the war was not over, as they had supposed; but they had still to wrestle both with flesh and blood, and with principalities and powers: So that temptations were on every side; and often temptations of such a kind, as they knew not how to speak in a class; in which persons of every sort, young and old, men and women, met together.

2. These, therefore, wanted some means of closer union; they wanted to pour out their hearts without reserve, particularly with regard to the sin which did still easily beset them, and the temptations which were most apt to prevail over them. And they were the more desirous of this, when they observed it was the express advice of an inspired writer: "Confess your faults one to another, and pray one for another, that ye may be healed."

3. In compliance with their desire, I divided them into smaller companies, putting the married or single men, and married or single women, together. The chief rules of these bands (that is, little companies; so that old English word signifies) run thus:—

"In order to 'confess our faults one to another,' and pray one for another that we may be healed, we intend, (1.) To meet once a week, at the least. (2.) To come punctually at the hour appointed. (3.) To begin with singing or prayer. (4.) To speak each of us in order, freely and plainly, the true state of our soul, with the faults we have committed in thought, word, or deed, and the temptations we have felt since our last meeting. (5.) To desire some person among us (thence called a Leader) to speak his own state first, and then to ask the rest, in order, as many and as searching questions as may be, concerning their state, sins, and temptations."

4. That their design in meeting might be the more effectually answered, I desired all the men-bands to meet me together every Wednesday evening, and the women on Sunday, that they might receive such particular instructions and exhortations as, from time to time, might appear to be most needful for them; that such prayers might be offered up to God, as their necessities should require; and praise returned to the Giver of every good gift, for whatever mercies they had received.

5. In order to increase in them a grateful sense of all his mercies, I desired that, one evening in a quarter, all the men in band, on a second, all the women, would meet; and on a third, both men and women together; that we might together "eat bread," as the ancient Christians did, "with gladness and singleness of heart," At these love-feasts (so we termed them, retaining the name, as well as the thing, which was in use from the beginning) our food is only a little plain cake and water. But we seldom return from them without being fed, not only with the "meat which perisheth," but with "that which endureth to everlasting life."

6. Great and many are the advantages which have ever since flowed from this closer union of the believers with each other. They prayed for one another, that they might be healed of the faults they had confessed; and it was so. The chains were broken, the hands were burst in sunder, and sin had no more dominion over them. Many were delivered from the temptations out of which, till then, they found no way to escape. They were built up in our most holy faith. They rejoiced in the Lord more abundantly. They were strengthened in love, and more effectually provoked to abound in every good work.

7. But it was soon objected to the bands, (as to the classes before,) "These were not at first. There is no Scripture for them. These are man's works, man's building, man's invention." I reply, as before, these are also prudential helps, grounded on reason and experience, in order to apply the general rules given in Scripture according to particular circumstances.

8. An objection much more boldly and frequently urged, is, that "all these bands are mere Popery." I hope I need not pass a harder censure on those (most of them at least) who affirm this, than that they talk of they know not what; they betray in themselves the most gross and shameful ignorance. Do not they yet know, that the only Popish confession is, the confession made by a single person to a Priest?—and this itself is in nowise condemned by our Church; nay, she recommends it in some cases. Whereas, that we practise it, the confession of several persons conjointly, not to a Priest, but to each other. Consequently, it has no analogy at all to Popish confession. But the truth is, this is a stale objection, which many people make against anything they do not like. It is all Popery out of hand.

VII. 1. And yet while most of these who were thus intimately joined together, went on daily from faith to faith; some fell from the faith, either all at once, by falling into known, wilful sin; or gradually, and almost insensibly, by giving way in what they called little things; by sins of omission, by yielding to heart-sins, or by not watching unto prayer. The exhortations and prayers used among the believers did no longer profit these. They wanted advice and instructions suited to their case; which as soon as I observed, I separated them from the rest, and desired them to meet me apart on Saturday evenings.

2. At this hour, all the hymns, exhortations, and prayers are adapted to their circumstances; being wholly suited to those who *did* see God, but have now lost sight of the light of his countenance; and who mourn after him, and refuse to be comforted till they know he has healed their backsliding.

3. By applying both the threats and promises of God to these real, but nominal, penitents, and by crying to God in their behalf, we endeavoured to bring them back to the great "Shepherd and Bishop of their souls;" not by any of the

fopperies of the Roman Church, although, in some measure, countenanced by antiquity. In prescribing hair-shirts, and bodily austerities, we durst not follow even the ancient Church; although we had unawares, both in dividing . . . , the believers, from the rest of the society, and in separating the penitents from them, and appointing a peculiar service for them.

VIII. 1. Many of these soon recovered the ground they had lost. Yea, they rose higher than before; being more watchful than ever, and more meak and lowly, as well as stronger in the faith that worketh by love. They now outran the greater part of their brethren, continually walking in the light of God, and having fellowship with the Father, and with his Son Jesus Christ,

2. I saw it might be useful to give some advices to all those who continued in the light of God's countenance, which the rest of their brethren did not want, and probably could not receive. So I desired a small number of such as appeared to be in this state, to spend an hour with me every Monday morning. My design was, not only to direct them how to press after perfection; to exercise their every grace, and improve every talent they had received; and to incite them to love one another more, and to watch more carefully over each other; but also to have a select company, to whom I might unbosom myself on all occasions, without reserve; and whom I could propose to all their brethren as a pattern of love, of holiness, and of good works.

3. They had no need of being incumbered with many rules; having the best rule of all in their hearts. No peculiar directions were therefore given to them, excepting only these three:—

First. Let nothing spoken in this society be spoken again. (Hereby we had the more full confidence in each other.)

Secondly. Every member agrees to submit to his Minister in all indifferent things.

Thirdly. Every member will bring, once a week, all he can spare toward a common stock.

4. Every one here has an equal liberty of speaking, there being none greater or less than another. I could say freely to these, when they were met together, "Ye may all prophesy one by one," (taking that word in its lowest sense,) "that all may learn, and all may be comforted." And I often found the advantage of such a free conversation, and that "in the multitude of counsellors there is safety." Any who is inclined so to do is likewise encouraged to pour out his soul to God. And here especially we have found, that "the effectual fervent prayer of a righteous man availeth much."

IX. 1. This is the plainest and clearest account I can give of the people commonly called *Methodists*. It remains only to give you a short account of those who serve their brethren in love. These are Leaders of classes and bands, (spoken of before,) Assistants, Stewards, Visitors of the sick, and Schoolmasters.

2. In the third part of the "Appeal," I have mentioned how we were led to accept of Lay-Assistants. Their office is, in the absence of the Minister, (1.) To expound every morning and evening. (2.) To meet the united society, the bands, the select society, and the penitents, once a week. (3.) To visit the classes once a quarter. (4.) To hear and decide all differences. (5.) To put the disorderly back on trial, and to receive on trial for the bands or society. (6.) To see that the Stewards, the Leaders,

and the Schoolmasters faithfully discharge their several offices. (7.) To meet the Leaders of the bands and classes weekly, and the Stewards, and to overlook their accounts.

X. 1. But, long before this, I felt the weight of a far different care, namely, care of temporal things. The quarterly subscriptions amounted, at a mean computation, to above three hundred pounds a year. This was to be laid out, partly in repairs, partly in other necessary expenses, and partly in paying debts. The weekly contributions fell little short of eight pounds a week; which was to be distributed as every one had need. And I was expected to take thought for all these things: But it was a burden I was not able to bear; so I chose out first one, then four, and after a time, seven, as prudent men as I knew, and desired them to take charge of these things upon themselves, that I might have no incumbrance of this kind.

2. The business of these Stewards is, To manage the temporal things of the society. To receive the subscriptions and contributions. To expend what is needful from time to time. To send relief to the poor. To keep an exact account of all receipts and expenses. To inform the Minister if any of the rules of the society are not punctually observed. To tell the Preachers in love, if they think anything amiss, either in their doctrine or life.

3. The rules of the Stewards are, (1.) Be frugal. Save everything that can be saved honestly. (2.) Spend no more than you receive. Contract no debts. (3.) Have no long accounts. Pay everything within the week. (4.) Give none that asks relief, either an ill word or an ill look. Do not hurt them, if you cannot help. (5.) Expect no thanks from man.

4. They met together at six every Thursday morning; consulted on the business which came before them; sent relief to the sick, as every one had need; and gave the remainder of what had been contributed each week to those who appeared to be in the most pressing want. So that all was concluded within the week; what was brought on Tuesday being constantly expended on Thursday. I soon had the pleasure to find, that all these temporal things were done with the utmost faithfulness and exactness; so that my cares of this kind were at an end. I had only to revise the accounts, to tell them if I thought anything might be amended, and to consult how deficiencies might be supplied from time to time; for these were frequent and large, (so far were we from abundance,) the income by no means answering the expenses. But that we might not faint, sometimes we had unforeseen helps in times of the greatest perplexity. At other times we borrowed larger or smaller sums: Of which the greatest part has since been repaid. But I owe some hundred pounds to this day. So much have I gained by preaching the gospel!

XI. 1. But it was not long before the Stewards found a great difficulty with regard to the sick. Some were ready to perish before they knew of their illness; and when they did know, it was not in their power (being persons generally employed in trade) to visit them so often as they desired.

2. When I was apprized of this, I laid the case at large before the whole society; showed how impossible it was for the Stewards to attend all that were sick in all parts of the town; desired the Leaders of classes would more carefully inquire, and more constantly inform them, who were sick; and asked, "Who among you is willing, as well as able, to supply this lack of service?"

3. The next morning many willingly offered themselves. I chose six-and-forty of them, whom I judged to be of the most tender, loving spirit; divided the town into twenty-three parts, and desired two of them to visit the sick in each division.

4. It is the business of a Visitor of the sick, To see every sick person within his district thrice a week. To inquire into the state of their souls, and to advise them as occasion may require. To inquire into their disorders, and procure advice for them. To relieve them, if they are in want. To do any thing for them, which he (or she) can do. To bring in his accounts weekly to the Stewards.

Upon reflection, I saw how exactly, in this also, we had copied after the primitive Church. What were the ancient Deacons? What was Phebe the Deaconess, but such a Visitor of the sick?

5. I did not think it needful to give them any particular rules beside these that follow.—(1.) Be plain and open in dealing with souls. (2.) Be mild, tender, patient. (3.) Be cleanly in all you do for the sick. (4.) Be not nice.

6. We have ever since had great reason to praise God for his continued blessing on this undertaking. Many lives have been saved, many sicknesses healed, much pain and want prevented or removed. Many heavy hearts have been made glad, many mourners comforted: And the Visitors have found, from Him whom they serve, a present reward for all their labour.

XII. 1. But I was still in pain for many of the poor that were sick; there was no great expense, and so little profit. And first, I resolved to try, whether they might not receive more benefit in the hospitals. Upon the trial, we found there was indeed less expense, but no more good done, than before. I then asked the advice of several Physicians for them; but still it profited not. I saw the poor people pining away, and several families ruined, and that without remedy.

2. At length I thought of a kind of desperate expedient. "I will prepare, and give them physic myself." For six or seven and twenty years, I had made anatomy and physic the diversion of my leisure hours, though I never properly studied them, unless for a few months when I was going to America, where I imagined I might be of some service to those who had no regular Physician among them. I applied to it again. I took into my assistance an Apothecary, and an experienced Surgeon; resolving, at the same time, not to go out of my depth, but to leave all difficult and complicated cases to such Physicians as the patients should choose.

3. I gave notice of this to the society; telling them, that all who were ill of chronical distempers (for I did not care to venture upon acute) might, if they pleased, come to me at such a time, and I would give them the best advice I could, and the best medicines I had.

4. Many came: (And so every Friday since:) Among the rest was one William Kirkman, a weaver, near Old Nichol-street. I asked him, "What complaint have you?" "O Sir," said he, "a cough, a very sore cough. I can get no rest day nor night."

I asked, "How long have you had it?" He replied, "About threescore years: It began when I was eleven years old." I was nothing glad that this man should come first, fearing our not curing him might discourage others. However, I looked up to God, and said, "Take this three or four times a day. If it does you no good, it will do you no harm." He took it two or three days. His cough was cured, and has not returned to this day.

5. Now, let candid men judge, does humility require me to deny a notorious fact? If not, which is vanity? to say, I by my own skill restored this man to health; or to say, God did it by his own almighty power? By what figure of speech this is called boasting, I know not. But I will put no name to such a fact as this. I leave that to the Rev. Dr. Middleton.

6. In five months, medicines were occasionally given to above five hundred persons. Several of these I never saw before; for I did not regard whether they were of the society or not. In that time seventy-one of these, regularly taking their medicines, and following the regimen prescribed, (which three in four would not do,) were entirely cured of distempers long thought to be incurable. The whole expense of medicines during this time, was nearly forty pounds. We continued this ever since, and, by the blessing of God, with more and more success.

XIII. 1. But I had for some years observed many who, although not sick, were not able to provide for themselves, and had none who took care to provide for them: These were chiefly feeble, aged widows. I consulted with the Stewards, how they might be relieved. They all agreed, if we could keep them in one house, it would not only be far less expensive to us, but also far more comfortable for them. Indeed we had no money to begin; but we believed He would provide "who defendeth the cause of the widow:" So we took a lease of two little houses near; we fitted them up, so as to be warm and clean. We took in as many widows as we had room for, and provided them with things needful for the body; toward the expense of which I set aside, first, the weekly contributions of the bands, and then all that was collected at the Lord's supper. It is true, this does not suffice: So that we are considerably in debt, on this account also. But we are persuaded, it will not always be so; seeing "the earth is the Lord's, and the fulness thereof."

2. In this (commonly called The Poor House) we have now nine widows, one blind woman, two poor children, two upper-servants, a maid and a man. I might add, four or five Preachers; for I myself, as well as the other Preachers who are in town, diet with the poor, on the same food, and at the same table; and we rejoice herein, as a comfortable earnest of our eating bread together in our Father's kingdom.

3. I have blessed God for this house ever since it began; but lately much more than ever. I honour these widows; for they "are widows indeed." So that it is not in vain, that, without any design of so doing, we have copied after another of the institutions of the Apostolic age. I can now say to all the world, "Come and see how these Christians love one another!"

XIV. 1. Another thing which had given me frequent concern was, the case of abundance of children. Some their parents could not afford to put to school: So they remained like "a wild ass's colt." Others were sent to school, and learned, at least, to read and write; but they learned all kind of vice at the same time: So that it had been better for them to have been without their knowledge, than to have bought it at so dear a price.

2. At length I determined to have them taught in my own house, that they might have an opportunity of learning to read, write, and cast accounts, (if no more,) without being under almost a necessity of learning Heathenism at the same time: And after several unsuccessful trials, I found two such Schoolmasters as I

wanted; men of honesty and of sufficient knowledge, who had talents for, and their hearts in, the work.

3. They have now under their care near sixty children: The parents of some pay for their schooling; but the greater part, being very poor, do not; so that the expense is chiefly defrayed by voluntary contributions. We have of late clothed them too, as many as wanted. The rules of the school are these that follow:—

First. No child is admitted under six years of age. Secondly. All the children are to be present at the morning sermon. Thirdly. They are at school from six to twelve, and from one to five. Fourthly. They have no play-days. Fifthly. No child is to speak in school, but to the masters. Sixthly. The child who misses two days in one week, without leave, is excluded the school.

4. We appointed two Stewards for the school also. The business of these is, to receive the school subscriptions, and expend what is needful; to talk with each of the masters weekly; to pray with and exhort the children twice a-week; to inquire diligently, whether they grow in grace and in learning, and whether the rules are punctually observed; every Tuesday morning, in conjunction with the masters, to exclude those children that do not observe the rules; every Wednesday morning to meet with and exhort their parents, to train them up at home in the ways of God.

5. A happy change was soon observed in the children, both with regard to their tempers and behaviour. They learned reading, writing, and arithmetic swiftly; and at the same time they were diligently instructed in the sound principles of religion, and earnestly exhorted to fear God, and work out their own salvation.

XV. 1. A year or two ago, I observed among many a distress of another kind. They frequently wanted, perhaps in order to carry on their business, a present supply of money. They scrupled to make use of a pawnbroker; but where to borrow it they knew not. I resolved to try if we could not find a remedy for this also. I went, in a few days, from one end of the town to the other, and exhorted those who had this world's goods, to assist their needy brethren. Fifty pounds were contributed. This was immediately lodged in the hands of two Stewards; who attended every Tuesday morning, in order to lend to those who wanted any small sum, not exceeding twenty shillings, to be repaid within three months.

2. It is almost incredible, but it manifestly appears from their accounts, that, with this inconsiderable sum, two hundred and fifty have been assisted, within the space of one year. Will not God put it into the heart of some lover of mankind to increase this little stock? If this is not "lending unto the Lord," what is? O confer not with flesh and blood, but immediately "Join hands with God, to make a poor man live!"

3. I think, Sir, now you know all that I know of this people. You see the nature, occasion, and design of whatever is practised among them. And, I trust, you may be pretty well able to answer any questions which may be asked concerning them; particularly by those who inquire concerning my revenue, and what I do with it all.

4. Some have supposed this was no greater than that of the Bishop of London. But others computed that I received eight hundred a-year from Yorkshire only. Now, if so, it cannot be so little as ten thousand pounds a-year which I receive out of all England!

5. Accordingly, a gentleman in Cornwall (the Rector of Redruth) extends the calculation pretty considerably. "Let me see," said he: "Two millions of Methodists; and each of these paying two-pence a week." If so, I must have eight hundred and sixty thousand pounds, with some odd shillings and pence, a-year.

6. A tolerable competence! But be it more or less, it is nothing at all to me. All that is contributed or collected in every place is both received and expended by others; nor have I so much as the "beholding thereof with my eyes." And so it will be, till I turn Turk or Pagan. For I look upon all this revenue, be it what it may, as sacred to God and the poor; out of which, if I want anything, I am relieved, even as another poor man. So were originally all ecclesiastical revenues, as every man of learning knows: And the Bishops and Priests used them only as such. If any use them otherwise now, God help them!

7. I doubt not, but if I err in this, or any other point, you will pray God to show me his truth.

To have "a conscience void of offence toward God and toward man" is the desire of, Reverend and dear Sir, Your affectionate brother and servant,

John Wesley

SOCIAL POLICY AND ADMINISTRATION

Riot Act, 1715

1 Geo. 1, c. 5   *Statutes at Large*, XIII, 142-46.

This act was passed in the face of the Jacobite threat. It provided a mechanism for local handling of unlawful assemblies of twelve or more persons.

I. Whereas of late many rebellious riots and tumults have been in divers parts of this kingdom, to the disturbance of the publick peace, and the endangering of his Majesty's person and government, and the same are yet continued and fomented by persons disaffected to his Majesty, presuming so to do, for that the punishments provided by the laws now in being are not adequate to such heinous offences; and by such rioters his Majesty and his administration have been most maliciously and falsly traduced, with an intent to raise divisions, and to alienate the affections of the people from his Majesty; therefore for the preventing and suppressing of such riots and tumults, and for the more speedy and effectual punishing the offenders therein; be it enacted by the King's most excellent majesty, by and with the advice and consent of the lords spiritual and temporal and of the commons, in this present parliament assembled, and by the authority of the same, That if any persons to the number of twelve or more, being unlawfully, riotously, and tumultuously assembled together, to the disturbance of the publick peace, at any time after the last day of July in the year of our Lord one thousand seven hundred and fifteen, and being required or commanded by any one or more justice or justices of the peace, or by the sheriff of the county, or his under-sheriff, or by the mayor, bailiff or bailiffs, or other head-officer, or justice of the peace of any city or town corporate, where such assembly shall be, by proclamation to be made in the King's name, in the form herein after directed, to disperse themselves, and peaceably to depart to their habitations, or to their lawful business, shall, to the number of twelve or more (notwithstanding such proclamation made) unlawfully, riotously, and tumultuously remain or continue together by the space of one hour after such command or request made by proclamation, that then such continuing together to the number of twelve or more, after such command or request made by proclamation, shall be adjudged felony without benefit of clergy, and the offenders therein shall be adjudged felons, and shall suffer death as in case of felony without benefit of clergy.

II. And be it further enacted by the authority aforesaid, That the order and form of the proclamation that shall be made by the authority of this act, shall be as hereafter followeth (that is to say) the justice of the peace, or other person authorized by this act to make the said proclamation shall, among the said rioters, or as near to them as he can safely come, with a loud voice command, or cause to be commanded silence to be, while proclamation is making, and after that, shall openly and with loud voice make or cause to be made proclamation in these words, or like in effect:

> Our sovereign Lord the King chargeth and commandeth all persons, being assembled, immediately to disperse themselves, and peaceably to depart to their habitations, or to their lawful business, upon the pains contained in the act made in the first year of King George, for preventing tumults and riotous assemblies. God save the King.

And every such justice and justices of the peace, sheriff, under-sheriff, mayor, bailiff, and other head-officer, aforesaid, within the limits of their respective jurisdictions, are hereby authorized, impowered and required, on notice or knowledge of any such unlawful, riotous and tumultuous assembly, to resort to the place where such unlawful, riotous, and tumultuous assemblies shall be, of persons to the number of twelve or more, and there to make or cause to be made proclamation in manner aforesaid.

III.   And be it further enacted by the authority aforesaid, That if such persons so unlawfully, riotously, and tumultuously assembled, or twelve or more of them, after proclamation made in manner aforesaid, shall continue together and not disperse themselves within one hour, That then it shall and may be lawful to and for every justice of the peace, sheriff, or under-sheriff of the county where such assembly shall be, and also to and for every high or petty constable, and other peace-officer within such county, and also to and for every mayor, justice of the peace, sheriff, bailiff, and other head-officer, high or petty constable, and other peace-officer of any city or town corporate where such assembly shall be, and to and for such other person and persons as shall be commanded to be assisting unto any such justice of the peace, sheriff or under-sheriff, mayor, bailiff, or other head-officer aforesaid (who are hereby authorized and impowered to command all his Majesty's subjects of age and ability to be assisting to them therein) to seize and apprehend, and they are hereby required to seize and apprehend such persons so unlawfully, riotously and tumultuously continuing together after proclamation made, as aforesaid, and forthwith to carry the persons so apprehended before one or more of his Majesty's justices of the peace of the county or place where such persons shall be so apprehended, in order to their being proceeded against for such their offences according to law; and that if the persons so unlawfully, riotously and tumultuously assembled, or any of them, shall happen to be killed, maimed or hurt, in the dispersing, seizing or apprehending, or endeavouring to disperse, seize or apprehend them, by reason of their resisting the persons so dispersing, seizing or apprehending, or endeavouring to disperse, seize or apprehend them, that then every such justice of the peace, sheriff, under-sheriff, mayor, bailiff, head-officer, high or petty constable, or other peace-officer, and all and singular persons, being aiding and assiting to them, or any of them, shall be free, discharged and indemnified, as well against the King's Majesty, his heirs and successors, as against all and every other person and persons, of, for, or concerning the killing, maiming, or hurting of any such person or persons so unlawfully, riotously and tumultuously assembled, that shall happen to be so killed, maimed or hurt, as aforesaid.

IV. And be it further enacted by the authority aforesaid, That if any persons unlawfully, riotously and tumultuously assembled together, to the disturbance of the publick peace, shall unlawfully, and with force demolish or pull down, or begin to demolish or pull down any church or chapel, or any building for religious worship certified and registred according to the statute made in the first year of the reign of the late King William and Queen Mary, intituled, *An act for exempting their Majesty's protestant subjects dissenting from the church of England from the penalties of certain laws,* or any dwelling-house, barn, stable, or other outhouse, that then every such demolishing, or pulling down, or beginning to demolish, or pull down, shall be adjudged felony without benefit of clergy, and the offenders therein shall be adjudged felons, and shall suffer death as in case of felony, without benefit of clergy.

V. Provided always, and be it further enacted by the authority aforesaid, That if any person or persons do, or shall, with force and arms, wilfully and knowingly oppose, obstruct, or in any manner wilfully and knowingly lett, hinder, or hurt any person or persons that shall begin to proclaim, or go to proclaim according to the proclamation hereby directed to be made, whereby such proclamation shall not be made, that then every such opposing, obstructing, letting, hindering or hurting such person or persons, so beginning or going to make such proclamation, as aforesaid, shall be adjudged felony without benefit of clergy, and the offenders therein shall be adjudged felons, and shall suffer death as in case of felony, without benefit of clergy; and that also every such person or persons so being unlawfully, riotously and tumultuously assembled, to the number of twelve, as aforesaid, or more, to whom proclamation should or ought to have been made if the same had not been hindred, as aforesaid, shall likewise, in case they or any of them, to the number of twelve or more, shall continue together, and not disperse themselves within one hour after such lett or hindrance so made, having knowledge of such lett or hindrance so made, shall be adjudged felons, and shall suffer death as in case of felony, without benefit of clergy.

VI. And be it further enacted by the authority aforesaid, That if after the said last day of July one thousand seven hundred and fifteen, any such church or chapel, or any such building for religious worship, or any such dwelling-house, barn, stable, or other out-house, shall be demolished or pulled down wholly, or in part, by any persons so unlawfully, riotously and tumultuously assembled, that then, in case such church, chapel, building for religious worship, dwelling-house, barn, stable or out-house, shall be out of any city or town, that is either a county of itself, or is not within any hundred, that then the inhabitants of the hundred in which such damage shall be done, shall be liable to yield damages to the person or person injured and damnified by such demolishing or pulling down wholly or in part; and such damages shall and may be recovered by action to be brought in any of his Majesty's courts of record at Westminster, (wherein no essoin, protection or wager of law, or any imparlance shall be allowed) by the person or persons damnified thereby, against any two or more of the inhabitants of such hundred, such action for damages to any church or chapel to be brought in the name of the rector, vicar or curate of such church or chapel that shall be so damnified, in trust for applying the damages to be recovered in rebuilding or repairing such church or chapel; and that judgment being given for the plaintiff or plaintiffs in such action, the damages so to be recovered shall, at the request of such plaintiff or plaintiffs, his or their executors or administrators, be raised and levied on the inhabitants of such hundred, and paid to such plaintiff or plaintiffs, in such manner and form, and by such ways and means, as are provided by the statute made in the seven and twentieth year of the reign of Queen Elizabeth, for reimbursing the person or persons on whom any money recovered against any hundred by any party robbed, shall be levied: and in case any such church, chapel, building for religious worship, dwelling-house, barn, stable or out-house so damnified, shall be in any city or town that is either a county of itself, or is not within any hundred, that then such damages shall and may be recovered by action to be brought in manner aforesaid (wherein no essoin, protection or wager of law, or any imparlance shall be allowed) against two or more inhabitants of such city or town; and judgment being given for the plaintiff or plaintiffs in such action, the damages so to be recovered shall, at the request of such plaintiff or plaintiffs, his or their executors or administrators, made to the justices of the peace of such city or town at any quarter-sessions to be holden for the said city or town, be raised and levied on the inhabitants of such city or town, and paid to such plaintiff or plaintiffs, in such manner and form, and by such ways and means, as are provided by the said statute made in the seven and twentieth year of the reign of Queen Elizabeth, for reimbursing the person or persons on whom any money recovered against any hundred by any party robbed, shall be levied.

VII.   And be it further enacted by the authority aforesaid, That this act shall be openly read at every quarter-session, and at every leet or law-day.

VIII.   Provided always, That no person or persons shall be prosecuted by virtue of this act, for any offence or offences committed contrary to the same, unless such prosecution be commenced within twelve months after the offence committed. . . .

Poor Relief Act, 1722

9 Geo. 1, c. 7   *Statutes at Large*, XV, 28-33.

This act empowered parishes to maintain workhouses for the relief of the poor.

Whereas by an act of parliament, made and passed in the third and fourth years of the reign of their late majesties King William and Queen Mary, it was provided, That in every parish a book or books should be kept, wherein the names of all persons, who did or might receive collections should be registred, with the time when they were first admitted to such relief, and the occasion which brought them under that necessity; and that no such person should be allowed to have or receive collection at the charge of the parish, but by authority, or under the hand of one justice of peace residing in such parish, or if none there dwelling, in the parts near or next adjoining, or by order of the justices at their quarter-sessions, except in case of pestilential diseases, plague or small-pox: and whereas under colour of the proviso in the said act, many persons have applied to some justices of peace, without the knowledge of any officers of the parish, and thereby, upon untrue suggestions, and sometimes upon false or frivolous pretences, have obtained relief, which hath greatly contributed to the encrease of the parish-rates: for remedy whereof, be it enacted by the King's most excellent majesty, by and with the advice and consent of the lords spiritual and temporal and commons, in this present parliament assembled, and by the authority of the same, That from and after the twenty fifth day of March which shall be in the year of our Lord one thousand seven hundred and twenty three, no justice of peace shall order relief to any poor person dwelling in any parish, until oath be made before such justice of some matter which he shall judge to be a reasonable cause or ground for having such relief, and that the same person had by himself, herself or some other, applied for relief to the parishioners of the parish, at some vestry or other publick meeting of the said parishioners, or to two of the overseers of the poor of such parish, and was by them refused to be relieved, and until such justice hath summoned two of the overseers of the poor to shew cause why such relief should not be given, and the person so summoned hath been heard or made default to appear before such justice; any thing in the said proviso, or any law to the contrary notwithstanding.

II. And be it further enacted by the authority aforesaid, That the person whom any such justices of peace shall think fit to order to be relieved, shall be entred in such book or books so to be kept by the parish, as one of those who is to receive collection, as long as the cause for such relief continues, and no longer; and that no officer of any parish shall (except upon sudden and emergent occasions) bring to the account of the parish any monies he shall give to any poor person of the same parish, who is not registred in such book or books to be kept by the said parish, as a person entitled to receive collection, on paid of forfeiting the sum of five pounds, to be levied by distress and sale, by warrant of any two or more justices of the peace of the same county, who shall have examined into and found him guilty of such offence; which said sum shall be applied to and for the use of the poor of the said parish, by direction of the said justice or justices of the peace.

III. And for the greater ease of justices of the peace, whom his Majesty or his successors hath or shall be commission authorize to act as a justice of the peace for any county of this realm; be it enacted by the authority aforesaid, That if any such justice of peace shall happen to dwell in any city, or other precinct that is a county of itself, situate within the county at large, for which he shall be appointed justice of peace, although not within the same county, it shall and may be lawful for any such justice of peace to grant warrants, take examinations, and made orders for any matters, which any one or more justice or justices of the peace may act in, at his own dwelling-house, altho' such dwelling-house be out of the county where he is authorized to act as a justice of peace, and in some city or other precinct adjoining, that is a county of itself; and that all such warrants, orders and other act or acts of any justice of peace, and the act or acts of any constable, tithingman, headborough, overseer of the poor, surveyor of the highways or other officer, in obedience to any such warrant or order, shall be as valid, good and effectual in the law, although it happen to be out of the limits of the proper precinct or authority: provided always, That nothing in this act contained shall extend to give power to the justices of peace for the counties at large, to hold their general quarter-sessions of the peace in the cities or towns which are counties of themselves, nor to impower justices of peace, sheriffs, bailiffs, constables, headboroughs, tithingmen, borsholders or any other peace-officers of the counties at large, to act or intermeddle in any matters or things arising within the cities or towns which are counties of themselves, but that all such actings and doings shall be of the same force and effect in law, and none other, as if this act had never been made.

IV. And for the greater ease of parishes in the relief of the poor, be it further enacted by the authority aforesaid, That it shall and may be lawful for the churchwardens and overseers of the poor in any parish, town, township or place, with the consent of the major part of the parishioners or inhabitants of the same parish, town, township or place, in vestry, or other parish or publick meeting for that purpose assembled, or of so many of them as shall be so assembled, upon usual notice thereof first given, to purchase or hire any house or houses in the same parish, township or place, and to contract with any person or persons for the lodging, keeping, maintaining and employing any or all such poor in their respective parishes, townships or places, as shall desire to receive relief or collection from the same parish, and there to keep, maintain and employ all such poor persons, and take the benefit of the work, labour and service of any such poor person or persons, who shall be kept or maintained in any such house or houses, for the better maintenance and relief of such poor person or persons, who shall be there kept or maintained; and in case any poor person or persons of any parish, town, township or place, where such house or houses shall be so purchased or hired, shall refuse to be lodged, kept or maintained in such house or houses, such poor person or persons so refusing shall be put out of the book or books where the names of the persons, who ought to receive collection in the said parish, town, township or place, are to be registred, and shall not be entitled to ask or receive collection or relief from the churchwardens and overseers of the poor of the same parish, town or township; and where any parish, town or township shall be too small to purchase or hire such house or houses for the poor of their own parish only, it shall and may be lawful for two or more such parishes, towns or townships or places, with the consent of the major part of the parishioners or inhabitants of their respective parishes, town, township or places, in vestry or other parish or publick meeting for that purpose assembled, or of so many of them as shall be so assembled, upon usual notice thereof first given, and with the approbation of any justice of peace dwelling in or near any such parish, town or place, signified under his hand and seal, to unite in purchasing, hiring, or taking such house, for the lodging, keeping and maintaining of the poor of the several parishes, townships or places so uniting, and there to keep, maintain and employ the poor of the respective parishes so uniting, and to take and have the benefit of the work, labour or service of any poor there kept and maintained, for the better maintenance and relief of the poor there kept, maintained and employed; and that if any poor person or persons in the respective parishes, townships or places so uniting, shall refuse to be lodged, kept and maintained in the house, hired or taken for such uniting parishes, townships or places, he, she or they so refusing, shall be put out of the collection-book, where his, her or their names were registred, and shall not be entitled to ask or demand relief or collection from the churchwardens and overseers of the poor in their respective parishes, townships or places; and that it shall and may be lawful for the churchwardens and overseers of the poor of any parish, township or place, with the consent of the major part of the parishioners or inhabitants of the said parish, township or place where such house or houses is, are, or shall be purchased or hired for the purposes aforesaid, in vestry, or other parish or publick meeting, for that purpose assembled, or of so many of them as shall be so assembled, upon usual notice thereof first given, to contract with the church-wardens and overseers of the poor of any other parish, township or place, for the lodging, maintaining or employing, of any poor person or persons of such other parish, township or place, as to them shall seem meet; and in case any poor person or persons of such other parish, township or place, shall refuse to be lodged, maintained and employed in such house or houses, he, she or they so refusing, shall be put out of the collection-book of such other parish, township or place, where his, her or their names were registred, and shall not be entitled to ask, demand or receive any relief or collection from the church-wardens and overseers of the poor of his, her or their respective parish, township or place: provided always, That no poor person or persons, his, her or their apprentice, child or children, shall acquire a settlement in the parish, town or place, to which he, she or they are removed by virtue of this act, but that his, her or their settlement, shall be and remain in such parish, town or place, as it was before such removal; any thing in this act to the contrary notwithstanding.

V. And be it further enacted by the authority aforesaid, That from and after the twenty fifth day of March which shall be in the year of our Lord one thousand seven hundred and twenty three, no person or persons shall be deemed, adjudged or taken, to acquire or gain any settlement in any parish or place, for or by virtue of any purchase of any estate or interest in such parish or place, whereof the consideration for such purchase doth not amount to the sum of thirty pounds, bona fide paid, for any longer or further time than such person or persons shall inhabit in such estate, and shall then be liable to be removed to such parish or place, where such person or persons were last legally settled, before the said purchase and inhabitancy therein.

VI. And be it further enacted by the authority aforesaid, That no person or persons whatsoever, who from and after the twenty fifty day of March in the year of our Lord one thousand seven hundred and twenty three, shall be taxed, rated or assessed to the scavenger or repairs of the highway, and shall duly pay the same, shall be deemed or taken to have any legal settlement in any city, parish, town or hamlet, for or by reason of his, her or their paying to such scavenger's rate or repairs of the highway as aforesaid; any law to the contrary in any wise notwithstanding.

VII. And whereas there was a clause in the statute made in the eighth and ninth years of his late majesty King William the Third, intituled, *An act for the supplying some defects in the law for the relief of the poor of this kingdom,* whereby it was enacted, That after the first day of May one thousand six hundred ninety seven, all appeals against any order for the removing of any poor persons, should be heard at the quarter-sessions of the county or division, wherein the parish or place, from whence such person should be removed, doth lie, and not elsewhere, except the liberty of Saint Albans; be it enacted by the authority aforesaid, That it shall and may be lawful for the justices of the peace, within the liberty of the borough of Saint Peter and hundred of Nassaborough in the county of Northampton, to hear and determine all appeals to them made, against any order made for removal of any poor person, in their quarter-sessions, as they might have done before the making of the said last mentioned act; any thing therein or in this present act contained to the contrary thereof in any wise notwithstanding.

VIII.   And whereas several disputes and controversies have arisen and been concerning the time of notice to be given of appeals from orders of removals of poor persons, to prevent the same, as much as may be for the future, be it enacted by the authority aforesaid, That from and after the said twenty fifth day of March one thousand seven hundred and twenty three, no appeal or appeals from any order or orders of removal of any poor person or persons whatsoever from any parish or place to another, shall be proceeded upon in any court or quarter-sessions, unless reasonable notice be given by the church-wardens or overseers of the poor of such parish or place, who shall make such appeal unto the church-wardens or overseers of the poor of such parish or place, from which such poor person or persons shall be removed, the reasonableness of which notice shall be determined by the justices of the peace at the quarter-sessions, to which the appeal is made; and if it shall appear to them that reasonable time of notice was not given, then they shall adjourn the said appeal to the next quarter-sessions, and then and there finally hear and determine the same.

IX.   And for the preventing vexatious removals, be it further enacted by the authority aforesaid, That from and after the twenty fourth day of June in the year of our Lord one thousand seven hundred and twenty three, if the justices of the peace shall, at their quarter-sessions, upon an appeal before them there had concerning the settlement of any poor person, determine in favour of the appellant, that such poor person or persons was or were unduly removed, that then the said justices shall, at the same quarter-sessions, order and award to such appellant so much money, as shall appear to the said justices to have been reasonably paid by the parish, or other place, on whose behalf such appeal was made for or towards the relief of such poor person or persons, between the time of such undue removal, and the determination of such appeal; the said money so awarded to be recovered in the same manner, as costs and charges upon an appeal are prescribed to be recovered by the said statute made in the ninth year of his late majesty King William the Third, intituled, *An act for supplying some defects in the laws for the relief of the poor of this kingdom.*

Act for regulating elections within the City of London, 1724

11 Geo. 1, c. 18   *Statutes at Large*, XV, 221-27.

This measure gave the right of election within the City of London to freemen who were £10 householders, thus insuring the dominance of wealthy merchants.

Whereas of late years great controversies and dissentions have arisen in the city of London at the elections of citizens to serve in parliament, and of mayors, aldermen, sheriffs, and other officers of the said city, and many evil-minded persons, having no right of voting, have unlawfully intruded themselves into the assemblies of the citizens, and presumed to give their votes at such elections, in manifest violation of the rights and privileges of the citizens, and of the freedom of their elections, and to the disturbance of the publick peace: And whereas great numbers of wealthy persons, not free of the said city, do inhabit, and carry on the trade of merchandize and other imployments, within the said city, and refuse or decline to become freemen of the same, by reason of an antient custom within the said city restraining the freemen of the same from disposing of their personal estates by their last wills and testaments: And whereas great dissentions have arisen between the aldermen and commons of the common council of London, in or concerning the making or passing of acts, orders or ordinances in common council, which if not timely settled and determined, may occasion great obstructions of the publick business and concerns of the said city, and create many expensive controversies and suits at law, and be attended with other dangerous consequences: Now to the intent that suitable remedies may be provided for preserving the privileges of the city of London, and the freedom of elections therein, and for settling the right of such elections, and putting a stop to the aforesaid controversies and dissentions, and the ill consequences of the same, and that a constant supply may be had of able officers, capable of supporting the dignity of and maintaining good order and government within that antient, populous, and loyal city, which is of the greatest consequence to the whole kingdom; be it enacted by the King's most excellent majesty, by and with the advice and consent of the lords spiritual and temporal and commons, in this present parliament assembled, and by the authority of the same, That at all times, from and after the first day of June in the year of our Lord one thousand seven hundred and twenty five, upon every election of a citizen or citizens to serve for the said city of London in parliament, and upon all elections of mayors, sheriffs, chamberlains, bridge-masters, auditors of chamberlains and bridge-masters accounts, and all and every other officer and officers to be chosen in and for the said city, by the liverymen thereof, and upon all elections of aldermen and common council-men chosen at the respective wardmotes of the said city, the presiding officer or officers at such elections shall, in case a poll be demanded by any of the candidates, or any two or more of the electors, appoint a convenient number of clerks to take the same, which clerks shall take the said poll in the presence of the presiding officer or officers, and be sworn by such officer or officers truly and indifferently to take the same, and to set down the name of each voter, and his place of residence or abode, and for whom he shall poll, and to poll no person who shall not be sworn, or being a quaker, shall not affirm according to the direction of this act: and every person before he is admitted to poll at any election of any citizen or citizens to serve in parliament, or of any officer or officers usually chosen by the liverymen of the said city as aforesaid, shall take the oath herein after mentioned, or being one of the people called quakers, shall solemnly affirm the effect thereof, that is to say,

> You do swear, That you are a freeman of London, and a liveryman of the company of   and have so been for the space of twelve kalendar months; and that the place of your abode is at   in   and that you have not polled at this election, So help you God.

And in case of any election of any alderman or common council-man, every person, before he is admitted to poll, shall take the oath herein after mentioned, or, being one of the people called quakers, shall solemnly affirm the effect thereof, that is to say,

> You do swear, That you are a freeman of London, and an householder in the ward of   and have not polled at this election. So help you God.

And if any person or persons shall refuse or neglect to take the oaths hereby respectively appointed to be taken, or being a quaker shall refuse or neglect to make such solemn affirmation as aforesaid, then and in every such case the poll or vote of such person or persons so neglecting or refusing shall be, and the same is hereby declared to be null and void, and as such shall be rejected and disallowed.

II. And be it further enacted by the authority aforesaid, That at all times from and after the said first day of June in the year of our Lord one thousand seven hundred and twenty five, upon every election of such citizen or citizens, officer or officers, by the liverymen of the said city, and upon every election of such officer or officers at any wardmote of the said city as aforesaid, all and every person and persons having a right to vote or poll at such election or elections shall, before he be admitted to vote or poll thereat (if required by any of the candidates, or any two or more of the electors) first take the oaths in and by an act made in the first year of his Majesty's reign, intituled, *An act for the further security of his Majesty's person and government, and the succession of the crown in the heirs of the late princess Sophia, being protestants, and for extinguishing the hopes of the pretended prince of Wales, and his open and secret abettors,* appointed to be taken, or being one of the people called quakers shall, if required as aforesaid, solemnly affirm the effect thereof; and if any person or persons shall, being required thereunto as aforesaid, refuse or neglect to take the said oaths by the said act appointed to be taken, or to affirm the effect thereof as aforesaid, That then the poll or vote of such person or persons so neglecting or refusing shall be, and the same is hereby declared to be null and void, and as such shall be rejected and disallowed; and the presiding officers at all and every the respective elections aforesaid, and such sworn clerks as shall be by them appointed, are hereby respectively authorized and impowered to administer the above-mentioned oaths and affirmations; and if any such presiding officer or officers, sworn clerk or clerks, shall neglect or refuse so to do, or shall otherwise offend in the premises, contrary to the true intent and meaning of this act, every such officer and sworn clerk shall for every such offence forfeit the sum of sixty pounds of lawful money of Great Britain, besides costs of suit.

III. And it is hereby further enacted, That if any person or persons shall wilfully, falsly and corruptly take the said oaths or affirmations set forth and appointed in and by this act, or either of them, and be thereof lawfully convicted by indictment or information, or if any person or persons shall corruptly procure or suborn any other person to take the said oaths or affirmations, or either of them, whereby he shall wilfully and falsly take the said oaths or affirmations, or either of them, and the person so procuring or suborning shall be thereof convicted by indictment or information, every person so offending shall for every such offence incur and suffer such penalties, forfeitures and disabilities, as persons convicted of wilful and corrupt perjury at the common law are liable unto.

IV. And to the intent that the poll at every such election may be expeditiously and duly taken; be it further enacted by the authority aforesaid. That if a poll shall be demanded at any of the elections before-mentioned, after the said first day of June in the year of our Lord one thousand seven hundred and twenty five, the presiding officer or officers at such election shall begin such poll the day the same shall be demanded, or the next day following at the furthest, unless the same shall happen on a Sunday, and then on the next day after, and shall duly and orderly proceed thereon from day to day (Sundays excepted) until such poll be finished, and shall finish the poll at elections by the liverymen within seven days, exclusive of Sundays, and the poll at the wardmote within three days, exclusive of Sunday, after the commencing the same respectively, and shall, upon adjourning the poll on each day, at all and every the elections aforesaid, seal up the poll-books with the seals, and in the presence of such of the respective candidates, or persons deputed by them, as shall desire the same, and the said poll-book shall not be opened again but at the time and place of meeting, in pursuance of such adjournment; and after the said poll is finished, the said poll-books, being sealed as aforesaid, shall within two days after be publickly opened at the place of election, and be duly and truly cast up, and within two days after such casting up the numbers of the votes or polls for each candidate shall be truly, fairly and publickly declared to the electors at the place of election, by the officer or officers presiding at such election; and if a scrutiny shall, upon such declaration made, be lawfully demanded, the same shall be granted and proceeded upon, and the respective candidates shall immediately nominate to the presiding officer or officers at such elections, any number of persons qualified to vote at such election not exceeding six, to be scrutineers for and on behalf of the candidate or candidates on each side, to whom the presiding officer or officers at such election shall, within six days next after such scrutiny shall be demanded, upon request and at the charge of the candidate or candidates, or any the scrutineers on his or their behalfs, deliver or cause to be delivered to him or them a true copy, signed by such officer or officers, of the poll taken at such election; and all and every the scrutinies to be had or taken upon any election to be made by the liverymen of the said city, shall begin within ten days after the delivery of the copies of the said polls, and be proceeded on day by day (Sundays excepted) and shall be finished within fifteen days after the commencement of such scrutiny; and thereupon the presiding officer or officers shall, within four days after the finishing such scrutiny, publickly declare at the place of such election, which of the candidates is or are duly elected, and the number of legal votes for each candidate appearing to him or them upon such scrutiny; and on the election of any officer or officers at the respective wardmotes of the said city, if a scrutiny be demanded, the candidates, or scrutineers nominated on their behalfs respectively shall, within ten days next after the receipt of the copy or copies of the polls taken at such election, deliver or cause to be delivered to the presiding officer or officers, the names in writing of the several persons who have polled in the said election, against whose votes they shall object, with the particular objections against each respective name; and the presiding officer or officers shall thereupon, within three days then next following, at the request and charges of any candidate or candidates, or the scrutineers named on his or their behalfs, deliver or cause to be delivered to him or them, one or more true copy or copies (signed as aforesaid) of the paper containing such names and objections as aforesaid; and the said presiding officer or officers, within ten days then next following (exclusive of Sundays) after having fully heard such of the said candidates as shall desire the same, or some person appointed by him or them, touching such objections, shall, at or in the place of election, openly and publickly declare which of the said candidates is or are duly elected, and the number of legal votes for each candidate appearing to him or them upon such scrutiny; and if the said presiding officer or officers, or any other person or persons, shall offend in the premises, every such offender shall forfeit for every such offence the sum of two hundred pounds of lawful money of Great Britain, with full costs of suit, over and above all other penalties and forfeitures inflicted by any other act or acts of parliament.

V.   And be it further enacted by the authority aforesaid, That after any election made, and scrutiny taken, as is herein before provided and directed, the presiding officer or officers at such election and scrutiny shall deliver, under his or their hand or hands, a true list of the voters by him or them disallowed upon such scrutiny, to any of the candidates who shall, upon the final declaration of the election as aforesaid, demand the same, within six days after such demand made, such candidate paying for the same: provided always, That no such list as is hereby directed to be given, nor any thing therein contained, shall be admitted to be given in evidence on any action or occasion whatsoever.

VI.   And be it further enacted by the authority aforesaid, That the mayor of the city of London for the time being, upon request to him made by any candidate or candidates, his or their agent or agents, at any election of a citizen or citizens to serve in parliament for the said city, or of a mayor, or any other officer or officers to be chosen by the liverymen thereof, where a scrutiny is demanded and granted, shall issue his precepts, as has been usual, requiring the masters and wardens of the livery companies of the said city respectively, to cause their clerks forthwith to return to him two true lists of all the liverymen of their respective companies; and the said clerks shall return such their respective lists upon oath within three days after the receipt of any such precepts, one of which lists so returned the said mayor shall, and he is hereby required forthwith to deliver or cause to be delivered to the candidate or candidates on each side at such election, or to his or their agent or agents respectively.

VII. And whereas divers controversies and disputes have arisen in the said city of London touching the right of election of aldermen and common council-men for the respective wards of the said city; for quieting all such disputes and controversies for the future, it is hereby further enacted by the authority aforesaid. That from and after the said first day of June in the year of our Lord one thousand seven hundred and twenty five, the right of election of aldermen and common council-men for the several and respective wards of the said city shall belong and appertain to freemen of the said city of London, being householders, paying scot as herein after is mentioned and provided, and bearing lot, when required, in their several and respective wards, and to none other whatsoever.

VIII. Provided nevertheless, That the houses of such householders be respectively of the true and real value of ten pounds a year at the least; and that such householders be respectively the sole occupiers of such houses, and have been actually in the possession respectively of a house of such value in the ward wherein the election is made, by the space of twelve calendar months next before such election.

IX. Provided also, and for the better ascertaining what are the rates and taxes to which such householders ought to contribute and pay their scot, the same as hereby declared and enacted to be a rate to the church, to the poor, to the scavenger, to the orphans, and to the rates in lieu of or for the watch and ward, and to such other annual rates, as the citizens of London, inhabiting therein, shall hereafter be liable unto, other than and except annual aids granted or to be granted by parliament; and in case any such householder, within the space aforesaid, shall have been rated and charged, and contributed and paid his scot to all the said rates or taxes, or thirty shillings a year to all or some of them, except as aforesaid, every such person shall be deemed and taken to be a person paying of scot.

X. [Provided always, That such householder, within the space aforesaid, shall have been rated or charged, and contributed or paid his scot to all and singular the rates and taxes (other than and except annual aids granted by parliament) whereunto the citizens of London, inhabiting therein, are or shall be liable, or shall have paid in the whole to the said rates and taxes, or some of them, except as aforesaid, thirty shillings a year at least;] and in case any two or more partners carry on a joint trade in any such house together, and shall have been householders of such house by such space of time as aforesaid, such partners shall, paying their scot in manner aforesaid, and bearing their respective proper lots, if required, have votes at the elections aforesaid; so as such house, wherein such partners carry on their trade, be of the true and real yearly value of as many respective sums of ten pounds a year, computed together, as there are partners.

XI. Provided also, That where two persons and no more, not being partners, shall have by the space aforesaid severally inhabited in the same house, such two persons severally paying their scots, and bearing their respective lots as aforesaid, shall have votes at the elections aforesaid; so as such house, wherein such two persons inhabit, be of the true and real yearly value of twenty pounds or upwards, and that each of the said persons doth pay the yearly rend of ten pounds at the least for his respective part of such house.

XII. Provided always, That nothing in this act contained shall extend, or be construed to extend, to oblige any person or persons to pay any scot or bear any lot, from the doing of which they are or shall be exempted and discharged by act of parliament, charter or writ of privilege; but that such person and persons so exempted and discharged shall and may vote at any election of any alderman, common council-man or other officer usually chosen at the wardmotes of the said city, notwithstanding he or they shall not have born such lot, or paid such scot, in such manner as he or they should or might have done, in case this act had not been made, and no otherwise. . . .

Juries Act, 1730

3 Geo. 2, c. 25   *Statutes at Large*, XVI, 161-70.

This act laid down a procedure for choosing jurors and introduced other reforms of the jury system.

Whereas many evil practices have been used in corrupting of jurors returned for the trial of issues joined to be tried before the justices of assize or *Nisi prius,* and the judges of the great sessions in Wales, and the judge or judges of the sessions for the counties palatine of Lancaster, Chester or Durham, and many neglects and abuses have happened in making up the lists of freeholders, who ought to serve on such trials, and many persons being lawfully summoned to serve on juries have neglected to appear, to the great injury of many persons in their properties and estates; in order to prevent the like practices, neglects and abuses: be it enacted by the King's most excellent majesty, by and with the advice and consent of the lords spiritual and temporal and commons in this present parliament assembled, and by the authority of the same, That from and after the first day of September one thousand seven hundred and thirty, the person or persons required by a statute made in the seventh and eighth years of the reign of his late majesty King William the Third, intituled, *An act for the ease of jurors, and better regulating of juries,* and by a clause in another act made in the third and fourth years of the reign of the late Queen Anne, intituled; *An act for making perpetual an act for the more easy recovery of small tithes; and also an act for the more easy obtaining partition of lands in coparcenary, joint tenancy and tenancy in common; and also for making more effectual and amending several acts relating to the return of jurors,* to give in, or who are by virtue of this act to make up, true lists in writing of the names of persons qualified to serve on juries, in order to assist them to complete such lists, pursuant to the intent of the said act, shall (upon request by him or them made to any parish officer or officers who shall have in his or their custody any of the rates for the poor or land tax in such parish or place) have free liberty to inspect such rates, and take from thence the name or names of such freeholders, copyholders or other persons qualified to serve on juries, dwelling within their respective parishes or precincts for which such list is to be given in and returned, pursuant to the said acts; and shall yearly and every year, twenty days at least before the feast of Saint Michael the Archangel, upon two or more Sundays, fix upon the door of the church, chapel and every other publick place of religious worship within their respective precincts, a true and exact list of all such persons intended to be returned to the quarter-sessions of the peace, as qualified to serve on juries, pursuant to the directions of the said act, and leave at the same time a duplicate of such list with a churchwarden, chapelwarden or overseer of the poor of the said parish or place, to be perused by the parishioners without fee or reward, to the end that notice may be given of persons so qualified who are omitted, or of persons inserted by mistake who ought to be omitted out of such lists; and if any person or persons, not being qualified to serve on juries, shall find his or their name or names mentioned in such list, and the person or persons required to make such list shall refuse to omit him or them, or think it doubtful whether he or they ought to be omitted, it shall and may be lawful to and for the justices of the peace for the county, riding or division at their respective general quarter-sessions, to which the said lists shall be so returned, upon satisfaction from the oath of the party complaining, or other proof, that he is not qualified to serve on juries, to order his or their name or names to be struck out or omitted in such list, when the same shall be entred in the book to be kept by the clerk of the peace for that purpose, pursuant to the said act.

II. And be it further enacted, That if any person or persons required by the said acts to return or give in, or by virtue of this act to make up any such list, or concerned therein, shall wilfully omit out of any such list any person or persons whose name or names ought to be inserted, or shall wilfully insert any person or persons who ought to be omitted, or shall take any money or other reward for omitting or inserting any person whatsoever, he or they so offending shall, for every person so omitted or inserted in such list, contrary to the meaning of this act, forfeit the sum of twenty shillings for every such offence, upon conviction before one or more justice or justices of the peace of the county, riding or division where such offender shall dwell, upon the confession of the offender, or proof by one or more credible witness or witnesses on oath, one half thereof to be paid to the informer, and the other half to the poor of such parish or place for which the said list is returned; and in case such penalty shall not be paid within five days after such conviction, the same shall be levied by distress and sale of the offender's goods, by warrant or warrants from one or more justice or justices of the peace, returning the overplus, if any there be; and the said justice or justices, before whom such person shall be convicted of such offence, shall, in writing under the hands, certify the same to the justices at their next general quarter-sessions which shall be held for the county in which the person or persons so omitted or inserted shall dwell, which justices shall direct the clerk of the peace for the time being to insert or strike out the name or names of such person or persons as shall by such certificate appear to have been omitted or inserted in such lists, contrary to the meaning of this act; and duplicates of the said lists, when delivered in at the quarter-sessions of the peace, and entred in such book to be kept by the clerk of the peace for that purpose, shall, during the continuance of such quarter-sessions, or within ten days after, be delivered or transmitted by the clerk of the peace to the sheriff of each respective county, or his under sheriff, in order for his returning of juries out of the said lists; and such sheriff or under sheriff shall immediately take care, that the names of the persons contained in such duplicates shall be faithfully entred alphabetically, with their additions and places of abode, in some book or books to be kept by him or them for that purpose; and that every clerk of the peace neglecting his duty therein shall forfeit the sum of twenty pounds to such person or persons as shall inform or prosecute for the same, until the party be thereof convicted upon an indictment before the justices of the peace at any general quarter-sessions of the peace to be holden for the same county, riding, division or precinct.

III. And be it further enacted, That in case any sheriff, under sheriff, bailiff or other officer to whom the return of juries shall belong, shall summon and return any person or persons to serve on any jury in any cause to be tried before the justices of assize or *Nisi prius*, or judges of the said great sessions, or the judge or judges of the sessions for the said counties palatine, whose name is not inserted in the duplicates so delivered or transmitted to him or them by such clerk of the peace, if any such duplicate shall be delivered or transmitted, or if any clerk of assize, judge's associate or other officer shall record the appearance of any person so summoned and returned as aforesaid, who did not really and truly appear, then and in such case any judge or justice of assize or *Nisi prius,* or judge or judges of the said great sessions, or the judge or judges of the sessions for the said counties palatine, shall and may, upon examination in a summary way, set such fine or fines upon such sheriff or under sheriff, clerk of the assize, judge's associate or other officer, for every such person so summoned and returned as aforesaid, and for every person whose appearance shall be so falsely recorded, as the said judge or justice of assize, *Nisi prius,* or of the said great sessions, or the judge or judges of the sessions for the said counties palatine shall think meet, not exceeding ten pounds, and not less than forty shillings.

IV. And for preventing abuses by sheriffs, under sheriffs, bailiffs or other officers concerned in the summoning or returning of jurors; be it enacted by the authority aforesaid, That no persons shall be returned as jurors to serve on trials at any assizes or *Nisi prius*, or at the said great sessions, or at the sessions for the said counties palatine, who have served within the space of one year before in the county of Rutland, or four years in the county of York, or of two years before in any other county, not being a county of a city or town; and if any such sheriff shall wilfully transgress therein, any judge or justice of assize or *Nisi prius,* or of the said great sessions, or the judge or judges of the sessions for the said counties palatine, may and is hereby required on examination and proof of such offender as he shall think meet, not exceeding five pounds for any one offence.

V. And be it further enacted, That the sheriff, under sheriff or other officer to whom the return of juries shall belong, shall from time to time enter or register in a book to be kept for that purpose the names of such persons as shall be summoned, and shall serve as jurors on trials at any assizes or *Nisi prius,* or in the said courts of great sessions, or sessions for the said counties palatine, together with their additions and places of abode alphabetically, and also the times of their services;

and every person so summoned and attending or serving as aforesaid, shall (upon application by him made to such sheriff, under sheriff or other officer) have a certificate testifying such his attendance or service done, which certificate the said sheriff, under sheriff or other officer is hereby directed and required to give without fee or reward; and the said book shall be transmitted by such sheriff, under sheriff or other officer, to his or their successor or successors, from time to time.

VI. And be it further enacted, That no sheriff, under sheriff, bailiff or other officer or person whatsoever, shall directly or indirectly take or receive any money or other reward to excuse any person from serving or being summoned to serve on juries, or under that colour or pretence, and that no bailiff or other officer appointed by any sheriff or under sheriff to summon juries, shall summon any person to serve thereon other than such whose name is specified in a mandate signed by such sheriff or under sheriff, and directed to such bailiff or other officer; and if any sheriff, under sheriff, bailiff or other officer shall wilfully transgress in any the cases aforesaid, any judge or justice of assize, *Nisi prius* or great sessions aforesaid, or the judge or judges of the sessions for the said counties palatine, may and is hereby required, on examination and proof of such offence, in a summary way, to set a fine or fines upon any person or persons so offending as he shall think meet, not exceeding ten pounds, according to the nature of the offence.

VII. And whereas by the said act of the seventh and eighth years of the reign of his late majesty King William the Third, and also by another act made in the third and fourth years of the reign of her late majesty Queen Anne, all constables, tythingmen and headboroughs are obliged to give in true lists at the respective general quarter-sessions of the peace holden for each county, riding or division, of the names and places of all persons within their respective precincts or places qualified to serve on juries, to the justices of the peace in open court, which hath by experience been found inconvenient and expensive to several constables, tythingmen and headboroughs, such quarter-sessions being often held at a great distance from their abode: for remedy whereof be it enacted by the authority aforesaid, That from and after the said first day of September one thousand seven hundred and thirty, it shall be lawful and sufficient for all or any constables, tythingmen or headboroughs after they shall have made and compleated such lists of persons qualified to serve on juries for their respective parishes or precincts, according to the manner directed by the before mentioned acts and this present act, to subscribe the same in the presence of one or more justice or justices of the peace for each respective county or place, and also at the same time to attest the truth of such lists upon oath to the best of their knowledge or belief, which oath such justice or justices respectively are hereby impowered and required to administer; and the said lists shall (being first signed by the said justices respectively, before whom the same shall be attested on oath, and subscribed as aforesaid) be delivered by the said constables, tythingmen or headboroughs to the chief or high constables of the hundreds or divisions whereunto the same shall respectively belong, who are hereby directed and required to deliver in such lists to the justices of the peace for the county, riding or division at their respective general quarter-sessions in open court, attesting at the same time upon oath their receipt of such lists from the constables, tythingmen or headboroughs respectively, and that no alteration hath been therein made since their receipt thereof; and the said lists, so delivered in and attested, shall be deemed as effectual, as if they had been delivered in by the constables, tythingmen or headboroughs for their respective parishes or precincts.

VIII. And be it further enacted by the authority aforesaid, That from and after the twenty fifth day of December one thousand seven hundred and thirty, every sheriff or other officer to whom the return of the *Venire facias juratores,* or other process for the trial of causes before justices of assize or *Nisi prius* in any county in England, doth or shall belong, shall, upon his return of every such writ of *Venire facias* (unless in causes intended to be tried at bar, or in cases where a special jury shall be struck by order or rule of court) annex a panel to the said writ, containing the christian and sur-names, additions and places of abode of a competent number of jurors named in such lists as qualified to serve on juries, the names of the same persons to be inserted in the panel annexed to every *Venire facias,* for the trial of all issues at the same assizes in each respective county; which number of jurors shall be not less than forty eight in any county, nor more than seventy two, without direction of the judges appointed to go the circuit and sit as judges of assize or *Nisi prius* in such county, or one of them, who are hereby respectively impowered and required, if he or they see cause, by order under his or their respective hand or hands, to direct a greater or lesser number, and then such number, as shall be so directed shall be the number to serve on such jury; and that the writs of *Habeas corpora juratorum,* or *Distringas,* subsequent to such writ of *Venire facias juratores,* need not have inserted in the bodies of such respective writs the names of all the persons contained in such panel, but it shall be sufficient to insert in the mandatory part of such writs respectively, *Corpora separalium personarum in panello huic brevi annexo nominatarum,* or words of the like import, and to annex to such writs respectively panels containing the same names as were returned in the panel to such *Venire facias,* with their additions and places of abode, that the parties concerned in any such trials may have timely notice of the jurors who are to serve at the next assizes, in order to make their challenges to them, if there be cause; and that for the making the returns and panels aforesaid, and annexing the same to the respective writs, no other fee or fees shall be taken than are now allowed by law to be taken for the return of the like writs and panels annexed to the same; and that the persons named in such panels shall be summoned to serve on juries at the then next assizes or sessions of *Nisi prius* for the respective counties to be named in such writs, and no other.

IX. And be it further enacted, That every sheriff or other officer, to whom the return of juries for the trial of causes in the court of grand sessions in any county of Wales do or shall belong, shall, at least eight days before every grand sessions, summon a competent number of persons qualified to serve on juries, out of every hundred and commote within every such county, so as such number be not less than ten or more than fifteen, without the directions of the judge or judges of the grand sessions held for such county, who is and are hereby impowered, if he or they shall see cause, by rule or order of court, to direct a greater or lesser number to be summoned out of every such hundred and commote respectively; and that the said officer and officers who shall summon such persons, shall return a list containing the christian and surnames, additions and places of abode of the persons so summoned to serve on juries, the first court of the second day of every grand sessions; and that the persons so summoned or a competent number of them, as the judge or judges of such grand sessions shall direct, and no other, shall be named in every panel to be annexed to every writ of *Venire facias juratores, Habeas corpora juratorum,* and *Distringas,* that shall be issued out and returnable for the trial of causes in such grand sessions.

X.   And be it further enacted by the authority aforesaid, That every sheriff or other officer to whom the return of the *Venire facias juratores,* or other process for the trial of causes before the justices of the courts or sessions to be held for the counties palatine of Chester, Lancaster or Durham doth belong, shall, fourteen days at the least before the said courts or sessions shall respectively be held, summon a competent number of persons qualified to serve on juries, so as such number be not less than forty eight nor more than seventy two, without the direction of the judge or judges of the courts or sessions to be held for such counties palatine respectively, and shall, eight days at the least before such courts or sessions shall respectively be held, make or cause a list to be made of the persons so summoned to serve on juries, containing their christian and surnames, additions and places of abode; and the list so made shall forthwith be publickly hung up in the sheriff's office, to be inspected and read by any person or persons whatsoever; and that the persons named in such list and no other, shall be summoned to serve on juries at the next courts or sessions to be held for the said respective counties palatine; and the said sheriff or other officer is hereby required to return such list on the first day of the court or sessions to be held for the said counties palatine respectively; and the persons so summoned, or a competent number of them, as the judge or judges of such courts or sessions respectively shall direct, and no other, shall be named in every panel to be annexed to every writ of *Venire facias juratores, Habeas corpora juratorum* and *Distringas,* that shall be issued out and returnable for the trial of causes in such courts or sessions respectively.

XI.   And be it further enacted by the authority aforesaid, That the name of each and every person who shall be summoned and impanelled as aforesaid, with his addition, and the place of his abode, shall be written in several and distinct pieces of parchment or paper, being all as near as may be, of equal size and bigness, and shall be delivered unto the marshall of such judge of assize or *Nisi prius,* or of the said great sessions, or of the sessions for the said counties palatine, who is to try the causes in the said county, by the under sheriff of the said county, or some agent of his; and shall by direction and care of such marshal be rolled up all as near as may be, in the same manner, and put together in a box or glass to be provided for that purpose; and when any cause shall be brought on to be tried, some indifferent person, by direction of the court, may and shall in open court draw out twelve of the said parchments or papers one after another; and if any of the persons whose names shall be so drawn, shall not appear, or be challenged and set aside, then such further number, until twelve persons be drawn who shall appear, and after all causes of challenge shall be allowed as fair and indifferent; and the said twelve persons so first drawn and appearing, and approved as indifferent, their names being marked in the panel, and they being sworn, shall be the jury to try the said cause; and the names of persons so drawn and sworn shall be kept apart by themselves in some other box or glass to be kept for that purpose, till such jury shall have given in their verdict, and the same is recorded, or until such jury shall, by consent of the parties or leave of the court, be discharged; and then the same names shall be rolled up again and returned to the former box or glass, there to be kept with the other names remaining at that time undrawn, and so *toties quoties,* as long as any cause remains then to be tried.

XII. Provided always, That if any cause shall be brought on to be tried in any of the said courts respectively, before the jury in any other cause shall have brought in their verdict, or be discharged, it shall and may be lawful for the court to order twelve of the residue of the said parchments or papers, not containing the names of any of the jurors who shall not have so brought in their verdict, or be discharged, to be drawn in such manner as is aforesaid, for the trial of the cause which shall be so brought on to be tried.

XIII. And be it further enacted, That every person or persons, whose name or names shall be so drawn as aforesaid, and who shall not appear after being openly called three times, upon oath made by some credible person that such person so making default had been lawfully summoned, shall forfeit and pay for every default in not appearing upon call as aforesaid (unless some reasonable cause of his absence be proved by oath or affidavit, to the satisfaction of the judge, who sits to try the said cause) such fine or fines not exceeding the sum of five pounds, and not less than forty shillings, as the said judge shall think reasonable to inflict or assess for such default.

XIV. Provided always, That where a view shall be allowed in any cause, that in such case six of the jurors named in such panel, or more, who shall be mutually consented to by the parties or their agents on both sides, or if they cannot agree, shall be named by the proper officer of the respective courts of king's bench, common pleas, exchequer at Westminster, or the grand session in Wales, and the said counties palatine, for the causes in their respective courts, or if need be, by a judge of the respective courts where the cause is depending, or by the judge or judges, before whom the cause shall be brought on to trial respectively, shall have the view, and shall be first sworn, or such of them as appear, upon the jury to try the said cause, before any drawing as aforesaid, and so many only shall be drawn to be added to the viewers who appear, as shall after all defaulters and challenges allowed, make up the number of twelve to be sworn for the trial of such cause.

XV. And whereas some doubt hath been conceived touching the power of his Majesty's courts of law at Westminster, to appoint juries to be struck before the clerk of the crown, master of the office, prothonotaries, or other proper officer of such respective courts, for the trial of issues depending in the said courts, without the consent of the prosecutor or parties concerned in the prosecution or suit then depending, unless such issues are to be tried at the bar of the same courts: be it declared and enacted by the authority aforesaid, That it shall and may be lawful to and for his Majesty's courts of king's bench, common pleas and exchequer at Westminster respectively, upon motion made on behalf of his Majesty, his heirs or successors, or on the motion of any prosecutor or defendant in any indictment or information for any misdemeanor, or information in the nature of a *Quo warranto,* depending or to be brought or prosecuted in the said court of king's bench, or in any information depending or to be brought or prosecuted in the said court of exchequer, or on the motion of any plaintiff or plaintiffs, defendant or defendants in any action, cause or suit whatsoever, depending or to be brought and carried on in the said courts of king's bench, common pleas and exchequer, or in any of them, and the said courts are hereby respectively authorized and required, upon motion as aforesaid, in any of the cases before-mentioned, to order and appoint a jury to be struck before the proper officer of each respective court, for the trial of any issue joined in any of the said cases, and triable by a jury of twelve men, in such manner as special juries have been, and are usually struck in such courts respectively, upon trials at bar had in the said courts, which said jury so struck as aforesaid, shall be the jury returned for the trial of the said issue.

XVI. And it is hereby further enacted, That the person or party who shall apply for such jury to be struck as aforesaid, shall bear and pay the fees for the striking such jury, and shall not have any allowance for the same, upon taxation of costs.

XVII. Provided always, and it is hereby further enacted, That where any special jury shall be ordered by rule of any of the said courts to be struck by the proper officer of such court, in the manner aforesaid, in any cause arising in any city, or county of a city or town, the sheriff or sheriffs, or under sheriff of such city, or county of a city or town shall be ordered by such rule to bring, or cause to be brought before the said officer, the books or lists of persons qualified to serve on juries within the same, out of which juries ought to be returned by such sheriff or sheriffs, in like manner as the freeholders book hath been usually ordered to be brought, in order to the striking of juries for trials at the bar, in causes arising in counties at large, and in every such case the jury shall be taken and struck out of such books or lists respectively.

XVIII. And be it enacted by the authority aforesaid, That any person or persons having an estate in possession in land in their own right, of the yearly value of twenty pounds or upwards, over and above the reserved rent payable thereout, such lands being held by lease or leases for the absolute term of five hundred years or more, or for ninety nine years or any other term determinable on one or more life or lives, the names of every such person or persons shall and may, and are hereby directed and required to be inserted in the respective lists as aforesaid, in order to their being inserted in the freeholders book; and the persons appointed to make such lists are hereby directed to insert them accordingly; and such leaseholder or leaseholders shall and may be summoned or impanelled to serve on juries in like manner as freeholders may be summoned and impanelled by virtue of this or any other act or acts of parliament for that purpose, and be subject to the like penalties for non-appearance, any law, statute, use or custom to the contrary notwithstanding.

XIX. And be it further enacted by the authority aforesaid, That the sheriffs of the city of London for the time being, shall not impanel or return any person or persons to try any issue joined in any of his Majesty's courts of king's bench, common pleas and exchequer, or to be or serve on any jury at the sessions of *Oyer* and *Terminer*, gaol-delivery or sessions of the peace, to be had or held for the said city of London, who shall not be an housholder within the said city, and have lands, tenements or personal estate, to the value of one hundred pounds; and the same matter and cause alledged by way of challenge, and so found, shall be taken and admitted as a principal challenge, and the person or persons so challenged, shall and may be examined on oath of the truth of the said matter.

XX.   And be it further enacted by the authority aforesaid, That the sheriffs or other officers, to whom the returning of juries doth or shall belong, for any county, city or place respectively, shall not impanel or return any person or persons to serve on any jury for the trial of any capital offence, who at the time of such return would not be qualified in such respective county, city or place, to serve as jurors in civil causes for that purpose; and the same matter and cause alledged by way of challenge, and so found, shall be admitted and taken as a principal challenge, and the person or persons so challenged, shall and may be examined on oath of the truth of the said matter.

XXI.   And be it enacted, That this act shall be openly read once in every year at the general quarter-sessions to be holden for every county, city or place, within that part of Great Britain called England and Wales, next after the twenty fourth day of June.

XXII.   And be it further enacted by the authority aforesaid, That this act shall continue and be in force until the first day of September one thousand seven hundred and thirty three, and from thence to the end of the then next session of parliament, and no longer.

Contemporary description of certain London artisans and tradesmen, 1747

R. Campbell, *The London Tradesmen: Being a Compendious View of All the Trades, Professions, Arts, Both Liberal and Mechanic, now Practised in the Cities of London and Westminster* (London, 1747), 255-71.

Chap. LVI
Of the Shagreen-Case-Maker, and Trunk-Maker

Sect. 1. Of the Shagreen-Case-Maker

The first of these Tradesmen is employed in making Shagreen Cases for Watches, Tweezers, etc. and Chests for Plate. There is some Ingenuity in the Business, and it affords reasonable Profits to the Master: The Journeymen earn Fifteen or Sixteen Shillings a Week, and are pretty constantly employed. It requires neither much Strength, nor any previous Education; a Youth may be bound to it about Fourteen Years of Age.

Sect. 2. Of the Trunk-Maker

The Trunk-Maker is a very noisy Trade: Besides Trunks, Portmanteaus, etc. they generally make Leather-Buckets; and between both return reasonable Profits. The Genius required to fit a Lad for this Trade has nothing particular in it: He must be a mere Dunce who cannot acquire it in less than seven Years. A moderate Share of Strength is necessary: A Lad may be bound about fourteen or fifteen Years of Age, and when out of his Time may earn from Twelve to Fifteen Shillings a Week.

Sect. 3. Of the Box-Maker

The Box-Maker is no more than a bungling Joiner: He is employed chiefly in making Boxes and Cases for packing up all manner of dry Goods. He requires more Strength than Brains; and a Journeyman earns the common Joiner's Wages, about Fifteen Shillings a Week.

Chap. LVII
Of the Needle and Pin-Maker

Sect. 1. Of the Needle-Maker

This Tradesman does not require to be so acute as the Instruments he makes; the Needle-Maker's Skill consists in the just Temper of his Steel; the mechanical Part requires neither much Strength nor Skill. The Steel is drawn in Wire to the Fineness of the Needle designed, cut into Lengths, then the Eye is struck with an Instrument proper for that Use and the Point is filed down.

Sect. 2. Of the Pin-Maker

The Pin-Maker makes his Pins of Brass Wire drawn by the Wire-Drawers, and imported from Abroad; one Hand is employed in cutting it into different Lengths according to the Size of the Pins, another in making the Heads, a fourth in putting them on, and a fifth in Pointing; by the Number of different Hands employed, this Work is quickly dispatched, otherwise it could scarce afford a living Profit; as it is, it turns out but a poor Business, and a Journeyman earns no more than a common Labourer.

Chap. LVIII
Of the Cork-Cutter

This Tradesman's Name implies his Business; the Cork is the Bark of a Tree of that Name of the Product of Spain; it requires no great Head-piece, but a sharp Knife to execute this Business; Women are mostly employed, and earn Seven or Eight Shillings a Week at so much a Dozen of Corks. It is soon acquired, and worth no Boy's While to serve an Apprenticeship to learn the Mistery.

Chap. LIX
Of the Brush-Maker

Sect. 1. The Brush-Maker

It is easy to comprehend the Nature of this Tradesman's Business; he makes Hair Brooms and Brushes of all Sorts: His chief Materials are Hogs Bristles, which he combs, picks, and cuts in Lengths fit for the various Sorts of Brushes he makes; he cuts and forms the wooden Part of the Brush, with an Instrument much of the Nature of that used by the Last-Maker. It requires no great Genius to become fully Master of this Mistery, and but a moderate Degree of Strength: It is not over and above profitable to the Master, and the Journeyman earns from Twelve to Fifteen Shillings a Week. The Trade is pretty much overstocked with Hands, which is no great Encouragement for Apprentices to bind. The Age fit for binding to the Trade, is from Twelve Years of Age and upwards, and their Education has no Influence upon their Art, whether Liberal or not.

Sect. 2. The Broom-Maker

As we are upon the Article of Brushes and Hair Brooms, I must not forget Birch Brooms, which make no inconsiderable Figure in Trade; I am told some employ Four or Five Hundred Pounds in this Article; however I do not find any of these great Masters take Apprentices, or that their Mistery requires great Talents: They generally employ Women and common Labourers to do their Work.

Sect. 3. Mop-Maker

There are a Sort of Mops made by the Birch Broom-Makers, of Woollen Rags, and a Class of People who live by picking up and selling Rags for this Purpose; and another Sort of Mops made of woollen Thrumbs. This last is a profitable Branch; those who make them may earn Twelve or Fifteen Shillings a Week. As I have mentioned Rags, I must here take notice, that these Rag-Men who buy up Linnen Rags for the Paper Mills, employ some Thousands, and make a very genteel Living by it.

Chap. LIX
Of the Weavers in General

Sect. 1. Of Narrow-Weavers, viz Ribbon, Livery-Lace, Incle-Weavers, etc.

The Weaving Business is very extensive, and divided into innumerable Branches; as many as there are different Fabricks of wrought Goods: They may be divided into the Narrow and Broad Weavers, and again into Silk, Cloth, and Linnen Weavers, and each of these into as many Branches as there are different Sorts of Commodities made of these Materials. The Narrow Weavers are such as are employed in weaving Livery Laces for Beds, Ribbons, plain, flowered and brocaded, Tapes, Incles, etc. etc. There are Engine-Looms for making some of these Narrow Goods, wherein Ten or a Dozen of Pieces can be made at once, but Goods made on those Looms are not so good as those made by Hand; the Reason is, it is impossible to find Thread of any Sort, every way equal. These Engines bestow an equal Pressure upon all Threads alike, whereas the Workman when weaving by Hand, increases or diminishes the Strength of his Pull, according to the Coarseness or Fineness of the Thread; and by that Means conceals all Difference in the Wast of Warp.

We have treated of some of the Narrow Weavers elsewhere, as of the Orrice-Weaver; see Chapter XXXth, Sect. 5th. The whole Tribe of Narrow Weavers make but poor Bread, and less in Proportion to the Coarseness of the Materials they use. The common Run of them may earn about Nine Shillings a Week; the Classes most employed in London, are the Livery-Lace-Weavers, and the Ribbon-Weaver. The greatest Number employed in the other Articles work in the Country, and send up their Goods to the London Market, at a much cheaper Rate than they can be afforded to be manufactured here.

Sect. 2. *The Several Tribes of Broad Weavers*

As to those in the Broad Way, the Silk Weaver is most employed in London; Stuffs, Broad Cloaths and Woollen Goods are chiefly made in the Cloathing Counties of England, and the Linnen is the Manufacture of Scotland, Ireland, France and Germany. The Spittlefield Weavers, who all work in the Silk Manufacture, are a numerous Body. The plain Silk Weaver requires but little Ingenuity, but the Weavers of flowered Silks, Damasks, Brocades and Velvets are very ingenious Tradesmen: These ought to learn Drawing to design their own Patterns; the Want of which gives the French Workmen the greatest Advantage over us. Were our Weavers as expert at designing as their Rivals, the Weavers in Spittlefields need not be obliged to send to Paris for new Patterns: A Man acute with his Pen in Drawing, could strike out new Fancies as well as the Frenchman; for I cannot apprehend there can be any general natural Difference between Workmen, if they have equal Advantages of Education and Experience in their Business.

As to the Construction of a Loom for these rich Manufactures, it is the same with that designed for coarser Goods; all Looms have some Principles common to them, but it is impossible to give the Reader an Idea of that which constitutes the Difference among them without a Plate or Model.

Sect. 3. *Wages of a Silk-Weaver*

The Journeyman Weaver in most Branches in the Silk Way may earn a Guinea or Eighteen Shillings a Week, if constantly employed; it requires moderate Strength: A Boy may be bound about Eleven or Twelve Years of Age. They are employed younger, but more for the Advantage of the Master, than any thing they can learn of their Trade in such Infant Years.

Sect. 4. *Of the Silk-Man*

The Tradesman buys raw Silk from the Importer, and sometimes imports it himself and sells it to the Manufacturer. If we consider him a Ware-House-Keeper and Retailer, he requires no great Genius to acquire the Mistery of His Trade; if as a Merchant, we refer him to that Chapter where his Qualifications are comprehended under the general Description of a Merchant.

Sect. 5. *The Silk-Throwster*

The Silk-Throwster, by a Mill calculated for that Purpose, throws the Silk, and prepares it for the various Uses of the Weaver; he employs mostly Women, to whom he gives but small Wages: It is a very profitable Business for the Master, and requires but a small Share of Ingenuity. Spinning the hard Silk and winding it employs a great Number of Female Hands, who may make good Bread of it, if they refrain from the common Vice of Drinking and Sotting away their Time and Senses.

Chap. LX
Of Dyers of All Sorts

Sect. 1. Dyers of All Sorts

In London there are Dyers of all Sorts; some dye only Wool, others Silk; some confine themselves to particular Colours, such as Scarlet and Blues; the Scarlet Dyer is by much the most ingenious and profitable Branch of the Dying Business; the best Dyes that are struck of that Colour are done upon the River Severn; the Water of that River has some Influence upon the Operation, which renders Cloths finished there preferable to those made any where else in Europe. The Business of a Dyer in the Woollen Way in general is very laborious and chilly; they are constantly dabbling in Water hot and cold. The Silk Dyers have not so much Labour as the other, but all Classes require a moderate Degree of Strength; a Youth ought not to be bound until Fourteen or Fifteen Years of Age. The general Wages among Dyers is Half a Crown and Three Shillings a Day.

The Woollen-Dyers besides Copperas and the Fulling Mill, which is an Engine moved by a Horse for milling the Cloth, have a Hot-Press to give it a Gloss. The Silk-Dyers, instead of a Press, use an Engine called a Mangle or Calendar. The Silk when dyed and dry is rolled round a Roller, and put upon a smooth Plain, under a great Weight moved backward and forward by the Interposition of a Wheel and a Horse.

Sect. 2. Of Calendars

These Tradesmen keep Calendars or Mangles, being heavy Engines moved by Horses, or Men, for pressing chiefly Linnen Cloths of all Sorts. It requires more Strength than Ingenuity, and I do not understand that they take Apprentices; the few that are Masters about Town employ Labourers, who earn from Nine to Twelve Shillings a Week, and by Degrees learn to be expert in the Business, so as to confine themselves to that Work alone.

Sect. 3. Of Dry-Salters

This is a Shop-keeping Business who deals in Dyes or Colours for the Dyers mostly. They sometimes differ little from the Oil-Shop, and in no Case it requires much Ingenuity to acquire their Mistery.

Sect. 4. Of Starch-Makers

Starch is mostly made in the Country, it is made of the finest Flour soaked in Water and afterwards dried; we make very good here, but they esteem the Poland Starch best. It is a laborious Business enough, and tolerably profitable. Journeymen earn from Nine to Fifteen Shillings a Week.

Sect. 5. Of Blue-Makers

This Tradesman makes a Species of Blue-Dye, mostly used by the Callico-Printers, and generally keeps a Shop something like a Dry-Salter's, where he sells Dyes and Starch, but they generally use Labourers and seldom take Apprentices for the making of Blue. Such Apprentices as they take are in the Shop-keeping Way.

Chap. LXI
Of the Soap-Boiler

Soap is composed of Lime, Salt of Vegetables, and the Fat of Animals; a Lee or Lixivium is made of Kelp, that is, the Salt of Sea Weed obtained by burning, or of the white Ashes of other Vegetables, into which is added a Quantity of Lime-water. When the Lee has stood long enough in the Fatts to extract all the Salts from the Ashes, it is then drained off and put into a Boiler, with a Proportion of Tallow, (if for hard Soap) or of Oil (if for soft Soap), where it is allowed to boil until the Tallow or Oil is sufficiently incorporated with the strong Lee, and is become of one thick Consistence; it is then taken out with Ladles and poured into Chests; before it is cool they pour over it some Blue, which penetrates through the Mass; when it is cold, it is taken out of the Chests, and cut into Lengths with a Wire, and laid up to dry; It is a laborious nasty Business, but abundantly profitable, and requires no great Share of Ingenuity; if the Master and one Man in the House understands the Business, the whole Work may be performed by Labourers. The Wages given such a Foreman depends upon the Business of the Boiler, and is in proportion to the Largeness of his Dealing; the others concerned are paid as other Labourers, from Nine to Twelve Shillings a Week.

Chap. LXIII
Of the Brewer and Distiller

Sect. 1. Brewer

The Brewers in London, as far as I can learn, seldom take Apprentices; his Work is carried on by Labourers, who have acquired their Knowledge by Experience; and those who intend to set up the Business have either been acquainted with it, by being Son or Relation to some Man in the Trade, or take their Chance, by depending on the Skill and Honesty of the Clerks and Servants: The Business of a Brewer requires a large Stock of Ready Money to set up with, and the Profits returned are proportionably considerable.

Sect. 2. Of the Copper-Smith

The Copper-Smith makes Coppers, Boilers for the Brewers, and all Manner of large Vessels of Copper. This differs only from the Brazier, who likewise makes Copper Utensils, that his Work is the largest and the most laborious. Their Journeymen and Apprentices ought to have as much Strength as any Mechanic I know, and he and they ought to live by themselves, for they are very noisy

Neighbours. The Wages of a Journeyman is from Twelve to Twenty Shillings a Week.

Sect. 3. Of the Back-Maker

This Tradesman makes Backs for the Brewer to cool his Liquors in, is something between the Cooper and the Carpenter, and requires more Strength than Ingenuity, and their Wages is from Twelve to Fifteen Shillings a Week.

Sect. 4. Of the Iron Cooper

This is a Class of Smiths employed in making Iron Hoops for the large Vessels belonging to Brewers and Distillers, is a laborious and not very profitable Branch of that numerous Craft. Their Wages is like that of the other Classes.

Sect. 5. Distilling in General

The London Distillery is now arrived at a very great Perfection, though not near so much as it is to be hoped it may. We make ten times the Quantity of Spirits we made Forty Years ago; the Consumption has increased prodigiously and I believe the Goodness of the Commodity has received some Improvement. It brings in a large Revenue to the Crown; the Dealers get great Estates, but I am afraid it has contributed to debauching the Morals, and debilitating the Strength of the common People. The Cheapness of Home-made Spirits encourages the Vulgar to drink. It lays a Temptation in their Way; they have now got the Habit, which daily increases upon them with such Rapidity, that if the Evil increases in the next ten Years as it has done in the last, Drunkenness must become the Characteristick of the People, they must live upon Spirits, and forget Labour and Sobriety. The Children must be born in Gin, brought up in a Gin-shop, live in Drunkenness, and kick out of the World without having enjoyed one sober Thought; but private Vices are public Benefits, and while they continue such, we have no great Hopes of redressing those many Calamities that attend national Drunkenness.

Sect. 6. The Malt Distiller

The Malt Distiller is the Father of all the other Classes, as he furnishes them with the Chief of their Materials. To distil Malt, the Process is as follows; the Malt is grinded and mashed in the same Manner as if you intended to brew Strong Beer; the Worts are taken off without mixing any Hops, and put to cool in Backs; when cold, they are drawn out of the Backs into working Fatts, and fomented with Yeast; they keep constantly stirring about the Worts in the Fatts until they are thoroughly fermented, and the Barm begins to fall to the Bottom; they are then ready for singling, and are called Wash. They are put into a Still about three Parts full; the Fire is kept pretty brisk till the Wash is near upon the boil; when the Head of the Still is put on, and luted to the Worm in the Worm-tub; then the Fire is allowed to decrease until the Still begins to run; it is kept in a constant flow Heat until the Whole is singled. The first Production is called Low Wines. These Low Wines are again put into the Still, which with the Worm ought to be well cleaned, and are distilled a second Time, and are now pure Spirits of Malt.

Sect. 7. The Compound Distiller

The Malt Distiller proceeds no farther, but sells his Malt Spirits to the Compound Distillers: They put a Quantity of Juniper Berries, Anniseed, or other Materials, with which they mean to flavour their Spirits, into a Still, with a Quantity of Malt Spirit, lowered with Water, and proceed to distill as before. This produces those bewitching Liquors called Gin, Anniseed, ect.

Sect. 8. Molasses Spirits

Molasses Spirits are distilled from Treacle, by the Compound Distillers; the Molasses are diluted with Water to a proper Thinness, then warmed, fermented and wrought in the same Manner as the Malt Wash. When thoroughly fermented, it is singled into Low Wines and re-drawn into Spirits in the same Manner as Malt.

The several Classes of Distillers, notwithstanding the high Duty, have a Secret of making large Profits: How they can pretend to pay the Revenue, and sell sound Spirits for so small a Price as they do, I own is a Mistery past finding out by my shallow Apprehension; but the Fact is true, that they all get Estates, and yet the poor Man may get drunk for Two-pence. It is soon enough to bind a Lad Apprentice to a Distiller at Fifteen; but I believe it is not very common to take Apprentices in that Branch; nor does it require much Ingenuity. I wish they had all of them more Conscience and Honesty, and believed, that they were answerable to God and their Country for the Mischief they do by selling distilled Poison under the fictitious Names of Gin, Anniseed, etc. The Distiller, no doubt, increases the Revenue, and vends the Farmers Product, and in that Respect may be looked upon as a beneficial Member of the Society; but the Evil arising from his Trade to Individuals, in my Opinion, over-balances all the Good he does the Public.

I could wish either that he distilled none but good Spirits, and took a high Price for them; or that there were as few Distillers in our Days as in those of Queen Elizabeth, when our Countrymen had Spirits without Gin, and the Expence of the Publick was defrayed without debauching the Morals of the People.

Sect. 9. Of the Maltster

Malt is made of Barley, Oats, Rye, Pease and Beans, but for the most Part of Barley; though the other Grains may be malted, they are not so commonly used. To make Malt of Barley, the Maltster steeps in a Steep-full of Water, large in Proportion to his Malt Barn; it lies in steep till the whole Grain is equally soft, and that you may bruise it, by holding the Grain between your Finger and Thumb endways; it is then taken out of the Steep and laid in the rot Heap until it begins to put forth a Spire at one End. When it has spired enough, the Heap is spread every Day larger, until it is spread into a Floor, and covers all the Malt Barn; they keep turning it every five or six Hours, until the Grain is perfectly dry. When it is put upon the Kiln and dried by a slow constant Fire, it is then taken off and is ready for the Market. It requires great Care and Judgment to make Malt properly, and is attended with reasonable Profits; but little Malt is made in London in proportion to the Consumption; the most of it is made in the Country, shipped for London and sold at Bear-Key.

Chap. LXIV
Of the Wine-Cooper and Vintner

The Trade of a Wine-Cooper is all a Mistery, his original Business was to take care of the Wine-Cellar, to mix Wines of different Growths, to answer the Flavour and Taste required by the different Palates of his Customers; to fine them down, purge them from their Lees, and render them fit for Drinking; to cure the several Diseases to which Wines are liable; to recover them when pricked, and preserve them when on the Fret; to renew their Flavour and Colour when lost by Age or any Accident. He tastes the Wine at the Keys, knows the Products of different Countries, and the special Qualities of particular Vineyards: This is the honest Part of his Business, and requires a nice Palate and great Labour and Experience to become fully Master of, but of late Years he has gone a Step farther, he is not contented with compounding Wine with Wine to produce different Flavour, Taste and Body; to cure the common Faults of real Wine and prepare them for Use; but he attempts to perform the Miracle of turning Water into Wine; he converts Cyder and several more noxious Materials to a Resemblance of Port, Sack, Canary, and other real Products of the Vine, and is become so alert at deceiving, that few People know when they drink the true Juice of the Grape, or some sophisticated Stuff brewed by the Wine-Cooper. As to the Honesty of this Trade, according to the present Practice, I believe few will be an Advocate for it; but the Profits arising from the Knowledge and Practice of these Misteries are so large, that it is in vain for Conscience to interpose or perswade the Dealers to leave it off, or others not to learn the pernicious Art. A Lad designed for a Wine-Cooper, must have naturally a nice distinguishing Palate; if he has naturally a Taste, Experience teaches him the peculiar Properties and Flavour of Wine, but without it all the Experience on Earth cannot make a Wine-Cooper of him. He may be bound about Fourteen or Fifteen, having only the common Education of a middling Tradesman. A Wine-Cooper, in the Employs of a Wine-Merchant, has generally a Guinea a Week besides Perquisites, which are very large.

The Vintner every Body knows, if he deals honestly, buys neat Wines, and his Profits arise from the Difference between buying and selling, but few of them are contented with that reasonable Profit. They for the most Part dabble at the business of the Wine-Cooper, and Re-brew in their Cellars what had been before Brewed in the Wine-Vaults. A Lad, who is to serve his Time to a Vintner, must be an acute, active Fellow, quick of Apprehension, nimble in in his Heels, ready handed and complaisant in his Disposition; he ought to read and write, and may be bound about Twelve Years of Age; some of them even as Drawers made very good Bread of it. The Trade of the Master, by the general bad Repute he has brought upon Wine, is neither so large no so certain as formerly. Tradesmen are now got more into the Taste of Malt Liquor, and we find our Taverns either shut up or converted into Alehouses; so that I cannot think there is much Encouragement to serve Seven Years Apprenticeship to this Trade.

Chap. LXV
Of the Tallow and Wax-Chandler

Tallow Candles are made two Ways; in order to make the common Store Candles the Tallow is first rendered and strained from the Skin and all Impurities in the Fat. The Wicks are made of Cotton spun for that Use; the Workmen cut them into proper Lengths; the Tallow is melted and put into a Fat of boiling Water, which keeps it in constant Flow; the Wicks are ranged five or six upon a long small Stick, and placed upon Stands near the Fat; the Candle-Maker takes one of these Sticks by both Ends, plunges it into the Fat and takes it out again; this he lays down upon the Stands, and takes up another, until he has dipped them all; then he begins with the first and dips it again, and continues dipping them one after another till they are of the Thickness wanted.

Mould Candles are made thus; they have Moulds made of Lead, Tin, or Glass, of different Sizes, according as they intend to make Candles; the Wick is prepared of Cotton, the same as for Store-Candles, and fixed in the middle of the Mould. When all the Moulds are wicked, the Tallow already rendered, is melted and poured into the Moulds, and is allowed to stand some time till the Tallow is perfectly congealed and cold, and then the Candle is drawn out.

It is a nauseous greasy Business, but the Profits attone for that Inconvenience; it is a healthy Business enough, few of them die of Consumptions; yet pthisicky People, not used to it, find much Difficulty to breathe near the Scent of a Tallow-Chandler's Work-House. Journeymen earn the common Wages. A Youth may be bound about Thirteen or Fourteen Years of Age without any extraordinary Education, or any particular Genius.

Wax Candles are made after a different Manner, they are neither cast in Moulds nor dipped, but rolled and drawn. They make Sealing Wax and Wafers, and Flambeaus, Links, etc. The Business is still more profitable than that of the Tallow-Chandler, and reckoned a more genteel Trade. Journeymen earn the common Wages from Twelve to Fifteen Shillings. A Youth may be bound about Fourteen Years of Age, without any particular Genius or Education.

A Nation Transformed
1760-1830

A Nation Transformed
1760-1830

Economic historians have, with some justification, begun to denigrate the term *Industrial Revolution*. Between 1760 and 1830—the dates frequently assigned to the classic phases of the Industrial Revolution—the economy did not advance as quickly as the word *revolution* connotes. The social transformations that leaped over ancient barricades were spasmodic. The degree of impersonality in capital-labor relationships varied considerably from industry to industry. People's lives changed dramatically, but not with great frequency. Yet modifications of the synoptic view can be misleading also. For revolution or no revolution, these were the most important seventy years in Britain's history, and for economic reasons. The process of industrialization was unparalleled in world history. It provided Britain with the unique opportunity to establish a base of international ascendancy; this remained impregnable for almost a century.

From 1760 on ripples of economic transformation began to swirl through every crevice of national life. Factory organization increased in scope, consolidation of land moved apace, and steam power replaced water power. The framework of economic activity underwent fundamental changes. The limited market economy of parish and village was replaced by national and subsequently international markets, sensitive to the slightest fluctuations in supply and demand. Many aspects of economic activity were integrated. Turnpike trusts and canal commissioners were established on profit bases to initiate innovations in transportation. Canal building, symbolized in particular by the opening of the duke of Bridgewater's canal (1761), marked the commencement of an era of low-priced goods and movable resources. Population, inventiveness, and productivity—all accelerated in conformance with market forces unleashed by the lure of profits. The level of investment increased significantly and on a regular basis, so as to meet the desiderata of an expanding economy. Consumer demand, tempted into existence by cheap prices, penetrated into the core of the country's economic life. Growth industries connected with the production of food, the manufacture of cotton cloth, and the exploitation of coal and iron emerged, producing many social side effects.

It is difficult to catalog the stages of this economic metamorphosis, and even more difficult to construct a convincing explanation for it. The central government did not play a positive role. Private industry was encouraged, but the state incurred no specific obligations to private entrepreneurship. On the other hand, population

323

increase (stimulated initially by rising material standards), growing private demand (the result of international as well as domestic factors), and a decreasing rate of interest (itself the product of complex political and economic factors) were all causes. There were additional factors: a spate of technological innovations, the internal dynamics of change, and greater emphasis upon science. In the final analysis, the industrialization of 1760-1830 cannot be explained satisfactorily by reference to a single strand of behavior. It resulted from the coalescence of a series of convergent efforts that erupted spontaneously into a new volcanic "mix."

Industrialization and urbanization influenced virtually every sphere of activity. Even the impact of the French Revolution—with its welter of unsettling ideas and aspirations and its thrust towards democracy—was modified, in Britain, by economic forces. The two revolutions—political and economic—merged from the 1790s onwards to generate a continuing dynamic for reform. Political life underwent fundamental transformations, demands for educational reform became more strident, an unsettling religious dimension was introduced into national controversy, and constitutional developments of previous decades were accentuated in unforeseen ways. All of these changes, and more, occurred—for example, the beginning of a shift from a nonprofessional state to one that was active and interventionist, prepared to redefine its attitudes towards social policies and to comprehend the dynamics of industrial expansion.

Reform was the keynote of this period. New social and psychological relationships matured, and new forms of expression evolved. Commercial groups felt themselves devoid of proper political authority and agitated for a reduction of government patronage—as in the Economical Reform movement of 1779-80—and for a bevy of political and financial reforms. Aroused by the eccentric peregrinations of John Wilkes and the propaganda of Major John Cartwright, artisans called for changes that would enhance their status in an uncertain world. Nonconformists and Catholics paraded their grievances (exacerbated in the instance of the latter by the "No Popery" Gordon Riots of 1780) and secured, by the repeal of the Test and Corporation Acts (1828-29), a considerable measure of practical freedom. And the unskilled and illiterate poor—Burke's "great unwashed"—became increasingly sensitive to their deprivations. More than any other group, they were jogged into an evolving consciousness by the spasms of revolutions abroad and unrest at home.

The 1790s were a breakwater in the history of reform. Admittedly, there is no direct connection between the Wilkesite agitation of the 1760s and the emergence of the London Corresponding Society in 1792. Wilkes involved himself with a potpourri of issues including general warrants, parliamentary reporting, and the right of the Commons to determine its membership; the LCS expressed artisan demands for radical social reform and undiluted manhood suffrage. Yet more than a tenuous link existed between the reform agitation of earlier periods, championed by Wilkes, Christopher Wyvill (leader of the Yorkshire petitioning movement), Major Cartwright, and Charles James Fox, the Whig libertarian, and that of the decade of the French Revolution.

But whereas political dissent was tolerated in earlier periods, it became distinctly unfashionable in the 1790s. The Pitt government, hitherto sympathetic to political "improvement," boldly attacked the artisan reformers by means of a combination act, the suspension of habeas corpus, stringent regulations upon printers, and restrictions on public meetings. Not unpredictably, these policies led to greater polarization and strengthened the reformers' commitment to their cause. The reorientation of parliamentary forces in 1792, with Edmund Burke and other opponents of the government now joining Pitt's new Tory party, further increased tension. In an age which had not yet experienced the stabilizing influence of party discipline, the balance of power shifted to new forces that agitated outside the parliamentary arena.

The end of the Napoleonic wars signalled a new period of widespread unrest in Britain and revolution became *the* conservative bugbear. Economic dislocations caused by the war distorted the pace of industrialization; the conversion from wartime to peacetime production put considerable strains on the economy. Middle-class urban pressure groups secured repeal of the income tax in 1815. (It was reimposed permanently by Peel in 1842.) Landed interests passed a corn law that made the importation of foreign grain prohibitively dear, setting the stage for a convulsive struggle between powerful groups over the issue of protection.

Moreover, those who wielded less economic and political weight than the propertied classes agitated for more fundamental changes. Artisans, outworkers, craftsmen, and poor shopkeepers renewed and kept up pressure for an extension of the franchise and for legislation to correct the abuses of the factory system. Their political illusions were shattered in St. Peter's Field, Manchester, in August 1819 when local militiamen contributed to the pantheon of working-class martyrology by participating in the "Peterloo massacre." The Liverpool government responded by passing legislation that reduced the freedom to dissent—the "Six Acts" (1819). This repressive policy cast a shadow across the few substantial reforms that were introduced during this period as, for example, the Factory Act (1819), which limited the hours of work for children in textile mills.

Education posed continual and sometimes critical problems throughout the period. The growth of an urban society sensitized popular cultural awareness and stimulated a desire for literacy. The gradual dissemination of the reading habit and the effective use of a cheap press for educational and propaganda purposes, as in the period 1815-19, posed the possibility of subversion of the political system. The response to this educational challenge took several forms. The educational endeavors of Churchmen (for example, the writings of Hannah More), Dissenters, and secular reformers like the Benthamites co-opted the device of reading for propagandizing conservative ideals. Another reaction was the more heavyhanded one of repression, as can be seen in the continuation of legal restrictions and taxes upon the press. These controls were effectual in the short term: even William Cobbett, the peerless popular journalist, was compelled to flee to America for two years and to increase the price of his *Political Register* in 1820. But they were not permanent solutions. Spectacular conflicts over state provision for schooling and the struggle for a free press remained to be fought out in succeeding decades.

Although its full thrust came after 1830, the beginnings of the modern administrative state are discernible during these years. Disciples of Jeremy Bentham, factory reformers, evangelical moralists, and others championed varying degrees of state intervention. Their motives differed; the results were the same. Local power structures gave way to the central government and checks were set upon private enterprise. The time-honored authority of justices of the peace was undermined by new officials who looked to the central state for succour. Yet—and this is a paradox that runs through the administrative history of the succeeding century—the *dominant* strain of economic policy was anticollectivist. Parliament delivered telling strokes of the axe to mercantilist regulations; laissez-faire received a crucial fillip. With the exception of the 1815 Corn Law (and even it was diluted by an act passed in 1828), tariffs were reduced and navigation statutes were repealed.

By 1830 Britain stood on the verge of momentous administrative changes. The relationships of landlord, capitalist, and worker within a hitherto traditional society were about to be permanently transformed. Yet even in 1830, Britain—with her massive concentration of population, her smoking chimneys, her consumer products, and her modern urban culture—was being shaped out of all recognition.

FIRST INDUSTRIAL REVOLUTION

Contemporary description of the duke of Bridgewater's canal, c. 1764

The History of the Inland Navigations, Particularly Those of the Duke of Bridgewater, in Lancashire and Cheshire, and the Intended one Promoted by Earl Gower and other Persons of Distinction in Staffordshire, Cheshire, and Derbyshire (London: T. Lowndes, 1766), 23-31, 36 41.

The third duke of Bridgewater (Francis Egerton, 1736-1803) was a pioneer of inland navigation in Britain. This canal, built between 1759 and 1764, forged a link between his collieries at Worsley and the Manchester market. By reducing substantially the price of coal, it gave a spectacular impetus to canal building.

Observations on the proposed Navigation

The river Mersey, by its communication with the Western Sea, is by nature navigable, in springtides, from Liverpool to Warrington bridge.

By an act of parliament, passed in the year 1720, certain undertakers were empowered to make the rivers Mersey and Irwell navigable from Liverpool to Manchester, and to take a tonnage of 3s. 4d. per ton for all goods navigated between Bank Quay (being near three miles below Warrington bridge) and Manchester.

The freight and tonnage upon those rivers, between Liverpool and Manchester, is 12s. per ton; and between Warrington and Manchester 10s. per ton.

The town of Manchester being supplied with coals by land-carriage, at the expence of from 9s. to 10s. per ton upon a medium, and there being no communication by water, from any collieries to the rivers Mersey or Irwell above Warrington, the duke of Bridgwater [*sic*], who has considerable coal mines in his estate at Worsley, about four miles north of the river Irwell, hath been enabled, by two acts of parliament, passed in the years 1759 and 1760, to make a navigable canal from Worsley mill to Manchester, and to extend a branch of it to Longford bridge, (about three miles from Manchester, upon the great road between that town and Cheshire) and to take a tonnage of 2s. 6d. per ton.

The applications for these Acts were supported by petitions from several parts of the country; the public utility of the undertakings never controverted, and the practicability is fully evinced, by compleating the navigation from Worsley over the river Irwell to Longford bridge, and within two miles of Manchester.

The duke is now proceeding in the further execution of the navigation; and, in order to drain and convey his coals from the mine, is driving up a subterraneous sough upon the level of his canal, which communicates with it, and carries boats of six or seven tons burden.

327

It is found, upon proper surveys, to be practicable to extend this navigation from Longford bridge through a populous part of the county of Chester, to communicate to the river Mersey at the Hempstones, above eight miles below Warrington bridge, from whence there is a natural tide navigation to Liverpool; and the duke is willing to make this extension, without any further tonnage than the 2s. 6d. granted by the former Acts: but to this scheme many objections have been made.

Objection I

That the land-owners will suffer by having their lands cut through and separated, and that a great number of acres will, by this new navigation, be covered with water, and for ever lost to the public.

Answer

Full compensation is to be made for all lands before they can be used for the purposes of the bill, and for all consequential and unforeseen damages; and the duke is obliged to provide proper bridges, and other conveniencies, for the accommodation of the owners and occupiers of lands.

With respect to the loss of lands, by a number of acres being covered with water, whoever knows the great extent of moss and barren land through which the intended canal is to be cut, and has seen the methods practised upon the duke's canal, already finished, by back-drains and aqueducts made under the canal, will be perfectly satisfied, that the lands in general will be drained, and greatly improved, and the back drains will entirely prevent any prejudice from the ouzing through the banks; and satisfaction for any particular and temporary damage, it is presumed, is fully provided for: and the admission of all sorts of manure tonnage free, will furnish an additional means of improvement the the land-owners.

Objection II

That there is no necessity for this new navigation, as the old one upon the rivers Mersey and Irwell is compleat, and sufficient to answer all the purposes of the public, and to carry more goods than the present trade will supply.

Answer

The old navigation is very imperfect, expensive, and precarious, as no vessels can be brought up from the Hempstones into their first lock above Warrington bridge but at springtides, there never having been any attempt to improve that part of the navigation; and between that place and Manchester there are many shallows, which it is very difficult to pass with loaded vessels, and in times of floods the whole is impassable.—These defects occasion great delays and uncertainties in the delivery of goods, which are very inconvenient to trade, and lay the merchants under a necessity of sending very great quantities of goods weekly between Manchester and Liverpool by land-carriage, at the expence of 30s. or 40s. per ton.

The duke's new intended navigation will be above nine miles nearer than the old one, and passable at all times, there being a sufficiency of water at the Hempstones to bring up boats of 40 or 50 tons burthen at the lowest neap tides; the passage from thence to Manchester will be easy and secure, as there will be no shallows or streams to contend with, or floods to obstruct it; and by means of this navigation, goods will be carried from Manchester to Liverpool for 6s. per ton, including freight and tonnage; which, besides the great advantage of expedition and certainty in the delivery, will save one half of the present expence, upon all goods carried by water between Liverpool and Manchester, (that is to say, at the rate of 6s. instead of 12s.) and above four fifth parts of the present expence upon that great quantity of goods now necessarily carried by land, (that is to say, at the rate of 6s. instead of 30 or 40s.) and be the means of conveying many useful commodities, such as coal, timber, slate, stone, and many other things of small value, which cannot afford so great an expence as 12s. per ton.

Objection III

That the new navigation runs parallel with, and in many places very near, the old one, and can therefore extend no advantage to the public but what they already receive from the old navigation.

Answer

The old navigation affords little or no advantage to the country through which it runs, the freight and tonnage being so heavy, and the course of it being in deep low ground, accessible but in few places, and there not being a wharf or quay between Manchester and Warrington bridge, which is upwards of 26 miles by water.

Although the duke's navigation may, in some parts, run parallel with the old one between Manchester and the Hempstones, yet, for the greatest part of its course, it will be two, three, or four miles from it, and the communication with the adjacent country more easy, as it will be made on higher ground than the old navigation, and cross many public highways which do not lead to it, and will save a land-carriage of nine or ten miles for many hundred tons per week, passing between Cheshire and Manchester.

From Worsley to Altrincham, the new navigation will lie in a different direction to the old one, as it will be carried over the rivers Irwell and Mersey, and will save a land-carriage of many thousand tons of coals every year, for upwards of thirteen miles, through bad roads, to supply the inhabitants of that part of the county of Chester, which borders upon the county of Lancaster.

These are advantages which the country can in no wise receive from the old navigation.

Objection IV

That the water which is to supply the new navigation, is proposed to be taken from the old rivers, and will be a great prejudice, if not a total obstruction of the old navigation in dry seasons.

Answer

The duke cannot take any water, either from the Irwell or Mersey, into his navigation, as both those rivers lye considerably below the level of his present and intended canal.—His Grace's present canal is chiefly supplied with two streams of water flowing from springs cut by him and his ancestors in the bowels of their estate, by driving up soughs to drain the mines, and the waters from thence are still increasing by the progress of the works, the deepest of those soughs being now carrying on with great expedition; which waters, it is apprehended, may with great propriety be called his own, and which at present will be sufficient to fill upwards of 18 locks in 24 hours, being many more than is requisite to answer all the trade that the country can possibly supply on both navigations.

By measuring and comparing the quantities of water used in the old and new navigation, the disproportion will appear so great, that if the quantity used in the new one was to be added to, or diverted from the old one, it would not vary the perpendicular depth a fortieth part of an inch, and could make no sensible difference in the navigation of vessels; at the driest seasons the waters from the duke's soughs and springs producing above 66 cube feet per minute, and the waters in the Irwell and Mersey producing, in the driest seasons, 7700 cube feet per minute, as appears from the most accurate measures and observations which have been taken.

But in order to preserve a due circulation of water in the canal, and to supply any loss which may be sustained by leakage in the course of that work, it is proper that power should be given to the duke to make use, if necessary, of contiguous streams. Yet the exercise of this power cannot be detrimental to the old navigation, as supposing no leakage, the waste waters, which by the bill are directed to be turned into the river, will not only be equal to the streams and waters so taken in, but encreased by the above surplus of the water produced by the soughs and springs; and all this water will be also let off into the river at as high, and in most cases a higher level than the streams and waters, if not so diverted, would in their natural course fall in. And supposing a leakage, yet the old navigation cannot be prejudiced, as the water carried off by such leakage will naturally find its way into the bed of the river; but as the duke is desirous that every necessary provision should be inserted in the bill for obliging him to make a full and ample satisfaction to the proprietors of the old navigation, and all other persons, for any damage they may sustain by the loss of the water to be so diverted; it is apprehended, there cannot remain the least shadow of an objection.

Objection V

That as the proprietors of the old navigation have advanced large sums of money, and as they undertook it upon the faith of parliament, they have acquired such a property in it as ought not to be taken from them, without a full compensation.

Answer

The parliament, in passing the act for the old navigation, had only in view the advantage of the public, and could not mean to give the undertakers an exclusive right to this mode of carriage, if a better and more advantageous conveyance could be afterwards found.—The undertakers were voluntary adventurers: they were for many years disappointed in their expectations: several who had advanced money thought proper to forfeit the sums paid, rather than hazard a further disbursement; and others, who had compleated their payments, amounting to about 41*l.* per share, sold out at 12*l.*—At last, a sort of navigation was compleated, after eighteen years had elapsed: a navigation tedious, expensive, and liable to great interruption: a navigation in which the hopes of the legislature, and the expectations of the public, and the undertakers, were in a great measure baffled: a navigation, the defects whereof a turnpike road was made to supply.—Meritorious as the first design might have been, the difficulties in the execution, and in the use of it, plainly demonstrate it to have been mistaken, or an ill executed scheme. And is the public to be denied a more expeditious, safe, and, in every respect, a better navigation, because this was attempted? and not to have the advantage of carriage for 6s. per ton, because the proprietors of the old navigation cannot carry for less than 12s.?

Though they have been in possession of this river above 40 years, and the use of the navigation above 20 years; and though they are in the greatest apprehension of ruin from the proposed scheme, (the strongest proof of its utility) they may, if that scheme was to take effect, have 30*l.* for every share, that originally cost about 41*l.* And if their dividends have not, in so many years, made up to them considerably more than the difference, with the interest upon the whole, it is submitted, If that is not a very striking proof, that their undertaking has been of very small importance in this manufacturing country.

The creditors upon turnpike acts are adventurers, with respect to the money advanced, in the same manner as the undertakers of navigations.—They are merely adventurers, without having the advantage of making the roads in the cheapest manner, placing the turnpikes, or collecting the tolls, and without any chance of benefit from the increase of trade. They hazard the whole, and can only receive a certain stipulated interest, with the principal.—The undertakers of navigations have the direction of the works, the collection of the tonnage, and all the advantages that may arise from an increase of carriage.—At the head of artificial navigations, made under the authority of parliament, warehouses have been erected, and wharfs provided, at a great expence, for the benefit of navigation: and yet parallel turnpikes have been made, whereby the security of the creditors of the former turnpikes have been much endangered; and navigations have been extended, whereby such warehouses and wharfs have been in a great measure rendered useless, without any compensation being directed to be made by parliament, for any damages they might sustain by the execution of those new laws, calculated for the benefit of the publick.

This mode of navigation is new in its kind; and, from the experiments already made, carries the most promising appearance of success; and may, if the completion thereof is allowed, be the means of introducing into many other trading parts of the kingdom, a more easy, cheap, and expeditious conveyance than can otherwise be obtained.

New schemes and proposals have, from the novelty of the thing, or the local and particular interests of private persons, frequently met with difficulties and obstructions: but it is unnecessary to enumerate the great advantages that have accrued to the trade and commerce of this kingdom, from the attention and encouragement the legislature hath, for many years, given to every attempt where public utility was the object. . . .

A Particular Account of the duke of Bridgwater's Navigation
In a Letter to the Printer of the St. James's Chronicle

Manchester,
Sept. 30, 1763

Sir,

'Tis not long since I viewed the artificial curiosities of London, and now have seen the natural wonders of the Peak; but none of them have given me so much pleasure as I now receive in surveying the duke of Bridgwater's navigation in this country. His projector, the ingenious Mr. Brindley, has indeed made such improvements in this way, as are truly astonishing. At Barton bridge he has erected a navigable canal in the air; for it is as high as the tops of trees. Whilst I was surveying it with a mixture of wonder and delight, four barges passed me in the space of about three minutes, two of them being chained together, and dragged by two horses, who went on the terras of the canal, whereon, I must own, I durst hardly venture to walk, as I almost trembled to behold the large river Irwell underneath me, across which this navigation is carried by a bridge, which contains upon it the canal of water, with the barges in it, drawn by horses, which walk upon the battlements of this extraordinary bridge. This navigation begins at the foot of some hills, in which the duke's coals are dug, from whence a canal is cut through rocks, which day-light never enters. By this means large boats are hauled to the innermost parts of those hills, and being there filled with coals, are brought out by an easy current, which supplies the whole navigation, for the space of about ten miles. At the mouth of the cavern is erected a water-bellows, being the body of a tree, forming a hollow cylinder, standing upright: upon this a wooden bason is fixed, in the form of a funnel, which receives a current of water from the higher ground. This water falls into the cylinder, and issues out at the bottom of it, but at the same time carries a quantity of air with it, which is received into tin pipes, and forced to the innermost recesses of the coal-pits, where it issues out, as if from a pair of bellows, and rarifies the body of thick air, which would otherwise prevent the workmen from subsisting on the spot where the coals are dug.

From Barton I steered my course towards this place, and in my way saw the navigation carried sometimes over the public roads, and in some places over bogs, but generally by the side of hills; by which means it has a firm natural bank on one side, while the other, composed of earth and gravel thrown up, is about eight yards broad. At proper distances, soughs are formed near the top of the canal, which prevents it from overflowing during immoderate rains.

In some places, where Mr. Brindley has been forced to carry his navigation across a public road, being obliged to keep the water on a level, he has sunk the road gradually, so as to pass under his canal, which forms a bridge over the road; the carriages, by an easy descent, going down on one side, and by the same easy ascent, coming up again on the other. Near this town, where Cornebrook comes athwart the duke's navigation, the current of the brook is stopped, and let into a large bason, from whence it falls gradually into a smaller one that is within it, and is open at the bottom; by which means the water sinks into a drain, and is conveyed under-ground to the other side of the canal, where it rises into its old channel.

At this place, which is about a mile from Manchester, the duke's agents have made a wharf, and are selling coals at three-pence halfpenny per basket, which is about seven score weight; and next summer they intend to land them in this town.

Many gentlemen of this neighbourhood are reaping the benefit of Mr. Brindley's inventions; he having taught them a method of draining coal-pits by a fire-engine, constructed at the expence of 150*l.* which no one before knew how to make at less than 500*l.* In these he uses wooden chains, which are preferable to iron ones, and cylinders made of deal, which supply the place of those which were usually made of cast iron. Channels are now cutting also in many other coal-pits, and boats are used instead of sledges, to convey the coals to the mouths of the pits.

I am yours, etc.

T. L.

A Second Letter

July 1, 1765

Sir,

I now send you some additional observations on the duke of Bridgwater's extraordinary navigation which I made yesterday at Stretford, where I found four hundred men at work, (though it was Sunday) in putting the finishing stroke to about two hundred yards of the canal, which reached nearly to the Mersey; and on drawing up the flood-gates, was to receive last night a proper quantity of water, with a number of loaded barges, and some things which I can ill describe. One of these appeared like the hull of a collier, with its deck all covered after the manner of a cabin, and having an iron chimney in the center; this, on inquiry, proved to be the carpentry, but was shut up, being Sabbath-day, as was another barge, which contained the smith's forge. Other vessels were loaded with soil, which was put into troughs, fastened together, and rested on boards that lay across two barges; between each of these was room enough to discharge the loading, by loosening some iron pins at the bottom of the troughs: other barges lay loaded with the foundation stones of the navigation canal or bridge, which is to hold the duke's barges of coals and merchandize, intended to be carried across the Mersey. Near two thousand oak piles are already driven to strengthen the foundation of this Bridge. The carpenters on the Lancashire side were preparing the center frame; and on the Cheshire, all hands, and I may say, all the water, at work in bringing down the soil, and beating the ground adjoining to the foundation of the bridge, which is designed to be covered with stone in a month, and finished in ten days more.

I surveyed the duke's men for two hours, and think the industry of bees, or labour of ants, is not to be compared with them. Each man's work seemed to depend, and be connected with his neighbour's, and the whole posse appeared, as I conceive did that of the Tyrians, when they wanted houses to put their heads in, and were building Carthage.

This bridge, when finished, will unite the Lancashire and Cheshire parts of the duke's navigation, and next year he will be able to sell coals at Dunham in Cheshire. He has finished the cut quite across Sale Moor, and will soon compleat it over the meadows on each side of the River Mersey; the entrance of which, from the low and boggy situation, was, by men of common understanding, deemed his *ne plus ultra*. At this place, Mr. Brindley caused trenches to be made, and placed deal balks in an erect position, backing and supporting them on the outside with other balks laid in rows, and screwed fast together; and on the front-side, he threw the earth and clay, in order to form his navigation canal. After thus finishing forty yards of his artificial river, he removed the balks, and placed them again where the canal was designed to advance. In order to feed that end of the navigation which is near Manchester, he has raised, and, as it were, swallowed up the river Medlock, where he last year erected some stoneworks; and in order to keep its bed dry for his workmen, he turned off the chief part of the water by a cut through the rock, and invented an engine called a spoon, which he worked at the end of a lever by a horse. When this spoon dips into the water, a kind of flap door, made of leather, is pressed open, and admits the water till full, and on being weighed up, the pressure of the water within closes the door, and as the lever rises, it runs off into a channel cut at the end of the spoon handle. From the wharf, at this place, the poor of Manchester fetch great quantities of coal in wheelbarrows; and Mr. Brindley, in order to remove the inconvenience of carrying them up Castle hill, is driving a large tunnel through the center of this hill, into which he intends to inroduce his barges, and by a crane, which is to be worked by a box-water-wheel, he proposes to land the coals close to this town. That branch of the canal which is finished, and on which coals are already brought to Manchester, is about ten miles long, and the Cheshire branch already finished is about nine miles, which is computed to be executed, on an average, at one thousand guineas a mile; from which I may venture to prophecy, that though this be the first still navigation in England, it will not be the last, as by this means a communication may be made with most rivers; and trading towns may now have navigations far superior to those of rivers, made by little more than the waste water that runs from their pumps, etc.

T. L.

Act to punish persons who destroy mills, engines, mines, bridges, or fences used for enclosing fields, 1768

9 Geo. 3, c. 29   *Statutes at Large*, XXVIII, pt. 1, 211-12.

This statute provided the death penalty for machine breaking and related offenses. It illustrates the tensions involved in the processes of industrialization and enclosure.

Whereas by an act passed in the first year of the reign of his late majesty King George the First, intituled, *An act for preventing tumults and riotous assemblies, and for the more speedy and effectual punishing the rioters,* it is, among other things, enacted, That if any persons unlawfully, riotously, and tumultuously assembled together, to the disturbance of the publick peace, shall unlawfully and with force demolish or pull down, or begin to demolish or pull down, any church or chapel, or any building for religious worship, certified and registered according to the statute made in the first year of the reign of the late King William and Queen Mary, intituled, *An act for exempting their Majesties protestant subjects dissenting from the church of England from the penalties of certain laws,* or any dwelling-house, barn, stable, or other out-house; that then, every such demolishing or pulling down, or beginning to demolish or pull down, shall be adjudged felony without benefit of clergy; and the offenders therein shall be adjudged felons, and shall suffer death as in cases of felony without benefit of clergy: and whereas some doubts have arisen whether the said act extends to the pulling down and demolishing of mills: therefore, for remedying the mischiefs which may ensue therefrom, and for the more effectual punishment of such offenders, be it enacted by the King's most excellent majesty, by and with the advice and consent of the lords spiritual and temporal, and commons, in this present parliament assembled, and by the authority of the same, That if any person or persons unlawfully, riotously, and tumultuously assembled together, to the disturbance of the public peace, shall, at any time after the first day of July, one thousand seven hundred and sixty nine, unlawfully and with force demolish or pull down, or begin to demolish or pull down, any wind saw mill, or other wind mill, or any water mill, or other mill which shall have been or shall be erected, or any of the works thereto respectively belonging; that then every such demolishing or pulling down, or beginning to demolish or pull down, shall be adjudged felony without benefit of clergy, and the offenders therein shall be adjudged felons, and shall suffer death as in case of felony without benefit of clergy.

II. And whereas no effectual provision hath heretofore been made for preventing the burning of mills, be it therefore enacted by the authority aforesaid, That if any person or persons shall from and after the first day of July, one thousand seven hundred and sixty nine, wilfully or maliciously burn, or set fire to, any wind saw mill, or other wind mill, or any water mill, or other mill; such person so offending, being lawfully convicted thereof, shall be adjudged guilty of felony without benefit of clergy, and shall suffer death as in case of felony without benefit of clergy.

III. And for more effectually preventing the destroying of engines for draining collieries, coal mines, and other mines, and bridges and waggon ways used in conveying coals, lead, and other minerals from thence; and also fences made or to be made for inclosing lands by virtue of acts of parliament; be it further enacted by the authority aforesaid, That if any person or persons shall at any time after the first day of July, one thousand seven hundred and sixty nine, wilfully or maliciously set fire to, burn, demolish, pull down, or otherwise destroy or damage, any fire engine or other engine erected, or to be erected, for draining water from collieries or coal mines; or for drawing coals out of the same; or for draining water from any mine of lead, tin, copper, or other mineral; or any bridge, waggon way, or trunk erected, or to be erected, for conveying coals from any colliery or coal mine, or straith for depositing the same; or any bridge or waggon way erected, or to be erected, for conveying lead, tin, copper, or other mineral, from any such mine; or any fence or fences that are or shall be erected, set up, provided, or made, for dividing or inclosing any common waste or other lands or grounds, in pursuance of any act or acts of parliament; every such person, being lawfully convicted of any or either of the said several offences, or of causing or procuring the same to be done, shall be adjudged guilty of felony, and shall be subject to the like pains and penalties as in cases of felony; and the court by or before whom such person shall be tried, shall have power and authority to transport such felon for the term of seven years, in like manner as other felons are directed to be transported by the laws and statutes of this realm.

    IV. Provided always, That no person or persons shall be prosecuted by virtue of this act for any offence or offences committed contrary to the same, unless such prosecution be commenced within eighteen months after the offence committed.

General Consolidating Act for the establishment of turnpike trusts, 1773

13 Geo. 3, c. 78   *Statutes at Large*, XI, 846-55.

This act stimulated the improvement of public roads by facilitating the establishment of local trusts empowered to collect tolls for upkeep and amendment.

    Whereas the Laws now in being for the Amendment and Preservation of the Highways of that Part of Great Britain called England require some Explanation and Amendment may it therefore please your Majesty that it may be enacted; and be it enacted by the King's most Excellent Majesty, by and with the Advice and Consent of the Lords Spiritual and Temporal, and Commons, in this present Parliament assembled, and by the Authority of the same, That from henceforth, upon the Twenty-second Day of September, in every Year, unless that Day shall be Sunday, and then on the Day following, the Constables, Headboroughs, Tythingmen, Churchwardens, Surveyor of the Highways, and Householders, being assessed to any Parochial or Publick Rate of every Parish, Township, or Place, shall assemble together at the Church or Chapel of such Parish, Township, or Place, or if there shall be no Church or Chapel, then at the usual Place of publick Meetings for such Parish, Township, or Place, at the Hour of Eleven in the Forenoon: And the major Part of them, so assembled, shall make a List of the Names of at least Ten Persons living within such respective Parishes, Townships, or Places, who each of them have an Estate in Lands, Tenements, or Hereditaments, lying within such respective Parish, Township, or Place, in their own Right, or in the Right of their Wives, of the Value of Ten Pounds by the Year; or a personal Estate of the Value of One hundred Pounds; or are Occupiers or Tenants of Houses, Lands, Tenements, or Hereditaments, of the yearly Value of Thirty Pounds: And if there shall not be Ten Persons having such Qualifications as aforesaid, then they shall insert in such List the Names of so many of such Persons as are so qualified, as above required, together with the Names of so many of the most sufficient and able Inhabitants of such Parish, Township, or Place, not so qualified, as shall make up the Number Ten, if so many can be found; if not, so many as shall be there resident, to serve the Office of Surveyor of the Highways: And the Constable, Headborough, or Tythingman, of such Parish, Township, or Place, shall, within Three Days after such Meeting, transmit a Duplicate of such List to One of the Justices of the Peace within the Limit of the County, Riding, Division, Hundred, City, Corporation, Precinct, or Liberty, where such Parish, Township, or Place, shall lie, living in or near the same; and shall also return and deliver the original List, made and agreed upon at such Meeting, to the Justices of the Peace, at their Special Sessions to be held for the Highways within that Limit, in the Week next after the Michaelmas General Quarter Sessions of the Peace in every Year; and shall also, within Three Days after making the said List, give personal Notices to, or cause Notices in Writing to be left at, the Places of Abode of the several Persons contained in such List, informing them of their being so named, to the Intent that they may severally appear before the Justices at the said Special Sessions to accept such Office, if they shall be appointed thereto, or to shew Cause, if they have any, against their being appointed: And the said Justices are hereby authorised and required to hold such Special Sessions at such convenient Place or Places within their respective Limits, as they in their Discretion shall judge proper; and to give Notice of the Time and Place where they intend to hold the same to the Constables, Headboroughs, or Tythingmen, of every such Parish, Township, or Place, at least Ten Days before the holding of the said Session; and the said Justices, then and there, from the said Lifts, according to their Discretion, and the Largeness of the Parish, Township, or Place respectively, by Warrant under their Hands and Seals, shall appoint One, Two, or more of such Persons, as aforesaid, if he or they shall, in the Opinion of such Justices, be qualified for the Office of Surveyor, if not, One, Two, or more of the other substantial Inhabitants or Occupiers of Lands, Tenements, Woods, Tithes, or Hereditaments, within such Parish, Township, or Place, living within Three Miles thereof, and within the same County, fit and proper to serve the Office of Surveyor of the Highways for such Parish, Township, or Place, if any such can be found; which Appointment shall, by the Constables, Headboroughs, or Tythingmen, aforesaid, be notified to every Person so appointed by the said Justices, within Three Days after such Appointment, by serving him with the said Warrant, or by leaving the same, or a true Copy thereof, at his House, or usual Place of Abode; and every Person so appointed, if he accepts the said Office, shall be Surveyor of the Highways for the said Parish, Township, or Place, for the Year ensuing, and shall take upon him and duly execute the Office aforesaid; and the said Justices shall then and there give such of the said Surveyors as shall personally appear before them a Charge, for the better Performance of their Duty, according to the Directions of this Act: And if any of the said Persons, so appointed, whose Names were contained in such List, and who were served with the said Notice, shall refuse or neglect to appear at the said Special Sessions, and accept the said Office, if appointed thereto, in

Manner aforesaid, or shall not, within Six Days after being served with such Warrant of Appointment, signify his Acceptance thereof, either in Person, or by Writing, to One of the said Justices, he shall forfeit the Sum of Five Pounds; and in case any Person so appointed by the said Justices, whose Name was not contained in such List, shall refuse or neglect to accept the said Office, or shall not, within Six Days after being served with such Appointment, shew to One of the Justices signing such Appointment, sufficient Cause why he should not serve such Office, he shall forfeit the Sum of Fifty Shillings: Provided that no Person who hath been appointed and served the Office of Surveyor for One Year, shall be liable to be appointed Surveyor for the same Parish, Township, or Place, within Three Years from the Time of such first Appointment and Service, unless he shall consent thereto; but if no such List shall be made and returned, or if the said Justices shall make such Appointment, as aforesaid, and the Person or Persons so appointed shall refuse to serve the said Office, the said Justices, or any Two of them, shall and may, and are hereby required, at the said Special Sessions, or at some subsequent Special Sessions, to be held within One Month after, to nominate and appoint some other Person or Persons to be Surveyor of such Parish, Township, or Place, whom they shall judge proper to execute that Office, and shall and may fix such Salary to be paid to such Surveyor, to be appointed as herein last before mentioned, out of the said Forfeitures, and all other Forfeitures, Fines, Penalties, Assessments, and Compositions, to be paid, levied, and raised, under the Authority of this Act, within such Parish, Township, or Place respectively, as such Justices shall think fit, not exceeding One-eighth Part of what shall have been raised by an Assessment of Sixpence in the Pound, for the Use of the Highways within such Parish, Township, or Place, where any such Assessment shall have been raised, and observing the same Restriction as near as they can, from the best Information they shall be able to get of the probable Amount of such an Assessment, where none hath been already made; and the said Justices shall and may, if they think fit, require the Constables, Headboroughs, Tythingmen, and Surveyor, of every such Parish, Township, and Place, or any of them, to return to them, at such Time and Place as they shall appoint, an Account, in Writing, of the Sum which such Assessment of Sixpence in the Pound hath raised, or will, in his or their Opinion, raise, within such Parish, Township, or Place: And if the Constables, Headboroughs, Tythingmen, Churchwardens, Surveyors of the Highway, and such Householders as aforesaid, of any Parish, Township, or Place, shall neglect or refuse to make such List as aforesaid; or if the Constable, Headborough, or Tythingman, of any Parish, Township, or Place, shall not return the said List of Names when made, and such Duplicate thereof, as aforesaid, and give such Notice or Notices, and serve such Warrant or Warrants, as in this Act is directed; or if the said Constable, Headborough, Tythingman, and Surveyor, or any of them, shall neglect to return such Account of the Amount of such Assessment, as aforesaid, when so required as aforesaid; every Constable, Headborough, Tythingman, Churchward, or Surveyor, so neglecting or refusing, in any of the said Cases, shall, for every such Default respectively, forfeit the Sum of Forty Shillings.

II. And be it further enacted, That in all Cases where the said Justices, upon Neglect or Refusal of the Person so nominated Surveyor as aforesaid to accept the said Office, shall appoint any other Person for such Surveyor, with a Salary as aforesaid, the said Justices shall, and are hereby required to appoint One substantial Inhabitant of such Parish, Township, or Place, for Assistant to such Surveyor in the several Matters, and for the several Purposes hereafter mentioned, until the next annual Appointment of Surveyors, according to the Directions of this Act; and if the Person so appointed Assistant shall, upon Notice of such Appointment, refuse to accept that Office, he shall forfeit the Sum of Fifty Shillings: And in that Case, it shall and may be lawful for such Justices to appoint any other substantial Inhabitant of such Parish, Township, or Place, for Assistant to such Surveyor, in Manner and for the Time aforesaid; and if such Second appointed Assistant shall decline or refuse to accept the said Office, he shall, in like Manner, forfeit the Sum of Fifty Shillings; and the said Justices shall and may appoint any other Person, inhabiting in such Parish, Township, or Place, Assistant to such Surveyor, who shall be intitled to the said Forfeitures herein last before mentioned; and also to some further Allowance by way of Salary, (to be paid as the Surveyor's Salary is hereby directed to be paid), if the said Justices shall think any such Salary necessary, and shall order the same, which they are hereby authorised to do: Provided that no Person so appointed Assistant for One Year shall be liable to be appointed Assistant for the same Parish, Township, or Place, within Three Years next following such First Appointment, without his Consent.

III. And be it further enacted, That the Surveyor of every Parish, Township, or Place, who shall not reside therein, but shall be appointed with such Salary as aforesaid, shall, if required by the Churchwarden, Overseer of the Poor, or any principal Inhabitant of the Parish, Township, or Place, for which he shall be so appointed Surveyor, at the Time of his Appointment, or within Fourteen Days after, give a Bond upon Paper, without Stamp thereupon, to some proper Person within such Parish, Township, or Place, to be nominated by the said Justices, with sufficient Surety, to account for the Money which shall come to his Hands as Surveyor, according to the Directions of this Act; which Bond shall be good and effectual in Law.

IV. And be it further enacted, That the Assistant, so to be nominated and appointed, shall, and is hereby required, to the best of his Skill and Judgement, to assist the said Surveyor, whenever requested by him, in calling in and attending the Performance of the Statute Duty; in collecting the Compositions, Fines, Penalties, and Forfeitures; in making and collecting the Assessments; in making out and serving the Notices authorised by this Act; and in such other Matters and Things as shall be reasonably required of him by the Surveyor, in the Execution of his Office as Surveyor, pursuant to this Act: And the said Assistant shall justly and truly account with, and pay to, the said Surveyor, or to his Order, from Time to Time, according to the Directions of this Act, all the Money which shall come to his Hands as Assistant, by the Means aforesaid; and, in Default thereof, he shall forfeit Double the Value of the Money by him so received, and not so paid and accounted for; and if the said Assistant shall wilfully neglect or make Default in the Performance of any of the Duty required from him by this Act, he shall forfeit, for every such Offence, any Sum not exceeding Five Pounds, nor less than Forty Shillings, at the Discretion of the Justice or Justices of the Limit within which such Assistant shall be appointed: And the said Surveyor shall, and is hereby required to send Orders, in Writing, upon the said Assistant, for the Payment of all Sums due to any Person or Persons, for Work or Materials, by virtue of this Act, which amount to Forty Shillings, or upwards; and the said Surveyor shall not be responsible for any Sum or Sums of Money which shall be received by the said Assistant, and shall not be actually paid to such Surveyor, or to his Order, as aforesaid.

V. Provided always, and be it further enacted, That if Two Parts out of Three of those so to be assembled in any such Parish, Township, or Place, for the Nomination of Surveyors, as aforesaid, shall agree in the Choice of any particular Person of Skill and Experience, to serve the said Office of Surveyor for such Parish, Township, or Place, and in the settling of a certain Salary for his Trouble therein, and shall return the Name of such Person, together with the List herein-before directed, to the Justices of the Peace at their said Sessions, to be held in the Week next after the Michaelmas Quarter Sessions; that then, and in every such Case, it shall and may be lawful for the said Justices, if they shall think proper to appoint such Person to be Surveyor for such Parish, Township, or Place, and allow him the Salary mentioned in such Agreement, which shall be raised and paid in the same Manner as the Salary herein-before mentioned is directed to be raised and paid; and in case any Surveyor to be appointed under the Authority of this Act shall die, or become incapable of executing that Office, before such next Special Sessions for appointing Surveyors, the said Justices, or any Two of them, shall and may, at some Special Sessions, nominate and appoint such Person or Persons as they shall think proper, to execute the said Office, until such next Special Sessions for appointing Surveyors as aforesaid; and if such deceased Surveyor had a Salary, they may allow the same Salary to his Successor, in Proportion to the Time he shall serve the said Office; and if the said Justices of the Peace, at their said Special Sessions, or at any Time afterwards, pursuant to the Powers of this Act, shall appoint more than one Person for Surveyor of any Parish, Township, or Place, all and every Person or Persons so appointed, shall be comprehended under the Word Surveyor in every Part of this Act.

VI. And be it further enacted, That no Tree, Bush, or Shrub, shall be permitted to stand or grow, in any Highways, within the Distance of Fifteen Feet from the Centre thereof, (except for Ornament or Shelter to the House, Building, or Court-yard of the Owner thereof), or hereafter to be planted within the Distance aforesaid; but the same shall respectively be cut down, grubbed up, and carried away, by the Owner or Occupier of the Land or Soil where the same doth or shall stand or grow, within Ten Days after Notice to him, her, or them, or his, her, or their Steward or Agent, given by the said Surveyors, or any of them, on Pain of forfeiting for every Neglect, the Sum of Ten Shillings.

VII. And be it further enacted, That the Possessors of the Land next adjoining to every Highway shall cut, prune, and plash their Hedges, and also cut down or prune and lop the Trees growing in or near such Hedges or other Fences, (except those Trees planted for Ornament or Shelter, as aforesaid), in such Manner that the Highways shall not be prejudiced by the Shade thereof respectively, and that the Sun and Wind may not be excluded from such Highway to the Damage thereof; and that if such Possessor shall not, within Ten Days after Notice given by the Surveyor for that Purpose, cut, prune, and plash, such Hedges, and cut down or prune and lop such Trees, in Manner aforesaid, it shall and may be lawful for the Surveyor, and he is hereby required, to make Complaint thereof to some Justice of the Peace of the Limit where such Highway shall be, who shall summon the Possessor of the said Lands to appear before the Justices at some Special Sessions for that Limit, to answer to the said Complaint; and if it shall appear to the Justices, at such Special Sessions, that such Possessor had not complied with the Requisites of this Act, it shall and may be lawful for the said Justices, upon hearing the Surveyor and the Possessor of such Land, or his Agent, (or in Default of his Appearance, upon having due Proof of the Service of such Summons), and considering the Circumstances of the Case, to order such Hedges to be cut, plashed, and pruned, and such Trees to be cut down, or pruned in such Manner, as may best answer the Purposes aforesaid; and if the Possessor of such Lands shall not obey such Order, within Ten Days after it shall have been made, and he shall have had due Notice thereof, he shall forfeit the Sum of Two Shillings for every Twenty-four Feet in Length of such Hedge which shall be so neglected to be cut and plashed, and the Sum of Two Shillings for every Tree which shall be so neglected to be cut down or pruned, and lopped; and the Surveyor, in case of such Default made by the Possessor, shall, and is hereby required to cut, prune, and plash such Hedges, and to cut down or prune and lop such Trees, in the Manner directed by such Order; and such Possessor shall be charged with, and pay, over and above the said Penalties, the Charges and Expences of doing the same; or, in Default thereof, such Charges and Expences shall be levied, together with the said Forfeiture, upon his or her Goods and Chattels by Warrant from a Justice of Peace, in such Manner as is authorised for Forfeitures incurred by virtue of this Act.

VIII. And be it further enacted, That Ditches, Drains, or Watercourses, of a sufficient Depth and Breadth, for the keeping all Highways dry, and conveying the Water from the same shall be made, scoured, cleansed, and kept open, and sufficient Trunks, Tunnels, Plats, or Bridges, shall be made and laid where any Cartways, Horseways, or Footways, lead out of the said Highways into the Lands or Grounds adjoining thereto, by the Occupier or Occupers of such Lands or Grounds; and every Person or Persons who shall occupy any Lands or Grounds adjoining to, or lying near such Highway through which the Water hath used to pass from the said Highway, shall, and is hereby required, from Time to Time, as often as Occasion shall be, to open, cleanse, and scour, the Ditches, Watercourses, or Drains, for such Water to pass without Obstruction; and that every Person making Default in any of the Matters or Things aforesaid, after Ten Days Notice to him, her, or them, given of the same, by the said Surveyor, shall, for every such Offence, forfeit the Sum of Ten Shillings.

IX. And be it further enacted, That if any Person or Persons, shall lay, in any Highway, any Stone, Timber, Straw, Dung, or other Matter, or in making, scouring, or cleansing the Ditches or Watercourses, shall permit the Soil or Earth, dug out of such Ditches, Drains, or Watercourses, to remain in such Highway, in such Manner as to obstruct or prejudice the same, for the Space of Five Days after Notice thereof given by the Surveyor of the Highways; every Person or Persons offending in any of the said Cases, shall, for every such Offence, forfeit and pay the Sum of Ten Shillings.

X. And be it further enacted, That if any Stone or Timber, or any Hay, Straw, Stubble, or other Matter, for the making of Manure, or on any other Pretence whatsoever, not tolerated by this Act, shall be laid in any Highway, within the Distance of Fifteen Feet from the Centre thereof, and shall not, within Five Days after Notice given by the Surveyor, or some Person aggrieved thereby, be removed, it shall and may be lawful for the Owner or Possessor of the Lands adjacent, or any other Person or Persons whomsoever, by Order from some Justice of Peace, to clear the said Highways, by removing the said Stone, Timber, Hay, Straw, Dung, or other Matter, and to have, take, and dispose of the same, to his and their own Use.

XI. And, for preventing Obstructions in the said Highways, be it enacted, That if any Person shall wilfully set, place, or leave, any Waggon, Cart, or other Carriage, or any Plough or Instrument of Husbandry, in any of the said Highways, (except only with respect to such Waggon, Cart, or Carriage, during such reasonable Time as the same shall be loading or unloading, and standing as near the Side of such Highway as conveniently may be), so as to interrupt or hinder the free Passage of any other Carriage, or of His Majesty's Subjects; every Person so offending shall forfeit the Sum of Ten Shillings for every such Offence.

XII. And be it further enacted, That the Surveyors of the Highways, to be appointed by virtue of this Act, shall, at all such Times and Seasons as they shall judge proper, view all the common Highways, Trunks, Tunnels, Plats, Hedges, Ditches, Banks, Bridges, Causeways, and Pavements, within the Parish, Township, or Place, for which they shall be appointed Surveyors; and in case they shall observe any Nuisances, Incroachments, Obstructions, or Annoyances, made, committed, or permitted in, upon, or to the Prejudice of them, or any of them, contrary to the Directions of this Act, they shall, from Time to Time, as soon as conveniently may be, given, or cause to be given, to any Person or Persons, doing, committing, or permitting the same, personal Notice, or Notice in Writing, to be left at his, her, or their usual Place or Places of Abode, specifying the Particulars wherein such Nuisances, Defaults, Obstructions, or Annoyances, consist; and if such Nuisances, Obstructions, or Annoyances, shall not be removed, and the Ditches, Drains, Gutters, and Watercourses aforesaid effectually made, scoured, cleansed, and opened, and such Trunks, Tunnels, Plats, and Bridges, made and laid, and such Hedges properly cut and pruned, within Twenty Days after such Notice of the same respectively given as aforesaid, then the said Surveyors shall be, and they are hereby fully authorised and impowered, forthwith to remove such Nuisances, Obstructions, or Annoyances, and open, cleanse, and scour such Ditches, Gutters, and Watercourses, and make or amend such Trunks, Tunnels, Plats, or Bridges, and cut and prune such Hedges, for the Benefit and Improvement of the said Highways, to best of their Skill and Judgement, and according to the true Intent and Meaning of this Act; and the Person or Persons so neglecting to make, or open and cleanse such Ditches, Gutters, or Watercourses, or to cut or prune such Hedges, during the Time aforesaid, after such Notice given, shall forfeit for every Foot in Length which shall be so neglected, the Sum of One Penny; and the said Surveyors shall be reimbursed what Charges and Expences they shall be at in removing such Nuisances, Obstructions, or Annoyances, and making or opening, cleansing and scouring, such Ditches, Gutters, and Watercourses, and in making or amending such Trunks, Tunnels, Plats, or Bridges, and in cutting and pruning such Hedges respectively, by the Person or Persons who ought to have done the same, over and above the said Forfeiture; and in case such Person or Persons shall, upon Demand, refuse or neglect to pay the said Surveyor his Charges and Expences occasioned thereby respectively, and also the said Forfeiture of One Penny per Foot, then the said Surveyor shall apply to any Justice of the Peace; and, upon making Oath before him of Notice being given to the Defaulter in Manner aforesaid, and of the said Work being done by such Surveyor, and of the Expences attending the same, the said Surveyor shall be repaid by such Person or Persons all such his said Charges as shall be allowed to be reasonable by the said Justice; or, in Default of Payment thereof on Demand, the same shall be levied in such Manner as the Penalties and Forfeitures hereby inflicted are directed to be levied.

XIII. Provided nevertheless, That no Person or Persons, shall be compelled, nor any Surveyor permitted, by virtue of this Act, to cut or prune any Hedge at any other Time than between the last Day of September and the last Day of March; and that nothing herein contained shall extend, or be construed to oblige any Person or Persons to sell any Timber Trees growing in Hedges at any Time whatsoever, except where the Highways shall be ordered to be enlarged, as herein-after mentioned, or to cut down or grub up any Oak Trees growing within such Highway, or in such Hedges, except in the Months of April, May, or June, or any Ash, Elm, or other Trees, in any other Months than in the Months of December, January, February, or March.

XIV. And be it further enacted, That where the Ditches, Gutters, or Watercourses, which have been usually made, or which are herein-before directed to be made, cleansed, and kept open, shall not be sufficient to carry off the Water which shall lie upon and annoy the Highways; that then, and in every such Case, it shall and may be lawful for the said Surveyors, by the Order of any One or more of the said Justices, to make new Ditches and Drains in and through the said Lands and Grounds adjoining, or lying near to such Highways, or in and through any other Lands or Grounds, if it shall be necessary, for the more easy and effectually carrying off such Water from the said Highways, and also to keep such Ditches, Gutters, or Watercourses, scoured, cleansed, and opened; and the said Surveyors, and their Workmen, are hereby authorised to go upon the said Lands for the Purposes aforesaid: Provided, that the said Surveyors make proper Trunks, Tunnels, Plats, Bridges, or Arches, over such Ditches, Gutters, or Watercourses, where the same shall be necessary, for the convenient Use and Enjoyment of the Lands or Grounds through which the same shall be made, and, from Time to Time, keep the same in Repair; and do also make Satisfaction to the Owner or Occupier of such Lands which are not Waste or Common, for the Damages which he, she, or they, shall sustain thereby; to be settled and paid in such Manner as the Damages for getting Materials in several or inclosed Lands or Grounds are hereafter directed to be settled and paid.

XV. And be it further enacted, That the said Surveyors of the Highways shall, and they are hereby required to make, support, and maintain, or cause to be made, supported, and maintained, every publick Cartway leading to any Market Town, Twenty Feet wide at the least; and every publick Horseway or Driftway, Eight Feet wide at the least, if the Ground between the Fences inclosing the same will admit thereof.

XVI. Provided always, and be it further enacted, That where it shall appear, upon the View of any Two or more of the said Justices of the Peace, that the Ground or Soil of any Highway between the Fences thereof is not of sufficient Breadth, and may be conveniently widened and enlarged, or that the same cannot be conveniently enlarged, and made commodious for Travellers, without diverting and turning the same; such Justices shall, and they are hereby impowered, within their respective Jurisdictions, to order such Highways respectively to be widened and enlarged, or diverted and turned, in such Manner as they shall think fit, so that the said Highways, when enlarged and diverted, shall not exceed Thirty Feet in Breadth; and that neither of the said Powers do extend to pull down any House or Building, or to take away the Ground of any Garden, Park, Paddock, Court, or Yard; and for the Satisfaction of the Person or Persons, Bodies Politick or Corporate, who are seised or possessed of, or interested in their own Right, or in Trust for any other Person or Persons, in the said Ground that shall be laid into the said Highways respectively, so to be enlarged, or through which such Highway, so to be diverted and turned, shall go, the said Surveyor, under the Direction, and with the Approbation of the said Justices, shall, and is hereby impowered to make an Agreement with him, her, or them, for the Recompence to be made for such Ground, and for the making such new Ditches and Fences as shall be necessary, according and in Proportion to the several and respective Interests therein, and also with any other Person or Persons, Bodies Politick or Corporate, that may be injured by the enlarging, altering, or diverting such Highways respectively, for the Satisfaction to be made to him, her, or them respectively, as aforesaid: And if the said Surveyor under the Direction, and with the Approbation, of the said Justices, cannot agree with the said Person or Persons, Bodies Politick or Corporate, or if he, she, or they, cannot be found, or shall refuse to treat, or take such Recompence or Satisfaction as shall be offered to them respectively by such Surveyor; then the Justices of the Peace, at any General Quarter Sessions to be holden for the Limit wherein such Ground shall lie, upon Certificate in Writing, signed by the Justices making such View as aforesaid, of their Proceedings in the Premises, and upon Proof of Fourteen Days Notice in Writing having been given by the Surveyor of such Parish, Township, or Place, to the Owner, Occupier, or other Person or Persons, Bodies Politick or Corporate, interested in such Ground, or to his, her, or their Guardian, Trustee, Clerk, or Agent, signifying an Intention to apply to such Quarter Sessions for the Purpose of taking such Ground, shall impanel a Jury of Twelve disinterested Men out of the Persons returned to serve as Jurymen, at such Quarter Sessions; and the said Jury shall, upon their Oaths, to the best of their Judgments, assess the Damages to be given, and Recompence to be made, to the Owners and others interested as aforesaid in the said Ground, for their respective Interests, as they shall think reasonable, not exceeding Forty Years Purchase for the clear yearly Value of the Ground so laid out, and likewise such Recompence as they shall think reasonable, for the making of new Ditches and Fences on the Side or Sides of the said Highways that shall be so enlarged or diverted, and also Satisfaction to any Person or Persons, Bodies Politick or Corporate, that may be otherwise injured by the enlarging or diverting the said Highways respectively: And upon Payment or Tender of the Money so to be awarded and assessed to the Person or Persons, Bodies Politick or Corporate, intitled to receive the same, or leaving it in the Hands of the Clerk of the Peace of such Limit, in case such Person or Persons, Bodies Politick or Corporate, cannot be found, or shall refuse to accept the same, for the Use of the Owner of, or others interested in, the said Ground, the Interest of the said Person or Persons, Bodies Politick or Corporate, in the said Ground, shall be for ever divested out of them, and the said Ground, after such Agreement or Verdict as aforesaid, shall be esteemed and taken to be a publick Highway, to all Intents and Purposes whatsoever; saving nevertheless to the Owner or Owners of such Ground all Mines, Minerals, and Fossils, lying under the same, which can or may be got without breaking the Surface of the said Highway; and also all Timber and Wood growing upon such Ground, to be fallen and taken by such Owner or Owners within One Month after such Order shall have been made, or in Default thereof, to be fallen by the said Surveyor or Surveyors within the respective Months aforesaid, and laid upon the Land adjoining, for the Benefit of the said Owner or Owners: And where there shall not appear sufficient Money in the Hands of the Surveyor or Surveyors, for the Purposes aforesaid, then the said Two Justices, in case of Agreement, or the said Court of Quarter Sessions, after such Verdict as aforesaid, shall order an equal Assessment to be made, levied, and collected, upon all and every the Occupiers of Lands, Tenements, Woods, Tithes, and Hereditaments, in the respective Parishes, Townships, or Places, where such Highways shall lie, and direct the Money to be paid to the Person or Persons, Bodies Politick or Corporate, so interested in such Manner as the said Justices, or Court of Quarter Sessions respectively, shall direct and appoint: And the Money thereby raised shall be employed and accounted for, according to the Order and Direction of the said Justices, or Court of Quarter Sessions respectively, for and towards the purchasing the Land to enlarge or divert the said Highways, and for the making the said Ditches and Fences, and also Satisfaction for the Damages sustained thereby; and the said Assessment, if not paid within Ten Days after Demand, shall, by Order of the said Justices, or Court of Quarter Sessions respectively, be levied by the said Surveyor, in the manner herein-after mentioned: Provided, that no such Assessment to be made in any One Year shall exceed the Rate of Sixpence in the Pound of the yearly Value of the Lands, Tenements, Woods, Tithes, and Hereditaments, so assessed.

XVII. And be it further enacted, That when any such new Highways shall be made as aforesaid, the old Highway shall be stopped up, and the Land and Soil thereof shall be sold by the said Surveyor, with the Approbation of the said Justices, to some Person or Persons whose Lands adjoin thereto, if he, she, or they, shall be willing to purchase the same, if not, to some other Person or Persons, for the full Value thereof: But if such old Road shall lead to any Lands, House, or Place which cannot in the Opinion of such Justices respectively be accommodated with a convenient Way and Passage from such new Highway, which they are hereby authorised to order and lay out, if they find it necessary; then, and in such Case, the said old Highway shall only be sold subject to the Right of Way and Passage to such Lands, Houses, or Place respectively, according to the ancient Usage in that Respect; and the Money arising from such Sale, in either of the said Cases, shall be applied towards the Purchase of the Land where such new Highway shall be made: And upon Payment or Tender of the Money so to be agreed for as aforesaid, and upon a Certificate being signed by the said Two Justices, or by the Chairman of the said Court of Quarter Sessions, in case the same shall be determined there, describing the Lands so sold, and expressing the Sum so agreed for, and directing to whom the same shall be paid; and upon the Purchaser's taking a Receipt for such Purchase-money from the Person intitled to receive the same, by an Indorsement on the Back of such Certificate, the Soil of such old Highway shall become vested in such Purchaser and his Heirs; but all Mines, Minerals, and Fossils, lying under the same, shall continue to be the Property of the Person or Persons who would from Time to Time have been intitled to the same, if such old Highway had continued there.

XVIII. And be it further enacted, That in case such Jury shall give in and deliver a Verdict for more Monies, as a Recompence for the Right, Interest, or Property, of any Person or Persons, Bodies Politick or Corporate, in such Lands or Grounds, or for the making such Fence, or for such Damage or Injury to be sustained by him, her, or them respectively, as aforesaid, than what shall have been proposed and offered by the said Surveyor, before such Application to the said Court of Quarter Sessions, as aforesaid; that then, and in such Case, the Costs and Expences attending the said several Proceedings shall be borne and paid by the Surveyor of the said Highway, out of the Monies in his or their Hands, or to be assessed and levied by virtue and under the Powers of this Act; but if such Jury shall give and deliver a Verdict for no more, or for less Monies than shall have been so offered and proposed by the said Surveyor, before such Application to the said Court or Quarter Sessions; that then the said Costs and Expences shall be borne and paid by the Person or Persons, Bodies Politick or Corporate, who shall have refused to accept the Recompence and Satisfaction so offered to him, her, or them, as aforesaid.

XIX. And be if further enacted, That when it shall appear, upon the View of any Two or more of the said justices of the Peace, that any publick Highway, not in the Situation herein-before described, or publick Bridleway, or Footway, may be diverted, so as to make the same nearer or more commodious to the Publick, and the Owner or Owners of the Lands and Grounds through which such new Highway, Bridleway, or Footway, is proposed to be made, shall consent thereto by Writing under his or their Hand and Seal, or Hands and Seals, it shall and may be lawful, by Order of such Justices, at some Special Sessions, to divert and turn, and to stop up such Footway, and to divert, turn, and stop up, and inclose, sell, and dispose of such old Highway or Bridleway, and to purchase the Ground or Soil for such new Highway, Bridleway, or Footway, by such Ways and Means, and subject to such Exceptions and Conditions, in all Respects, as herein-before mentioned with regard to Highways to be widened or diverted; and where any such Highway, Bridleway, or

Footway, herein last before described, shall be so ordered to be stopped up or inclosed, and such new Highway, Bridleway, or Footway, set out and appropriated in lieu thereof, as aforesaid, it shall and may be lawful for any Person or Persons injured or aggrieved by any such Order or Proceeding, or by the Inclosure of any Road or Highway, by virtue of any Inquisition taken upon any Writ of *Ad quod damnum*, to make his or their Complaint thereof, by Appeal to the Justices of the Peace at the next Quarter Sessions, which shall be holden within the Limit where the same shall lie, after such Order made or Proceeding had, as aforesaid, upon giving Ten Days Notice in Writing of such Appeal to the Justices of the Peace at the next Quarter Sessions, which shall be holden within the Limit where the same shall lie, after such Order made or Proceeding had, as aforesaid, upon giving Ten Days Notice in Writing of such Appeal to the Surveyor and Party interested in such Inclosure, if there shall be sufficient Time for that Purpose; if not, such Appeal may be made upon the like Notice to the next subsequent Quarter Sessions of the Peace, which Courts of Quarter Sessions are hereby respectively authorised and impowered to hear and finally determine such Appeal; and if no such Appeal be made, or, being made, such Order and Proceedings shall be confirmed by the said Court, the said Inclosures may be made, and the said Ways stopped, and the Proceedings thereupon shall be binding and conclusive to all Persons whomsoever; and the new Highway, Bridleway, or Footway, so to be appropriated and set out, shall be, and for ever after continue, a publick Highway, Bridleway, or Footway, to all Intents and Purposes whatsoever; but no Inclosures of such old Highways or Bridleway, or Stoppage of such Footway, shall be made, until such new Highways, Bridleway, or Footway, shall be compleated and put into good Condition and Repair, and so certified by Two Justices of the Peace, upon View thereof; which Certificate shall be returned to the Clerk of the Peace, and by him inrolled amongst the Records of the said Court of Quarter Sessions; but from and after such Certificate, such old Highways, Bridleway, or Footway, shall and may be stopped up, and the Soil of such old Highways or Bridleway sold, in the Manner, and subject to the Reservations and Restrictions herein-before mentioned with respect to Highways to be enlarged or diverted by virtue of this Act: And where any Highway, Bridleway, or Footway, hath been diverted and turned above Twelve Months, either from Necessity, where the same have been destroyed by Floods, or Slips of the Ground on which they were made, or from other Causes and Motives, if new Highways, Bridleways, or Footways, have been made in lieu thereof, nearer or more commodious to the Publick, and the same have been acquiesced in, and no Suit or Prosecution hath been commenced for the diverting or turning the same, every new Highway, Bridleway, or Footway, set out and used in the Place of that so diverted and turned, shall from henceforth be the publick Highway, Bridleway, or Footway, to all Intents and Purposes whatsoever; and all Persons liable to the Repair of any such old Highways, Bridleway, or Footway, so diverted and turned, or to be diverted and turned, as aforesaid, shall, in the same Manner, be and continue liable to the Repair of such new Highways, Bridleway, or Footway, except where any Agreement shall have been made relative to such Repairs, between the Parties interested therein, which hath laid the Burthen thereof, or of any Part thereof, upon any other Person or Persons in which Case the same shall be observed.

XX. Provided nevertheless, and be it further enacted, That no common Land, lying between the Fences of any old Highway to be stopped up or inclosed by virtue of this Act shall be inclosed; and where the Land lying between the Fences of such Highway, not being common Land, shall, upon a Medium, exceed Thirty Feet in Breadth, and not extend to Fifty Feet in Breadth, the same shall not be stopped up or inclosed, until Satisfaction shall be made to the Owner of such Land, for so much thereof as shall exceed the said Breadth of Thirty Feet; and if the Parties cannot agree in the Satisfaction so to be made, the same shall be adjusted by the said Justices, or the Jury, if a Jury shall be impanalled; and if the Land between the Fences inclosing such Highways, not being common Land, shall exceed Fifty Feet in Breadth upon a Medium, or if the said old Road, so to be diverted or turned shall lie through the open Field or Ground belonging to any particular Person or Persons, such Person or Persons, and also the Person or Persons intitled to the Land between the Fences on the Side of such Highway, shall respectively hold and enjoy the Land and Soil of such old Highway, and pay to the Surveyor, for the Use of the Highways, so much Money as shall be agreed upon between the Parties; or if they cannot agree, so much as shall be deemed and adjudged by the said Justices, or Jury, if such Jury shall be impanelled, as aforesaid, to be adequate to the Purchase of it, estimating such Highway at Thirty Feet in Breadth, upon an Average.

XXI. And be it further enacted, That where any Footway shall be diverted by virtue of this Act, through the Land belonging to the same Person who owned the Land through which such old Footway lay, the same shall be adjudged and deemed an Exchange only, and no Satisfaction or Compensation shall be made, unless the Land to be used for such new Footway shall be of greater Length, and of greater Value, than the Land used for such old Footway; and where the said Footway shall not be turned through the Lands belonging to the same Person, the Damage occasioned by such old Footway to the Lands through which it lay, if the Parties interested shall not agree in adjusting the same, shall be adjudged by Two indifferent Persons, the One to be named by the Owner of the Land, and the other by the said Two Justices; and if the Persons so to be nominated cannot agree therein, they shall chuse some Third Person to adjudge the same, whose Determination shall be final; and the Money at which such Damages shall be assessed shall be applied in making Satisfaction to the Owner or Owners of the Land through which such new Footway shall be made.

XXII. And be it further enacted, That if in any Parish, Township, or Place, where any Highway shall be diverted and turned by virtue of this Act, it shall appear to the Justices who are hereby authorised to view or inquire into the same, that there are other Highways within such Parish, Township, or Place, besides that so to be diverted and turned, which may, without Inconvenience to the Publick, be diverted into such new Highway hereby authorised to be made, or into any other Highway or Highways within such Parish, Township, or Place, and the Charge of repairing such Highway or Highways may be thereby saved to such Parish, Township, or Place, it shall and may be lawful for such Justices to order such Highway or Highways, which shall appear to them unnecessary, to be stopped up, and the Soil thereof sold, in such Manner, and subject to such Restrictions, and such Right of Appeal to the

Party or Parties aggrieved thereby, as are herein-before respectively directed and given concerning the Highways, to be stopped up or inclosed.

XXIII. And be it further enacted, That every Surveyor shall and may, from Time to Time, give Information upon Oath to the said Justices, or any Two or more of them, or all such Highways, and of all Bridges, Causeways, or Pavements, upon such Highways, as are out of Repair, and ought to be repaired by any Person or Persons, Bodies Politick or Corporate, by reason of any Grant, Tenure, Limitation, or Appointment, of any charitable Gift, or otherwise howsoever; and the said Justices shall limit a Time for repairing the same, of which Notice shall be given by the said Surveyor to the Occupier or Occupiers of the Lands or Tenements liable to the Burthen of such Repairs or to such other Person or Persons, Bodies Politick or Corporate, as are chargeable with the same; and if such Repairs shall not be effectually made within the Time so limited, the said Justices shall, and are hereby required to present such Highways, Bridges, Causeways, or Pavements, so out of Repair, together with the Person or Persons, Bodies Politick or Corporate, liable to repair the same, at the next General Quarter Sessions of the Peace for the Limit wherein such Highway shall lie, and the Justices at such Quarter Sessions may, if they see just Cause, direct the Prosecution to be carried on at the general Expence of such Limit, and to be paid out of the general Rates within the same.

XXIV. And be it further enacted, That every Justice of Assize, Justices of the Counties Palatine of Chester, Lancaster, and Durham, and of the Great Sessions in Wales, shall have Authority by this Statute, upon his or their own View, and every Justice of the Peace, either upon his own View, or upon Information upon Oath to him given by any Surveyor of the Highways, to make Presentment, at their respective Assizes or Great Sessions, or in the open General Quarter Sessions, of such respective Limit of any Highway, Causeway, or Bridge, not well and sufficiently repaired and amended, or of any other Default or Offence committed and done contrary to the Provision and Intent of this Statute; and that all Defects in the Repair thereof shall be presented in such Jurisdiction where the same do lie, and not elsewhere; and that no such Presentment, nor any Indictment for any such Default or Offence, shall be removed by *Certiorari*, or otherwise, out of such Jurisdiction, till such Indictment or Presentment be traversed, and Judgement thereupon given, except where the Duty or Obligation of repairing the said Highways, Causeways, or Bridges, may come in Question; and that every such Presentment made by any such Justice of Assize, Counties Palatine, Great Sessions, or of the Peace, upon his own View, or upon such Information having been given to such Justice of the Peace, upon the Oath of such Surveyor of the Highways, as aforesaid, shall be as good, and of the same Force, Strength, and Effect, in the Law, as if the same had been presented and found by the Oaths of Twelve Men; and that for every such Default or Offence so presented, as aforesaid, the Justices of Assize, Counties Palatine, and Great Sessions, at their respective Courts, and the Justices of Peace, at their General Quarter Sessions, shall have Authority to assess such Fines as to them shall be thought meet: Saving to every Person and Persons that shall be affected by any such Presentment, his, her, or their lawful Traverse to the same Presentment, as well with respect to the Fact of Nonrepair as to the Duty or Obligation of repairing the said Highways, as they might have had upon any

Indictment of the same, presented and found by a Grand Jury; and the Justices of the Peace, at their General Quarter Sessions, or the major Part of them, may, if they see just Cause, direct the Prosecutions upon such Presentments as shall be made at the Quarter Sessions, as aforesaid, to be carried on at the general Expence of such Limit, and to be paid out of the general Rates within the same.

XXV. And be it further enacted, That the said Justices of the Peace, at any Special Sessions to be held by virtue of this Act, may, by Writing under their Hands and Seals, order and appoint those Highways, (not being Turnpike Road), which in their Opinion do most want Repair within their Jurisdiction, to be first amended, and at what Time, and in what Manner, the same shall be amended; according to which Order, if such there be, all and singular the respective Surveyors of the said Highways are hereby required to proceed within their respective Liberties.

XXVI. And for the better Convenience of Travellers, where several Highways meet, be it further enacted, That the said Justices, at some Special Sessions to be held for the Purposes of this Act, shall issue their Precept to the Surveyor of the Highways for any Parish, Township, or Place, where several Highways meet, and there is no proper or sufficient Direction Post, or Stone, already fixed or erected, requiring him forthwith to cause to be erected or fixed, in the most convenient Place where such Ways meet, a Stone or Post, with Inscriptions thereon, in large legible Letters, painted on each Side thereof, containing the Name or Names of the next Market Town or Towns, or other considerable Place or Places, to which the said Highways respectively lead; and also at the several Approaches or Entrances to such Parts of any Highways as are subject to deep or dangerous Floods, graduated Stones or Posts, denoting the Depth of Water in the deepest Part of the same, and likewise such Direction Posts or Stones, as the said Justices shall judge to be necessary, for the guiding of Travellers in the best and safest Tract through the said Floods or Waters; and the said Surveyor shall be reimbursed the Expences of providing and erecting the same respectively out of the Monies which shall be received by him or them, pursuant to the Directions of this Act; and in case any Surveyors shall, by the Space of Three Months after such Precept to him directed and delivered, neglect or refuse to cause such Stones or Posts to be fixed, as aforesaid, every such Offender shall forfeit the Sum of Twenty Shillings.

XXVII. And for the better repairing, and keeping in Repair, the said Highways, and providing of Materials for that Purpose, be it enacted, That it shall and may be lawful to and for every Surveyor, to be appointed as aforesaid, to take and carry away, or cause to be taken and carried away, so much of the Rubbish or Refuse Stones, of any Quarry or Quarries, lying and being within the Parish, Township, or Place, where he shall be Surveyor, (except such as shall have been got by the Surveyor of any Turnpike Road), without the Licence of the Owner or Owners of such Quarries, as they shall judge necessary, for the Amendment of the said Highways, but not to dig or get Stone in such Quarry without Leave of the Owner thereof; and also that it shall and may be lawful for every such Surveyor, for the Use aforesaid, in any waste Land or common Ground, River, or Brook, within the Parish, Township, or Place, for which he shall be Surveyor, or within any other Parish, Township, or Place, wherein Gravel, Sand, Chalk, Stone, or other Materials are respectively likely to be found, (in case sufficient cannot be conveniently had within the Parish, Township, or Place, where the same are to be employed, and sufficient shall be left for the Use of the Roads in such other Parish, Township, or Place), to search for, dig, get, and carry away the same, so that the said Surveyor doth not thereby divert or interrupt the Course of such River or Brook, or prejudice or damage any Building, Highway, or Ford, nor dig or get the same out of any River or Brook within the Distance of One hundred Feet above or below any Bridge, nor within the like Distance of any Dam or Wear; and likewise to gather Stones lying upon any Lands or Grounds within the Parish, Township, or Place, where such Highway shall be, for such Service and Purpose, and to take and carry away so much of the said Materials as by the Discretion of the said Surveyor shall be thought necessary to be employed in the Amendment of the said Highways, without making any Satisfaction for the said Materials; but Satisfaction shall be made for all Damages done to the Lands or Grounds of any Person or Persons, by carrying away the same, in the Manner herein-after directed for getting and carrying Materials in inclosed Lands or Grounds; but no such Stones shall be gathered without the Consent of the Occupier of such Lands or Grounds, or a Licence from a Justice of Peace for that Purpose, after having summoned such Occupier to come before him, and heard his Reasons, if he shall appear and give any, for refusing his Consent.

XXVIII. Provided always, and be it further enacted by the Authority aforesaid, That nothing in this Act contained, relative to the gathering or getting of Stones, shall extend to any Quantity of Land, (being private Property), covered with Stones thrown up by the Sea, commonly called Beach.

XXIX. And be it further enacted, That it shall and may be lawful for every such Surveyor, for the Use aforesaid, to search for, dig, and get Sand, Gravel, Chalk, Stone, or other Materials, if sufficient cannot conveniently be had within such waste Lands, common Grounds, Rivers, or Brooks, in and through any of the several or inclosed Lands or Grounds of any Person or Persons whomsoever, within the Parish, Township, or Place where the same shall be wanted, or by Licence from two Justices of the Peace, at a Special Sessions within any other Parish, Township, or Place, adjoining or lying near to the Highway for which such Materials shall be required, if it shall appear to such Justices that sufficient Materials cannot be conveniently had in the Parish, Township, or Place, where such Highways lie, or in the waste Lands, or common Grounds, Rivers, or Brooks, of such adjacent Parish, Township, or Place, and that a sufficient Quantity of Materials will be left for the Use of the Parish, Township, or Place, where the same shall be, (such Lands or Grounds not being a Garden, Yard, Avenue to a House, Lawn, Park, Paddock, or inclosed Plantation), and to take and carry away so much of the said Materials as by the Discretion of the said Surveyor shall be thought necessary to be employed in the Amendment of the said Highways; the said Surveyor making such Satisfaction for the Damage to be done to such Lands or Grounds by the getting and carrying away the same, as shall be agreed upon between him and the Owner, Occupier, or other Person interested in such Lands or Ground respectively, in the Presence and with the Approbation of Two or more substantial Inhabitants of such Parish, Township, or Place; and in case they cannot agree, then such Satisfaction and Recompence shall be settled and ascertained by Order of One or more Justice or Justices of the Peace of the Limit where such Land or Ground shall lie: And in such Places, where, from the want of other Materials, burnt Clay may be substituted in the Place thereof, it shall and may be lawful for the Surveyor to dig Clay in such Places as he is hereby authorised to dig Chalk or Gravel, and to dry the same upon the Lands adjoining, and to burn the same upon any waste Lands or common Grounds, and to carry such Clay in such Manner as other Materials are allowed to be carried by this Act, upon making such Satisfaction for the Damages within the several inclosed Lands or Grounds where such Clay shall be placed or carried, as herein directed with regard to other Materials: Provided, that when the Owner of any such inclosed Lands shall have Occasion for any such Materials lying within the same, for the Repair of any Highway, or other Roads or Ways upon his Estate, or which he shall be under Obligation to repair, and shall give Notice to such Surveyor that he apprehends there will not be sufficient for those Purposes, and also for the Use of the publick Highways; then, and in every such Case, the Surveyor shall not be permitted to dig or take such Materials without the Consent of such Owner, or an Order of Two Justices of the Peace, after having summoned and heard the said Owner or Occupier, or his Steward or Agent; which Justices are hereby authorised to inquire into the Nature and Circumstances of the Case, and to permit or restrain such Power, in such Manner, and under such Directions, as to them shall seem just. . . .

"National Debt," an article from Arthur Young's *Annals of Agriculture*, 1784

Arthur Young, *Annals of Agriculture, and other Useful Arts* (1784), I, 51-70.

In this essay Arthur Young (1741-1820), a propagandist for an improved agriculture, urges the cultivation of wasteland.

Let us therefore examine, if this policy, of which the late experience has so fully manifested the folly, cannot be changed—and if the cultivation of those 13 millions of acres of waste land in Great Britain cannot be attempted, upon principles highly favourable to every valuable interest of the state, and more practicable than the old system of colonizing.

The wastes which disgrace this country, are many of them in our richest counties, and on the most fertile soils. They are scattered over the whole kingdom under the name of commons, greens, forests, chaces, moors, bogs, marshes, etc. Where the soil is good they yield little more benefit to the community than the poorest, for want of being cleared of the spontaneous growth, and drained; and are, besides, so overstocked with cattle, so irregularly and so improperly, that three fourths of their value is usually reaped by the stocks of a few great farmers adjoining. As to the benefit to the poor, it is perfectly contemptible; where it tempts them to become owners of cattle or sheep usually ruinous. Some speculative writers who have passed their lives by a fire side, have attempted to persuade the public, that the inclosure of commons starved the poor, and was the reason of the great rise in all the products of land, but the depreciated value of all those articles in 1778, 1779, and 1780, proved the folly of their idea more completely than a thousand arguments could have done.

To bring into culture all wastes of every donomination which are now uncultivated, not because the soil is bad, but because cursed with the rights of commonage, I consider as the very greatest object of British policy. There may be difficulties in the arrangement of the business, but no doubt of its propriety.

With above eight millions of waste acres in England, and five in Scotland, and with from 1 to 200,000 able hands discharged by the peace, there appears to be ample materials for a statesman to work with. The enquiry is how to contrive the business at the least national expence, a considerable one is certainly necessary; and he who objects to the plan upon that account, would do well to recollect what we have hitherto spent on colonies, and what is yet actually spending.

In all undertakings of this kind, the less that is done immediately by the execution of government the better—as far as private industry could be made the means of carrying into effect such plans, the cheaper and more advantageous is usually the whole operation.

Sir William Osborne, in Ireland, executed an idea that ought to make his name respected in his country as long as it has an existence. The mountains above Clonmel belong to him. He once met a fellow with a wife and several children all in rags and miserably poor, that asked charity of him. The athletic form of the man seemed to reproach him for his business; but he said he could get no work. A happy thought then struck Sir William, *I suppose,* said he, *you are idle and will not work for others; but will you work for yourself? There is a tract of waste,* (pointing to his mountains) *if you will settle on it I will assist you.* The plan was no sooner sketched than executed. The man went up the mountain, Sir William gave him a roof for his cabin, (which is 30 or 40 shillings) he planted his potatoes, and thrived. I viewed some years afterwards his works, he was then a moderate farmer, and surrounded by several more, who, with no other encouragement than having land for nothing, (a black mountain hid for weeks together in the clouds,) the roof of a cabin, and some lime given them—from ragged beggars became farmers possessing good stocks of cattle.—All arising from the single principle, one of the most powerful that actuates the human bosom, that if you give property in land you will create the industry that shall improve it. It is this only that spread America with cultivation, and filled her woods with people.

Sir William Osborne had idle beggars, and the mountain, and he had the genius to combine those two ideas, and to produce every thing that flows from active industry. England has the wastes and the hands, let her also combine them.

But how?—Not so impracticable as may at first blush be thought. Let us consider, in the first place, the expence. I should assign a dwelling and ten acres of lands to every family: the first is the chief article of cost; but the practice of many of the English counties of lodging the poorest people in houses of fifty, sixty, and even eighty pounds, expence must be set aside, being in truth one of the greatest obstacles to population. In Ireland the whole burthen of the habitation being the roof, which is dear from the scarcity of timber, the object of the dwelling is a meer trifle; nor is it credible what an encouragement to population this single circumstance proves in that kingdom, and also in America. Poor labourers and soldiers that have been used to hardships, would be comfortable in such dwellings as could be raised at a trifling expence. They might afterwards improve them with their own labour. Ten pounds is allowance sufficient, and too much of the mud walls of Ireland (by far the warmest I ever met in cottages) were to be adopted: I would add forty shillings for the absolute necessaries of furniture. The inclosure of the field is requisite, the labour would be too heavy on the man, for tho' four lots were thrown together, so that the fences of separation would serve double purposes, yet they would amount to 480 perch, or 120 per lott; for this article I shall allow one shilling a perch or six pounds, and ten shillings for a gate.—Live stock comes next, which a poor man could not buy without assistance; I would give every man a cow with a calf, which may generally be bought for six pounds six shillings and I think it might not be amiss to let him have two ewe sheep, though in some situations a hog would be preferable; we may allow 16 shillings for these. Three sacks of potatoes for seed are essential; the success of the undertaking would depend more on the culture of this root (demanding neither plough nor teams) than perhaps on any other branch of their industry. I would also give him one sack of corn for seed, the sort best adapted to the soil; if we reckon 30 shillings for these two articles, we shall have raised the whole expence to 27 *l*. 2 *s*. Let us suppose it 30 *l*. Many more things would be necessary to establish a regular farm, but we give him that which must do all the rest, *encouragement to be industrious*. Sir William Osborne's mountaineers had scarcely a tenth part of what is here minuted, yet they succeeded, and out of a miserable soil formed good farms. But, as a still further encouragement, they should have a lease for three lives, and by act of parliament be freed from all demands of tythe, poor rates, or any parish charges, being by reciprocity cut off from all right, in case of misfortunes, of being themselves or posterity burthensome to the parish. Requiring no other rent-service or return than the exertions of their industry, promoting the national interests by advancing their own. One observation, however, I must make on an advantage of another sort which might acrue to the state, and that is the encouragement in case of a war, which might be held out and faithfully performed, that all soldiers and sailors who served through the war, survived it, and were discharged, should thus be provided for; many, doubtless, of the men who would now be settled would succeed and thrive greatly, and be a constant spectacle to others, of the reward that should attend the service of their country. I am mistaken if these alone might not in time preclude all necessity of pressing.

In the next place, as to the fund from whence to supply the expence.

Less than half a million a year thus expended, would make the business of so long duration, that the State would not feel the effect soon enough to prove the vast advantages that would result from the plan. The sum is large, but it would make probable a much better return than any other expence the nation ever yet incurred. That sum would thus provide for 16,666 men, establishing as many families and farms, and bringing every year into cultivation 166,600 waste acres. At 40 shillings an acre (and I would easily shew that it would not be less) there would be a created produce of 333,320*l*. a year increasing income.

Years	Acres	Produce
1st	166,660	000,000
2d	333,320	332,320
3d	499,980	666,640
4th	666,640	999,960
5th	833,300	1,333,280
6th	999,960	1,666,600
7th	1,166,620	1,999,920
8th	1,333,280	2,333,240
9th	1,499,940	2,666,560
10th	1,666,600	2,999,880
	9,166,300	14,998,400

By which time 166,600 men would be settled, and at five per house, there would be a population of 833,300 souls added to the kingdom. Credit might be taken perhaps for the whole, for the increase of population in a country where employments are full is very small and gradual, but depends totally on the *increase* of demand, employment, and subsistence. This establishment would be a new colony where the principles of American population would be brought into these desart parts of Britain. Fifteen millions of produce would in ten years be created, and an *income* of 3,333,200*l.* a year. And all this for a less sum than it now costs us to keep Gibraltar, a barren rock of impregnable defence indeed, the possession of which gives us little more benefit than results from the knowledge of our having a post which cannot be taken from us, while we can find so gallant a hero as an Elliot to defend it: Or than Minorca did cost us, which is taken from us. Comparing it with the expence we have been at for colonies, it is but a drop of water to the ocean.

In providing for this expence, it would not, perhaps, be improper to take if from the bounties and drawbacks paid at the Custom-house. It is supposed that frauds alone, in those articles, amount to little short of half a million a year; but, without supposing it to arise simply from a saving of these, if some of them are admitted to be necessary or useful, there can be little doubt but this sum, thus diverted from a doubtful service to the most beneficial one ever yet undertaken, would yield abundantly more to the wealth, income, and even *commerce* of the kingdom. But, if neither bounties nor drawbacks existed, the plan ought not, therefore, to be laid aside; but this revenue, raised by temporary taxes for a purpose so essentially necessary in creating those resources, by means of which alone the nation can support the burthen of future wars.

It must not be imagined that the expence is an unproductive one relative even to the public revenue. I before shewed, that an income from land, trade, and manufacture, of something more than 100 millions, pays at present in Great Britain taxes to the amount of above 13 millions, or about an eighth.—It is a very fair conclusion, that all similar income to be created will also pay an eighth; indeed it is a fact capable of equal proof with most of the postulata in the political science. Now it is highly worthy of attention, that in the 13th year of the undertaking, the public expence would cease altogether, because it would, by receiving an eighth in taxes, draw back the full amount of the annual expenditure, or half a million. This is too clear to be doubted; but, if it was twenty years before that entire re-action took place, still it would be a most comfortable and promising resource, to see the execution of such a splendid project, at an expence sure to be drawn back with ample profit. Some calculators erroneously I conceive, think that all taxes fall ultimately on land alone, or at least the income from it pays a much greater share than from commerce or manufactures; if so, the nation would draw back her expence much sooner, as the proportion of the income would be more than an eighth.

Upon this system it would take but a short period to improve the eight millions and upwards of waste acres in England, which would then yield an annual produce of sixteen millions, the public revenue would be increased two millions a year; and population receive an addition of between 6 and 700,000 souls, in the proportion of 40 to 1000 pounds product. And all this immense resource of wealth and strength would be created at no greater expence than six millions and an half expended in thirteen years.

It may be no impertinence to observe, that such a creation of internal produce of 16 millions, paying two millions in taxes, would be a much greater addition to our wealth, income, population, and strength, than we now receive from our brilliant oriental dominions of Bengal, Bahar, and Orixa, though an empire as large as France—and that the one would be perfectly secure, while the other is hazardous in proportion to its consequence, is what must strike the most careless imagination. Would any man hesitate at the expence of half a million a year, for 13 years, in order to regain the territory of North America? Yet, most assuredly, that dominion never paid us in power, wealth, or population, half of what such a plan as I have sketched would do. Would any man permit small difficulties, or objections that did not amount to the full proof of impracticability, to be urged against a system that should produce advantages equal to these, by means of East or West Indian, or colonial schemes. If we were to judge by all our former, and much of our present policy, certainly he would not; yet, is the possession of these resources in the center of our own territory, or double the advantage and security that could attend them in any distant region.

Political calculators abound with idle and visionary schemes for the payment of the national debt; they would have been better employed in teaching the nation the easiest way to bear it. The true secret is to *increase* your income, and in proportion to the effecting that, you virtually *lessen* the debt. If 32 millions of cultivated acres, with the manufactures and commerce attendant, are able to bear a debt of 200 millions: double the cultivation to 64 millions of acres, and then the debt becomes but as 100 millions; or, in other words, you might bear one of 400 with as much ease as you now support that of 200. This is the plainest, most obvious, and by much the most practical method of lessening the debt.

I wish I was a king, said a farmer's boy: why, what would you do if you was a king? *I would swing upon the gate, and eat bacon all day long.* So I also may wish I was a king: if I did, it would be for the pleasure of executing such a plan as this for a personal amusement. I would send a message to the House of Commons, desiring to be invested with a power, on my own personal examination in any progresses I might make through my dominions, of ordering the necessary inclosures, buildings, and expenditures for the establishment of farms in tracts now waste. And I should be very well assured that my faithful Commons would not refuse it. They would, on the contrary, be happy in promoting the royal pleasures that had for their end the cultivation, improvement, and population of the kingdom. They would rejoice to see the presence of their sovereign diffusing industry; making barren desarts smile with cultivation—and peopling joyless wastes with the grateful hearts of men, who, through these efforts, had exchanged the miseries of poverty for chearfulness, content, and competence; rearing the quiet cottage of private happiness, and the splendid turrets of public prosperity. These should be my amusements; doubtless they are such as kings would look down upon with a contempt equal to mine at the swinging and bacon of a country boy. But I should feel an enjoyment as refined, perhaps, as that which arises from desolated though conquered provinces, from the triumphs that military glory erects on the ruin and sufferings of humanity. And when I died, my memory would have the honour of being forgotten; for I should rank with those kings of ancient days, *dignes sans doute de nos éloges puisque l'histoire ne les a pas nommes.*

As every plan in a free country which affects the property of any one, must be prepared in such a manner as to remove the objections that may be supposed to arise, we must consider the interest of the persons who at present have any sort of property in these wastes proposed in this manner to be cultivated. A considerable part, the royal forests, would be free from all objections, as to the rights of landlords. Other tracts in which these have a claim, but subject to rights of commonage, are of so little real value to the owners, that they would, beyond all doubt, be ready to let the public lott them out in farms free of rent for three lives, provided they reverted back to them at the termination of those lives, built, inclosed, and cultivated, and free from tythe and poor rates. The great advantage of such an arrangement to this class of men, is too obvious to need insisting on. Where the rights to the waste were complex, from the variety of landlords, lords of manors, etc. concerned, the reversionary right to the lotts should be assigned to each upon the same principles as govern a parliamentary inclosure: with this difference, that the obstinacy or folly of individuals should not be allowed to prevent the operation of a plan so decidedly advantageous to the whole community. With regard to the cottagers adjoining, who enjoyed a right of commonage of which they made any use, relief to them would be exceedingly easy, for they should be chosen in preference for peopling the new farms, a recompence so much superior to any thing they could before possess, as to remove every objection that could arise, were they deprived of any rights, or even advantages. To oppress any industrious poor people in a plan, the great feature of which, is to encourage their efforts, and add to their happiness, would be not only a contradiction but a useless one.

Upon the whole, I see no objections that might not be overcome with great ease. Where there are such ample materials with which to satisfy every claimant after the duration of the leases, no one concerned could be really apprehensive of injury. No injuries could be inflicted without a quadruple restitution. But as to the opposition that arose through caprice, obstinacy, and the wrong-headedness of a few individuals, they should be disregarded in the same manner as they are in inclosures, by the common operation of an act of parliament. Indeed I think so very few objections could arise from the parties concerned, that it would be probably adviseable to begin upon these private properties which would not preclude the sale or other application of the crown lands.

As to the method of executing this scheme, many objections would doubtless arise, but by no means insuperable. Probably it would be found most adviseable to make the men themselves the principle executors of the work, with this single caution, not to trust them with money. Returns being gained of the computed number of waste acres in every path of the kingdom from the assessors of the land tax, the men might be distributed proportionably, as near as possible to the place of their legal settlement; and billeted on the parish, till their cottages were erected, and their fences made, in the manner prescribed by the act of parliament. Perhaps it would not be impracticable to trust the execution to the parish officers, under the control of two justices of the peace *viewing the premises.* No money to be allowed in reimbursement, till satisfactory proof was made, that it was actually expended as prescribed by the act. The men having an interest for their lives in the new farm, they would be very active in checking any sinister designs against them. Parish officers are intrusted with the expenditure of much larger sums, and though certainly not without abuses, yet being in accounts vastly more complex and various than could arise from the simplicity of a few articles under a very easy control, the execution of such a plan in their hands, would be much less liable to abuses than the business already in it.—It would, however, be proper to give to the men themselves the absolute choice of the spot in the waste where they were to be settled, to avoid a very obvious motive that might lead to their injury.

There are, doubtless, other modes of executing the idea, but perhaps not so readily, nor at so small an expence, nor in which the men themselves would have so much to do—and the more depended on them, the better chance for their being well treated. The men, and the future inhabitants of the houses, being cut off from ever becoming chargeable to the parish, would prevent the establishment from being viewed with evil eyes.

Operations to so great an extent must necessarily spread into all parts of the kingdom, and consequently could not be put under the direction of a few active and well chosen managers. A very obvious way of conducting smaller undertakings of this sort, would be to fix such a manager in the center of a forest chace or moor, to build, inclose, and fix the men in their farms, upon the regular and orderly plan of a new colony. Such an establishment in the midst of the moors of Northumberland, another in Durham, another in Devonshire, etc. would be doing the business speedily, effectually, and free from imposition or abuses; but the scale would be trifling on comparison with what I have proposed.

The favourite object of my ideal agriculture, was always the improvement of waste lands. I once sketched a plan of conducting a great work of this sort, for spreading cultivation over a waste in the speediest manner possible. Those who have not turned their thoughts to such subjects, would scarcely believe what an extent of country, even to the amount of the largest forest, the works under one man's direction would in a few years cloath.

I was young enough then to think some plan of that sort might be embraced, and that my enquiries, pursuits, and practice, united with the activity I knew myself capable of, might have contributed, without the instigation of any mean or unworthy motive, to the execution of such a design. I am now much older, and I hope too wise to imagine, that I have any talents that can ever be of use beyond the limits of my own farm. The years of retirement in which I have lived, have perfectly quieted all such expectations, and convinced me, that to think such pursuits and employments, as I have delighted in, were adapted to public use in this age and country, were truly amongst the follies of my younger days. Throughout these papers, therefore, I have been studiously attentive to propose no plan that would not in its progress execute itself. No managers, no conductors, no inspectors are necessary: one explicit, decided, and vigorous act of parliament, that made the private interest of every one concerned the means of execution, would effect the whole.

Let us, however, suppose, that the idea of difficulties should get the better of all the true vigour and spirit which ought to animate the minds of men, when the public benefit is so nearly and greatly concerned. Could no other plan be adopted that would force the improvement of some portion of these enormous wastes that are such a disgrace to the kingdom? Much might certainly be done by a bounty per acre given for their culture, upon the plan delineated in the following advertisement of the Society of Arts, suggested to them by me.

> For the improvement of the greatest number of acres of waste moor-land, not less than one hundred; a piece of plate of the value of 100 *l.* with a suitable inscription. It is required that the land, before improvement, be absolutely uncultivated, in a great measure useless, not let to any tenant, and without any building upon it except cottages or huts. That, in its improved state, it shall be enclosed, cultivated, and divided into fields of not more than ten acres each, with buildings erected thereon sufficient for the use and residence of a tenant, and let on lease to one who occupies no other land.

The words *not let to any other tenant*, do not include rights of commonage let with the adjoining farms.

Such a plan as this might easily be adapted to the different purport of an act of parliament. If the bounty was 3 *l.* per acre, a right of inclosure, and the exemption for ever from tythe and poor rates, 500,000 *l.* would improve 167,000 acres annually. No difficulties in this plan could arise that might not be obviated in a moment. If different claims or properties interfered in a waste, they might be settled by commissioners chosen by the parties; who should be obliged to name them, though only one declared his intention of claiming the bounty, in order that such single person's share might be set out, and the owner permitted to execute the works prescribed by the act. The cottagers who made use of their rights of commonage, should be recompensed by small lots of land thrown to their dwellings, and contiguous to them. The execution of such an act of parliament would be a most decisive measure, and, if continued, would carry a very high degree of cultivation into every waste and neglected corner of the island.

There is a motive for bringing into cultivation the waste lands of the kingdom, which can scarcely fail of making an impression. If corn of all sorts was so permanently cheap as to keep the markets too low, it might be said that we have enough already, and that cultivating great additional tracts of land, would be only adding in that respect to an evil; but such is the superior increase of our people to the increase of our culture, that the price is generally high—so high as to occasion clamour and complaint. And the register of our export and import, will shew that our consumption is so much greater than our growth, that no apprehensions of that fort can reasonably take place. It should also be considered, that the execution of such works as are here sketched, would, by the great increase of employment, yield people to consume some of the products raised.

By that register, it appears, that reckoning wheat and rye to yield 2½ qrs. per acre, oats 4, and beans and pease 3½, we have, in 11 years, imported the product of 179,084 acres of wheat and rye, 673,177 acres of oats, and 19,433 acres of pease and beans, in all 871,694 acres, or per annum 79,245 acres. The imports exceeding our exports in

Wheat	343,682 Qrs.
Oats	2,692,708
Rye	104,028
Beans and Pease	68,016

I am very far from finding fault with importations that connect nations together, and assist the mutual intercourse which ought to subsist between them; but I think the object of such imports, should be commodities which other climates yield in preference to our own, rather than such as are the common produce of our whole territory. This regular import of an article which we formerly exported to a vast amount, shews that the state of cultivation has not kept a due pace with the increase of our people and consumption.

Lawsuit concerning James Watt's patent for the steam engine, 16 May 1795

James P. Muirhead, *The Origin and Progress of the Mechanical Inventions of James Watt: Illustrated by his correspondence with his friends and the specifications of his patents* (London: John Murray, 1854), III, 164-81.

The Scottish mechanical engineer James Watt (1736-1819) invented the modern condensing steam engine in 1765 and later effected various improvements on it. In 1775 he formed a partnership with Matthew Boulton (1728-1809) and they manufactured steam engines at Birmingham until 1800. Although the decision concerning his patent in this case was inconclusive, Watt's patent was validated in 1799.

Special Case in the Court of Common Pleas, and Opinions of the Judges thereon,
in the cause Matthew Boulton and James Watt (Plaintiffs)
versus Edward Bull (Defendant)

This was an action upon the case, for unlawfully infringing the privilege declared by an Act of Parliament made in the fifteenth year of his present Majesty's reign, intituled, "An Act for vesting in James Watt, engineer, his executors, administrators, and assigns, the sole use and property of certain Steam-engines, commonly called Fire-engines, of his invention, described in the said Act, throughout his Majesty's dominions, for a limited time," to be vested in the plaintiff James Watt, his executors, administrators, and assigns, of making, constructing, and selling certain engines, in the said Act particularly described, for the term of twenty-five years, by the defendant's making, constructing, and selling engines, in imitation of the said engines invented by the plaintiff James Watt, and secured to him and his assigns by the said Act, and of the like nature and kind as the said kind of engine so invented by the plaintiff James Watt, and by using and putting in practice the invention of the plaintiff James Watt, in the said Act mentioned, within the kingdom of Great Britain, during the said term; two-third parts of which said privileges had been granted and assigned by the plaintiff James Watt to the plaintiff Matthew Boulton; to which action the defendant pleaded the general issue, not guilty, and issue was thereupon joined.

This cause came on to be tried at the sittings after Trinity term, one thousand seven hundred and ninety-three, held at Westminster-hall, in and for the county of Middlesex, before the Right Hon. the Lord Chief Justice Sir James Eyre, knight, and a special jury; when a verdict was given for the plaintiff, subject to the opinion of the Court on the following Special Case:—

"His present Majesty, by letters patent dated the fifth day of January, in the ninth year of his reign, did give and grant unto the plaintiff James Watt his special licence, full power, sole privilege and authority, that he the plaintiff James Watt, his executors, administrators, and assigns, should and lawfully might, during the term of fourteen years therein mentioned, use, exercise, and vend, throughout that part of his Majesty's kingdom of Great Britain called England, the dominion of Wales, and town of Berwick-upon-Tweed, and also in his Majesty's colonies and plantations abroad, the said James Watt's new-invented method of lessening the consumption of steam and fuel in fire engines; with a proviso for the said James Watt, by writing under his hand and seal, to cause a particular description of the nature of the said invention to be enrolled in his Majesty's High Court of Chancery within four calendar months after the date of the said letters patent.

"The plaintiff James Watt, in pursuance of the said proviso, did, by writing under his hand and seal, cause a specification or description of the nature of the said invention to be enrolled in his Majesty's High Court of Chancery, within the said time limited for that purpose; which description is particularly set forth in the said Act of Parliament.

"In the fire engines referred to in the said specification, and which were in use prior to the patent in question, motion was given to the piston by the pressure of the atmosphere acting upon one side thereof, while a vacuum, or certain degree of exhaustion, was produced on the other side, within the steam vessel denominated the cylinder, by means of the injection of cold water, whereby the steam was condensed; which operation, prior to the invention of the said James Watt, was always performed in the steam vessel or cylinder itself.

"When the steam had been condensed, and the piston had descended, such portions of air and water as remained under it within the steam vessel or cylinder were expelled through valves by the next succeeding steam from the boiler, and that steam, counterbalancing the pressure of the atmosphere at the open end of the cylinder, allowed the piston to rise up with that end of the lever to which it was attached, while the other end of the lever, and the matters attached thereto, descended, by reason of their greater comparative weight, and thus the engine was restored to that state in which it was previous to the first condensation.

"The steam was for this purpose, as occasion required, admitted through a pipe from a distinct vessel called the boiler, where it was generated, which occasionally communicated with the cylinder by means of a valve, which was opened and shut by the action of the engine.

"The injection of cold water was in like manner admitted, as occasion required, into the cylinder, through a pipe from another distinct vessel containing cold water, called the injection cistern, by means of a cock or valve, which was also opened and shut by the action of the engine, and such pumps as were used in these engines were also wrought by the engines themselves.

"The construction and use of pumps for drawing out air, elastic vapour, or water from places or vessels where a vacuum or exhaustion was required, were known and practised before the obtaining the letters patent abovementioned, but had not been applied to the cylinders or condensers of steam engines.

"The said invention of the said James Watt, was at the time of making the said letters patent, a new and an useful invention; and the said privilege, vested by the said Act of Parliament in the said James Watt and his assigns, *was infringed by the defendant in manner charged upon him by the declaration.*

"The said specification made by the said James Watt is of itself sufficient to enable a mechanic, acquainted with the fire engines previously in use, to construct fire engines, producing the effect of lessening the consumption of fuel and steam in fire engines, upon the principle invented by the said James Watt.

"The questions for the opinion of the Court are,

"First, *Whether the said patent is good in law, and continued by the Act of Parliament above mentioned.*

"Second, *Whether the above specification of the plaintiff James Watt is, in point of law, sufficient to support the above patent.*

"If the opinion of the court shall be in favour of the plaintiff upon both these questions, then the above verdict for the plaintiffs is to stand:

"If not, then a verdict is to be entered for the defendant instead of the verdict given for the plaintiffs."

On Saturday the sixteenth of May, one thousand seven hundred and ninety-five, this special case stood in the paper for judgment, when the Lord Chief Justice Eyre took notice that the court were divided upon the case, and would therefore deliver their opinions *seriatim.*

Rooke, J.—In this cause of Boulton and Watt v. Bull, there is a special case stated for the opinion of the court; and the case is this. [*Reads the case.*]

From this state of the case, and from the admission of counsel on both sides, I assume the following facts. That the plaintiff Watt is the inventor of a new and useful improvement in fire engines, whereby the consumption of steam, and consequently of fuel, is considerably lessened: that the improvement is of such a nature that it may legally be the object of protection by royal patent: that a patent has been granted to the inventor on the condition of a specification of the nature of the invention: that a specification has been made sufficient to enable a mechanic to construct fire engines containing the improvement invented by the patentee: and that the legislature, six years after the patent had been granted, thought proper to extend the duration of the patent from eight years then to come to twenty-five years. The patent was granted the fifth of January, the ninth of the present King; the statute was the fifteenth of the present King.

Under these circumstances I think I conform to the spirit of the statute of 21 James I., cap. 3, sec. 6, if I incline to support this patent; provided it may be supported without violating any rule of law: and I think so for these two reasons; first, because the patentee is substantially entitled to the protection of the patent; and, secondly, because the public are sufficiently instructed and will be duly benefited by the specification.

Against this claim of the patentee certain objections have been taken, which, it is contended, deprive him of all legal right to protection from it.

First, it is objected that the patent is not for fire engines upon the particular construction containing this new improvement, but for a new-invented method of lessening the consumption of steam and fuel.

Secondly, that no particular engine is described in this specification, but that the patentee only sets forth the principles.

And the last objection is, that the statute has not duly prolonged the patent, because the patent is for a method, and the statute for an engine.

It is to be observed that these objections are merely formal; they do not affect the substantial merits of the patentee, nor the meritorious consideration which the public have a right to receive, in return for the protection which the patentee claims.

As to the first objection, it is, that the patent is not for a fire engine of a particular construction, but for a new-invented method. The patent presupposes the existence of the fire engine, and gives a monopoly to the patentee of his new-invented method of lessening the consumption of steam and fuel in fire engines: the obvious construction of these words is, that he has made an improvement in the construction of fire engines; for what does *method* mean but mode or manner of effecting? what method can there be of saving steam or fuel in engines, but by some variation of the construction of them? A new-invented method, therefore, conveys to my understanding the idea of a new mode of construction. I think those words are tantamount to fire engines of a newly-invented construction; at least I think they will bear this interpretation, if they do not necessarily exclude every other.

The specification shows this was the meaning of the words as understood by the patentee, for he has specified a new and particular mode of constructing fire engines. If he has so understood it, and if the words will bear this interpretation, then I think this objection, which is merely verbal, is answered: to which I add, that patents for a method, or art of doing particular things, have been so numerous, according to the lists left with us, that *method* may be considered as a common expression in instruments of this kind; it would, therefore, be extremely injurious to the interests of patentees to allow this verbal objection to prevail.

As to the second objection, that no particular engine is described, that no model or drawing is set forth, I hold this not to be necessary, provided the patentee so describes the improvement as to enable artists to adopt it when his monopoly expires. The jury find that he has so described it.

It is objected that he professes to set forth *principles* only; but we are not bound by what he professes to do, but by what he has really done: had he professed to set forth a full specification of his improvement, and had not set it forth intelligibly, his specification would have been insufficient, and his patent void. It seems, therefore, but reasonable that, if he sets forth his improvement intelligibly, his specification shall be supported, though he professes only to set forth the principle.

The term *principle* is equivocal: it may denote the *summum genus*, or the radical elementary truths of a science, or it may denote those consequential axioms which are founded on radical truths, but which are used as fundamental truths by those who do not find it expedient to have recourse to first principles.

The radical principles on which all steam engines are formed are the natural properties of steam, its expansiveness and condensibility: whether the machines are formed in one shape or another, whether the machines are formed in one shape or another, whether the cylinder is kept hot or suffered to cool, whether condensed in one vessel or another, still the radical principles are the same.

When the present patentee set his inventive faculties to work, he found fire engines already in existence, and the two natural qualities of steam already known and mechanically used: he only invented an improvement in the mechanism by which they might be employed to greater advantage. There is no newly-discovered natural principle as to steam, nor any new mechanical principle in his machine: the only invention is a new mechanical employment of principles already known.

As to the specification, some part of it, so much as represents the future intentions of the patentee, may be considered, according to the language of the specification, as theoretical only; but the greater part described a practical use of improved mechanism, the basis on which the improvement is founded.

The object of the patentee was to condense the steam without cooling the cylinder: the means adopted to effectuate this were to enclose the cylinder in a case which will confine the heat, or transmit it slowly, to surround it with steam or other heated bodies, and to suffer neither water or any other substance colder than the steam to enter or touch it during that time. These means are set forth.

The objection is, there is no drawing or model of a particular engine; but where is the necessity of such drawing or model, if the specification is intelligible without it? Had a drawing or model been made, and any man had copied the improvement and made a machine in a different form, no doubt that would have been an infringement of the patent. Why? Because the mechanical improvement would have been introduced into the machine, though the form was varied. It follows from thence that a mechanical improvement, and not the form of the machine, is the object of the patent; and if the mechanical improvement is intelligibly specified, of which a jury must be the judges, whether the patentee calls it a principle, invention, or method, or by whatever appellation, we are not bound to consider his terms, but the real nature of his improvement, and the description he has given of it, and we may, I think, protect him without violating any rule of law.

As to the articles of the specification which denote intention only, and do not state the thing to be applied, I do not think he could maintain an action for breach of these articles, for he cannot anticipate the protection before he is entitled to it by practical accomplishment. But the patent is for a method already adopted, and the two first and most material articles are set forth as already accomplished; and the case states it was new and useful at the time of making this patent. I therefore consider the most essential parts of the patent—the keeping the cylinder hot, enclosing it in a case, and surrounding it with steam—as carried into practical effect at the time of the patent; and the defendant has infringed this, and I will presume, after a verdict where nominal damages only are given, that the evidence was applied to and the damages given for those articles only which are well specified. Now, if he has infringed on those articles from an action because he has been guilty of an additional infringement on that which is specified as matter of intention only.

Upon the objection of the want of a drawing or model, that at first struck me as of great weight. I thought it would be difficult to ascertain what was an infringement of a method, if there was no *additional* representation of the improvement or thing methodized; but I have satisfied my mind thus: *infringement or not*—is the question for the jury. In order to decide this, they must understand the nature of this improvement or thing infringed. If they can understand this without a model, I am not aware of any rule of law which requires a model or a drawing to be set forth, or which makes void an intelligible specification of a mechanical improvement, merely because no drawing or model is annexed. In the present case I do not hear that the want of a drawing or a model occasioned any difficulty to this jury; they have expressly decided that Mr. Watt has the merit of a new and an useful invention, and that this invention was infringed by the defendant: how can I say that they could not understand this for want of a drawing, especially when the jury have added that the specification is sufficient to enable a mechanic, acquainted with the fire engines previously in use, to construct fire engines producing the effect of lessening the consumption of fuel and steam in fire engines, upon the principle invented by the plaintiff?

For these reasons I think the second objection, that no particular engine is set forth, is not of sufficient weight to destroy the effect of the patent.

As to the third, though the patent is for a method, and the statute for fire engines of his invention, if I am right in my opinion that the expression "new-invented method of lessening the consumption of steam and fuel in fire engines" is tantamount to fire engines of a new construction to lessen the consumption of steam and fuel, it follows, that the patent and the statute are, in grammatical construction, for one and the same thing: that the patentee and the legislature intended they should be so, there can be no doubt. I consider the statute as a legislative comment on the patent, and I think it tends to illustrate and fortify, rather than invalidate the privilege which the plaintiffs claim.

The arguments on the part of the defendant have not suggested to me any other objections which require a direct answer; the objections I have already noticed are, to my understanding, satisfactorily answered: I am therefore of opinion that the verdict ought to stand.

Heath, J.—This patent is expressly for a new-invented method of lessening the consumption of steam and fuel in fire engines. It appears that the invention of the patentee is original, and may be the subject of a patent; but the question is, inasmuch as this invention is to be put in practice by the means of machinery, whether this patent ought not to have been for one or more machines, etc., or whether this is such a specification as entitles him to the monopoly of a method.

If method and machinery had been used by the said patentee as convertible terms, and the same consequence would result from both, it might be too strong to say the inventor should lose the benefit of his patent by the misapplication of his term: in truth it is not so; his counsel have contended for the exclusive monopoly of a method of lessening the consumption of steam and fuel in fire engines, and that, therefore, would better answer the purposes of the patentee, for the method is a principle reduced to practice; it is in the present instance the general application of a principle to an old machine.

There is no doubt that the patentee might have obtained a patent for his machinery, because the Act of Parliament he obtained acknowledged his patent, and he himself, in one thousand seven hundred and eighty-two, procured a patent for his invention of certain new improvements upon steam and fire engines for raising water, etc., which contained new pieces of mechanism applicable to the same.

Upon this statement the following objections arise to the patent, which I cannot answer: namely, that if there may be two different species of patents, the one for an application of a principle to an old machine, and the other for a specific machine, one must be good and the other bad. The patent that admits the most lax interpretation should be bad, and the other alone conformable to the rules and principles of common law, and to the statute on which patents are founded.

The statute of 21 James I. prohibited all monopolies, reserving to the King, by an express proviso, so much of his ancient prerogative as shall enable him to grant letters patent and grants of privilege for the term of fourteen years or under, of the sole working or making of any manner of new manufactures within this realm, to the true and first inventor and inventors of such manufactures.

What then falls within the scope of the proviso are such manufactures as are reducible to two classes:—the first machinery; the second includes medicines formed by chemical and other processes, where the vendible substance is the thing produced, and that which operates preserves no permanent form.

In the first class the machine, and in the second class the substance produced, are the subjects of the patent.

I approve of the term *manufacture* in the statute, because it precludes all nice refinement; it gives us to understand the reason of the proviso, that it was introduced for the benefit of trade: that which is the subject of a patent ought to be specified, and it ought to be that which is vendible, otherwise it cannot be a manufacture.

This is a new species of manufacture; the novelty of the language is sufficient to excite alarm. It has been urged that other patents have been litigated and established; for instance, Dollond's, which was for a refracting telescope. I consider that as substantially an improved machine: a patent for an improvement of a refracting telescope, and a patent for an improved refracting telescope, are in substance the same. The same specification would serve for both patents. The organization of parts is the same in both.

I asked, in the argument, for an instance of a patent for a method   *   *   *   *   *   and none such could be produced. I was then pressed with patents for chemical processes, many of which are for a method; but that is from an inaccuracy of expression, because the patent, in truth, is for a vendible substance, neither of which were produced in a new way.

To pursue this train of reasoning still further, I shall consider how far the arguments in support of this patent will apply to the invention of original machinery founded on a new principle. The steam engine furnishes an instance. The Marquis of Worcester discovered, in the last century, the expansive force of steam, and first applied it to machinery. As the original inventor, he was clearly entitled to a patent: would the patent have been good to be applied to all machinery, or to the machine to which he had discovered it might be applied? The patent decides the matter.

It must be for the vendible matter, and not for the principle.

Another objection, may be urged against the patent, upon the application of the principle to an old machine, which is, that whatever machinery may be hereafter invented would be an infringement of the patent, if it be founded on the same principle. If this were so, it would reverse the clearest positions of law respecting patents for machinery, by which it has been always held that the organization of a machine may be the subject of a patent, but principles cannot be so.

If the argument for the patentee could be correct, it would follow, that, where a patent was obtained for the principle, the organization would be of no consequence; therefore the patent for the application of the principle must be as bad as the patent for the principle itself.

It has been urged for the patentee, that the patentee could not specify all the cases to which his machinery could be applied: the answer seems obvious, that what he cannot specify he has not invented.

The finding of the jury, that steam engines may be made upon the principle stated by the patentee, by a mechanic acquainted with the fire engines previously in use, is not conclusive.

This patent extends to all machinery that may be made on this principle, so that he has taken a patent for more than he has specified; and as the subject of his patent is an entire thing, the want of a full specification is a breach of the conditions, and avoids the patent. Indeed it seems impossible to specify a principle and application to all cases, and that furnishes an argument that it cannot be the subject of a patent.

It has been usual to examine the specification as a condition on which the patent has been granted. I shall now consider it in another point of view; for it is a clear principle that the subject of every grant must be certain. The usual mode has been for the patentee to describe the subject of it by the specification. The patent and the specification should contain a full description. Then in this, as in most other cases, the patent would be void, for the uncertain description of the thing granted, if it were not aided by the statute. The grant of a method is not good, because uncertain; the specification of [a] method or application of principle is equally so, for the reasons I have alleged. . . .

General Enclosure Act, 2 July 1801

41 Geo. 3, c. 109   *Statutes at Large,* LXIII, 322-31, 338-40.

The enclosure of open fields and commons was the most significant change in the agrarian economy during this period. Between 1760 and 1840 over five million acres of land were enclosed and several thousand enclosure acts were passed. The General Enclosure Act (1801) considerably facilitated the process.

Whereas, in order to diminish the expence attending the passing of acts of inclosure, it is expedient that certain clauses usually contained in such acts should be comprised in one law, and certain regulations adopted for facilitating the mode of proving the several facts usually required by parliament on the passing of such acts; may it therefore please your Majesty, that it may be enacted; and be it enacted by the King's most excelleng majesty, by and with the advice and consent of the lords spiritual and temporal, and commons, in this present parliament assembled, and by the authority of the same, That no person shall be capable of acting as a commissioner in the execution of any of the powers to be given by any act hereafter to be passed for dividing, alloting, or inclosing any lands or grounds, except the power of signing and giving notice of the first meeting of the commissioner or commissioners for executing any such act, and of administering the oath or affirmation herein-after directed, until he shall have taken and subscribed the oath or affirmation following:

I A. B. do swear [or, being one of the people called Quakers, do solemnly affirm], That I will faithfully, impartially, and honestly, according to the best of my skill and ability, execute and perform the several trusts, powers, and authorities vested and reposed in me as a commissioner, by virtue of an act for [here insert the title of the act] according to equity and good conscience, and without favour or affection, prejudice or partiality, to any person or persons whomsoever. So help me God.

Which oath or affirmation it shall be lawful for any one of the commissioners, where more than one shall be appointed by any such act, or any one justice of the peace for the county within which the said lands or grounds shall be situated, where only one commissioner shall be so appointed, to administer, and they are hereby respectively required to administer the same; and the said oath or affirmation, so to be taken and subscribed by each commissioner or commissioners, and a copy of the inrolment thereof shall be admitted as legal evidence.

II. And be it further enacted, That every person appointed a commissioner in or by virtue of any such act, who shall refuse or decline to act as such, shall forthwith give notice in writing to the other commissioner or commissioners of his intention to refuse or decline acting as a commissioner: provided always, That no such commissioner shall be capable of being a purchaser of any part or parts of the lands, tenements, or hereditaments within any parish in which the lands and grounds intended to be inclosed are situate, either in his own name, or in the name or names of any person or persons, until five years after the date and execution of the award to be made by any such commissioner or commissioners.

III. And whereas disputes or doubts may arise, concerning the boundaries of parishes, manors, hamlets, or districts, to be divided and inclosed, and of parishes, manors, hamlets or districts, adjoining thereto; be it therefore enacted, That the commissioner or commissioners appointed in or by virtue of any such act shall, and he or they is and are hereby authorised and required, by examination of witnesses upon oath or affirmation (which oath or affirmation any one of such commissioners is hereby impowered to administer), and by such other legal ways and means as he or they shall think proper, to enquire into the boundaries of such several parishes, manors, hamlets, or districts; and in case it shall appear to such commissioner or commissioners that the boundaries of the same respectively are not then sufficiently ascertained and distinguished, such commissioner or commissioners shall, and he or them is and are hereby authorised and required to ascertain, set out, determine, and fix the same respectively; and after the said boundaries shall be so ascertained, set out, determined, and fixed, the same shall and are hereby declared to be, the boundaries of such parishes, manors, hamlets, or districts: provided always, That such commissioners or commissioners (before he or they proceed to ascertain and set out the boundaries of such parishes, manors, hamlets, or districts) shall, and he or they is and are hereby required to give publick notice, by writing under his or their hands to be affixed on the most publick doors of the churches of such parishes, and also by advertisement to be inserted in some newspaper to be named in such act, and also by writing to be delivered to or left at the last or usual places of the abode of the respective lords or stewards of the lords of the manors in which the lands and grounds to be inclosed shall be situate, and of such adjoining manor or manors ten days at least before the time of setting out such boundaries, of his or their intention to ascertain, set out, determine, and fix the same respectively; and such commissioner or commissioners shall, within one month after his or their ascertaining and setting out the same boundaries, cause a description thereof in writing to be delivered to or left at the places of abode of one of the churchwardens or overseers of the poor of the respective parishes, and also of such respective lords or stewards: provided always, That if any person or persons interested in the determination of the said commissioner or commissioners respecting the said boundaries, shall be dissatisfied with such determination, such person or persons may appeal to the justices of the peace acting in and for the county in which such lands or grounds shall be situate at any general quarter session of the peace to be holden within four calendar months next after the aforesaid publication of the said boundaries, by delivering or leaving such description as aforesaid, the party or parties making such appeal, giving eight days notice of such appeal and of the matter thereof in writing to the commissioners; and the decision of the said justices therein shall be final and conclusive, and shall not be removed or removeable by *Certiorari* or any other writ or process whatsoever, into any of his Majesty's courts of record at Westminster, or elsewhere.

IV. And be it further enacted, That a true, exact, and particular survey, admeasurement, plan, and valuation, of all the lands and grounds to be divided, allotted, and inclosed by any such act, and also of all the messuages, cottages, orchards, gardens, homesteads, ancient inclosed lands and grounds, within any such parish or manor, shall be made and reduced in writing, by such commissioner or commissioners, or by such other person or persons as he or they shall nominate and appoint, as soon as conveniently may be, for the purposes of such act, and the number of acres and decimal parts of an acre, in statute measure, contained in all the lands and grounds directed or authorised to be divided, allotted, and inclosed, and also in all the ancient inclosed lands, grounds, and homesteads aforesaid, and of each and every proprietor's distinct property in the same respectively, at the time of making such survey and admeasurement, shall be therein set forth and specified; and that the said survey, admeasurement, plan, and valuation, shall be kept by such commissioner or commissioners; and the person or persons who shall make such survey, admeasurement, plan, and valuation, shall verify the same upon oath or affirmation, at any meeting to be held after the making thereof (which oath or affirmation the commissioners, or any one of them, are and is hereby empowered and required to administer); and the proprietors and their respective agents, and all persons interested therein, shall at all seasonable times have liberty to peruse and inspect such admeasurement and plan only, and to take copies thereof and extracts therefrom respectively.

V. And be it further enacted, That for surveying, admeasuring, and valuing all the said lands and grounds, and for other like purposes of such act, it shall be lawful for such commissioner or commissioners, every or any of them, or the person or persons to be appointed by him or them, to make such survey, admeasurement, plan, and valuation, together with their and every of their assistants and servants, at any time or times whatsoever, until such division shall be completed, to enter, view, and examine, survey and admeasure, all and every part of the lands and grounds intended to be divided and allotted, and also all the ancient inclosed lands, grounds, and homesteads, directed to be surveyed, and to do or cause to be done any act or thing necessary for putting such act into execution: provided always, That any map or survey made at the time of passing any such act, which shall be tendered to such commissioner or commissioners, and which shall be in his or their judgement, and to his or their satisfaction a just and true map or survey, proper for the purpose of carrying such act into execution, may be used for that purpose, if the said commissioner or commissioners shall think fit, without any new map or survey being made of such part of the lands and grounds, as shall be comprised in any such approved map or survey as aforesaid.

VI. And be it further enacted, That all persons, and bodies corporate or politick, who shall have or claim any common or other right to or in any such lands so to be inclosed, shall deliver or cause to be delivered to such commissioner or commissioners, or one of them, at some one of such meetings as the said commissioner or commissioners shall appoint for the purpose (or within such further time, if any, as the said commissioner or commissioners shall for some special reason think proper to allow for that purpose) an account or schedule in writing, signed by them, or their respective husbands, guardians, trustees, committees, or agents, of such their respective rights or claims, and therein describe the lands and grounds, and the respective messuages, lands, tenements, and hereditaments, in respect whereof they shall respectively claim to be entitled to any and which of such rights in and upon the same or any part thereof, with the name or names of the person or persons then in the actual possession thereof, and the particular computed quantities of the same respectively, and of what nature and extent such right is, and also in what rights, and for what estates and interests they claim the same respectively, distinguishing the freehold from the copyhold or leasehold; or on non-compliance therewith, every of them making default therein shall, as far only as respects any claim so neglected to be delivered, be totally barred and excluded of and from all right and title in or upon such lands so to be divided respectively, and of and from all benefit and advantage in or to any share or allotment thereof; all which said claims or accounts shall, at all seasonable times until after the execution of the said award, be open to the inspection and perusal of all parties interested or claiming to be interested in the premises, their respective agents or attornies, who may take copies thereof, or extracts therefrom respectively; and if any person or persons, or body politick or corporate interested, or claiming to be interested in the premises, shall have any objection to offer to any such account or claim, the particulars of such objection shall be reduced into writing, and signed by them or their respective husbands, guardians, trustees, committees, or agents, and shall be delivered to the said commissioner or commissioners, at or before some other meeting of such commissioner or commissioners, to be by him or them appointed for that purpose; and no such objection shall afterwards be received, unless for some legal disability or special cause to be allowed by the said commissioner or commissioners.

VII. Provided also, and be it further enacted, That nothing herein contained shall authorise such commissioner or commissioners to hear and determine any difference or dispute which may arise, touching the right or title to any lands, tenements, or hereditaments, but such commissioner or commissioners shall assign and set out the several allotments directed to be made unto the person or persons, who, at the time of the division and inclosure, shall have the actual seisin or possession of the lands, tenements, or hereditaments, in lieu or in right whereof such allotment shall be respectively made: provided also, That no difference or suit, touching the title to any lands, tenements, or hereditaments, shall impede or delay the commissioner or commissioners in the execution of the powers vested in him or them, by virtue of any such act; but the division or inclosure directed to be made shall be proceeded in, notwithstanding such difference or suit.

VIII. And be it further enacted, That such commissioner or commissioners shall, and he or they is and are hereby authorised and required, in the first place, before he or they proceed to make any of the divisions and allotments directed in and by any such act, to set out and appoint the publick carriage roads and highways, through and over the lands and grounds intended to be divided, allotted, and inclosed, and to divert, turn, and stop up, any of the roads and tracts, upon and over, all, or any part of the said lands and grounds, as he or they shall judge necessary, so as such roads and highways shall be, and remain thirty feet wide at the least, and so as the same shall be set out in such directions as shall, upon the whole, appear to him or them most commodious to the publick, and he or they are hereby further required to ascertain the same by marks and bounds, and to prepare a map in which such intended roads shall be accurately laid down and described, and to cause the same, being signed by such commissioners, if only one, or the major part of such commissioners, to be deposited with the clerk of the said commissioner or commissioners, for the inspection of all persons concerned; and as soon as may be after such carriage roads shall have been so set out, and such map so deposited, to give notice in some newspaper to be named in such bill, and also by affixing the same upon the church door of the parish, in which any of the lands so to be inclosed shall lie, of his or their having set out such roads, and deposited such map, and also of the general lines of such intended carriage roads, and to appoint in and by the same notice, a meeting to be held by the said commissioner or commissioners, at some convenient place, in or near to the parish or township within which the said inclosure is to be made, and not sooner than three weeks from the date and publication of such notice, at which meeting, it shall and may be lawful, for any person who may be injured or aggrieved by the setting out of such roads to attend; and if any such person shall object to the setting out of the same, then such commissioner or commissioners, together with any justice or justices of peace, acting in and for the division of the county in which such inclosure shall be made, and not being interested in the same, who may attend such meeting, shall hear and determine such objection, and the objections of any other such person, to any alteration that the said commissioner or commissioners, together with such justice or justices, may in consequence propose to make, and shall, and he or they are hereby required, according to the best of their judgment upon the whole, to order and finally direct how such carriage roads shall be set out, and either to confirm the said map, or make such alterations therein as the case may require: provided always, That in case such commissioner or commissioners shall by such bill be empowered to stop up any old or accustomed road, passing or leading through any part of the old inclosures in such parish, township, or place, the same shall in no case be done without the concurrence and order of two justices of the peace, acting in and for such division, and not interested in the repair of such roads, and which order shall be subject to an appeal to the quarter sessions, in like manner and under the same forms and restrictions as if the same had been originally made by such justice as aforesaid.

IX. And be it further enacted, That such carriage roads so to be set out as aforesaid, shall be well and sufficiently fenced on both sides, by such of the owners and proprietors of the lands and grounds intended to be divided, allotted, and inclosed, and within such time as such commissioner or commissioners shall, by any writing under his or their hands, direct or appoint, and that it shall not be lawful for any person or persons to set up or erect any gate across any such carriage road, or to plant any trees in or near to the hedges on the sides thereof, at a less distance from each other than fifty yards; and such commissioner or commissioners shall, and he or they is and are hereby empowered and required, by writing under his or their hands, to nominate and appoint one or more surveyor or surveyors, with or without a salary, for the first forming and completing such parts of the said carriage roads as shall be newly made, and for putting into complete repair such part of the same as shall have been previously made, which salary (if any) and also the expence of forming, completing, and repairing such roads respectively, over and above a proportion of the statute duty on the roads so to be repaired, shall be raised in like manner as the charges and expences of obtaining and passing any such act, and of carrying the same into execution, shall be thereby directed to be raised, and shall be paid to such surveyor or surveyors on or before the execution of the award of such commissioner or commissioners; and in case the same shall be thereby provided to be raised by sale of any part of the lands so to be divided and inclosed, that then such commissioner or commissioners shall make a conditional rate upon the owners and proprietors of the same, in case the produce of such sale should prove insufficient for the purposes aforesaid; and such surveyor or surveyors shall, and he or they is and are hereby directed to be in all respects subject to the jurisdiction and controul of the justices of the peace acting in and for the county in which such roads shall respectively lie, and shall account to such justices in like manner for all monies so to be by him or them received and expended, and for the re-payment of any surplus which may remain in his or their hands to such persons as shall have been made liable to contribute thereto, according to the proportion so as above ascertained by such commissioner or commissioners; and such justices shall have the like powers of levying any such rate as may by them be thought necessary for the purposes aforesaid, according to the proportions previously ascertained by such commissioner or commissioners, as if such surveyor or surveyors had been appointed under or by virtue of the general highway act passed in the thirteenth year of the reign of his present Majesty; and in case such surveyor or surveyors shall neglect to complete and repair such roads respectively within the space of two years after such award, unless a further time, not exceeding one year, shall for that purpose be allowed by such justices, and then within such further time, he or they shall forfeit the sum of twenty pounds, and the inhabitants at large of the parish, township, or place wherein such roads shall be respectively situate, shall be in no wise charged or chargeable towards forming or repairing the said roads respectively, except such proportion of such statute duty as aforesaid, till such time as the same shall, by such justices in their special sessions, be declared to be fully and sufficiently formed, completed, and repaired, from which time, and for ever thereafter, the same shall be supported and kept in repair by such persons, and in like manner as the other public roads within such parish, township, or place, are by law to be amended and kept in repair.

X. And be it further enacted, That such commissioner or commissioners shall, and he or they is and are hereby empowered and required to set out and appoint such private roads, bridleways, footways, ditches, drains, watercourses, watering places, quarries, bridges, gates, stiles, mounds, fences, banks, bounds, and land marks, in, over, upon, and through or by the sides of the allotments to be made and set out in pursuance of such act, as he or they shall think requisite, giving such notice and subject to such examination as to any private roads or paths, as are above required in the case of publick roads, and the same shall be made, and at all times for ever thereafter be supported and kept in repair, by and at the expence of the owners and proprietors for the time being of the lands and grounds directed to be divided and inclosed, in such shares and proportions as the commissioner or commissioners shall in and by his or their award order and direct.

XI. And be it further enacted, That after such publick and private roads and ways shall have been set out and made, the grass and herbage arising thereon shall for ever belong to and be the sole right of the proprietors of the lands and grounds which shall next adjoin the said roads and ways on either side thereof, as far as the crown of the road; and all roads, ways, and paths, over, and through, and upon such lands and grounds which shall not be set out as aforesaid, shall be for ever stopped up and extinguished, and shall be deemed and taken as part of the lands and grounds to be divided, allotted, and inclosed, and shall be divided, allotted, and inclosed accordingly: provided, That nothing herein contained shall extend, or be construed to extend, to give such commissioner or commissioners any power or authority to divert, change, or alter any turnpike road that shall or may lead over any such lands and grounds, unless the consent of the majority of the trustees of such turnpike road, assembled at some publick meeting called for that purpose on ten days notice, be first had and obtained.

XII. And be it further enacted, That such commissioner or commissioners in making the several allotments directed by any such act, shall have due regard as well to the situation of the respective houses or homesteads of the proprietors, as to the quantity and quality of the lands and grounds to be allotted to them respectively, so far as may be consistent with the general convenience of the said proprietors; and that such commissioner or commissioners in making the said allotments shall have particular regard to the convenience of the owners or proprietors of the smallest estates in the lands and grounds directed to be allotted and exchanged.

XIII. And whereas the proprietors and persons interested in open common fields, meadows, pastures, commons, and waste lands, directed to be divided and allotted, whose allotments thereof will be small, and expensive to inclose, may be desirous of stocking and depasturing their allotments in common, and of sharing such produce as may grow thereon, under proper regulations; be it therefore further enacted, That such commissioner or commissioners shall be, and he or they is and are hereby fully authorised and empowered, on application of the parties interested at their first or second meeting for receiving claims, and on an attentive view and full consideration of the premises, to award, order, and direct any such allotments to be laid together and ring-fenced, and to be stocked and depastured in common, and to make such orders and regulations for the equitable enjoyment thereof, and for the participation of any produce growing or to grow thereon, as such commissioner or commissioners may think beneficial and proper for the said several parties interested therein.

XIV. And be it further enacted, That the several shares of and in any lands or grounds which shall upon any such division be assigned, set out, allotted, and applied, unto and for the several persons who shall be entitled to the same, shall, when so allotted, be and be taken to be in full bar of and satisfaction and compensation for their several and respective lands, grounds, rights of common, and all other rights and properties whatsoever, which they respectively had or were entitled to, in and over the said lands and grounds, immediately before the passing of any such act; and that from and immediately after the making the said division and allotments, and the execution of the award of such commissioner or commissioners, or at any other time as such commissioner or commissioners shall, by writing under his or their hands, to be affixed on the principal door of the church of the parish in which the lands and grounds shall be situate, direct or appoint, all rights of common, and all rights whatsoever, by such act intended to be extinguished, belonging to or claimed by any person or persons whomsoever, bodies politick or corporate, in, over, or upon such lands or grounds, shall cease, determine, and be for ever extinguished.

XV. And be it further enacted, That such commissioner or commissioners shall, and he or they is and are hereby authorised, to set out, allot, and award any messuages, buildings, lands, tenements, hereditaments, new allotments, or old inclosures, within such parish or manors, in lieu of or in exchange for any other messuages, buildings, lands, tenements, hereditaments, new allotments, or old inclosures within the said parish or manors, or within any adjoining parish or place; so as that all such exchanges be made with the consent of the respective owners, proprietors, or other persons, seised of the lands, hereditaments, and premises which shall respectively be so exchanged as aforesaid, or of the husbands, guardians, trustees, committees or attornies acting for or on behalf of such owners, proprietors, or other persons respectively, who are under coverture, minors, lunaticks, or beyond the seas, or under any other disability or incapacity of acting for themselves (such consent to be testified by writing under their respective hands); and so that all such exchanges be ascertained, specified, and set forth in the award of such commissioner or commissioners; and so that all such exchanges of any lands, tenements, or hereditaments, belonging to or held in right of any church, chapel, or ecclesiastical benefice, shall also be made with the like consent, in writing, of the bishop of the diocese, and of the patron of any church, chapel, or ecclesiastical benefice for the time being; and all such exchanges so made as aforesaid shall be for ever good, valid, and effectual in the law, to all intents and purposes whatsoever.

XVI. And whereas it may happen that some of the proprietors of messuages, cottages, tenements, or lands, in any such parish or manor, and persons entitled to allotment or allotments to be made by virtue of any such act, may be seized thereof or entitled thereto in joint tenancy, or as coparceners or tenants in common, and cannot, by reason or infancy, settlement, or absence beyond the seas make any effectual division thereof; be it therefore further enacted, That it shall be lawful for any such commissioner or commissioners, and he or they is and are hereby authorised and empowered (upon the request in writing of such joint tenants or coparceners, or tenants in common, or any or either of them, or of the husbands, guardians, trustees, committees, or attorneys of such as are under coverture, minors, lunaticks, or under any other incapacity as aforesaid, or absent beyond seas) to make partition and division of the messuages, cottages, tenements, lands, and allotment or allotments, to such of the said owners or proprietors who shall be entitled to the same as joint tenants, coparceners, or tenents in common, and to allot the same accordingly to such owners and proprietors in severalty; and from and immediately after the said allotments shall be so made and declared, the same shall be holden and enjoyed by the person or persons to whom the same shall be allotted in severalty, in such and the same manner, and subject to such and the same uses, as the undivided parts or shares of such estates would have been held in case such partion and division had not been made.

XVII. And be it further enacted, That all and every person or persons, to whom any allotment or allotments shall be made by virtue of any such act, shall, and he, she, or they is and are hereby required to accept his, her, and their respective allotments within the space of two calendar months next after the execution of the award, directed to be made in and by any such act; and in case any person or persons shall neglect or refuse to accept of his, her, or their share or allotment within the time before mentioned, such person or persons so neglecting or refusing shall be totally excluded from having or receiving any estate or interest, or right of common whatsoever, in any part of the lands and grounds to be divided and inclosed by virtue of any such act.

XVIII. Provided always, and be it further enacted, That it shall and may be lawful for the respective guardians, husbands, trustees, committees, or attorneys of any person or persons being minors, femes covert, lunaticks, beyond the seas, or otherwise incapable by law to accept any such allotment as shall be made by virtue of any such act, to and for the use of such person or persons so incapacitated as aforesaid; and also that any person or persons entitled to any allotment or allotments as tenant or tenancts for life or lives, shall be, and he, she, and they is and are hereby respectively enabled and enquired to accept of and take such allotments or allotments respectively; and every such acceptance respectively shall be and is hereby declared to be valid and effectual, to all intents and purposes whatsoever: provided further, That the non-claim or non-acceptance of any such guardian, husband, trustee, committee, or attorney, shall not exclude or in any way prejudice the right of any infant, feme covert, lunatick, or other person or persons being under any disability or incapacity as aforesaid, or absent beyond the seas, who shall claim or accept such share or allotment within twelve calendar months next after such disability or incapacity shall be removed, or of any person entitled as heir in remainder after the death of any person dying during such incapacity or disability, who shall claim or accept the same within one year next after his, her, or their right, title or interest shall have accrued, descended, or vested, or be known so to be.

XIX. And be it further enacted, That after the allotments shall be set out by such commissioner or commissioners, and at any time before the execution of his or their award, it shall be lawful for any person or persons to whom any allotment or allotments shall be so made, and staked or marked out, by and with the consent of such commissioner or commissioners in writing under his or their hands, to ditch, fence off, and inclose their respective allotments, in such manner as such commissioner or commissioners shall so direct and appoint. . . .

XXXIII. And, for the better enabling such commissioner or commissioners to determine the several matters and things by this or any such act referred to his or their determination, be it enacted, That it shall be lawful to and for the said commissioner or commissioners from time to time, as he or they shall see occasion, by any writing or writings under his or their hand or hands, to summon and require any person or persons to appear before them at any time and place in such writing to be appointed, to testify the truth touching the matter in dispute between any proprietors or interested persons, or otherwise relating to the execution of the powers given by this or any such act, and to cause a copy of such writing to be served on such person or persons required to give evidence, or to be left at his, her, or their usual or last place of abode; and every person or persons so summoned, who shall not appear before the said commissioner or commissioners pursuant to such summons (without assigning some reasonable excuse for not appearing) or appearing shall refuse to be sworn or examined on oath or affirmation, which oath or affirmation the said commissioner or commissioners is and are hereby empowered and required to administer, (such person or persons having been paid or tendered to him, her, or them, the reasonable charges of his, her, or their attendance) and being thereof convicted before one of his Majesty's justices of the peace of the county or district in which such lands are situated, upon information thereof upon oath made before any such justice, shall, for every such neglect or refusal, forfeit and pay such sum of money, not exceeding ten pounds, nor less than five pounds, as such justice or justices shall think fit and order.

XXXIV. Provided always, and be it further enacted, That no witness summoned to attend such commissioner or commissioners, shall be obliged to travel above eight miles from the boundary of the parish, manor, or district, by any such act intended to be inclosed.

XXXV. And be it further enacted, That as soon as conveniently may be after the division and allotment of the said lands and grounds shall be finished, pursuant to the purport and directions of this or any such act, the said commissioner or commissioners shall form and draw up, or cause to be formed and drawn up, an award in writing, which shall express the quantity of acres, roods, and perches, in statute measure, contained in the said lands and grounds, and the quantity of each and every part and parcel thereof which shall be so allotted, assigned, or exchanged, and the situations and descriptions of the same respectively, and shall also contain a description of the roads, ways, footpaths, watercourses, watering places, quarries, bridges, fences, and land marks, set out and appointed by the said commissioner or commissioners respectively as aforesaid, and all such other rules, orders, agreements, regulations, directions, and determinations, as the said commissioner or commissioners shall think necessary, proper, or beneficial to the parties; which said award shall be fairly ingrossed or written on parchment, and shall be read and executed by the commissioner or commissioners, in the presence of the proprietors who may attend at a special general meeting called for that purpose, of which ten days notice at least shall be given in some paper to be named in such act and circulating in the county, which execution of such award shall be proclaimed the next Sunday in the church of the parish in which such lands shall be, from the time of which proclamation only and not before, such award shall be considered as complete; and shall, within twelve calendar months after the same shall be so signed and sealed, or so soon as conveniently may be, be inrolled in one of his Majesty's courts of record at Westminster, or with the clerk of the peace for the county in which such lands shall be situated, to the end that recourse may be had thereto by any person or persons interested therein, for the inspection and perusal whereof no more than one shilling shall be paid; and a copy of the said award, or any part thereof, signed by the proper officer of the court wherein the same shall be inrolled, or by the clerk of the peace for such county, or his deputy, purporting the same to be a true copy, shall from time to time be made and delivered by such officer or clerk of the peace for the time being as aforesaid, to any person requesting the same, for which no more shall be paid than two-pence for every sheet of seventy-two words; and the said award, and each copy of the same, or of any part thereof, signed as aforesaid, shall at all times be admitted and allowed in all courts whatever as legal evidence; and the said award or instrument, and the several allotments, partitions, regulations, agreements, exchanges, orders, directions, determinations, and all other matters and things therein mentioned and contained, shall, to all intents and purposes, be binding and conclusive, except where some provision to the contrary is herein and shall be by any such act contained, unto and upon the said proprietors, and all parties and persons concerned or interested in the same, or in any of the lands, grounds, or premises aforesaid; and also that the said respective commissioners, if they think it necessary, shall form or draw, or cause to be formed and drawn, on parchment or vellum, such maps or plans of the said lands and grounds, the better to describe the several new allotments or divisions to be made, and premises that shall be exchanged by virtue of this act, and which shall express the quantity of each allotment in acres, roods, and perches, together with the names of the respective proprietors at the time of such division and allotment; which said maps and plans shall be annexed to and inrolled with the said respective award, and shall be deemed and construed in every respect as and for part of the said award. . . .

Evidence before the Select Committee to Adjust Differences in the Cotton Industry, March 1804

Parliamentary Papers, 1803-04, V, Cmd. 150, 6-9, 13-15.

Working conditions in the Lancashire cotton trade are well described in the following testimony of James Mason, a journeyman calico printer, and James Ellison, a print cutter.

Mr. James Mason, a Journeyman Callico Print at Manchester; Called in, and Examined, 16 March 1804

Can you give a comparative Statement of Journeymen and Apprentices in the counties and places mentioned in the Petition?—Yes; the total number of Journeymen in Lancashire, Cheshire, Derby, and Stafford, is 1,495, and 893 Apprentices; this Statement was taken at Christmas last.

Can you give a like Statement for London and its neighbourhood?—I have not had the opportunity of taking all, but have taken the number of 14 Shops; 216 Journeymen and 37 Apprentices.

Point out how the practice of taking Apprentices without Indenture is injurious to the Petitioners?—By their being at liberty to quit their Masters on trifling occasions; not being held by Indentures, they have an easier opportunity of so doing; and by that means, when they make application at another place, they have always the preference to a Journeyman; they are not Journeymen till they have served out their time of seven years.

How have they the preference?—Because they will work for less Wages.

How do the country Apprentices serve their time in general?—Generally by having stipulated days work. I went apprentice for 3s. 6d. per week the first year, for 4s. the second, 4s. 6d. the third, 5s. the fourth, 6s. the fifth, and for 7s. the sixth and seventh years; the work I did in the first year, each week, was 42 Colours.

What was the value of the Work per week you did that year at Journeymen's prices?—It would have amounted to £.1. 11s. 6d. at 5s. 3d. per day; in my second year, I did 36 Colours per week of a more difficult sort, worth 5s. per day at Journeymen's prices; the other five years on an average I should have earned, at Journeymen's prices, 25s. per week: the reason why it appears less in these last years is that the Work required more skill, and therefore we had easier day's work set us.

Was the Work before mentioned you did, as stipulated by your Master?—Yes, and I was enforced by him to do it.

In what manner does the heat of the Printing Shops affect the Workmen so as to debilitate their constitutions?—By promoting too great a quantity of perspiration in the first instance, as Printers are in general obliged to work nearly naked, and are confined nearly 11 or 12 hours in the day in general, which has a tendency to weaken the constitution in such a manner as to disable them from procuring a livelihood at any out-door work.

Does the effluvia of the drugs add to the bad effects of the heat?—Yes, very materially; and the reason I assign for it is, being of an asthmatic habit of myself, I feel a difficulty of breathing when I am confined in a shop over-hot, and where large quantity of work is dried; and I do not feel such sensations in any other place of equal heat, such as in dressing rooms, or in other parts of the business.

What other Branches of the Trade are affected by an overstock of hands, and how?—There are two other Branches, namely, Print-cutters and Pattern-drawers.

When there is a scanty quantity of Work, who are discharged?—The Journeymen: I have been discharged twice myself; once for five weeks and another time for eighteen weeks; the Apprentices were at work: at the shop I worked at that time, there were seven Apprentices and five Journeymen; three of us were discharged all at once, as being newest hands.

How much have you worked at your Trade for the last two years?—All the time, except when engaged in this business as Agent.

When you were in your Apprenticeship, were you not paid something more for working over-hours?—Yes, I was paid at the rate of half Journeymen's price for over-work; sometimes I could have got 1s. per day, and sometimes I could not do my stipulated work.

Did you ever find any difficulty of obtaining Work when you applied for it?—Yes, since I have been a Journeyman.

When you applied for Work did you first apply to the Master or to the Journeymen?—In general to the Journeymen; the reason is, that there are very often disturbances between Journeymen and Masters at shops as to prices, or very often a scarcity of Work, which makes the Journeymen working at the shop afraid that the Masters, seeing so many Apprentices, would either be more severe with them, or discharge some of them.

Do not those disturbances about Wages arise generally when there is the most Work to be done, and the Masters have the most occasion for their Labour?—I cannot say.

Did you ever know Journeymen strike on these disturbances?—Yes, I have known the Journeymen turn out several times; these Turn-outs have as often happened upon an attempt to reduce Wages.

Did the Apprentices ever go with the Journeymen when they struck Work?—Yes; because in many instances the rates of Apprentice work are regulated by that of Journeymen; and they feel a diminution of Journeymen's work must affect them.

Have you not known that the Journeymen have given these Apprentices money to subsist on while from their Masters?—I do not know any such instance; I have heard that it has been done.

Did you ever know that the Journeymen have received money themselves from any particular Fund?—Yes; but it was long since, not within these four years, raised by voluntary subscription.

Was you ever asked to subscribe to that Fund?—I have been solicited to give any sum I thought proper.

What do you mean by Apprentices Wages being affected by those of the Journeymen?—There are some shops in our business, where the Apprentices are bound to earn 20s. per week at Journeymen's prices, for which they receive their indentured Wages; consequently, if a diminution takes place in the Journeymen's Wages, the Apprentices will have more Work for the same sum.

Suppose a Master has no Work to give out, must he not pay the stipulated Wages to his Apprentices?—Yes, he must; but before the Apprentice becomes a Journeyman, he is obliged to make up all loss of time; some have been known to serve 10 years, owing to want of Work from their own neglect.

If an Apprentice does not gain 20s. per week at Journeymen's prices, does his Master pay him his indentured Wages?—Yes; but before he is allowed to earn any over work, he must make up his loss of time.

What is the average Price of Journeymen's Wages?—He is paid according to his Work; the ordinary average of a good Journeyman is about 25s. per week.

Do you depend upon your own employment for your support?—Yes.

In what way was you supported during the time you was out of employment?—From my own means, or my friends.

What do you mean by your Friends?—Private friends and relations.

Did you receive any Money at that time from any Funds?—No.

Would you have liked to have taken Employment if it had been objectionable to the Journeymen to whom you first applied?—Yes, I did do it, contrary to the wish of some of the Journeymen.

Do not you know some instances of Workmen having turned out, in consequence of Masters having employed persons not approved of by the Journeymen?—Not from my own personal knowledge; I have heard so.

When the Apprentices came back to the Masters, having gone off with the Journeymen, in what way did the Masters conduct themselves towards those Apprentices?—They have generally put them into gaol, in the instances I have heard of.

Have you known of any Turn-outs of the Journeymen in consequence of such proceeding on the part of the Master?—Yes, I have heard of it.

Upon your subscribing to the Funds alluded to before, did you receive any Ticket, or other written Document?—Not at the Time of subscribing.

At what other Time?—We receive a Ticket in general when we leave a shop, whether we leave of our own accord, or are discharged, which Ticket entitles us to receive a halfpenny from every shop to carry us on to the next.

Do you not know instances of Journeymen having been obstructed in obtaining employment, by other Journeymen, in consequence of not being able to produce a Ticket?—Yes.

Have you not known of standings out on the part of the Journeymen at a time when they might have obtained full Employment, and when there was a great demand on the part of the Masters?—I cannot say exactly, unless they have refused on account of the diminution of the Prices.

Do you remember formerly, when Journeymen out of Employment, having a Ticket, would have received Money from the Fund?—Yes.

At what period did the alteration take place of the Halfpenny Contributions, which were granted from Journeymen, on application from those out of Employment?—At Christmas 1800.

Was not that alteration made in consequence of the passing of the Combination Act?—The relinquishment of Funds did take place from the Combination Act; the Halfpenny Subscription arose to do away the practice of Men out of work sending in private Petitions to the Shops, when some Men might give 6d. and some none at all.

Did not the Halfpenny Contribution take place immediately after abandoning the assistance given from the Funds?—I do not recollect exactly the time of the abandonment of the Funds.

Have the Journeymen suffered in consequence of too many Apprentices coming into the Trade?—Yes.

Have not the Wages of Journeymen been progressively increasing since you became a Journeyman?—Yes; they have increased.

If no increase of Hands had been introduced into the Trade, would the important Cotton Manufacture have flourished to the same extent it has done; or could the Pieces manufactured have been printed?—No, certainly not.

How long has the increase of Apprentices existed of which you complain?—Since 1790.

Mr. James Ellison, of Oakenshaw, near Blackburn, Print Cutter; Called in, and Examined, 22 March 1804

How long were you serving your Apprenticeship, and what were your wages?—Seven years; for the first year at 3*s.* per week; 3*s.* 6*d.* the second; 4*s.* the third; 5*s.* the fourth; 6*s.* the fifth; and 7*s.* the sixth and seventh.

At what time does the Work of the Apprentices come to be of equal value to the Masters with the Journeymen's?—In the second year of my Apprenticeship I frequently did Journeymen's Work.

How many Printers can one Cutter employ?—Eight or 10 on an average.

How many Cutters can one Drawer employ?—About 8 or 10 on an average.

Can you state what Number of Cutters and Drawers are employed as Apprentices and Journeymen at a House at Sabden?—From the last information I had, there were 4 Journeymen Cutters and 13 Apprentices; 2 Journeymen Drawers and 8 Apprentices.

What additional Number of Journeymen Cutters and Drawers have been thrown into the trade at Church Works by their taking Apprentices?—At Church Bank, in 23 years, 58 Cutters and 23 Drawers, total 81; since then 12 dead; 23 working elsewhere; 16 turned to other businesses; 30 still employed there; 51 overplus.

Does the new method of cutting Prints by brassing, employ more or less hands?—It requires less hands by brassing, because the brass Prints are more durable than wood: a brass Print may perhaps do 3 or 400 hundred Pieces, a cut, or wood print, perhaps only 100 to 150: the length of time to make these Instruments nearly equal.

Do you know of any Journeymen Cutters being discharged from an overstock of hands?—I have known frequent instances; I wish to mention my own as one: in the year 1799 I was without Work, and in 1800 I had very little Work from January to September, and was totally without from September to August 1802; during that time I frequently applied to Mr. Berry at Sabden, and was told he had no Work to spare for Journeymen; his Apprentices could do all he had. I had taught some of those Apprentices he had at that time, and they did the Work which I was promised to have, having been promised Work as long as they had a job to give to a Cutter.

Can you give an account of the distresses of the Journeymen Cutters?—With respect to myself, my distresses were very great, inasmuch as I had no Work; I was under the necessity of weaving Callicoes, and my earnings were so small, I found it impossible to maintain myself and family from starving.

During the time you were out of employ in September 1800 and August 1802, did you receive no relief from any Fund from the Journeymen?—No.

Did you ever go round to any of the Cutters to get relief?—No.

Do you know on whose applications the children are taken Apprentices?—It frequently happens the Masters apply, and sometimes the Parents; I have known it both ways.

Do not you know that there are a great many Cutters and Drawers wanted at different Print Grounds in Cheshire?—I know nothing of that.

How long since you were in the employ of the House at Sabden?—The last Work I had from there was in the beginning of September 1800.

Were there not a number of Journeymen Cutters employed when you said you wanted Work at Berry's?—Yes.

Did not your Master complain that you did your Work imperfectly?—Never.

Did you not work at several Grounds after you left Berry's?—No, not till August 1802.

Did you not sometimes wait for Work at those grounds when other Journeymen were in full employ?—One instance I can relate of it: I lived at a distance from Sabden at that time; the Journeymen Cutters on the ground were Mr. Berry's tenants mostly, and their families were employed with them.

Were there not a number of Journeymen employed at Open Shaw when you were weaving at that place?—There were none of them that had full Work during the time I was weaving.

At what ages are Apprentices generally taken?—At different ages, from 14 to 18 years.

Is there not at this moment a great demand for Cutters?—I have not heard of it.

Is there any difference in the Wages of Journeymen Cutters?—It depends on the goodness of the workman's hand.

What are the greatest Wages you have known a Journeymen Cutter to earn per week?—Perhaps for an odd week he may get 30s.

What is the lowest in full employ?—About a guinea.

What have you earned per week in full work?—About 25s.; I never had less than a guinea; I have sometimes earned 30s.

At the period you have mentioned your distress, were there hands adequate to the Work going on?—Yes.

From what circumstance did your distress arise?—From want of Work

Do you suppose that any of the hands then employed did not earn more than a guinea a week?—Yes, possibly they might.

Do you believe that the different Houses that employed the Workmen at the time of your distress, made a selection of the best Workmen only?—No.

Do not you believe that the Distress you mention was owing to an inferiority of Workmanship?—No.

When you was distressed, did you apply to Masters?—Yes; I was at Mr. Duxbury's, at Cross Hall, and at Mr. Reddish's, at Brinscow Hall.

Did you apply to those you have mentioned personally for Work?—Yes; their answer was that they had none to spare.

Do not you know that the Wages of Cutters have lately increased?—Yes, a little.

GEORGE III AND THE CONSTITUTION

Speech by George III upon his accession to the throne, 25 November 1760

Parliamentary History, XV, 981-85.

The King, being seated on the throne, adorned with his crown and regal ornaments, and attended by his officers of state; the Lords being in their robes; the Gentleman Usher of the black rod received his Majesty's commands, to let the Commons know, "It is his Majesty's pleasure, they attend him immediately, in this House." Who being come, with their Speaker; his Majesty was pleased to speak as follows:

My Lords and Gentlemen; The just concern which I have felt in my own breast, on the sudden death of the late king my royal grandfather, makes me not doubt but you must all have been deeply affected with so severe a loss: the present critical and difficult conjuncture has made this loss the more sensible, as he was the great support of that system, by which alone the liberties of Europe, and the weight and influence of these kingdoms, can be preserved; and gave life to the measures conducive to those important ends.

I need not tell you the addition of weight which immediately falls upon me, in being called to the government of this free and powerful country at such a time, and under such circumstances: my consolation is in the uprightness of my own intentions; your faithful and united assistance; and the blessing of heaven upon our joint endeavours, which I devoutly implore.

Born and educated in this country, I glory in the name of Briton; and the peculiar happiness of my life will ever consist in promoting the welfare of a people, whose loyalty and warm affection to me, I consider as the greatest and most permanent security of my throne; and I doubt not but their steadiness in these principles will equal the firmness of my invariable resolution, to adhere to and strengthen this excellent constitution in Church and State, and to maintain the Toleration inviolable. The civil and religious rights of my loving subjects are equally dear to me with the most valuable prerogatives of my crown: and, as the surest foundation of the whole, and the best means to draw down the Divine favour on my reign; it is my fixed purpose to countenance and encourage the practice of true religion and virtue.

I reflect with pleasure on the successes with which the British arms have been prospered this last summer. The total reduction of the vast province of Canada, with the city of Montreal, is of the most interesting consequence, and must be as heavy a blow to my enemies, as it is a conquest glorious to us; the more glorious because effected almost without effusion of blood, and with that humanity which makes an amiable part of the character of this nation.

Our advantages gained in the East Indies have been signal; and must greatly diminish the strength and trade of France in those parts, as well as procure the most solid benefits to the commerce and wealth of my subjects.

In Germany, where the whole French force has been employed, and combined army, under the wise and able conduct of my general prince Ferdinand of Brunswick, has not only stopt their progress, but has gained advantages over them, notwithstanding their boasted superiority, and their not having hitherto come to a general engagement.

My good brother and ally the king of Prussia, although surrounded with numerous armies of enemies, has, with a magnanimity and perseverance almost beyond example, not only withstood their various attacks, but has obtained very considerable victories over them.

Of these events I shall say no more at this time, because the nature of the war in those parts has kept the campaign there still depending.

As my navy is the principal article of our natural strength, it gives me much satisfaction to receive it in such good condition; whilst the fleet of France is weakened to such a degree, that the small remains of it have continued blocked-up by my ships in their own ports: at that same time, the French trade is reduced to the lowest ebb; and, with joy of heart, I see the commerce of my kingdoms, that great source of our riches, and the fixed object of my never-failing care and protection, flourishing to an extent unknown in any former war.

The valour and intrepidity of my officers and forces both at sea and land have been distinguished so much to the glory of this nation, that I should be wanting in justice to them, if I did not acknowledge it. This is a merit which I shall constantly encourage and reward; and I take this occasion to declare, that the zealous and useful service of the militia, in the present arduous conjuncture, is very acceptable to me.

In this state I have found things at my accession to the throne of my ancestors: happy in viewing the prosperous part of it; happier still should I have been, had I found my kingdoms, whose true interest I have entirely at heart, in full peace: but, since the ambition, injurious encroachments, and dangerous designs of my enemies, rendered the war both just any necessary; and the generous overture made last winter, towards a congress for a pacification, has not yet produced a suitable return; I am determined, with your cheerful and powerful assistance, to prosecute this war with vigour, in order to that desirable object, a safe and honourable peace: for this purpose, it is absolutely incumbent upon us to be early prepared; and I rely upon your zeal and hearty concurrence to support the king of Prussia and the rest of my allies; and to make ample provision for carrying on the war, as the only means to bring our enemies to equitable terms of accommodation.

Gentlemen of the House of Commons, The greatest uneasiness which I feel at this time is, in considering the uncommon burthens necessarily brought upon my faithful subjects: I desire only such supplies as shall be requisite to prosecute the war with advantage, be adequate to the necessary services, and that they may be provided for in the most sure and effectual manner: you may depend upon the faithful and punctual application of what shall be granted.

I have ordered the proper estimates for the ensuing year to be laid before you; and also an accompt of the extraordinary expences, which, from the nature of the different and remote operations, have been unavoidably incurred.

It is with peculiar reluctance that I am obliged, at such a time, to mention any thing which personally regards myself; but, as the grant of the greatest part of the Civil List revenues is now determined, I trust in your duty and affection to me, to make the proper provision for supporting my civil government with honour and dignity: on my part, you may be assured of a regular and becoming economy.

My Lords, and Gentlemen, The eyes of all Europe are upon you. From your resolutions the Protestant interest hopes for protection; as well as all our friends, for the preservation of their independency; and our enemies fear the final disappointment of their ambitious and destructive views. Let these hopes and fears be confirmed and augmented, by the vigour, unanimity, and dispatch, of your proceedings.

In this expectation I am the more encouraged, by a pleasing circumstance, which I look upon as one of the most auspicious omens of my reign. That happy extinction of divisions, and that union and good harmony which continue to prevail amongst my subjects, afford me the most agreeable prospect: the natural disposition and wish of my heart are to cement and promote them: and I promise myself, that nothing will arise on your part, to interrupt or disturb a situation so essential to the true and lasting felicity of this great people.

Then his Majesty was pleased to retire; and the Commons withdrew.

Leading article by John Wilkes in No. 45 of *The North Briton,* 23 April 1763

The North Briton, II, 227-40.

This famous article by John Wilkes (1727-97) attacking the king's speech on opening Parliament touched off a series of prosecutions. It propelled Wilkes to the leadership of the reform movement and undercut the popularity of George III.

The North Briton makes his appeal to the good sense, and to the candour of the English nation. In the present unsettled and fluctuating state of the *administration,* he is really fearful of falling into involuntary errors, and he does not wish to mislead. All his reasonings have been built on the strong foundation of *facts*; and he is not yet informed of the whole interior state of government with such *minute precision*, as now to venture the submitting his crude ideas of the present political crisis to the discerning and impartial public. The Scottish minister has indeed *retired*. Is his influence at an end? or does he still govern by the *three* wretched tools of his power, who, to their indelible infamy, have supported the most odious of his measures, the late ignominious *Peace*, and the wicked extension of the arbitrary mode of *Excise?* The North Briton has been steady in his opposition to a *single*, insolent, incapable, despotic minister; and is equally ready, in the service of his country, to combat the *triple-headed, Cerberean* administration, if the Scot is to assume that motley form. By him every arrangement *to this hour* has been made, and the notification has been as regularly sent by letter under his Hand. *It therefore* seems clear to a demonstration, that he intends only to retire into that situation, which he held before he first took the seals; I mean the dictating to every part of the king's administration. The North Briton desires to be understood, as having pledged himself a firm and intrepid assertor of the rights of his fellow-subjects, and of the liberties of Whigs and Englishmen.

Genus Oratonis *atrox*, & *vehemens*, cui opponitur *lenitatis* & *mansuetudinis*. Cicero.

The *King's Speech* has always been considered by the legislature, and by the public at large, as the *Speech of the Minister*. It has regularly, at the beginning of every session of parliament, been referred by both houses to the consideration of a committee, and has been generally canvassed with the utmost freedom, when the minister of the crown has been obnoxious to the nation. The ministers of this free country, conscious of the undoubted privileges of so spirited a people, and with the terrors of parliament before their eyes, have ever been cautious, no less with regard to the matter, than to the expressions, of *speeches*, which they have advised the sovereign to make from the throne, at the *opening* of each session. They well knew that an honest house of parliament, true to their trust, could not fail to detect the fallacious arts, or to remonstrate against the daring acts of violence, committed by any minister. The Speech at the *close* of the session has ever been considered as the most *secure* method of promulgating the favourite court creed among the vulgar; because the parliament, which is the constitutional guardian of the liberties of the people, has in this case no opportunity of remonstrating, or of impeaching any wicked servant of the crown.

This week has given the public the most abandoned instance of ministerial effrontery ever attempted to be imposed on mankind. The *minister's speech* of last Tuesday, is not to be paralleled in the annals of this country. I am in doubt, whether the imposition is greater on the sovereign, or on the nation. Every friend of his country must lament that a prince of so many great and amiable qualities, whom England truly reveres, can be brought to give the sanction of his sacred name to the most odious measures, and to the most unjustifiable, public declarations, from a throne ever renowned for truth, honour, and unsullied virtue. I am sure, all foreigners, especially the king of Prussia, will hold the minister in contempt and abhorrence. He has made our sovereign declare,

> My expectations have been fully answered by the happy effects which the several allies of my crown have derived from this salutary measure of the definitive Treaty. The powers at war with my good brother, the King of Prussia, have been induced to agree to such terms of accommodation, as that great prince has approved; and the success which has attended my

negociation, has necessarily and immediately diffused the blessings of peace through every part of Europe.

The infamous fallacy of this whole sentence is apparent to all mankind: for it is known, that the King of Prussia did not barely *approve*, but absolutely *dictated*, as conqueror, every article of the terms of peace. No advantage of any kind has accrued to that magnanimous prince from *our negociation*, but he was basely deserted by the *Scottish* prime-minister of *England*. He was known by every court in Europe to be scarcely on better terms of friendship *here*, than at *Vienna*; and he was betrayed by us in the *treaty of peace*. What a strain of insolence, therefore, is it in a minister to lay claim to what he is conscious all his efforts tended to prevent, and meanly to arrogate to himself a share in the same and glory of one of the greatest princes the world has ever seen? The king of *Prussia*, however, has gloriously kept *all* his former *conquests*, and stipulated security for all his allies, even for the *elector of Hanover*. I know in what light this great prince is considered in Europe, and in what manner he has been treated here; among other reasons, perhaps, from some contemptuous expressions he may have used of the *Scot*: expressions which are every day ecchoed by the whole body of *Englishmen* through the southern part of this island.

The *Preliminary Articles of Peace* were such as have drawn the contempt of mankind on our wretched negociators. All our most valuable conquests were agreed to be restored, and *the East-India company* would have been infallibly ruined by a single article of this fallacious and baneful negociation. No hireling of the minister has been hardy enough to dispute this; yet the minister himself has made our sovereign declare, "the satisfaction which he felt at the approaching re-establishment of peace upon conditions so honourable to his crown, and so beneficial to his people." As to the *entire approbation* of parliament, which is so vainly boasted of, the world knows how that was obtained. The large debt on the *Civil List*, already above half a year in arrear, shews pretty clearly the transactions of the winter. It is, however, remarkable, that the minister's speech dwells on the *entire approbation* given by parliament to the *Preliminary Articles*, which I will venture to say, he must by this time be ashamed of; for he has been brought to confess the total want of that knowledge, accuracy and precision, by which such immense advantages both of trade and territory, were sacrificed to our inveterate enemies. These gross blunders are, indeed, in some measure set right by the *Definitive Treaty*; yet, the most important articles, relative to *cessions, commerce*, and the Fishery, remain as they were, with respect to the *French*. The proud and feeble *Spaniard* too does not renounce, but only desists *from all pretensions, which he may have formed, to the right of Fishing*—where? only *about the island of* Newfoundland—till a favourable opportunity arises of *insisting* on it, *there, as well as elsewhere*.

The minister cannot forbear, even in the *King's Speech*, insulting us with a dull repetition of the word *economy*. I did not expect so soon to have seen that word again, after it had been so lately exploded, and more than once, by a most numerous audience, *hissed* off the stage of our *English* theatres. It is held in derision by the *voice of the people*, and every tongue loudly proclaims the universal contempt, in which these empty professions are held by *this* nation. Let the public be informed of a single instance of *economy*, except indeed in the household. Is a regiment, which was completed as to its compliment of officers on the *Tuesday*, and broke on the *Thursday*, a proof of *economy?* Is the pay of the *Scottish Master Elliot* to be voted by an *English* parliament, under the head of *economy?* Is this, among a thousand others, one of the convincing proofs of a *firm resolution to form government on a plan of strict economy?* Is it not notorious, that in the reduction of the army, not the least attention has been paid to it. Many unnecessary expences have been incurred, only to encrease the power of the crown, that is, to create more lucrative jobs for the creatures of the minister? The *staff* indeed is broke, but the discerning part of mankind immediately comprehended the mean subterfuge, and resented the indignity put upon so brave an officer, as marshal *Ligonier*. That step was taken to give the whole power of the army to the crown, that is, to the minister. Lord *Ligonier* is now no longer at the head of the army; but lord *Bute* in effect is: I mean that every preferment given by the crown will be found still to be obtained by *his* enormous influence, and to be bestowed only on the creatures of the *Scottish* faction. The nation is still in the same deplorable state, while *he* governs, and can make the tools of *his* power pursue the same odious measures. Such a retreat, as he intends, can only mean that personal indemnity, which, I hope, guilt will never find from an injured nation. The negociations of the late inglorious *peace*, and the *excise*, will haunt him, wherever he goes, and the terrors of the just resentment, which he must be to meet from a brave and insulted people, and which must finally crush him, will be for ever before his eyes.

In vain will such a minister, on the soul dregs of his power, the tools of corruption and despotism, preach up in *the speech* that *spirit of concord, and that obedience to the laws, which is essential to good order*. They have sent the *spirit of discord* through the land, and I will prophecy, that it will never be extinguished, but by the extinction of their power. Is the *spirit of concord* to go hand in hand with the Peace and Excise thro' this nation? Is it to be expected between an insolent Exciseman, and a *peer, gentleman, freeholder,* or *farmer,* whose private houses are now made liable to be entered and searched at pleasure? *Gloucestershire, Herefordshire,* and in general all the *Cyder* counties, are not surely the *several counties* which are alluded to in the *speech*. The *spirit of concord* hath not gone forth among them; but the *spirit of liberty* has, and a noble opposition has been given to the wicked instruments of oppression. A nation as sensible as the *English,* will see that a *spirit of concord,* when they are oppressed, means a tame submission to injury, and that a *spirit of liberty* ought then to arise, and I am sure ever will, in proportion to the weight of the grievance they feel. *Every* legal *attempt of a contrary tendency* to the *spirit of concord* will be deemed a justifiable resistance, warranted by the *spirit of the English constitution*.

A despotic minister will always endeavour to dazzle his prince with high-flown ideas of the *prerogative* and *honour* of the *crown,* which the minister will make a parade of *firmly maintaining*. I wish as much as any man in the kingdom to see *the honour of the crown* maintained in a manner truly becoming *Royalty*. I lament to see it sunk even to prostitution. What a shame was it to see the security of this country, in point of military force, complimented away, contrary to the opinion of

Royalty itself, and sacrificed to the prejudices and to the ignorance of a set of people, the most unfit from every consideration to be consulted on a matter relative to the security of the *house of Hanover*? I wish to see *the honour of the crown* religiously asserted with regard to our allies, and the dignity of it scrupulously maintained with regard to foreign princes. Is it possible such an indignity can have happened, such a sacrifice of *the honour of the crown of England,* as that a minister should already have kissed his majesty's hand on being appointed to the most insolent and ungrateful court in the world, without a previous assurance of that reciprocal nomination which the meanest court in Europe would insist upon, before she proceeded to an act otherwise so derogatory to her honour? But *Electoral Policy* has ever been obsequious to the court of *Vienna*, and forgets the insolence with which *count Colloredo* left England. Upon a principle of *dignity* and *economy*, lord *Stormont*, a *Scottish* peer of the loyal house of *Murray*, kissed his majesty's hand, I think, on Wednesday in the *Easter* week; but this ignominious act has not yet disgraced the nation in the *London Gazette*. The ministry are not ashamed of doing the thing in private; they are only afraid of the publication. Was it a tender regard for the *honour* of the late king, or of his present majesty, that invited to court *lord George Sackville, in these first days of Peace,* to share in the general satisfaction, which all good courtiers received in the indignity offered to lord *Ligonier*, and on the advancement of—? Was this to shew *princely* gratitude to the eminent services of the accomplished general of the house of *Brunswic,* who has had so great a share in rescuing *Europe* from the yoke of *France*; and whose nephew we hope soon to see made happy in the possession of the most amiable princess in the world? Or, is it meant to assert *the honour of the crown* only against the united wishes of a loyal and affectionate people, founded in a happy experience of the talents, ability, integrity, and virtue of those, who have had the glory of redeeming their country from bondage and ruin, in order to support, by every art of corruption and intimidation, a weak, disjointed, incapable set of—I will call them any thing but *ministers*—by whom the *Favourite* still meditates to rule this kingdom with a rod of iron.

The *Stuart* line has ever been intoxicated with the slavish doctrines of the *absolute, independent, unlimited* power of the crown. Some of that line were so weakly advised, as to endeavour to reduce them into practice: but the *English* nation was too spirited to suffer the least encroachment on the ancient liberties of this kingdom. The *King of England* is only the first magistrate of this country; but is invested by law with the whole executive power. He is, however, responsible to his people for the due execution of the royal functions, in the choice of ministers, etc. equally with the meanest of his subjects in his particular duty. The personal character of our present amiable sovereign makes us easy and happy that so great a power is lodged in such hands; but the *favourite* has given too just cause for him to escape the general odium. The *prerogative* of the crown is to exert the constitutional powers entrusted to it in a way, not of blind favour and partiality, but of wisdom and judgment. This is the spirit of our constitution. The people too have their *prerogative*, and, I hope, the fine words of Dryden will be engraven on our hearts, "Freedom *is the English subject's* Prerogative."

Decision by Lord Chief Justice Pratt of the Court of Common Pleas upholding the validity of general warrants but releasing John Wilkes from imprisonment, 3 May 1763

Complete Collection of State Trials, XI, 304.

The use of a general warrant against Wilkes and his collaborators after the publication of The North Briton, No. 45, *produced a constitutional crisis. These warrants were subsequently ruled illegal, a decision upheld by Commons resolutions passed in 1766. Sir Charles Pratt (1714-94), later Earl Camden, became subsequently lord chancellor (1766) and president of the council (1782, 1784-94).*

Lord Chief Justice Pratt, after stating the warrant of commitment, said, there are *two* objections taken to the legality of this warrant, and a *third* matter insisted on for the defendant, is privilege of parliament.

The first objection is, that it does not appear to the court that Mr. *Wilkes* was charged by any evidence before the secretaries of state, that he was the author or publisher of the *North Briton, number* XLV. In answer to this, we are all of opinion, that it is not necessary to state in the warrant that Mr. *Wilkes* was charged by any evidence before the secretaries of state, and that this objection has no weight. Whether a justice of peace can *ex officio*, without any evidence or information, issue a warrant for apprehending for a crime, is a different question. If a crime be done in his fight, he may commit the criminal upon the spot; but where he is not present, he ought not to commit upon discretion. Suppose a magistrate hath notice, or a particular knowledge that a person has been guilty of an offence, yet I do not think it is a sufficient ground for him to commit the criminal; but in that case he is rather a witness than a magistrate, and ought to make oath of the fact before some other magistrate, who should thereupon act the official part, by granting a warrant to apprehend the offender; it being more fit that the accuser should appear as a witness, then act as a magistrate. But that is not the question upon this warrant. The question here is, whether it is an essential part of the warrant, that the information, evidence or grounds of the charge before the secretaries of state should be set forth in the warrant? And we think it is not. *Tho. Rudyard's* case, 2 *Vent.* 22. cannot be applied to this case; for in the case of a conviction it is otherwise. It was said that a charge by witness was the ground of a warrant; but we think it not requisite to set out more than the offence, and the particular species of it. It may be objected, if this be good, every man's liberty will be in the power of a justice of peace. But *Hale, Coke* and *Hawkins*, take no notice that a charge is necessary to be set out in the warrant. In the case of the *seven bishops*, their counsel did not take this objection, which no doubt but they would have done, if they had thought there had been any weight in it. I do not rely upon the determination of the judges who then presided in the *King's Bench*. I have been attended with many precedents of warrants returned into the *King's Bench*; they are almost universally like this; and in sir *William*

Wyndham's case, 1 *Stra.* 2, 3. this very point before us is determined. And *Hawkins*, in his 2 *Pl. Coron.* 120. *sect.* 17. says,

> It is safe to set forth that the party is charged upon oath; *but this is not necessary*; for it hath been resolved, that a commitment for treason, or for suspicion of it, without setting forth any particular accusation, or ground of suspicion, is good;

and cites sir *William Wyndham's* case, *Trin*, 2 *Geo. Dalt. cap.* 121. *Cromp.* 233. *b.*

The second objection is, that the libel ought to be set forth in the warrant in haec verbe, or at least so much thereof as the secretaries of state deemed infamous, seditious, etc. that the court may judge whether any such paper ever existed; or if it does exist, whether it be an infamous and seditious libel, or not. But we are all of a contrary opinion. A warrant of commitment for felony must contain the *spices* of felony briefly;

> as for felony for the death of *J. S.* or for burglary in breaking the house of J. S. etc. and the reason is, because it may appear to the judges upon the return of an *habeas corpus*, whether it be felony or not

The magistrate forms his judgment upon the writing, whether it be an infamous and seditious libel or not at his peril; and perhaps the paper itself may not contain the whole of the libel; *inuendo's* may be necessary to make the whole out. There is no other word in the law but *libel* whereby to express the true idea of an infamous writing. We understand the nature of a libel as well as a *species* of felony. It is said the libel ought to be stated, because the court cannot judge whether it is a libel or not without it; but that is matter for the *judge and jury* to determine at the trial. If the paper was here, I should be afraid to read it. We might perhaps be able to determine *that it was a libel,* but we could not judge *that it was not a libel,* because of *inuendo's,* etc. It may be said, that without seeing the libel we are not able to fix the *quantum* of the bail; but in answer to this, the nature of the offence is known by us. It is said to be an infamous and seditious libel, etc. it is such a misdemeanor as we should require good bail for, (moderation to be observed) and such as the party may be able to procure.

The third matter insisted upon for Mr. *Wilkes* is, that he is a member of parliament, (which has been admitted by the king's serjeants) and intitled to privilege to be free from arrests in all cases except *treason, felony, and actual breach of the peace,* and therefore ought to be discharged from imprisonment without bail; and we are all of opinion that he is intitled to that privilege, and must be discharged without bail. In the case of the seven bishops, the court took notice of the privilege of parliament, and thought the bishops would have been intitled to it, if they had not judged them to have been guilty of a *breach of the peace*; for three of them, *Wright, Holloway,* and *Allybone,* deemed a seditious libel to be an actual breach of the peace, and therefore they were ousted of their privilege most unjustly. If Mr. *Wilkes* had been described as a member of parliament in the return, we must have taken notice of the law of privilege of parliament, otherwise the members would be without remedy, where they are wrongfully arrested against the law of parliament. We are bound to take notice of their privileges, as being part of the law of the land. 4

Inst. 25. says, the privilege of parliament holds unless it be in three cases, *viz. treason, felony, and the peace:* these are the words of *Coke.* In the trial of the seven bishops, the word *peace* in this case of privilege is explained to mean where surety of the peace is required. Privilege of parliament holds in information for the king, unless in the cases before excepted. The case of an information against lord *Tankerville* for bribery, 4 *Anne, (a)* was within the privilege of parliament. See the resolution of lords and commons, *anno* 1675. We are all of opinion that a libel is not a breach of the peace. It tends to the breach of the peace, and that is the utmost, 1 *Lev.* 139. But that which only tends to the breach of the peace cannot be a breach of it. Suppose a libel be a breach of the peace, yet I think it cannot exclude privilege; because I cannot find that a libeller is bound to find *surety of the peace,* in any book whatever, nor ever was, in any case, except one, *viz.* the case of the seven bishops, where three judges said, that *surety of the peace* was required in the case *of a libel.* Judge *Powell,* the only honest man of the four judges, dissented; and I am bold to be of his opinion, and to say, that case is not law. But it shews the miserable condition of the state at that time. Upon the whole, it is absurd to require surety of the peace or bail in the case of a libeller, and therefore Mr. *Wilkes* must be discharged from his imprisonment; whereupon there was a loud *huzza* in *Westminster-hall.* He was discharged accordingly.

Letters from "Junius" to the *Public Advertiser*, **January 1769**

The Letters of Junius, ed. C. W. Everett, reprint of Henry Sampson Woodfall ed. (1772; London: Faber & Gwyer, 1927), 21-32.

The spectacular "Junius" letters, probably written by Philip Francis (1740-1818), criticizing political figures of the day, appeared in several journals from 1769 to 1772. They stimulated attacks upon the government and led to the downfall in 1770 of the ministry of the duke of Grafton (Augustus Henry Fitzroy, third duke, 1735-1811; first lord of the treasury and prime minister, 1768-1770; lord privy seal, 1771-75, 1782-83). These articles also gave a fillip to the emerging profession of journalism.

21 January 1769

Sir,

The submission of a free people to the executive authority of government, is no more than a compliance with laws which they themselves have enacted. While the national honour is firmly maintained abroad, and while justice is impartially administered at home, the obedience of the subject will be voluntary, chearful, and I might almost say, unlimited. A generous nation is grateful even for the preservation of its rights, and willingly extends the respect due to the office of a good prince into an affection for his person. Loyalty, in the heart and understanding of an

Englishman, is a rational attachment to the guardian of the laws. Prejudices and passion have sometimes carried it to a criminal length; and, whatever foreigners may imagine, we know that Englishmen have erred as much in a mistaken zeal for particular persons and families, as they ever did in defence of what they thought most dear and interesting to themselves.

It naturally fills us with resentment, to see such a temper insulted and abused. In reading the history of a free people, whose rights have been invaded, we are interested in their cause. Our own feelings tell us how long they ought to have submitted, and at what moment it would have been treachery to themselves not to have resisted. How much warmer will be our resentment, if experience should bring the fatal example home to ourselves!

The situation of this country is alarming enough to rouse the attention of every man, who pretends to a concern for the public welfare. Appearances justify suspicion; and, when the safety of a nation is at stake, suspicion is a just ground of inquiry. Let us enter into it with candour and decency. Respect is due to the station of ministers; and, if a resolution must at last be taken, there is none so likely to be supported with firmness, as that which has been adopted with moderation.

The ruin or prosperity of a state depends so much upon the administration of its government, that to be acquainted with the merit of a ministry, we need only observe the condition of the people. If we see them obedient to the laws, prosperous in their industry, united at home, and respected abroad, we may reasonably presume that their affairs are conducted by men of experience, abilities and virtue. If, on the contrary, we see an universal spirit of distrust and dissatisfaction, a rapid decay of trade, dissensions in all parts of the empire, and a total loss of respect in the eyes of foreign powers, we may pronounce, without hesitation, that the government of that country is weak, distracted and corrupt. The multitude, in all countries, are patient to a certain point. Ill-usage may rouse their indignaton, and hurry them into excesses, but the original fault is in government. Perhaps there never was an instance of a change in the circumstances and temper of a whole nation so sudden and extraordinary as that which the misconduct of ministers has, within these very few years, produced in Great Britain. When our gracious sovereign ascended the throne, we were a flourishing and a contented people. If the personal virtues of a king could have insured the happiness of his subjects, the scene could not have altered so entirely as it has done. The idea of uniting all parties, of trying all characters, and of distributing the officers of state by rotation, was gracious and benevolent to an extreme, though it has not yet produced the many salutary effects which were intended by it. To say nothing of the wisdom of such a plan, it undoubtedly arose from an unbounded goodness of heart, in which folly had no share. It was not a capricious partiality to new faces;—it was not a natural turn for low intrigue; nor was it the treacherous amusement of double and triple negotiations. No, Sir, it arose from a continued anxiety, in the purest of all possible hearts, for the general welfare. Unfortunately, for us, the event has not been answerable to the design. After a rapid succession of changes, we are reduced to that state which hardly any change can mend. Yet there is no extremity of distress, which of itself ought to reduce a great nation to despair. It is not the disorder, but the physician;—it is not a casual concurrence of calamitous circumstances, it is the pernicious hand of government, which alone can make a whole people desperate.

Without much political sagacity, or any extraordinary depth of observation, we need only mark how the principal departments of the state are bestowed, and look no farther for the true cause of every mischief that befalls us.

The finances of a nation, sinking under its debts and expenses are committed to a young nobleman already ruined by play. Introduced to act under the auspices of Lord Chatham, and left at the head of affairs by that nobleman's retreat, he became minister by accident; but, deserting the principles and professions which gave him a moment's popularity, we see him, from every honourable engagement to the public, an apostate by design. As for business, the world yet knows nothing of his talents or resolution; unless a wayward, wavering inconsistency be a mark of genius, and caprice a demonstration of spirit. It may be said, perhaps, that it is his grace's province, as surely it is his passion, rather to distribute than to save the public money, and that while Lord North is Chancellor of the Exchequer, the First Lord of the Treasury may be as thoughtless and as extravagant as he pleases. I hope, however, he will not rely too much on the fertility of Lord North's genius for finance. His lordship is yet to give us the first proof of his abilities: It may be candid to suppose that he has hitherto voluntarily concealed his talents; intending, perhaps, to astonish the world, when we least expect it, with a knowledge of trade, a choice of expedients, and a depth of resources equal to the necessities, and far beyond the hopes, of his country. He must now exert the whole power of his capacity, if he would wish us to forget, that, since he has been in office, no plan has been formed, no system adhered to, nor any one important measure adopted, for the relief of public credit. If his plan for the service of the current year be not irrevocably fixed on, let me warn him to think seriously of consequences before he ventures to increase the public debt. Outraged and oppressed as we are, this nation will not bear, after a six years' peace, to see new millions borrowed, without an eventual diminution of debt, or reduction of interest. The attempt might rouse a spirit of resentment, which might reach beyond the sacrifice of a minister. As to the debt upon the civil list, the people of England expect that it will not be paid without a strict enquiry how it was incurred. If it must be paid by parliament, let me advise the Chancellor of the Exchequer to think of some better expedient than a lottery. To support an expensive war, or in circumstances of absolute necessity, a lottery may perhaps be allowable; but, besides that it is at all times the very worst way of raising money upon the people, I think it ill becomes the Royal dignity to have the debts of a King provided for, like the repairs of a county bridge, or a decayed hospital. The management of the King's affairs in the House of Commons cannot be more disgraced than it has been. A leading minister repeatedly called down for absolute ignorance;—ridiculous motions ridiculously withdrawn;—deliberate plans disconcerted, and a week's preparation of graceful oratory lost in a moment, give us some, though not adequate idea of Lord North's parliamentary abilities and influence. Yet, before he had the misfortune to be Chancellor of the Exchequer, he was neither an object of derision to his enemies, nor of melancholy pity to his friends.

A series of inconsistent measures had alienated the colonies from their duty as subjects, and from their natural affection to their common country. When Mr. Grenville was placed at the head of the Treasury, he felt the impossibility of Great Britain's supporting such an establishment as her former successes had made indispensable, and at the same time of giving any sensible relief to foreign trade, and to the weight of the public debt. He thought it equitable that those parts of the empire, which had benefited most by the expenses of the war, should contribute something to the expenses of the peace, and he had no doubt of the constitutional right vested in parliament to raise that contribution. But, unfortunately for this country, Mr. Grenville was at any rate to be distressed, because he was minister, and Mr. Pitt and Lord Camden were to be the patrons of America, because they were in opposition. Their declarations gave spirit and argument to the colonies, and while perhaps they meant no more than the ruin of a minister, they in effect divided one half of the empire from the other.

Under one administration the stamp act is made; under the second it is repealed; under the third, in spite of all experience, a new mode of taxing the colonies is invented, and a question revived, which ought to have been buried in oblivion. In these circumstances a new office is established for the business of the plantations, and the Earl of Hillsborough called forth, at a most critical season, to govern America. The choice at least announced to us a man of superior capacity and knowledge. Whether he be so or not, let his despatches, as far as they have appeared, let his measures, as far as they have operated, determine for him. In the former we have seen strong assertions without proof, declamation without argument, and violent censures without dignity or moderation; but neither correctness in the composition, nor judgment in the design. As for his measures, let it be remembered, that he was called upon to conciliate and unite; and that, when he entered into office, the most refractory of the colonies were still disposed to proceed by the constitutional methods of petition and remonstrance. Since that period they have been driven into excesses little short of rebellion. Petitions have been hindered from reaching the throne; and the continuance of one of the principal assemblies rested upon an arbitrary condition, which, considering the temper they were in, it was impossible they should comply with, and which would have availed nothing as to the general question if it had been complied with. So violent, and I believe I may call it so unconstitutional, an exertion of the prerogative, to say nothing of the weak injudicious terms in which it was conveyed, gives us as humble an opinion of his lordship's capacity, as it does of his temper and moderation. While we are at peace with other nations, our military force may perhaps be spared to support the Earl of Hillsborough's measures in America. Whenever that force shall be necessarily withdrawn or diminished, the dismission of such a minister will neither console us for his imprudence, nor remove the settled resentment of a people, who, complaining of an act of the legislature, are outraged by an unwarrantable stretch of prerogative, and, supporting their claims by argument, are insulted with declamation.

Drawing lots would be a prudent and reasonable method of appointing the officers of state, compared to a late disposition of the secretary's office. Lord Rochford was acquainted with the affairs and temper of the southern courts: Lord

Weymouth was equally qualified for either department. By what unaccountable caprice has it happened, that the latter, who pretends to no experience whatsoever, is removed to the most important of the two departments, and the former by preference placed in an office, where his experience can be of no use to him? Lord Weymouth had distinguished himself in his first employment by a spirited, if not judicious, conduct. He had animated the civil magistrate beyond the tone of civil authority, and had directed the operations of the army to more than military execution. Recovered from the errors of his youth, from the distraction of play, and the bewitching smiles of Burgundy, behold him exerting the whole strength of his clear, unclouded faculties, in the service of the crown. It was not the heat of midnight excesses, nor ignorance of the laws, nor the furious spirit of the House of Bedford: No, Sir, when this respectable minister interposed his authority between the magistrate and the people, and signed the mandate on which, for aught he knew, the lives of thousands depended, he did it from the deliberate motion of his heart, supported by the best of his judgment.

It has lately been a fashion to pay a compliment to the bravery and generosity of the commander-in-chief, at the expense of his understanding. They who love him least make no question of his courage, while his friends dwell chiefly on the facility of his disposition. Admitting him to be as brave as a total absence of all feeling and reflection can make him, let us see what sort of merit he derives from the remainder of his character. If it be generosity to accumulate in his own person and family a number of lucrative employments— to provide, at the public expense, for every creature that bears the name of Manners; and, neglecting the merit and services of the rest of the army, to heap promotions upon his favourites and dependants, the present commander-in-chief is the most generous man alive. Nature has been sparing of her gifts to this noble lord; but, where birth and fortune are united, we expect the noble pride and independance of a man of spirit, not the servile, humiliating complaisance of a courtier. As to the goodness of his heart, if a proof of it be taken from the facility of never refusing, what conclusions shall we draw from the indecency of never performing? And if the discipline of the army be in any degree preserved, what thanks are due to a man, whose cares, notoriously confined to filling up vacancies, have degraded the office of commander-in-chief into a broker of commissions!

With respect to the navy, I shall only say, that this country is so highly indebted to Sir Edward Hawke, that no expence should be spared to secure to him an honourable and affluent retreat.

The pure and impartial administration of justice is perhaps the firmest bond to secure a chearful submission of the people, and to engage their affections to government. It is not sufficient that questions of private right and wrong are justly decided, nor that judges are superior to the vileness of pecuniary corruption. Jefferies himself, when the court had no interest, was an upright judge. A court of justice may be subject to another sort of bias, more important and pernicious, as it reaches beyond the interest of individuals, and affects the whole community. A judge under the influence of government, may be honest enough in the decision of private causes, yet a traitor to the public. When a victim is marked out by the ministry, this judge will offer himself to perform the sacrifice. He will not scruple to prostitute his dignity, and betray the sanctity of his office, whenever an arbitrary point is to be carried for government, or the resentments of a court are to be gratified.

These principles and proceedings, odious and contemptible as they are, in effect are no less injudicious. A wise and generous people are roused by every appearance of oppressive, unconstitutional measures, whether those measures are supported openly by the power of government, or masked under the forms of a court of justice. Prudence and self-preservation will oblige the most moderate dispositions to make common cause, even with a man whose conduct they censure, if they see him persecuted in a way which the real spirit of the laws will not justify. The facts, on which these remarks are founded, are too notorious to require an application.

This, Sir, is the detail. In one view, behold a nation overwhelmed with debt; her revenues wasted; her trade declining; the affections of her colonies alienated; the duty of the magistrate transferred to the soldiery; a gallant army, which never fought unwillingly but against their fellow subjects, mouldering away for want of the direction of a man of common abilities and spirit: and, in the last instance, the administration of justice become odious and suspected to the whole body of the people. This deplorable scene admits but of one addition—that we are governed by councils, from which a reasonable man can expect no remedy but poison, no relief but death.

If, by the immediate interposition of Providence, it were possible for us to escape a crisis so full of terror and despair, posterity will not believe the history of the present times. They will either conclude that our distresses were imaginary, or that we had the good fortune to be governed by men of acknowledged integrity and wisdom: they will not believe it possible that their ancestors could have survived, or recovered from so desperate a condition, while a Duke of Grafton was Prime Minister, a Lord North Chancellor of the Exchequer, a Weymouth and a Hillsborough Secretaries of State, a Granby Commander in Chief, and a Mansfield chief criminal judge of the kingdom.

Junius

26 January 1769

Sir,

The kingdom swarms with such numbers of felonious robbers of private character and virtue, that no honest or good man is safe; especially as these cowardly, base assassins, stab in the dark, without having the courage to sign their real names to their malevolent and wicked productions. A writer, who signs himself Junius, in the Public Advertiser of the 21st instant, opens the deplorable situation of this country in a very affecting manner; with a pompous parade of his candour and decency, he tells us, that we see dissensions in all parts of the empire, an universal spirit of distrust and dissatisfaction, and a total loss of respect towards us in the eyes of foreign powers. But this writer, with all his boasted candour, has not told us the real cause of the evils he so pathetically enumerates. I shall take the liberty to explain the cause for him. Junius, and such writers as himself, occasion all the mischiefs complained of, by falsely and maliciously traducing the best characters in the kingdom. For when our deluded people at home, and foreigners abroad, read the poisonous and inflammatory libels that are daily published with impunity, to vilify those who are in any way distinguished by their good qualities and eminent virtues; when they find no notice taken of, or reply given to these slanderous tongues and pens, their conclusion is, that both the ministers and the nation have been fairly described, and they act accordingly. I think it therefore the duty of every good citizen to stand forth, and endeavour to undeceive the public, when the vilest arts are made use of to defame and blacken the brightest characters among us. An eminent author affirms it to be almost as criminal to hear a worthy man traduced, without attempting his justification, as to be the author of the calumny against him. For my own part I think it a sort of misprision of treason against society. No man, therefore, who knows Lord Granby, can possibly hear so good and great a character most vilely abused, without a warm and just indignation against this Junius, this high priest of envy, malice, and all uncharitableness, who has endeavoured to sacrifice our beloved commander-in-chief at the altars of his horrid deities. Nor is the injury done to his lordship alone, but to the whole nation, which may too soon feel the contempt, and consequently the attacks of our late enemies, if they can be induced to believe that the person on whom the safety of these kingdoms so much depends, is unequal to his high station, and destitute of those qualities which form a good general. One would have thought that his lordship's services in the cause of his country, from the battle of Culloden to his most glorious conclusion of the late war, might have entitled him to common respect and decency at least; but this uncandid, indecent writer, has gone so far as to turn one of the most amiable men of the age, into a stupid, unfeeling, and senseless being; possessed indeed of a personal courage, but void of those essential qualities which distinguish the commander from the common soldier.

A very long, uninterrupted, impartial, and I will add, a most disinterested friendship with Lord Granby, gives me the right to affirm, that all Junius's exertions are false and scandalous. Lord Granby's courage, though of the brightest and most ardent kind, is among the lowest of his numerous good qualities; he was formed to excel in war by nature's liberality to his mind as well as person. Educated and instructed by his most noble father, and a most spirited as well as excellent scholar, the present Bishop of Bangor, he was trained to the nicest sense of honour, and to the truest and noblest sort of pride, that of never doing or suffering a mean action. A sincere love and attachment to his king and country, and to their glory, first impelled him to the field, where he never gained aught but honour. He impaired, through his bounty, his own fortune; for his bounty, which this writer would in vain depreciate, is founded upon the noblest of the human affections, it flows from a heart melting to goodness from the most refined humanity. Can a man, who is described as unfeeling, and void of reflection, be constantly employed in seeking proper objects on whom to exercise those glorious virtues of compassion and generosity? The distressed officer, the soldier, the widow, the orphan, and a long list besides, know that vanity has no share in his frequent donations; he gives, because he feels their distresses. Nor has he ever been rapacious with one hand to be bountiful with the other; yet this uncandid Junius would insinuate, that the dignity of the commander-in-chief is depraved into the base office of a commission broker; that is, Lord Granby bargains for the sale of commissions: for it must have this meaning, if it has any at all. But where is the man living who can justly charge his lordship with such mean practices? Why does not Junius produce him? Junius knows that he has no other means of wounding this hero, than from some missile weapon, shot from an obscure corner: He seeks, as all such defamatory writers do,

—spargere voces
In Vulgum ambiguas—

to raise suspicion in the minds of the people. But I hope that my countrymen will be no longer imposed upon by artful and designing men, or by wretches, who, bankrupts in business, in fame, and in fortune, mean nothing more than to involve this country in the same common ruin with themselves. Hence it is that they are constantly aiming their dark, and too often fatal, weapons against those who stand forth as the bulwark of our national safety. Lord Granby was too conspicuous a mark not to be their object. He is next attacked for being unfaithful to his promises and engagements: Where are Junius's proofs? Although I could give some instances, where a breach of promise would be a virtue, especially in the case of those who would pervert the open, unsuspecting moments of convivial mirth, into sly, insidious applications for preferment, or party systems, and would endeavour to surprise a good man, who cannot bear to see any one leave him dissatisfied, into unguarded promises. Lord Granby's attention to his own family and relations is called selfish. Had he not attended to them, when fair and just opportunities presented themselves, I should have thought him unfeeling, and void of reflection indeed. How are any man's friends or relations to be provided for, but from the influence and protection of the patron? It is unfair to suppose that Lord Granby's friends have not as much merit as the friends of any other great man: If he is generous at the public expense, as Junius invidiously calls it, the public is at no more expense for his lordship's friends than it would be if any other set of men possessed those offices. The charge is ridiculous!

The last charge against Lord Granby is of a most serious and alarming nature indeed. Junius asserts that the army is mouldering away for want of the direction of a man of common abilities and spirit. The present condition of the army gives the directest lie to his assertions. It was never upon a more respectable footing with regard to discipline, and all the essentials that can form good soldiers. Lord Ligonier delivered a firm and noble palladium of our safeties into Lord Granby's hands, who has kept it in the same good order in which he received it. The strictest care has been taken to fill up the vacant commissions with such gentlemen as have the glory of their ancestors to support, as well as their own, and are doubly bound to the cause of their king and country, from motives of private property as well as public spirit. The adjutant-general, who has the immediate care of the troops after Lord Granby, is an officer who would do great honour to any service in Europe, for his correct arrangements, good sense, and discernment upon all occasions, and for a punctuality and precision which give the most entire satisfaction to all who are obliged to consult him. The reviewing generals, who inspect the army twice a year, have been selected with the greatest care, and have answered the important trust reposed in them in the most laudable manner. Their reports of the condition of the army are much more to be credited than those of Junius, whom I do advise to atone for his shameful aspersions, by asking pardon of Lord Granby, and the whole kingdom, whom he has offended by his abominable scandals. In short, to turn Junius's own battery against him, I must assert, in his own words, "that he has given strong assertions without proof, declamation without argument, and violent censures without dignity or moderation."

William Draper

Proceedings of the Commons voiding the election of John Wilkes as MP for Middlesex County, 10 February-8 May 1769

Parliamentary History, XVI, 577-96.

Wilkes was elected to the Middlesex constituency four times before being admitted to his seat in 1774. The following expulsion proceedings were expunged from the Commons records in 1782.

Mr. Seymour moved, that the Resolution of the House of Friday last, relating to the Expulsion of John Wilkes, esq., then a member of this House, might be read. And the same being read accordingly; he also moved, "That, as the Resolution of this House by which John Wilkes, esq., then a member of this House, was expelled, contains a charge of accumulative offences, the said Resolution shall not be considered or used as a precedent for the future."

No arguments in favour of the motion were brought forward but such as were before made use of. But against the motion it was said, that it would be confessing the House to have done a very wrong thing a day or two before; that when a majority of the House had agreed to a measure, it became the measure of the House, and so ought not to be altered that session.

The motion was negatived without a division.

February 17

It was ordered, "That the deputy clerk of the crown do attend this House immediately, with the return to the writ for electing a knight of the shire to serve in this present parliament for the county of Middlesex, in the room of John Wilkes, esq., expelled this House." And the deputy clerk of the crown attending, according to order; the said writ and return were read. After which,

Lord Strange moved, "That John Wilkes, esq. having been, in this session of parliament, expelled this House, was, and is, incapable of being elected a member to serve in this present parliament."

Mr. James Townshend gave the House an account of the Middlesex election. He observed there were above 2000 freeholders of Middlesex present; that they proceeded in a calm, determinate manner, had unanimously chosen Mr. Wilkes; and should the House expel him again, he believed their full determination was to petition the King to dissolve this parliament, and call another.

Lord North called him to order for this, observing he had never heard such unparliamentary language in that House. He exclaimed, Would the people petition to dissolve this parliament? If they did, he hoped no person would be found hardy enough to set his name to such a petition, a proceeding which would bring any minister's head to the block; and would call for all the weight of avenging power.— He was called to order by

Captain Phipps, who declared he never could have imagined any minister so ignorant of the laws, as not to have read the Bill of Rights, in which it is expressed, that the subject has an undoubted right to petition the throne.

Mr. Townshend then continued. He was surprised to hear such threats thrown out in that House, when liberty of speech was its greatest privilege. That, however, threats of that nature had no effect on him. He would tell that minister who used them, that he believed there were thousands ready to set their hands to such a petition; but if no other could be found, he himself should never refuse to appear in name or person in support of so constitutional a measure.

Sir George Saville said, that as a representative of a large county, it was his duty to assert the rights of his constituents; he apprehended, but desired to be instructed by the House, if it was not legal for the people to petition the throne; and if it was legal, whether that right of petitioning did not extend to ask any thing in the power of the King to grant. This he looked on as the people's right, and that no threats thrown out in that House could or ought to alter the law.

Lord North then explained away all or most of his meaning, saying, that all he meant was, most probably parliament would resent such an affront on those who should sign such a petition.

In favour of the motion it was observed, that when a member is once expelled, it is the undoubted law of parliament not to admit that person to sit again in the same parliament; and the case was cited of Robert Walpole, who being re-elected for Lynn, the House of Commons determined that he could not be returned again that parliament; the Journals of the House being applied to, it appeared "That sir Robert Walpole, being expelled for bribery and corruption, is not capable of sitting in this parliament."

Mr. Dowdeswell then proposed an amendment to the motion, observing, that as the case of sir Robert Walpole was the only one that had ever happened, and much stress was laid on that precedent, we ought strictly to conform ourselves to it, and therefore proposed that the words of the vote by which Mr. Wilkes was expelled should be added to the motion. This would have entirely altered the case, as it would then have appeared that expulsion does not always infer the rendering a person incapable of being re-elected: but it passed without amendment—it would open such a door for expulsions that no man's seat was secure—there is one "worst" man in the House—turn him out. Is there not now a "worst" man left—turn him out too. In short, when will you stop?—You have turned one out for impiety and obscenity. Do half a dozen members of this House ever meet over a convivial bottle that their discourse is entirely free from obscenity—from impiety—or abusing government? Even in the cabinet, that pious, reforming society; was Mr. Wilkes there to be adjudged, and were the innocent man to throw the first stone, they would slink out one by one, and leave the culprit uncondemned.

The ministry used very few arguments, relying entirely on the ultimate ratio. And on the question being put it was carried against the amendment 228 to 102.

The main question of incapacity was then again discussed: the refusal of the amendment made many of those who would have voted for Mr. Wilkes's incapacity, now the question became general, vote against it; a member may be accused of writing a libel—the House expels him—but for being tried for that libel in the court of law he is found innocent—is that person never to be reinstated? How can you make that person amends for such expulsion? But, say the ministry, parliament will never expel a member but for just cause—when a ministry are to be judges, woe to their opposers.

Lord Strange said, if Mr. Wilkes put up again and again; if any person opposed him and had but 20 votes, he should be of opinion that person had carried his election. He was answered that now Mr. Wilkes's prophecy was near being accomplished: when the House had begun by voting who should not be members, the next step would be voting who should; and the right of the electors be entirely destroyed.

Then the main question being put, "That John Wilkes, esq., having been, in this session of parliament, expelled this House, was, and is, incapable of being elected a member to serve in this present parliament;" The House divided. Yeas 235; Noes 89. So it was resolved in the affirmative.

A motion being made, That the late election of a knight of the shire to serve in this present parliament for the county of Middlesex, is a void election, a member, in his place, informed the House, that he was present at the last election of a knight of the shire to serve in this present parliament for the said county; that there was no other candidate then the said Mr. Wilkes; that there was no poll demanded for any other person, nor any kind of opposition to the election of the said Mr. Wilkes.

Resolved, That the said election is a void election.

Ordered, "That Mr. Speaker do issue his warrant to the clerk of the crown; to make out a new writ for the electing of a knight of the shire to serve in this present parliament for the county of Middlesex, in the room of John Wilkes, esq., who is adjudged incapable of being elected a member to serve in this present parliament, and whose election for the said county has been declared void."

March 17

On the motion of lord North, it was ordered, "That the deputy clerk of the crown do attend this House immediately, with the return to the writ for electing a knight of the shire to serve in this present parliament for the county of Middlesex, in the room of John Wilkes, esq., adjudged incapable of being elected a member to serve in this present parliament, and whose election for the said county had been declared void." And the deputy clerk attending accordingly: the said writ and return were read. And it appearing by the return, that John Wilkes, esq., was elected, and returned to serve as a knight of the shire to serve in this present parliament for the said county of Middlesex; the House was moved, that the entries in the votes of the House, upon the 17th of February, of the proceedings of the House, upon the return to the writ for electing a knight of the shire to serve in this present parliament for the county of Middlesex, in the room of John Wilkes, esq., expelled this House, might be read.

And the same being read accordingly; a motion was made, and the question being proposed, That the election and return of John Wilkes, esq., who hath been by this House adjudged incapable of being elected a member to serve in this present parliament, are null and void; and the previous question being put, That that question be now put; it was resolved in the affirmative.

Then the main question being put:

Resolved, That the election and return of John Wilkes, esq., who hath been by this House adjudged incapable of being elected a member to serve in this present parliament, are null and void.

And a motion being made, That Mr. Speaker do issue his warrant to the clerk of the crown, to make out a new writ for the electing of a knight of the shire to serve in this present parliament, for the county of Middlesex, in the room of John Wilkes, esq., who hath been by this House adjudged incapable of being elected a member to serve in this present parliament, and whose election and return have been declared null and void;

And the House being informed, that Mr. John Smith, under sheriff of the county of Middlesex, attended at the door, who could give the House some account of the proceedings at the last election of a knight of the shire to serve in this present parliament for the county of Middlesex; he was called in; and, at the bar, informed the House, that he was present at the last election of a knight of the shire to serve in this present parliament for the county of Middlesex: that no other candidate was proposed but John Wilkes, esq.; and that no elector gave or tendered his vote for any other person than the said Mr. Wilkes.

Ordered, "That Mr. Speaker do issue his warrant to the clerk of the crown, to make out a new writ for the electing of a knight of the shire to serve in this present parliament for the county of Middlesex, in the room of John Wilkes, esq., who hath been adjudged incapable of being elected a member to serve in this present parliament, and whose election and return have been declared null and void."

April 7

Colonel Onslow rose and observed, that the election at Brentford was coming on; that he had reason to apprehend riots; that several freeholders durst not go there to give their votes. He therefore moved, that the sheriffs should be ordered to attend the House on the 10th instant, to take their instructions, how to prevent the riots.

The ministry seconded him, observing that the House should always interfere, especially in keeping the peace at elections, and that they had done it in a very recent instance.

In answer it was observed, that the instance alluded to was when a riot had actually happened, the poll interrupted, many books lost, and the sheriffs had come to take counsel of the House how they should proceed; that to suppose a riot, would probably be a means of making one; that it was encroaching on the powers of government to suppose the civil power not able to maintain itself, and to call the legislative to assist the executive; that however as the motion had been made, the House could not well reject it, lest if a riot should happen, the consequences would be objected to be the fault of those who voted against it.

Mr. Dowdeswell observed that the motion was in itself ridiculous; for when the sheriffs came, what should the House say to them? He thought it would be much more advisable to make an order that the sheriffs should use their endeavours to keep the peace, by making an additional number of constables, etc. This idea was adopted. When the debate grew a little warm,

Mr. Burke attacked the ministry as authors of the whole system of riots, by the various encouragements they had given. In the sailors riots, they had employed a person at the head of that mob, one captain Fall, and given him a pension for what he had done in that mob: the appointing leaders of mobs, was a sure method to encourage mobs, by shewing a countenance to the principles on which they were raised: the pardoning the murderers in the Brentford riot, was a very proper extension of the royal prerogative: yet the method in which it was done, by giving reasons drawn from the partial opinions of interested surgeons, tending to destroy that confidence that every man ought to have in the trial of juries, and to bring into contempt the authority of the laws, was so weak a measure, that nothing but the most impotent, ignorant, dispirited administration could give life to. A time must come, though the ministers might put it off as long as they could, when an account must be given to the people of the steps by which so great innovations had been made in the constitution, and the longer that account was deferred, by so much more weighty the load would fall upon them. Now was a proper time to begin such enquiry, and those persons, be they who they might, on whom the cause of the riots could properly be laid, should, as he thought, be held out for the detestation of all honest men, and the punishment of the crown.

The ministry observed, that the gentleman might begin by enquiring, if the House thought it necessary, but nobody would imagine they would join issue to bring about such enquiry. They denied they knew any thing of the employing captain Fall, they did not conceive the pardon granted to the rioters, let it have been done in what manner it would, would have met with universal approbation. The present way was equal in justice to any other.

Colonel Barré observed that the ministry were like a polypus: cut it into pieces it was a polypus still; one part of the ministry employed its talents in raising mobs; another part in quelling them; and a third knew nothing at all of the matter: but he wondered they were so ignorant of the old parliamentary systems, not to know that when a minister was so publicly attacked, he never would leave the House until he had cleared himself from the accusation; and congratulated them on the new method found out of putting a negative on enquiries of that nature, by voting them not necessary.

It was then ordered, "That the sheriffs of Middlesex do apply to the magistrates of the said county, and acquaint them, that it is the order of this House, That the said magistrates do attend the next election of a knight of the shire for the said county, and do appoint a proper number of constables, and take every other means in their power, to preserve the peace and freedom of the said election."

April 14

Mr. Onslow made a motion for the return of a knight of the shire for Middlesex, to be immediately brought up. This was opposed, as unjust to colonel Luttrell, as proceeding on the return might hinder his petition for an undue election. The freeholders, too, might petition, but by proceeding in this summary way both were prevented; that an enquiry into the return, must either be followed by a motion to vote in colonel Luttrell, perhaps contrary to his inclination, as not choosing to stand on such narrow ground, to be the member for a county against the opinion of so large a majority of freeholders, when, perhaps, he might have other more manly ground to stand on; or else it must be followed by declaring it a void election, which might be exceedingly unjust, as there were so many other candidates. Others observed, that putting off the enquiry for fourteen days would give time for petitions against the election, and could be attended with no bad consequences, as Mr. Wilkes had been declared incapable by this parliament, which perhaps was a measure not absolutely just, but it was a law of parliament that no resolution could be rescinded in the same session; the next session might probably think differently from this, and once more establish the right of the people on its just basis—that this had unfortunately become a dispute between the parliament and the people, which, so far from ending our unfortunate disturbances, would in all probability encrease them to an height destructive of the constitution.

On the other hand it was urged, that the dignity of the House was concerned in putting an end immediately to this affair; that having voted Mr. Wilkes incapable of being returned, the people had no right to give their votes to him—the sheriffs were guilty of an audacious insult on the House of Commons, and liable to censure for having returned him; that the proceeding so immediately, was following the exact steps taken by the House in the former case where he had been declared incapable of being elected. The return was therefore called for, and Mr. Wilkes's election declared void.

Mr. Onslow then moved that the sheriffs of Middlesex should immediately attend the House with the poll; which was agreed to; but the ministry having neglected to give the sheriffs notice, they were so long in coming that the House got into confusion and riot for two hours, and then the night was so far advanced that it became improper to enter into any new debate that night: a motion was made by the ministry to adjourn to next day, which was Saturday.

The Opposition opposed Saturday as contrary to the custom of parliament, which never did any thing of consequence on that day; that Saturday was dedicated to other business, or pleasure; that it seemed as if the hurrying on this business was such a measure of government, that unusual means were taken to insure its success; that precipitation might sooner inflame than quiet the minds of the people. However the Ministry were so eager to finish the affair, that they voted for Saturday by a majority of 207 to 115.

April 15

Mr. Onslow made a motion, "That Henry Lawes Luttrell, esq. ought to have been returned to knight of the shire to serve in this present parliament for the county of Middlesex." He produced an instance of a person who was first in the poll, but being incapable of being chosen by a refusal to take the oaths, the House of Commons considered him as no candidate, and voted in the person who was next on the poll. This instance he brought to shew, that when votes were given to a person incapable of being chosen, those votes were looked upon, by the House of Commons, as thrown away, and the person next on the poll always declared duly elected by the House: he talked a good deal of his motives for making this motion, as founded on the principles of whiggism and the revolution; that the law of parliament was the law of the land; and consequently Mr. Wilkes having been declared incapable by the House of Commons, this was a legal disqualification, and of course the same case as that before cited: the House ought therefore to proceed in the same manner they had hitherto done in cases of the same nature, and vote Mr. Luttrell in.

The Attorney General, on the same side, observed, that he looked upon Mr. Wilkes's disqualification, notified as it was in the writ to the sheriffs and freeholders, as absolutely conclusive on them; and, therefore, the sheriffs were guilty of a great impropriety, to say no worse, in returning Mr. Wilkes: that in the late infamous riot at St. James's, there was regularity, order, and a well laid design, and he was sorry to inform the House, that he could get no legal proof to bring any person to justice; he thought to take the advice of the House how he should proceed therein. It was observed, too, that the House had, at different times, by three votes, disqualified several ranks of men, as aliens, denizens, sheriffs, minors, or clergymen: that if they could disqualify bodies of men, they could do the same to a single person.

Sir Fletcher Norton spoke on the same side. He observed, that he could not say that it was illegal for the freeholders to offer their votes for Mr. Wilkes. It was not illegal for the sheriff to take those votes for Mr. Wilkes. It was not illegal for the sheriffs to return Mr. Wilkes, when chosen; but he thought it highly indecent to fly thus in the face of a resolution of the House of Commons. The sheriffs might have made other returns; they might have returned all the candidates; or they might have made a special return; or they might have returned Mr. Luttrell. That the Commons, acting in a judicial capacity, he thought their resolutions equal to a law. He instanced some members who were disqualified by such resolutions at different times; as, Hall, for libelling; sir E. Sawyer, Mr. Montague, for bribery, etc. If you have a right to expel, it would be of no use, if not able to keep out the person so expelled.

Lord North spoke long, but chiefly to the passions; he described Mr. Wilkes, and his actions, in a lively manner; shewed the variety of troubles he had given the ministry—that unless by voting in Mr. Luttrell, an end was put to this debate, the whole kingdom would be in confusion. Though he owned he did not think that measure would put an end to the distractions. He spoke much more to the expediency than the legality of the measure proposed.

Mr. Beckford observed, on the other side, that all the precedents they had mentioned were of persons disqualified by act of parliament, consequently not applicable to the present case; Mr. Wilkes being disqualified only by a vote of one part of the legislature—that the House of Commons, alone, cannot make a law, binding any body but themselves—if they, by a vote, can disqualify whom they please; the consequence of which must be the getting into their own hands the power of the whole government. He concluded with a story in scripture, of Rehoboam, the son of Solomon, when the ten tribes of Israel revolted from his government; which he recommended to the ministry to apply.

Serjeant Glynn spoke very ably, and fairly observed, that the disqualification of Mr. Wilkes not being the law of the land, the freeholders of Middlesex were not obliged to take notice of it—that the disqualifications of bodies of men, as clergy, aliens, etc., were all either by express laws, or by implication from the common law, and that the votes of the House to that effect, were only declaratory, but not enacting—that undoubtedly the House had a jurisdiction over its own members, and were judges of the rights of electors, but such judgments must be according to law, a natural consequence of every court of judicature in this kingdom—that the right of the freeholders of Middlesex, as well as the right of every citizen or burgess, was an inherent right in them, not derived from the House of Commons, and therefore could not be taken from them by the House, except in cases, where offending against law, they had forfeited a right to such privileges.

Mr. Burke drew a very moving picture of the present state of the nation, and the terrible consequences to be dreaded from this measure; shewing that this was not, as had been represented, a dispute between the House and the freeholders of Middlesex, but between the House and all the voters of England, who would easily perceive their franchises invaded by this vote. He accused the ministry of the steps they had taken to sow discord between the King and the people. He said, that the Addresses were libels on the people, accusing them of crimes the ministry had forced them into—that the court of examining surgeons, was a rank libel on the trial by juries, and that the dignity of the ministry was destroyed by a dispute they were obliged to enter into with a poor surgeon, who had publicly threatened them with a prosecution for defaming him, and had never dared to defend themselves.

Mr. Grenville made, this day, one of the best speeches that had been made in the House of Commons for many years. He shewed, from history, that the vote of the House of Lords respecting one of their own members, had been considered by the King's-bench as null and void, because contrary to law; and that the Judges had not been punished by the Lords for so doing (this was in the case of lord Banbury, Holt chief justice). He then shewed, that in the case of Ashby and White, a vote of the House of Commons, contrary to law, had also been disregarded by the courts below; and, from the premises, concluded, that a vote of the House might and did bind the House, the session it was made in; but, out of the House, except in matters of privilege, had no effect on the people. If the ministry, he said, will take such headstrong measures, the vengeance of a deluded, injured people, must fall on them
    The motion was then carried by 197 against 143.

April 29

A Petition of the freeholders of the county of Middlesex, was presented to the House and read; setting forth, "That the petitioners being informed by the votes of the House, that the return for the said county hath been amended by rasing out the name of John Wilkes, esq., and inserting the name of Henry Lawes Luttrell, esq. instead thereof, and that leave was given to petition this House, touching the election of Henry Lawes Luttrell, esq.; and representing to the House, that the said Henry Lawes Luttrell had not the majority of legal votes at the said election, nor did the majority of the freeholders, when they voted for John Wilkes, esq., mean thereby to throw away their votes, or to wave their right of representation, nor would they by any means have chosen to be represented by the said Henry Lawes Luttrell, esq.; the petitioners therefore apprehend he cannot sit as the representative of the said county in parliament, without manifest infringement of the rights and privileges of the freeholders thereof: the petitioners therefore hope that the House will give leave that they may be heard by their counsel against the said election and return, and grant them such further relief as they shall think meet."
    Ordered, That the matter of the said Petition, so far as the same relates to the election of Henry Lawes Luttrell, esq., be heard at the bar of this House, upon the 8th of May.

May 8

The House proceeded to the hearing of the matter of the Petition of the freeholders of the county of Middlesex.

And the counsel were called in, and the said Petition was read. And the order, made upon the 29th of April last, for hearing this day, at the bar of this House, the matter of the said Petition, so far as the same relates to the election of Henry Lawes Luttrell, esq., was also read.

And the standing order of the House made the 16th of January, 1735, for restraining the counsel, at the bar of this House, or before the committee of privileges and elections, from offering evidence touching the legality of votes for members to serve in parliament, for any county, shire, city, borough, cinque port, or place, contrary to the last determination in the House of Commons, was also read.

And the counsel for the petitioners were heard; and having proposed to produce evidence, to shew that the numbers upon the poll were for Mr. Wilkes 1143, and for Mr. Luttrell 296; the same was admitted by the counsel for the sitting member.

Then the counsel for the sitting member were heard. And one of the counsel for the petitioners having been heard by way of reply; the counsel on both sides were directed to withdraw.

And a motion being made, "That Henry Lawes Luttrell, esq. is duly elected a knight of the shire to serve in this present parliament for the county of Middlesex;" the House divided; Yeas 221; Noes 152. So it was resolved in the affirmative.

The following very able summary of the Arguments made use of during the Debates on the Expulsion of Mr. Wilkes, is taken from the Annual Register for 1769:

It was said by those who opposed the expulsion of Mr. Wilkes, That the right of the electors to be represented by men of their own choice, was so essential for the preservation of all their other rights, that it ought to be considered as one of the most sacred parts of our constitution. That the House of Commons was not a self-constituted power, acting by an inherent right; but an elected body, restrained within the limits of a delegated authority; hence, as they were chosen, they could not dispute the right of their constituents, without sapping the foundation of their own existence, and infringing the fundamental principles of the constitution. That the law of the land had regulated the qualifications of members to serve in parliament, and that the freeholders of every county had an indisputable right to return whom they thought proper, provided he was not disqualified by any of those known laws. That new restraints are not arbitrarily to be imposed at pleasure by the judgment of any court. The legislature alone, which is the united power of the state, King, Lords, and Commons, can enact new restraints. Courts of judicature, and houses of parliament acting as courts of judicature, have only the power of declaring them: and in the use of that power are bound by the law as it stands at the time of making that declaration. When usage is collected from the ancient, uniform, and uninterrupted practice of parliament, we have the custom of parliament; and that custom is the law of parliament. These restraints, therefore, do not stand solely on the decision of the House, or the judgment of a court having competent jurisdiction in the case: they are much better founded in the previous usage, and the repeated acquiescence of those who are affected by them.

These incapacities are generally known; they are enumerated by law-writers of the first authority, who expressly declare all other persons eligible; these grave writers could not conceive, that a resolution of the House of Commons could from time to time either create or declare new disqualifications. They are founded in good sense; analogous to the like restraints adjudged in other cases by the courts of law; and confirmed by usage. They are not occasional but fixed: to rule and govern the question as it shall arise; not to start up on a sudden, and shift from side to side, as the caprice of the day or the fluctuation of party shall direct. Our constitution does not know any court so supreme as to be above reason, nor so absolute as to be able to make a custom under pretence of declaring it. The doctrine here asserted is such as would maintain the resolution of the House to be the law of the land by virtue of its own authority only, notwithstanding it may have usage, reason, and justice to contend against.

Instances were given of former resolutions, repeatedly taken upon much deliberation, in opposition to good sense and reason, common usage, and the rights of the electors, It was said that a most salutary doctrine was to be drawn from the glaring inconsistency of these resolutions: that where power goes beyond right, it finds no resting place; it never knows where to stop; but that every part of its career shews the danger of passing the bound prescribed by law.

Besides the original disqualifications, founded on reason and the common law, and which are as ancient as the constitution, and from their nature must be as permanent, restraints have at different times been laid on by the statute law, and founded therefore in the consent of the whole community. These are arbitrary, take their rise from expediency, and are liable to be changed from time to time, by that authority which gave them being. If these restraints could have been established by any authority less than that of an act of parliament, it is not to be imagined that the House of Commons would have applied to the other branches of the legislature, in a matter which entirely concerned itself, and its constituents in their elections; though every application risked at least the mortification of a refusal; and that in our own times place-bills, and pension-bills, have been tendered at the bar of the House of Lords from year to year, though their only object was the independency of the House of Commons. That the great patriots who tendered those bills, never dreamed of the doctrine now set up, which tells us, that any restraint declared by the House, derives sufficient authority from that declaration, and is good in law.

That instances may be brought of experiments made, how far a vote of the House might be effectual, where the vote has been afterwards dropped, and the effect obtained by an act of parliament. That in particular, April 2, 1677, the House came to a resolution to prevent expences in elections after the teste of the writ, much in the same words as in the act afterwards passed, 7 Will. 3. This was made the standing order of the House at that time. It was renewed and confirmed as such, May 28, and October 21, 1678. But, to give it effect, it became necessary to pass an act of parliament for that purpose, six years after the Revolution.

That the House of Commons has the right, incidental to its judicature, of declaring what incapacities are legal. But it behoves the House to take care, that, instead of exercising the powers which it has, it assume not those which it has not; that from the temperate and judicious use of a legal power, vested in it for the benefit of the people, it swell not to the utmost pitch of extravagance and despotism, and make the law, under pretence of declaring it.

It was shewn that Mr. Wilkes was not, by any construction whatever, under any legal disability. That there are an infinite number of cases, in which the expediency of new powers in magistrates, courts of justice, and either House of Parliament, are apparent. But these powers cannot be assumed. They must be derived from a superior authority to an inferior; from the legislature to either House of Parliament. That there is a manifest difference between expulsion and disability; and that we must totally forget the common sense and meaning of words, if we can persuade ourselves that expulsion, which is the less degree of punishment, involves disability, which is the greater; and that the same difference between the sense of these words in common language, has in a parliamentary sense been constantly observed by the House of Commons.

The causes of expulsion were examined; it was said, that the charge against Mr. Wilkes, was so accumulated, that it was difficult to say precisely for what he was expelled; and that it was probable, if the question had been put separately for each offence contained in that charge, judgment of expulsion might not have passed for either. That the first offence contained in the general charge, was the publication of the North-Briton; which had been taken up by a former parliament, and for which he had been then punished by expulsion. That being punished by a former parliament, he could not be brought a second time to punishment in this parliament for the same offence, and that it would be an imputation on the justice of the House to suppose it. The second offence, was the publication of an impious and obscene libel, which had been taken up by the House of Lords in a former parliament, and for which he had been convicted and punished; but which was no offence against the House of Commons, nor in any respect within its criminal jurisdiction. The third and last offence, was the libel contained in the introductory preface to lord Weymouth's letter: however this may be understood as a libel, it was said not to be one of those offences, which are within the criminal jurisdiction of the House of Commons.

The precedents of disability founded upon former resolutions, were strictly examined; it was shewn that some of them overthrow themselves; that nobody can rely on the authority of proceedings in which there appears a manifest abuse, a daring illegality, and a slavish submission to power: such proceedings are vicious in the whole as well as in part; and ought never to be quoted in order to be followed. That others were established in the most violent times, when every day produced new invasions of the constitution. That in the year 1642, the precedents grow upon us so abundantly, as to lose all pretence to authority. That 49 members were expelled in two months only of that year, and most or all of them rendered incapable of sitting: that the majority then were clearing the House of their obnoxious brethren; and that to render their policy complete, and better secure to their order of incapacity the effect intended, new writs were seldom issued at the time of the expulsion; and frequently were not issued at all.

That order arose out of this confusion; and that from the Restoration to the present time, the sentence or punishment has never gone beyond expulsion, except in a few instances of members disabled from being elected at particular boroughs, on proof of a corrupt influence obtained in them.

That the power of expulsion is sufficiently great: it may be used to disgrace, to harass, to ruin an individual; but it carries with it no public danger. If the House abuse its power in the execution of it, the electors have their remedy, by re-electing the expelled member. But when incapacity of being re-elected is super-added to the expulsion, it is no longer the case of an individual; the rights of the electors are most materially affected. A stop is put to the freedom of their election. The number of persons open to their choice is diminished; and though that diminution is in one only, that single person may be their first favourite, and perhaps on that account rendered incapable. Nor does the evil stop here. The elected learn to taste the sweets of culling their company, not only by removing troublesome opponents, but barring their re-entry; and by putting a negative on the first interest in any place, make room for the second. That reason cries aloud against such a power in any set of men whatever. Happily she is opposed by no considerable list of precedents, except in 18 years of confusion from 1642 to 1660. That when we see this power so seldom exercised in old times, so grossly abused when it was, and so entirely abandoned since, we cannot but conclude that usage disclaims the power as much as reason protests against it, and that it does not exist in our constitution.

Such were a few of the many arguments urged with great force and energy on this side of the question. On the other side it was said, That the House of Commons had long been allowed a power of expelling their own members, and that unless the person expelled was to be excluded, the power of expulsion was wholly useless, and tended rather to expose the House of Commons to contempt, than to increase its dignity or importance. That the right claimed by the freeholders of Middlesex, was no other than the right of doing wrong, of sending a member to parliament, who was certainly ineligible in the eye of reason, however he might be deemed returnable in the judgment of the law. That if the House was obliged by the constitution to receive all persons who were returned by a majority of freeholders, and who were qualified according to law, the freeholders were equally bound not to return improper persons. That the law could not foresee all possible cases; but that if it could have been thought, that the freeholders would have made an injudicious, improper, or dangerous use, of this great privilege of election, the constitution would not have entrusted them with it. That our wise ancestors by no means intended, that infidels should be the guardians of our religion, beggars the protectors of our property, or convicts the framers of our laws.

That the House of Commons is the sole court of judicature in all cases of election. That this authority is derived from the first principles of our government; viz. the necessary independence of the three branches of the legislature. Did any other body of men possess this power, members might be obtruded upon the House, and their resolutions might be influenced under colour of determining elections. They have therefore an exclusive jurisdiction, and must be in all these cases the dernier resort of justice. That the House in the present case is the competent judge of disability, and that their decision on it is final; that if in this, or any other instance, its decisions were found to be attended with prejudice, the united branches of the legislature in their supreme and collective capacity, might interpose, and by passing a law regulate such decisions for the future; but that nothing less could restrict their authority.

It is asked, under what head of legal disability, is the present expulsion to be found? How are the electors to know it? The answer is easy: the records of parliament will inform them. How have they learnt, that judges of the superior courts cannot be chosen representatives of the people? How are aliens? How are clergymen disqualified? The House has adjudged them incapable as the several questions occurred.

It was said, that a very extraordinary principle had been adopted in the course of this debate, as if the Commons wanted to infringe upon the liberties of the people, without recollecting, that the Commons and the people are virtually the same, and that any endeavour to make them separate bodies, is no less dangerous than it is preposterous. If the Commons in their representative capacity have privileges which render them important, that importance increases the consequence of the people in their capacity of delegation; the people cannot be secure, unless the Commons are secure; they are inseparably connected both in interest and in freedom; and though upon some occasions the privilege of parliament may be a seeming oppression to individuals, the loss of it would be attended with very fatal effects to the whole community. That if the House of Commons had not in their collective capacity a title to peculiar privileges, no one member in his individual character could claim them with the smallest degree of propriety; yet individuals hourly claimed them with confidence, and they were admitted by the law of the land.

That nothing could be more misrepresented, than by saying that this measure was an injury to the freeholders of Middlesex. That on the contrary the injury was attempted on their side, who would obtrude an improper person on the House as a member, and obstinately persevere in this attempt, though all England was open to them for the choice of a proper person. That the supposed violation of right, in returning a person with a manifest inferiority of votes, will vanish, if the subject is properly considered, and a liberal construction put upon the law. That those who obstinately and wilfully persevere in voting for an unqualified person, are to be considered as not voting at all; their right of suffrage is acknowledged; but if the elector obstinately refuses to exercise this right according to law, he wantonly suspends his own right for the time, and his act being illegal is consequently void, and he is only in the situation of a man who had neglected to attend; he suffers no injury, he knows the consequence of what he does, and if he chuses to indulge his humour, it cannot even be counted a hardship. That an unqualified candidate can be no candidate; and that it is so evident that votes given to a person incapable by law of receiving them, must in their nature be null and void, that it is surprising how any body can dispute it.

These arguments were supported by a long train of precedents, shewing the usage of the House in a number of cases under the two heads of exclusion and expulsion. The former cases came generally within the line which has before been animadverted upon; the inferences drawn from the latter were greatly controverted, and in some instances, particularly the case of sir Robert Walpole, were shewn to overthrow the principle which they were brought to establish.

Commons debates on the unauthorized printing of parliamentary speeches and the apprehension of the printers responsible, 8 February-25 March 1771

Parliamentary History, XVII, 59-71, 73-77, 96-105, 109-10, 113-14, 120-24, 139-49, 155.

The failure of the Commons to enforce its privileges in this area led to the de facto legalization of parliamentary reporting from this time onward.

Colonel George Onslow made a Complaint to the House, of the printed Newspapers, entitled, "The Gazetteer and New Daily Advertiser, Friday, February 8, 1771," printed for R. Thompson; and also of the printed Newspaper, intituled, "The Middlesex Journal, or Chronicle of Liberty, from Tuesday, February 5, to Thursday, February 7, 1771," printed for J. Wheble; as misrepresenting the Speeches, and reflecting on several of the members of this House, in contempt of the order, and in breach of the privilege, of the House. He read a paragraph from the said Papers, in which he was said to have made a motion to stop the liberty of the press, by preventing the Speeches of the members being printed during the session. He moved that it might be read, and the printers brought to justice for infringing a standing order of the House, against printing, in newspapers, the transactions of the House of Commons. It was observed, that this practice had got to an infamous height; that members were represented to the world as saying what they did not say; and that their interests in their boroughs were often hurt by it: that it had never been done in former times; even in the most violent opposition to sir Robert Walpole, no transaction or speeches were published, except during the intervals of parliament, and then only in a decent manner. That it was now absolutely necessary either to punish the offenders severely, or revise the standing order.

The gentlemen in the minority acknowledged the abuse of the press in the present instance, but observed, that Cinna, and some other ministerial writers, were amongst the foremost in abusing, personally, the most respectable gentlemen who differed from them. That prosecutions of this nature would only promote the sale of the libels, not put an end to the practice, as was seen in the case of Bingley: that perhaps it might be difficult to found a prosecution for publishing the Speeches of members of parliament which never were made, and therefore were no speeches: that this was far from a new practice, having been authorized by Charles 1, whose minister, lord Clarendon, had made speeches, and published them as made by members of parliament, merely to misrepresent those members: that the practice of letting the constituents know the parliamentary behaviour of their representatives, was founded on the truest principles of the constitution, who even ought to know the particular votes they gave in every case, as the constituents had no other powers over their representatives, when once chosen, but to determine whether they were proper to be re-elected. That misrepresentations of any member were infamous, but ought to be punished legally by the member so affected, and not by the hand of power and weight of the legislature, whose exercise of power was always odious and oppressive.

The question being put, that the said Papers be delivered in at the table, the House divided. The Yeas went forth.

Tellers

Yeas { Colonel Onslow
      { Mr. Dundas   } 90

Noes { Sir William Meredith }
     { Mr. Turner   } 55

So it was resolved in the affirmative. And the said papers were delivered in at the table accordingly; and several paragraphs therein were read.

Ordered, That the said R. Thompson and J. Wheble do attend this House upon Monday next.

February 26

The several orders of the day, for the attendance of R. Thompson and J. Wheble, being read; and the said R. Thompson and J. Wheble not attending, according to order, the messenger, to whom the said orders were delivered, being called upon, to give an account of the service thereof, acquainted the House, that he went to the house of the said J. Wheble, in Paternoster-row, on Thursday evening last; and being informed by his servant that he was not at home, he shewed the said servant the original order for the attendance of the said J. Wheble, and left a copy thereof with the said servant, and desired him to give the same to his master when he came home; which the said servant promised to do.

The said messenger also acquainted the House, That he went to the house of the said R. Thompson, in Newgate-street, on Thursday evening last; that he was told he was not at home; and that then he shewed the original order for the attendance of the said R. Thompson to, and left a copy thereof with, his servant, and desired him to give the same to his master; which he likewise promised to do.

A motion was made, "That the said John Wheble be, for his contempt, in not obeying the order of this House, for his attendance on the House this day, taken into the custody of the Serjeant at Arms, or his deputy, attending this House."

This was opposed, as vindicating a matter bad in itself, and impolitic in the present situation of affairs, when every violent exercise of power met with the detestation of all good men; that those powers of the House to punish had been usurped by the House at times when they were principally made use of to preserve the independence of it from the crown, and at a time when the short duration of parliaments made that power less dreaded than the present.—The short answer was, that the House having made the order, it must be vindicated.

March 4

The deputy Serjeant at Arms being called upon to give an account of the service of the orders of the House of Tuesday last, for taking into custody John Wheble and

R. Thompson, acquainted the House, that, though he had been several times at their respective houses, and had made diligent search after them, in order to take them into custody, he had not yet been able to meet with either of them.

On the motion of Colonel Onslow, it was resolved, That an humble Address be presented to his Majesty, that he will be graciously pleased to issue his royal proclamation, for apprehending the said John Wheble and R. Thompson, with a promise of reward for the same.

March 12

Colonel Onslow finding himself disappointed in his attempt to punish the two printers, rose this day in his place, and said he had three brace of printers more. He then made complaint to the House, of the printed news-paper, intituled, The Morning Chronicle, and London Advertiser, Monday, March 4, 1771, printed for William Woodfall; The St. James's Chronicle, or British Evening Post, from Thursday, March 7, to Saturday March 9, 1771, printed by Henry Baldwin; The London Packet, or New Evening Post, from Wednesday, February 27, to Friday March 1, 1771, printed for T. Evans; The Whitehall Evening Post, from Thursday, February 28, to Saturday, March 2, 1771, printed and sold by T. Wright; The General Evening Post (London) from Thursday, March 7, to Saturday, March 9, 1771, sold by S. Bladon; and The London Evening Post, from Thursday, March 7, to Saturday March 9, 1771, printed for J. Miller; as containing the Debates, and misrepresenting the Speeches of several of the members, of this House, in contempt of the orders, and in breach of the privilege, of this House. He then moved, "That the paper, intituled, The Morning Chronicle, and London Advertiser, Monday, March 4, 1771, printed for William Woodfall, be delivered in at the table and read."

The minority opposed this with great earnestness: they wished the ministry to consider, that they had already attempted to punish two printers who had hitherto eluded their vigilance, and probably would in the end gain a victory over the House; that the honour and dignity of parliament should never be committed on so slight a ground as that of a general order; that the House ought to consider well before it took the first step, as on that depended the whole success; that the speeches printed, were no disgrace to the members for whom they were made, and as those members did not make any particular complaint of the injuries done them, the House in general had no reason to take it up; that many of the papers were disguised with blanks, disguised names, etc. which the House were not yet enabled to fill up; that the whole news-writers in every part of England, were liable to the same prosecutions, and their number was near 200; if all were prosecuted, what possible time could the House have to do any other business, than that of indulging the hon. gentleman's inclination for persecution; that he had something the appearance of the character of sir Gregory Gazette in the play, whose passion for newspapers made him exclaim, "What 100 newspapers in one day!" that this was attacking a hive of bees or an hydra, who would sprout 100 heads for one cut off. However, the House divided. The Yeas went forth.

Tellers

Yeas	{ Mr. Onslow { Mr. Cooper	}	140
Noes	{ Sir Joseph Mawbey { Mr. Hussey	}	43

So it was resolved in the affirmative. And the said paper was delivered in at the table accordingly; and several paragraphs therein were read.

Ordered, That the said William Woodfall do attend this House upon Thursday next.

March 16

J. Miller, printer of the London Evening Post, was, between the hours of two and three in the afternoon, assaulted and made a prisoner in his own house, by William Whittam, a messenger of the House of Commons. He sent directly for a constable, to whom he gave the messenger in charge, and the messenger did the same by him. They proceeded together, and with several other persons who were witnesses of the transaction, to Guildhall: but the sitting justice, Mr. Alderman Wilkes, having dispatched the business of the day, and signed the rota book, was gone to the Mansion-house. They went immediately there, and made application to the lord mayor, who was in his bed-chamber ill of the gout. The messenger desired that he might have leave to send to John Clementson, esq. deputy serjeant at arms, which was granted; and the lord mayor adjourned the hearing of the business till six in the evening. At that hour the lord mayor, and the aldermen Wilkes and Oliver, heard the cause in his lordship's bed-chamber, Mr. Clementson being present, as well as the messenger, the printer, Robert Morris, esq. as his counsel, and many other persons. Mr. Clementson said, he came from the Speaker of the House of Commons, to demand both the messenger and Mr. Miller, the printer; which demand was refused by the lord mayor, and the refusal minuted down by the serjeant in a book. The lord mayor demanded of the messenger, what his accusation was against Miller, and by what right he had apprehended one of his citizens; and if he was a peace-officer in the city. The messenger declared, that he did not accuse Miller of any thing criminal, but had taken him into custody by virtue of an order of the House of Commons. The lord mayor demanded to see the order, which, after much altercation, was given in by Mr. Clementson. Mr. Morris then argued the whole cause very ably, and insisted particularly on the invalidity of such a warrant. Mr. Clementson desired to confine himself to its being signed by sir Fletcher Norton, Speaker of the House of Commons, and to the two demands he then made, of the messenger and Mr. Miller being delivered to him. The lord mayor then, and the aldermen Wilkes and Oliver, discharged Mr. Miller from the custody of the messenger. They proceeded next to the complaint of the publisher for the assault and false imprisonment, which was clearly proved by the evidence of John Topping, and Robert and Henry Page. The messenger called no witness, and Mr. Clementson admitted the facts. The lord mayor then asked the messenger for bail to answer the complaint; but he said he had none; and Mr. Clementson declared, that the messenger should not give bail. On this refusal the lord mayor and the two aldermen signed the Mittimus of the messenger of the House of Commons to the Compter. As soon as this was done, Mr. Clementson said, "I waited for this: and now I see the warrant of commitment actually signed, I will offer bail;" upon which the messenger was bound over for his appearance in a recognizance of 40*l.* with two sureties in 20*l.* each, and the printer in a recognizance of 40*l.* to prosecute for the assault and false imprisonment. Almost every man in the room offered to be bail for the messenger. The Mansion-house was exceedingly full of people, but not the least confusion or disturbance happened.

March 18

Mr. Speaker acquainted the House, that he having, in pursuance of the order of the House of Thursday last, issued his warrant to the Serjeant at Arms, or his deputy, attending this House, to take into custody J. Miller; the messenger, to whom the said warrant was delivered, had, by virtue thereof, arrested the said J. Miller on Friday last; and that thereupon the said messenger having been charged in custody of a constable by the said J. Miller, as having committed an assault on the person of the said J. Miller, the said messenger was carried before the lord mayor of the city of London, by the said constable; when the deputy Serjeant at Arms attending this House acquainted the said lord mayor, that the said arrest of the said J. Miller was made by the said messenger under a warrant signed by the Speaker of the House of Commons, which warrant was there produced, and shewn to the said lord mayor; and demanded of the said lord mayor, that the said messenger should be discharged, and the said J. Miller delivered up to the custody of the said messenger; and that the said lord mayor, after such information and demand as aforesaid, having heard the several parties so brought before him, and seen the warrant signed by the Speaker for the apprehension of the said J. Miller, declared it to be his opinion, that the said warrant was illegal, and that the said J. Miller ought to be discharged, and ordered him to be discharged accordingly; and that a warrant of commitment was also signed by the said lord mayor and two aldermen of the city of London, to commit the said messenger for the assault pretended to be made on the said J. Miller; and that the said messenger had given security for his appearance to answer the said charge at the next general quarter sessions of the peace to be held for the city of London.

The Deputy Serjeant at Arms was called in. The following is the substance of his examination.

It appeared that on the 15th of March, 1771, the deputy-serjeant of the House of Commons went to the Mansion-house, and was introduced to the lord-mayor in his bed-chamber: he told him he understood that a messenger of the House of Commons, to whom a warrant for apprehending one Miller, a printer, was directed, was taken up by a constable, and charged with an assault: he therefore desired to know, if the messenger had been brought before him. The lord mayor said, he had been told that a person, who was called a messenger of the House of Commons, had been brought there, and charged with an assault, but that he had put it off till six o'clock. The deputy serjeant waited in an ante-room till six o'clock. The messenger came, and Miller, and a constable (John Downe), and a large concourse of people: then they went into my lord mayor (alderman Wilkes and alderman Oliver were there with him.) The lord mayor asked what was the purpose of their coming thither; Miller said he charged Whitham, the messenger, with an assault: on this, Mr. Robert Morris appeared, and said he was counsel for Miller, the prosecutor; he said, that Miller had been violently assaulted, and falsely imprisoned, by an illegal warrant. Downe, the constable, (who was asked for by the lord mayor) said, Miller had applied to him about one or two o'clock, and had complained of an assault committed on him in his own house, by the messenger, and charged him to take the messenger into custody; he therefore took him into custody, in order to carry him before a proper magistrate.

Miller was then called upon, who said, that a person, who called himself a messenger of the House of Commons, came to him, and took him into custody, by virtue of a pretended warrant. Miller was then sworn by the lord mayor, and said upon his oath, that what he had before said was true: he went on, and said he had refused to go with the person; that the person had used violence, and had seized hold of him, and was pulling him along. The lord mayor asked the messenger what offence Miller had committed, or what authority he had for assaulting Miller in this manner: the messenger said, he had the Speaker's warrant directed to him to take Miller into custody. The lord mayor asked where the warrant was; the deputy serjeant told Whitham to open it and read it himself. The lord mayor, or Mr. Morris (the deputy could not tell which), said, that it must be produced; the deputy objected to it for some time; but the lord mayor saying it could not be taken notice of, if not produced, the deputy serjeant delivered it to the lord mayor, on his promising to deliver it back to him again. The deputy waited till that time to see the nature of the assault charged on Whitham; and finding that it was for executing the warrant for taking Miller into custody, he then told the lord mayor, that he appeared before him as deputy serjeant at arms of the House of Commons; that he came there by the Speaker's directions, and that he had his commands to demand not only Whitham the messenger, but likewise Miller, his prisoner, and that he made that demand in the most solemn manner he was able. Mr. Morris, on this, desired that the deputy might be sworn as an evidence: he declared that he would not be sworn, and said, he did not come as an evidence, but as an officer of the House of Commons, to execute the commands given him by the Speaker. The lord mayor said, he could not take notice of any thing in his magisterial capacity that was not given upon oath. The deputy was then asked by Mr. Morris, if he refused to be examined to any of the facts or circumstances within his knowledge: the deputy doubted at first what answer to give to that; but on recollection he said, if there was the least doubt either of the warrant being signed by the Speaker, or of his having the Speaker's commands to demand Whitham the messenger, and Miller his prisoner, he was ready to be sworn to the truth of those matters, but that he would not be sworn generally. Finding that to be his resolution, Mr. Morris declined swearing him as to those matters; but the deputy again repeated, that if there was any doubt as to those matters, he was ready to swear to them.

The lord mayor asked Whitham, if he was a peace-officer, or a constable? He said, he was not; and further, if he had applied to any city magistrate to back his warrant? He said, he had not. Upon this, the lord mayor declared, that it was very extraordinary for any citizen to be taken up in the city of London, without the knowledge or authority of the lord mayor, or some other magistrate of the city; and that if this was permitted to be the case, it would be trampling on the laws, and there would be an end of the rights of this city.

Then Miller was examined as to his being a liveryman of the city of London. The lord mayor said, it was his opinion, that no warrant but from him, or some other magistrate of the city, was good and valid to take up any citizen; that he thought himself bound, so long as he held the great office of chief magistrate of the city of London, to take notice of a proceeding of this sort; and that it was his duty to defend the citizens of London, and their rights and liberties, to the last extremity. He said, he was of opinion, the messenger had no right to take up Miller, who was a citizen, not being charged with any felony, trespass, or breach of the peace.

Mr. Morris then made four objections to the warrant. 1st, That the words (House of Commons) was not a sufficient description of the power which had passed the vote.—That it should have been the House of Commons in parliament assembled. 2dly, That J. Miller was no sufficient description of the person. 3dly, That the offence was not inserted; and therefore that it was illegal, and without colour of law. 4thly, That it did not appear that Flr. Norton, Speaker, who signed the warrant, was the sir Fletcher Norton who was Speaker of the House of Commons.

The lord mayor then asked Whitham, if he intended to carry Miller away as his prisoner? Whitham said, he did.

The lord mayor then said, he thought the warrant was illegal; and therefore he discharged Miller out of the custody of the messenger; and said at the same time, This citizen comes here to claim a citizen's protection of me, and I think he is entitled to it.

Then the lord mayor proceeded on the assault.—Miller proved, that Whitham had laid hold of his arm, and pulled him; and that in about five minutes afterwards the constable came.—After this three persons were produced to prove the assault. These persons were, Henry Page, of Newgate-street, printer: John Topping, of the Old Bailey, printer; Robert Page, of Newgate-street, printer. They proved that Whitham laid hold of Miller's arm, and said, he was his prisoner; and that Miller said he should not go, or did not choose to go—That Whitham said, you must go, and Miller said he should not; and then Whitham charged every body present to assist him. After this the constable was brought, and the constable charged all present to assist him.

The lord mayor on this gave it as his opinion, That the assault was fully proved, and that Whitham must give security to appear at the next session for the city of London, to answer such indictments as should be then found against him, for the assault and false imprisonment; himself in forty, and two sureties in twenty pounds each; and Miller was to be bound to appear, and make out the charge.—Mr. Morris, and many others present, were ready to be bail for Whitham—Whitham was very much frightened, and was ready to offer bail: but the deputy serjeant insisted he should not give bail. The lord mayor desired it might be noticed, that bail was offered, but not accepted by Whitham.

Then the lord mayor directed a warrant to be made out for committing Whitham to the Compter. On this Mr. Morris desired, that the other two aldermen might sign the warrant, as well as his lordship; else it might be supposed that they did not concur in opinion with his lordship. The lord mayor said, he did not desire any body else to sign it; though the two aldermen declared themselves ready to do it. The warrant, however, was directed to be altered, by the clerk, into the plural number, and was signed by aldermen Wilkes and Oliver. He (the deputy) then asked the lord mayor, if it was signed by them all? The lord mayor said it was; and directions were given by him and Mr. Wilkes, to the constable, that he might be used kindly in prison. Just before they were going to take him away, the deputy said, he thought that this being a commitment he had gone far enough; and then he offered bail. The lord mayor grew warm at this, and said, he found that this proceeding was meant to exaggerate the offence. After this was done, the deputy went back immediately to the Speaker, and told him all that had happened.

March 19

The lord mayor came from the city, attended by a great crowd of respectable people, as the supporter of their liberties.

The evidence, which was yesterday given to the House by the Deputy Serjeant at Arms attending this House, was read; and the said Deputy Serjeant at Arms was further examined by the said lord mayor.

And then the *Lord Mayor* was heard in his place as follows: At the time I was admitted an alderman of the city of London, I took a solemn oath, that I would protect the city of London in their franchises and rights: I have ever done so to the best of my abilities. When I was admitted into the office of lord mayor, I was sworn in the same manner. This brought to my remembrance what a charge I had taken upon myself, to defend the people who were under my particular jurisdiction. I knew that my government, in discharge of the office I was chosen into, was to be from the laws and charters, granted, from time to time, to the citizens of London. By these charters it appears, that no warrant, commands, process, or attachment, shall be executed within the city of London, but by the ministers of the same city. At the time the messenger was brought before me, I asked him particularly, if he was a constable of the city of London, or a peace officer? He said he was not. I then asked him, whether he had applied to any alderman of the city of London to back the warrant, that it might be properly executed? He said he had not. The several charters granted to the city of London have been confirmed by act of parliament, made in the reign of William and Mary. I knew extremely well, that if I had not acted in the manner I did, in discharging that person, I should have been guilty of perjury, or of a breach of my oath; I therefore thought it too conscientious a matter, which was the reason of my acting as I did. Next to supporting and executing the duties of my office of chief magistrate, the duty I owe is to this House: and I should be as tender as any member of this House of the liberties of the Commons of England. But when I knew that my first and grand tie was that of a magistrate of the city of London; that I thought was, by the oath I had taken, my first duty. I think I have done no more than my duty. I hope this House will be of that opinion. With respect to the commitment, I did sign such a warrant; but at the same time, I rather desired the person might be admitted to bail, which I much pressed. But your officer refused to give bail, though several gentlemen, then present at the Mansion-house, offered to become bail. As this is the state of the matter, I entirely submit to the justice of the House of Commons; but, at the same time, I must glory in my own breast, in having executed what I was sworn to do, at the time of my first becoming a magistrate. If I had gone no further than discharging Miller, and had not proceeded to commit the messenger for the assault, I apprehend I was liable to be called upon in the court of King's-bench, for not executing my duty as a magistrate. This House will, I am persuaded, be very tender, when they find on what motive I acted—I mean the obligation, by the oath I took when I first appointed a magistrate.

[March 20]

The order of the day being read, for the attendance of John Wilkes, esq. alderman of London,

Sir Joseph Mawbey said: When I made the motion originally for the attendance of Mr. Wilkes, I did it without any communication, directly or indirectly, with him on the subject, and without knowing whether it would or would not be agreeable to him. I desired this attendance, because he appeared to me to be equally criminal, if any criminality had been incurred, which I deny, with the worthy chief magistrate, who has been ordered to attend in his place: he was aiding, assisting, and advising in the steps that led to the commitment of the messenger for an assault, which has given such umbrage to the House. I will go farther, and say, though it has not yet come out in evidence before the House, that every gentleman knows, that after this House had addressed the crown to advertise a reward for apprehending the printers, and when, in consequence of a proclamation for that purpose, one of them was so apprehended, Mr. Wilkes first began the insult on what you call your privilege, discharged the printer, and bound the person over in a recognizance to answer for such apprehension. If any thing criminal has been done, he is certainly the greatest criminal; and yet gentlemen who have felt so much for the honour and privilege of the House, betrayed a disposition to take no sort of notice of him. I thought he should be ordered to attend, and, in consequence, he was directed to attend this day. I have not seen him since; but when I came to attend my duty here, I had this letter put into my hands in the lobby, by a gentleman sent by him, which is now unopened, and which I was desired to deliver to the Speaker in the name of Mr. Wilkes: I deliver it accordingly, and desire it may be read.

Mr. Speaker.—I must complain to the House of the hon. gentleman's disrespect to me personally, and of the indignity offered to the House, in not delivering sooner the letter into my hands; he ought in candour to have given it me earlier in the day; I will not look at the contents, it shall not be opened now—it is using me with want of respect; and I submit to the House, whether the hon. gentleman's conduct does not deserve reprehension. How can I tell whether the letter be proper or not to be communicated to the House till I have read it? I have received many letters lately, the contents of which have been very improper. . . .

The following is a Copy of Mr. Wilkes's Letter to the Speaker:

London, March 20, 1771

Sir; I this morning received an order, commanding my attendance this day in the House of Commons. I observe that no notice is taken of me in your order as a member of the House, and that I am not required to attend in my place. Both these circumstances, according to the settled form, ought to have been mentioned in my case, and I hold them absolutely indispensible. In the name of the freeholders of Middlesex I again demand my seat in parliament, having the honour of being freely chosen, by a very great majority, one of the representatives for the said county. I am ready to take the oaths, prescribed by law, and to give in my qualification as knight of the shire. When I have been admitted to my seat, I will immediately give the House the most exact detail, which will necessarily comprehend a full justification of my conduct relative to the late illegal proclamation, equally injurious to the honour of the crown, and the rights of the subject, and likewise the whole business of the printers. I have acted entirely from a sense of duty to this great city, whose franchises I am sworn to maintain, and to my country, whose noble constitution I reverence, and whose liberties, at the price of my blood, at the last moment of my life, I will defend and support.

I am, Sir, your most humble servant,

John Wilkes

March 25

The several orders of the day being read, for the attendance of Brass Crosby, esq. lord mayor of London, and Richard Oliver, esq. alderman of the city of London, in their places;

And the *Lord Mayor* attending accordingly in his place, acquainted the House, that he had received the Resolution of this House of Friday last, for allowing him liberty to be heard, by his counsel, upon all such points as do not controvert the privileges of this House; but that finding the counsel were, by that Resolution, restrained from speaking to many points material to his defence, and that the counsel he could depend upon, and whom he wished to employ, were on the circuit; he therefore would not give the House the trouble of hearing counsel on this occasion.

Then the evidence, which, upon Monday last, was given to the House, by the deputy Serjeant at Arms attending this House, was read; and the minutes of what the lord mayor had offered to the House, in his defence, upon Tuesday last, were also read.

And the original Charter, granted to the city of London, upon the 6th of March, in the first year of Edward 3, was produced, and read.

And the House being informed, that a person attended at the door, with a book, containing the oaths taken by the magistrates of the city of London; he was called in; and the book being produced, the copy of the oath taken by an alderman of the city of London, and also the oath of the lord mayor, were read. And then the lord mayor was further heard.

His lordship said, The House had now heard read the oaths he had taken as a magistrate of the city of London: he appealed to those oaths when he was here before; and he thought the House, now they had heard them read, would be satisfied that he could act no otherwise than he did, in doing right to every man who was brought before him: he gloried in having done that, and he was persuaded that every member of the House would be of the same opinion. But he must still further appeal, if it was necessary, that he had acted agreeably to the laws and constitution of his country, in protecting the liberties of the subject, which he saw most manifestly invaded. As he said before, he said then, that he appealed to the justice of the House.

Mr. Welbore Ellis then began. He observed, that the privileges in question were essential to the very being of this House, as without them the House could neither act in its judicial, legislative, or inquisitorial capacity; that they were a check to the power of the other branches of the legislature; that the cause of liberty was the cause of this House; if the powers of this House were weakened, liberty would be so too. As this power was necessary, so it was always acknowledged by the courts below, who always confirmed or did not dispute this power; that the practice of parliament was invariably the same; the ground of doubt was the charter of London, which gave or could give no power not inherent in the crown, and that the crown had no power over the privileges of this House; that the general order concerning the printers not printing the debates of the House was not a new thing; that it had been begun in 1641, and at different times renewed to this House. He then moved, "That the discharging out of the custody of one of the messengers of this House, J. Miller, (for whom the newspaper, entitled, 'The London Evening Post, from Thursday, March 7, to Saturday, March 9, 1771,' purports to be printed, and of which Paper a complaint was made in the House of Commons, on the 12th day of this instant March, and who, for his contempt, in not obeying the order of this House, for his attendance on the House upon Thursday the 14th instant, was ordered to be taken into the custody of the Serjeant at Arms, or his deputy, attending this House; and who, by virtue of the Speaker's warrant, issued under the said order, had been taken into the custody of the said messenger) is a breach of the privilege of this House."

Sir G. Savile opposed this motion, as the House had already gone too far, and what they had done tended to overturn the just power of the House. That the House of Commons might best be trusted with such a great power, but if the House was not the true representatives of the people, by so much the worse was any power in them. By denying counsel, or granting a meeting of counsel, the proceeding had been unjust and vitiated ab initio: that in this state he could not decide on the question now before the House, and should therefore move the previous question, to give time to the House, to revise their proceedings. He hoped, that whilst they were thus employed in underpinning or propping up the powers of the House, it would not tumble about their ears.

Alderman Townsend observed, that this question was between the people and their representatives; had he been in the lord mayor's situation, he would have done the same; that though this might be within the prerogative privileges of the House; whenever the former were extended at the expence of the people, he hoped the people would tear them from the House. He observed, that the King claimed also more prerogative to himself, as did also the House of Lords, witness their late illegal commitment and fine on Woodfall the printer; that all those prerogatives, joined to those claimed by the Commons would leave the people scarcely the shadow of liberty. It was the opinion of chief justice Holt, that the parliament at large could not create privileges against law, much less can the House of Commons. When the Commons used their privileges against the crown, the people joined with the parliament in supporting them, and at that time they had the force of laws; the same in their disputes with the House of Lords; but when used against the people, the people discontented would be alarmed for their liberty, "and by opposing end them." He apprehended there was a settled intention in government to root out the people's liberties; it had begun in modelling the House, and now extended to the liberty of the press, and shutting up courts of justice. There was a power greater than that of the King, which had of late controverted all administration, that of the princess of Wales, into whose influence over our councils the House ought to make enquiry.

The ministry opposed the previous question, observing, that the necessity of a power to send for persons, papers, and records, constituted the essence of the House of Commons; that their privileges were the privileges of the people, and to lessen them would ruin their liberty; that so long ago as 1641, the House had made resolutions in respect of publishing their proceedings or debates, which had been confirmed in after times at different periods; that as to counsel being heard, it would have been a new supposition in the House, which was so jealous of their privileges, as never to allow any discussion of them any where but in the House.

The House being informed of a tumultuous crowd, in Palace-yard, and in the passages leading to the House, who interrupted members in their coming into the House, the high constable of the city of Westminster was called in, and examined as to the said tumultuous crowd; and he acquainted the House, that he had done every thing in his power to disperse them, with the assistance of a great number of the constables of Westminster; but that all his endeavours had been in vain.

The House was moved, that the entry in the Journal of the House, of the 27th of February 1699, of the proceedings of the House, in relation to the information given to the House, of a crowd of people being got together, in a tumultuous and riotous manner, in the Palace-yard, Westminster-hall, and the passages to this House, might be read. And the same being read accordingly; and the House being informed, that several of the justices of the peace of Middlesex and Westminster attended, they were called in; and, at the bar, Mr. Speaker, by order of the House, acquainted them, that the House had received information of the said tumultuous crowd; and that the House did expect that they should, together with the other magistrates now sitting at the Guildhall of the city of Westminster, forthwith do every thing in their power to disperse that riotous crowd; and that they should, as soon as they were able, return, and inform the House what they had done in this matter. And then they withdrew.

And, after some time, the House being informed, that the said justices were again attending, they were called in; and, at the bar, acquainted the House, that they had, in obedience to the orders of the House, in a great measure dispersed the crowd, and cleared the passages for the members coming into the House; but that there was still a great crowd in the Court of Requests; and Mr. Speaker directed them still to attend, and to continue and use their endeavours to keep every thing quiet. And then they again withdrew.

The Lord Mayor then acquainting the House, that he found himself extremely ill; and therefore hoped that the House would dispense with his further attendance at present; but hoped the matter might go on in his absence; and that he should submit himself to every thing the House should do; he, with leave of the House, withdrew.

Then the said previous question being put, That the first proposed question be now put; the House divided. The Noes went forth.

Tellers

Yeas	Mr. Onslow	212	
	Mr. Charles Fox		
Noes	Mr. Byng	90	
	Mr. Seymour		

So it was resolved in the affirmative.

Then the main question being put;

Resolved, 1. That the discharging out of the custody of one of the messengers of this House J. Miller (for whom the newspaper, intituled, "The London Evening Post, from Thursday, March 7, to Saturday, March 9, 1771," purports to be printed, and of which paper a complaint was made in the House of Commons, on the 12th day of this instant March, and who, for his contempt, in not obeying the order of this House, for his attendance on the House upon Thursday the 14th day of this instant March, was ordered to be taken into the custody of the Serjeant at Arms, or his deputy, attending this House, and who, by virtue of the Speaker's warrant issued under the said order, had been taken into the custody of the said messenger) is a breach of the privilege of this House.

2. That the signing a warrant against the said messenger, for having executed the said warrant of the Speaker, is a breach of the privilege of this House.

3. That the holding the said messenger to bail, for having executed the said warrant of the Speaker, is a breach of the privilege of this House.

Mr. Wallace then proposed to proceed against Mr. Alderman Oliver.

Colonel Barré observed, that it was then near one in the morning; that no court of judicature in the world would proceed on a new trial at this hour: he therefore moved to adjourn.

The House divided. The Noes went forth.

Tellers

Yeas	{ Mr. Walsingham	}	97
	{ Mr. Baker		
Noes	{ Dr. Burrel	}	214
	{ Mr. Jolliffe		

So it passed in the negative.

Mr. Dunning: Sir; the hon. and learned gentleman who spoke last, has, in my opinion, misapprehended the ground of the debate: he concludes, because we have an authority to seize and commit in cases of treason, that we must necessarily have an equal authority in cases of less importance: but this reasoning is self-refutory to the meanest apprehension; for the punishment of particular crimes is left to the established courts of law, and we never interpose but in times of particular exigence, where there is a conspiracy against the state, or some reasonable ground of general alarm for the nation. To quit the legislative for the judicial character, upon trivial occasions, and to check the operations of law by the exercise of privilege, must ultimately sap the very foundation of the laws, undermine the pillars of legal rectitude, and overturn the glorious fabric of the constitution.

Sir, the great advantage of a legal government consists in the general knowledge which the people have of those ordinances by which they are governed. On this account Cicero, and the wisest of the ancient statesmen, condemned the ostracism of the Athenians, and those wanton exertions of privilege among the Romans, which, like our bills of attainder, left him to be punished by laws, which were instituted subsequent to the particular crime of which he was accused.

Sir, the principle at present adopted by the House, operates, in my opinion, as a perpetual bill of attainder. The subject does an action which he conceives to be innocent, because it is not prohibited by any specified law; the House of Commons disapproves this action, they order the man to be seized, commit him indefinitely to prison, and when he applies for redress to the courts of law, the judges are deaf to his complaint, because he has been oppressed by the privilege of parliament.

I know, Sir, it is urged, that without a power of punishing every contempt which is offered to your authority, there must be a speedy termination of your weight, if not of your actual existence. Give me leave, however, to observe, that while your authority is constitutionally exerted, it will always be implicitly obeyed; while you consult the good of the people, the people will consult your honour; but when you once manifest a spirit of despotism, they will manifest a spirit of resistance: the English are to be governed, but never to be oppressed: they are, in the language of the vulgar, to be led, but not driven; and they will always resist when they see a palpable attack upon the constitution.

As I speak, Sir, to support the cause of justice, and not to advance the views of any party whatever, I shall readily acknowledge, that the courts of law have acquired through necessity, a right of punishing contempts, because, without such an authority, there would be a total end of their jurisdiction. But even in the courts of law, I do not hesitate to pronounce the power contradictory to the principles of Magna Charta. The necessity, however, induces us to tolerate the invasion, for without such a toleration, every man would claim a privilege of obeying, or disobeying, the decision of our judges at his own discretion, and all, as the poet says, would consequently be "anarchy and uproar."

But, Sir, if punishing contempts in court, is a power which ought to be exercised with the nicest circumspection, and if nothing but the most indispensible necessity can thus properly make the benches of justice, judge and jurors in their own cause, how careful should we be, not to grant this power where the necessity does not exist, and where the exercise of it is as plainly repugnant to the letter of our laws, as to the spirit of our constitution. The hon. and learned member who spoke before me, says, that in England there are several kinds of law, and that when your messenger was apprehended by one law, he was discharged by another: this he insists to be apparently inequitable: but why will not gentlemen, when they talk about legal equity, tell us openly what it is? If we have privileges that must not be violated, in God's name let us tell the people what they are, that they may avoid the violation.

Sir; the House is, I own, in many cases the sole judge of its own privileges, but there are many others, in which if they come incidentally before a court, the judge must inevitably take them under his cognizance. Suppose, for instance, that the serjeant at arms, in executing your warrant upon the printers, had been killed, and that the homicides were afterwards tried for the fact; will any man say, Sir, that in such a case your privileges would not be cognizable before another jurisdiction? Will any man say, that the judge was not to enquire whether the warrant under which the serjeant acted was legal or illegal, or whether the homicide was a justifiable defence, or an absolute murder? Surely no man, who wishes to retain the constitutional mode of trying by jury, will be hardy enough to assert any thing like this; and if nothing like this is to be asserted, what becomes of the fashionable doctrine, that the Commons upon all occasions are the only expounders of their own privileges?

Sir, our whole constitution is a political kind of chaos, and depends upon the preservation of opposing elements; the King has his prerogative—the Peers their jurisdiction—and we our privileges: we are equal in legislative importance, even to the two hereditary estates, but we are not superior; we are independent with respect to them, but not so with relation to the people; the people were the original spring from which the three streams of government proceeded, and must in fact be paramount to all. They will therefore naturally enquire how we, their representatives particularly, have executed our trust, and will as naturally execrate our names.

If once we vilely turn that very power,
Which we derive from popular esteem,
To sap the bulwarks of the public freedom.

Sir; the people have already opposed us by their magistrates, and they will oppose us farther by their juries; though were we in fact as much respected as we are already despised; as much esteemed as we are universally detested, the establishment of tyranny in ourselves, who are appointed for no purpose but to repel it in others, would expose us to the abhorrence of every good Englishman. Let us, therefore, stop where we are; let us not justify oppression by oppression, nor forget our own posterity, if we are regardless of our country. Let even the abject principle of self, which actuates, I fear, too many of my auditors, for once operate in the cause of virtue. We have sons and we have daughters to leave behind us; they will have children, and these children will have their successive generations. Shackle them not, therefore, before they are born.

Sir; the best inheritance, which we can possibly bequeath our race, is freedom; in robbing our constituents of this inestimable blessing, we in fact take it away from our descendants, and make the creatures of their own hands the masters of their fortunes and their lives. It is a plausible argument, that the voice of the nation is only to be heard in this House; but plausibility does not necessarily imply justice, nor does this House constitute a real representative of the kingdom. The metropolis, for instance, which contains at least a sixth part of the people, has no more than four members; and many of the principal trading towns are wholly without a member: when this is recollected, Sir, and when it is moreover recollected, that the inadequacy of parliamentary representation is a subject of universal complaint, there is but a slender basis for asserting that our voice is the voice of the kingdom, and that as such it should be decisive in every deliberation.

I readily grant, Sir, that the sense of this House, whether agreeable or disagreeable to the sense of the people, is generally submitted to, and that the nation will endure much before it attempts to shake the load of oppression from its shoulders. The public is an unwieldy body; its operations are slow, and nothing can rouse it into action, but the most urgent call of necessity; yet, for this very reason, when it does move, its motion is a very serious circumstance; the more the subject is inclined to bear, the more we should be alarmed at his sensibility; when his patience is exhausted, we may conclude that his reasons for discontent are ample, and in proportion as he shews himself unwilling to murmur, in the same proportion we should shew our readiness to remove every source of his dissatisfaction.

Sir; the friends of administration, besides the fallacious mode of reasoning which I have here exposed, recur to another specious fallacy to countenance the oppression of government. We are told, that the various petitions presented to the throne for the dissolution of this parliament, are by no means to be regarded, because the majority of counties have not petitioned for this purpose. On the contrary, it is inferred that as the majority of counties have been silent, the complaints of those who have really talked of grievances must be considered only as the effusions of faction, fomented by the interested, and supported by the misled; that they are on the one hand excited by ambition, and on the other composed of ignorance, but on both repugnant to reason, and injurious to the real happiness of the kingdom. Superficial enquirers into the nature of public transactions, may, Sir, be deluded by a logic of this kind, yet it will have very little weight with those who have made a close examination into facts. The bulk of the people, Sir, is not to be estimated by the extent of miles, or the multiplication of counties. The metropolis, as I have already observed, contains in itself a sixth of our inhabitants, and if we reckon the petitioners, by the more rational criterion of the land tax, we shall find that they exceed the supposed friends of the ministry in numbers, by so considerable a sum as 25,000*l*. a year.

Why, then, Sir, are we to imagine, that the language of the late petitions is not the language of our constituents at large? Are there no murmurs, no discontents in the silent counties? Or have our gracious rulers practised no arts, to keep their uneasiness from the ear of their sovereign? We may labour to deceive ourselves, Sir, but our labours to deceive the public will be ineffectual. The minister will not meet that complaisance without doors, which he is so certain of meeting within; the very motion before the House is a proof of our being generally abhorred. The magistrates of London would not dare to resist our resolutions, if the nation was not evidently warmed with their sentiments, and thoroughly persuaded, that the existence of their freedom depends upon a determined opposition to the unwarrantable exercise of our authority. Perhaps, Sir, it may be said, our privileges are the privileges of those we represent, and that the political importance of the elector must be diminished, if the importance of the elected undergoes the smallest diminution. Let me again exhort gentlemen not to deceive themselves. Whenever the interest of the representative and the represented are one, their views must be one also. At present, however, their interests are as contrary as their views, and nothing but the very soul of absurdity could possibly affirm, that our encroachment on the rights of the subject, was absolutely requisite for the maintenance of his necessary weight in the constitution.

Sir; gentlemen are exceedingly indignant at the supposed temerity of the two magistrates, now labouring under the displeasure of the House; and ask, with a tone of resentful surprise, if the corporation of London is to be independent of the Commons regularly assembled in parliament? Why not, Sir, if the law has made them so? If the law has indulged the citizens with particular immunities, why are these immunities to be invaded? We sit here for the professed purpose of guarding the laws, not for the professed purpose of trampling them under foot: we ourselves are the creatures, not the masters of the constitution: we have no existence but a legal one; we can have no existence but a legal one, and consequently it is as weak as it is wicked in us to overleap the established bounds of legality.

Mr. Charles Fox: Sir; notwithstanding what the hon. gentleman who spoke last has been pleased to urge relative to the divided views, and the divided interests of the Commons and the people, he has not been able to convince me, either that the authority of this House is not the best security of the national freedom, or that our welfare can possibly be separated from the welfare of the public.

Sir; the hon. gentleman is pleased to say, that the voice of this House is not the voice of the people, and he sets the language of clamour without doors in opposition to our deliberations, as if we were not particularly appointed by the constitution, the only revealers of the national mind, the only judges of what ought to be the sentiments of the kingdom. I say, Sir, what ought to be, because many laws are highly necessary for the public safety, which excite the discontent of the people. If we were never to pass a law, till it obtained the sanction of popular approbation, we should never have a settled revenue to support either the establishment of our domestic policy, or to defend ourselves against the invasion of a foreign enemy. You never see a tax instituted, Sir, without hearing loud impeachments of parliamentary integrity. The uninformed zealots, who seem animated with an enthusiastic love for their country, generally charge us with having sold them to the minister; and we are accused of venality for imposing those burdens, which we know to be absolutely necessary, and to which we ourselves, if the House of Commons is supposed an assembly of the first property in the state, must always be the largest contributors.

Sir; it will possibly appear strange, that a representative of the people should not deem it more meritorious to comply with the wishes of his constituents, than to counteract them; and it may possibly be urged, that it is his duty, upon all occasions, to act in conformity to those wishes, however repugnant they may be to the sense of his own conviction. Sir, I will not differ with the hon. gentleman about the idea he annexes to his term of "the people;" I will, for argument sake, allow that nine tenths of the people are at this moment in opposition to government. But I shall at the same time insist, that we have higher obligations to justice, than to our constituents; we are chosen the delegates of the British electors for salutary not for pernicious purposes; to guard, not to invade the constitution: to keep the privileges of the very freemen we represent, as much within their proper limits, as to controul any unwarrantable exertion of the royal authority. We are bound to promote their true interests in preference to the dearest desires of their hearts, and the constitution makes us the sole arbiters of those interests, notwithstanding the imaginary infallibility of the people.

To shew, Sir, the propriety of this reasoning, let us suppose that the people, instead of this mixed monarchy, which we celebrate as equally the pride and envy of the universe, should instruct us, their representatives, to introduce a democratical form of government; should we act as good subjects to our king, or as faithful guardians to our country, if we complied with so dangerous an advice? We have sworn to maintain this constitution in its present form; to maintain the privileges of parliament as a necessary part of that constitution, and neither to encroach upon the legal jurisdiction of the peers, nor the just prerogatives of the sovereign. Shall we, then, do what we are sensible is wrong, because the people desire it? Shall we sacrifice our reason, our honour, and our conscience for fear of incurring the popular resentment, and while we are appointed to watch the Hesperian fruit of liberty with a dragon's eye, be ourselves the only slaves of the whole community?

Perhaps the hon. gentleman will tell me, that nothing but the "soul of absurdity" could suspect the people of a design against their own happiness. Sir, I do not suspect the people of any such design, but I suspect their capacity to judge of their true happiness. I know they are generally credulous, and generally uninformed; captivated by appearances, while they neglect the most important essentials, and always ridiculously ready to believe, that those men who have the greatest reason from their extensive property, to be anxious for the public safety, are always concerting measures for the oppression of their own posterity. Sir, if I misrepresent the people, whence spring those eternal terrors of being ruined, in the midst of the most unbounded prosperity? Have not we tottered, if popular clamour must be credited, upon the verge of ruin, since the first moment of our existence as a nation. Indeed, at the Revolution, patriotism itself acknowledges we were saved; yet from that period let us only read the works of our greatest politicians, and we shall find ourselves utterly undone. Even our glorious Deliverer was scarcely seated upon the throne, when the grateful people, whose liberties he had restored, began to consider him as an enemy to the constitution. In every succeeding reign we were destroyed, and at this moment, while exulting in all the pride of a felicity never known to our ancestors, we are planted in the deepest abyss of destruction.

Let us look around, Sir, let us survey the monuments of our ruin, and then ask what credit is due to the representations of our political screech-owls? Observe the magnificence of our metropolis—the extent of our empire—the immensity of our commerce and the opulence of our people; Survey the unfortunate citizens of London, Sir, and you will find every shop-keeper of any consideration, with his elegant villa, and his variety of equipages. Consider only the present opposition of the city to the whole body of the British legislature, and then judge how it must be oppressed! To shew you farther the ruined state of the kingdom, let me remind you that our territories occupy no more than the largest, the most valuable space of any European dominion in the four quarters of the globe; that our trade is proportioned to this superiority of empire, and that our subjects from the burning regions of Indostan, to the chilling mountains of Canada, exceed the subjects of every other power in greatness of wealth, and certainty of freedom. These, Sir, are the proofs of our declining fortune; may our calamities of this kind hourly encrease, though the people should still continue to murmur! and may we always remain the happiest nation under heaven, however offended our patriots may be, because we are not happier than is consistent with the lot of humanity!

From what I have advanced, Sir, with respect to our duty as representatives of the people, it naturally follows, that we are by no means to act against our own judgment merely to gratify the resentments of their ill-humour, or the whimsies of their caprice. In Charles the 1st's time the unlimited indulgence of the popular wish, was the destruction of the constitution; and, if the present allegations of popularity deserve the least weight, they shew what incompetent judges the people are of the public prosperity. The last parliament, Sir, was as obnoxious to the people, as this, in which we are now sitting, they approved what it is fashionable to term an 'infamous' peace, and they expelled a profligate libeller of their lawful sovereign; yet with all this weight of delinquency upon their heads, reviled and execrated as they were by the people, look round, and see who the people have chosen in their room. If we except deaths and promotions, Sir, are not the former traitors to a man, again the representative body of the legislature, again trusted with the freedom of the subject, and again the express election of the people? When we see these things, Sir, we are immediately struck with this alternative, either that the people are not judges of their own welfare, or that they have sold themselves for an infamous price to their members. In either case, the conclusion proves the little regard which should be paid to their complaints against the sense of our conviction. If they are virtuous, they are not wise; and if they possess wisdom, they have no right to find fault, since every oppression they groan under, is the natural result of their own scandalous dishonesty.

It is urged, Sir, with great gravity, by many gentlemen in opposition, that the House of Commons, as the creatures of the people, have no right whatever to exercise an authority over their constituents. This position, Sir, breathes the spirit of freedom with a vengeance, for it lays the axe to the root of all subordination at once, and puts an entire end to the whole system of constitutional government.

No doctrine, Sir, was ever yet broached in this kingdom, either so dangerous, or so ridiculous, as that which seriously insists that the House of Commons, because elected, is without jurisdiction, and that the people, because the origin of all power, must therefore be exempt from all obedience. The people make the laws, as well as the legislators; but will any advocate of licentiousness presume to say, because they are the fountain of authority, that they are of consequence discharged from a submission to legal institutions? The law, Sir, is as much the creature of their formation as this House; yet surely it will not be said, that they are to tread it under foot, or to launch out into the barbarisms of their natural state, after solemnly forming a compact of civil society.

The only point, therefore remaining to be discussed is, Whether the people at large, or this House, are the best judges of the public welfare? For my own part, Sir, I shall not hesitate to pronounce positively in favour of this House. What acquaintance have the people at large with the arcana of political rectitude, with the connections of kingdoms, the resources of national strength, the abilities of ministers, or even with their own dispositions? If we are to believe the very petitions which they have lately presented to the throne, they are unequal to those powers which the constitution has trusted to their hands. They have the power of electing their representatives; yet you see they constantly abuse this power, and appoint those as the guardians of their dearest rights, whom they accuse of conspiring against the interests of their country. For these reasons, Sir, I pay no regard whatever to the voice of the people: it is our duty to do what is proper, without considering what may be agreeable: their business is to chuse us; it is our business to act constitutionally, and to maintain the independency of parliament: whether it is attacked by the people or by the crown, is a matter of little consequence; it is the attack, not the quarter it proceeds from, which we are to punish; and if we are to be controuled in our necessary jurisdiction, can it signify much, whether faction intimidate us with a rabble; or the King surround us with his guards? If we are driven from the direct line of justice, by the threats of a mob, our existence is useless in the community. The minority within doors, need only assault us by their myrmidons without, to gain their ends upon every occasion. Blows will then carry what their arguments cannot effect, and the people will be their own agents, though they elect us to represent them in parliament. What must the consequence be? Universal anarchy, Sir. Therefore as we are chosen to defend order, I am for sending those magistrates to the Tower who have attempted to destroy it; I stand up for the constitution, not for the people; if the people attempt to invade the constitution, they are enemies to the nation. Being, therefore, Sir, convinced that we are to do justice, whether it is agreeable or disagreeable, I am for maintaining the independency of parliament, and will not be a rebel to my king, to my country, or my own heart, for the loudest huzza of an inconsiderate multitude. . . .

The question being put, that the words, "committed to the Tower of London," stand part of the question. The House divided. The Yeas went forth.

Tellers

Yeas { Mr. Onslow / Mr. Whately } 170

Noes { Mr. Pulteney / Mr. Hussey } 38

So it was resolved in the affirmative; and the House adjourned at half past three on the morning of the 26th.

Speech by Edmund Burke proposing a plan for reform of civil and other establishments, House of Commons, 11 February 1780

Parliamentary History, XXI, 11-18, 28-41, 63-72.

The abortive plan of retrenchment presented by Edmund Burke (1729-97) reflected widespread demands for a reduction of political patronage and of royal privileges.

These desires of the people of England, which come far short of the voluntary concessions of the king of France, are moderate indeed. They only contend that we should interweave some economy with the taxes with which we have chosen to begin the war. They request, not that you should rely upon economy exclusively, but that you should give it rank and precedence, in the order of the ways and means of this single session.

But if it were possible, that the desires of our constituents, desires which are at once so natural, and so very much tempered and subdued, should have no weight with a House of Commons, which has its eye elsewhere; I would turn my eyes to the very quarter to which theirs are directed. I would reason this matter with the House, on the mere policy of the question; and I would undertake to prove, that an early dereliction of abuse, is the direct interest of government; of government taken abstractedly from its duties, and considered merely as a system intending its own conservation.

If there is any one eminent criterion, which, above all the rest, distinguishes a wise government from an administration weak and improvident, it is this:—"well to know the best time and manner of yielding, what it is impossible to keep."—There have been, Sir, and there are, many who choose to chicane with their situation, rather than be instructed by it. Those gentlemen argue against every desire of reformation, upon the principles of a criminal prosecution. It is enough for them to justify their adherence to a pernicious system, that it is not of their contrivance; that it is an inheritance of absurdity, derived to them from their ancestors; that they can make out a long and unbroken pedigree of mismanagers that have gone before them. They are proud of the antiquity of their house; and they defend their errors, as if they were defending their inheritance: afraid of derogating from their nobility; and carefully avoiding a sort of blot in their scutcheon, which they think would degrade them for ever.

It was thus that the unfortunate Charles the 1st defended himself on the practice of the Stuart who went before him, and of all the Tudors; his partizans might have gone to the Plantagenets.—They might have found bad examples enough, both abroad and at home, that could have shewn an ancient and illustrious descent. But there is a time, when men will not suffer bad things because their ancestors have suffered worse. There is a time, when the hoary head of inveterate abuse will neither draw reverence nor obtain protection. If the noble lord in the blue ribbon pleads "Not guilty," to the charges brought against the present system of public economy, it is not possible to give a fair verdict by which he will not stand acquitted. But pleading is not our present business. His plea or his traverse may be allowed as an answer to a charge when a charge is made. But if he puts himself in the way to obstruct reformation, then the faults of his office instantly become his own. Instead of a public officer in an abusive department, whose province is an object to be regulated, he becomes a criminal who is to be punished. I do most seriously put it to administration, to consider the wisdom of a timely reform. Early reformations are amicable arrangements with a friend in power; late reformations are terms imposed upon a conquered enemy: early reformations are made in cool blood; late reformations are made under a state of inflammation. In that state of things the people behold in government nothing that is respectable. They see the abuse, and they will see nothing else.—They fall into the temper of a furious populace provoked at the disorder of a house of ill fame; they never attempt to correct or regulate; they go to work by the shortest way.—They abate the nuisance, they pull down the house.

This is my opinion with regard to the true interest of government. But as it is the interest of government that reformation should be early, it is the interest of the people that it should be temperate. It is their interest, because a temperate reform is permanent; and because it has a principle of growth. Whenever we improve, it is right to leave room for a further improvement. It is right to consider, to look about us, to examine the effect of what we have done. Then we can proceed with confidence, because we can proceed with intelligence. Whereas in hot reformations, in what men, more zealous than considerate, call making clear work, the whole is generally so crude, so harsh, so indigested; mixed with so much imprudence, and so much injustice; so contrary to the whole course of human nature, and human institutions, that the very people who are most eager for it, are among the first to grow disgusted at what they have done. Then some part of the abdicated grievance is recalled from its exile in order to become a corrective of the correction. Then the abuse assumes all the credit and popularity of a reform. The very idea of purity and disinterestedness in politics falls into disrepute, and is considered as a vision of hot and inexperienced men; and thus disorders become incurable, not by the virulence of their own quality, but by the unapt and violent nature of the remedies. A great part therefore, of my idea of reform, is meant to operate gradually; some benefits will come at a nearer, some at a more remote period. We must no more make haste to be rich by parsimony, than by intemperate acquisition.

In my opinion, it is our duty when we have the desires of the people before us, to pursue them, not in the spirit of literal obedience, which may militate with their very principle, much less to treat them with a peevish and contentious litigation, as if we were adverse parties in a suit. It would, Sir, be most dishonourable for a faithful representative of the Commons, to take advantage of any inartificial expression of the people's wishes, in order to frustrate their attainment of what they have an undoubted right to expect. We are under infinite obligations to our constituents, who have raised us to so distinguished a trust, and have imparted such a degree of sanctity to common characters. We ought to walk before them with purity, plainness, and integrity of heart; with filial love, and not with slavish fear, which is always a low and tricking thing. For my own part, in what I have meditated upon that subject, I cannot indeed take upon me to say I have the honour to follow the sense of the people. The truth is, I met it on the way, while I was pursuing their interest according to my own ideas. I am happy beyond expression to find that my intentions have so far coincided with theirs, that I have not had cause to be in the least scrupulous to sign their petition, conceiving it to express my own opinions, as nearly as general terms can express the object of particular arrangements.

I am therefore satisfied to act as a fair mediator between government and the people, endeavouring to form a plan which should have both an early and a temperate operation. I mean, that it should be substantial; that it should be systematic. That it should rather strike at the first cause of prodigality and corrupt influence, than attempt to follow them in all their effects.

It was to fulfil the first of these objects (the proposal of something substantial) that I found myself obliged at the outset, to reject a plan proposed by an honourable and attentive member of parliament, (Mr. Gilbert) with very good intentions on his part, about a year or two ago. Sir, the plan I speak of was the tax of 25 per cent. moved upon places and pensions during the continuance of the American war.— Nothing, Sir, could have met my ideas more than such a tax if it was considered as a practical satire on that war, and as a penalty upon those who led us into it; but in any other view it appeared to me very liable to objections. I considered the scheme as neither substantial nor permanent, nor systematical, nor likely to be a corrective of evil influence. I have always thought employments a very proper subject of regulation, but a very ill-chosen subject for a tax. An equal tax upon property is reasonable; because the object is of the same quality throughout. The species is the same, it differs only in its quantity; but a tax upon salaries is totally of a different nature; there can be no equality, and consequently no justice, in taxing them by the hundred in the gross.

We have, Sir, on our establishment, several offices which perform real service—we have also places that provide large rewards for no service at all. We have stations which are made for the public decorum; made for preserving the grace and majesty of a great people—we have likewise expensive formalities, which tend rather to the disgrace than the ornament of the state and the court. This, Sir, is the real condition of our establishments. To fall with the same severity on objects so perfectly dissimilar, is the very reverse of a reformation. I mean a reformation framed, as all serious things ought to be in number, weight and measure.—Suppose, for instance, that two men receive a salary of 800*l.* a year each.—In the office of one there is nothing at all to be done; in the other, the occupier is oppressed by its duties.—Strike off 25 per cent. from these two offices, you take from one man 200*l.* which in justice he ought to have, and you give in effect to the other 600*l.* which he ought not to receive. The public robs the former, and the latter robs the public; and this mode of mutual robbery is the only way in which the office and the public can make up their accounts.

But the balance in settling the account of this double injustice, is much against the state. The result is short. You purchase a saving of 200*l.* by a profusion of six. Besides, Sir, whilst you leave a supply of unsecured money behind, wholly at the discretion of ministers, they make up the tax to such places as they wish to favour, or in such new places as they may choose to create. Thus the civil list becomes oppressed with debt; and the public is obliged to repay, and to repay with an heavy interest, what it has taken by an injudicious tax. Such has been the effect of the taxes hitherto laid on pensions and employments, and it is no encouragement to recur again to the same expedient.

In effect, such a scheme is not calculated to produce, but to prevent, reformation. It holds out a shadow of present gain to a greedy and necessitous public, to divert their attention from those abuses, which in reality are the great causes of their wants. It is a composition to stay enquiry; it is a fine paid by mismanagement, for the renewal of its lease. What is worse, it is a fine paid by industry and merit, for an indemnity to the idle and the worthless. But I shall say no more upon this topic, because (whatever may be given out to the contrary) I know that the noble lord in the blue ribbon perfectly agrees with me in these sentiments.

After all that I have said on this subject, I am so sensible, that it is our duty to try every thing which may contribute to the relief of the nation, that I do not attempt wholly to reprobate the idea even of a tax. Whenever, Sir, the incumbrance of useless office (which lies no less a dead weight upon the service of the state, than upon its revenues) shall be removed;—when the remaining offices shall be classed according to the just proportion of their rewards and services, so as to admit the application of an equal rule to their taxation; when the discretionary power over the civil list cash shall be so regulated, that a minister shall no longer have the means of repaying with a private, what is taken by a public hand—if after all these preliminary regulations, it should be thought that a tax on places is an object worthy of the public attention, I shall be very ready to lend my hand to a reduction of their emoluments.

Having thus, Sir, not so much absolutely rejected, as postponed, the plan of a taxation of office,—my next business was to find something which might be really substantial and effectual. I am quite clear, that if we do not go to the very origin and first ruling cause of grievances, we do nothing. What does it signify to turn abuses out of one door, if we are to let them in at another? What does it signify to promote economy upon a measure, and to suffer it to be subverted in the principle? Our ministers are far from being wholly to blame for the present ill order which prevails.

Whilst institutions directly repugnant to good management are suffered to remain, no effectual or lasting reform can be introduced.

I therefore thought it necessary, as soon as I conceived thoughts of submitting to you some plan of reform, to take a comprehensive view of the state of this country; to make a sort of survey of its jurisdictions, its estates, and its establishments. Something, in every one of them, seemed to me to stand in the way of all economy in their administration, and prevented every possibility of methodizing the system. But being, as I ought to be, doubtful of myself, I was resolved not to proceed in an arbitrary manner, in any particular which tended to change the settled state of things, or in any degree to affect the fortune or situation, the interest or the importance, of any individual. By an arbitrary proceeding, I mean one conducted by the private opinions, tastes, or feelings, of the man who attempts to regulate. These private measures are not standards of the exchequer, nor balances of the sanctuary. General principles cannot be debauched or corrupted by interest or caprice; and by those principles I was resolved to work.

Sir, before I proceed further, I will lay these principles fairly before you, that afterwards you may be in a condition to judge whether every object of regulation as I propose it, comes fairly under its rule. This will exceedingly shorten all discussion between us, if we are perfectly in earnest in establishing a system of good management. I therefore lay down to myself seven fundamental rules; they might indeed be reduced to two or three simple maxims, but they would be too general, and their application to the several heads of the business before us, would not be so distinct and visible. I conceive then,

1st, That all jurisdictions which furnish more matter of expence, more temptation to oppression, or more means and instruments of corrupt influence, than advantage to justice or political administration, ought to be abolished.

2ndly, That all public estates which are more subservient to the purposes of vexing, overawing, and influencing those who hold under them, and to the expence of perception and management, than of benefit to the revenue, ought, upon every principle, both of revenue and of freedom, to be disposed of.

3dly, That all offices which bring more charge than proportional advantage to the state; that all offices which may be engrafted on others, uniting and simplifying their duties, ought, in the first case, to be taken away; and in the second, to be consolidated.

4thly, That all such offices ought to be abolished, as obstruct the prospect of the general superintendant of finance; which destroy his superintendency, which disable him from foreseeing and providing for charges as they may occur; from preventing expence in its origin, checking it in its progress, or securing its application to its proper purposes. A minister under whom expences can be made without his knowledge, can never say what it is that he can spend, or what it is that he can save.

5thly, That it is proper to establish an invariable order in all payments; which will prevent partiality; which will give preference to services, not according to the importunity of the demandant, but the rank and order of their utility or their justice.

6thly, That it is right to reduce every establishment, and every part of an establishment (as nearly as possible) to certainty, the life of all order and good management.

7thly, That all subordinate treasuries, as the nurseries of mismanagement, and as naturally drawing to themselves as much money as they can, keeping it as long as they can, and accounting for it as late as they can, ought to be dissolved. They have a tendency to perplex and distract the public accounts, and to excite a suspicion of government even beyond the extent of their abuse.

Under the authority and with the guidance of those principles, I proceed; wishing that nothing in any establishment may be changed, where I am not able to make a strong, direct, and solid application of those principles, or of some one of them. An economical constitution is a necessary basis for an economical administration. . . .

I come next to the great supreme body of the civil government itself. I approach it with that awe and reverence with which a young physician approaches to the cure of the disorders of his parent. Disorders, Sir, and infirmities, there are—such disorders, that all attempts towards method, prudence, and frugality, will be perfectly vain, whilst a system of confusion remains, which is not only alien, but adverse to all economy; a system, which is not only prodigal in its very essence, but causes every thing else which belongs to it to be prodigally conducted.

It is impossible, Sir, for any person to be an economist where no order in payments is established; it is impossible for a man to be an economist, who is not able to take a comparative view of his means, and of his expences, for the year which lies before him; it is impossible for a man to be an economist, under whom various officers in their several departments may spend,—even just what they please,—and often with an emulation of expence, as contributing to the importance, if not profit, of their several departments. Thus much is certain; that neither the present, nor any other first lord of the Treasury, has been ever able to take a survey, or to make even a tolerable guess, of the expences of government for any one year; so as to enable him with the least degree of certainty, or even probability, to bring his affairs within compass. Whatever scheme may be formed upon them, must be made on a calculation of chances. As things are circumstanced, the first lord of the Treasury cannot make an estimate. I am sure I serve the king, and I am sure I assist administration, by putting economy at least in their power. We must class services; we must (as far as their nature admits) appropriate funds; or every thing, however reformed, will fall again into the old confusion.

Coming upon this ground of the civil list, the first thing in dignity and charge that attracts our notice, is the royal household. This establishment, in my opinion, is exceedingly abusive in its constitution. It is formed upon manners and customs that have long since expired. In the first place, it is formed, in many respects, upon feudal principles. In the feudal times, it was not uncommon, even among subjects, for the lowest offices to be held by considerable persons; persons as unfit by their incapacity, as improper from their rank, to occupy such employments. They were held by patent, sometimes for life, and sometimes by inheritance. If my memory does not deceive me, a person of no slight consideration held the office of patent hereditary cook to an earl of Warwick—the earl of Warwick's soups, I fear, were not the better for the dignity of his kitchen. I think it was an earl of Gloucester, who officiated as steward of the household to the archbishops of Canterbury. Instances of the same kind may in some degree be found in the Northumberland house-book, and other family records. There was some reason in ancient necessities, for these ancient customs. Protection was wanted; and the domestic tie, though not the highest, was the closest.

The king's household has not only several strong traces of this feudality, but it is formed also upon the principles of a body corporate; it has its own magistrates, courts, and by-laws. This might be necessary in the ancient times, in order to have a government within itself, capable of regulating the vast and often unruly multitude which composed and attended it. This was the origin of the ancient court called the Green Cloth—composed of the marshall, treasurer, and other great officers of the household, with certain clerks. The rich subjects of the kingdom, who had formerly the same establishments (only on a reduced scale) have since altered their economy; and turned the course of their expence from the maintenance of vast establishments within their walls, to the employment of a great variety of independent trades abroad. Their influence is lessened; but a mode of accommodation, and a style of splendour, suited to the manners of the times, has been increased. Royalty itself has insensibly followed; and the royal household has been carried away by the resistless tide of manners: but with this very material difference—private men have got rid of the establishments along with the reasons of them; whereas the royal household has lost all that was stately and venerable in the antique manners, without retrenching any thing of the cumbrous charge of a gothic establishment. It is shrunk into the polished littleness of modern elegance and personal accommodation; it has evaporated from the gross concrete, into an essence and rectified spirit of expence, where you have tuns of ancient pomp in a vial of modern luxury.

But when the reason of old establishments is gone, it is absurd to preserve nothing but the burthen of them. This is superstitiously to embalm a carcass not worth an ounce of the gums that are used to preserve it. It is to burn precious oils in the tomb; it is to offer meat and drink to the dead,—not so much an honour to the deceased, as a disgrace to the survivors. Our palaces are vast inhospitable halls. There are bleak winds, there "Boreas, and Eurus, and Caurus, and Argestes loud," howling through the vacant lobbies, and clattering the door of deserted guardrooms, appal the imaginations, and conjure up the grim spectres of departed tyrants—the Saxon, the Norman, and the Dane; the stern Edwards and fierce Henries—who stalk from desolation to desolation, through the dreary vacuity, and melancholy succession of chill and comfortless chambers. When this tumult subsides, a dead, and still more frightful silence would reign in this desert, if every now and then the tacking of hammers did not announce, that those constant attendants upon all courts in all ages, jobs, were still alive; for whose sake alone it is, that any trace of ancient grandeur is suffered to remain. These palaces are a true emblem of some governments; the inhabitants are decayed, but the governors and magistrates still flourish. They put me in mind of Old Sarum, where the representatives, more in number than the constituents, only serve to inform us, that this was once a place of trade, and sounding with "the busy hum of men," though now you can only trace the streets by the colour of the corn; and its sole manufacture is in members of parliament.

These old establishments were formed also on a third principle, still more adverse to the living economy of the age. They were formed, Sir, on the principle of purveyance, and receipt in kind. In former days, when the household was vast, and the supply scanty and precarious, the royal purveyors, sallying forth from under the gothic portcullis, to purchase provision with power and prerogative, instead of money, brought home the plunder of a hundred markets, and all that could be seized from a flying and hiding country, and deposited their spoil in a hundred caverns, with each its keeper. There, every commodity, received in its rawest condition, went through all the process which fitted it for use. This inconvenient receipt produced an economy suited only to itself. It multiplied offices beyond all measure; buttery, pantry, and all that rabble of places, which, though profitable to the holders, and expensive to the state, are almost too mean to mention.

All this might be, and I believe was, necessary at first; for it is remarkable, that purveyance, after its regulation had been the subject of a long line of statutes (not fewer, I think, than twenty-six) was wholly taken away by the 12th of Charles the 2nd; yet in the next year of the same reign, it was found necessary to revive it by a special act of parliament, for the sake of the king's journies. This, Sir, is curious; and what would hardly be expected in so reduced a court as that of Charles the 2nd, and so improved a country as England might then be thought. But so it was. In our time, one well filled and well covered stage-coach requires more accommodation than a royal progress; and every district, at an hour's warning, can supply an army.

I do not say, Sir, that all these establishments, whose principle is gone, have been systematically kept up for influence solely: neglect had its share. But this I am sure of, that a consideration of influence has hindered any one from attempting to pull them down. For the purposes of influence, and for those purposes only, are retained half at least of the household establishments. No revenue, no not a royal revenue, can exist under the accumulated charge of ancient establishment, modern luxury, and parliamentary political corruption.

If therefore we aim at regulating this household, the question will be, whether we ought to economise by detail, or by principle? The example we have had of the success of an attempt to economize by detail, and under establishments adverse to the attempt, may tend to decide this question.

At the beginning of his Majesty's reign, lord Talbot came to the administration of a great department in the household. I believe no man ever entered into his Majesty's service, or into the service of any prince, with a more clear integrity, or with more zeal and affection for the interest of his master; and I must add, with abilities for a still higher service. Economy was then announced as a maxim of the reign. This noble lord, therefore, made several attempts toward a reform. In the year 1777, when the King's civil list debts came last to be paid, he explained very fully the success of his undertaking. He told the House of Lords, that he had attempted to reduce the charges of the King's tables, and his kitchen.—The thing, Sir, was not below him. He knew that there is nothing interesting in the concerns of men, whom we love and honour, that is beneath our attention.—"Love," says one of our old poets, "esteems no office mean;" and with still more spirit, "entire affection scorneth nicer hands." Frugality, Sir, is founded on the principle, that all riches have limits. A royal household, grown enormous, even in the meanest departments, may weaken and perhaps destroy all energy in the highest offices of the state. The gorging a royal kitchen may stint and famish the negociations of a kingdom. Therefore the object was worthy of his, was worthy of any man's attention.

In consequence of this noble lord's resolution, (as he told the other House) he reduced several tables, and put the persons entitled to them upon board wages, much to their own satisfaction. But unluckily, subsequent duties requiring constant attendance, it was not possible to prevent their being fed where they were employed—and thus this first step towards economy doubled the expence.

There was another disaster far more doleful than this. I shall state it, as the cause of that misfortune lies at the bottom of almost all our prodigality. Lord Talbot attempted to reform the kitchen; but such, as he well observed, is the consequence of having duty done by one person, whilst another enjoys the emoluments, that he found himself frustrated in all his designs. On that rock his whole adventure split.—His whole scheme of economy was dashed to pieces; his department became more expensive than ever;—the civil list debt accumulated— Why? It was truly from a cause, which, though perfectly adequate to the effect, one would not have instantly guessed;—It was because the "turnspit in the king's kitchen was a member of parliament." The king's domestic servants were all undone; his tradesmen remained unpaid, and became bankrupt—because the turnspit of the king's kitchen was a member of parliament. His majesty's slumbers were interrupted, his pillow was stuffed with thorns, and his peace of mind entirely broken—because the king's turnspit was a member of parliament. The judges were unpaid; the justice of the kingdom bent and gave way; the foreign ministers remained inactive and unprovided; the system of Europe was dissolved; the chain of our alliances was broken; all the wheels of government at home and abroad were stopped—because the king's turnspit was a member of parliament.

Such, Sir, was the situation of affairs, and such the cause of that situation, when his Majesty came a second time to parliament, to desire the payment of those debts which the employment of its members in various offices, visible and invisible, had occasioned. I believe that a like fate will attend every attempt at economy by detail, under similar circumstances, and in every department. A complex operose office of account and controul, is, in itself, and even if members of parliament had nothing to do with it, the most prodigal of all things. The most audacious robberies, or the most subtle frauds, would never venture upon such a waste, as an over careful, detailed guard against them will infallibly produce. In our establishments, we frequently see an office of account, of 100*l.* a year expence, and another office of an equal expence, to controul that office, and the whole upon a matter that is not worth twenty shillings.

To avoid, therefore, this minute care which produces the consequences of the most extensive neglect, and to oblige members of parliament to attend to public cares, and not to the servile offices of domestic management, I propose, Sir, to economize by principle, that is, I propose to put affairs into that train which experience points out as the most effectual, from the nature of things, and from the constitution of the human mind. In all dealings where it is possible, the principles of radical economy prescribe three things; first, undertaking by the great; secondly, engaging with persons of skill in the subject matter; thirdly, engaging with those who shall have an immediate and direct interest in the proper execution of the business.

To avoid frittering and crumbling down the attention by a blind unsystematic observance of every trifle, it has ever been found the best way to do all things which are great in the total amount, and minute in the component parts, by a general contract. The principles of trade have so pervaded every species of dealing, from the highest to the lowest objects; all transactions are got so much into system, that we may, at a moment's warning, and to a farthing value, be informed at what rate any service may be supplied. No dealing is exempt from the possibility of fraud. But by a contract on a matter certain, you have this advantage—you are sure to know the utmost extent of the fraud to which you are subject. By a contract with a person in his own trade, you are sure you shall not suffer by want of skill. By a short contract you are sure of making it the interest of the contractor to exert that skill for the satisfaction of his employers.

I mean to derogate nothing from the diligence or integrity of the present, or of any former board of green-cloth. But what skill can members of parliament obtain in that low kind of province? What pleasure can they have in the execution of that kind of duty? And if they should neglect it, how does it affect their interest, when we know that it is their vote in parliament, and not their diligence in cookery or catering, that recommends them to their office, or keeps them in it?

I therefore propose, that the King's tables (to whatever number of tables, or covers to each, he shall think proper to command) should be classed by the steward of the household, and should be contracted for, according to their rank, by the head or cover;—that the estimate and circumstance of the contract should be carried to the Treasury to be approved; and that its faithful and satisfactory performance should be reported there previous to any payment; that there, and there only, should the payment be made. I propose, that men should be contracted with only in their proper trade; and that no member of parliament should be capable of such contract. By this plan, almost all the infinite offices under the lord steward may be spared; to the extreme simplification, and to the far better execution of every one of his functions. The king of Prussia is so served. He is a great and eminent (though indeed a very rare) instance of the possibility of uniting in a mind of vigour and compass, an attention to minute objects, with the largest views, and the most complicated plans. His tables are served by contract, and by the head. Let me say, that no prince can be ashamed to imitate the king of Prussia; and particularly to learn in his school, when the problem is—"The best manner of reconciling the state of a court with the support of war?" Other courts, I understand, have followed him with effect, and to their satisfaction.

The same clue of principle leads us through the labyrinth of the other departments. What, Sir, is there in the office of the great wardrobe (which has the care of the King's furniture) that may not be executed by the Lord Chamberlain himself? He has an honourable appointment? He has time sufficient to attend to the duty; and he has the vice chamberlain to assist him. Why should not he deal also by contract, for all things belonging to this office, and carry his estimates first, and his report of the execution in its proper time, for payment, directly to the board of Treasury itself? By a simple operation (containing in it a treble controul) the expences of a department, which for naked walls, or walls hung with cobwebs, has in a few years cost the crown 150,000*l.* may at length hope for regulation. But, Sir, the office and its business are at variance. As it stands, it serves not to furnish the palace with its hangings, but the parliament with its dependent members.

To what end, Sir, does the office of removing wardrobe serve at all? Why should a jewel office exist for the sole purpose of taxing the King's gifts of plate? Its object falls naturally within the Chamberlain's province; and ought to be under his care and inspection without any fee. Why should an office of the robes exist, when that of groom of the stole is a sinecure, and that this is a proper object of his department?

All these incumbrances, which are themselves nuisances, produce other incumbrances, and other nuisances. For the payment of these useless establishments, there are no less than three useless treasures; two to hold a purse, and one to play with a stick. The treasurer of the household is a mere name. The cofferer, and the treasurer of the chamber receive and pay great sums, which it is not at all necessary they should either receive or pay. All the proper officers, servants, and tradesmen, may be inrolled in their several departments, and paid in proper classes and times with great simplicity and order, at the exchequer, and by direction from the treasury.

The Board of Works, which in the seven years preceding 1777, has cost towards 400,000*l.*; and (if I recollect rightly) has not cost less in proportion from the beginning of the reign, is under the very same description of all the other ill-contrived establishments, and calls for the very same reform. We are to seek for the visible signs of all this expence.—For all this expence, we do not see a building of the size and importance of a pigeon-house. Buckingham-house was reprised by a bargain with the public for 100,000*l.*;—and the small house at Windsor has been, if I mistake not, undertaken since that account was brought before us. The good works of that board of works, are as carefully concealed as other good works ought to be; they are perfectly invisible. But though it is the perfection of charity to be concealed, it is, Sir, the property and glory of magnificence, to appear and stand forward to the eye.

That board, which ought to be a concern of builders, and such like, and of none else, is turned into a junto of members of parliament. That office too has a treasury, and a paymaster of its own; and lest the arduous affairs of that important exchequer should be too fatiguing, that paymaster has a deputy to partake his profits, and relieve his cares. I do not believe, that either now or in former times, the chief managers of that board have made any profit of its abuse. It is, however, no good reason that an abusive establishment should subsist, because it is of as little private as of public advantage. But this establishment has the grand radical fault, the original sin, that pervades and perverts all our establishments; the apparatus is not fitted to the object, nor the workmen to the work. Expences are incurred on the private opinion of an inferior establishment, without consulting the principal; who can alone determine the proportion which it ought to bear to the other establishments of the state, in the order of their relative importance.

I propose, therefore, along with the rest, to pull down this whole ill-contrived scaffolding, which obstructs, rather than forwards our public works; to take away its treasury; to put the whole into the hands of a real builder, who shall not be a member of parliament; and to oblige him by a previous estimate and final payment, to appear twice at the treasury before the public can be loaded. The King's gardens are to come under a similar regulation.

The Mint, though not a department of the household, has the same vices. It is a great expence to the nation, chiefly for the sake of members of parliament. It has its officers of parade and dignity. It has its treasury too. It is a sort of corporate body; and formerly was a body of great importance; as much so on the then scale of things, and the then order of business, as the Bank is at this day. It was the great centre of money transactions and remittances for our own, and for other nations; until king Charles the 1st, among other arbitrary projects, dictated by despotic necessity, made it withhold the money that lay there for remittance. That blow (and happily too) the Mint never recovered. Now it is no bank; no remittance-shop. The Mint, Sir, is a manufacture, and it is nothing else; and it ought to be undertaken upon the principles of a manufacture; that is, for the best and cheapest execution, by a contract upon proper securities, and under proper regulations.

The Artillery is a far greater object; it is a military concern; but having an affinity and kindred in its defects with the establishments I am now speaking of, I think it best to speak of it along with them. It is, I conceive, an establishment not well suited to its martial, though exceedingly well calculated for its parliamentary purposes.—Here there is a treasury, as in all the other inferior departments of government. Here the military is subordinate to the civil, and the naval confounded with the land service. The object indeed is much the same in both. But when the detail is examined, it will be found that they had better be separated. For a reform of this office, I propose to restore things to what (all considerations taken together) is their natural order: to restore them to their just proportion, and to their just distribution. I propose, in this military concern, to render the civil subordinate to the military; and this will annihilate the greatest part of the expence, and all the influence belonging to the office. I propose to send the military branch to the army, and the naval to the admiralty: and I intend to perfect and accomplish the whole detail (where it becomes too minute and complicated for legislature, and requires exact, official, military, and mechanical knowledge) by a commission of competent officers in both departments. I propose to execute by contract, what by contract can be executed; and to bring, as much as possible, all estimates to be previously approved, and finally to be paid by the Treasury.

Thus, by following the course of nature, and not the purposes of politics, or the accumulated patchwork of occasional accommodation, this vast expensive department may be methodized; its service proportioned to its necessities, and its payments subjected to the inspection of the superior minister of finance;—who is to judge of it on the result of the total collective exigencies of the state. This last is a reigning principle through my whole plan; and it is a principle which I hope may hereafter be applied to other plans.

By these regulations taken together—besides the three subordinate treasuries in the lesser principalities, five other subordinate treasures are suppressed. There is taken away the whole establishment of detail in the household; the Treasurer;—the Comptroller (for a comptroller is hardly necessary where there is no treasurer) the Cofferer of the Household; the Treasurer of the Chamber; the Master of the Household; the whole Board of Green Cloth;—and a vast number of subordinate offices in the department of the Steward of the Household;—the whole establishment of the Great Wardrobe;—the Removing Wardrobe;—the Jewel Office;—The Robes; the Board of Works; almost the whole charge of the civil branch of the Board of Ordnance are taken away. All these arrangements together will be found to relieve the nation from a vast weight of influence, without distressing, but rather by forwarding every public service. When something of this kind is done, then the public may begin to breathe. Under other governments, a question of expence is only a question of economy, and it is nothing more; with us, in every question of expence, there is always a mixture of constitutional considerations.

It is, Sir, because I wish to keep this business of subordinate treasuries as much as I can together, that I brought the Ordnance-office before you, though it is properly a military department. For the same reason I will now trouble you with my thoughts and propositions upon two of the greatest under treasuries, I mean the office of Paymaster of the Land Forces, or Treasurer of the Army; and that of the Treasurer of the Navy. The former of these has long been a great object of public suspicion and uneasiness. Envy too has had its share in the obloquy which is cast upon this office. But I am sure that it has no share at all in the reflections I shall make upon it, or in the reformations that I shall propose. I do not grudge to the honourable gentleman who at present holds the office, any of the effects of his talents, his merit, or his fortune. He is respectable in all these particulars. I follow the constitution of the office without persecuting its holder. It is necessary in all matters of public complaint, where men frequently feel right and argue wrong, to separate prejudice from reason; and to be very sure, in attempting the redress of a grievance, that we hit upon its real seat, and its true nature. Where there is an abuse in office, the first thing that occurs in heat is to censure the officer. Our natural disposition leads all our enquiries rather to persons than to things. But this prejudice is to be corrected by maturer thinking.

Sir, the profits of the Pay-office (as an office) are not too great, in my opinion, for its duties, and for the rank of the person who has generally held it. He has been generally a person of the highest rank; that is to say, a person of eminence and consideration in this House. The great and the invidious profits of the Pay-office are from the bank that is held in it. According to the present course of the office, and according to the present mode of accounting there, this bank must necessarily exist somewhere. Money is a productive thing; and when the usual time of its demand can be tolerably calculated, it may, with prudence, be safely laid out to the profit of the holder. It is on this calculation that the business of banking proceeds. But no profit can be derived from the use of money, which does not make it the interest of the holder to delay his account. The process of the Exchequer colludes with this interest. Is this collusion from its want of rigour and strictness, and great regularity of form? The reverse is true. They have in the Exchequer brought rigour and formalism to their ultimate perfection. The process against accountants is so rigorous, and in a manner so unjust, that correctives must, from time to time, be applied to it. These correctives being discretionary, upon the case, and generally remitted by the barons to the lords of the Treasury, as the best judges of the reasons for respite, hearings are had; delays are produced; and thus the extreme of rigour in office (as usual in all human affairs) leads to the extreme of laxity. What with the interested delay of the officer; the ill-conceived exactness of the court; the applications for dispensations from that exactness; the revival of rigorous process, after the expiration of the time; and the new rigours producing new applications, and new enlargements of time, such delays happen in the public accounts, that they can scarcely ever be closed.

Besides, Sir, they have a rule in the Exchequer, which, I believe, they have founded upon a very ancient statute, that of the 51st of Henry 3, by which it is provided, "That when a sheriff or bailiff hath began his account, none other shall be received to account until he that was first appointed hath clearly accounted, and that the sum has been received." Whether this clause of that statute be the ground of that absurd practice, I am not quite able to ascertain. But it has very generally prevailed, though I am told that of late they began to relax from it. In consequence of forms adverse to substantial account,we have a long succession of paymasters and their representatives, who have never been admitted to account, although perfectly ready to do so. . . .

I have now finished all that for the present I shall trouble you with on the plan of reduction. I mean next to propose to you the plan of arrangement, by which I mean to appropriate and fix the civil list money to its several services according to their nature; for I am thoroughly sensible, that if a discretion, wholly arbitrary, can be exercised over the civil list revenue, although the most effectual methods may be taken to prevent the inferior departments from exceeding their bounds, the plan of reformation will still be left very imperfect. It will not, in my opinion, be safe to permit an entirely arbitrary discretion even in the first lord of the Treasury himself; it will not be safe to leave with him a power of diverting the public money from its proper objects, of paying it in an irregular course, or of inverting perhaps the order of time, dictated by the proportion of value, which ought to regulate his application of payment to service.

I am sensible too, that the very operation of a plan of economy which tends to exonerate the civil list of expensive establishments, may in some sort defeat the capital end we have in view, the independence of parliament; and that in removing the public and ostensible means of influence, we may increase the fund of private corruption. I have thought of some methods to prevent an abuse of surplus cash under discretionary application; I mean the heads of secret service, special service, various payments, and the like; which I hope, will answer, and which in due time I shall lay before you. Where I am unable to limit the quantity of the sums to be applied, by reason of the uncertain quantity of the service, I endeavour to confine it to its line; to secure an indefinite application to the definite service to which it belongs; not to stop the progress of expence in its line, but to confine it to that line in which it professes to move.

But that part of my plan, Sir, upon which I principally rest, that, on which I rely for the purpose of binding up, and securing the whole, is to establish a fixed and invariable order in all its payments, which it shall not be permitted to the first lord of the Treasury, upon any pretence whatsoever, to depart from. I therefore divide the civil list payment into nine classes, putting each class forward according to the importance or justice of the demand, and to the inability of thy persons entitled to enforce their pretentions; that is, to put those first who have the most efficient offices, or claim the justest debts; and, at the same time, from the character of that description of men, from the retiredness, or the remoteness of their situation, or from their want of weight and power to enforce their pretensions, or from their being entirely subject to the power of a minister, without any reciprocal power of aweing, ought to be the most considered, and are the most likely to be neglected; all these I place in the highest classes: I place in the lowest those whose functions are of the least importance, but whose persons or rank are often of the greatest power and influence.

In the first class I place the judges, as of the first importance. It is the public justice that holds the community together; the ease, therefore, and independence of the judges, ought to supersede all other considerations, and they ought to be the very last to feel the necessities of the state, or to be obliged either to court or bully a minister for their right: they ought to be as weak solicitors on their own demands, as strenuous assertors of the rights and liberties of others. The judges are, or ought to be, of a reserved and retired character, and wholly unconnected with the political world.

In the second class I place the foreign ministers. The judges are the links of our connections with one another; the foreign ministers are the links of our connection with other nations. They are not upon the spot to demand payment, and are therefore the most likely to be, as in fact they have sometimes been, entirely neglected, to the great disgrace, and perhaps the great detriment of the nation.

In the third class, I would bring all the tradesmen who supply the crown by contract, or otherwise.

In the fourth class, I place all the domestic servants of the king, and all persons in efficient offices, whose salaries do not exceed 200*l.* a year.

In the fifth, upon account of honour, which ought to give place to nothing but charity and rigid justice, I would place the pensions and allowances of his Majesty's royal family, comprehending of course the Queen, together with the stated allowance of the privy purse.

In the sixth class, I place those efficient offices of duty, whose salaries may exceed the sum of 200*l.* a year.

In the seventh class, that mixed mass the whole pension list.

In the eighth, the offices of honour about the King.

In the ninth, and the last of all, the salaries and pensions of the first lord of the Treasury himself, the Chancellor of the Exchequer, and the other commissioners of the treasury.

If by any possible mismanagement of that part of the revenue which is left at discretion, or by any other mode of prodigality, cash should be deficient for the payment of the lowest classes, I propose, that the amount of those salaries where the deficiency may happen to fall, shall not be carried as debt to the account of the succeeding year, but that it shall be entirely lapsed, sunk, and lost; so that government will be enabled to start in the race of every new year, wholly unloaded, fresh in wind and in vigour. Hereafter no civil list debt can ever come upon the public. And those who do not consider this as saving, because it is not a certain sum, do not ground their calculations of the future on their experience of the past.

I know of no mode of preserving the effectual execution of any duty, but to make it the direct interest of the executive officer that it shall be faithfully performed. Assuming, then, that the present vast allowance to the civil list is perfectly adequate to all its purposes, if there should be any failure, it must be from the mismanagement or neglect of the first commissioner of the treasury; since, upon the proposed plan, there can be no expence of any consequence, which he is not himself previously to authorize and finally to controul. It is therefore just, as well as politic, that the loss should attach upon the delinquency.

If the failure from the delinquence should be very considerable, it will fall on the class directly above the first lord of the Treasury, as well as upon himself and his board. It will fall, as it ought to fall, upon offices of no primary importance in the state; but then it will fall upon persons, whom it will be a matter of no slight importance for a minister to provoke—it will fall upon persons of the first rank and consequence in the kingdom; upon those who are nearest to the king, and frequently have a more interior credit with him than the minister himself. It will fall upon masters of the horse, upon lord chamberlains, upon lord stewards, upon grooms of the stole, the lords of the bed-chamber. The household troops form an army, who will be ready to mutiny for want of pay, and whose mutiny will be really dreadful to a commander in chief. A rebellion of the thirteen lords of the bed-chamber would be far more terrible to a minister, and would probably affect his power more to the quick, than a revolt of thirteen colonies. What an uproar such an event would create at court! What petitions and committees, and associations, would it not produce! Bless me! what a clattering of white sticks and yellow sticks would be about his head—what a storm of gold keys would fly about the ears of the minister—what a shower of Georges, and Thistles, and medals, and collars of S.S. would assail him at his first entrance into the antichamber, after an insolvent Christmas quarter. A tumult which could not be appeased by all the harmony of the new year's ode. Rebellion it is certain there would be; and rebellion may not now indeed be so critical an event to those who engage in it, since its price is so correctly ascertained at just a thousand pound.

Sir, this classing, in my opinion, is a serious and solid security for the performance of a minister's duty. Lord Coke says, that the staff was put into the treasurer's hand to enable him to support himself when there was no money in the exchequer, and to beat away importunate solicitors. The method, which I propose, would hinder him from the necessity of such a broken staff to lean on, or such a miserable weapon for repulsing the demands of worthless suitors, who, the noble lord in the blue ribbon knows, will bear many hard blows on the head, and many other indignities, before they are driven from the treasury. In this plan, he is furnished with an answer to all their importunity; an answer far more conclusive than if he had knocked them down with his staff—"Sir, (or my lord), you are calling for my own salary—Sir, you are calling for the appointments of my colleagues who sit about me in office—Sir, you are going to excite a mutiny at court against me—you are going to estrange his majesty's confidence from me, through the chamberlain, or the master of the horse, or the groom of the stole."

As things now stand, every man, in proportion to his consequence at court, tends to add to the expence of the civil list, by all manner of jobs, if not for himself, yet for his dependents. When the new plan is established, those who are now suitors for jobs, will become the most strenuous opposers of them. They will have a common interest with the minister in public economy. Every class, as it stands low, will become security for the payment of the preceding class; and thus the persons whose insignificant services defraud those that are useful, would then become interested in their payment. Then the powerful, instead of oppressing would be obliged to support the weak; and idleness would become concerned in the reward of industry. The whole fabric of the civil economy would become compact and connected in all its parts; it would be formed into a well-organised body, where every member contributes to the support of the whole; and where even the lazy stomach secures the vigour of the active arm.

This plan, I really flatter myself, is laid, not in official formality, nor in airy speculation, but in real life, and in human nature, in what "comes home (as Bacon says) to the business and bosoms of men." You have now, Sir, before you, the whole of my scheme, as far as I have digested it into a form, that might be in any respect worthy of your consideration.—I intend to lay it before you in five Bills. [Titles of the Bills read.] The plan consists, indeed, of many parts, but they stand upon a few plain principles. It is a plan which takes nothing from the civil list without discharging it of a burthen equal to the sum carried to the public service. It weakens no one function necessary to government; but on the contrary, by appropriating supply to service, it gives it greater vigour. It provides the means of order and foresight to a minister of finance, which may always keep all the objects of his office, and their state, condition, and relations, distinctly before him. It brings forward accounts without hurrying and distressing the accountants; whilst it provides for public convenience, it regards private rights. It extinguishes secret corruption almost to the impossibility of its existence. It destroys direct and visible influence equal to the offices of at least fifty members of parliament. Lastly, it prevents the provision for his Majesty's children, from being diverted to the political purposes of his minister.

These are the points, on which I rely for the merit of the plan: I pursue economy in a secondary view, and only as it is connected with these great objects. I am persuaded, that even for supply this scheme will be far from unfruitful, if it be executed to the extent I propose it. I think it will give to the public, at its periods, 2 or 300,000*l.* a year; if not, it will give them a system of economy, which is itself a great revenue. It gives me no little pride and satisfaction, to find that the principles of my proceedings are, in many respects, the very same with those which are now pursued in the plans of the French minister of finance. I am sure, that I lay before you a scheme easy and practicable in all its parts. I know it is common at once to applaud and to reject all attempts of this nature. I know it is common for men to say, that such and such things are perfectly right—very desirable; but that, unfortunately, they are not practicable. Oh! no, Sir, no. Those things which are not practicable, are not desirable. There is nothing in the world really beneficial, that does not lie within the reach of an informed understanding, and a well-directed pursuit. There is nothing that God has judged good for us, that he has not given us the means to accomplish, both in the natural and the moral world. If we cry, like children, for the moon, like children we must cry on.

We must follow the nature of our affairs, and conform ourselves to our situation. If we do, our objects are plain and compassable. Why should we resolve to do nothing, because what I propose to you may not be the exact demand of the petition; when we are far from resolved to comply even with what evidently is so? Does this sort of chicanery become us? The people are the masters. They have only to express their wants at large and in gross. We are the expert artists; we are the skilful workmen, to shape their desires into perfect form, and to fit the utensil to the use. They are the sufferers, they tell the symptoms of the complaint; but we know the exact seat of the disease, and how to apply the remedy according to the rules of art. How shocking would it be to see us pervert our skill, into a sinister and servile dexterity, for the purpose of evading our duty, and defrauding our employers, who are our natural lords, of the object of their just expectations. I think the whole not only practicable, but practicable in a very short time. If we are in earnest about it, and if we exert that industry, and those talents in forwarding the work, which I am afraid may be exerted in impeding it—I engage, that the whole may be put in complete execution within a year. For my own part, I have very little to recommend me for this or for any task, but a kind of earnest and anxious perseverance of mind, which, with all its good and all its evil effects, is moulded into my constitution. I faithfully engage to the House, if they choose to appoint me to any part in the execution of this work, which (when they have made it theirs by the improvements of their wisdom, will be worthy of the able assistance they may give me) that by night and by day, in town or in country, at the desk, or in the forest, I will, without regard to convenience, ease, or pleasure, devote myself to their service, not expecting or admitting any reward whatsoever. I owe to this country my labour, which is my all; and I owe to it ten times more industry, if ten times more I could exert. After all I shall be an unprofitable servant.

At the same time, if I am able, and if I shall be permitted, I will lend an humble helping hand to any other good work which is going on. I have not, Sir, the frantic presumption to suppose, that this plan contains in it the whole of what the public has a right to expect, in the great work of reformation they call for. Indeed it falls infinitely short of it. It falls short even of my own ideas. I have some thoughts not yet fully ripened, relative to a reform in the customs and excise, as well as in some other branches of financial administration. There are other things too, which form essential parts in a great plan for the purpose of restoring the independence of parliament. The Contractors' Bill of last year it is fit to revive; and I rejoice that it is in better hands than mine. The Bill for suspending the votes of Custom-house officers, brought into parliament several years ago, by one of our worthiest and wisest members, (would to God we could along with the plan revive the person who designed it!) But a man of very real integrity, honour, and ability, will be found to take his place, and to carry his idea into full execution. You all see how necessary it is to review our military expences for some years past, and, if possible, to bind up and close that bleeding artery of profusion: but that business also, I have reason to hope, will be undertaken by abilities that are fully adequate to it. Something must be devised (if possible) to check the ruinous expence of elections.

Sir, all or most of these things must be done. Every one must take his part.

If we should be able by dexterity or power, or intrigue, to disappoint the expectations of our constituents, what will it avail us? We shall never be strong or artful enough to parry, or to put by the irresistible demands of our situation. That situation calls upon us, and upon our constituents too, with a voice which will be heard. I am sure no man is more zealously attached than I am to the privileges of this House, particularly in regard to the exclusive management of money. The Lords have no right to the disposition, in any sense, of the public purse; but they have gone further in self-denial than our utmost jealousy could have required. A power of examining accounts, to censure, correct, and punish, we never, that I know of, have thought of denying to the House of Lords. It is something more than a century since we voted that body useless; they have not voted themselves so. The whole hope of reformation is at length cast upon us; and let us not deceive the nation, which does us the honour to hope every thing from our virtue. If all the nation are not equally forward to press this duty upon us, yet be assured, that they will equally expect we should perform it. The respectful silence of those who wait upon your pleasure, ought to be as powerful with you, as the call of those who require your service as their right. Some, without doors, affect to feel hurt for your dignity, because they suppose that menaces are held out to you. Justify their good opinion, by shewing that no menaces are necessary to stimulate you to your duty.—But, Sir, whilst we may sympathise with them, in one point, who sympathise with us in another, we ought to attend no less to those who approach us like men, and who, in the guise of petitioners, speak to us in the tone of a concealed authority. It is not wise to force them to speak out more plainly, what they plainly mean.—But the petitioners are violent. Be it so. Those who are least anxious about your conduct, are not those that love you most. Moderate affection, and satiated enjoyment, are cold and respectful; but an ardent and injured passion is tempered up with wrath, and grief, and shame, and conscious worth, and the maddening sense of violated right. A jealous love lights his torch from the firebrands of the furies.—They who call upon you to belong wholly to the people, are those who wish you to return to your proper home; to the sphere of your duty, to the post of your honour, to the mansion-house of all genuine, serene, and solid satisfaction. We have furnished to the people of England (indeed we have) some real cause of jealousy. Let us leave that sort of company which, if it does not destroy our innocence, pollutes our honour: let us free ourselves at once from every thing that can increase their suspicions, and inflame their just resentment; let us cast away from us, with a generous scorn, all the love-tokens and symbols that we have been vain and light enough to accept;—all the bracelets, and snuff-boxes, and miniature pictures, and hair devices, and all the other adulterous trinkets that are the pledges of our alienation, and the monuments of our shame. Let us return to our legitimate home, and all jars and all quarrels will be lost in embraces. Let the Commons in parliament assembled, be one and the same thing with the commons at large. The distinctions that are made to separate us, are unnatural and wicked contrivances. Let us identify, let us incorporate ourselves with the people. Let us cut all the cables and snap the chains which tie us to an unfaithful shore, and enter the friendly harbour, that shoots far out into the main its moles and jettees to receive us—"War with the world, and peace with our constituents." Be this our motto, and our principle. Then indeed, we shall be truly great. Respecting ourselves we shall be respected by the world. At present all is troubled, and cloudy, and distracted, and full of anger and turbulence, both abroad and at home; but the air may be cleared by this storm, and light and fertility may follow it. Let us give a faithful pledge to the people that we honour, indeed, the crown; but that we belong to them; that we are their auxiliaries, and not their task-masters; the fellow-labourers in the same vineyard, not lording over their rights, but helpers of their joy: that to tax them is a grievance to ourselves, but to cut off from our enjoyments to forward theirs, is the highest gratification we are capable of receiving. I feel with comfort, that we are all warmed with these sentiments, and while we are thus warm, I wish we may go directly and with a cheerful heart to this salutary work.

Sir, I move for leave to bring in a Bill,

> For the better regulation of his Majesty's Civil Establishments, and of certain Public Offices; for the limitation of pensions, and the suppression of sundry useless, expensive, and inconvenient places; and for applying the monies saved thereby to the public service.

Commons debate on John Dunning's motion for limiting the influence of the crown, 6 April 1780

Parliamentary History, XXI, 340-53.

The acceptance by the Commons of John Dunning's (1731-83) famous resolution that the influence of the crown "has increased, is increasing, and ought to be diminished" had no legal impact on the monarch but it revealed a deep level of dissatisfaction with George III.

The House, according to order, resolved itself into a committee of the whole House, to consider of the Petition of the gentlemen, clergy, and freeholders of the county of York, respecting an Economical Reform, and also the several other petitions referred to the consideration of the said committee. The titles of the said petitions being read, in all about forty in number,

Mr. Dunning rose, and said, it was unnecessary to observe that the subject matter to be taken into consideration, was the subject matter contained in the petitions. Independent of the great objects which the petitions recommended to the care and attention of parliament, which had been according to the particular ideas of the several classes of petitioners of a various nature, there was one great fundamental point on which they hinged, that of setting limits or paring down the increased, dangerous, and alarming influence of the crown, and an economical expenditure of the public money. In one point of view, both these objects might be fairly consolidated into one great principle. For instance, if the public money was faithfully applied, and frugally expended, that would reduce the influence of the crown; if, on the other hand, the influence of the crown was restrained within its natural and constitutional limits, it would once more restore that power which the constitution had vested in that House, the enquiring into and controuling the expenditure of public money; but nevertheless, though the principle embraced one great object, a necessity arose, that the principle should be divided; that is, the remedy should, in pursuance of the objects held forth and recommended in the petitions, be directed to two points.

Before he proceeded any further, therefore, he should take it for granted, because the fact stood so stated in the petitions on the table, that a reform of the public expenditure, and limiting and restraining the increasing influence of the crown, were the two great objects which must draw the attention of that House, and necessarily force those two important subjects into discussion.

These being the evils set forth in the petitions, it was his duty, however unequal he might be to the task he had undertaken, to apply what he deemed specific and distinct remedies to them both; that was, to propose some remedy, or frame some resolution, which would serve as a basis, on which he might afterwards erect a system of measures, to answer the purpose, and comply with the wishes of the petitioners.

Before he proceeded any further, it would be necessary for him to state and remind the House of what had been done, as it was supposed, in consequence of the petitions now on the table, and how far those attempts had or had not succeeded; because such an enquiry would partly point out the resistance already made and avowed to the great objects of the petitions; and would have this important effect; it would shew, that no redress could be, or was meant to be given to the petitioners, by the modes already tried; and at the same time prove precisely, nay literally, in what particulars those who were supposed to lead and direct the majorities of that House, meant to resist and defeat the prayers of the petitions.

An hon. gentleman behind him (Mr. Burke) had produced a Bill partly upon the plan of the petitions. It might not embrace every object described, or pointed to in the petitions. But he believed no person, on any side of the House, would dispute with him, that the Bill contained nothing but what was consonant to the letter and spirit of the petitions, nor excluded or determined against a syllable of their contents. He should not attempt to do that gentleman justice for his unwearied endeavours on that occasion, because, with the very best disposition to do it, he found himself totally unequal to the undertaking. He knew it would be painful to his hon. friend to hear his sentiments while present; but as an act of duty, which he thought himself bound to discharge, however irksome to his hon. friend, he could not pass over in silence, what must remain as a monument to be handed down to posterity, of the uncommon zeal, unrivalled industry, astonishing abilities, and invincible perseverance of the hon. gentleman. He had undertaken a task big with labour and difficulty; a task that embraced a variety of the most important objects, extensive, various, and complicated; yet such was the eminent and unequalled abilities, so extraordinary the talents and ingenuity, and such the fortunate frame of the hon. gentleman's mind, his vast capacity and happy conception, that in his hands, what must have proved a vast heap of ponderous matter, composed of heterogeneous ingredients, discordant in their nature, and opposite in principle, was so skilfully arranged as to become quite simple as to each respective part, dependent on each other; and the whole, at the same time, so judiciously combined, as to present nothing to almost any mind tolerably intelligent to divide, puzzle, or distract it. This was a true description of his hon. friend's Bill. He trusted that he would permit him to use that appellation, and it was his peculiar pride to be permitted to do so.

But what was the consequence of such a Bill, brought forward by such a man? Upon its being first proposed, the united approbation of, he believed, every individual in that House. The highest, and, in his opinion, the best deserved eulogiums of every part; and he believed most sincerely, its genuine sentiments at the time, for he could safely make a distinction between the real sentiments of that House permitted to act according to its own immediate feelings, and the impressions afterwards made upon it arising from without. The House, he believed, expressed the former, on the occasion alluded to; when other opinions seemed to prevail, he most sincerely believed, and was firmly persuaded, that the latter temper and disposition which appeared towards his hon. friend's Bill, originated out of that House, and not within these walls.

Such being the reception of the Bill, or of the proposition for introducing it, what was its reception when it was introduced? Doubts were immediately started as soon as it made its appearance. A shew of candour, a kind of mock approbation was to be preserved. It might contain some matter worthy of consideration; but it was shortly avowed by the noble lord, who is supposed to lead the majorities of this House, that the Bill, as to the great objects which it proposed to attain, was fundamentally wrong. What were those objects? Almost the very objects proposed to be obtained by the petitions now on your table; a reduction of the undue and unconstitutional influence of the crown, and an enquiry into the expenditure of the civil list, the abolishing sinecure places, exorbitant salaries, etc. Whatever dexterity may have been used, some matters came out in the course of this contest, which have in fact been the occasion of the trouble I am now going to give this House.

In the course of this very important discussion, two fundamental points came into controversy; but more of that as I proceed. The first clause in the hon. gentleman's Bill relative to the office of a third Secretary of State, pursued the idea of the petitions; it went to the reduction of the public expenditure, and to the abolishing of an useless office. The noble lord in the blue ribbon, and an hon. gentleman of great abilities, and of great supposed weight in this House, met both principles fairly, in argument; but at the same time contended, that the place was not useless. The noble lord in the blue ribbon said, that the influence of the crown was not too great; another noble lord (Nugent) contended, that the influence of the crown, as stated in argument, was constitutional and necessary; and the hon. gentleman to whom I have just alluded (Mr. Rigby) met the other point insisted on in the petitions, the enquiry into the expenditure of his Majesty's civil list revenue, by saying it was not competent to this House. The hon. gentleman was challenged to bring his question forward; the noble lord shrunk from the contest, under the same pretext that I foresee he will endeavour to defeat, or evade the resolution which I shall have the honour to move; and the hon. gentleman seemed himself not so sanguine, when the matter was decided by a question moved to take the sense of the House. Be that as it may, my hon. friend's clause was lost, under the pretence that the office proposed to be abolished was not useless, or, if it was, that no evidence of its being useless had appeared. I foresee, likewise, that I shall be called on, for evidence of the truth of what I shall move in this committee.

The next clause, relative to the abolition of the Board of Trade, was opposed on the same ostensible ground, of its not being useless. The minister however, besides the ostensible ground, maintained both the other doctrines, that the influence of the crown was not too much, and that the parliament had no right to controul the civil list expenditure; but the House was not to be drove. The House revolted, and the clause was carried by a small majority.

What was the fate of the next clause? That was openly opposed in principle; which principle was supported, in one shape or other, by a great majority of this House. The King's household was deemed sacred, it was not to be touched; a distinction was made by those who gave the minister that majority; useless places which relate to the functions of the state may be abolished, but the King's revenue for the support of his household is his own private personal revenue, with which parliament neither have, nor can have, any thing to do. Here, I may say, my hon. friend's Bill was put an end to.

The next attempt made in pursuance of the prayers of the petitions, was by an hon. friend of mine, (colonel Barré) with whom I have long lived in habits of the greatest intimacy and friendship. My hon. friend suggested the propriety of instituting a committee of accounts. This went to another part of the prayer of the petitions, the mode of collecting, transmitting, receiving, and issuing the public monies. My hon. friend, with great labour and indefatigable attention, aided by the ability and experience he is confessedly known to possess, spared no pains to render his plan as perfect as possible. A very few days had not intervened, before the noble lord in the blue ribbon, foreseeing that many things extremely irksome and unpleasant to his lordship might come out, should such a commission be instituted, run a race with my hon. friend for the Bill; and without any private communication or previous information, snatched the Bill from out of the hands of my hon. friend, where it had been placed by the unanimous voice and approbation of the House. But my hon. friend by this act, which wore in its first aspect a very suspicious appearance, and in every respect a very uncandid ungentlemanlike appearance, had no reason to complain. Neither should I think, or care about who performed the duty to the public, so that it was well and faithfully performed. Was that the case? By no means. It is true his lordship has brought in a Bill, but what is it? A Bill appointing commissioners to inspect the public accounts, not the accounts in general, but some particular accounts, something relative to balances. Who, again, are to be the commissioners appointed to execute this business? Not members of this House; but persons out of it, to be appointed by the noble lord himself. A Bill of a similar nature was passed in the 2nd of William and Mary. In that Bill it was provided, that all the public accounts, including the civil list, should be enquired into, the privy purse and secret service money alone excepted; and this exception not to extend to persons in this House enjoying pensions. Here the civil list expenditure is totally omitted; and though it were not, no enquiry could extend to members enjoying pensions here, because the list of those pensions have been already denied by the noble lord.

Another effort was made to diminish the influence of the crown, in this House, by an hon. gentleman (sir P. J. Clerke) by excluding persons holding contracts, made privately with any of the official boards, which was attended with more success than either of the other two I have mentioned; so that the whole of what has been done in consequence of that pile of parchment now on your table, containing the sentiments, the prayers, and petitions of above 100,000 electors, amounts, in the whole, to a single clause in my hon. friend's Bill, which standing naked, as it does, is of little or no importance; the proposition snatched out of my other hon. friend's hands, by the noble lord, and only snatched to insult you in this House, and mock your constituents out of it, and the Contractors' Bill, which ministers, or at least their friends and confidents, pretend to predict, will miscarry in another place; or, should that not happen to be the case, boast that it will answer no one purpose of those who have framed and supported it. Such is the manner the dutiful and respectful petitions of the people of England has been treated. I trust, however, that the people of England, knowing how they have been treated, will resent the insult put upon them by those, who, to oppression and neglect, have added mockery and contempt.

I would add a word or two, respecting my hon. friend below me, (colonel Barré), for the faithful and disinterested performance of his duty in this House; how has he been treated by some of his opponents? He has been called a dependant; I presume, alluding to the honour he enjoys in the friendship and intimacy of a certain noble lord, a member of the other House (lord Shelburne.) If that intimacy and friendship be a state of dependance, I am happy in classing myself among that noble lord's dependants. I will assure those who have alluded to what they call dependance, that it is a state of dependance, accompanied with perfect freedom. It is true, my hon. friend has been honoured with the noble lord's friendship, for upwards of 20 years; but I think I know the frame of mind and disposition of my hon. friend too well, to be persuaded that he would purchase any man's intimacy upon any terms short of a perfect equality, and mutual confidence; and I think I may likewise add, that if any person should attempt to purchase the noble lord's friendship, by mean or improper concessions, there is not a man on earth would more readily see through or despise it. I know the noble lord to be a great private, as well as public character. I know my hon. friend to possess a spirit of true independence. I am persuaded of the noble lord's great and acknowledged talents as a senator and a politician; and I can add, great as he may appear in a public light, that his private character is no less amiable and worthy of general admiration.

Having endeavoured, as far as lay in my power, to describe what the petitioners mean, and what administration mean; on the other hand, give me leave to recur to the ground of my present proposed resolutions. I have already observed, that the great objects of the petitioners have been resisted both in argument and by public avowals, by the minister and his friends. They have told you that the influence of the crown is not too much, and ought not of course to be lessened; the petitioners have asserted the direct contrary. Ministers have told you, that it is not competent for this House to enquire into the expenditure of the civil list; the direct contrary are the sentiments of the petitioners. To talk of petitions or redress is vain, idle, nugatory, and ineffectual, while these two points are maintained by those who have the majority of the House. To bring both these points fairly to issue, I mean to frame two propositions, abstracted from the petitions on your table, and take the sense of the committee upon them. I mean that they shall be short, and as simple as possible, so as to draw forth a direct affirmative or negative. If the committee should agree with me in the resolutions, I mean to follow them up with real, substantive, practicable measures; but should they disagree or dissent, or endeavour to evade or procrastinate, there will be at once an end of the petitions, and a full answer to the petitioners.

It may be asked, are my propositions to be taken from the petitions on the table? Are they to be worded in the language of this or that petition? By no means. Some may be more extensive, others may be more full and specific; it will suffice that my propositions will not differ from any, as to the principle, though copied from none. My first resolution will be,

> That it is the opinion of this committee, that it is necessary to declare, that the influence of the crown has increased, is increasing, and ought to be diminished.

My second,

> That it is competent to this House, to examine into, and to correct, abuses in the expenditure of the civil list revenues, as well as in every other branch of the public revenue, whenever it shall appear expedient to the wisdom of this House so to do.

He then proceeded to argue the question on the ground of notoriety, that the influence of the crown was increased, and ought to be diminished, having first regularly moved it. He supported his argument, not upon proof, which he said it was idle to require, and must be decided by the consciences of those who as a jury were called upon to determine what was or was not within their own knowledge. He quoted Mr. Hume to prove, that he foresaw the increasing influence so early as the year 1742; and also quoted judge Blackstone as an authority for its existence. He cited a passage from Hume's Essays, to shew that that able writer had prophesied, that arbitrary monarchy would one day or other be the euthanasia of the British constitution. He could affirm upon his own knowledge, and pledge his honour to the truth of the assertion, that he knew upwards of fifty members in that House who voted always in the train of the noble lord in the blue ribbon; that confessed out of the House, that the influence of the crown was increased, and dangerously increased. He adduced several arguments of a similar nature, and sat down, he said, with this consolation, that neither the minority of that House, nor the people at large, would be any longer mocked and insulted with this or that management or trick, this or that evasion; for the certain alternative would be, that the decision on the question now proposed by him would declare, whether the petitions were to be really attended to, or finally and totally rejected.

Earl Nugent observed, that the hon. gentleman had founded his motion upon the petitions then lying on the table. He had, from time to time, attended to the contents of the said petitions, and did not recollect any part which accorded with the two resolutions stated by the hon. gentleman. He acknowledged, that some of the petitions stated one grievance, and some another, but none of them any thing resembling the proposition moved, or the other proposition opened by the learned gentleman. The propositions did not go so far as many of the petitions, and they went farther than others. Some of the petitions were confined merely to the economical expenditure of public money; some to the abolition of sinecure places, unmerited pensions, exorbitant salaries, etc. and many of them proceeded on the idea, that the influence of the crown had increased to a degree dangerous to the liberties of the people. Such being the real state of the petitions on the table, he recommended the learned gentleman to modify his motion, so as to take up the specific prayer of some one petition, or frame it so as to make it an aggregate of them all; otherwise, the resolution now moved must be considered to be the learned gentleman's own opinion on the subject, and not that of any one set or class of petitioners. In the course of discussing the resolution therefore, it would not admit of the matter contained in the said petitions being more than collaterally introduced into the debate. Would the hon. gentleman say, that the influence of the crown was, or was not, dangerous to the liberties of the people? If not, the proposition, which he called upon the committee to resolve, could not be considered in any other light than as the individual opinion of the learned gentleman.

Mr. Dunning said, he thought he had sufficiently explained himself in the course of his speech. His own sentiments, he assured the noble lord, went the full length of such of the petitions as asserted, that the influence of the crown had increased to a degree dangerous to the liberties of the people. Some other petitions did not go so far; but he believed, nine out of ten of the petitions on the table contained this general proposition, that the influence of the crown was increased, and improperly and unconstitutionally increased; and that a reform in the expenditure of the civil list revenue was become absolutely necessary. So far, therefore, his two propositions were meant to go; namely, to the prayer of every petition, and to contradict none. They contained an abstract of the whole of the petitions on the table, and formed a great principle of union, importing, in the gross, what was prayed for by each separately. Such as the propositions were, he was perfectly satisfied with them. He was much obliged to the noble lord for his proffered aid upon the present occasion, though, for the reasons both before and now given, he must decline making use of it. The proposition before the committee, and now moved by the way of resolution, must stand or fall upon its own merit; it was not an abstracted proposition; though, as he foresaw at the opening, he should not be surprised to hear it called an abstract proposition.

Earl Nugent said, he thought the resolution now moved, clearly an abstract proposition. The learned gentleman had said, that he would not inform the House what further measures he intended to graft upon his two intended resolutions. This he always understood to be the true definition of an abstract question. There were, to be sure, instances in the records of parliament, in which abstract questions were moved and agreed to, but they were very improper precedents to be followed; but in general, even then they related to some previous proceeding in the House, some disputed point, some subject of controversy under discussion, in which the sense of the House was particularly called for. When this happened not to be the case, the person who came to desire the House to vote an abstract question, having a prospective view to measures which were to be ingrafted on it, was bound by the nature of the requisitions thus made, to explain to the House what those measures were intended to be; otherwise, one of those two things might happen, that either the House might agree to an abstract question, to no manner of purpose, or, having resolved it, might be obliged to negative the measure so engrafted, though it bore a strong seeming relation to the antecedent resolution agreed to. It was the established usage of parliament to do so; it was a duty in point of candour incumbent on the member who made it; and it was every way agreeable to the wisdom and justice of that House.

In this point of view, the question now proposed was an abstract one, because it was not connected with any one measure whatever; it pointed to no remedy, nor was it apparently designed to avert any evil. For instance, many gentlemen in that House might think, that the influence of the crown was increased; some, that it was increasing; and others, that it ought to be diminished. Nevertheless, if the proposition should be resolved, when the measure which the learned gentleman meant to follow it up with came to be considered and divided upon, the same gentlemen, who agreed with the question in abstract, might totally disapprove of the remedy to be applied; whereas, if the measure of correction accompanied the fact of abuse, the same gentlemen who might vote the question in abstract, would many of them probably reject it, when they should be acquainted with the use or end proposed by voting it to be true.

Upon the proposition itself, he could fairly say, it was not founded. He had more than once given it as his sincere opinion, that the influence of the crown was not increased, neither comparatively increased, or improperly increased. He had long sat in parliament, and he could affirm, he never recollected a period in which influence was less felt, that since his noble friend in the blue ribbon came into his present situation; but allowing that the influence of the crown had been gradually on the increase since the period alluded to by the learned gentleman, as quoted from the words of an ingenious political writer (Mr. Hume) would the learned gentleman, or any other gentleman, lay his hand fairly on his heart, and declare, that he thought this was the time, and peculiarly the time, which called for its immediate diminution? At a time when America was lost—he would speak out—he feared irretrievably lost. [A loud cry of hear him! hear him!] He was willing to repeat his words, America was lost. The American war proved a wrong measure. He supported the war. He was not ashamed to own that he was wrong himself.

[Another loud cry from the opposition benches.] He did not mean to say that it was wrong in principle, for in a similar situation he should adhere to his former conduct; but what he wished to convey to his auditors was, that from a succession of untoward accidents, that it was wrong, because the event proved unfortunate. But after such a series of disappointments, followed by a war with France, and closely followed again by a war with Spain, with great loans, heavy taxes, and all the unpopular consequences incident to such a state of things, to contend that the influence of the crown was increasing, and ought to be diminished, was, in his opinion, to the last degree preposterous. The people were heavily burthened; they foresaw an increase of those burthens daily approaching; they felt the loss of America; they were disappointed and out of temper; consequently, it was idle to talk of the dangerous influence of the crown. But supposing the argument which he had heard frequently urged in that House of late, that the increase of taxes, of the influence arising from a state of war, in the military departments of government, had thrown a sudden weight into the hands of the crown; would not every gentleman present acknowledge that this influence could only have temporary duration; that it must cease with the cause, the continuance of the war; and that as soon as peace was restored, things would flow into their old channel? Yet those who maintain the propriety of reducing the influence of the crown, are so absurd to apply a remedy which they mean shall operate perpetually, while they acknowledge that the chief cause of the evil is but of a temporary nature, and will cease to operate with the duration of the present war.

The learned gentleman has produced a proposition, that the influence of the crown "has increased, is increasing, and ought to be diminished." Has he produced, or so much as promised, a tittle of evidence of the facts so alleged? Not a word of that: but he has said a great deal about the opinions of speculative men, of an eminent lawyer lately deceased, and of two ingenious political writers (Hume and Blackstone.) The former says, the influence of the crown began to shew itself in or about the year 1742. I was in parliament before that period, and remember that clamours and speculations of that kind prevailed long before the year 1742; but I protest that I thought then, as I think now, that they were totally unfounded; and I can fairly affirm, that I never felt it myself, nor gave a single vote under any influence whatever, but what was necessary for the support of government. But I will go one step further, and take the two first assertions in the hon. gentleman's proposition as proved, that the influence of the crown has increased, and is increasing; will the learned gentleman's conclusion follow? May not this increased influence be necessary? Has he ventured to state that it is not? By no means; he declines the fair allegation that it is imporper or unconstitutional, and takes a leap to his conclusion, by inferring that it ought to be diminished.

On the whole, the learned gentleman has desired the committee to vote an abstract question, declaring his intention of holding back the point which should be the proper subject of debate; he has taken facts as proved, without offering any species of proof whatever: and finally, he has drawn a conclusion not by any means deducible from the premises stated in the resolution. It is true, he has argued much on the ground of notoriety; far the greater part depending on the authority of the writers which I have mentioned; a very extraordinary medium of proof, in my opinion, to found a resolution of parliament upon: and the hon. gentleman has further adduced the contradiction between the conduct of gentlemen in that House, who vote with the ministers, with the language held by the same persons out of it. He says, that they vote within these walls that no such unconstitutional influence exists; and without them, acknowledge that it does exist to a dangerous degree. I do not know well how to contradict this assertion of the hon. gentleman; but this I will affirm, that if there be such abandoned wretches within these walls, that they merit the contempt of every honest man within and without this House, and the indignation, reprobation, and detestation of mankind: they are wretches indeed; they are no less profligate than shameless; they at once convict themselves, and glory in their infamy. I hope there are not any such, not only in this House, but in any other place; for I am sure they are not fit for human society. I am inclined to hope, that the learned gentleman is rather mistaken, or has exaggerated their number. This I will say, however, that if there be any such on this side of the House, I hope they will, in the course of the evening, go over to the other side: for I shall ever be of opinion, that the cause which is supported by such men ought to be abandoned; and, as one, I say to them, "Go you worst of men, be your hearts and motives ever so corrupt, preserve some appearance of principle and decency, and support those tentiments in public, which you approve of and secretly avow in private."

Mr. *Dunning* thought it his duty to say a word or two in answer to what had fallen from the noble lord. His lordship doubted the fact relative to the contradictory sentiments entertained by some gentlemen in that House. He believed it would be extremely improper to mention names; but though he confined his description to fifty, he believed he might with truth extend it to a much greater number. He mixed much with mankind; his habits of life and profession gave him frequent opportunities of being acquainted with the sentiments of many persons in that House, when they were out of it; and he could declare upon his honour, that he was fully warranted in the assertion he had made, that he knew fifty members in that House, and the most of them within his hearing, who totally reprobated and condemned, out of the House, the measures they supported and voted for in it; and though no man held private conversation more sacred than he did, if the issue of the present debate was to depend upon naming them, and it was the pleasure of the House to desire it, he could and would name them.

Place Act, 1782

22 Geo. 3, c. 41   *Statutes at Large*, XXXIV, 48-50.

This measure disenfranchised revenue and excise officers.

For the better securing the freedom of elections of members to serve in parliament, be it enacted by the King's most excellent majesty, by and with the advice and consent of the lords spiritual and temporal, and commons, in this present parliament assembled, and by the authority of the same, That, from and after the first day of August, one thousand seven hundred and eighty-two, no commissioner, collector, supervisor, gauger, or other officer or person whatsoever, concerned or employed in the charging, collecting, levying, or managing the duties of excise, or any branch or part thereof; nor any commissioner, collector, comptroller, searcher, or other officer or person whatsoever, concerned or employed in the charging, collecting levying, or managing the customs, or any branch or part thereof; nor any commissioner, officer, or other person concerned or employed in collecting, receiving, or managing, any of the duties on stamped vellum, parchment, and paper, nor any person appointed by the commissioners for distributing of stamps; nor any commissioner, officer, or other person employed in collecting, levying, or managing, any of the duties on salt; nor any surveyor, collector, comptroller, inspector, officer, or other person employed in collecting, managing, or receiving, the duties on windows or houses; nor any postmaster, postmasters general, or his or their deputy or deputies, or any person employed by or under him or them in receiving, collecting, or managing the revenue of the post-office, or any part thereof, nor any captain, master, or mate, of any ship, packet, or other vessel, employed by or under the postmaster or postmasters general in conveying the mail to and from foreign ports, shall be capable of giving his vote for the election of any knight of the shire, commissioner, citizen, burgess, or baron, to serve in parliament for any county, stewartry, city, borough, or cinque port, or for chusing any delegate in whom the right of electing members to serve in parliament, for that part of Great Britain called Scotland, is vested: and if any person hereby made incapable of voting as aforesaid, shall nevertheless presume to give his vote, during the time he shall hold, or within twelve calendar months after he shall cease to hold or execute any of the offices aforesaid, contrary to the true intent and meaning of this act, such votes so given shall be held null and void to all intents and purposes whatsoever, and every person so offending shall forfeit the sum of one hundred pounds, one moiety thereof to the informer, and the other moiety thereof to be immediately paid into the hands of the treasurer of the county, riding, or division, within which such offence shall have been committed, in that part of Great Britain called England; and into the hands of the clerk of the justices of the peace of the counties or stewartries, in that part of Great Britain called Scotland, to be applied and disposed of to such purposes as the justices at the next general quarter session of the peace to be held for such county, stewartry, riding, or division, shall think fit; to be recovered by any person that shall sue for the same, by action of debt, bill, plaint, or information, in any of his Majesty's courts of record at Westminster, in which no essoin, protection, privilege, or wager of law, or more than one imparlance, shall be allowed; or by summary complaint before the court of session in Scotland; and the person convicted on any such suit shall thereby become disabled and incapable of ever bearing or executing any office or place of trust whatsoever under his Majesty, his heirs and successors.

   II.   Provided always, and be it enacted, That nothing in this act contained shall extend, or be construed to extend, to any person or persons for or by reason of his or their being a commissioner or commissioners of the land tax, or for or by reason of his or their acting by or under the appointment of such commissioners of the land tax, for the purpose of assessing, levying, collecting, receiving, or managing the land tax, or any other rates or duties already granted or imposed, or which shall hereafter be granted or imposed by authority of parliament.

III. Provided also, and be it further enacted, That nothing in this act contained shall extend, or be construed to extend, to any office now held, or usually granted to be held, by letters patent for any estate of inheritance or freehold.

IV. Provided always, and be it enacted by the authority aforesaid, That nothing herein contained shall extend to any person who shall resign his office or employment on or before the said first day of August, one thousand seven hundred and eighty-two.

V. Provided also, and be it enacted, That no person shall be liable to any forfeiture or penalty by this act laid or imposed, unless prosecution be commenced within twelve months after such penalty or forfeiture shall be incurred.

Commons debate on the resignation of the North government, 20 March 1782

Parliamentary History, XII, 1214-21.

Frederick North (1732-92; called Lord North; second earl of Guilford, 1790) was George III's chancellor of the exchequer (1767-82) and first lord of the treasury (1770 82). Under increasing pressure as a result of his unsuccessful American policies, he resigned before a motion could be put to that effect.

Ever since the beginning of the session, there never were so many members in the House, as appeared there this day; and the crowds of spectators were in proportion greater than usual. At a quarter after four, when the House was ready to enter upon the great business of the day, and the Speaker had called to gentlemen to take their places, the earl of Surrey, the member who was to have made the motion, stood up: and just at the same moment lord North got upon his legs: and each noble lord seemed determined not to give way to the other: this created a great deal of confusion, one side of the House crying out loudly for earl Surrey to speak first; the other side as loudly calling out lord North. At last,

Mr. Baker rose to speak to order. He thought it indecent in the noble lord in the blue ribbon to rise at a time, when he knew the noble earl had a motion of the greatest importance to submit to the House.

Lord North said that it was not through disrespect for the noble lord that he had risen; but merely to save him the trouble of making, and the House that of discussing a question, which at present he might say was become totally unnecessary.

Mr. Baker called the noble lord again to order: he said that he had no right to know of what nature or complexion the motion was, or would be, which his noble friend had not yet made; and that therefore it was highly unparliamentary to say that it was become totally unnecessary.

Lord North insisted, that it was not disorderly in him to suppose he knew, or to say he knew, what was the substance of the motion, which the noble lord was then going to make; for it had been publicly announced to the House some days ago by an hon. member that a motion would be made on this day, similar to that which had been rejected on Friday last: and therefore having all the information which he could derive from such a notice, it was perfectly competent for him to rise, if he pleased, to move to adjourn, in order to prevent the discussion of a question, which he no longer thought necessary. His reason for thinking it was no longer necessary was, that as the object of the motion was to remove his Majesty's ministers, he could take upon him to say, that his Majesty's ministers were no more; and therefore the object being already attained, the means by which gentlemen had intended to obtain it, could no longer be necessary.

The other side of the House called out for lord Surrey! lord Surrey! accompanied with the words "No adjournment! no adjournment."

Mr. Hopkins obtained a hearing, and said, though he was ready to address the noble lord in the blue ribbon had he been out of order before, he had been most thoroughly out of order in what he had then said. The noble lord had no right to presume what was the tendency of any motion, before it was made; every syllable, therefore, that he had said relative to the motion to be expected from the noble lord near him, was clearly out of order.

A clamour prevailed here, in consequence of an infinite number of members of both sides rising to speak at once, but Mr. Pitt obtained the preference after lord North had said, "I did not put a question of adjournment, I merely informed the House, what I meant to have done, had I been heard when I first rose;" to which sir Fletcher Norton assented.

Mr. W. Pitt then said, he was sorry to see that the noble lord in the blue ribbon had attempted to excite the attention of the House, before a matter of such universal expectation as the motion, which it was known for some days past would be made by the noble lord near him, was heard, and more so that this had given rise to so much heat, eagerness, and disorder. He should have conceived the regular mode for the noble lord in the blue ribbon to have proceeded, would have been to have waited till the other noble lord had made his motion, and then, if he had thought it right or proper, to have moved his question of adjournment upon that, to state, in his speech, his reasons for urging such adjournment. By so doing, the House would have seen their way clearly and distinctly, and would have been able to have formed a judgment fitted to the occasion, without shewing any of that heat and eagerness, which was in no case proper, but least of all in a moment like the present.

Mr. Fox finding that the House was in very great confusion, thought that the best way to produce order was by moving, that lord Surrey be allowed to make his motion; and he thought this the more necessary, as the House could not place any confidence in the word of the minister; and therefore, ought not to believe upon that word, that the King's ministers were no more; the House ought to take care, and it had it in its power effectually to take care, that the ministers should be no more; a vote of that House would suffice; and while they had it in their power to pass such a vote, they ought not to omit it. He therefore concluded with moving, "That the earl of Surrey do first speak." This motion being read from the chair,

Lord North rose and said, that he had now a right to speak to the question. The noble lord began with declaring, that he had been extremely surprised to hear from an hon. gentleman who spoke last but one, that what he had risen to say, should have occasioned so much heat and disorder. Nor was he less surprised at being told, that he knew not the purport of the noble lord's intended motion, and that it was impossible for him to have known it, till it had been regularly made. Did gentlemen recollect that the House had been expressly informed, when notice was given of that motion, that it was a motion somewhat differing in point of form, but essentially the same in substance, as the motion of Friday last, and the motion of Friday se'nnight? Would any gentleman assert, that the tendency of the motion was a secret? Would any gentleman go so far as to say, that it was not a motion, the object of which was a vote of the House, expressing it to be the desire of parliament, that his Majesty's ministers should be removed? Did he stand liable to contradiction, when he declared, that he conceived such to be the object of the intended motion, and that he did not imagine he stood alone in the knowledge, that such was its object? Such, then, being the case, where was the impropriety, where was the irregularity, where was the error in his rising to say, that the object of the motion was already accomplished; and that no debate was necessary? Nor could he imagine, that what he was about to have said, had it been agreeable to the House to have suffered him to go on, would, by any means, have occasioned either heat, or eagerness, or disorder in the House, as the hon. gentleman had been pleased to say, it would have done. It would be very extraordinary, indeed, to hold, as an argument, that a declaration of the business being already done, which it was the object of the motion of the day to effect, would give rise to heat, to eagerness, or to disorder. The House would remember, that in the debates which had taken place repeatedly within those walls, in the course of the past three weeks, it had been again and again declared, that the country was in a state of distraction and confusion, that there was no administration, that every thing was at a stand, and that he was the obstacle to good government and good order being restored. He had come down that day, therefore, to assure the House, that he was no longer the obstacle he had been described to be. His lordship said, he would not mention names, but he could with authority assure the House, that his Majesty had come to a full determination to change his ministers. This intelligence he had conceived, would have been sufficient to have induced the House to be of opinion, that it would be altogether unnecessary to debate a question, which had for its object a removal already effected; and with that view it was, that he had offered himself so early to the notice of the chair.

He could pledge himself to that House that his Majesty's ministry was at an end. Before, however, he took leave of his situation entirely, he felt himself bound to return his most grateful thanks to the House for the very kind, the repeated, and the essential support, he had for so many years received from the Commons of England, during his holding a situation to which he must confess he had at all times been unequal. And it was, he said, the more incumbent on him to return his thanks in that place, because it was that House which made him what he had been. His conduct within those walls had first made him known, and it had been in consequence of the part he had taken in that House, that he became recommended to his sovereign. He thanked the House therefore for their partiality to him, on all, and—he would use the phrase—for their forbearance on many occasions. Certainly he could not be pleased at their not thinking him any longer worthy of the confidence of parliament, nor for their wishing to vote his removal, but their general support of him, through a service of many years continuance, claimed his fullest acknowledgments and his warmest gratitude; and he ever should hold it in his memory as the chief honour of his life, to have been so supported. A successor of greater abilities, of better judgment, and more qualified for his situation, was easy to be found; a successor more zealous for the interests of his country, more anxious to promote those interests, more loyal to his sovereign, and more desirous of preserving the constitution whole and entire, he might be allowed to say, could not so easily be found. The crown had resolved to choose new ministers, and he hoped to God, whoever those ministers were, they would take such measures as should tend effectually to extricate the country from its present difficulties, and to render us happy and prosperous at home, successful and secure abroad.

Having said so much, his lordship declared, that unless the motion of the noble lord was not what he supposed it to be, that it did not go to any new point, nor aim at more than the bare removal of ministers, he saw no reason for putting it then. At any rate, let the motion extend ever so far, there could be no necessity for being in such a hurry about it, as to insist on putting it that day. Having for so many years held a public situation, and been entrusted with the management of public affairs, he was perfectly conscious he was responsible for his conduct, and whenever his country should call upon him to answer, it was his indispensible duty to answer for every part of that conduct. For which reason, he pledged himself to the House that he would not run away; and neither the noble lord who intended to make the motion, nor any other hon. gentleman who meant to have supported it, need be at all apprehensive, that if it were not made that day, it would not be made while he was to be come at. He did assure the House he should remain to be found, as much as ever, and would on no account avoid any enquiry that might be thought necessary with regard to him. Upon these grounds, his lordship moved the question of adjournment, on the question moved by the hon. gentleman opposite to him. He confessed that at present the adjournment could not be of any other consequence than to put off the question till to-morrow; and his wish was to adjourn for a longer period, in order to give his Majesty time to make the necessary arrangements for a new administration: however, as there was another motion before the House, the adjournment could take place only for one day; and, to-morrow, he should propose a further adjournment for a few days. There was, indeed, another mode of proceeding, and that was by delivering a message from his Majesty to both Houses, desiring that they would adjourn for a few days, until he should have time to form a new administration; but the reason why he had not adopted that mode was, that there were several Bills before the House of Lords, which would be necessary to have passed before the recess; and therefore it was necessary that the Upper House should remain sitting; the same reason, however, did not subsist for the Lower House continuing to sit. He concluded, therefore, by moving "That the House do not adjourn."

Mr. Wm. Pitt rose to explain what the noble lord had so very much misunderstood. He had not charged the noble lord with pretending to know more of the motion intended to be made, than any other member of that House must be supposed to know from the notice that had been given of it; he had merely alluded to the heat and disorder, evident in the House, and had said, that he had conceived, as he still did, that it would have been more regular for the noble lord to have waited, till the motion that was expected, had been made, and then to have risen and moved an adjournment, for the reasons the noble lord had stated. A great deal that had fallen from the noble lord in the blue ribbon, certainly was material, and would doubtless have its due weight with the House; if, however, gentlemen were inclined to rely on the noble lord's declaration, and the other noble lord should on that account consent to postpone his motion, it at least was necessary to have that declaration accurately, clearly, and correctly defined, so that the House might fully comprehend to what extent the noble lord pledged himself, and that his declaration of that day was not merely a plea for getting rid of the motion, in order that they might be put out of possession of their majority.

Lord John Cavendish begged to be heard a few words. The noble lord's declaration had great weight in his mind; at the same time, he thought the noble lord had not said enough. He had not told the House for what they were to adjourn, nor to what day. As to going into a detail at large, of the circumstances alluded to by the noble lord, he was perfectly aware, that it would be highly improper, and indeed, that it was from motives of delicacy not to be desired. All he wished for was, that the noble lord and the House might perfectly understand each other's meaning before it was agreed to withdraw, or rather to postpone the motion, intended to have been made that day.

Lord North rose again, and said, had he been permitted to have spoken when he first rose, and before any question was put, he should have made the declaration, which the House had heard, and followed it up with a motion for an adjournment of a few days. A question having, however, been moved before he could do so, and the chair being in possession of that question, the noble lord and the House must be aware, that he could do no otherwise than barely move to adjourn, which of course meant no more than an adjournment till morning. With regard to a fuller and more explicit detail of the particulars to which he had alluded when he was up before, the noble lord who spoke last, had confessed he was aware that it was a matter neither proper in itself, nor to be expected by the House. This much, however, he would venture to say, that those persons who had for some time conducted the public affairs, were no longer his Majesty's ministers. They were no longer to be considered as men holding the reins of government and transacting measures of state, but merely remaining to do their official duty, till other ministers were appointed to take their places. The sooner those new ministers were appointed the better it would be, in his opinion for the public, and the better for the country in general.

Mr. Fox said that it did not seem to be a matter of any great importance, whether the motion of his noble friend the earl of Surrey should be put, or they should trust to the solemn declaration made by the noble lord. He could have wished, perhaps, that the motion were put and carried, because it would then manifestly appear to the nation at large, that the ministers of the crown did not retire either from the caprice of this or that minister, or from their wishing to go out, or from their being tired of their situations, or for any of the common reasons which ordinarily occasion the resignment of ministers, but because it was the sense of parliament, that they should retire, because that House had expressly called upon the crown for their dismission, and because the good of the country made it absolutely necessary. These were the reasons which impelled him to wish the motion put and carried. On the other hand, they had the less weight with him, because it was, he trusted, already sufficiently known, that the sense of parliament was against them, and although the motions of Friday last and the Friday before, had not actually been carried, yet he considered that motions debated in such full houses, and where the minister had so small a majority as nine or ten, were in effect carried, and in all reasonable construction, as much carried, as if there had not been such a majority against them. The great end, therefore, of carrying the motion of his noble friend, was already, in his mind, and he believed, in the consideration of the whole country, effectually answered. For which reason, he begged, that, let who would be the persons who should be called on by their sovereign to form the new administration, they might ever hold it in their minds, that his Majesty's late ministers were dismissed, because parliament disapproved of the system of their government, and that it was evident from parliament having gone so far to effect a removal of ministers, that it would be expected their successors should act upon different principles, and in a manner totally opposite. He declared, it had given him great pleasure, the preceding evening, to hear an hon. member say in a thin House, that he hoped, if his Majesty's ministers were removed, those who should be appointed in their room, would no longer govern by influence and corruption, and that if persons who had been in opposition came in, they would religiously adhere to their opposition principles, and not let it be a mere change of hands, without a change of measures. He enlarged a good deal on this idea, and in a warm manner declared, that he should ever hold those men infamous, be they who they might, who altered their principles on obtaining power; and that as the House had solemnly determined by their late conduct, that they rejected and abhorred a government of influence, the new ministers must always remember that fact, and remember also, that they owed their situations to that House. Mr. Fox concluded with advising his noble friend, not to make his intended motion that day, but to reserve it for Monday, in case the noble lord's declaration should fall short of its expected completion. He also agreed to withdraw his own motion.

Commons debate rescinding the 1769 expulsion of John Wilkes as MP for Middlesex County, 8 May 1782

Parliamentary History, XXII, 1407-11.

Mr. Wilkes said; Mr. Speaker: I think myself peculiarly happy at the present moment, that I have the honour of submitting to the House an important national question respecting the rights of election when the friends and favourites of the people enjoy, with the smiles of our sovereign, the offices of trust and power in the state, accompanied with that fair influence, which is necessarily created by great ability, perfect integrity, the purest political virtue, and the remembrance of their former upright conduct in the cause of the people. If the people of England, Sir, have at any period explicitly and fully declared an opinion respecting a momentous constitutional question, it has been in regard to the Middlesex election in 1768, and the subsequent most profligate proceedings of an administration, hostile by system to the rights of this country, and every part of the British empire. An instance cannot be found in our history of a more general concurrence of sentiment among the freeholders of England, and they were joined by almost every borough and corporation in the southern part of the island. I am satisfied therefore that I now shall find the real friends of the people determined and zealous in the support of their just claims and undoubted privileges.

Hitherto, Sir, every attempt for the recovery of this invaluable franchise has been rendered fruitless by the arts and machinations of power in the hands of wicked men; and I may with truth assert, that the body of the people long addressed, petitioned, and remonstrated with manly firmness and perseverance, but without the least effect, or even impression. The full redress demanded by this injured nation seems reserved to distinguish the present propitious aera of public liberty among the early and blooming honours of an administration, which possesses the confidence, and daily conciliates the affections, of a brave and sensible people. Their voice was never heard in a more clear and distinct manner than on this point of the first magnitude for all the electors of the kingdom, and I trust will now be heard favourably. The general resentment and indignation ran so high against the House of Commons, which committed the outrage, that their immediate dissolution became the prayer of numberless petitions to the throne. No man scrupled to declare them unworthy to exist in their political capacity. The public pronounced them guilty of sacrificing and betraying the rights, which they were called upon by every tie of justice and duty to defend. The noble spirit of the freeholders of Middlesex, persevering in the best of causes, undaunted by all the menaces of power, was the subject of the most general applause and admiration. The voice of the people was then in the harsh and sharp tone of passion and anger against ministers. It will, I am persuaded, soon be in the soft and pleasing accents of joy and thankfulness to our deliverers.

It is scarcely possible, Sir, to state a question in which the people of this free country are more materially interested than in the right of election, for it is the share, which they have reserved to themselves in the legislature. When it was wrested from them by violence, the constitution was torn up by the roots. I have now the happiness of seeing the Treasury bench filled with the friends of the constitution, the guardians and lovers of liberty, who have been upwearied and uniform in the defence of all our rights, and in particular of this invaluable franchise. I hail the present auspicious moment, and with impatience expect the completion of what I have long and fervently desired for my friends and country, for the present age, and a free posterity. The former conduct of those now in power affords me the most sanguine hopes of this day seeing justice done to a people, to whom they have so frequently appealed, who now look up to them with ardent expectation, with pleasure and esteem. Consistency, Sir, has drawn the right line of their political conduct to this period. It will now point out the same path of public virtue and honour. May I be indulged in a hint, which I mean to extend much beyond the business of the day, when I say that consistency will be attended with that stability and perfect security which are the objects of every good man's wishes for them? They have given us a fair earnest of their reverence for the constitution by their support of two Bills, essentially necessary to restore the purity and independency of parliament; I mean, the Bill for preventing contractors sitting in the House of Commons, and the Bill for disabling officers of the revenue from voting at elections—[Mr. Wilkes was here interrupted by a message by sir Francis Molyneux, gentleman usher of the Black Rod, desiring the immediate attendance of the House of Commons in the House of Lords. The Speaker then went up to the House of Peers: and after his return and report of what had passed, Mr. Wilkes said] I return my thanks to the Black Rod for so luckily interposing in favour of this House, when I might possibly have again tired them with the important, however stale, case of the Middlesex election, which their patient ear has for several years with much good nature suffered. I will now make some return for their indulgence, in profiting by the circumstance of this happy interruption, and not saying a single word about Walpole or Wollaston, Coke or Blackstone. I will not detain the House longer than by moving, That the entry in the Journal of the House of the 17th of February, 1769, of the resolution, "That John Wilkes, esq. having been in this session of parliament expelled this House, was and is incapable of being elected a member to serve in this present parliament," might be read. The same being read, Mr. Wilkes next moved, "That the said Resolution be expunged from the Journals of this House, as being subversive of the rights of the whole body of electors of this kingdom."

Mr. Byng seconded the motion.

Mr. Fox opposed it; but said that it was not from any false pride, or fear of being thought inconsistent. He had turned the question often in his mind, and he was still convinced that the resolution which gentlemen wanted to expunge, was founded on proper principles: it was for the good of the people of England that the House should have a power of expelling any man, whom the representatives of the people of England thought unworthy to sit among them: this was a privilege too valuable to be given up. He supposed some cases in which the public utility of it would be felt and acknowledged: if the Bill for excluding contractors from seats in that House, had been rejected in the other; and the House of Commons should come to a resolution of their own, that no person holding a contract should sit amongst them, the present contractors losing their seats, might be re-elected, and then if not prevented by this inherent privilege of the House to expel, the very men whom the House should have pronounced improper to sit among them, might be returned again. However, though he opposed the motion, he felt very little anxiety for the event of the question, for when he found the voice of the people was against the privilege, as he believed was the case at present, he would not preserve the privilege, to make use of it against the people, which was originally intended for the preservation of their liberties. Moreover, he did not think it was of great consequence to retain the privilege, when the power to enforce it was gone: the power was undoubtedly gone; for gentlemen might remember, that when two members of that House had, as magistrates of London, grossly violated the privilege, the natural punishment ought to have been expulsion: but the House was afraid to proceed to that length: the public no longer acknowledged the privilege; they had associated, they had declared their sentiments to parliament, and had taught parliament to listen to the voice of their constituents. The mere expunging of the resolution, however, would not be of any great use; the doctrine would remain just as before; unless a Bill should be brought in, which should put the matter beyond all dispute.

The Lord Advocate opposed the motion also: but he spoke principally to Mr. Fox's idea of excluding any one from a seat in that House by a mere resolution of the House, and without the concurrence of the other branches of the legislature: such a resolution would be contrary to all law, and to the very spirit of the constitution, according to which no one right or franchise of an individual was to be taken from him, but by law. He animadverted also on the doctrine of associations, which he condemned as dangerous to the last degree, if ten or twelve gentlemen should associate, so might ten thousand; and God only knew where such associations, once formed, would end; that House had seen an association of 20,000 men, with blue cockades, and their excesses were but too well remembered. In a word, from such meetings would arise confusion: and from confusion would spring up, not liberty, but the rankest tyranny and despotism.

Lord Mahon, lord Surrey, sir P. J. Clerke, and the Secretary at War spoke also for the motion: the House at last divided, when there appeared for expunging, 115; against it 47. The same was expunged by the clerk accordingly. It was then ordered,

> That all the declarations, orders, and resolutions of this House respecting the election of John Wilkes, esq. for the county of Middlesex, as a void election, the due and legal election of Henry Lawes Luttrell, esq. into parliament for the said county, and the incapacity of John Wilkes, esq. to be elected a member to serve in the said parliament, be expunged from the Journals of this House, as being subversive of the rights of the whole body of electors of this kingdom.

The same were likewise expunged by the clerk at the table.

The Regency crisis: Exchange between William Pitt, the prime minister, and Charles James Fox, House of Commons, 10 December 1788

Parliamentary History, XXVII, 705-13.

William Pitt (1759-1806; chancellor of the exchequer, 1782; first lord of the treasury and prime minister, and chancellor of the exchequer, 1783-1801, 1804-06) and his chief Whig opponent, Charles James Fox (1749-1806; foreign secretary, 1782, 1783, 1806), debated the provisions to be made for the royal power during the illness of George III. Fox argued for a much larger exercise of sovereignty by the Prince of Wales, the proposed regent.

Mr. *Pitt* said, that the paper from the privy council, which had been already placed upon the table, as well as the more regular examinations of which the House had just heard the contents, afforded them sufficient information, both with regard to the melancholy subject which had occasioned them to assemble, and the opinions of the physicians thereon; and must fill their minds with a reasonable hope, that a happier moment would arrive than the present, although the faculty who had been consulted, were still unable to declare the precise time of its arrival. Gratified, however, as the House must be in that expectation, yet the uncertainty how long it might be protracted, rendered it their indispensable duty to proceed with every degree of dispatch, and in the most respectful manner, to take those intermediate steps which the unfortunate exigency of the moment required, in order to provide for the present serious situation of affairs, with a view to guard the liberties of the people from danger, and secure the safety of the country; that his Majesty might have the gratification of knowing, when the happy moment of his recovery should arrive, that the people whom he had loved and protected, had suffered as little as possible by his illness. The point to be agitated on this occasion, involved in it whatever was dear to the interests of the country, whatever was valuable to the people, whatever was important in the fundamental principles of our free constitution. The steps to be taken, therefore, preliminary to the discussion of this interesting subject, were such as he could not conceive likely to create any difference of opinion. That the House might have the advantage of the wisdom of their ancestors to guide their proceedings, and act upon the fullest information, he should move for the appointment of a committee to examine into, search for, and report precedents, from which report they would be enabled to see, what had been the steps taken in former moments of difficulty and danger, whence they might proceed with the greater security in providing for the present melancholy circumstances of the country. He conceived the report of such a committee might be made in the course of the present week. He then moved; "That a committee be appointed to examine and report precedents of such proceedings as may have been had, in case of the personal exercise of the royal authority being prevented or interrupted, by infancy, sickness, infirmity, or otherwise, with a view to provide for the same."

Mr. Fox having premised that he was happy to feel a coincidence of sentiments with those of the right hon. gentleman in most parts of his speech, added, that undoubtedly it was their duty to lose no time in proceeding to provide some measure for the exigency of the present moment, but that exigency was so pressing in point of time, that he, for one, would willingly dispense with the motion then made. If the motion were carried, it must be considered, that it was loss of time. What were they going to search for? Not precedents upon their journals, not parliamentary precedents, but precedents in the history of England. He would be bold to say, nay they all knew, that the doing so would prove a loss of time, for there existed no precedent whatever, that could bear upon the present case. The circumstance to be provided for did not depend upon their deliberations as a house of parliament; it rested elsewhere. There was then a person in the kingdom different from any other person that any existing precedents could refer to—an heir apparent of full age and capacity to exercise the royal power. It behoved them, therefore, to waste not a moment unnecessarily, but to proceed with all becoming diligence to restore the sovereign power and the exercise of the royal authority. When the unfortunate situation of his Majesty was first made known to that House, by a presentation of the minute of the Privy Council, some gentlemen had expressed a doubt whether the House could make such a paper a ground of parliamentary proceedings. Mr. Fox reminded the House that he had gone farther, and declared he thought the Report of the Privy Council was not an authentic document, nor such as that House could make the ground of its proceedings. That defect had now been remedied, and the House was, in consequence of the regular examination which his Majesty's physicians had undergone before a committee of their own, in possession of the true state of the King's health. That being known to the House, and through them to the nation at large, he contended that it was then, and then only, the precise point of time for the House to decide, and that not a single moment ought to be lost. In his firm opinion, his royal highness the Prince of Wales had as clear, as express a right to assume the reins of government, and exercise the power of sovereignty, during the continuance of the illness and incapacity with which it had pleased God to afflict his Majesty, as in the case of his Majesty's having undergone a natural and perfect demise: and, as to this right, which he conceived the Prince of Wales had, he was not himself to judge when he was entitled to exercise it; but the two Houses of Parliament, as the organs of the nation, were alone qualified to pronounce when the Prince ought to take possession of, and exercise, his right. He thought it candid, entertaining this opinion, to come forward fairly, and avow it at that instant; and therefore, under such an idea, he conceived that as short a time as possible ought to intervene between the Prince of Wales's assuming the sovereignty, and the present moment. He justified the Prince's not making this his indubitable claim himself, by imputing his desire of waving the open advancement of it, to his having been bred in those principles which had placed his illustrious House on the throne, and to his known reverence and regard for those principles, as the true fundamentals of our glorious constitution, in the maintenance of which, his family had flourished with so much prosperity and happiness, as sovereigns of the British empire. Hence it was, that his Royal Highness chose rather to wait the decision of Parliament, with a patient and due deference to the constitution, than to urge a claim, that, he trusted, a majority of that House, and of the people at large, admitted; and which, he was persuaded, could not be reasonably disputed. But, ought he to wait unnecessarily? Ought his Royal Highness to wait while precedents were searched for, when it was known that none, that bore upon the case which so nearly concerned him, existed? Take it for granted, the House agreed to the motion, and proceeded by their committee to search for precedents. What precedents did the wording of the motion point to? It spoke in general and indefinite language. Possibly it might mean parliamentary precedents, referring to such contingencies as the present. If that were its meaning, the words "parliamentary precedents" ought to have been expressed in it. He should not oppose the motion, but he thought it his duty to say, that it was incumbent on the House to lose no time in restoring the third estate. His Royal Highness, he was convinced, must exercise the royal prerogative during, and only during, his Majesty's illness. With regard to the examination of the physicians, he would not take up the time of the House with commenting on the particular answers and opinions of each. However the physicians might have delivered opinions, that might, in the minds of some men, impress one turn of idea, and, in the minds of others, a very different turn of idea, three points were, he thought, undeniable inferences from the whole of their examinations, in which he had assisted above stairs. These three points formed the result, and must be the substratum on which that House would necessarily raise the superstructure, whatever it might be, that they should deem it expedient to erect. He took the three points to be these: 1. That his Majesty was incapable of meeting his Parliament, or proceeding to business. 2. That there was a great prospect, and a strong probability, of his recovery. 3. But that with respect to the point of time when that recovery would take place, they were left in absolute doubt and uncertainty. Upon this occasion, Mr. Fox said, that he could not avoid expressing his hopes that the House would agree with him, that these three points formed the true, fair, uncoloured result of the examination of his Majesty's physicians. He recapitulated the general heads of his speech; and, after repeating his willingness to accede to every proposition that was consistent with the due solemnity of their proceeding, upon so serious an occasion, and declaring that he did not impute any desire to create delay, or unnecessarily avoid dispatch, to the right hon. gentleman who spoke last, added, that he certainly would not resist the motion, although he had thought it incumbent on him to give his opinion on the subject freely and unreservedly.

Mr. Pitt said, he must take the liberty to observe, that the right hon. gentleman had thrown out an idea which, whatever he might have generally thought of him, as to his penetration and discernment, as to his acquaintance with the laws and general history of the country, and as to his knowledge of the theory of the constitution— however he might repeatedly have found occasion to differ with him in respect to his measures and opinions in his practice under it—he defied all his ingenuity to support, upon any analogy of constitutional precedent, or to reconcile to the spirit and genius of the constitution itself. The doctrine advanced by the right hon. gentleman was itself, if any additional reason were necessary, the strongest and most unanswerable for appointing the Committee he had moved for, that could possibly be given. If a claim of right was intimated (even though not formally) on the part of the Prince of Wales, to assume the government, it became of the utmost consequence to ascertain, from precedent and history, whether this claim was founded; which, if it was, precluded the House from the possibility of all deliberation on the subject. In the mean time, he maintained, that it would appear, from every precedent and from every page of our history, that to assert such a right in the Prince of Wales, or any one else, independent of the decision of the two Houses of Parliament, was little less than treason to the constitution of the country. He did not mean then to enter into the discussion of that great and important point; because a fit occasion for discussing it would soon afford both the right hon. gentleman and himself an ample opportunity of stating their sentiments upon it. In the mean time, he pledged himself to this assertion, that in the case of the interruption of the personal exercise of the royal authority, without any previous lawful provision having been made for carrying on the government, it belonged to the other branches of the legislature, on the part of the nation at large, the body they represented, to provide, according to their discretion, for the temporary exercise of the royal authority, in the name, and on the behalf of the sovereign, in such manner as they should think requisite; and that, unless by their decision, the Prince of Wales had no more right (speaking of strict right) to assume the government, than any other individual subject of the country. What Parliament ought to determine on that subject, was a question of discretion. However strong the arguments might be on that ground, in favour of the Prince of Wales, which he would not enter into at present, it did not affect the question of right; because, neither the whole, nor any part, of the royal authority could belong to him in the present circumstances, unless conferred by the Houses of Parliament.—As to the right hon. gentleman's repeated enforcement of the Prince of Wales's claim, he admitted that it was a claim entitled to most serious consideration; and thence, argued, that it was the more necessary to learn how the House had acted in cases of similar exigency, and what had been the opinion of Parliament on such occasions. He would not allow that no precedent analogous to an interruption of the personal exercise of the royal authority, could be found, although there might possibly not exist a precedent of an heir apparent in a state of majority, during such an occurrence, and in that case, he contended, that it devolved on the remaining branches of the legislature, on the part of the people of England, to exercise their discretion in providing a substitute. From the mode in which the right hon. gentleman had treated the subject, a new question presented itself, and that of greater magnitude even than the question which was originally before them, as matter of necessary deliberation. The question now was, the question of their own rights, and it was become a doubt, according to the right hon. gentleman's opinion, whether that House had, on this important occasion, a deliberative power. He wished, for the present, to wave the discussion of that momentous consideration; but, he declared that he would, at a fit opportunity, state his reasons for advising what step Parliament ought to take in the present critical situation of the country, contenting himself with giving his contradiction of the right hon. gentleman's bold assertion, and pledging himself to maintain the opposite ground against a doctrine so irreconcileable to the spirit and genius of the constitution. If the Report of the Committee had not proved the necessity of the motion he had made, the right hon. gentleman had furnished the House with so strong an argument for inquiry, that if any doubt had existed, that doubt must vanish. Let it not, then, be imputed to him, that he offered the motion, with a view to create delay; indeed, the right hon. gentleman had not made any such imputation. In fact, no imputation of that sort could be supported; since no longer time had been spent, after the first day of their meeting, than was absolutely necessary to ensure as full an attendance as the solemnity of the occasion required; since that time, every day had been spent in ascertaining the state of his Majesty's health, and now the necessity of the case was proved, it behoved them to meet it on the surest grounds. Let them proceed, therefore, to ascertain their own rights; let every man in that House, and every man in the nation, who might hear any report of what had passed in the House that day, consider, that on their future proceedings depended their own interests, and the interest and honour of a sovereign, deservedly the idol of his people. Let the House not, therefore, rashly annihilate the authority of Parliament, in which the existence of the constitution was so intimately involved.

Mr. Fox begged the House would permit him to rise again to explain. The right hon. gentleman had, though he believed unintentionally, misrepresented what he had said; at least, an expression which the right hon. gentleman had used, might, if not explained, have the effect of a misrepresentation, on account of its equivocal meaning. The right hon. gentleman had charged him with something like treason to the constitution, for having asserted that the Prince of Wales had a right, from law, to the government, which the two Houses could not take away from him: the right hon. gentleman, however, in stating the position, instead of the words "the two Houses," substituted the equivocal word "Parliament:" it was this word which required explanation. If by parliament the right hon. gentleman meant the three branches of the legislature, consisting of King, Lords, and Commons, he would agree with him that such a position would be treasonable; for no doubt the parliament, in that sense, could alter or limit the succession, or place such restrictions as it pleased upon the exercise of the sovereign power. But if by parliament he meant the two Houses without the king, then he would be bold to say, such a parliament, if such could be entitled to that name, could not legally deprive the Prince of Wales of the regency during the incapacity of his father, and during that period only, or place any restrictions upon him in the exercise of the sovereign power in the name of his father, So far would it be from being treason in him to assert, "that the two Houses could alter the succession, or restrain the exercise of the sovereign power," that if he should be daring enough to support such a proposition, the King's attorney-general would prosecute him for uttering such a doctrine, and would show that he was open to the penalties of a praemunire for maintaining it.— Every one knew, he said, that he was no advocate for the antiquated and exploded doctrine of indefeasible hereditary right; but it had been declared that the crown of England was not elective. Now, if for the purpose of guarding against the discussion and anarchy of an elective government, the crown was by law declared to be hereditary, why should it not be inferred from analogy, that the exercise of the sovereign power was also hereditary. Such an inference was necessary to give life and spirit to the letter of the law, declaring the hereditary descent of the crown; and consequently the claim of the Prince of Wales to the right of assuming the government, during his father's illness, ought to be admitted. Indeed, he was astonished to find any one bold enough to dispute it. Some time ago, the Speaker had, from the chair, expressed his doubts, whether in the present state of affairs, the House had legally the power of ordering writs, even for the purpose of rendering its own representation complete; and yet the right hon. gentleman would contend, that it had a right to exercise the highest power, that of vesting, though for a time, sovereign authority in the person of a regent. In truth, it was matter of serious doubt whether, under the present circumstances, the House to which he was then speaking, was really a House of Parliament. Those meetings from which the country had derived the blessings of a free constitution, as settled at the Revolution, knew too well what they were, to call themselves a parliament; they called themselves by their true name, a convention, for they were no more, until a third estate was created. And perhaps the two Houses at present might be more truly styled a convention than a parliament, until the third estate was restored, by the recognition of the heir apparent's right, the declaration of the two Houses, or even an appointment of a regency under their authority.—He had said before, that the Prince's right to the Regency was indisputable: he would now go farther, and assert that it so belonged of right, during what he would call the civil death of the king, that it could not be more completely or legally his, by the ordinary and natural demise of the crown. The prince, therefore, who maintained that right, and yet forebore to assume it, was entitled to the thanks of his country. He was actuated by a respectful regard to the principles that had placed his illustrious family upon the throne: he waited to be informed of the sense of the people, before he would assume what no man had a right to take from him, what the law and the constitution had given him a right to take, without waiting for a declaration of either House of Parliament. It was not decent, therefore, to trifle with a prince, whose conduct was marked with such meritorious forbearance, by instituting an inquiry into precedents, that had nothing to do with the case. It was the duty of the two Houses to restore the royal authority, and that immediately; and he denied the right hon. gentleman, acute as he was, to contradict that assertion; but if the two Houses of Parliament took advantage of the present calamitous state of the country, to arrogate to themselves a power to which they had no right, they acted contrary to the spirit of the constitution, and would be guilty of treason.

Mr. Pitt wished it to be known what the point was, upon which the right hon. gentleman and he were at issue. He asserted, that to make a provision for the executive power of the government, during an interruption of the personal exercise of the royal authority, by sickness, infirmity, or otherwise, did rest with the remaining existing branches of the legislature. It was a matter entirely in their discretion; what that discretion was, he should not then discuss, but should only say, if the right hon. gentleman's doctrine was what he understood it to be, namely, that the two Houses had no such discretion, but that his Royal Highness had a claim to the exercise of the sovereign power, which superseded the right of either House to deliberate on the subject, there was an essential difference between their respective arguments, and that difference constituted the point upon which they were at issue.

Curwen's Act, 19 June 1809

49 Geo. 3, c. 118   *Statutes at Large*, XXI, 914-15.

This act sought to reduce bribery and other corrupt practices in parliamentary elections.

Whereas it is expedient to make further Provision for preventing corrupt Practices in the procuring of Elections and Returns of Members to sit in the House of Commons: And Whereas the giving, or procuring to be given, or promising to give or to procure to be given any Sum of Money, Gift, or Reward, or any Office, Place, Employment, or Gratuity, in order to procure the Return of any Member to serve in Parliament, if not given to or for the Use of some Person having a Right or claiming to have a Right to act as Returning Officer, or to vote at such Election, is not Bribery within the Meaning of an Act passed in the Second Year of King George the Second, intituled, *An Act for the more effectual preventing Bribery and Corruption in the Election of Members to serve in Parliament,* but such Gifts or Promises are contrary to the ancient Usage, Right, and Freedom of Elections, and contrary to the Laws and Constitution of this Realm; Be it declared and enacted by the King's most Excellent Majesty, by and with the Advice and Consent of the Lords Spiritual and Temporal, and Commons, in this present Parliament assembled, and by the Authority of the same, That if any Person or Persons shall, from and after the passing of this Act, either by himself, herself, or themselves, or by any other Person or Persons for or on his, her, or their Behalf, give or cause to be given, directly or indirectly, or promise or agree to give any Sum of Money, Gift, or Reward, to any Person or Persons, upon any Engagement, Contract, or Agreement, that such Person or Persons to whom, to whose Use, or on whose Behalf such Gift of Promise shall be made, shall, by himself, herself, or themselves, or by any other Person or Persons whatsoever at his, her, or their Solicitation, Request or Command, procure or endeavour to procure the Return of any Person to serve in Parliament for any County, Stewartry, City, Town, Borough, Cinque Port, or Place, every Person so having given or promised to give, if not returned himself to Parliament for such County, Stewartry, City, Town, Borough, Cinque Port, or Place, shall for every such Gift or Promise forfeit the Sum of One thousand Pounds, to be recovered in such Manner as is herein-after provided, with respect to the Sum of Five hundred Pounds; and every such Person so returned and so having given or so having promised to give, or knowing of and consenting to such Gifts or Promises, upon any such Engagement, Contract, or Agreement, shall be and is hereby declared and enacted to be disabled and incapacitated to serve in that Parliament for such County, Stewartry, City, Town, Borough, Cinque Port, or Place, and that such Person shall be deemed and taken, and is hereby declared and enacted to be deemed and taken to be no Member of Parliament, and enacted to be, to all Intents, Constructions, and Purposes, as if he had never been returned or elected a Member in Parliament; and any Person or Persons who shall receive or accept of, by himself, herself, or themselves, or by any other Person or Persons in trust for or to the Use or on the Behalf of him, her, or them, any such Sum of Money, Gift, or Reward, or any such Promise upon any such Engagement, Contract, or Agreement, shall forfeit to His Majesty the Value and Amount of such Sum of Money, Gift, or Reward, over and above the Sum of Five hundred Pounds, which said Sum of Five hundred Pounds he, she, or they shall forfeit to any Person who shall sue for the same, to be recovered with such Costs of Suit by Action of Debt, Bill, Plaint, or Information, in any of His Majesty's Courts of Record at Westminster, if the Offence be committed in that Part of the United Kingdom called England and Wales, and in any of His Majesty's Courts of Record at Dublin, if the Offence be committed in Ireland, wherein respectively no Essoign or Wager of Law, or more than One Imparlance shall be allowed; and if the Offence be committed in Scotland, then to be recovered with full Costs of Suit by summary Action or Complaint before the Court of Session, or by Prosecution before the Court of Justiciary there.

II. Provided always, and be it further enacted, That nothing in this Act contained shall extend, or be construed to extend, to any Money paid or agreed to be paid to or by any Person, for any legal Expence bona fide incurred at or concerning any Election.

III. And be it further enacted, That if any Person or Persons shall, from and after the passing of this Act, by himself, herself, or themselves, or by any other Person or Persons for or on his, her, or their Behalf, give or procure to be given, or promise to give or procure to be given, any Office, Place, or Employment, to any Person or Persons whatsoever, upon any express Contract or Agreement that such Person or Persons, to whom or to whose Use or on whose Behalf such Gift or Promise shall be made, shall by himself, herself, or themselves, or by any other Person or Persons at his, her, or their Solicitation, Request, or Command, procure or endeavour to procure the Return of any Person to serve in Parliament for any County, Stewartry, City, Town, Borough, Cinque Port, or Place, such Person so returned, and so having given or procured to be given, or so having promised to give or procure to be given, or knowing of and consenting to such Gift or Promise upon any such express Contract or Agreement, shall be and is hereby declared and enacted to be disabled and incapacitated to serve in that Parliament for such County, Stewartry, City, Town, Borough, Cinque Port, or Place, and that such Person shall be deemed and taken, and is hereby declared and enacted to be deemed and taken to be no Member of Parliament, and enacted to be to all Intents, Constructions, and Purposes as if he had never been returned or elected a Member in Parliament; and any Person who shall receive or accept of, by himself, herself, or themselves, or by any other Person or Persons in trust for or to the Use or on the Behalf of such Persons, any such Office, Place, or Employment, upon such express Contract or Agreement, shall forfeit such Office, Place, or Employment, and be incapacitated for holding the same, and shall forfeit the Sum of Five hundred Pounds, which said Sum of Five hundred Pounds shall be recovered as is hereinbefore enacted; and any Person holding any Office under His Majesty, who shall give such Office, Appointment, or Place, upon any such express Contract or Agreement, that the Person to whom or for whose Use such Office, Appointment, or Place shall have been given, shall so procure or endeavour to procure the Return of any Person to serve in Parliament, shall forfeit the Sum of One thousand Pounds, to be recovered in such Manner as is herein-before provided.

IV. And be it further enacted, That no Person shall be made liable to any Forfeiture or Penalty by this Act created or imposed, unless some Prosecution, Action, or Suit, for the Offence committed, shall be actually and legally commenced against such Person within the Space of Two Years next after such Offence against this Act shall be committed, and unless such Person shall be actually and legally arrested, summoned, or otherwise served with any original or other Writ or Process within the same Space of Time, so as such Arrest, Summons, or Service of any original or other Writ or Process shall not be prevented by such Person absconding or withdrawing out of the Jurisdiction of the Court out of which such original or other Writ or Process shall have issued; and in case of any such Prosecution, Suit, or Process as aforesaid, the same shall be proceeded in and carried on without any wilful Delay; and that all Statutes of Jeofails and the Amendments of the Law whatever shall and may be construed to extend to all Proceedings in any such Prosecution, Action, or Suit.

Regency Act, 5 February 1811

51 Geo. 3, c. 1   *Statutes at Large*, LXV, 1-6.

George III became permanently insane in 1810. The Prince of Wales, later George IV (1820-30), was appointed regent but temporary restrictions were placed on his right to grant peerages, places, and pensions.

Whereas by reason of the severe Indisposition with which it hath pleased God to afflict the King's Most Excellent Majesty, the Personal Exercise of the Royal Authority by His Majesty is, for the present, so far interrupted, that it becomes necessary to make Provision for assisting His Majesty in the Administration and Exercise of the Royal Authority, and also for the Care of his Royal Person during the continuance of His Majesty's Indisposition, and for the Resumption of the Exercise of the Royal Authority by His Majesty; Be it therefore enacted by the King's Most Excellent Majesty, by and with the Advice and Consent of the Lords Spiritual and Temporal, and Commons, in this present Parliament assembled, and by the Authority of the Same, That His Royal Highness George Augustus Frederick Prince of Wales shall have full Power and Authority, in the Name and on the Behalf of His Majesty, and under the Stile and Title of "Regent of the United Kingdom of Great Britain and Ireland," to exercise and administer the Royal Power and Authority to the Crown of the United Kingdom of Great Britain and Ireland belonging, and to use, execute and perform all Authorities, Prerogatives, Acts of Government and Administration of the same, which lawfully belong to the King of the said United Kingdom to use, execute and perform; subject to such Limitations, Exceptions, Regulations and Restrictions, as are hereinafter specified and contained; and all and every Act and Acts which shall be done by the said Regent, in the Name and on the Behalf of His Majesty, by virtue and in pursuance of this Act, and according to the Powers and Authorities hereby vested in him, shall have the same force and Effect to all Intents and Purposes as the like Acts would have if done by His Majesty himself, and shall to all Intents and Purposes be full and sufficient Warrant to all Persons acting under the Authority thereof; and all Persons shall yield Obedience thereto, and carry the same into Effect, in the same manner and for the same Purposes as the same Persons ought to yield Obedience to and carry into Effect the like Acts done by His Majesty himself; any Law, Course of Office, or other Matter or Thing to the contrary notwithstanding.

II. And be it further enacted, That as to all Authorities given and Appointments made in the Name and on the Behalf of His Majesty, and all other Acts, Matters and Things usually done under the Authority of the Royal Sign Manual, the Signature of the Regent in the Form following; that is to say, *George P. R.* or in cases where the Royal Signature has usually been affixed in Initials only, then in the Form *G. P. R.,* shall be as valid and effectual, and have the same Force and Effect as His Majesty's Royal Sign Manual, and shall be deemed and taken to be to all Intents and Purposes His Majesty's Royal Sign Manual, and be obeyed as such.

III. And be it further enacted, That when His Majesty shall by the Blessing of God be restored to such a State of Health as to be capable of resuming the Personal Exercise of his Royal Authority, and shall have declared his Royal Will and Pleasure thereupon, as hereinafter provided, all and every the Powers and Authorities given by this Act, for the Exercise and Administration of His Royal Power and Authority, or for the using, executing and performing the Authorities, Prerogatives, Acts of Government and Administration of the same, which belong to the King of the United Kingdom of Great Britain and Ireland to use, execute and perform, or for the Care of His Majesty's Royal Person, shall cease and determine; and no Act, Matter or Thing, which, under this Act, and previous to such Declaration might be done in the Administration of His Majesty's Royal Power and Authority, or in the using, exercising or performing any such Authorities, Prerogatives, Acts of Government or Administration as aforesaid, or in the Care of His Majesty's Royal Person, by virtue and in pursuance of this Act, shall, if done after such Declaration of His Majesty's Royal Will and Pleasure, be thenceforth valid or effectual.

IV. Provided always, and be it further enacted, That all Persons holding any Offices or Places, or Pensions during His Majesty's Pleasure, at the time of such Declaration, under any Appointment or Authority of the Regent, or Her Majesty, under the Provisions of this Act, shall continue to hold the same, and to use, exercise and enjoy all the Powers, Authorities, Privileges and Emoluments thereof, notwithstanding such Declaration of the Resumption of the Royal Authority by His Majesty, unless and until His Majesty shall declare his Royal Will and Pleasure to the contrary; and all Orders, Acts of Government or Administration of His

Majesty's Royal Authority, made, issued or done by the said Regent, before such Declaration, shall be and remain in full Force and Effect, until the same shall be countermanded by His Majesty.

V. Provided also, and be it further enacted, That no Acts of Regal Power, Prerogative, Government or Administration of Government, of what Kind or Nature soever, which might lawfully be done or executed by the King's Most Excellent Majesty, personally exercising his Royal Authority, shall, during the Continuance of the Regency by this Act established, be valid and effectual, unless done and executed in the Name and on the Behalf of His Majesty, by the Authority of the said Regent, according to the Provisions of this Act, and subject to the Limitations, Exceptions, Regulations and Restrictions hereinafter contained.

VI. And be it further enacted, That the said Regent, before he shall act or enter upon his said Office of Regent, shall take the following Oaths:

I do sincerely promise and swear, That I will be faithful and bear true Allegiance to His Majesty King George. So help me God.

I do solemnly promise and swear, That I will truly and faithfully execute the Office of Regent of the United Kingdom of Great Britain and Ireland, according to an Act of Parliament passed in the Fifty first Year of the Reign of His Majesty King George the Third, intituled, An Act [*here insert the Title of this Act*]; and that I will administer, according to Law, the Power and Authority vested in me by virtue of the said Act; and that I will in all Things, to the utmost of my Power and Ability, consult and maintain the Safety Honour and Dignity of His Majesty and the Welfare of his People. So help me God.

I do faithfully promise and swear, That I shall inviolably maintain and preserve the Settlement of the true Protestant Religion, with the Government, Worship, Discipline, Rights and Privileges of the Church of Scotland, as established by the Laws made there in Prosecution of the Claim of Right, and particularly by an Act, intituled, *An Act for securing the Protestant Religion, and Presbyterian Church Government*, and by the Acts passed in the Parliament of both Kingdoms, for Union of the Two Kingdoms. So help me God.

Which Oaths shall be taken before His Majesty's most Honourable Privy Council; who are hereby required and empowered to administer the same, and to enter the same in the Books of the said Privy Council.

VII. And be it further enacted, That the said Regent shall, at the time of his taking such Oaths as aforesaid, and before the Members of the Privy Council administering the same, make, subscribe, and audibly repeat the Declaration mentioned in an Act made in the Thirtieth Year of King Charles the Second, intituled, *An Act for the more effectual preserving the King's Person and Government, by disabling Papists from sitting in either House of Parliament*; and shall produce a Certificate of his having received the Sacrament of the Lord's Supper in any of the Royal Chapels, signed by the Person administering the same; which Certificate shall be sufficient Evidence of the said Regent's having received the Sacrament; and such Declaration and Certificate shall respectively be registered in the Books of the Privy Council.

VIII. Provided always, and be it enacted, That until after the First Day of February One thousand eight hundred and twelve, if Parliament shall be then assembled, and shall have been sitting for Six Weeks immediately previous to the said First Day of February One thousand eight hundred and twelve, or if Parliament shall be then assembled, but shall not have been so sitting for Six Weeks, then until the Expiration of Six Weeks after Parliament shall have been so assembled and been sitting; or if Parliament shall not then be assembled, then until the Expiration of Six Weeks after Parliament shall have been assembled and sitting, next after the said First Day of February One thousand eight hundred and twelve, the Regent shall not have or exercise any Power or Authority to grant, in the Name and on the Behalf of His Majesty, any Rank, Title or Dignity of the Peerage, by Letters Patent, Writ of Summons, or any other manner whatever, or to summon any Person to the House of Lords by any Title to which such Person shall be the Heir Apparent, or to determine the Abeyance of any Rank, Title or Dignity of Peerage, which now is or hereafter shall be in Abeyance, in favour of any of the Coheirs thereof by Writ of Summons, or otherwise.

IX. Provided also, and be it further enacted, That the said Regent shall not, until after the said First Day of February One thousand eight hundred and twelve, or the Expiration of such Six Weeks as aforesaid, have Power or Authority to grant, in the Name or on the Behalf of His Majesty, any Office or Employment whatever, in Reversion, or to grant for any longer Term than during His Majesty's Pleasure, any Office, Employment, Salary or Pension whatever, except such Offices and Employments in Possession for the Term of the natural Life, or during the good Behaviour of the Grantee or Grantees thereof respectively, as by Law must be so granted: Provided always, that nothing herein contained, shall in any manner affect or extend to prevent or restrain the granting of any Pensions under the Provisions of an Act passed in the Thirty ninth Year of the Reign of His present Majesty, intituled, *An Act for the Augmentation of the Salaries of the Judges of the Courts in Westminster Hall, and also of the Lords of Session, Lords Commissioners of Justiciary, and Barons of Exchequer in Scotland; and for enabling His Majesty to grant Annuities to Persons in certain Offices in the said Courts of Westminster Hall, on their Resignation of their respective Offices;* and of another Act passed in the Forty eighth Year of His present Majesty, intituled, *An Act for enabling His Majesty to grant Annuities to the Judges of the Courts of Session, Justiciary and Exchequer in Scotland, upon the Resignation of their Offices;* and of another Act passed in Ireland, in the Fortieth Year of the Reign of His present Majesty, intituled, *An Act to enable His Majesty to grant Annuities to the Lord High Chancellor, and to the Judges of the Courts of Common Pleas and Exchequer, Judge or Commissary of the Court of Prerogative, the Judge of the Court of Admiralty, the Chairman of the Quarter Sessions of the County of Dublin and Assistant Barristers of the several other Counties, on the Resignation of their respective Offices;* and to amend an Act passed in the Thirty sixth Year of His present Majesty, intituled, *An Act for encreasing the Salaries of the Chief and other Judges of the Courts of King's Bench and Common Pleas, and of the Chief Baron* *and other Barons of the Court of Exchequer in this Kingdom;* or to prevent or restrain the granting of any Pensions out of the Revenues of the British Territories in the East Indies, under the Provisions of any Act or Acts of Parliament now in force, to such Persons as may have held the Office of Chief Justice or other Judge in the Supreme Courts of Judicature at Fort William in Bengal and at Madras, and the Office of Recorder of Bombay.

X. Provided also, and be it further enacted, That nothing in this Act contained, shall in any manner affect or extend to prevent or restrain the granting of any Pensions under the Provisions of an Act passed in the Forty first Year of the Reign of His present Majesty, intituled, *An Act for the better Regulation of His Majesty's Prize Courts in the West Indies and America, and for giving a more speedy and effectual Execution to the Decrees of the Lords Commissioners of Appeals,* and of another Act passed in the Forty third Year of His present Majesty, intituled, *An Act for the Encouragement of Seamen, and for the better and more effectual manning His Majesty's Navy; for regulating the Payment of Prize Money, and for making Provision for the Salaries of the Judges of the Vice Admiralty Courts in the Island of Malta, and in the Bermudas and Bahama Islands;* and also of another Act passed in the Forty fifth Year of His present Majesty, intituled, *An Act for the Encouragement of Seamen, and for the better and more effectually manning of His Majesty's Navy.*

XI. And be it enacted, That nothing in this Act contained shall extend or be construed to extend to empower the said Regent, in the Name and on the Behalf of His Majesty, to give the Royal Assent to any Bill or Bills in Parliament, for repealing, changing, or in any respect varying the Order and Course of Succession to the Crown of this Realm, as the same stands now established by an Act passed in the Twelfth Year of the Reign of King William the Third, intituled, *An Act for the further Limitation of the Crown, and better securing the Rights and Liberties of the Subject;* or to any Act for repealing or altering the Act made in the Thirteenth Year of the Reign of King Charles the Second, intituled, *An Act for the Uniformity of Public Prayers and Administration of Sacraments, and other Rites 'and Ceremonies, and for establishing the Form of making, ordaining and consecrating Bishops, Priests and Deacons in the Church of England;* or the Act of the Fifth Year of the Reign of Queen Anne, made in Scotland, intituled, *An Act for securing the Protestant Religion and Presbyterian Church Government.*

XII. Provided also, and be it enacted, That if His said Royal Highness George Augustus Frederick Prince of Wales shall not continue to be resident in the United Kingdom of Great Britain and Ireland, or shall at any time marry a Papist, then and in either of such cases, all the Powers and Authorities vested in His said Royal Highness by this Act, shall cease and determine.

XIII. And whereas it is expedient that the Care of His Majesty's Royal Person should be committed to the Queen's Most Excellent Majesty, together with the sole Direction of such Portion of His Majesty's Household as shall be deemed requisite and suitable for the due Attendance on His Majesty's Sacred Person, and the Maintenance of his Royal Dignity; Be it therefore enacted, That the Care of His Majesty's Royal Person, and the disposing, ordering and managing of all Matters and Things relating thereto, shall be, and the same are hereby vested in the Queen's

Most Excellent Majesty, during the Continuance of His Majesty's Indisposition; and that the sole Direction of His Majesty's Household, except the Lord Chamberlain of His Majesty's Household, the Captain of the Yeomen of His Majesty's Guard, and the Captain of the Honourable Band of Gentlemen Pensioners shall be and is hereby vested in Her Majesty; and Her said Majesty shall have the full and sole Power and Authority, by any Instrument or Instruments in Writing signed and sealed by Her Majesty, to nominate and appoint, in case of any Vacancies arising by Resignation or Death, all the Officers and Persons belonging to His Majesty's Household, in the respective Departments thereof, whose Appointment, Nomination or Removal have heretofore been made by His Majesty; except the Lord Chamberlain of His Majesty's Household, and the Gentlemen and Grooms of His Majesty's Bedchamber, His Majesty's Equerries, the Captain of the Yeomen of His Majesty's Guard, and the Captain of the Honourable Band of Gentlemen Pensioners; and the Nomination and Appointment by Her Majesty, in Manner and Form aforesaid, shall be valid and effectual to all Intents and Purposes as if the same had been made or done by His Majesty in the accustomed manner; and the several Persons so appointed shall be entitled to the like Precedence, Privileges, Salaries, Wages, Profits and all other Emoluments, as the several Persons now holding and enjoying the same Offices are respectively entitled to: Provided always, that the Power and Authority given by this Act to Her Majesty, to nominate and appoint such Persons of His Majesty's Household as are not hereinbefore excepted, shall continue in force until the said first Day of February, or the Expiration of such Six Weeks as aforesaid, and no longer: Provided also, that Her said Majesty shall not have any Power or Authority to remove any Officer in any Department of His Majesty's Household, by this Act made subject to the Nomination or Appointment of Her Majesty, who shall have been nominated and appointed by His Majesty: Provided also, That until the Expiration of such Period as aforesaid, no Appointment shall be made to the Office of Lord Chamberlain of His Majesty's Household, now vacant, but that all the Duties of the said Office shall be performed by the Vice Chamberlain; and that during such Period as aforesaid, no Person holding the Office of Gentleman or Groom of His Majesty's Bedchamber, or being One of His Majesty's Equerries, shall be subject to be removed; and no Vacancy which shall arise by Death or Resignation of any of the Grooms or Gentlemen of His Majesty's Bedchamber, or of His Majesty's Equerries, shall be supplied or filled up, or any Appointment or Nomination made to supply any such Vacancy. . . .

BEGINNING OF THE REFORM MOVEMENT

John Wilkes's motion for "a just and equal representation of the people of England in Parliament," House of Commons, 21 March 1776

Parliamentary History, XVIII, 1287-97.

Although this motion was rejected by the Commons, it was the first of its kind to be introduced in the eighteenth century.

Mr. Speaker; all wise governments, and well-regulated states, have been particularly careful to mark and correct the various abuses, which a considerable length of time almost necessarily creates. Among these, one of the most striking and important in our country is, the present unfair and inadequate state of the representation of the people of England in parliament. It is now become so partial and unequal from the lapse of time, that I believe almost every gentleman in the House will agree with me in the necessity of its being taken into our most serious consideration, and of our endeavouring to find a remedy for this great and growing evil.

I wish, Sir, my slender abilities were equal to a thorough investigation of this momentous business. Very diligent and well-meant endeavours have not been wanting to trace it from the first origin. The most natural and perfect idea of a free government is, in my mind, that of the people themselves assembling to determine by what laws they chuse to be governed, and to establish the regulations they think necessary for the protection of their property and liberty against all violence and fraud. Every member of such a community would submit with alacrity to the observance of what had been enacted by himself, and assist with spirit in giving efficacy and vigour to laws and ordinances, which derived all their authority from his own approbation and concurrence. In small inconsiderable states, this mode of legislation has been happily followed, both by ancient and modern times. The extent and populousness of a great empire seems scarcely to admit it without confusion or tumult: and therefore our ancestors, more wise in this than the ancient Romans, adopted the representation of the many by a few, as answering more fully the true ends of government. Rome was enslaved from inattention to this very circumstance, and by one other fatal act, which ought to be a strong warning to the people, even against their own representatives, the leaving power too long in the hands of the same persons, by which the armies of the republic became the armies of Sylla, Pompey and Caesar. When all the burghers of Italy obtained the freedom of Rome, and voted in public assemblies, their multitudes rendered the distinction of the citizen of Rome and the alien impossible. Their assemblies and deliberations became disorderly and tumultuous. Unprincipled and ambitious men found out the secret of turning them to the ruin of the Roman liberty and commonwealth. Among us this evil is avoided by representation, and yet the justice of the principle is preserved. Every Englishman is supposed to be present in parliament, either in person, or by a deputy chosen by himself, and therefore the resolution of parliament is taken to be the resolution of every individual, and to give the public the consent and approbation of every free agent of the community.

According to the first formation of this excellent constitution, so long and so justly our greatest boast and best inheritance, we find that the people thus took care no laws should be enacted, no taxes levied, but by their consent, expressed by their representatives in the great council of the nation. The mode of representation in ancient times being tolerably adequate and proportionate, the sense of the people was known by that of parliament, their share of power in the legislature being preserved, and founded in equal justice. At present it is become insufficient, partial, and unjust.

From so pleasing a view as that of the equal power, which our ancestors had, with great wisdom and care, modelled for the Commons of this realm, the present scene gives us not very venerable ruins of that majestic and beautiful fabric, the English constitution. As the whole seems in disorder and confusion, all the former union and harmony of the parts are lost or destroyed. It appears, Sir, from the writs remaining in the King's remembrancer's office in the exchequer, that no less than 22 towns sent members to the parliament in the 23rd, 25th, and 26th of Edward I, which have long ceased to be represented. The names of some of them are scarcely known to us, such as those of Canebrig and Bamburg in Northumberland, Pershore and Brem in Worcestershire, Jarvall and Tykhull in Yorkshire. What a happy fate, Sir, has attended the boroughs of Gatton and Old Sarum, of which, although *ipsae perière ruinae,* the names are familiar to us, the clerk regularly calls them over, and four respectable gentlemen represent their departed greatness, as the knights at a coronation represent Aquitaine and Normandy! The little town of Banbury, "petite ville, grand renom," as Rabelais says of Chinon, has, I believe, only 17 electors, yet gives us in its representative, what is of the utmost importance to the majority here, a first lord of the Treasury, and a chancellor of the Exchequer. Its influence and weight on a division, I have often seen overpower the united force of the members for London, Bristol, and several of the most populous counties. East Grinstead too, I think, has only about 30 electors, yet gives a seat among us to that brave, heroic lord (George Germaine) at the head of a great civil department, now very military, who has fully determined to conquer America—but not in Germany! It is not, Sir, my purpose to weary the patience of the House by the researches of an antiquary into the ancient state of our representation, and its variations at different periods. I shall only remark shortly on what passed, in the reign of Henry 6, and some of his successors. In that reign, sir John Fortescue, his chancellor, observed that the House of Commons consisted of more than 300 chosen men; various alterations were made by succeeding kings till James 2. No change has happened since that period. Great abuses, it must be owned, contrary to the primary ideas of the English constitution, were committed by our former princes, in giving the right of representation to several paltry boroughs, because the places were poor, and dependent on them, or on a favourite overgrown peer. The land marks of the constitution have often been removed. The marked partiality for Cornwall, which single county still sends, within one, as many members as the whole kingdom of Scotland, is striking. It arose from yielding to the crown in tin and lands a larger hereditary revenue than any other English county, as well as from the duchy being in the crown, and giving an amazing command and influence. By such abuses of our princes the constitution was wounded in its most vital part. Henry 8 restored two members, Edward 6 twenty, queen Mary four, queen Elizabeth twelve, James 1 sixteen, Charles 1 eighteen, in all seventy-two. The alterations by creation in the same period were more considerable, for Henry 8 created thirty-three, Edward 6 twenty-eight, queen Mary seventeen, queen Elizabeth forty-eight, James 1 eleven; in all 173. Charles 1 made no new creation of this kind. Charles 2 added two for the county, and two for the city of Durham, and two for Newark on Trent. This House is at this hour composed of the same representation it was at his demise, notwithstanding the many and important changes which have since happened. It becomes us therefore to enquire, whether the sense of parliament can be now, on solid grounds, from the present representation, said to be the sense of the nation, as in the time of our forefathers. I am satisfied, Sir, the sentiments of the people cannot be justly known at this time from the resolutions of a parliament, composed as the present is, even though no undue influence was practised after the return of the members to the House, even supposing for a moment the influence of all the baneful arts of corruption to be suspended, which, for a moment, I believe, they have not been, under the present profligate administration. Let us examine, Sir, with exactness and candour, if the representation is fair and perfect; let us consider of what the efficient parts of this House are composed, and what proportion they bear, on the large scale, to the body of the people of England, who are supposed to be represented.

The southern part of this island, to which I now confine my ideas, consists of about five millions of people, according to the most received calculation. I will state by what numbers the majority of this House is elected, and I suppose the largest number present of any recorded in our Journal, which was in the famous year 1741. In that year the three largest divisions appear on our Journals. The first is that of the 21st of January, when the numbers were 253 to 250; the second on the 28th of the same month, 236 to 235; the third on the 9th of March, 244 to 243. In these divisions the members for Scotland are included; but I will state my calculations only for England, because it gives the argument more force. The division therefore, I adopt, is that of January 21. The number of members present on that day were 503. Let me, however, suppose the number of 254 to be the majority of members, who will ever be able to attend in their places. I state it high, from the accidents of sickness, service in foreign parts, travelling and necessary avocations. From the majority of electors only in the boroughs, which return members to this House, it has been demonstrated, that this number of 254 is elected by no more than 5,723 persons, generally the inhabitants of Cornish, and other very insignificant boroughs, perhaps by not the most respectable part of the community. Is our sovereign, then, to learn the sense of his whole people from these few persons?

Are these the men to give laws to this vast empire, and to tax this wealthy nation? I do not mention all the tedious calculations, because gentlemen may find them at length in the works of the incomparable Dr. Price, in Postlethwaite, and in Burgh's Political Disquisitions. Figures afford the clearest demonstration, incapable of cavil or sophistry. Since Burgh's calculations only one alteration has happened. I allude to the borough of Shoreham in Sussex. By the Act of 1771, all the freeholders of 40s. per annum in the neighbouring rape or hundred of Bramber are admitted to vote for that borough; but many of the old electors were disfranchised. It appears likewise, that 56 of our members are elected by only 364 persons. Lord Chancellor Talbot supposed that the majority of this House was elected by 56,000 persons, and he exclaimed against the injustice of that idea. More accurate calculations than his lordship's, and the unerring rules of political arithmetic, have shewn the injustice to be vastly beyond what his lordship even suspected.

When we consider, Sir, that the most important powers of this House, the levying taxes on, and enacting laws for, five millions of persons, is thus usurped and unconstitutionally exercised by the small number I have mentioned, it becomes our duty to restore to the people their clear rights, their original share in the legislature. The ancient representation of this kingdom, we find, was founded by our ancestors in justice, wisdom, and equality. The present state of it would be continued by us in folly, obstinacy, and injustice.

This evil has been complained of by some of the wisest patriots our country has produced. I shall beg leave to give that close reasoner Mr. Locke's ideas in his own words. He says, in the treatise on Civil Government,

> Things not always changing equally, and private interest often keeping up customs and privileges, when the reasons of them are ceased, it often comes to pass, that in governments, where part of the legislative consists of representatives chosen by the people, that in tract of time this representation becomes very unequal and disproportionate to the reasons it was at first established upon. To what gross absurdities the following of a custom, when reason has left it, may lead, we may be satisfied, when we see the bare name of a town, of which there remains not so much as the ruins, where scarce so much housing as a sheep-cote, or more inhabitants than a shepherd, is to be found, sends as many representatives to the grand assembly of law-makers, as a whole county, numerous in people, and powerful in riches. This strangers stand amazed at, and every one must confess, needs a remedy.

After so great an authority as that of Mr. Locke, I shall not be treated on this occasion as a mere visionary; and the propriety of the motion I shall have the honour of submitting to the House, will scarcely be disputed. Even the members for such places as Old Sarum and Gatton, who, I may venture to say at present *stant nominis umbrae*, will, I am persuaded, have too much candour to complain of the right of their few constituents, if indeed they have constituents, if they are not self-created, self-elected, self-existent, of this pretended right being transferred to the county, while the rich and populous manufacturing towns of Birmingham, Manchester, Leeds, Sheffield, and others, may have at least an equitable share in the formation of those laws by which they are governed. My idea, Sir, in this case, as to the wretched and depopulated towns and boroughs in general, I freely own, is amputation. I say with Horace, "Inutiles ramos amputans, feliciores inserit."

This is not, Sir, the first attempt of the kind to correct, although in an inconsiderable degree, this growing evil. Proceedings of a similar nature were had among us above a century past. The clerk will read from our Journals what passed on the 26th of March, 1668, on a Bill to enable the county palatine of Durham to send two knights for the county, and two citizens for the city of Durham. [The Clerk reads.] In a book of authority, Anchitell Grey's Debates, we have a more particular account of what passed in the House on that occasion. He says, that "Sir Thomas Meres moved, that the shires may have an increase of knights, and that some of the small boroughs, where there are but few electors, may be taken away, and a Bill for that purpose." We find afterwards, "on a division, the Bill was rejected, 65 to 50." This division, however, alludes only to the Bill then before the House, respecting the county and city of Durham. I desire to add the few remarkable words of sir Thomas Strickland in this debate, because I have not seen them quoted on the late important American questions. "The county palatine of Durham was never taxed in parliament by ancient privilege before king James's time, and so needed no representatives; but now being taxed, it is but reasonable they should have." Such sentiments, Sir, were promulgated in this House even so long ago as the reign of Charles 2.

I am aware, Sir, that the power, *de jure*, of the legislature to disfranchise a number of boroughs, upon the general grounds of improving the constitution, has been doubted; and gentlemen will ask, whether a power is lodged in the representative to destroy his immediate constituent? Such a question is best answered by another. How originated the right, and upon what ground was it at first granted? Old Sarum and Gatton, for instance, were populous towns, and therefore the right of representation was first given them. They are now desolate, and of consequence ought not to retain a privilege, which they acquired only by their extent and populousness. We ought in every thing, as far as we can, to make the theory and practice of the constitution coincide. The supreme legislative body of a state must surely have this power inherent in itself. It was *de facto* lately exercised to its full extent by parliament in the case of Shoreham with universal approbation, for near a hundred corrupt voters were disfranchised, and about twice that number of freeholders admitted from the county of Sussex.

It will be objected, I foresee, that a time of perfect calm and peace throughout this vast empire is the most proper to propose internal regulations of this importance; and that, while intestine discord rages in the whole northern continent of America, our attention ought to be fixed upon that most alarming object, and all our efforts employed to extinguish the devouring flame of a civil war. In my opinion, Sir, the American war is in this truly critical area one of the strongest arguments for the regulation of our representation, which I now submit to the House. During the rest of our lives, likewise, I may venture to prophesy, America will be the leading feature of this age. In our late disputes with the Americans, we have always taken it for granted, that the people of England justified all the iniquitous, cruel, arbitrary, and mad proceedings of administration, because they had the approbation of the majority of this House. The absurdity of such an argument is apparent, for the majority of this House we know speak only the sense of 5,723 persons, even supposing, according to the laudable constitutional custom of our ancestors, that the constituent had been consulted on this great national point, as he ought to have been. We have seen in what manner the acquiescence of a majority here is obtained. The people in the southern part of this island amount to upwards of five millions. The sense, therefore, of five millions cannot be ascertained by the opinion of not 6,000, even supposing it had been collected. The Americans with great reason insist, that the present war is carried on contrary to the sense of the nation, by a ministerial junto, and an arbitrary faction, equally hostile to the rights of Englishmen, and the claims of Americans. The various addresses to the throne from most numerous bodies, praying that the sword may be returned to the scabbard, and all hostilities cease, confirm this assertion. The capital of our country has repeatedly declared, by various public acts, its abhorrence of the present unnatural civil war, begun on principles subversive of our constitution. Our history furnishes frequent instances of the sense of parliament running directly counter to the sense of the nation. It was notoriously of late the case in the business of the Middlesex election. I believe the fact to be equally certain in the grand American dispute, at least as to the actual hostilities now carrying on against our brethren and fellow subjects. The proposition before us will bring the case to an issue; and from a fair and equal representation of the people, America may at length distinguish the real sentiments of freemen and Englishmen.

I do not mean, Sir, at this time, to go into a tedious detail of all the various proposals which have been made for redressing this irregularity in the representation of the people. I will not intrude on the indulgence of the House, which I have always found favourable and encouraging. When the Bill is brought in, and sent to a committee, it will be the proper time to examine all the minutiae of this great plan and to determine on the propriety of what ought now to be done, and to consider what formerly was actually accomplished. The Journals of Cromwell's parliaments prove that a more equal representation was settled, and carried by him into execution. That wonderful, comprehensive mind embraced the whole of this powerful empire. Ireland was put on a par with Scotland. Each kingdom sent 30 members to a parliament, which consisted likewise of 400 from England and Wales. It was to be triennial. Our colonies were then a speck on the face of the globe; now they cover half the new world. I will at this time, Sir, only throw out general ideas, that every free agent in this kingdom should, in my wish, be represented in parliament; that the metropolis, which contains in itself a 9th part of the people, and the counties of Middlesex, York, and others, which so greatly abound with inhabitants, should receive an increase in their representation; that the mean, and insignificant boroughs, so emphatically styled "the rotten part of our constitution," should be lopped off, and the electors in them thrown into the counties; and the rich, populous, trading towns, Birmingham, Manchester, Sheffield, Leeds, and others, be permitted to send deputies to the great council of the nation.

The disfranchising of the mean, venal, and dependent boroughs would be laying the axe to the root of corruption and treasury influence, as well as aristocratical tyranny. We ought equally to guard against those, who sell themselves, or whose lords sell them. Burgage tenures, and private property in a share of the legislature, are monstrous absurdities in a free state, as well as an insult on common sense. I wish, Sir, an English parliament to speak the free, unbiassed sense of the body of the English people, and of every man among us, of each individual, who may justly be supposed to be comprehended in a fair majority. The meanest mechanic, the poorest peasant and day-labourer, has important rights respecting his personal liberty, that of his wife and children, his property, however inconsiderable, his wages, his earnings, the very price and value of each day's hard labour, which are in many trades and manufactures regulated by the power of parliament. Every law relative to marriage, to the protection of a wife, sister, or daughter, against violence and brutal lust, to every contract or agreement with a rapacious or unjust master, is of importance to the manufacturer, the cottager, the servant, as well as to the rich subjects of the state. Some share therefore in the power of making those laws, which deeply interest them, and to which they are expected to pay obedience, should be reserved even to this inferior, but most useful, set of men in the community. We ought always to remember this important truth, acknowledged by every free state, that all government is instituted for the good of the mass of the people to be governed; that they are the original fountain of power, and even of revenue, and in all events the last resource.

The various instances of partial injustice throughout this kingdom will likewise become the proper subjects of enquiry in the course of the Bill before the committee. Of this nature are the many freeholds in the city of London, which are not represented in this House. These freeholds being within the particular jurisdiction of the city, are excluded from giving a vote in the county of Middlesex, and by act of parliament only liverymen can vote for the representatives of the city of London. These, and other particulars, I leave. I mention them now, only to shew the necessity of a new regulation of the representation of this kingdom.

My enquiries, Sir, are confined to the southern part of the island. Scotland I leave to the care of its own careful and prudent sons. I hope they will spare a few moments from the management of the arduous affairs of England and America, which are now solely entrusted to their wisdom, and at present so much engross their time, to attend to the state of representation among their own people, if they have not all emigrated to this warmer and more fruitful climate. I am almost afraid the 45 Scottish gentlemen among us represent themselves. Perhaps in my plan for the improvements of the representation of the inhabitants of England, almost all the natives of Scotland may at this time be included. I shall only remark, that the proportion of representation between the two countries cannot be changed. In the 22nd article of the treaty of Union, 45 is to be the proportion of the representative body in the parliament of Great-Britain for the northern part of this island. To increase the members for England and Wales beyond the number, of which the English parliament consisted at the period of that treaty in 1706, would be a breach of public faith, and a violation of a solemn treaty between two independent states. My proposition has for its basis the preservation of that compact, the proportional share of each kingdom in the legislative body remaining exactly according to its present establishment.

The monstrous injustice and glaring partiality of the present representation of the Commons of England has been fully stated, and is, I believe, almost universally acknowledged, as well as the necessity of our recurring to the great leading principle of our free constitution, which declares this House of Parliament to be only a delegated power from the people at large. Policy, no less than justice, calls our attention to this momentous point; and reason, not custom, ought to be our guide in a business of this consequence, where the rights of a free people are materially interested. Without a true representation of the Commons our constitution is essentially defective, our parliament is a delusive name, a mere phantom, and all other remedies to recover the pristine purity of the form of government established by our ancestors would be ineffectual, even the shortening the period of parliaments, and a place and pension Bill, both which I highly approve, and think absolutely necessary. I therefore flatter myself, Sir, that I shall have the concurrence of the House with the motion, which I have now the honour of making, "That leave be given to bring in a Bill for a just and equal Representation of the People of England in Parliament."

Take Your Choice by Major Cartwright, a tract on the "present rotten parliamentary system," 1776

Take Your Choice (London: J. Almon, 1776), ix-xxv.

In this influential tract the "father of reform," Major John Cartwright (1740 1824), argued the case for annual parliaments.

TAKE YOUR CHOICE!

Representation	Imposition
and	and
Respect:	Contempt.
Annual Parliaments	Long Parliaments
and	and
Liberty:	Slavery.

INTRODUCTION

Having proposed to urge upon you, my countrymen! a reformation, both as to the length, and as to the constituting of your parliaments; it seems but proper, previously to state some of the inconveniencies and evils, which I apprehend to be the necessary consequences of, and inseparable from, our present rotten parliamentary system.

All men will grant, that the lower house of parliament is elected by only a handful of the commons, instead of the whole; and this, chiefly by bribery and undue influence. Men who will employ such means are villains; and those who dupe their constituents by lying promises, are far from honest men. An assembly of such men is *founded* on *iniquity*: consequently, the fountain of legislation is poisoned. Every stream, how much soever mixed, as it flows with justice and patriotism, will still have poison in its composition.

Nor will it be denied me, that, in consequence of the long duration of a parliament, the members, as soon as seated, feel themselves too independent on the opinion and good will of their constituents, even where their suffrages have not been extorted nor bought; and that, of course, they despise them.

From the first of these data, it will follow, that we are subject to have the House of Commons filled by men of every bad description that can be thought of, and that strict integrity, which ought to be the strongest of all recommendations, amounts to a positive exclusion; except it happen indeed to be united with a capital fortune and great county connections.

From the first and second jointly; our representatives, who are in fact our deputed servants, are taught to assume the carriage and haughtiness of despotic masters; to think themselves unaccountable for their conduct; and to neglect their duty.

Whether, indeed, the house of commons be in a great measure filled with idle school-boys, insignificant coxcombs, led-captains and toad-eaters, profligates, gamblers, bankrupts, beggars, contractors, commissaries, public plunderers, ministerial dependants, hirelings, and wretches, that would sell their country, or deny their God for a guinea, let every one judge for himself. And whether the kind of business very often brought before the house, and the usual manner of conducting it, do not bespeak this to be the case; I likewise leave every man to form his own opinion: particularly that independent and noble-minded few, who experience the constant mortification of voting and speaking without even a hope of being able thereby to serve their country.

But without insisting on these things as fact, and only admitting the possibility of them from the combined causes already assigned, of long parliaments, undue influence and bribery, it is natural to expect, as indeed all experience shews it must happen, that a country, whose affairs are *subject to fall* into such hands must be ruined, sooner or later, by those very men who shall be in the office of its guardians and preservers; except it shall make an alteration in this particular.

And accordingly, we find our own country in a condition which shews that its affairs have long been in such hands. It has passed through all the stages of abuse, and is at length arrived at a precipice tremendous to look from. The current of corruption is smooth and flattering; and it meanders for a while through scenes not unpleasant to the careless passengers: but it is deceitful, and sure to terminate in a Niagarian fall; and to dash its navigators headlong into the abyss of slavery and wretchedness, unless they take warning in time and will manfully exert themselves. Our giddy vessel of state is swiftly gliding down this current; and, by the velocity with which the passing shores of our fair provinces fly from our wondering eyes and are lost to sight, we may know that we are in the dreadful vortex, and we may hear the very roaring of the cataract. But yet, we need not perish, except the character of our nation hath forsaken us. The English sailor, whether naval or political, is imprudent and thoughtless enough, God knows; but when dangers surround him, or an enemy comes in sight, he shews that he is neither a coward nor a lubber; he knows how to deal with either of them. We should, on this occasion do no more than right, were we to begin our work with putting the law of *Oleron* in execution, by throwing overboard our besotted pilots: not but that I think, there will be more magnanimity in suffering even those wretches to share in the general preservation.

But, dropping these metaphors, let us proceed with the proposed detail of the most material public inconveniencies and evils which may be attributed to the usage of long parliaments.

I.   The kingdom, under long (and always meaning corrupt) parliaments, hath been proverbial for making war without wisdom, and peace without policy. And yet, one of the pretences against annual parliaments hath been, that they would occasion such ministerial instability and incertitude of national councils, that foreign powers would not confide in your treaties nor alliances. But this, so far as *we* have any business with the argument, is diametrically opposite to the truth. Annual parliaments will always adhere to the true interests of the nation; and upon all alliances formed upon that basis, foreigners would most assuredly rely, sooner than upon the faith of kings. But annual parliaments would not, it is true, suffer ministers to negociate away the blood and treasure of this kingdom, in order to flatter the weaknesses or partialities of the prince, nor to gratify their own avarice or ambition. Such parliaments would, moreover, give stability and permanency to administrations, by extinguishing party and faction, and leaving a minister of state nothing to do but to attend to the duties of his office and the preparing of plans for the public good. He would no longer have the greatest part of his time taken up in forming and conducting one faction, and opposing the rest: nor would his station then have those charms for an unprincipled man which it has at present. It would only be desirable to men of a generous ambition for serving their country by their personal labours, and who could content themselves with no more power than should be consistent with the liberties of their fellow citizens. Such men would be too estimable in the opinion of the public, and consequently in the judgment of an annual parliament, ever to be disturbed with an ill-intended opposition to their wise and honest measures. Opposition, from which alone we find protection against tyranny in the present corrupt state of things, is in itself an evil: but one that would vanish together with long parliaments; for to them it owes its being, and with them must die. An annual parliament properly chosen, would not be composed of two or three contending factions, each aiming at power by the overthrow of its rivals; but would be in fact, as in theory it is called, a national council. The opinion of every individual (making some allowances for oratory) would have its weight, in proportion to its solidity: and it would be the desire of a very great majority of the members to assist the minister in perfecting his plans of government by sage advice; not to oppose nor to support, right or wrong, according to pay or party.

II.   It has been owing to the constant sacrifices which have been made of the national interests to the separate interests of the court, that so many continental connections and subsidiary engagements have been formed by our ministers under the sanction of long parliaments. Besides the lavish waste of money which have been occasioned, the demands upon us for troops, have brought us to imagine a very considerable army necessary to us. Hence in a great measure it is, that our military establishment is so large, and so kept up, as to be but half a step from a standing army in the worst sense of those words.

III. And it has been in order to answer ministerial, not national purposes, that an army has been kept in our colonies during peace. So far from their being for the protection of the colonies against the irruptions of the savages, the troops never were seen upon the borders; but were quartered in the chief towns along the sea coast, for the tyrannical purpose of keeping the people in awe.

IV. Our country, fertile as it is by nature, enriched by commerce, and inhabited by a people characteristically active and industrious, is nevertheless mortgaged like the estate of a prodigal. We groan under the burthen of an enormous debt; no less than 137 millions sterling: while our ministers are still going on in the ways of waste and profusion. This debt is not only a grievous evil in itself; but it is a fruitful parent of other evils. Amongst the most considerable, are its making so many people creatures of the crown, by being dependent for a livelihood on the manifold arrangements respecting our funds. Hereby a very powerful and united party is formed against every reformation in finance. Moneyed property in the funds also converts whole herds of men into drones, who contribute nothing towards the public stock; but, on the contrary, are a dead weight on the industry of the nation.

Under annual parliaments (always supposing them to have contained a full representation of the commons) these evils would not have been known: or if any temporary debt had been unavoidably contracted, it would as certainly have been speedily discharged. The nation would consequently be in no danger of bankruptcy from any untoward event, as it is at present; and would have been at all times ready to repel the attacks of its enemies. But the *feelings* of the great bulk of the nation, are not the same with the *feelings* of *long parliaments* founded in corruption: nor will the *language* of such parliaments to their prince, ever express *the sense of the people*.

V. Are not our sanguinary statutes, by which we year by year spill rivers of blood, a reproach to the political knowledge, to the humanity, to the religion of our island? And are not our prisons and our treatment of prisoners shocking and foolish?

VI. Are we not suffering from the distress and idleness of the poor, and from a visible depopulation; and do we not leave millions of acres uncultivated?

VII. Is not the metropolis and the whole kingdom over-run with vagrants and beggars, notwithstanding our astonishing provisions against want?

VIII. Is not every city, town and village, crowded with alehouses, those hotbeds of idleness and vice? And are not gaming and adultery, amongst the higher ranks of the people, become such enormities in a civilized community, as to cry aloud for the attention of the legislature?

IX. Are we not alienating the affections of the people from the crown by injuries and insults? Are we not grieving and provoking peaceable subjects, and thereby nourishing sects and schisms by adhering to their detriment to trifles and to nonsense in church government; instead of sacrificing them to good sense and charity, and forming a new pale for our church on the foundations of reason and truth?

But when will any national evil ever be taken into consideration, and corrected by the *spontaneous* act of a long parliament? Men who are too ignorant to legislate for a tavern club, or who are voluptuaries and debauchees, or whose whole thoughts are engrossed by the loaves and fishes, are they to watch over the good of a great nation, to remark its deviations into political error, and to recal it by wise institutions? Is it not known by too melancholy an experience, that the proposer of any individual improvement, is first received with the coldness of a miser to a beggar of alms; and if his zeal for the public be too strong to be damped by such usage, that he is then opposed and baited in parliament as a mad enthusiast? Who can tell me of any the least improvement in our laws and policy that hath been made of late years by long parliaments, which has not been the sole effect of some very spirited exertion in individuals, favoured by the circumstances of the day, and backed by some pressing and urgent evil which could no longer be endured? What sort of an idea does this give one of *a national council?* 10, 100, 1000, 10,000. But to recite, one by one, the evils proceeding from long parliaments, would require volumes. And it is to be noted that there is not a public evil existing, which would have been prevented or would now be remedied by an annual, that ought not to be placed to the account of a long parliament. The reader, if he wishes to go deep into that enquiry, will do well to peruse the political disquisitions of the late Mr. Burgh. I will only further say in general, that, to the extreme venality of the boroughs and the prostitution in parliament, to the barefaced pillage of the public treasure practised by ministers, and their prefering men without the smallest regard to decency in point of character, are originally owing without doubt, that sordid devotion to avarice which hath generally infected the people from the highest to the lowest, and that almost universal insensibility to the public good which accompanies it. Instead of counteracting the natural ill effects of luxury proceeding from wealth and prosperity, and giving it a beneficial turn by wise and humane laws; it has been the business of *government* (which "in almost every age and country," says Burgh "has been the principal *grievance* of the people") to debauch and corrupt the manners and morals of the people, by every possible invention; in order to remove every obstacle in the way to absolute power. It beats up and bids high for volunteers in iniquity. The greater felons, who are ready at its command to destroy their country, are caressed and rewarded: but little ones, indeed, who take a purse or steal a sheep, are hanged without remorse, for not being proof against example and temptation. Is not every man taught to sell himself, his honour, his conscience, his soul, for a price! And is not he who hath a scruple, the butt of ministerial ridicule! We should justly esteem that mariner mad, who, in order to carry a leaky ship to the end of a long voyage, should be continually boring fresh holes in her bottom. Is there less madness in corrupting the parliament, in order to carry on the business of government? He who knows no better mode of governing than that, is fit to govern no where but in the infernal regions.

This has been more or less the condition of our government ever since we have had long parliaments. "We see the same corrupt or impolitic proceedings going on in the administration of a *Harley,* a *Walpole,* a *Pelham,* a *Pitt,* a *Bute,* a *Grafton,* a *North;* and we see every parliament implicitly obeying the orders of the minister. Some ministers we see more criminal, others less; some parliament more slavish, others less; but we see all ministers and all parliaments, *the present always excepted,* guilty; inexcusably guilty, in suffering the continual and increasing prevalency of corruption, from ministry to ministry, and from parliament to parliament." But there never has been a time when these descriptions were so applicable as they are at present. Are not men of the most blasted characters the confidential servants of the crown? Are not the scales of council weighed down with ministerial ayes and noes instead of solid and weighty arguments; and is not all parliamentary debate become a mockery? Have not millions of your unoffending brethren in America been devoted by mercenary majorities to slavery or to slaughter? Is not your commerce put to the hazard on a cast, whether or not it shall be ruined? And are you not inviting an unequal war; all to no one end or purpose, but because two or three desperate ideots will have it so, rather than abandon the vicious schemes of ambition they had once formed? Have not defaulters of millions upon millions constantly escaped parliamentary vengeance! And fiends who have fattened on the famine and butchery of the inoffensive *Asiatics,* are they not amongst your legislators, respected and honoured!—What national depravity, what extremes of wickedness, and what public calamities must we not experience, while the fountain of legislation and the springs of government are so impure!—

So ruinous a system needs must, in its progress, grow worse and worse. The chariot of corruption, (if I may be allowed a new metaphor) under the guidance of rotten whigs would soon enough have arrived, without the whip, at the goal of despotism: but now, that furious tories have seized the reins, 'tis lashed onward with impetuous haste; nor do they seem sensible to their danger, though its axles are already on fire with its rapidity. The ministers of the present reign have daringly struck at your most sacred rights, have aimed through the sides of America a deadly blow at the life of your constitution, and have shewn themselves hostile, not only to the being, but to the very name of liberty. The word itself has been proscribed the court; and for any one who dared to utter it, the gentlest appellations have been Wilkite, republican and disturber of the peace. Facts recent in every one's memory I have no need to repeat. I will only therefore just mention the atrocious violation of the first principle of the constitution in the never-to-be forgotten business of the Middlesex election. An enumeration of all their crimes would shew them to be deserving of the highest punishments. And yet, the sum of all the evils they have brought upon us, added to all those which former ministers had intailed upon the nation, are light and trivial in comparison of the *one great evil of a long parliament.* Feast the fowls of the air with such ministers, but leave your legislature unreformed; and you will only add a few inglorious days to the period of your expiring liberties. Succeeding ministers might be more circumspect; but, with the aid of a prostitute parliament, they would at length succeed. "Could we have had every one of our corrupt ministers impeached, and even convicted, would a corrupt parliament filled with their obsequious tools, have punished them? If we did nothing toward a radical cure of grievances, and obliging the succeeding to be honester than the foregoing; what should we have gained by such prosecutions? The greatest part of the *Roman* emperors was massacred, and so are many of *Asiatic* and *African* tyrants, But did the *Romans* or do the *Turks,* and the people of *Algiers,* gain any additional liberty by the punishment of their oppressors? We know they did not. Nor shall we by clamouring, nor even by punishing; any more than we stop robbing on the highway by hanging, unless we put it out of the *power* of ministers to go on abusing us and trampling upon our liberties; and this can only be done restoring independency to parliament." It is downright quixotism to imagine, that so long as your parliament remains corrupt, you can ever have a patriot minister: and, except parliament be reformed, 'tis a matter of very great indifference who are *in* and who are *out.* I will not utterly deny the possibility of your having a patriot minister prior to a parliamentary reformation; but I do not myself conceive how such a man is to arrive at such a station. One of that stamp could not go through thick and thin, and wade through all the miry paths that lead to it: nor have I any great expectation of a miraculous conversion of any one, who hath once passed through those ways to the seat of power. Neither do I see the prudence of waiting for so rare a phenomenon as a patriot minister, to do that for you which you can do for yourselves; and thereby put things in such a state, that a patriot minister will no longer be a phenomenon, but a natural and common appearance.

The revolution which expelled the tyrant James from the throne, glorious as it was to the character, and essential to the safety of this nation, was yet a very defective proceeding. It was effected in too anxious a moment, and in too precipitate a manner, to lay a lasting foundation for the security of public freedom and prosperity. *William* the deliverer was but half the friend to liberty which he pretended to be. Had he been a truly patriot prince, his share in the expulsion of a tyrant would have been his smallest merit; and he would have embraced the opportunity afforded him by his own success and the tide of reformation being set in, to have guarded the constitution against every conceivable danger towards which it had any tendency to be exposed in process of time. When the immortal and blessed *Alfred* had overthrown the oppressors of his country, he thought the work of a king only begun; and devoted the rest of his reign to the correcting abuses, the establishing of justice, and laying the broad foundations of liberty and happiness. But history shews *William* to have been a cold-hearted Dutchman, ungrateful to a people who had given him a crown, and more fond of power than of squaring his government with the principles of the constitution. And this was one of the best of our kings. Then put not your trust in princes: neither have confidence in ministers! Whether they covet inordinate power for its own sake, or for the sake of lucre, they will have it if possible. And when one lusts for gold, the other for dominion, they will be reciprocally the pimps to each other passion. The prince will invade the people's property, in order to enrich his minister; the minister will violate their liberties, in order to render his master absolute. For one *Alfred*, there are a thousand *Charleses*; for one *Falkland*, a thousand *Walpoles*. Trust not, I say, in princes nor in ministers; but trust in *yourselves,* and in representatives chosen by *yourselves* alone!

The State of the Prisons in England and Wales by John Howard, 1777

The State of the Prisons in England and Wales, with preliminary observations, and an account of some foreign prisons (Warrington: William Eyres, 1777), 7-24, 49-77.

John Howard (1726?-90), the reformer, here presents a descriptive account of the horrifying conditions prevailing in prisons and suggests specific remedies for their improvement.

There are prisons, into which whoever looks will, at first sight of the people confined there, be convinced, that there is some great error in the management of them: the sallow meagre countenances declare, without words, that they are very miserable: many who went in healthy, are in a few months changed to emaciated dejected objects. Some are seen pining under diseases, "*sick and in prison*;" expiring on the floors, in loathsome cells, of pestilential fevers, and the confluent small-pox: victims, I must not say to the cruelty, but I will say to the inattention, of sheriffs, and gentlemen in the commission of the peace.

The cause of this distress is, that many prisons are scantily supplied, and some almost totally unprovided with the necessaries of life.

There are several Bridewells (to begin with them) in which prisoners have no allowance of *Food* at all. In some, the keeper farms what little is allowed them: and where he engages to supply each prisoner with one or two pennyworth of bread a day, I have known this shrunk to half, sometimes less than half the quantity, cut or broken from his own loaf.

It will perhaps be asked, does not their work maintain them? for every one knows that those offenders are committed to *hard labour*. The answer to that question, though true, will hardly be believed. There are very few Bridewells in which any work is done, or can be done. The prisoners have neither tools, nor materials of any kind; but spend their time in sloth, profaneness and debauchery, to a degree which, in some of those houses that I have seen, is extremely shocking.

Some keepers of these houses, who have represented to the magistrates the wants of their prisoners, and desired for them necessary food, have been silenced with these inconsiderate words, *Let them work or starve.* When those gentlemen know the former is impossible, do they not by that sentence, inevitably doom poor creatures to the latter?

I have asked some keepers, since the late act for preserving the health of prisoners, why no care is taken of their sick: and have been answered, that the magistrates tell them *the act does not extend to Bridewells.*

In consequence of this, at the quarter sessions you see prisoners, covered (hardly covered) with rags; almost famished; and sick of diseases, which the discharged spread wherever they go, and with which those who are sent to the County-Gaols infect these prisons.

The same complaint, *want of food*, is to be found in many *County-Gaols*. In about half these, debtors have no bread; although it is granted to the highwayman, the house-breaker, and the murderer; and medical assistance, which is provided for the latter, is withheld from the former. In many of these Gaols, debtors who would work are not permitted to have any tools, lest they should furnish felons with them for escape or other mischief. I have often seen those prisoners eating their water-soup (bread boiled in mere water) and heard them say, "We are locked up and almost starved to death."

As to the relief provided for Debtors by the benevolent act, 32d of George II. (commonly called the lords act, because it originated in their house) I did not find in all England and Wales (except the counties of Middlesex and Surrey) *Twelve Debtors* who had obtained from their creditors the four-pence a day, to which they had a right by that act: the means of procuring it were out of their reach. In one of my journeys I found near six hundred prisoners, whose debts were under twenty pounds each: some of them did not owe above three or four pounds: and the expence of sueing for the aliment is in many places equal to those smaller debts; for which some of these prisoners had been confined several months.

At Carlisle but one debtor of the forty-nine whom I saw there had obtained his groats: and the gaoler told me that during the time he had held that office, which was fourteen years, no more than four or five had received it; and that they were soon discharged by their creditors neglecting to pay it. No one debtor had the aliment in York Castle, Devon, Cheshire, Kent, and many other counties. The truth is, some debtors are the most pitiable objects in our gaols.

To their wanting necessary food, I must add not only the demands of gaolers, etc. for fees; but also the extortion of bailiffs. These detain in their houses (properly enough denominated *spunging-houses*) at an enormous expence, prisoners who have money. I know there is a legal provision against this oppression; but the mode of obtaining redress (like that of recovering the groats) is attended with difficulty: and the abuse continues. The rapine of these extortioners needs some more effectual and easy check: no bailiff should be suffered to keep a public house; the mischiefs occasioned by their so doing, are complained of in many parts of the kingdom.

Here I beg leave to mention the hard case of prisoners confined on exchequer processes; and those from the ecclesiastical courts: the latter are excluded from the privilege of bail; and the former from the benefit of insolvent acts.

Felons have in some Gaols two pennyworth of bread a day; in some three halfpennyworth; in some a pennyworth; in some a shilling a week: the particulars will be seen here-after in their proper places. I often weighed the bread in different prisons, and found the penny loaf 7½ to 8½ ounces, the other loaves in proportion. It is probable that when this allowance was fixed by its value, near double the quantity that the money will now purchase, might be bought for it: yet the allowance continues unaltered: and it is not uncommon to see the whole purchase, especially of the smaller sums, eaten at breakfast: which is sometimes the case when they receive their pittance but once in two days; and then on the following day they must fast.

This allowance being so far short of the cravings of nature, and in some prisons lessened by farming to the gaoler, many criminals are half starved: such of them as at their commitment were in health, come out almost famished, scarce able to move, and for weeks incapable of any labour.

Many prisons have *No Water*. This defect is frequent in Bridewells, and Town-Gaols. In the felons courts of some County-Gaols there is no water: in some places where there is water, prisoners are always locked up within doors, and have no more than the keeper or his servants think fit to bring them: in one place they are limited to three pints a day each—a scanty provision for drink and cleanliness!

And as to *Air*, which is no less necessary than either of the two preceding articles, and given us by Providence quite *gratis*, without any care or labour of our own; yet, as if the bounteous goodness of Heaven excited our envy, methods are contrived to rob prisoners of this *genuine cordial of life*, as Dr. Hales very properly calls it: I mean by preventing that circulation and change of the salutiferous fluid, without which animals cannot live and thrive. It is well known that air which has performed its office in the lungs, is seculent and noxious. Writers upon the subject shew, that a hogshead of it will last a man only an hour: but those who do not choose to consult philosophers, may judge from a notorious fact. In 1756, at Calcutta in Bengal, out of 170 persons who were confined in a hole there one night, 154 were taken out dead. The few survivors ascribed the mortality to their want of fresh air, and called the place, from what they suffered there, *Hell in miniature*!

Air which has been breathed, is made poisonous to a more intense degree by the effluvia from the sick; and what else in prisons is offensive. My reader will judge of its malignity, when I assure him, that my cloaths were in my first journeys so offensive, that in a post-chaise I could not bear the windows drawn up: and was therefore often obliged to travel on horseback. The leaves of my memorandum-book were often so tainted, that I could not use it till after spreading it an hour or two before the fire: and even my antidote, a vial of vinegar, has after using it in a few prisons, become intolerably disagreeable. I did not wonder that in those journies many gaolers made excuses; and did not go with me into the felons wards.

From hence any one may judge of the probability there is against the health and life of prisoners, crowded in close rooms, cells, and subterraneous dungeons, for fourteen or sixteen hours out of the four and twenty. In some of those caverns the floor is very damp: in others there is sometimes an inch or two of water; and the straw, or bedding is laid on such floors, seldom on barrack bedsteads. Where prisoners are not kept in underground cells, they are often confined to their rooms, because there is no court belonging to the prison, which is the case in most City and Town-Gaols: or because the walls round the yard are ruinous, or too low for safety: or because the gaoler has the ground for his own use. Prisoners confined in this manner, are generally unhealthy. Some Gaols have no *Sewers;* and in those that have, if they be not properly attended to, they are, even to a visitant, offensive beyond expression: how noxious then to people constantly confined in those prisons!

One cause why the rooms in some prisons are so close, is perhaps the window-tax, which the gaolers have to pay: this tempts them to stop the windows, and stifle their prisoners.

In many Gaols, and in most Bridewells, there is no allowance of *Straw* for prisoners to sleep on; and if by any means they get a little, it is not changed for months together, so that it is almost worn to dust. Some lie upon rags, other upon the bare floors. When I have complained of this to the keepers, their justification has been, "The county allows no straw; the prisoners have none but at my cost."

The evils mentioned hitherto affect the *health* and *life* of prisoners: I have now to complain of what is pernicious to their *Morals;* and that is, the confining all sorts of prisoners together: debtors and felons; men and women; the young beginner and the old offender: and with all these, in some counties, such as are guilty of misdemeanors only; who should have been committed to Bridewell, to be corrected by diligence and labour; but for want of food, and the means of procuring it in those prisons, are in pity sent to such County-Gaols as afford these offenders prison-allowance.

Few prisons separate men and women in the day-time. In some counties the Gaol is also the Bridewell: in others those prisons are contiguous, and the yard common. There the petty offender is committed for instruction to the most profligate. In some Gaols you see (and who can see it without pain?) boys of twelve or fourteen eagerly listening to the stories told by practised and experienced criminals, of their adventures, successes, stratagems, and escapes.

I must here add, that in some few Gaols are confined idiots and lunatics. These serve for sport to idle visitants at assizes, and other times of general resort. The insane, where they are not kept separate, disturb and terrify other prisoners. No care is taken of them, although it is probable that by medicines, and proper regimen, some of them might be restored to their senses, and to usefulness in life.

I am ready to think, that none who give credit to what is contained in the foregoing pages, will wonder at the havock made by the *Gaol-Fever*. From my own observations in 1773 and 1774, I was fully convinced that many more were destroyed by it, than were put to death by all the public executions in the kingdom. This frequent effect of confinement in prison seems generally understood, and shews how full of emphatical meaning is the curse of a severe creditor, who pronounces his debtor's doom to *Rot in Gaol*. I believe I have learned the full import of this sentence, from the vast numbers who to my certain knowledge, some of them before my eyes, have perished in our Gaols.

But the mischief is not confined to prisons. Not to mention now the number of *sailors,* and of *families* in America, that have been infected by transports, since this mode of punishment is by a late act suspended. Multitudes catch the distemper by going to their relatives and acquaintance in the Gaols: many others from prisoners discharged: and not a few in the courts of judicature.

In Baker's *Chronicle,* page 353, that historian mentioning the Assize held in Oxford Castle 1577 (called from its fatal consequence the *Black Assize*) informs us, that "all who were present died within forty hours: the Lord Chief Baron, the Sheriff, and about three hundred more." Lord Chancellor Bacon ascribes this to a disease brought into court by the prisoners; and Dr. Mead is of the same opinion.

The first of these two authors, Lord Bacon, observes, that

the most pernicious infection next the plague, is the smell of the jail; when the prisoners have been long and close and nastily kept: whereof *we have had, in our time, experience twice or thrice;* when both the judges that sat upon the jail, and numbers of those who attended the business, or were present, sickened upon it and died.

At the Lent Assize in Taunton, 1730, some prisoners who were brought thither from Ivelchester Gaol, infected the court; and Lord Chief Baron Pengelly; Sir James Sheppard, Serjeant; John Pigot, Esq. Sheriff, and some hundreds besides, died of the gaol-distemper. At Axminster, a little town in Devonshire, a prisoner discharged from Exeter Gaol in 1755, infected his family with that disease: of which two of them died; and many others in that town afterwards. The numbers that were carried off by the same malady in London in 1750, two judges, the lord mayor, one alderman, and many of inferior rank, are too well known to need the mentioning further particulars.

Sir John Pringle observes, that "jails have often been the cause of malignant fevers;" and he informs us, that in the late rebellion in Scotland, above 200 men of one regiment were infected with the jail-fever, by some deserters brought from prisons in England.

Dr. Lind, Physician to the Royal Hospital at Haslar, near Portsmouth, shewed me in one of the wards a number of sailors ill of the gaol-fever; brought on board their ship by a man who had been discharged from a prison in London. The ship was laid up on the occasion. That gentleman, in his *Essay on the Health of Seamen*, asserts, that "The source of infection to our armies and fleets are undoubtedly the jails; we can often trace the importers of it directly from them. It often proves fatal in impressing men on the hasty equipment of a fleet. The first English fleet sent last war to America, lost by it above 2000 men." In another place he assures us, that "the seeds of infection were carried from the guard-ships into our squadrons—and the mortality, thence occasioned, was greater than by all other diseases or means of death put together."

It were easy to multiply instances of this mischief; but those which have been mentioned are, I presume, sufficient to shew, even if no mercy were due to prisoners, that the Gaol-Distemper is a national concern of no small importance.

The general prevalence and spread of wickedness in prisons, and abroad by the discharged prisoners, will now be as easily accounted for, as the propagation of disease. It is often said, "A prison pays no debts;" I am sure it may be added, that a prison mends no morals. Sir John Fielding observes, that "a criminal discharged—generally by the next sessions after the execution of his comrades, becomes the head of a gang of his own raising." Improved, no doubt, in skill by the company he kept in gaol: and petty offenders who are committed to Bridewell for a year or two, and spend that time, not in hard labour, but in idleness and wicked company, or are sent for that time to County-Gaols, generally grow desperate, and come out fitted, for the perpetration of any villainy. How directly contrary this to the intention of our laws with regard to these offenders; which certainly is to correct and reform them! Instead of which, their confinement doth notoriously promote and increase the very vices it was designed to suppress. Multitudes of young creatures, committed for some trifling offence, are totally ruined there. I make no scruple to affirm, that if it were the wish and aim of Magistrates to effect the destruction present and future of young delinquents, they could not devise a more effectual method, than to confine them so long in our prisons, those seats and seminaries (as they have been very properly called) of idleness and every vice.

Shall these irregularities, the sources of misery, disease, and wickedness, be endured in a nation celebrated for good sense and humanity; and who from these principles, do treat one sort of prisoners with tenderness and generosity? I mean prisoners of war. These have provision in plenty; some to spare and sell to the soldiers on guard. We frequently saw their stated allowance hung up for their inspection. Some prisons had large areas for them to walk in; and at night every man had a hammock to himself. It is the farthest thing in the world from my wish to deprive captives of any one of these benefits—I am only desirous of seeing the same humanity shewn to our own countrymen in distress; so that a consistent and uniform practice may prove our benevolence to be a firm and steady principle; and that those who are censorious may find no occasion for ascribing our kind usage of foreigners to a less amiable motive.

Here it will be said, prisoners of war are not felons, nor yet debtors; and government is sometimes at the end of a war, reimbursed the expence of maintaining them. This latter I believe is fact; and the former is true without dispute: we do not look upon foreign enemies, nor they upon us, as delinquents: we cut one another to pieces in battle.

But it may be said, enough of the declamatory kind has been written by others. Much it is true, has been written: yet I beg leave to transcribe, a few lines from a celebrated author, which may be thought to come under that description. After representing the calamitous case of prisoners, he goes on to this purpose,

> The misery of Gaols is not half their evil; they are filled with every corruption which poverty and wickedness can generate between them; with all the shameless and profligate enormities that can be produced by the impudence of ignominy, the rage of want, and the malignity of despair. In a prison the awe of the public eye is lost, and the power of the law is spent; there are few fears, there are no blushes. The lewd inflame the lewd, the audacious harden the audacious. Every one fortifies himself as he can against his own sensibility, endeavours to practise on others the arts which are practised on himself; and gains the kindness of his associates by similitude of manners.

Besides the grievances already mentioned; there are several *bad customs* in Gaols, and relating to them, which aggravate the distress of prisoners. I shall enumerate these distinctly, yet briefly. . . .

Regulations

Without a due attention to the economy and government of a Prison, it is evident that no contrivance of structure can secure it from being the abode of wickedness, disease, and misery; I shall therefore offer a few hints for the better regulation of a Gaol.

The first care must be to find a good man for a Gaoler; one that is honest, active, and humane. Such was *Abel Dagge*, who was formerly keeper of Bristol Newgate. I regretted his death, and revere his memory.

This officer must be sober himself, that he may, by example, as well as authority, restrain drunkenness, and other vices in his prison. To remove a strong temptation to the contrary, it is highly requisite that no Gaoler, Turnkey, or other servant be suffered to hold the *Tap*; or to have any connexion, concern, or interest whatever in the sale of liquors of any kind. Gaolers who hold, or let, the tap, find their account in not only conniving at, but promoting drunkenness and midnight revels. What profligate and debauched company of both sexes, do we see let into our Gaols, that the *Tap* may be kept running! Besides this, the Gaoler's interest in the sale of liquors, may prompt him to be partial in his behaviour to his prisoners; to treat at least with neglect, those who are poor and have nothing to spend; which is the case of far the greater number: while he shall caress dishonest debtors, who take shelter in a prison, in order to live there in riot upon the property of their creditors.

I know that by the statute of 32d George II. a Debtor has a right to send out of the Gaol for liquor and other necessaries. This is a very judicious provision; and very beneficial to prisoners where they have the full and free use of it. But some Gaolers there are, who find ways to restrain this privilege, for the profits of their tap: whereas if Gaolers were prohibited from all concern in the sale of liquor, this would not only remove that check, and restore to prisoners the free enjoyment of the liberty they are entitled to; but would also be the means of suppressing much *Intemperance*; and perhaps of entirely abolishing *Garnish*, as well as *Clubs* or night associations.

That it is necessary to deprive Gaolers of all profits arising from the *Tap*, I am convinced, not by mere speculation, but by what I have learned from conversation with *Gaolers* themselves. I asked two of them, whom I found candid and intelligent, "what they thought would be the most likely means of effecting a thorough reformation in Gaols." The answer I had from both, was to this purpose, "Let no licences be granted for selling beer or wine in Gaols: let it be made some other way worth our while to keep them."

Gaolers should have salaries proportioned to the trust and trouble; since no office, if *faithfully* and *humanely* administered, better deserves an adequate encouragement: yet not so much as to raise them above attention to their duty, and the daily inspection of their Gaols.

The *Gaol-Committee,* which I have mentioned before, in their Report of the Marshalsea Prison, 14 May 1729, after enumerating many mischiefs which they found had been occasioned by the Gaoler's holding or letting the tap, draw the following conclusion; "This shews the inconveniency of the Keepers having the advantage of the Tap-house, since to advance the rent thereof, and to consume the liquors there vended, they not only encourage riot and drunkenness, but also prevent the needy prisoner from being supplied by his friends with the meer necessaries of life, in order to encrease an exorbitant gain to their tenants."

When I was in Ireland (January 1775) I found, not without some surprise, that no liquors were sold in any of the prisons which I saw. Upon inquiry, I learned that there is an Act against it, made in the third year of his present Majesty.

No Prisoner should be a Turnkey. It is the Gaoler's duty to inspect the wards himself every day, and not to leave this to servants. The *Magistrates* of Glasgow have expressly ordered that "The Gaoler every morning and evening, at the opening of, and before the shutting up the prison, shall personally visit every room and place therein."

He must encourage and promote cleanliness. For this reason an old or infirm man should not be a Gaoler: when that is the case, all is commonly dirty. He should be compassionate to the sick. If he is ordered to distribute the allowance, he must do justice to the county or city, and to his prisoners, by giving to the latter the full stated quantity.

I have said before, a Gaoler should not live at a distance from his prison. He should not only reside on the spot, but be constantly at home. Prisoners generally take advantage from his absence. For this reason, no Keeper of a Prison should be a *Sheriff's Officer*. Such are very often abroad; and some of them have acknowledged to me, that their business as Officers was incompatible with their duty as Gaolers.

I had the pleasure to find a Chaplain appointed to most of the County-Gaols; in consequence of the Act made 13th of his present Majesty. When this office is vacant, it behoves Magistrates not to take the first Clergyman who offers his service, without regarding his real character. They should choose one who is in principle a *Christian*: who will not content himself with officiating in public; but will converse with the prisoners; admonish the profligate; exhort the thoughtless; comfort the sick; and make known to the condemned that *Mercy* which is revealed in the *Gospel*.

In the Life of *Bernard Gilpin*, page 173, the writer, speaking of his labours, informs us, that "where-ever he came, he used to visit all the Jails and places of confinement; few in the kingdom having at that time any appointed Minister." And by his affectionate address "he is said to have reformed many very abandoned persons in those places."

In some prisons where there is a Chaplain appointed, no worship is fixed for Sunday: in some where that day is fixed, the Chaplain, choosing his hours, comes sometimes too soon in the morning, sometimes between morning and evening service, at the prisoners dinner-time: in some there is no fixed day at all. It would be proper to have sermon and prayers once at least on the Lord's Day: and prayers two fixed days in the week besides. And if a Chapter of the *New Testament* were read daily in order by one of the prisoners to the rest, or by the Gaoler, before the distribution of prison allowance, the time would not be mispent. The reader, if a prisoner, might be allowed a small weekly pension. The Gaoler should not, as some do, hinder any prisoner from attending divine service. He ought to remove every hindrance: and, on Sunday especially, no visitants should be admitted during that time. Visitants who are there before, should go out or attend.

Upon asking at more places than one, "why there were so few prisoners at prayers," I have been answered, "they are drinking with their friends." The Gaoler should be constant at Chapel with his prisoners; and set a good example for them to follow. The Chaplain who officiates in the Gaol may also be employed at the *Bridewell*, where the distance will allow; and preach once a Sunday in each prison.

It perhaps will be said, that I propose a great deal of duty to these gentlemen. The Act just recited allows a sum *not exceeding fifty pounds a year* for their services. Many counties have fixed that salary; but I should hope that Clergymen might be found who would act from a much nobler motive, a regard to the most important interests of their fellow-creatures.

The late Act for *preserving the health of prisoners* requires that an *experienced Surgeon or Apothecary* be appointed to every Gaol: a man of repute in his profession. His business is, in the first place, to order the immediate removal of the sick to the Infirmary. Their irons should be taken off; and they should have, not only medicines, but also diet suitable to their condition. He must diligently and daily visit them himself; not leaving them to journeymen and apprentices. He should constantly inculcate the necessity of cleanliness and fresh air; and the danger of crowding prisoners together. I need not add, that he must report to the Justices at each Quarter Sessions, a state of the health of the prisoners under his care.

At Newgate there are commonly about two hundred prisoners. Here the danger to them, and to the city from them, is great. To this capital prison in the metropolis, the Magistrates would, in my humble opinion, do well to appoint a *Physician*, a *Surgeon*, and *Apothecary*. One of the two latter to visit each ward in the prison *every day*. The two Compters are near enough to be taken care of by the same gentlemen; and they need to be visited as constantly. This attention would, in all probability, prevent the spread of any infectious disease in those Gaols; and stop the mouths of County-Gaolers, who, when their prisons are infected, tell you (as I have often heard them) "The distemper was brought from *Newgate* by prisoners removed from thence by *habeas corpus*."

No Prisoner should be subject to any demand of *Fees*. The Gaoler should have a salary in lieu of them; and so should the Turnkeys. Their wages should not be included in the Gaoler's salary: and not only their pay, but the number of them necessary for each prison, should be determined by the Magistrates. Neither of those articles should be left to the interested appointment of a Gaoler. If fees be not abolished, I am sure they should be reduced; and so should the Chamber Rents for Master-side Debtors. In this matter (of the Chambers) another regulation is also needful; that is, no middle-sized room should have more beds than two. The bedding and other furniture should be specified as to articles and value.

For *Common-side Debtors* there should be a ward entirely free: they should not be subject to any demand of rent; as in many prisons they are. These prisoners should either be alimented by their creditors without expence and delay; or have from the county the same allowance of every kind (at least) as felons: food, bedding, and medicine.

In order to *Cleanliness,* than which scarce any thing in the whole economy of a Gaol is of more importance, every ward and room should be well scraped; and then washed with lime and water during the act of effervescence, at least twice a year; just after the Lent and Summer Assize. Each ward and room should be swept, and washed, *every day,* by the respective inhabitant; and some times with hot vinegar. Idle Gaolers affect to excuse their negligence in this respect, by pretending that daily washing would make the rooms too damp, and endanger the health of prisoners. This is mere pretence: the effect is directly contrary. There is not in England a prison more healthy, considering the number of prisoners of the lowest sort, than *Tothillfields Bridewell*; where the rooms are washed every day. The prisoners do the work by turns: and the healthiness of the prison is a demonstration, that no inconvenience, but great benefit, is the consequence. In *Newgate*, the prisoner who sweeps the ward has a double allowance of bread. Every prisoner should be obliged to wash his hands and face before he comes for his daily allowance; and to keep himself as neat as circumstances will admit. I have said before, there should be plenty of water in a prison; and need not add now, that prisoners should constantly have free and easy access to it.

Every prisoner who comes to Gaol dirty, should be washed in the cold or warm bath; and his cloaths should be put into the oven, in a sack on a pair of iron dogs. He should be provided with coarse washing cloaths to wear while his own are thus purifying: washing cloaths should be kept ready in the Gaol for this purpose. Each prisoner should have a clean shirt once a week. There should be in each ward a towel on a roller clean every day. Pails, mops, brooms, soap, vinegar, and fuel for the oven, should be supplied by the county or town: otherwise Gaols will never be kept clean and wholesome.

No stable or dunghill should be suffered in the yard; nor any fowls kept there, which I have often seen not only in the yards, but also in the rooms of many prisons. Sweepings, ashes, etc. should be taken away every week.

If the bedding is straw, it should be put in coarse canvass; if it is not so enclosed, it ought to be changed every week. Each bed should have a coarse coverlid or two.

Prisoners should not remain in the day-time in the little rooms or cabins in which they sleep: they should have a common ward, day-room or kitchen.

Those who drink only water, and have no nutritious liquor, ought to have at least a pound and half of bread every day. The bread should be one day old, and then honestly weighed to them. If once a week (suppose on Sunday) some of the coarser pieces of beef were boiled in the copper, and half a pound of the meat without bone given to each prisoner, with a quart of the broth, and then only one pound of bread, this Sunday Dinner might be made an encouragement to peaceable and orderly behaviour: the turbulent and refractory should not have it. Such an allowance, might help to remove a bad custom that obtains too generally, the pretence of refreshing prisoners with better food and drink on Sunday; upon which many are admitted into the Gaols, and keep the prisoners from Chapel.

I state the allowance in *weight*, not money, because of the variable price. Besides that quantity of bread, each prisoner should have a penny a day in money for cheese, butter, potatoes, pease, or turnips: or he should have a pennyworth of one of those articles.

Here, as in the tap, I must insist upon it as highly necessary, that every Gaoler, Bridewell-Keeper, Turnkey, etc. be excluded from all concern in the prisoners allowance; from all profit arising *directly* or *indirectly* from the sale of their bread, or other food. Whoever distributes it, should be free from all temptation to fraud; and be subject to a strong check. The whole allowance of prisoners should never be given them in money.

The Reader will plainly see, that I am not an advocate for *extravagant and profuse allowance* to prisoners. I plead only for necessaries, in such a moderate quantity, as may support health and strength for labour. The law allows the *poor* debtor who is detained in prison, two shillings and four-pence per week (I wish it were more easily obtained) and the government allowance to assize convicts under sentence of transportation is a little more, viz. two shillings and six-pence; which the Sheriff charges to Government in his bill of cravings, presented at the expiration of his office. And I believe upon the average price of bread, potatoes, etc. the allowance I have mentioned does not exceed those sums. I presume it may be thought rather incongruous to allow prisoners before trial (on which some of them may be found not guilty) less than is given to those that are convicted.

No *Fighting* should be suffered in a Gaol: no quarreling, or abusive language; nor the frequent occasion of them, gaming. If any one be injured, let him complain to the Keeper, who should hear both parties face to face, decide the matter, and punish the aggressor by closer confinement. Faults that deserve more severe animadversion, should be reserved for the cognizance of the Magistrates, or an inspector: of whom presently.

Money sent, collected, or bequeathed, should be distributed by the Magistrates. Some of it might be laid out in tools, etc. for such debtors as will work.

The mention of *Legacies* reminds me of the need there is of a list of them painted legibly on a board; which should be hung up so as to be read by the prisoners. Very few Gaols have such a table: and for want of it many Legacies have been entirely lost; and the charitable intention of the Testators frustrated. Yet care of legacies is expressly required by the Act 32d George II.

In the like conspicuous manner should be hung up in every Gaol an authentic *Table of Fees,* till they are abolished. This also is expressly required by the same Act. Yet in many Gaols it is totally disregarded, and they have no such tables.

In the Act 24th George II. which prohibits the use of spirituous liquors in Prisons or Workhouses, it is expressly required, that every Gaoler, Keeper, Master, etc. shall procure one or more copies of the three clauses which contain the several articles of the prohibition, to be printed or fairly written, and hung up in one of the most public places of the Prison or Work-house, and renewed as occasion required, under the penalty of forty shillings for every default.

There should also be a list of the *Allowance* to prisoners: for want of which I have known them defrauded of a considerable part of their food: the whole of which is no where more than sufficient. The same list should exhibit the particulars of bedding, or straw.

The Act for preserving the health of prisoners requires that it be painted on a board, etc. as aforesaid: not merely written or printed on paper, because that is more perishable, and liable to be torn. The Rules for Cleanliness, and Orders against Garnish, Gaming, Drunkenness, Quarreling, Profaneness and Obscenity, should also be visibly exhibited; with the penalties for each of those crimes. The penalties should be fixed by the Magistrates, or by law. The table should also shew the hours of opening and shutting the several wards; and of attending public worship. Besides setting down these hours in a table, notice should be given of them by a bell, as in the dock-yards. I have known prisoners absent from Chapel, who said they would have been there, but did not know the service was performing.

It is expressly required by the Act 32d George II. that Rules and Orders made, signed, and confirmed, as the Table of Fees, be drawn up for every Prison, and hung up *conspicuously* in it for inspection of prisoners. Yet in many Prisons neither Fees nor Orders are to be seen: the latter in very few.

Finally, The care of a Prison is too important to be left wholly to a Gaoler; paid indeed for his attendance, but often tempted by his passions, or interest, to fail in his duty. To every prison there should be an Inspector appointed; either by his colleagues in the magistracy, or by Parliament. Sheriffs and Magistrates have indeed this power already; and prisons are their immediate care. But some Sheriffs excuse themselves from attention to this part of their duty, on account of the short duration, expence, and trouble of their office: and those Gentlemen, as well as Gentlemen in the Commission of the Peace, have no doubt been fearful of the consequence of looking into prisons. But the danger from such inspection is in great measure removed: and it may be expected that Sheriffs will now engage in this business; and that among Justices, and Town-Magistrates, there may always be found one man generous enough to undertake this important service. Or if the constant trouble be thought too much for one person, it may proceed by annual, quarterly, or monthly rotation. The Inspector should make his visit once a week, or at most in a fortnight; changing his days. He should take with him a memorandum of all the rules, and inquire into the observance or neglect of them. He should (as is done in some of our Hospitals) look into every room, to see if it be clean, etc. He should speak with every prisoner; hear all complaints; and immediately correct what he finds manifestly wrong: what he doubts of, he may refer to his brethren in office, at their next meeting. A good Gaoler will be pleased with this scrutiny: it will do him honour, and confirm him in his station. In case of a less worthy Gaoler, the examination is more needful, in order to his being reprimanded; and, if he be incorrigible, to his being discharged. This Honourable Delegate should have *no salary*: he should engage from the noble motive of doing justice to prisoners, and service to his country.

I have often inquired of Gaolers whether the Sheriffs, Justices, or Town-Magistrates inspected their Gaols. Many of the oldest have answered, "None of those Gentlemen ever looked into the dungeons, or even the wards of my Gaol." Others have said, "Those Gentlemen think that if they came into my Gaol, they should soon be in their graves." Others, "The Justices think the inside of my House too close for them; they satisfy themselves with viewing the outside." Now if Magistrates continue thus negligent of their duty, a general thorough reformation of our Prisons must be despaired of: what has been already obtained will soon be lost, and all will sink again into the former dreadful condition.

Bridewells

If our Bridewells be not more properly conducted, sending prisoners from them to County-Gaols will defeat all the care of the most attentive Gaolers, and the whole intention of the Act for preserving the health of prisoners; and discharged offenders will spread disease and vice. . . . Few or none of the windows should have glass; only shutters; and these should be open several hours in the day. In the court-yard (for such is necessary in every prison) there should be a pump, or some other provision for water in plenty. And prisoners should be permitted to walk about, when they have done working.

For in work they ought, most certainly, to be employed. This is indispensibly requisite. *Not one* who is not sick should be idle. Where the prisoners are numerous, there should be several work-rooms; and but few prisoners in one room. Those who work by compulsion are more likely to be seduced to idleness in large companies, than when they are more by themselves. The Keeper should be a master of some manufacture; a man of activity, prudence, and temper. And he should keep his prisoners at work ten hours a day; meal-times included.

For women, especially those that have children with them, and sometimes at the breast, there should be a chimney in one or two rooms: and in winter firing should be allowed. I have known infants starved to death for want of this. In some prisons the smoke has no vent but at the doors and windows. In some Bridewells there should be a separate little room or two for faulty apprentices, as at *Tothillfields*, and *Clerkenwell*. In all, two airy wards for the sick, with medical relief. Men and women should have work-shops, as well as night-rooms, separate. There should be baths, and an oven, for the same purposes as in the Gaols. In some County-Bridewells there are from twenty to thirty prisoners, and in Tothillfields and Clerkenwell many more. Great care should be taken to prevent infection; to keep the House clean, and well aired; and invariably to adhere to strict rules of sobriety and diligence, in order to correct the faults of prisoners, and make them for the future useful to society. Gentle discipline is commonly more efficacious than severity; which should not be exercised but on such as will not be amended by lenity. These should be punished by solitary confinement on bread and water, for a time proportioned to their fault. The Keeper should, by all means, reside in the House. He should not be suffered to farm any part of the allowance; nor to sell liquor, or any thing else. The whole management should be frequently inquired into, in the same manner as that of a Gaol, and by the same Inspectors.

I know not any reason why a House of Correction may not be conducted with as much regularity, as any other house where the family is equally numerous. Some foreign Bridewells are so conducted. Let the sober and diligent be distinguished by some preference in their diet, or lodging; or by shortening the term of their confinement; and giving them, when discharged, a good character. This last will be a strong incitement to good behaviour. The common diet should be *at least* as good and as much as that of felons in a Gaol. The hours of rising, of reading a chapter in the bible, of prayers, of meals, or work, etc. should all be fixed by the magistrates, and notice of them given by a bell.

A Bridewell under proper regulation would contribute not a little towards its own maintenance. An exact account should be kept of the profit of the work; and all of it applied to common benefit; not left to the disposal of Keepers: for some of them in the few Bridewells where work is done, keep to themselves a sixth part, some half and some the whole of the prisoners earnings; giving them only the short county-allowance, and sometimes but part of that. When I said all the earnings should go to common stock, I meant it of the stated hours for working. Those who will employ themselves in extra-hours, should have the profit to themselves. And perhaps it might be an encouragement to diligence in the stated hours, to give them some small portion of the profit of these also. With regular economy, Prisoners would be better nourished, and fitter for labour, than they now are; and yet the county not burthened with much, if any, additional expence. But a building fit for the intention ought first to be provided.

The charge of this, as well as of a proper Gaol, will no doubt, be complained of. But if that be weighed against the benefit that will accrue to the public, it will be found but light. Besides that ought not to be allowed as a valid objection, the occasion of which should have been removed long ago. Why have some Prisons been suffered to become ruinous; so that many rooms in them are unsafe, and prisoners are crowded together in the few that remain? Why were not the walls of the yards repaired in time, that prisoners might with safety be allowed the proper use of them? Money, to the amount of thousands is not witheld when Shire-halls and Town-halls are wanted. These we often see grand and elegant Edifices. Why should it be spared when the morals and lives of multitudes are at stake; and when it is impossible the design of the Legislature should be answered without it? I mean amending the manners of Petty Offenders; preventing the increase of felonies, and the spread of diseases. That the two latter, instead of being prevented, are promoted by the present irregularity of Bridewells, is notorious. Prescription founded on culpable negligence should not be admitted in bar of a demand, which every principle of equity, humanity, and utility conspires to enforce.

I have only farther to add under this head, that the management of Bridewells is now a matter of more than ordinary concern, since offenders are at present committed to them for terms so long as from *three* to *ten years*. Most of these persons would probably have been sentenced to *transportation* when that mode of punishment was in use.

I had taken some pains to make inquiries concerning the state of *transports*, with regard to whom many cruelties and impositions were commonly practised, and whose condition was in many respects equally contrary to humanity and good policy: I flattered myself that I had discovered means of remedying these evils in a considerable degree, and of disburthening the counties of a heavy expence with which they were charged; and was preparing to lay them before the Public, when a new turn was given to the matter by Act of Parliament.

Since this has taken place, I suppress what I had written; and shall only give, at the end of my book, a list of the numbers delivered from Newgate for transportation in the course of three years. This will shew, in a very alarming light, the danger there may be in future of crowding our prisons, so as to produce the most destructive consequences.

I cannot conclude this Section without attempting to obviate some objections that may occur to the improvements proposed in it. It may be said, that from the many conveniences suggested in the structure of Gaols, and the removal of those hardships which rendered them so terrible, the dread of being confined in them will in great measure be taken off, and the lower classes of people will find them more comfortable places of residence than their own houses. But let it be considered, in the first place, that although I have indeed recommended such attentions in the construction and management as may free them from the *diseases* and *hardships* under which they have laboured, I have proposed nothing to give them an air of *elegance*, or *pleasantness*. On the contrary, I have censured the plan of some modern Gaols as too shewy and splendid; and nothing abroad struck me more with regard to these buildings, than the perfect *plainness* and *simplicity* of their appearance. Then, with respect to the more humane treatment of the prisoners in the articles of food, lodging, and the like, I venture to assert, that if to it be joined such strict regulations in preventing all dissipation and riotous amusement, as I have inculcated, confinement in a prison, though it may cease to be destructive to health and morals, will not fail to be sufficiently irksome and disagreeable, especially to the idle and profligate.

Commons debate on a Yorkshire petition for reduction of public expenditures, 8 February 1780

Parliamentary History, XX, 1371-82.

The Yorkshire petitioning movement, led by the Reverend Christopher Wyville (1740-1822), provided a popular base for the campaign to reduce crown patronage.

Sir George Savile presented the following Petition:

To the Honourable the Commons of Great Britain in Parliament assembled: the Petition of the Gentlemen, Clergy, and Freeholders of the County of York,

Sheweth; That this nation hath been engaged for several years in a most expensive and unfortunate war; that many of our valuable colonies, having actually declared themselves independent, have formed a strict confederacy with France and Spain, the dangerous and inveterate enemies of Great Britain; that the consequence of those combined misfortunes hath been, a large addition to the national debt, a heavy accumulation of taxes, a rapid decline of the trade, manufactures, and land-rents of the kingdom.

Alarmed at the diminished resources and growing burthens of this country, and convinced that rigid frugality is now indispensibly necessary in every department of the state, your petitioners observe with grief, that notwithstanding the calamitous and impoverished condition of the nation, much public money has been improvidently squandered, and that many individuals enjoy sinecure places, efficient places with exorbitant emoluments, and pensions unmerited by public service, to a large and still increasing amount; whence the crown has acquired a great and unconstitutional influence, which, if not checked, may soon prove fatal to the liberties of this country.

Your petitioners conceiving that the true end of every legitimate government is not the emolument of any individual, but the welfare of the community; and considering that by the constitution of this realm, the national purse is intrusted in a peculiar manner to the custody of this honourable House; beg leave further to represent, that until effectual measures be taken to redress the oppressive grievances herein stated, the grant of any additional sum of public money, beyond the produce of the present taxes, will be injurious to the rights and property of the people, and derogatory from the honour and dignity of parliament.

Your petitioners therefore, appealing to the justice of this honourable House, do most earnestly request that before any new burthens are laid upon this country, effectual measures may be taken by this House to enquire into and correct the gross abuses in the expenditure of public money; to reduce all exorbitant emoluments; to rescind and abolish all sinecure places and unmerited pensions; and to appropriate the produce to the necessities of the state in such manner as to the wisdom of parliament shall seem meet. And your petitioners shall ever pray, etc.

Sir George Savile apoligized for speaking in a low tone of voice: he had got a cold: there was a soreness in his throat, which he was afraid might prevent him from speaking in so audible a manner as to be heard by this great assembly. [The House was remarkably still and attentive. The character of the speaker, the importance of the subject, the novelty of the occasion, fully counterbalanced the distemper that would have proved fatal to the eloquence of a member less popular speaking on a lighter subject: such was the deep silence that prevailed on both sides of the House, that the venerable patriot was heard without much difficulty.] He had the honour to represent a very extensive, a very populous, a very mercantile, manufacturing, and rich county. In such a county, it must naturally be imagined, that many private interests might be made objects of parliamentary bounty, if either the represented or representatives, like some others, were more attentive to inclosure bills, to road bills, and others of the same stamp, than to the great concerns of the nation. This is now the last day of receiving private petitions. I have waited until I think they are all given in. I have no private petition to present, though in such a county as Yorkshire, new bridges, roads, and havens, would not be unworthy the consideration of the legislature. I have here a petition which has swallowed up the consideration of all private objects, and superseded all private petitions. A petition subscribed by 8,000 freeholders and upwards. The people have heard that a regard to private interest, in this House, is a great enemy to the discharge of our public duty. They feel severely the pressure of heavy taxes, yet, they are told, the money which they can so ill spare, is wasted profusely, without producing any good, nay, and to the production of many bad effects. They beg that enquiry may be made into the expenditure of that money, that if there are any exorbitant salaries, they may be reduced: that if there are any useless places or unmerited pensions, they may be abolished. These things are represented calmly and with moderation. Nothing is said of the conduct of ministers, it may have been good or bad, for ought that appears in the petition. Never, surely, were petitioners to parliament more cool and dispassionate. They confine themselves to one object, the expenditure of the public money. They make no strictures on the past management of ministry; though candour obliges me to acknowledge, that it is pretty plainly hinted or implied in the petition, that they who have hitherto managed our public affairs, shall manage them no more. I hope no objection will be made to the receiving of this petition. Indeed that is not what I fear. Ministry dare not refuse to give the petition a hearing. But it is an easy matter to hear a petition, and to put it off without complying with the prayer of it. The noble lord, if he had a mind (looking towards lord North) could by one nod induce a majority of this House to grant the prayer of this petition; or if he pleases, he can put it off with abundance of ingenuity and address. He will probably have no objection to hear the petition read; he may profess great regard to the petitioners, an anxious concern for their interest; he may even go so far as to consent to enquire into the alledged grievances, and fix a time and a committee for that purpose. Yet still it may be his secret purpose to defeat the end of the petition. I therefore now call upon the noble lord to speak out like a man, and to declare whether he means to countenance and support the petition or not. Such an open and manly declaration of his intentions, will save us much time and trouble, and will better become a man of his consequence, than any arts of ministerial craft and juggling. I hope he will seriously consider this petition, what is the importance of it, who were the instigators of it, by whom, as well as by how many it is subscribed. I make no threats; this petition is not presented by men with swords and muskets. It is a legal, a constitutional petition. It is the right of the British subjects to petition. But petitions of the kind that have often been presented here and elsewhere, and as often disregarded, I own, were nugatory, and must be ineffective. The request of the petitioners is here so reasonable, that they cannot but expect that it will be granted; but should it be refused—here I leave a blank, that blank let the consciences, let the feelings, let the reason of ministers supply. Nor will palliations, excuses, partial expedients, be sufficient. Mock enquiries will not answer our purpose. If the parliament mock the people, the people will learn not to respect the parliament. In order to detract from the weight of petitions, it is not uncommonly insinuated, that they are procured by underhand arts, or by publicly canvassing for them; or it is alledged, that the petitioners are of no great importance, their petition may be rejected with impunity; neither of these insinuations would be just in the present case. Such a petition as this could not be instigated by a few incendiaries operating on simple and credulous people in hedge ale-houses; it is the result of the common feelings of a numerous people; the cause is as general as the effect; it is the same voice that sounds in Yorkshire, which will soon be heard in other parts of the country. I was not a little surprized to find, that my hon. friend near me (Mr. Burke) had drawn up a plan to be proposed to this House within two days, founded on ideas so similar to those that dictated this petition. There was no communication that I know of between that gentleman and the petitioners of Yorkshire. The universality of the sentiments on this subject, is no contemptible proof of their justness. I wish that this House may consider, I repeat it, from whom this petition comes. It was first moved in a meeting of 600 gentlemen and upwards; in the hall where this petition was conceived, there was more property than within the walls of this House. [Here sir George threw down upon the table, with a good deal of vehemence, a list of the gentlemen's names.] But, he continued, they are not to abandon the petition, whatever may be its fate in this House; there is a committee appointed to correspond on the subject of the petition with the committees of other counties. [Here he in like manner threw down on the table a list of the names of the committee.] The subscribers are between 8 and 9,000, as appears from the petition itself.—A motion being made for leave that the petition might be read, it was read accordingly.

Sir George rose again to explain and enforce the prayer of the petition. The petitioners had not presumed to dictate any particular mode of enquiry or redress of the grievances complained of; how far parliament were to go, or what particular steps they ought to take, would be pointed out by a disposition to comply with the petition, if that disposition should exist. The following observation, however, fell from sir George, that something more was expected than what he had seen in the propositions to be made to the House by his hon. friend, Mr. Burke.

Lord North said, that the hon. gentleman need not have taken so much pains to convince the House that the petition ought to be received; nor to have expatiated on so obvious a truth, as that it was not to be dreaded that any man, or set of men, would dare to reject it. No man in his senses, who sat in that House, was ignorant that the right of petitioning belonged to all British subjects. He had been called upon to declare whether he would oppose or forward the object of the petition. The petition was now before the House; it had been read, and it should have his consent to lie on the table for some time, as was usual in such cases, for the perusal of the members: the House, he doubted not, would take it into their serious consideration; and after enquiring into the facts alledged, after examining the merits of the case, freely and impartially decide, according to the best of their judgment, in such a manner, as to consult the good of the petitioners, without losing sight of that of the country in general. A petition properly introduced, would always, he hoped, meet with a fair and candid attention. With respect to the threats that had been broadly hinted by the hon. gentleman, he hoped they would have no effect on the minds of the judges one way or the other. He had been threatened with unknown but severe consequences, if he should so much as delay granting the requested redress, until an enquiry should be made into the existence, nature, and extent of the alledged grievances. Truly, I must say, said his lordship, that the petition suffers not a little by a prohibition from all enquiry into the facts on which it is founded. [Here sir George Savile rose to explain what he had said. He was not against an enquiry, but against the semblance of an enquiry, a mock enquiry. He had taken the liberty to ask the noble lord, whether he would make an enquiry, *bona fide,* for the purpose of answering or frustrating the end of the petition.] To my ear, continued lord North, what fell from the hon. gentleman had the appearance of a caveat against any kind of enquiry. He insinuates that the enquiry will be undertaken with sinister and partial views. How far this is fair and candid, nay how far such suppositions, in a case of this kind, are parliamentary, I submit to the judgment of the House. The hon. gentleman has said, that the ideas and sentiments that gave birth to the petition, are very universal; as a proof of this he observes, and he is surprized to observe, so wonderful a similarity between the ideas of gentlemen in Yorkshire on the subject of the petition, and those of an hon. gentleman, who is soon to make a motion on that subject in this House. With regard to that matter, he would only say, that what seemed so surprizing to the hon. gentleman, did not surprize him in the least. He concluded by telling the House, that they must not consider his proceeding in raising the necessary supplies as any disrespect to the petition. The petition was neither formally nor virtually negatived, although the consideration of it was not preferred to all other business. The supplies had been voted, and it would be necessary, without much longer delay, to enter on the subject of ways and means.

Mr. Fox said, that he did not intend to speak at this time on the subject of the petition before the House; but he could not refrain from making some observations on the positions that had now been made by the noble lord. The consideration of the petition, says he, may very fitly be postponed till after that of the ways and means for raising the supplies. Compare this language with the generous and magnanimous admiration of ministry, when they applauded and admired the conduct of the associations in Ireland, who refused to grant supplies for more than one half year, before their grievances should be redressed, before the prayer of their petition for a free trade should be granted. Is there one law for the associations in Ireland, and another for those of England? No. The noble lord is a man of accuracy and consistency. He must therefore mean, whatever he may have said in the heat and hurry of debate, that the associations in England, in imitation of those in Ireland, ought to grant no supplies, to pay no taxes, until their petition find a proper respect; until its prayer be fully granted. I am at a loss to conjecture the threats that the noble lord says have been hinted by the hon. gentleman, meaning thereby to fix a stigma on this and other petitions. The people are not in arms, they do not menace civil war. They have in their power, legal, constitutional, peaceable means of enforcing their petition. It is to these means the hon. gentleman alludes, when the noble lord supposes that he throws out threats of another kind. No, Sir, let not the mild but firm voice of liberty be mistaken for the dismal and discordant accents of blood and slaughter. The evil the hon. gentleman presages, if this or other petitions are spurned with contempt and insolence, is of another, though not of a less formidable nature. The people will lose all confidence in their representatives, all reverence for parliament. The consequences of such a situation I need not point out: let not the contemplation of necessary effects be considered as a denunciation of vengeance. I wish most anxiously that gentlemen would consider what they are when they sit in this House. Insignificant of themselves, they derive their importance from the appointment of their constituents. It is the duty of members of parliament to conform to the sentiments, and in some degree, even to the prejudice of the people. In their legislative capacity, the wishes and wants of the people, ought in this land of liberty to be their grand rule of conduct. I say in their legislative capacity; for I make a distinction between that and their judicial capacity; in which last they must give judgment according to the letter of the law, and in this, too, they consult the interests of liberty. Suppose the people should be of opinion that there is no longer any need of a very expensive Board of Trade and Plantations, when that trade and those plantations, for the sake of which the Board was first established, no longer exist, would it not become the noble lord's duty, to sacrifice his particular opinion to theirs, and to act agreeably to their notions and instructions? The noble lord has been very severe upon the hon. gentleman, upon the supposition that he had entered his caveat against even taking time to enquire into the allegations contained in the petition. The hon. gentleman has himself sufficiently repelled the attacks of his noble opponent, by reminding him that what he apprehended was not a real but a mock enquiry. But one thing, said Mr. Fox, I cannot but remark. The ideas of an enquiry, and an intention to defeat its object, seem so intimately connected in the noble lord's mind, that it is not in his power to disjoin them: so closely associated, that he cannot think on the one, without confounding it with the other. I cannot imagine, continued this ingenious and animated speaker, that any objection can possibly be made to the petition. But some may say, "Are we sinners above all that went before us? like those on whom the tower of Siloam fell? Are we more corrupt than other parliaments who were never pestered with petitions of this kind?" No, I do not suppose you are; but though former parliaments were as bad as you, and you know the severity of that comparison, yet the people did not know it. Now they do not perhaps see it, but they feel it; they feel the pressure of taxes; they beg you would not lay your hand so heavily on them, but be as economical as possible. We on this side of the House recommend and enforce their applications. Let ministry hearken to the petitions of the people, even though they are recommended to their favourable regard by members in opposition. Let them grant their requests, and the whole glory of so popular a compliance will be theirs. Their praises were sounded in loud strains for granting to the people of Ireland, what that people made good for themselves by their own muskets. I will put the controversy between the ministry and gentlemen on this side of the House, on the same issue on which the wisest of men, Solomon, rested the determination of the dispute between the two women, each of whom claimed the living child, and disavowed the dead one. We say to ministry, You misapply the public money; nay, you do worse, you apply it to bad purposes: ministry say to us, You want our places; and thus the charge of corruption is given and retorted. Come now, let us see whose child corruption is; opposition are willing, are desirous, that it should be sacrificed; ministry have often made similar professions; the time is come to prove the sincerity of both; see who will now acknowledge; see who will father this dear but denied child, corruption! On the whole, economy will strengthen the hands of government, relieve the people from hardships, be a source of fame and triumph to ministry over their adversaries; for who will dare to say, or who will not be abhorred for saying any thing to the prejudice of so honest and upright an administration, as those men who shall redress in so satisfactory a manner the grievances of an oppressed people? The people of England only pray to be on a footing with the subjects of France, whose government voluntarily rescinded unnecessary places, thus opening a source of strength in a tender and in a wise plan of economy.

Mr. Turner said, he held in his hand a petition from the city of York, signed by 990 burgesses, almost the whole of his constituents, of a similar nature to that which had been just presented in the name of the county. The importance of the petition had already been explained, and the necessity of complying with the prayer very ably inculcated; he would only assure the House, that the petition originated with the people themselves; no influence had been used, on his part, to instigate it; he considered it as the duty of members, not to lead, but to follow the sentiments of their constituents. Several of the gentlemen who had opposed the petition were his most dear and intimate friends; they knew that he never solicited their voices in behalf of the petition; he neither would dictate to his voters in any public measure, nor submit to the meanness of asking them to chuse him member to represent them in parliament. Rather than stoop to such a conduct, he would be content to go about the city carrying stones on his back. This much, however, he told all his voters, that if they wished to support the present ministry, not to elect him their representative. The petition, he declared on his honour, had never been promoted by him. It is the genuine voice of my constituents, said he; their numbers, their property, their unanimity, I hope, will give it some weight. Let it be remembered, that the petitions now presented to parliament, are not ordinary petitions; for you may hear of them again, if you should not think proper to forward their object.

Lord George Gordon begged to remind the House, that a reformation should begin with religion. Associations were forming against the toleration of Papists in every part of the British empire; Ireland, Scotland, and England, were alike averse to the measure; the most dreadful consequences were to be apprehended, if the ministry obstinately persisted in it. He reminded the House, that the most bigotted tyrants had sunk beneath the weight of a Protestant army. He paid the highest compliments to his worthy friends (sir G. Savile and Mr. Burke); said he was convinced that they had supported the Bill from the purest motives; and his lordship expressed his sincere concern, that policy, in any one instance, should render the most unlimited toleration dangerous to a free state; but where the happiness of the people was concerned, the interest of individuals should always give way.

The Petition was ordered to lie on the table.

Address of the Society for Constitutional Information, 14 January 1785

A Third Address from the Society for Constitutional Information to the People of Great Britain and Ireland (London, 1785), 8-page pamphlet.

This association was founded by Major John Cartwright in April 1780 to agitate for parliamentary reform. It issued many tracts and broadsides on the subject.

A period of five years is now nearly elapsed, since this society first took upon itself the task of distributing constitutional information among the people of these kingdoms.—It must be confessed, that the time, when we commenced our labours in the public service, was peculiarly favourable to our undertaking. The nation had then just begun to feel the complicated disgraces and miseries of a war, waged against all the dearest interest of justice and humanity. The splendid successes of our former contests with the house of Bourbon, fresh in the memory of the people, served only to embitter the series of inauspicious events, which attended our war with America. And, though at the commencement of those unfortunate disputes, the people, dazzled with the lustre of former victories, intoxicated with prosperity, and impatient of controul, scorned the dictates of reason or of justice, the humiliating circumstances which had since taken place, had not a little contributed to dispose them to listen somewhat more willingly to the voice of admonition. Accumulated taxes, the certain consequences of a long and expensive war, had naturally put the nation upon considering, whether the war, in which they were then engaged, were just and necessary, or the result of misguided ambition.

Different, however, as were the opinions on this subject, and various as were the arguments by which they were respectively defended, yet the honest advocates on every side of the question, agreed in one point; that is to say, in the necessity of a speedy and substantial reform in the expenditure of the public money—wisely considering, that that measure was equally necessary, either to carry on a burthensome war with effect, to restore our finances already almost irremediably disordered, or to diminish the exorbitant influence of the crown.

The opposition, which an economical reform experienced from a venal ministry, even after the people universally groaned under the intolerable burthens of the war, and after the influence of the crown had been complained of by parliament itself, excited a general spirit of discontent and enquiry. The most probable means of carrying this popular measure against the united efforts of interest and power, and of preserving the nation from again experiencing similar calamities, were questions which engrossed the attention of the people at large, and increased the thirst for political knowledge. The most obvious and most radical preservative, which then presented itself, was a Reformation of Parliament. This opened a most extensive, though not a new field, as well of speculative as of practical discussion. In these useful political speculations, the industry of many publicspirited writers was employed with so much assiduity and success, and every species of constitutional information was caught by the public with such eagerness and avidity, that perhaps the grounds of just government, and the principles of the English constitution are now better understood by *the nation*, than at any former period.

The unremitting zeal, manifested by this society on all those important questions, cannot be forgotten by the public. It cannot be forgotten, how loudly we lifted up our voice against the baneful American war; how earnestly we urged a reform, as well economical as parliamentary. And we rejoice to find that our labours have not been in vain. We please ourselves in the reflection, that we have been in some degree instrumental in kindling that flame, which hath extended its influence to the remotest corners of our island. The sacred fire of liberty hath even burst the barriers of the ocean, and spread far and wide over our sister kingdom. Nor shall its force abate, until our purified constitution shall emerge from the flame, with all its ancient vigor and renovated lustre.

But, while we indulge these pleasing hopes, what is our concern to see the prospect clouded by repeated attacks upon the most valuable parts of our constitution, the Trial by Jury, and the Liberty of the Press! we should be wanting to our fellow citizens, we should be wanting to ourselves, and to the engagements, which, by associating, we entered into with the public, were we to suffer such events to pass without animadversion, without exposing their dangerous tendency, and pointing out their only remedy.

In Ireland we have beheld a daring infringement on both these inestimable privileges, by an act passed in the last session of the parliament of that kingdom, which has in certain cases drawn the cognizance of the crime of publishing of a libel from the ancient constitutional tribunal of a jury, to the summary jurisdiction of justices appointed by the crown. Let not our brethren in Ireland console themselves with the lenity of the punishment inflicted by that statute. Every invasion of the rights of mankind hath appeared at first in its least odious form, and time only hath discovered all its natural deformity. Let them be assured, that this apparent lenity is but a lure to reconcile them to the principle of the bill. Let them permit this parliament to chastise them with whips: future parliaments will chastise them with scorpions. The same necessity, which is said to call for this dangerous innovation, will be made the pretext in future for arming it with new terrors, for increasing its penalties, and multiplying its punishments. *Obsta principiis*, as hath been well observed, is the only safe rule of practical policy.

But can we be surprized at this attempt in a remoter part of the empire, when, in the very metropolis of this kingdom, in the case of the dean of St. Asaph, the most alarming doctrines have been held forth to the public, by the majority of the judges of our court of King's Bench? We are well aware, that in no very modern times, prerogative judges, have maintained that the jury had no right to decide whether the paper in question were or were not a libel. But we are certain that this doctrine is of no high antiquity—and, on the contrary, that the most ancient, and most authoritative writers on the English law, have maintained the right of the jury to find a general verdict. We mean not, however, here to enter upon the discussion of a point of positive municipal law; we shall only say, that, if the law be as the court have in this instance declared it, there is an end of trial by jury in matters of libel: there is an end of the liberty of the press: the English constitution is no more.

You may, perchance, be told by some courtly lawyer, that the present judges have said and done no more than their predecessors have said and done before them. It is fit, however, that you should be informed, that the doctrine now held forth is infinitely more extensive, and infinitely more dangerous than all that has been laid down by the most arbitrary ministers of justice in former times. Their adjudications extended only to matters of libel. Their decisions could affect only the property, the liberty, or the reputation of the subject. We are now for the first time told, that the crimes of forgery and writing an incendiary letter are exactly in the same predicament with that of publishing a libel. We now learn, that not only the property, the liberty, and the reputation, but even the life, of the subject are at the disposal of fixed magistrates appointed by the crown.

But, as if these measures and these doctrines were not sufficient to awaken the attention of the public, it is still more strongly called upon by some recent transactions, in which, with complicated mischief, the trial by jury is abolished, the right of popular assemblies is violated, and an inquisitorial power of extorting evidence from a prisoner against himself is established. We mean the late unprecedented prosecutions by attachment in Ireland. That any man should be treated as a criminal for convening the people at their own request, to deliberate on the mode of attaining a redress of their grievances, is not a little extraordinary. That this act, if done by a sheriff, should be deemed a contempt of the court of king's bench, is still more incomprehensible. But that a person suspected of a crime should be compelled by duress of imprisonment to become his own accuser, is indeed a subject of the most serious alarm. If such a mode of proceeding be tolerated in any part of the British dominions, there is an end of all the boasted pre-eminence of our system of criminal jurisprudence. In France, the preliminary torture no longer exists. In Spain and Portugal, we hear no more of the severity of the inquisition. And in England and Ireland, where it is a settled principle of criminal law, that no man is bound to accuse himself, that a confession extorted by threats, or even by promises, is of no avail against a prisoner, shall we suffer ourselves to be compelled to answer interrogatories upon oath, framed by an incensed attorney-general, for the avowed illegal purpose of making us criminate ourselves? In our own history we read, that the rack was not unfrequently used against state prisoners, during the tyrannical reigns of the Tudors, and the first of the Stewarts. But in vain will all the judges of England have declared their abhorrence of so detestable a practice, in vain will they have exclaimed, that no such punishment was known or allowed by our law, if, by submitting to the process of attachment, we acquiesce in the principle of torture. For where is the mighty difference between extorting a confession by the rack or by imprisonment? Nay, is not the former best suited to the generous and courageous spirit of a Briton? Would he not prefer the short but dreadful trial, where he may shew the vigor of his mind unsubdued by all the violence of the rack, rather than languish out his days in the gloomy and servile horrors of a prison?

Nor suffer yourselves to be told, that the method of examining the delinquent upon oath in matters of contempt, is of "high antiquity, and by long and immemorial usage is become the law of the land" [Black. Com. IV, 288]. A bad custom ought to be abolished. High antiquity and immemorial usage can never make it to be the law of the land; but furnish an unanswerable argument for its speedy abrogation.

Nor let our countrymen of Great Britain imagine themselves uninterested in the concerns of the people of Ireland. The liberties of our sister kingdom, the remaining hope of Britain, united to us by all the ties of long connection, vicinity, similarity of language, of manners, and of laws, can never be to us an object of small importance. Every precedent of law adduced in support of this extraordinary doctrine, may be cited in our own courts with equal propriety and justice. English judges may perhaps be found (perhaps they have already existed) to support the same doctrines and the same practice. Let our countrymen reflect, that in this case the same law prevails in both kingdoms. Our liberties are inseparably connected with those of our brethren in Ireland. We must stand or fall together; or, at least, we shall not long survive them.

Such are the facts, which we submit to your consideration: and such are the motives, which compel us to declare, that Your Liberties Are in Danger: that Your Constitution Is Shaken to the Foundation: and that, unless a speedy and substantial exertion take place on the part of the people, It Will Fall to Rise No More.

To hope that parliament, as it is now constituted, would even offer to remove, one by one, the causes of our complaints, would indeed be a vain and visionary expectation. Parliament itself is in too corrupt and miserable a state to attempt to reform grievances. And, were our legislature to undertake, and even to accomplish, so laudable a purpose, we are sorry to say, it is by no means certain, that the result would be answerable to the hopes of the people. New grievances will still arise, as wounds will continually break out, where the cure is incomplete.

Let us then intreat you by your property, your liberties, your lives, by all that is dear to you as men and as citizens, for a while to suspend your attention to these lesser, though grievous, wounds to the constitution. Let us, for the present, direct our united force against those intolerable badges of slavery, the sources of all our calamities, the unconstitutional duration of parliament, and a defective representation of the people—a representation so totally mangled and absurd, as to subject us to the pity or the ridicule of all foreign nations. No more let us boast of our freedom at home, our glories abroad. Our glories are tarnished: our liberties are fled: and, if we lose the golden moment, will never more return.

In the whole course of our endeavours to obtain a reformation of parliament, never did any opportunity present itself so favourable as at present. At what former period of our exertions were the people of England so strongly supported by the voice of their brethren in Scotland and Ireland? When had we a minister bound down by so many solemn engagements to promote a parliamentary reform, and at the same time so powerfully enabled to enforce it? Who can remember an opposition more strongly disposed to second our endeavours? Nothing remains to be wished for, but a vigorous support of our friends in parliament, by numerous applications on the part of the people: and this we trust will not long be wanting.

When this grand national grievance shall be done away, when the people shall again have acquired their just weight in the scale of legislation, then, and not till then, shall we behold our rights restored, our liberties re-established, and all the detail of lesser abuses corrected and removed. Then only will our apprehensions of danger from the power of the nobles and the prerogative of the crown be wholly dispelled. Then only shall we feel, that the rights and privileges of the commons' house of parliament are *in fact* the rights and privileges of the people of Great Britain. And, if our late heavy calamities have deprived us of the hopes of ever repossessing that dazzling splendor (seldom, alas! productive of substantial good), which once encircled the British name, we may at least insure Domestic Happiness and Liberty to ourselves and our posterity.

Speech by William Pitt, the prime minister and chancellor of the exchequer, introducing a motion for parliamentary reform, House of Commons, 18 April 1785

Parliamentary History, XXV, 432-50.

Pitt's plan for an extension of the parliamentary suffrage and a redistribution of seats was defeated by 84 votes.

Mr. Chancellor Pitt rose to call the attention of the House to the important subject of a Reform in the Representation of the People. He said it was unnecessary for him to point out how much this subject ought to engage the attention of gentlemen, and how nearly it was connected with every other interest which could be important to Englishmen. In entering upon this subject, he said, he was aware of the division of sentiment, and of the pertinacity with which some men adhered to opinions inimical to every species of reform. But he rose with hopes infinitely more sanguine than he ever felt before, and with hopes which he conceived to be rationally and solidly founded. There never was a moment when the minds of men were more enlightened on this interesting topic than now; there never was a moment when they were more prepared for its discussion. A great many objections which from time to time had been adduced against reform, would not lie against the propositions which he intended to submit to the House; and the question was in truth new in all its shape to the present parliament.

He was sensible of the difficulty there was now, and ever must be, in proposing a plan of reform. The number of gentlemen who were hostile to reform, were a phalanx, which ought to give alarm to any individual upon rising to suggest such a measure. Those who, with a sort of superstitious awe, reverence the constitution so much as to be fearful of touching even its defects, had always reprobated every attempt to purify the representation. They acknowledged its inequality and corruption, but in their enthusiasm for the grand fabric, they would not suffer a reformer, with unhallowed hands, to repair the injuries which it suffered from time. Others, who, perceiving the deficiencies that had arisen from circumstances, were solicitous of their amendment, yet resisted the attempt, under the argument, that when once we had presumed to touch the constitution in one point, the awe which had heretofore kept us back from the daring enterprize of innovation might abate, and there was no foreseeing to what alarming lengths we might progressively go, under the mask of reformation. Others there were, but for these he confessed he had not the same respect, who considered the present state of representation as pure and adequate to all its purposes, and perfectly consistent with the first principles of representation. The fabric of the House of Commons was an ancient pile, on which they had been all taught to look with reverence and awe: from their cradles they had been accustomed to view it as a pattern of perfection; their ancestors had enjoyed freedom and prosperity under it; and therefore an attempt to make any alterations in it would be deemed, by some enthusiastic admirers of antiquity, as impious and sacrilegious. No one reverenced the venerable fabric more than he did; but all mankind knew that the best institutions, like human bodies, carried in themselves the seeds of decay and corruption, and therefore he thought himself justifiable in proposing remedies against this corruption, which the frame of the constitution must necessarily experience in the lapse of years, if not prevented by wise and judicious regulations.

To men who argued in this manner, he did not presume to address his propositions, for such men he despaired of convincing; but he had well-grounded hopes, that in what he should offer to the House, he should be able to convince gentlemen of the former descriptions, that though they had argued so strongly against general and unexplained notions of reform, their arguments would not weigh against the precise and explicit proposition which it was his purpose to submit to them. The objection to reform, under the idea of innovation, would not hold good against his suggestion, for it was not an innovation on any known and clear principle of the constitution. Their objection to reform, because it might introduce habits of change and alteration, of which no man could foresee the extent or termination, would be equally inapplicable to his plan, for in his mind it would be complete and final. In his mind, it would comprehend all that a rational reformer would think it necessary now or at any time to do, and would therefore give no licence to future or more extensive schemes. The argument, that no alteration of the number of members composing the House ought at any time to be suffered, and that no reform of the representation in what was emphatically called the corrupt parts, ought to be accomplished by an act of power, would be equally inapplicable; for, by his proposition, he meant to lay it down as a first principle, that the number of the House ought to remain the same, and that the reform of decayed boroughs ought not to proceed on disfranchisement. This, he said, was the third effort made by him since he had the honour of a seat in parliament, to prevail upon the legislature to adopt a reform in the representation of the people. He had twice failed in his endeavours to effect this salutary purpose, and yet he was not discouraged from renewing them this day: he was encouraged by two circumstances which he had not in his favour on the former occasions. The reform which he now meant to propose, was more consistent with the views of the best and most moderate men; and this was a new House of Commons, that had never been consulted on the subject of reform, and consequently had not, like the two last, negatived a proposition made for introducing it. Therefore, though the subject might be thought stale by the public, as it had been so frequently agitated, it was perfectly new to the House of Commons which he had then the honour to address.

That gentlemen should have set themselves against general and unqualified notions of reform, he did not much wonder; and that they should be still more inimical to the vague, impracticable, and inconclusive chimeras which had been thrown out at different times by different reformers, he was not astonished. Reverencing the constitution, and feeling all the pride of an Englishman on the experience of its beauty, even with all its blemishes, it was no wonder that gentlemen should be alarmed at suggestions which were founded on no principle, and which admitted of no limit. But there were certain propositions, in which he had reason to think that all men must coincide. If there were any specific means of purifying the state of representation on its first principle, without danger of altering the fabric, and without leaving it either in uncertainty or disorder, such means ought, with becoming caution, to be used. On this clear and indisputable proposition it was that he wished to go. It was because he imagined that a plan might be formed, congenial with the first principles of representation, which would reform the present inadequate state, and provide in all future times for as adequate and perfect a state of representation as they could expect to arrive at, in the present circumstances of the country. He was aware, when he spoke in this manner, that the idea of general and complete representation so as to comprehend every individual, and give him his personal share in the legislature of the country, was a thing incompatible with the population and state of the kingdom. The practical definition of what the popular branch of our legislature was at this day, he took to be precisely this: An assembly freely elected, between whom and the mass of the people there was the closest union and most perfect sympathy. Such a House of Commons it was the purpose of the constitution originally to erect, and such a House of Commons it was the wish of every reformer now to establish. Those who went farther—those who went to ideas of individual representation, deluded themselves with impossibilities, and took the attention of the public from that sober and practicable path in which they might travel safely and with ease, to launch them into an unbounded sea, where they had no pilot to direct, and no star to guide them.

Solicitous as he was of reform, he never could countenance vague and unlimited notions. It was his wish to see the House adopt a sober and practicable scheme, which should have for its basis the original principle of representation, and should produce the object which every lover of our constitution must have in view—a House of Commons between whom and the people there should exist the same interest, and the most perfect sympathy and union. It was his purpose to see an arrangement made, which, while it corrected the present inadequate state of representation, should keep it adequate when made so, and should give to the constitution purity, consistency, and, if possible, immortality. Such was the sanguine idea which he entertained from his project, and such he trusted would be the sentiment of the House upon its exposition. Whatever argument might be adduced against its practicability, and what against its expediency, he trusted that the old argument of innovation would not be alleged. As he had said, it was not an innovation; and he was sure that gentlemen would agree with him in this sentiment, when they turned their eyes with him back to the earliest periods of our history, and traced the practice of our ancestors in the purest days.

He considered it, on such a review, as one of the most indisputable doctrines of antiquity, that the state of representation was to be changed with the change of circumstances. As far back as the period of the reign of Edward I. which was the first time when they could trace distinct descriptions of men in the representation, the doctrine of change was clearly understood. The counties were not uniform; the number of members was frequently varied; and from that period to the reign of Charles II. there were few reigns in which representation was not varied, and in which it did not undergo diminutions or fluctuations of some kind or other. Those changes were owing to the discretion which was left in the executive branches of the legislature, to summon or not to summon whom they pleased to parliament. The executive branch of the legislature was vested with this discretion on no other principle, than that the places, which might for the time being have such a share in the general scale of the people, as should entitle them, or rather subject them, to the duty of sending members to the representative body, might be appointed to do so. In this very discretionary power the principle of alteration was visible, and it manifested the original notion which our forefathers had of representation to be this:—That whereas it was impossible that every individual of a populous country could make choice of a representative, the task should be committed to such bodies of men as might be collected together in communities in the several districts of the kingdom: and as such communities must from their nature be fluctuating and moveable, that the Crown should have the discretion of pointing out which of them were proper from their size and scale, to execute this duty for the rest. Every man must acknowledge that to have exercised this discretion otherwise than soundly, must have been a high grievance; and he needed not to say, that if it were now vested in the Crown, and that ministers might fix on such places as they pleased for the choice of members, there was not a man in England who would not consider the liberties of his country as extinguished. Such discretion, however, did exist; and he mentioned it to shew, that principles in representation had been departed from, and had their existence no longer. The argument against change was an argument against the experience of every period of our history. There had not been of late any addition to the county share in the representation, except indeed of the palatines, of the principality of Wales, and of another addition which had been made since the period at which it was common to say that our constitution was fixed, the Revolution, namely, the addition of all that part of the united kingdom called Scotland.

But in the borough representation the changes had been infinitely more common. Gentlemen had undoubtedly read, that, of the boroughs which used formerly to send members to parliament, seventy-two had been disfranchised, that was to say, that the Crown had ceased to summon them at general elections to return burgesses to the House of Commons. After the restoration, thirty-six of these boroughs petitioned parliament to be restored to the exercise of their ancient franchise; their prayer was granted, and to this day they continue to enjoy it. But the other thirty-six, not having presented any petition on the subject, had not recovered their lost franchise. Upon this he would be bold to say, that, considering the restoration of the former, and the continued deprivation of the latter, the spirit of the constitution had been grossly violated, if it was true, (but which he denied) that the extension to one set of boroughs of the franchise of returning members to parliament, and the resumption of it from others, was a violation of the constitution. For if the numbers could not originally have been constitutionally increased, so they could not constitutionally have been diminished. But having been once diminished, to restore them might by some be said to make an innovation; and if the parliament had any authority to restore the franchise, the principle of restoration ought to have been extended to the seventy-two boroughs, and not confined to one half of them. Here then it appeared manifest, that the whole was governed by a principle which militated directly against the modern doctrine, that to do what had been constantly done for ages, by the wisest of our ancestors, was to innovate upon the constitution. The seventy-two boroughs in question had discontinued to return members, because they had fallen into decay. Thirty-six of them afterwards recovered their franchise, when they recovered their former wealth and population; but the other thirty-six, not having renovated their former vigour and consequence in the state, remained to this day deprived of the franchise which had been taken from them, when they lost the wealth and population, on account of which they had originally obtained it.

Why then was there a greater objection to any change in the representation of certain boroughs now, than there had been in former periods? Why were they more sacred now than the thirty-six boroughs which had been disfranchised, and which had no share at present in the representation of the country? The arguments that influenced gentlemen against any change at this time, would have equally operated against the thirty-six boroughs which had from time to time been extinguished, as well as against the same number, which, having been abolished, were, from a change of their circumstances, re-instated in their privilege. In those earlier periods, such was the notion of representation, that as one borough decayed, and another arose, the one was abolished, and the other invested with the right; and alterations took place from accident or caprice, which, however, so far as they went, stood good and valid. The alterations were not made by principle; they did not arise from any fixed rule laid down and invariably pursued, but they were founded in that notion which gave the discretionary power to the Crown, viz. that the principle places, and not the decayed boroughs, should be called upon to exercise the right of election.

He contended, therefore, that the same notion should now prevail, but that it should be rescued from that accident and caprice in which it had before been involved; that the alteration should be made on principle; and that they should establish this as a clear and external axiom in representation—that it should always be the same—that it should not depend upon locality or name, but upon number and condition, and that a standard should be fixed for its size. He would submit to the world which of the two was most anxious for the preservation of the original principle of the constitution, he who was for maintaining the exterior, and name of representation, when the substance was gone, or he who, preferring the substance and reality of representation to the name and exterior, was solicitous of changing its seat from one part of the country to another, as one place might flourish and another decay? It was his idea, that if they could deduce any good principles from theory, and apply them to practice, it was their duty to do so. It was then the theory, and it had been the practice, in all times, to adapt the representation to the state of the country; and this was exactly what it was his intention to recommend to the House. Now and in all future time to adapt the representation to the state of the country, was the idea of reform which he entertained.

Perhaps gentlemen would be apt to exclaim that this contradicted the declaration with which he set out, viz. that the plan which he meant to propose would be final and complete. When they came, however, to hear the whole of his idea, he trusted they would find that his proposition had in view not only an immediate reform, but that it comprehended an arrangement which must operate in all future time, and provide for the changes which in the nature of things must incessantly arise in a country like Britain. He wished to establish a permanent rule to operate like the discretion, out of which our present constitution had sprung. That discretion would be very improper to exist now, though in ruder times it was not so dangerous, when representation was rather a burthen than a privilege, rather a duty than an object of ambition. For that discretion he was no advocate; but he wished to remind gentlemen, that that discretionary power had never been wrested from the hands of the executive branch of the legislature, and that to this day there existed but the Act of Union to prevent the Crown from adding to or diminishing the number of that House. By the Act of Union, the proportionate numbers for the two parts of the kingdom were fixed, and from the date of that Act, but not till that Act, the discretion of the Crown was at an end.

The argument of withstanding all reformation, from the fear of the ill consequences that might ensue, made gentlemen come to a sort of compromise with themselves. "We are sensible of certain defects; we feel certain inconveniencies in the present state of representation; but fearing that we may make it worse by alteration, we will be content with it as it is." This was a sort of argument to which he could not give his countenance. If gentlemen had at all times been content with this doctrine, the nation would have lost much of that excellence of which our constitution now had to boast. Who would say but that the excellence of the constitution was the fruit of constant improvement? To prove this fact required but little illustration. It was, for instance, a first principle in our constitution, that parliament should meet as frequently as the exigencies of the state should require. This was a clear principle, but the periods were not fixed. Practice, however, had improved on this principle, and now it was established that parliament should annually meet.

Something like that which he meant now to recommend, did take place in very early periods of our history. It was remarkable that James I, a prince who mounted the throne with high ideas of prerogative, and who was not to be suspected of being too partial to the liberties of the subject, stated, in his first proclamation for calling a parliament, that the sheriffs of the counties should not direct such boroughs to send members, as were so utterly ruined as to be incapable or unentitled to contribute their share to the representation of the country. At another period of our history, which, whatever objection he might have to its general principles, had given rise to many salutary laws; he meant in the days of Cromwell; it was declared by the Protector that there should be a greater proportion of knights than of burgesses in the House of Commons. He mentioned this authority (for which he had, in the general, no great reverence, seeing that his opposition to Charles I, began in licentiousness, and proceeded, as licentiousness always did, to tyranny,) because it would shew, that whatever was his respect for the constitution of the country, his opinion evidently was, that representation should be proportioned to the people represented. Lord Clarendon, in speaking of the plan of Cromwell, had said, and it was to be found in his writings, "that it was worthy of a more warrantable authority, and of better times." From these circumstances, he thought that a doubt could not be left on the mind, but that it always had been the principle of representation that it should change with the changes which the country might endure, and that it should not be merely governed by exterior and local considerations.

Feeling, therefore, that this was the clear principle of representation, he begged the House to remember, that he had told them, in the outset, that his plan was free from the objection of altering the number of the House, and also from the objection of making any change in the boroughs by disfranchisement: his plan consisted of two parts: the one was more immediate than the other, but they were both gradual. The first was calculated to procure an early, if not an immediate change of the representation of the boroughs; and the second was intended to establish a rule, by which the representation should change with the changes of the country. It was the clear and determined opinion of every speculatist, that there should be an alteration of the present proportion between the counties and boroughs, and that, in the change, a larger proportion of members should be given for the populous places, than for places that had neither property nor people.

It was therefore his intention to submit to the House to provide, that the members of a certain number of boroughs of the last description, that is, of boroughs decayed, should be distributed among the counties. He would take the criterion, by which he should judge what boroughs were decayed, from the number of houses; and this was a mode of judgment which was not liable to error, and which he conceived to be perfectly consistent with the original principle of representation. He should propose, that these members should be transferred to the counties, beginning with those that stood in the greatest need of addition. Such a reform as this was in its nature limited; for, if once the standard for the lowest county was fixed, the proportion for all must be the same, and it would be impossible to add more for any one county than for the rest. In this view of the business, he imagined, that the House would agree with him in thinking, that there were about thirty-six boroughs so decayed, as to come within the scheme of such an operation. Seventy-two would therefore be the number of members to be added to the counties, in such proportion as the wisdom of parliament might direct, and this number it was his intention to propose should be fixed and unalterable. The operation should be gradual, as he intended that the boroughs should be disfranchised on their own voluntary application to parliament. Gentlemen must be aware that a voluntary application to parliament was not to be expected without an adequate consideration being given to the boroughs; and he trusted that gentlemen would not start at the idea of such a consideration being provided for. A reform could only be brought about by two means—by an act of power, or by an adequate consideration which might induce bodies or individuals to part with rights which they considered as a species of valuable inheritance, or of personal property. To reform by violence, he, and he was sensible many others, had an insurmountable objection; but he considered a reform in the representation of the people an object of such value and importance, that he did not hesitate in his own mind to propose and to recommend to the House the establishment of a fund for the purpose of purchasing the franchise of such boroughs as might be induced to accept of it under the circumstances which he had mentioned.

It might be asked what the consideration could be for such a franchise. He knew there was a sort of squeamish and maiden coyness about the House in talking on this subject; they were not very ready to talk in that House, on what, at the same time it was pretty well understood, out of doors they had no great objection to negociate, the purchase and the sale of seats. But he would fairly ask gentlemen, if these sort of franchises were not capable of being appreciated? and whether, notwithstanding all the proud boast of its being an insult to an Englishman to ask him to sell his invaluable franchise, there were not abundance of places where, without imputing immortality to any individual, such franchise might be purchased? Could it not be proved, that in this country estates so situated as to command an influence in a decayed or depopulated borough, and to have the power of returning two members to parliament, sold for more money than they would have done if situated in any other place, however luxuriant the soil might be, however productive its harvests? Unless, indeed, its harvests could occasionally produce a couple of members, its intrinsic value was less. There were many reasons why men might be induced to surrender this franchise. In some instances, where the right of returning members was attached to the possession of an estate, and where it might be considered as an inheritance, giving to the possessor the power of doing so much good to his country, he might warrantably and honourably accept of a valuable consideration, since by the use of the equivalent, he might be equally serviceable to the community. In some instances, persons enjoyed the franchise in consequence of a life-right; and enjoying it only for the lives, interest would naturally induce them to accept of a consideration: others enjoyed it by a still more temporary tenure, merely by the circumstance of local residence; and to them, therefore, it must be an opportunity which they would covet to embrace. Seeing the matter, therefore, in these points of view, he had no doubt in his own mind, but that the boroughs to which he alluded would voluntarily surrender their franchise to parliament, on such consideration being given. He should propose that the fund to be established should be divided into two parts, and that it should be stipulated that a larger sum should be given for perpetuities than for temporary rights. He had stated before, that this operation would not be immediate, at least to the full extent; for he had reason to believe that it would neither be slow nor distant.

The second part of his plan was to provide, that, after the full and final operation of the first proposition, that is, after the extinction of 36 boroughs, and the transfer of their members to the county representation, if there still should remain any borough so small and so decayed as to fall within the size to be fixed on by parliament, such borough should have in its power to surrender its franchise on an adequate consideration, and that the right of sending the members to parliament should be transferred to such populous and flourishing towns as might desire to enjoy the right; and that this rule should remain good, and operate in all future time, and be applied to such boroughs as, in the fluctuating state of a manufacturing and commercial kingdom, might fall into decay in one part of the country, and rise into condition in another. These propositions, taken together, comprehended what he conceived to be a final and complete system, and which would ease the minds of gentlemen with respect to any future scheme of reform being attempted, or being necessary. This was not a plan of reform either fluctuating or changeable. It was not subject to the argument, that the stirring of this question would lead to endless innovations, and that when once involved in change, there was no foreseeing where we might stop: nor was it subject to the objection that it was an innovation; for he had very much failed in making his own ideas intelligible to the House, if he had not shewn them that it was a plan in every respect congenial, not only with the first principle, but with the uniform practice of the constitution. These arguments, therefore, he trusted, would not be brought against his plan. The argument whether his propositions were practicable, whether they were susceptible of an easy and early execution, he should be happy to hear and to discuss. But all the arguments that had from time to time been brought against general and unexplained notions, as they were not applicable, he trusted they would not be adduced.

He anticipated several objections, which, when the propositions came to be discussed in the detail, he should be happy to meet and to combat. The first, he supposed, would be the argument of the expense. Certainly it would always be wise and proper for that House to guard against wild and chimerical schemes and speculations, which might involve their constituents in additional burthens; but he did not believe that, in a matter so dear and important to Englishmen, they would be intimidated from embracing it by the circumstance of the cost. He conceived it to be above price: it was a thing which the people of England could not purchase too highly. Let gentlemen set the question in its proper point of view; let them oppose to the expense, however great, the probable, and indeed the almost certain, advantages to accrue from it, and then they would see how little the argument of economy ought to weigh against the purification of the popular branch of the legislature. If there always had been a House of Commons who were the faithful stewards of the interests of their country, the diligent checks on the administration of the finances, the constitutional advisers of the executive branch of the legislature, the steady and uninfluenced friends of the people, he asked, if the burthens which the constituents of that House were now doomed to endure, would have been incurred? Would the people of England have suffered the calamities to which they had lately been made subject? And feeling this great and melancholy truth, would they consider the divestment of any sum as an object, when by doing so, such a House of Commons might be ascertained? He did not, therefore, think that the argument of the expense would be much insisted on, nor indeed would the expense be so great as, on the first blush of the matter, gentlemen might be apt to imagine.

Another objection that he foresaw was, that the operation would be but gradual, and its full and final accomplishment at least be distant. This, however, was not an objection that could have much weight. He did not believe that the operation would either be so slow or very distant: he had stated to the House several reasons, to shew that the different descriptions of men would have an interest in accepting the conditions to be offered by parliament; and in the fluctuating state of property, and in the almost constant necessities of men, he argued, that the offer of the consideration would from time to time be irresistible. He was sanguine, perhaps, in saying, that, before next parliament, the benefit of this plan might be felt, and in the mean time, this objection of the plan being gradual, would be less regarded, from the confidence which the people of England had in their present representatives. They would wait with patience for the operation of this arrangement, from the confidence which they had in the truth and character of the present parliament. It was elected under circumstances which made it dear to Englishmen; it had not yet forfeited the confidence of the country; and he was warranted in presuming that, with such a House of Commons, the constituent body would not be eager for the immediate accomplishment of this reform.

He said, that in the proposed change of representation, and in adding seventy-two members to the counties, he forgot in the proper place to mention, that it was his wish to add to the number of the electors in those counties. There was no good reason why copyholders should not be admitted to the exercise of the franchise as well as freeholders. Their property was as secure, and, indeed, in some instances, more so than that of the freeholders; and such an accession to the body of electors would give an additional energy to representation. He conceived that the addition of seventy-two members would be as much as it would be proper to give to the proportion between county and borough. These seventy-two members would be divided between the counties and the metropolis, as nothing could be more evident than that the cities of London and Westminster, as well as the counties, had a very inadequate share in the representation of the kingdom. To give to the counties and the metropolis a greater addition than seventy-two members, or thereabouts, would be the means of introducing disorders into the election more injurious than even its present inadequacy.

He needed not, he believed, enumerate the arguments that presented themselves to his mind in favour of a reform. Every gentleman, who had taken pains to investigate the subject, must see that it was most materially wanted. To conquer the corruption that existed in those decayed boroughs, would be acknowledged an impossible attempt. The temptations were too great for poverty to resist, and the consequence of this corruption was so visible, that some plan of reforming the boroughs had clearly become absolutely necessary. In times of calamity and distress, how truly important was it to the people of this country that the House of Commons should sympathise with themselves, and that their interests should be indissoluble? It was most material that the people should have confidence in their own branch of the legislature; the force of the constitution, as well as its beauty, depended on that confidence, and on the union and sympathy which existed between the constituent and representative. The source of our glory and the muscles of our strength were the pure character of freedom, which our constitution bore. To lessen that character, to taint it, was to take from our vitals a part of their vigour, and to lessen not only our importance, but our energy with our neighbours.

If we looked back to our history, we should find that the brightest periods of its glory and triumph were those in which the House of Commons had the most complete confidence in their ministers, and the people of England the most complete confidence in the House of Commons. The purity of representation was the only true and permanent source of such confidence: for though occasionally bright characters had arisen, who, in spite of the general corruption and depravity of the day in which they lived, had manifested the superior influence of integrity and virtue, and had forced both parliament and people to countenance their administration; yet it would be unwise for the people of England to leave their fate to the chance of such characters often arising, when prudence must dictate that the certain way of securing their properties and freedom was to purify the sources of representation, and to establish that strict relation between themselves and the House of Commons, which was the original idea of the constitution to create. He hoped that the plan which he had mentioned was likely to re-establish such a relation; and he recommended to gentlemen not to suffer their minds to be alarmed by unnecessary fears. Nothing was so hurtful to improvement as the fear of being carried farther than the principle on which a person set out.

It was common for gentlemen to reason with themselves, and to say that they would have no objection to go so far, and no farther, if they were sure that, in countenancing the first step, they might not either be led themselves, or lead others farther than they intended to go. So much they were apt to say was right—so far they would go—of such a scheme they approved—but fearing that it might be carried too far, they desisted from doing even what they conceived to be proper. He deprecated this conduct, and hoped that gentlemen would come to the consideration of this business, without fearing that it would lead to consequences that would either ruin or alarm us. He begged pardon for having troubled the House so long—he wished to put them in possession of all his ideas on the important subject, though he was aware, that until the matter came to be argued in the detail, it was impossible for him to foresee all the objections that might be started. He should therefore conclude with moving, "That leave be given to bring in a Bill to amend the Representation of the People of England in Parliament."

Declaration and address of the Society of the Friends of the People, 26 April 1792

Resolutions of the Society of the Friends of the People Associated for the Purpose of Obtaining Parliamentary Reform (London, 1792), 7-14.

This society was formed in April 1792 by Charles Grey (1764-1845; later second earl, 1807; and prime minister, 1830-34), Charles James Fox, and other aristocratic supporters of reform. Its objectives were an extension of the franchise and more frequent parliamentary elections.

DECLARATION

A number of persons having seriously reviewed and considered the actual situation of public affairs, and state of the Kingdom, and having communicated to each other their opinions on these subjects, have agreed and determined to institute a society, for the purpose of proposing to parliament, and to the country, and of promoting, to the utmost of their power, the following constitutional objects, making the preservation of the constitution, on its true principles, the foundation of all their proceedings.

First,—To restore the freedom of election, and a more equal representation of the people in parliament.

Secondly,—To secure to the people a more frequent exercise of their right of electing their representatives.

The persons who have signed their names to this agreement, think that these two fundamental measures will furnish the power and the means of correcting the abuses, which appear to them to have arisen from a neglect of the acknowledged principles of the constitution, and of accomplishing those subordinate objects of reform, which they deem to be essential to the liberties of the people, and to the good government of the kingdom.

[100 signatures]

ADDRESS TO THE PEOPLE OF GREAT BRITAIN

No man, who is not ready to express his concurrence in our principles, by signing the declaration, can be admitted into our Society. The objects of it, as we conceive, are of a nature at all times fit to be pursued and recommended to the country. At different periods they have heretofore been avowed and supported by the highest authorities in this kingdom; by eminent individuals, and considerable bodies of men; by Mr. Locke and Judge Blackstone; by the late Earl of Chatham, and Sir George Savil; by the Duke of Richmond, the Marquis of Lansdowne, Mr. Pitt, and Mr. Fox; by petitions from several counties, and by repeated declarations from the city of London. In appealing to the avowed opinions of men of established reputation, or of distinguished rank in their country, we do not mean to strengthen the reason, or inforce the necessity of the measure we propose, so much as to obviate all personal imputations, which the enemies of the cause will be ready to throw upon those who support it. It is not that, on our own account, we dread the effect or regard the impression, which such imputations may produce. But we think it material to the credit and success of our proceedings to shew, that we are not aiming at Reforms unthought of by wise and virtuous men: that our opinions neither possess the advantage, nor are liable to the objection of novelty; and that we cannot be accused or suspected of factious motives, or dangerous designs, without extending the same accusation or suspicion to men, whose situation and property, independent of their character and principles, have given them an important stake in the peace and good government of the kingdom. Convinced by our own reflections, by experience, and by authority, that the thing we propose to do, is fit to be done, we have, with equal deliberation, weighed the reasons that may recommend, or be objected to the present time, as the most or least proper for bringing it forward. On this point, we have no address to make to the determined enemies of a Reform of every kind; their objection, whether valid or not, is to the substance of the measure, and cannot be abated by circumstances. To those, who concur generally in the principle, but who may be inclined by particular reasons to defer the attempt, we seriously wish to submit the following considerations:—That if this be, as we believe it is, a season of general tranquillity in the country, it is, on that account, the more proper for temperate reflection, and prudent exertions to accomplish any necessary improvement, and when practical measures for that purpose are most likely to be adopted with discretion and pursued with moderation. If we are persuaded to wait for other times, of a different complexion, for times of public complaint, or general discontent, we shall then be told, that general remedies are not fit to be proposed in the moment of particular disorder, and that it is our duty to wait for the return of quiet times, unless we mean to create or increase confusion in the country. The result of this dilemma, if it be suffered to prevail, is pure and absolute inactivity at present, and for ever. On the other hand, if it be true, as we are convinced it is, that, in this general appearance of tranquillity, there is some mixture of discontent, as well as of strong and well grounded opinion, on the subject of abuses in the Government, and corruptions of the Constitution, we wish it to be considered by men, whose judgement has been formed or enlightened by experience, and whose actions are most likely to be directed by prudence, whether, in taking proper measures to remove the cause and objects of such discontent and opinion, the choice of the time be not a material part of the measure; and whether the earliest time, that can be taken, for preventing the encrease of an existing evil, be not the safest and the best? The example and experience of another kingdom, are held out to deter us from innovations of any kind. We say, that the Reforms we have in view are not innovations. Our intention is, not to change, but to restore; not to displace, but to re-instate the Constitution upon its true principles and original ground. In the conduct of persons most likely to reproach us with a spirit of innovation, we see a solid ground for retorting the imputation. Their professions of admiration of the beauty and of zeal for the security of the Constitution, appear to us too lavish to be sincere, especially when compared with those practical violations, with which they suffer this beautiful system to be invaded, and to which they never refuse to give their concurrence. They will not innovate, but they are no enemies to gradual decay, as if the changes insensibly produced by time, and nourished by neglect, were not in effect the most dangerous innovations. But what security have we, that the dispositions of such men are not something worse than passive? that, in praising the Constitution, they have no other meaning but to adorn a victim, which they wish to sacrifice, or to flatter the beauty they are endeavouring to corrupt? Let their intention be what it may, we answer their accusation in the words of one of the wisest of mankind: "That time is the greatest innovator; and if time of course alters things to the worse, and if wisdom and counsel shall not alter them to the better, what shall be the end?"

By the Reform proposed by Lord Chatham [22 January 1770], he declared in the House of Lords, that he meant *to infuse a portion of new health into the Constitution*. The Duke of Richmond has declared [17 January 1783], that his reasons in favour of a Parliamentary Reform were formed on the experience of twenty-six years, which, whether in or out of Government, had equally convinced him, "that the restoration of a genuine House of Commons, by a renovation of the Rights of the People, was the only remedy against that system of corruption, which had brought the nation to disgrace and poverty, and threatened it with the loss of liberty."

Other authorities, in favour of a Parliamentary Reform, as direct and explicit as these, might be quoted in abundance. The public is possessed of them. We rather wish to encounter, because we are sure we can efface, in every rational mind, the impression, which may have been made by a view of those events, which have attended a total change in the Constitution of France. We deny the existence of any resemblance whatever between the cases of the two kingdoms; and we utterly disclaim the necessity of resorting to similar remedies. We do not believe that, at this day, an absolute avowed despotism, in the hands of the executive power, would be endured in this country. But who can say, to what conclusion the silent unresisted operation of abuses, incessantly acting and constantly increasing, may lead us hereafter; what habits it may gradually create; what power it may finally establish? The abuses in the government of France were suffered to gather and accumulate, until nothing but an eruption could put an end to them. The discontent of the people was converted into despair. Preventive remedies were either not thought of in time, or they were not proposed until it was too late to apply them with effect. The subversion of the ancient government ensued. The inference from this comparison is at once so powerful and so obvious, that we know not by what argument to illustrate or enforce it. We mean to avert for ever from our country the calamities inseparable from such convulsions. If there be, as it is said, in any part of this kingdom, a disposition to promote confusion, or even to arrive at improvement by unconstitutional and irregular courses, we hold ourselves as strictly pledged to resist that disposition, wherever it may appear, as to pursue our own objects by unexceptionable methods. If, on the contrary, it be true, that the mass of the people are satisfied with the present state of things, or indifferent about it; if they approve of the representation as it stands, the form of election, and the duration of the trust; or if, condemning these things, they are determined, from indolence or despair, not to attempt to correct them; then indeed the efforts of individuals may be ineffectual, but they cannot be injurious to the peace of the community. If the spirit of the Constitution be dead in the hearts of the people, no human industry can revive it. To affirm, that extensive mischief may be done by a statement of facts or arguments, which make no general impression on the public mind, is a proposition that contradicts itself, and requires no refutation. We trust it will be proved by experiment, that these inconsistent assertions are equally unfounded, and that the people of this country are no more disposed to submit to abuses without complaint, than to look for redress in any proceedings repugnant to the laws, or unwarranted by the constitution. Between anarchy and despotism, speaking for ourselves, we have no choice to make;—we have no preference to give. We neither admit the necessity, nor can we endure the idea of resorting to either of these extremities as a refuge from the other. The course we are determined to pursue, is equally distant from both. It must be blindness not to see, and treachery not to acknowledge [Blackstone], "*that the instruments of power, though not so open and avowed as they formerly were, are not the weaker on that account;*" that many circumstances have added to the power of the crown, and that, *in particular, the increase of the national debt and taxes has, in its natural consequences, thrown such a weight into the executive scale of government, as could not have been foreseen or intended by our ancestors at the Revolution.* Our general object is to recover and preserve the true balance of the Constitution.

These are the principles of our association, and, on our steady adherence to them, we look with a just confidence to the approbation and support of the people in the prosecution of our object. A measure, so likely to be opposed by the united strength of various interests, can never succeed, but by the declared and hearty concurrence of the nation.

Commons debate on Charles Grey's unsuccessful motion for parliamentary reform, 30 April 1792

Parliamentary History, XXIX, 1300-24.

Mr. Grey rose to give notice of a motion which, in the course of the next session, he should have the honour to submit to their consideration, the object of which was a reform in the representation of the people. On a subject of such importance, he could not content himself with merely stating his notice, but would trouble the House by saying a few words upon it. The necessity of such reform had been often asserted by eminent men both in that and the other house of parliament: it had been acknowledged by the right hon. gentleman over the way (Mr. Pitt) and by his right hon. friend (Mr. Fox); from the influence of different interests, however, every attempt to introduce a reform had hitherto proved unsuccessful. That the proposition had been relinquished by the right hon. gentleman, and had never since been brought forward, he rather attributed to its failure of success on former occasions, than to any change of opinion on the subject. He meant not to throw imputations on any gentleman, or to censure them for a desertion of the cause which he supported; so far from entertaining such an idea, he hoped and trusted he should find them forward friends and advocates of the proposition. He was fully convinced that since the subject had been last brought forward, a considerable change had taken place in the minds of the people, and that the necessity of a reform was at present pretty generally acknowledged. Abuses had been permitted to creep into the constitution through neglect, or had been introduced into it by corruption, and those abuses were of a nature so dangerous, that they threatened the very existence of the constitution itself. A reform, therefore, he was persuaded, was the only mode of preserving it from rapid decay, and that on that measure the security of the country, and the continuance of its freedom, depended. The times were critical, and the minds of the people agitated. It was to do away every cause of complaint, and to preserve the peace of the public and the general tranquillity, that he wished a reform to take place in the representation. Within the two last years the privileges of that House had been curtailed and infringed, in a greater degree, than in any preceding period of equal duration. In his mind it was a point of the utmost importance that the House should enjoy the good opinion of the public, and possess their confidence as a true representation of the people. If the House was not considered as the true representatives of the people, the worse of dangers were to be apprehended. The loss of that character might produce all the miseries of civil commotion, with which God forbid this nation should ever be afflicted! If there were those who wished to promote confusion and excite mischief, he exceedingly regretted it; he disclaimed all connexion with such persons, and must ever reprobate their conduct. He was convinced, however, that the evils which threatened the constitution, could only be corrected by a timely and temperate reform; and, in his mind, the measure demanded the serious consideration of every friend to his country, and would be found deserving of his support. He trusted, therefore, that between the present day, and that on which he should bring forward the proposition, gentlemen would weigh well the question and give it their most deliberate attention; and in that interval he hoped the sentiments of the people on the subject would be fully ascertained.

Mr. Pitt said, he believed it was not strictly regular to enter into any observations upon a mere notice of a motion; and therefore he was under the correction of the chair, whether or not he should articulate a syllable.—[Go on! Go on! was echoed from different parts of the House.] He then proceeded. If ever there was an occasion, in which the mind of every man, who had any feeling for the present, or hope for the future happiness of this country, should be interested, the present was the time for its exertion. The present was the time in which the whole House should lose sight of form in the regulation of debate, and apply at once to the substance of the subject. Nothing could be said upon this subject, at this time, that did not involve the questions of the most serious and lasting importance to the people of this country, to the very being of the state. He had other motives, he confessed, besides the general importance of the subject, to say a few words now upon it. It was a question on which he had thought attentively. He was unwilling to weary the House with many observations upon his own conduct, or what seemed not exactly to correspond with what he had professed in the earliest part of his public character; because he was convinced that the question to be brought forward on this subject, would involve something more than the character, the fortune, the connexion, the liberty, or the life of any individual. It might affect the peace and tranquillity which, under the favour of Providence, this country had, for a long time, enjoyed, in a superior degree, perhaps, to any part of the habitable globe. It might affect us, who, from the time of general darkness and bondage to the present hour, had sat quietly, perceiving other powers struggling with tyranny and oppression, while we enjoyed our freedom it might even bring us into anarchy and confusion worse, if possible, than if we had to contend with despotism itself.—He thought the country should know what the opinions of public men were upon the subject now before them, and how they felt at this moment. He confessed they had a peculiar right to know from him his opinion on the subject of parliamentary reform. He could have wished that a subject of this immense importance had been brought forward at a time when he was personally more able to take an active part in a debate than at present, but above all, on a day on which the House had no other matter to attend to. He wished, also, the hon. gentleman would bring it forward on some distinct proposition stated to the House, that they might, early in the next session of parliament, take the whole question into consideration; in which case he should, perhaps, have reserved himself until the day appointed for the consideration of the subject: but as this was a general notice, without any specific proposition, he must say he felt no difficulty in asserting, in the most decisive terms, that he objected both to the time and the mode in which this business was brought forward. He felt this subject so deeply, that he must speak on it without any reserve. He would therefore confess, that, in one respect, he had changed his opinion upon this subject, and he was not afraid to own it. He retained his opinion of the propriety of a reform in parliament, if it could be obtained without danger or mischief, by a general concurrence, pointing harmlessly at its object. But he confessed he was afraid, at this moment, that if agreed on by that House, the security of all the blessings we enjoyed would be shaken to the foundation. He confessed, he was not sanguine enough to hope that a reform at this time could safely be attempted. His object always had been, but now most particularly so, to give permanence to that which we actually enjoy, rather than remove any subsisting grievances. He conceived that the beautiful system of our constitution, and the only security we had for the continuance of it, was in the House of Commons; but he was sorry to confess, that that security was imperfect, while there were persons who thought that the people were not adequately represented in parliament. It was essential to the happiness of the people, that they should be convinced that they, and the members of that House, felt an identity of interest: that the nation at large, and the representatives of the people, held a conformity of sentiment: this was the essence of a proper representative assembly; under this legitimate authority, a people could be said to be really free; and this was a state in which the true spirit of proper democracy could be said to subsist. This was the only mode by which freedom and due order could be well united. If attempts were made to go beyond this, they ended in a wild state of nature that mocked the name of liberty, and by which the human character was degraded, instead of being made free. He once thought, and still thought, upon the point of the representation of the Commons, that if some mode could be adopted, by which the people could have any additional security for a continuance of the blessings which they now enjoy, it would be an improvement in the constitution of this country. That was the extent of his object; farther he never wished to go; and if this could be obtained without the risk of losing what we have, he should think it wise to make the experiment. When he said this, it was not because he believed there was any existing grievance in this country that was felt at this hour. On the contrary, he believed that at this moment we actually did enjoy as much happiness as we should, or that a rational man ought to hope for. He believed that we were in a state of prosperity and progressive improvement rarely equalled, never excelled, by any nation at any period in the history of the world.—He now came to the time and mode of bringing this subject forward. Upon these points, every rational man had two things to consider. These were, the probability of success, and the risk to be run by the attempt. Upon the latter consideration he owned, his apprehensions were very great: he feared the corruptions that might follow the attempt; and looking at it in both views, he saw nothing but discouragement. He saw no chance of succeeding in the attempt in the first place, but saw great danger of anarchy and confusion in the second. He saw no wisdom in attempting any thing, without a united and careful attention to the probable consequences, with fear and dread. It was true, he had made some attempts upon this subject himself—but at what time? What were the circumstances in which he did so? There was then a general apprehension, which now, thank God, was referred to rather as a matter of history than any thing else; all fear of danger was entirely removed; but there was then a general feeling, that we were upon the verge of a national bankruptcy, and a strong sense was entertained of practical grievances:—this was at the conclusion of the American war; succeeding a period, when the influence of the crown was declared to have increased, to be increasing, and that it ought to be diminished. Many thought, and he was of the number that unless there was a better connexion between the parliament and the people, and a uniformity of sentiment between them, the safety of this country was endangered. Many moderate men at that time admitted, there were abuses that ought to be corrected; but, having weighed the whole state of the case, even as it stood then, they were of opinion, that although some evil was to be met with, yet that, on the whole, the good preponderated, and, therefore, from a fear of possible consequences, they voted against his plan of reformation. If in such a time, and under such circumstances, moderate men thought in this way, what would they think under the present circumstances? He put it not only to that House, but also to the country at large; and he would ask all moderate men in it, what were their feelings on this subject at this moment? He believed that he could anticipate the answer—"This is not a time to make hazardous experiments." Could we forget what lessons had been given to the world within a few years? Could we suppose that men felt the situation of this country, as now happily contrasted with others, to be in a deplorable condition? Could we expect that these moderate men would become converts to the new system attempted in another country—a system which all men would reject? He hoped that such doctrine would not find many proselytes among the moderate and the peaceable; if not, there could be no hope of success, and consequently, no wisdom in the attempt. But it seemed that there were a great number of persons in this country who wished for a reform in parliament, and they were increasing daily. That their number was great, he was happy enough to doubt: what their interest or their vigour would be, if called upon to exert themselves, against the good sense and courage of the sober part of the community, did not occasion him much apprehension. He did not mean to allude to the sentiments of any particular member of that House for the purpose of being severe; but when they came in the shape of advertisements in newspapers, inviting the public as it were to repair to their standard and to join them, they should be reprobated, and the tendency of their meetings exposed to the people in their true colours. He was willing, as long as he could to give gentlemen the best construction that could be put upon their actions; but the advertisements he alluded to in the public newspapers, were sanctioned with the very name of the gentleman who had given the present notice. He would say, that there should be a great deal of activity on the part of the friends of our constitution, to take pains properly to address the public mind, and to keep it in that state which was necessary to our present tranquillity. He had seen with concern that those gentlemen of whom he spoke, who were members of that House, were connected with others, who professed not reform only, but direct hostility to the very form of our government. This afforded suspicion, that the motion for a reform was nothing more than the preliminary to the overthrow of the whole system of our present government; and if they succeeded, they would overthrow what he thought the best constitution that was ever formed on the habitable globe. These considerations led him to wish the House to take great care that no encouragement should be given to any step that might sap the very foundation of our constitution. When he saw these opinions published, and knew them to be connected with opinions that were libels on the form of our government,—the hereditary succession to the throne—the hereditary titles of our men of rank—and the total destruction of all subordination in the state, he confessed he felt no inclination to promise his support to the proposed motion for a parliamentary reform. It was to follow a madness which had been called liberty in another country—a condition at war with freedom and good order—a state to which despotism itself was preferable—a state in which liberty could not exist for a day; if it appeared in the morning, it must perish before sunset.—He begged leave to assure the House, that he thought it his duty, to the last hour of his life, to oppose, to the utmost of his power, attempts of this nature. So much did he disapprove of the present attempt, that, if he were called to choose either to hazard this, or for ever abandon all hopes or desire to have any reform at all, he would say he would have no reform whatever; and he believed that as a member of parliament, as an Englishman, and as an honest man, it was his duty to make that declaration at once. He wished the hon. gentleman to reflect on his character, the stake he had in the country, and the hazard to which he might expose himself.—All, all might be lost by an indiscreet attempt upon the subject! He could not help lamenting that this notice had been given. He had then made, he said, a sort of compendium of all the objections he should submit to the House if the motion should ever be made, and concluded with an encomium on the constitution of this country—a monument of human wisdom, which had hitherto been the exclusive blessing of the English nation.

Mr. Fox said, he understood that they were in some measure to consider themselves as debating some part of the subject in the present stage of it, and the question now was, whether this subject should, or should not, be brought forward early in the next session of parliament? He felt additional difficulty from the speech he had just heard, and he was sorry to find it received so much of the approbation of the House. He knew that within the walls of that House, the words "parliamentary reform" were completely unpopular. The public, he believed, regarded it in a very different view; and therefore he should state to the House what the feelings of his mind were upon the subject. First of all he begged it to be remembered, that he never professed to be so sanguine upon this subject as the right hon. gentleman who had just spoken; but, although less sanguine, he happened to be a little more consistent in this case; for he had, early in his public life, formed an opinion of the necessity of a parliamentary reform, and he remained to this hour as fully convinced as ever of that necessity. The danger which then existed, still existed to the liberty of the people. The chancellor of the exchequer had, year after year, made speeches in favour of a parliamentary reform. He had followed it up to the year 1785, when at last his ardour forsook him. The cause for this reform had, so far from being diminished been progressively increasing, and most of all in the two last sessions of parliament. He had given his reason upon this subject before; he would not now say that there must be a parliamentary reform; he was almost forbidden to talk of it from the speech he had just heard; but, unless something was done—he knew it was not agreeable to the House to hear it—but he would repeat, that, unless something was done to quiet the minds of the people, there would be some difficulty in preserving the interal tranquillity of this kingdom for any great length of time. The misfortune was, that the proceedings of that House often were at variance with the opinion of the public. Of the truth of this the armament against Russia was a striking instance. The declaration of the House was, that we should proceed to hostilities; the declaration of the people was, that we should not; and so strong was that declaration, that it silenced and overawed the minister, with his triumphant majority; he was obliged to relinquish his plan at a time when he had a confiding and implicit majority. What was the consequence? That the people of England were at this moment paying the expense of an armament for which they never gave their consent; and that, as far as that went, they paid their money for not being represented in parliament; that their sentiments were not spoken in parliament; and, what was still worse, that, when a complaint was made of the impropriety of this, those who called themselves the representatives of the people, refused to inquire into the subject at all; they did not think it worth while to clear up to the people any part of the transaction, so as to show them the folly of their opinion, and the wisdom of their representatives. These were the points that disgusted the public with the proceedings of parliament. The truth was, that the principle on which this, as well as other votes, had been given by that House, was wrong in itself; it was the confidence which had been so implicitly given to the minister, and that too, not merely to him from experience of his probity and talents, but because he was minister; the doctrine was, that the agent of the executive power for the time being, be he who he might, was entitled to confidence; and if he afterwards committed what the people called a blunder, no inquiry should be had into his conduct. As to the other part of the right hon. gentleman's speech, which related to the allies of his hon. friend, he thought he should give it a complete answer, by saying to the minister, pray, who will you have for yours? On our part there are infuriated republicans—on yours, there are the slaves of despotism; both of them unfriendly, perhaps, to some part of the constitution of their country, but there was no comparison between them in point of real hostility to the spirit of freedom; the one, by having too ardent a desire for liberty, lost sight of the true medium by which it was to be preserved; the other detested the thing itself, and were pleased with nothing but tyranny and despotism.

As to the books that had been lately published upon the principles of government, and to which the minister alluded, when he talked of dangerous doctrine against monarchy, he could only say, that he had not read many of them: there were two well-known pamphlets, written by a gentleman, who had distinguished himself as an author, during the American war, a native of that country, of the name of Paine. One of these pamphlets he had read; the other he had not seen; and he must say, that whatever merit might be met with in that publication, he could not suppose we were so far reduced, as to be in any great danger from the abuse of a foreigner; nor because, perhaps, (he did not remember seeing it, by-the-by), the word "reform" was to be seen in the "Rights of Man," that therefore all those who thought a reform necessary, agreed with the general tendency of that book; the truth was, that the book, called "Rights of Man," was a performance totally different from all ideas of reform in our government. It went the length of changing the form of it. Why, then, should those who professed reverence for the constitution of this country, be charged with having taken up the sentiments contained in a book that was a libel on it? As to the fear of innovation, he confessed there appeared to him to be very little in it; at least it could not be well urged, by the right hon. the chancellor of the exchequer, because upon that point he must argue against himself; if innovation was wrong now, it must have been so always, when the right hon. gentleman brought it forward. In short, the longer the reform had been delayed, the more urgent it became, and care should be taken that the disease should not be permitted to increase, until it required a desperate remedy.

In short, upon the word "innovation" he must take the liberty of repeating what he had uttered almost the first time he addressed that House; an observation which some thought quaintly expressed, "That the greatest innovation that could be introduced in the constitution of England was, to come to a vote, that there should be no innovation in it." The greatest beauty of the constitution was, that in its very principle it admitted of perpetual improvement, which time and circumstances rendered necessary. It was a constitution, the chief excellence of which was, that of admitting a perpetual reform.

He saw nothing in any human institution so very sacred as not to admit of being touched or looked at; in his opinion, the permanency of the constitution must depend upon what the people thought of it, and before they could have any great reverence for it, it was necessary they should be convinced that the voice of their representatives was in unison with their own. He did not choose to make any invidious reference to past circumstances. If it was to be understood that the House of Commons should be the organ of the public voice, he must say that he could not help wishing that no minister might again advise the sovereign to disregard the address of the House of Commons, because it did not speak the voice of the people. Mr. Fox here alluded to the chancellor of the exchequer's conduct in the year 1784, when the House of Commons addressed the king not to dissolve the parliament at that alarming crisis. He could not, he said, conceive any thing more dangerous than such a practice. He here took a view of the present administration, and the history of it, as applicable to the present subject, and confessed that there was a great deal of the right hon. gentleman's speech that he did not understand, when compared with some of his former declarations.

Much had been insisted, although obliquely, as to the supposed terrific situation of France, upon which he should observe, that the old government was so detestable, that the most moderate man he ever heard in his life had agreed, that if it could be proved that great improvements might not be introduced into it, the whole of it ought to be overthrown at once; the revolution therefore was justified, and therefore there did not appear to him so much danger from the supposed contagion of their example; to dread similar danger we should be in similar circumstances, which was nothing like the case. Why, then should we shut the door against reform? Whenever he heard speeches on the dreadful situation of the French (tolerably well exaggerated by the way, in the accounts we received of their calamities, and of the defectiveness of the present form of their government), he always thought they preceded expressions of disapprobation of all reform in this country. If it was true that the people of this country felt grievances and really wished for a parliamentary reform, they had a right to have it; if, on the contrary, there were no such grievances, nor any such wishes, his hon. friend was in the right to give this notice; it afforded time to inquire into the facts, and called on the public for attention to the object. At all events, attention should be called to these things, and he believed it would turn out to be the general opinion, that a reform was wanting; for he believed it to be a principle which attended all human institutions, that unless they were amended, they would naturally become worse—that whatever was not improved must naturally degenerate.

He might be asked, Mr. Fox said, why his name was not in the list of the society for reform? His reason was, that though he saw great and enormous grievances, he did not see the remedy. Had his hon. friend consulted him, he should have hesitated before he recommended him to take the part he had taken; having, however, taken it, he could not see why the present period was improper for the discussion. The right hon. gentleman, he thought, had in his warmth out-run himself, when he held forth Great Britain as the only power exempted from despotism and anarchy, and in possession of undisturbed liberty. France, Mr. Fox said, had entirely changed a detestable government. Poland, he hoped the right hon. gentleman would not maintain, was under a despotism; and he would make a false statement if he asserted that America was not in the full enjoyment of liberty—a liberty which had produced justice, commerce, wealth, and prosperity. The world he believed to be rapidly improving in science, in knowledge, and in virtue; and as philosophy was spreading her light around every part of the globe, England alone, he hoped, would not remain without improvement, and enveloped in the darkness of bigotry. Our constitution he admired, and particularly that principle of it which admitted of every improvement being grafted upon it safely. The crown, Mr. Fox said, had been curtailed of its prerogative, the lords had had their privileges abridged, and the Commons, within his memory, had also had their privileges abridged; he saw no danger, therefore, in continued reform, and had no difficulty in declaring himself a friend to improvement of every kind. He concluded with observing, that he wished the public to know the real object of this notice, namely, to call their attention to the subject of a reform in the representation of the people in parliament.

The Speaker reminded the House, that they had no motion before them, but said if it was their pleasure to proceed, he should submit entirely to their judgment.

Mr. Burke began by saying, that there were few subjects indeed, which would have induced him to come down, and deliver his opinions in that House, but this was certainly one which he thought he was in duty bound not to pass over in silence. He was now an old man, and there was still a stronger reason for his not engaging in the discussion of public questions—he had received from his best friends the best advice that they could have given to him; it was, to retire. His friends judged right, and he certainly thought himself unfit for business, when he recollected that he had lost such friends, as any man must have been proud to associate with and with whom he had so long acted with the most fervent and mutual sincerity. That being the case, the advice and the conduct of his friends, as well as twenty-seven years experience in parliament, was a warning for him how to guide his future proceedings in that House, or in other words, a warning to retire, considering himself at the same time as one who had done his duty, and had become old and infirm in the service of his country. Yet, while he left the more active concerns of life to the conduct of men more vigorous in years and in understanding, he still would put in his claim, as a friend to the country, to use his utmost exertions in its service, whenever an attack was made upon the constitution, and to defend its real interests against every attempt to overturn it. As invalids, therefore, were always put upon garrison duty, and though not the first for foreign service, were those who ought first to move when the garrison was attacked, it became his duty now to come forward; they ought especially to be foremost in the defence, because if they were worsted, they left behind them those who were possessed of more strength and greater power to defend it effectually.

In this view, he looked upon the present notice, which, taking it merely as a notice, he considered to be fraught with mischievous consequences; not that he meant to ascribe any wrong motives or intentions to those who brought it forward, because he knew well that there were amongst them many for whom he had the highest respect, and most sincere friendship; but, he must contend, that though their motives might be as pure and patriotic as could be, still, by acting upon an erroneous system, the consequences might be dangerous. He was happy to see, and to congratulate the House and the country upon one thing, and that was, that two very great, and deservedly very great men, both in the opinion of that House and of the country, gave similar opinions, and entertained similar sentiments upon this subject, with this only difference, that the right hon. gentleman opposite to him had stated his belief that no such grievances existed as ought to induce the House to agree to this idea of reform, and the other right hon. gentleman thought that if those grievances did exist, the friends to a reform had not proposed or held forth any thing like a remedy for them, because he was convinced that a parliamentary reform would not be an effectual remedy, if such grievances existed. He did not think that the word reform ought to carry that weight with it which some gentlemen seemed to allow. If a reform was necessary, the way to prove that it ought to be agreed to was first by stating the grievance, and then pointing out the specific remedy This, however, had not been done in the present case. The friends to this plan of reform seemed to address the people in the same manner, as if a physican were to say to a patient, "You labour under a terrible disease, and must take any and every remedy we prescribe for you; whether it be opium, an emetic, a blistering plaister, or all together, you must take them, however discordant in effects, because, depend upon it, you are in such a desperate situation that you must do it." Similar was the present mode of telling the people, "You are unhappy, ought to be discontented, and call for a reform, though we do not even pretend to specify or show what reform is proper, or such as might be of any service to you." Mr. Burke said, he considered giving a vote in that House upon any subject as very different to joining an association for making converts to a cause by holding out to the people the necessity of complaining, when they themselves felt no cause for complaint. The present reformers appeared in the light of quacks, rather than regular physicians; they held out preventives when no disease was dreaded, and wished to cram them down the throats of the people, and make them complain, when they were not sensible of grievances, and when the public voice was completely different from what those friends to reformation stated it to be. He would ask, if the sense of the people had been consulted, whether this association would have been formed? Were there any petitions from the people stating their grievances? If this was not the case, was it good and constitutional doctrine to hold out to them, that the House of Commons was in itself a grievance? That there was in its formation something intrinsically corrupt? Let democracy get to its greatest extent in this country, or in that House, still it would be found that there were, and would continue to be, great men in that House upon different sides of any question, that must and ought to have influence. He regretted being obliged to notice what a right hon. friend of his had said, relative to the proceedings in the year 1784; their mischievous tendency he allowed as much as the right hon. gentleman; but what had arisen from the conduct of the difference societies and clubs that associated in 1780, in various parts of the kingdom? These societies, in associating, were obliged to admit amongst their numbers men of very different principles, and reformers of various denominations; the consequence was, that no system could be thought of that suited the views of all, of course many were dissatisfied, and in the end they dropt every idea of their own reform. This failure, however, he could not ascribe to the right hon. gentleman opposite (Mr. Pitt), who did every thing he could to bring about a reform, and seemed as eager and zealous to effect it, as he enforced it with all the natural eloquence and energy that he possessed.

At that period, the acquiescence of the people was considered necessary, as he trusted it ever would, and it was found then, and he believed it would be found now, that the people had no such idea in their heads. They did not then, nor would they now, call for a parliamentary reform. What next did the right hon. gentleman say? Why, that they must make the people feel the grievances they laboured under, if they could not discover them themselves, and excite them to complaints which they knew no cause for; and all this they would do from the following argument that they know some reform is necessary, and that by putting it into the hands of such men as are, from their rank, fortunes, character, and respectability in the country, the most likely to propose a temperate and adequate reform, having much at stake themselves, they will study the more the interests of the people. As to the characters of the men, he would not hesitate a moment to pronounce them entitled to every encomium that could be bestowed on them; but would they pledge their characters and their consequence in the country, that when they have once raised a strong spirit of reformation and innovation amongst the people, they will have the power to guide their opinions, and prevent excesses, when the ideas of the people, may probably carry them to an ungovernable length, upon a subject of which they understand so little? If the hon. gentleman who proposed this could guide and regulate the public opinion as they could their own, the case would be different; but that was not possible, and therefore he thought there could be no such thing as a temperate reform. Let them recollect, that in the days of Hampden, Hyde, and other reformers, and at different periods of the English history, it was almost invariably found that it ended. This was one strong reason why they should not countenance any indefinite reform; for in fact they never could know its extent and its consequences.

He agreed perfectly with his right hon. friend, that this country had been for a very long time in a perpetual state of innovation and progressive reform, and though kings had reigned who rather checked than encouraged improvements of the constitution, yet it was found that improvements had, from time to time, taken place, and they were uniformly found to be rather in defence of the real constitution than innovations. It was likewise true, that we had at different times cut off certain branches of the prerogative, when those branches were found to be inimical to the welfare of the people; but we had always kept the lamp of the constitution burning, and supplied it occasionally with necessary assistance, without ever attempting to alter its former nature; we had seen a reformation, a revolution, and, on an abdication of the crown, we had seen a new family seated upon the throne; but we had never, at any one period, touched upon an alteration in the representation of the people till very lately. If we are in slavery, if in anarchy and confusion, if, in short, we labour under any grievance whatever, let us look if it proceeds from the representation of the people in parliament. Is the landed or commercial interest affected? does any one interest overpower or act against another in this country? can it be proved that such are the effects of the present representation of the people? He really believed not. The Russian armament had been mentioned, and certainly that was a subject upon which the opinion of the people was very decided, though that opinion differed widely from the opinion of that House. The people were decidedly against the measure, but yet they did not go so far as to say that the measure, ought to destroy the minister; and this, he contended, was generally the case with the people of England, whoever was minister at the time. It had been so with sir Robert Walpole, and would be so with every future minister.

He came next to what had been said on Paine's book, which he thought had been very properly termed by the right hon. gentleman a libel of the most infamous kind against the constitution of this country. He would ask those who supported those visionary schemes of reform, what it was they had to dread? Could they point out any person in that House who was the avowed friend to despotism? or could they suggest any thing like a conspiracy against the privileges of the people? He believed it was impossible; but he thought there was no difficulty in saying there were those in the country who were avowed enemies to the constitution [A cry of, Name them, name them!] He begged gentlemen not to distress themselves by the repetition of calls, with which he could not comply. He would ask, whether he had called upon them in a similar way, when they had made allusions much stronger than he had done! however he would satisfy their curiosity on this point, by stating what the declared opinions of that night warranted him in doing, which was, that Paine's pamphlet was an infamous libel upon the constitution, and therefore that those clubs and societies who recommended that book to be read by the people, were the avowed enemies of the constitution, by prescribing to the people, what was admitted by the first men in that House, to be a libel on the constitution, and tending, by its contents, to subvert and overturn it. Mr. Paine had been called a stranger, a foreigner, not an Englishman, a Frenchman, nor an American. In short, he seemed to be a man who knew just enough of all countries to confuse and distract all, without being of the least use to any. There were in this country men who scrupled not to enter into an alliance with a set in France of the worst traitors and regicides that had ever been heard of—the club of the Jacobins. Agents had been sent from this country, to enter into a federation with that iniquitous club, and those agents were men of some consideration in this country; the names he alluded to were Thomas Cooper and James Watt. Here Mr. Burke read the address presented to the club of the Jacobins by those gentlemen on the 16th of April. He said, this was nothing of fancy or invention, but an avowal that there were clubs in this country, who bound themselves, by a federation with those regicides, to approve their conduct and act in concert with them. He likewise could name others who avowed similar principles; for instance, Mr. Walker of Manchester. And what did those people do? did they only give their own sentiments? No. By the answer of the Jacobin club, it appeared that those worthies of Manchester undertook—from what authority he knew not—to represent all England. This led him to state, that, however upright the motives of the hon. gentleman near him might be, they must necessarily, in order to succeed in their object, unite themselves with some of the worst men in the kingdom.

Mr. Burke ridiculed the idea of a moderate or temperate reform as impossible, nor could he look upon the present schemes as if there were two parties, one for a temperate reform, and the other for a subversion of the constitution. And he would ask those hon. gentlemen, if they could answer for all who might join them on this occasion, and were sure that they would be satisfied with moderate measures? He then observed, that France was not in a situation for reform, but was distracted by a violent party. He described the national assembly as consisting of seven hundred members, four hundred of whom were lawyers, three hundred of no description that he could name: and out of the whole he believed there were not six of them that possessed in any one way a hundred pounds per annum. Having treated the national assembly and their conduct with great contempt, he asked if this was a time for encouraging visionary reforms in this country? He said, though he had generally objected to the reforms formerly proposed, it was because the mode did not meet his approbation; and he never had resisted reform when he thought it likely to be useful; for instance, the reform moved by the right hon. gentleman opposite seemed to him, if it had been agreed to, productive of good effects, without risk of any harm; but in the year 1780, the associations in different parts of the country would have defeated any temperate reform. The noble duke who was then a reformer had proposed one mode, and the right hon. gentleman another, and he stated what the difference between them was. He adverted to the county meetings, which he thought not the most probable or quiet way of obtaining the sense of the people, or even knowing the true sense of those meetings. He made some remarks on confidence in ministers, which had been too much enlarged, both in 1784 and 1792, towards the right hon. gentleman opposite, as had been stated by his right hon. friend. He then declared his fixed admiration of that constitution which gave us freedom without losing order; and which, by increasing its order, increased its liberty; and which, he hoped and trusted, he ever should see a continuance of, unmolested and secure against every attack. Theories ought to be founded on experience, and instead of adapting the constitution to a theory, the theory he wished to see grow out of the constitution. He concluded, by putting it to the House to say, whether they knew of any existing grievance that warranted the risk, that must inevitably attend the proposed motion for a parliamentary reform.

Mr. *Fox* said, that he must explain, in a few words, three points on which the right hon. gentleman had misunderstood him. The first was not very material: it was, that, though he mentioned Paine's book as a libel on the constitution, he had not used the terms infamous and seditious, etc. which the right hon. gentleman applied to it. The next was, that when he had mentioned confidence, it was without any personal allusion to the right hon. gentleman opposite, but to the king's ministers for the time; conceiving the confidence of late so much required by the executive power, as very unconstitutional and destructive. The third was, that he had not said that a parliamentary reform could be no remedy to existing grievances, but that he had heard of no specific mode of reform that he was convinced would be a proper remedy.

Address of the London Corresponding Society, 19 November 1792

Address of the London Corresponding Society to the other Societies of Great Britain, united in obtaining a reform in Parliament (London, 1792), 10-page pamphlet.

The LCS was composed of artisans who favored universal manhood suffrage and other radical reforms. Thomas Hardy (1752-1832), secretary of the society, was arrested for treason in 1793 but acquitted. The LCS was suppressed in 1799.

Friends and Fellow Countrymen!
      Unless we are greatly deceived, the Time is approaching when the Object for which we struggle is likely to come within our Reach.—That a Nation like Britain should be free, it is requisite only that Britons should will it to become so; that such should be their Will, the Abuses of our Original Constitution, and the Alarm of our Aristocratic Enemies, sufficiently witness.—Confident in the Purity of our Motives, and in the Justice of our Cause, let us meet Falsehood with Proofs, and Hypocrisy with Plainness: Let us presevere in declaring our Principles, and Misrepresentation will meet its due Reward—Contempt.
      In this View the Artifices of a late Aristocratic Association, formed on the 20th Instant, call for a few Remarks, on account of the Declaration they have published relative to other Clubs and Societies formed in this Nation. It is true that this Meeting of Gentlemen (for so they style themselves) have mentioned no Names, instanced no Facts, quoted no Authorities; but they take upon themselves to assert, that Bodies of their Countrymen have been associated professing Opinions favourable to the Rights of Man, to Liberty, and Equality; and moreover that those Opinions are conveyed in the Terms No King! No Parliament!—So much for their Assertions.
      If this be intended to include the Societies to which we respectively belong, we here in the most solemn Manner deny the latter Part of the Charge; while in admitting the former, we claim the Privilege, and glory in the Character, of Britons. Whoever shall attribute to us (who wish only the Restoration of the lost Liberties of our Country) the expressions of No King! No Parliament! or any Design of invading the Property of other Men, is guilty of a wilful, and impudent, and a malicious Falsehood.

We know and are sensible that the Wages of every Man are his Right; that Difference of Strength, of Talents, and of Industry, do and ought to afford proportional Distinctions of Property, which, when acquired and confirmed by the Laws, is sacred and inviolable. We defy the most slavish and malevolent Man in the Meeting of the 20th Instant, to bring the remotest Proof to the Contrary: If there be no Proof, we call upon them to justify an insidious Calumny, which seems invented only to terrify Independent Britons from reclaiming the Rightful Constitution of their Country.

We admit and we declare, that we are Friends to Civil Liberty, and therefore to Natural Equality, both of which we consider as the Rights of Mankind—Could we believe them to be "in direct Opposition to the Laws of this Land," we should blush to find ourselves among the Number of its Inhabitants; but we are persuaded that the Abuses of the Constitution will never pass current for its true Principles, since we are told in its first Charter that all are Equal in the Sight of the Law, which "shall neither be sold, nor refused, nor delayed, to any Free Man whatsoever." Should it ever happen that "Right and Justice" are opposed by Expence, by Refusal, or by Delay, *then is this Principle of Equality violated, and we are no longer Freemen.*

Such are our Notions of those Rights, which it is boldly maintained are "inconsistent with the Well-being of Society." But let us not suffer Men, who avow no Principles of Liberty, whose favourite Cry is Inequality of Property, to estrange others of our Countrymen from aiding us in serving the Community, and from recovering to the Nation that Share of its Sovereignty, which has unhappily been sacrificed to Corrupt Courtiers and intriguing Bourough-mongers.

If our Laws and Constitution be just and wise in their Origin and their Principle, every Deviation from them as first established must be injurious to the People, whose Persons and Property were then secured; if, at the Revolution, this Country was adequately represented, it is now so no longer; and therefore calls aloud for Reform.

If it be true that the People of Britain are superior to other Nations, is it that our Taxes are less burthensome, or that our Provisions are less expensive? Is it from the various Productions of our soil that we are rich? Is it owing to the Majority of our Numbers that we are strong? Certainly not! France has the Advantage in all these Respects, and up to this Period she has never been our superior in Wealth, in Power, in Talents, or in Virtues. But let us not deceive ourselves, the Difference between us and that Nation was, formerly, that our Monarchy was limited while their's was absolute; that the Number of our Aristocracy did not equal the Thousandth Part of their's; that we had Trial by Jury while they had none; that our Persons were protected by the Laws, while their Lives were at the Mercy of every titled Individual. We therefore had that to fight for which to them was unknown, since we were Men while they were Slaves.

The scene indeed has changed: Like our brave Ancestors of the last Century, they have driven out the Family that would have destroyed them; they have scattered the Mercenaries who invaded their Freedom, "and have broken their Chains on the Heads of their Oppressors." If during this Conflict with military Assassins and domestic Traitors, Cruelty and Revenge have arisen among a few Inhabitants of the Capital, let us lament these Effects of a bloody and tyrannous

Manifesto; but let us leave to the hypocritical Pretenders to Humanity the Talk of blackening the Misfortune, and attributing to a whole Nation the Act of an enraged Populace.

As we have never yet been cast so low at the Foot of Despotism, so is it not requisite that we should appeal to the same aweful Tribunal with our Brethren on the Continent. May our Enmities be written in Sand, but may our Rights be engraven on Marble! We desire to overthrow no Property but what has been raised on the Ruins of Our Liberty! We look with Reverence on the landed and commercial Interests of our country; but we view with Abhorrence that Monopoly of Burgage Tenures, unwarranted by Law or Reason in this or any other Nation in Europe.

Let us then continue, with Patience and Firmness, in the Path which is begun; let us then wait and watch the ensuing Parliament, from whom we have much to hope and little to fear. The House of Commons may have been the Source of our Calamity, it may prove that of our Deliverance. Should it not, we trust we shall not prove unworthy of our Forefathers, Whose Exertions in the Cause of Mankind So Well Deserve Our Imitation.

The Spithead mutiny, April 1797

Parliamentary History, XXXIII, 493-501.

In 1797, against the background of war with revolutionary France, two naval mutinies occurred: one in the English Channel fleet at Spithead, and the other in the North Sea fleet at Nore. The seamen at Spithead sent petitions for better conditions and pay to the House of Commons and the Board of Admiralty; these, and the ensuing exchanges, concluding with a royal proclamation pardoning the mutinous seamen, follow.

THE SEAMEN'S PETITION TO THE HOUSE OF COMMONS
18 APRIL 1797

To the Right Hon. and the Hon. Knights, Citizens, and Burgesses, in Parliament assembled. The humble Petition of the Seamen and Mariners on board his Majesty's Ships, in behalf of themselves,

Humbly sheweth;

That your Petitioners relying on the candour and justice of your honourable House, make bold to lay their grievances before you, hoping, that when you reflect on them, you will please to give redress, as far as your wisdom shall deem necessary.

We beg leave to remind your August Assembly, that the act of parliament passed in the reign of king Charles the 2nd, wherein the wages of all seamen serving on board his majesty's fleet was settled, passed at a time when the necessaries of life, and slops of every denomination, were at least 30 per cent cheaper than at the present time, which enabled seamen and mariners to provide better for their families, than we can now do with one half advance.

We therefore request your honourable House will be so kind as to revise the act before-mentioned, and make such amendments therein, as will enable your petitioners and their families to live in the same comfortable manner as seamen and mariners did at that time.

Your petitioners, with all humility, laid their grievances before the honourable earl Howe, and flattered ourselves with the hopes that his lordship would have been an advocate for us, as we have been repeatedly under his command, and made the British flag ride triumphantly over that of our enemies. But to our great surprise, we find ourselves unprotected by him, who has seen so many instances of our intrepidity, in carrying the British flag into every part of the seas with victory and success.

We profess ourselves as loyal to our sovereign, and zealous in the defence of our country as the army and militia can be, and esteem ourselves equally entitled to his majesty's munificence, therefore with jealousy we behold their pay augmented, and their out-pensions of Chelsea-college increased to thirteen pounds per annum, while we remain neglected, and the out-pensioners of Greenwich have only seven pounds per annum.

We, your petitioners, therefore humbly implore that you would take these matters into consideration, and with your accustomed goodness and liberality, comply with the prayer of this petition, and your petitioners, as in duty bound, will ever pray, etc.

We, the delegates of the fleet, hereunto sign our names for the ships' companies:

Royal George—Valentine Joyce, John Morrice.
Queen Charlotte—Patrick Glynn, John Udleson.
Royal Sovereign—Joseph Green, John Richardson.
London—Alexander Harding, Wm. Ruly.
Glory—Patrick Dugan, John Bethell.
Duke—Michael Adams, W. Anderson.
Mars—Thomas Allen, James Blithe.
Marlborough—John Vassia, Wm. Senator.
Ramilies—Charles Berry, George Clear.
Robust—David Wilson, John Scrivener.
L'Impeteux—John Witna, William Porter.
Defence—Geo. Galaway, James Barerick.
Terrible—Mark Turner, George Salked.
La Pompé—William Potts, James Melvin.
Minotaur—Dennis Lawley, G. Crosland.
Defiance—John Saunders, J. Husband.

THE SEAMEN'S PETITION TO THE ADMIRALTY BOARD
18 APRIL 1797

To the Right Hon. the Lords Commissioners of the Admiralty.

My Lords; We, the seamen of his majesty's navy, take the liberty of addressing your lordships, in an humble Petition, showing the many hardships and oppressions we have laboured under for many years, and which we hope your lordships will redress as soon as possible: we flatter ourselves that your lordships, together with the nation in general, will acknowledge our worth and good services, both in the American war, as well as the present; for which good service your lordships' petitioners do unanimously agree in opinion, that their worth to the nation, and laborious industry in defence of their country, deserve some better encouragement than that we meet with at present, or from any we have experienced.

We, your petitioners, do not boast of our good services for any other purpose than that of putting you and the nation in mind of the respect due to us, nor do we ever intend to deviate from our former character; so far from any thing of that kind, or that an Englishman or men should turn their coats: we likewise agree in opinion, that we should suffer double the hardships we have hitherto experienced before we would suffer the Crown of England to be in the least imposed upon by that of any other power in the world; we therefore beg leave to inform your lordships of the grievances which we at present labour under.

We, your humble petitioners, rely that your lordships will take into early consideration the grievances of which we complain, and do not in the least doubt but your lordships will comply with our desires, which are every way reasonable.

The first grievance which we have to complain of is, that our wages are too low, and ought to be raised, that we might be the better able to support our wives and families in a manner comfortable, and whom we are in duty bound to support as far as our wages will allow, which we trust will be looked into by your lordships and the honourable House of Commons in parliament assembled.

We, your petitioners, beg that your lordships will take into consideration the grievances of which we complain, and now lay before you:

1. That our provisions be raised to the weight of sixteen ounces to the pound, and of a better quality, and that our measures may be the same as those used in the commercial trade of this country.
2. That your petitioners request your honours will be pleased to observe there should be no flour served while we are in harbour, in any port whatever, under the command of the British flag; and also, that there might be granted a sufficient quantity of vegetables of such kind as may be the most plentiful in the ports to which we go; which we grievously complain, and lay under the want of.
3. That your lordships will be pleased seriously to look into the state of the sick on board his majesty's ships, that they may be better attended to, and that they may have the use of such necessaries as are allowed for them in time of their sickness, and that these necessaries be not on any account embezzled.

4.   That your lordships will be so kind as to look into this affair, which is no wise unreasonable, and that we may be looked upon as a number of men standing in defence of our country, and that we may in some wise have grant and opportunity to taste the sweets of liberty on shore, when in any harbour, and when we have completed the duty of our ship, after our return from sea; and that no man may encroach upon his liberty, there shall be a boundary limited, and those trespassing any farther, without a written order from the commanding officer, shall be punished according to the rules of the navy, which is a natural request, and congenial to the heart of man, and certainly to us, that you make the boast of being the guardians of the land.

5.   That if any man is wounded in action, his pay be continued until he is cured, and discharged; and if any ship has any real grievances to complain of, we hope your lordships will readily redress them, as far as is in your power, to prevent any disturbances.

It is also unanimously agreed by the fleet, that from this day no grievances shall be received, in order to convince the nation at large, that we know when to cease to ask, as well as to begin, and that we ask nothing but what is moderate, and may be granted without detriment to the nation, or injury to the service.

Given on board the Queen Charlotte, by the Delegates of the Fleet, this 18th day of April, 1797.

(Signed by the same names as the Petition to the House of Commons.)

THE ADMIRALTY BOARD'S ANSWER TO THE PETITIONS
18 APRIL 1797

By the Commissioners for executing the Office of Lord High Admiral of Great Britain and Ireland, etc.

Having taken into consideration the Petitions transmitted by your lordship, from the crews of his majesty's ships under your command, and having the strongest desire to attend to all complaints of the seamen in his majesty's navy, and to grant them every just and reasonable redress, and having considered the difference of the price of the necessaries of life, at this and at that period when the pay of seamen was established, we do hereby require and direct your lordship to take the speediest method of communicating to the fleet;

That we have resolved to recommend it to his majesty, to propose to parliament to increase the wages of seamen in his majesty's navy in the following proportions, viz.

To add four shillings per month to the wages of petty officers and able seamen; three shillings per month to the wages of ordinary seamen, and two shillings per month to the wages of landmen.

That we have resolved, that seamen wounded in action shall be continued in pay until their wounds are healed, or until, being declared unserviceable, they shall receive a pension, or be received into the Royal Hospital at Greenwich, and that having a perfect confidence in the zeal, loyalty, and courage of all the seamen in the fleet, so generally expressed in their Petition, and in their earnest desire of serving their country, with that spirit which always so eminently distinguished British seamen, we have come to this resolution the more readily, that the seamen may have, as early as possible, an opportunity of showing their good dispositions, by returning to their duty, as it may be necessary that the fleet should speedily put to sea to meet the enemy of the country.

Given under our hands, at Portsmouth, the 18th day of April, 1797.

Spencer
Arden
W. Young

To the Right Hon. Lord Bridport, K. B. Admiral, of the White, Commander in Chief of a squadron of his Majesty's ships employed in the Channel service.

THE SEAMEN'S REPLY
19 APRIL 1797

We received your lordships' answer to our Petition; and, in order to convince your lordship and the nation in general of our moderation, beg leave to offer the following remarks to your consideration, viz.

That there never has existed but two orders of men in the navy—able and ordinary; therefore the distinction between ordinary and landmen is totally new. We therefore humbly propose to your lordships, that the old regulations be adhered to; that the wages of able seamen be raised to one shilling per day, and that of petty officers and the ordinary in the usual proportion; and, as a farther proof of our moderation, and that we are actuated by a true spirit of benevolence towards our brethren, the marines, who are not noticed in your lordships' answer, we humbly propose that their pay be augmented while serving on board, in the same proportion as ordinary seamen; this, we hope and trust, will be a convincing proof to your lordships that we are not actuated by a spirit of contradiction, but that we earnestly wish to put a speedy end to the present affair. We beg leave to state to your lordships, that the pensions from Greenwich College, which we earnestly wish to be raised to ten pounds per annum; and in order to maintain which, we humbly propose to your lordships, that every seaman employed in the merchant service, instead of sixpence per month, which they now pay, shall hereafter pay one shilling per month, which, we trust, will raise a fund fully adequate to the purpose; and as this, in time of peace, must be paid by your petitioners, we trust it will give a convincing proof of our disinterestedness and moderation. We would also recommend that this regulation be extended to the seamen in the service of the East-India Company, as we know by experience that there are few sailors employed by them but what have been in the royal navy, and we have seen them with our own eyes, after sickness or other accident has disabled them, without any hope of relief or support but from their former services in the navy.

As to provisions, that they be augmented to sixteen ounces to the pound of bread and meat, cheese, butter, and liquor in proportion, and of a better quality, and a sufficient quantity of vegetables, and that no flour be served with fresh beef. And we farther beg leave to inform your lordships, that it is unanimously agreed, that, until the grievances before stated are redressed, and an act of amendment passed, we are determined not to life an anchor; and the grievances of particular ships must be redressed.

Given under our hands, the Delegates of the fleet, on board the Queen Charlotte, at Spithead, April 19, 1797.

RESOLUTION OF THE ADMIRALTY BOARD
20 APRIL 1797

By the Commissioners for executing the Office of Lord High Admiral of Great Britain and Ireland, etc.

Having taken into consideration a paper containing several representations from the seamen of his majesty's ships at Spithead, respecting an advance of their wages, and being desirous of granting them every request that can, with any degree of reason, be complied with, we have resolved to recommend it to his majesty, that an addition of five shillings and sixpence per month be made to the wages of petty officers and seamen belonging to his majesty, which will make the wages of able seamen one shilling per day, clear of all deductions; an addition of four shillings and sixpence per month to the wages of every ordinary seaman; and an addition of three shillings and sixpence to the wages of the landmen; and that none of the allowance made to the marines, when on shore, shall be stopped, on their being embarked on board any of his majesty's ships. We have also resolved, that all seamen, marines, and others, serving in his majesty's ships, shall have the full allowance of provisions, without any deductions, for leakage or waste; and that until proper steps can be taken for carrying this into effect, short-allowance money shall be paid to the men in lieu of the deduction heretofore made; and that all men wounded in action shall receive their full pay until their wounds shall be healed, or until, being declared incurable, they shall receive a pension from the chest at Chatham, or shall be admitted into the Royal Hospital at Greenwich. And your lordship is hereby required and directed to communicate this our determination to the captain of each of his majesty's ships under your orders, directing him to make it known to the ship's company under his command, and to inform them, that should they be insensible to the very liberal offers now made to them, and persist in their present disobedience, they must no longer expect to enjoy those benefits to which by their former good conduct they were entitled: that in such case, all the men now on board the fleet at Spithead shall be incapable of receiving any smart-money or pension from the chest of Chatham, or of being admitted at any time into the Royal Hospital at Greenwich; and that they must be answerable for the dreadful consequences which will necessarily attend their continuing to transgress the rules of the service in open violation of the laws of their country. On the other hand, he is to inform them, that we promise the most perfect forgiveness of all that has passed on this occasion to every ship's company, who, within one hour after the communication to them of the above-mentioned resolutions, shall return to their duty in every particular, and shall cease to hold farther intercourse with any men who continue in a state of disobedience and mutiny.

Given under our hands, at Portsmouth, the 20th of April, 1797.

Spencer
Arden
W. Young

To the Right hon. Lord Bridport, K. B. Admiral of the White, Commander in Chief of his Majesty's ships to be employed in the Channel, Soundings, etc.

By the Command of their Lordships,
Wm. Marsden

THE SEAMEN'S REPLY
22 APRIL 1797

To the Right Hon. the Lords Commissioners of the Admiralty.

We, the seamen and marines in and belonging to his majesty's fleet, now lying at Spithead, having received with the utmost satisfaction, and with hearts full of gratitude, the bountiful augmentation of pay and provisions, which your lordships have been pleased to signify shall take place in future in his majesty's royal navy, by your order, which has been read to us this morning, by the command of admiral lord Bridport:

Your lordships having thus generously taken the prayer of our several Petitions into your serious consideration, you have given satisfaction to every loyal and well-disposed seaman and marine belonging to his majesty's fleet; and, from the assurance which your lordships have given us respecting such other grievances as we thought right to lay before you, we are thoroughly convinced, should any real grievance or other cause of complaint arise in future, and the same be laid before your lordships in a regular manner, we are perfectly satisfied that your lordships will pay every attention to a number of brave men, who ever have, and ever will be, true and faithful to their king and country.

But we beg leave to remind your lordships, that it is a firm resolution, that until the flour in port be removed, the vegetables and pensions augmented, the grievances of private ships be redressed, an act passed, and his majesty's gracious pardon for the fleet now lying at Spithead be granted, that the fleet will not lift an anchor; and this is the total and final answer.—*April 22.*

THE KING'S PROCLAMATION PARDONING THE SEAMEN
22 APRIL 1797

For pardoning such Seamen and Marines of the squadron of his Majesty's Fleet, stationed at Spithead, as have been guilty of an act of Mutiny or Disobedience of Orders, or any Breach or Neglect of Duty, and who shall, upon Notification of such Proclamation on board their respective Ships, return to the regular and ordinary discharge of their Duty.

> *George R.*
> Upon report of the lords commissioners of the Admiralty of the proceedings of the seamen and marines of the squadron of our fleet stationed at Spithead, and of the measures taken by the said lords commissioners in consequence thereof; and, in order to manifest our desire to give due encouragement to all those who shall return to the regular and ordinary discharge of their duty, according to the rules and practice of the navy; we have thought fit, by the advice of our privy council, to issue this our royal proclamation, and do hereby promise our most gracious pardon to all seamen and marines serving on board the said squadron, who shall, upon notification hereof on board their respective ships, return to the regular and ordinary discharge of their duty: and we do hereby declare, that all such seamen and marines, so returning to their duty, shall be discharged and released from all prosecutions, imprisonments, and penalties, incurred by reason of any act of mutiny or disobedience of orders, or any breach or neglect of duty, previously committed by them, or any of them.
> Given at our Court at Windsor, the 22nd day of April, 1797, and in the 37th year of our reign.—God save the King!

Speech by Charles Grey introducing a motion for parliamentary reform, House of Commons, 26 May 1797

Parliamentary History, XXXIII, 644-53.

Grey's famous motion for parliamentary reform was rejected, 256-91. Supporters of Grey and of Charles James Fox, his Whig ally, then seceded from the Commons and ceased to participate in its debates for several years.

Mr. Grey rose, in pursuance of the notice which he had given, to move for a Reform in the Representation of the people. In bringing forward a notice of such a nature, he said, he laid his account, from past experience, in exposing himself to many uncharitable imputations. If, in their resistance to the destructive system of ministers—if in their endeavours to check them in their ruinous career—if in their efforts to control them in their profuse and extravagant waste of public money, he and his friends had incurred imputations of a wish to gratify personal interest and private ambition, and of a wanton desire to thwart executive government, they could not in the present instance expect to escape similar, or still more odious imputations. It was some consolation, however, that though their exertions were not well received in that House, the public might pass a different decision upon them; and to the public would the eventual decision belong. It might, perhaps, be deemed presumption in him, to call the attention of the House to the conduct of an individual so insignificant as he was. They would do him the justice, however, to allow that, in his propositions for a reform in parliament, he had never proceeded on any speculation of natural and imprescriptible rights. The measures which he had the honour to bring forward were founded, not on speculative, but on practical grounds. Both the speculative and the practical defects of the present system had been so largely discussed and so often repeated, that his labour on the present occasion was much abated without injury to the cause. His views, he repeated, had proceeded on practical grounds, and not on grounds of right; because no man could claim any particular form of government upon a ground of right. Here, however, he begged not to be misunderstood when he stated this proposition: he avowed that there was no man more warmly attached to, or who would more steadily support, the natural and imprescriptible rights of mankind—these were liberty and security; and when liberty and security were not properly guaranteed by any particular system of government, either in consequence of original or accidental defects, the people who lived under it, had a right to demand, either that it should be changed or amended. But, on the other hand, the advocates for universal suffrage, before they demanded that their plan should be adopted, were bound to show, that it was for the good of the people that it should be adopted. It would be also recollected, that he had never grounded his motion for reform upon the inequality of the present misrepresentation. Inequality of representation of itself he did not consider as a sufficient ground of reform. For instance he never had argued, that there should be a reform in the representation of the people, because Cornwall sent as many representatives to parliament as all the counties of Scotland together, and because there were some boroughs with a few houses and a handful of inhabitants, which returned as many members to the House of Commons as the opulent and extensive county of York. Though this sounded strange in theory, yet if it was not shown, that in practice, it was injurious to the rights of Englishmen, their defence was good, who contended that the nation, under its present system of government had enjoyed much prosperity, and a large portion of happiness, and who argued against the expediency of a change from the chance of endangering the existence of the system, and of giving birth to evils of a much more serious nature than those which were experienced under it.

Having thus stated his general principles upon the subject, Mr. Grey proceeded to inquire what was the end and the use of the House of Commons, and what was the present state of the representation of the people. When he considered what it ought to be, the questions naturally occurred, whether it had acted for the interest of the people? whether it had watched the conduct of ministers? whether it had controlled the executive government in its operations? and, above all, whether, in the exercise of its appropriate duty, it had been a faithful guardian to the public purse? When he considered what it was, suggestions of a different nature occurred. Instead of attention, he was afraid there had been negligence; instead of inquiry, there had been confidence; instead of control, there had been obedience; and instead of economy, there had been profusion. But if it had thus failed in its duty, and if misfortunes, numerous and dreadful had been the consequence of the failure, whatever difference of opinion there might be respecting the time and mode of reform, he was convinced there could be little or no objection to the measure, considered abstractedly. How, then, did they stand? It was now five years since he first made a motion for a reform in parliament. At that time the country was described as being in a state of great prosperity, and the public were induced fondly to entertain the prospect of a prolongation of the term of peace. When he looked back, however, for thirty years; when he reflected on the wars in which it had been engaged, and when he reviewed the conduct of the different administrations during these wars; when, in particular, he considered the conduct of the American war, and the embarrassments into which the country was brought in consequence of the profuse expenditure which marked the administration of that period; when, moreover, he beheld a new aera arising in France, which threatened a great and momentous change in the political system of Europe—from all these considerations he was induced to bring forward a measure, which in his opinion, would tend to prevent those evils from again recurring which the nation had formerly had occasion to lament, and which might withstand the influence of new opinions. In a short time after we engaged in a war with France. Our prosperity was still stated to be undiminished. One campaign was to decide the contest, and the triumphant march to Paris was for ever to check the insolence of the enemy. A noble lord [the earl of Mornington] then argued for the prosperity of the country, from the comparative statement of our exports and imports, and concluded a most eloquent description of our increased resources with saying, that we had risen from the lowest state of humiliation and adversity,

> More glorious and more dread than from no fall,
> And trusted we might fear no second fate.

That argument he considered as deficient, because he did not advert to the causes which had produced that state of adversity from which we had just emerged; and he proposed at the time a measure by which the nation might have been guarded against a second humiliation. Whether the remedy would or would not have been effectual, he knew not; but this he knew, that the remedy was rejected, and that the country was again reduced to a state of calamity which made the effects of the American war, when compared with it, trifling, and our situation after it enviable. If, as the noble lord contended, the prosperity of the country was matter of credit to the House of Commons, and if it was an argument against any change in the constitution of that assembly, the disasters which it had lately suffered, and the state of adversity to which it was now reduced, were to the full as good an argument either against its wisdom or its virtue, and in favour of a change of constitution. In stating the evils arising from universal suffrage, the noble lord instanced the government of France, under which that mode of election obtained, and the profuse expenditure consequent upon it. Here again Mr. Grey contended, that he had the advantage of the noble lord in argument; for its extravagance and prodigality were fairly charged as objections to the constitution of the government of France, would not the same objection apply with equal force to the profuse expenditure of public money in this country, the guardianship of which immediately belonged to the House of Commons? What, since that time, had been our situation? We had been reduced from a state of unparalleled prosperity, to a state, if not of despondency, at least of imminent danger and deep distress. Under the pressure of great and accumulated calamities, how had the House of Commons conducted itself? Had they shown either vigilance of inquiry or independence of spirit? Had they investigated the origin of their misfortunes, or checked ministers in their mad and ruinous career? Nay, the very reverse! In a war, remarkable only for misfortune, and distinguished, on our part, solely by disgrace, they had suffered ministers to go on from failure to failure, adding misconduct to misfortune, and madness to folly, without either investigation or inquiry. When attacks were made on the liberties and even the lives of the subject, the House of Commons did not interpose in behalf of freedom invaded, or innocence assaulted. When the shores of our sister kingdom were laid open and defenceless to the fleets of an invading enemy, no inquiry was instituted into the cause of such gross and criminal neglect. When, by the mandate of the privy council, the Bank of England stopped payment, and a shock unequalled at any other time was given to public credit, the minister was absolved, upon his own excuses, from any kind of censure.

Having stated the effects of the system, it was needless to enter upon the mode of election. But, was it not notorious to every one, that men without holding any communion with the people, without either property or talents, merely by throwing themselves on the patronage of a great man, got seats in parliament, not for the purpose of consulting the good of the commonwealth, and defending the rights of the people, but for the purpose of promoting their own interest, by betraying the trust reposed in them? As a remedy for these evils, he proposed to alter the system from which they flowed. Had he implicitly followed the dictates of his own private judgment, he should have adopted the mode of moving for a committee to inquire into the nature and extent of the evil, and to have found out a remedy suitable and proportionate to it. Though that appeared to him to be the better mode of proceeding, when he proposed it before at different times, there was always one objection offered to it, which, on the present occasion, he was desirous of obviating. It was objected, "Would you loosen the confidence of the people in the present House of Commons, by acknowledging the defects of its constitution without proposing a remedy, by showing how it might be constituted better?" To obviate this objection, he should state the outline of the plan which he conceived might remedy the evil of which he complained. His object, then, was to obtain for the people, a full, fair, and free representation in the House of Commons. He wished to alter no part of the constitution. It was his desire that it, should remain as it had been established composed of King, Lords, and Commons. He did not wish to alter any thing which could remain in its present state consistently with the attainment of his object, which as he before stated, was nothing more than a full, free, and fair representation of the people. He should propose, therefore, that the same number of members should serve in parliament as at present. He should propose that the country representation should remain nearly upon the same footing. There were a few alterations, however, which he thought should take place. Instead of 92 county members, which there were at present, he thought that in future, in order to put an end to the inequalities that now existed, there should be 113. For instance, instead of two for the county of York, as there were at present, he thought there should be two for each riding; and so in other counties, where the present representation was not proportionate to the extent of soil and population. The next alteration which he submitted to the House, referred to the mode of return. In order to put an end to compromises, etc. he should propose, that each county or riding should be divided into grand divisions, each of which should return one representative. The only other alteration which he had to propose in the county representation, related to the qualification of electors. The right of election, instead of being confined to freeholders, as it now was, he thought should be extended to copyholders and leaseholders, who were bound to pay a certain annual rent a certain number of years. These were all the alterations which he had to propose in the county representation. The reform which he had to propose in the other branch of representation, was of a much more extensive nature. He should propose, that the remaining 400 members should be returned by one description of persons, which were householders. He did not conceive that it would be difficult in the present, as it had been found easy in other instances, to ascertain the various proportions of population in the different counties. He did not propose, however, that these proportions should be accurately observed, but that they should be regulated by local circumstances; for instance, that great towns, such as the metropolis, should require a greater number of electors to return a representative, than in places where the population was more scattered; otherwise the populous towns would obtain a too great local ascendancy. It was a part of his plan, that the country should be divided into different divisions, and that, if possible, one person should not be permitted to vote for more than one member of parliament. This scheme necessarily involved a great number of subordinary details, into which it was impossible for him to enter. In order to prevent expense, the poll ought to be taken through the whole kingdom at one time.

This was the general outline of the plan which he had to propose. To state that it could obtain any thing like exactness at once, or that it was not liable to great difficulties in the execution, would be presumptuous and foolish in the extreme. But he flattered himself it was not liable to any insuperable or fundamental objections. Upon this plan, the land-owner would find his property suitably represented; the merchant would find support in the householders; and men of respectability and talents in the different professions, would find a fair door open for getting into parliament. The only persons whom he would wish to exclude from that House, were men who were neither possessed of landed property, nor engaged in commercial enterprise, nor professors of any particular science; but men who, without property, without industry, and without talents, obtained seats in the House of Commons by the influence of great men, for the purpose, as he had said before, not of consulting for the good of the people, but of promoting their own interests. If such as he had described were the situation of the electors, what would be the situation of the elected? They would hold their seats, not on the basis of universal suffrage, but of universal representation. The qualification would be so fixed, that no man, however mean, might not hope, by honest industry and fair exertions, to obtain a seat in the House of Commons. And he begged to say, that a man, arrived at the respectable situation of being father, and consequently master of a family, having given hostages, as it were, to society, as an assurance of his interest in its welfare, was not unworthy of a share in the legislation of his country. In order to carry this plan into effect, he should move for leave to bring in a bill, which he should not propose to pass this session, but which should be brought in, lie over for discussion during the summer, and be decided upon in the course of next session. There was still another topic upon which he had not touched, namely, the duration of parliament. If the reform in the representation was adopted, but not otherwise, it occurred to him, that the duration of parliament should be limited to three years.

Having thus stated the outline of the plan, there remained little more for him to trouble the House with. One objection had always beem made to a motion for a reform, when he had brought it forward, namely, that it was an improper time to agitate the question. So far from this appearing to him to be an objection on the present occasion, that the time was one of the greatest inducements he had for bringing it forward. If he had had any doubts before upon this point, they would have been removed by the change which had taken place in the sentiments of many persons of respectability, who formerly disapproved of the substance of the measure, and doubted much its propriety, and whose support he looked for on this evening. But there were considerations of much greater weight. In what situation were we placed? In prosperity we were told, that there was no need for reform; and though the right hon. gentleman (Mr. Pitt) at one time contended for the necessity of reform, if we would shun the recurrence of the evils of the American war, he forgot his promise upon coming into power. At present, we were in a state which, God knows! was far, very far, removed from prosperity. He would ask, then, whether, in the present state of unexampled calamity, the country could go on in its present scale of expense without a check being given to those who had the direction of public affairs? If the present House of Commons had brought us near the end of our resources, what could prevent our ruin, but a change in the constitution of that House? When he looked abroad, and surveyed the face of Europe, there was no object which to him appeared so desirable to an Englishman, attached to the constitution of his country as a respectable and independent House of Commons, speaking the sentiments, and consulting for the interest of the nation at large. In France, a revolution had taken place; the principles, at least, in which it originated, whatever others might think of them, he should always defend. Stained it certainly had been with enormities, but ministers themselves had confessed that order was restored, and that they had asked pardon of God and man. For his own part, he entertained a sanguine hope, that, in the end, it would tend to the diffusion of liberty and rational knowledge all over the world. With this revolution, then, how ought the people of this country to be governed? The constitution ought to be restored to them; and when every abuse was reformed, the system would leave them nothing to regret. If you look to Ireland, you find the affairs in that country were every day becoming more alarming. God grant that a convulsion may not happen, but it can only be prevented by measures of reform and conciliation. If such an event should unfortunately take place in that country, would it not be wise to prevent all ground for discontent in this, by removing in time every just cause of complaint? How was it possible that the House could possess the confidence of the people, after having brought the country to suffer disgrace after disgrace; after being brought to the verge, if not into the gulf of bankruptcy, without witnessing one effort, on the part of its representatives, to wipe off the stains it had received, or to save it from approaching ruin? Was it believed that the debates in that House were conducted with a view to the public good? He admitted, for the sake of argument, that the side of the House with which he had the honour to act, were no more actuated than the other by motives of a pure disinterested nature; though, while he made the admission, his conscience acquitted him of the crime. Was it not in every one's mouth that the object of the one party was to keep their places, and of the other to supplant them? And if such an opinion was entertained, how was it compatible with respect?

These were the motives which induced him to submit to the House the motion which he should have the honour to propose. There was one other point, which was personal to himself, and upon which, perhaps, he ought not at all to trouble the House. As long as he held a seat in that House, he should think himself bound to perform the duty he owed to his constituents; but he considered it as unnecessary any longer to expose himself to that obloquy which he had sustained in acting the part which he found himself called upon to take in the discussions of that House. Seeing calamity succeed calamity, and that every effort of his had hitherto been ineffectual in stemming the tide of misfortune, he despaired of a continuance of his efforts being more successfull. Though he should always be present, therefore, in future, to vote for or against any measures by which the interests of his constituents might be affected, after that night, he should not think proper to trouble the House with any observations. Mr. Grey concluded with moving, "That leave be given to bring in a bill, to amend and regulate the Election of Members to serve in the Commons House of Parliament."

FINANCIAL POLICY OF WILLIAM PITT

Speech by William Pitt, the prime minister and chancellor of the exchequer, on establishing a Sinking Fund to repay the National Debt, House of Commons, 29 March 1786

Parliamentary History, XXV, 1294-1312.

Pitt's great first ministry (1783-1801) witnessed important fiscal and administrative reforms which gave stability to the financial structure. In his Sinking Fund scheme, Pitt was following along the lines laid out by Robert Walpole seventy years earlier.

Sir; The object I have to refer to this committee is, to consider of the means of decreasing the national debt. To attempt to recommend this purpose by any words, would surely be quite superfluous: the situation of this country, loaded with an enormous debt, to pay the interest of which every nerve has been stretched, and every resource nearly drained, carries with it a stronger recommendation than any arguments I could possibly adduce. That something should be done to relieve the nation from the pressure of so heavy a load, is indeed acknowledged by all: and, I trust, that in this House there is only one feeling upon the subject. To you do the public turn their eye, justly expecting, that from the trust you hold, you will think it your duty to make the most serious efforts, in order to afford them the long-wished-for prospect of being relieved from an endless accumulation of taxes, under the burthen of which they are ready to sink. Upon the deliberation of this day do they place all their hopes of a full return of prosperity, and that public security, which will give confidence and vigour to those exertions in trade and commerce, upon which the flourishing state of this country so much depends. Yet not only the public and this House, but other nations look to the business of this day; for, by the establishment of what is now proposed, our rank will be decided among the Powers of Europe. To behold this country emerging from a most unfortunate war, which added such an accumulation to sums before immense, that is was the belief of surrounding nations, and of many among ourselves, that our powers must fail us, and we should not be able to bear up under it; to behold this nation, instead of despairing at its alarming condition, looking boldly its situation in the face, and establishing upon a spirited and permanent plan the means of relieving itself from all its incumbrances, must give such an idea of our resources, and of our spirit of exertion, as will astonish the nations around us, and enable us to regain that pre-eminence to which we are on many accounts so justly entitled. The propriety and the necessity of adopting a plan for this purpose is not only universally allowed, but it is also admitted that immediate steps ought to be taken to make provision for this purpose. And I am persuaded, that whatever differences of opinion we may have in this House, no difference will this day be entertained that effectual provision be immediately made to reduce the debt of this nation.

The chief subject then before the committee is, not whether the recommendation in his Majesty's Speech should be complied with; nor even is it a matter of dispute what sum ought to be allotted for this purpose; for it seems agreed, by common consent of all, that one million annually ought to be laid aside as the means of gradually accomplishing this desirable purpose. The great points which we have to consider are:—In the first place, what measures ought to be taken to acquire a million for this purpose. Secondly, what is the way of applying it. I must here congratulate the nation upon the arrival of this wished-for-day, when all despondency and gloomy fear may be laid aside, and our prospects brightened with joy and hope. With how much pleasure am I able to add, that this can be carried into effect without laying any heavy new burthens upon the people. This is beyond the hopes of almost every man, and is indeed a subject of the greatest rejoicing to every friend of this country.

In order to be acquainted with our real situation, to see what we have and what we want, I mean to state to the committee the annual income and the annual expenditure of the nation, as the ground upon which we are to proceed with regard to the object before us. This has already been done by the select committee, who were appointed for the purpose of examining into the subject, and whose reports are now upon your table. It is a matter of much satisfaction that this mode has been taken to ascertain the sums of the revenue, and the expense of the nation. You have not the word of an individual, but the report of a committee of this House, who have given an authentic, an accurate, and a clear statement of the whole. This has been long enough published to have put it in the power of ever gentleman to examine it with attention, and I hope none have neglected it. It is so much better that every thing of that kind, every thing that contains so many figures, should be stated on paper, than be trusted to the memory, that it will not be necessary for me to detain the House long with that part of the subject.

The committee have very properly arranged their inquiries under two heads, taken from different periods. The first is, from Michaelmas 1784 to Michaelmas 1785; and the second, from the 5th of January 1785 to the 5th of January 1786. In the first period the annual receipt appears to be 15,379,182*l*.; in the second period, in the year ending the 5th of Jan. 1786, the amount is 15,397,471*l*. There never was a report upon any subject, nor upon such a subject as this, of so much consequence to the nation. The manner to which it has been drawn up, speaks the praise of the committee much higher than I am able to do by any words I could use. The clear, the precise, the accurate mode they have observed throughout the whole; the great attention which they have paid to the object for which they were appointed, deserves the highest encomiums. The care with which they have avoided all sanguine conclusions from the premises before them, can never be too much applauded. Rigorous in calculating all contingencies which might arise to baulk the hopes of the nation, and tend to disappoint their hopes of the expected surplusses; most faithful to their trust, most scrupulous with regard to the truth of their statements, shewing at once their respect for the House, their sense of the importance of the business into which they had been deputed to examine, they have proceeded to deliver in a report; which, in point of clearness, precision, just and fair deduction, stands eminently distinguished above every report I have ever seen.

The first sum they have stated as the whole revenue that has been received into the Exchequer from the 5th of January 1785 to the 5th of January 1786, is 12,499,916*l*. After this, next follow two sums, which they have thought proper to deduct from this sum, which has been received into the Exchequer. First are the arrears due from the East India Company, which ought to have been paid before, but had been respited to them, and amounts to 401,118*l*. The other sum, which in the same manner is deducted, is the excess of the window duties, but which, from the alteration of the assessments, will not be paid any longer. These two articles, therefore, being considered only as contingencies, are not reckoned as part of the yearly revenue. These two sums, then, amounting to about 457,200*l*. being deducted, leave a remainder of 12,042,690*l*. This sum, which has been paid into the Exchequer, is considered as a part of our stated yearly income, it being, each article of it, made up by taxes which are payable every year.

The rest of the sums which they have stated as the amount of the public revenue, which is something above 3,300,000*l*. arises from taxes, which, though payable yearly, have not yet been all received into the Exchequer in such a manner as to have with them their proper vouchers; but the committee thought right to add them to the sums that had been received. Of these sums there can be little doubt or uncertainty. They are collected by the officers in different parts of the kingdom, according to assessments made and returned to them: where, therefore, these taxes have not actually been received, the assessments are taken, and a calculation made from them, with which there is the greatest human probability of their agreeing; indeed, no other method more clear and conclusive could have been suggested. Of this kind is the additional Window-tax, commonly known by the name of the Commutation-tax: this amounts to 380,000*l*. from Michaelmas 1784 to Michaelmas 1785, and 253,000*l*. from the 5th of Jan. 1785 to the 5th of Jan. 1786. The additional tax also upon two-wheel and four-wheel carriages, 107,000*l*. for the latter, and 59,281*l*. for the former. The added duty on male servants, 42,000*l*. for the latter period, and 26,000*l*. for the former. Farther duty on horses, waggons, and carts, 73,601*l*. to Jan, 1786, and 59,829*l*. to Michaelmas 1785. It is impossible to say all these taxes have been received; but they have stated them in so cautious and guarded a manner, that there is little reason to doubt of their equalling, if not exceeding, the statement.

After these follow the taxes which have not been all received into the Exchequer; those which were laid on in 1784 and 1785, and not having had time for their fair and full operation. The produce of those laid on in the year 1784, at Michaelmas, amounted to 103,000*l*., and in January to 22,000*l*.; the produce of those laid on in 1785, at Michaelmas last, including the improvement of the medicine duty, amounts to 265,000*l*., and at the 5th of January to 242,000*l*. To these is added the sum of 14,000*l*. which is yearly paid at the Excise and Alienation-office in part of the civil list; and also the Land and Malt-tax, which being yearly voted, came under this head, and amount to 2,600,000*l*. All these sums added, made together, at Michaelmas 1785, 3,365,000*l*., which, added to the receipts for that year, viz. 11,874,000*l*. would produce a sum of 15,379,000*l*. But, in January 1786, the whole of the sums amounted to 3,354,000*l*., which, added to the amount of the receipts for the year, made 15,397,000*l*., only a difference of about 20,000*l*.

This, then, is the annual income of this country, and upon the true statement of which there is every reason to rely. There is, indeed, a small difference in the two statements, the one ending at Michaelmas, and the other at January; but, although I should take the smallest, it would not make any difference in the deductions I shall draw from this subject. Indeed, it is well known to those who, from their official situations, have had an opportunity of observing, that it is some time before new taxes can fairly operate. So many evasions are at first formed, and so many frauds committed, that it generally takes some time before they can be levied to their full extent; and it is owing to this circumstance chiefly that there is a difference between the two terms.

Many of the taxes laid on in the year 1784, and almost all those in 1785, are under the description I have given: and I have the greatest reason to believe they will greatly increase in their produce, when evasions are detected, and more effectual means made use of to collect them fully; and although none of them have been actually paid into the Exchequer, nor is it possible from receipt to form any judgment with regard to them, yet I am persuaded that the particular character which the committee have maintained, will appear, with regard to them, that they are stated cautiously, and within their true limits. There is one tax which I may just mention as an instance of the truth of what I have observed with regard to new taxes; that is the duty on game licences, which has produced 20,000*l*. more since the alterations it received. There is only one error that I can perceive, and that is 4,140*l*., which ought to be deducted from the produce of the taxes imposed in 1785. Surely, on a subject of this kind, the sum of 4,000*l*. is not a great deal. Some of the taxes in 1785 are stated upon very sure ground, and from what has been received since January, though not received soon enough to be laid before the committee, give reason to believe they will produce more than they are rated at. Among these particularly is the Shop-tax, the House-tax, and the Servants'-tax; the other taxes are stated on more uncertain grounds, such as the duty on pawnbrokers, and some others. Upon the whole, I do conceive, that we may rely upon this account as the real revenue of the country. The committee have stated every thing upon the best grounds the nature of the case admitted; and I have stated their results more for the sake of recalling them to gentlemen's minds than to add any thing new. My object is to shew that it is a fair deduction, and may be taken as the produce of the year from January 1785 to January 1786.

Whether or not we can rely upon this as an annual income, to continue at the same rate to this nation, is another question. I do think we may rely upon it so far as to look upon this annual income as a fund for an annual decrease of our debt; yet I do not look upon it as a certain income. Events may happen to swell this produce beyond the most sanguine calculation; and it may also happen that a disappointment may take place upon subjects so complicated in their nature. The trade and wealth of the nation is too fluctuating to admit that any average can be taken. A sudden disaster may blast all our hopes; and it may happen even that, without any disastrous event to this country, we may cut a poor figure for a year, or a number of years. I therefore do not take the liberty to make any other statement but what the committee have made, and would therefore read what the committee have said at the beginning of their report. For the reasoning stated by the committee, you (as much as they expect) have reason to conclude that this flourishing condition of our revenue will continue. We have nothing indeed to fear. We may lay despondent thoughts aside. Every thing depends upon the spirit of this House, and the resolution, the good sense, and the industry of the country, to put these things out of all doubt. It was more than could be thought possible, that, within a single year, such a success would happen. But it is not confined to one year; ever since the happy aera of the restoration of the peace, this has been more or less the case. The increase was slow at first, but constant; and the happy progress of last year shews, from pleasing experience, that we have no reason to fear its being stationary, or becoming retrograde. A great part of this flourishing appearance which trade has of late put on, and the great influx into the Exchequer, have been owing to the regulations that have been taken to crush clandestine trade. This was the more to be believed, as the increase of revenue chiefly appeared from the customs; and this gave room to hope that further great and essential improvements of the revenue might arise from wholesome regulations with regard to articles of illicit traffic. Driven from its strong hold of tea, it lurks in other petty trenches, from whence it may be effectually chased. Every thing that is done to effect this, as introducing a permanent source of revenue by making trade return into a regular channel. What has been done in this way cannot as yet have had its full operation, because, as great capitals were employed in this clandestine business, the occupation will subsist for a while, even although it is a losing trade. The measures taken two years ago, under the articles of tobacco and spirits, have caused the smuggling of these to subside to a great degree, and have much increased our revenue. In the article of salt the frauds are very considerable, and ought immediately to be redressed. But, with regard to wines, the frauds arise to so great, to so enormous a pitch, that, if we will take the effectual measures to repress them, all the deficiencies will be made up in what is stated as the annual progress of the revenue. If we have the means of doing this in our power, and do not make use of them, we must certainly suffer just blame. I intend, for my part, to bring forward very soon a plan for that purpose, which I mean to submit to the consideration of the House, and flatter myself, that, if it meets with their approbation, it will occasion a very great increase to the revenue of the kingdom. After having in this manner represented every thing in the fairest light I am able, to enable you to form a just view of the whole of the real and probable sources of our national income, I shall now proceed upon the idea that this is a true statement of our revenue, which has been laid upon your table by the committee, and that we may expect (with as much certainty as can attend any thing of this kind) that we shall enjoy an increasing revenue of 15,397,000*l.* per annum.

The next subject of our discussion is, what may be the annual expenditure of the nation. This the committee have also stated, and it amounts to 14,478,181*l.* There is a great part of the particular items, of which this sum is made up, that the committee have omitted to mention, because the sums charged have been previously stated by act of parliament. This they considered as permanent expenses, and therefore distinguish them from what is fluctuating. In the former description they considered the interest of the national debt, which is 9,275,769*l.* and with the Exchequer bills,make a sum of 9,532,000*l.*: this part contains also the civil list, 900,000*l.*; the charges on the aggregate fund, 64,000*l.*; and the appropriated duties, 66,500*l.*: the whole of this division is 10,554,000*l.* The other class of expenses include the different establishments for the defence of the nation; as the army, the navy, the ordnance, and the militia. There may be extraordinary charges for these purpose: but that the committee had not any thing to do with in the present estimate; they have stated the expense only that must be occasioned by a peace establishment, and this they have done on a very enlarged and liberal footing.

They have allowed for the navy, during peace, 18,000 men, which is more than ever had been kept up during any peace; and they allowed for this 1,800,000*l.* It must be observed that the committee did not go to state what ought to be the expense of our navy, but only what, after the deduction of all our expenses, would remain as a surplus; and therefore their business is to state every thing on the largest probable footing. They have taken the army upon the same mode of reasoning; and they allow for the charge of it a sum of 1,600,000*l.*, much greater than was in the peace establishment before the last war, when we had so numerous, but distant possessions to defend: and it is extremely probable that this may be reduced, in a short time, considerably under the sum stated in the report. The ordnance, also, is stated largely: this, however, we shall be under the necessity of keeping up: it was found that we were much wanting in this respect in the beginning of the last war; and it would be very hazardous to allow ourselves to run a similar risk in any other.

The miscellaneous services are taken upon an average of some years back; but I think it is very probable that they too have been stated higher than they will be found to be: these arose chiefly from addresses of this House to the King, for particular grants, and also from the establishments of our colonies abroad, and from bills of exchange drawn by their governors upon the treasury: these services were stated at 74,274*l.* Deducting the whole of the expenditure from the annual income, there remained a surplus of 900,000*l.*

This, then, is the sum which remains to be applied to the purpose of decreasing the annual debt: but, as the fund for this purpose ought to be a million annually, I shall move, in this committee, such taxes as will produce the sum of 100,000*l.* And I am happy to say that this may be done without laying fresh burthens upon the people. I shall move that an additional duty be laid upon spirits: they were formerly charged in what is called the wash, with 7*d.* per gallon, that was afterwards decreased to 5*d.*; I shall now raise it to 6*d.* per gallon, which will produce about 70,000*l.*, without being any encouragement to smuggling. Another I mean to lay is only a modification of a tax; a duty upon the importation of two species of timber, deals and battens: I will rate this at 30,000*l.* I shall lay another upon an article of mere luxury; upon perfumery and hair powder: these I will rate at 15,000, or 20,000*l.* So that, altogether, the sum wanted to complete the million will be made up.

I must here observe, that although this is stated to be the annual expenditure, some time must intervene before the expenditure can be reduced to this point. It must be attended to, that we are only just emerged from the most ruinous and expensive war in which this country was ever engaged. Many of the heavy burthens we incurred during that war, had not ended with the conclusion of it, but still continued, and must be expected some time to continue to hang upon us. Under the head of the navy, many ships that had been laid upon the stocks were to be finished. They have been built too far to allow them to go back, and to be lost to the public; and they were, besides, necessary to increase our naval strength to an equality with our powerful neighbours. This was so considerable, that, although the committee had stated the peace establishment of the navy at 1,800,000*l.* yet the expense attending this present year was 600,000*l.* above it, though it may not, perhaps, be more than 560,000*l.* In the army also, the exceedings were much above the common run of the expense on that establishment; and this amounted to nearly 300,000*l.* This is chiefly expended in a way where justice and humanity forbid economy—to the reduced officers on half-pay, and to the widows of officers; a part of the navy extraordinary is taken up in the same way. These two sums would go almost to annihilate the surplus, if it was to be applied to these purposes within the year. But in truth and fact they are not annual charges, they are only the remaining sums of the expenses of last war, and must cease altogether in a few years. It would, therefore, be unfair and unwise to charge them as annual expenditures. In four years the great burthen of them, that of the ship-building, will cease: nor can this be effected sooner. I conceive, therefore, that you must look to a future average to come at your expense. It appears to me that this may be done with great safety; and I have not a doubt but that resources are to be found that will justify this mode of proceeding, and be sufficient to keep every thing well without burthening the nation. And if we judge in this manner, the expectations raised by the public will doubtless be amply satisfied.

Now, therefore, I wish to call the attention of the committee to this object. I am clear that we immediately appropriate this million to the payment of the debt, even although the time when we shall have this surplus free from all other expenses, cannot be exactly ascertained. I myself am persuaded, that, as I have already intimated, we have certain extraordinary resources to which we may apply to liquidate this sum, without the addition of new taxes. Let us then examine what sums they are for which we have to provide the means of payment. This extraordinary expense chiefly arises from the navy: and it was occasioned by the very large contracts into which we had entered for the building of ships. On this account 2,400,000*l.* had been called for this year, as the extraordinary expense of the navy; but this would not continue to be required after the ships now building were completed. This would decrease each year, and would be, in every probability, reduced to a standing sum for a peace establishment in the year 1790. This expense, and the very liberal establishment of 1,800,000*l.* would enable us to possess a marine the most flourishing this country ever beheld. As the estimate for the navy stands this present year, it is 600,000*l.* above what is stated at the settled peace expense in the year 1790. But it is to be noticed, that, after two new ships have been completed, which will be in the course of this year, this extra sum will be reduced to 400,000*l.*; this, in four years, amounts to the sum of 1,600,000*l.*, and, with the additional expense of this year, to 1,800,000*l.*

With regard to the army, the expenses also had been very great, but were of a nature which also tended to diminish, in time, but which it was impossible to restrict. What this chiefly arose from was, as I mentioned before, from pensions to officers widows, and to officers upon half pay; and this sum amounted to about 260,000*l.* Under this head of expense comes also that occasioned by bills of exchange from our colonies abroad: these amounted to very considerable extra sums of late years. But when we recollect, that we are not now obliged to keep up the immense establishments abroad that we have been accustomed to do, we may expect these will diminish very rapidly. Our chief expense at present arises from Canada; and from the well-known prudence, honour, economy, and disinterested spirit of the gallant officer who is now appointed to that command, we have every reason to hope that a very considerable saving of expense will be produced. I need only mention his name to enforce conviction of whatever I say in his praise; the great and gallant officer I speak of is sir Guy Carleton. Those who are acquainted with his military talents and military conduct, deservedly hold him high indeed. But from his no less acknowledged disposition to economy, from his vigilance and activity, we may say, that, whatever can be done by care and attention will be effected. And at present, even the extraordinary expense is not very considerable, as far as it has come to our knowledge; but we have reason to think that a saving may be produced on this establishment.

Another matter of expense comes properly under this head; and it is what the House have already acknowledged to be a just demand upon the justice and generosity of this nation, that is, a provision for the American sufferers. Their situation demands the most tender consideration. Nor would I choose to mention any sum for this purpose: if it was a great one, it would raise the expectations of those unhappy people; and I would not wish to say any thing more to them than that I hope there will be a generous and liberal regard paid to their melancholy and unfortunate circumstances. Another matter of extra expense under this head, is the ordnance; but as Parliament have not decided what is to be the expense of it, and have already disapproved going into large additions to this part of the national establishment, I shall not say what sum will be necessary for this purpose. All these different subjects of expense are, in a great measure, uncertain; nor is it possible at present to say, with minute accuracy, to what particular sum they will amount: but I think a sum of 300,000*l.* is likely to be the call for those purposes, and to be provided for in the course of two or three years.

There is another matter of expense which the committee have not mentioned in their reports, and which is the subject of the King's message this day; this will be a matter before Parliament. The impossibility of reducing the civil list within the sum of 900,000*l.* allowed by Parliament, proceeded chiefly from that part being mortgaged for the payment of certain Exchequer-bills, by annual payments of 50,000*l.,* which reduced it from 900,000 to 850,000*l.* Of these Exchequer-bills there remains due about 180,000*l.;* and there was besides, an arrear against the civil list of about 30,000*l.* more. The Crown had long been embarrassed by this incumbrance; and that it may be entirely removed, I shall move, on this day se'nnight, when his Majesty's message shall be taken into consideration, for the sum of 210,000*l.*

The whole, therefore, that we are now to find the means of providing for is, the extra expenses of the navy and army, which I have stated liberally at 3,000,000*l.*

This is to be accounted for in the course of four years, after which time we shall have a clear annual surplus of a million, unincumbered with any demands upon the national income. Although this sum should be funded, and ways and means found to answer the interest, it would not occasion any great burthen upon the people; but the state of this country at present is so very flourishing, that I am happy to say that it will not be necessary to burthen the people with any taxes upon this account, but certain extraordinary resources are to be found within ourselves that will abundantly answer what is here required. The committee first make mention of Lotteries; which are, indeed, a resource that Government can have recourse to, but which is in itself so encouraging to a spirit of gambling, that it is doubtful whether it ought to be adopted. The spirit of gambling is indeed so deeply rooted, that I am afraid it is of little consequence whether a lottery be withholden or not, and it is always a resource equal to 140,000*l.*; however, as it is not resolved by Government whether there shall be one this year, I shall not put it to account.

The next head they mention is that of Army Savings, and this bears the appearance of being very considerable: and indeed a very considerable sum under this description had been paid into the Exchequer; this consisted chiefly of money that had been appropriated to different services and which had not been expended. This had been very considerable in the peace following the war before the last; and from the extent of the immense grants during this war, we might expect much more. Of these sums, together with the surplus of several funds, the amount of 450,000*l.* had already been paid into the Exchequer. There are, besides this, immense sums in the hands of former paymasters, which, it is to be expected, we shall be able in a little time to come at. The mode, hitherto, of keeping the army accounts has been extremely open to abuse; and accordingly paymasters have taken every advantage to keep the public money in their hands. Notwithstanding this, it is to be hoped that as soon as the commissioners have time to call in the out-standing accounts, they will be enabled to collect a very great sum: this is justified as far as they have gone; but the labour is extremely great, as they have to go through no less than one hundred and eighteen regiments of foot, and as many regiments of horse and dragoons, whose accounts for non-effective men had not been examined into for twenty years together. One regiment they had gone through already had produced 22,000*l.* for the use of Government; and although I cannot be so sanguine as to hope that every regiment will produce as much, yet I think I may state the total, including contracts and other articles of abuse, at the sum of 100,000*l.*

The next source mentioned by the committee, is a balance due from the East India Company for the subsistence of troops in India, and on account of victualling the navy. This amounted to 600,000*l.*; and there was a probability of its being paid in a very short time. The committee also mentioned the Unclaimed Dividends in the funds, that a part of them might be applied consistently with the safety of the public creditors to the public use. The Crown lands are also a source of produce; but as it is not determined how to dispose of them, I will not mention them in the account; and that perhaps it might be thought right to apply them to the relief of the American loyalists.

The great article upon which the committee dwell, and upon which they founded their expectations of a permanent surplus, is the improvement of our revenue by proper regulations to discourage smuggling, and give room to the fair trader to reap those advantages which are due to his labours, and which must in every light add to the amount of the customs; this, both by encouraging the legal merchant, and bringing those goods to a regular entry that would have been clandestinely disposed of. The regulations which had been already made in this respect, had not had room for their full operation, and yet they have occasioned a very great addition to the revenue of the nation, and might be expected still to increase, as this increase is regular and progressive, and not the sudden effect of the suppression of our warlike operations. It is indeed not easy to be conceived, by those not conversant in those subjects, how numerous and how artful the frauds are which are daily put in practice in every subject of the national revenue. One article, that of wine, required immediate remedy; and I flatter myself with very great sums indeed from this branch. The consumption of wine in this country is not diminished, and yet it does not appear that the average of last year compared with the year 1746, is equal to it in produce of revenue, so far that it sinks below it no less than 240,000*l.* Without laying a burthen upon the country, there are many regulations to be made in the article of spirits that will increase the revenue from that branch of trade. The article of tobacco is another object that attention must be paid to: and I have no doubt that from the regulations that will be proposed in these articles, at least 300,000*l.* annually may be produced. In another session of parliament I intend also to bring about a consideration of the customs, which will undoubtedly add greatly to the produce of the revenue: we shall not, however, enter upon this at present; I have stated enough to the House. Those who compare our annual sums with our annual expenditure, may here see sums equal to apply to the deficiencies without any new demands, or any new burthens upon the people. I have stated what these deficiencies may be, as matters of uncertainty; but if it be about 3,000,000*l.* the whole may be provided for without any new burthens of any sort. Why, it may be said, do I not fund this? For this good reason; that I shall not, in all probability, have occasion to raise it: even if it were funded now, there could be little hazard of its being made good.

I may now proceed to lay apart the million: but before I enter upon that part of the discussion which relates to the particular mode of applying this annual sum, it will be proper to consider the effect it will have. If this million, to be so applied, is laid out, with its growing interest, it will amount to a very great sum in a period that is not very long in the life of an individual, and but an hour in the existence of a great nation: and this will diminish the debt of this country so much as to prevent the exigencies of war from raising it to the enormous height it has hitherto done. In the period of 28 years the sum of a million, annually improved, would amount to four millions per annum. But care must be taken that this fund be not broken in upon: this has hitherto been the bane of this country: for if the original Sinking Fund had been properly preserved, it is easy to be proved that our debts at this moment would not have been very burthensome: this has hitherto been, in vain, endeavoured to be prevented by acts of parliament: the minister has uniformly, when it suited his convenience, gotten hold of this sum, which ought to have been regarded as most sacred. What then is the way of preventing this? The plan I mean to propose is this: that this sum be vested in certain commissioners, to be by them applied quarterly to buy up stock; by this means, no sum so great will ever lie ready to be seized upon any occasion, and the fund will go on without interruption. Long, and very long has this country struggled under its heavy load, without any prospect of being relieved: but it may now look forward to an object upon which the existence of this country depends; it is, therefore, proper it should be fortified as much as possible against alienation. By this manner of paying 250,000*l.* quarterly into the hands of commissioners, it would make it impossible to take it by stealth; and the advantage would be too well felt ever to suffer a public act for that purpose. A minister could not have the confidence to come to this House and desire the repeal of so beneficial a law, which tended to directly to relieve the people from their burthens.

The persons who should be appointed to this commission should be of rank and distinction, to secure them from suspicion, and to give, as far as character could go, a belief of their discharging it with faithfulness. In the first place, I think it right that the respectable commoner, whoever he shall be, who fills the chair of this House, should be placed at the head of it. Parliament, in instituting a commission of so much importance towards the support of national credit and prosperity, could not more solemnly, nor more pointedly promulgate its high sense of the duty by which that commission is bound, than by appointing the first member of this House to be at the head of it. I think also, without ascribing any thing to myself, that the person who holds an office so intimately connected with finance as the Chancellor of the Exchequer, ought to have a place in this commission. There is another person, who, from his high rank, as well as from his virtues and reputation, I think ought to have a share in this business, and he is also, at present, a member of this House: this is the Master of the Rolls. The governor and the deputy-governor of the Bank of England I think ought also to be of the number. Also the accountant-general of the high court of Chancery, who, by virtue of his office, was already employed in the money of all suitors and wards in the funds, and increasing, by that means, the capital, by the accumulation of compound interests. Such as these persons I shall propose to be appointed to this trust, when the Bill comes before the committee. There might be some difficulty in determining how to regulate the conduct of the commissioners in the purchase of stock; but that might, perhaps, be left to their own discretion. But, although it might be proper to leave the manner of doing this to their own prudence, it would not be so proper, by any means, to leave to them the regulation of the time when they were to purchase: this, I think, ought to be on every transfer day in the quarter, at regular periods, and in equal sums.

I am very far from ascribing any merit to myself in suggesting this scheme; but, I cannot but think myself peculiarly happy in having a task to perform so very different from any of my predecessors, and that, instead of expending the money of the public, I should have the great good fortune to be led to set about to diminish our burthens. This plan, which I have now the honour to bring forward, has long been the wish and hope of all men; and I am proud to flatter myself that my name may be inscribed on that firm column now about to be raised to national faith and national prosperity. I shall not detain the House longer, because I am persuaded that they must be already tired of the tedious detail upon which I have been under the necessity of entering. The time when the operation of this fund is to begin. I think should be upon the 5th of July. At that time let 250,000*l.* be paid into the hands of the commissioners for this purpose; and after that, continued quarterly: this will make 750,000*l.* to be expended during the three quarters. I shall just mention upon what I found the expectations of having a surplus this year, of 750,000*l.* after paying the current expenses of the year; by which there will appear a surplus over and above the stipulated annual one of some hundred thousand pounds.

	£
The House had voted for Seamen	936,000
Ordinary of Navy	1,645,000
Extraordinary	800,000
	3,281,000
Army Plantations, Extraordinaries, etc.	1,966,261
Ordnance	333,000
Civil List, etc. making the sum voted	8,956,261
Exchequer Bills	2,500,000
Sum not yet voted	810,824
The total of the supplies would then be	12,477,085

The Ways and Means are as follow:

Land and Malt tax	2,750,000
Exchequer Bills	5,500,000
Surplus of the Sinking Fund, in hand	582,000
Estimated produce of 1786	3,444,000
Arrears from East India Company Life Annuities, etc.	1,086,000
Amount of Ways and Means for the current year 1786	13,362,480
From which deduct the surplus, as above	12,477,085
Remainder	00,885,395
From this sum deduct the three quarterly payments, beginning on the 5th of July, of 250,000*l.* per quarter, for the reduction of our debts, amounting to	750,000
And there would be a neat surplus of	135,395
But if, as the Committee stated, the revenue do rise according to the latest experience, there would still be a farther difference in our favour of	313,699
Making in this case a clear excess accruing at Christmas next, (above the regular surplus) of the sum of	449,093

I shall now move, "That it is the opinion of this committee, that the sum of one million per annum be granted to his Majesty, to be vested in Commissioners, and to be by them applied to the reduction of the National Debt, and that the same be charged upon, and made payable out of the surplusses, excesses, overplus monies, and other revenues, composing the fund commonly called the Sinking Fund."

Speech by William Pitt, the prime minister and chancellor of the exchequer, proposing consolidation of the customs and excise duties, House of Commons, 25 February 1787

Parliamentary History, XXVI, 626-33.

Mr. Pitt rising again, observed, that it would be unnecessary for him to dwell upon the great importance of the subject, and the advantages which must inevitably result from it; they were in themselves so obvious, that it was more difficult to account for its having been delayed so long, than to prove the propriety of now adopting it. The increasing commerce of the country on one hand, and the accumulated burthens on the other; the various additions which it had been found necessary to make to the national income, by augmenting almost every subsisting duty, and the concomitant progression of the resources from whence that income was supplied, had so widely exceeded the expectations of our ancestors and all the grounds of calculation, on which they founded their system of finance, that the principles which they adopted, as suited to the narrow and confined scale of their public exigency and resources, were no longer applicable to the present state either of the trade or the revenue of the country. The consequences of thus retaining the old principles under the altered circumstances of the country, were, in several points of view, highly detrimental to the interests of the nation. In the first and most material instance, they were productive of great inconvenience to individuals, as well to the merchants as to the officers of the customs, from the difficulty they occasioned in calculating and ascertaining the amount of the several sums to be paid by the former; and they were also, in some degree attended with an actual loss to the revenue. Mr. Pitt went very much at length into the origin and progress of our revenue, as it at present stands, and particularly that branch which arises from the customs, stating, that the first institution of the present subsisting duties of custom, was made by statute the 12th of Charles 2, under the names of tonnage and poundage—the first of those was an imposition on wines, laid on by the quantities imported; and the other was a proportional duty calculated by value on all other articles. This last duty of poundage, calculated on the value of the several articles, was of a nature liable to great inaccuracy and irregularity—the value of the goods was ascertained by a book of rates, and computed on the quantities of the goods either with respect to gage, to weight, or to *taille*—it was not a real value that was fixed upon them, so that the duty should bear a certain proportion to that real value, but an arbitrary value, perhaps according to their actual standard at the time of imposing the duty, yet which must, from the natural fluctuations of trade and manufactures, be necessarily liable to many changes and alterations. The consequence of such a mode of taxation when it was laid on by bulk, was, that in goods of one general description the duty was always the same, whether upon the more perfect or the coarser manufacture, by which means it either operated as a prohibition to the latter, or was not at all felt by the former. There was, besides, another mode by which duties were imposed; which was by a proportion to the value on goods not rated, and this was the real and actual value of the goods, as sworn to by the importer. This principle of taxation, being once adopted, was pursued in every fresh subsidy which had been granted for the payment of the interest of the several loans that were raised from time to time. In some instances it had operated by imposing additional duties, calculated by a per-centage on the duty at present paid; in others it had laid a farther duty on a different denomination of the commodity, either with respect to its value, its bulk, its weight, or its number; and proceeding in this manner from period to period, it had at length, by the numerous additions so made, and the unbounded increase of the articles of commerce, produced that mass of confusion, which was now so universally complained of, as productive of such an infinity of inconvenience and delay to those whom it was the interest of the country to have as free from all unnecessary embarrassments as possible—the mercantile part of the nation.

Adverting next to the nature and extent of those inconveniences which hence arose to the merchants, Mr. Pitt represented to the committee, that almost all of the additional subsidies had been appropriated to some specific fund, for the payment of certain specific annuities, and that there must therefore be a separate calculation made at the Custom-house for each of the different subsidies; and that from the great complexity of the whole system, scarcely any one merchant could be acquainted, by any calculations of his own, with the exact amount of what he was to pay. It was, at first view, perhaps to be wondered at, that consequences seriously bad, had not as yet resulted from this evil; but there were two causes by which that circumstance might be accounted for. The first was, that some persons employed in the Custom-house, whose whole time being dedicated to the business, were more conversant with it than any merchant could be supposed to be—had, for the ease and convenience of the traders and merchants, arranged a general view of the Customs, in the form of a book of rates, which was, to a certain degree, found to be useful; but the utility arising from such a compilation, could not be of any very long standing, when it was considered that there was, every session of parliament, some alteration or another made in several of the duties, and each of those alterations following the old principle, totally unhinged and overturned the use of every preceding printed calculation. But even if this disadvantage did not attend the Custom-house officers book of rates, it yet only tended to relieve, in a very inconsiderable degree, the grievance complained of; for although the calculations contained in the book might have been ever so accurate, yet the merchant could not go to the Custom-house and enter his goods immediately, by paying down the sum stated in the book of rates, but must wait, as if such book never existed, until all the usual calculations on each subsidy had been made, the several acts by which such subsidies had been granted having so directed; and thus, in point of time, nothing was saved by the merchant. The other cause, by which the inconvenience was in a degree obviated, was one to which, for many very good reasons, as speedy a stop as possible should be put. The officers of the Customs, having, from constant practice and experience, acquired a greater facility in making the necessary calculations than the merchant could be supposed to have done, were the only persons to whom the merchant could apply for assistance and direction. Thus, the merchant was not only in a great degree left at the mercy of the officers, but the officers themselves, who were intended to be a check upon the merchants, were forced to become their agents—a procedure repugnant to every principle of reason and policy. Those abuses which he had stated to exist in the Customs, obtained also, though not to the same extent, in the Excise, and, in a certain degree, in one other great branch of revenue, the Stamps. He should therefore include them in his general plan.

The mode by which he proposed to remedy this great abuse was, by abolishing all the duties which now subsisted in this confused and complex manner, and to substitute in their stead, one single duty on each article, amounting as nearly as possible to the aggregate of all the various subsidies already paid; only in general where a fraction was found in any of the sums, to change the fraction for the nearest integral number, usually taking the higher, rather than the lower. There could, he said, be no great objection to this very trifling rise in the amount of the duties, as either such rise, or an equivalent diminution must take place, or the confusion consequent on fractions still continue. This advantage from the fractions to the integral would produce an increase in the revenue to the amount of about 20,000*l.* per annum, and would lay upon the public a burthen most amply compensated by the great relief which the merchant would experience from the whole of the plan. Still there would be some diminution of revenue in certain branches of it, where it might be found expedient to substitute the lower instead of the higher integral number in place of the fraction. He here enlarged on the advantages of the plan, as well with regard to the convenience which the merchant and officers of the Custom-house would experience, as the benefit which must result to the revenue by freeing it from the clogs and fetters with which it was loaded, and instead of the obscurity which it now laboured under, rendering it so clear and distinct, that no mistake or error could possibly take place in any future inquiries which might be had upon the subject. In some few articles it was his intention to introduce regulations of much greater extent than what he had stated, particularly in certain species of timber, which he would explain more at length to the committee when he came to the resolution on that head. And in respect to the duty on drugs he should propose to make a very considerable reduction, as the duties on those articles were so high as almost to drive the fair trader out of the market, and throw the whole into the hands of the smuggler. On such goods as were not to be rated, in consequence of this new system, it was his intention to propose certain duties proportioned to the sworn value of the articles, which duties, in general, would not exceed the sum of 27½ per cent.

It might now be proper to observe in what degree the consolidation of the duties might affect the security of the public creditor. As many of the subsidies which it was proposed to abolish were particularly appropriated to the payment of certain specified annuitants, and as some of the annuitants were entitled to a valuable priority of payment, it was doubted whether such right of priority might not be infringed upon by abolishing those funds from which such prior payments were to issue, and consolidating them all into one general mass. But, this valuable priority it was by no means his intention to affect, as the plan which he should adopt would leave it at the option of all persons enjoying such right of priority to continue in possession of it, or relinquish it, as they might think proper. This priority of payment arose from the terms of the several loans by which certain funds were raised for the payment of the interest of such loans, and the surplusses of those funds to go to the aggregate fund, out of which aggregate fund other annuities were to be paid. The right of priority might as well be maintained by paying them all out of one general fund, as by paying first one set of annuitants out of several funds, and the remaining annuitants out of the surplusses of those funds, provided that, out of that general fund, the first payments were actually made to those annuitants entitled to that priority. No injury could possibly arise to the public credit by such an arrangement; and no real benefit resulted to those who enjoyed the right of prior payment, the resources of the country being equally bound for the payment of the whole; and the payments already made to the annuitants were not paid out of the respective funds appropriated to the different annuities; but the whole of that business was, at this moment, conducted at the bank, nearly in the same manner as it would be, when the whole of the revenue was to be consolidated into one general fund. The State, he apprehended, had a right, consistent with its good faith to its creditors, to make such alterations in the nature of its securities as it should see to be convenient and necessary, provided that on every such alteration it took care to substitute such a security as should be substantially equivalent to that which was so changed; and he challenged the attention of the committee to a most particular observance of every part of the plan that was in any way connected with the public faith, in order that it might be most religiously adhered to: but to dispute this right of the Legislature, to modify the security which it afforded to the public creditors, would, if carried to its full extent, absolutely preclude the possibility of ever making any alteration in any tax which might be once adopted. There could not, however, he flattered himself, be any ground of objection, on the head of public faith, to the system which he meant to propose; for, he should recommend, that not only all the several funds then consolidated should become chargeable with the public debt, but that every other resource of the country of any description whatsoever, should be a collateral security for the payment of those debts—even the aids of the current year. Yet, notwithstanding his opinion of this right of the Legislature to modify its own securities, he was still of opinion, that it ought not to be done, if it could possibly be avoided, without the consent of the several creditors, which it had been the constant practice of Parliament to take, whenever it proceeded upon any such measure. This consent was to be taken by allowing a proper time for the public creditors to make their objections; and, if in that time none were made, to construe their silence into acquiescence. This mode he was desirous to adopt in the present instance. On the subject of the funds, he contended, that none of them could possibly be affected in any disadvantageous manner by the new modification.

Having thus, he hoped, clearly demonstrated the eligibility of this plan, as well from the advantages likely to result from it to trade and revenue, as from its being completely free from any objection in respect to public credit; having, he trusted, made it perfectly intelligible to every gentleman, he should proceed to explain how he proposed to carry it into execution. He was persuaded, that every gentleman who approved of the plan, would feel a desire to co-operate with him as strenuously as possible to carry it into effect, and in so very complicated and detailed a subject would be willing to dispense with as much form as possible towards its speedy completion. He should not, therefore, enter at present into the detail of all the several resolutions by which the plan was to be supported, but should satisfy himself with having them all understood as having been read *pro forma*; proposing, however, on such of them as were of most consequence, and likely to be attended with the greatest variety of opinion, to trouble the House with his sentiments more at large, and pledging himself that he would not suffer any resolution of the whole volume (for they amounted to nearly three thousand in number) which appeared to him of considerable importance to pass, without calling the attention of the committee particularly to it—that a subject of such importance might have the most ample discussion in all its essential points. He had given no ordinary share of attention to this business—he had not left one unconsulted from whom any information could be obtained—the plan had been referred to the Board of Revenue, and had received their perfect approbation—the greatest diligence had been used to circulate it among the most diligent and respectable of those persons who were most immediately concerned in its operation—the trading interest; and he was happy to say, that it was received by them all with the highest satisfaction, and he flattered himself that he came forward on the subject, supported by the best of all possible authorities, the information of the most enlightened persons on all parts of the business, and the universal consent of those who were most interested in the event. But as it was a question of such great importance, and ran into so very extensive a detail, he recommended it to gentlemen to pay it their most serious attention in all its branches, that the good intentions of those who were instrumental in framing it might not be in any instance frustrated by those mistakes, inaccuracies, or even clerical errors, to which so very complicated a subject must necessarily be liable. He should content himself for the present with barely moving a general preliminary resolution, by which the committee would go no farther than the adoption of the main principle, and the discussion of the more minute questions which must arise upon it, would be left open to their future judgment; and as many of those questions would require a very ample consideration, he should not wish to proceed farther in the committee until the ensuing Thursday. He concluded by moving a resolution to the following purport:—"That all duties of Customs, Excise, and certain duties of Stamps, do cease and determine, and that other duties be substituted in their stead."—In the motion were included certain specific exceptions, as the duties on malt, mum, cyder, perry, etc.

Speech by William Pitt, the prime minister and chancellor of the exchequer, on the state of public finances, House of Commons, 17 February 1792

Parliamentary History, XXIX, 816-30, 833-38.

The paragraph in his majesty's speech which has been referred to this committee, has already announced to us, and to the public, the most welcome intelligence which it was possible for us to receive; it has raised the pleasing expectation, that, after all the difficulties with which we have struggled, the period is at length arrived, when, by the flourishing state of our finances, we may be enabled to enter on a system which will afford immediate and substantial relief to a large proportion of our constituents, and at the same time give additional security and effect to that important, and, I trust, inviolable system which has been adopted for the reduction of the national debt.

In proceeding to detail the measures which I shall propose with a view to these important objects, I shall consider it as my first and most indispensable duty to state, as distinctly as possible, every circumstance which can be necessary for enabling the committee, not only to form a satisfactory judgment on the general result of our situation, but to examine the various calculations and reasonings on which that result is founded; and in attempting to execute so extensive a task, it is no small relief to my mind to reflect, that the repeated discussions which have taken place on questions of finance, have rendered them, in a great degree, familiar to the House and to the public; and that, by the measures which have been adopted for simplifying the nature and form of the public accounts, they are at length freed from that obscurity and intricacy in which they were formerly involved, and are rendered so clear and intelligible, that there is no man who may not, with a small degree of attention, become as fully master of the subject, as those whose official duty has led them to make it their peculiar study. The first point to which I wish to call the attention of the committee, is the amount of what may be considered as the probable future income of the country; and I shall begin by recapitulating the result of the accounts for different years, which have been already stated. The produce of the permanent taxes in the last year, from the 5th of Jan. 1791, to the 5th of Jan. 1792, appears to have been 14,132,000*l.*; which, with the addition of 2,558,000*l.* (being the average amount of the annual duties, on land and malt, as stated by the select committee last year), will make the total revenue of the year 16,690,000*l.* To this there must be added a sum, which in the accounts on the table, has been included in the produce of the separate and temporary taxes imposed last year, for the purpose of defraying the expense of the Spanish armament, but which, in fact, makes part of the general and permanent revenue. It will be recollected that an addition was made last year to the duties on bills and receipts, and the addition was consolidated with the old duty. The whole of this consolidated duty has been carried to the account of the separate fund; but only the excess beyond the former produce can be considered as arising from the additional duty; and a sum equal to the former produce, being about 40,000*l.*, is to be added to the other sums which I have stated, making the total revenue for the last year 16,730,000*l.* The produce of the year preceding was 16,437,000*l.* after deducting the produce of a fifty-third week, which was included in the account of that year. The principal branches of the revenue being paid from the respective offices into the exchequer, by weekly payments, on a stated day, a fifty-third weekly payment in the course of a year, recurs nearly in the proportion of once in every period of six years. In judging, therefore, of the probable future amount of the revenue, the produce of the fifty-third week ought not to be included in any one particular year, and it is therefore here deducted; but, on the other hand, one-sixty part of its amount, being about 32,000*l.*, ought to be added to the average formed on any number of years. The average formed on the two last years, without this addition, would be 16,583,000*l.*, and with it 16,615,000*l.* The produce of the year ending on the 5th of January, 1790, was 15,991,000*l.*, and the average of the last three years (making the same allowance for the fifty-third week) amounts to 16,418,000*l.* The produce of the year ending the 5th of January, 1789, was 15,565,000*l.*, and the average formed on the last four years, amounts to 16,212,000*l.* It appears, therefore, that the actual produce of the year 1791, being 16,730,000*l.*, exceeds by above 500,000*l.* the average formed on the last four years;—that it exceeds the average formed on the last two years by above 100,000*l* —the average on the last three years by nearly 300,000*l.*, and the actual produce of the last year but one, by nearly the same sum. If, then, I form my calculation of our future revenue, not on the separate amount of any one of these particular years, but upon the average amount of four years, during which there has been a constant increase, I am certainly not attempting to lead the committee into too favourable an opinion; but I am rather wishing to recommend that degree of caution, which the importance of the subject always deserves, and particularly at the present moment, when we are holding out hopes of relief, in which, above all things, we should be careful to avoid the chance of disappointment. I propose therefore to rest my computation upon this average produce of four years, being 16,212,000*l.*, and this sum, on a general view of the subject, we may safely assume, as not being likely to exceed the permanent annual revenue of the country.

I shall next desire the committee to compare the statement of the annual revenue, with that of the permanent annual expenditure; and I shall take as the basis of this comparison, the estimates contained in the report of the committee appointed in the last session to examine the public income and expenditure, only making such corrections as arise from certain additions on the one hand, and reductions on the other, which at that time were not foreseen. The whole permanent expenditure as stated by the committee, (including therein the interest of the national debt, the million annually issued for the reduction of debt, the civil list, and all the permanent charges on the consolidated fund, as well as all the establishments which are annually voted) is 15,969,00*l.*; to which there was added in the course of the last session (but subsequent to the report of the committee) the sum of 12,000*l.* charged on the consolidated fund, for the establishment of the duke of Clarence; and a further sum of about 12,000*l.* for defraying the expense of the separate government of the province of Upper Canada. Besides this, some further provisions will be necessary for the establishment of the duke of York, on the happy event of his marriage; and this may probably occasion an addition of 18,000*l.* The amount of these additional charges is 42,000*l.*

I have next to state those reductions which, as far as we can at present judge, may be expected to take place in our permanent establishments, although they cannot operate to their full extent in the persent year. The first article of reductions is under the head of the naval service, in which I am inclined to hope that the number of seamen may be reduced to 16,000, being 2,000 less than last year. This will produce a saving of 104,000*l.*, and a further saving of about 10,000*l.* may probably be made in the estimate for the works to be carried on in the dockyards.— In the actual establishment of the army, (after allowing for the proposed additions, which were explained when the army estimate was voted), there may probably be a diminution of about 50,000*l.;* and 36,000*l.* will be saved in consequence of the expiration of the treaty for the Hessian subsidy, which, under the present circumstances, his majesty has not thought it necessary to renew. If, therefore, allowance is made on the one hand for the addition of 42,000*l.*, and for the reductions in the army and navy, amounting together to about 200,000*l.*, the estimate of the permanent annual expenditure will stand at 15,811,000*l.;* the amount of the income of the last year, as I have before stated it, exceeds this sum by 919,000*l.;* the average of the amount of the two last years exceeds it by 804,000*l.;* the average of the three years by 607,000*l.;* and that of the four years on which I rest my calculations, by 401,000*l.* This, then, is the comparative view which I take of the permanent income and expenditure; and; according to the lowest of these calculations, there remains a disposable annual surplus of about 400,000*l.*, after defraying the expense of all the establishments, and applying the annual million to the reduction of the public debt.

Before I submit to the committee the manner in which I would propose to distribute this surplus in future, I wish to advert to the supply, and ways and means for the present year, because in these there will be found some additional articles both of expenditure and of receipt. The supply for each year, as gentlemen are aware, includes all the establishments and the charges for the various branches of the public service, together with all incidental charges which are defrayed by annual grants. It is independent of the interest and charges of the national debt, of the million annually issued to the commissioners of the civil list, and of the other charges on the consolidated fund. The amount of all these articles is 11,391,000*l.*, and being permanently fixed, forms no part of the supply voted in each year. For the navy we have voted this year 16,000 seamen, of which the charge is 832,000*l.;* for what is called the ordinary of the navy, 672,000*l.;* and for the extraordinary building and repairs (including the work in the dockyards) 350,000*l.* We have also voted 131,000*l.* towards the reduction of the navy debt, which is sufficient for defraying the whole of the extra expenses of the naval department in the last year, (including those of the armament) as far as they have not been already defrayed by the surplus arising from former grants. These sums together make 1,985,000*l.*—The establishment of the army for the present year is 1,474,000*l.;* the extraordinaries 277,000*l.;* besides 63,000*l.*, advanced for the troops in India, which will ultimately be repaid by the company. The total voted for the army is 1,814,000*l.*—For the ordinary expenses of the ordnance there has been voted 221,000*l.*; for the extraordinaries nearly 157,000*l.*; and under the head of services performed in former years, but unprovided for, 44,000*l.*, making in the whole the sum of 422,000*l.* The estimates for the colonies and plantations, amount to about 31,000*l.* Various miscellaneous services, including the expense of African forts, the Mint, the roads in Scotland, the maintenance and transportation of convicts, the sum paid for printing Journals, and some other articles, (particularly a compensation to the owners of African vessels for losses sustained in consequence of the late regulations, and likewise to the settlers removed in the year 1786 from the Mosquito shore), amount in the whole to 114,000*l.*—There are two other articles which always form part of the annual statement of the supply, under the heads of deficiency of grants, and estimated deficiency of the land and malt, the nature of which is fully explained in the report of the committee of the last session, and for which allowance is made, though in a different shape, in the comparison of the permanent income and expenditure. The amount of the deficiency of grants is 436,000*l.*, which includes in it the sum of 123,000*l.* repaid to the bank, in consequence of the diminution of their floating balance, out of which 500,000*l.* had been advanced for the supply of last year; and the deficiency on the land and malt may be estimated at 350,000*l.* To these articles I shall propose to add two others; the first is 100,000*l.* out of the supplies of the present year, to be applied towards the discharge of the exchequer bills issued on account of the Spanish armament; by which means we shall be enabled to repeal immediately the additional duty on malt, the produce of which for the present year was appropriated to the separate fund created for that purpose. The second is an additional sum to be issued in this particular year, beyond the annual million, for the reduction of the national debt; and, on the comparison of the supply with the ways and means for the year, I think it will appear, that this sum may be safely stated at 400,000*l.* I have now enumerated all the articles of the supply, except the debentures to the American loyalists. These I omit, because they are nearly balanced by the profit on the lottery, which I do not mean to include in the statement of ways and means.

The first article of the estimated ways and means for the present year is the amount of the annual duties on land and malt, which may here be taken at 2,750,000*l.*, because exchequer bills will be issued on the credit of these duties to that amount; and the deficiency in the actual produce of the duties will, according to the usual practice, become a charge on the supply of future years, as the deficiency of the produce of former years is a charge on the supply of the present year. The next article consists of the sums which may be expected to be applied towards defraying the supply of the year out of the produce of the consolidated fund. This fund includes in it the whole amount of all thy permanent taxes, and is applicable, in the first instance, to the payment at the end of each quarter of the permanent charges which I have before had occasion to enumerate. Any surplus which remains after payment of those charges is, from time to time, disposeable by parliament; and a sum equal to the expected amount of that surplus in the course of a year is always voted as an article of ways and means. In voting the ways and means, it has for some time been the practice to calculate from the 5th of April in the current year, to the 5th of April following; so that the grants for the supply of each particular year are not expected to be completed till the expiration of the first quarter in the subsequent year. In the present instance, however, there remained a sum of 155,000*l.* out of the actual surplus of the consolidated fund on the 5th of January, 1792, after making good the whole sum granted for the service of the year 1791, which had not been estimated to be completed till the quarter ending the 5th of April, 1792. The increase of the revenue having defrayed the whole charge, and furnished this actual surplus, as early as on the 5th of January last, and the 5th of April next, will yield a further surplus (after paying the interest of the debt, and other fixed charges) which instead of being applied, as was estimated, to the service of the year 1791, will be applicable to the supply of the present year, and to this is to be added the growing produce of the consolidated fund for the succeeding twelve months, from the 5th of April, 1792, to the 5th of April, 1793.

The expected amount of the disposeable surplus on the 5th of April next, I state at 486,000*l.*; and in forming this calculation, I suppose the whole produce of the permanent taxes, during the current quarter, to be equal to the average formed from the corresponding quarters in each of the last four years, which amounts to 2,970,000*l.* To this is to be added the expected produce, during this quarter, of the temporary taxes appropriated to defray the expenses of the Spanish armament, because, up to the 5th of April, those taxes are directed to be carried to the consolidated fund, and the proportion of the expense of the Spanish armament, which was charged on the supply of 1792, has been already defrayed out of the produce of the revenue up to the 5th of January. Supposing these taxes to yield in this quarter a sum equal to their average produce in the three quarters since they have taken effect, their amount will be nearly 200,000*l.*, and this, added to the sum before stated, will make a total of 3,170,000*l.* From this is to be deducted the amount of the interest of debt, and other fixed charges on the consolidated fund for this quarter, which is about 2,684,000*l.* leaving a remainder of 486,000*l.*

The further amount of the sum, which may be expected to arise from the surplus of the consolidated fund, between the 5th of April, 1792, and the 5th of April, 1793, I propose to estimate in like manner on the average of the four last years, making the necessary deduction on account of the taxes which I shall on this day propose to you to repeal.

The total amount of the revenue on that average, exclusive of land and malt, was 13,654,000*l.* The annual amount of the taxes proposed to be repealed is about 223,000*l.*: but as some arrears will be received from these taxes subsequent to their repeal, the sum to be deducted on this account in the present year, will not be to that amount, and may be estimated at about 163,000*l.* The total amount of the interest of debt and other fixed charges on the consolidated fund is (as I have already stated) 11,391,000*l.* There will, therefore, on these suppositions, remain a disposeable surplus of 2,100,000*l.*, to which is to be added a sum of 200,000*l.* which there is good ground to suppose will be re-paid to the public during this year from the balances of different accounts. These articles of ways and means added together amount to 5,691,000*l.* The articles of supply which I have enumerated, amount in the whole to 5,654,000*l.*, so that the ways and means exceed this supply by 37,000*l.*

I have already observed that, in the supply of the present year, there are some articles included, which exceed considerably the estimate of the permanent annual expenditure in the several branches of the public service; these consist principally of the additional sum of 400,000*l.* proposed to be issued to the commissioners; the sum of 100,000*l.* granted in lieu of the malt duty; the sum granted for the navy debt; that repaid to the bank; the advance on account of the troops in India, and some excess in the army estimate; in the unprovided estimate of the ordnance; in the miscellaneous services and the deficiency of grants; and they all appear peculiar to the present year, and not likely to recur in future, except as far as an annual addition may hereafter be made to the sums issued for the reduction of the national debt.

In speaking however of the future expenditure, I am aware that contingencies may occasionally arise, which cannot at present be foreseen; but, as far as I have now the means of judging, I am not aware of any specific article in which there is likely to be an excess beyond the permanent estimate, except in the amount of the small sums which may be still necessary for completing the works for the protection of the dock-yards at home, and the expense of carrying into execution the plan of fortifications in the West Indies, which will be a subject of separate consideration. And with a view to these articles, or to other contingencies that may arise, I have the satisfaction of thinking, that they will probably be fully balanced by extraordinary resources, beyond the calculated amount of the present income. On the result, then of these different statements, I think there is no reason to doubt, that we may, in the present year, apply an additional sum of 400,000*l.* to the reduction of the national debt, and repeal the temporary duty on malt, at the same time allowing for the repeal of permanent taxes to the amount of about 200,000*l.* and for the application of nearly an equal annual sum in future, as a permanent addition to the fund for the discharge of the national debt.

The next point for consideration, is, the propriety of the general principle which I have assumed as the foundation of my plan; that of distributing the surplus of our revenue, and applying it in equal proportions to the diminution of taxes, and the reduction of debt. I have thought this the wisest plan which we can adopt, because, by combining present relief with permanent credit and security, it seems most likely to prevent any temptation hereafter to break in, with a rude hand, on the system for the gradual reduction of our debt. At the same time, this addition to the sinking fund, with the aid of a further sum from a distant source, which I shall mention presently, and, independent of any further increase of revenue, will enable us to make a rapid progress in this important work, and in a very short space of time to reach a point, which perhaps not long since was thought too distant for calculation.

I shall beg the indulgence of the committee while I state this rather more at large, because it is connected with other considerations which may lead to important measures for enforcing and strengthening our system for the discharge of the national debt. In attempting to form any calculations of the proportion of debt which may be discharged at any particular time, there are some contingencies which can only be stated hypothetically. They may, however, now be reduced to a narrower point than they have been in any former period. One material circumstance which has necessarily been considered as uncertain, is the price of the funds; but, as far as relates to the 3 per cents, this uncertainty seems to be in a great measure removed, with a view to the question under consideration; for, supposing the present state of prosperity to continue, no calculation can reasonably be formed on the idea of paying off any large portion of this stock but at par. Under such circumstances, the principal question would be, whether the fund for the reduction of debt ought to be applied to the redemption or purchase of the 3 per cents, with a view to the reduction of interest on the 4 per cents, and on the 5 per cents? or, whether it should be applied to the redemption, first, of the 4 per cents, and afterwards (as soon as they become redeemable) of the 5 per cents? Without entering into minute disquisitions on this point, I will only state, that, according to the most accurate calculations which I have seen, the mode of applying the sinking fund to the purchase of the 3 per cents, and making use of the general improvement of credit in order to reduce the interest of the 4 per cents, and of the 5 per cents (when redeemable), and to carry the saving of interest as an addition to the sinking fund, will, on the whole, be quicker in its operation than the other mode, though not in any very considerable degree. I shall therefore suppose, in the first instance, that an addition of 400,000*l.* should be applied in the present year to the reduction of debts, and an annual addition, from the revenue for the next four years, of 200,000*l.* When the debentures to the American loyalists shall be discharged (which will be in about four years subsequent to the present) the profits arising from the lottery, which, as I have already stated, are now set against this article of expenditure, will be left free, and will form an addition to the annual surplus. If the addition shall be distributed in the same manner as is now proposed, with respect to the present surplus, and if the tickets should continue to bear their present price, a further annual sum of 150,000*l.* (after allowing for the repeal of taxes to the same amount) will be applicable to the reduction of debt. Previous to this period, the 4 per cents may naturally be supposed to have been reduced in the first instance to 3½, and ultimately to 3 per cent.; and the saving by this reduction of interest will amount at first to about 160,000*l.,* and when completed, to about 320,000*l.* By the operation of the present sinking fund, and of these additions to the redemption of the 3 per cents at par, it may be expected that 25 millions of three per cents will have been paid off in the year 1800, after which the 5 per cents become redeemable; and supposing the 3 per cents to continue at par, a further saving may then in a short time be made, by converting the 5 per cents to 3 per cents, which will amount in the whole to above 360,000*l.* and which I likewise suppose to be carried to the aid of the present sinking fund. The material question which on these suppositions it is natural to ask, is, when will the sinking fund arise to the amount of 4 millions per annum, which is the limit after which, according to the act of 1786, it is no longer to accumulate, but the interest of the capital which it thenceforth may redeem, is to be left open for the disposition of parliament? It will amount to that sum, on the suppositions which I have stated, in 1808, a period of about fifteen years from the present time.

I am not, indeed, presumptuous enough to suppose, that when I name fifteen years, I am not naming a period in which events may arise, which human foresight cannot reach, and which may baffle all our conjectures. We must not count with certainty on a continuance of our present prosperity during such an interval; but unquestionably there never was a time in the history of this country, when, from the situation of Europe, we might more reasonably expect fifteen years of peace, than we may at the present moment. But in looking forward to this very period, there arises one of the considerations to which I have referred, and which may lead us still to amend and enforce our system for the reduction of debt.

When the sum of four millions was originally fixed as the limit for the sinking fund, it was not in contemplation to issue more annually from the surplus revenue than one million; consequently the fund would nor rise to four millions till a proportion of debt was paid off, the interest of which, together with the annuities which might fall in in the interval, should amount to three millions. But as, on the present supposition, additional sums beyond the original million are to be annually issued from the revenue, and applied to the aid of the sinking fund, the consequence would be that, if that fund (with these additions carried to it) were still to be limited to four millions, it would reach that amount, and cease to accumulate, before as great a portion of the debt is reduced as was originally in contemplation. This effect would be more considerable, if, instead of an annual addition of 350,000l. in the whole, which is the amount on which I have calculated, the further increase of the revenue should admit, (as it probably may) of the application of a larger surplus; and in either of these cases, although the ultimate amount of the sinking fund would be equal to what was originally intended, and it would reach that point sooner, yet it would bear a less proportion to the capital of the debt, which it would afterwards have to discharge, than it would have done according to the original plan. In order to avoid this consequence, which would, as far as it went, be a relaxation in our system, I should propose, that whatever may be the additional annual sums applied to the reduction of debt, the fund should not cease to accumulate till the interest of the capital discharged, and the amount of expired annuities should, together with the annual million only, and exclusive of any additional sums amount to four millions.

But I confess, that, in the present situation of the country, I am inclined to think that we ought not to stop here. What we did in 1786 was, perhaps, as much as could be attempted under the circumstances of that time. At present we ought not to confine our views to the operation of the sinking fund, compared with the debt now existing. If our system stops there, the country will remain exposed to the possibility of being again involved in those embarrassments, which we have, in our own time, severely experienced, and which, apparently, brought us almost to the verge of bankruptcy and ruin. We ought therefore to look forward, in order to provide a permanent remedy against the danger of fresh accumulation of debt, in consequence of future contingencies. And this, as I shall explain more particularly on some future occasion, may, I am persuaded, be effected without the danger of any inconvenience or embarrassment, which can counterbalance the magnitude of the object. The measure which I have in view is, to enact, that whenever any loan should take place in future, unless raised by annuities which would terminate in a moderate number of years, there should of course be issued out of the consolidated fund, to the commissioners for the reduction of the national debt, an additional annual sum, sufficient to discharge the capital of such loan, in the same period as the sinking fund, after reaching its largest amount, will discharge what would then remain of the present debt. The committee will recollect, that the idea which I am now stating is not new to my mind, though I have never before proposed it as a permanent regulation. Two years from this time, when I had the mortification of thinking that the country might be engaged in an expensive war, in consequence of our discussions with the court of Spain, I gave notice that I should propose to follow, very nearly, this system, with respect to any loans which might then be necessary. I will not, however, enlarge further on this subject at present. I have already stated enough to show that the system which I wish to propose is calculated to provided effectually for the discharge of the public debt, at the same time that it diminishes the burthens of the people; and that, in consulting our own immediate ease, we cannot be accused of sacrificing the permanent interests of posterity.

Supposing therefore, that the distribution which I have suggested should appear to the House fit to be adopted, and that taxes to the amount of 200,000*l.* per annum should now be taken off, I will beg leave next, for the purpose of bringing the whole subject under consideration, to state the particular taxes, which if nothing preferable is suggested by others, I should propose to repeal. And, in making this selection, there are two objects which I wish principally to keep in view. The first, to which it is very material to attend, is, that the actual relief felt by the public should be proportioned to the amount of revenue which is relinquished. Under these descriptions those taxes seem most clearly to be included, which are raised by the mode of assessment, because as they are paid directly out of the pocket of the individual, and do not pass through circuitous channels like taxes upon the articles of consumption, where the tax is often blended with the price of the commodity, there can be little doubt that the relief intended to be given will in these instances be effectual to its fullest extent. The other object which I naturally have in view, is, that the relief intended should apply peculiarly to that class, to whom, on every account, it ought first to be extended,—I mean the most necessitous, and the most industrious part of the community.

Combining these objects, the first article to which I have directed my attention is, the temporary duty on malt, imposed in the last session. The three next taxes which I shall state, are permanent taxes, which fall under the description of being raised by assessment, and which have also the further advantage of extending relief widely, and where we must most wish it to be extended.—The first is the tax upon female servants, which is certainly paid by the poorer class of house-keepers, and which is charged upon about 90,000 different families; the amount is 31,000*l.* The next is, the tax upon carts and waggons, which applies to the whole of the yeomanry of the country, to all those who are occupied in agriculture, who pay in this shape a sum not indeed very considerable, but which perhaps is felt, from the inconvenience and trouble which it occasions, more than from the burthen itself. About 90,000 persons are affected by this tax also, of which the amount is nearly 30,000*l.* The third tax applies to the poorest of all the orders of the community,—I mean the tax on houses having less than seven windows, which are exempted from the payment of any other tax, but that of three shillings. The amount of the sum is small, but to those who are the objects of it, its repeal will be a substantial relief and comfort, and it will at least be a pledge and earnest of the attention of parliament to their interests. It extends, I believe, to between three and four hundred thousand houses, and its amount of about 56,000*l.* The next and last which I have to mention is the last additional tax of a halfpenny per pound on the article of candles, which presses more, perhaps, than any other tax on consumption, upon the class of whom I have been speaking; and if this tax is repealed from a given day, and the duty upon the stock in hand is allowed to all the manufacturers and dealers in that article, I believe there can be no question that the reduction of the price will be in proportion to the duty repealed: its amount is about 106,000*l.;* and the total of all these taxes is 223,000*l.* . . . .

Having gone thus far, having stated the increase of revenue, and shown that it has been accompanied by a proportionate increase of the national wealth, commerce, and manufactures, I feel that it is natural to ask, what have been the peculiar circumstances to which these effects are to be ascribed? The first and most obvious answer which every man's mind will suggest to this question, is, that it arises from the natural industry and energy of the country: but what is it which has enabled that industry and energy to act with such peculiar vigour, and so far beyond the example of former periods?—The improvement which has been made in the mode of carrying on almost every branch of manufacture, and the degree to which labour has been abridged, by the invention and application of machinery, have undoubtedly had a considerable share in producing such important effects. We have besides seen, during these periods, more than at any former time, the effect of one circumstance which has principally tended to raise this country to its mercantile preeminence—I mean that peculiar degree of credit, which, by a two-fold operation, at once gives additional facility and extent to the transactions of our merchants at home, and enables them to obtain a proportional superiority in markets abroad. This advantage has been most conspicuous during the latter part of the period to which I have referred; and it is constantly increasing, in proportion to the prosperity which it contributes to create. In addition to all this, the exploring and enterprising spirit of our merchants has been seen in the extension of our navigation and our fisheries, and the acquisition of new markets in different parts of the world; and undoubtedly those efforts have been not a little assisted by the additional intercourse with France, in consequence of the commercial treaty; an intercourse which, though probably checked and abated by the distractions now prevailing in that kingdom, has furnished a great additional incitement to industry and exertion.

But there is still another cause, even more satisfactory than these, because it is of a still more extensive and permanent nature; that constant accumulation of capital, that continual tendency to increase, the operation of which is universally seen in a greater or less proportion, whenever it is not obstructed by some public calamity, or by some mistaken and mischievous policy but which must be conspicuous and rapid indeed in any country which has once arrived at an advanced state of commercial prosperity. Simple and obvious as this principle is, and felt and observed as it must have been in a greater or less degree, even from the earliest periods, I doubt whether it has ever been fully developed and sufficiently explained, but in the writings of an author of our own times, now unfortunately no more (I mean the author of a celebrated treatise on the Wealth of Nations), whose extensive knowledge of detail, and depth of philosophical research, will, I believe, furnish the best solution to every question connected with the history of commerce, or with the systems of political economy. This accumulation of capital arises from the continual application of a part at least, of the profit obtained in each year, to increase the total amount of capital to be employed in a similar manner, and with continued profit in the year following. The great mass of the property of the nations is thus constantly increasing at compound interest; the progress of which, in any considerable period, is what at first view would appear incredible. Great as have been the effects of this cause already, they must be greater in future: for its powers are augmented in proportion as they are exerted. It acts with a velocity continually accelerated, with a force continually increased, "Mobilitate viget, viresque acquirit eundo." It may indeed, as we have ourselves experienced, be checked or retarded by particular circumstances—it may for a time be interrupted or even overpowered; but, where there is a fund of productive labour and active industry, it can never be totally extinguished. In the season of the severest calamity and distress, its operations will still counteract and diminish their effects;—in the first returning interval of prosperity, it will be active to repair them. If we look to a period like the present, of continued tranquillity, the difficulty will be to imagine limits to its operation. None can be found, while there exists at home any one object of skill or industry short of its utmost possible perfection;—one spot of ground in the country capable of higher cultivation and improvement; or while there remains abroad any new market that can be explored, or any existing market that can be extended. From the intercourse of commerce, it will in some measure participate in the growth of other nations, in all the possible varieties of their situations. The rude wants of countries emerging from barbarism, and the artificial and increasing demands of luxury and refinement, will equally open new sources of treasure, and new fields of exertion, in every state of society, and in the remotest quarters of the globe. It is this principle which, I believe, according to the uniform result of history and experience, maintains on the whole, in spite of the vicissitudes of fortune, and the disasters of empires, a continued course of successive improvement in the general order of the world.

Such are the circumstances which appear to me to have contributed most immediately to our present prosperity. But these again are connected with others yet more important. They are obviously and necessarily connected with the duration of peace, the continuance of which, on a secure and permanent footing, must ever be the first object of the foreign policy of this country. They are connected still more with its internal tranquillity and with the natural effects of a free but well regulated government. What is it which has produced, in the last hundred years, so rapid an advance, beyond what can be traced in any other period of our history? What but that, during that time, under the mild and just government of the illustrious princes of the family now on the throne, a general calm has prevailed through the country, beyond what was ever before experienced: and we have also enjoyed, in greater purity and perfection, the benefit of those original principles of our constitution, which were ascertained and established by the memorable events that closed the century preceding? This is the great and governing cause, the operation of which has given scope to all the other circumstances which I have enumerated. It is this union of liberty with law, which, by raising a barrier equally firm against the encroachments of power, and the violence of popular commotion, affords to property its just security, produces the exertion of genius and labour, the extent and solidity of credit, the circulation and increase of capital; which forms and upholds the national character, and sets in motion all the springs which actuate the great mass of the community through all its various descriptions. The laborious industry of those useful and extensive classes (who will, I trust, be in a peculiar degree this day the object of the consideration of the House) the peasantry and yeomanry of the country; the skill and ingenuity of the artificer; the experiments and improvements of the wealthy proprietor of land; the bold speculations and successful adventures of the opulent merchant and enterprising manufacturer; these are all to be traced to the same source, and all derive from hence both their encouragement and their reward. On this point therefore let us principally fix our attention, let us preserve this first and most essential object, and every other is in our power! Let us remember, that the love of the constitution, though it acts as a sort of natural instinct in the hearts of Englishmen, is strengthened by reason and reflection, and every day confirmed by experience; that it is a constitution which we do not merely admire from traditional reverence, which we do not flatter from prejudice or habit, but which we cherish and value, because we know that it practically secures the tranquillity and welfare both of individuals and of the public, and provides, beyond any other frame of government which has ever existed, for the real and useful ends which form at once the only true foundation and only rational object of all political societies.

I have now nearly closed all the considerations which I think it necessary to offer to the committee. I have endeavoured to give a distinct view of the surplus arising on the comparison of the permanent income (computed on the average which I have stated) with what may be expected to be the permanent expenditure in time of peace, and I have also stated the comparison of the supply, and of the ways and means of this particular year. I have pointed out the leading and principal articles of revenue in which the augmentation has taken place, and the corresponding increase in the trade and manufactures of the country; and finally, I have attempted to trace these effects to their causes, and to explain the principles which appear to account for the striking and favourable change in our general situation. From the whole result, I trust I am entitled to conclude, that the scene which we are now contemplating is not the transient effect of accident, not the short-lived prosperity of a day, but the genuine and natural result of regular and permanent causes. The season of our severe trial is at an end, and we are at length relieved, not only from the dejection and gloom which, a few years since, hung over the country, but from the doubt and uncertainty which, even for a considerable time after our prospect had begun to brighten, still mingled with the hopes and expectations of the public. We may yet, indeed, be subject to those fluctuations which often happen in the affairs of a great nation, and which it is impossible to calculate or foresee; but as far as there can be any reliance on human speculations, we have the best ground from the experience of the past, to look with satisfaction to the present, and with confidence to the future. "Nunc demum redit animus, cum non spem modo ac votum securitas publica, sed ipsius voti fiduciam et robur assumpserit." This is a state not of hope only, but of attainment; not barely the encouraging prospect of future advantage, but the solid and immediate benefit of present and actual possession.

On this situation and this prospect, fortunate beyond our most sanguine expectations, let me congratulate you, and the House, and my country! And before I conclude, let me express my earnest wish, my anxious and fervent prayer, that now in this period of our success, for the sake of the present age and of posterity, there may be no intermission in that vigilant attention of parliament to every object connected with the revenue, the resources, and the credit of the state, which has carried us through all our difficulties, and led to this rapid and wonderful improvement;—that, still keeping pace with the exertions of the legislature, the genius and spirit, the loyalty and public virtue of a great and free people, may long deserve, and (under the favour of Providence) may ensure the continuance of this unexampled prosperity; and that Great Britain may thus remain for ages in the possession of these distinguished advantages under the protection and safeguard of that constitution, to which, as we have been truly told from the throne, they are principally to be ascribed, and which is indeed the great source, and the best security of all that can be dear and valuable to a nation.—Mr. Pitt concluded with moving his first resolution, viz. "That it is the opinion of this committee, that, from and after the 5th of April 1792, the duties charged by an act, made in the 31st of his present majesty, intituled, 'An Act for granting to his majesty additional duties upon malt,' do cease and determine."

Bank Restriction Act, 3 May 1797

37 Geo. 3, c. 45   *Statutes at Large*, XLI, 210-16.

This act confirmed the suspension of cash payments by the Bank of England as proclaimed in an Order in Council of 24 February 1797. The drain of bullion due to heavy war expenditures led to this inflationary and controversial measure. Cash payments were resumed in 1821.

Whereas, by minute of his Majesty's privy council, made on the twenty-sixth day of *February* one thousand seven hundred and ninety-seven, upon the representation of the chancellor of the exchequer, stating, that from the result of the information which he had received, and of the enquiries which it had been his duty to make respecting the effect of the unusual demands for specie that have been made upon the metropolis, in consequence of ill-founded or exaggerated alarms in different parts of the country, it appeared, that unless some measure was immediately taken, there might be reason to apprehend a want of a sufficient supply of cash to answer the exigencies of the publick service; it was declared to be the unanimous opinion of the board, that it was indispensably necessary for the publick service, that the directors of the bank of *England* should forbear issuing any cash in payment until the sense of parliament could be taken on that subject, and the proper measures adopted thereupon for maintaining the means of circulation and supporting the publick and commercial credit of the kingdom at this importunate conjuncture; and it was ordered, that a copy of the said minute should be transmitted to the directors of the bank of *England*, and they were thereby required, on the grounds of the exigency of the case, to conform thereto until the sense of parliament could be taken as aforesaid: and whereas, in pursuance of the said minute, the said governor and company of the bank of *England*, have since the said twenty-sixth day of *February* one thousand seven hundred and ninety-seven, forborne to issue cash in payments, except for purposes for which the issue of cash was deemed unavoidable; and it is necessary that the restriction contained in the said minute, although not warranted by law, should be confirmed, and should be continued for a limited time by the authority of parliament: be it enacted by the King's most excellent majesty, by and with the advice and consent of the lords spiritual and temporal, and commons, in this present parliament assembled, and by the authority of the same, That all acts done by the said governor and company of the bank of *England*, or by their order or direction, in pursuance of the said minute of council, shall be, and the same are hereby ratified and confirmed; and that all and every persons and person who have or hath been concerned in doing any such acts, or any matter or thing relating thereto, shall be, and are and is hereby saved harmless, indemnified, and discharged, in respect thereof, as well against the King's majesty, his heirs and successors, as against all and every other persons and person; and that all suits and proceedings whatsoever touching or concerning any matter discharged by this act, shall be, and the same are hereby made void and of no effect to all intents and purposes; any law, statute, or usage to the contrary notwithstanding.

II.   And be it further enacted by the authority aforesaid, That, from and after the passing of this act, it shall not be lawful for the said governor and company to issue any cash in payment of any debt or demand whatsoever, except according to the provisions herein-after contained; and that during the continuance of the restriction hereby imposed on payments by the said governor and company in cash, no action or suit shall be prosecuted against the said governor and company to compel payment of any note of the said governor and company expressed to be payable on demand, or to compel payment of any note of the said governor and company made payable otherwise than on demand, which the said governor and company shall be willing to exchange for any note or notes of equal amount expressed to be payable on demand, or to compel payment of any sum of money whatsoever by the said governor and company, which the said governor and company shall be willing to pay in notes of the said governor and company expressed to be payable on demand; and it shall be lawful for the said governor and company during the continuance of the restriction aforesaid on payments in cash, to apply to the court wherein any action or suit shall be brought, or shall be depending, against the said governor and company, to stay proceedings therein, in a summary way; and in case such action or suit shall be brought to compel payment of any note or notes of the said governor and company made payable on demand, it shall be lawful for the said governor and company to apply to the said court to stay all proceedings in such action or suit until the expiration of the time herein-after limited for the continuance of such restriction as aforesaid, and such court shall stay all proceedings accordingly; and in like manner it shall be lawful for the said governor and company to apply to any court in which any action or suit shall be brought or depending for the purpose of compelling payment by the said governor and company of any note of the said governor and company payable otherwise than on demand, or of any other debt or demand whatsoever, to stay all proceedings against the said governor and company in such action or suit, on payment of such sum of money as shall appear to be justly due, or which might be recovered in such action or suit, by delivery of notes of the said governor and company for the amount thereof expressed to be payable on demand, if the party or parties to whom such money shall appear to be due shall be willing to accept payment thereof in such notes, and thereupon such court shall order all proceedings to be stayed accordingly; but if the party or parties entitled to any such money shall refuse to accept payment thereof by delivery of such notes of the said governor and company, expressed to be payable on demand as aforesaid, the said court shall order all proceedings against the said governor and company in such action or suit to be stayed until the expiration of the time herein-after limited for the continuance of such restriction on payments in cash as aforesaid: provided always, That if it shall appear to such court to be necessary for the purpose of ascertaining the amount of any demand on the said governor and company, or otherwise for the furtherance of justice, that any proceedings should be had for any such purpose, it shall be lawful for the said court to permit proceedings to be had in any such action or suit for such necessary purpose only, or to ascertain the amount of such demand, in a summary way, as the nature of the particular case may require, and as shall be consistent with the restriction on payments in cash hereby imposed: provided also, That no costs shall be recovered against the said governor and company, in any action or suit which, during the continuance of the restriction aforesaid, shall be brought or prosecuted for the purpose of compelling payment by the said governor and company of any debt or demand, unless the court wherein the same shall be brought or prosecuted shall be of opinion that the same was necessary for the purpose of ascertaining the amount of such debt or demand, or the title thereto, and in such case such court may direct the payment of such costs by the said governor and company in their notes expressed to be payable on demand, if the party or parties entitled to such costs shall be willing to accept such notes; and if such party or parties shall refuse to accept such notes, then such court shall stay all proceedings to compel payment of such costs until after the expiration of the restriction on payments by the said governor and company in cash, herein contained.

III. Provided always, and it is hereby enacted by the authority aforesaid, That nothing in this act contained shall extend to restrain the said governor and company from issuing any sum of money less than twenty shillings in cash in payment of any debt or demand not amounting to twenty shillings, or in payment of so much of any larger debt or demand as shall be a fractional part of twenty shillings over and above the residue of such debt or demand; or from issuing any sum of money in cash for the services of the army, navy, or ordnance, in pursuance of an order of his Majesty's privy council, stating the special purpose for which such issue shall be required, and the necessity for the same; all which orders of council shall be laid before both houses of parliament within three days after the date of each of such order, if parliament shall be then sitting, and if not, then within three days after the sitting of parliament.

IV. Provided always, and be it enacted, That it shall not be lawful for the said governor and company, during the continuance of the restriction on payments of cash imposed by this act, to issue any sum of money in cash, or in notes of the said governor and company, by way of loan or advance, for or on account of the publick service, except to an amount not exceeding six hundred thousand pounds, on the credit of exchequer bills, to be issued by virtue of an act of the present session of parliament for raising the sum of eighteen millions by way of annuities; any law, usage, or statute, to the contrary notwithstanding.

V. Provided always, and be it further enacted by the authority aforesaid, That, from and after the seventh day of *April* one thousand seven hundred and ninety-seven, during the continuance of the restriction by this act imposed on payments by the said governor and company in cash, it shall nevertheless be lawful for the said governor and company to accept, from any person or persons whatsoever, any sum or sums of money, in cash, not being less than five hundred pounds, in exchange for notes of the said governor and company, of equal amount, upon an engagement from the said governor and company to pay to such person or persons, during the continuance of such restriction as aforesaid, cash in exchange for any note or notes of the said governor and company, payable on demand, to such an amount, not exceeding in the whole three fourths of the sum of money which shall have been so paid by such person or persons to the said governor and company in cash, and in such proportions, and at such intervals, as shall be expressed in such engagement; and it shall be lawful for the said governor and company to pay in cash such sum and sums of money as shall be required to be so paid, according to the terms of such engagement, to the amount, in the proportions, at the times, and in the manner therein to be expressed; any thing in this act contained to the contrary notwithstanding.

VI. Provided always, and be it further enacted by the authority aforesaid, That it shall be lawful for the said governor and company, notwithstanding the restriction imposed by this act, to advance, for the accommodation of the persons dealing as bankers in *London, Westminster*, and the borough of *Southwark*, in cash, any sums of money, not exceeding one hundred thousand pounds in the whole, to be paid to such persons, at such times, in such proportions, and in such manner, as to the said governor and company shall seem expedient.

VII. Provided always, and be it further enacted, That it shall and may be lawful to and for the said governor and company of the bank of *England*, upon application being made to them, by or on the behalf of the treasurer of the bank called *The Bank of Scotland*, established by an act of the parliament of *Scotland*, in one thousand six hundred and ninety-five, or by or on the behalf of the cashier of the bank called *The Royal Bank of Scotland*, incorporated by royal charter, dated the thirty-first day of *May* one thousand seven hundred and twenty-seven, to issue and pay to such treasurer or cashier respectively, or to such person or persons as they shall respectively appoint to receive the same, for the sole use of the said banks, such sum or sums of money, in gold or silver, as may be required, not exceeding the sum of twenty-five thousand pounds for each of the said banks; any thing herein contained to the contrary thereof in anywise notwithstanding.

VIII. And be it further enacted by the authority aforesaid, That all payments in notes of the said governor and company expressed to be payable on demand, which have been made since the said twenty-sixth day of *February* one thousand seven hundred and ninety-seven, or which shall be made during the restriction on payments by the said governor and company in cash, herein contained, shall be deemed payments in cash if made and accepted as such; any law, statute, or usage, to the contrary thereof notwithstanding. . . .

X. And be it further enacted by the authority aforesaid, That, during the continuance of the restriction on payments by the said governor and company in cash, by this act imposed, all sums of money which now are or shall become payable for any part of the publick revenue, shall be accepted by the collectors, receivers, and other officers of the revenue, authorised to receive the same, in notes of the said governor and company, expressed to be payable on demand, if offered to be so paid (fractional parts of the sum of twenty shillings only excepted).

XI. Provided always, and be it enacted, That it shall and may be lawful for the governor and company of the bank of *England*, during the continuance of this act, to issue cash, out of any cash which shall have come into the hands of the said governor and company subsequent to the twenty-sixth day of *February* last, and which shall be at their disposal, in payment of any debt or demand whatsoever, or of any part or proportion of any debt or demand whatsoever, upon their giving five days notice in writing to the speaker of the house of commons of their intention so to do, any thing in this act to the contrary thereof in anywise notwithstanding; which notice the speaker of the house of commons is hereby required to cause forthwith to be inserted in the *London Gazette*, and a copy thereof to be affixed on the *Royal Exchange* in *London*.

XII. And be it further enacted by the authority aforesaid, That this act shall be in force and have continuance, so far as the same restrains the said governor and company from issuing cash in payments, until the twenty-fourth day of *June* one thousand seven hundred and ninety-seven.

XIII. And be it further enacted by the authority aforesaid, That this act, or any clause, matter, or thing herein contained, may be repealed, altered, or varied, in any manner whatsoever, during the present session of parliament.

PITT'S INCOME TAX

Pitt's proposal for a temporary graduated income tax to finance war expenditure was adopted. The unpopular tax was abolished in 1816, but reintroduced permanently in 1842.

Speech by William Pitt, the prime minister and chancellor of the exchequer, House of Commons, 3 December 1798

Parliamentary History, XXXIV, 1-21

Before I proceed to submit to the committee the very important matters which form the subject of this day's consideration, I conceive it necessary to state the amount of the total services of the present year, and of the ways and means applicable to those services. The total sum voted for the ordinaries and extraordinaries of the navy and transport services amounts to 13,642,000*l.* being the same sum, within a very small amount, as was granted last session. The next head of expense is the army, the estimates of which amount to 8,840,000*l.* The extraordinaries, to be incurred in 1798, were stated at 3,200,000*l.* There was also a vote of credit for one million, applicable to unforseen expenses. This vote of credit will cover all the extraordinary expenses to the end of the year. But with respect to the vote of credit for this year, one million will be wanted to discharge that amount issued in exchequer bills. Under the article, then, of army expenditure, there remain the extraordinary services of the year 1799, which I may put at two millions. Thus the total amount, under the head of army will be 8,840,000*l.* including the one million for the discharge of exchequer bills issued, and two millions for the extraordinary services of 1799. Under the head of ordnance services there has been voted 1,570,000*l.* The above sums, with the addition of the miscellaneous services, swell the total of the supply to 29,272,000*l.*

Towards raising this supply the same resources will be applicable as are applicable at all periods, whether of peace or of war. The land and malt have always been taken at 2,750,000*l.* There remains the lottery, 200,000*l.* and the growing produce of the consolidated fund, which I take at 1,500,000*l.* In addition to this, a tax was laid in the last session upon the exports and imports founded upon the peculiar situation of our trade, as it then stood. The tax has not only yielded to the full amount of what I estimated it at, but has even exceeded it. That duty I estimate at 1,700,000*l.* The above articles form a total of 6,150,000*l.* The remainder must be raised either by a tax within the year, in the same manner as the assessed tax bill of last year, or by a loan. The sum to be provided for is upwards of 23 millions. Gentlemen will recollect, that, in the debates upon the subject of the assessed taxes last session, two fundamental principles were established as the rule by which we should be guided in providing for the supplies for the service of the year. These were, first, to reduce the total amount to be at present raised by a loan; and next, as far as it was not reducible, to reduce it to such a limit, that no more loan should be raised than a temporary tax should defray within a limited time. In the first place, the tax acceded to by the House last session was for the purpose of providing for the supplies of the year; and in the next place, for the purpose of extinguishing the loan raised in that year. From the modifications, however, which that measure underwent, the produce was considerably diminished. Other means, indeed, were adopted to remedy the deficiency thus occasioned. The voluntary and cheerful efforts which, so honourably to the country, came in aid of the deficit of the assessed taxes, and the produce of the exports and imports beyond the estimate, brought the amount of the sums raised to that at which they had been calculated. The different articles were estimated at 7½ millions, and this sum is fully covered by the actual receipt under the different heads. The produce of the assessed taxes, under all the modifications, and all the tricks and evasions, is yet four millions. I had taken it at four and a half after the modifications were adopted. This deficiency is supplied by the excess on the head of voluntary contributions. Instead of 1,500,000*l.* the voluntary contributions already exceed two millions; and the sum of 7½ millions for which credit was taken, has been effective to the public service.

Satisfactory as it must be to review the circumstances to which we owe these advantages, and the benefits which the mode of raising the supplies to a considerable extent adopted last session has produced, it is unnecessary for me to state, that, however the principle may deserve our approbation, it is much to be desired that its effects should be more extensive, and its application more efficient. By the causes to which I have alluded, the full advantage of the principle has not been obtained. The wishes and the interest of individuals, I am sure, must unite in demanding a more comprehensive, a more equal and a more vigorous application of a principle, the rare advantages of which we have been able to ascertain, if we have not yet been so fortunate as to enjoy. Last session those who acknowledged the importance of the principle of raising a considerable part of the supplies within the year, confined their objections to the proportion fixed upon the scale of the assessed taxes, as unequal in its application, and liable to great evasion in practice. Though not insensible of the weight of the objection, I then felt it my duty, convinced as I was of the immense advantages of the system to adopt some visible criterion by which to estimate and to regulate the extent of contribution, if it was not possible to devise means of embracing fully every class of property, and every source of contribution. I felt it materially important to follow some durable, some apparent and sensible criterion, by which to apportion the burthen. At the same time I felt, that although the assessed taxes furnished the most comprehensive and efficient scale of contribution, there necessarily must be much income, much wealth, great means, which were not included in its application. It now appears that not by any error in the calculation of our resources, not by any exaggeration of our wealth, but by the general facility of modification, by the anxiety to render the measure as little oppressive as possible, a defalcation has arisen which ought not to have taken place. Yet, under the disadvantage and imperfections of an unequal and inadequate scale of application, the effects of the measure have tended to confirm our estimates of its benefits, and to encourage us to persevere in its principle. Every circumstance in our situation, every event in the retrospect of our affairs, demonstrates the advantages of the system of raising a considerable part of the supplies within the year, and ought to induce us to enforce it more effectually to prevent those frauds, which an imperfect criterion and a loose facility of modification have introduced; to repress those evasions so disgraceful to the country, so injurious to those who honourably discharge their equal contribution, and, above all, so detrimental to the great object of national advantage which it is intended to promote. In these sentiments, our leading principle should be to guard against all evasion, to endeavour by a fair and strict application, to realize that full tenth, which it was the original purpose of the measure of the assessed taxes to obtain, and to extend this as far as possible in every direction, till it may be necessary clearly to mark the modification, or to renounce, in certain instances, the application of it altogether. If, then, the committee assent to this principle, they must feel the necessity of following it up, by more efficient provisions. They will perceive the necessity of obtaining a more specific statement of income than the loose scale of modification, which, under the former measure, permitted such fraud and evasion. If such a provision be requisite to correct the abuses of collection, to obviate the artifices of dishonesty, to extend the utility of the whole system, it will be found that many of the regulations of the old measure will be adapted to a more comprehensive and efficient application of the principle. If regulations can be devised to prevent an undue abatement, and to proportion the burthen to the real ability, means must be employed to reach those resources which it is impossible under the present system of the assessed taxes to touch. Experience proves that we must correct and remedy, in order to secure the advantages which the measure is calculated to afford. It is in our power to make them our own. I think I can show that whatever benefit the principle upon which we have begun to act, is fitted to bestow, may by a liberal, fair, and efficient application, be carried to an extent far greater than has yet been obtained, an extent equal to every object of great and magnanimous effort, to every purpose of national safety and glory, to every advantage of permanent credit and of increased prosperity.

Impressed, then, with the importance of the subject, convinced that we ought, as far as possible, to prevent all evasion and fraud, it remains for us to consider, by what means these defects may be redressed, by what means a more equal scale of contribution can be applied, and a more extensive effect obtained. For this purpose it is my intention to propose, that the presumption founded upon the assessed taxes shall be laid aside, and that a general tax shall be imposed upon all the leading branches of income. No scale of income indeed which can be devised will be perfectly free from the objection of inequality, or entirely cut off the possibility of evasion. All that can be attempted is, to approach as near as circumstances will permit to a fair and equal contribution. I trust that the opinion of the country will concur with the disposition of parliament to give that energy to our exertions, to give that stability to our resources, which our present situation and our future prosperity demand. I trust that all who value the national honour and the national safety, will co-operate in the desirable purpose of obtaining by an efficient and comprehensive tax upon real ability, every advantage which flourishing and invigorated resources can confer upon national efforts. The details of a measure which attempts an end so great and important, must necessarily require mature deliberation. At present all that I can pretend to do is, to lay before the committee an outline of a plan which endeavours to combine every thing at which such a measure ought to aim. This outline I shall now proceed to develope to the committee as clearly and distinctly as I am able.

It will occur to every one to inquire what species of commissioners shall be vested with the power of fixing the rate of assessment under a measure which must leave a considerable discretionary power. In such commissioners several qualifications are in a particular manner desirable. They ought to be persons of a respectable situation in life; as far as possible removed from any suspicion of partiality, or any kind of undue influence; men of integrity and independence. From the experience we have had of the benefits derived from the voluntary exertions of such a body of commissioners, we may be able to ascertain in what classes to look for men qualified for the important functions which the office would impose. Still, however, I should consider it necessary to vary somewhat from the mode pursued in forming the commissioners of the land tax. After much consideration, it occurs to me that, out of the commissioners appointed under the act for assessing the land-tax, a certain proportion should be taken with given qualifications; and that no man should be admitted to act as commissioner for the purposes to be afterwards specified, who does not possess 300*l.* per annum. To these, other persons of similar qualifications should be added, and the list so framed should be referred to the grand jury, or those who have served on the two last grand juries to form the commissioners. In case the party is dissatisfied with the decision of these commissioners, another body of commissioners should be formed, to whom an appeal may be carried. In commercial towns some special provisions will be necessary, adapted to the nature of circumstances.

The next point for consideration, is the mode of contribution which shall be adopted. On this head it is my intention to propose, that no income under 60*l.* a year shall be called upon to contribute, and that the scale of modification up to 200*l.* a year, as in the assessed taxes, shall be introduced with restriction. The quota which will then be called for ought to amount to a full tenth of the contributor's income. The mode proposed of obtaining this contribution differs from that pursued in the assessed taxes, as instead of trebling their amount, the statement of income is to proceed from the party himself. In doing this it is not proposed that income shall be distinctly laid open, but it shall only be declared that the assessment is beyond the proportion of a tenth of the income of the person on whom it is imposed. In this way, the disclosure at which many may revolt will be avoided, and at the same time every man will be under the necessity of contributing his fair and equal proportion. How then it will be asked, is evasion and fraud to be checked? Knowing the difficulty of guessing what a man's real ability is, I do not think that the charge of fixing what is to be the rate, ought to be left to the commissioners. It would, I am persuaded, be most acceptable to the general feeling, to make it the duty of a particular officer, as surveyor, to lay before the commissioners such grounds of doubt, as may occur to him on the fairness of the rate at which a party may have assessed himself. These doubts, and the reasons on which they are founded, are then to be transmitted by the surveyor to the commissioners, in order that they may call for farther explanation from the person concerned. When in the case of the assessed taxes we have had so much experience of the evasions which have taken place; when we see the consequences which have resulted from a vague rule of exemption, and an indefinite principle of deduction: when we see that, by the different modes by which exemptions were regulated, persons, who probably would have shrunk from a direct fraud, have been able by different pretences to disguise the fair and adequate proportion which they ought to have contributed, it becomes more than ever necessary to render every case of exemption precise, and to guard every title to deduction from the danger of being abused. At the same time, under every disadvantage of the unrestricted application of deduction, and the easy commission of fraud, we have yet ample proof of our national wealth and general honesty. To prevent the country from suffering by dishonesty, to prevent the willing contributor from being taxed to the utmost proportion of his means, while his wealthy neighbour owes his exemption to meanness, it is necessary to guard with greater strictness against every chance of evasion. When doubts are entertained that a false statement has been given, it shall be competent for the commissioners to call for a specification of income. It will be necessary to simplify and to state with precision the different proportions of income arising from land, from trade, annuity, or profession, which shall entitle to deduction. The commissioners are then to say whether they are satisfied with the statement which has been given. The officer or surveyor is to be allowed to examine and to report whether there appears reason to believe that the assessment is adequate. When the day of examination arrives, the commissioners shall hear what the surveyor and the party have to allege in support of the objection and the assessment, and examine other individuals. The schedule, which shall be drawn up in such a manner as accurately to define every case of exemption or deduction, shall be presented by the party, with his claim clearly specified. To the truth of the schedule he shall make oath. The party, however, shall not be compelled to answer; his books shall not be called for, nor his confidential clerks or agents examined. If, however, he declines to submit to the investigation of his books, and the examination of his clerks, and other means of ascertaining the truth, it shall be competent for the commissioners to fix the assessment, and their decision shall be final, unless he appeals to the higher commissioners. No disclosure is compulsory; but if the party is unwilling to disclose, he must acquiesce in the decision of the commissioners, who shall not be authorized to relieve without a full disclosure.

This, I am perfectly ready to admit, gives to the commissioners considerable power; but I think I have stated enough to show to the committee, that, unless some such powers be afforded under this act, the real and substantial effect of the measure will be entirely defeated. I think, too, I have proved, that commissioners, selected in the manner I have described, are as likely to be as free from all undue influence, and to act with as much integrity and honour, as any other set of men whatever. If, however, a better mode should be suggested, so far from opposing it, I shall consider it as a melioration and improvement of my plan. With respect to the information which may be communicated to the commissioners, I should propose that they shall be strictly sworn not to disclose such information, nor to avail themselves of it for any other purpose separate from the execution of the act. If any statement, however, should be made upon oath, which the commissioners shall think to be false, and which they may wish to bring to a trial, it must be obvious to the committee that then there ought to be afforded the means of carrying on a prosecution for perjury. But on no other ground should there be any disclosure of facts by the commissioners, or any of the other officers appointed to carry the act into execution.

Having laid down these general principles and outlines, I cannot feel, that if commissioners of the description I have alluded to can be found, bound to execute their duty fairly and impartially, and sworn to secrecy—I say, if such men can be selected, I cannot feel, however strong the objections may be against the disclosure of circumstances, that any statement made to such commissioners is liable to the general objection against public disclosures of the incomes and circumstances of individuals in a commercial country; at least, I am sure there is every disposition in the plan to guard against it. There is little danger, I conceive, that such commissioners will act partially, or conduct themselves vexatiously; and, in my opinion, there does not remain any fair ground for jealousy in individuals, that a disclosure to such men will give to persons in the same line of life any advantages over them.—Perhaps, however, Sir, there is once class of men to whom it may be for the committee to determine whether they ought not to remain exceptions to the act. Among the descriptions of persons to whom it may remain for the committee to consider whether a disclosure would not be detrimental, is the class which includes the poorest persons engaged in mercantile concerns; a class whose gains are most precarious, whose credit may be most doubtful, and most injured by a disclosure—I speak of the persons engaged in retail trades, to whom the assessed tax bill of last session gave great indulgencies, considering that the relief of abatement was one of which they could not avail themselves, without greater inconvenience and injury to them, perhaps, than to a higher description of mercantile traders. I wish, therefore, the committee to consider whether it may not be as well to leave that class to pay on the mitigated rate of assessment to which they are liable under the assessed tax bill, as to subject them to the general rate of the present bill. It will also naturally enter into the consideration of the committee, what allowances or exemptions ought to be extended to other descriptions of persons. In the last act, certain allowances and abatements were granted to persons with large families. That principle it will certainly be proper to extend to this measure; and the only doubt which I entertain upon the subject is, whether it was carried far enough in the bill of last year. If this suggestion be admitted, it will naturally be a matter of doubt, whether the principle in the last bill, with respect to persons having no families, ought not to be extended. It will also very reasonably occur to the minds of the committee, that it is of the utmost importance to the due execution of the act, that, as far as the general principles can be laid down for establishing a rate of landed property, or what may be the proper average of incomes which are subject to average, the rates in the last act should be subject to correction and improvement. By the operation of these powers, and by the influence of these rules, we may expect to arrive more nearly at that fair proportion which each man ought to contribute towards the exigencies of the country.

The next consideration is one liable to more difficulty and doubt, upon which gentlemen will be aware that every thing must be conjectural, but in which we are still not without lights to guide us—I mean as to the probable amount of a tax of this kind. The committee must be convinced, that what I shall state will be with doubt and uncertainty. I shall, however, submit to the view of the House the information I have collected, the authorities with which I am fortified, and the grounds upon which I proceed. And first, Sir, I shall proceed to state what is the first great object of income. I mean the property derived from land. Upon this point I have consulted the best opinions, and authors of the most acknowledged merit. Upon the subject of the rent of the land of this country, sir William Petty is the earliest author I have consulted. At the time he wrote, the rent of land was stated at eight millions. In a subsequent period, in the beginning of this century, and in the reign of queen Anne, two writers of credit, Davenant and King, represented the rental of the land to be 14,000,000l. However they differed on other points, on this they both agreed. Posterior to that time it was a received opinion, that the land-tax of four shillings in the pound was equivalent to about two shillings of what would be collected on the real rents of the kingdom, which were stated to amount to twenty millions. Full twenty years ago this was said by a writer, who was also a member of this House, and who in a work he wrote, expressly recommended the very principle which I have submitted to the committee this day. The same estimate was stated, and the same opinion was countenanced, by the celebrated author of the Wealth of Nations, Adam Smith. He received it as a statement generally admitted, and sufficiently proved, that the rent of the land in the kingdom was twenty millions yearly. In a work published as long ago as the year 1774, Mr. Arthur Young, who had made agricultural pursuits his study, advanced the same opinion. I mention all these authorities, to show what has been supposed to be the amount of the rental of the land at different periods. I have also had the advantage of other inquiries made expressly by a body who have made the cultivation of the land their peculiar province—I mean the Board of Agriculture. I allude more particularly to one report published by a person who made this part of the subject his study, the report drawn up by Mr. Middleton. All these, checked with other examinations, state the cultivated land of the country to amount to little less than forty millions of acres. Any attempt to state what is the average value of these forty millions of acres, must be extremely uncertain. Many persons most conversant on the subject believe the average value to be fifteen shillings per acre. I shall, however, take it at no more than twelve shillings and six-pence. I will put the average value at twenty-five millions a year. And gentlemen will see, that when I take the number of acres at forty millions, and the average value at only twelve shillings and six-pence per acre, the result is only an increase of five millions beyond what it was twenty years ago, and that therefore I cannot be considered as a sanguine calculator. However, in this part of the subject, I desire the committee to bear in mind, that it will be proper to propose a reduction for all under 60l. a year, and that the same modifications be admitted into this act as in the Assessed Tax bill—I mean the scale of income from 60l. to 200l. a year, and rising from a 120th part to a tenth. I mean on this account to assume a deduction of one fifth, and to state the taxable property at only twenty millions.

I shall next proceed to state that part of income from land which belongs to the tenant. I propose to value every man according to his rent, making only a deduction for repairs. What I shall suggest for the further consideration of the committee, is three-fourths of the rack rend which the tenant pays to the landlord. The value of the income from land which belongs to the tenant I take at nineteen millions; the income to the landlord at twenty-five millions. Instead of deducting only one-fifth, as I have suggested with respect to the landlord, I shall propose with respect to the tenant, to deduct two-thirds, leaving five millions as the taxable property of the tenants. The next income arising from land, is an income which is received neither by the landlord, nor by the tenant,—I mean what is received from tithes. This is an income enjoyed, either by lay impropriators, or by the clergy. The statements of the amount of the tithes are different; but I estimate the value of them to be five millions. If gentlemen suppose the amount of the cultivated land in the country to be forty millions of acres, and the average value to be twenty-five millions, they will find my valuation to be very moderate: it is also Mr. Arthur Young's statement. Upon this subject of tithes, I propose to allow a deduction of one-fifth, though perhaps I may be considered as stating the reduction too largely, but gentlemen will consider the allowance to be made for poor livings—Another species of property is that which arises from mines, and from shares in canals. There is also another property which I have not included in the rents of land, I mean the property arising from the sale of timber. I take all these three, the mines, canals, and timber, at three millions. Another species of rent is that received for houses. I propose to proceed upon the rate which was followed in the act of last session. To establish accurately the rent of houses has ever been found impracticable, particularly of houses of the higher description of rent, which have always been undervalued. Out of 700,000 houses, 250,000 are calculated to pay to the assessed taxes; I shall therefore take the rent of houses at no more than six millions. In the early statements to which I have alluded, the profits gained by the professors of the law alone are estimated at one million and a half; I cannot suppose that they are at all diminished. Allowing, besides, for all the branches of the medical profession, I conceive that two millions is a very small sum as the amount of the incomes arising from the professions.

The next head of income relates to the profits of retail trade: but there are persons of a certain description, with respect to whom it will be necessary to make some allowance. The reduction I shall propose to take at one-eighth of the nett [*sic*] sum of the profits of the trade of Great Britain, after which there will remain a sum of 5,000,000*l*. applicable to the general operation of the tax. There will then remain another article of taxation, which is the income spent in this country by persons who derive it from other parts of the world; and unquestionably all who reside in this kingdom, and draw their means from sources out of it, cannot be dissatisfied at contributing to their own support and protection. Of this description, the only persons I shall think it necessary to estimate are those whose incomes arise from their having property in Ireland, and who reside in this country, and persons owning estates in the West Indies, or receiving the interest of mortgages on estates in that part of the world. With respect to those persons whose incomes arise from Ireland, I believe it is the generally received opinion, that the property of persons of this description amounted to at least 1,000,000*l*., a considerable time since, and now, from the increase of rents, it may reasonably be estimated far beyond that sum. With respect to the incomes of estates in the West Indies, the total amount cannot be estimated at less than 7,000,000*l.* sterling, and far the greater amount is produced from the property of persons residing in Great Britain, who either own estates, or have mortgages upon them for which they receive interest. From that are to be deducted the amount of the exports carried out, and the charge of cultivating the estates in the West Indies; after which deduction, I estimate the produce of income in the West Indies at four millions. Thus I think I may fairly estimate at five millions the whole produce of income arising beyond seas, and enjoyed by persons in this country.

The next description of property is the income of persons not in trade. Under this head will be included annuities of all kinds, public and private mortgages, and income arising from money lent upon securities under various denominations. At the same time the committee will go along with me in seeing that, in estimating the general rental of the land of England, I have taken it with all its burthens, and consequently have included the mortgages. In the practical detail of the measure, it will come to be decided whether it shall fall on the land owner, or on the mortgagee. In respect, therefore, of this description of property, I do not now make any distinct estimate. With respect to private annuities of another kind, it is also difficult to ascertain their amount. Not so with regard to public annuities; we have no difficulty in ascertaining the exact amount of the annuities paid by the public to individuals, and I shall have no hesitation in submitting to the committee, that when a general assessment upon income is to take place, no distinction ought to be made as to the sources from which that income may arise. There can be no fair objection taken by the stockholder upon the occasion; there can be no question of a breach of good faith with the public creditor, by thus imposing upon him what every other subject of the realm is to incur. The public creditor enjoys his security under the most sacred obligations of the state, and whenever an idea has been started of imposing upon the stockholders, separately and distinctly, any sort of tax, I have reprobated the attempt, as utterly inconsistent with the good faith of public engagement. Parliament has always gone along with me in the feeling that no such tax ought to be levied upon them, and they have uniformly acted upon this feeling, on the principle, that, as the public creditors came forward and lent their money to the state in the moment of its necessity, while at the same time they bore, in common with every other description of his majesty's subjects, the taxes on consumption, they were to be secured against any imposts, distinctly levelled at them as annuitants of the public; and the parliament has felt this more particularly from the recollection of the duty which they owe to persons who had embarked so much, and identified themselves so intimately with the state. Against any direct tax upon the stockholder, then, I am sure the committee would set themselves in opposition; but the matter is materially reversed, when a tax is to be levied upon the income of every description of persons in the realm; when it is no longer in the power of the stockholder to say, I could avoid this tax by removing my property from the funds to landed security, or to trade; every argument against including him in the assessment is withdrawn. The protection yielded to the stockholder, is the same as to the landholder, the merchant, and the manufacturer. The duty, therefore, is the same, and every other description of persons in the country would have a right to complain, if, when they are called upon for a sacrifice of this extraordinary nature, so numerous a body of persons were to be exempted from the assessment. I am confident, therefore, that every gentleman who hears me, will agree that the principle of the measure is not liable to any imputation of breach of faith. It cannot be called a resumption of the annuity that has been granted to the public creditors, nor an infringement of the contract that was originally made with them. They are, in this instance, only to do that which every other body of men in the kingdom are to do; they are to make a sacrifice of part of their income to the necessities of the state, upon the principle of giving security to all which they possess. I should say to the stockholder, as one of the public, "if you expect from the state the protection which is common to us all, you ought also to make the sacrifice which we are called upon to make. It is not peculiar to you to make. It is not peculiar to you; it does not belong to the quality of your income; but it is made general, and required from all; you could not embark your capital in any other species of security in which it would not be subject to the same charge." I do not know what objection the stockholder could make to this appeal. I include, therefore, the public annuitants in the view of the proposed tax, and there is no difficulty in estimating the amount of this species of income. At the same time, it is to be taken into consideration, that all that part of the public annuities which have been redeemed by the nation, is to be exempted from the charge of the tax. Taking the amount of the redemption, therefore, at what it now appears to be, the rental of the public annuitants may be estimated at 15,000,000*l.*; but here, as in all the other cases, both of the land and rental, and of other sources of property, there will, of course, be admitted the same exemptions to all annuitants who have less than 60*l.* a year, and the same modifications to all who possess from 60*l.* to 200*l.* a year. At the same time it is to be considered, that these exemptions and modifications are only to apply to those individuals whose whole income amounts to less than 200*l.* a year. If persons possess incomes from various sources, they are to be calculated in the aggregate; for the exemption or the modification will not apply, if the whole income should not be under the stipulated sum. I am sure, that I shall over-rate the amount of these exemptions and modifications, when I deduct one-fifth from the sum that I have stated the public annuities to be; but I do not admit that deduction, and therefore state the total of the income from the public funds at 12,000,000*l.*

There now remain the other great sources of trade to the inhabitants of this country;—the produce of trade, foreign and domestic: and this branch of income is, in its nature, more difficult of estimate than any other. We have, however, lights and aids by which we may come to a knowledge of a material part, at least, of this source of national wealth, I mean the produce of our foreign trade. The capital employed in this way is certainly not less than 80,000,000*l.* sterling. Assuming this as the capital, the next question is, what we ought to take as the profit to all the description of persons employed in carrying on this branch of our trade? In estimating this, we must necessarily include in our view, not merely the merchant who exports, but all the orders and descriptions of persons from the manufacturer upwards, who are in any way connected with our export trade. Under this head come in the profits of brokerage, wharfage, and carriage, with all the other contributory trades connected with foreign commerce; and I am sure I make a moderate calculation, when I estimate the average of the profits upon the capital of 80,000,000*l.* at 15 per cent. I take, therefore, 12,000,000*l*, as the income of all the persons connected with the foreign trade of this kingdom.

There now remains that which more than any other branch of our income baffles the power of scrutiny, and affords even very limited grounds for conjecture: I mean the profits arising from domestic trade and manufacture. Here the many descriptions of persons whose skill and industry are the source of income in all the progress of our arts and manufactures, from the first preparation of the rude and raw material to its state of perfection, serve to make calculation almost impossible from their variety and extent. Even here, however, we have some means of forming an idea. Of the general capital of 80,000,000*l.* employed in the foreign trade, it has been pretty accurately determined, that about 30,000,000*l.* are destined and employed in the export of the leading manufactures of England. I am sure, then, that the committee will go along with me in saying, that the amount of the capital and sum employed in internal trade must be four times the amount of our export of British manufacturers. When we look at the vast machine of trade in all its parts, let any gentleman ask himself whether, in the woollen manufactures, cotton, linen, hardware, pottery, and in all the other great and leading branches of manufacture, there can be a less sum employed than four times the amount of that which is appropriated by the merchant for the purpose of exportation? Viewing all the enormous capital invested in domestic manufacture. I cannot take it at less than 120,000,000*l.* and upon this capital I estimate the gain at no more than 15 per cent, making a sum of 18,000,000*l.* per annum of income.—There is one other description of income which, though it embraces a vast variety of individuals, is reducible to none of the former heads, but comes naturally to be included in the article of domestic trade; I mean artisans, architects, brewers, distillers, builders, brickmakers, masons, carpenters, and all that innumerable class of persons who, by skill in their professions, draw their incomes from the general prosperity of the country. The committee will at once perceive how numerous and how varied this class of persons must be, and how impossible it is to arrive at an accurate criterion of the general amount of their gains. I am sure, however, they will agree with me that I understate it, when I take it at 10,000,000*l.* per annum. I thus estimate the whole amount of our internal manufactures and trade at 28,000,000*l.* a year.

I have thus rapidly gone through all the distinct branches of national rental, and of national profits, from which we have to derive the tax that I mean to propose to you. I have through the whole, been anxious to understate the amount of the estimate, and to overrate the exemptions and deductions that it would be necessary to make from each. I make the whole annual rental and profits, after making the deductions which I think reasonable, 102,000,000*l.* sterling. For the sake of greater clearness, I will recapitulate the several heads:

	£
Land rental, after deducting one-fifth	20,000,000
Tenant's rental of land, deducting two-thirds of the rack rent	6,000,000

Tythes, deducting one-fifth	£4,000,000
Mines, canal-navigation, etc. deducting one-fifth	3,000,000
Rental of houses, deducting one-fifth	5,000,000
Profits of professions	2,000,000
Rental of Scotland, taking it at one-eighth of that of England	5,000,000
Income of persons resident in Great Britain, drawn from possessions beyond seas	5,000,000
Annuities from the public funds, after deducting one-fifth for exemptions and modifications	12,000,000
Profits on the capital employed in our foreign commerce	12,000,000
Profits on the capital employed in domestic trade, and the profits of skill and industry	28,000,000
In all	£102,000,000

Upon this sum a tax of 10 per cent is likely to produce 10,000,000*l.* a year, and this is the sum at which I shall assume it. Now, supposing that ten millions is the sum thus collected, gentlemen will recollect that, in the last session of parliament, the assessed taxes were the only part of the public resources which were mortgaged for the sum of 8,000,000*l.* borrowed for the public service in 1797. I should think, therefore, that the sum now proposed to be raised in lieu of the assessed taxes, should, after its appropriation to the supplies of the present year, remain as a pledge for the discharge of that sum for which the assessed taxes were a security, and also for the discharge of the loan of the present year, beyond what will be paid out of the sinking fund. Taking the assessed taxes at four millions, they would have been mortgaged for two years after peace;—and thus the advantage of this measure is this, that no greater sums will be raised on any individuals than those which have been hitherto paid, at least by such as have rendered the measure of the legislature effectual; they will be relieved of a greater than a proportional share of their burthen, and the duration of the burthen will not be half the time. But it does not stop here; it looks anxiously to the alleviation of the burthens of the country, by a great temporary exertion; it looks to the quality of the tax, and the general efficacy of the measure, conscious that on them depends our success in the great cause in which we are engaged.—In the mode of applying the sum now to be raised, there are different ways. The sum which the assessed taxes were applied to discharge amounted last year to eight millions; it would be only to borrow a sum equal to the debt to supply the deficiency; but it occurs to me, that a more simple and direct mode is, to apply this sum, in the first instance, to the supplies of the year, but at the same time to enact, that the tax shall continue till it has discharged the debt for which the assessed taxes were mortgaged, and then to make a farther charge for what may be borrowed beyond what the sinking fund will discharge. Supposing this ten per cent on income produces 10,000,000*l.* the period when I should propose it to take effect would be the 5th of April next. I should propose the repeal of the former assessed taxes at the same period; but from the calculation I have made 4½ millions will be raised from the 1st Feb. 1798, to the 1st Feb. 1799. It would, therefore, be more beneficial to commence the operation of this new measure at an earlier period, because of the benefit of the increased rate of taxation; but there will be the addition of what will come in under the assessed taxes, which will amount to 700,000*l*. Thus there will be raised 10,700,000*l*. But this is not applicable to the whole of the subject; for gentlemen will recollect, that the interest of the 8,000,000*l*. was also charged on the assessed taxes. The interest will continue in the course of the present year, to which also is to be added the interest of whatever loan may be made this year. This will amount to about 1,500,000*l*., which leaves the sum of 9,200,000*l*. as applicable to the services of the present year. This aid would be all that is necessary to furnish the ways and means for the supplies, except as to the sum of 24 millions: 14 millions, therefore, is the sum necessary to be raised by loan, of which, however, 4½ millions is discharged by the operation of the sinking fund, consequently 9½ millions is the whole sum to be added to the national debt. I wish, therefore to lay this down as a principle, that 9½ millions is the sum to be raised this year, for which I should propose to charge as a mortgage the income tax, after discharging the former mortgage. After enlarging upon the benefits likely to result from the measure of raising a considerable portion of the supplies within the year, the right hon. gentleman concluded with moving the following Resolutions:

1. That it is the opinion of this committee, that so much of an act made in the last session of parliament, intituled, "An Act for granting to his Majesty an Aid and Contribution for the Prosecution of the War," as charges any person with an additional duty in proportion to the amount of the rates or duties to which, prior to the 5th day of April, 1798, such person was assessed, according to any assessment made in pursuance of any act of parliament in force at the time of passing the said act of the last session, be repealed.

2. That it is the opinion of this committee, that, towards raising the supply granted to his majesty, there be charged annually, during a term to be limited, the several rates and duties following, upon all income arising from property in Great Britain, belonging to any of his majesty's subjects, although not resident in Great Britain; and upon all income of every person residing in Great Britain, and of every body politic or corporate, or company, fraternity, or society of persons, whether corporate or not corporate, in Great Britain, whether any such income shall arise from lands, tenements, or hereditaments, wheresoever the same shall be situated in Great Britain, or elsewhere; or from any kind of personal property, or other property whatever; or from any profession, office, employment, trade, or vocation; that is to say.

One one-hundred-and-twentieth part of such income, if the same shall amount unto 60*l*. per annum, and shall be under 65*l*. per annum.

One ninety-fifth part of such income, if the same shall amount to 65*l*. but shall be under 70*l*.

One seventieth part of such income, if the same shall amount to 70*l*. but shall be under 75*l*.

One sixty-fifth part of such income, if the same shall amount to 75*l*. but shall be under 80*l*.

One sixtieth part of such income, if the same shall amount to 80*l*. but shall be under 85*l*.

One fifty-fifth part of such income, if the same shall amount to 85*l*. but shall be under 90*l*.

One fiftieth part of such income, if the same shall amount to 90*l*. but shall be under 95*l*.

One forty-fifth part of such income, if the same shall amount to 95*l*. but shall be under 100*l*.

One fortieth part of such income, if the same shall amount to 100*l*. but shall be under 105*l*.

One thirty-eighth part of such income, if the same shall amount to 105*l*. but shall be under 110*l*.

One thirty-sixth part of such income, if the same shall amount to 110*l*. but shall be under 115*l*.

One thirty-fourth part of such income, if the same shall amount to 115*l*. but shall be under 120*l*.

One thirty-second part of such income, if the same shall amount to 120*l*. but shall be under 125*l*.

One thirtieth part of such income, if the same shall amount to 125*l*. but shall be under 130*l*.

One twenty-eighth part of such income, if the same shall amount to 130*l*. but shall be under 135*l*.

One twenty-sixth part of such income, if the same shall amount to 135*l*. but shall be under 140*l*.

One twenty-fourth part of such income, if the same shall amount to 140*l*. but shall be under 145*l*.

One twenty-second part of such income, if the same shall amount to 145*l*. but shall be under 150*l*.

One twentieth part of such income, if the same shall amount to 150*l*. but shall be under 155*l*.

One nineteenth part of such income, if the same shall amount to 155*l*. but shall be under 160*l*.

One eighteenth part of such income, if the same shall amount to 160*l*. but shall be under 165*l*.

One seventeenth part of such income, if the same shall amount to 165*l*. but shall be under 170*l*.

One sixteenth part of such income, if the same shall amount to 170*l*. but shall be under 175*l*.

One fifteenth part of such income, if the same shall amount to 175*l*. but shall be under 180*l*.

One fourteenth part of such income, if the same shall amount to 180*l*. but shall be under 185*l*.

One thirteenth part of such income, if the same shall amount to 185*l*. but shall be under 190*l*.

One twelfth part of such income, if the same shall amount to 190*l.* but shall be under 195*l.*

One eleventh part of such income, if the same shall amount to 195*l.* but shall be under 200*l.*

And one-tenth part of such income, if the same shall amount to 200*l.* or upwards.

Speech by Henry Hobhouse opposing Pitt's income tax proposal, House of Commons, 4 December 1798

Parliamentary History, XXXIV, 24–26.

Mr. Hobhouse said, that between the evil of persevering longer in the funding system, and the evil of the present attempt to raise a great part of the supplies within the year, he could not well balance his mind; if, therefore, he had not other grounds for rejecting the present measure, he should feel himself at a loss to decide what vote he should give. Those grounds it was now his duty to state. He hoped he might be allowed to inquire, what would be the effect of making either expenditure, income, or property, the basis of taxation. If expenditure be made the criterion, then the avaricious capitalist would not pay his due proportion, but the weight would fall on him who, in consequence of having spent more than he could well afford, was least liable to support it. If income be taken as the test, then the tax would operate with glaring inequality. The man who had an income of 1,000*l.* per annum arising from capital, and the man who gained the same annual sum by a profession or by business, surely ought not to be assessed in the same degree. If two merchants had each 1,000*l.* a year from their commerce, they ought not to be taxed alike; because the one might be obliged to apply a greater proportion of his income than the other, to the repair of buildings or machinery. If property only be taxed, it might be argued, that those who had the greatest property might not have the greatest income; and that the necessary expenditure of two persons who had equal property might be very different. On these grounds he could not bring himself to believe that either property, income, or expenditure, should solely and exclusively be taxed. Such a basis of taxation would, in his opinion, be highly unjustifiable. The most unexceptionable one that could be laid, ought to be formed out of a combination of the three. The individual should be rated according to the property he possessed, the income it produced, and the degree of expenditure, which his situation in life, the size of his family, or other considerations might demand.—Besides this objection to a tax upon income, he had others extremely strong and forcible. It was a tax which would strike with peculiar force at industry and the fruits of industry, while indolence was left untouched and encouraged. And what must be the natural consequence of this discouragement of industry? Does it not tend to relax those springs which give life and activity to every branch of trade, commerce, agriculture, etc.? The merchant is accustomed annually to convert a part of his profits into capital. If the tax-gatherers call for a portion of those profits, he must devote less to the increase of his reproductive stock. Thus the progress of our trade would be obstructed. There was a passage in Steuart's Political Economy so appropriate that he would read it: "As to the pure profits on trade: although they appear to be income, yet I consider them rather as stock, and therefore they ought not to be taxed. They resemble the annual shoots of a tree which augment the mass of it; but are very different from the seed, or fruit which is annually produced, and is annually separated from it." These shoots the minister was now lopping, and thus the growth of the tree would be checked; a few years hence he would probably cut down the tree, that he might the more easily lay his hand upon the fruit.—He had not stated this tax to be a violation of the public faith to the stockholder, because he did not view it in that light. Undoubtedly there was a clause in all the loan acts, securing to the public creditor his dividends "free from all taxes, charges and impositions whatever." But from the moment the money had found its way into the pocket of the stockholder, from that moment it became liable to taxation. Neither had he insisted upon another case, namely, that all persons from 200*l.* per annum and upwards should pay a tenth part. Surely it was flagrantly unjust to take 10 per cent from the man who possessed but 200*l.* per annum, while he, who rioted in the enjoyment of 40,000*l.* yearly income, paid no more. As to the productiveness of this new financial project, he would not hesitate to say, that it was calculated, in some respects, to bring in more than the late act for augmenting the assessed taxes.

POLICY OF REPRESSION

French revolutionary ideals generated considerable waves of sympathy among British reformers as can be seen, for example, in the activities of the London Corresponding Society. The Pitt government responded to this growth of radicalism by introducing a series of repressive measures.

Account by Joseph Priestley of the Birmingham "Church and King" Riots, July 1791

Joseph Priestley, *An Appeal to the Public, on the Subject of the Riots in Birmingham: To which are added, Strictures on a pamphlet intitled "Thoughts on the late Riot at Birmingham"* (Dublin, 1792), 16-33.

In the document which follows, the Unitarian reformer Joseph Priestley (1733-1804) describes how his house and scientific laboratory in Birmingham were destroyed by a mob because of his sympathy with the French Revolution.

Being in London at the time of the first debate on the subject, I heard Mr. Pitt (whom, justly or unjustly, we had been led to consider as friendly to our cause) speak against it; and perceiving, as I thought, his total misapprehension of the subject, I addressed a *Letter* to him relating to the situation of Dissenters, and on other collateral subjects, especially the state of the established church, both here and in Ireland. This *Letter* gave great offence. But I appeal to the impartial public, whether, though written with some degree of indignation, at recent, and as we thought, unjust treatment, there be any thing in it unbecoming men and Englishmen, unjustly and ignominiously treated. This *Letter* was written, and published, while I was in London, and therefore had no particular reference to Birmingham. What I did there was as follows.

It being usual on the 5th of November to give our congregations a discourse on some subject relating to *religious liberty*, I made choice of that of the Test Act, and at the request of my hearers the discourse was published. But I will venture to say that it is one of the calmest, and most moderate, of all discourses that was ever written on a political subject.

What, now, was the conduct of the clergy throughout England, and especially at Birmingham, on this occasion? Endeavours were used to render the Dissenters the objects not only of exclusion from civil offices, but of general odium and punishment. Dr. *Croft's Sermon*, and that of Mr. Madan, both delivered at

Birmingham, are extant, and the spirit of them was the same with that of hundreds, I may say thousands, that were echoed from other pulpits, charging the Dissenters, in opposition to all history, and even to recent and existing facts, with principles inimical to the government of the country, and to the prince upon the throne; as pure republicans in their hearts, and who would scruple no means to overturn not the church only, but also the state.

Dr. Price and myself were particularly pointed out as seditious and dangerous persons; the very pests of society, and unworthy the protection of government. Such language as this is even held to this day, and in spite of the most explicit denial of what is thus laid to our charge, and of every possible species of evidence to the contrary, including the constant language of our serious writings, will, to all appearance, long continue to be held.

Being particularly pointed at by Mr. Madan, and both friends and enemies looking upon me as called upon to make some reply; I did it with great reluctance, as to a clergyman, whom, on other accounts, I truly respected, and whom, as living in the same town with me, I might occasionally meet; to say nothing of the farther acquaintance which I had once flattered myself I might make with him. This reply I made in a series of *Familiar Letters to the Inhabitants of Birmingham*, and I appeal to any person who has the least pretention to impartiality, whether they be not a mild and good-humoured reply to an unprovoked invective.

I there showed that the Dissenters were, and always had been, the best friends to the present government; that I had myself written much in defence and praise of it; and though, being a Dissenter, I, of course, could be no friend to the established church, with respect either to doctrine or discipline, I allowed others to judge and act, as I did, for themselves, and that I wished for no alterations but such as should have the general concurrence of the country, and those made in such a manner, as that no person living should be injured by them. This has been my constant language on the subject of reformation in church or state. Mr. Madan replied, without retracting any part of his charge. But notwithstanding this, I continued, and concluded my *Letters* with the same good-humour with which I began them.

These Letters were much read both in Birmingham and the neighbourhood, and indeed throughout England. But though they convinced many persons that the Dissenters had been ill used, and that we had much more to say for ourselves than they had imagined, they were far from conciliating the clergy, or the more violent sticklers for the established church.

Other attempts, and some of them of a very infamous kind, were made to render my character odious. Old calumnies were revived, and new ones invented, concerning my being an enemy to Christianity, and to religion in general; and a clergyman (as there is every reason to think) published an account of my having converted Mr. Silas Deane to atheism, and his confession of it upon his death-bed. This was represented in public prints, and the pamphlet containing the account was industriously circulated by some of the clergy in Birmingham and its neighbourhood. At first I neglected the idle story, as sufficiently contradicted by my writings and my whole conduct. Afterwards, however, at the instance of my friends, I published the clearest refutation of it. But even this did not appear to make any favourable impression on my enemies in Birmingham. The offence given by my *Familiar Letters* was never forgiven.

Mr. Burn also published a set of *Letters to me*, in which he charged me with rejecting the testimony of the Apostles concerning the person of Christ; and though I denied the charge, and shewed the absurdity of it, he replied without retracting it. In the *Preface to my Letters to Mr. Burn*, I gave my opinion with great freedom concerning the state of the Dissenters, and the clergy of the established church, warning them of the violence and folly of their conduct, and the probable consequences of it. But the use they made of this *Preface* was to print *Extracts from it*, so curtailed and arranged, as to represent me as a mover of sedition, and a dangerous member of society. This printed paper was sent to the bishops, and to all the members of the house of Commons the day before the last debate on the subject of the Test and Corporation Acts, so that it was impossible to counteract the effects of it: and being put into the hands of Mr. Burke, and declaimed upon by him, was of material disservice to our cause. I shewed the unfairness of this proceeding in a *printed letter* sent to the bishops, and all the members of the house of Commons, as theirs had been. But to all appearance, this complete justification only tended to exasperate my enemies, and they spared no pains to exasperate others.

The effect of this controversy upon the common people in Birmingham, who were made to believe that, some way or other, both the church and the state were in danger, and that my object was the utter destruction of both, was great and visible enough. On the walls of houses, etc. and especially where I usually went, were to be seen in large characters, "Madan for ever, Damn Priestley, No Presbyterians, Damn the Presbyterians," etc. etc. At one time I was followed by a number of boys, who left their play, repeating what they had seen on the walls, and shouting out, *Damn Priestley, damn him, damn him for ever, for ever, for ever*, etc. etc. This was, no doubt, a lesson which they had been taught by their parents, and what these, I fear, had learned from their superiors. Such things as these were certainly unpleasant to me; but I was conscious I had done nothing to deserve such treatment; and despising mere *obloquy*, I was far from suspecting that it would ever lead to the outrages which have since taken place.

In the exultation of the high church party on the defeat of our last application to Parliament, personal danger was apprehended to myself, by some of my more zealous friends; and a number of young men of my congregation came to tell me, that myself and my house were threatened, but that if I chose it, they would undertake to defend both me, and it, at the risk of their lives. I replied that I did not apprehend any danger, and that if any violence was offered to me on that account, I should make no resistance. It has always been my maxim, as may be seen in my writings, and what I have always maintained in conversation, that it becomes christians to bear every kind of insult and violence when it is offered on the account of *religion*, and that nothing but our *civil rights* are to be defended by the sword.

I took no notice of any of the particulars above-mentioned; and though I was told that some of the clergy of the town and neighbourhood were frequently preaching against the Dissenters, and often against myself by name, or by description, I never preached a single sermon on the subject, or wrote any thing more than the pieces above-mentioned, which are before the public, and may be examined at the reader's leisure, till the appearance of *Mr. Burke's Reflections on the French Revolution*, a work that has been more generally read than any publication in my time, and which has contributed more than any other to excite a spirit of party; the clergy almost universally approving it, and the low church party and Dissenters as generally condemning it.

My friends well know that I was far from having any intention of animadverting upon this performance, being at that time engaged in other pursuits, and having a real respect for the writer, till I was pressed to undertake it by several of my friends, who were pleased to think me better qualified than most others to reply to what Mr. Burke had advanced on the subject of *Civil Establishments of Christianity.* At their solicitation I wrote my *Letters to Mr. Burke*, and this publication, though a very temperate one, provoked the clergy, and the zealous friends of the establishment still more; and in consequence of this, their efforts to inflame the minds of the populace against the Dissenters in general, and myself in particular, were redoubled, and the prophane habit of drinking *Damnation and confusion to the Presbyterians*, at the convivial meetings of some persons of better fashion, as well as those of the lower order, was much increased.

So apparent were the marks of extreme bigotry, and the true spirit of persecution at this time, that upon occasion of preaching the *Hackney College Sermon*, in April last (and which my friends know that I long declined) I was led to say,

> In another respect, also, we are now in the situation of the primitive christians; as the friends of reformation have nothing to expect from *power*, or *general favour*; but must look for every species of abuse and persecution that the spirit of the times will admit of. If even burning alive was a sight that the country would now bear, there exists a spirit which would inflict that horrid punishment, and with as much cool indifference, or savage exultation, as in any preceding age of the world.

But though I saw this, and that the marks of this spirit were apparent in various other parts of England, I had no suspicion of its breaking out on the innocent occasion of celebrating the *French Revolution*, and therefore was far from being prepared for any such outrage.

The celebration of this great event by a public dinner at Birmingham was no measure of mine. Indeed, I am well known to all my friends to be averse to public entertainments, and never enjoy myself at them; my habits of life, too long confirmed to be easily altered, being quite opposite to every thing of this nature. However, when the friends of that Revolution proposed it, and wished to have my company, I did not decline their invitation, and we had a meeting or two, partly for *that* purpose, and partly to settle the rules of a Constitutional Society, such as that which is established at Manchester, the chief object of which was to promote a more equal representation of the people of this country in Parliament, and we had printed two copies of *general principles of government*, to be subscribed by all the members, and one copy of *particular rules* for our conduct, copied chiefly from those of Manchester; but we had not pleased ourselves with them, and nothing was absolutely settled.

Many persons in different parts of the kingdom, but more especially at Birmingham, thought the celebration of the French Revolution to be a right and a wise measure, in order to conciliate the French nation, and to promote a friendly and commercial intercourse with it. It is well known that the late *commercial treaty* is not popular in France, and it was thought to be impolitic to heighten the dislike of that nation to *this*, by refusing to partake of their joy, in what was known to give them the greatest satisfaction.

With the dinner itself I had, in a manner, nothing to do. I did not so much as suggest one of the proper and excellent toasts provided on the occasion, though it was natural for my friends to look to me for things of that kind, if I had interested myself much in it; and when opposition was talked of, and it was supposed that some insults would be offered to myself in particular, I yielded to the solicitations of my friends, and did not attend. Others, however, went on that very account; thinking it mean, and unbecoming Englishmen, to be deterred from a lawful and innocent act, by the fear of lawless insult; and accordingly they assembled, and dined, in number between eighty and ninety.

When the company met, a crowd was assembled at the door, and some of them hissed, and shewed other marks of disapprobation, but no material violence was offered to any body. Mr. Keir, a member of the church of England, took the chair; and when they had dined, drank their toasts, and sung the songs which had been prepared for the occasion, they dispersed. This was about five o'clock, and the town remained quiet till about eight. It was evident, therefore, that the *dinner* was not the proper cause of the riot which followed: but that the mischief had been pre-concerted, and that this particular opportunity was laid hold of for the purpose.

Some days before this meeting, a few copies of a printed *hand-bill* of an inflammatory nature, of which a copy is given in the *Appendix*. No. I. had been found in a public house in the town, and of this great use was made to inflame the minds of the people against the Dissenters, to whom, though without any evidence whatever, it was confidently ascribed. The thing itself did not deserve any notice, and paragraphs of as seditious a nature frequently appear in the public newspapers, and other publications, and (as would, no doubt, have been the case with this) are neglected and forgotten. But the magistrates of Birmingham, and other known enemies of the Dissenters, were loud in their exclamations against it, though perhaps fabricated for the use that was made of it; and a copy was officiously sent to the secretaries of state, who ordered a strict enquiry to be made after the author, printer, or distributor; and in consequence of this a reward of an hundred pounds was offered, for the discovery of any of them.

In consequence of all this preparation, we were informed that, though the trade of Birmingham had never been more brisk, so that hands could not be found to manufacture the goods that were ordered, many of the public-houses were that day full of people, whose horrid execrations against the Dissenters were heard into the streets; and it has been asserted that some of the master-manufacturers had shut up their work-shops, and thereby left their men at full liberty for any mischief.

It has since appeared that besides the dinner at the Hotel, there were also dinners of the opposite party on this fourteenth of July, and those not of the lowest class of the people, with whom the common ale-houses were filled. These did not rise from their entertainment so early, or with so much sobriety, as those who dined at the Hotel; and it was at the breaking up of *their* companies that the riots commenced. Let the impartial then judge to which of the dinners the riot that followed is to be ascribed.

Mr. Adam Walker, the ingenious and well known lecturer in natural Philosophy, was passing through the town with his wife and family, and dined with me at my own house, for the last time, on that day. Before dinner, I had walked to the town with him, and they left me in the evening. Some time after this, three of my intimate friends, whose houses were situated near the same road, and farther from the town than mine, called upon me to congratulate me, and one another, on the dinner having passed over so well; and after chatting chearfully some time on the subject, they left me just as it was beginning to be dark.

After supper, when I was preparing to amuse myself, as I sometimes did, with a game of backgammon, we were alarmed by some young men rapping violently at the door; and when they were admitted, they appeared to be almost breathless with running. They said that a great mob had assembled at the Hotel, where the company had dined; that after breaking the windows there, they were gone to the New Meeting, and were demolishing the pulpit and pews, and that they threatened me and my house. That they should think of molesting *me* I thought so improbable, that I could hardly give any credit to the story. However, imagining that perhaps some of the mob might come to insult me, I was prevailed upon to leave the house, and meant to go to some neighbour's at a greater distance from the town; but having no apprehension for the house itself, or any thing in it, I only went up stairs, and put some papers and other things of value, where I thought that any persons getting into the house would not easily find them. My wife did the same with some things of hers. I then bade the Servants keep the doors fastened; if any body should come, to say that I was gone, and if any stones should be thrown at the windows, to keep themselves out of danger, and that I did not doubt but they would go away again.

At this time, which was about half past nine o'clock, Mr. S. Ryland, a friend of mine, came with a chaise, telling us there was no time to lose, but that we must immediately get into it, and drive off. Accordingly, we got in with nothing more than the cloathes we happened to have on, and drove from the house. But hearing that the mob consisted only of people on foot, and concluding that when they found I was gone off in a chaise, they could not tell whither, they would never think of pursuing me, we went no farther than Mr. Russell's, a mile on the same road, and there we continued several hours, Mr. Russell himself, and other persons, being upon the road on horseback to get intelligence of what was passing. I also more than once walked about half way back to my own house for the same purpose; and then I saw the fires from the two meeting-houses, which were burning down.

About twelve we were told that some hundreds of the mob were breaking into my house, and that when they had demolished *it*, they would certainly proceed to Mr. Russell's. We were persuaded, therefore, to get into the chaise again, and drive off; but we went no further than Mr. Thomas Hawks's on Mosely-Green, which is not more than half a mile farther from the town, and there we waited all the night.

It being remarkably calm, and clear moon-light, we could see to a considerable distance, and being upon a rising ground, we distinctly heard all that passed at the house, every shout of the mob, and almost every stroke of the instruments they had provided for breaking the doors and the furniture. For they could not get any fire, though one of them was heard to offer two guineas for a lighted candle; my son, whom we left behind us, having taken the precaution to put out all the fires in the house, and others of my friends got all the neighbours to do the same. I afterwards heard that much pains was taken, but without effect, to get fire from my large electrical machine, which stood in the library.

About three o'clock in the morning the noises ceased, and Mr. Russell and my son coming to us, said that the mob was almost dispersed, that not more than twenty of them remained, and those so much intoxicated, that they might easily be taken. We therefore returned with him, and about four o'clock were going to bed at his house. But when I was undressing myself for that purpose, news came that there was a fresh accession of some hundreds more to the mob, and that they were advancing towards Mr. Russell's. On this we got into the chaise once more, and driving through a part of the town distant from the mob, we went to Dudley, and thence to my son-in-law's, Mr. Finch at Heath-Forge, five miles farther, where we arrived before breakfast, and brought the first news of our disaster.

Here I thought myself perfectly safe, and imagining that when the mischief was over (and I had no idea of its going beyond my own house) and supposing that, as the people in general would be ashamed, and concerned, at what had happened, I might return; thinking also that the area within the walls of the Meeting house might soon be cleared, I intended, if the weather would permit, to preach there the Sunday following, and from this text, *Father forgive them, for they know not what they do.*

At noon, however, we had an express from Stourbridge, to acquaint us that the mob had traced me to Dudley, and would pursue me to Heath. To this I paid no attention, not to another from Dudley in the evening to inform us of the same thing; and being in want of sleep, I went to bed soon after ten. But at eleven I was awaked, and told that a third express was just arrived from Dudley, to assure us that some persons were certainly in pursuit of me, and would be there that night. All the family believing this, and urging me to make my escape, I dressed myself, got on horseback, and with a servant rode to Bridgnorth, where I arrived about two in the morning.

After about two hours' sleep in this place, I got into a chaise, and went to Kidderminster, on my way to London. Here I found myself among my friends, and, as I thought, far enough from the scene of danger, especially as we continually heard news from Birmingham, and that the mischief did not extend beyond the town. Hearing, particularly, that all was quiet in Dudley, I concluded that there could be no real cause of apprehension at Heath; and being unwilling to go farther than was necessary, I took a horse, and arrived there in the evening.

There, however, I found the family in great consternation at the sight of me; and Mr. Finch just arriving from Dudley, and saying that they were in momentary expectation of a riot there, that the populace were even assembled in the street, and were heard to threaten the meeting-house, the house of the minister, and those of other principal Dissenters, and that all attempts to make them disperse had been in vain, I mounted my horse again, though much fatigued, and greatly wanting sleep.

My intention was to get to an inn about six miles on the road to Kidderminster, where I might get a chaise, and in it proceed to that town. No chaise, however, was to be had; so that I was under the necessity of proceeding on horseback, and neither the servant nor myself distinguishing the road in the night, we lost our way, and at break of day found ourselves on Bridgnorth race ground, having ridden nineteen miles, till we could hardly sit our horses.

Arriving at this place a second time, about three o'clock in the morning, we with some difficulty roused the people at an indifferent inn, and I immediately got into bed, and slept a few hours. After breakfast we mounted our horses, and I got a second time to Kidderminster. There, finding that if I immediately took a chaise, and drove fast, I might get to Worcester time enough for the mail-coach, I did so; and meeting with a young man of my own congregation, he accompanied me thither, which was a great satisfaction to me, as he acquainted me with many particulars of the riot, of which I was before ignorant. At Worcester I was just time enough for the coach, and fortunately there was one place vacant. I took it, and travelling all night, I got to London on Monday morning, July 18.

Alien Act, 1793

33 Geo. 3, c. 4   *Statutes at Large*, XXXIX, pt. 1, 10-16.

This act placed certain restrictions upon aliens.

Whereas a great and unusual number of persons, not being natural-born subjects of his Majesty, or denizens or persons naturalized by act of parliament, have lately resorted to this kingdom: and whereas, under the present circumstances, much danger may arise to the publick tranquillity from the resort and residence of aliens, unless due provision be made in respect thereof; be it therefore enacted by the King's most excellent majesty, by and with the advice and consent of the lords spiritual and temporal, and commons, in this present parliament assembled, and by the authority of the same, That, during the continuance of this act, the master or commander of every ship or vessel which shall arrive in any port or place of this kingdom, shall, immediately on his arrival, declare in writing to the collector and comptroller, or other chief officer of the customs, at or near such port or place, whether there are, to the best of his knowledge, any foreigners on board his said vessel; and shall, in his said declaration, specify the number of foreigners, if any, on board his said vessel, and also specify their names and respective rank, occupation, or description, as far as he shall be informed thereof.

II.   And be it further enacted by the authority aforesaid, That the master or commander of every ship or vessel, so arriving as aforesaid, who shall neglect or refuse to make such declaration as aforesaid, shall, for every such offence, forfeit and pay the sum of ten pounds, for each and every foreigner who shall have been on board at the time of the arrival of such ship or vessel as aforesaid, whom he shall have wilfully neglected or refused to declare as aforesaid; one moiety whereof shall be to the informer or informers, and the other moiety to the poor of the parish or place in which such offence shall have been committed, to be recovered before any one or more justice or justices of the peace acting in and for the division, city, town, or place, in which such offence shall have been committed, by the confession of the party, or on the oath of one or more credible witness or witnesses; and in case such master or commander as aforesaid shall neglect or refuse forthwith to pay such penalty as he shall be adjudged to pay in manner aforesaid, that it shall and may be lawful for the collector, comptroller, or other chief officer of the customs, to detain such ship or vessel as aforesaid, until the same shall have been paid.

III.   And be it further enacted by the authority aforesaid, That every alien who shall arrive in any port or place of this kingdom, on or after the tenth day of *January* one thousand seven hundred and ninety-three, shall, immediately after such arrival, declare in writing to the collector, comptroller, or other chief officer of the customs, at or near such port or place, his or her name and rank, occupation or description, or if a domestick servant, then also the name, rank, occupation, or description of his or her master or mistress, or shall verbally make to such officer as aforesaid such declaration, to be by him reduced to writing; and shall also in like manner declare the country or countries, place or places where he or she shall have principally resided for six calendar months next immediately preceding such arrival: and that every such alien who shall neglect to make declaration of the aforesaid particulars, or who shall wilfully make any false declaration thereof, shall, for every such offence, on conviction thereof in his Majesty's court of king's bench, or in any court of oyer and terminer, gaol delivery, or great sessions, or justiciary court in *Scotland*, be adjudged to depart out of this realm, and all other his Majesty's dominions, within a time to be limited in such judgement; and if he or she shall be found therein after such time in such judgement so limited, without lawful cause, he or she shall, being duly convicted thereof, be transported for life.

IV.   And be it further enacted by the authority aforesaid, That every such alien so arriving as aforesaid, shall obtain from the collector, comptroller, or other chief officer of the customs (and such officers are hereby respectively required to deliver the same) a certificate of his or her declarations, made in writing or verbally, containing all the particulars in such declaration contained.

V.   Provided always, and be it further enacted by the authority aforesaid, That nothing herein-before contained shall extend or be construed to extend to any mariner, whom the master or commander of any ship or vessel, arriving in any port or place in *Great Britain*, shall certify to such collector, comptroller, or other chief officer of the customs, in writing, subscribed by such master or commander, to be actually engaged and employed in the navigation of such ship or vessel, during the time that such mariner shall remain so actually engaged and employed; and which certificate in writing, so subscribed as aforesaid, every such master or commander as aforesaid is hereby required to give.

VI.   And be it further enacted by the authority aforesaid, That it shall not be lawful for any alien so arriving to import or bring into this kingdom, any weapons, arms, gunpowder, or ammunition whatever, other than as merchandize, subject to the laws now in force respecting the importation of such arms or ammunition respectively as merchandize; and that it shall be lawful for any of his Majesty's officers of the customs to take into his or their custody any weapons, arms, gunpowder, or ammunition which shall be attempted to be imported or brought into this kingdom, in any manner contrary to this act, taking an account thereof; which account shall specify the persons by whom the same were respectively brought; . . .

VII.   And be it further enacted by the authority aforesaid, That when and so often as his Majesty, his heirs and successors, shall think it necessary for the safety or tranquillity of the kingdom, by his or their proclamation or order in council, to direct that aliens of any description therein contained (not being alien merchants within the true intent and meaning of this act) shall not be landed in this kingdom, or shall not be landed, except at such places, and under such regulations, as shall be in such proclamation or order expressed, then and in every such case the master or commander of every ship, or vessel, or boat, having any such alien or aliens on board, shall not suffer any such alien or aliens to land within any part of this kingdom, contrary to such proclamation or order in council, unless by the express permission of his Majesty, signified under the hand of one of his Majesty's principal secretaries of state; and every such master or commander wilfully neglecting to conform to any of the directions or regulations contained in such proclamation or order, shall forfeit fifty pounds for every alien so landed, to be recovered before one or more of his Majesty's justices of the peace, one moiety thereof to be to the informer or informers, and the other moiety to the poor of the parish where such offence shall be committed, and such ship or vessel from on board of which any such alien or aliens shall so land, and every other vessel or boat used in landing any such alien or aliens, shall and may be seized by any officer or officers of the customs or excise, and the same shall respectively be forfeited, together with all tackle, apparel, ammunition, and furniture, thereunto respectively belonging.

VIII.   And be it further enacted by the authority aforesaid, That no alien so arriving shall depart from the place in which he or she shall have so arrived, except for the purpose of making such declaration as herein-before required to the collector, comptroller, or other chief officer of the customs as aforesaid, or for the purpose of obtaining such passport as is herein-after mentioned, without previously obtaining a passport from the mayor or other chief magistrate of such place, or from one justice of peace for the county or district in which the same may be situated; in which passport shall be expressed the name and rank, occupation or description, of such alien, as declared by him or her to such officer of the customs as aforesaid, and also the town or place to which such alien purposes to go; and such mayor, magistrate, or justice, is hereby required to give such passport on application made to him for that purpose, on production of the certificate of his or her declaration as aforesaid, provided that such town or place, to which such alien purposes to go, shall not be a town or place from which such alien is restrained from going by any such proclamation or order as is herein mentioned, and provided that such alien shall not have landed in this kingdom contrary to any such proclamation or order in council as is herein mentioned.

IX.   And be it further enacted by the authority aforesaid, That when and so often as any alien, except the domestick servants of any of his Majesty's natural-born subjects, or such as shall have had letters patent of denization, or been naturalized by act of parliament, being actually attendant on their respective masters, who shall have arrived in this kingdom since the first day of *January* one thousand seven hundred and ninety-two, or who shall arrive therein at any time during the continuance of this act, shall be desirous to change the place of his or her usual residence, or to quit the town or place at which such alien shall have arrived by virtue of his or her first passport, such alien shall obtain from the mayor or chief magistrate, or any justice of the peace for the county, town, place, or district, in which such alien shall be resident, a passport, in which shall be expressed the name and description of such alien in the manner herein-before provided, and also, unless such alien shall be an alien merchant, the name of the town or place to which such alien shall propose to remove; and such mayor, chief magistrate, or justice, is hereby required to give such passport, on application made to him for that purpose by such alien: provided always, That every such alien shall, at the time of making such application, exhibit to such magistrate or justice the passport, by virtue of which such alien arrived in such county, district, town, or place in which he or she shall be resident, or, if such alien shall not have arrived therein by virtue of any passport, a certificate from the magistrate or justice, or other person to whom such alien shall have delivered an account of his or her name and description, in the manner herein-after provided.

X. Provided also, and be it enacted by the authority aforesaid, That if it shall appear to the satisfaction of such mayor, magistrate, or justice, upon due examination upon oath of such alien, and also, if necessary, of any other person or persons, that such alien is an alien merchant, within the true intent and meaning of this act, it shall not be necessary to express in such passport the name of the town or place to which such alien shall propose to remove, but the same shall describe such alien to be an alien merchant within the true intent and meaning of this act, and give full liberty to such alien merchant to pass and repass to and from all parts of this kingdom.

XI. And be it further enacted by the authority aforesaid, That it shall and may be lawful to and for the mayor or chief magistrate, or for any justice of peace of any county, city, town, place, or district within this kingdom, to require of any alien who shall have arrived in this kingdom after the first day of *January* one thousand seven hundred and ninety-two, or shall arrive at any time during the continuance of this act, except such domestick servants as aforesaid, and who shall be passing through or be found in such county, city, town, place, or district, to exhibit to such mayor, magistrate, or justice, his or her passport, which he or she is hereby required to exhibit accordingly, and in default thereof, or in case it shall appear thereby that such alien not being therein described as an alien merchant, in the manner in this act mentioned, is not in his or her way to such town or place as is therein expressed, and such mayor, magistrate, or justice shall see cause to suspect that such alien is not *bona fide* proceeding to such town or place as aforesaid, or in case such mayor, magistrate or justice, shall see cause to suspect that such alien landed in this kingdom contrary to any such proclamation or order in council, as is herein mentioned, such mayor, magistrate, or justice may commit such alien to the common gaol, or other publick prison, or detain such alien in such custody as such mayor, magistrate, or justice may think proper, until notice thereof be sent, by such mayor, magistrate, or justice, to one of his Majesty's principal secretaries of state, which notice such mayor, magistrate, or justice is hereby required forthwith to transmit, and until sufficient time shall have been allowed for the transmission of his Majesty's commands thereupon; and unless his Majesty shall thereupon, within ten days in *England*, or fourteen days in *Scotland*, signify his pleasure that such alien shall be discharged, or shall direct, in manner herein-after mentioned, that such alien shall depart the realm, it shall and may be lawful for such mayor, magistrate, or justice, to cause such alien to be committed to the common gaol, without bail or mainprize, until he or she shall be delivered by due course of law.

XII.   And be it enacted by the authority aforesaid, That every alien whom his Majesty shall not so signify his pleasure to discharge, who shall have refused to exhibit his or her passport, or who shall have been found not *bona fide* proceeding to the town or place therein expressed, or who shall have wilfully landed in this kingdom contrary to any proclamation or order in council herein mentioned, and who shall be lawfully convicted thereof in his Majesty's court of king's bench, or any court of oyer and terminer, or gaol delivery, or great sessions, or court of justiciary in *Scotland*, shall be adjudged to suffer imprisonment for any time not exceeding one month, and at the expiration of the said term to depart out of the realm within a time to be limited in such judgement; and if such alien shall be found therein after such time in such judgement so limited, without lawful cause, such alien shall, being duly convicted, be transported for life.

XIII.   And be it further enacted by the authority aforesaid, That if any person or persons shall wilfully forge, counterfeit, or alter, or cause to be forged, counterfeited, or altered, or shall utter, knowing the same to be forged, counterfeited, or altered, any such passport or certificate as are by this act directed, or shall obtain such passport or certificate under any other name or description than that which he or she shall have declared to such custom house officer, or to any such mayor, magistrate, or justice as are herein mentioned, or shall falsely pretend to be the person mentioned in such passport or certificate, such person or persons shall, for every such offence, on conviction thereof in his Majesty's court of king's bench, or any court of oyer and terminer, gaol delivery, or great sessions, or in the justiciary court in *Scotland*, be adjudged to be imprisoned, and shall be imprisoned in the common gaol for any time not exceeding six calendar months, and at the expiration of that time to depart out of this realm, within a time to be limited by such judgement; and if such person or persons be found therein after such time in such judgement so limited, without lawful cause, he or she shall, being duly convicted, be transported for life.

XIV.   And be it further enacted by the authority aforesaid, That notices of the several regulations herein-before contained shall be printed in different languages, and shall be affixed in publick places in the different ports of this kingdom, and shall also be delivered by the custom house officers to all foreigners on their arrival in any port of this kingdom, in every case in which it can conveniently be done; but that it shall not be necessary for the conviction of any alien offending against this act, to prove such personal delivery of the said notices.

XV.   And be it further enacted by the authority aforesaid, That when and so often as his Majesty, his heirs and successors, shall, by his or their proclamation, or by his or their order in council, or order under his or their sign manual, direct that any alien being, or who may hereafter arrive within this realm during the continuance of this act, shall depart this realm within a time limited in such proclamation or orders respectively, and any alien shall knowingly neglect or refuse to pay due obedience to such proclamation or orders respectively, or shall be found in this kingdom contrary to such proclamation or orders, as the case may be, it shall and may be lawful for any of his Majesty's principal secretaries of state, or for any justice of the peace, or for any mayor or chief magistrate as aforesaid, to cause every such alien, so neglecting or refusing as aforesaid, to be arrested, and to be committed to the common gaol of the county or place where he or she shall be so arrested, there to remain, without bail or mainprize, until he or she shall be delivered by due course of law.

XVI. And be it further enacted by the authority aforesaid, That every such alien so disobeying or knowingly neglecting to pay due obedience to such proclamation or orders respectively, or being found in this kingdom contrary to such proclamation or orders respectively, who shall be lawfully convicted thereof in his Majesty's court of king's bench, or any court of oyer and terminer, gaol delivery, or great sessions, or court of justiciary in *Scotland*, shall be adjudged to suffer imprisonment for any time not exceeding one month, and at the expiration of the said term to depart out of the realm, within a time to be limited by such judgement, and if such alien shall be found therein, after such time in such judgement so limited, without lawful cause, such alien shall, being duly convicted, be transported for life.

XVII. And be it further enacted by the authority aforesaid, That it shall and may be lawful for any one of his Majesty's principal secretaries of state, in cases where he shall apprehend that immediate obedience will not be paid to such proclamation, or orders respectively, as aforesaid, by warrant under his hand and seal to give such alien in charge to one of his Majesty's messengers, or to such other person or persons to whom he shall think proper to direct such warrant, in order to his or her being conducted out of the kingdom, in such manner as shall be suitable to his or her rank and situation; and that in case any excuse shall be alledged by any such alien for not complying with such proclamation or orders respectively, it shall and may be lawful for the lords of his Majesty's privy council to judge of the validity of such excuse, and to allow or disallow the same; and such alien shall remain in the custody of such messenger, or such other person or persons as aforesaid, until the lords of his Majesty's privy council shall have signified their determination thereupon.

XVIII. And be it further enacted by the authority aforesaid, That it shall and may be lawful for his Majesty, his heirs and successors, by his or their proclamation, or order in council, or order under the royal sign manual, to order and direct any alien or aliens who shall have arrived within this kingdom since the first day of *January* one thousand seven hundred and ninety-two, or who shall arrive therein during the continuance of this act, other than alien merchants, and the domestick servants of any of his Majesty's natural-born subjects, or of such as shall have had letters patent of denization, or been naturalized by act of parliament, actually and *bona fide* employed in the service of their respective masters, to dwell and reside respectively in such district or districts as his Majesty, his heirs and successors, shall think necessary for the publick security; and if any such alien, except as herein-before excepted, being so ordered and directed, shall dwell or shall be found to be or have been in any part of this kingdom, other than such district or districts as aforesaid, in breach of such proclamation or orders respectively, it shall and may be lawful for any of his Majesty's principal secretaries of state, or for any justice of peace, or any such mayor or chief magistrate as aforesaid, to cause such alien to be arrested, and if it shall appear to such principal secretary of state, or to such justice, mayor, or chief magistrate, that such alien did knowingly and wilfully depart out of such district or districts, in breach of such proclamation or orders respectively, such alien shall be committed to the common gaol, there to be detained, without bail or mainprize, until he or she shall be delivered by due course of law: and if any such alien, except as herein-before excepted, shall be duly convicted in his Majesty's court of king's bench, or any court of oyer and terminer, gaol delivery, or great sessions, or court of justiciary in *Scotland*, of knowingly and wilfully dwelling or residing, or being found to be, or of having been in any place in this kingdom in breach of such proclamation or orders respectively as aforesaid, he or she shall be adjudged to be imprisoned, and shall be imprisoned for any time not exceeding one month. . . .

Habeas Corpus Suspension Act, 23 May 1794

34 Geo. 3, c. 54   *Statutes at Large*, XXXIX, pt. 2, 556-57.

This act empowered the government to detain without bail and on unspecified charges person suspected of treason and other serious crimes.

Whereas a traitorous and detestable conspiracy has been formed for subverting the existing laws and constitution, and for introducing the system of anarchy and confusion which has so totally prevailed in *France*: therefore, for the better preservation of his Majesty's sacred person, and for securing the peace and the laws and liberties of this kingdom; be it enacted by the King's most excellent majesty, by and with the advice and consent of the lords spiritual and temporal, and commons, in this present parliament assembled, and by the authority of the same, That every person or persons that are or shall be in prison within the kingdom of *Great Britain* at or upon the day on which this act shall receive his Majesty's royal assent, or after, by warrant of his said Majesty's most honourable privy council, signed by six of the said privy council, for high treason, suspicion of high treason, or treasonable practices, or by warrant, signed by any of his Majesty's secretaries of state, for such causes as aforesaid, may be detained in safe custody, without bail or mainprize, until the first day of *February* one thousand seven hundred and ninety-five; and that no judge or justice of the peace shall bail or try any such person or persons so committed, without order from his said Majesty's privy council, signed by six of the said privy council, till the said first day of *February* one thousand seven hundred and ninety-five; any law or statute to the contrary notwithstanding.

II. And be it further enacted by the authority aforesaid, That the act made in *Scotland* in the year of our Lord one thousand seven hundred and one, (intituled, *An act for preventing wrongous imprisonment, and against undue delays in trials*), in so far as the same may be construed to relate to cases of treason and suspicion of treason, be suspended until the said first day of *February* one thousand seven hundred and ninety-five; and that until the said day no judge, justice of peace, or other officer of the law in *Scotland*, shall liberate, try, or admit to bail, any person or persons that is, are, or shall be, in prison within *Scotland*, for such causes as aforesaid, without order from his said Majesty's privy council, signed by six of the said privy council: provided always, That, from and after the said first day of *February* one thousand seven hundred and ninety-five, the said persons so committed shall have the benefit and advantage of all laws and statutes any way relating to or providing for the liberty of the subjects of this realm, and that this present act shall continue until the said first day of *February* one thousand seven hundred and ninety-five, and no longer.

III. Provided always, and be it enacted, That nothing in this act shall be construed to extend to invalidate the ancient rights and privileges of parliament, or to the imprisonment or detaining of any member of either house of parliament during the sitting of such parliament, until the matter of which he stands suspected be first communicated to the house of which he is a member, and the consent of the said house obtained for his commitment or detaining.

Speech by Thomas Erskine at the Old Bailey defending Thomas Hardy and other radical leaders against charges of high treason, 31 October 1794

Howell's State Trials, XXIV, 938-70.

Hardy and his associates were arrested after attending in 1793 a British Convention of the Delegates of the People held in Edinburgh. Hardy was secretary of the London Corresponding Society at the time. Defended by Thomas Erskine (1750-1823), later first Baron Erskine, the defendants were acquitted by the jury.

Gentlemen, I declare that I am utterly astonished, on looking at the clock, to find how long I have been speaking; and that, agitated and distressed as I am, I have yet strength enough left for the remainder of my duty;—at every peril of my health it shall be exerted; for although, if this cause should miscarry, I know I shall have justice done me for the honesty of my intentions; yet what is that to the public and posterity?—What is it to them, when, if upon this evidence there can stand a conviction for high treason, it is plain that no man can be said to have a life which is his own?—For how can he possibly know by what engines it may be snared, or from what unknown sources it may be attacked and overpowered?—Such a monstrous precedent would be as ruinous to the king as to his subjects—We are in a crisis of our affairs; which putting justice out of the question, calls in sound policy for the greatest prudence and moderation.—At a time when other nations are disposed to subvert *their* establishments, let it be our wisdom to make the subject feel the practical benefits of *our own*: let us seek to bring good out of evil:—the distracted inhabitants of the world will fly to us for sanctuary, driven out of their countries from the dreadful consequences of not attending to seasonable reforms in government; victims to the folly of suffering corruptions to continue, till the whole fabric of society is dissolved and tumbles into ruin. Landing upon our shores, they will feel the blessing of security, and they will discover in what it consists; they will read this trial, and their hearts will palpitate at your decision:—they will say to one another, and their voices will reach to the ends of the earth; may the constitution of England endure for ever!—the sacred and yet remaining sanctuary for the oppressed:—here, and here only, the lot of man is cast in security:—what though authority, established for the ends of justice, may lift itself up against it;—what though the House of Commons itself should make an *ex-parte* declaration of guilt;—what though every species of art should be employed to entangle the opinions of the people, which in other countries would be inevitable destruction:— yet in England, in enlightened England, all this will not pluck a hair from the head of innocence;—the jury will still look steadfastly to the law, as the great polar star, to direct them in their course:—as prudent men they will set no example of disorder, nor pronounce a verdict of censure on authority, or of approbation or disapprobation beyond their judicial province:—but, on the other hand, they will make no political sacrifice, but deliver a plain, honest man, from the toils of justice.—When your verdict is pronounced, this will be the judgment of the world;—and if any amongst ourselves are alienated in their affections to government, nothing will be so likely to reclaim them:—they will say—Whatever we have lost of our control in parliament, we have yet a sheet-anchor remaining to hold the vessel of the state amidst contending storms:—we have still, thank God, a sound administration of justice secured to us, in the independence of the judges, in the rights of enlightened juries, and in the integrity of the bar;—ready at all times, and upon every possible occasion, whatever may be the consequences to themselves, to stand forward in defence of the meanest man in England, when brought for judgment before the laws of the country.

To return to this Scotch Convention.—Their papers were all seized by government.—What their proceedings were they best know: we can only see what parts they choose to show us: but, from what we have seen, does any man seriously believe, that this meeting at Edinburgh meant to assume and to maintain by force all the functions and authorities of the state?—Is the thing within the compass of human belief?—If a man were offered a dukedom, and twenty thousand pounds a year, for trying to believe it, he might say he believed it, as what will not man say for gold and honours? but he never in fact could believe that this Edinburgh meeting was a parliament for Great Britain:—how indeed could he, from the proceedings of a few peaceable, unarmed men, discussing, in a constitutional manner, the means of obtaining a reform in parliament; and who, to maintain the club, or whatever you choose to call it, collected a little money from people who were well disposed to the cause; a few shillings one day, and perhaps as many pence another?— I think as far as I could reckon it up, when the report from this great committee of supply was read to you, I counted that there had been raised, in the first session of this parliament, fifteen pounds, from which indeed you must deduct two bad shillings, which are literally noticed in the account.—Is it to be endured, gentlemen, that men should gravely say, that this body assumed to itself the offices of parliament?—that a few harmless people, who sat, as they profess, to obtain a full representation of the people, were themselves, even in their own imaginations, the complete representation which they sought for?—Why should they sit from day to day to consider how they might obtain what they had already got?—If their object was an universal representation of the whole people, how is it credible they could suppose that universal representation to exist in themselves—in the representatives of a few societies instituted to obtain it for the country at large?—If they were themselves the nation, why should the language of every resolution be, that reason ought to be their grand engine for the accomplishment of their object, and should be directed to convince the nation to speak to parliament in a voice that must be heard? The proposition, therefore, is too gross to cram down the throats of the English people, and this is the prisoner's security.—Here again he feels the advantage of our free administration of justice; this proposition on which so much depends, is not to be reasoned upon on parchment, to be delivered privately to magistrates for private judgment: no he has the privilege of appealing aloud, as he now appeals by me, to an enlightened assembly full of eyes, and ears, and intelligence where speaking to a jury is, in a manner, speaking to a nation at large, and flying for sanctuary to its universal justice.

Gentlemen, the very work of Mr. Paine, under the banners of which this supposed rebellion was set on foot, refutes the charge it is brought forward to support: for Mr. Paine, in his preface, and throughout his whole book, reprobates the use of force against the most evil governments; the contrary was never imputed to him.—If his book had been written in pursuance of the design of force and rebellion, with which it is now sought to be connected, he would, like the prisoners, have been charged with an overt act of high treason; but such a proceeding was never thought of.—Mr. Paine was indicted for a misdemeanor, and the misdemeanor was argued to consist not in the falsehood that a nation has no right to choose or alter its government, but in seditiously exciting the nation, without cause, to exercise that right.—A learned lord (lord chief baron Macdonald), now on this bench, addressed the jury as attorney-general upon this principle: his language was this:—The question is not, what the people have a right to do, for the people are, undoubtedly, the foundation and origin of all government; but the charge is, for seditiously calling upon the people, without cause or reason, to exercise a right which would be sedition, supposing the right to be in them: for though the people might have a right to do the thing suggested, and though they are not excited to the doing it by force and rebellion, yet, as the suggestion goes to unsettle the state, the propagation of such doctrines is seditious. There is no other way, undoubtedly, of describing that charge. I am not here entering into the application of it to Mr. Paine, whose counsel I was, and who has been tried already. To say that the people have a right to change their government, is indeed a truism; every body knows it, and they exercised the right, otherwise the king could not have had his establishment amongst us. If, therefore, I stir up individuals to oppose by force the general will, seated in the government, it may be treason; but to induce changes in a government, by exposing to a whole nation its errors and imperfections, can have no bearing upon such an offence:—the utmost which can be made of it is a misdemeanor, and that too depending wholly upon the judgment which the jury may form of the intention of the writer—The Courts, for a long time, indeed, assumed to themselves the province of deciding upon this intention, as a matter of law, conclusively inferring it from the act of publication: I say the Courts *assumed* it, though it was not the doctrine of lord Mansfield, but handed down to him from the precedents of judges before his time: but even in that case, though the publication was the crime, not, as in this case the intention, and though the quality of the thing charged, when not rebutted by evidence for the defendant, had so long been considered to be a legal inference, yet the legislature, to support the province of the jury, and in tenderness for liberty, has lately altered the law upon this important subject. If, therefore, we were not assembled, as we are, to consider of the existence of high treason against the king's life, but only of a misdemeanor for seditiously disturbing his title and establishment, by the proceedings for a reform in parliament, I should think the Crown, upon the very principle which, under the libel law, must now govern such a trial, quite as distant from its mark; because, in my opinion, there is no way by which his majesty's title can more firmly be secured, or by which (above all, in our times) its permanency can be better established, than by promoting a more full and equal representation of the people, by peaceable means; and by what other means has it been sought, in this instance, to be promoted?

Gentlemen, when the members of this convention were seized, did they attempt resistance?—Did they insist upon their privileges as subjects under the laws, or as a parliament enacting laws for others?—If they had said or done any thing to give colour to such an idea, there needed no spies to convict them; the crown could have given ample indemnity for evidence from amongst themselves: the societies consisted of thousands and thousands of persons, some of whom, upon any calculation of human nature, might have been produced: the delegates, who attended the meetings, could not be supposed to have met, with a different intention from those who sent them; and, if the answer to that is, that the constituents are involved in the guilt of their representatives, we get back to the monstrous position *from which I observed you before to shrink back, with visible horror, when I stated it*; namely, the involving in the fate and consequence of this single trial every man, who corresponded with these societies, or who, as a member of societies in any part of the kingdom, consented to the meeting which was assembled, or which was in prospect:—but, I thank God, I have nothing to fear from those hydras, when I see before me such just and honourable men to hold the balance of justice.

Gentlemen, the dissolution of this parliament speaks as strong a language as its conduct when sitting.—How was it dissolved? When the magistrates entered, Mr. Skirving was in the chair, which he refused to leave:—he considered and asserted his conduct to be legal, and therefore informed the magistrate he must exercise his authority, that the dispersion might appear to be involuntary, and that the subject, disturbed in his rights, might be entitled to his remedy.—The magistrate on this took Mr. Skirving by the shoulder, who immediately obeyed; the chair was quitted in a moment, and this great parliament broke up. What was the effect of all this proceeding at the time, when whatever belonged to it must have been best understood?—Were any of the parties indicted for high treason?—Were they indicted even for a breach of the peace in holding the Convention?—None of these things.—The law of Scotland, arbitrary as it is, was to be disturbed to find a name for their offence, and the rules of trial to be violated to convict them:—They were denied their challenges to their Jurors, and other irregularities were introduced, so as to be the subject of complaint in the House of Commons.—Gentlemen, in what I am saying, I am not standing up to vindicate all that they published during these proceedings, more especially those which were written in consequence of the trials I have just alluded to; but allowance must be made for a state of heat and irritation:— they saw men whom they believed to be persecuted for what they conceived to be innocent; they saw them the victims of sentences which many would consider as equivalent to, if not worse than, judgment of treason: sentences which, at all events had never existed before, and such as, I believe, never will again with impunity.— But since I am on the subject of *intention*, I shall conduct myself with the same moderation which I have been prescribing; I will cast no aspersions, but shall content myself with lamenting that these judgments were productive of consequences, which rarely follow from authority discreetly exercised. How easy is it then to dispose of as much of the evidence as consumed half a day in the anathemas against the Scotch Judges! It appears that they came to various resolutions concerning them: some good, some bad, and all of them irregular. Amongst others they compare them to Jeffries, and wish that they, who imitate his example, may meet his fate.—What then?—Irreverend expressions against Judges are not acts of high treason!—If they had assembled round the Court of Justiciary and hanged them in the execution of their offices, it would not have been treason within the statute.—I am no advocate for disrespect to Judges, and think that it is dangerous to the public order; but putting aside the insult upon the Judges now in authority, the reprobation of Jeffries is no libel, but an awful and useful memento to wicked men. Lord Chief Justice Jeffries denied the privilege of English law to an innocent man. He refused it to sir Thomas Armstrong, who in vain pleaded, in bar of his outlawry, that he was out of the realm when he was exacted—(an objection so clear, that it was lately taken for granted, in the case of Mr. Purefoy)—The daughter of this unfortunate person, a lady of honour and quality, came publicly into court to supplicate for her father; and what were the effects of her supplications, and of the law in the mouth of the Prisoner? "Sir Thomas Armstrong," said Jeffries, "you may amuse yourself as much as you please with the idea of your innocence, but you are to be hanged next Friday;"—and, upon the natural exclamation of a daughter at this horrible outrage against her parent, he said, "Take that woman out of court:" which she answered by a prayer, that God Almighty's judgments might light upon him. Gentlemen, they did light upon him; and when, after his death, which speedily followed this transaction, the matter was brought before the House of Commons, under that glorious Revolution which is asserted throughout the proceedings before you, the judgment against Sir Thomas Armstrong was declared to be a murder under colour of justice? Sir Robert Sawyer, the Attorney General, was expelled the House of Commons for his misdemeanour in refusing the writ of error,—and the executors of Jefferies were commanded to make compensation to the widow and the daughter of the deceased. These are great monuments of justice;—and, although I by no means approve of harsh expressions against authority, which tend to weaken the holdings of society, yet let us not go beyond the mark in our restraints nor suppose that men are dangerously disaffected to the government, because they feel a sort of pride and exultation in events, which constitute the dignity and glory of their country.

Gentlemen, this resentment against the proceedings of the Courts in Scotland, was not confined to those who were the objects of them; it was not confined even to the friends of a Reform in Parliament—a benevolent public, in both parts of the island, joined them in the complaint; and a gentleman of great moderation, and a most inveterate enemy to parliamentary reform, as thinking it not an improvement of the government, but nevertheless a lover of his country and its insulted justice, made the convictions of the delegates the subject of a public inquiry:—I speak of my friend Mr. William Adam, who brought these judgments of the Scotch Judges before the House of Commons—arraigned them as contrary to law, and proposed to reverse them by the authority of Parliament. Let it not then be matter of wonder, that these poor men, who were the immediate victims of this injustice, and who saw their brethren expelled from their country by an unprecedented and questionable judgment, should feel like men on the subject, and express themselves as they felt.

Gentlemen, amidst the various distresses and embarrassments which attend my present situation, it is a great consolation that I have marked from the beginning, your vigilant attention and your capacity to understand; it is, therefore, with the utmost confidence that I ask you a few plain questions, arising out of the whole of these Scotch proceedings.—In the first place, then, do you believe it to be possible, that, if these men had really projected the Convention as a traitorous usurpation of the authorities of Parliament, they would have invited the Friends of the People, in Frith-street, to assist them, when they knew that this Society was determined not to seek the reform of the constitution, but by means that were constitutional, and from whom they could neither hope for support nor concealment of evil purposes?—I ask you next, if their objects had been traitorous, would they have given them, without disguise or colour, to the public and to the government, in every common newspaper? and yet it is so far from being a charge against them, that they concealed their objects by hypocrisy or guarded conduct, that I have been driven to admit the justice of the complaint against them, for unnecessary inflammation and exaggeration.—I ask you farther, whether if the proceedings, thus published and exaggerated, had appeared to Government, who knew every thing belonging to them, in the light they represent them to you *to-day*, they could possibly have slept over them with such complete indifference and silence? For it is notorious, that after this Convention had been held at Edinburgh; after, in short, every thing had been said, written, and transacted, on which I am now commenting, and after Mr. Paine's book had been for above a year in universal circulation,—ay, up to the very day when Mr. Grey gave notice, in the House of Commons, of the intention of the

Friends of the People for a reform in Parliament, there was not even a single indictment on the file for a misdemeanor; but, from that moment, when it was seen that the cause was not beat down or abandoned, the proclamation made its appearance, and all the proceedings that followed had their birth.—I ask you, lastly, Gentlemen, whether it be in human nature, that a few unprotected men, conscious in their own minds, that they had been engaged and detected in a detestable rebellion to cut off the king, to destroy the administration of justice, and to subvert the whole fabric of the government, should turn round upon their country, whose ruin they had projected, and whose most obvious justice attached on them, complaining, forsooth, that their delegates, taken by magistrates, in the very act of high treason, had been harshly and illegally interrupted in a meritorious proceeding? The history of mankind never furnished an instance, nor ever will, of such extravagant, preposterous, and unnatural conduct! No, no, Gentlemen; all their hot blood was owing to their firm persuasion, dictated by conscious innocence, that the conduct of their delegates had been legal, and might be vindicated against the magistrates who obstructed them:—in that they might be mistaken;—I am not arguing that point at present: if they are hereafter indicted for a misdemeanor, and I am Counsel in that cause, I will then tell you what I think of it:—sufficient for the day is the good or evil of it,—it is sufficient, for the present one, that the legality or illegality of the business has no relation to the crime that is imputed to the Prisoner.

The next matter that is alleged against the authors of the Scotch Convention, and the societies which supported it, is, their having sent addresses of friendship to the convention of France. These addresses are considered to be a decisive proof of republican combination, verging closely in themselves upon an overt act of treason.—Gentlemen, if the dates of these addresses are attended to, which come no lower down than November 1792, we have only to lament, that they are but the acts of private subjects, and that they were not sanctioned by the state itself.—The French nation, about that period, under their new constitution, or under their new anarchy, call it which you will, were nevertheless most anxiously desirous of maintaining peace with this country.—But the king was advised to withdraw his ambassador from France, upon the approaching catastrophe of its most unfortunate prince;—an event which, however to be deplored, was no justifiable cause of offence to Great Britain.—France desired nothing but the regeneration of her own government; and if she mistook the road to her prosperity, what was that to us?—But it was alleged against her in parliament, that she had introduced spies amongst us, and held correspondence with disaffected persons, for the destruction of our constitution; this was the charge of our minister, and it was, therefore, held to be just and necessary, for the safety of the country, to hold France at arm's length, and to avoid the very contagion of contact with her at the risk of war.—But, gentlemen, this charge against France was thought by many, to be supported by no better proofs than those against the prisoner.—In the public correspondence of the ambassador from the French king, and upon his death, as minister from the convention, with his majesty's secretary of state, documents which lie upon the table of the House of Commons, and which may be made evidence in the cause, the executive council repelled with indignation all the imputations, which to this very hour are held out as the vindications of quarrel. "If there be such persons in

England," says monsieur Chauvelin—"has not England laws to punish them?—France disavows them—such men are not Frenchmen."—The same correspondence conveys the most solemn assurances of friendship down to the very end of the year 1792—a period subsequent to all the correspondence and addresses complained of.—Whether these assurances were faithful or otherwise,—whether it would have been prudent to have depended on them or otherwise,—whether the war was advisable or unadvisable,—are questions over which we have no jurisdiction;—I only desire to bring to your recollection, that a man may be a friend to the rights of humanity and to the imprescriptible rights of social man, which is now a term of derision and contempt, that he may feel to the very soul for a nation beset by the sword of despots, and yet be a lover of his own country and its constitution.

Gentlemen, the same celebrated person, of whom I have had occasion to speak so frequently, is the best and brightest illustration of this truth. Mr. Burke, indeed, went a great deal farther than requires to be pressed into the present argument; for he maintained the cause of justice and of truth, against all the perverted authority and rash violence of his country, and expressed the feelings of a christian and a patriot in the very heat of the American war; boldly holding forth our victories as defeats; and our successes as calamities and disgraces. "It is not instantly," said Mr. Burke,

> that I can be brought to rejoice, when I hear of the slaughter and captivity of long lists of those names which have been familiar to my ears from my infancy, and to rejoice that they have fallen under the sword of strangers, whose barbarous appellations I scarcely know how to pronounce. The glory acquired at the *White Plains* by colonel *Raille*, has no charms for me; and I fairly acknowledge, that I have not yet learned to delight in finding *Fort Kniphausen* in the heart of the British dominions.

If this had been said or written by Mr. Yorke at Sheffield, or by any other member of these societies, heated with wine at the Globe-tavern, it would have been trumpeted forth as decisive evidence of a rebellious spirit, rejoicing in the downfall of his country; yet the great author from whose writings I have borrowed, approved himself to be the friend of this nation at that calamitous crisis, and had it pleased God to open the understandings of our rulers, his wisdom might have averted the storms that are now thickening around us. We must not, therefore, be too severe in our strictures upon the opinions and feelings of men as they regard such mighty public questions.—The interests of a nation may often be one thing, and the interests of its government another; but the interest of those who hold government for the hour, is at all times different from either. At the time many of the papers before you were circulated on the subject of the war with France, many of the best and wisest men in this kingdom began to be driven by our situation to these melancholy reflections; and thousands of persons, the most firmly attached to the principles of our constitution, and who never were members of any of these societies, considered, and still consider, Great Britain as the aggressor against France; they considered, and still consider, that she had a right to choose a government for herself, and that it was contrary to the first principles of justice, and, if possible, still more repugnant to the genius of our own free constitution, to combine with despots for her destruction: and who knows but that the external pressure upon France may have been the cause of that unheard-of state of society which we complain of ?—who knows, but that, driven as she has been to exertions beyond the ordinary vigour of a nation, it has not been the parent of that unnatural and giant strength which threatens the authors of it with perdition? These are melancholy considerations, but they may reasonably, and at all events, be lawfully entertained.—We owe obedience to government in our *actions*, but surely our *opinions* are free.

Gentlemen, pursuing the order of time, we are arrived, at length, at the proposition to hold *another convention, which, with the supposed support of it by force, are the only overt acts of high treason charged upon this record.*—For, strange as it may appear, there is no charge whatever before you of any one of those acts or writings, the evidence of which consumed so many days in reading, and which has already nearly consumed my strength in only passing them in review before you.—If every line and letter of all the writings I have been commenting upon were admitted to be traitorous machinations, and if the convention in Scotland was an open rebellion, it is conceded to be foreign to the present purpose, unless as such criminality in them might show the views and objects of the persons engaged in them:—on that principle only the Court has over and over again decided the evidence of them to be admissible; and on the same principle I have illustrated them in their order as they happened, that I might lead the prisoner in your view up to the very point and moment when the treason is supposed to have burst forth into the overt act for which he is arraigned before you.

The transaction respecting this second convention, which constitutes the principal, or more properly the only overt act in the indictment, lies in the narrowest compass, and is clouded with no ambiguity.—I admit freely every act which is imputed to the prisoner, and listen not so much with fear as with curiosity and wonder, to the treason sought to be connected with it.

You will recollect that the first motion towards the holding of a second convention, originated in a letter to the prisoner from a country correspondent, in which the legality of the former was vindicated, and its dispersion lamented:—this letter was answered on the 27th of March 1794, and was read to you in the crown's evidence in these words:

March 27, 1794

Citizen;—I am directed by the London Corresponding Society to transmit the following Resolutions to the Society for Constitutional Information, and to request the sentiments of that society respecting the important measures which the present juncture of affairs seems to require.

The London Corresponding Society conceives that the moment is arrived, when a full and explicit declaration is necessary from all the friends of freedom—whether the late *illegal and unheard-of prosecutions and sentences* shall determine us to abandon our cause, or shall excite us to pursue a radical reform, with an ardour proportioned to the magnitude of the object, and with a zeal as *distinguished* on *our* parts as the *treachery of others in the same glorious cause is notorious.* The Society for Constitutional Information is therefore required to determine whether or no they will be ready, when called upon, to act in conjunction with *this and other societies to obtain a fair representation of the* People—*whether they concur with us in seeing the necessity of a speedy convention, for the purpose of obtaining, in a constitutional and legal method, a redress of those grievances under which we at present labour, and which can only be effectually removed by a full and fair representation of the people of Great Britain.* The London Corresponding Society cannot but remind their friends that the present crisis demands all the prudence, unanimity, and vigour, that may or can be exerted by Men and *Britons*; nor do they doubt but that manly firmness and consistency will finally, and they believe shortly, terminate in the full accomplishment of all their wishes.

I am, fellow citizen (in my humble measure), a friend of the rights of man.

T. Hardy, Secretary

They then resolve that there is no security for the continuance of any right but in equality of *laws*; not in equality of *property*, the ridiculous bugbear by which you are to be frightened into injustice;—on the contrary, throughout every part of the proceedings, and most emphatically in Mr. Yorke's speech, so much relied on, the beneficial subordinations of society, the security of property, and the prosperity of the landed and commercial interests, are held forth as the very objects to be attained by the reform in the representation which they sought for.

In examining this first moving towards a second convention, the first thing to be considered is, what reason there is, from the letter I have just read to you, or from any thing that appears to have led to it, to suppose that a *different sort* of convention was projected from that which had been before assembled and dispersed.—The letter says *another* British Convention; and it describes the same objects as the first—compare all the papers for the calling this second convention with those for assembling the first, and you will find no difference, except that they mixed with them extraneous and libellous matter, arising obviously from the irritation produced by the sailing of the transports with their brethren condemned to exile. These papers have already been considered, and separated, as they ought to be, from the charge.

I will now lay before you all the remaining operations of this formidable conspiracy up to the prisoner's imprisonment in the Tower. Mr. Hardy having received the letter just adverted to, regarding a second convention, the Corresponding Society wrote the letter of the 27th of March, and which was found in his hand-writing, and is published in the first Report, page 11. This letter, enclosing the Resolutions they had come to upon the subject, was considered by the Constitutional Society on the next day, the 28th of March, the ordinary day for their meeting, when they sent an answer to the Corresponding Society, informing them that they had received their communication, that they heartily concurred with them in the objects they had in view, and invited them to send a delegation of their members to confer with them on the subject.

Now, what were the objects they concurred in, and what was to be the subject of conference between the societies by their delegates? Look at the letter, which distinctly expresses its objects, and the means by which they sought to effect them:—had these poor men (too numerous to meet all together, and therefore renewing the cause of Parliamentary Reform by delegation from the societies) any reason to suppose, that they were involving themselves in the pains of treason, and that they were compassing the King's death, when they were redeeming (as they thought) his authority from probable downfall and ruin? Had treason been imputed to the delegates before?—Had the imagining the death of the King ever been suspected by any body?—Or when they were prosecuted for misdemeanors, was the prosecution considered as an indulgence conferred upon men whose lives had been forfeited?—And is it to be endured, then, in this free land, made free too by the virtue of our forefathers, who placed the King upon his throne to maintain this freedom, that forty or fifty thousand people, in the different parts of the kingdom, assembling in their little societies to spread useful knowledge, and to diffuse the principles of liberty, which the more widely they are spread, the surer is the condition of our free government, are in a moment, without warning, without any law or principle to warrant it, and without precedent or example, to be branded as traitors, and to be decimated as victims for punishment!—The Constitutional Society having answered the letter of the 27th of March, in the manner I stated to you;—committees, from each of the two societies, were appointed to confer together.—The Constitutional Society appointed Mr. Joyce, Mr. Kydd, Mr. Wardle, and Mr. Holcroft, all indicted; and Mr. Sharpe, the celebrated engraver, not indicted, but examined as a witness by the Crown;—five were appointed by the Corresponding Society to meet these gentlemen, viz. Mr. Baxter, Mr. Moore, Mr. Thelwall, and Mr. Hodgson, all indicted, and Mr. Lovett, against whom the bill was thrown out. These gentlemen met at the house of Mr. Thelwall on the 11th of April, and there published the resolutions already commented on, in conformity with the general objects of the two societies, expressed in the letter of the 27th of March, and agreed to continue to meet on Mondays and Thursdays for farther conference on the subject. The first Monday was the 14th of April, of which we have heard so much, and no meeting was held on that day;—the first Thursday was the 17th of April, but there was no meeting;—the 21st of April was the second Monday, but there was still no meeting;—the 24th of April was the second Thursday when the five of the Corresponding Society attended, but nobody coming to meet them from the other, nothing of course was transacted;—on Monday, the 28th of April, three weeks after their first appointment, this bloody and impatient band of conspirators, seeing that a Convention Bill was in projection, and that Hessians were landing on our coasts, at last assembled themselves;—and now we come to the point of action.—Gentlemen, they met;—they shook hands with each other;—they talked over the news and the pleasures of the day;—they wished one another a good evening, and retired to their homes;—it is in vain to hide it, they certainly did all these things—The same *alarming* scene was repeated on the three following days of meeting, and on Monday, May the 12th, would, but for the vigilance of Government, have probably again taken place:—but on that day Mr. Hardy was arrested, his papers seized, and the conspiracy which pervaded this devoted country was dragged into the face of day. To be serious, gentlemen, you have *literally* the whole of it before you in the meetings I have just stated; in which you find ten gentlemen, appointed by two peaceable societies, conversing upon the subject of a constitutional reform in parliament, publishing the result of their deliberations, without any other arms than one supper-knife; which, when I come to the subject of arms, I will, in form, lay before you.—Yet for this, and for this alone, you are asked to devote the prisoner before you, and his unfortunate associates, to the pains and penalties of death, and not to death alone, but to the eternal stigma and infamy of having conceived the detestable and horrible design of dissolving the government of their country, and of striking at the life of their Sovereign, who had never given offence to them, nor to any of his subjects.

Gentlemen, as a conspiracy of this formidable extension, which had no less for its object than the sudden annihilation of all the existing authorities of the country, and of every thing that supported them, could not be even gravely stated to have an existence, without contemplation of force to give it effect; it was absolutely necessary to impress upon the public mind, and to establish, by formal evidence, upon the present occasion, that such a force was actually in preparation.—This most important and indispensable part of the cause was attended with insurmountable difficulties, not only from its being unfounded in fact, but because it had been expressly negatived by the whole conduct of Government:—for although the motions of all these societies had been watched for two years together; though their spies had regularly attended, and collected regular journals of their proceedings; yet when the first Report was finished, and the Habeas Corpus Act suspended upon the foundation of the facts contained in it, there was not to be found, from one end of it to the other, even the insinuation of arms; I believe that this circumstance made a great impression upon all the thinking dispassionate part of the public, and that the materials of the first Report were thought to furnish but a slender argument to support such a total eclipse of liberty. No wonder, then, that the discovery of a pike in the interval between the two Reports, should have been highly estimated—I mean no reflections upon Government, and only state the matter, as a man of great wit very publicly reported it;—he said that the discoverer, when he first beheld the long-looked for pike, was transported beyond himself with enthusiasm and delight, and that he hung over the rusty instrument with all the raptures of a fond mother, who embraces her first-born infant, "*and thanks her God for all her travail past.*"

In consequence of this discovery, whoever might have the merit of it, and whatever the discoverer might have felt upon it, persons were sent by Government (and properly sent) into all corners of the kingdom to investigate the extent of the mischief; the fruit of this inquiry has been laid before you, and I pledge myself to sum up the evidence which you have had upon the subject, not by parts, or by general observations, but in the same manner as the Court itself must sum it up to you, when it lays the whole body of the proof with fidelity before you.—Notwithstanding all the declamations upon French anarchy, I think I may safely assert, that it has been distinctly proved, by the evidence, that the Sheffield people were for universal representation in a British House of Commons. This appears to have been the general sentiment, with the exception of one witness, whose testimony makes the truth and *bona fides* of the sentiments far more striking; the witness I allude to (George Widdison), whose evidence I shall state in its place, seems to be a plain, blunt, honest man, and by-the-by, which must never be forgotten of any of them, the Crown's witness—I am not interested in the veracity of any of them, for (as I have frequently adverted to) the Crown must take them for better for worse;—it must support each witness, and the whole body of its evidence throughout.—If you do not believe the whole of what is proved by a witness, what confidence can you have in part of it, or what part can you select to confide in?—If you are deceived in part,—who shall measure the boundaries of the deception?—This man says he was at first for universal suffrage; Mr. Yorke had persuaded him, from all the books, that it was the best; but that he afterwards saw reason to think otherwise, and was not for going the length of the Duke of Richmond: but that all the other Sheffield people were for the Duke's plan; a fact confirmed by the cross-examination of every one of the witnesses.—You have, therefore, positively and distinctly, upon the universal authority of the evidence of the Crown, the people of Sheffield, who are charged as at the head of a republican conspiracy, proved to be associated on the very principles which, at different times, have distinguished the most eminent persons in this kingdom; and the charge made upon them, with regard to arms, is cleared up by the same universal testimony.

You recollect that, at a meeting held upon the Castle-hill, there were two parties in the country, and it is material to attend to what these two parties were.—In consequence of the King's proclamation, a great number of honourable, zealous persons, who had been led by a thousand artifices to believe, that there was a just cause of alarm in the country, took very extraordinary steps for support of the magistracy.—The publicans were directed not to entertain persons who were friendly to a reform of Parliament, and alarms of change and revolution pervaded the country, which became greater and greater, as our ears were hourly assailed with the successive calamities of France.—Others saw things in an opposite light, and considered that these calamities were made the pretext for extinguishing British liberty;—heart-burnings arose between the two parties; and some, I am afraid a great many, wickedly or ignorantly interposed in a quarrel which zeal had begun.—The societies were disturbed in their meetings, and even the private dwellings of many of their members were illegally violated.—It appears by the very evidence for the Crown, by which the cause must stand or fall, that many of the friends of reform were daily insulted,—their houses threatened to be pulled down, and their peaceable meetings beset by pretended magistrates, without the process of the law.—These proceedings naturally suggested the propriety of having arms for self-defence, the first and most unquestionable privilege of man, in or out of society, and expressly provided for by the very letter of English law.—It was ingeniously put by the learned Counsel, in the examination of a witness, that it was complained of amongst them, that very little was sufficient to obtain a warrant from some magistrates, and that therefore it was as well to be provided for those who might have warrants as for those who had none. Gentlemen, I am too much exhausted to pursue or argue such a difference, even if it existed upon the evidence, because if the societies in question (however mistakenly) considered their meetings to be legal, and the warrants to disturb them to be beyond the authority of the magistrate to grant, they had a right, at the peril of the legal consequences, to stand upon their defence; and it is no transgression of the law, much less high treason against the King, to resist his officers when they pass the bounds of their authority. So much for the general evidence of arms; and the first and last time that even the name of the prisoner is connected with the subject, is by a letter he received from a person of the name of Davison. I am anxious that this part of the case should be distinctly understood, and I will, therefore, bring back this letter to your attention; the letter is as follows:

> Fellow-citizen;—The barefaced aristocracy of the present administration has made it necessary that we should be prepared to act on the defensive, against any attack they may command their newly armed minions to make upon us. A plan has been hit upon, and, if encouraged sufficiently, will, no doubt, have the effect of furnishing a quantity of pikes to the patriots, great enough to make them formidable. The blades are made of steel, tempered and polished after an approved form. They may be fixed into any shafts (but *fir* ones are recommended) of the girt of the accompanying hoops at the top end, and about an inch more at the bottom.
>
> The blades and hoops (more than which cannot properly be sent to any great distance) will be charged one shilling. Money to be sent with the orders.
>
> As the institution is in its infancy, immediate encouragement is necessary.
>
> *Orders may be sent to the Secretary of the Sheffield Constitutional Society.* [*Struck out.*]
>
> *Richard Davison*
>
> *Sheffield, April 24th,* 1794

Gentlemen, you must recollect (for if it should escape you, it might make a great difference) that Davison directs the answer to this letter to be sent to Robert Moody at Sheffield, to prevent post-office suspicion; and that he also encloses in it a similar one, which Mr. Hardy was to forward to Norwich, in order that the society at that place might provide pikes for themselves, in the same manner that Davison was recommending, through Hardy, to the people of London. Now what followed upon the prisoner's receiving this letter?—It is in evidence, by this very Moody, to whom the answer was to be sent, and who was examined as a witness by the crown, *that he never received any answer to the letter*; and, although there was an universal seizure of papers, no such letter, nor any other, appeared to have been written; and, what is more, the letter to Norwich, from Davison, enclosed in his letter to Hardy, was never forwarded, but was found in his custody when he was arrested, three weeks afterwards, folded up in the other, and unopened, as he received it.—Good God! what is become of the humane sanctuary of English justice—where is the sense and meaning of the term *proveably* in the statute of king Edward, if such evidence can be received against an English subject, on a trial for his life!—If a man writes a letter to me about pikes, or about any thing else, can I help it?—And is it evidence (except to acquit me of suspicion) when it appears that nothing is done upon it? Mr. Hardy never before corresponded with Davison—he never desired him to write to him.—How indeed could he desire him when his very existence was unknown to him?—He never returned an answer;—he never forwarded the enclosed to Norwich;—he never even communicated the letter itself to his own society, although he was its secretary, which showed he considered it as the unauthorized, officious correspondence of a private man;—he never acted upon it at all, nor appears to have regarded it as dangerous or important, since he neither destroyed nor concealed it. Gentlemen, I declare I hardly know in what language to express my astonishment, that the crown can ask you to shed the blood of the man at the bar upon such foundations.—Yet this is the whole of the written evidence concerning arms: for the remainder of the plot rests, for its foundation, upon the parole evidence, the whole of which I shall pursue with precision, and not suffer a link of the chain to pass unexamined.

William Camage was the first witness: he swore that the Sheffield societies were frequently insulted, and threatened to be dispersed; so that the people in general thought it necessary to defend themselves against illegal attacks:—that the justices having officiously intruded themselves into their peaceable and legal meetings, they thought they had a right to be armed; but they did not claim this right under the law of nature, or by theories of government, but as *English subjects*, under the government of *England*; for they say in their paper, which has been read by the crown that would condemn them, that they were entitled by the *Bill of Rights* to be armed. Gentlemen, they state their title truly.—The preamble of that statute enumerates the offences of king James 2nd; amongst the chief of which was, his causing his subjects to be disarmed, and then our ancestors claim this violated right as their indefeasible inheritance.—Let us therefore be cautious how we rush to the conclusion, that men are plotting treason against the king, because they are asserting a right, the violation of which has been adjudged against a king to be treason against the people; and let us not suppose that English subjects are a banditti, for preparing to defend their legal liberties with pikes, because pikes may have been accidentally employed in another country to destroy both liberty and law.—Camage says he was spoken to by this Davison about three dozen of pikes— What then?—He is *the Crown's witness, whom they offer to you as the witness of truth*, and he started with horror at the idea of violence, and spoke with visible reverence for the king; saying, God forbid that he should touch him; but he, nevertheless, had a pike for himself. Indeed, the manliness with which he avowed it, gave an additional strength to his evidence.—"No doubt," says he,

> I had a pike, but I would not have remained an hour a member of the society, if I had heard a syllable, that it was in the contemplation of any body to employ pikes or any other arms against the king or the government.—We meant to petition parliament, through the means of the convention of Edinburgh, thinking that the House of Commons would listen to this expression of the general sentiments of the people; for it had been thrown out, he said, in parliament, that the people did not desire it themselves.

Mr. Broomhead, whose evidence I have already commented upon, a sedate, plain, sensible man, spoke also of his affection to the government, and of the insults and threats which had been offered to the people of Sheffield: he says,

I heard of arms on the Castle-hill, but it is fit this should be distinctly explained: a wicked hand-bill, to provoke and terrify the multitude, had been thrown about the town in the night, which caused agitation in the minds of the people; and it was then spoken of, as being the right of every individual, to have arms for defence; but there was no idea ever started of *resisting*, much less of *attaching* [*sic*], the government. I never heard of such a thing. I fear God, [said the witness] and honour the king; and would not have consented to send a delegate to Edinburgh, but for peaceable and legal purposes.

The next evidence, upon the subject of arms, is what is proved by Widdison, to which I beg your particular attention, because, if there be any reliance upon his testimony, it puts an end to every criminal imputation upon Davison, through whom, in the strange manner already observed upon, Hardy could alone be criminated.

This man, Widdison, who was both a turner and hair-dresser, and who dressed Davison's hair, and was his most intimate acquaintance, gives you an account of their most confidential conversations upon the subject of the pikes, when it is impossible that they could be imposing upon one another; and he declares, upon his solemn oath, that Davison, without even the knowledge or authority of the Sheffield Society, thinking that the same insults might be offered to the London Societies, wrote the letter to Hardy, *of his own head, as the witness expressed it*, and that he, Widdison, made the pike-shafts, to the number of a dozen and a half.—Davison, he said, was his customer; he told him that people began to think themselves in danger, and he therefore made the handles of the pikes for sale, to the number of a dozen and a half, and one likewise for himself, without conceiving that he offended against any law. "I love the King," said Widdison, "as much as any man, and all the people I associated with did the same; I would not have stayed with them if they had not:—Mr. Yorke often told me privately, that he was for universal representation, and so were we all—*the duke of Richmond's plan was our only object.*"

This was the witness who was shown the duke's letter, and spoke to it as being circulated, and as the very creed of the societies.—This evidence shows, beyond all doubt, the genuine sentiments of these people, because it consists of their most confidential communications with one another; and the only answer, therefore, that can possibly be given to it is, that the witnesses, who deliver it, are imposing upon the Court—But this (as I have wearied you with reiterating) the crown cannot say: for, in that case, their whole proof falls to the ground together, since it is only from the same witnesses that the very existence of these pikes and their handles comes before us; and, if you suspect their evidence *in part*, for the reasons already given, it must be *in toto* rejected.—My friend is so good as to furnish me with this farther observation, that Widdison said he had often heard those who called themselves aristocrats say, that if an invasion of the country should take place, they would begin with destroying their enemies at home, that they might be unanimous in the defence of their country.

John Hill was next called: he is a cutler, and was employed by Davison to make the blades for the pikes; he saw the letter which was sent to Hardy, and knew that it was sent lest there should be the same call for defence in London against illegal attacks upon the societies; for that at Sheffield they were daily insulted, and that the opposite party came to his own house, fired muskets under the door, and threatened to pull it down; he swears that they were, to a man, faithful to the king, and that the reform proposed was in the Commons House of Parliament.

John Edwards was called, farther to connect the prisoner with this combination of force: but so far from establishing it, he swore, upon his cross-examination, that his only reason for going to Hardy's was, that he wanted a pike for his own defence, without connexion with Davison, or with Sheffield, and without concert or correspondence with any body. He had heard, he said, of the violences at Sheffield, and of the pikes that had been made there for defence; that Hardy, on his application, showed him the letter which, as has appeared, he never showed to any other person.—This is the whole sum and substance of the evidence which applies to the charge of pikes, after the closest investigation, under the sanction, and by the aid of parliament itself; evidence which, so far from establishing the fact, would have been a satisfactory answer to almost any testimony by which such a fact could have been supported: for in this unparalleled proceeding, the prisoner's counsel is driven by his duty to dwell upon the detail of the crown's proofs; because the whole body of it is the completest answer to the indictment which even a free choice itself could have selected.—It is farther worthy of your attention, that, as far as the evidence proceeds from these plain, natural sources, which the crown was driven to, for the necessary foundation of the proceedings before you, it has been simple,—uniform,—natural, and consistent; and that whenever a different complexion was to be given to it, it was only through the medium of spies and informers, and of men, independently of their infamous trade, of the most abandoned and profligate characters.

Before I advert to what has been sworn by this description of persons, I will give you a wholesome caution concerning them, and, having no eloquence of my own to enforce it, I will give it to you in the language of the same gentleman whose works are always seasonable, when moral or political lessons are to be rendered delightful. Look then at the picture of society, as Mr. Burke has drawn it, under the dominion of spies and informers: I say under their *dominion*, for a resort to spies may, on occasions, be justifiable, and their evidence, when confirmed, may deserve implicit credit: but I say under the *dominion* of spies and informers, because the case of the crown must stand alone upon their evidence, and upon their evidence, not only unconfirmed, but in *direct contradiction to every witness, not an informer or a spy,* and in a case too where the truth, whatever it is, lies within the knowledge of forty or fifty thousand people. Mr. Burke says—I believe I can remember it without reference to the book.

A mercenary informer knows no distinction. Under such a system, the obnoxious people are slaves, not only to the government, but they live at the mercy of every individual; they are at once the slaves of the whole community, and of every part of it; and the worst and most unmerciful men are those on whose goodness they most depend.

In this situation men not only shrink from the frowns of a stern magistrate, but are obliged to fly from their very species. The seeds of destruction are sown in civil intercourse and in social habitudes.—The blood of wholesome kindred is infected.—The tables and beds are surrounded with snares. All the means given by Providence to make life safe and comfortable, are perverted into instruments of terror and torment.—This species of universal subserviency that makes the very servant who waits behind your chair, the arbiter of your life and fortune, has such a tendency to degrade and abase mankind, and to deprive them of that assured and liberal state of mind which alone can make us what we ought to be, that I vow to God, I would sooner bring myself to put a man to immediate death for opinions I disliked, and so to get rid of the man and his opinions at once, than to fret him with a feverish being, tainted with the gaol distemper of a contagious servitude, to keep him above ground, an animated mass of putrefaction, corrupted himself, and corrupting all about him.

Gentlemen, let me bring to your recollection the deportment of the first of this tribe, Mr. Alexander,—who could not in half an hour even tell where he had lived, or why he had left his master.—Does any man believe that he had forgotten these most recent transactions of his life? Certainly not—but his history would have undone his credit, and must therefore be concealed.—He had lived with a linen draper, whose address we could scarcely get from him, and they had parted because they had words:—What were the words? We were not to be told that.—He then went to a Mr. Kellerby's, who agreed with him at twenty-five guineas a year.—Why did he not stay there?—He was obliged, it seems, to give up his lucrative agreement, because he was obliged to attend here as a witness.—Gentlemen, Mr. Kellerby lives only in Holborn, and was he obliged to give up a permanent engagement with a tradesman in Holborn, because he was obliged to be absent at the Old Bailey for five minutes in one single day? I asked him if he had told Mr. White, the solicitor for the Treasury, who would not have been so cruel as to deprive a man of his bread by keeping him upon attendance which might have been avoided by a particular notice.—The thing spoke for itself—he had never told Mr. White: but had he ever told Mr. Kellerby? for how else could he know that his place was inconsistent with his engagement upon this trial? No, he had never told him!—How then did he collect that his place was inconsistent with his duty here? This question never received any answer.—You saw how he dealt with it, and how he stood stammering, not daring to lift up his countenance in any direction,—confused,—disconcerted,—and confounded.

Driven from the accusation upon the subject of pikes, and even from the very colour of accusation, without the proof of arms, we have got this miserable, solitary knife, held up to us as the engine which was to destroy the constitution of this country; and Mr. Groves, an Old Bailey solicitor, employed as a spy upon the occasion, has been selected to give probability to this monstrous absurdity, by his *respectable* evidence.—I understand that this same gentleman has carried his system of spying to such a pitch as to practise it since this unfortunate man has been standing a prisoner before you, proffering himself, as a friend, to the committee preparing his defence that he might discover to the crown the materials by which he meant to defend his life.—I state this only from report, and I hope in God I am mistaken; for human nature starts back appalled from such atrocity, and shrinks and trembles at the very statement of it.—But as to the perjury of this miscreant, it will appear palpable beyond all question, and he shall answer for it in due season. He tells you he attended at Chalk Farm; and that there, forsooth, amongst about seven or eight thousand people, he saw two or three persons with knives:—he might, I should think, have seen many more, as hardly any man goes without a knife of some sort in his pocket.—He asked, however, it seems, where they got these knives, and was directed to Green, a hair-dresser, who deals besides in cutlery; and accordingly this notable Mr. Groves went (as he told us) to Green's, and asked to purchase a knife; when Green in answer to him said, "speak low, for my wife is a damn'd aristocrat."—This answer was sworn to by the wretch, to give you the idea that Green, who had the knives to sell, was conscious that he kept them for an illegal and wicked purpose, and that they were not to be sold in public.—The door, he says, being a-jar, the man desired him to speak low, from whence he would have you understand that it was because this aristocratic wife was within hearing.—This, gentlemen, is the testimony of Groves, and Green himself is called as the next witness; and called by whom? Not by me—I know nothing of him, he is the crown's own witness.—He is called to confirm Grove's evidence; but *not being a spy*, he declared solemnly upon his oath, and I can confirm his evidence by several respectable people, that the knives in question lie constantly, and lay then, in his open shop window, in what is called the show glass, where cutlers, like other tradesmen, expose their ware to public view; and that the knives differ in nothing from others publicly sold in the Strand, and every other street in London;—that he bespoke them from a rider, who came round for orders in the usual way; that he sold only fourteen in all, and that they were made up in little packets, one of which Mr. Hardy had, who was to choose one for himself, but four more were found in his possession, because he was arrested before Green had an opportunity of sending for them.

Gentlemen, I think the pikes and knives are now completely disposed of; but something was said also about guns; let us, therefore, see what that amounts to.—It appears that Mr. Hardy was applied to by Samuel Williams, a gun-engraver, who was not even a member of any society, and who asked him if he knew any body who wanted a gun—Hardy said he did not; and undoubtedly upon the crown's own showing, it must be taken for granted that if at that time he had been acquainted with any plan of arming, he would have given a different answer, and would have jumped at the offer:—about a fortnight afterwards, however (Hardy in the interval having become acquainted with Franklow), Williams called to buy a pair of shoes, and then Hardy, recollecting his former application referred him to Franklow, who had in the most public manner raised the forty men, who were called the Loyal Lambeth Association:—so that, in order to give this transaction any bearing upon the charge, it became necessary to consider Franklow's assocation as an armed conspiracy against the government;—though the forty people who composed it were collected by public advertisement;—though they were enrolled under public articles;—and though Franklow himself, as appears from the evidence, attended publicly at the Globe tavern in his uniform, whilst the cartouch boxes and the other accoutrements of these secret conspirators lay publicly upon his shop-board, exposed to the open view of all his customers and neighbours. This story, therefore, is not less contemptible than that which you must have all heard concerning Mr. Walker, whom I went to defend at Lancaster, where that respectable gentleman was brought to trial upon such a trumped-up charge, supported by the solitary evidence of one Dunn, a most infamous witness: but what was the end of that prosecution?— I recollect it to the honour of my friend, Mr. Law, who conducted it for the crown, who, knowing that there were persons whose passions were agitated upon these subjects at that moment, and that many persons had enrolled themselves in societies to resist conspiracies against the government, behaved in a most manly and honourable manner, in a manner, indeed, which the public ought to know, and which I hope it never will forget: he would not even put me upon my challenges to such persons, but withdrew them from the panel: and when he saw the complexion of the affair, from the contradiction of the infamous witness whose testimony supported it, he honourably gave up the cause.

Gentlemen, the evidence of Lynam does not require the same contradiction which fell upon Mr. Groves, because it destroys itself by its own intrinsic inconsistency;—I could not, indeed, if it were to save my life, undertake to state it to you.—It lasted, I think, about six or seven hours, but I have marked under different parts of it, passages so grossly contradictory, matter so impossible, so inconsistent with any course of conduct, that it will be sufficient to bring these parts to your view, to destroy all the rest. But let us first examine in what manner this matter, such as it is, was recorded.—He professed to speak from notes, yet I observed him frequently looking up to the ceiling whilst he was speaking;—when I said to him, Are you now speaking from a note? Have you got any note of what you are now saying? he answered; Oh no, this is from recollection.—Good God Almighty! recollection mixing itself with notes in a case of high treason:—He did not even take down the words—nay, to do the man justice, he did not even affect to have taken the words, but only the substance, as he himself expressed it—*O excellent evidence!—The substance of words taken down by a spy, and supplied, when defective, by his memory.* But I must not call him a spy; for it seems he took them *bona fide* as a delegate, and yet *bona fide* as an informer;—what a happy combination of fidelity! faithful to serve, and faithful to betray!—correct to record for the business of the society, and correct to dissolve and to punish it!—What after all do the notes amount to? I will advert to the parts I alluded to—they were, it seems, to go to Frith-street, to sign the Declaration of the Friends of the Liberty of the Press, which lay there already signed by between twenty and thirty members of the House of Commons, and many other respectable and opulent men, and then they were to begin civil confusion, and the king's head and Mr. Pitt's were to be placed on Temple-bar.—Immediately after which we find them resolving unanimously to thank Mr. Wharton for his speech to support the glorious Revolution of 1688, which supports the very throne that was to be destroyed! which same speech they were to circulate in thousands for the use of the societies throughout the kingdom.—Such incoherent, impossible matter, proceeding from such a source, is unworthy of all farther concern.

Thus driven out of every thing which relates to arms, and from every other matter which can possibly attach upon life, they have recourse to an expedient, which, I declare, fills my mind with horror and terror: it is this—The Corresponding Society had (you recollect), two years before, sent delegates to Scotland, with specific instructions, peaceably to pursue a parliamentary reform;—when the convention which they were sent to was dispersed, they sent no others—for they were arrested when only considering of the propriety of another convention. It happened that Mr. Hardy was the secretary during the period of these Scotch proceedings, and the letters consequently written by him, during that period, were all official letters from a large body circulated by him in point of form. When the proposition took place for calling a second convention, Mr. Hardy continued to be secretary, and in that character, signed the circular letter read in the evidence for the crown, which appears to have found its way, in the course of circulation, into *Scotland*. This single circumstance has been admitted as the foundation of receiving in evidence against the prisoner, a long transaction imputed to one Watt, at Edinburgh, whose very existence was unknown to Hardy.—This Watt had been employed by government as a spy, but at last caught a Tartar in his spyship; for, in endeavouring to urge innocent men to a project, which never entered into their imaginations, he was obliged to show himself ready to do what he recommended to others; and the tables being turned upon him, he was hanged by his employers.—This man Watt read from a paper designs to be accomplished, but which he never intended to attempt, and the success of which he knew to be visionary.—To suppose that Great Britain could have been destroyed by such a rebel as Watt, would be, as Dr. Johnson says, to expect that a great city might be drowned by the overflowing of its kennels. But whatever might be the peril of Watt's conspiracy, what had Hardy to do with it? The people with Watt were five or six persons, wholly unknown to Hardy, and not members of any society of which Mr. Hardy was a member; I vow to God, therefore, that I cannot express what I feel, when I am obliged to state the evidence by which he is sought to be affected.—A letter, viz. the circular letter signed by Hardy for calling another convention, is shown to George Ross, who says he received it from one Stock, who belonged to a society which met in Nicholson-street, in Edinburgh, and that he sent it to Perth, Strathaven, Paisley, and other places in Scotland; and the single unconnected evidence of this public letter, finding its way into Scotland, is made the foundation of letting in the whole evidence, which hanged Watt, against Hardy, who never knew him.—Government hanged its own spy in Scotland upon that evidence, and it may be sufficient evidence for that purpose: I will not argue the case of a dead man, and, above all, of such a man; but I will say, that too much money was spent upon this performance, as I think it cost government about fifty thousand pounds.—M'Ewan says, that Watt read from a paper to a committee of six or seven people, of which he, the witness, was a member, that gentlemen, residing in the country, were not to leave their habitations, under pain of death; that an attack was to be made in the manner you remember, and that the lord justice Clerk, and the judges, were to be cut off by these men in buckram; and then an address was to be sent to the king, desiring him to dismiss his ministers and to put an end to the war, or that he might expect bad consequences. *What is all this to Mr. Hardy?* How is it possible to affect *him* with any part of this? Hear the sequel, and then judge for yourselves.—Mr. Watt said (*i.e.* the man who is hanged, said), after reading the paper, that he, Watt, wished to correspond with Mr. Hardy in a safe manner;—so that because a ruffian and a scoundrel, whom I never saw or heard of, chooses, at the distance of four hundred miles, to say, that he *wishes to correspond with me,* I am to be involved in the guilt of his actions! It is not proved, or insinuated, that Mr. Hardy ever saw, or heard of, or knew, that such men were in being as Watt or Downie:—nor is it proved, or asserted, that any letter was, in fact, written by either of them to Hardy, or to any other person—No such letter has been found in his possession, nor a trace of any connexion between them and any member of any English society;—the truth I believe is, that nothing was intended by Watt but to entrap others to obtain a reward for himself, *and he has been amply and justly rewarded.* Gentlemen, I desire to be understood to be making no attacks upon government;—I have wished, throughout the whole cause, that good intentions may be imputed to it, but I really confess, that it requires some ingenuity for government to account for the original existence of all this history, and its subsequent application to the present trial. They went down to Scotland, after the arrest of the prisoners, in order, I suppose, that we might be taught the law of high treason by the lord justice Clerk of Edinburgh, and that there should be a sort of rehearsal to teach the people of England to administer English laws; for, after all this expense and preparation, no man was put upon his trial, nor even arraigned under the special commission in Scotland, but these two men; one for reading this paper, and the other for not dissenting from it when it was read; and, with regard to this last unfortunate person, the crown thought it indecent, as it would indeed have been indecent and scandalous, to execute the law upon him; as a gentleman upon his jury said he would die, rather than convict Downie without a recommendation of mercy, and he was only brought over to join in the verdict, under the idea that he would not be executed, and accordingly he has not suffered execution. If Downie, then, was an object of mercy, or rather of justice, though he was in the very room with Watt, and heard distinctly the proposition, upon what possible ground can they demand the life of the prisoner at the bar, on account of a connexion with the very same individual, *though he never corresponded with him, nor saw him, nor heard of him,—to whose very being he was an utter stranger?*

Gentlemen, it is impossible for me to know what impression this observation makes upon you, or upon the Court; but I declare I am deeply impressed with the application of it.—How is a man to defend himself against such implications of guilt?—Which of us all would be safe, standing at the bar of God or man, if he were even to answer for all his *own* expressions, without taking upon him the crimes or rashnesses of *others?* This poor man has, indeed, none of his own to answer for: yet how can he stand safely in judgment before you, if, in a season of alarm and agitation, with the whole pressure of government upon him, your minds are to be distracted with criminating materials brought from so many quarters, and of an extent which mocks all power of discrimination?—I am conscious that I have not adverted to the thousandth part of them; yet I am sinking under fatigue and weakness.—I am at this moment scarcely able to stand up whilst I am speaking to you, deprived as I have been, for nights together, of every thing that deserves the name of rest, repose, or comfort.—I, therefore, hasten, whilst yet I may be able, to remind you once again of the great principle into which all I have been saying resolves itself.

Gentlemen, my whole argument then amounts to no more than this, that before the crime of compassing *the king's death* can be found *by you, the jury,* whose province it is to judge of its existence, it must be *believed by you* to have existed in point of fact.—Before you can adjudge *a fact*, you *must believe it*—not suspect it—or imagine it, or fancy it,—*but believe it*;—and it is impossible to impress the human mind with such a reasonable and certain belief, as is necessary to be impressed, before a christian man can adjudge his neighbour to the smallest penalty, much less to the pains of death, without having such evidence as a reasonable mind will accept of, as the infallible test of truth. And what is that evidence?—Neither more nor less than that which the constitution has established in the courts for the general administration of justice; namely, that the evidence convinces the jury, beyond all reasonable doubt, that the criminal *intention*, constituting the crime, existed in the mind of the man upon trial, and was the main spring of his conduct. The rules of evidence, as they are settled by law, and adopted in its general administration, are not to be overruled or tampered with.—They are founded in the charities of religion—in the philosophy of nature—in the truths of history, and in the experience of common life; and whoever ventures rashly to depart from them, let him remember that it will be meted to him in the same measure, and that both God and man will judge him accordingly.—These are arguments addressed to your reasons and consciences, not to be shaken in upright minds by any precedent, for no precedents can sanctify injustice;—if they could, every human right would long ago have been extinct upon the earth.—If the state trials in bad times are to be searched for precedents, what murders may you not commit;—what law of humanity may you not trample upon;—what rule of justice may you not violate;—and what maxim of wise policy may you not abrogate and confound? If precedents in bad times are to be implicitly followed, why should we have heard any evidence at all? You might have convicted without any evidence, for many have been so convicted, and in this manner murdered, even by acts of parliament. If precedents in bad times are to be followed, why should the Lords and Commons have investigated these charges, and the crown have put them into this course of judicial trial? since, without such a trial, and even after an acquittal upon one, they might have attainted all the prisoners by act of parliament;—they did so in the case of lord Strafford.—There are precedents, therefore, for all such things:—but such precedents as could not for a moment survive the times of madness and distraction, which gave them birth, but which, as soon as the spurs of the occasions were blunted, were repealed and execrated even by parliaments, which, little as I may think of the present, ought not to be compared with it: parliaments sitting in the darkness of former times,—in the night of freedom,—before the principles of government were developed, and before the constitution became fixed.—The last of these precedents, and all the proceedings upon it, were ordered to be taken off the file and burnt, to the intent that the same might no longer be visible in after ages; an order dictated, no doubt, by a pious tenderness for national honour, and meant as a charitable covering for the crimes of our fathers.—But it was a sin against posterity; it was a treason against society,—for, instead of commanding them to be burnt they should rather have directed them to be blazoned in large letters upon the walls of our courts of justice, that, like the characters decyphered by the prophet of God, to the Eastern tyrant, they might enlarge and blacken in your sights, to terrify you from acts of injustice.

In times, when the whole habitable earth is in a state of change and fluctuation,—when deserts are starting up into civilized empires around you,—and when men, no longer slaves to the prejudices of particular countries, much less to the abuses of particular governments, enlist themselves, like the citizens of an enlightened world, into whatever communities in which their civil liberties may be best protected; it never can be for the advantage of this country to prove, that the strict, unextended letter of her laws, is no security to its inhabitants.—On the contrary, when so dangerous a lure is every where holding out to emigration, it will be found to be the wisest policy of Great Britain to set up her happy constitution,— the strict letter of her guardian laws, and the proud condition of equal freedom, which her highest and her lowest subject ought alike to enjoy;—it will be her wisest policy to set up these first of human blessings against those charms of change and novelty which the varying condition of the world is hourly displaying, and which may deeply affect the population and prosperity of our country—In times, when the subordination to authority is said to be every where but too little felt, it will be found to be the wisest policy of Great Britain, to instil into the governed an almost superstitious reverence for the strict security of the laws; which, from their equality of principle, beget no jealousies or discontent;—which, from their equal administration, can seldom work injustice; and which, from the reverence growing out of their mildness and antiquity, acquire a stability in the habits and affections of men, far beyond the force of civil obligation:—whereas severe penalties, and arbitrary constructions of laws intended for security, lay the foundations of alienation from every human government, and have been the cause of all the calamities that have come, and are coming upon the earth.

Gentlemen, what we read of in books makes but a faint impression upon us, compared to what we see passing under our eyes in the living world.—I remember the people of another country, in like manner, contending for a renovation of their constitution, sometimes illegally and turbulently, but still devoted to an honest end;—I myself saw the people of Brabant so contending for the ancient constitution of the good Duke of Burgundy;—how was this people dealt by?—All, who were only contending for their own rights and privileges, were supposed to be of course disaffected to the Emperor:—they were handed over to courts constituted for the emergency, as this is, and the Emperor marched his army through the country till all was peace;—but such peace as there is in Vesuvius, or Etna, the very moment before they vomit forth their lava, and roll their conflagrations over the devoted habitations of mankind:—when the French approached, the fatal effects were suddenly seen of a government of constraint and terror;—the well-affected were dispirited, and the disaffected inflamed into fury.—At that moment the Archduchess fled from Brussels, and the Duke of Saxe-Teschen was sent express to offer the *joyeuse entrée* so long petitioned for in vain: but the season of concession was past;—the storm blew from every quarter, and the throne of Brabant departed for ever from the House of Burgundy. Gentlemen, I venture to affirm, that, with other councils, this fatal prelude to the last revolution in that country, might have been averted. If the Emperor had been advised to make the concessions of justice and affection to his people, they would have risen in a mass to maintain their prince's authority, interwoven with their own liberties; and the French, the giants of modern times, would, like the giants of antiquity, have been trampled in the mire of their own ambition. In the same manner a far more splendid and important crown passed away from his Majesty's illustrious brows:—*the imperial crown of America.*—The people of that country too, for a long season, contended as subjects, and often with irregularity and turbulence, for what they felt to be their rights: and, O gentlemen! that the inspiring and immortal eloquence of that man, whose name I have so often mentioned, had then been heard with effect?—what was his language to this country when she sought to lay burdens on America,—not to support the dignity of the Crown, or for the increase of national revenue, but to raise a fund for the purpose of corruption;—a fund for maintaining those tribes of hireling skipjacks, which Mr. Tooke so well contrasted with the hereditary nobility of England!—Though America would not bear this imposition, she would have borne any useful or constitutional burden to support the parent state.—"For that service, for all service," said Mr. Burke,

whether of revenue, trade, or empire, my trust is in her interest in the British constitution. My hold of the colonies is in the close affection which grows from common names, from kindred blood, from similar privileges, and equal protection. These are ties which, though light as air, are as strong as links of iron. Let the colonies always keep the idea of their civil rights associated with your government, they will cling and grapple to you, and no force under heaven will be of power to tear them from their allegiance. But let it be once understood, that your government may be one thing, and their privileges another; that these two things may exist without any mutual relation; the cement is gone; the cohesion is loosened; and every thing hastens to decay and dissolution. As long as you have the wisdom to keep the sovereign authority of this country as the sanctuary of liberty, the sacred temple consecrated to our common faith, wherever the chosen race and sons of England worship freedom, they will turn their faces toward you. The more they multiply, the more friends you will have; the more ardently they love liberty, the more perfect will be their obedience. Slavery they can have any where. It is a weed that grows in every soil. They may have it from Spain, they may have it from Prussia. But until you become lost to all feeling of your true interest and your natural dignity, freedom they can have from none but you. This is the commodity of price, of which you have the monopoly. This is the true act of navigation, which binds to you the commerce of the colonies, and through them secures to you the wealth of the world. Is it not the same virtue which does every thing for us here in England? Do you imagine then, that it is the land-tax act which raises your revenue? that it is the annual vote in the Committee of Supply, which gives you your army? or that it is the Mutiny Bill which inspires it with bravery and discipline? No!

surely no! It is the love of the people; it is their attachment to their government, from the sense of the deep stake they have in such a glorious institution, which gives you your army and your navy, and infuses into both that liberal obedience, without which your army would be a base rabble, and your navy nothing but rotten timber.

Gentlemen, to conclude—My fervent wish is, that we may not conjure up a spirit to destroy ourselves, nor set the example here of what in another country we deplore.—Let us cherish the old and venerable laws of our forefathers.—Let our judicial administration be strict and pure; and let the Jury of the land preserve the life of a fellow-subject, who only asks it from them upon the same terms under which they hold their own lives, and all that is dear to them and their posterity for ever.—Let me repeat the wish with which I began my address to you, and which proceeds from the very bottom of my heart;—may it please God, who is the Author of all mercies to mankind, whose providence, I am persuaded, guides and superintends the transactions of the world, and whose guardian spirit has for ever hovered over this prosperous island, to direct and fortify your judgments. I am aware I have not acquitted myself to the unfortunate man, who has put his trust in me, in the manner I could have wished;—yet I am unable to proceed any farther; exhausted in spirit and in strength, but confident in the expectation of justice.— There is one thing more, however, that (if I can) I must state to you, namely, that I will show, by as many witnesses, as it may be found necessary or convenient for you to hear upon the subject, that the views of the societies were what I have alleged them to be;—that whatever irregularities or indiscretions they might have committed, their purposes were honest;—and that Mr. Hardy's, above all other men, can be established to have been so. I have, indeed, an Honourable Gentleman (Mr. Francis) in my eye, at this moment, to be called hereafter as a witness, who being desirous in his place, as a member of Parliament, to promote an inquiry into the seditious practices complained of, Mr. Hardy offered himself voluntarily to come forward, proffered a sight of all the papers, which were afterwards seized in his custody, and tendered every possible assistance to give satisfaction to the laws of his country, if found to be offended. I will show likewise his character to be religious, temperate, humane, and moderate, and his uniform conduct all that can belong to a good subject, and an honest man.—When you have heard this evidence, it will, beyond all doubt, confirm you in coming to the conclusion which, at such great length (for which I entreat your pardon), I have been endeavouring to support.

Treasonable and Seditious Practices Act, 18 December 1795

36 Geo. 3, c. 7   *Statutes at Large*, XL, 561-64.

We, your Majesty's most dutiful and loyal subjects, the lords spiritual and temporal, and commons of *Great Britain*, in this present parliament assembled, duly considering the daring outrages offered to your Majesty's most sacred person, in your passage to and from your parliament at the opening of this present session, and also the continued attempts of wicked and evil disposed persons to disturb the tranquillity of this your Majesty's kingdom, particularly by the multitude of seditious pamphlets and speeches daily printed, published, and dispersed, with unremitting industry, and with a transcendent boldness, in contempt of your Majesty's royal person and dignity, and tending to the overthrow of the laws, government, and happy constitution of these realms, have judged, that it is become necessary to provide a further remedy against all such treasonable and seditious practices and attempts: We, therefore, calling to mind the good and wholesome provisions which have at different times been made by the wisdom of parliament for the averting such dangers, and more especially for the security and preservation of the persons of the sovereigns of these realms, do most humbly beseech your Majesty that it may be enacted; and be it enacted by the King's most excellent majesty, by and with the advice and consent of the lords spiritual and temporal, and commons, in this present parliament assembled, and by the authority of the same, That if any person or persons whatsoever, after the day of the passing of this act, during the natural life of our most gracious sovereign lord the King, (whom Almighty God preserve and bless with a long and prosperous reign,) and until the end of the next session of parliament after a demise of the crown, shall within the realm or without, compass, imagine, invent, devise, or intend death or destruction, or any bodily harm tending to death or destruction, maim, or wounding, imprisonment or restraint, of the person of the same our sovereign lord the King, his heirs and successors, or to deprive or depose him or them from the stile, honour, or kingly name, of the imperial crown of this realm, or of any other of his Majesty's dominions or countries; or to levy war against his Majesty, his heirs and successors, within this realm, in order, by force or constraint, to compel him or them to change his or their measures or counsels, or in order to put any force or constraint upon, or to intimidate, or overawe, both houses, or either house of parliament; or to move or stir any foreigner or stranger with force to invade this realm, or any other his Majesty's dominions or countries, under the obeisance of his Majesty, his heirs and successors; and such compassings, imaginations, inventions, devices, or intentions, or any of them, shall express, utter, or declare, by publishing any printing or writing, or by any overt act or deed; being legally convicted thereof, upon the oaths of two lawful and credible witnesses, upon trial, or otherwise convicted or attainted by due course of law, then every such person and persons, so as aforesaid offending, shall be deemed, declared, and adjudged, to be a traitor and traitors, and shall suffer pains of death, and also lose and forfeit as in cases of high treason.

II.   And be it further enacted by the authority aforesaid, That if any person or persons within that part of *Great Britain* called *England*, at any time from and after the day of the passing of this act, during three years from the day of passing this act, and until the end of the then, next session of parliament, shall maliciously and advisedly, by writing, printing, preaching, or other speaking, express, publish, utter, or declare, any words or sentences to excite or stir up the people to hatred or contempt of the person of his Majesty, his heirs or successors, or the government and constitution of this realm, as by law established, then every such person and persons, being thereof legally convicted, shall be liable to such punishment as may by law be inflicted in cases of high misdemeanors; and if any person or persons shall, after being so convicted, offend a second time, and be thereupon convicted, before any commission of oyer and terminer, or gaol delivery, or in his Majesty's court of king's bench, such person or persons may, on such second conviction, be adjudged, at the discretion of the court, either to suffer such punishment as may now by law be inflicted in cases of high misdemeanors, or to be banished this realm, or to be transported to such place, as shall be appointed by his Majesty for the transportation of offenders; which banishment or transportation shall be for such term as the court may appoint, not exceeding seven years.

III. And be it further enacted, That if any offender or offenders, who shall be so ordered by any such court as aforesaid to be banished the realm, or transported beyond the seas, in manner aforesaid, shall be afterwards at large within any part of the kingdom of *Great Britain*, without some lawful cause, before the expiration of the term for which such offender or offenders shall have been ordered to be banished, or transported beyond the seas as aforesaid, every such offender being so at large as aforesaid, being thereof lawfully convicted, shall suffer death, as in cases of felony without benefit of clergy; and such offender or offenders may be tried, either before justices of assize, oyer and terminer, great sessions, or gaol delivery, for the county, city, liberty, borough, or place, where such offender or offenders shall be apprehended and taken, or from whence he, she, or they, was or were ordered to be banished or transported; and the clerk of assize, clerk of the peace, or other clerk or officer of the court, having the custody of the records where such orders of banishment or transportation shall be made, shall, at the request of the prosecutor, or any other person on his Majesty's behalf, make out and give a certificate, in writing, signed by him, containing the effect and substance only (omitting the formal part) of every indictment and conviction of such offender or offenders, and of the order for his, her, or their banishment or transportation, to the justices of assize, oyer and terminer, great sessions, or gaol delivery, where such offender or offenders shall be indicted (not taking for the same more than two shillings and sixpence;) which certificate shall be sufficient proof of the conviction and order for banishment or transportation of such offender or offenders.

IV. Provided always, That no person or persons, by virtue of this present act, shall for any misdemeanor incur any the penalties herein-before mentioned, unless he, she, or they, be prosecuted within six calendar months next after the offence committed, and the prosecution brought to trial or judgment within the first term, sittings, assizes, or sessions, in which, by the course of the court wherein such prosecution shall be depending, the prosecutor could bring on such trial, or cause such judgement to be entered, or in the term, sittings, assizes, or session, which shall next ensue, unless the court in which such prosecution shall be depending, or before which such trial ought to be had, shall, on special ground stated by motion in open court, think fit to enlarge the time for the trial thereof, or unless the defendant shall be prosecuted to or towards an outlawry; and that no person shall, upon trial, be convicted by virtue of this act, for any misdemeanor, but by the oaths of two credible witnesses.

V. Provided always, and be it further enacted, That all and every person or persons that shall at any time be accused, or indicted, or prosecuted, for any offence made or declared to be treason by this act, shall be entitled to the benefit of the act of parliament, made in the seventh year of his late majesty King *William* the Third, intituled, *An act for regulating of trials in cases of treason and misprison of treason*; and also to the provisions made by another act of parliament, passed in the seventh year of her late Majesty Queen *Anne*, intituled, *An act for improving the union of the two kingdoms.*

VI. Provided also, and be it enacted, That nothing in this act contained shall extend, or be construed to extend, to prevent or affect any prosecution by information or indictment at the common law, for any offence within the provisions of this act, unless the party shall have been first prosecuted under this act.

Corresponding Societies Act, 12 July 1799

39 Geo. 3, c. 79   *Statutes at Large*, XLII, 309-15, 318-21.

This act was designed to suppress societies "established for seditious and treasonable" purposes, including the London Corresponding Society. It imposed restrictions on printers and required the registration of printing presses.

Whereas a traiterous conspiracy has long been carried on, in conjunction with the persons from time to time exercising the powers of government in *France*, to overturn the laws, constitution, and government, and every existing establishment, civil and ecclesiastical, both in *Great Britain* and *Ireland*, and to dissolve the connection between the two kingdoms, so necessary to the security and prosperity of both: and whereas, in pursuance of such design, and in order to carry the same into effect, divers societies have been of late years instituted in this kingdom, and in the kingdom of *Ireland*, of a new and dangerous nature, inconsistent with publick tranquillity, and with the existence of regular government, particularly certain societies calling themselves *Societies of United Englishmen, United Scotsmen, United Britons, United Irishmen,* and *The London Corresponding Society*: and whereas the members of many of such societies have taken unlawful oaths and engagements of fidelity and secrecy, and used secret signs, and appointed committees, secretaries, and other officers, in a secret manner; and many of such societies are composed of different divisions, branches, or parts, which communicate with each other by secretaries, delegates, or otherwise, and by means thereof maintain an influence over large bodies of men, and delude many ignorant and unwary persons into the commission of acts highly criminal: and whereas it is expedient and necessary that all such societies as aforesaid, and all societies of the like nature, should be utterly suppressed and prohibited, as unlawful combinations and confederacies, highly dangerous to the peace and tranquillity of these kingdoms and to the constitution of the government thereof as by law established: be it enacted by the King's most excellent majesty, by and with the advice and consent of the lords spiritual and temporal, and commons, in this present parliament assembled, and by the authority of the same, That, from and after the passing of this act, all the said societies of *United Englishmen, United Scotsmen, United Irishmen,* and *United Britons,* and the said society commonly called *The London Corresponding Society,* and all other societies called *Corresponding Societies,* of any other city, town, or place, shall be, and the same are hereby utterly suppressed and prohibited, as being unlawful combinations and confederacies against the government of our sovereign lord the King, and against the peace and security of his Majesty's liege subjects.

II. And be it further enacted by the authority aforesaid, That, from and after the passing of this act, all and every the said societies, and also every other society now established, or hereafter to be established, the members whereof shall, according to the rules thereof, or to any provision or agreement for that purpose, be required or admitted to take any oath or engagement, which shall be an unlawful oath or engagement within the intent and meaning of an act, passed in the thirty-seventh year of his Majesty's reign, intituled, *An act for more effectually preventing the administering or taking of unlawful oaths,* or to take any oath not required or authorised by law; and every society, the members whereof, or any of them, shall take, or in any manner bind themselves by any such oath or engagement, on becoming or in consequence of being members of such society; and every society, the members whereof shall take, subscribe, or assent, to any test or declaration not required by law, or not authorised in manner herein-after mentioned; and every society, of which the names of the members, or of any of them, shall be kept secret from the society at large, or which shall have any committee or select body so chosen or appointed, that the members constituting the same shall not be known by the society at large to be members of such committee or select body, or which shall have any president, treasurer, secretary, delegate, or other officer so chosen or appointed, that the election or appointment of such persons to such offices shall not be known to the society at large, or of which the names of all the members, and of all committees or select bodies of members, and of all presidents, treasurers, secretaries, delegates, and other officers, shall not be entered in a book or books to be kept for that purpose, and to be open to the inspection of all the members of such society; and every society which shall be composed of different divisions or branches, or of different parts, acting in any manner separately or distinct from each other, or of which any part shall have any separate or distinct president, secretary, treasurer, delegate, or other officer, elected or appointed by or for such part, or to act as an officer for such part; shall be deemed and taken to be unlawful combinations and confederacies; and every person, who from and after the passing of this act, shall become a member of any such society, or who being a member of any such society, at the passing of this act, shall afterwards act as a member thereof; and every person who, after the passing of this act, shall directly or indirectly maintain correspondence or intercourse with any such society, or with any division, branch, committee, or other select body, president, treasurer, secretary, delegate, or other officer, or member thereof as such, or who shall, by contribution of money or otherwise, aid, abet, or support such society, or any members or officers thereof as such; shall be deemed guilty of an unlawful combination and confederacy.

III. Provided always nevertheless, and be it enacted, That nothing herein contained shall extend to any declaration to be taken, subscribed, or assented to by the members of any society, in case the form of such declaration shall have been first approved and subscribed by two or more of his Majesty's justices of the peace for the county, stewartry, riding, division, or place, where such society shall ordinarily assemble, and shall have been registered with the clerk of the peace, or his deputy, for such county, stewartry, riding, division, or place, for which there shall be paid a fee of one shilling and no more; but that such approbation of the justices as aforesaid shall remain valid and effectual no longer than until the next general session for such county, stewartry, riding, division, or place, unless the same shall, on application made by the parties concerned, be confirmed by the major part of the justices present at such general session; and if the same shall not be then and there so confirmed, the provisions of this act shall from thenceforth extend to such declaration, and to all societies or persons subscribing the same, in so far as may relate to all acts which may be done by them, or any of them, subsequent to the holding of such general session.

IV. Provided also, and be it enacted, That no person who, at or before the passing of this act, shall be, or shall have been a member of any such society, shall be liable to any pain or penalty for having been a member of such society at or before the passing of this act, in case such person shall not in any manner act as a member of such society at any time after the passing of this act.

V. And whereas certain societies have been long accustomed to be holden in this kingdom under the denomination of *Lodges of Free Masons*, the meetings whereof have been in great measure directed to charitable purposes; be it therefore enacted, That nothing in this act shall extend to the meetings of any such society or lodge which shall, before the passing of this act, have been usually holden under the said denomination and in conformity to the rules prevailing among the said societies of free masons.

VI. Provided always, That this exemption shall not extend to any such society, unless two of the members composing the same shall certify upon oath, (which oath any justice of the peace or other magistrate is hereby empowered to administer), that such society or lodge has, before the passing of this act, been usually held under the denomination of a *Lodge of Free Masons*, and in conformity to the rules prevailing among the societies or lodges of free masons in this kingdom; which certificate duly attested by the magistrate before whom the same shall be sworn and subscribed by the persons so certifying, shall, within the space of two calendar months after the passing of this act, be deposited with the clerk of the peace for the county, stewartry, riding, division, shire, or place, where such society or lodge hath been usually held: provided also, That this exemption shall not extend to any such society or lodge, unless the name or denomination thereof, and the usual place or places, and the time or times of its meetings, and the names and descriptions of all and every the members thereof, be registered with such clerk of the peace as aforesaid, within two months after the passing of this act, and also on or before the twenty-fifth day of *March* in every succeeding year.

VII. And be it enacted, That the clerk of the peace, or the person acting in his behalf, in any such county, stewartry, riding, division, shire, or place, is hereby authorised and required to receive such certificate, and make such registry as aforesaid, and to enrol the same among the records of such county, stewartry, riding, division, shire, or place, and to lay the same, once in every year, before the general session of the justices for such county, stewartry, riding, division, shire, or place; and that it shall and may be lawful for the said justices, or for the major part of them, at any of their general sessions, if they shall so think fit, upon complaint made to them, upon oath, by any one or more credible persons, that the continuance of the meetings of any such lodge or society is likely to be injurious to the publick peace and good order, to direct that the meetings of any such society or lodge within such county, stewartry, riding, division, shire, or place, shall from thenceforth be discontinued; and any such meeting held, notwithstanding such order or discontinuance, and before the same shall, by the like authority, be revoked, shall be deemed an unlawful combination and confederacy under the provisions of this act.

VIII. And be it further enacted, That every person who, at any time after the passing of this act, shall in breach of the provisions thereof, be guilty of any such unlawful combination and confederacy, as in this act is described, shall and may be proceeded against for such offence in a summary way, either before one or more justice or justices of the peace for the county, stewartry, riding, division, city, town, or place, where such person shall happen to be, or by indictment to be preferred in the county, riding, division, city, town, or place, in *England*, wherein such offence shall be committed, or by indictment in the court of justiciary, or in any of the circuit courts in *Scotland*, if the offence shall be committed in *Scotland*; and every person being convicted of any such offence, on the oath of one or more credible witness or witnesses, by such justice or justices as aforesaid, shall be by him or them committed to the common gaol or house of correction for such county, stewartry, riding, division, city, town, or place, there to remain without bail or mainprize, for the term of three calendar months, or shall be by such justice or justices adjudged to forfeit and pay the sum of twenty pounds, as to such justice or justices shall seem meet; and in case such sum of money shall not be forthwith paid into the hands of such justice or justices, he or they shall by warrant under his or their hand and seal, or hands and seals, cause the same to be levied by distress and sale of the offender's goods and chattels, together with all costs and charges attending such distress and sale, and, for want of sufficient distress, shall commit such offender to the common gaol or house of correction of such county, stewartry, riding, division, city, town, or place, as aforesaid, for any time not exceeding three calendar months; and every person convicted of any such offence upon indictment by due course of law, shall and may be transported for the term of seven years, in the manner provided by law for transportation of offenders, or imprisoned for any time not exceeding two years, as the court before whom such offender shall be tried shall think fit; and every such offender, who shall be ordered to be transported, shall be subject and liable to all laws concerning offenders ordered to be transported.

IX. Provided always, That it shall be lawful for the justice or justices of the peace, by or before whom any person shall, in pursuance of this act, be convicted of any unlawful combination or confederacy, and such justice or justices is and are hereby authorised and empowered (if he or they shall see cause) to mitigate and lessen the punishment herein-before directed to be inflicted upon any offender against this act, so convicted as aforesaid, so as the punishment be not thereby reduced to less than one third of the punishment hereby directed to be inflicted as aforesaid, whether such punishment shall be by imprisonment or fine.

X. Provided also, and be it further enacted, That any person who shall be prosecuted before any justice or justices of the peace, in a summary way, for any offence against this act, and shall be convicted or acquitted by such justice or justices, shall not afterwards be prosecuted, or be liable to be prosecuted, by indictment or otherwise, for the same offence; and so in like manner any person who shall be convicted or acquitted upon any indictment for any offence against this act, shall not afterwards be prosecuted, or be liable to be prosecuted before any justice or justices of the peace, in a summary way, for the same offence.

XI. Provided also, That nothing in this act contained shall extend to prevent any prosecution by indictment, or otherwise, for any thing which shall be an offence within the intent and meaning of this act, and which might have been so prosecuted if this act had not been made, unless the offender shall have been prosecuted for such offence under this act, and convicted or acquitted of such offence; save only that no person shall be prosecuted for having been, before the passing of this act, a member of any society hereby declared to be an unlawful combination and confederacy, if such person shall not in any manner have acted as a member of such society after the passing of this act.

XII. Provided always, That nothing herein contained shall extend to discharge any person in custody at the passing of this act, or who, having been in custody, shall have been discharged, on bail or recognizance, from any prosecution which might have been had against such person if this act had not been made.

XIII. And be it further enacted, That if any person shall knowingly permit any meeting of any society hereby declared to be an unlawful combination or confederacy, or of any division, branch, or committee of such society, to be held in his or her house or apartment, such person shall, for the first offence, forfeit the sum of five pounds, and shall, for any such offence committed after the date of his or her conviction for such first offence, be deemed guilty of an unlawful combination and confederacy in breach of this act.

XIV. And be it further enacted, That it shall be lawful for any two or more justices of the peace acting for any county, stewartry, riding, division, city, town, or place, upon evidence on oath that any meeting of any society, hereby declared to be an unlawful combination and confederacy, or any meeting for any seditious purpose, hath been held, after the passing of this act, at any house, room, or place, licensed for the sale of ale, beer, wine, or spirituous liquors, to adjudge and declare the licence or licences for selling ale, beer, wine, or spirituous liquors, granted to the person or persons keeping such house, room, or place, to have been forfeited; and the person or persons so keeping such house, room, or place, shall, from and after the day of the date of such adjudication and declaration, be subject and liable to all and every the penalties and forfeitures for any act done after that day, which such person or persons would be subject and liable to, if such licence or licences had expired, or otherwise determined on that day.

XV. And whereas divers places have of late been used for delivering lectures or discourses, and holding debates, which are not within the provisions of the act, passed in the thirty-sixth year of his Majesty's reign, for the more effectually preventing seditious meetings and assemblies, but which lectures, discourses, or debates, have in many instances been of a seditious and immoral nature; and other places have of late been used for seditious and immoral purposes, under the pretence of being places of meeting for the purposes of reading books, pamphlets, newspapers, or other publications; be it further enacted, That every house, room, field, or other place, at or in which any lecture or discourse shall be publickly delivered, or any publick debate shall be had on any subject whatever, for the purpose of raising or collecting money, or any other valuable thing from the persons admitted, or to which any person shall be admitted by payment of money, or by any ticket or token of any kind delivered in consideration of money or any other valuable thing, or in consequence of paying or giving, or having paid or given, or having agreed to pay or give, in any manner, any money or other valuable thing, or where any money or other valuable thing shall be received from any person admitted either under pretence of paying for any refreshment or other thing, or under any other pretence, or for any other cause, or by means of any device or contrivance whatever; and every house, room, or place, which shall be opened or used as a place of meeting, for the purpose of reading books, pamphlets, newspapers, or other publications, and to which any person shall be admitted by payment of money, or by any ticket or token of any kind delivered in consideration of money or other valuable thing, or in consequence of paying or giving, or having paid or given, or having agreed to pay or give, any money or other valuable thing, or where any money or other valuable thing shall be received from any person admitted either under pretence of paying for any refreshment or other thing, or under any other pretence, or for any other cause, or by means of any device or contrivance whatever; shall be deemed a disorderly house or place within the intent and meaning of the said act, passed in the thirty-sixth year of his Majesty's reign, for the more effectually preventing seditious meetings and assemblies, unless the same shall have been previously licensed in manner herein-after mentioned; and the person by whom such house, room, field, or place, shall be opened or used, for any of the purposes aforesaid, shall forfeit the sum of one hundred pounds, for every day or time that such house, room, field, or place, shall be opened or used as aforesaid, to such person as will sue for the same, and be otherwise punished as the law directs in cases of disorderly houses; and every person managing or conducting the proceedings, or acting as moderator, president, or chairman, at such house, room, field, or place, so opened or used as aforesaid, or therein debating, or delivering any discourse or lecture, or furnishing or delivering any book, pamphlet, newspaper, or other publication as aforesaid; and also every person, who shall pay, give, collect, or receive, or agree to pay, give, collect, or receive any money, or any thing, for or in respect of the admission of any person into any such house, room, field, or place, or shall deliver out, distribute, or receive any such ticket or tickets, or token or tokens as aforesaid, knowing such house, room, field, or place to be opened or used for any such purpose as aforesaid, shall, for every such offence, forfeit the sum of twenty pounds. . . .

XXIII. And whereas many societies, established of late years for treasonable and seditious purposes, and especially the said societies of *United Englishmen, United Scotsmen, United Irishmen,* and *United Britons,* and the said society called *The London Corresponding Society,* and other corresponding societies, have at various times caused to be published, in great quantities, divers printed papers of an irreligious, treasonable, and seditious nature, tending to revile our holy religion, and to bring the profession and worship thereof into contempt among the ignorant, and also to excite hatred and contempt of his Majesty's royal person, government, and laws, and of the happy constitution of these realms, as by law established, and utterly to eradicate all principles of religion and morality; and such societies have dispersed such printed papers among the lower classes of the community, either *gratis*, or at very low prices, and with an activity and profusion beyond all former example: and whereas all persons printing or publishing any papers or writings are by law answerable for the contents thereof, but such responsibility hath of late been in a great degree eluded by the secret printing and publication of such seditious, immoral, and irreligious papers or writings as aforesaid, and it is therefore highly important to the publick peace that it should in future be known by whom any such papers shall be printed; be it enacted, That, from and after the expiration of forty days from the day of passing this act, every person having any printing press, or types for printing, shall cause a notice thereof, signed in the presence of and attested by one witness, to be delivered to the clerk of the peace acting for the county, stewartry, riding, division, city, borough, town, or place, where the same shall be intended to be used, or his deputy, according to the form prescribed in the schedule hereunto annexed; and such clerk of the peace, or deputy respectively, shall, and he is hereby authorised and required to grant a certificate in the form prescribed in the schedule hereunto annexed, for which such clerk of the peace, or deputy, shall receive the fee of one shilling, and no more, and such clerk of the peace, or his deputy, shall file such notice, and transmit an attested copy thereof to one of his Majesty's principal secretaries of state; and every person who, not having delivered such notice, and obtained such certificate as aforesaid, shall, from and after the expiration of forty days next after the passing of this act, keep or use any printing press or types for printing, or having delivered such notice, and obtained such certificate as aforesaid, shall use any printing press or types for printing in any other place than the place expressed in such notice, shall forfeit and lose the sum of twenty pounds.

XXIV. Provided also, That nothing herein contained shall extend to his Majesty's printers of *England* and *Scotland*, or to the public presses belonging to the universities of *Oxford* and *Cambridge* respectively.

XXV. And be it further enacted, That, from and after the expiration of forty days after the passing of this act, every person carrying on the business of a letter founder, or maker or seller of types for printing, or of printing presses, shall cause notice of his or her intention to carry on such business to be delivered to the clerk of the peace of the county, stewartry, riding, division, city, borough, town, or place, where such person shall propose to carry on such business, or his deputy, in the form prescribed in the schedule to this act annexed; and such clerk of the peace, or his deputy, shall, and he is hereby authorised and required thereupon to grant a certificate in the form also prescribed in the said schedule, for which such clerk of the peace, or his deputy, shall receive a fee of one shilling, and no more, and shall file such notice, and transmit an attested copy thereof to one of his Majesty's principal secretaries of state; and every person who shall, after the expiration of the said forty days, carry on such business, or make or sell any type for printing, or printing press, without having given such notice, and obtained such certificate, shall forfeit and lose the sum of twenty pounds.

XXVI. And be it further enacted, That every person who shall sell types for printing, or printing presses, as aforesaid, shall keep a fair account in writing, of all persons to whom any such types or presses shall be sold, and shall produce such accounts to any justice of the peace who shall require the same; and if such person shall neglect to keep such account, or shall refuse to produce the same to any such justice, on demand in writing to inspect the same, such person shall forfeit and lose, for such offence, the sum of twenty pounds.

XXVII. And be it further enacted, That, from and after the expiration of forty days after the passing of this act, every person who shall print any paper or book whatsoever, which shall be meant or intended to be published or dispersed, whether the same shall be sold or given away, shall print upon the front of every such paper, if the same shall be printed on one side only, and upon the first and last leaves of every paper or book which shall consist of more than one leaf, in legible characters, his or her name, and the name of the city, town, parish, or place, and also the name (if any) of the square, street, lane, court, or place, in which his or her dwelling house or usual place of abode shall be; and every person who shall omit so to print his name and place of abode on every such paper or book printed by him, and also every person who shall publish or disperse, or assist in publishing or dispersing, either *gratis* or for money, any printed paper or book, which shall have been printed after the expiration of forty days from the passing of this act, and on which the name and place of abode of the person printing the same shall not be printed as aforesaid, shall, for every copy of such paper so published or dispersed by him, forfeit and pay the sum of twenty pounds.

XXVIII. And be it further enacted, That nothing in this act contained shall extend, or be construed to extend, to any papers printed by the authority and for the use of either house of parliament.

XXIX. And be it further enacted, That every person who, from and after the expiration of forty days after the passing of this act, shall print any paper for hire, reward, gain, or profit, shall carefully preserve and keep one copy (at least) of every paper so printed by him or her, on which he or she shall write, or cause to be written or printed, in fair and legible characters, the name and place of abode of the person or persons by whom he or she shall be employed to print the same; and every person printing any paper for hire, reward, gain, or profit, who shall omit or neglect to write, or cause to be written or printed as aforesaid, the name and place of his or her employer on one of such printed papers, or to keep or preserve the same for the space of six calendar months next after the printing thereof, or to produce and shew the same to any justice of the peace, who, within the said space of six calendar months, shall require to see the same, shall, for every such omission, neglect, or refusal, forfeit and lose the sum of twenty pounds.

XXX. And be it further enacted, That it shall be lawful for any person, to whom or in whose presence any printed paper, not having the name and place of abode of any person printed thereon, in manner herein-before directed, or having a fictitious or false name or place of abode printed thereon, shall be sold, or offered for sale, or shall be delivered *gratis*, or offered so to be, or shall be pasted, fixed, or left in any publick place, or in any other manner exposed to publick view, to seize and detain the person so selling or offering to sell, or delivering or offering to deliver, or pasting, fixing, or leaving in any publick place, or in any other manner exposing to publick view, any such printed paper as aforesaid, and forthwith to take and convey him or her before some justice of the peace for the county, stewartry, riding, division, city, borough, town, or place, where such person shall be seized, or to deliver him or her to some constable or other peace officer, to be taken and conveyed before such justice as aforesaid, to the intent that such justice may hear and determine whether such person hath been guilty of any offence against this act.

XXXI. Provided always, That nothing herein contained shall extend to the impression of any engraving, or to the printing by letter press, of the name, or the name and address, or business or profession, of any person, and the articles in which he deals, or to any papers for the sale of estates or goods by auction, or otherwise.

XXXII. Provided also, That nothing herein contained shall extend, or be construed to extend, to alter or vary any rule, regulation, or provision contained in any act of parliament now in force respecting the printing, publishing, or distributing any printed newspaper, or other printed paper.

XXXIII. And be it further enacted, That if any justice of the peace, acting for any county, stewartry, riding, division, city, borough, town, or place, shall, from information upon oath, have reason to suspect that any printing press or types for printing is or are used or kept for use without notice given and certificate obtained as required by this act, or in any place not included in such notice and certificate, it shall be lawful for such justice, by warrant under his hand and seal, to direct, authorise, and empower any constable, petty constable, borsholder, headborough, or other peace officer, in the day time, with such person or persons as shall be called to his assistance, to enter into any such house, room, and place, and search for any printing press or types for printing; and it shall be lawful for every such peace officer, with such assistance as aforesaid, to enter into such house, room, or place, in the day time accordingly, and to seize, take, and carry away, every printing press found therein, together with all the types and other articles thereto belonging, and used in printing, and all printed papers found in such house, room, or place.

XXXIV. Provided always, That no person shall be prosecuted or sued for any penalty imposed by this act, unless such prosecution shall be commenced, or such action shall be brought, within three calendar months next after such penalty shall have been incurred.

Combination Act, 29 July 1800

40 Geo. 3, c. 106   *Statutes at Large*, XLII, 847-55.

Although this act prohibited the formation of trade unions, it modified an even more stringent act passed in 1799. It did not succeed entirely in suppressing trade unions and was effectively repealed by the acts of 1824 and 1825.

Whereas it is expedient to explain and amend an act, passed in the thirty-ninth year of the reign of his present Majesty, intituled, *An act to prevent unlawful combinations of workmen*; be it therefore enacted by the King's most excellent majesty, by and with the advice and consent of the lords spiritual and temporal, and commons, in this present parliament assembled, and by the authority of the same, That from and after the passing of this act, the said act shall be repealed; and that all contracts, covenants, and agreements whatsoever, in writing or not in writing, at any time or times heretofore made or entered into by or between any journeymen manufacturers or other persons within this kingdom, for obtaining an advance of wages of them or any of them, or any other journeymen manufacturers or workmen, or other persons in any manufacture, trade, or business, or for lessening or altering their or any of their usual hours or time of working, or for decreasing the quantity of work, (save and except any contract made or to be made between any master and his journeyman or manufacturer, for or on account of the work or service of such journeyman or manufacturer with whom such contract may be made), or for preventing or hindering any person or persons from employing whomsoever he, she, or they shall think proper to employ in his, her, or their manufacture, trade, or business, or for controlling or anyway affecting any person or persons carrying on any manufacture, trade, or business, in the conduct or management thereof, shall be and the same are hereby declared to be illegal, null, and void, to all intents and purposes whatsoever.

II.   And be it further enacted, That no journeyman, workman, or other person shall at any time after the passing of this act make or enter into, or be concerned in the making of or entering into any such contract, covenant, or agreement, in writing or not in writing, as herein-before declared to be an illegal covenant, contract, or agreement; and every journeyman and workman or other person who, after the passing of this act, shall be guilty of any of the said offences, being thereof lawfully convicted, upon his own confession, or the oath or oaths of one or more credible witness or witnesses, before any two justices of the peace for the county, riding, division, city, liberty, town, or place where such offence shall be committed, (which oath either of such justices is hereby authorised and empowered to administer in such case, and in all other cases where an oath is to be taken before any justices of the peace in pursuance of this act), within three calendar months next after the offence shall have been committed, shall, by order of such justices, be committed to and confined in the common gaol within his or their jurisdiction, for any time not exceeding three calendar months, or at the discretion of such justices shall be committed to some house of correction within the same jurisdiction, there to remain and to be kept to hard labour for any time not exceeding two calendar months.

III.   And be it further enacted, That every journeyman or workman, or other person, who shall at any time after the passing of this act enter into any combination to obtain an advance of wages, or to lessen or alter the hours or duration of the time of working, or to decrease the quantity of work, or for any other purpose contrary to this act, or who shall, by giving money, or by persuasion, solicitation, or intimidation, or any other means, wilfully and maliciously endeavour to prevent any unhired or unemployed journeyman or workman, or other person, in any manufacture, trade, or business, or any other person wanting employment in such manufacture, trade, or business, from hiring himself to any manufacturer, or tradesman, or person conducting any manufacture, trade, or business, or who shall, for the purpose of obtaining an advance of wages, or for any other purpose contrary to the provisions of this act, wilfully and maliciously decoy, persuade, solicit, intimidate, influence, or prevail, or attempt or endeavour to prevail, on any journeyman or workman, or other person hired or employed, or to be hired or employed in any such manufacture, trade, or business, to quit or leave his work, service, or employment, or who shall wilfully and maliciously hinder or prevent any manufacturer or tradesman, or other person, from employing in his or her manufacture, trade, or business, such journeymen, workmen, and other persons as he or she shall think proper, or who, being hired or employed, shall, without any just or reasonable cause, refuse to work with any other journeyman or workman employed or hired to work therein, and who shall be lawfully convicted of any of the said offences, upon his own confession, or the oath or oaths of one or more credible witness or witnesses, before any two justices of the peace for the county, riding, division, city, liberty, town, or place, where such offence shall be committed, within three calendar months next after the offence shall have been committed, shall, by order of such justices, be committed to and be confined in the common gaol within his or their jurisdiction, for any time not exceeding three calendar months; or otherwise be committed to some house of correction within the same jurisdiction, there to remain and to be kept to hard labour for any time not exceeding two calendar months.

IV. And for the more effectual suppression of all combinations amongst journeymen, workmen, and other persons employed in any manufacture, trade or business, be it further enacted, That all and every persons and person whomsoever, (whether employed in any such manufacture, trade, or business, or not), who shall attend any meeting had or held for the purpose of making or entering into any contract, covenant, or agreement, by this act declared to be illegal, or of entering into, supporting, maintaining, continuing, or carrying on any combination for any purpose by this act declared to be illegal, or who shall summons, give notice to, call upon, persuade, entice, solicit, or by intimidation, or any other means, endeavour to induce any journeyman, workman, or other person employed in any manufacture, trade, or business, to attend any such meeting, or who shall collect, demand, ask, or receive any sum of money from any such journeyman, workman, or other person, for any of the purposes aforesaid, or who shall persuade, entice, solicit, or by intimidation, or any other means, endeavour to induce any such journeyman, workman, or other person to enter into or be concerned in any such combination, or who shall pay any sum of money, or make or enter into any subscription or contribution, for or towards the support or encouragement of any such illegal meeting or combination, and who shall be lawfully convicted of any of the said offences, upon his own confession, or the oath or oaths of one or more credible witness or witnesses, before any two justices of the peace for the county, riding, division, city, liberty, town, or place where such offence shall be committed, within three calendar months next after the offence shall have been committed, shall, by order of such justices, be committed to and confined in the common gaol within his or their jurisdiction, for any time not exceeding three calendar months, or otherwise be committed to some house of correction within the same jurisdiction, there to remain and be kept to hard labour for any time not exceeding two calendar months.

V. And be it further enacted, That no person (whether employed as a journeyman or workman in any manufacture, trade, or business, or not) shall at any time after the passing of this act wilfully pay or give any sum of money as a subscription or contribution for the purpose of paying expences incurred or to be incurred by any person or persons acting contrary to the provisions of this act, by payment of money, or other means, support or maintain any journeyman, workman, or other person, or contribute towards his support or maintenance, for the purpose of inducing him to refuse to work, or to be hired or employed in any manufacture, trade, or business; and every person, who shall be guilty of any such offence shall forfeit and lose any sum not exceeding the sum of ten pounds; and every journeyman, workman, and other person, who shall collect or receive any money or valuable thing for any of the purposes aforesaid, shall forfeit and lose any sum not exceeding the sum of five pounds; such penalties of ten pounds and five pounds respectively to be forfeited, one moiety to his Majesty, and the other moiety to the informer and the poor of the parish where such offence has been committed, to be equally divided between them; and all and every of the said offences shall be heard and determined in a summary way, before two justices of the peace for the county, riding, division, city, liberty, town, or place, where such offence shall be committed, and the conviction for the same may be had and made upon the oath or oaths of one or more credible witness or witnesses; and the amount of the forfeiture or penalty for every such offence shall be fixed and determined by such justices, but not exceeding the severa! sums herein-before mentioned; and in case any such forfeiture or penalty shall not be forthwith paid pursuant to such conviction, such justices shall, by warrant under their hands, cause the same to be levied by distress and sale of the offender's goods and chattels, together with all costs and charges attending such distress and sale; and in case no sufficient distress can be had, such justices shall, by warrant under their hands, commit the offender to the common gaol within his or their jurisdiction, there to remain, without bail or mainprize, for any time not exceeding three calendar months nor less than two calendar months; or otherwise, at the discretion of such justices, to some house of correction within their jurisdiction, there to remain and be kept to hard labour for any time not exceeding two calendar months.

VI. And be it further enacted, That all sums of money which at any time heretofore have been paid or given as a subscription or contribution for or towards any of the purposes prohibited by this act, and shall, for the space of three calendar months next after the passing of this act, remain undivided in the hands of any treasurer, collector, receiver, trustee, agent, or other person, or placed out at interest, and all sums of money which shall at any time after the passing of this act, be paid or given as a subscription or contribution for or towards any of the purposes prohibited by this act, shall be forfeited, one moiety thereof to his Majesty, and the other moiety to such person as will sue for the same in any of his Majesty's courts of record at *Westminster*; and any treasurer, collector, receiver, trustee, agent, or other person in whose hands or in whose name any such sum of money shall be, or shall be placed out, or unto whom the same shall have been paid or given, shall and may be sued for the same as forfeited as aforesaid.

VII. And, for the better discovery of all sums of money which have been or shall be paid or given by way of subscriptions or contribution for any purpose prohibited by this act, be it further enacted, That all and every the persons and person who shall or may be liable by virtue of this act to be sued for the same, shall be obliged and compellable to answer upon oath to any information which shall or may be preferred against them or him in any court of equity, by or in the name of his Majesty's attorney general on the part of his Majesty, or at the relation of any informer, for discovering the sum and sums of money so paid or given for any of the prohibited purposes aforesaid, and such court shall and may make such orders and decrees therein as to such court shall seem just, and no person shall demur to or refuse to answer such information by reason of any penalty or forfeiture to which such person may be liable in consequence of any discovery which may be sought thereby.

VIII. Provided always, and be it enacted, That upon payment into the court in which such information shall be filed of all the money paid or given unto any such treasurer, collector, receiver, trustee, agent, or other person for any of the prohibited purposes aforesaid, and remaining in his hands at the time of filing such informations, and upon making a full discovery of all the securities or upon which all such money which shall not be so remaining in his hands shall have been placed out or invested, the person or persons paying such money into court and making such discovery shall be acquitted and discharged from all forfeitures and penalties which shall or may have been incurred by him or them by reason of having collected or received such money, or otherwise acted concerning the same, and from all actions and other suits respecting the same by any person or persons whomsoever, any statute, law, or usage, or any thing in this act contained to the contrary thereof in anywise notwithstanding; nor shall any person be liable to any forfeiture or penalty or to any prosecution whatsoever, for or in respect of any sum of money which such person shall discover to have been paid, received, or given by any answer to any such information as aforesaid.

IX. And be further enacted, That all and every persons and person who shall or may offend against this act, shall and may, equally with all other persons, be called upon and compelled to give his or her testimony and evidence, as a witness or witnesses on behalf of his Majesty, or of the prosecutor or informer, upon any information to be made or exhibited under this act against any other person or persons, not being such witness or witnesses as aforesaid; and that in all such cases, every person having given his or her testimony or evidence as aforesaid shall be and hereby is indemnified of, from, and against any information to be laid, or prosecution to be commenced against him or her for having offended in the matter wherein or relative to which he, she, or they shall have given testimony or evidence as aforesaid.

X. And, for the more effectually enforcing and carrying into execution the provisions of this act, be it further enacted, That on complaint and information on oath before any one or more justice or justices of the peace, of any offence having been committed against this act, within his or their respective jurisdictions, such justice or justices are hereby authorised and required to summon the person or persons charged with being an offender or offenders against this act, to appear before any two such justices, at a certain time or place to be specified, and if any person or persons so summoned shall not appear according to such summons, then such justices (proof on oath having been first made before them or him of the due service of such summons upon such person or persons, by delivering the same to him or them personally, or leaving the same at his or their usual place of abode, provided the same shall be so left twenty-four hours at the least before the time which shall be appointed to attend the said justices upon such summons) shall make and issue their or his warrant or warrants for apprehending the person or persons so summoned and not appearing as aforesaid, and bringing him or them before such justices, or it shall be lawful for such justices, if they shall think fit, without issuing any previous summons, and instead of issuing the same, upon such complaint and information on oath as aforesaid, to make and issue their warrant or warrants for apprehending the person or persons by such information charged to have offended against this act, and bringing him or them before such justices; and upon the person or persons complained against appearing upon such summons, or being brought by virtue of such warrant or warrants before such justices, or upon proof on oath of such person or persons absconding, so that such warrant or warrants cannot be executed, then such justices shall, and they are hereby authorised and required forthwith to make enquiry touching the matters complained of, and to examine into the same, by the oath or oaths of any credible persons, as shall be requisite, and to hear and determine the matter of every such complaint, and upon confession by the party, or proof by one or more credible witness or witnesses, upon oath, to convict or acquit the party or parties against whom complaint shall have been made as aforesaid.

XI. And be it further enacted, That it shall be lawful for the justices of the peace before whom any such complaint and information shall be made as aforesaid, and they are hereby authorised and required, at the request in writing of any of the parties, to issue his or their summons to any witness or witnesses to appear and give evidence before such justices at the time and place appointed for hearing and, determining such complaint, and which time and place shall be specified in such summons; and if any person or persons so summoned to appear as a witness or witnesses as aforesaid, shall not appear before such justices at the time and place specified in such summons, or offer some reasonable excuse for the default, or appearing according to such summons, shall not submit to be examined as a witness or witnesses, and give his or their evidence before such justices touching the matter of such complaint, then and in every such case it shall be lawful for such justices, and they are hereby authorised, (proof on oath in the case of any person not appearing according to such summons having been first made before such justice or justices of the due service of such summons on every such person, by delivering the same to him or her, or by leaving the same twenty-four hours before the time appointed for such person to appear before such justices, at the usual place of abode of such person), by warrant under the hands of such justices, to commit such person or persons so making default in appearing, or appearing and refusing to give evidence, to some prison within the jurisdiction of such justices, there to remain without bail or mainprize, until such person or persons shall submit himself, herself, or themselves to be examined, and give his, her, or their evidence before such justices as aforesaid.

XII. And be it further enacted, That the justices before whom any person or persons shall be convicted of any offence against this act, or by whom any person shall be committed to prison for not appearing as a witness, or not submitting to be examined, shall cause all such convictions, and the warrants or orders for such commitment to be drawn up in the form, or to the effect set forth in the first schedule to this act.

XIII. And be it further enacted, That the justices before whom any such conviction shall be had, shall cause the same (drawn up in the form or to the effect herein-before directed) to be fairly written on parchment, and transmitted to the next general sessions or general quarter sessions of the peace to be holden for the county, riding, division, city, liberty, town, or place wherein such conviction was had, to be filed and kept amongst the records of the said general sessions or general quarter sessions; and in case any person or persons shall appeal, in manner herein-after mentioned, from the judgement of the said justices to the said general sessions or general quarter sessions, the justices in such general sessions or general quarter sessions, are hereby required, upon receiving such conviction, to proceed to the hearing and determination of the matter of the said appeal, according to the directions of this act.

XIV. Provided always, and be it enacted, That nothing in this act contained shall extend, or be construed to extend, to repeal, take away, or abridge the powers and authorities given to any justice or justices of the peace in and by any act or acts of parliament heretofore made and now in force touching any combinations of manufacturers, journeymen, or workmen, or for settling and adjusting disputes or differences between masters and their journeymen, workmen, or other persons employed by them in any manufacture, trade, or business, or the rate or amount of wages to be paid to such journeymen, workmen, or other persons, or the mode or time of their working or being employed, or the quantity of work to be done, or touching any matter whatsoever also provided for by this act; but that all justices of the peace shall continue to use, exercise, and execute all the powers and authorities given to them in and by such acts of partliament, or any of them, in such and the same manner as they could or might have done if this act had not been made; any thing herein contained to the contrary in anywise notwithstanding.

XV. Provided always, That this act shall not extend to authorise or empower any person or persons carrying on any manufacture, trade, or business, to employ therein any journeyman or workman contrary to the regulations and provisions contained in any act or acts of parliament which hath or have been heretofore made, and is and are now in force, for settling, regulating, or directing the manner or method of conducting, managing or carrying on any particular manufacture, trade, or business, or the work or service of the persons employed therein, without the previous licence and consent in writing, of one justice of the peace for the county, riding, division, city, liberty, town, or place in which such manufacture, trade, or business shall be carried on, expressing the cause or reason of giving or granting the same; which licence it shall be lawful for one such justice to grant whenever the qualified journeymen or workmen usually employed in any manufacture, trade, or business, shall refuse to work therein for reasonable wages, or to work for any particular person or persons, or to work with any particular persons, or shall, by refusing to work, for any cause whatsoever, or by misconducting themselves when employed to work, in any manner impede or obstruct the ordinary course of any manufacture, trade, or business, or endeavour to injur the person or persons carrying on the same.

XVI. Provided also, and be it further enacted by the authority aforesaid, That no justice of the peace, being also a master in the particular trade or manufacture in or concerning which any offence is charged to have been committed under this act, shall act as such justice under this act; any thing herein contained, or any former statute, law, usage, or custom to the contrary thereof in anywise notwithstanding.

XVII. And be it further enacted, by the authority aforesaid, That all contracts, covenants, and agreements whatsoever, in writing or not in writing, made or to be made by or between any masters or other persons, for reducing the wages of workmen, or for adding to or altering the usual hours or time of working, or for increasing the quantity of work, shall be, and the same are hereby declared to be illegal, null, and void, to all intents and purposes whatsoever; and all and every such masters, being thereof lawfully-convicted by the oath or oaths of one or more credible witness or witnesses, before any two justices of the peace for the county, riding, division, city, liberty, town or place, where such offence shall have been committed, within three calendar months next after the offence shall have been commited, shall forfeit and lose the sum of twenty pounds, one moiety thereof to his Majesty, and the other moiety in equal shares to the informer and the poor of the parish where such offence has been committed; and in case any such forfeiture or penalty shall not be forthwith paid pursuant to such conviction, such justices shall, by warrant under their hands cause the same to be levied by distress and sale of the offender's goods and chattels, together with all costs and charges attending such distress and sale; and in case no sufficient distress can be had, such justices shall, by warrant under their hands, commit the offender to the common gaol or some house of correction within their jurisdiction, for any time not exceeding three calendar months nor less than two calendar months. . . .

SPREAD OF LITERACY

Village Politics by Hannah More, c. 1790s

The Works of Hannah More, 2 vols. (New York: Harper & Brothers, 1835), I, 58-63.

Hannah More (1745-1833), who propagated her evangelical views in cheap books and tracts, was one of the first writers to grasp the potential of a mass readership. Village Politics *was the first of her famous "Cheap Repository Tracts."*

ADDRESSED TO ALL THE MECHANICS, JOURNEYMEN, AND LABOURERS, IN GREAT BRITAIN

By Will Chip, a Country Carpenter

It is a privilege to be prescribed to in things about which our minds would otherwise be tost with various apprehensions. And for pleasure, I shall profess myself so far from doating on that popular idol, Liberty, that I hardly think it possible for any kind of obedience to be more painful than an unrestrained liberty. Were there not true bounds, of magistrates, of laws, of piety, of reason in the heart, every man would have a fool, nay, a mad tyrant to his master, that would multiply him more sorrows than the briars and thorns did to Adam, when he was freed from the bliss at once, and the restraint of Paradise, and became a greater slave in the wilderness than in the enclosure.—*Dr. Hammond's Sermon.*

A Dialogue between Jack Anvil, the Blacksmith, and Tom Hod, the Mason

Jack. What's the matter, Tom? Why dost look so dismal!

Tom. Dismal, indeed! Well enough I may.

Jack. What! is the old mare dead? or work scarce?

Tom. No, no, work's plenty enough, if a man had but the heart to go to it.

Jack. What book art reading? Why dost look so like a hang dog?

Tom. (*Looking on his book.*) Cause enough. Why I find here that I'm very unhappy, and very miserable; which I should never have known if I had not had the good luck to meet with this book. Oh 'tis a precious book!

Jack. A good sign though; that you can't find out you're unhappy without looking into a book for it! What is the matter?

677

Tom. Matter? Why I want liberty.

Jack. Liberty! That's bad indeed! What! has any one fetched a warrant for thee? Come, man, cheer up, I'll be bound for thee. Thou art an honest fellow in the main, though thou dost tipple and prate a little too much at the Rose and Crown.

Tom. No, no, I want a new constitution.

Jack. Indeed! Why I thought thou hadst been a desperate healthy fellow. Send for the doctor directly.

Tom. I'm not sick; I want liberty and equality, and the rights of man.

Jack. O, now I understand thee. What! thou art a leveller and a republican, I warrant!

Tom. I'm a friend to the people. I want a reform.

Jack. Then the shortest way is to mend thyself.

Tom. But I want a *general reform.*

Jack. Then let every one mend one.

Tom. Pooh! I want freedom and happiness, the same as they have got in France.

Jack. What, Tom, we imitate them? We follow the French! Why they only began all this mischief at first in order to be just what *we* are already; and what a blessed land must this be, to be in actual possession of all they ever hoped to gain by all their hurly-burly. Imitate them indeed!—why I'd sooner go to the negroes to get learning, or to the Turks to get religion, than to the French for freedom and happiness.

Tom. What do you mean by that? ar'n't the French free?

Jack. Free, Tom! ay free with a witness. They are all so free that there's nobody safe. They make free to rob whom they will, and kill whom they will. If they don't like a man's looks, they make free to hang him without judge or jury, and the next lamp-post serves for the gallows; so then they call themselves free, because you see they have no law left to condemn them, and no king to take them up and hang them for it.

Tom. Ah, but Jack, didn't their king formerly hang people for nothing too? and besides, were they not all papists before the revolution?

Jack. Why, true enough, they had but a poor sort of religion; but bad is better than none, Tom. And so was the government bad enough too; for they could clap an innocent man into prison, and keep him there too as long as they would, and never say, with your leave or by your leave, gentlemen of the jury. But what's all that to us?

Tom. To us! Why don't many of our governors put many of our poor folks in prison against their will? What are all the jails for? Down with the jails, I say; all men should be free.

Jack. Harkee, Tom, a few rogues in prison keep the rest in order, and then honest men go about their business in safety, afraid of nobody; that's the way to be free. And let me tell thee, Tom, thou and I are tried by our peers as much as a lord is. Why the *king* can't send me to prison if I do no harm; and if I do, there's reason good why I should go there. I may go to law with sir John at the great castle yonder; and he no more dares lift his little finger against me than if I were his equal. A lord is hanged for hanging matter, as thou or I should be; and if it will be any comfort to thee, I myself remember a peer of the realm being hanged for killing his man, just the same as the man would have been for killing *him*. [Lord Ferrers was hang'd in 1760, for killing his steward.]

Tom. A lord! Well, that is some comfort to be sure. But have you read the Rights of Man?

Jack. No, not I: I had rather by half read the *Whole Duty of Man*. I have but little time for reading, and such as I should therefore only read a bit of the best.

Tom. Don't tell me of those old-fashioned notions. Why should not we have the same fine things they have got in France? I'm for a *constitution*, and *organization*, and *equalization*, and *fraternization*.

Jack. Do be quiet. Now, Tom, only suppose this nonsensical equality was to take place; why it would not last while one could say Jack Robinson; or suppose it could—suppose in the general division, our new rulers were to give us half an acre of ground a-piece; we could to be sure raise potatoes on it for the use of our families; but as every other man would be equally busy in raising potatoes for *his* family, why then you see if thou wast to break thy spade, I, whose trade it is, should no longer be able to mend it. Neighbour Snip would have no time to make us a suit of clothes, nor the clothier to weave the cloth; for all the world would be gone a digging. And as to boots and shoes, the want of some one to make them for us, would be a still greater grievance than the tax on leather. If we should be sick, there would be no doctor's stuff for us; for doctors would be digging too. And if necessity did not compel, and if inequality subsisted, we could not get a chimney swept, or a load of coal from pit, for love or money.

Tom. But still I should have no one over my head.

Jack. That's a mistake: I'm stronger than thou; and Standish, the exciseman, is a better scholar; so that we should not remain equal a minute. I should out-*fight* thee, and he'd out*wit* thee. And if such a sturdy fellow as I am, was to come and break down thy hedge for a little firing, or take away the crop from thy ground, I'm not so sure that these new-fangled laws would see thee righted. I tell thee, Tom, we have a fine constitution already, and our forefathers thought so.

Tom. They were a pack of fools, and had never read the Rights of Man.

Jack. I'll tell thee a story. When sir John married, my lady, who is a little fantastical, and likes to do every thing like the French, begged him to pull down yonder fine old castle, and build it up in her frippery way. No, says sir John, what shall I pull down this noble building, raised by the wisdom of my brave ancestors; which outstood the civil wars, and only underwent a little needful repair at the revolution; a castle which all my neighbours come to take a pattern by—shall I pull it all down, I say, only because there may be a dark closet, or an awkward passage, or an inconvenient room or two in it? Our ancestors took *time* for what they did. They understood *foundation* work; no running up your little slight lath and plaster buildings, which are up in a day, and down in a night. My lady mumpt and grumbled; but the castle was let stand, and a glorious building it is; though there may be a trifling fault or two, and though a few decays want stopping; so now and then they mend a little thing, and they'll go on mending, I dare say, as they have leisure, to the end of the chapter, if they are let alone. But no pull-me-down works. What is it you are crying out for, Tom?

Tom. Why for a perfect government.

Jack. You might as well cry for the moon. There's nothing perfect in this world, take my word for it: though sir John says, we come nearer to it than any country in the world ever did.

Tom. I don't see why we are to work like slaves, while others roll about in their coaches, feed on the fat of the land, and do nothing.

Jack. My little maid brought home a story-book from the charity school t'other day, in which was a bit of a fable about the belly and the limbs. The hands said, I won't work any longer to feed this lazy belly, who sits in state like a lord and does nothing. Said the feet I won't walk and tire myself to carry him about; let him shift for himself; so said all the members; just as your levellers and republicans do now. And what was the consequence? Why the belly was pinched to be sure, and grew thin upon it; but the hands and the feet, and the rest of the members, suffered so much for want of their old nourishment, which the belly had been all the time administering, while they accused him of sitting in idle state, that they all fell sick, pined away, and would have died, if they had not come to their senses just in time to save their lives, as I hope all you will do.

Tom. But the times—but the taxes, Jack.

Jack. Things are dear to be sure, but riot and murder is not the way to make them cheap. And taxes are high; but I'm told there's a deal of old scores paying off, and paying off, by them who did not contract the debt neither, Tom. Besides things are mending, I hope; and what little is done is for us poor people; our candles are somewhat cheaper, and I dare say, if the honest gentleman who has the management of things, is not disturbed by you levellers, things will mend every day. But bear one thing in mind: the more we riot, the more we shall have to pay: the more mischief is done, the more will the repairs cost: the more time we waste in meeting to redress public wrongs, the more we shall increase our private wants. And mind too, that 'tis working, and not murmuring, which puts bread in our children's mouths, and a new coat on our backs. Mind another thing too, we have not the same ground of complaint; in France the poor paid all the taxes, as I have heard 'em say, and the quality paid nothing.

Tom. Well, I know what's what, as well as another; and I'm as fit to govern—

Jack. No, Tom, no. You are indeed as good as another man, seeing you have hands to work, and a soul to be saved. But are all men fit for all kind of things? Solomon says; "How can he be wise whose talk is of oxen?" Every one in his way. I am a better judge of a horse-shoe than Sir John; but he has a deal better notion of state affairs than I; and I can no more do without his employ than he can do without my farriery. Besides, few are so poor but they may get a vote for a parliament-man; and so you see the poor have as much share in the government as they well know how to manage.

Tom. But I say all men are equal. Why should one be above another?

Jack. If that's thy talk, Tom, thou dost quarrel with Providence, and not with government. For the woman is below her husband, and the children are below their mother, and the servant is below his master.

Tom. But the subject is not below the king: all kings are "crown'd ruffians:" and all governments are wicked. For my part, I'm resolved I'll pay no more taxes to any of them.

Jack. Tom, Tom, if thou didst go oft'ner to church, thou wouldst know where it is said "Render unto Caesar the things that are Caesar's;" and also, "Fear God, honour the king." *Your* book tells you that we need obey no government but that of the people; and that we may fashion and alter the government according to our whimsies: but *mine* tells me, "Let every one be subject to the higher powers, for all power is of God, the powers that be are ordained of God; whosoever therefore resisteth the power, resisteth the ordinance of God." Thou say'st, thou wilt pay no taxes to any of them.—Dost thou know who it was that worked a miracle, that he might have money to pay tribute with, rather than set you and me an example of disobedience to government? an example, let me tell thee, worth an hundred precepts, and of which all the wit of man can never lessen the value. Then there's another thing worth minding, when St. Paul was giving all those directions, in the epistle to the Romans, for obedience and submission; what sort of a king now dost think they had? Dost think 'twas a *saint* which he ordered them to obey?

Tom. Why it was a kind, merciful, charitable king to be sure; one who put nobody to death or to prison.

Jack. You was never more out in your life. Our parson says he was a monster—that he robbed the rich, and murdered the poor—set fire to his own town, as fine a place as London—fiddled to the flames, and then hanged and burnt the Christians, who were all poor, as if they had burnt the town. Yet there's not a word about rising.—Duties are fixed, Tom.—Laws are settled; a Christian can't pick and choose, whether he will obey or let it alone. But *we* have no such trials.—We have a king the very reverse.

Tom. I say we shall never be happy, till we do as the French have done.

Jack. The French and we contending for liberty, Tom, is just as if thou and I were to pretend to run a race; thou to set out from the starting-post when I am in already; thou to have all the ground to travel when I have reached the end. Why we've got it man! we've no race to run! we're there already! Our constitution is no more like what the French one was, than a mug of our Taunton beer is like a platter of their soup-maigre.

Tom. I know we shall be undone, if we don't get a new *constitution*—that's all.

Jack. And I know we shall be undone if we *do*. I don't know much about politics, but I can see by a little, what a great deal means. Now only to show thee the state of public credit, as I think Tim Standish calls it. There's farmer Furrow, a few years ago he had an odd fifty pounds by him; so to keep it out of harm's way, he put it out to use, on government security, I think he calls it; well, t'other day he married one of his daughters, so he thought he'd give her that fifty pounds for a bit of a portion. Tom, as I'm a living man, when he went to take it out, if his fifty pounds was not almost grown to an hundred! and would have been a full hundred, they say, by this time, if the gentlemen had been let alone. [This was written before the war, when the funds were at the highest.]

Tom. Well, still as the old saying is—I should like to do as they do in France.

Jack. What, shouldest like to be murdered with as little ceremony as Hackabout, the butcher, knocks down a calf? or shouldest like to get rid of thy wife for every little bit of tiff? And as for liberty of *conscience*, which they brag so much about, why they have driven away their parsons (ay, and murdered many of 'em) because they would not swear as they would have them. And then they talk of liberty of the press; why, Tom, only t'other day they hanged a man for printing a book against this pretty government of theirs.

Tom. But you said yourself it was sad times in France, before they pulled down the old government.

Jack. Well, and suppose the French were as much in the right as I know them to be in the wrong; what does that argue for *us*?—Because my neighbour Furrow, t'other day pulled down a crazy old barn, is that a reason why I must set fire to my tight cottage?

Tom. I don't see for all that why one man is to ride in his coach and six, while another mends the highway for him.

Jack. I don't see why the man in the coach is to *drive over* the man on foot, or hurt a hair of his head, any more than you. And as to our great folks, that you levellers have such a spite against, I don't pretend to say they are a bit better than they should be; but that's no affair of mine; let them look to that they'll answer for that in another place. To be sure, I wish they'd set us a better example about going to church, and those things; but still *hoarding's* not the sin of the age; they don't lock up their *money*—away it goes, and every body's the better for it.—They do spend too much, to be sure, in feastings and fandangoes; and so far from commending them for it, if I was a parson I'd go to work with 'em, but it should be in another kind of way; but as I am only a poor tradesman, why 'tis but bringing more grist to my mill. It all comes among the people. Their very extravagance, for which, as I said before, their parsons should be at them, is a fault by which, as poor men, we are benefitted; so you cry out just in the wrong place. Their coaches and their furniture, and their buildings, and their planting, employ a power of tradesmen and labourers. Now in this village, what should we do without the castle? Though my lady is too rantipolish, and flies about all summer to hot water and cold water, and fresh water and salt water, when she ought to stay at home with sir John: yet when she does come down, she brings such a deal of gentry that I have more horses than I can shoe, and my wife more linen than she can wash. Then all our grown children are servants in the family, and rare wages they have got. Our little boys get something every day by weeding their gardens, and the girls learn to sew and knit at Sir John's expense, who sends them all to school of a Sunday besides.

Tom. Ay, but there's not Sir Johns in every village.

Jack. The more's the pity. But there's other help. 'Twas but last year you broke your leg, and was nine weeks in the Bristol Infirmary, where you was taken as much care of as a lord, and your family was maintained all the while by the parish. No poor-rates in France, Tom; and here there's a matter of two million and a half paid for the poor every year, if 'twas but a little better managed.

Tom. Two million and a half!

Jack. Ay, indeed, Not translated into ten-pences, as your French millions are, but twenty good shillings to the pound. But when this levelling comes about, there will be no infirmaries, no hospitals, no charity-schools, no Sunday-schools, where so many hundred thousand poor souls learn to read the word of God for nothing.— For who is to pay for them? *Equality* can't afford it; and those that may be willing won't be able.

Tom. But we shall be one as good as another for all that.

Jack. Ay, and bad will be the best. But we must work as we do now, and with this difference, that no one will be able to pay us. Tom! I have got the use of my limbs, of my liberty, of the laws, and of my Bible. The two first I take to be my *natural* rights; the two last my *civil* and *religious* rights: these, I take it, are the *true Rights of Man,* and all the rest is nothing but nonsense, and madness, and wickedness. My cottage is my castle; I sit down in it at night in peace and thankfulness, and "no man maketh me afraid." Instead of indulging discontent, because another is richer than I in this world (for envy is at the bottom of your equality works) I read my Bible, go to church, and look forward to a treasure in Heaven.

Tom. Ay, but the French have got it in *this* world.

Jack. 'Tis all a lie, Tom. Sir John's butler says his master gets letters which *say* 'tis all a lie. 'Tis all murder, and nakedness, and hunger, many of the poor soldiers fight without victuals, and march without clothes. These are your *democrats!* Tom.

Tom. What then, dost think all the men on our side wicked?

Jack. No—not so neither—If some of the leaders are knaves, more of the followers are fools. Sir John, who is wiser than I, says the whole system is the operation of fraud upon folly. They've made fools of most of you, as I believe. I judge no man Tom; I hate no man. Even republicans and levellers, I hope, will always enjoy the protection of our laws; though I hope they will never be our law *makers.* There are many true dissenters, and there are some hollow churchmen; and a good man is a good man, whether his church has got a steeple to it or not.—The new fashioned way of proving one's religion is to *hate* somebody. Now, though some folk pretend that a man's hating a papist, or a presbyterian, proves him to be a good *churchman,* it don't prove him to be a good *Christian,* Tom. As much as I hate republican works, I'd scorn to *live* in a country where there was not liberty of conscience; and where every man might not worship God in his own way. Now that liberty they had not in France: the Bible was shut up in an unknown and heathenish tongue.—While here, thou and I can make as free use of ours as a bishop: can no more be sent to prison unjustly than the judge who tries us; and are as much taken care of by the laws as the parliament-man who makes them.—Then, as to your thinking that the new scheme will make you happy, look among your own set and see if any thing can be so dismal and discontented as a leveller.—Look at France. These poor French fellows used to be the merriest dogs in the world; but since equality came in, I don't believe a Frenchman has ever laughed.

Tom. What then dost thou take French *liberty* to be?

Jack. To murder more men in one night, than ever their poor king did in his whole life.

Tom. And what dost thou take a *democrat* to be?

Jack. One who lives to be governed by a thousand tyrants, and yet can't bear a king.

Tom. What is *equality?*

Jack. For every man to pull down every one that is above him: while, instead of raising those below him, to his own level, he only makes use of them as steps to raise himself to the place of those he has tumbled down.

Tom. What is the *new Rights of Man?*

Jack. Battle, murder, and sudden death.

Tom. What is it to be *an enlightened people?*

Jack. To put out the light of the Gospel, confound right and wrong, and grope about in pitch darkness.

Tom. What is *philosophy,* that Tim Standish talks so much about?

Jack. To believe that there's neither God, nor devil, nor heaven, nor hell: to dig up a wicked old fellow's [Voltaire] rotten bones, whose books, Sir John says, have been the ruin of thousands; and to set his figure up in a church and worship him.

Tom. And what is a *patriot* according to the new school?

Jack. A man who loves every other country better than his own, and France best of all.

Tom. And what is *Benevolence?*

Jack. Why, in the new fangled language, it means contempt of religion, aversion to justice, overturning of law, doating on all mankind in general, and hating every body in particular.

Tom. And what mean the other hard words that Tim talks about— *organization* and *function,* and *civism,* and *incivism,* and *equalization,* and *inviolability,* and *imperscriptible,* and *fraternization?*

Jack. Nonsense, gibberish, downright hocus-pocus. I know 'tis not English; sir John says 'tis not Latin; and his valet de sham says 'tis not French neither.

Tom. And yet Tim says he never shall be happy till all these fine things are brought over to England.

Jack. What! in this christian country, Tom? Why dost know they have no *Sabbath* in France? Their mob parliament meets on a Sunday to do their wicked work, as naturally as we do to go to church. [Since this they have crammed ten days into the week, in order to throw Sunday out of it.] They have renounced God's word and God's day, and they don't even date in the year of our Lord. Why dost turn pale, man? And the rogues are always making such a noise, Tom, in the midst of their parliament-house, that their speaker rings a bell, like our penny-post man, because he can't keep them in order.

Tom. And dost thou believe they are as cruel as some folks pretend?

Jack. I am sure they are, and I think I know the reason. We christians set a high value on life, because we know that every fellow-creature has an immortal soul: a soul to be saved or lost, Tom—Whoever believes that, is a little cautious how he sends a soul unprepared to his grand account. But he who believes a man is no better than a dog, who make no more scruple of killing one than the other.

Tom. And dost thou think our Rights of Man will lead to all this wickedness?

Jack. As sure as eggs are eggs.

Tom. I begin to think we're better off as we are.

Jack. I'm sure on't. This is only a scheme to make us go back in every thing. 'Tis making ourselves poor when we are getting rich, and discontented when we are comfortable.

Tom. I begin to think I'm not so very unhappy as I had got to fancy.

Jack. Tom, I don't care for drink myself, but thou dost, and I'll argue with thee, not in the way of principle, but in thy own way; when there's all equality there will be no *superfluity*; and levelling will rob thee of thy ale more than the malt tax does.

Tom. But Standish says, if we had a good government, there'd be no want of any thing.

Jack. He is like many others, who take the king's money and betray him: let him give up the profits of his place before he kicks at the hand that feeds him.—Though I'm no scholar, I know that a good government is a good thing. But don't go to make me believe that *any* government can make a bad man good, or a discontented man happy.—What art musing upon, man?

Tom. Let me sum up the evidence, as they say at 'sizes—Hem! To cut every man's throat who does not think as I do, or hang him up at a lamp-post!—Pretend liberty of conscience, and then banish the parsons only for being conscientious!—Cry out liberty of the press, and hang up the first man who writes his mind!—Lose our poor laws!—Lose one's wife perhaps upon every little tiff! —March without clothes, and fight without victuals!—No trade!—No Bible! No Sabbath nor day of rest!—No safety, no comfort, no peace in this world—and no world to come!—Jack, I never knew thee tell a lie in my life.

Jack. Nor would I now, not even against the French.

Tom. And thou art very sure we are not ruined?

Jack. I'll tell thee how we are ruined. We have a king, so loving, that he would not hurt the people if he could: and so kept in, that he could not hurt the people if he would. We have as much liberty as can make us happy, and more trade and riches than allows us to be good. We have the best laws in the world, if they were more strictly enforced; and the best religion in the world if it was but better followed. While old England is safe, I'll glory in her, and pray for her, and when she is in danger, I'll fight for her, and die for her.

Tom. And so will I too, Jack, that's what I will, (*Sings*) *"O the roast beef of old England!"*

Jack. Thou art an honest fellow, Tom.

Tom. This is Rose and Crown night, and Tim Standish is now at his mischief; but we'll go and put an end to that fellow's work, or he'll corrupt the whole club.

Jack. Come along.

Tom. No; first I'll stay to burn my book, and then I'll go and make a bonfire and—

Jack. Hold, Tom. There is but one thing worse than a bitter enemy—and that is an imprudent friend. If thou would'st show thy love to thy king and country, let's have no drinking, no riot, no bonfires: put in practice this text, which our parson preached on last Sunday, "Study to be quiet, work with your own hands, and mind your own business."

Tom. And so I will, Jack—Come on.

Dr. Thomas James on the Rugby curriculum from 1778 to 1794

Dr. Thomas James, Letter to Dr. Samuel Butler, in *The Life and Letters of Dr. Samuel Butler, Head-Master of Shrewsbury School 1798-1836, and afterwards bishop of Lichfield in so far as they illustrate the Scholastic, Religious, and Social life of England, 1790-1840* (London: John Murray, 1896), I, 25-30.

In 1798 Dr. Thomas James (1748-1804) wrote the first of three "letters of advice" describing the "Rugby System" under his headmastership. Consisting mainly of the lessons set in each form, these letters throw great light on the working of a public school at the close of the eighteenth century. The letter which follows provides the daily lessons of the fifth and sixth forms and some general remarks. It begins without a salutation.

[14 October 1798?]

Fifth and Sixth Forms

Monday, at 7—Watts' *Scripture History*, sixteen pages, or Goldsmith's *Roman History* (2 vols., 8vo), sixteen pages at a lesson at least, or twenty pages at most; or *History of England* in a series of letters, with geography and chronology of each lesson. Ingles does geography instead of this lesson in its *turn*, as after *Roman History* finished in one volume; then again after second volume and Watts finished.

Perhaps twelve pages of Watts may be full enough at first.

At 10—Thirty-five lines of the *Iliad*, twice construed and parsed. The next lesson in the same book is always set after doing present lesson. Take *Selecta ex Iliade* by W. Holwell, if it can be got. But at Christmas you may come to Worcester and mark your Homer and Virgil by my books.

At 3—About fifty lines in *Scriptores Romani*, twice construed. Set Tuesday's translation.

At 5—Thirty-eight lines in Virgil, or rather *Selecta e Virgilio*. 38 x 2 = 76 construed in the week, less fifty repeated Friday, leaving twenty-six. (See Friday's lessons at seven and three.)

Tuesday, at 7—Thirty lines of Tully's *Offices* repeated. Themes looked over.

Note—I should set translation of Tully one week, the next some English to be translated into Latin (as Willymot's *Peculiars*, or my Erasmus Englished), and then translation of Tully or English theme alternately, always rendering English into Latin once a fortnight.

At 10—Thirty-five lines of *Poetae Graeci*. Verse theme set and English translation for this day.

Half-Holiday—Absence [roll-call] at three and five, or half after five in summer.

Exercise—One week English theme or English translation. The next week translate English into Latin. This English was Erasmus translated by me, but

Willymot's *Peculiars* will do. Lock up at . . . different times between six and eight, according to the season. The earlier Prayers are the better.

Wednesday, at 7—Translation or English theme looked over. Repeat Tuesday's *Poetae Graeci.*

At 10—Thirty-five lines of *Scriptores Graeci.*

At 3 and 5—The same as Monday; but a selection *ex Cicerone,* or his letters (at the end of the book), were construed on Monday, and *Selecta e Livio, Tacito* (you may leave out perhaps *e Paterculo*) were construed on a Wednesday.

Exercise Latin Verses—Lowest number of lowest fifth is sixteen.

Note—Tully repeated for themes and Ovid for verses is good, but sometimes Greek grammar must be said, instead of these lessons—at least the principal parts of it.

Thursday, at 7—Latin verses looked over. Thirty lines of *Selecta ex Ovidio* repeated, or Greek grammar.

At 10—Homer as on Monday.

Half-Holiday—In honour of one or even two (perhaps one of these from the fifth form) of the best praepostor's exercises.

Thursday's exercise—Lyrics of various sorts: Iambics, Sapphics, Asclep., Alc., Trochaics. Two upper praepostors make Greek.

Friday, at 7—Thirty-five lines of Homer repeated (or Thursday's Homer); *or* sometimes twenty-five lines of Homer and twenty-six lines of Virgil have been said, which compleats the repetition of all the Virgil of the week.

At 10—Sixty lines in Horace's *Satyrs* [*sic*] and *Epistles* and *Ars Poetica* were construed, or Juvenal, *Sat.* 1, 3, 10, 14, or Persius, *Sat.* 5.

N.B.—Horace and Juvenal are thus finished in two and a half years.

At 3—Fifty lines of Monday's and Wednesday's Virgil repeated. Horace lesson of the morning construed a second time.

N.B.—If twenty-six lines of Virgil be said on Friday morning, then all the Virgil construed will be said.

At 5—Thirty lines in Tully's *Offices* once construed, which are to be repeated in the following week, and also thirty lines in *Selecta ex Ovidio* once construed and once hastily read off in English, which are to be repeated *in the next following week.* Ingles's fifth form assistant teaches the fifth form the Tully and *Selecta ex Ovidio,* while he teaches *Funebres Orationes* or Pindar, or etc., for this lesson; but these lessons are perfectly academic, and rather beyond the power of young boys, unless they be already accomplished scholars.

Saturday—Sixty lines of Friday's Horace repeated. The head-master, having no exercise, examines a lower form. Ingles takes his sixth and fifth form repetition (which is made to an assistant), etc.

At 10—Fifty lines in Greek play or fifty lines in Demosthenes twice construed; or if time be wanted read it off hastily a second time into English. Latin theme for Monday set now.

Third lesson of Saturday at twelve—Thirty-five lines in select parts of Milton (suppose the printed *Elegant Extracts of Poetry,* by Dr. Knox, were used). This also would be a reading book or a library of poetry to a schoolboy. Now also Mathematics were done, which was my utter ruin at the time; or speeches rehearsed, which I advise you to avoid altogether, as being the most painful and laborious instruction that can be given. Nothing wears a man out so much.

Saturday is a half-holiday, and of course (like other half-holidays) is for writing, dancing, French, drawing, or even fencing—as it is now taught at Rugby.

Sunday—Absence at nine, at breakfast.

At 10—Do not use Secker, which works the master, not the scholar; but use Greek Testament and work the scholar, and throw in any supplementary explanation—even the contents of all Secker on the commandments if you will. Or, if you have any Sunday's duty to do, make the boys abridge in writing two pages of Secker.

N.B.—In abridgements made at Rugby (for they now abridge Watts's *History* instead of answering orally—which is an alteration, but not an improvement), Ingles calls on this or that boy to read four or five lines of his own written abridgement, and so hears the whole of the lesson to be abridged read over by the boys in such little parts once or twice over. This saves the master, and is right if he has other duty on a Sunday.

Call absence after church in the church, or let the senior monitor prick down absentees; or the form praepostors may do this severally. When you come to see me (of which, however, I must have notice, as I expect some relations for some time at Christmas), I can furnish you with verses, themes, and hints, and with Latin themes—themes, etc., which you can copy if you will.

Horace's *Odes* and *Epodes* are divided into four equal parts, one part is construed in each half-year—being construed over regularly a first time at each lesson, and read over quickly into English for a second construing over; and thus the whole of the *Odes* is finished in two years. You may mark twelve divisions in your Horace, when you come to see me at Christmas; and then bring your Homer and Virgil and Milton for the same purpose.

Odes are read for about four weeks and not more, or not five weeks altogether, each half-year. Four lessons are construed in them in each week—viz. sixty lines Monday at three; sixty lines Monday at five; sixty lines Tuesday at ten; sixty lines Wednesday at five.

N.B.—Virgil is dropped during the four weeks of Ode-time, and such other lessons as belong to the Ode school-times.

The above four lessons (or 4 x 60 = 240 lines) in *Odes* are thus repeated: forty lines Tuesday at seven; forty lines Wednesday at seven; forty lines Thursday at seven; thirty lines on Friday at seven, together with twenty-five lines in Homer or twenty-five lines *Poetae Graeci*, as may seem best according to the important matter contained in either lesson for the week; sixty lines on Friday at three; thirty lines at third morning lesson at twelve on Saturday (dropping the Milton in Ode-time).

In all two hundred and forty lines repeated in the week; or repeated three forties, two thirties, and one double of thirty, or sixty.

Geography, or the four quarters, with Antient [*sic*] Greece and Italy—done for the second and fourth exercise of the week (on Tuesdays and Thursdays)—is done once over in a year, and is done for nine exercises. For geography Cellarius in octavo, and Guthrie's last edition by Dilly in octavo, with my geography, will do.

My geography may be had at Rowel's for a shilling a book (by your application to Ingles, who has hacked and hewed my book and reprinted it), and it will suit your purpose still. I have much improved it indeed, but I have not inclination now to print it.

Make a library for your boys, as I did—every boy giving something at coming to school, and also on going away; at least a crown coming, and perhaps double going away. Buy Knox's *Elegant Extracts in Poetry—in Prose—*and *of Epistles*; L'Emprière's *Classical and Historical Dictionary*; Johnson's *Dictionary* (in 2 vols., 8vo), with *Beauties of Pope* (in 2 vols., 12mo, 7s.), *Beauties of Spectators, Tatlers, and Guardians* (2 vols., 12 mo, 7s.); *Beauties of Adventurer, Connoisseur, Rambler, and Idler* (2 vols., 7s.). These may be got immediately by a sufficient subscription among the boys.

Two declamations *pro* and *con* are made once in an half-year. Each declamation is divided into two exercises, and made as two Latin themes: *Exordium* and *Prima Pars Probationis*, for one theme; and for a second theme, *Secunda Pars Probationis* and *Peroratio.*

Greek Plays— Burgess's *Pentalogia*, with a Latin translation printed and sold by Mr. C. Dilly in the Poultry; but the Greek *Pentalogia* is out of print and not to be had for a school, wherefore the five following plays—printed separately by Mr. Pote of Eton—are now used in schools, and may be easily had. 'Tis laughingly called Pote's *Pentalogia.*

Euripides	(1) *Hippolytus*
	(2) *Medea*
Sophocles	(3) *Philoctetes*
Aeschylus	(4) *Prometheus*
Aristophanes	(5) *Plutus*

These plays are 3s. each, and great is the advantage (to keep parents in good humour) of purchasing each half-year only what the boy uses;—as you will find. Keep down expences.

If no translations are printed to these (for the boys at Eton do now, I believe, depend for construing the plays on tutors), then you may get two or three old editions with Latin translations for a few shillings and lend them to the boys, as I did.

The above plays are a good and sufficient specimen. Read also Demosthenes and Pindar, as you read Greek plays.

If you should want more, 'tis probable more plays will be printed at Eton, by the time you will have finished the above.

If you provide books (as Heyrick of Leicester and many masters do), then I recommend C. Dilly in the Poultry as an honest man for your bookseller—who will allow you twelve per cent on books, and perhaps more on paper, pens, pencils, etc., etc. If you do not provide books, give the profit to an assistant (it will help to pay his salary), or at least give it to your writing master, unless borough interest requires you to deal with a Shrewsbury bookseller.

Avoid giving a whole holiday after five weeks completed as the worst of plagues, for you are sure of having a large school. The three half-holidays on Tuesday, Thursday, and Saturday are excellent things both for master and boy, leaving exercises and masters of accomplishments to fill them up. If you are obliged to give a whole holiday, suffer it not to pass without a regular exercise, by way of rider to direct it and preserve it from wild schemes and excursions.

Candles allowed till a quarter before ten for fifth and sixth forms, and till nine for all below. A quarter clock saves much bell-ringing. Boys are locked up from a quarter after six to eight, by increases or decreases of a quarter of an hour according to the season.

Bed-room doors are opened in the morning at half after six, and on Sunday or a whole holiday at seven—and there is absence at breakfast at nine as well as at other meals.

It is a cheap plan and a good one to take in the fourth form Dalzel's *Collectanea Minora*, instead of Greek Aesop and Greek Testament; for it contains many parts of Greek Aesop—of [Poikile Historia]—with various poetic selections; so that one purchase serves for many books both in prose and poetry. It is equally good to take Dalzel's *Collectanea Majora* for the fifth form in two vols. octavo, the one volume being prose according to *Scriptores Graeci,* the other volume being poetry and answering to our *Poetae Graeci,* and both contain many the same things with those our Eton books: and Dalzel's publication is of such sort as to serve even instead of the purchase of Homer's *Odyssey,* and *Poetae Graeci* too; for there is much of the *Odyssey* at least in it—of the *Iliad,* I believe none. You may begin at least with a purchase of this in your school library. The saving expence in books is a great consideration; and the scale is easily enlarged at any time. Dalzel's notes are an excellent companion for a boy or master too, in such parts of *Scriptores Graeci* and *Poetae Graeci* as are common to Dalzel and those Eton books. Dalzel has no Latin, but excellent and scholar-like notes in English; but this mode of teaching Greek without Latin is now prevalent in many places, as at the Charterhouse in London, Mr. Innes's at Warwick, and, I have heard, at Winchester. There is no objection to it, but the despair it may occasion to dull boys, who, it is answered, must rely on the brighter boys after all. You will judge, therefore, what you will do in this matter, after purchasing one set of either of the above, which will cost you but little, and nothing if bought for the boys' library. I send this to assure you that I am not forgetful of you, and will prepare you another sheet as soon as I can—in a very few days. I have just placed one son at Rugby in the upper fourth, and one son in the fourth at Charterhouse, to which I was invited by a voluntary and unsolicited offer of Lord Dartmouth, whose sons, the two Legges, I educated. It is now an exceeding great benefit—£40 a year to the Bachelor at College, and £60 a year to the Master of Arts—being an eight years' benefit after leaving school, and the education is almost for nothing.

I heartily give you and Mrs. Butler joy, in which Mrs. James joins with me. I thank you for your kind invitation; but I shall hope at Christmas to have all my children with me, now scattered. Mrs. James and I shall be glad to see you for three or four days, and Mrs. Butler, if you travel our way at Christmas, and indeed whenever you may come. In the meantime I will satisfy your wishes by writing; being your faithful friend,

T. James

Improvements in Education by **Joseph Lancaster, 1803**

Improvements in Education: Abridged, containing a complete epitome of the system of education, invented and practised by the author (London: J. Lancaster, 1808), 1-18, 22-33.

A Quaker, Joseph Lancaster (1778-1838) opened a school in 1801 and provided free education to the poor by organizing corps of older boys as monitors to oversee and instruct. By 1832 this "monitorial system" of instruction was widely used as a cheap way of educating the poor.

METHOD OF ARRANGING A SCHOOL
INTO CLASSES

First, The object in view, in forming a School into classes, is to promote improvement. If only four or six scholars should on examination be found in a school *learning the same thing*, as A. B. C. ab, addition, subtraction, etc. they should be formed into a class, as their proficiency will be nearly doubled, by being classed, and studying in conjunction A class may consist of any number of scholars, more or less without limitation to any particular number.

The Rule by Which Classes
Are to Be Formed

Any number of boys, whose proficiency is nearly equal in what they are learning, should be *classed*, and taught together. Of course the whole school must be arranged into classes.

Of the Two Kinds of Classes

As there are two descriptions of boys in every school, viz. those who are *learning*, and those who have *learned*, so there are two kinds of classes. To the first, the object of study is a progressive series of lessons, rising step by step, to that point, where children may take an interest in, and store their minds with knowledge for use in future life: to the last, the different branches of learning, are not so much objects of *study* as mediums of *mental improvement*.

I intend in the course of this tract, to point out a series of lessons adapted to both descriptions of scholars.

Gradation of Classes in Learning to Read

Class 1   A, B, C
     2   Two letters, as ab, etc.

3   Three letters
4   Four letters
5   Five and six letters
6   Testament, or selection of Scripture lesson
7   Bible
8   A selection of the best proficients in Reading

The Children learning the alphabet as hereafter described, may learn to *print* their letters in the sand, or on a slate.

After a learner has improved beyond the first class, *whatever* class he may be in, he must learn to make his *writing* alphabet on the slate.

After having learned the writing alphabet, *whatever class* the scholar *may be in*, he must write on the slate *the same* as he reads or spells in his reading or spelling lesson. If in the two letter class, he will write words of two letters; if in the three letter class, words of three letters, etc. etc.

Gradation of Classes in Learning to Write

Class 1   Printing A, B, C
2   Writing alphabet, or words of two letters
3   Words of three letters
4   Four letters
5   Five and Six letters
6   Two syllables, etc.
7
8   } A particular series of spelling lessons, published by J.L.

The mode of tuition in writing, being connected with the new method of spelling, will be hereafter described under the head spelling.

Gradation of Classes in Learning Arithmetic

Class 1   Pupils who are learning to make and combine, units, tens, etc.
2   Addition
3   Compound ditto
4   Subtraction
5   Compound ditto
6   Multiplication
7   Compound ditto
8   Division
9   Compound ditto
10   Reduction
11   Rule of Three
12   Practice

The Mode of Examining Pupils for, and Arranging Them into Classes, To Learn Reading, and Writing

On the entry of a Scholar, the Superintendent should examine his proficiency in distinguishing the letters of the printed alphabet; if he does not know them all, he must be placed in the first Class.

If the superintendent finds the pupil knows his alphabet *perfectly*, he must place him in the Second class.

If the scholar can perfectly repeat all the lessons belonging to the second class, he must be placed in the third, if he can repeat well all the lessons appropriated to the third class, he must be placed in the fourth: the same rule to be observed in forming the fifth, sixth, and seventh classes.

The eighth class to be a selection from the best readers in the seventh; they may be admitted to the use of Books, for the improvement of their minds, which the other classes are not allowed; on this subject more will be said in the sequel.

Of Writing in Classes

By the usual method of teaching to write, the art of writing is totally distinct from reading or spelling. On the new plan, spelling and writing are connected, and equally blended with reading. When a boy is classed for learning to read by the arrangement of reading classes, he is consequently classed for learning to write at the same time.

On the admission of every Scholar, the Superintendent will enter the name, residence, and every other particular relative to him, under its proper head, in a School-list; a printed plan of which, is annexed.

On Forming a School into Arithmetical Classes

On the new plan, the first great care of the Master, must be wholly to discard the numeration table, and the practice of learning numeration by it, as it is entirely superseded by the new method, which teaches the same thing, in a much shorter, and more practical way.

Whenever a pupil is admitted into the School, and has never before learned any arithmetic, he must be placed in the first class. If he has made any *apparent* progress, unless that progress be found on examination to be *real*, he must begin again at the first class. In forming a new School with the above exception, it will be best for *all* the pupils to begin Arithmetic, from the first class.

Of the Arrangement of Lessons for Classes

In the course of this epitome, an abridged specimen of the lessons for the classes will be given. At present it is only requisite to say, that on my new system of education, there is a series of lessons to be pasted on boards, adapted to each class, as the classes rise above each other, progressively. These lessons being regularly numbered, should be placed on the school-walls, on nails, numbered, in like manner. The card lesson, No. 1 (for the 2nd or any other class) to be placed on the nail No. 1. Lesson No. 2 on the nail No. 2, etc. Each series of lessons to be placed by itself. Each class to study *only* that series of lessons adapted to it; this rule must be invariably attended to, or the classes which are learning, will be particularly liable to confusion. When pupils are removed from one class to another, it is then only, they may enter on a new series of lessons.

The method of rewards attached to this plan of classification will be detailed by itself.

CHAP. 2ND
OF MONITORS WHO TEACH, AND THE QUALIFICATIONS REQUISITE FOR THAT DUTY, AND MODE OF ASCERTAINING THOSE QUALIFICATIONS

On this head, the duty of the superintendent or master, will be, to ascertain that each monitor is *fully competent*, to teach the lessons of the class he is appointed to. This certainty can be obtained only by actually examining the *intended* monitor in the lessons he will be required to teach. The master must never appoint a new monitor without such examination. I have known some persons who *pretend* to teach on my plan, appoint a boy as a monitor, merely because they judged him to be a good reader; no master should appoint monitors by *guess*, when an actual certainty is in his power: but this cannot be attained without an examination and progressive series of lessons on my plan adapted to the mode of tuition.

The necessity for such examination is more urgent, as in the minor lessons, the sounds of letters often vary from soft to hard, and a number of words admit of different meanings, and are consequently pronounced different ways. A pupil may read well in general, and yet either not know, or may forget after some time such local variations. If then, he is not carefully examined by the superintendent he will teach some words improperly.

As it respects Arithmetic, the superintendent should ascertain by individual examination, whether the pupil he selects as a monitor, is fully master of each particular sum, or lesson appointed to be taught to his class. The *monitors of reading, and spelling,* should not *only be able, as scholars*, to understand and perform the lessons they are appointed to teach, but be *instructed* under the inspection of the superintendent; in the mode of teaching, and any locality, which may be attached to particular lessons.

It should be considered that monitors on the new plan are of two descriptions, those for *tuition,* and those for *order*. Duties, which, as will be shewn in the sequel, are in *some* instances, wholly distinct from each other.

To these, we must add a third description, who are called Inspecting Monitors. Of these, even in a very large school, but *few* are requisite.

Monitors of every kind are sometimes *stated*, and sometimes *occasional*.

Monitors are stated, when they are appointed to attend the regular duties of the school, in tuition, order, or inspection. Monitors are occasional, when acting as *substitutes* for regular monitors, whom ill health, or any other cause, may detain from school.

Rules for Appointing Monitors of Tuition

Firstly, the monitors appointed, must understand and be quite perfect in the lessons they are to teach, as to good reading and spelling.

Secondly, they must understand the *mode* of teaching.

Thirdly, in the first five classes, monitors may be appointed from the next superior class to teach the one immediately below it. Thus, the second or two letter class will furnish monitors who may teach the first, or alphabet class, the third will supply monitors for the second, the fourth for the third, and the fifth for the fourth, the sixth class will supply a choice of monitors for the fifth, for itself, and for the order of the *school. Before* the seventh class, each class will supply boys to teach the class below it; this will ground the monitors in the lessons they have themselves last learned, by the act of teaching them. From the sixth class upwards, the classes will supply boys to act as monitors and teach themselves; the teachers of the sixth, seventh, and eighth classes, may be chosen out of the said classes, as any boy who can read can teach, and the art of tuition, in those classes, depends only on the knowledge of reading and writing. The system of inspection of progress in learning, as respects the scholar, is *only* on *his* part mental, neither inspection nor the mode of instruction, require any other qualification on the part of the teacher than the mere art of reading and writing, united with orderly behaviour.

Of Monitors Tickets, Superintendent's Lists, and the Office of Monitor-General

Every monitor should wear in school, a printed or leather ticket gilt, and lettered thus—Monitor of the first class—Reading Monitor of the second class—Monitor of the third class, with variations for arithmetic, reading, spelling, etc.

Each of these tickets to be numbered. A row of nails with numbers on the wall marking the place of each ticket, to be placed in every school-room. The nail numbered one, being the place for the ticket, No. 1. When school begins, the monitors are to be called to take their tickets, every ticket left on a nail, will shew a regular monitor *absent*, when an occasional monitor must of course be chosen.

One monitor of order, to be appointed by the master, to see what monitors are absent daily, and to appoint others in their place for the occasion; this in a *large* school, will be found a great relief to the master.

As nothing should in any case be left to the Monitor, the Superintendent should in the first instance appoint every stated monitor himself, he should then examine the school to find a number of boys fit to be occasional monitors, of these he should make two lists, one for himself, and one for the lad appointed as monitor-general, and from that list he will appoint substitutes. The monitor-general's office is merely *to take an account of monitors present and absent*, and to appoint substitutes from the Superintendent's list of boys fit for the different offices of monitors.

Of the Duties of Monitors

In large schools on the old plan of education, the burden of the master's duty increases in a great degree, with the increase of numbers, till it becomes *insupportable*. On the new plan, the burden increases in a very small degree in comparison of the number, and admits of dividing the master's labour among many, which would otherwise rest only on himself. Some classes in a school will occasionally be *extinct* in consequence of the improvement of the scholars. If all the children who are in the alphabet class, improve so as to be removed to the second, the alphabet class must be extinct, unless fresh scholars are admitted. The same, if all the boys in the subtraction class become masters of that rule, they must be removed to another class and there will be no subtraction class in the school, until more boys are admitted, or are brought forward from an inferior class. Where children continue at school for some time, and no new scholars are admitted, it appears possible, the whole of the minor classes may become extinct, and not be revived till an admission of new scholars.

In a very large school, more monitors are wanted than in a smaller one; the system remains the same, only the number of agents for effecting it are greater. In a small school, some duties may be done by the master, because they relate to a few pupils or monitors, and are immediately under his own eye. In a small school of 100 children, no monitor-general will be needed, as from the fewness of the monitors, that duty may be performed by the master, but in a large school, it becomes an alleviation of the master's labour, to appoint such a monitor.

All the monitors should have a written or printed paper of their "Duties," which they should particularly study, and repeat once a week. Those duties which are the same in all schools, and which apply generally to the mode of teaching, may be *had printed, as see the Appendix, containing a list of things wanting in the outfit of a new school.* These duties each monitor should paste in the books belonging to his class. The larger series of papers on the duties of monitors, should be read for a class lesson by all boys selected as regular, or auxiliary monitors, in order to prepare them, by a knowledge of their duty, for the proper discharge of it.

Assistant Monitors are only needful when a class is more than 20, or 25, then the monitor should be relieved from continual attention to his class, to give him time for his studies, but the class must by no means be divided between two equal monitors, both acting at the same time.

OF THE METHOD OF TEACHING THE ALPHABET, OR FIRST CLASS

Auxiliary Method of Teaching the Alphabet, by Printing in Sand

The first, or lower class of scholars, are those who are yet unacquainted with their alphabet. This class may consist of ten, twenty, an hundred, or any other number of children, who have not made so much progress as to know how to distinguish all their letters at first sight. If there are only twenty of this description in the school, one monitor can govern and teach them; if double the number, if will require two teachers, and so in proportion for every additional twenty boys. The reader will observe, that, in this and every other class described in the succeeding plan and arrangement, the monitor has but one plain duty to do, and the scholars the same to learn. This simplicity of system defines at once the province of each monitor in tuition. The very name of each class imports as much—and this is called the first, or A, B, C, class. The method of teaching is as follows: a bench for the boys to sit on, is fixed to the floor; another, about a foot higher, is placed for them to print on. On the desk before them are placed deal ledges (a pantile lath, nailed down to the desk, will answer the same purpose) thus:

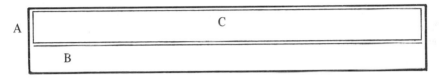

The letter A, shows the entire surface of the desk, which is supported by two, three, or more legs, as usual for such desks, and according to the size. B, is a vacant space, where the boys lean their left arms, while they write or print with the right hand. The sand is placed in the space C. [The space C, is painted black; the sand mostly used, is whitish: when the children trace the letters in the white sand, the black ground shews them to more advantage.] The double lines represent the ledges (or pantile laths) which confine the sand in its place: sand of any kind will do, but it must be *dry*. The boys print in the sand, with their *fingers*: they all print at the *command* given by their monitor. A boy who knows how to print, and distinguish some of his letters, is placed by one who knows few with a view to assist him; and, particularly, that he may copy the form of his letters, from *seeing* him make them. We find this copying one from another a great step towards proficiency. In teaching the children to print the alphabet, the monitor first makes a letter on the sand before any child who does not know anything about it; the child is then required to *retrace* the same letter, which the monitor has made for him with his fingers, and thus he is to continue employed, till he can make the letter himself, without the monitor's assistance. Then he may go on to learn another letter. None but the first class write in sand.

The letters are taught in courses: they are arranged in *three courses* according to their similarity of form. There are three simple examples, which regulate the formation of the whole alphabet. *First*, a line, as in the letters I, H, T, L, E, F, i, l: *Second*, depending upon the formation of an angle; as, A, V, W, M, N, Z, K, Y, X,— v, w, k, y, z, x: a circle or a curve; as, O, U, C, J, D, P, B, R, Q, S,—a, o, b, d, p, q, g, e, m, n, h, t, u, r, s, f, j. These courses of letters are soon acquired, on account of the similarity of form. The greatest difficulty in teaching the letters occurs in those, the form of which are exactly alike, and are only distinguished by change of position; p, q, and b, d, are frequently mistaken for each other; but by *making* the two letters at the same time, the children readily learn to distinguish them. Then again, they are all employed in printing at once; and it is both curious and diverting to see a number of little creatures, many not more than four or five years old, and some hardly that, stretching out their little fingers with one consent, to make the letters. When this is done, they sit quietly till the sand is smoothed by the monitor, with a *flat-iron*, such as is commonly used for ironing linen. The sand being dry, the iron meets no resistance, and thus all the letters made in a very short time, by each boy, are, in as short a time, obliterated by the monitor; and the boys again apply their *fingers* to the sand, and proceed as before. . . .

Improved Method of Teaching Spelling by Writing

This following method of spelling is excellent, being entirely an *addition* to the regular course of studies, without interfering with, or deranging them in the least. It commands the attention; gratifies the active disposition of youth, and is an excellent introduction and auxiliary to writing. It supersedes, in a great measure, the use of books in tuition, while (to speak moderately) it doubles the actual improvement of the children. It is as simple an operation as can well be imagined.—Thus, supply twenty boys with slates and pencils, and pronounce any word for them to write, suppose it is the word "and," or the word, "re-so-lu-tion;" they are obliged to listen with attention, to catch the sound of every letter as it falls from their teacher's lips; again, they have to retrace the idea of every letter, and the pronunciation of the word, as they write it on the slates. If we examine ourselves when we write letters, we shall find, this is so much connected with orthography, that we cannot write a word without spelling as we write, and habitually correcting any inaccuracy that may occur.

Now these twenty boys, if they were at a common school, would each have a book; and, one at a time, would read or spell to their teacher, while the other nineteen were looking at their books, or about them, as they pleased; or, if their eyes are rivetted on their books, by terror and coercion, can we be sure that their attention is engaged, as appearance seems to indicate it is? On the contrary when they have slates, the twentieth boy may read to the teacher, while the other nineteen are spelling words on the slate, instead of sitting idle. [It will be seen in the article Reading, I do not approve of solitary reading, one by one; it raises no emulation.] The class, by this means, will spell, write, and read, every word. In addition to this, the same trouble which teaches twenty, will suffice to teach sixty or an hundred, by employing some of the senior boys to inspect the slates of the others, they not omitting to spell the word themselves; and, on a signal given by them to the principal teacher, that the word is finished by all the boys they overlook, he is informed when to dictate another to the class. This experiment has been tried with some hundreds of children, and it has been found they could all write from, by one boy's dictating the words written. The benefit of this mode of teaching, can only be limitted by the school-room being so large, that they can not be heard distinctly, for if seven hundred boys were all in one room, *as one class*, learning the same thing, they could all write and spell by this method at the dictation of one monitor. I hope the candour and good sense of every reader, will justly appreciate the benefit and importance of this method of teaching. The *repetition* of one word by the monitor, serves to rivet it firmly on the minds of each one of the class, and also on his own memory; thus *he* cannot possibly teach the class without improving *himself* at the same time. We reflect with pleasure that by this invention, a boy who is associated in a class of an hundred others, not only reads as much as if he was a solitary individual under the master's care, but he will also spell sixty or seventy words of four syllables, in less than two hours; by writing them on the slate, when this additional number of words, spelt by each boy daily is taken into account, the aggregate will amount to repetitions of many thousands of words annually; when not a word would be written or spelt, and nothing done by nineteen twentieths of the scholars at the same time. Thus, it is entirely an improvement, an addition, and introduction to their other studies, without the least additional trouble on the part of the teacher; without deranging or impeding his attention to other studies, as is usually the case with the study of extra lessons; at least more than doubling the advances of each individual towards a proficiency, at the same time; and, possessing all these advantages, it prevents idleness, and procures that great desideratum of schools, *quietness*, not by terror, but by commanding attention: for, as it requires much writing, but few boys can write and talk at the same time. In this case, nothing is wholly committed to the pupil or monitor; in the usual mode some degree of mental exertion, may or may not be made, by the pupil and omission remain undetected; but this is so visible, that every boy's attention to his lesson may be seen on his slate, and detection immediately follows idleness, or an indifferent performance! It is simple in itself, and abounding with many advantages; of this I am well convinced by daily experience of its utility; in particular, the great practice it affords in writing

Boys who learn by the new mode, have six times the usual practice; but, in the old way, the expense is, at the *first cost*, 5½d per month, for writing books, pens, and ink each boy: this will be six times increased, if it is desired to give both classes of boys equal practice; the usual cost for sixty boys is 16*l*. 10*s*. per annum.

Old Way
Six times the usual charge for writing paper, etc.   £99
New Way
If they have not slates already provided sixty slates will cost   £1
Allow a hundred slate pencils per annum, each boy, at 8d, per
  hundred   __2__
                                                                     __3__
Balance, in favour of the new mode   £96

The many hundreds of respectable characters, among the nobility, gentry, and clergy, who have visited the institution, can bear witness, that the progress of the boys by this method of writing spelling, is astonishing! Not of one, or a few boys, but of the whole school. By the practice of writing on the slate, they learn to humour their pencils, so as to write just like a pen, in making the up and down strokes of the letters. About one hundred and fifty boys have writing books, and their writing on the slate, is a *fac simile* of their writing in books: which they seldom do, more than four times in a week, and then only a single copy, which fills a quarto page, each time.

The boy may always make his pencil good by cutting it to a proper point, this will not easily apply to quills or pens. It will be found where there is much practice in writing, that a good plain hand for use, and not for show depends more on *much practice* than on the manner of holding the pen; and that a good body to the letters equally proportioned to down strokes, or up strokes, depends more on the application of the point of the pencil to the slate, or the pen to the paper, than on the length of either pencil or pen, or the position and play of the finger, which can only give command of hand in long strokes, whereas the most of the letters in the alphabet are formed of short strokes, which neither reach above nor below the line.

All the school, being classed according to their proficiency in reading, their spelling in this mode is united with their reading. It is a mode so useful as to *need* no addition to it, and is complete of itself, as it stands; *spelling* connected with *writing*.

All the classes are placed in regular progression one above another, from the first to the eighth. Every class is employed under its own monitor, spelling by writing words which the different monitors dictate to each class. The monitor of a class does no other duty but dictate, or see that one of the boys in the class dictates words for the class to spell, the boy dictating a word, writing it *himself*, the monitor writing it also, and inspecting the performance of each boy in his class being responsible for any mistakes they commit, and preparing them for the superintendent's inspection.

A METHOD OF TEACHING TO SPELL AND READ, WHEREBY ONE BOOK WILL SERVE INSTEAD OF SIX HUNDRED BOOKS

It will be remembered, that the usual mode of teaching requires every boy, to have a book; yet each boy can only read or spell one lesson at a time, in that book. Now, all the other parts of the book are in wear, and liable to be *thumbed* to pieces; and, while a child is learning a lesson on the one part of the book, the other parts are useless. Whereas, if a spelling book contains twenty or thirty different lessons, and it were possible for thirty scholars to read the thirty lessons in that book, it would be equivalent to thirty books for its utility. To effect this, it is desirable the whole of the book should be printed three times larger that the common size of type, which would make it equal in size and cost to three common spelling books, value from eight-pence to a shilling each. Again, it should be printed with only one page to a leaf, which would again double the price, and make it equivalent in bulk and cost to five or six common books; its different parts should be pasted on pasteboard or deal boards cut on purpose, and suspended by a string, to a nail in the wall, or other convenient place: one board should contain the alphabet; others, words and syllables of from two, to six letters. The reading lessons gradually rising from words of one syllable, in the same manner, till they come to words of five or six letters, or more, preparatory to the Testament lessons. There is a circumstance, very seldom sufficiently regarded, in the introductory lessons which youth usually have to perform before they are admitted to read in the Testament. A word of six letters or more, being divided by hy-phens, reduces the syllables, which compose it, to three, or four, letters each; of course, it is as easy to read syllables, as words of four letters: and the child, who can read or spell the one, will find the other as easy attainable.

In the preparatory lessons I have published the words are thus di-vi-ded which forms a more natural introduction to the Testament.

When the cards are provided, as before mentioned, from six to eight boys may stand in a circle round each card, and clearly distinguish the print to read or spell, as well or better than if they had a common spelling book in each of their hands. If one spelling book was divided into thirty different parts or lessons, and each lesson given to a different boy, it would only serve thirty boys, changing their lessons among themselves, as often as needful; and the various parts would be continually liable to be lost or torn. But, every lesson placed on a card, will serve for six or eight boys at once: and, when that six or eight have repeated the whole lesson, as many times over as there are boys in the circle, they are dismissed to their spelling on the slate, and another like number of boys *may* study the same lesson, in *succession*: indeed *two hundred boys* may all repeat their lessons from *one* card, in the space of *three hours*. Each class reads and spells in this manner by drafts of six or eight boys, each beginning at number one, and going on to the highest number in the class, those pupils, in day schools, who unavoidably come in at irregular hours, being called for to read, or spell about half an hour before school closes, so that even those, who come too late to read in proper order, do not miss their lessons. If the value and importance of this plan, for saving paper and books in teaching to read and spell, will not recommend itself, all I can say in its praise, from experience, will be of no avail.

When standing in circles, to read or spell, the boys wear their numbers, tickets, pictures, etc. as described under the head, Emulation and Reward; and give place to each other, according to merit, as mentioned in the account of the two first classes.

Evidence before the Select Committee on Education of the Poor, concerning schools in Spitalfields, 1816

Parliamentary Papers, 1816, IV, *Third Report,* Cmd. 495, 187-95.

Mr. John Tacey, called in, and Examined

What school are you connected with?—A British and Foreign Society's school.

Have you the superintendence of a school?—Yes.

Where is it situate?—North-street, City Road.

How many children are taught there?—The total number at present is 605.

How long have you been in it?—Three years and three months.

Were you taught at the Borough-road school?—Yes, I was apprenticed to Mr. Lancaster.

You have heard the evidence of the last Witness?—Yes.

As far as your experience and observation goes, do you agree with him?—Yes, I agree with him in every thing he has mentioned.

How long have you been engaged in this system of education, altogether?—Six years, in three different schools.

What is the annual expense of your school?—The annual expense, not including the rent of premises or ground-rent, is about 160*l*.

What is the school rent?—The building is partly purchased for 1800*l*. which is to be paid by instalments of 300*l*.

How many children can it accommodate?—About 800.

What is the reason it is not full?—There is no want of schools in that district; the means of educating the poor is principally wanted; there are no more applications for admission.

Do you mean, that there are no poor children in your neighbourhood uneducated?—None without the means of being educated.

What other schools are there in that district, besides your own?—I do not know exactly.

Upon what is your opinion founded, that there are the means of education for all the poor in your neighbourhood?—The room being so commodious for the education of a greater number of children, and having no applications, at least not enough to fill the school, and there being many other charities in the same neighbourhood.

Is it a poor neighbourhood?—I do not know much of the neighbourhood.

Is it a very populous neighbourhood?—Yes.

Do you know any thing of Sunday schools?—I do not; but there are upwards of 500 of my children attend at Sunday schools.

Mr. Thomas Harrod, called in, and Examined

What school are you connected with?—Spitalfields British and Foreign School.

How many children are educated there?—500.

How many is the school capable of educating?—About 700; it was built for 1000, and at the first two years of the establishment there were about from 700 to 800 daily attended, but there was not sufficient room to accommodate those conveniently; we were obliged to reduce the number of desks, which reduced the number of boys; it will now accommodate about 600.

To what do you ascribe your not being full?—For want of means, the parents have not the means of paying.

How much do the children pay at your school?—Thirteen pence per quarter; it was opened at first for a number of free scholars, but the funds were so low, that without the assistance of the boys it could not have gone on, and therefore they were obliged to stop admitting free scholars, and the children were obliged to pay.

Are the poor in that neighbourhood unprovided with the means of education?—Yes, from that reason.

Can you form an estimate of the number of poor children there may be uneducated?—Within the immediate neighbourhood of Spitalfields, I should suppose there are 400 or 500 boys uneducated, and without the means of education.

In how large a district do you consider there are that number?—Taking in only the parishes of Spitalfields and Bethnal Green.

What is the population of those two parishes?—I really do not know; I judge from an inquiry that I made last week in only a few streets, and I found the number in each family very considerable who were remaining in the house, and whose parents were very anxious to get them, now they were out of employment, into schools; those boys had been formerly for a short time in this school, but were taken out in consequence of their parents being in full employ, which is not the case now, and which makes them anxious to have them re-admitted, if they could, without any expense, not being able to pay themselves.

Do the parents seem desirous of the education of their children?—Very.

How long have you been engaged in education upon the new plan?—About fifteen years.

Have you heard the last two Witnesses examined?—I have.

Do you agree with them?—Yes; only that in Sunday schools they are not able to do any thing more, in the time stated, than read.

How long do you think they take to learn to read in Sunday schools, if they have no other means of instruction?—About two or three years, I should imagine.

Mr. William Crawford, called in, and Examined

Are you a member of the committee of the Spitalfields Lancasterian school in Spicer-street?—I am.

Have any measures been lately taken to ascertain the extent of the want of education among the poor in the neighbourhood of Spitalfields?—Inquiries have been made in the neighbourhood of Spitalfields, and it appears that in 2,091 families that have been visited, and containing 5,953 children, there were 2,565 children, from six to fourteen years of age, without any education.

Who made those inquiries?—Several gentlemen were called together for the purpose.

Did you make your inquiries in the poorest part of Spitalfields, or in a part where the poor did not so much abound?—Generally all over Spitalfields; we selected various districts.

Would those districts be a fair sample of the neighbourhood of Spitalfields in general?—I think they would.

What portion of that neighbourhood do they include; a third, fourth, fifth, or what?—They include the whole of Spitalfields, and some part of the immediate neighbourhood.

Do you mean the whole of Spitalfields?—Yes, and some part of the parishes immediately adjoining.

In what parish or parishes was that part of the neighbourhood?—A part in Bethnal Green, and, I think, part in Shoreditch.

Was the district examined, too extensive for the attendance of children on one school, or was it not?—I think it was too extensive for the children to attend one school.

What school is there now in that district or neighbourhood?—I have a list of the schools for the instruction of the poor in Spitalfields, the Old Artillery Ground, and Norton Falgate; which embraces nearly the whole of the district which has been examined.

[It was delivered in, and read, as follows:]

List of Schools for the Instruction of the Children of the Poor, in Spitalfields, the Old Artillery Ground, and Norton Falgate

Place	Description	Day School		Sunday School		Clothed	Treasurer	Master or Mistress	Expenditure	
		Boys	Girls	Boys	Girls					
Spitalfields	Parochial	56	54	–	–	Clothed	E. Merrick Esq.	Master & Mistress	450.	In this School the Committee hire Teachers, and give as rewards to the children articles of Clothing.
D°	D°	–	–	70	100	- -	Mr. Brown	- - -	80.	
Raven-row	Methodists	–	–	254	227	–	–	–	–	
Montague-street	British System	–	100	–	–	- -	Mrs. Buxton	Mistress	–	
D°	Protestant Dissenters	–	–	200	200	–	–	–	–	
Wood-street	D°	50	50	–	–	Clothed	- - -	Master & Mistress	450.	The Teachers in this School subscribe towards its support.
White's-row	D°	–	–	–	100	- -	Miss Good	- - -	30.	
Hope-street Chapel	D°	–	–	100	120	- -	Mr. Stirtevant	- - -	10.	
Artillery-street	D°	–	–	–	90	–	–	–	–	
Crispin-street	D°	–	–	–	70	–	–	–	–	
Steward-street	D°	21	21	–	–	Clothed	J. Wilson, Esq.	Master & Mistress	–	On Sundays a Dinner is provided at the School-house for the Children.
Elder-street	Sir George Wheler's Chapel	–	36	–	–	D° - -	Mr. Fouche	Mistress	100.	
Spicer-street Spitalfields	British System	350	–	–	–	- -	Mr. Gurney Barclay	- - -	140.	This School can accommodate 700;–but owing to the embarrassed state of its finances, the Committee do not admit any children gratuitously; the pay is one penny per week.
Total		477	261	670	907					

Are any of those schools out of that district?—Not any.

Did you find the want of education to be chiefly among the very poorest?—Yes.

In what proportion among the very poorest, should you apprehend?—About seven eighths.

What reason do the parents allege, in general, for not sending their children to school?—They allege principally poverty.

What other reasons do they also allege? —In some cases the necessity of employing the children during the day.

Were those cases numerous, in which they spoke of the necessity of employing the children during the day?—Not very numerous; the silk trade at present is very dull, and does not now afford much employment for children.

Do you imagine that in a good state of the trade there would be an objection to children going to school, in that neighbourhood, from the wish of the parents to employ them?—I believe a considerable number in that neighbourhood would be kept by their parents from attending the school on that account.

Do the parents in general seem very desirous of education for their children?—Very desirous.

Do they make any stipulations about it, and say they should not like such and such a sort of school?—Not in any case, among the families I visited.

But seem satisfied with good education, in whatever shape it might be presented?—Exactly so; they appeared anxious in their inquiries when schools would be opened.

Did they make any inquiries about the clothing of their children, as if they expected that would be a necessary condition in their appearance?—Not generally.

Did any considerable number? Not any considerable number.

In what state did the children appear, in cases in which the want of education which you have mentioned was expressed; did they appear dirty and miserable?—In a very miserable condition.

Was there any great deficiency in their manners; were they uncivil?—There seemed considerable wildness in the manners of the uneducated children, and their persons were generally very dirty.

Their looks were not like those of children who were accustomed to go to school?—Certainly not.

There was a want of that civility and propriety of behaviour which is amongst those children who go to school?—Yes.

Most of those children are employed in the silk business, when at work?—The greater proportion of them.

In the Lancasterian school, mentioned in the paper just delivered in, as capable of accommodating 700, but as having but 350 children, do you conceive that the pay of a penny per week per child, demanded in that school, is the reason that it is not full?—I believe it is the reason with many parents for not sending their children to that school.

Have you reason to think it would be full if no pay were asked of the children?—I think it would. I beg leave to observe, that many of the parents are very ignorant and insensible of the advantages of early instruction, and are therefore apt to neglect sending their children; or, if they are sent, their attendance is very irregular; another cause of non-attendance is the distress which now prevails in Spitalfields, which is beyond description; many of the children are kept from school from the want of clothing and shoes.

Have any of the other schools, contained in the above paper, room for more children than at present belong to them?—I believe the Sunday schools have; the others are parish schools, or charity schools.

Can you state in what degree they have room for more, respectively?—No, I cannot.

Have you reason to think that, taken collectively, they would hold considerably more children than are now in them?—I think they would.

Do you imagine that their not being full is owing to the same cause you have mentioned, in speaking of the Lancasterian school?—In some cases the schools will not accommodate a greater number.

But in those schools which would admit a greater number, do you imagine that the present deficiency in numbers is owing to the causes that you stated as operating in preventing the Lancasterian school from being full?—I am not prepared to answer that question.

When you speak of 350 children as now belonging to the Lancasterian school, you mean to speak of the number on the books?—No, the number actually attending.

Do you know how many are upon the books of the school?—I am not exactly prepared to say what that number is.

Do you know of any measure in contemplation to remedy the non-attendance of the children belonging to it?—With respect to the indifference of parents, and the want of clothing, I apprehend that if district associations were established on the principle recommended by the British and Foreign School Society for their associations, those difficulties would in a great measure be removed. It has been proposed that local societies be formed in districts containing from four hundred to five hundred poor children, and that schools should be established for the accommodation of that number; the most reputable characters among the lower orders would be invited to co-operate with their more affluent neighbours, in visiting from house to house, and from apartment to apartment, in order to impress upon the poor the benefits which schools impart; such of the poor as could afford it, would be encouraged to subscribe one penny per week; weekly visits to the poor, to collect the pence, would serve to interest their feelings in the education of their children, and keep the subject constantly before their minds. Frequent communications with the poor, on subjects connected with the welfare of their children, have a beneficial tendency on the minds of the parents.

Has this plan been tried in any district you are acquainted with?—It has not been adopted in London; but an association has been formed upon this principle at Northampton, which has completely succeeded.

When was it formed?—About eighteen months ago.

Do you know whether a similar system has been adopted in any other quarter?—An auxiliary school society has been established in Southwark, for the purpose of forming associations of this description; but this society is not yet in action.

Have you had any experience of the comparative effects of day schools and Sunday schools in imparting learning to the poor?—I have been for some years a teacher in a Sunday school in Bishopsgate parish, and I have been in the habit of attending a day school on the British and Foreign system.

What have been your conclusions from what you have seen, as to the comparative progress?—I consider that a boy would learn to read, write, and cipher, at a day school on the British and Foreign system, in one fourth part of the time in which he would learn to read only at a Sunday school.

What did you find the average time requisite to teach children to read at Sunday schools, who have not had the advantage of attending day schools?—About four years.

In that time would they read fluently? —I think they would.

What are the comparative effects on the manners of the children who attend the Sunday schools and day schools?—In general the children who attend the day schools attend Sunday schools; but there certainly is a considerable difference in the habits of those who attend Sunday schools only, to the disadvantage of the latter.

If a child attended a day school and also a Sunday school for a year and a half, and another child attended only a day school for four or five years, which should you think would have the advantage, with reference to the effects produced on manners and habits? —I should think the child who attended the day school, from the restraint which the day school would impose on him.

Do you ground your opinion on instances now in your mind, or on your general impression of what would be likely to be the effect?—From personal observation, and from the impression which has been made on my mind, from being in the habit of attending both schools

Do you find from your experience that almost all the children who attend day schools, also attend Sunday schools?—I think they do, generally. There is a numerous class of children whom it is very difficult to get to school; I allude to the children of the very lowest description of poor; these children may be seen wandering in the streets, without shoes or stockings, and generally exhibit a miserable appearance; their habits may be traced to parental neglect; many of these children are turned into the streets in the morning by their parents, and dare not return in the evening unless they take with them a certain sum, the fruits either of mendicity or of crime. There are other children, who are quite deserted by their parents. In Covent Garden market there are between thirty and forty boys, who are accustomed to sleep under the sheds and baskets every night, and when they rise in the morning have no other means of procuring subsistence but by the commission of crime. I submit to the Committee, that these children can only be benefited by institutions which combine employment with instruction. If schools of industry could be established in the most populous districts of the Metropolis, they would be the means of saving a number of destitute youth, who are training up in the most dangerous habits, and are often impelled as it were into the commission of crime.

Are those children, in general, in a state of complete ignorance?—It is very rarely indeed that any of those children can read.

Would their parents send them to a school if one was open, without pay, to receive them?—In some cases I do not think they would.

For what reason?—I have repeatedly called on the parents of children of this description, in the hope of inducing them to send their children to school, but I have often been unable to succeed in my endeavours.

For what reason?—They allege the want of clothing for the children, and the necessity of employing them during the day.

Are those parents in the lowest condition of life?—The very lowest.

Do they derive a profit from the mendicity of their children?—In many cases they do.

Do the parents avow this, when you mention it to them?—The parents do not avow it, but the children acknowledge it.

Can you guess how much a child may make by begging for its parents, in a day?—I should apprehend about two shillings a day by begging; the profits however which they have derived from begging have been much lessened since the publication of the Report on Mendicity.

Are there many children of the description you have now alluded to, in the Metropolis?—I should apprehend that there are between four and five thousand.

Do you consider that those children are withheld by their parents from schools, for the reason you have given?—I do; but I consider that if the children could earn a livelihood by attending schools of industry, their parents, in a number of cases, would cheerfully send them.

How much could a child earn at the schools of industry you refer to?—That entirely depends upon the manufacture they are engaged in; in some trades, the profits of children are very considerable.

Do they ever amount to 2s. a day?—They frequently do.

Do you think children would earn more by those employments than they do by begging and thieving?—I think they would by begging, but not by thieving.

Then do you apprehend that those parents, whom you have described, would prefer having their children earn less by an honest calling, than more by a dishonest one?—In a number of cases I think that the parents would prefer placing their children at schools of industry, though with less profit, from a fear of the punishment attendant on the commission of crime.

Do you allude to those parents whom you have already described as having the 4 or 5000 children you have mentioned?—I do.

Do you conceive there is any considerable proportion of these parents who would prefer having their children earn more by begging and thieving, and would refuse to send them to the schools alluded to?—I believe that proportion would not be very considerable.

Do you conceive that nothing short of compulsion would induce such parents to send their children to school?—I think that nothing short of compulsion would effect that object, with such persons.

In estimating the number you have mentioned, do you include the Borough and Surrey side of the River generally?—I do.

Mr. Thomas Heaver, called in, and Examined
What are you?—I am a member of the British and Foreign School Society, and a director of the Spicer-street school, Spitalfields; I have been a member of the committee of the Spicer-street school ever since its formation.

You have heard the latter part of the last Witness's examination?—I have.

Do you agree with him in his account of poor children?—I do.

Have you had occasion to examine any of the gangs of juvenile depredators who have been lately confined in Newgate?—Very frequently, for the last twelvemonth.

Are you a member of any committee for the purpose of that examination?—I am a member of an association for inquiring into the causes of juvenile delinquency

How many of those persons may you have examined?—I have examined individually about one hundred in prison, and a considerable number out of prison.

What has been the result of that examination?—I found them very generally in a complete state of ignorance, having no idea either of religion or morality.

Of what class of society were they, generally speaking? —Principally children of the lowest description, frequently abandoned by their parents.

Can you form any estimate of the probability of such parents allowing their children to go to school, if the means of instruction for nothing were provided?—I think if schools were opened gratuitously, that the greatest portion of such parents might be induced to send their children to them; but yet there are some so insensible to the advantages resulting from instruction, that no persuasion would effect it.

State any further information upon this subject which you may have procured, relating to these young delinquents above referred to?—I have generally found that their prepossession for street gambling, and associating with lads of the same loose character as themselves, have deluded their minds so strongly as to make them insensible to any dispositions except those of the most depraved description; but yet, when opportunity has offered to select some from the group or gang, and to reason with them tenderly upon the excellence of religion, they have been made sensible of the error of their ways; when kept separate for a time, the most pleasing results have arisen; I know of upwards of twenty boys who have been snatched from these vile associations, and are now in a fair way of being restored to society; but I have always found it expedient to take them from their parents, where the parents had been the cause of the delinquency of the child. The free use of spirits by the parents appears to me to be one of the primary causes of that laxity of moral principle which is now so evidently prevalent among the lower orders of the community.

Did you perceive any indisposition to education in the children themselves?— At first I did; but after conversing with them seriously on the advantages to be derived from education, they admitted it, and said they should rejoice to go to school.

Mr. Samuel Bevington, and Mr. Charles Beavitt, called in, and Examined

(To Mr. Bevington.) Have you paid a great deal of attention to schools in your neighbourhood?—I have been treasurer to the one in our parish some time.

What school is that?—Bermondsey and St. John's.

(To Mr. Beavitt.) What are you?—Schoolmaster to the above-mentioned school.

(To Mr. Bevington.) What is the nature of that school?—It is on the British and Foreign system, and supported by voluntary contributions.

How many is it calculated to hold?—Four hundred.

Boys and girls?—Only boys.

How many are there who attend it at the present time?—The average attendance is 260, but we are increasing daily.

Is there any clothing found?—We have given shoes and stockings by way of rewards for their merit tickets.

How do you account for there being only 260, if your school would contain 400?—We have not taken sufficient pains, till the present time, to inform the poor that their children might come; we found that out by inquiries made within the last few days; yet within another week our school will be quite full.

How long has the school been established?—I think this is the fourth year.

Have you an account with you of the expenses attending that school?—No, I have not; but they have averaged about 200 *l.* a year.

Do you recollect the items of that expense?—Rent, 80 *l.* a year; master, 100 *l.*; rewards and incidental expenses, 20 *l.*; it has been rather more than 200 *l.* I would observe, that the attendance at the school is only 260, the number on the books is about 320; and from the short time that is necessary for each boy, we have on education as many as 400 in the year; 100 go out, and 100 come in.

Do you limit the admission to any particular age?—No; as soon as a boy is competent to take his form in the sand class we admit him.

How long, upon the average, do you find it necessary to continue them in this school, coming in in the sand class?—We have never been so full as to be obliged to discharge any, but I suppose we shall soon. There are seven or eight boys under seven years of age, who have not been in the school more than one year and a half, who can read the Testament sufficiently well for their parents to understand them, although they did not know their letters when they came in.

How long have you been engaged in superintending the new system of education?—About four years.

Have you any information respecting the free school in Grange Road?—I received this paper from Mr. Nottage, the treasurer. [It was delivered in.]

Can you give the Committee any information respecting a free school in Cheerygarden-steet?—Yes; there is a Sunday school for 200 girls, out of which 60 are selected for daily instruction, and six of those are clothed; and twenty boys put under the care of the schoolmaster for daily instruction: it is done by voluntary contributions, and is under the superintendence of Mrs. Townshend.

Is this a school in which the British and Foreign plan of instruction is introduced?—No, it is not.

Are the master and mistress persons who are paid for their attendance?—Yes.

Do the children who are educated in your school upon the British and Foreign plan, attend divine service regularly on a Sunday?—Yes; those whose parents state a wish for their going to church, are always taken there by the master; and care is taken that all the others attend some place of worship, which is generally under the superintendence of the Sunday school.

Do you recollect the proportion of boys and girls who attend church, and those who go to other places of worship?—About 70 to church, out of the 360; there is a National school, which has diminished our number of church boys.

The remainder all attend meeting?—Yes.

Is it any particular meeting they attend?—No, they go to some Sunday school or other; there are three principal ones that take them.

Have you found any repugnance on the part of Church of England people to send their children to the schools?—No.

Can you give the Committee any information as to the proportion of the Dissenters to the Church of England people in the district, generally?—No, I cannot; our population is 20,000, and the church will only hold 1200, galleries and all: there is a large Methodist meeting in the parish, but it is attended very much by those not belonging to the parish.

Do you find any reluctance on the part of the lower orders to send their children to school?—No, not at all.

Have you in your neighbourhood many very poor persons?—Not of the lowest order; lodging is too dear; it is a manufacturing neighbourhood, where a great deal is earned.

Have the lower orders of your neighbourhood sufficient means of education?—They have not sufficient means generally; but I expect, for a populous parish, it is the nearest competent of any parish round London. The boys and girls together are 900, between five and fourteen years old, who do not receive any education. I should wish to observe generally, that the order and regularity necessary to be sustained by so large a number, is perhaps of more use to the habits of the children, than even the instruction we give them.

Description of the endowed grammar schools at Reading and Macclesfield, 1818

Nicholas Carlisle, *A Concise Description of the Endowed Grammar Schools in England and Wales* (London: Baldwin, Cradock, and Joy, 1818), 1, 36-41, 117-22.

Nicholas Carlisle (1771-1847) was a noted antiquary and librarian.

READING

In the year 1445, according to Leland, John Thorne, Abbot of the Monastery of Reading, having suppressed an old Alms-house for poor Sisters, near St. Lawrence's Church, which had, probably, been founded by one of his predecessors, employed the revenues of it to the use of the Almoner. But Henry the Seventh, being here soon after, was offended with the Abbot, for converting the funds of a Religious House, to purposes so foreign to the intentions of the donor, and ordered him to settle the house and lands on some Charitable Establishment.

In consequence of this intimation from His Majesty, the Abbot made it a Grammar School; in which benevolent design he was seconded by one William Dene, an officer in the Abbey, who gave two hundred marks towards the advancement of the Foundation, as Leland collected from his Tomb in the Abbey

Church. But the Abbot dying soon afterwards, in 1486, the settlement was not completed; though it appears to have been begun, as, after the Dissolution, the sum of £10. *per annum* was paid to the Master by The Crown.

But, in the reign of Queen Elizabeth, the Corporation undertook to pay the Master's salary, in return for certain lands bestowed upon them by Her Majesty, and then amounting to about £41 9s 7d. *per annum.*

By this Charter, which bears date the 23d of September, 1560, they were authorized to nominate and appoint the Master.

In the subsequent reign of Charles the First, Archbishop Laud, by his will, gave lands at Bray, then of the annual value of £20, as an addition to the Master's salary; which sum, by the increase of rent, has been augmented to £50 a year.

It is remarkable, that there are no Statutes belonging to this School, to regulate the conduct of the Masters and Scholars; such as are usually annexed to the Foundation of all other Schools. The Charter of Queen Elizabeth only reciting, that "a School, or Grammar School, founded and built by Our Predecessors, is in the Borough, *for educating the Boys of the Inhabitants of the said Borough, and others, in Literature.*"

The want of a systematic foundation is probably the cause of this omission: as Henry the Seventh merely left general directions for the establishment of the School, without contributing any thing to the Master's stipend: which was paid by the Abbot of Reading, until the Dissolution, as may be inferred from Cox's dedication of his "Art or Crafte of Rhetoryke;" and, afterwards, it was charged upon the Manor of *Cholsey* by Henry the Eighth.

Archbishop Laud was the most liberal Benefactor to the School; but, not considering himself as it's [*sic*] Founder, he did not draw up any Statutes for it's government. This worthy Prelate, however, appointed Three Visitors; viz.—The Vice-Chancellor of the University of Oxford, The President of St. John's, and The Warden of All Souls College; and left the interest of a sum of £24, for the expenses of their reception and entertainment. They visit the School every *third* year.

It has been customary, besides occasional examinations in Classical learning, for the Scholars to recite Speeches, or to perform Plays, at the time of this Triennial Visitation. The first Play on record is that of *Cato*, in 1731. The present Master, The Rev. Dr. Valpy, has paid great attention to the Theatrical Representations, and has purified and altered some Plays of Plautus and of Shakespeare, for the use of his Scholars. Of these Plays, four of Shakespeare have been published, viz., King John, the Second Part of Henry the Fourth, The Roses, from the Third Part of Henry the Sixth, and The Merchant of Venice, Four Plays of Plautus, The Amphitruo, The Aulularia, The Captives, and The Rudens, have likewise been printed for the use of Schools. Some Plays of Sophocles and Euripides have also been performed by the Scholars, with the strict costume of ancient Greece. The amount of money received at these Representations is very laudably bestowed upon some deserving object of Public Charity.

There are two Scholarships in St. John the Baptist's College, Oxford, belonging to this School, which were founded by Sir Thomas White, in 1557. In the Statutes of the College, as drawn up by himself, Sir Thomas observes;—

Seeing that there is nothing in the whole society of man more divine; nothing more analogous to our nature, than to be liberal and bountiful towards those, to whom we conceive ourselves most beholden: Neither are we tied by stricter bonds of friendship to any, more than to the citizens of London; among whom we have been, not only long conversant, and brought up almost from our infancy, but also have attained and gotten the greatest part of such goods and commodities, as now, by Divine permission, we enjoy; Wherefore, being moved with that love and piety, which we bear towards our Fellow Citizens, we do appoint, ordain, and will, that Forty-three of the poorer Scholars, who, either within London, or the suburbs thereof, shall bestow their time diligently in Grammar, may be admitted into this our College, founded and endowed at our costs and charges, and they shall enjoy all such advantages as the present scholars possess:—

Also, each of the following Schools, viz., Coventry, Bristol, and Reading, shall send Two Scholars, who shall partake of the same advantages and privileges, as the others enjoy. One, also, shall be chosen out of Tunbridge School, in the County of Kent:—

And now, to the end that there may be some certainty appointed, concerning the nominating and electing of these Seven Scholars, whom we will have equal to the others, in all the advantages and privileges of the College;—

As often as any place of these Seven shall become void, we will, that within forty days after such vacancy, The President and Fellows shall certify and advise, by Letters, signed with their own hands, the Mayors and Aldermen of those places, out of which such Scholars are to be named and chosen, that is to say, Coventry, Bristol, Reading, and Tunbridge, out of which Two Scholars each are to be elected, except out of Tunbridge, from which, out of respect to the great love we bore to Sir Andrew Judd, Knight, Founder of the Grammar School there, we do ordain and will, that One Scholar shall be nominated and elected, as often as the place assigned for this School shall be void. And they shall take care to send such out of their Schools, to The College, as either they themselves shall know, or in the judgment of others, shall believe to be fit to learn Logic. And we do decree, ordain, and will, that this nomination, assignation, evocation, and election, of Forty-three Scholars, and Six Choristers, by the Worshipful Men, The Master, Wardens, and Assistants, and The President, and Vice-President, and Two of the Chief Senior Fellows; And also, the nomination, evocation, and election, of those Seven Scholars, by The Mayors and Aldermen of those places, of which we made mention before, be made and kept for ever: neither shall it be lawful at any time, for The President and Fellows, which now are, or for their successors, to invert, change, break, or weaken the form of electing Scholars, which we have prescribed, nor to expound, or interpret otherwise than the true, natural, and grammatical sense of the words do bear, under pain of expulsion out of The College: Neither shall they at any time consent, either in word or deed, to them that do otherwise.

These Scholarships, at the end of two years, regularly lead to Fellowships.

The School-room for many years occupied the lower part of the Great Hall of The Hospital of St. John; the upper part being used as a Town-hall. When the Town-hall was re-built, the School continued for some time in it's old situation. But, as it had been found subject to many inconveniences, the present Master, in the year 1790, built a new School-room, fifty-two feet in length, *at his own expense.*

The Master's House, remarkable for the convenience and salubrity of the situation, was built by Mr. Hiley, a former Master, for the reception of his Boarders, and rented by his successor, Mr. Spicer; who, in 1771, set on foot a subscription for purchasing and annexing it to the School, for the residence of the Master:—liberal contributions were made by The Corporation, by St. John's College, and by the neighbouring Gentry, particularly such as had been educated in the School;—but, it was not until the year 1784, that the intention was carried into effect, and the House purchased of Dr. Addington, the Son-in-Law of Mr. Hiley, and vested in The Corporation, as Trustees. Here again we experience the liberality of Dr. Valpy, who has considerably enlarged and improved the House, particularly by the addition of a spacious Hall and Library.

As the School was founded *for the Sons of the Inhabitants and others,* it is open to all who conform to the Regulations of the Establishment.

At *Nineteen,* boys are superannuated for the Foundation at St. John's College.

The Latin and Greek Grammars in use, are those written by the present Master. The system of Education, with such alterations as expedience and locality render necessary, is formed upon those of Westminster, Eton, and Winchester Colleges.

This School is deservedly in great repute, under the excellent management of the present learned Master, Richard Valpy, D.D.

Besides the Head Master, some of the Assistants receive Boarders, on different terms, according to the numbers which they accommodate.

Cardinal Wolsey is said, on the authority of Archbishop Parker, to have been a short time Master of this School.

Among the eminent Persons, who have received their Education in this Seminary of Learning, besides many distinguished living Characters, may be enumerated,—Archbishop Laud; John Blagrave, the Mathematician; James Merrick, the Translator of the Psalms; The Rev. Charles Coates, M.A., Author of the History of Reading; Thomas Turner, D.D., Dean of Canterbury; William Davies Shipley, Dean of St. Asaph; Francis Annesley, LL.D., First Master of Downing College; Robert Vansittart, LL.D., Professor of Law at Oxford; Ambrose Serle, Esq.; John Loveday, Esq.; The Rev. W. Benwell.

MACCLESFIELD

Sir John Percyvale, Knight, some time Lord Mayor of London, and who was born "fast by the Town of Maxfield," founded a Free School here, that "gentil mens sonnes and other good mennes children *in Maxfield, and the Countre thereabouts*, might be taught Grammar," and to "pray for his soule, etc." And, by his Will, bearing date the 25th of Jany., 1502, he directed, that Lands of the yearly value of Ten Pounds should be purchased for it's endowment.

The Foundation of this School has, however, generally been attributed to King Edward the Sixth, who, by his Letters Patent bearing date the 25th of April, 1552, "upon the Petition, as well of the Inhabitants of Macclesfield, as of many other of his Subjects of the whole neighbouring Country," ordained, "that thenceforth there should be one Grammar School in Macclesfield aforesaid, which should be called The Free Grammar School of King Edward the Sixth, for the Education, Institution, and Instruction of Children and Youth in the Grammar,"—and "to be continued for ever under one Master or Tutor, and one Sub-Tutor or Usher."

And that his intention might take the better effect, and that the Lands and Revenues to be granted for the maintenance of the School, might be the better governed, His Majesty directed, "that thenceforth there should be, within the *Vill* of Macclesfield and Parish of Prestbury aforesaid, Fourteen of the most discreet and honest Inhabitants of the same Vill and Parish, which should be for the time being, and should be called Governors of the Possessions, Revenues, and Goods, of the said School, called and to be called "The Free Grammar School of King Edward the Sixth in Macclesfield;" constituting them a Body Corporate, by the name of "The Governors of the Possessions, Revenues, and Goods, of The Free Grammar School of King Edward the Sixth in Macclesfield," with perpetual Succession; and endowing the same with Sixteen acres of land near Chester, and several Crofts, Closes, Meadows, and Houses, in and near that City, being parcel of the possessions of The College of Saint John the Baptist, called "*The Prebend's Lands*; together with all the lands and Houses which had belonged to the Chantry, called "*The Pettie Canon*," then or late in the occupation of Richard Brereton, Esq., with other Messuages and Lands; and also "His said Majesty's one tenement, called "*The School House*," with all their appurtenances situate, lying, and being in Macclesfield, Broken Cross, Mottram, and Prestbury, or elsewhere, within the said County of Chester, which were *thentofore* given, granted, assigned, or appointed, for the maintenance of The Grammar School in Macclesfield aforesaid;" to be holden of His Majesty and his successors, as of his Manor of East Greenwich, rendering to His Majesty, his heirs and successors, Twenty-five Shillings at his Court of Augmentation of the Revenues of his Crown, at the Feast day of St. Michael the Archangel, every year, to be paid for all rents, services, and demands whatsoever:—That the Governors might from thenceforth have a Common Seal, might sue and be sued, and should have full power and authority to nominate and appoint a Master and Usher of the School, as often as the same should be void:— That, with the advice of the Bishop of the Diocese for the time being, they might make fit and wholesome Statutes and Ordinances, in writing, concerning the ordering and directing of the Master and Usher, and Scholars, and the preservation and disposition of the Rents and Revenues, and sustaining of the School; which Statutes so to be made, his Majesty commanded inviolably to be observed from time to time:—That the Governors might further receive of any person lands or other hereditaments not exceeding the clear yearly value of £20, above and besides the former grant, the Statute of Mortmain or any other Statute to the contrary notwithstanding:—And, "that all the issues, rents, and revenues of the aforesaid lands, tenements, and possessions, by the said Letters Patent granted, and thenafter to be given and assigned to the sustentation of the aforesaid School, from time to time, should be converted to the sustaining the Master and Usher of the said School for the time being, and not otherwise, or to any other uses or intentions."

In the year 1750, the Governors sold the ancient School-house and some lands; purchased a capital messuage for the School, which was repaired and altered for that purpose; and made some other purchases, and exchanges.

As a sanction to these proceedings, and for the purpose of procuring further powers, which the expected increase of the Revenues rendered desirable, it was deemed requisite to apply for an Act of Parliament, which was obtained in the 14 Geo. III., 1774.

This Act, besides confirming the above purchases and exchanges, and a Rent-charge on the Chester Canal, which had been given in lieu of some land taken by the Proprietors, empowered The Governors to sell certain houses, and to lay out the money arising from the sale, in lands; to grant building or repairing leases; "to appoint such or so many person or persons as shall be proper and necessary to be Master or Masters, with suitable Salaries, to be paid out of the Revenues of the said School, to teach and instruct the Children and Youth educated at the said School, not only in Grammar and Classical Learning, but also in writing, arithmetick, geography, navigation, mathematicks, the modern languages, and other branches of Literature and Education," as shall from time to time, in the judgment of the Governors, be proper and necessary, "to render the said Foundation of the most general use and benefit, and as the state of the Revenues of the said School will admit;" there being always a Head Master, whose Salary must not be less than £100; and an Usher, whose salary must not be less than £40; the salaries to be increased at discretion; to dismiss Masters for Immorality, Incapacity, wilful neglect of their Duty, or any other just and reasonable cause, with the approbation of the Bishop; and, in case of Incapacity, by the Visitation of God, in the Head Master, to allow him a Pension.

At the time of passing this Act, the Revenues of the School, which were then £170 *per annum*, were expected, on the expiration of certain Leases, to be raised to £600 *per annum*, and upwards. They now amount to upwards of £800 a year; and, in a few years, on the dropping in of old leases, may amount to nearly £1000 *per annum*.

The School is open to Boys of the Parish of Prestbury indefinitely, free of expense, except as to French, and writing and accompts. They are admitted as soon as they can read English correctly, and may remain as long as their Parents please. There is no particular form of admission; application to the Head Master being the usual mode, which is always successful. The Children of indigent persons are *not excluded*, as has been supposed; but, from the expense of books and the little attention paid to the minor branches of Learning in comparison with the Classics, such Children are seldom sent to the Grammar School.

The Master is empowered to take after the rate of 10*s*. 6*d per* Quarter from Day-scholars for learning French, and the like sum for learning writing and accompts.

The Eton Latin and Greek Grammars were used for many years, but those of Dr. Valpy have lately been substituted.

The first object of Macclesfield School is Classical Literature, which comprehends the English, Latin, and Greek languages. The Higher Forms are likewise instructed in the Elements of Algebra, and Euclid;—The Lower and Middle Classes, in Writing, Arithmetic, and the use of the Globes, modern and ancient Geography, etc. The French language is introduced to a certain extent, in every department of the School, and is further substituted in the place of Greek, for the benefit of those Pupils who are not intended for College or Professions. A suitable collection of English Authors is appropriated to each Class, and the greatest attention is paid to correct Elocution and Classical Composition.

There are no Exhibitions belonging to this School; but the Head Master has recommended to the Governors to found Exhibitions, whenever the Revenues of the Institution will allow.

Boys from this School are usually sent to Brasen-Nose College Oxford, where a preference is given to them; Sir Richard Sutton, one of the Founders of that College, having been born in the Parish of Prestbury.

The School at present consists of *Thirty* Boarders, and *Nineteen* Day-Scholars.

The present Head Master is, David Davies, D.D., whose Salary is £200 *per annum*, and a spacious House, clear of taxes. This Gentleman takes Pupils, his Terms being,

For Entrance, Five Guineas.

Board and Education, { in the Lower Forms, 35 guineas a year.
{ in the Higher Forms, 40 guineas a year.

A single Bed, if required, Four guineas a year.

Extra Charges:—Dancing, Fencing, Drawing, One guinea a quarter each.

N.B. Three months' notice is expected before the removal of any Young Gentleman.

The Salary of the Second Master is £150 *per annum*.

The Salary of the Writing Master is £100 *per annum*.

The Salary of the French Master is £50 *per annum*.

John Brownswerd, a celebrated Grammarian and Latin Poet, was Master of this School in the reign of Queen Elizabeth. He lies buried in the Chancel of the Parochial Chapel, where there is a tablet to his memory, with a Latin Inscription, which was written by his Scholar, Thomas Newton.

The History of the Fairchild Family by **Mrs. Sherwood, 1818-47**

The History of the Fairchild Family; or, the Child's Manual (London: James Nisbet, 1875), 10-18.

This famous book, the first part of which was published in 1818, was reprinted many times in Great Britain and the United States. The excerpt which follows is an illustration of the popular religious fiction of the period. Mrs. Mary Sherwood

(1775-1851) was an evangelical propagandist who wrote many tracts for young people and indulged in numerous works of charity.

Man before the Fall

"It is Lucy's birthday," said Mr. Fairchild, as he came into the parlour one fine morning in May; "we will go to see John Trueman, and take some cake to his little children, and afterwards we will go on to visit Nurse, and carry her some tea and sugar."

Nurse was a pious old woman, who had taken care of Lucy when she was a baby, and now lived with her son and his wife Joan in a little cottage not far distant, called Brookside Cottage, because a clear stream of water ran just before the door.

"And shall we stay at Nurse's all day, papa?" said the children.

"Ask your mamma, my dears," said Mr. Fairchild.

"With all my heart," said Mrs. Fairchild; "and we will take Betty with us to carry our dinner."

So when the children had breakfasted, and Betty was ready, they all set out. And first they went down the lane towards John Trueman's cottage. There is not a pleasanter lane near any village in England; the hedge on each side is of hawthorn, which was then in blossom; and the grass was soft under the feet as a velvet cushion; on the bank, under the hedge, were all manner of sweet flowers, violets, and primroses, and the blue vervain.

Lucy and Emily and Henry ran gaily along before their papa and mamma, and Betty came after with the basket. Before they came up to the gate of John Trueman's cottage, the children stopped to take the cake out of Betty's basket, and to cut shares of it for John's little ones. Whilst they were doing this, their papa and mamma had reached the cottage, and were sitting down at the door when they came up.

I must make my reader acquainted with John Trueman. He was a poor working man, and had a wife and six children. But I should not call him poor; I should rather call him rich; for he had cause to hope that his wife and all his children (that is, all who were old enough to inspire such hopes) had been brought to the knowledge of God; and as for John himself, there was reason to think that he was one of the most faithful servants of God in all the country round.

John Trueman's cottage was a neat little place, standing in a garden, adorned with pinks and rosemary, and southernwood. John himself was gone out to his daily work when Mr. and Mrs. Fairchild came to his house; but his wife Mary was at home, and was just giving a crust of bread and a bit of cheese to a very poor woman who had stopped at the gate with a baby in her arms.

"Why, Mary," said Mr. Fairchild, "I hope it is a sign that you are getting rich, as you have bread and cheese to spare."

"Sir," she answered, "this poor woman is in want, and my children will never miss what I have given her."

"You are very right," answered Mrs. Fairchild. " 'He that giveth to the poor lendeth to the Lord,' and the Lord will pay it again;" and at the same time she slipped a shilling into the poor woman's hand.

John and Mary Trueman had six children; the eldest, Thomas, was working in the garden; and little Billy, his youngest brother, who was but three years old, was carrying out the weeds as his brother plucked them up. Mary, the eldest daughter, was taking care of the baby; and Kitty, the second, sat sewing, whilst her brother Charles, a little boy of seven years of age, read the Bible aloud to her. They were all neat and clean, though dressed in very coarse clothes.

When Lucy and Emily and Henry divided the cake amongst the poor children, they looked very much pleased; but they said that they would not eat any of it till their father came in at night. "If that is the case," said Mrs. Fairchild, "you shall have a little tea and sugar, to give your father with your cake;" so she gave them some out of the basket. Mary Trueman first thanked God, and then Mr. and Mrs. Fairchild, for these good things, and she, with all her children, followed Mr. and Mrs. Fairchild with curtseys and bows to the corner of the lane.

As Mr. and Mrs. Fairchild and their children passed through the village, they stopped at the schools, and found everything as they could wish—the children all clean, neat, cheerful, and busy; and the master and mistress very attentive. They were much pleased to see everything in such good order in the schools; and having passed this part of the village, they turned aside into a large meadow, through which was the path to Nurse's cottage. Many sheep, with their lambs, were feeding in this meadow, and here, also, were abundance of primroses, cowslips, daisies, and buttercups, and the songs of the birds which were in the hedgerows were exceedingly delightful.

As soon as the children came in sight of Nurse's little cottage, they ran on before to kiss Nurse, and to tell her that they were come to spend the day with her. The poor woman was very glad, because she loved Mr Fairchild's children very dearly; she therefore kissed them, and took them to see her little grandson Tommy, who was asleep in the cradle. By this time Mr. and Mrs. Fairchild and Betty were come up; and whilst Betty prepared the dinner, Mr. and Mrs. Fairchild sat talking with Nurse at the door of the cottage.

Their discourse ran upon the mercy and goodness of God to his people, and poor Nurse especially was full of gratitude for what had been lately done for her son; for this young man had for a short time past given evidence of a great change of heart, insomuch that he made his mother and wife extremely happy, whereas he had formerly given them great uneasiness. "These are blessings," said Mr. Fairchild to Nurse, "for which you cannot be too thankful."

Betty and Joan laid the cloth upon the fresh grass before the cottage-door; and when Joan had boiled some potatoes, Mr. and Mrs. Fairchild sat down to dinner with the children; after which the children went to play in the meadow, by the brookside, till it was time for them to be going home. But before they parted from Nurse, I should tell you that Mr. Fairchild read a chapter in the Bible aloud; and afterwards they all prayed together, that God would bless them until they should meet again; and Mrs. Fairchild having given Nurse the tea and sugar, the good old woman kissed the dear children, and they returned home with their papa and mamma.

"What a happy day we have had!" said Lucy, as she walked home between her papa and mamma; "everything has gone well with us since we set out; and every one we have seen has been kind and good to us; and the weather has been so fine, and everything looks so pretty all around us!"

"It is very true," said Mr. Fairchild, "that we have had a happy day, my dear; for we have conversed with no persons to-day but those who live in the fear of God. If everybody in this world feared God, the world would again become nearly such as it was before Adam sinned; but by 'reason of sin all lands mourn.' "

"Was the world very pretty, papa," said Emily, "before wickedness came into it?"

"It is written in the first chapter of Genesis," said Mr. Fairchild, "that when God had made all things, He looked on them, and behold, they were very good. Adam and Eve were made in the image of God; they were, no doubt, most lovely to look upon; and they had no angry, wicked passions to disturb them. They were placed in a garden watered by four streams, and in which was every kind of tree pleasant to the sight, or good for food. There were no evil beasts then in the world; no sickness or sorrow, no pain, no death; but when Adam sinned all these evils came into the world."

"If men were to leave off being wicked, papa," said Lucy, "would pain and sorrow leave them?"

"Men can never leave off sinning, my dear," said Mr. Fairchild, "because sin is in our hearts, and will continue to trouble us to our dying day; but in proportion as the people of any town, or village, or house, believe in the Lord Jesus Christ, and love Him, they will become more and more happy; and, in proportion as people give way to sin, they become more miserable. In those heathen countries where God is not known to all, the people are poor, miserable, cruel, and dirty: they do not know what it is to be happy: the fields look barren and desolate, and the very beasts share their misery. I remember a time when Nurse and her son did not love God! and then they were not happy, but were always quarrelling and miserable: their little cottage did not look clean and orderly and pleasant, as it now does, but was always in uproar and confusion: but, now that God has given them clean hearts, you see how happy they are. We must have clean hearts, before we could be happy even in heaven; 'without holiness, no man shall see the Lord.' " (Heb. xii. 14.)

By this time Mr. and Mrs. Fairchild, with their children, had arrived at home; and they were very tired, for they had walked a long way that day.

General Depravity of Mankind in all Countries after the Fall

Mr. Fairchild had a little tame hare, which he kept in his study. He had had it many years. This hare had a little wooden house, with a small door, in the study; and whenever anything frightened it, it used to run into its house, where it remained in safety. Emily and Lucy and Henry used to go every morning into the garden, to get parsley and other green things for the hare. One day, when they came in with the hare's food, they saw their papa sitting at his study table, examining a large round ball, or globe, which was fixed upon a stand before him. The children had never seen this before, because it was just come from London, a present from Mr. Fairchild's uncle.

"Oh! papa! papa! what pretty thing is that?" said the children: "pray let us see it!"

"It is a globe, my dears," said Mr. Fairchild; "your kind uncle sent it from London, for your use."

"Oh, that was good, papa!" said Lucy; "it is very pretty."

"Yes, it is very pretty, indeed," said Henry; "but I do not understand its use."

"My little people, come here," said Mr. Fairchild, "and stand round the table, and I will try to make you understand what is the use of the globe."

So the children gave the hare his parsley, and gathered round their papa.

"Of what shape is this thing, my dears?" said Mr. Fairchild.

"It is round, papa," said Lucy; "round like an apple."

"This thing, my dears," said Mr. Fairchild, "is called a globe; it is the shape of the world in which we live, and upon it are drawn, as in a picture, all the countries of the world."

"Oh, papa, how pretty!" said Emily; "and is the world in which we live round like this?"

Mr. Fairchild. "Yes, my dears; and it hangs in the heavens as the moon does, kept there by the almighty power of God."

"Papa," said Henry, "will you teach us where all the countries are upon the globe?"

Mr. Fairchild. "Yes, my dear; you shall come into my study, and I will teach you a little every day; and we will talk about the various nations and peoples who live on this globe."

The next morning the children came again into Mr. Fairchild's study, and he gave them the instruction he had promised them. And first he taught them that the globe was divided, by general agreement, into four unequal parts—namely, Europe, Asia, Africa, and America. "Asia is that part of the world," said Mr. Fairchild, "in which the garden of Eden, or Paradise, was supposed to have been placed, where the first man, Adam, had lived."

"Oh, papa!" said Emily, "show us where the garden of Eden was."

"Here it was," said Mr. Fairchild, "as is supposed, upon the borders of the river Euphrates, which was one of the four rivers of Paradise.

"Paradise, my dears," continued Mr. Fairchild, "was a most lovely place, such as we never saw; for there is no place in this world in which the ruin caused by sin does not appear. But when Adam and Eve were tempted by the devil to eat the forbidden fruit, they were cast out of Paradise; their bodies became subject to sickness and death; and their hearts became exceedingly corrupt, and all their children, who have since been born in their likeness, are utterly and entirely sinful: so that of ourselves we cannot do a good thing, or think a good thought."

"Papa," said Lucy, "may we say some verses, about mankind having bad hearts?"

"Yes, my dear," answered Mr. Fairchild.

Then each of the children repeated a verse from the Bible to prove that the nature of man, after the fall of Adam, is utterly and entirely sinful.

Lucy's verse. "And God saw that the wickedness of man was great in the earth, and that every imagination of the thoughts of his heart was only evil continually;

and it repented the Lord that he had made man on the earth, and it grieved him at his heart. The earth also was corrupt before God; and the earth was filled with violence. And God looked upon the earth, and behold it was corrupt; for all flesh had corrupted his way upon the earth." (Gen. vi. 5, 6, 11, 12.)

Emily's verse. "And Noah builded an altar unto the Lord, and took of every clean beast, and of every clean fowl, and offered burnt offerings on the altar. And the Lord smelled a sweet savour: and the Lord said in his heart, I will not again curse the ground any more for man's sake: for the imagination of man's heart is evil from his youth; neither will I again smite any more everything living as I have done." (Gen. viii. 20, 21.)

Henry's verse. "For I know that in me, that is, in my flesh, dwelleth no good thing." (Rom. vii. 18.)

"You find by these verses, my dear children," said Mr. Fairchild, "that the heart of every man is entirely and utterly corrupt; that there is no good in us whatever: so that we cannot, without God's help, think even one good thought. This is the dreadful state into which Adam brought himself and his children by his disobedience; he made us children of wrath and heirs of hell. But at the very time that Adam fell and was turned out of Paradise, God, in his very great goodness, gave him a promise to be his comfort: this promise was, that one born among his children should destroy his enemy the devil, and save his brethren."

"I know who that is," said Lucy, "who was to be born amongst the children of Adam to destroy the works of the devil: it is the Lord Jesus Christ: who, though He is God, took the body of a man, and was born like a baby, and died for us all."

"Oh!" said Henry, "I wish I could love the Lord Jesus Christ more than I do; but my wicked heart will not let me."

"Ah! my boy," said Mr. Fairchild, "we may all say the same: but there is one comfort, that we could not wish to love Him, if He did not put this wish into our hearts. And now, my dears," said Mr. Fairchild, "let us pray that God will give us a knowledge of the exceeding wickedness of our hearts; that we may, knowing our wretched state, look up to the dear Saviour, who can only save us from hell."

Story on the Commandments

The next morning, at the time fixed by Mr. Fairchild, the children went into the study; and Mr. Fairchild showed them more places on the globe, and taught them many things which they did not know before. I shall put down what he taught them in this place, as you may perhaps like to read it.

"After Adam and Eve were turned out of Paradise," said Mr. Fairchild, "on account of their disobedience to God, they had many children born; and these children had children, and children's children, till, at the end of two thousand years, they had multiplied exceedingly; but these people were very wicked; so very wicked, that it repented God that He had made them; and He sent a flood of water to destroy all the people that were upon the face of the earth, excepting only one person and his family."

Henry. "And that was Noah, who was saved in the ark."

"The account of Noah's preservation is given us in Heb. xi. 7," said Mr. Fairchild. Mr. Fairchild then showed to his children, upon the globe, a mountain in Asia, which he said was Ararat, where Noah's ark rested after the flood. And he showed them also a place not very far distant, to which Noah's children travelled after they began to multiply upon the face of the earth, called the "Plain of Shinar."

"Oh!" said Emily; "and I know what the children of Noah did in the Plain of Shinar."

"Let us hear, then," said Mr. Fairchild, "if you can repeat the account from the Bible."

Emily. "Yes, papa. 'And the whole earth was of one language and of one speech. And it came to pass, as they journeyed from the east, that they found a plain in the land of Shinar, and they dwelt there. And they said one to another, Go to, let us make brick, and burn them thoroughly. And they had brick for stone, and slime had they for mortar. And they said, Go to, let us build us a city, and a tower whose top may reach unto heaven; and let us make us a name, lest we be scattered abroad upon the face of the whole earth. And the Lord came down to see the city and the tower, which the children of men builded. And the Lord said, Behold, the people are one, and they have all one language; and this they begin to do: and now nothing will be restrained from them which they have imagined to do. Go to, let us go down, and there confound their language, that they may not understand one another's speech. So the Lord scattered them abroad from thence upon the face of all the earth, and they left off to build the city: therefore is the name of it called Babel; because the Lord did there confound the language of all the earth: and from thence did the Lord scatter them abroad upon the face of all the earth.' " (Gen. xi. 1-9.)

"Very well, my dear," said Mr. Fairchild. "From this place, which is called Babel, or Babylon, to this day, the families of the children of Noah spread themselves all over the face of the earth; some going one way, and some another, and settling themselves in different countries: some going towards the north, where it is extremely cold, and the fields are covered with frost and snow, and others towards the south, where the sun has immense power, and the earth is in some seasons scorched with burning heat.

"But wherever the families of the children of Noah had settled themselves," added Mr. Fairchild, "they have, from the time of Noah, even till now, filled the earth with violence and wickedness. How many nations have, for ages past, forgotten the name of the true God, and have made to themselves vile gods of wood and of stone! 'changing the glory of the incorruptible God into an image made like to corruptible man, and to birds, and four-footed beasts, and creeping things.' " (Rom. i. 23.)

Mr. Fairchild then stated to his children this awful truth, which few understand, or duly consider: that, vile and abominable as the heathen are, there is another order of people to be found too commonly in countries calling themselves Christian, whose condemnation in the world to come, it is to be feared, will be greater than even that of the heathen themselves. "And these," he said, "are those persons who, having the opportunity of reading their Bible, and hearing the Gospel preached, yet live in utter neglect of the great salvation prepared for them; people who think of little or nothing but enjoying what they call pleasure, gathering together riches, or making themselves great in the world. Even England," added Mr. Fairchild, "this happy country, in which there are many who preach the pure Gospel, in which there are numbers of holy books daily within our reach, in which the Bible is found in almost every house, is full of those persons who neglect and despise religion; and though it would be thought very shameful in this country for a man plainly to say, 'I do not love my Saviour—I do not believe in the Holy Spirit!' yet there are thousands who show as much by their careless lives and vain conversation."

"Papa," said Lucy, "I fear, from what you say, that there are very few real Christians in the world, and that a very great part of the human race will be finally lost."

"My dear child," replied Mr. Fairchild, "it is not the will of God that one should be lost; neither is it our business to decide upon this matter; this we know, that a way of salvation has been pointed out to us, and that it will be our own fault if we do not accept this great salvation; the great sins of mankind are pride and unbelief; this is the natural state of man's heart, and it is the work of the Holy Spirit of God to convince us of this unbelief, and to bring us to a knowledge of our unhappy state by nature, and of that which the blessed Saviour has done for us. From the beginning of the world until this present day, there always have been some who have been thus convinced of sin, and brought to the knowledge of God. These are those blessed persons who are now called in Scripture the children of God; and these are those who are described in Rev. xiv. 1-5, also in Heb. xi. 4-6 and 32-40.

"From these verses we may learn, my dear children," said Mr. Fairchild, "that all people who are not brought to believe in God the Father, God the Son, and God the Holy Ghost, the Blessed and Holy Trinity, as they are shown to us in the Bible, remain in their sins, and are in a state of condemnation; but that those who have a right faith will receive a new nature from God, and will be saved through the Lord Jesus Christ."

"Oh, papa, papa!" said the children, "pray for us, that we may not be wicked and go to hell."

"I would have you remember, my dear children," said Mr. Fairchild, "that there is no such thing as being saved, except by the Lord Jesus Christ, through his death; nothing you can do yourselves can save you. Even if you could, from this time forward, live without sin, yet you are condemned already for your past sins. Neither can you keep even one of God's commandments without the help of the Holy Spirit."

"Papa," said Lucy, "we will pray to the Holy Spirit to help us, and then we shall get better."

"Ask your mamma, to-morrow," said Mr. Fairchild, "to tell you a story of something which happened to her when she was young, by which you will better understand what is meant when I say you cannot be good without the help of the Spirit."

Speech by Henry Brougham introducing his bill for a national system of education, House of Commons, 11 July 1820

Hansard, n.s., II, 365-66.

The Whig reformer Henry Brougham (1778-1868), afterwards Baron Brougham and Vaux (1830), was a founder of the Edinburgh Review *(1802) and of the University of London. His abortive proposal for a national education system grew out of inquiries into the misappropriation of charitable funds for popular education, first instituted by Brougham in 1816 as chairman of the Select Committee on the Education of the Lower Orders.*

[Education of the Poor Bill.] Mr. Brougham brought in his bill, "for better providing the means of Education for his Majesty's Subjects," which was read a first time.

Mr. Brougham, in rising to move, that it be read a second time to-morrow, said, he wished to notice, and to allay an alarm which, he understood, his bill had excited amongst two very numerous and highly respectable classes of his majesty's subjects—the Protestant Dissenters and the Roman Catholics. The House would hardly believe the extent to which this alarm had gone, especially when they recollected the observations with which he had introduced the plan. It was supposed, in consequence of the system being connected with the Protestant ecclesiastical establishment, that it was intended to compel children of various denominations to attend Protestant worship. This feeling had operated so powerfully, that some members of these two respectable bodies had addressed queries to him on the subject. It was asked by one party, whether it was not true (a point, he begged leave to observe, directly contradicted by the report) that it was intended to compel Roman Catholics to send their children to Protestant schools and Protestant worship? and certain dissenters seemed to consider this as a bill introduced for the purpose of "rooting out the last remains of religious liberty in this country." With respect to the Test act, as it affected dissenters, he would offer no observations on this occasion. But he thought the expression "to root out the last remains of religious liberty in this country," was exceedingly strong, when the dissenters were allowed, by an annual indemnity act, to get rid of the sacramental test. He would, however, tell those individuals, and if any of them happened to be present, he hoped they would recollect the declaration, that there was not a man in the House, nor in the country, more decidedly adverse to any thing harsh or intolerant than he was. Nor was there an individual who had a stronger dislike to tests, except where their abrogation might interfere with the existence of the government. He was the last man to keep up tests, unless they were absolutely necessary; and much less would he assist in extending them.—He would now state, that he had omitted in the present bill the sacramental test to schoolmasters, which he had originally contemplated. The bill still provided that the schoolmaster should be a member of the established church; but it dispensed with the ceremony of his receiving the sacrament a month before his election. He made this alteration, as he knew persons who were averse from taking the sacrament (not from any objection to it, but, on the contrary, from a reverence for the ceremony), because they did not think it was fitting to receive it as the passport to a civil office. Making every allowance for the conscientious scruples of those individuals, on the point he had stated, he had consented to give up that part of the bill. He could assure those most worthy and respectable, and infinitely-respected friends to religious liberty, the Protestant Dissenters of England—whose regard for civil and religious liberty was only equalled by their loyalty to the Crown, and their good disposition towards the constitution as by law established—that he had neither done nor said any thing that could form a just ground for such an alarm. He had deemed it necessary to observe thus much, in order to prevent the possibility of misrepresentation.

Address by Dr. George Birkbeck at the opening of the London Mechanics' Institution, 20 February 1824

Mechanics' Magazine, Museum, Register, Journal and Gazette (28 February 1824), 418-21.

Birkbeck (1776-1841) was the founder of the adult education movement which sought to popularize scientific knowledge through mechanics' institutes. The London institute had an initial membership of thirteen hundred and served as a model for numerous provincial associations.

Gentlemen;—With feelings of exultation, unutterable, I rise to offer my warmest, heartfelt congratulations, on this momentous occasion. This hour is witness to hopes, long, ardently, and anxiously cherished by me, now rapidly realizing in the visible and effective existence of *A Mechanics' Institution* in the emporium of the world.

Had you, Gentlemen, beheld the small number of artizans, who, in a large and flourishing city, were willing to accept the earliest invitation to enter the temple of science, this striking scene would be contemplated with gratitude and delight, still more lively and enthusiastic; with gratitude, arising from the permission to behold the extended impulsive operation of the growing appetite for knowledge, one of the noblest propensities of man; with delight, from perceiving that the mighty spirit of the age, which has been pervading the whole rational creation, has at length fructified the intellectual mass, and roused it from death-like slumber, to animation and activity. The inquiring spirit of the age has loudly demanded that the door of Science should be thrown open, and that its mysteries should be revealed to all mankind. This demand has been answered here as well as elsewhere, without reference to age, occupation, or condition; and, judging from the aspect of this thronged assembly, the result must be most auspicious to the progress of knowledge. "There is a *time*," the wisest of mortals has declared, "for all things;" and the ardour with which the present project has been embraced, proves beyond the possibility of question, that this is the time for the universal diffusion of the blessings of knowledge. "There is a *tide* in the affairs of men," one of the most splendid examples of human genius has affirmed, "which, taken at the flood, leads on to fortune." The tide of knowledge, within a recent period, has been rapidly rolling on towards this elevation; and if we do not neglect the golden opportunity, we shall achieve that intellectual fortune, in which consists, alike, individually and aggregately, the most substantial riches and the most substantial glory.

It is not my intention to place before you the vast and varied results of this projected union of science and art; or, in other words, of this combination of the discoveries of the philosophic mind, with the inventions of mechanic genius: the objects and the effects of this combination will be far more intelligibly and impressively depicted, by the liberal and enlightened Professor to whom you will soon have the pleasure and advantage of directing your attention. [Professor Millington was to deliver an Introductory Lecture on the Elementary Principles of Mechanical Science.] I shall content myself with advancing and illustrating the position, that knowledge, by whomsoever obtained, like virtue, which it strikingly resembles, is its own reward; that, therefore, the pleasure flowing from mental exercise, and the satisfaction resulting from the attainment of truth, are sufficient compensations for the labour of study, when unattended by pecuniary or commercial advantage. The independent benefits resulting from these pursuits, I cannot better illustrate than by adopting the language of a distinguished divine, whose energetic eloquence has occasionally been heard within these walls. "Knowledge in general," says the Rev. Robert Hall,

expands the mind, exalts the faculties, refines the taste of pleasure, and opens innumerable sources of intellectual enjoyment. By means of it we become less dependent for satisfaction upon the sensitive appetites; the gross pleasures of sense are more easily despised; and we are made to feel the superiority of the spiritual to the material part of our nature. Instead of being continually solicited by the influence and irritation of sensible objects, the mind can retire within herself, and expatiate in the cool and quiet walks of contemplation. The Author of nature has wisely annexed a pleasure to the exercise of our active powers, and particularly to the pursuit of truth, which, if it be in some instances less intense, is far more durable than the gratifications of sense: and this duration, to say nothing of its other properties, renders it incomparably more valuable. It may be repeated without satiety, and pleases afresh with every reflection upon it. These are self-created satisfactions, always within our reach, not dependent upon events; not requiring a peculiar combination of circumstances to produce or maintain them; they rise from the mind itself, and inhere, so to speak, in its very substance. Let the mind but retain its proper functions, and they spring up spontaneously, unsolicited, unborrowed, and unbought. Even the difficulties and impediments which obstruct the pursuit of truth, serve, according to the economy under which we are placed, to render it more interesting. The labour of intellectual search resembles and exceeds the tumultuous pleasures of the chace [*sic*] and the consciousness of overcoming a formidable obstacle, or of lighting upon some happy discovery, gives all the enjoyments of a conquest, without those corroding reflections by which the latter must be impaired. Can we doubt [he adds], that Archimedes, who was so absorbed in his contemplations, as not to be diverted from them by the sacking of his native city, and was killed in the very act of meditating a mathematical theorem, did not, when he exclaimed, "I have found it! I have found it!" feel a transport as genuine as was ever experienced after the most brilliant victory.

Whilst I thus refer several important explanations to Professor Millington, it would, I am aware, be satisfactory, and may even be expected, that a sketch of the design and progress of the London Mechanics' Institution should here be introduced, supplying information on topics, which hitherto have been very inadequately comprehended by the public. This delineation I defer at present, in compliance with the suggestions of the committee, for the purpose of connecting with it some notice of our financial concerns, and some other matters of interest, in order that you may be made acquainted with them before the next general meeting of the subscribers, the regular channel for such communications.

One advantage which may perhaps be produced by the introduction of science amongst the operative classes, some recent legislative movements induce me to mention. The wisdom of our present rulers is likely soon to explode certain restrictive measures, by which, the want of wisdom or the superabundance of its spurious representative in their long extinct predecessors, had fettered the artizan. To accomplish this purpose, it is probable that the most splendid talents of both the great parties in the state will be united; and it can scarcely be doubted, that they will succeed in repealing those laws, which prohibit the exportation of machinery, the emigration of the artizan, and the combination of workmen for purposes which they may deem essential to their prosperity. Now, extensive emigration, one probable consequence of such repeals, we must deplore; because with this portion of our population, the strength and the wealth of the nation must depart from our shores. If by improving the means of production and increasing the sources of his comfort, we render the artizan better satisfied with the fruits of his labour and more strongly attached to his native land, we shall effectually restrain his disposition to wander by the influence of his free choice, without the operation of statutes to which he reluctantly submits. Unless allured by very strong temptations, the English mechanic will seldom quit the home of his fathers: he clings to the spot which gave him birth with the fondest affection; and although occasionally disturbed by discontent, or crossed by hopeless anticipation, is ready to exclaim with Cowper, a poet replete with the pure and unsophisticated sentiments of a Briton,

> England, with all thy faults, I love thee still.
> My country! and, while yet a nook is left

Where English minds and manners may be found,
Shall be constrained to love thee. Though thy clime
Be fickle, and thy year most part deformed
With dripping rains, or withered by a frost,
I would not yet exchange thy sullen skies
And fields without a flower, for warmer France
With all her vines; nor for Ausonia's groves
Of golden fruitage, and her myrtle bowers.

Far, however, be it from me to advocate the retention within the circumference of our Island, of the Arts and Sciences, which are our best possessions, and our brightest ornaments. Over the western world, now in her sublime career of independence calling for their aid, I would have them liberally diffused: thus, indeed, in part atoning for those wrongs which followed in the train of the genius and enterprise of Columbus. Let European arts and European science freely cross the western main, to enrich the gay savannahs, and the vast mountain plains, in regions distinguished alike by their sublimity and inexhaustible fertility, until all that can be wafted by the winds, or that can be impelled by all-conquering steam, excepting European vices and European warriors, may be found

Where Andes, giant of the western star,
Looks from his throne of clouds o'er half the world.

It ought likewise ever to be remembered, that a relationship, and even a close alliance, has been established betwixt this country and all the habitable portions of the globe; enforcing the duty of reciprocal service, and demanding from us a full performance of good offices, whenever and wheresoever we may appear. Especially, if as represented by the eloquent Secretary for Foreign Affairs, on a late festive occasion in this city, we form with other nations, however remote, but one great family. "We ought never to forget," says he, "that at all periods the field of our native glory is that sea, which disjoins all other countries from each other, and unites them all to England."

Before I conclude this introductory address, permit me, Gentlemen, to repel some apprehensions or insinuations, which, in the cautious but mischievous mode of hinting a fault, or hesitating dislike, have been opposed to our proceedings. From the want of being well known, we certainly have not obtained full credit for the *singleness* of our purpose; and we have been, somewhat illiberally it must be granted, suspected of having more in our designs than has been allowed to meet the ear. For myself, who, although not the originator of this Institution, took the earliest counsel with its earliest effectual projectors, I can boldly declare, that the scientific cultivation of the mind of the mechanic, was and still continues to be, *my only object.* For my friends Mr. Robertson and Mr. Hodgskin, your original temporary secretaries, who first gave currency to the plan, and were the powerful means of organizing our first public movements, I can with equal confidence answer. But what need of any voucher here for them? They are always before you. *The Mechanic's Magazine*, the most valuable gift which the hand of science has ever yet offered to the artizan, of which they are the intelligent Editors, carries along with it incontestible evidence of the inflexible resolution with which they can pursue their sole objects, your amelioration and your instruction. For several individuals who took an active part in the public proceedings, and for the Committee to whom you have entrusted the management of your concerns, I can without hesitation, make a similar avowal. All *intention* of interference with political questions we do therefore disclaim; and, not less cheerfully than advantageously, do we resign them to that "patriot-eloquence," which can shake the senate, and flash down fire upon our country's foes. If indirectly we shall be supposed to exercise any influence,—and education may extend the views of the Mechanic,—I am persuaded that we shall invigorate the attachment which must ever exist to every wise and well-constructed system of legislation. Such at least was the opinion of "the great political unknown," as the following quotation will testify. "The submission," says Junius,

> of a free people to the executive authority of government, is no more than a compliance with laws which they themselves have made. While the national honour is firmly maintained abroad, and while justice is impartially administered at home, the obedience of the subject will be voluntary, cheerful, and I might almost say unlimited. A generous nation is grateful even for the preservation of its rights; and willingly extends the affection due to the office of a good prince into an affection for his person. Loyalty in the heart and *understanding* of an Englishman is a *rational* attachment to the guardian of the laws.

Whilst we also determine to avoid all direct interference with another subject of importance still more vital and profound, we feel confident that by the light which we propose to diffuse, we shall strengthen rather than invalidate its sanctions. That system of morality, which has for the basis of its social regulations the plain, comprehensive, practical, and persuasive injunction, to "do unto others, that which we wish others should do unto us;" and that system of religion, which assures us that "this mortal shall put on immortality;" which imparts to us a knowledge

> Of things above this world, and of their being
> Who dwell in Heaven;

and which promises, after the best and happiest employment of this transitory condition, an endless progression in knowledge and felicity, never can be defrauded of their paramount influence upon the heart of man, by measures which are calculated to enlarge his intellectual possessions. By looking abroad through nature, it is obvious likewise, that our conceptions of the stupendous power of its Omniscient Author, must be improved, enlarged, and exalted; and a frequent reverential scrutiny during the search after final causes, into the designs of creation, will gradually and impressively unfold their wisdom and benevolence: thereby unavoidably augmenting our instinctive and acquired feelings, of gratitude and veneration towards Omnipotence. "Every man," says the late candid and distinguished theologian Dr. Paley,

> has some particular train of thought, which, more than any other, determines his character. This train may be more or less judiciously fixed;

but, in a moral view, there is no contradiction, that if one train be more desirable than another, it is that which regards the phenomena of nature, with a constant reference to a supreme, intelligent Author. To have made this the habitual sentiment of our minds, is to have laid the foundation of every thing which is religious. The world from thence becomes a temple, and life itself one continued act of adoration.

REVIVAL OF RADICALISM

Sir Francis Burdett's protest against the imprisonment of John Gale Jones, a radical orator, 23 March 1810

Sir Francis Burdett to his Constituents; Denying the power to the House of Commons to imprison the People of England (London: R. Bagshaw, 1810), 8-page pamphlet.

The House of Commons committed Burdett (1770-1844) to the Tower for reprinting this speech, an event which touched off considerable unrest in London. A champion of free speech, he entered the House of Commons in 1796. He advocated both parliamentary and prison reform, the removal of Catholic disabilities, and the abolition of flogging in the army.

[Piccadilly]

Gentlemen; The House of Commons having passed a Vote, which amounts to a declaration, that an Order of theirs is to be of more weight than Magna Charta and the Laws of the Land, I think it my duty to lay my sentiments thereon before my Constituents, whose characters as free-men, and even whose personal safety, depend, in so great a degree, upon the decision of this question—a question of no less importance than this: Whether our liberty be still to be secured by the laws of our fore-fathers, or be to lay at the absolute mercy of a part of our fellow-subjects, collected together by means which it is not necessary for me to describe.

In order to give to this subject all the attention to which it is entitled; and to avoid the danger to be apprehended from partial views and personal feeling, it will be advisable to argue the question on its own merits, putting the individual (however we may deplore his present sufferings) out of view; though at the same time, every man ought to consider the case his own; because, should the principle, upon which the Gentlemen of the House of Commons have thought proper to act in this instance, be once admitted, it is impossible for any one to conjecture how soon he himself may be summoned from his dwelling, and be hurried, without trial, and without oath made against him, from the bosom of his family into the clutches of a jailor. It is, therefore, now the time to resist the doctrine upon which Mr. Jones has been sent to Newgate; or, it is high time to cease all pretensions to those Liberties which were acquired by our forefathers, after so many struggles and so many sacrifices.

Either the House of Commons is authorised to dispense with the Laws of the Land; or it is not. If the Constitution be of so delicate a texture, so weak a frame, so fragile a substance, that it is to be only spoken of in terms of admiration, and to be viewed merely as a piece of curious but unprofitable workmanship; if Magna

Charter and all the wholesome Laws of England be a dead-letter: in that case, the affirmative of the proposition may be admitted; but, if the Constitution lives, and is applicable to its ends; namely, the happiness of the community, the perfect security of the life, liberty and property of each member and all the members of the society; then the affirmative of the proposition can never be admitted; then must we be freemen; for we need no better security, no more powerful protection for our Rights and Liberties, than the Laws and Constitution. We seek for, and we need seek for, *nothing new*; we ask for no more than what our fore-fathers insisted upon as their own; we ask for no more than what they bequeathed unto us; we ask for no more than what they, in the Testament which some of them had sealed, and which the rest of them were ready to seal, with their blood, expressly declared to be "*the Birthright* of the People of England;" namely, "*The Laws Of England*". To these Laws we have a right to look, with confidence, for security—to these laws the individual now imprisoned has, through me, applied for redress, in vain. Those, who have imprisoned him, have refused to listen to my voice, weakly expressing the strong principles of the Law, the undeniable claims of this Englishman's "*Birth-right.*" Your voice may come with more force; may command greater respect; and, I am not without hope, that it may prove irresistible, if it proclaim to this House of Commons in the same tone as the tongues of our ancestors proclaimed to the Kings of old, "*Nolumus Leges Angliae Mutari*"; or, in our own more clear and not less forcible language; "*The Laws of England Shall Not Be Changed.*"

The Principle, fellow-citizens, for which we are now contending, is the same Principle, for which the people of England have contended from the earliest ages, and their glorious success in which contests are now upon record in the Great Charter of our Rights and Liberties, and in divers other subsequent Statutes of scarcely less importance. It was this same great Principle, which was again attacked by Charles the First. In the measure of Ship Money, when again the people of England and an uncorrupted House of Commons renewed the contest; a contest which ended in the Imprisonment, the Trial, the Condemnation, and the Execution of that ill-advised King. The self same Principle it was, that was so daringly violated by his Son James the Second; and for which violation he was compelled to flee from the just indignation of the people, who not only stript him of his Crown, but who prevented that Crown from descending to his family. In all these contests, the courage, perseverance, and fortitude of our ancestors, conspicuous as they were, were not more so than their wisdom; for, talk as long as we will about Rights, Liberties, Franchises, Privileges and Immunities, of what avail are any, or all of these together, if our Persons can, at the sole will and command of any man, or set of men, be seized on, thrown into prison, and there kept during the pleasure of that man, or set of men? If every one of you be liable, at any time, to be sent to jail without trial, and without oath made against you, and there to be detained as long as it pleases the parties sending you there (perhaps to the end of your life), without any Court to appeal to, without any means of redress: if this be the case, shall we still boast of the Laws and of the Liberties of England? Volumes have been written by Foreigners as well as by our own countrymen in praise of that part of our Law, which in so admirable a manner, provides for our personal safety against any attacks of men in power. This has, indeed, been, in all ages, the pride of our country; and it is the maintenance of this principle which enabled us to escape that bondage, in which all the States and Kingdoms in Europe were enthralled by abandoning and yielding it up; and, we may be assured, that if we now abandon it, the bright days of England's glory will set in the night of her disgrace.

But, I would fain believe that such is not to be our fate. Our Fore-fathers made stern grim-visaged *Prerogative* hide his head: they broke in pieces his sharp and massy sword. And, shall we, their Sons, be afraid to enter the lists with undefined *Privilege*, assuming the powers of Prerogative?

I shall be told, perhaps, that there is not much danger of this power being *very frequently* exercised. The same apology may be made for the exercise of any power, whatever. I do not suppose that the Gentlemen of the House of Commons will send any of you to jail, when you do not displease them. Mr. Yorke did not move for the sending of Mr. Jones to jail, until Mr. Jones displeased him; but, it is not a very great compliment to pay to any Constitution, to say, that it does not permit a man to be imprisoned, unless he has done something to displease persons in power. It would be difficult, I should suppose, to find any man upon earth, however despotic his disposition, who would not be contented with the power of sending to prison, during his pleasure, every one who should dare to do any thing to displease him. Besides, when I am told, that there is little danger that the Gentlemen in the House of Commons will *often* exercise this power, I cannot help observing, that, though the examples may be few, their effect will, naturally, be great and general. At this moment, it is true, we see but one man actually in jail for having displeased those Gentlemen; but the fate of this one man (as is the effect of all punishments) will deter others from expressing their opinions of the conduct of those who have had the power to punish him. And, moreover, it is in the nature of all power, and especially of assumed and undefined power, to increase as it advances in age; and, as Magna Charta and the Law of the Land have not been sufficient to protect Mr. Jones; as we have seen him sent to jail for having described the conduct of one of the members as an *outrage upon public feeling*, what security have we, unless this power of Imprisonment be given up, that we shall not see other men sent to jail for stating their opinion respecting Rotten Boroughs, respecting Placemen and Pensioners sitting in the House; or, in short, for making any declaration, giving any opinion, stating any fact, betraying any feeling, whether by writing, by word of mouth, or by gesture, which may displease any of the Gentlemen assembled in St. Stephen's Chapel?

Then, again, as to the *kind* of punishment; why should they stop at sending persons to jail? If they can send whom they please to jail; if they can keep the persons, so sent, in jail as long as they please; if they can set their prisoners free at the end of the first hour, or keep them confined for seven years: if, in short, their absolute Will is to have the force of Law, what security can you have, that they will stop at *Imprisonment*? If they have the absolute power of imprisoning and releasing, why may they not send their prisoners to York-Jail as well as to a jail in London? Why not confine men in solitary cells, or load them with chains and bolts? They have not gone these lengths yet; but, what is there to restrain them, if they are to be the sole judges of the extent of their own powers, and if they are to exercise those powers without any controul, and without leaving the parties, whom they choose to punish, any mode of appeal, any means of redress?

That a Power such as this should exist in any country it is lamentable to be obliged to believe; but, that it should be suffered to exist, and that its existence should be openly and even boastfully avowed, in a country, whose chief glory has been its free constitution of government, is something too monstrous to be believed, if the proof were not before our eyes. Had the least doubt hung upon my mind of the illegality of the proceedings in the present case, it would have been altogether removed by the answers given to the references made by me to the Great Luminaries of our Law and to the Laws themselves. The Argument, by which I endeavoured to convince the Gentlemen of the House of Commons, that their acts, in the case of Mr. Jones, were illegal, I shall now lay before you, in a more full and connected way than it could possibly be done by the Parliamentary Reporters; and, in doing this, I shall do all that now remains in my power towards the correction of this, as I deem it, most enormous Abuse of Power, and most dangerous of all encroachments upon the Rights and Liberties of Englishmen.

> I remain, Gentlemen, Your most
> obedient, humble Servant,

Francis Burdett

Speech by Lord Byron opposing the Frame Work Bill, House of Lords, 27 February 1812

Hansard, n.s., XXI, 966-72.

This bill provided the death penalty for machine breaking, and was passed in response to outbreaks of industrial sabotage in the Midlands and Yorkshire. The Luddite movement, as it came to be known, was lead by stockingers, croppers, and other handworkers who feared replacement by the machine. Byron (1788-1824) spoke only twice in the House of Lords; this was his maiden speech.

My Lords; the subject now submitted to your lordships for the first time, though new to the House, is by no means new to the country. I believe it had occupied the serious thoughts of all descriptions of persons, long before its introduction to the notice of that legislature, whose interference alone could be of real service. As a person in some degree connected with the suffering county, though a stranger not only to this House in general, but to almost every individual whose attention I presume to solicit, I must claim some portion of your lordships' indulgence, whilst I offer a few observations on a question in which I confess myself deeply interested.

To enter into any detail of the Riots would be superfluous: the House is already aware that every outrage short of actual bloodshed, has been perpetrated, and that the proprietors of the Frames obnoxious to the rioters, and all persons supposed to be connected with them, have been liable to insult and violence. During the short time I recently passed in Nottinghamshire, not twelve hours elapsed without some fresh act of violence; and on the day I left the county I was informed that forty frames had been broken the preceding evening, as usual, without resistance and without detection.

Such was then the state of that county, and such I have reason to believe it to be at this moment. But whilst these outrages must be admitted to exist to an alarming extent, it cannot be denied that they have arisen from circumstances of the most unparalleled distress: The perseverance of these miserable men in their proceedings, tends to prove that nothing but absolute want could have driven a large, and once honest and industrious, body of the people, into the commission of excesses so hazardous to themselves, their families, and the community. At the time to which I allude, the town and county were burthened with large detachments of the military; the police was in motion, the magistrates assembled, yet all the movements civil and military had led to—nothing. Not a single instance had occurred of the apprehension of any real delinquent actually taken in the fact, against whom there existed legal evidence sufficient for conviction. But the police, however useless, were by no means idle: several notorious delinquents had been detected; men, liable to conviction, on the clearest evidence, of the capital crime of Poverty; men, who had been nefariously guilty of lawfully begetting several children, whom, thanks to the times! they were unable to maintain. Considerable injury has been done to the proprietors of the improved Frames. These machines were to them an advantage, inasmuch as they superseded the necessity of employing a number of workmen, who were left in consequence to starve. By the adoption of one species of Frame in particular, one man performed the work of many, and the superfluous labourers were thrown out of employment. Yet it is to be observed, that the work thus executed was inferior in quality; not marketable at home, and merely hurried over with a view to exportation. It was called in the cant of the trade, by the name of "Spider work." The rejected workmen in the blindness of their ignorance, instead of rejoicing at these improvements in arts so beneficial to mankind, conceived themselves to be sacrificed to improvements in mechanism. In the foolishness of their hearts they imagined, that the maintenance and well doing of the industrious poor, were objects of greater consequence than the enrichment of a few individuals by any improvement, in the implements of trade, which threw the workmen out of employment, and rendered the labourer unworthy of his hire. And it must be confessed that although the adoption of the enlarged machinery in that state of our commerce which the country once boasted might have been beneficial to the master without being detrimental to the servant; yet, in the present situation of our manufactures, rotting in warehouses, without a prospect of exportation, with the demand for work and workmen equally diminished; Frames of this description, tend materially to aggravate the distress and discontent of the disappointed sufferers. But the real cause of these distresses and consequent disturbances lies deeper. When we are told that these men are leagued together not only for the destruction of their own comfort, but of their very means of subsistence, can we forget that it is the bitter policy, the destructive warfare of the last 18 years, which has destroyed their comfort, your comfort, all mens' comfort? That policy, which, originating with "great statesmen now no more," has survived the dead to become a curse on the living, unto the third and fourth generation! These men never destroyed their looms till they were become useless, worse than useless; till they were become actual impediments to their exertions in obtaining their daily bread. Can you, then, wonder that in times like these, when bankruptcy, convicted fraud, and imputed felony are found in a station not far beneath that of your lordships, the lowest, though once most useful portion of the people, should forget their duty in their distresses, and become only less guilty than one of their representatives? But while the exalted offender can find means to baffle the law, new capital punishments must be devised, new snares of death must be spread for the wretched mechanic who is famished into guilt. These men were willing to dig, but the spade was in other hands: they were not ashamed to beg, but there was none to relieve them: their own means of subsistence were cut off, all other employments pre-occupied, and their excesses, however to be deplored and condemned, can hardly be subject of surprise.

It has been stated that the persons in the temporary possession of Frames connive at their destruction; if this be proved upon enquiry, it were necessary that such material accessories to the crime, should be principals in the punishment. But I did hope, that any measure proposed by his Majesty's government, for your lordships' decision, would have had conciliation for its basis; or, if that were hopeless, that some previous enquiry, some deliberation would have been deemed requisite; not that we should have been called at once without examination, and without cause, to pass sentences by wholesale, and sign death-warrants blindfold. But, admitting that these men had no cause of complaint; that the grievances of them and their employers were alike groundless; that they deserved the worst, what inefficiency, what imbecility has been evinced in the method chosen to reduce them! Why were the military called out to be made a mockery of, if they were to be called out at all? As far as the difference of seasons would permit, they have merely parodied the summer campaign of major Sturgeon; and, indeed, the whole proceedings, civil and military, seemed on the model of those of the Mayor and Corporation of Garratt.—Such marchings and counter marchings! from Nottingham to Bullwell, from Bullwell to Banford, from Banford to Mansfield! and when at length the detachments arrived at their destination, in all "the pride, pomp, and circumstance of glorious war," they came just in time to witness the mischief which had been done, and ascertain the escape of the perpetrators, to collect the "spolia opima" in the fragments of broken frames, and return to their quarters amidst the derision of old women, and the hootings of children. Now, though in a free country, it were to be wished, that our military should never be too formidable, at least to ourselves, I cannot see the policy of placing them in situations where they can only be made ridiculous. As the sword is the worst argument that can be used, so should it be the last. In this instance it has been the first; but providentially as yet only in the scabbard. The present measure will, indeed, pluck it from the sheath; yet had proper meetings been held in the earlier stages of these riots, had the grievances of these men and their masters (for they also had their grievances) been fairly weighed and justly examined, I do think that means might have been devised to restore these workmen to their avocations, and tranquillity to the county. At present the county suffers from the double infliction of an idle military and a starving population. In what state of apathy have we been plunged so long, that now for the first time the House has been officially apprized of these disturbances? All this has been transacting within 130 miles of London, and yet we, "good easy men, have deemed full sure our greatness was a ripening," and have sat down to enjoy our foreign triumphs in the midst of domestic calamity. But all the cities you have taken, all the armies which have retreated before your leaders are but paltry subjects of self congratulation, if your land divides against itself, and your dragoons and your executioners must be let loose against your fellow citizens.—You call these men a mob, desperate, dangerous, and ignorant; and seem to think that the only way to quiet the "Bellua multorum capitum" is to lop off a few of its superfluous heads.— But even a mob may be better reduced to reason by a mixture of conciliation and firmness, than by additional irritation and redoubled penalties. Are we aware of our obligations to a mob? It is the mob that labour in your fields and serve in your houses, that man your navy, and recruit your army, that have enabled you to defy all the world, and can also defy you when neglect and calamity have driven them to despair. You may call the people a mob, but do not forget, that a mob too often speaks the sentiments of the people. And here I must remark with what alacrity you are accustomed to fly to the succour of your distrest allies, leaving the distressed of your own country to the care of Providence or—the Parish. When the Portuguese suffered under the retreat of the French every arm was stretched out, every hand was opened, from the rich man's largess, to the widow's mite, all was bestowed to enable them to rebuild their villages and replenish their granaries. And at this moment, when thousands of misguided but most unfortunate fellow-countrymen are struggling with the extremes of hardships and hunger, as your charity began abroad it should end at home. A much less sum, a tithe of the bounty bestowed on Portugal, even if those men (which I cannot admit without enquiry) could not have been restored to their employments, would have rendered unnecessary the tender mercies of the bayonet and the gibbet. But doubtless our friends have too many foreign claims to admit a prospect of domestic relief; though never did such objects demand it. I have traversed the seat of war in the peninsula, I have been in some of the most oppressed provinces of Turkey, but never under the most despotic of infidel governments did I behold such squalid wretchedness as I have seen since my return in the very heart of a Christian country. And what are your remedies? After months of inaction, and months of action worse than inactivity, at length comes forth the grand specific, the never failing nostrum of all state physicians, from the days of Draco to the present time. After feeling the pulse and shaking the head over the patient, prescribing the usual course of warm water and bleeding, the warm water of your maukish police, and the lancets of your military, these convulsions must terminate in death, the sure consummation of the prescriptions of all political Sangrados. Setting aside the palpable injustice and the certain inefficiency of the Bill, are there not capital punishments sufficient in your statutes? Is there not blood enough upon your penal code, that more must be poured forth to ascend to Heaven and testify against you? How will you carry the Bill into effect? Can you commit a whole county to their own prisons? Will you erect a gibbet in every field and hang up men like scarecrows? or will you proceed (as you must to bring this measure into effect) by decimation? place the county under martial law? depopulate and lay waste all around you? and restore Sherwood forest as an acceptable gift to the crown, in its former condition of a royal chase and an asylum for outlaws? Are these the remedies for a starving and desperate populace? Will the famished wretch who has braved your bayonets, be appalled by your gibbets? When death is a relief, and the only relief it appears that you will afford him, will he be dragooned into tranquillity? Will that which could not be effected by your grenadiers, be accomplished by your executioners? If you proceed by the forms of law where is your evidence? Those who have refused to impeach their accomplices, when transportation only was the punishment, will hardly be tempted to witness against them when death is the penalty. With all due deference to the noble lords opposite, I think a little investigation, some previous enquiry would induce even them to change their purpose. That most favourite state measure, so marvellously efficacious in many and recent instances, temporizing, would not be without its advantages in this. When a proposal is made to emancipate or relieve, you hesitate, you deliberate for years, you temporise and tamper with the minds of men; but a death-bill must be passed offhand, without a thought of the consequences. Sure I am from what I have heard, and from what I have seen, that to pass the Bill under all the existing circumstances, without enquiry, without deliberation, would only be to add injustice to irritation, and barbarity to neglect. The framers of such a Bill must be content to inherit the honours of that Athenian lawgiver whose edicts were said to be written not in ink but in blood. But suppose it past; suppose one of these men, as I have seen them,— meagre with famine, sullen with despair, careless of a life which your lordships are perhaps about to value at something less than the price of a stocking-frame—suppose this man surrounded by the children for whom he is unable to procure bread at the hazard of his existence, about to be torn for ever from a family which he lately supported in peaceful industry, and which it is not his fault that he can no longer so support, suppose this man, and there are ten thousand such from whom you may select your victims, dragged into court, to be tried for this new offence, by this new law; still, there are two things wanting to convict and condemn him; and these are, in my opinion,—Twelve Butchers for a Jury, and a Jefferies for a Judge!

Description by Robert Owen of his reforms at New Lanark, 1812

Robert Owen, *A Statement Regarding the New Lanark Establishment* (Edinburgh: John Muir, 1812), 23-page pamphlet.

Robert Owen (1771-1858), the Welsh reformer, purchased the New Lanark cotton mills in Scotland and initiated a comprehensive plan for ameliorating the conditions of his workers. Owen subsequently developed a social theory based on small villages of cooperation and became one of the most influential British thinkers of the nineteenth century.

About twenty-six years ago, the late Mr David Dale of Glasgow, whose benevolence and philanthropy are well known, commenced an extensive spinning establishment near the Falls of the Clyde, and he founded it on the combined principles of public and private advantage.

It was continued by him for upwards of thirteen years, when, having no sons to succeed him, and being far advanced in life, he sold it to some English merchants, and myself, who married his eldest daughter.

These gentlemen remained in partnership with me ten years, when some of them resold their interest in it to merchants resident in Glasgow, who still hold these shares. But from the first sale by Mr Dale, until midsummer last, the management of the establishment was under my direction. At the commencement of that period, I arranged the outline of a plan, on a principle on which I had previously acted in a different part of the kingdom for several years; which was intended to unite and bring into action all the local advantages of the situation; to produce the greatest ultimate profits to the proprietors, with the greatest comfort and improvement to the numerous population to whom it afforded employment; that the latter might be a model and example to the manufacturing community, which, without some essential change in the formation of their characters, threatened, and now still more threatens, to revolutionize and ruin the empire. The plan was founded on the simple and evident principle, that any characters, from the savage to the sage or intelligent benevolent man, might be formed, by applying the proper means, and that these means are to a great extent at the command and under the controul of those who have influence in society; and, although mankind are generally unconscious of these important powers, there are few things admitting of any doubt, which are so easy as this, of full and complete demonstration. This system has been pursued at these works, without a single exception from the principle stated, for 13 years, and the result has been precisely that which was calculated. The population originally brought to the establishment was, with a few exceptions, a collection of the most ignorant and destitute from all parts of Scotland, possessing the usual characteristics of poverty and ignorance. They were generally indolent, and much addicted to theft, drunkenness, and falsehood, with all their concomitant vices, and strongly experiencing the misery which these ever produce. But by means so gradually introduced, as to be almost imperceptible to them, they have been surrounded with those circumstances which were calculated, first to check, and then to remove their inducements to retain these inclinations; and they are now become conspicuously honest, industrious, sober, and orderly; so that an idle individual, one in liquor, or a thief, is scarcely to be seen from the beginning to the end of the year; and they are become almost a new people, and quite ready to receive any fixed character which may be deemed the most advantageous for them to possess.

I was proceeding in preparing the means for accomplishing *this* object, when those gentlemen, who had lately become part proprietors with me of the Establishment, and who rather wished to employ their capital for a more immediate return of profit, objected to this system being pursued, and, alarmed at the events of the times, they would not consent to the temporary expenditure required for carrying it into execution.

I have said, temporary expenditure, because a comparatively small sum to that which had been expended; and a short period of time would have enabled me to complete the great outline of the plan; and in one year more, this latter part alone would have repaid the extra expense, besides giving important permanent advantages to the establishment.

In justice, however, to these gentlemen, it is necessary to state, that they are almost all strangers to the establishment and business; and that during the short period they have been part proprietors with me of the concern, they have not drawn any profits beyond the interest of their capital out of it; for, owing to our foreign political relations, which had created unknown difficulties in the commercial world, it had become necessary to reinvest these in the improvements, to place the concern beyond the risk of similar events, and enable it to meet them with success; and, in consequence of the profits being so expended, a permanent saving, exceeding six thousand pounds per annum, has been effected, and a considerable progress has also been made towards the reduction of a still larger annual sum. The contract of the company, however, vested the legal direction of the business in a majority of the shares, and they held a majority, although I possess a greater number of shares than any other individual; and, for the reasons previously stated, they came to a resolution of putting a stop to all those plans which I had in progress for the farther improvement of the community, and ultimate profit to the concern; and which, by the facts they would have established, had the plan been continued, would have soon created a very beneficial change in society, rendering that which now appears inconsistent and uncontroulable [sic] among the ignorant, plain, evident, and of easy direction. Under these circumstances, rather than be the active means of destroying a system which promises such important public as well as private advantages, and which had cost me many years close application and study, and much individual expense, I resigned the management; and the other proprietors are now endeavouring to conduct the establishment; but as they do not understand the principles on which it has been formed, and by which it is yet supported, I see the whole in their hands will soon become a manufacturing concern, similar to others in the kingdom; but I fear it will prove too extensive for them to manage with success on any other principles than those on which it has hitherto proceeded, as all its parts have been arranged to form a complete whole. In consequence, I have inquired if they will sell the interest they hold in the business, and have been given to understand, that they are willing to dispose of it on the same terms they purchased about two years ago; and if the system hitherto adopted shall be persevered in, those terms cannot fail to prove highly advantageous to the parties purchasing. I have, therefore, now to consider what is the best practicable plan for carrying these important objects into execution; for my own means are inadequate to so extensive an undertaking. But it may be said, that new schemes are hourly brought forward in all parts of the kingdom, and that ninety-nine of these out of every hundred prove visionary.

This is true; and, in reply to a fact so well known, I have to state, that this establishment has now existed upwards of twenty-six years; that besides the profits which the first proprietor derived from it, during thirteen years from its commencement, but which I have not the means of ascertaining, the latter proprietors have received, over and above five per cent. per annum upon all the capital employed in it, upwards of fifty thousand pounds; besides supporting above two thousand individuals, without any employment, for four months, at an expense exceeding seven thousand pounds. And in the same period, improvements have been carried on and finished out of the profits, which have now increased the powers of produce at the establishment to five times their original extent, and at an annual reduction of prime cost of nearly sixty thousand pounds, with a great improvement of quality in the material produced; and a considerable progress has also been made towards completing six times the extent, at an annual reduction of prime cost, exceeding eighty-five thousand pounds, which will be the state of the establishment at the end of next year. In the same period, also, an addition has been made to the village, forming part of the establishment, to contain from eleven to twelve hundred more inhabitants, which have been added to its population; and these, with the former occupiers of the houses, have been provided with all manner of public conveniencies and external comforts; and the most ample means were in preparation, and far advanced, to give their children the most beneficial education for their station in the community, and effectually to train them to habits which could not fail to make them valuable members of society. In consequence, likewise, of this system having been adopted and persevered in, the establishment, in a mercantile view, while supported by an adequate capital, is now put beyond the risk of ordinary circumstances; for the produce of it is of the nature of a raw material, applicable to the common purposes of male and female clothing in all ranks of life; it is of course in general demand, and will be always required; and although these improvements have cost upwards of eighty thousand pounds, it can now be produced, covering that expense, as low,—and, in a few months, when the arrangements in progress, which include the daily supply of fuel, food, clothes, and employment, for the whole population, shall be completed,—will be produced lower than it can be at any other establishment: Its success, therefore, becomes as certain as that of any mercantile or manufacturing concern in the kingdom, and so soon as peace shall again take place, very abundant profits may be reasonably expected, while an immediate return of ten per cent. on the capital to be advanced, may be confidently calculated upon. But to those who feel a deep interest in the well-being of their fellow-creatures, it will be considered of far more importance, that the slothful are become diligent, the thief honest, the drunkard sober, the licentious temperate, the wretched and diseased healthy, and comparatively happy; that poors' rates and litigation are banished from the community; and that the rising generation are now acquiring those habits and that knowledge which give the most heartfelt gratification to all who visit them. In consequence the village and works, which have been created at an expense probably of two hundred thousand pounds, have now more the appearance of a national benevolent institution, than of manufacturing works founded by an individual; and in fact it has become a national establishment of high interest to the community; for it may now be justly said to be the best model in practice of a charitable institution, which, in lieu of debasing the character of the poor, and impoverishing the rich, directs and enables the former to support themselves in comfort and independence, and, by their industry and good conduct, to add essentially to the national wealth and resources.

If, then, the principles on which this system has been founded, have already effected these beneficial changes, of which all may now satisfy themselves, allow me to say, on the credit of that which has been accomplished, that those parts of it which were in progress, and are to follow, would yet effect far more extensive and important improvements, and give the whole stability.

But it may be necessary to explain more particularly what I mean by those plans which I had in progress, for the further improvement of the community, and ultimate profit to the concern.

They were intended to *increase* the population, diminish its expense, *add* to its domestic comforts, and greatly improve its character. Towards effecting these purposes, a building has been erected, which may be termed the "*New Institution,*" situated in the centre of the establishment, with an inclosed area before it. The objects intended to be accomplished by which are, *first,* To obtain for the children, from the age of two to five, a play-ground, in which they may be easily superintended, and their young minds properly directed, while the time of the parents will be much more usefully occupied, both for themselves and the establishment. This part of the plan arose from observing, that the tempers of children among the lower orders are generally spoiled, and vicious habits strongly formed, previous to the time when they are usually sent to school; and, to create the characters desired, these must be prevented, or as much as possible counteracted. The area is also to afford a place of meeting for the children, from the age of five to ten, previous to and after school hours, and to serve the boys for a drill-ground. It likewise contains conveniencies calculated to give the children such habits as will enable the master of police to keep the village in a decent, clean state; and this is no small difficulty to overcome, where other habits have always obtained.

Secondly, To procure a large store-cellar, which was much wanted, and, by this arrangement, has been placed in the most advantageous situation for both the works and village; and it will be found to be of much use to the establishment.

Thirdly, A kitchen upon a large scale, in which food may be prepared of a better quality, and at a much lower rate, than individual families can now obtain it; for, under this arrangement, two or three fires, and half a dozen attendants, will supersede the necessity of several hundred fires, and as many attendants, particularly in summer; and the provisions will be prepared of the most wholesome and nutritious materials, obtained at the cheapest rates, aided by every known conveniency, and the best information which can be collected on the subject. It is obvious, that most of the families among the working class, are unusually destitute of all these advantages.

Fourthly, An eating-room immediately adjoining the kitchen, one hundred and ten feet by forty within, in which those to whom it may be convenient may take all their regular meals. As several of the young persons employed at the works, reside at the county town of Lanark, more than a mile distant, and from which their meals are regularly sent at considerable trouble and expense; and as a still greater number *lodge* in the village, and now inconveniently board themselves, these will all find an immediate benefit from both the kitchen and eating-room, and they afford so many substantial advantages to the general inhabitants of the place, that it is to be feared the space allotted for the eating-room, ample as it may appear, will soon be found too circumscribed.

Fifthly, The eating-room, by an immediate removal of the tables to the ceiling, will afford space in which the younger part of the adults of the establishment may dance three nights in a week during winter, one hour each night; and which, under proper regulations, is expected to contribute essentially to their health. This part of the plan is considered of some importance, because, during the short days of winter, the young people have no means of enjoying exercise in the open air, and this can be obtained as a substitute, at a trifling expense; and this change of motion, from their constant occupations, will be most favourable for their spirits, and a strong source of attachment to the works.

Sixthly, Another room, the whole length of the building, being 140 feet long, 40 wide, and 20 high, which is to be the general education-room and church for the village, and those who attend the works. In this it was intended, that the boys and girls were to be taught to read well, and to understand what they read; to write expeditiously a good legible hand, and to learn correctly; so that they may comprehend and use with facility the fundamental rules of arithmetic. The girls were also to be taught to sew, cut out, and make up useful family garments; and, after becoming perfect in these, they were to attend in rotation in the kitchen and eating-room, to learn to cook cheap and nutritious food, and to clean and keep a house neat and in order. And the boys were to be taught in the drill-ground the manual exercise, and as much of the principles of military tactics as would enable them, with a little previous practice, at any future period of their lives, aided also by the sentiments they would acquire, to render the most effectual defence to their country.

Seventhly, This room was intended to be arranged, not only in the most convenient manner for the several branches of useful education enumerated, but also to serve for a lecture-room and church. The lectures were to be given in winter three nights a week, alternately with dancing, and to be familiar discourses to instruct the population in their domestic economy, particularly in the methods they should adopt in training up their children, and forming their habits from their earliest infancy, in which, at present, they are deplorably ignorant. By these lectures they were also to be taught how to expend their earnings to the most advantage, and to appropriate the surplus, which will arise to them in consequence, to create a well-regulated competency; thus relieving them from the anxious fear of want under any circumstances, or at any period, and giving them that rational independence arising from their own exertions and superior conduct, without which, consistency of character, or domestic comfort, are not to be expected. The church was intended to be a general one, so that no part of the population may be excluded from it, and open occasionally to every sect of Christians in their turn. But the great leading principles of its regular doctrines, were, to inculcate the healing of all religious differences,—a real respect for each others sentiments, on the ground that every individual, from one cause or other, which in general may be easily explained, must conscientiously deem his own the best, and which, indeed, is the only reason why they are entertained. And, above all, to enforce that most important precept, which, when fully comprehended, will be found alone sufficient to direct all our social intercourse, which is, "That there is no other way by which mankind can obtain general and continued happiness, than by training every individual from its infancy, to exert itself in promoting, with sincerity, the happiness of every other individual within its circle of action." And, by adopting the *proper* means, this may be universally taught with ease and with certainty.

And, *lastly,* The plan also included the improvement of the road from the works and village to the old town of Lanark, which is now almost impassable for young children in winter, and in such a state as to prevent in a great measure the population of the latter from being available for the manufacturing purposes of the former, and from deriving any benefit from its institutions, which are calculated to educate the whole of the children in the neighbourhood, as well as the works are to give them employment afterwards.

Beneficial as these arrangements, connected with the *New Institution,* must be to the individuals employed at the works, they will be at least equally advantageous, in a pecuniary view, to the proprietors of the establishment; for the whole expense of these combined operations will not exceed six thousand pounds, three thousand of which have been already expended; and, so far as my former experience enables me to judge of the consequences to arise from them, they cannot save less to the establishment than as many thousand pounds per annum, but probably much more.

First, By the improvement of the road between the old and new towns of Lanark, by shortening and widening it, and forming a good foot-path, making the distance easy and pleasant even for the youngest children from the former, to attend the schools and works at the latter, and which, with the conveniency of the public kitchen and eating-room, will make the population of the old town nearly as available for the objects of the establishment as that of the new is at present; giving a double supply of operatives for the same demand, and of course, constituting a perpetual check against any sudden and great advance of labour, which, in its consequences, is usually as injurious to those employed as to their employers.

Secondly, The kitchen and eating-room will enable the proprietors to support the population of the village, now exceeding 2200 individuals, at 1s. 6d. per week less than the expense at which they now feed themselves; which alone will constitute a saving of £8580 per annum, to be divided between the proprietors and population of both towns.

Thirdly, By the arrangements formed for the education of the children, they will be trained regularly for their employment, and all their habits, bodily and mental, formed to carry them to a high state of perfection; and this alone, in its consequences, will be of incalculable advantage to the concern; for to these people are entrusted the care and use of nice and valuable machinery, with a very great variety of materials requisite for the business, with all the varied operations of the manufacture of the establishment through all its processes to the annual value of two hundred thousand pounds, the cost and perfection of which depend essentially on their conduct; and a saving of one penny per lb. on the manufacture is now upwards of £6000 per annum, and in a short period, will be near £8000 per do.;— while hitherto, the works have been supplied with operatives from among strangers from all parts of the country, who have been instructed in the business at an almost incalculable loss and expense to the proprietors, besides keeping the establishment in a comparative stake of inferiority.

Advantageous, however, as these arrangements will be to the individuals employed at the works, and to the proprietors of the establishment, they will yet prove of far higher importance in a national view by the principles they will establish, and the consequences which will arise from them. For now, the manufacturing population of this country is feelingly alive to its apparent interests, extremely active, and that activity encreased to the highest pitch by the present state of commerce, requiring all their exertions for their support; but they are also, with partial exceptions, so ignorant as to be easily misdirected, and their numbers exceed the half of the population of the kingdom. Can such a combination of circumstances be contemplated without a conviction, that, if they shall be permitted to continue much longer without an effectual remedy being applied, very fatal consequences must be the result?

The principles on which the arrangements which have been explained have been formed, point out that remedy, and the experience of more than 20 years on an extended scale, prove them to be practically correct; and if they shall be generally adopted, the consequences will be, that not only our manufacturing but our entire population will gradually change its character; and if the means recommended shall be persevered in, it will ultimately become so well instructed, as to distinguish clearly between its true and apparent interests, and to detect the fallacy of those who might attempt to mislead them from the former. Poor's rates, the bane of the lower orders, would cease, foresight and temperance would generally prevail, their industry would be directed by intelligence, and the happiness they would soon experience in consequence, would render them a far more efficient and powerful population for their numbers than has ever yet existed, and with the resources which this country possesses, would make it impenetrable to foreign attack, however formidable it might be. Thus, if this plan had been pursued at these works but for one year longer, a population of from two to three thousand individuals would have been placed in a more happy situation than is to found in any manufacturing class at present known; and, from the singular success which their superior conduct must give to the establishment in a pecuniary view, permanence would be given to the system. And, that the advantages of such a system being seen upon an extended scale in practice, may not be lost to our country and the world in general,—

I propose, that an association of some of the leading and most patriotic characters in the country, should be formed, either by charter or otherwise, for the purpose of giving such weight and influence to the system, as would ensure its speedy and general adoption; for, as many of the most intelligent and enlightened men in the kingdom, of all sects and parties, who have seen it in practice, as well as several foreigners of the first distinction, who have also minutely inspected it, have, without one exception, given it their unqualified approbation, I consider it now ready to undergo the most severe scrutiny and investigation.

To conclude. I do not hesitate to say, that this experiment is the most important that has ever yet been attempted for the general happiness of society; and that, conscious of the security of the grounds on which I have proceeded, and mean to proceed, I am ready to pledge my life for its ultimate, full, and complete success.

"To the Journeymen and Labourers of England, Wales, Scotland, and Ireland" by William Cobbett, 2 November 1816

Cobbett's Weekly Political Register, 2 November 1816.

William Cobbett (1763-1835) was a popular journalist of extraordinary power and style. He wrote numerous tracts, books, and broadsides on a variety of subjects, but it was in his Political Register *(1802-35) that he achieved maximum influence as a reformer. In the following address he pinpointed the paper money system and heavy taxation as grievances productive of much of the distress of the period.*

Friends and Fellow Countrymen, Whatever the pride of rank, of riches, or of scholarship may have induced some men to believe, or to affect to believe, the real strength and all the resources of a country, ever have sprung and ever must spring, from the *labour* of its people; and hence it is, that this nation, which is so small in numbers and so poor in climate and soil compared with many others, has, for many ages, been the most powerful nation in the world: it is the most industrious, the most laborious, and therefore, the most powerful. Elegant dresses, superb furniture, stately buildings, fine roads and canals, fleet horses and carriages, numerous and stout ships, warehouses teeming with goods; all these, and many other objects that fall under our view, are so many marks of national wealth and resources. But all these spring from *labour*. Without the Journeyman and the labourer none of them could exist; without the assistance of their hands, the country would be a wilderness, hardly worth the notice of an invader.

As it is the labour of those who toil which makes a country abound in resources, so it is the same class of men, who must, by their arms, secure its safety and uphold its fame. Titles and immense sums of money have been bestowed upon numerous Naval and Military Commanders. Without calling the justice of these in question, we may assert that the victories were obtained by *you* and your fathers and brothers and sons in co-operation with those Commanders, who, with *your* aid have done great and wonderful things; but, who, without that aid, would have been as impotent as children at the breast.

With this correct idea of your own worth in your minds, with what indignation must you hear yourselves called the Populace, the Rabble, the Mob, the Swinish Multitude; and, with what greater indignation, if possible, must you hear the projects of those cool and cruel and insolent men, who, now that you have been, without any fault of yours, brought into a state of misery, propose to narrow the limits of parish relief, to prevent you from marrying in the days of your youth, or to thrust you out to seek your bread in foreign lands, never more to behold your parents or friends? But suppress your indignation, until we return to this topic, after we have considered the *cause* of your present misery and the *measures* which have produced that cause.

The times in which we live are full of peril. The nation, as described by the very creatures of the government, is fast advancing to that period when an important change must take place. It is the lot of mankind, that some shall labour with their limbs and others with their minds; and, on all occasions, more especially on an occasion like the present, it is the duty of the latter to come to the assistance of the former. We are all equally interested in the peace and happiness of our common country. It is of the utmost importance, that in the seeking to obtain those objects, our endeavours should be uniform, and tend all to the same point. Such an uniformity cannot exist without an uniformity of sentiment as to public matters, and, to produce this latter uniformity amongst you is the object of this address.

As to the *cause* of our present miseries, it is the *enormous amount of the taxes*, which the government compels us to pay for the support of its army, its placemen, its pensioners, etc. and for the payment of the interest of its debt. That this is the *real* cause has been a thousand times proved; and, it is now so acknowledged by the creatures of the government themselves. *Two hundred and five* of the Correspondents of the Board of Agriculture ascribe the ruin of the country to *taxation*. Numerous writers, formerly the friends of the Pitt System, now declare, that taxation has been the cause of our distress. Indeed, when we compare our present state to the state of the country previous to the wars against France, we must see that our present misery is owing to no other cause. The taxes then annually raised amounted to about 15 millions: they amounted last year to 70 millions. The nation was then happy: it is now miserable.

The writers and speakers, who labour in the cause of corruption, have taken infinite pains to make the *labouring classes* believe, that *they* are *not taxed*; that the taxes which are paid by the landlords, farmers, and tradesmen, do not affect the journeymen and labourers; and that the tax-makers have been *very* lenient towards *you*. But, I hope, that you see to the bottom of these things now. You must be sensible, that, if *all* your employers were *totally* ruined in one day, you would be *wholly* without employment and without bread; and, of course, in whatever *degree* your employers are deprived of their means, they must withold means from you. In America the most awkward common labourer receives five shillings a day, while provisions are cheaper in that country than in this. Here a carter, boarded in the house, receives about seven pounds a year; in America he receives about thirty pounds a year. What is it that makes this difference? Why in America the whole of the taxes do not amount to more than about *ten shillings* a head upon the whole of the population; while in England they amount to nearly *six pounds* a head. *There*, a journeyman or labourer may support his family well and save from thirty to sixty pounds a year: *here*, he amongst you is a lucky man, who can provide his family with food and with decent clothes to cover them, without any hope of possessing a penny in the days of sickness, or of old age. *There* the chief Magistrate receives 6000 pounds a year: *here* the civil list surpasses a million of pounds in amount, and as much is allowed to each of the *Princesses* in one year, as the chief Magistrate of America receives in two years though that country is nearly equal to this in population.

A Mr. Preston, a lawyer of great eminence, and a great praiser of Pitt, has just published a pamphlet in which is this remark: "It should always be remembered that every eighteen pounds a year paid to any placeman or pensioner, withdraws from the public the means of giving active employment to one individual as the head of a family; thus depriving five persons of the means of sustenance from the fruits of honest industry and active labour, *and rendering them paupers.*" Thus this supporter of Pitt acknowledges the great truth, that the taxes are the cause of a people's poverty and misery and degradation. We did not stand in need of this acknowledgment; but, it is good for us to see the friends and admirers of Pitt brought to make this confession.

It has been attempted to puzzle you with this sort of question: "If *taxes* be the cause of the people's misery, how come it that they were not so miserable *before* the taxes were reduced as they are *now*?" Here is a fallacy, which you will be careful to detect. I know that the taxes have been reduced; that is to say, *nominally* reduced, but not so in fact, on the contrary they have, in reality, been greatly augmented. This has been done by *the slight-of-hand of paper-money.* Suppose, for instance, that four years ago, I had 100 pounds to pay in taxes, *then* 130 bushels of wheat would have paid my share. If I have *now* seventy-five pounds to pay in taxes, it will require 190 bushels of wheat to pay my share of taxes. Consequently, though my taxes are *nominally* reduced, they are, in reality, greatly augmented. This has been done by the legerdemain of paper-money. In 1812, the pound note was worth only thirteen shillings in silver. It is now worth twenty shillings. Therefore, when we now pay a pound note to the tax-gatherer, we really pay him twenty shillings where we before paid him thirteen shillings; and the fundholders who lent pound notes worth thirteen shillings each, are now *paid* their interest in pounds worth twenty shillings each. And, the thing is come to what Sir Francis Burdett told the Parliament it would come to. He told them, in 1811, that if they ever attempted to pay the interest of their debt in gold and silver, or in paper-money equal in value to gold and silver, the farmers and tradesmen must be ruined, and the journeymen and labourers be reduced to the last stage of misery.

Thus, then, it is clear, that it is the weight of the taxes, under which you are sinking, which has already pressed so many of you down into the state of paupers, and which now threatens to deprive many of you of your existence. We next come to consider, what have been *the causes of this weight of taxes.* Here we must go back a little in our history, and you will soon see, that this intolerable weight has *all proceeded from the want of a Parliamentary Reform.*

In the year 1764, soon after the present king came to the throne, the annual interest of the debt amounted to about 5 millions, and the whole of the taxes to about nine millions. But, soon after this a war was entered on to compel the Americans to submit to be taxed by the Parliament *without being represented in that Parliament.* The Americans triumphed, and, after the war was over, the annual interest of the Debt amounted to about 9 millions and the whole of the taxes to about 15 millions. This was our situation, when the French people began their Revolution. The French people had so long been the slaves of a despotic government, that the friends of freedom in England rejoiced at their emancipation. The cause of *reform*, which had never ceased to have supporters in England for a great many years, now acquired new life, and the Reformers urged the Parliament to *grant reform*, instead of going to war against the people of France. The

Reformers said: "Give the nation *reform*, and you need fear no *revolution*." The Parliament, instead of listening to the Reformers, *crushed them*, and went to war against the people of France; and the consequence of these wars is, that the annual interest of the Debt now amounts to 45 millions, and the whole of the taxes, during each of the last several years, to 70 millions. So that these wars have *Added* 36 millions a year to the interest of the Debt, and 55 millions a year to the amount of the whole of the taxes! This is the price that we have paid for having checked (for it is only *checked*) the progress of liberty in France; for having forced upon that people the family of Bourbon, and for having enabled another branch of that same family to restore the bloody Inquisition which Napoleon had put down.

Since the restoration of the Bourbons and of the old government of France, has been as far as possible, the grand result of the contest; since this has been the *end* of all our fightings and all our past sacrifices and present misery and degradation; let us see (for the enquiry is now very full of interest,) what sort of government that was, which the French people had just destroyed when our government began its wars against that people.

If, only 28 years ago, any man in England had said, that the government of France was one that ought to be suffered to exist, he would have been hooted out of any company. It is notorious, that that government was a cruel despotism; and that we and our forefathers always called it such. This description of that government is to be found in all our histories, in all our Parliamentary debates, in all our books on government and politics. It is notorious, that the family of Bourbon have produced the most perfidious and bloody monsters that ever disgraced the human form. It is notorious, that millions of Frenchmen have been butchered and burnt and driven into exile by their commands. It is recorded even in the history of France, that one of them said, that the putrid carcass of a protestant smelt sweet to him. Even in these latter times, so late as the reign of Louis XIV. it is notorious, that hundreds of thousands of innocent people were put to the most cruel death. In some instances they were burnt in their houses; in others they were shut into lower rooms, while the incessant noise of kettle drums over their heads, day and night, drove them to raving madness. To enumerate all the infernal means employed by this tyrant to torture and kill the people would fill a volume. *Exile* was the lot of those who escaped the swords, the wheels, the axes, the gibbets, the torches of his hell-hounds. England was the place of refuge for many of these persecuted people. The grand-father of the present Earl of Radnor, and the father of the venerable Baron Masseres, were amongst them; and, it is well known that England owes no inconsiderable part of her manufacturing skill and industry to that atrocious persecution. Enemies of freedom, wherever it existed, this family of Bourbon, in the reign of Louis XIV. and XV. fitted out expeditions for the purpose of restoring the Stuarts to the throne of England, and thereby caused great expense and bloodshed to this nation; and, even the Louis, who was beheaded by his subjects, did in the most perfidious manner, make war upon England, during her war with America. No matter what was the nature of the cause, his conduct was perfidious; he professed *peace* while he was preparing for war. His object could not be to assist freedom, because his own subjects wery slaves.

Such was the *family* that were ruling in France, when the French Revolution began. After it was resolved to go to war against the people of France, all the hirelings of corruption were to set to work to gloss over the character and conduct of the old government, and to paint in the most horrid colours the acts of vengeance which the people were inflicting on the numerous tyrants, civil and military, and ecclesiastical, whom the change of things had placed at their mercy. The people's turn was now come, and, in the days of their power, they justly bore in mind the oppressions which they and their forefathers had endured. The *taxes*, imposed by the government, became, at last, intolerable. It had contracted a *great Debt* to carry on its wars. *In order to be able to pay the interest of this debt and to support an enormous standing army in time of peace*, it laid upon the people burdens, which they could no longer endure. It *fined* and *flogged fathers* and *mothers* if their *children* were detected in smuggling. Its courts of justice were filled with cruel and base judges. The nobility treated the common people like dogs; these latter were compelled to serve as *soldiers*, but were excluded from all share, or chance, of *honour* and *command*, which were *engrossed by the nobility*.

Now, when the time came for the people to have the power in *their* hands, was it surprizing, that the first use they made of it was to take vengeance on their oppressors? I will not answer this question myself. It shall be answered by Mr. Arthur Young, the present *Secretary of the Board of Agriculture*. He was in France at the time, and, living upon the very spot, and having examined into the causes of the revolution, he wrote and published the following remarks, in his *Travels*, Vol. I. page 603.

It is impossible to justify the excesses of the people on their taking up arms; they were certainly guilty of cruelties; it is idle to deny the facts, for they have been proved too clearly to admit of doubt. But is it really *The People*, to whom we are to impute the whole?—Or to *Their Oppressors*, who had kept them so long in a state of bondage? He who chooses to be served by slaves, and by ill treated slaves, must know that he holds both his property and his life by a tenure far different from those who prefer the service of well treated freemen; and he who *dines to the music of groaning sufferers*, must not, in the moment of insurrection, complain that his daughters are ravished, and then destroyed; and that his sons' throats are cut. When such evils happen, they surely are *more imputable to the tyranny of the master*, than to the cruelty of the servant. The analogy holds with the French peasants. The murder of a Seigneur, (a Lord,) or a country seat in flames, is recorded in every newspaper; the rank of the person who suffers, attracts notice; but where do we find *the registers of that seigneur's oppressions of his peasantry*, and his exactions of feudal services, *from those whose children were dying around them for want of bread*? Where do we find the minutes that assigned these starving wretches to some vile petty-fogger, to be fleeced by impositions, *and Mockery of Justice*, in the seigneural courts (petty courts of justice)? Who gives us the awards of the Intendant (Head Tax-collector) and his *sub-delegues*, which took off the taxes of a man of fashion, and laid them with accumulated weight, on the poor, who were so unfortunate, as to be his neighbours? Who has dwelt sufficiently upon explaining all the ramifications of despotism, *regal, aristocratical, and ecclesiastical*, pervading the *whole mass of the people*; reaching like a circulating fluid, the *most distant capillary tubes of poverty and wretchedness?* In these cases the sufferers are too ignoble to be known; and the mass *too indiscriminate to be pitied*. But, should a philosopher feel and reason thus? Should he mistake *the cause* for the *effect?* and giving all his pity *to the few*, feel no compassion *for the many*, because they suffer in his eyes, not individually, but *by millions?* The excesses of the people cannot, I repeat, be justified; it would undoubtedly have done them credit, both as men and as Christians, if they had possessed their new acquired power with moderation. But, let it be remembered, that the populace in no country ever use power with moderation; excess is inherent in their aggregate constitution: and as every government in the world knows, that violence infallibly attends power in such hands, it is doubly bound in common sense, and for common safety, so to conduct itself, that the people may not find an interest in public confusions. They will always *suffer much and long*, before they are effectually roused; nothing, therefore, can kindle the flame, but such oppressions of some classes or order in Society as give able men the opportunity of seconding the general mass; discontent will diffuse itself around; and if the government *Take Not Warning in Time*; it is *Alone answerable for all the burnings and all the plunderings and all the devastation and all the blood that follow.*

Who can deny the justice of these observations? It was the government *Alone* that was justly chargeable with the excesses committed in this early stage, and, in fact, in every other stage, of the revolution of France. If the government had given way *in Time*, none of these excesses would have been committed. If it had listened to the complaints, the prayers, the supplications, the cries, of the cruelly treated and starving people; if it had changed its conduct, reduced its expences, it might have been safe under the protection of the peace officers, and might have disbanded its standing army. But, it persevered; it relied upon the bayonet, and upon its judges and hangmen. The latter were destroyed, and the *former went over to the side of the people*. Was it any wonder that the people burnt the houses of their oppressors, and killed the owners and their families?—The country contained thousands upon thousands of men that had been ruined by taxation, and by judgments of infamous courts of justice, "a mockery of justice;" and, when these ruined men saw their oppressors at their feet, was it any wonder that they took vengeance upon them? Was it any wonder that the son, who had seen his father and mother flogged, because he, when a child, had smuggled *a handful of salt*, should burn for an occasion to shoot through the head the ruffians who had thus lacerated the bodies of his parents? Moses slew the insolent Egyptian who had smitten one of his countrymen in bondage. Yet Moses has never been called either a *murderer* or a *cruel wretch* for this act; and the bondage of the Israelites was light as a feather, compared to the tyranny under which the people of France had groaned for ages.

Moses resisted oppression in the only way that resistance was within his power. He knew that his countrymen had *no chance of justice in any court*; he knew that petitions against his oppressions were all in vain; and, "looking upon the *burdens*" of his countrymen, he resolved to begin the only sort of resistance that was left him. Yet, it was little more than a mere *insult* that drew forth his anger and resistance; and, if Moses was justified, as he clearly was, what needs there any apology for the people of France?

It seems, at first sight, very strange, that the government of France should not have "*taken warning in time.*" But, it had *so long* been in the habit of *despising the people*, that its mind was incapable of entertaining any notion of danger from the oppressions heaped upon them. It was surrounded with panders and parasites, who told it nothing but flattering falsehoods; and, it saw itself supported by 250,000 *bayonets*, which it thought irresistible; though it found in the end, that those, who wielded those bayonets were not long so base as to be induced, either by threats or promises, to butcher their brothers and sisters and parents.— And, if you ask me how the *Ministers* and the *Noblesse* and the *Priesthood*, who generally know pretty well how to take care of themselves; if you ask me, how it came to pass, that *they* did not "*take warning in time*," I answer, that they *did take warning*, but, that, seeing, that the change which was coming *would deprive them of a great part of their power and emoluments*, they resolved to *resist the change*, and to *destroy* the country, if possible, *rather than not have all its wealth and power to themselves*. The ruffian, whom we read of, a little time ago, who stabbed a young woman, because she was breaking from him to take the arm of another man whom she preferred, acted upon the principle of the Ministers, the Noblesse and the Clergy of France. They could no longer unjustly *possess*, therefore they would *destroy*. They saw that if a just government were established; that, if the people were fairly represented in a national council; they saw, that if this were to take place, they would no longer be able to wallow in wealth at the expence of the people; and, seeing this, *they resolved to throw all into confusion*, and, if possible, to make a heap of ruins of that country, which they could no longer oppress, and the substance of which they could no longer devour.

Talk of *violence* indeed! Was there any thing too violent, any thing too severe, to be inflicted on these men? It was *they* who produced confusion; it was *they* who caused the massacres and the guillotinings; it was *they* who destroyed the kingly government; it was *they* who brought the King to the block. They were answerable for *all* and for every single part of the mischief, as much as Pharaoh was for the plagues in Egypt, which history of Pharaoh seems, by the bye, to be intended as a lesson to all future tyrants. He "set task-masters over the Israelites to afflict them with burdens; and he made them build treasure cities for him; he made them serve with rigour; he made their lives bitter with hard bondage, in morter and in brick, and in all manner of service of the field; he denied them straw, and insisted upon their making the same quantity of bricks, and because they were unable to obey, the task-masters called them *idle* and *beat* them." Was it too much to scourge, and to destroy all the first born, of men who could tolerate, assist, and uphold a tyrant like this? Yet was Pharaoh less an oppressor than the old government of France.

Thus, then, we have a view of the former state of that country by wars against the people of which we have been brought into our present state of misery. There are many of the hirelings of corruption, who actually insist on it, that we ought now to go to war again for the restoring of *all* the cruel despotism which formerly existed in France. This is what cannot be done, however. Our wars have sent back the Bourbons; but the *tythes*, the *Seigneurs* (the Lords), and many other curses, have not been restored. The French people still enjoy much of the benefit of the revolution; and great numbers of their antient petty tyrants have been destroyed. So that, even were things *to remain as they are*, the French people have gained greatly by their revolution. But things cannot remain as they are. Better days are at hand.

In proceeding now to examine the *remedies* for your distresses, I shall first notice some of those, which foolish, or cruel and insolent men have proposed. Seeing that the *cause* of your misery is the *weight of taxation*, one would expect to hear of nothing but a *reduction of taxation* in the way of remedy; but, from the friends of corruption, never do we hear of any such remedy. To hear them, one would think, that *you* had been the guilty cause of the misery you suffer; and that you, and you alone, ought to be made answerable for what has taken place. The emissaries of corruption are now continually crying out against the *weight* of the *poor-rates*, and they seem to regard all that is taken in that way as a *dead loss to the Government!* Their project is, to deny relief to all who are *able to work.* But what is the use of your being *able* to work, if no one will, or can, give you work? To tell you that you must work for your bread, and, at the same time, not to find any work for you, is full as bad as it would be to order you to make bricks without straw. Indeed, it is rather more cruel and insolent; for Pharaoh's task-masters did point out to the Israelites that they might go into the fields and get *stubble*. The *Courier* newspaper, of the 9th October, says, "we must thus be *cruel* only to be *kind.*" I am persuaded, that you will not understand this kindness, while you will easily understand the cruelty. The notion of these people seems to be, that every body that receives money out of the taxes have *a right* to receive it, *except you*. They tremble at the fearful amount of the poor-rates: they say, and very truly, that those rates have risen from *two and a half* to *eight* or *ten* millions since the beginning of the wars against the people of France; they think, and not without reason, that these rates will soon swallow up nearly all the rent of the land. These assertions and apprehensions are perfectly well founded; but how can *you* help it? You have not had the management of the affairs of the nation. It is not *you* who have ruined the farmers and tradesmen. You want only food and raiment: you are ready to work for it; but you cannot go naked and without food.

But the complaints of these persons against you are the more unreasonable, because they say not a word against the sums paid to *Sinecure Placemen and pensioners*. Of the five hundred and more correspondents of the Board of Agriculture, there are scarcely ten, who do not complain of the weight of the poor-rates, of the immense sums taken away from them by the *poor*, and many of them complain of the *idleness* of the poor. But not one single man complains of the immense sums taken away to support *Sinecure Placemen*, who do *nothing* for their money, and to support pensioners, many of whom are *women* and *children*, the wives and daughters of the nobility and other persons in high life, and who can do nothing and never can have done any thing, for what they receive. There are of these places and pensions all sizes, from *twenty pounds* to *thirty thousand* and nearly *forty thousand pounds a year!* And, surely, these ought to be done away before any proposition be made to take the parish allowance from any of you, who are unable to work, or to find work to do. There are several individual placemen, the profits of *each* of which would maintain *a thousand families*. The names of the *Ladies* upon the pension list would, if printed one under another, fill a sheet of paper like this. And is it not, then, base and cruel at the same time in these Agricultural Correspondents to cry out so loudly against the charge of supporting the unfortunate *Poor*, while they utter not a word of complaint against the Sinecure Places and Pensions?

The unfortunate journeymen and labourers and their families have a right, they have a *just claim*, to relief from the purses of the rich. For, there can exist no riches and no resources, which they by their labour, have not *assisted to create*. But, I should be glad to know how the sinecure placemen and lady pensioners have assisted to create food and raiment, or the means of producing them. The labourer who is out of work, or ill, to-day, may be able to work, and set to work to-morrow. While those placemen and pensioners never can work; or, at least, it is clear that they never *intend* to do it.

You have been represented by the *Times* newspaper, by the *Courier*, by the *Morning Post*, by the *Morning Herald*, and others, as the *Scum* of society. They say, that you have *no business at public meetings*; that you are *rabble*, and that you *pay no taxes*. These insolent hirelings, who wallow in wealth, would not be able to put their abuse of you in print were it not for *your labour*. You create all that is an object of taxation; for even the *land* itself would be good for nothing without your labour. But, are you *not taxed*? Do you pay *no taxes*? One of the Correspondents of the Board of Agriculture has said, that care has been taken to lay *as little tax as possible* on the articles used by *you*. One would wonder how a man could be found impudent enough to put an assertion like this upon paper. But, the people of this country have so long been insulted by such men, that the insolence of the latter knows no bounds.

The *tax-gathers* do not, indeed come to *you* and demand money of you; but, there are few articles which you use, in the purchase of which you do not pay *a tax*.

On your shoes,

        Salt,
        Beer,
        Malt,
        Hops,
        Tea,
        Sugar,
        Candles,
        Soap,
        Paper,
        Coffee,
        Spirits,
        Glass of your windows,

Bricks and tiles,
Tobacco.

On all these, and many other articles, you pay *a tax*, and even on your *loaf* you pay a tax, because every thing is taxed from which the loaf proceeds. In several cases the tax amounts to more than one half of what you pay for the article itself; these taxes go, in part, to support Sinecure Placemen and Pensioners; and, the ruffians of the hired press call you the *Scum* of society, and deny that you have any right to show your faces at any public meeting to petition for a reform, or for the removal of any abuse whatever!

Mr. Preston, whom I quoted before, and who is a *Member of Parliament* and has a large estate, says, upon this subject, "Every family, even of the poorest labourer, consisting of five persons, may be considered as paying, in *indirect taxes*, at least *ten pounds a year*, or more than half his wages at seven shillings a week!" And yet the insolent hirelings call you the *mob*, the *rabble*, the *scum*, the *swinish multitude*, and say that your voice is nothing; that you have no business at public meetings; and that *you* are, and ought to be, considered as nothing in the body politic!—Shall we *never* See the day when these men will change their tone! Will they never cease to look upon you as brutes! I trust they will change their tone, and that the day of the change is *at no great distance!*

The weight of the Poor-rate, which must increase while the present system continues, alarms the Corrupt, who plainly see, that what is paid to relieve you *they* cannot have. Some of them, therefore, hint at your *early marriages* as a great evil, and a *Clergyman*, named Malthus, has seriously proposed measures for *checking* you in this respect; while one of the Correspondents of the Board of Agriculture complains of the *Increase of bastards*, and proposes severe *punishment* on the parents! How hard these men are to please! What would they have you do? As some have called you the *swinish multitude*, would it be much wonder if they were to propose to serve you as families of young pigs are served? Or, if they were to bring forward the measure of Pharaoh, who ordered the midwives to kill all the male children of the Israelites?

But, if you can restrain your indignation at these insolent notions and schemes, with what feelings must you look upon the condition of your country, where the increase of the people is now looked upon as a curse! Thus, however, has it always been, in all countries, where taxes have produced excessive misery. Our Countryman, Mr. Gibbon, in his history of the *Decline and Fall of the Roman Empire*, has the following passage:

> The horrid practice of *murdering their new-born infants* was become every day more frequent in the provinces. It was the effect of *distress*, and the distress was principally occasioned by the *intolerable burden of taxes*, and by the *vexatious as well as cruel prosecutions of the officers of the Revenue* against their insolvent debtors. The less opulent or less industrious part of mankind, instead of rejoicing at an increase of family, deemed it an act of paternal tenderness to release the children from the impending miseries of a life which they themselves were unable to support.

But, that which took place under the base Emperor Constantine will not take place in England. You will not murder your new-born infants, nor will you, to please the corrupt and the insolent, debar yourselves from enjoyments to which you are invited by the very first of nature's laws. It is, however, a disgrace to the country, that men should be formed in it capable of putting ideas so insolent upon paper. So then, a young man, arm-in-arm with a rosy-cheeked girl, must be a spectacle of evil omen! What! and do they imagine, that you are thus to be *extinguished*, because some of you are now (without any fault of yours) unable to find work? As far as you were wanted to labour, to fight, or to pay taxes, you were welcome, and they boasted of your numbers; but, now that the country has been brought into a state of misery, these corrupt and insolent men are busied with schemes *for getting rid of you*. Just as if you had not as good a right to live and to love and to marry as they have! They do not propose, far from it, to check the breeding of Sinecure Placemen and Pensioners, who are supported in part by the taxes which you help to pay. They say not a word about the *whole families*, who are upon the pension list. In many cases, there are sums granted in trust for *the children* of such a Lord or such a Lady. And, while labourers and journeymen who have large families too, are actually paying taxes for the support of these Lords' and Ladies' children, these cruel and insolent men propose that they shall have no relief, and that their having children ought to be *checked!* To such a subject no *words* can do justice. You will *feel* as you ought to feel; and to the effect of your feelings I leave these cruel and insolent men.

There is one more scheme to notice, which, though rather less against nature is not less hateful and insolent, namely, *to encourage you to emigrate to foreign countries*. This scheme is distinctly proposed to the government by one of the Correspondents of the Board of Agriculture. What he means by *encouragement* must be to *send away* by force, or by *paying for the passage*; for a man who has *money* stands in no need of relief. But, I trust, that not a man of you *will move*, let the *encouragement* be what it may. It is impossible for *many* to go, though the prospect may be ever so fair. We must stand by our country, and it is base not to stand by her, as long as there is a chance of seeing her what she ought to be. But, the proposition is, nevertheless, base and insolent. This man did not propose to *encourage* the Sinecure Placemen and Pensioners to emigrate; yet, surely, you who help to maintain them by the taxes which you pay, have as good a right to remain in the country as they have! You have fathers and mothers and sisters and brothers and children and friends as well as they; but, this base projector recommends that you may be encouraged to leave your relations and friends for ever; while he would have the Sinecure Placemen and Pensioners remain quietly where they are!

No: you will not leave your country. If you have suffered much and long, you have the greater right to remain in the hope of seeing better days. And I beseech you not to look upon yourselves as the *scum*; but, on the contrary, to be well persuaded, that a great deal will depend upon *your exertions;* and, therefore, I now proceed to point out to you what appears to me to be the line of conduct which Journeymen and Labourers ought to pursue in order to obtain *effectual relief*, and to assist in promoting tranquillity and restoring the happiness of their country.

We have seen, that the cause of our miseries is the *burden of taxes* occasioned by wars, by standing armies, by sinecures, by pensions, etc. It would be endless and useless to enumerate all the different heads or sums of expenditure. The *remedy* is what we have now to look to, and that remedy consists wholly and solely of such a *reform* in the Common's, or People's, House of Parliament, as shall give to every payer of *direct taxes* a vote at elections, and as shall cause the Members to be *elected annually*.

In a late Register I have pointed out how easily, how peaceably, how fairly, such a parliament might be chosen. I am aware, that it may, and not without justice, be thought wrong to deprive those of the right of voting, who pay *indirect* taxes. Direct taxes are those which are directly paid by any person into the hands of the taxgatherer, as the assessed taxes and rates. Indirect taxes are those which are paid indirectly through the maker or seller of goods, as the tax on soap or candles or salt or malt. And, as no man ought to be taxed *without his consent*, there has always been a difficulty upon this head. There has been no question about the *right* of every man, who if free to exercise his will, who has a settled place in society, and who pays a tax of *any sort*, to vote for Members of Parliament. The difficulty is in taking the votes by any other means than by the *Rate Book*; for, if there be no *list* of tax-payers in the hands of *any person*, mere menial servants, vagrants, pick-pockets and scamps of all sorts might not only come to poll, but they might poll in several parishes or places, on one and the same day. A corrupt rich man might employ scores of persons of this description, and in this way would the purpose of reform be completely defeated. In America, where one branch of the Congress is elected for *four* years and the other for *two years*, they have still adhered to the principle of *direct taxation*, and, in some of the states, they have made it necessary for a voter to be worth a hundred pounds. Yet they have, in that country, duties on goods, custom duties and excise duties also; and, of course, there are many persons, who really *pay taxes*, and who, nevertheless, are not permitted to vote. The people do not complain of this. They know, that the number of votes is so great, that no corruption can take place, and they have no desire to see livery servants, vagrants and pickpockets take part in their elections. Nevertheless, it would be very easy for a *reformed parliament*, when once it had taken root, to make a just arrangement of this matter. The most likely method would be to take off the indirect taxes, and to put a small direct tax upon every master of a house, however low his situation in life.

But, this and *all other good things*, must be done by a *reformed Parliament.—* We must have *that first*, or we shall have nothing good; and, any man, who would, *before hand*, take up your time with the detail of what a reformed parliament ought to do in this respect, or with respect to any changes in the form of government, can have no other object than that of defeating the cause of reform, and, indeed, the very act must show, that *to raise obstacles* is his wish.

Such men, now that they find you justly initiated, would persuade you, that, because things have been perverted from their true ends, there is *nothing good* in our *constitution and laws*. For what, then, did Hampden die in the field, and Sydney on the scaffold? And, has it been discovered, at last, that England has *always* been an enslaved country from top to toe? The Americans, who are a very wise people, and who love liberty with all their hearts, and who take care to *enjoy* it too, took special care not to part with any of the great principles and laws which they derived from their fore-fathers. They took special care to speak with reverence of, and to preserve, Magna Charta, the Bill of Rights, the Habeas Corpus, and not only all the body of the Common Law of England, but most of the rules of our courts, and all our form of jurisprudence. Indeed, it is the greatest glory of England that she has thus supplied with sound principles of freedom those immense regions, which will be peopled, perhaps by hundreds of millions.

I know of no enemy of reform and of the happiness of the country so great as that man, who would persuade you, that we possess *nothing good*, and that *all* must be torn to pieces. There is no principle, no precedent, no regulation (except as to mere matter of detail), favourable to freedom, which is not to be found in the Laws of England or in the example of our Ancestors. Therefore, I say, we may ask for, and we want *nothing new*. We have great constitutional laws and principles, to which we are immovably attached. We want *great alteration*, but we want *nothing new*. Alteration, modification to suit the times and circumstances; but, the great principles ought to be and must be, the same, or else confusion will follow.

It was the misfortune of the French people, that they had no great and settled principles to refer to in their laws or history. They sallied forth and inflicted vengeance on their oppressors; but, for want of settled principles, to which to refer, they fell into confusion; they massacred *each other*; they next flew to a military chief to protect them even *against themselves*; and the result has been what we too well know. Let us, therefore, congratulate ourselves, that we have great constitutional principles and laws, to which we can refer, and to which we are attached.

That *Reform* will come I know, if the people do their duty; and all that we have to guard against is *confusion*, which cannot come if Reform take place *in time*. I have before observed to you, that when the friends of corruption in France saw that they could not prevent a *change*, they bent their endeavours to produce *confusion*, in which they fully succeeded. They employed numbers of unprincipled men to go about the country proposing all sorts of mad schemes. They produced, first a confusion in men's minds, and next a civil war between provinces, towns, villages, and families. The tyrant Robespierre, who was exceeded in cruelty only by some of the Bourbons, was proved to have been in league with the open enemies of France. He butchered all the real friends of freedom whom he could lay his hands on, except Paine, whom he shut up in a dungeon till he was reduced to a skeleton. This monster was, at last, put to death himself; and his horrid end ought to be a warning to any man, who may wish to walk in the same path. But I am, for my part, in little fear of the influence of such men. They cannot cajole *you*, as Robespierre cajoled the people of Paris. It is, nevertheless, necessary for you to be on your guard against them, and, when you hear a man talking big and hectoring about projects which *go farther than a real and radical reform of the Parliament*, be you well assured, that that man would be a second Robespierre if he could, and that he would make use of you, and sacrifice the life of the very last man of you; that he would ride upon the shoulders of some through rivers of the blood of others, for the purpose of gratifying his own selfish and base and insolent ambition.

In order effectually to avoid the rock of confusion, we should keep steadily in our eye, not only what we *wish* to be done, but what *can* be done *now*. We know that such a reform as would send up a Parliament, chosen by all the payers of direct taxes, is not only just and reasonable, but *easy of execution*. I am, therefore, for accomplishing that object first; and I am not at all afraid, that a set of men who would really hold the purse of the people, and who had been just chosen freely by the people, would very soon do every thing that the warmest friend of freedom could wish to see done.

While, however, you are upon your guard against false friends, you should neglect no opportunity of doing all that is within your power to give support to the cause of Reform. *Petition* is the channel for your sentiments, and there is no village so small that its petition would not have some weight. You ought to attend at every public meeting within your reach. You ought to read to, and to assist each other in coming at a competent knowledge of all public matters. Above all things, you ought to be unanimous in your object, and not to suffer yourselves to be *divided*.

The subject of *religion* has nothing to do with this great question of reform. A reformed parliament would soon do away all religious distinctions and disabilities. In their eyes, a Catholic and a Protestant would both appear in the same light.

The *Courier*, the *Times*, and other emissaries of Corruption, are constantly endeavouring to direct your wrath against Bakers, Brewers, Butchers, and other persons, who deal in the necessaries of life. But, I trust, that you are not to be stimulated to such a species of violence. These tradesmen are as much in distress as you. They cannot help their malt and hops and beer and bread and meat being too dear for you to purchase. They all sell as cheap as they can without being absolutely ruined. The beer you drink is more than half *tax*, and when the tax has been paid by the seller, he must have payment back again from you who drink, or he must be ruined. The Baker has numerous taxes to pay, and so has the Butcher, and so has the Miller, and the Farmer. Besides all men are *eager to sell*, and, if they could sell *cheaper*, they certainly would, because that would be the sure way of *getting more custom*. It is the weight of the taxes, which press us *all* to the earth, *except those who receive their incomes out of those taxes*. Therefore I exhort you most earnestly not to be induced to lay violent hands on those, who really suffer as much as yourselves.

On the subject of *lowering wages*, too, you ought to consider, that your employers cannot give to you, that which they have not. At present corn is *high in price*, but that high price is no benefit to the farmer, because it has arisen from that *badness of the crop*, which Mr. Hunt foretold at the Common Hall, and for the foretelling of which he was so much abused by the hirelings of the press, who, almost up to this very moment, have been boasting and thanking God for *the goodness of the crop!* The farmer, whose corn is half destroyed, gains nothing by selling the remaining half for *double* the price at which he would have sold the whole. If I grow 10 quarters of wheat, and, if I save it all, and sell it for 2 pounds a quarter, I receive as much money as if I sold the one half of it for 4 pounds a quarter. And, I am better off in the former case, because I want wheat for *seed* and because I want some to *consume myself*. These matters I recommend to your serious consideration; because, it being *unjust* to fall upon your employers to force from them to give that which they have not to give, your conduct in such cases must tend to weaken the great cause, it which we ought all now to be engaged; namely, *the removal of our burdens through the means of a reformed parliament*. It is the interest of vile men of all descriptions to set one part of the people against the other part; and, therefore, it becomes you to be constantly on your guard against their allurements.

When journeymen find their wages reduced, they should take time *to reflect on the real cause*, before they fly upon their employers, who are, in many cases, in as great, or greater, distress than themselves. How many of those employers have, of late, gone to jail for debt, and left helpless families behind them! The employer's trade falls off. His goods are reduced in price. His stock loses the half of its value. He owes money. He is ruined; and how can he continue to pay *high wages?* The cause of his ruin, is the *weight of the taxes*, which presses so heavily on us all, that we lose the power of purchasing goods. But, it is certain, that a great many, a very large portion, of the farmers, tradesmen, and manufacturers, have, by their *supineness* and want of *public spirit*, contributed towards the bringing of this ruin upon themselves and upon you. They have *skulked* from their public duty. They have kept aloof from, or opposed, all measures for a redress of grievances; and, indeed, they still *skulk*, though ruin and destruction stare them in the face. Why do they not *now* come forward and *explain* to you the *real cause* of the reduction of your wages? Why do they not put themselves at your head in *Petitioning* for redress? This would secure their property much better than the *calling in of troops*, which can never afford them more than a short and precarious security. In the days of their prosperity, they were *amply warned* of what has now come to pass; and the far greater part of them abused and calumniated those who gave them the warning. Even if they would *now* act the part of men worthy of being relieved, the relief to us all would speedily follow. If they will not; if they will still *skulk*, they will merit all the miseries which they are destined to suffer.

Instead of coming forward to apply for a reduction of those taxes which are pressing them as well as you to the earth, what are they doing? Why, they are applying to the government to add to their receipts by passing *Corn-Bills*, by preventing *foreign wool* from being imported; and many other such silly schemes. Instead of asking for a *reduction of taxes*, they are asking *for a means of paying taxes!* Instead of asking for the abolition of Sinecure Places and Pensions, they pray to *be enabled to continue to pay the amount of those places and pensions*. They know very well, that the salaries of the judges and of many other persons were greatly raised, some years ago, on the ground of the rise in the price of *labour* and *provisions*; why, then, do they not ask to have those salaries *reduced* now that *labour* is reduced? Why do they not apply to the case of the judges and others, the arguments which they apply to *you*? They can talk boldly enough to you; but, they are too great cowards to talk to the government, even in the way of *Petition!* Far more honourable is it to be a ragged pauper than to be numbered among such men.

These people call themselves the *respectable* part of the nation. They are, as they pretend, the *virtuous* part of the people, because they are *quiet*; as if virtue consisted in *immobility!* There is a canting Scotchman, in London, who publishes a paper called the "*Champion*," who is everlasting harping upon the virtues of the "*fire-side*," and who inculcates the duty of quiet submission. Might we ask this Champion of the tea-pot and milk-jug, whether Magna Charta and the Bill of Rights were won by the fire-side? Whether the tyrants of the House of Stuart and of Bourbon were hurled down by fire-side virtues? Whether the Americans gained their independence, and have preserved their freedom, by quietly sitting by the fire-side? Oh, no! these were all atchieved by *action*, and amidst bustle and noise. *Quiet*, indeed! Why, in this quality, a log, or a stone, far surpasses even the pupils of this "*Champion*" of quietness; and the chairs round his fire-side exceed those who sit in them. But, in order to put these quiet, fire-side, respectable people to the *test*, let us ask them, if they approve of drunkenness, breaches of the peace, black-eyes, bloody-noses, fraud, bribery, corruption, perjury, and subornation of perjury; and, if they say *No*, let us ask them whether they are not going on all over the country at every general election. If they answer *Yes*, as they must, unless they be guilty of wilful falsehood, will they then be so good as to tell us, how they reconcile their *inactivity* with sentiments of *virtue*? Some men, in all former ages, have been held in esteem for their wisdom, their genius, their skill, their valour, their devotion to country, etc. but, never, until this age was *quietness* deemed a quality to be extolled. It would be no difficult matter to show, that the quiet, fire-side, gentry are the most callous and cruel, and, therefore, the most wicked, part of the nation. Amongst them it is that you find all the peculators, all the blood-suckers of various degrees, all the borough-voters and their offspring, all the selfish and unfeeling wretches, who rather than risk the disturbing of their ease for one single month, rather than go a mile to hold up their hand at a public meeting, would see half the people perish with hunger and cold. The *humanity*, which is continually on their lips, is all *fiction*. They weep over the tale of woe in a novale but, round their "decent fire-side," never was compassion felt for a real sufferer, or indignation at the acts of a powerful tyrant.

The object of the efforts of such writers is clearly enough seen. Keep all *quiet*! Do not *rouse*! Keep *still*! Keep *down*! Let those who perish, perish in *silence*! It will, however, be out of the power of these Quacks, with all their laudanum, to allay the blood which is now boiling in the veins of the people of this kingdom; who, if they are doomed to perish, are, at any rate, resolved not to perish *in silence*. The writer, whom I have mentioned above, says, that he, of *course*, does not count "the *lower classes*, who, under the *pressure of need*, or under the influence of *ignorant prejudice*, may blindly and weakly *rush upon certain and prompt punishment;*" but that "the security of every *decent* fire-side, every *respectable* father's best hopes for his children, still connect themselves *with the Government*." And by *Government* he clearly means, all the mass as it now stands. There is nobody so callous and so insolent as your sentimental quacks and their patients. How these "decent fire-side" people would stare, if, some morning, they were to come down and find them occupied by uninvited visitors! I hope they never will. I hope that things will never come to this pass: but if one thing, more than any other, tends to produce so sad an effect, it is the cool insolence with which such men as this writer treats the most numerous and most suffering classes of the people.

Long as this Address already is, I cannot conclude without some observations on the "*Charity Subscriptions*" at the *London Tavern*. The object of this Subscription professes to be to afford relief to the *distressed Labourers*, etc. About *forty thousand pounds* have been subscribed, and there is not much probability of its going much further. There is an *absurdity* upon the face of the scheme; for, as all parishes are *compelled by law* to afford relief to every person in distress, it is very clear, that, as far as money is given by these people to relieve the poor, there will be so much *saved in the parish rates*. But, the folly of the thing is not what I wish you most to attend to. Several of the Subscribers to this fund receive each of them more than *ten thousand pounds*, and some more than *thirty thousand pounds* each out of these taxes, which you help to pay, and which emoluments not a man of them proposes to give up. The *Clergy* appear very forward in this Subscription. An Archbishop and a Bishop assisted at the forming of the scheme. Now, then, observe, that there has been given *out of the taxes*, for several years past, *a hundred thousand pounds a year*, for *what*, think you? Why, for the relief of the *Poor Clergy*! I have no account at hand later than that delivered *last year*, and there I find this sum!—For the *Poor Clergy*! The *rich* Clergy do not pay this sum; but, it comes out of those taxes, part, and a large part, of which *you* pay on your *beer, malt, salt, shoes*, etc. I dare say, that the "*decent* fire-sides" of these "Poor Clergy" still "connect themselves with the government." The decent fire-sides would be great fools if they did not so connect themselves! Amongst all our misery we have had to support the intolerable disgrace of being an object of the *charity* of a *Bourbon Prince*, while we are paying for supporting that family upon the throne of France. Well! But, is this all? We are taxed, at the very same moment, for the support of *French Emigrants*! And, you shall now see to what amount. Nay, not only *French*, but *Dutch* and others, as appears from the forementioned account, laid before parliament last year.—The sum, paid out of the taxes, in one year for the *Relief* of *Suffering French Clergy and Laity, St. Domingo Sufferers, Dutch Emigrants, Corsican Emigrants*, was 187,750*l.*, yes, *one hundred and eighty-seven thousand, seven hundred and fifty pounds*, paid to this set in one year out of those taxes, of which *you* pay so large a share, while you are insulted with a Subscription to relieve you, and while there are projectors who have the audacity to recommend schemes for preventing you from marrying while young, and to induce you to emigrate from your country! I'll venture my life, that the "decent fire-sides" of all this swarm of French Clergy and Laity and Dutch and Corsicans and St. Domingo *sufferers* "still connect themselves closely with the government;" and, I will also venture my life, that you do not stand in need of one more word to warm every drop of blood remaining in your bodies! As to the money subscribed by *Regiments of Soldiers*, whose pay arises from taxes, in part paid by you, though it is a most shocking spectacle to behold, I do not think so much of it. The soldiers are your fathers, brothers, and sons. But, if they were *all* to give their *whole pay*, and if they amount to *one hundred and fifty thousand men*, it would not amount to *one half* of what is now paid in Poor-rates and, of course would not add half a pound of bread to every pound, which the unhappy paupers now receive. All the *expences* of the *Army* and *Ordnance* amount to an enormous sum. To sixteen or eighteen millions; but they pay of 150,000 men, at one shilling a day each, amounts to no more than *two millions, seven hundred and twelve thousand, and five hundred pounds*. So that, supposing them all to receive one shilling a day each the soldiers receive only about a third part of the sum now paid annually in Poor-rates.

I have no room, nor have I any desire, to appeal to your passions upon this occasion. I have laid before you, with all the clearness I am master of, the causes of our misery, the measures which have led to those causes, and I have pointed out what appears to me to be the only remedy—namely, a reform of the Commons, of People's, House of Parliament. I exhort you to proceed in a peaceable and lawful manner, but, at the same time, to proceed with zeal and resolution in the attainment of this object. If the *Skulkers* will not join you, if the "decent fire-side" gentry still keep aloof, proceed by yourselves. Any man can draw up a petition, and any man can *carry* it up to London, with instructions to deliver it into trusty hands to be presented whenever the House shall meet. Some further information will be given as to this matter in a future Number. In the meanwhile, I remain Your Friend,

Wm. Cobbett

Eyewitness account by John Taylor of the "Peterloo massacre," 1819

J. E. Taylor, *Notes and Observations, critical and explanatory, on the papers relative to the internal state of the country, recently presented to Parliament* . . . (London: Effingham Wilson, 1820), 164-76.

The "Peterloo massacre" occurred at St. Peter's Fields in Manchester on 16 August 1819, when a huge gathering of reformers was dispersed by the yeomanry. Eleven people were killed and over five hundred wounded, and the incident became a famous rallying cry for discontented reformers. Taylor (1791-1844) subsequently founded the Manchester Guardian *(1821).*

Mr. Philips's account of the meeting itself is very short, and does not contain much, except in the way of inference or supposition, to which it is possible to object. The regularity of approach to St. Peter's, the marching in military array (if it must be called so,) but which I could only recognize as the adoption of that plan of proceeding to the place of meeting, which was the farthest removed from any thing having at all the appearance of tumult; the flags, the music, the sticks, are all, with some minor differences of detail, characteristics, the exhibition of which, at the meeting, is admitted by every one.

With respect to the sticks: I saw a column pass down Mosley Street, (I do not know whether it was the same that Mr. Philips had seen at Ardwick, though, from the route by which it came upon the ground, that is not improbable.) Of the persons who composed it, however, I calculated at the time, that about one in ten, certainly not two in ten, had sticks; and I only saw one, which, from its appearance of freshness, seemed to have been provided specially for the occasion. I did not observe any which, according to the sagacious conclusion of Mr. Wheeler, were "shouldered as representative of muskets;" nor if I had, should I have considered it as of importance, any more than if they had been bestrode, "as representative of" horses. The friends of alarm, knowing that "walking-stick" is not a term which would excite much terror, endeavour to make the formidable weapons of the weavers appear more fearful, by calling them "clubs and bludgeons." They were, however, nothing but common walking-sticks; and indeed I was much surprised to see so few even of them, for every one at all conversant with the habits of country-people hereabouts knows, that when they have far to walk, they seldom omit taking one with them.

To my view, the whole manner and appearance of the people, and I saw most of the different bodies, shewed that they attached a degree of serious importance to the business, about which they were assembled. That their objects and intentions were peaceable, was proved to demonstration, by their bringing with them to the meeting, so many women and children; nor did I see an action, or hear a word, in the slightest degree obnoxious to the laws of the land. None, indeed, of the most bitter opponents of the meeting, none of the most anxious or the most acute defenders of the magistrates, have *yet* ventured to assert, that any the slightest act of violence had taken place before the charge of the cavalry. All that Mr. Hay could express at the time, was a conviction that the meeting "bore the appearance of insurrection." All that Mr. Francis Philips yet alleges, is a conviction of its *"revolutionary tendency."* In this state of perfect peace and quietness the assembly still continued; when the yeomanry cavalry came very rapidly upon the ground. The speed of their progress was such, even at some distance from the field, that a woman was knocked down, her child fell from her arms and was killed; an old man, considerably upwards of seventy years of age, was rode over, and both his arms were broken, as they turned the corner of the cottage wall. In describing the advance of the cavalry towards the hustings, Mr. Philips says, he "did not see a sword used." I am not aware that any person has ever asserted that he did. He "solemnly believes, that had the crowd given way to them, (the yeomanry,) no cuts would have been given." I know of no law, which authorizes a yeoman to sabre me, because I may not give way to him quite so soon as he wishes that I should. Besides, the density of the crowd, and the suddenness and impetuosity of the irruption of the cavalry, rendered it impossible for the people to open a passage. There is an unconscious simplicity about the remainder of the sentence, which is quite amusing: "a great dust arose, when they (the yeomanry) quickened their speed, so that I could not distinguish all that passed; and certainly, I did not see one person struck with the sabre." Why not? Mr. Philips shall answer for himself. Because "I could not distinguish all that passed." The letting-off of this negative evidence, reminds me of the story of the Irishman, who, when half a score persons swore, that they had seen him commit a certain theft, claimed to be acquitted upon his trial, because he could produce ten times as many who did not see him: like Mr. Philips, I did not see "one person struck with the sabre," though, it was not the "dust" which prevented it, but a more potent reason; inasmuch as I had left the ground some minutes before the yeomanry came. The number of sabre wounds that I have since seen, is, however, ample proof that many were given. And several persons, whose credibility is to not be impeached, at least, by Mr. Philips's negative evidence, have distinctly sworn, either that they were wounded themselves, or saw wounds inflicted upon others, before the cavalry arrived at the hustings. There is no evidence, which deserves a serious refutation, to prove that any stones were thrown at the cavalry, before they reached the hustings; though it is assumed by Mr. Philips, as a point established, (page 58) that "no lives would have been lost, if opposition had not been made to the civil and military powers." What! did Mr. Ashworth oppose them? Did Mrs. Parkinson oppose them? But I ask for proof, that such "opposition" was made. Mr. Wheeler's story of the "long brats that contain pockets," is too ridiculous to obtain credit; like the parliamentary tales of the two cart-loads of stones, and the thrice-read riot act. It bears falsehood upon the face of it; for the same money which would purchase "a brewer's brat," would have sufficed to provide some more efficient weapons of offence, than a pocket full of stones. Besides, nothing could give an air of tolerable plausibility to such a preparation, since no reason for it would exist, except an opinion on the part of the people, that they should be attacked. Had they anticipated the probability of that event, they would doubtless, either have come much better prepared for it, or kept at home; believing however, as they did, that their meeting was legal, they could have no expectation of being disturbed. That any person should gravely assert, or, asserting, expect to obtain credit, that an unarmed multitude, amongst whom were many women and children, should attack a body of cavalry, armed with swords and pistols, is indeed to me astonishing.

But by what right were the yeomanry brought upon the field? I think I have, in my remarks upon the parliamentary documents, proved, that the meeting was legal. That it was peaceable, I presume, will not now be questioned.

If therefore, the object were merely to arrest Mr. Hunt and his companions, why, but for the very determination to produce the consequences that ensued, were such instruments employed, or such a period chosen? Mr. Hunt might doubtless have been found with ease when the meeting was over, and none of his companions who were named in the warrant, were likely to abscond to avoid its being served upon them; indeed it is morally impossible that they could in any way be aware of its existence. Nor is the execution of a warrant for misdemeanour (the warrant does not, I am assured, allege *any* distinct fact of illegality,) a matter of such importance as to justify the putting in danger the lives of such an immense multitude of people. But, even if Mr. Hunt and his companions be guilty to the full extent to which crime is imputed to them, I cannot think that the consciences of the Magistrates would have been less at ease, whilst I am sure that the feelings of the country would have been less outraged, if the yeomanry had not been ordered to assault the people; and to arrest Mr. Hunt, without assaulting them, was under the then existing circumstances absolutely impossible. Again, if it were after mature deliberation thought necessary to arrest Mr. Hunt during the meeting, why was not the civil power in the first instance employed? No attempt was made to execute the warrant by its agency, and it would have been thought time enough by any discreet, or humane, or constitutionally disposed persons to call in a military force, when the civil power had been found unable to do its duty, or had been obstructed in the performance of it. Taking, therefore, all the circumstances together, I cannot but conclude, that it was *ab initio* intended to dissolve the meeting by force, and that the arrest of Mr. Hunt and his associates was merely the pretext by which the attack was to be justified. But, even though the meeting should hereafter be shewn to have been illegal, still it was illegally dispersed. That the Riot Act was not read I have proved (so far as a negative can be proved) already; and Mr. Philips admits he "did not hear it," but adds that he has "no doubt of its having been read, from the respectable testimony he has heard on that point; but certainly, it was heard only very partially." If Mr. Philips meant, that the country should take his statement as evidence of this fact, he ought to have told us, on the authority of this "respectable testimony," not merely that the Riot Act was read, but how, where, when, and by whom? The mere assertion, without a full and satisfactory explanation of all these points, is worse than trifling, because it aims at deception; and if the forms and intentions of the law had been complied with, the opportunity of proving that such was the fact, must, I conceive, have been anxiously desired and eagerly embraced. The time has been, that evidence upon that point would have been most beneficial to the Magistrates; but, though the police office has vomited forth its dregs to bear testimony in their favour, the reading of the Riot Act yet remains unproved.

It is not necessary for me to repeat the horrifying description of the scenes that ensued after the prisoners were arrested. They can never be obliterated from the memories of those who were fated to witness them. But Mr. Philips justly observes, that "For any individual to give a correct account of all the circumstances of that eventful meeting, from his own actual knowledge, is impossible." As I only witnessed the dispersion of it from a distance, I shall therefore, content myself with stating its results; simply adding, that I can never forget the deep expression of terror and surprise depicted in the countenances of the poor creatures as they ran by me; apparently scarce knowing where they were, or whither they should fly for safety. There are now upon the books of the Committee for the relief of the sufferers, 579 cases of injury, sustained on that day. Of these, 421 have already been authenticated by the strictest personal investigation, and the sufferers relieved. Amongst this latter number, there are 161 cases of sabre wounds. In every case in which the name of individuals has been put upon the list of the Committee, the injuries sustained were so severe, as for a greater or less period to render the parties unable to follow their employment. Amongst the wounded are 104 girls and women, and of these, a considerable proportion received sabre wounds, many of which were very serious. Of the parties who were wounded on that day, ten are known to have died, and as is believed in consequence of the injury they sustained. One man, who was severely wounded, has become insane, and one woman, who was also wounded, in a fit of insanity cut her throat. That the number actually wounded was much greater than that which the list of the Committee exhibits, there can be no doubt, because many persons have endeavoured, from an apprehension of personal consequences, to conceal the circumstance of their having been present at the meeting. Several instances have indeed come under the notice of the Committee, where the knowledge of that fact, by employers, has caused to the poor sufferers the loss of their work.

Such then are the immediate consequences—such is the direct result, of the *glorious* victory of the 16th of August,—a victory obtained over whom? over our fellow-countrymen and neighbours; the most industrious—the most numerous, and the most useful class of our population—that class to whom we owe all our strength in war, from whom we must derive all our prosperity in peace.

Hitherto, my opinion of the conduct of the magistrates must be gathered from incidental observations, rather than from any direct or general statement. Of the yeomanry I have not yet spoken; but as Mr. Philips's pamphlet professes to be an exposure of the calumnies circulated, etc. against the Magistrates and yeomanry cavalry of Manchester and Salford; and as I have undertaken the task of answering that pamphlet, my opinion must necessarily be given. That I write under circumstances of considerable restraint, will be sufficiently obvious. It is an ungracious task, at all times, publicly to blame those who are our neighbours and fellow-townsmen; but at the present time to start a doubt of the humanity, of the prudence, of the impartiality, of the constitutional spirit, or of the sound judgment, of the magistrates, will almost be held to be seditious. However nauseous and fulsome the adulation which may be offered as incense to their vanity, it may yet be imprudent to reply to it; and when the rage of political hostility has instigated human passions to a deep and stern vibration, the "small still voice of truth," prompting to manly and independent investigation, is scarcely ever heard amid the storm.

The comments which I have made upon the parliamentary documents, will exhibit my opinion of the conduct of some of the Magistrates in individual cases. With respect, specifically, to the transactions of the 16th of August, it is generally understood, and I am assured it is capable of proof, (though for that, I do not pledge myself) that there was a considerable difference of opinion amongst the Magistrates themselves, as to the propriety of calling in the military *unless some actual breach of the peace were committed.* Certainly, my estimation of the character of some individuals amongst them has been very erroneous, if the deeds of that day received their *unanimous* approbation. But, however that fact may be, that there are amongst the Magistrates, individuals of the most violent political character—men, who most unwillingly concede to those who differ from them the liberty of manifesting their opinions, and who sometimes use language upon the bench more fit for the orgies of a Pitt-club—is beyond dispute. That there are some, whose circumstances rander it but too probable, that they look to the good things at the disposal of Ministers, as the reward of their devoted services, is also undeniable. That there are some, the avowed founders and patrons of Orange Societies, the organizers and supporters of a system of *espionage* of extent far greater, and of consequences more tremendous, than in any other district in the kingdom, is also too true; whilst that there are *any* distinguished for the possession of clear and comprehensive judgments, of sound constitutional information, of liberal and enlightened opinions, of superior acquired knowledge, or of great natural talents, I have yet to learn.

But though there can be no doubt, that the Magistrates sanctioned the proceedings of the 16th of August, I am inclined to believe, that it is not to them that we are to look, as the original instigators of the tragedy of that day. There is a committee appointed, I know not how, and consisting of I know not whom; but which arrogates to itself the title of the "Committee to strengthen the Civil Power." Judging of this body from its conduct, I am led to believe, that it consists principally of the waning remnant, or the few apt successors, of those whose bigotry and prejudices caused the riots of 1791 and 1792. That bigotry and those prejudices now, however, operate differently, for they have no longer the populace of their side. But as the people are not now to be incited to violence against the friends of freedom, it is an effort worthy of the same actors, to stir up prejudice, and suspicion, and distrust, against the people themselves. I do not mean to say, that these persons do not think they are "doing the state some service;" but I am sure we in this district were in a much more tranquil condition before they afflicted us by the incumbrance of their protection. However honestly disposed they may be, their acts render it sufficiently evident, that they are men of the most violent party feelings; that they do not possess that cool and discerning judgment which is requisite, by a scrupulous and diligent investigation of the nature of evidence, to enable them to elicit the truth;—that they are not nice as to the description of agents they employ, being predisposed to decide against the people; and finally, that they assume to themselves the most improper and unconstitutional power, actually placing the whole neighbourhood in a state of complete and hitherto unheard of *surveillance.*

From this anomalous self-constituted committee, many of the affidavit-makers, on the 16th of August, were, I believe, taken. Of its members, was the meeting which thanked the Magistrates and Yeomanry for their conduct, in part composed. Being heartily desirous that tranquillity and confidence may be restored amongst us, I entreat, as a preliminary measure, that the members of the committee will rest from the labours.

With respect to the conduct of the Yeomanry, on the 16th of August, I am decidedly of opinion, that considerable misapprehension has existed. That the greater part of the corps are actually incapable of acting with deliberate cruelty, it gives me pleasure to state my belief; but it is at the same time necessary to add, that by far the greater proportion of those cases, in which it is ascertained by what body of military wounds were inflicted, the yeomanry are the corps named. In order to account for this, it may be remarked, that they were first upon the field—they alone went up to the hustings—they alone took the flags and caps of liberty—and they alone were known to, and consequently can be identified by, the people. It is also beyond question, that there are in the corps individuals, whose political rancour approaches to absolute insanity; who before the meeting threatened what they would do; and who, reeking from the field, boasted of the feats they had achieved; who have openly avowed that their intention was to assassinate Mr. Hunt, and expressed their regret at not having effected their purpose. My decided opinion, therefore, is, that a few individuals inflicted all the wounds which have been attributed to the Yeomanry as a body. It is also true, notwithstanding the extraordinary gratuitous disclaimer of Col. Dalrymple, that in several instances both officers and privates of the hussars did interfere to stop the carnage. At least, this fact has been vouched to me by so many persons, totally unconnected with, and unknown to, each other; and as having occurred at such different parts of the ground, that I cannot for a moment hesitate to say, I am fully assured of the fact.

I have omitted to mention, that after the field was cleared (this fact I now introduce, because it has not been dwelt upon so much as it appears to me to deserve,) the yeomanry mustered again near Mr. Buston's house, waved their swords and cheered in token of triumph. That waving of swords I saw, those cheers I heard, and the sight and the sound smote heavy on my heart. For I could not have supposed, but that the dispersion of the assembled multitude would have least have been felt as a painful duty. I could not have supposed that the wounds and sufferings they had been the agents to inflict of their unarmed countrymen, would have been regarded by the Manchester yeomanry as a matter of exultation and rejoicing. . . .

Speech by George Tierney opposing the Seditious Meetings Prevention Bill, one of the "Six Acts," House of Commons, 29 November 1819

Hansard, n.s., XLI, 401-12.

The "Act for more effectually preventing Seditious Meetings and Assemblies" (60 Geo. 3, c. 6) was one of the "Six Acts" designed in the aftermath of Peterloo to discourage popular agitation and halt the spread of discontent. Tierney (1761-1830) was the leader of the Whigs in opposition between 1817 and 1821.

Mr. Tierney observed, that the awful denunciation by the noble lord [Viscount Castlereagh], of many of the principles which he (Mr. Tierney) had been accustomed to hold most sacred, must of course occasion him to rise under considerable embarrassment; but that embarrassment would be greater if he imagined that after the statement of the noble lord, the House would expect him on the sudden to be prepared to go into a general argument upon the question. Great variety of matter had been introduced, the greater part of which, to him at least, was perfectly new. When he came down to the House he had not the most distant conception that the noble lord would advert to many of the points on which he had dwelt at large. He assured the House, that he attended in his place, (and he hoped the noble lord would believe him), with a very sincere inclination to listen calmly and dispassionately to all that was to be advanced; he felt not the slightest prejudice on any of the points (on some it was impossible that he should feel any, as he was totally ignorant of them); but after what he had heard, he was conscious that he should not discharge his duty, if he did not trouble the House with a few, and a very few, observations. The noble lord had stated, that members on the opposition side of the House, on the first day of the session, had in substance agreed with all parts of the address relating to the seditious spirit pervading the manufacturing districts. It was almost needless to remind the House that the noble lord had no authority for that statement; for his own part, he (Mr. Tierney) had expressly asserted his agreement with the allegations in the address, as far only as they should be established by evidence to be produced. It was really astonishing that the noble lord, who could be candid enough on the first day of the session, should now, for some purpose of his own, not only state that which went even beyond the address, but attempt to ratify that statement by a supposed confirmation derived from the other side of the House. He (Mr. Tierney) had said then, and he repeated it now, that the measures to be adopted must depend upon the necessity, and that necessity could only be ascertained by due inquiry. He did not say that a possible case might not arise where new laws might be required; that a House of Commons in the discharge of its duty might not entertain projects of this kind, but what he maintained was that they ought not to do so until the necessity had been clearly and unequivocally made out. He denied that necessity at starting: no such case had been made out that justified such measures as had been proposed, even supposing, upon examination, it should turn out that the safety of the country required them. All the House had before it was the notoriety of certain proceedings; but the grounds of those proceedings, their motives, and extent, was only to be gathered from the papers communicated by the Prince Regent. Without meaning to anticipate the debate of to-morrow, to be introduced by his noble friend, he would say, that a more garbled, mutilated account was never presented to the House of Commons The noble lord had stated what undoubtedly was very consolatory, but for the comment with which it was accompanied—that the main body of the nation was sound and loyal; that in principle it was attached to the law and the constitution. Even in the disaffected districts, it had been admitted to-night, that the great mass of the population was untouched and untainted by disaffection, and that they were prepared to stand by the law and the constitution; nay, the noble lord went further; he had stated what would have astonished him, if any thing could astonish him from the present ministry on the subject of finance,—that the internal state of the country was perfectly prosperous; that in our foreign trade there was nothing to apprehend, but from the distress of America; that all our manufactures found their accustomed vent on the continent; and that it was the condition of America alone that restrained the commercial industry of the nation. Certainly, if the representations of the noble lord were to be believed in opposition to the evidence of our own senses, the country ought to be in a very happy condition; but how was it then that, as if the nature of the people had changed, as if they had become blind, obstinate, and perverse, it turned out that the nation was to be called upon to sacrifice its constitution on the altar of public security? The subjects of the realm were now told, that the old laws of England were not sufficient to guarantee protection to property; that what they had been accustomed to venerate as their safeguards were inadequate; that not only 10,000 additional soldiers were to be placed over them, but that those soldiers were to be backed by corps of yeomanry, and by statutes hitherto unknown; and after all this, they were to be assured that their condition was fortunate, and their finances flourishing! The noble lord had maintained, that by the amendment, he (Mr. Tierney) had marked his sense of the schemes by which the lower orders were misled. He admitted it; he meant to mark his opinion decisively, that those schemes were dangerous to the constitution, injurious to the public quiet, and most of all injurious to those who were deluded by them. If those unfortunate men could now look into the House, they would see the result of their endeavours; let them abuse the Whigs as violently, and stand by their champion Hunt as firmly as they pleased, if they could now witness the proceedings of parliament, they would see to what a miserable pass their leaders had reduced them, bound hand and foot, and delivered into the hands of those who, by new laws, and new troops, were establishing an inquisition upon the ruins of the constitution. A right hon. gentleman had said on a former night, that the Whigs had been for 50 years excluded from power. It was true, and here was the fruit of that exclusion. After the lapse of 50 years of rule, what had the opponents of the Whigs done for the nation? They had brought it to such a condition of discontent and disaffection, that in a period of profound peace, the tranquillity of the country could not be maintained without new laws, not consistent with the spirit of the constitution. The noble lord had opened five bills to the House.

The first was against Seditious and Tumultuous Assemblies—the second against Drilling—the third against the Possession of Arms—the fourth was against Traversing—the fifth branched out into two or three heads; and was aimed at the liberty of the press. With respect to the right of traverse, he freely confessed that his mind was open to information. He did not profess to be acquainted with all the grounds on which that right had originally been conceded to the subject; inconveniences might have arisen from it, and the remedies of the noble lord might be applied without danger. Yet with fear and trembling he should undertake to change an established principle of the common law, founded upon almost immemorial usage; and though he did not undertake to pronounce peremptorily against it, he approached it with a degree of awe, and would not change it until the necessity should be sufficiently established. If by the power of searching for arms the noble lord meant to go the length of saying that an Englishman was not to be allowed to have weapons for self-defence in his possession, a most grave case indeed must be made out before he could consent to the proposition. Going about in armed bodies from place to place was already illegal but between that and the established constitutional principle that a man had a right to have arms for his own defence he took a wide and material distinction. He begged of the House to pause before it sanctioned a measure which directly violated that privilege, in which twenty years ago men would have shuddered had it been even hinted that an alteration was intended. As a temporary measure it might under some circumstances be necessary; such as that large bodies of men were arming themselves in a way dangerous to the community. What was the fact? The papers upon the table merely proved, that certain persons had been making a limited number of pikes, that certain other persons had obtained some pistols and that a few more were in search of other fire-arms, if they could obtain them at a cheap rate. It was only pretended that Lancashire, Cheshire, a small part of Scotland, though thickly populated, and some districts of Yorkshire, were in a disturbed state: yet upon no better testimony than this the whole people of England were to be deprived of arms. [Lord Castlereagh said, across the table, that the Arms' bill was only to be local.] What then were the districts to which the law was to apply? [Lord Castlereagh replied, "Those included in the Watch and Ward act."] As he (Mr. Tierney) had not that measure precisely in his memory, he would not waste time by observations upon it. As to the law against drilling, he had heard with great astonishment, that such practices were not already against law; that no punishment could now be inflicted upon men who drilled and trained at night, and formed themselves into military array. If this were not so, he was, ready to submit to a new law on this subject. If it could be worded so as to meet the exigencies of the case, he honestly admitted that he had no objection to it; guarding himself with this observation, that it must be drawn so as not to go a single step beyond the necessity of the case, and that it was established that the men were drilling themselves evidently for the purpose of military operations. He next came to what in his mind was the great question of all—the new regulations against seditious and tumultuous meetings. Upon this subject the noble lord had asserted, that all the learned gentlemen on the other side of the House had very carefully abstained from giving any opinion whether assemblies of a particular description were or were not illegal. If he had understood his learned friends, their difficulty was this—that the question must depend upon particular circumstances; and until the facts of a case were laid before them, it was impossible to give an opinion upon it. No doubt a case might be shown in which it would be highly improper for the magistracy not to exert themselves by preventing a projected meeting, to preserve the public peace, a breach of which might threaten the safety of the country. Here the only question was, whether the particular circumstances under which the Manchester meeting was held were of such a description as that nothing but a military force could have put an end to its proceedings? To this he answered, that a meeting as large, or nearly as large, had taken place in Yorkshire; bodies of men had marched to Hunsletmoor of the same description as those that had attended at Manchester, with flags flying, and what had been termed an appearance of military array. What had become of it? The mayor of Leeds had felt no disposition to interfere; he had taken the proper precautions for the security of the peace, in the event of danger, though he did not think it right to make an ostentatious display of those precautions until a justifiable cause (which he did not apprehend) should be afforded for resorting to them. Such a cause did not occur. The persons assembled dispersed quietly; and from first to last, in Yorkshire, there had been no symptom of confusion. In Scotland, also, the magistrates had exercised a sound discretion; they had let the feeling of animosity waste itself; it did waste itself; and no such proceedings as those of Manchester had occurred there. And now the noble lord came forward, and assumed it as indisputable, that meetings must be confined within some other limitations, than those which at present existed, either numerical or local! The noble lord's plan appeared to be this—that no meeting should be allowed in any county, unless convened by the sheriff, the lord lieutenant, or by five magistrates: in certain towns, it must be called by the mayor; or if called by individuals, that no man could discuss and deliberate upon any public question out of his own parish. If such were the plan, there was at once an end of all the old wholesome spirit of the law upon this important subject. It would really seem from the cheers, as if the noble lord was restoring that old wholesome spirit, and that he (Mr. Tierney) was resisting it. Yet under that old wholesome spirit this country had flourished more than it would under the sage administration of the noble lord if he were to live for a century. Whether in former times any meetings as numerically great as those of which the noble lord complained had been held, he did not know; but every page and every corner of every page of our history showed that assemblies had been convened, where men were allowed to harangue in any times of alarm. Mr. Burke had well called them the safety-valve of the constitution, by which all the foul air was permitted to escape. This safety-valve with all his fears, the noble lord would destroy, and while he exclaimed that his only purpose was to preserve the constitution, no man could fail to see that he was preventing the exercise of an accustomed constitutional right. This attempt was to be viewed with the utmost jealousy; it was to introduce an entirely new system, and that not merely temporarily, but permanently. When the bills came before the House, many opportunities would be afforded for objections in detail, and he was much mistaken if they would not be found in every corner of every measure: he was now objecting only to the principle, and it ought not to be forgotten, that these acts were not to be local; they were to extend to England, Scotland, and Ireland. When the noble lord mentioned that he should open a whole system, he had flattered himself that a part of that system would be conciliation. It was now seen, however, that nothing but rigour and coercion were to be resorted to: a blow was struck at the very vitals of fair and free discussion, and did the House really believe that in following the steps of the noble lord it would not be treading upon very dangerous ground? Did it believe that the danger arising from the state of the country was as great as it was represented, or that the refusal of what the noble lord demanded, and a reliance upon the venerable laws of the kingdom, would not be the least hazardous experiment? Would not the new bills rather exasperate than repress? If there were these large bodies of men in a state of dangerous effervescence, which he much doubted, would not the peril be doubled, when they were told that they must expect nothing but coercion—that new laws should be invented to put them down, and that none of their grievances, whether real or imaginary, should receive a moment's attention? If parliamentary reform were mentioned in any shape, the immediate answer was—"Now you are going to innovate." Yet ministers were to make what innovations they pleased; they were to invade the most dear and settled rights of the people; to infringe upon privileges that the practice of many centuries had confirmed; and if a charge of innovation were made against them, they met it with a look of astonishment and a cheer of surprise. What must be the event? Would not those who were now agitated be worked to a state of madness or desperation, instead of being quelled and subdued? He warned the House how it consented to steps that might be attended with the most baleful consequence, and neglected the voice of the people; not merely of those who were enthusiastic on parliamentary reform, but of sober thinking men, whose experience gave them this unanswerable demonstration—that something was wrong here, and that something must be altered. Ministers might fancy that they could control the distressed by overawing them with 10,000 men; but they would find it impossible. A dead silence in the country might for a season be produced by soldiers and penal laws, but nothing could reconcile the people to the loss of their rights, or compel them to submit quietly to that grievous deprivation. The number of armed men might, in time, be rendered greater than the unarmed, and then, instead of venting their feelings by becoming spouters at public meetings, the discontented would be converted from empty boasters in public places, into real conspirators in dark corners. These matters well merited the attention of the House, and especially of that portion of it who thought of nothing (and he did not blame them for it) but of the preservation of property. Property never could be exposed to greater danger ultimately than for a popular representation, as this House called itself, to pass nothing but acts of rigour, and omit all attempts at kindness and conciliation. The right of meeting was not only to be taken away, but what the noble lord had called the broad liberty of the press was to be invaded. As to the cheap publications as they were called, no one viewed with greater disgust than he did their effusions, as well on the subject of religion as in vilification of the best characters in the country; and his chief astonishment had arisen from observing, that for three or four years together no attempt had been made to put a stop to them. The noble lord had observed that complaints had been made against the number of *ex-officio* informations, and it was true: they had been objected to as arbitrary and needless; but could any man read but the tenth part of the cheap publications, and not be persuaded that grand juries would have found true bills, and petty juries verdicts of guilty against their authors? Did ministers by this abstemiousness of prosecution mean to bring the matter to a crisis like the present? Did they contemplate a time when the vast accumulation of the evil would warrant them in this new infringement? If the libels had been brought before juries, ministers seemed to apprehend that the existing law would have been found sufficient, and they would thus have been deprived of one main ground on which their measure rested. As to the question of the liberty of the press, if he were to enter into it, a wide field indeed would be opened to him; but though he might lament the excess to which that liberty had in some instances been carried, he was persuaded that the old and recognized laws were adequate to restrain it. Upon this point the case was as defective as upon others; and as nothing was more valuable than the preservation of the liberty hitherto enjoyed, he hoped the nation would feel it, and that before the noble lord's bill passed into a law, depriving the people of their ancient privileges, they would assemble without fear, and pour in upon the House a tide of remonstrances which even the noble lord would not be able to resist. It was unnecessary for him on the present occasion to say more. The liberty of the press was as yet in safe hands—in the hands of the press itself: which would no doubt speedily throw light enough on the subject to show what the real causes were of the licentiousness of the few, that was to be made the ground for encroaching on the liberty of all. He had come down to the House with a sincere inclination to listen impartially to what the noble lord might suggest, and disposed to concur in the measures proposed, rather than to oppose them; but he had then no notion of the extent to which the demand would be made. He might have been willing to concede something if a necessity had been shown, but nothing would satisfy the noble lord but an attack upon the very vital principles of the British constitution. Were we to live in entirely new times? Were we now to hold up the world, that the constitution which we had hitherto venerated for its antiquity, and loved for the blessings it had conferred, was of no value? Formerly, when foreigners asked in what way we became possessed of such and such institutions that attracted their admiration, we could reply, that we were indebted for them to the right which the people of England enjoyed of thinking and speaking freely. But now another lesson was taught by the noble lord, who would convince us, that what had been the salvation of our liberties was the destruction of our happiness—that what we and our forefathers had believed, was false and foolish; and that to preserve freedom and property, the constitution must undergo a change which, in his conscience he (Mr. Tierney) believed it could not survive. He said fairly and openly that suspecting as he did the administration from which these measures emanated, he considered them as only the advanced guard of the array of bills which they were to direct against the constitution. He saw on the part of the government an evident determination to resort to nothing but force; they thought of nothing else; they dreamt of nothing else; they would try no means of conciliation, they would make no attempt to pacify and reconcile; force—force—force, and nothing but force that was their cry, and it had been the same for years: one measure of coercion had been, and would be, followed up by another, and the result would justify what he asserted, that 10,000 men would not answer their purpose; one measure of violence must succeed another, and what they gained by force they must retain by the same detestable means. The people would never rest until they were allowed to live under laws equally administered; until their honest industry could procure them the means of maintaining their families, and until they should again enjoy the blessings of that constitution which their ancestors intended they should partake. If not, discontent would increase to disaffection, and distress would produce discontent, notwithstanding the bold assertions of the noble lord, that the nation was prosperous, and had no wants but those which arose out of the present condition of America. If the noble lord had confined himself to the grant of 10,000 men, he should have deemed it a strong measure in a time of profound peace. Was any evidence offered that a body of the military had been overpowered, or even that it had not always been sufficient to the dispersion of any meeting? But if the country gave him more troops to put down new meetings, surely it was somewhat hard that he should also ask it for new laws, that were to prevent the possibility of new meetings. If the noble lord thought that the new laws would be effectual, where was the occasion for the 10,000 men? It was clear that the noble lord felt that his new laws were more likely to exasperate than to conciliate, and the best comment upon all the noble lord had advanced in favour of his new projects, was his declaration, "I want 10,000 men into the bargain." His sincere belief was, that the noble lord would want many more than 10,000 men, and what a melancholy prospect did that hold out to the country! It might be said that he used violent language. He admitted it; and all he could say in answer was, that he did not utter a single syllable that he did not on his honour, believe. He was an alarmist, he felt alarm, because he was compelled to trust to men who would rely on nothing against the people but brute force. He was alarmed because an attempt was to be made, under false pretences, to destroy all that was valuable in the constitution, unless it were defended by the free spirit of a yet free nation. Therefore it was, that he indulged a hope, that while the right of meeting remained, the people would meet and express their opinions with such effect that the threats and measures of coercion might be abandoned. He had hoped that a more moderate course would have been pursued, because, with the exception of the disturbed districts, as they were called, there was no part of Great Britain where assemblies might not be held, even by the admission of ministers, without the slightest danger to the public peace. He trusted that the country would thoroughly understand the nature of these novel laws, that the real objects of government would be evident, and that those objects by the public voice would be for ever defeated. If the country abstained from that course, and if the House, without any evidence to warrant those innovations, should consent to follow the noble lord in his desperate and adventurous course, all he could say was that he should witness it with the deepest and most sincere regret. He should then have lived long enough, and could no longer be of use to his country in that House. He saw an hon. gentleman on a bench below him smile. If that hon. gentleman expected him to secede, he should tell him that it was contrary to his principles to do so. He did not mean to retire from parliament—he would still attend, and by his vote oppose the progress of laws destructive of a nation's rights, but he should not feel bound, after the people had shown such apathy, to sacrifice for them as he had hitherto done, his time and his health. He hoped that all members would give the subject their most deliberate attention. The new laws were not such as the public exigency required; the extent, or even the existence of disaffection was not proved; and until it should be so, it was the duty of every honest man to pause. At least, attention ought to be paid to this point—whether some course of conciliation might not be adopted; whether steps ought not to be taken to satisfy the people, and to prove that, while the House was willing to repress sedition, it had a fixed determination to listen to their grievances, and, as far as possible, to apply a remedy.

Newspaper Stamp Duties Act, 30 December 1819

60 Geo. 3, c. 9   *Statutes at Large*, LX, 33-40.

Another of the "Six Acts," this statute applied the fourpence newspaper stamp duty to virtually all cheap publications. It was the most extreme of the "taxes on knowledge" and, although modified considerably in 1836, was not finally repealed until 1855.

Whereas Pamphlets and printed Papers containing Observations upon public Events and Occurrences, tending to excite Hatred and Contempt of the Government and Constitution of these Realms as by Law established, and also vilifying our holy Religion, have lately been published in great Numbers, and at very small Prices; and it is expedient that the same should be restrained: May it therefore please Your Majesty that it may be enacted; and be it enacted by The King's Most Excellent Majesty, by and with the Advice and Consent of the Lords Spiritual and Temporal, and Commons, in this present Parliament assembled, and by the Authority of the same, That from and after Ten Days after the passing of this Act, all Pamphlets and Papers containing any Public News, Intelligence or Occurrences, or any Remarks or Observations thereon, or upon any Matter in Church or State, printed in any Part of the United Kingdom for Sale, and published periodically, or in Parts or Numbers, at Intervals not exceeding Twenty six Days between the Publication of any Two such Pamphlets or Papers, Parts or Numbers, where any of the said Pamphlets or Papers, Parts or Numbers respectively, shall not exceed Two Sheets, or shall be published for Sale for a less Sum than Sixpence, exclusive of the Duty by this Act imposed thereon, shall be deemed and taken to be Newspapers . . .; and be subject to such and the same Duties of Stamps, with such and the same Allowances and Discounts, as Newspapers printed in *Great Britain* and *Ireland* respectively now are subject unto under and by virtue of the said recited Acts of Parliament, and shall be printed, published and distributed under and subject to all such and the like Rules, Regulations, Restrictions, Provisions, Penalties and Forfeitures, as are contained in the said recited Acts or either of them, or in any other Act or Acts of Parliament now in force in *Great Britain* or *Ireland* respectively, relating to Newspapers printed, published, dispersed or made public in the United Kingdom; and the said recited Acts of Parliament, and all other Acts of

Parliament now in force in *Great Britain* or *Ireland* respectively, relating to the printing, publishing, dispersing or making public in *Great Britain* or *Ireland* respectively, any Newspapers, or containing any Regulations relating thereto, and all the Clauses, Provisions, Regulations, Restrictions, Penalties and Forfeitures therein respectively contained, and in force at the passing of this Act, shall (except where the same may be altered by this Act) be applied and put in force in relation to all such Pamphlets and printed Papers aforesaid, as fully and effectually as if all such Clauses, Provisions, Regulations, Restrictions, Penalties and Forfeitures were respectively severally and separately re-enacted in and made Part of this Act; and the said recited Acts, and all other such Acts of Parliament as aforesaid, and this Act, shall, as to all the Purposes of carrying this Act into Execution, be construed as one Act. . . .

IV. And be it further enacted, That all Pamphlets and Papers containing any Public News, Intelligence or Occurrences, or any such Remarks or Observations as aforesaid, printed for Sale, and published periodically, or in Parts or Numbers, at Intervals exceeding Twenty six Days between any Two such Pamphlets or Papers, Parts or Numbers, and which said Pamphlets, Papers, Parts or Numbers respectively, shall not exceed Two Sheets, or which shall be published for Sale at a less Price than Sixpence, shall be first published on the First Day of every Calendar Month, or within Two Days before or after that Day, and at no other Time; and that if any Person or Persons shall first publish or cause to be published any such Pamphlet, Paper, Part or Number aforesaid, on any other Day or Time, he or they shall forfeit for every such Offence the Sum of Twenty Pounds.

V. And be it further enacted, That upon every Pamphlet or Paper containing any Public News, Intelligence or Occurrences, or any Remarks or Observations thereon, or upon any Matter in Church or State, printed in any Part of the United Kingdom for Sale, and published periodically, or in Parts or Numbers, at Intervals not exceeding Twenty six Days between the Publication of any Two such Pamphlets or Papers, Parts or Numbers, and upon every Part or Number thereof, shall be printed the full Price at which every such Pamphlet, Paper, Part or Number shall be published for Sale, and also the Day on which the same is first published for Sale, and also the Day on which the same is first published; and if any Person shall publish any such Pamphlet, Paper, Part or Number, without the said Price and Day being printed thereon, or if any Person shall at any Time within Two Months after the Day of Publication printed thereon as aforesaid, sell or expose to Sale any such Pamphlet, Paper, Part or Number, or any Portion or Part of such Pamphlet, Paper, Part or Number, upon which the Price so printed as aforesaid shall be Sixpence, or above that Sum, for a less Price than the Sum of Sixpence, every such Person shall for every such Offence forfeit and pay the Sum of Twenty Pounds.

VI. Provided always, and be it further enacted, That nothing in this Act contained shall extend or be construed to extend to subject any Person publishing any Pamphlet or Paper to any Penalty for any Allowance in Price made by the Person for whom and on whose behalf, and for whose Profit, Benefit or Advantage, the same shall have been first published, to any Bookseller or Distributor, or other Person to whom the same shall be sold for the Purpose of retailing the same.

VII. And be it further enacted, That all Pamphlets and Papers which are by this Act declared to be subject to the Stamp Duties upon Newspapers, shall be freed and discharged from all the Stamp Duties and Regulations contained in any Act of Parliament relating to Pamphlets.

VIII. And be it further enacted, That no Person, from and after Thirty Days after the passing of this Act, shall print or publish for Sale any Newspaper, or any Pamphlet or other Paper containing any Public News, Intelligence or Occurrences, or any Remarks or Observations thereon, or upon any Matter in Church or State, which shall not exceed Two Sheets, or which shall be published for Sale at a less Price than Sixpence, until he or she shall have entered into a Recognisance before a Baron of the Exchequer, in *England, Scotland* or *Ireland* respectively, as the Case may be, if such Newspaper or Pamphlet, or other Paper aforesaid, shall be printed in *London* or *Westminster*, or in *Edinburgh* or *Dublin*, or shall have executed in the Presence of, and delivered to some Justice of the Peace for the County, City or Place where such Newspaper, Pamphlet or other Paper shall be printed, if printed elsewhere, a Bond to His Majesty, His Heirs and Successors, together with Two or Three sufficient Sureties, to the Satisfaction of the Baron of the Exchequer taking such Recognisance, or of the Justice of the Peace taking such Bond, every Person printing or publishing any such Newspaper or Pamphlet or Paper aforesaid, in the Sum of Three hundred Pounds, if such Newspaper, Pamphlet or Paper shall be printed in *London* or within Twenty Miles thereof, and in the Sum of Two hundred Pounds, if such Newspaper, Pamphlet or Paper shall be printed elsewhere in the United Kingdom, and his or her Sureties in a like Sum in the whole, conditioned that such Printer or Publisher shall pay to His Majesty, His Heirs and Successors, every such Fine or Penalty as may at any Time be imposed upon or adjudged against him or her, by reason of any Conviction for printing or publishing any blasphemous or seditious Libel, at any Time after the entering into such Recognisance or executing such Bond; and that every Person who shall print or first publish any such Newspaper, Pamphlet or other Paper, without having entered into such Recognisance, or executed and delivered such Bond with such Sureties as aforesaid, shall, for every such Offence, forfeit the Sum of Twenty Pounds. . . .

XIII. And Whereas the Printer or Publisher of any Newspaper, and of any Pamphlet and Paper hereby enacted to be deemed and taken to be a Newspaper, will, after the passing of this Act, be bound, under and by virtue of the Provisions contained in the said Acts made and passed in the Thirty eighth and Fifty fifth Years of His Majesty's Reign respectively, to deliver to the Commissioners of Stamps in *Great Britain* and *Ireland* respectively, or some Distributor of Stamps or other Officer, on the Day on which the same is published, or within a certain Time afterwards, One of the Newspapers, Pamphlets or Papers so published, signed as in the said Acts is respectively directed: And Whereas it is expedient that the same or similar Provisions and Regulations should extend and be applied to all Pamphlets and Papers, whether published periodically or not, and which shall contain any Public News, Intelligence or Occurrence, or any Remarks or Observations thereon, or upon any Matter in Church or State, and which shall not exceed Two Sheets as aforesaid, or which shall be published for Sale at a less Price than Sixpence; Be it therefore enacted, That from and after Ten Days after the passing of this Act, the Printer or Publisher of any Pamphlet or other Paper for Sale, containing any Public News, Intelligence or Occurrences, or any Remarks or Observations thereon, or on any Matter in Church or State, shall, upon every Day upon which the same shall be published, or within Six Days after, deliver to the Commissioners of Stamps for *Great Britain* and *Ireland* respectively, at their Head Offices, or to some Distributor or Officer to be appointed by them to receive the same, and whom they are hereby required to appoint for that Purpose, One of the Pamphlets or Papers so published upon each such Day, signed by the Printer or Publisher thereof, in his Handwriting, with his Name and Place of Abode; and the same shall be carefully kept by the said Commissioners, or such Distributor or Officer as aforesaid, in such manner as the said Commissioners shall direct; and such Printer or Publisher shall be entitled to demand and receive from the Commissioners, or such Distributor or Officer, the Amount of the Retail Price of such Pamphlet or Paper so delivered; and in every Case in which the Printer and Publisher of such Pamphlet or Paper shall neglect to deliver One such Pamphlet or Paper in the manner hereinbefore directed, such Printer and Publisher shall, for every such Neglect respectively, forfeit and lose the Sum of One hundred Pounds.

XIV. Provided always, and be it further enacted, That in case the said Commissioners, or such Distributor or Officer aforesaid, shall refuse to receive or pay for any Copy of such Pamphlet or Paper offered to be delivered to them or him as aforesaid, for or on account of the same not being within the true Intent and Meaning of this Act, such Commissioners, Distributor or Officer shall, if required so to do, give and deliver to such Printer or Publisher a Certificate in Writing that a Copy of such Pamphlet or Paper had been by him duly offered to be delivered; and such Printer or Publisher shall thereupon be freed and discharged from any Penalty for not having delivered such Copy as aforesaid.

XV. And be it further enacted, That if any Person shall sell or expose to Sale any Pamphlet or other Paper not being duly stamped, if required to be stamped, such Person shall, for every such Offence, forfeit the Sum of Twenty Pounds.

XVI. And be it declared and enacted, That it shall be lawful for any of His Majesty's Courts of Record at *Westminster* or *Dublin* or of Great Session in *Wales*, or any Judge thereof respectively, or for any Court of Quarter or General Sessions of the Peace, or for any Justice of the Peace before whom any Person charged with having printed or published any blasphemous, seditious or malicious Libel, shall be brought for the purpose of giving Bail upon such Charge, to make it a Part of the Condition of the Recognisance to be entered into by such Person and his or her Bail, that the Person so charged shall be of good Behaviour during the Continuance of such Recognisance.

XVII. And be it further enacted, That all Fines, Penalties and Forfeitures by this Act imposed, shall be recovered by Action of Debt, Bill, Plaint or Information in any of His Majesty's Courts of Record at *Westminster* or *Dublin*, or the Courts of Great Session in the Principality of *Wales*, or the Courts of the Counties Palatine of *Chester, Lancaster* and *Durham*, or in the Court of Session or Court of Exchequer in *Scotland* (as the Case shall require), wherein no Essoign, Privilege, Protection, Wager of Law or more than One Imparlance shall be allowed; or before any Two

Justices of the Peace of the County, Riding, Stewartry, City or Place where the Offence shall be committed: Provided always, that no larger Amount in the Whole than One hundred Pounds shall be recoverable or recovered before any Justices of the Peace, for any such Penalties incurred in any one Day; any thing in this Act or any other Acts of Parliament contained to the contrary notwithstanding.

XVIII. And be it further enacted, That it shall be lawful for any Two or more Justices of the Peace, in all Cases in which they are authorised to hear and determine any Offence or Offences which shall be committed against this Act, or any other Act or Acts of Parliament which are by this Act required to be construed therewith as Part thereof, upon Information exhibited or Complaint made in that behalf, within Three Months after any such Offence committed, to summon the Party accused, and also the Witnesses on either Side; and upon the Appearance, or Contempt of the Party accused in not appearing, to proceed to the Examination of the Witness or Witnesses upon Oath (which Oath they are hereby empowered to administer), and to give Judgment for the Penalty or Penalties incurred; and in case the Party shall not immediately pay the said Penalty or Penalties, to commit the Offender to Prison, there to remain for any Time not exceeding Six Months, unless such pecuniary Penalty or Penalties shall be sooner paid and satisfied; and if any Party shall find himself or herself aggrieved by the Judgment of any such Justices, then he, she or they may, upon giving Security to the Amount or Value of the Penalty or Penalties adjudged, together with such Costs as may be awarded in case such Judgment shall be affirmed, appeal to the Justices of the Peace at the next Quarter or General Sessions of the Peace for the County, Riding, Division or Place wherein such Offence shall be committed, who are hereby empowered to summon and examine Witnesses upon Oath, and finally to hear and determine the same, and in case the Judgment shall be affirmed, it shall be lawful for such Justices to order the Person or Persons making such Appeal, to pay such Costs occasioned by such Appeal, as to them shall seem meet: Provided nevertheless, that it shall and may be lawful for the said respective Justices, where they shall see Cause, to mitigate or lessen any such Penalty or Penalties, in such manner as they in their Discretion shall think fit; the reasonable Costs and Charges of the Officers or Informers being always allowed over and above such Mitigation; and so as such Mitigation does not reduce the Penalty to less than One fourth Part thereof, over and above the said Costs and Charges. . . .

Speech by Henry Brougham in defense of Queen Caroline, House of Lords, 3 October 1820

Hansard, n.s., III, 112-31.

Caroline of Brunswick (1768-1821), wife of George IV, resided apart from her husband for many years, but returned to England in 1820 in order to claim the title of queen. A Bill of Pains and Penalties was introduced in the House of Lords on the grounds of her adultery. Many reformers leaped to her defense and she became for a time a symbol of opposition to the crown. Henry Brougham, a leading Whig reformer, was her attorney general in trial and conducted her defense successfully until her sudden death in 1821.

May it please your Lordships—The time is now come when I feel that I shall truly stand in need of all your indulgence. It is not merely the august presence of this assembly which embarrasses me; for I have oftentimes had experience of its condescension—nor the novelty of this proceeding that perplexes me; for the mind gradually gets reconciled to the strangest things—nor is it the magnitude of this cause that oppresses me; for I am borne up and cheered by that conviction of its justice, which I share with all mankind; but, my lords, it is the very force of that conviction, the knowledge that it operates universally, the feeling that it operates rightly, which now dismays me with the apprehension, that my unworthy mode of handling it, may, for the first time, injure it; and, while others have trembled for a guilty client, or been anxious in a doubtful case, or crippled with a consciousness of some hidden weakness, or chilled by the influence, or dismayed by the hostility, of public opinion, I, knowing that here there is no guiltiness to conceal, nor any thing, save the resources of perjury to dread, am haunted with the apprehension, that my feeble discharge of this duty may for the first time cast that cause into doubt, and may turn against me for condemnation those millions of your lordships countrymen, whose jealous eyes are now watching us, and who will not fail to impute it to me, if your lordships should reverse the judgment which the Case for the Charge has extorted from them. And I feel, my lords, under this weight so troubled, that I can hardly at this moment, with all the reflection which the indulgence of your lordships has accorded to me, compose my spirits to the discharge of my professional duty, under the weight of that grave responsibility which accompanies it. It is no light addition to this feeling, that I foresee, though at some distance, happily, that, before these proceedings close, it may be my unexampled lot to discharge a duty, in which the loyalty of a good subject may, among the ignorant, among the thoughtless—certainly not with your lordships for a moment—suffer an impeachment.

My lords; the princess Caroline of Brunswick arrived in this country in the year 1795—the niece of our sovereign, the intended consort of his heir apparent, and herself not a very remote heir to the crown of these realms. But I now go back to that period, only for the purpose of passing over all the interval which elapsed between that arrival and her departure in 1814. I rejoice that, for the present at least, the most faithful discharge of my duty permits me to draw this veil; but I cannot do so without pausing for an instant, to guard myself against a misrepresentation to which I know this cause may not unnaturally be exposed, and to assure your lordships most solemnly, that if I did not think that the cause of the Queen, as attempted to be established by the evidence against her, not only does not require recrimination at present—not only imposes no duty of even uttering one whisper by way of attack, by way of insinuation, against the conduct of her illustrious husband—but that it prescribes to me, for the present, silence upon this great and painful head of the case—I solemnly assure your lordships, that but for this conviction, my lips on that branch would not be closed; for, in discretionally abandoning the exercise of that power which I feel I have, in postponing for the present the statement of that case of which I am possessed, I feel confident that I am waving a right which I have, and abstaining from the use of materials which are mine. And let it not be thought, my lords, that if either now I did conceive, or if hereafter I should so far be disappointed in my estimate of the failure of the Case against me, as to feel it necessary to exercise that right—let no man vainly suppose, that not only I, but that any, the youngest member of the profession would hesitate one moment in the fearless discharge of that duty. I once before took leave to remind your lordships—which was unnecessary, but there are many whom it may be needful to remind—that an advocate, by the sacred duty of his connection with his client, knows, in the discharge of that office, but one person in the world, that client and none other. To save that client by all expedient means—to protect that client at all hazards and costs to all others, and among others to himself—is the highest and most unquestioned of his duties; and he must not regard the alarm, the suffering, the torment, the destruction, which he may bring upon any other; nay, separating even the duties of a patriot from those of an advocate, he must go on reckless of the consequences, if his fate it should unhappily be, to involve his country in confusion for his client.

But, my lords, I am not reduced to this painful necessity. I feel that if I were to touch that branch of the Case now, until any event shall afterwards show that unhappily I am deceiving myself—I feel that if I were now to approach that branch of the Case, I should seem to give up the higher ground of innocence on which I put it; I should seem to be justifying when I plead not guilty; I should seem to argue in extenuation and in palliation of offences, or levities, or improprieties, the least and the lightest of which I stand here to deny. For it is false, as has been said—it is foul and false as those who dared to say, who, pretending to discharge the higher duties to God, have shown, that they know not the first of their duties to their fellow-creatures—it is foul and false and scandalous in those who have said (and they know that it is so who have dared to say), that there are improprieties admitted to be proved against the Queen. I deny that the admission has been made. I contend that the evidence does not prove them. I will show you that the evidence disproves them. One admission, doubtless, I do make; and let my learned friends who are of counsel for the Bill take all the benefit of it, for it is all that they have proved by their evidence. I grant that her majesty left this country, and went to reside in Italy. I grant that her society was chiefly foreign. I grant that it was an inferior society to that in which she once moved in this country. I admit, my lords, that while here, and while happy in the protection—not perhaps, of her own family, after the fatal event which deprived it of its head; but while enjoying the society of your lordships, and the families of your lordships, I grant that the Queen moved in a more choice, in perhaps a more dignified society, than he did in Italy. And the charge against her is, that she has associated with Italians, instead of her own countrymen and countrywomen; and that, instead of the peeresses of England, she has sometimes associated with Italian nobility, and sometimes with persons of the commonalty of that country. But, who are they that bring this charge? Others may accuse her—others may blame her for going abroad—others may tell tales of the consequences of living among Italians, and of not associating with the women of her country, or of her adopted country; but it is not your lordships that have any right to say so. It is not you, my lords, that can fling this at her majesty. You are the last person in the world—you, who now presume to judge her, are the last persons in the world so to charge her; for you are the witnesses whom she must call to vindicate her from that charge. You are the last persons who can so charge her; for you, being her witnesses, have been also the instigators of that only admissible crime. While she was here, she courteously opened the doors of her palace to the families of your lordships. She graciously condescended to mix herself, in the habits of most familiar life, with those virtuous and distinguished persons. She condescended to court your society— and, as long as it suited purposes not of hers—as long as it was subservient to views not of her own—as long as it served interests in which she had no concern—she did not court that society in vain. But when changes took place—when other views arose—when that power was to be retained which she had been made the instrument of grasping—when that lust of power and place was to be continued its gratification, to the first gratification of which she had been made the victim—then her doors were opened in vain; then that society of the peeresses of England was withholden from her; then she was reduced to the alternative humiliating indeed, for I say that her condescension was no humiliation. She was only lowering herself, by omitting the distinction of rank to enjoy the first society in the world. But then it pleased you to reduce her to what was really humiliation—either to acknowledge that you had deserted her, to seek the company of those who now made it a favour, which she saw they unwillingly granted, or to leave the country and have recourse to other company. I say then, my lords, that it is not here that I must be told—it is not in the presence of your lordships I must expect to hear any one lift his voice to complain, that the princess of Wales went to reside in Italy, and associated with those whose society she neither ought to have chosen, nor perhaps would have chosen—certainly would not have chosen—perhaps I may say ought not to have chosen—had she been in other or happier circumstances.

In the midst of this, and of so much suffering as to an ingenuous mind such conduct could not fail to cause, she still had one resource, and which, for a space, was allowed to remain to her—I need hardly say I mean the comfort of knowing that she still possessed the undiminished attachment and grateful respect of her justly respected and deeply lamented daughter. An event took place which, of all others, most excites the feelings of a parent—that daughter was about to form a union upon which the happiness—upon which, alas! the Queen knew too well how much the happiness—or the misery of future life depended. No announcement was made to her majesty of the projected alliance. All England occupied with the subject— Europe looking on with an interest which it certainly had in so great an event— England had it announced; Europe had it announced—but the one person to whom no notice of it was given, was the mother of the bride who was to be espoused; and all that she had done then to deserve this treatment was, with respect to one of the illustrious parties, that she had been proved, by his evidence against her, to be not guilty of the charge; and, with respect to his servants, that they had formerly used her as the tool by which their ambition was to be gratified. The marriage itself was consummated. Still, no notice thereof was communicated to the Queen. She heard it accidentally by a courier who was going to announce the intelligence to the Pope, that ancient, intimate, much-valued ally of the Protestant Crown of these realms. A prospect grateful to the whole nation, interesting to all Europe, was now afforded, that the marriage would be a fruitful source of stability to the royal family of these realms. The whole of that period, painfully interesting to a parent as well as to a husband, was passed without the slightest communication; and if the princess Charlotte's own feelings had prompted her to open one, she was in a state of anxiety of mind and of delicacy of frame, in consequence of that her first pregnancy, which made it dangerous to have a struggle between power and authority on the one hand, and affection and duty on the other. An event truly fatal followed, which plunged the whole of England into grief and gloom; in which all our foreign neighbours sympathized: and while, with a due regard to the feelings of those foreign allies, and even of strange powers and princes, with whom we had no alliance, that event was speedily communicated by particular messengers to each, the person in all the world who had the deepest interest in that event—the person whose feelings, above those of all the rest of mankind, were most overwhelmed and stunned by it, was left to be stunned and overwhelmed by it accidentally; as she had, by accident, heard of the marriage. But, if she had not heard the dreadful news by accident, she would, ere long, have felt it; for the decease of the princess Charlotte was communicated to her mother, by the issuing of the Milan Commission and the commencement of the proceedings for the third time against her character and her life.

See, my lords, the unhappy fate of this illustrious woman! It has been her lot always to lose her surest stay, her best protector, when the dangers most thickened around her; and, by a coincidence almost miraculous, there has hardly been one of her defenders withdrawn from her, that his loss has not been the signal of an attack upon her existence. Mr. Pitt was her earliest defender and friend in this country. He died in 1806; and, but a few weeks afterwards, the first inquiry into the conduct of her royal highness began. He left her a legacy to Mr. Perceval, her firm, dauntless, most able advocate. And, no sooner had the hand of an assassin laid Mr. Perceval low, than she felt the calamity of his death, in the renewal of the attacks, which his gallantry, his skill, and his invariable constancy had discomfited. Mr. Whitbread then undertook her defence; and, when that castastrophe happened, which all good men lament, without any distinction of party or sect, again commenced the distant grumbling of the storm; for it then, happily, was never allowed to approach her, because her daughter stood her friend, and there were who worshipped the rising sun. But, when she lost that amiable and beloved daughter, all which might have been expected here—all which might have been dreaded by her if she had not been innocent—all she did dread—because, who, innocent or guilty, loves persecution; who delights in trial, when character and honour are safe?—all was at once allowed to burst upon her head; and the operations commenced by the Milan Commission. And, my lords, as if there were no possibility of the Queen losing a protector without some most important act being played in this drama against her, the day which saw the venerable remains of our revered sovereign consigned to the tomb—of that sovereign who, from the first outset of the princess in English life, had been her constant and steady defender—that same sun ushered the ringleader of the band of perjured witnesses into the palace of his illustrious successor! Why, my lords, do I mention these things? Not for the sake of making so trite a remark, as that trading politicians are selfish—that spite is twin-brother to ingratitude—that nothing will bind base natures—that favours conferred, and the duty of gratitude neglected, only make those natures the more malignant. My lords, the topic would be trite and general, and I should be ashamed to trouble your lordships with it; but I say this once more, in order to express my deep sense of the unworthiness with which I now succeed such powerful defenders, and my alarm lest my exertions should fail to do what theirs, had they been living, must have accomplished.

My lords; I pray your attention for a few moments, to what all this has resulted in. It has ended in the getting up of a story, to the general features of which I am now first about to direct the attention of your lordships. But I must begin by praying you to recollect what the Evidence has not only proved, but is very likely to have discharged from the memory of your lordships—I mean the Opening of my learned friend, the Attorney-General. Now, he shall himself describe, in his own words, the plan and the construction of that opening statement. It is most material for your lordships to direct your attention to this; because much of the argument rests on this comparative view. He did not then make a general speech, without book, without direction or instruction; but his speech was the spoken evidence; it was the transcript of that which he had before him; and the way in which that transcript was prepared, I leave your lordships, even uninformed to a certain degree as you now must needs be, to conjecture. "I will," said my learned friend—and every one who heard him make the promise, and who knows his strictly honourable nature, must have expected its accurate fulfilment—"I will most conscientiously state nothing which I do not, in my conscience, believe I shall be able to substantiate in proof; but I will withhold nothing, upon which I have the same conviction." I believed the attorney-general when I heard him promise. I knew that he spoke from his conscience; and now that I see he has failed in the fulfilment, I equally well know that there is but one cause for the failure—that he told you what he had in his brief, which he had got into his brief from the mouths of the witnesses. He could get it in no other way but that. The witnesses who had told falsehoods before, were scared from repeating them here, before your lordships. Now, I will give your lordships one or two specimens of this; because I think these samples will enable you to form a pretty accurate estimate, not only of the value of that evidence, where it comes up to my learned friend's Opening, but also to form a pretty good guess of the manner in which that part of it which did succeed was prepared for that purpose. I will merely take one or two of the leading witnesses, and compare one or two of the matters which my learned friend opened, and will not tire you with the manner in which they told the story.

First, my learned friend said, that the Evidence of the Queen's improper conduct would come down almost "until the time at which I have now the honour of addressing your lordships." I am quoting the words of my learned friend, from the short-hand writer's notes. In fact, by the Evidence, that "*almost*" means up to the present time, all but three years; that is to say, all but a space of time, exactly equal to that space of time over which the other part of the Evidence extends.—At Naples, where the scene is laid which is first so sedulously brought before your lordships, as if the first connection between the two parties began upon that occasion—as if that were the night when the guilty intentions, which they long had been harbouring, but for want of opportunity had not been able to fulfil, were at length gratified—at Naples—I pray your lordships to attend to the manner in which he opened this first and most important branch of his whole case, and which if it fails, that failure must affect the statement of circumstances, not only in this part in the Evidence, but in all the subsequent stages of it—How does my learned friend open that part of his case? "I shall show you," says he, "that there are clear, decisive marks of two persons having slept in the bed—the night that the Queen came home, the second night she was at Naples, she returned early from the Opera; she went to her own room, from thence she repaired to Bergami's room, where Bergami himself was—the next day she was not visible till an unusually late hour, and was inaccessible to the nobility of Naples. Every one of these assertions, rising one above another in succession and importance, but even the lowest of them of great moment to the case against her majesty—every one of them not only is false, but is negatived by the Witness produced to support them. Demont gives no "decisive marks;" she gives a doubtful and hesitating case. With one exception, there is nothing specific, even in what she swears; and with that I shall afterwards come to deal. But she denies that she knew where the Queen went when she first left her own bed-room. She denies that she knew where Bergami was at that time. She says affirmatively that the next morning the Queen was up and alert by the usual time. Not one tittle of evidence does she give, or any body else, of her having refused access to any one person who called; nor is any evidence given (to make it more complete) that any body called that morning.

Then come we to that which my learned friend opened with more than even his wonted precision. We know that all the rest was from his instructions. It could be from no other source. He had never been in Italy. Neither he nor my learned friend, the solicitor-general, have given us any idea of their knowing what sort of a country it is—that they know any thing of a masquerade—that they know any thing of a Cassino. My learned friend has represented as if the being black-balled at that Cassino is ruin to a person's character; forgetting who may be the members of the society at that Cassino—that there may be a colonel Browne—that it is held at the very place where the Milan Commission was held. "But," says my learned friend, the solicitor-general, "who ever heard of the wife of a royal prince of this country going disguised to a masquerade?" Who would have thought that, being disguised, and being on her way to a masquerade, she did not go in her own state coach, with her livery servants, with a coachman bedizened with lacquays plaistered, with all the "pomp, pride, and circumstance" of a court or a birth-day, but that she went in a common hired carriage, without the royal arms, without splendor and garb, out at the back-door, instead of issuing out of the front door, with all the world spectators. Nay, I only wonder that my learned friend did not state, that she went to a masquerade in a domino, and a false face! My lords, it was not, therefore, from their own personal observation, certainly not from having been present at these royal recreations of Murat's court, that my learned friends obtained their knowledge of this cause; but they have it from Demont or Majoochi; the witnesses who have been examined again and again; and who have again and again told the same story; but which story being founded in fact, they now recollected only the part that was true, and forgot what was untrue.

"Then," says my learned friend, in this instance which I am now going to state, leaving us to our general suspicions as to where he got his knowledge upon the other circumstances, and coming to something more specific, "I am instructed to state," and in another instance, "the witness says," so and so, showing he was reading the witness's deposition. "I am instructed to state, that the dress which the princess had assumed, or rather the want of it in part, was extremely indecent and disgusting;" and he adds afterwards, in commenting upon it, that it was of the "most indecent description;" so that she was, on account of that indecency, on account of the disgusting nature of it, by those who actually saw it, hooted from the public theatre. Your lordships will recollect what it came to—that the princess was there in a dress that was exceedingly ugly—the maid Demont said, in a "very ugly" dress; and that was all my learned friend could get her now to assert—that it was without form, and ugly—masques came about her, and she, unknown in her own masque—for, strange as it may appear to my learned friend, a person at a masquerade endeavours to be disguised—was attacked from joke or from spite—oftener from joke than from spite; her own dress being of that ugly description—from what reason is left to this moment unexplained.

My lords; I should fatigue your lordships if I were to go over other instances, I shall only mention that at Messina. Voices are said to have been heard. The attorney-general opened, that at Messina he should prove, that the princess and Bergami were locked up in the same room and were heard speaking together. That is now reduced, by the evidence, to certain voices being heard, she cannot say whose. At Savona, where my learned friend gives you, as he generally does in his speech, the very day of the month, the 12th of April, he stated, that the only access to the princess's room was through Bergami's, where there was no bed, but that in the princess's room there was a large bed. The witness proved only one of those particulars out of three.

Passing over a variety of particulars, I shall give only one or two instances from Majoochi's and Sacchi's evidence. "The princess remained in Bergami's room a very considerable time," the night that Majoochi swore she went into his room, "and there the Witness heard them kissing each other," says the attorney-general. Majoochi says, she remained there one of the times ten minutes, the other fifteen; and that he only heard a whispering. Now, as to Sacchi. The story as told by my learned friend, from the brief in his hand, and which I have no doubt my learned friend has in his papers, and that Sacchi had told before at Milan, is, that a courier one night returned from Milan, that is, that he, Sacchi, returned as a courier from Milan, for it was he whom he meant—that finding Bergami out of his own room, he looked about and saw him come out of the Queen's room undressed—that all the family were in bed—that he observed him—that he spoke to him—and that Bergami explained it by saying, he had gone, hearing his child cry, to see what was the matter; and desired him not to mention any thing about it.—Sacchi negatives this, as far as a man speaking to so unusual a circumstance, which if it had happened, must have forcibly impressed his recollection, can do so. He denies it as strongly as a man can, by denying all recollection of any such particulars, although not for want of examination; for my learned friend, the solicitor-general, questions him over and over again, and he cannot get him to come within a mile of such a fact.

Then come we to the disgraceful scenes, as the attorney-general described them, at the Barona; which he said—and if they had been as they were represented to him, I doubt not he used a very fair expression—he did not tell us what they were, but "they were so disgraceful, that it rather made that house deserve the name of a brothel, more than that of a palace, or a place fit for thr reception of her majesty, or a person of the least virtue or delicacy." Here, there is a most entire failure of proof from all the witnesses.

Then we are told, that at Naples the attendants were shocked and surprised by the conduct of the Queen—that in Sicily no doubt was entertained by them, from what they saw of the familiarities between the parties, that a criminal intercourse was going on there. Not one of those attendants describes that effect to have been produced upon their minds by what they saw. I shall afterwards come to what they did see; but they do not tell you this, though frequently prompted to do it. Then, as to the visiting of the nobility—that the Queen's society was given up by the ladies of rank of her own country, from the moment she left this country—that they all fell away—in short, that she was treated abroad, I know not from what motive, with something of the same abandonment with which she was treated in this country; I well know from what motive. All this is disproved by the evidence. How came my learned friend to forget the fact of that most respectable woman, lady Charlotte Lindsay, joining her at Naples, after her conduct had been observed by all the servants; with which servants lady Charlotte Lindsay naturally lived on terms of intimacy, and between which servants, I have no idea that any thing of that grave-like secrecy existed, which each of them has represented to have existed between themselves up to the time they came to the Cotton Garden depot, and up to the moment that they brought from that depot to your lordships' bar, the resources of their perjury. Lady Charlotte Lindsay, lord and lady Glenbervie, Mrs. Falconet and others had no doubt some intercourse with those Neapolitan servants, all of whom are represented as having been perfectly astounded with the impropriety, nay the indecency of the conduct of their royal mistress; and yet those persons are proved to have joined her, some at Naples, some at Rome, others at Leghorn, and to have associated with her, in spite of all this open and avowed indecorum.

But, even to a much later period, and in higher quarters, the Queen's company has been proved, by my learned friend's case, not to have been treated abroad with the neglect which it experienced here. She has been, in the first place; courteously received, even after her return from the long voyage, by the legitimate sovereign prince of Baden, a prince with a legitimate origin, though with a revolutionary accession to his territory. Equally well received was she by the still more legitimate Bourbons at Palermo; but courted was her society by the legitimate Stuarts of Sardinia, the heirs legitimate as contra-distinguished from the heirs of liberty and of right, to the throne of this realm—the illegitimate heirs I call them; but the true legitimates of the world, as some are disposed to call them who do not hold that allegiance, at least who disguise that allegiance, to the house of Brunswick, which, as good subjects, we all cherish. Nay, even a prince who, I doubt not, will rank, in point of antiquity and family, even higher than the legitimate Bourbons and Stuarts—I mean his highness the dey of Tunis, received her majesty as if she was respected by all his lighter-coloured brethren in the other parts of the globe. And she was also received, in the same respectful manner, by the representative of the king at Constantinople. So that wherever she has gone, she has met from all ranks, the only persons of authority and note whom she could have had as her vindicators. She was received by all those persons of authority and note, not only not as my learned friend expected to prove, but in the very reverse manner, and as from the evidence I have now described her.

Suffer me now, my lords, to solicit your lordships indulgence, while I look a little more narrowly into the case which was thus opened, and not proved by the attorney-general. The first remark which must strike any one who attends to this discussion, is one which pervades the whole case, and is of no small importance. Is it not remarkable, that such a case, possessed as they are of such witnesses, should have been left so lame and short as they must admit it to be left, when contrasted with their Opening? Was ever a case of criminal conversation brought into court under such favourable auspices? Who are your witnesses? The very two who, of all man and woman kind, must know must of this offence, not only if it were in the daily course of being committed, but if committed at all—I mean, the body servants of the two parties, the valet of the man, and the lady's own waiting maid. Why, in common cases, there are the very witnesses the counsel are panting to have and bring into court. From the form of the action, they can hardly ever venture to bring the man's servant; but if they can get hold of one by good fortune, they consider their case must be proved; and then the only question comes to be as to mitigation of damages—for as to proving the fact, no defendant would hold out. And if you believe any part of their case, it was not from any over caution of the parties—it was not from any great restraint they imposed on themselves, and, knowing that they were watched, that they took care to give the world nothing to see; because, if you believe the evidence, they had flung off all regard to decorum, all trammels of restraint, all ordinary prudence; and had given way to this guilty passion, as if they were still in the hey-day of youthful blood, and as if they were justified by those ties which render its indulgence a virtue rather than a crime. Yet, with all this want of caution—all these exhibitions of want of circumspection—the man's serving man, and the ladies waiting woman have not been able to prove more than these facts which, it is pretended, make out the charge. When I said, however, there was no caution or circumspection, I mis-stated the case. If you believe the evidence—and it is the great circumstance of improbability to which I solicit your attention—if you believe the evidence, there was every caution used by the parties themselves, to insure discovery, which the wishes and ingenuity of their most malignant adversary could have devised to promote his own designs. Observe how every part of the case is subject to this remark; and then I leave to your lordships confidently the inference that must arise from it. You will even find, that just in proportion as the different acts alleged are of a suspicious or of an atrocious nature, in exactly the same proportion do the parties take especial care that there shall be good witnesses, and many of them, in order to prove it. It would be a horrible case, if such features did not belong to it; but such features we have here abundantly; and if the witnesses are to be believed, no mortal ever acted as the Queen is represented to have done. Walking arm and arm is a most light thing; it seldom takes place except in the presence of witnesses, and many of those speaking most accurately respecting it; but sitting together in an attitude of familiar proximity which is somewhat less equivocal, is proved by several witnesses; and those who state it to have been done by the aid of placing the arms round the neck, or behind the back, and which accordingly raises it a step higher—these witnesses show you this happened when the doors were open, in the height of the sun, in a villa where hundreds of persons are walking, and when the house and villa were filled with common workmen. Several salutes were given; and, as this is still higher in the scale, it appears that never was a kiss to pass between these lovers without especial pains being taken, that a third person should be by to tell the story to those who did not see it. One witness is out of the room, while Bergami is about to take his departure on a journey from the Queen, while in Sicily. They want until he comes in, and then they kiss. When at Terracina Bergami is going to land, the whole party are on deck. The princess and Bergami retire to a cabin, and wait till Majoochi enters, and then the act is perpetrated. Sitting on a gun, or near the mast of the ship, on the knees of the paramour, is an act still higher in the scale of licentiousness—It is only proved scantily by one witness, but of that hereafter—care is taken that it should be perpetrated before eleven persons. But sitting upon a gun with the arms entwined, is such an act as leaves nothing to the imagination, except the granting of the last purposes of desire—This must be done in the presence of all the crew, of all the servants, and all the companions, by day and in the evening. The parties might be alone at night: then it was not done; but, at all other times, it is done before all the passengers and all the crew.

But the case is not left here. As your lordships might easily suppose, with persons so wary against themselves, such firm and useful allies of their accusers, such indispensable proofs of the case against them are not wanting to prove the last favour in the presence of good witnesses; and accordingly, sleeping together is not only said to have taken place habitually and nightly in the presence of all the company and all the passengers on board, but always, by land as well as by sea, did every body see it, that belonged to the party of pilgrims to Jerusalem. Nay, so far is this carried, that Bergami cannot retire into the anti-chamber where the princess is to change her clothes, or for any other purpose, without special care being taken, that the trusty, silent, honest, unintriguing Swiss waiting-maid shall be placed at the door of that anti-room, and told, "You wait here: we have occasion to retire for an hour or two and be naked together;" or at least, she is at liberty to draw what inferences she pleases from the fact.

But, my lords, I wish I could stop here. There are features of peculiar enormity in the other parts of this case; and in proportion as these disgusting scenes are of a nature to annoy every one, however unconcerned in the case, who hears them; to disgust and almost contaminate the mind of every one who is condemned to listen to them—in that proportion is especial care taken that they shall not be done in a corner. The place for them is not chosen in the hidden recesses of those receptacles of abomination which the continent have too many of, under the degraded and vilified name of palaces—the place is not taken in the hidden haunts which lust has degraded to its own purposes—some island where vice concealed itself from the public eye of ancient times—it is not in those palaces, in those Capreae of old, that the parties chose to commit such abominations; but they do it before witnesses in open day-light, when the sun is at the meridian. And that is not enough: the having them in the public high-ways is not enough: but they must have a courier of their own to witness them, without the veil of any one part of the furniture of a carriage, or of their own dress, to conceal from his eye their disgraceful situation! My lords, I ask your lordships whether vice was ever known before so unwary; whether folly was ever known so extravagant; whether unthinking passion, even in the most youthful period, when the passions swell high, and the blood boils in the veins, was ever known to act so thoughtlessly, so recklessly, so foolishly, as this case compels me to fancy? And when your lordships have put the facts to your minds, let this consideration dwell there, and let it operate as a check, when you come to examine the evidence by which the case is supported.

But all this is nothing. Their kindness to the enemy—their faithfulness to the plot against themselves, would be left short indeed, if it had gone no further than this; for it would then depend upon the good fortune of that adversary in getting hold of that witness; at least it might be questionable, whether the greater part of their precautions for their own ruin might not have been thrown away. Therefore, every one of these witnesses, without any exception, is either dismissed without a cause—for I say the causes are mere flimsinesses personified—or is refused to be taken back, upon his earnest and humble solicitations, when there was every human inducement to restore them to favour.—My lords, this is not all. Knowing what she had done; recollecting her own contrivances; aware of all these cunning and elaborate devices towards her own undoing; having before her eyes the pictures of all those schemes to render detection inevitable and concealment impossible; reflecting that she had given the last finishing stroke to this conspiracy of her own, by turning off these witnesses causelessly, and putting them into the power of her enemy; knowing that that enemy had taken advantage of her; knowing the witnesses were here to destroy her, and told that if she faced them she was undone; and desired and counselled and implored, again and again, to bethink her well before she ran so enormous a risk—the Queen comes to England, and is here, on this spot, and confronts these witnesses whom she had herself enabled to undo her. Menaced with degradation and divorce, knowing that was not an empty threat that was held out, and seeing it was about to be accomplished, up to this hour she refuses all endeavours towards a compromise of her honour and her rights; she refuses a magnificent retreat and the opportunity of an unrestrained indulgence in all her criminal propensities, and even a safeguard and protection from the court of England, and a vindication of her honour by the two Houses of parliament. If, my lords, this is the conduct of guilt—if these are the lineaments by which vice is to be traced in the human frame—if these are the symptoms of that worst of all states, dereliction of principle carried to excess, when it almost becomes a mental disease— then I have misread human nature; then I have weakly and groundlessly come to a conclusion—for I have always understood, that guilt was wary, and innocence alone unwary.

Attend now, my lords, I beseech you, with these comments upon the general features of the case, to the sort of evidence by which such a case is attempted to be established. I should exhaust myself, besides fatiguing your lordships, if I were to pause here and make a few of the cogent remarks which offer themselves, upon the connection of that part of the case which I have now gone through, with the part I am coming to. But there are one or two points so material, that I cannot omit all mention of them before I proceed further. I will make one observation, that, if an ordinary case could not be proved by such evidence as I am not to comment upon—if it would require very different proofs in the most common story, if there were no improbabilities such as I have shown—a case such as that I have now described, ought to be proved by the most convincing the most pure and immaculate testimony.

My lords; I do not intend to assert I have no interest in stating it—that a conspiracy has been formed against the Queen, by those who are the managers of the present proceeding. I say not such a thing. I only will show your lordships, that if there had been such a measure resorted to; that if any persons had been minded to ruin her majesty by such a device, they could not have taken a better course, and probably they would not have taken a different course, from that which I think the case of the prosecution proves them already to have pursued. In any such design, the first thing to be looked to is the agents, who are to make attacks against the domestic peace of an individual, and to produce evidence of misconduct, which never took place. Who are those persons I am fancying to exist if their existence be conceivable—who are those that they would have recourse to, to make up a story against the victim of their spiteful vengeance? First of all, they would get the servants who have lived in the house. Without them, it is almost impossible to succeed: with them, there is a most brilliant prospect of a triumphant result. Servants who have lived in the family were, in fact, all that could be desired—But, if those servants were foreigners, who were to be well tutored in their part abroad, and had to deliver their story where they were unknown, to be brought to a place to which they might never return all their days, and to speak before a tribunal which knew no more of them than they cared for it—whose threat they had no reason to dread, whose good opinion they were utterly careless of; living in a country to which they did not care two rushes whether they returned or not, and knew they never could return—those were the very identical persons such conspirators would have recourse to. But, there is a choice among foreigners. All foreigners are not made of the same materials; but, if any one country under heaven is marked out more than all the rest as the *Officina* for such a race, I say that country is the country of Augustus and Borgia. I speak of its perfidies, without imputing them to the country at large; but there in all ages perfidy could be had for money, while there was interest to be satisfied, or spite to be indulged. . . .

Every Woman's Book by **Richard Carlile, the first published British tract to advocate contraception, 1826**

Every Woman's Book; or, What is Love? (London: Richard Carlile, 1826), 34-48.

Carlile's (1790-1843) pioneering birth-control tract was written under the influence of the reformer Francis Place (1771-1854). It was reprinted several times and had a readership in the United States. Although Carlile wrote and published numerous controversial tracts on such subjects as republicanism, freethought, and insanity, Every Woman's Book *aroused the greatest storm of protest.*

This, like every other question, has its relations of connection and dependency. Plighted troth should not be broken for the mere love of change. Deceptions should not be practised. Successful concealments should never be made the substitutes of propriety. True chastity is that of the mind, which can examine itself and be satisfied as to the purity and utility of its motives.

The subject of love is wholly misunderstood, both in theory and practice, and must of existing human pain is the consequence of that misunderstanding. It is no more associated with sin than any other kind of commerce between individuals.

It is a fact that can hardly have escaped the notice of any one, that women who have never had sexual commerce begin to droop when about twenty-five years of age, that they become pale and languid, that general weakness and irritability, a sort of restless, nervous fidgettyness takes possession of them, and a sort of absorbing process goes on, their forms degenerate, their features sink, and the peculiar character of the old maid comes on. A state of health succeeds which makes their very existence in many cases a burthen to them, and in all cases produces melancholy sensations in those who know whence the cause proceeds.

The physical check, if once brought into general use, would remove this mass of evil; there would then be no such persons; for every young woman would then have a husband. Women, if we may be allowed the expression, would be in much greater demand, as every young man would take a wife, and women would be all but infinitely more respected than they are now.

It is not possible to anticipate the happiness likely to result from the physical check when once in general use.

There is an ill-founded notion current, that to produce an unlimited number of children is beneficial to society. A more erroneous notion was never formed. Like every other circumstance, it has its relations of good and evil. It is only a benefit to children, to be produced, when they can be made healthy and happy. It is only a benefit to parents, when they can produce them with the preservation of health and happiness. It is only a benefit to society, when children become conducive to the improvement of its state. It is an evil when they become a burthen to pre-existing members; an evil when they become a burthen to the parents; an evil when they are not healthy and happy.

All states of animal being are states of pleasure or pain. Pleasure is the absence or abatement of pain. All states of pain are evil: all states of pleasure are good. The greater amount of animal life is a state of pain, and the duty of humanity, virtue, or what is called morality, is to lessen the amount of pain. Whether this is done in lessening the number of sufferers, or in lessening the quantity of suffering in each individual, the good accomplished, or the real amount of pleasure generated, is the same; and the principle of preventing painful conceptions is a positive good to society.

But in this recommendation of the prevention of painful conceptions, in this newly-stated view of the subject of love, other objects are aimed at: we desire not only to prevent the existence of unhappy children that make parents and friends unhappy; but we aim a blow at all the unnatural propensities which either sex has associated with the passion of love. We seek the annihilation of prostitution and of the venereal disease, and he, who proposes a means equal to the eradication of this wide-spreading, this almost universal disease, will become the greatest benefactor of mankind. The unnatural propensities, of which prostitution may be justly ranked as one, are many: they are common to both male and female, and consist of self-excitements and unnatural gratifications, such as onanism, pederasty, and other substitutions for the accomplishment of seminal excretions in the male, and the appeasings of lascivious excitement in the females by artificial means. We desire to bring about a cessation from all these bad and disease producing practices by the recommendation of natural and healthy commerce between the sexes. We recommend chaste and proper commerce in preference to all the artificial and unnatural means that are extensively in use, to subdue, for the moment, the passion of love. We encourage the reality and decry the base artifice. The former promotes health and happiness; the latter generates disease, and all that is painful and disgraceful to those who practise it. A piece of sponge is set up for its extensive utility against the *condam,* the *baudruche,* the *dildo,* and whatever other invention custom has introduced or habit has dictated; against the whole series of artificial or unnatural gratification. The important discovery is, that if, before sexual intercourse, the female introduces into her vagina a piece of sponge as large as can be pleasantly introduced, having previously attached a bobbin or bit of narrow riband to withdraw it, it will, in most cases, be found a preventive to conception, that shall neither lessen the pleasure of the female nor injure her health. When convenient, the sponge should be dipped in warm water, or even in cold water rather than in none, as its property and purpose is to absorb the semen of the male, and it absorbs best when so far damp as to have been dipped in water and pressed with the hand.

The practice is common with the females of the more refined parts of the continent of Europe, and with those of the Aristocracy of England. An English Duchess was lately instanced to the writer, who never goes out to a dinner without being prepared with the sponge. The French and Italian women wear them fastened to their waists, and always have them at hand. One thing should be observed, and that is, *the most strict cleanliness,* never to use one bit of sponge a second time with a proper washing. The writer has been informed by those who have made experiments upon the matter, that the sponge is not felt by either party during the act of coition, and that no portion of the pleasure is abated; while, on the other hand, the pleasure is increased in the removal of all dread of evil consequences. One gentleman has made an experiment of using the sponge unknown to the female, of which she was ignorant until it was shewn to her; so that, it is clear, there is nothing unpleasant in its use for so important a purpose.

The use of the sponge is the female's safeguard; but there are other means, by which conceptions are avoided, to be practised by the male. One is, to wear the skin, or what, in France, is called *the bardruche*, in England, commonly, *the glove*. These are sold in London at brothels, by waiters at taverns, and by some women and girls in the neighbourhood of places of public resort, such as Westminster Hall, etc. Another is, not to inseminate the female, by observing a partial or complete withdrawing at the moment of seminal emission. This latter is the more certain means, and some women, particularly those of the Continent, will make it a part of the contract for intercourse, and look upon the man as a dishonest brute who does not attend to it.

A third means has been adopted and recommended to others by certain anatomists in London, which is, to emit the semen in the cavity below the womb, instead of into the womb, by lying in a parallel line on the female, leg on leg, at the time of emission. The theory of this practice can only be understood by anatomists, or explained by anatomical plates. It certainly has been asserted by some of them to be efficacious; but, upon the whole, it seems questionable, since it infers the necessity of emitting semen into the womb to produce a conception.

The theories of conception are by no means certain. The precise process is as much unknown to modern anatomists and physiologists, as it was to Galen, Hippocrates, or Aristotle. Hitherto, it has eluded all research, and there is scarcely a hope of discovering it, since women are not anatomists, and since their own experience is not equal to an explanation. It is a question, whether all women are impregnated by precisely the same means as to insemination, and none of the theories of conception have accounted for the production of twins or three children at one gestation and birth. The precise means by which the ovarium of the female is conveyed to the womb is not well explained.

In consequence of our imperfect knowledge of the process of conception, we can rely on nothing but experience, as to the means of preventing it. The piece of sponge has been questioned, as to its efficacy, in some cases; in others, it has been found certain; and the inference is, that variance in habit or construction of parts may vary its effects. Complete withdrawing before emission is certainly effectual in all cases; but not so easily to be observed by all persons. Partial withdrawing is effectual on some women; but not so with all. There is no certain rule, should the vagina be inseminated, and experience must decide which of the precautions is necessary.

There is so much of mental misery and bodily suffering to be avoided, by preventing conceptions, where there are injurious and not desired, that all persons interested should make it a peculiar study and observance. There is nothing unnatural in the circumstance, further than it is unnatural to use precautions against any other natural evil, such as a fever, a storm, or a beast of prey. Healthy human beings so far differ from the generality of other animals, that their desires and modes of living lead them to a constant intercourse at all seasons; and where debility is not produced by excess, health is confirmed by the stimulating and pleasing excitement.

To destroy a conception is an offence against the laws of the country. To aid or assist in destroying it is the same offence. A mother is not permitted to destroy her offspring, even while it be in the womb. The law protects the foetus, as it protects the born infant, and punishment would follow where the act of destruction was detected. Conception, therefore, should not be risked, with any view to subsequent destruction, as the prevention is alike moral and legal, and has no similarity to the destruction.

The notions of indecency and immorality, which the unreasoning minds of this day and this country attach to all discussions about sexual commerce, may be combated by referring to the history of mankind, and by shewing that through all the varied customs of different nations upon the subject, whatever was the prevailing custom was always the moral right of the matter. In some countries, and in former ages, the first principle of hospitality was to give the visitor the free use of the females of the house, and the wife first and in particular. An American Indian has been known to caress his visitor for the gratification of his wife, even when seeing them in the act of commerce. The Grecians and Romans had their Temple of Venus, where young people could appease their passions under the form of worship; and well would it be if such were the religion of every country. We should not see every third female sickly, consumptive, or wretched for want of sexual commerce. In no other respect than in this Temple and worship of Venus would we recommend a return to the customs of ancient nations upon the subject of sexual commerce. We desire an improvement upon their customs. We would encourage genuine love, wherever it can be made conducive to the happiness of either sex. We would not call upon the females of this day to join in a procession with a Phallus at their head; nor upon Christian ladies to preserve the cross as the standard of their faith, since that cross is but the mathematical emblem of that Phallus, and that Phallus, the male organ of generation, the emblem of the vivifying power of animal and vegetable matter, an emblem on which the deified principle of reason always was and always will be periodically crucified, have a temporary death and rise to life again. While we would preserve the moral spirit of love, we would have it to be the only religion of the State, as it admits of no sectarianism. We would purify whatever in it is gross and remove every gross idea from it, every idea that is not most refined and alike wise and moral.

It is the tact of those who are wedded to customs, to treat, as immoral, all theories and all practices which are opposed to them; but we, who introduce new theories and new practices or revive old ones which we think should not have been put aside, would beg a truce with you and ask you to examine before you condemn, to think, consider, and deliberate well before you decide; and where you cannot shew the contrary, pray give us credit for good motives.

It is known to all who have any thing like an extensive knowledge of mankind, that all sorts of schemes and even outrages upon the body of the female have been used, to render conceptions abortive; but here is the grand preventive which may be used by the one party without being discovered by the other.

The great end is, not to let the semen of the male remain in the genital vessels of the female. Such is the only clean and safe means of preventing conceptions. A variety of herbs and leaves have been used as draughts; but, however powerful as poisons, they are not to be depended on; and, must, in every case, injure the health of the female; beside this, every woman who resorts to these means feels degraded in her own opinion, from the consciousness that she has destroyed life. Here it is clear, that there is no life destroyed, nothing injurious to health, nothing but what must promote health, by removing all dread from the necessary practice of intercourse between the sexes. Nor is it to be called an indecent matter. The men, who have been instrumental in making this matter known in this country, are all elderly men, fathers of families of children grown up to be men and women, and men of first-rate moral characters, of first-rate learning, and some of the first politicians and philosophers that ever lived in this or in any other country: men, who are known as above described, in almost every country in Europe and America, and who look upon this as the most important discovery that has yet been made among mankind: important in every relation of popular morals, popular politics, domestic happiness, and social economy.

The great utility and importance of this measure may be summed up under the following heads:—

1st. That no married couple shall have more children than they wish to have and can maintain.

2nd. That no unhealthy woman shall bear children, that cannot be reared, and which endanger her own life in the parturition: that ineffectual pregnancy shall never be suffered.

3d. That there be no illegitimate children, where they are not desired by the mother.

4th, and finally. That sexual commerce, where useful and desired, may be made a pleasure, independent of the dread of a conception that blasts the prospects and happiness of the female.

If these reasons be not sufficient to satisfy the most fastidious mind, then the ignorance, the unfeeling ignorance under which that mind labours is to be pitied. We are all apt to be shocked at having long-established notions controverted. We value such notions as parts of our existence. We dislike the first examination of all controverting doctrines. But it is consistent with the current character of the things about us, that we be exposed to incessant change of habits and of doctrines: and all that is necessary to make us wise, is, that we freely examine every system, opinion, and thing that comes in our way, so as to interest or to shock us. "Prejudices," says Lequinio, an elegant French writer, in his work entitled *Les Prejuges Detruits*, "arise out of ignorance and the want of reflection; these are the bases on which the system of despotism is erected, and it is the master-piece of art in a tyrant, to perpetuate the stupidity of a nation, in order to perpetuate its slavery and his own dominion."

Boulanger has said most truly, "Every man is proud of having discovered a new truth." We are proud of this discovery. All men and all women will yet be proud of it. The prejudices of many may be offended by this book; but we trust to time and assuredly good intentions to wear away both offence and prejudice.

This book is not like one of those vile, mischievous, misleading, and fraudulent books, commonly on sale for the gratification of ignorantly-diseased appetites. It is not like the lascivious books which are secretly though extensively sold by almost every bookseller. Those books are printed solely for a corrupt and corrupting money-getting purpose, and exhibit nothing but bad examples; while this book, recommended to every woman, and most properly called "Every Woman's Book," is a book of instruction on one of the most interesting subjects, not only to the female, but to the male, to families and friends individually, and to society at large. It is a book of physical, philosophical, and moral instruction, and not only deserves the appellation of *every woman's book, but that of being a book for every man, woman, and child at the age of puberty.*

The sexes have never, before the publication of this book, had any fair, open, and honest instruction on the subject of love, on the regulation of that passion which is of the very first importance as to their health and happiness through life. A contemptible book, called "Aristotle's Master-Piece," has been bought up by thousands and tens of thousands throughout the country, under the notion that it affords instruction upon the subject of love. The book has no such instruction, has been published from no good motive, and is altogether a piece of ignorant quackery and deception. It was high time that something useful should be presented to the public, and it is presumed, that this is now done in this book, *in explaining the subject of love to every woman.*

FACTORIES AND POOR RELIEF

Act for the better regulation of chimney sweepers and their apprentices, 1788

28 Geo. 3, c. 48   *Statutes at Large*, XXXVI, 518-23.

Whereas the laws now in being respecting masters and apprentices do not provide sufficient regulations, so as to prevent various complicated miseries, to which boys employed in climbing and cleansing of chimneys are liable, beyond any other employment whatsoever, in which boys of tender years are engaged: and whereas the misery of the said boys might be much alleviated, if some legal powers and authorities were given for the regulation of chimney sweepers, and their apprentices: may it therefore please your Majesty that it may be enacted; and be it enacted by the King's most excellent majesty, by and with the advice and consent of the lords spiritual and temporal, and commons, in this present parliament assembled, and by the authority of the same, That, from and after the fifth day of *July* one thousand seven hundred and eighty-eight, it shall and may be lawful to and for the churchwardens and overseers of the poor, for the time being, of the several and respective parishes, townships, or places, within the kingdom of *Great Britain*, by and with the consent and approbation of two or more of his Majesty's justices of the peace, acting in and for any county, riding, city, town corporate, borough, or division, within *Great Britain*, (such consent and approbation to be signified by such justices in writing, under their hands, according to the form prescribed by the indenture contained in the schedule hereunto annexed) to bind or put out any boy, or boys, who is, are, or shall be of the age of eight years, or upward; and who is, are, or shall be chargeable, or whose parents are or shall become chargeable to the parish or parishes, or places, where they shall so be; or who shall beg for alms; or by and with the consent of the parent or parents of such boy or boys, to be apprentice and apprentices to any person or persons using or exercising the trade, business, or mystery of a chimney sweeper, for so long time, and until such boy or boys shall attain or come to the age of sixteen years; and such binding out any such apprentice and apprentices, shall be as effectual in the law, to all intents and purposes, as if such boy or boys was or were of full age, and by indenture had bound himself or themselves an apprentice or apprentices.

II. And, to the end that the time of the continuance of the service of such apprentice or apprentices may plainly and certainly appear; be it further enacted, That the age of every such boy or boys, so to be bound apprentice or apprentices, shall be mentioned and inserted in such indenture, being taken truly from the copy of the entry in the register book, wherein the time of his or their being baptized is or shall be entered (where the same can or may be had); which copy shall be given and attested by the minister, vicar, or curate of such parish or parishes or places wherein such boy or boys baptism shall be registered, without fee or reward, and may be written upon paper or parchment, without any stamp or mark; and where no such copy of such boy or boys being baptized can be had, such justices of the peace shall, as fully as they can, inform themselves of his or their age or ages, and from such information shall insert the same in the said indenture; and the age of such boy or boys, so inserted and mentioned in the said indenture (in relation to the continuance of his or their service) shall be taken to be his and their true age and ages, without any further proof thereof.

III. And, to the end and intent that there may be no doubt or uncertainty as to the form of the indenture, by which such boy or boys shall be bound apprentice or apprentices as aforesaid, and that the stipulations and agreements to be made and entered into by the said master or mistress may plainly and fully appear; be it enacted by the authority aforesaid, That such indenture shall be made and written out according to the form in the schedule hereunto annexed, and that the same shall not be charged with or liable to the payment of any higher or other stamp duty, than is now charged upon indentures for binding out poor children by their respective parishes or places; any law or statute to the contrary notwithstanding.

IV. And be it further enacted by the authority aforesaid, That all indentures, covenants, promises, and bargains hereafter to be made, or taken, of or for the having, taking, employing, retaining, or keeping of any boy or boys, as or in the nature of an apprentice or apprentices, or servant or servants, employed in the capacity of a climbing boy or chimney sweeper, who shall be under the age of eight years as aforesaid, than is by this act limited, ordained, and appointed, shall be absolutely void in the law to all intents and purposes· and that every person who shall from henceforth have, take, employ, retain, or keep any such boy or boys as or in the nature of an apprentice or apprentices, or servant employed in the capacity of a climbing boy or chimney sweeper as aforesaid, who shall be under the age of eight years as aforesaid, contrary to the tenor and true meaning of this act, and being convicted thereof, as herein-after mentioned, shall forfeit and pay for every such apprentice or servant, so by him or her had, taken, employed, retained, or kept, any sum not exceeding ten pounds, nor less than five pounds.

V. And whereas, in many large parishes within this realm, there are several townships or villages, and overseers of the poor are chosen and appointed within and for each such township or village respectively; be it therefore further enacted by the authority aforesaid, That the overseers of the poor of every such township or village shall and may from time to time, within every such township or village, do, perform and execute, all and every the acts, powers, and authorities hereby enacted or directed to be done, performed, or executed by the churchwardens or overseers of the poor of a parish or place; any thing herein, or in any other law or laws, contained to the contrary in any wise notwithstanding.

VI. And be it further enacted by the authority aforesaid, That it shall and may be lawful for one or more such justice or justices, or he or they shall have full power and authority, and is and are hereby authorised and impowered to inquire into and examine, hear, and determine, as well all complaints of hard or ill usage from the several and respective masters or mistresses, to whom such apprentice and apprentices shall be so bound as aforesaid, as also all complaints of such boys as already have, or who shall at any time hereafter voluntarily put themselves apprentices to such trade, business, or mystery of a chimney sweeper as aforesaid; and in like manner also to enquire into and examine, hear, and determine all complaints of masters or mistresses against such apprentice and apprentices,.and to make such orders therein respectively, as he or they is or are now enabled by law to do in other cases between masters and apprentices.

VII.   And be it further enacted by the authority aforesaid, That no person or persons using or exercising the trade, business, or mystery of a chimney sweeper, shall retain, keep, or employ any more than six apprentices at one and the same time; and that the name of every person so taking or receiving an apprentice or apprentices as aforesaid, and also the place of his or her abode, shall be marked or put upon a brass plate, to be set or affixed in the front of a leathern cap, which every master or mistress shall provide for each such apprentice, and which he shall wear when out upon his duty; and that every master or mistress shall forfeit for every apprentice so retained, kept, or employed by him or her beyond the number limited by this act, or for neglecting to provide each such apprentice with such leathern cap, and brass plate to be so affixed thereupon, and marked with his or her name and place of abode as aforesaid, contrary to the true intent and meaning of this act, any sum not exceeding the sum of ten pounds, nor less than five pounds.

VIII.   And be it further enacted by the authority aforesaid, That is any such master or mistress shall misuse or evil treat his or her apprentice, or that the said apprentice shall have any just cause to complain of the forfeiture or breach of any of the covenants, clauses, or agreements, to be expressed and contained in such indenture, made and written out according to the form in the schedule hereunto annexed, on the part and behalf of such master or mistress, then, and in such case, such master or mistress, being convicted thereof in manner herein-after mentioned, shall forfeit and pay, for every such offence, any sum not exceeding ten pounds, nor less than five pounds.

IX.   And be it further enacted, That no person or persons using or exercising the trade, business, or mystery of a chimney sweeper, shall let out to hire, or lend by the day or otherwise, to any other person for the purpose of sweeping of chimneys, any boy or boys that are already apprentice or apprentices, or that shall hereafter be bound apprentice or apprentices, under the directions of this act, nor shall cause such boy or boys to call the streets before seven of the clock in the morning, nor after twelve of the clock at noon, between *Michaelmas* and *Lady-day*, nor before five of the clock in the morning, nor after twelve of the clock at noon, between *Lady-day* and *Michaelmas*; and that if any master or mistress shall, after the passing of this act, offend in any of the cases aforesaid, he or she shall forfeit and pay, for every such offence, any sum not exceeding ten pounds, nor less than five pounds.

X.   And be it further enacted by the authority aforesaid, That all convictions for penalties and forfeitures, by this act imposed for any offence against the same, shall be made before one or more justice or justices of the peace, acting for the county, riding, city, town, borough, or division, where such offence was committed, either by confession of the offender, or upon the oath of one or more credible witness or witnesses; and for that purpose it shall be lawful for one or more such justice or justices, upon complaint made to him or them thereof, to summon the person or persons so offending before him or them to answer to such complaint, in such manner as he or they is and are authorised to do in any other matter cognizable before a magistrate.

XI. And be it further enacted by the authority aforesaid, That all penalties and forfeitures by this act imposed for any offence, neglect, or default against the same, and all costs and charges to be allowed and ordered by the authority of this act, shall be levied by distress and sale of the goods and chattels of the offender, or person liable or ordered to pay the same respectively, by warrant under the hand and seal of one or more such justice or justices of the peace, acting for the county, riding, city, town, borough, or division, where such offence, neglect, or default shall happen; and such order for payment of such costs or charges shall be made, rendering the overplus of such distress and sale (if any) to the party or parties, after deducting the charges of making the same; which warrant such justice or justices is and are hereby impowered and required to grant, upon conviction of the offender, by confession, or upon the oath of one or more credible witness or witnesses, or upon order made as aforesaid; and the penalties and forfeitures, costs and charges, when so levied, shall be paid, the one half to the informer, and the other half to the overseers of the poor of the parish, township, or place, where the master or mistress of such apprentice shall dwell and inhabit; and in case such distress cannot be found, and such penalties and forfeitures, or the said costs or charges shall not be forthwith paid, it shall and may be lawful for such justice or justices, and he and they is and are hereby authorised and required, by warrant under his or their hand and seal, or hands and seals, to commit such offender or offenders, or person or persons liable to pay the same respectively, to the common gaol or house of correction of the county, riding, city, town, borough, or division, where the offence shall be committed, or such order as aforesaid shall be made, for any time not exceeding three months, unless the said penalty, forfeiture, costs or charges, shall respectively be sooner paid.

XII. Provided nevertheless, That no warrant of distress shall be issued for levying any penalty or forfeiture, costs or charges, until six days after the offender shall have been convicted, and an order made and served upon him or her for payment thereof.

XIII. And be it further enacted by the authority aforesaid, That where any distress shall be made for any sum or sums of money, to be levied by virtue of this act, the distress itself shall not be deemed unlawful, nor the party or parties making the same be deemed a trespasser or trespassers, on account of any default, or want of form in any proceedings relating thereto; nor shall the party or parties distraining be deemed a trespasser or trespassers *ab initio*, on account of any irregularity which shall be afterwards done by the party or parties distraining; but the person or persons aggrieved by such irregularity may recover a full satisfaction for the special damage in an action on the case.

XIV. Provided always, That no plaintiff or plaintiffs shall recover in any action for any such irregularity, trespass, or wrongful proceedings, if tender of sufficient amends shall be made by or on the behalf of the party or parties who shall have committed, or caused to have been committed, any such irregularity or wrongful proceedings, before such action brought: and in case no such tender shall have been made, it shall and may be lawful for the defendant in any such action, by leave of the court where such action shall depend, at any time before issue joined, to pay into court such sum of money as he or they shall see fit, whereupon such proceedings or orders and judgements shall be had, made, and given, in and by such court, as in other actions where the defendant is allowed to pay money into court.

XV. And be it further enacted, That where any oath is hereby required and directed to be taken, the justice or justices of the peace of the county, riding, city, town, borough, or division, where the offence shall be committed, shall administer, and he or they is and are hereby respectively impowered to administer the same.

XVI. Provided always, and be it further enacted, That if any person shall think himself or herself aggrieved by any thing done by any justice or justices of the peace, in pursuance of this act, such person may appeal to the justices of the peace at the next general or quarter sessions of the peace to be holden for the county, riding, city, town, borough, or division wherein the cause of such complaint shall arise, having first entered into a recognizance, with sufficient surety, before such justices, to prosecute and abide by the order or orders that shall be made on such appeal, and also giving, or causing to be given, to the justice by whose act or acts such person shall think himself or herself aggrieved, notice in writing of his or her intention to bring such appeal, and of the matter thereof, within six days after the cause of such complaint shall have arisen.

XVII. And be it further enacted by the authority aforesaid, That this act shall be deemed, adjudged, and taken to be a publick act; and be judicially taken notice of as such, by all judges, justices, and other persons whomsoever, without specially pleading the same.

[Schedule omitted]

The Speenhamland decision, 6 May 1795

Berkshire Sessions Order Book (1791-95), 434-36.

This decision by the local Berkshire magistrates was widely adopted throughout England and had a momentous effect on poor law policy. Outdoor relief was introduced and recipients became eligible for direct supplements to their wages, calculated on the price of bread. Though more humane than the previous system, which relied heavily on workhouse relief, the Speenhamland system was inefficient and basically unworkable. It was replaced by the Poor Law Amendment Act (1834).

At a General Meeting of the Justices of this County, together with several discreet persons assembled by public advertisement, on Wednesday the 6th day of May 1795, at the Pelican Inn in Speenhamland (in pursuance of an order of the last Court of General Quarter Sessions) for the purpose of rating Husbandry Wages, by the day or week, if then approved of, Charles Dundas, Esq., in the Chair [nineteen names follow],

Resolved unanimously, That the present state of the Poor does require further assistance than has been generally given them.

Resolved, That it is inexpedient for the Magistrates to grant that assistance by regulating the Wages of Day Labourers, according to the directions of the Statutes of the 5th Eliz. and 1st of James: But the Magistrates very earnestly recommend to the Farmers and others throughout the county, to increase the pay of their Labourers in proportion to the present Price of Provisions; and agreeable thereto, the Magistrates now present have unanimously Resolved, That they will, in their several divisions, make the following calculations and allowances for relief of all poor and industrious Men and their families, who to the satisfaction of the Justices of their Parish, shall endeavour (as far as they can) for their own support and maintenance. That is to say,

When the Gallon Loaf of Second Flour, weighing 8 lb. 11 ozs. shall cost 1s.

Then every poor and industrious Man shall have for his own support 3s. weekly, either produced by his own or his family's labour, or an allowance from the poor rates, and for the support of his Wife and every other of his family, 1s. 6d.

When the Gallon Loaf shall cost 1s. 4d.

Then every poor and industrious Man shall have 4s. weekly for his own, and 1s. 10d. for the support of every other of his family.

And so in proportion, as the price of Bread rises or falls (that is to say) 3d. to the Man, and 1d. to every other of the family, on every 1d. which the loaf rises above 1s.

Factory Act, 22 June 1802

42 Geo 3, c. 73   *Statutes at Large*, XLIII, 632-36.

This landmark act, the first attempt by the central government to regulate the hours of work and conditions of employment in factories, was promoted by Robert Peel (1750-1830), a Lancashire cotton manufacturer and father of the future prime minister. The act applied to parish apprentices employed in textile mills and was not applicable to "free" child labor.

Whereas it hath of late become a practice in cotton and woollen mills, and in cotton and woollen factories, to employ a great number of male and female apprentices, and other persons, in the same building; in consequence of which certain regulations are become necessary to preserve the health and morals of such apprentices and other persons; be it therefore enacted by the King's most excellent majesty, by and with the advice and consent of the lords spiritual and temporal, and commons, in this present parliament assembled, and by the authority of the same, That from and after the second day of *December* one thousand eight hundred and two, all such mills and factories within *Great Britain* and *Ireland*, wherein three or more apprentices, or twenty or more other persons, shall at any time be employed, shall be subject to the several rules and regulations contained in this act; and the master or mistress of every such mill and factory is hereby strictly enjoined and required to pay due attention to and act in strict conformity to the said rules and regulations.

II. And be it enacted, That all and every the rooms and apartments in or belonging to any such mill or factory shall, twice at least in every year, be well and sufficiently washed with quick lime and water over every part of the walls and cieling [*sic*] thereof; and that due care and attention shall be paid by the master and mistress of such mills or factories, to provide a sufficient number of windows and openings in such rooms or apartments, to insure a proper supply of fresh air in and through the same.

III. And be it further enacted, That every such master or mistress shall constantly supply every apprentice, during the term of his or her apprenticeship, with two whole and complete suits of cloathing, with suitable linen, stockings, hats, and shoes; one new complete suit being delivered to such apprentice once at least in every year.

IV. And be it further enacted, That no apprentice that now is or hereafter shall be bound to any such master or mistress, shall be employed or compelled to work for more than twelve hours in any one day, (reckoning from six of the clock in the morning to nine of the clock at night), exclusive of the time that may be occupied by such apprentice in eating the necessary meals: provided always, that, from and after the first day of *June* one thousand eight hundred and three, no apprentice shall be employed or compelled to work upon any occasion whatever, between the hours of nine of the clock at night and six of the clock in the morning.

V. And be it further enacted, That in any mill or factory, wherein not less than one thousand nor more than fifteen hundred spindles are constantly used in the carrying on of the manufacture, it shall and may be lawful for the owner or owners of such mill to employ his apprentices in the night until the twenty-fifth day of *December* one thousand eight hundred and three; and in any mill or factory wherein more than fifteen hundred spindles shall be employed, it shall and may be lawful for the owner of such mill to employ his apprentices in the night until the twenty-fifth day of *June* one thousand eight hundred and four; any thing herein contained to the contrary notwithstanding.

VI. And be it further enacted, That every such apprentice shall be instructed, in some part of every working day, for the first four years at least of his or her apprenticeship, which shall next ensue from and after the second day of *December* one thousand eight hundred and two, if he or she is an apprentice on the said second day of *December* one thousand eight hundred and two, and for the first four years at least of his or her apprenticeship, if his or her apprenticeship commences at any time after the said second day of *December* one thousand eight and two, in the usual hours of work, in reading, writing, and arithmetick, or either of them, according to the age and abilities of such apprentice, by some discreet and proper person, to be provided and paid by the master or mistress of such apprentice, in some room or place in such mill or factory to be set apart for that purpose; and that the time hereby directed to be allotted for such instruction as aforesaid, shall be deemed and taken on all occasions as part of the respective periods limited by this act during which any such apprentice shall be employed or compelled to work.

VII. And be it further enacted, That the room or apartment in which any male apprentice shall sleep, shall be entirely separate and distinct from the room or apartment in which any female apprentice shall sleep; and that not more than two apprentices shall in any case sleep in the same bed.

VIII. And be it further enacted, That every apprentice, or (in case the apprentices shall attend in classes), every such class shall, for the space of one hour at least every *Sunday*, be instructed and examined in the principles of the Christian religion, by some proper person to be provided and paid by the master or mistress of such apprentice; and in *England* and *Wales*, in case the parents of such apprentice; and in *England* and *Wales*, in case the parents of such apprentice shall be members of the church of *England*, then such apprentice shall be taken, once at least in every year during the term of his or her apprenticeship, to be examined by the rector, vicar, or curate of the parish in which such mill or factory shall be situate; and shall also after such apprentice shall have attained the age of fourteen years, and before attaining the age of eighteen years, be duly instructed and prepared for confirmation, and be brought or sent to the bishop of the diocese to be confirmed, in case any confirmation shall, during such period, take place in or for the said parish; and in *Scotland* where the parents of such apprentice shall be members of the established church, such apprentice shall be taken once at least in every year,, during the term of his or her apprenticeship, to be examined by the minister of the parish; and shall after such apprentice shall have attained the age of fourteen years, and before attaining the age of eighteen years, be carried to the parish church to receive the sacrament of the Lord's supper, as the same is administered in churches in *Scotland*; and such master or mistress shall send all his or her apprentices under the care of some proper person, once in a month at least, to attend during divine service in the church of the parish or place in which the mill or factory shall be situated, or in some other convenient church or chapel where service shall be performed according to the rites of the church of *England*, or according to the established religion in *Scotland*, as the case may be, or in some licensed place of divine worship; and in case the apprentices of any such master or mistress cannot conveniently attend such church or chapel every *Sunday*, the master or mistress, either by themselves or some proper person, shall cause divine service to be performed in some convenient room or place in or adjoining to the mill or factory, once at least every *Sunday* that such apprentices shall not be able to attend divine service at such church or chapel; and such master or mistress is hereby strictly enjoined and required to take due care that all his or her apprentices regularly attend divine service, according to the directions of this act.

IX. And be it further enacted, That the justices of the peace for every county, stewartry, riding, division, or place, in which any such mill or factory shall be situated, shall, at the *Midsummer* sessions of the peace to be holden immediately after the passing of this act for such county, stewartry, riding, division, or place, and afterwards yearly at their annual *Midsummer* sessions of the peace, appoint two persons, not interested in, or in any way connected with, any such mills or factories, to be visitors of such mills or factories in such county, stewartry, riding, division, or place; one of whom shall be a justice of peace for such county, stewartry, riding, division, or place, and the other shall be a clergyman of the established church of *England* or *Scotland*, as the case may be; and in case it shall be found inconvenient to appoint one such justice and one such clergyman as aforesaid, it shall be lawful to and for such justices, and they are hereby required to appoint two such justices or two such clergymen; and the said visitors, or either of them, shall have full power and authority from to time throughout the year, to enter into and inspect any such mill or factory, at any time of the day, or during the hours of employment, as they shall think fit; and such visitors shall report from time to time in writing, to the quarter sessions of the peace, the state and condition of such mills and factories, and of the apprentices therein, and whether the same are or are not conducted and regulated according to the directions of this act, and the laws of the realm; and such report shall be entered by the clerk of the peace among the records of the session in a book kept for that purpose: provided always, that in case there shall be six or more such mills or factories within any one such county, riding, division, or place, then it shall be lawful for such justices to divide such county, riding, division or place, into two or more districts or parts, and to appoint two such visitors as aforesaid for each such districts or parts.

X. And be it further enacted, That in case the said visitors or either of them shall find that any infectious disorder appears to prevail in any mill or factory as aforesaid, it shall be lawful for them or either of them to require the master or mistress of any such mill or factory to call in forthwith some physician, or other competent medical person, for the purpose of ascertaining the nature and probable effects of such disorder, and for applying such remedies and recommending such regulations as the said physician, or other competent medical person, shall think most proper for preventing the spreading of the infection and for restoring the health of the sick; and that such physician, or other competent medical person, shall report to such visitors, or either of them, as often as they shall be required so to do, their opinion in writing of the nature, progress, and present state of the disorder, together with its probable effects; and that any expences incurred in consequence of the provisions aforesaid for medical assistance, shall be discharged by the master or mistress of such mill or factory.

XI. And be it further enacted, That if any person or persons shall oppose or molest any of the said visitors in the execution of the powers intrusted to them by this act, every such person or persons shall for every such offence forfeit and pay any sum not exceeding ten pounds nor less than five pounds.

XII. And be it further enacted, That the master or mistress of every such mill or factory shall cause printed or written copies of this act to be hung up and affixed in two or more conspicuous places in such mill or factory, and shall cause the same to be constantly kept and renewed, so that they may at all times be legible and accessible to all persons employed therein.

XIII. And be it further enacted, That every master or mistress of any such mill or factory who shall wilfully act contrary to or offend against any of the provisions of this act, shall for such offence, (except where otherwise directed), forfeit and pay any sum not exceeding five pounds nor less than forty shillings, at the discretion of the justices before whom such offender shall be convicted as after mentioned; one half whereof shall be paid to the informer, and the other half to the overseers of the poor in *England* and *Ireland*, and to the minister and elders in *Scotland*, of the parish or place where such offence shall be committed, to be by them applied in aid of the poor rate, in *England*, and *Ireland*, and for the benefit of the poor in *Scotland*, of such parish or place: provided always, that all informations for offences against this act, shall be laid within one calendar month after the offence committed, and not afterwards.

XIV. And be it further enacted, That every such master or mistress shall, at the *Epiphany* sessions in every year, make, or cause to be made, an entry in a book to be kept for that purpose by the clerk of the peace of the county, riding, or division in which any mill or factory shall be situate, of every such mill or factory occupied by him or her wherein three or more apprentices or twenty or more persons, shall be employed; and the said clerk of the peace shall receive for every such entry the sum of two shillings and no more.

XV. And be it further enacted, That all offences for which any penalty is imposed under this act, shall and may be heard before any two or more justices of the peace, acting in or for the place where the offence shall be committed; and all penalties and forfeitures by this act imposed, and all costs and charges attending the conviction of any such offender or offenders, shall and may be levied by distress and sale of the offenders goods and chattels, by warrant under the hand and seal of any two or more justices of the peace acting for the county, stewartry, riding, division, or place where such offence shall be committed, rendering the overplus (if any) to the party or parties offending; and which warrant such justices are hereby empowered and required to grant, upon conviction of the offender, either by confession, or upon the oath of one or more credible witness or witnesses (which oath such justices are hereby empowered to administer); and in case such distress cannot be found, and such penalties, forfeitures, and costs shall not be forthwith paid, it shall and may be lawful for such justices, and they are hereby empowered and required, by warrant under their hands and seals, to commit such offender or offenders to the common gaol or house of correction of the county, stewartry, riding, division, or place where the offence shall be committed, for any time not exceeding two calendar months, unless the said penalty, forfeiture, and costs, shall respectively be sooner paid and satisfied; provided always, that no warrant of distress shall be issued for levying any such penalty, forfeiture, or costs, until six days after the offender shall have been convicted, and an order made upon him or her for payment thereof; and no such conviction shall be removeable by *certiorari* or bill of advocation into any court whatsoever. . . .

Factory Act, 2 July 1819

59 Geo. 3, c. 66   *Statutes of the United Kingdom*, 1819, 418-19.

This measure applied to cotton mills. It prohibited the employment of children under nine, and set a maximum workday of twelve hours for children under sixteen. No adequate mechanism for enforcing the act was devised.

Whereas an Act was made in the Forty second Year of the Reign of His present Majesty, intituled *An Act for the Preservation of the Health and Morals of*

Apprentices and others employed in Cotton and other Mills, and Cotton and other Factories: And Whereas it is expedient that some further Provision should be made for the Regulation of Mills, Manufactories and Buildings, employed in the Preparation and spinning of Cotton Wool: Be it therefore enacted by The King's Most Excellent Majesty, by and with the Advice and Consent of the Lords Spiritual and Temporal, and Commons, in this present Parliament assembled, and by the Authority of the same, That from and after the First Day of *January* One thousand eight hundred and twenty, no Child shall be employed in any Description of Work, for the spinning of Cotton Wool into Yarn, or in any previous Preparation of such Wool, until he or she shall have attained the full Age of Nine Years.

II.   And be it further enacted, That no Person, being under the Age of Sixteen Years, shall be employed in any Description of Work whatsoever, in spinning Cotton Wool into Yarn, or in the previous Preparation of such Wool, or in the cleaning or repairing of any Mill, Manufactory or Building, or any Millwork or Machinery therein, for more than Twelve Hours in any one Day, exclusive of the necessary time for Meals; such Twelve Hours to be between the Hours of Five o'Clock in the Morning and Nine o'Clock in the Evening.

III.   And be it further enacted, That there shall be allowed to every such Person, in the course of every Day, not less than Half an Hour to Breakfast, and not less than One full Hour for Dinner; such Hour for Dinner to be between the Hours of Eleven o'Clock in Forenoon and Two o'Clock in the Afternoon.

IV.   Provided nevertheless, and be it further enacted, That if at any time, in any such Mill, Manufactory or Buildings as are situated upon Streams of Water, time shall be lost in consequence of the Want of a due Supply, or of an Excess of Water, then and in every such Case, and so often as the same shall happen, it shall be lawful for the Proprietors of any such Mill, Manufactory or Building, to extend the before mentioned time of daily Labour, after the Rate of one additional Hour *per* Day, until such lost time shall have been made good, but no longer.

V.   And be it further enacted, That the Ceilings and interior Walls of every such Mill, Manufactory or Building shall be washed with Quick Lime and Water Twice in every Year.

VI.   And be it further enacted, That in a conspicuous Part of every such Mill, Manufactory or Building, a Copy of this Act, or a full and true Abstract of the Regulations provided hereby, shall be hung up and affixed, and signed by the Proprietors, Manager or Overseer of such Mill, Manufactory or Building; and that such Copy or Abstract shall be kept and renewed, so that the same shall be at all times legible.

VII.   And be it further enacted, That every Master or Mistress of any such Cotton Mill, Manufactory or Building, who shall wilfully act contrary to or offend against any of the Provisions of this Act, or any of the Provisions of the above recited Act, shall for every such Offence forfeit and pay any Sum not exceeding Twenty Pounds, nor less than Ten Pounds, at the Discretion of the Justices before whom such Offender shall be convicted; One Half whereof shall be paid to the Informer, and the other Half to the Overseers of the Poor in *England*, to the Churchwardens in *Ireland*, and to the Ministers and Elders in *Scotland*, of the Parish or Place where such Offence shall be committed; to be by them applied in aid of the Poor Rate in *England*, and for the Benefit of the Poor in *Ireland* and *Scotland*, of such Parish or Place: Provided always, that all Informations for Offences against the said recited Act or this Act, shall be laid within Three Calendar Months subsequently to the Offence being committed, and not after the Expiration of such Three Calendar Months: Provided also, that all Penalties inflicted by this Act shall be levied, recovered and applied in manner directed by the said recited Act.

VIII.   And be it enacted, That this Act shall be deemed and taken to be a Public Act, and shall be judicially taken Notice of as such by all Judges, Justices and others, without specially pleading the same.

ADMINISTRATIVE AND LEGAL REFORMS

Westminster Paving Act, 1761

2 Geo. 3, c. 21   *Statutes at Large*, XXVI, 150-53.

This act provided for paving, cleaning, and lighting squares and streets of the city of Westminster. It was the first statute in this area that did not place the burden upon householders.

Whereas the several squares, streets, and lanes, within the city and liberty of *Westminster*, the parishes of *Saint Giles in the Fields, Saint George the Martyr, Saint George Bloomsbury*, that part of the parish of *Saint Andrew Holborn* which lies in the county of *Middlesex*, the several liberties of the *Rolls* and *Savoy*, and that part of the duchy of *Lancaster* which lies in the county of *Middlesex*, are in general, very ill paved and cleansed, and not duly lighted: and whereas the present methods prescribed by law for paving, cleansing, and lighting the said squares, streets, and lanes, are ineffectual: and whereas it would tend greatly to the benefit and safety of the inhabitants of the said squares, streets, and lanes, and of all persons passing through the same, if the pavements thereof were properly laid and regulated, and the said squares, streets, and lanes, kept clean, free from obstructions, and annoyances, and duly lighted: may it therefore please your Majesty, that it may be enacted; and be it enacted, etc, etc.

Commissioners appointed for carrying this act into execution.

15, or more, at their first meeting, to elect by ballot 20 other persons to be associated with them in the trust.

11, or more, giving 14 days notice, may fill up vacancies occasioned by the death, or refusal to act, of any of the commissioners, except of such as are *ex officio*.

Commissioners holding any office, or interested in any contract under the trust, are disqualified from acting, as such.

3, or more, are to hold their first meeting at *Westminster Bridge* office, on the Thursday sevennight after passing the act; and they are then to adjourn, and meet afterwards; as they shall think proper. On failure of a sufficient number of commissioners at any meeting to act and adjourn, the clerk is to appoint another meeting, giving 10 days notice; or, on his death, neglect or refusal, 2 commissioners may appoint one: they are to bear their own expences at all their meetings.

Qualification of commissioners, 300*l. per annum*, or 10,000*l.* etc.

Penalty 100*l.* on their acting, if not qualified, and they are to prove their qualification, if prosecuted, or pay the penalty.

11, or more, at their second or any subsequent meeting may appoint one, or more clerks, treasurers, and receivers; and also surveyors; and such other officers as they, or any 7 or more of them, shall think necessary; taking proper security; and they may remove them, and appoint others. Rates to be paid to the receivers. Officers, and others, to render an account upon oath, at the times and in the manner, 7 or more commissioners shall direct; and pay over the money in their hands to the order of 5 or more commissioners.

2 commissioners may administer the oath; and any person refusing to render such an account, or to verify the same, or to produce and deliver up the vouchers, and pay over the ballance, etc. may be sued, by action brought in the names of 2 or more commissioners, or complaint may be brought against him before 2 or more justices, who are impowered to hear and determine the matter in a summary way; and to levy by distress and sale the money, that shall appear to be in such persons hands; and for want of sufficient distress, to commit such offender, until he render an account and payment, or shall compound with 5 or more commissioners, and have paid the composition, or delivered up the writings, etc. 11 or more, commissioners may appoint officers salaries, and make allowance to such others as have aided or assisted the execution of this act.

Officers taking any fee or reward, other than their salaries, for doing their duty, or being concerned in interest in any bargain made by the commissioners for the purposes of this act, are disqualified from ever serving, or being employed under this act, and forfeit also 100*l*.

Treasurer to pay over, from time to time, the monies he receives, as soon as the same amount to 300*l*. into the bank, in the name of the commissioners; which is to be disposed of by an order of 5, or more, of them.

3, or more, commissioners are impowered from time to time, to order any of the publick squares, streets and lanes, within the said city, being thorough fares for wheel carriages, etc. to be paved, altered, cleansed, and lighted, etc.

And also such gravel, stones, and other materials, to be dug out of, or brought into the same, and such artificers and workmen to be employed, and money issued; and all other acts conducive to the designs of this act, to be done, as they shall think fit.

Clause in the act 5 *Eliz.* repealed, with respect to persons employed in consequence of this act, in paving, etc. Five, or more, commissioners may contract for the paving, cleansing, and lighting the squares and streets, etc. giving 14 days previous notice for persons to deliver in proposals.

Contractors for cleaning the streets may, by leave and order of two or more justices, and making satisfaction, lodge their dirt, for the accommodation of country carts, in such places as shall not appear to be intended to be built upon.

3, or more, commissioners may order all works done in pursuance of this act, to be inspected by their surveyor; and where any shall be found not well and duly performed, may sue the contractors for the penalties; to be applied for the purposes of this act.

Agreement between landlord and tenant touching the paving, lighting, and cleansing the streets, not vacated by this act; but the rates made by the commissioners are to be paid in lieu thereof; and all disputes concerning such agreements are to be settled by 5 or more commissioners.

Commissioners, or persons authorized by them, may inspect and take copies of the books kept for cleansing, paving, or lighting the streets and places in *London, Westminster*, or *Middlesex*.

Property of all materials for the purposes of this act vested in the commissioners: 3 may bring actions, or prefer indictments against any persons who shall steal any part thereof; and persons wilfully damaging the same, forfeit for the 1st offence, not exceeding 40s. nor less than 10s. and for the 2d and every other offence, not exceeding 3*l*. nor less than 20s. to be levied by distress and sale; and for want of distress, the offender to be committed to the house of correction, not exceeding two months, nor less than 10 days.

5 or more commissioners may sell the old materials, and apply the money to the purposes of this act.

Payments taken up by the workmen of any of the water companies, are to be repaired by the commissioners paviour, at the expence of such company; but where any of the pipes or plugs shall be raised, sunk, or altered for the purposes of this act, the expences shall be defrayed out of the rates.

5 or more of the commissioners may contract with the said companies for relaying such pavements.

Pavements taken up by the commissioners of sewers are to be relaid, at their expence, by the commissioners paviour.

5 or more commissioners may contract with the commissioners of sewers for relaying such pavements.

No alteration to be made in the form of the streets, etc. without the consent of 5 or more commissioners, on penalty of 5*l*. over and above all expences of reinstating the same.

5,000*l*. to be issued and applied out of the aids granted to his Majesty for the service of the year 1762, to be paid to 5 or more commissioners, or to their order, and applied in new paving the said squares, streets, and lanes.

Receiver to account quarterly to the commissioners, copies of the said accounts, and of the proceedings of the commissioners, to be delivered in every sessions to parliament, within 30 days after the opening.

Penalty of laying ashes or other annoyances in the streets, before the scavenger comes to carry away the same, is for the 1st offence 5s. for the 2d 10s. and for the 3d and every other offence 20s.

Obstruction, nuisance, or incroachment occasioned by setting out any carriages, timber, or other material, matter, or thing in the streets, etc. or by carts, etc, suffered to remain longer therein than is necessary for the loading or unloading thereof, may be removed, by order of 3 commissioners upon complaint thereof, at the charges of the offender, he paying moreover a sum not exceeding 40s.

No inclosure for building or repairing houses, to be made in any of the streets, etc. which shall be compleated by virtue of this act, without the consent of 3 or more commissioners, on penalty of forfeiting, not exceeding 20s. for every 12 hours such nuisance shall remain.

A rate, not exceeding 1s. 6d. in the pound to be made on all houses, etc. by 5 or more commissioners, half yearly or oftener, for defraying the expences of paving, repairing, cleansing, and lighting the streets, to be ascertained by the poor-rate of the respective parishes, and to be paid quarterly.

Receivers authorized by an order of 3 or more commissioners, may inspect the parish books concerning their poor's rate; and take copies thereof.

Where houses are lett out in lodgings to divers tenants, the owners are to be assessed, but the rate may be levied on the occupiers, which is to be allowed them in their rent.

Where houses, etc. shall be empty, untenanted or unoccupied, the owners are to be charged with one half of the said rates, and the premises are to remain a security for the arrears.

Where houses, etc. are occupied by foreign ministers, or others not liable by law to pay the rates, the owners are to pay the same; and the premises to remain a security for the arrears; and an action may be brought against the owner.

Tenants and occupiers are to pay the rates, and deduct the proportion paid on account of the owner or proprietor out of their rent.

All publick buildings, dead walls, and void spaces of ground to be rated by the square yard.

The rates for parish churches, chapels, and church yards, to be paid by the church or chapel wardens; and for other places, by the respective proprietors.

Where the rates shall not be paid within 10 days after demand, the receiver by warrant of two justices, with the assistance of a constable, may levy the same, with all charges, by distress and sale.

All the monies rasied and appropriated by this act are vested in the commissioners, to be applied for the purposes of the act only.

Penalties and forfeitures in general to be levied by distress and sale, by warrant of a justice, and to be paid to the commissioners treasurer.

Ballance of money received, and not paid over at the time of the receiver's death, is to be paid by the executors of the deceased's estate; and the receipt of 3 or more commissioners is a sufficient discharge for the same; but on nonpayment within 21 days after demanded, the treasurer may sue the executors.

Where persons shall quit their houses, etc. before they have paid the rates, the receiver by warrant of 2 justices for *Middlesex*, or city and liberty of *Westminster*, (the same being first backed by some magistrate for the place, where the distress is to be made) may levy the rates, and all charges by distress and sale.

No rate to be made upon any place, till the pavement is compleated; and all contracts before made (except between landlord and tenant) for paving, cleansing, or lighting the streets are then to cease. Persons paying to these rates are exempted from all other charges and penalties on account thereof.

As soon as any rate shall be made by virtue of this act, the owners or occupiers of houses, etc. assessed thereto, are discharged from payment of like rates made in pursuance of former acts.

Inhabitants of St *James's Square*, being included in an act of 12 *Geo.* II. *Lincoln's Inn Fields*, in an act of 8 *Geo.* II. and *Golden Square*, in an act of 24 *Geo.* II. are exempted out of this act.

This act not to extend to such parts of streets, etc. as are already directed to be paved, lighted, or cleansed, by any road act; nor to *Deans Yard*, and places adjoining to the south and west doors of *Westminster Abbey*.

Seven or more commissioners may make a new passage, or widen the old one, from *Drury Lane* into *Great Queen Street*, at the *Devil's Gap*; and purchase houses and ground for that purpose, etc. not exceeding 6 in number; and if they make a new one, may inclose and sell the old passage for building upon; and may pave, repair, and cleanse the same, in like manner as the squares and streets, etc. before mentioned.

No part of the rate, or money granted by parliament, to be applied in the purchase of the said houses or ground.

Persons aggrieved, where no other method of relief is appointed, may appeal to the quarter sessions within three months; giving 12 days notice of such appeal to the clerk or treasurer, and entering into recognizance, with security, to try the same, etc. justices to determine such appeal in a summary way, and award costs.

Distress not to be deemed unlawful, nor the party making it a trespasser, for want of form in the proceedings; nor the party distraining a trespasser *ab initio*, on account of any subsequent irregularity.

Party to recover full satisfaction only for the damage, in an action on the case: but where sufficient tender shall have been made, before the action brought, the plaintiff is not to recover. Defendant, with leave may pay money into court, etc.

Contracts and other writings not chargeable with any duty.

Orders and proceedings of the commissioners to be entered in books, and signed by the clerk; which may be produced and read in evidence.

No act of the commissioners valid, unless done at a publick meeting.

Proceedings against offenders not liable to be qualified for want of form; or removeable by *certiorari*. Limitation of actions. General issue. Treble costs.

Fox's Libel Act, 1792

32 Geo. 3, c. 60   *Statutes at Large*, II, 148-49.

This measure, promoted by Charles James Fox, enabled jurors in libel actions to pronounce a general verdict on the libel. Previously, the jury was restricted to a determination of the truth or falsity of a published statement, and only the judge could decide whether the publication was libellous.

Whereas doubts have arisen whether on the trial of an indictment or information for the making or publishing any libel, where an issue or issues are joined between the King and the defendant or defendants, on the plea of not guilty pleaded, it be competent to the jury impanelled to try the same to give their verdict upon the whole matter in issue: Be it therefore declared and enacted by the King's most excellent Majesty, by and with the advice and consent of the lords spiritual and temporal, and commons, in this present Parliament assembled, and by the authority of the same, that on every such trial the jury sworn to try the issue may give a general verdict of guilty or not guilty upon the whole matter put in issue upon such indictment or information, and shall not be required or directed by the court or judge before whom such indictment or information shall be tried to find the defendant or defendants guilty merely on the proof of the publication by such defendant or defendants of the paper charged to be a libel, and of the sense ascribed to the same in such indictment or information.

2. Provided always, that on every such trial the court or judge before whom such indictment or information shall be tried shall, according to their or his discretion, give their or his opinion and directions to the jury on the matter in issue between the King and the defendant or defendants in like manner as in other criminal cases.

3. Provided also, that nothing herein contained shall extend or be construed to extend to prevent the jury from finding a special verdict, in their discretion, as in other criminal cases.

4. Provided also, that in case the jury shall find the defendant or defendants guilty it shall and may be lawful for the said defendant or defendants to move in a rest of judgement, on such ground and in such manner as by law he or they might have done before the passing of this Act, any thing herein contained to the contrary notwithstanding.

First census of the population of Great Britain, 1801

Parliamentary Papers, 1801-02, VII, Cmd. 112, iii-iv, app. 502-03.

The following are from the Abstract of the Answers and Returns *published on 22 February 1802.*

QUESTIONS

To which, by Directions of an Act passed in the Forty-first Year of the Reign of His Majesty King George the Third, intituled, *An Act for taking an Account of the Population of* Great Britain*, and of the Increase or Diminution thereof*, written Answers were to be returned to the Rector, Vicar, Curate, or Officiating Minister, and Overseers of the Poor, or (in Default thereof) by some other substantial Householder, or every Parish, Township, and Place (including those Places also which are Extra-parochial) in *England*; and by the School-masters or other Persons appointed under the said Act for every Parish in *Scotland*; signed by them respectively, and attested upon Oath or Affirmation by the said Overseers, or (in Default thereof) by such other substantial House-holders as aforesaid, in *England*, and by the Schoolmasters or such other Persons as aforesaid in *Scotland*; for which Purpose they were directed to attend the Justices of the Peace, within their respective Jurisdiction, at such Times and Places as the said Justices of the Peace appointed, on Pain of incurring the Penalties imposed by the said Act for every wilful Default or Neglect.

1st. How many Inhabited Houses are there in your Parish, Township, or Place; by how many Families are they occupied; and, how many Houses therein are Uninhabited?

2d. How many Persons (including Children of whatever Age) are there actually found within the Limits of your Parish, Township, or Place, at the Time of taking this Account, distinguishing Males and Females, and exclusive of Men actually serving in His Majesty's Regular Forces or Militia, and exclusive of Seamen either in His Majesty's Service or belonging to Registered Vessels?

3d. What Number of Persons, in your Parish, Township, or Place, are chiefly employed in Agriculture; how many in Trade, Manufactures, or Handicraft; and, how many are not comprized in any of the preceding Classes?

4th. What was the Number of Baptisms and Burials in your Parish, Township, or Place, in the several Years 1700, 1710, 1720, 1730, 1740, 1750, 1760, 1770, 1780 and each subsequent Year, to the 31st Day of *December* 1800, distinguishing Males from Females?

5th. What has been the Number of Marriages in your Parish, Township, or Place, in each Year, from the Year 1754 inclusive to the End of the Year 1800?

6th. Are there any Matters which you think it necessary to remark in Explanation of your Answers to any of the preceding Questions?

In this Abstract are collected the Answers returning to the First, Second, Third, and Sixth Questions.

SUMMARY OF ENUMERATION

M.DCCC.I

	Houses			Persons		Occupations			Total of Persons
	Inhabited	By how many Families occupied	Uninhabited	Males	Females	Persons chiefly employed in Agriculture	Persons chiefly employed in Trade Manufactures, or Handicraft	All other Persons not comprized in the Two preceding Classes	
England · · · · · · · · · · · · ·	1,467,870	1,778,420	53,965	3,937,935	4,343,499	1,524,227	1,789,531	4,606,530	8,331,434
Wales · · · · · ·	108,053	118,303	3,511	237,178	284,368	189,062	53,822	266,573	541,546
Scotland · · · · ·	294,553	364,079	9,537	734,581	864,487	365,516	293,373	833,914	1,599,068
Army, including the Militia · · ·	—	—	—	198,351	—	—	—	—	198,351
Navy, including Marines · · · · ·	—	—	—	126,279	—	—	—	—	126,279
Seamen in Registered Shipping · ·	—	—	—	144,558	—	—	—	—	144,558
Convicts, on Board the Hulks · · ·	—	—	—	1,410	—	—	—	—	1,410
Total · · · · · · · · · ·	1,870,476	2,260,802	67,013	5,450,292	5,492,354	2,135,805	2,136,726	5,707,017	10,942,646

OBSERVATIONS

1. The Total Population of Great Britain must exceed the Number of Persons specified in the above Summary, inasmuch as there are some Parishes from which no Returns have been received.

2. The Number of Houses in Ireland has been nearly ascertained by the Collection of a Hearth-Money Tax; and therefrom it has been computed that the Population of that Part of the United Kingdom somewhat exceeds Four Millions of Persons.

3. The Islands of Guernsey, Jersey, Alderney, and Sark, the Scilly Islands, and the Isle of Man, are not comprized in this Enumeration. The Total Population of these Islands has been usually estimated at about Eighty Thousand Persons.

[Appended charts, prepared by John Rickman, Population Office, Whitehall, 8 December 1801]

CITIES OF LONDON AND WESTMINSTER, AND COUNTIES OF MIDDLESEX AND SURREY

	Houses			Persons		Occupations			Total of Persons
	Inhabited	By how many Families occupied	Uninhabited	Males	Females	Persons chiefly employed in Agriculture	Persons chiefly employed in Trade Manufactures, or Handicraft	All other Persons not comprized in the Two preceding Classes	
Out Parishes in Middlesex and Surrey									
St. Ann at Limehouse	755	1,046	11	2,336	2,342	10	1,292	3,276	4,678
Artillery Ground and Norton Falgate Liberty	437	767	13	1,424	1,756	1	947	2,232	3,180
Christ Church, in Southwark	1,530	2,563	56	4,541	5,392	19	2,501	7,413	9,933
Christ Church, in Spital Fields	1,876	4,205	145	6,894	8,197	4	6,166	8,921	15,091
St. Dunstan, Stepney	3,918	6,241	110	11,119	14,141	128	4,498	17,242	25,260
St. George in Bloomsbury	916	1,726	16	3,409	4,329	–	1,321	6,417	7,738
St. George in the East	4,029	5,771	119	9,231	11,939	21	2,414	19,292	21,170
St. George by Queen Square	721	1,481	15	2,522	3,751	–	1,023	5,250	6,273
St. Giles in the Fields	2,792	6,889	137	13,005	15,759	–	5,150	23,614	28,764
St. James and St. John, Clerkenwell . . .	3,320	6,288	107	11,094	12,551	27	4,967	18,651	23,645
St. John, at Hackney	2,050	2,420	84	5,422	7,308	44	897	11,789	12,730
St. John, at Wapping	998	1,574	38	2,717	3,172	5	1,427	4,457	5,889
St. Katherine near the Tower, and Tower Liberty .	587	782	20	1,461	1,754	–	632	2,583	3,215
St. Leonard, in Shoreditch	5,732	9,224	381	15,775	18,991	2,339	5,937	26,490	34,766
St. Luke, in Middlesex	3,776	7,033	61	12,500	14,381	38	6,728	20,115	26,881
St. Mary, at Islington	1,665	2,228	80	4,189	6,023	115	892	9,205	10,212
St. Mary, at Lambeth	4,790	8,813	220	12,400	15,585	955	5,148	21,875	27,985
St. Mary Magdalen, Bermondsey	3,137	4,283	66	7,986	9,183	94	3,959	13,116	17,169
St. Mary, at Newington Butts, Surrey . . .	2,865	3,740	75	6,450	8,397	119	1,965	12,763	14,847
St. Mary, at Rotherhithe	1,680	2,394	16	4,787	5,509	65	2,059	8,172	10,296
St. Mary Matsellon, at Whitechapel . . .	3,497	6,141	192	11,102	12,564	11	4,522	19,133	23,666
St. Matthew, at Bethnell Green	3,586	5,630	234	9,913	12,397	16	4,214	18,080	22,310
St. Paul, at Shadwell	1,550	2,647	48	3,622	5,206	–	973	7,855	8,828
	56,207	93,886	2,244	163,899	100,627	5,011	69,632	287,941	364,526

City and Liberties of Westminster

	Houses			Persons		Occupations			Total of Persons
	Inhabited	By how many Families occupied	Uninhabited	Males	Females	Persons chiefly employed in Agriculture	Persons chiefly employed in Trade Manufactures, or Handicraft	All other Persons not comprized in the Two preceding Classes	
St. Ann, Westminster, near Soho	1,294	2,471	88	5,249	6,388	—	3,477	8,160	11,637
St. Clement Danes, including the Duchy of Lancaster . . .	1,694	3,341	62	6,403	6,932	—	3,672	9,653	13,335
St. George by Hanover Square	4,344	9,170	91	15,799	21,661	163	5,989	32,288	38,440
St. James, Westminster	3,430	10,448	169	15,224	18,238	7	8,668	25,787	34,462
St. John the Evangelist	1,268	2,546	121	3,613	4,762	42	1,827	6,506	8,375
St. Margaret	2,367	4,956	97	7,131	10,377	43	2,792	14,673	17,508
St. Martin in the Fields	2,791	5,888	112	12,053	13,699	—	6,043	19,709	25,752
St. Mary le Strand	166	425	9	796	908	—	494	1,210	1,704
The Precinct of the Savoy	38	77	2	144	176	—	101	219	320
St. Paul, in Covent Garden	598	1,239	22	2,202	2,790	—	1,910	3,082	4,992
Verge of the Palaces of Whitehall and St. James's	241	272	11	707	978	23	58	1,604	1,685
	18,231	40,833	784	71,301	86,909	278	35,031	122,891	158,210
Inns of Court, Extra Parochial	1,230	816	62	1,293	614	—	46	1,682	1,907

[Appended charts, prepared by John Rickman, Population Office, Whitehall, 8 December 1801–*Continued*]

MIDDLESEX

Parishes not within the Bills of Mortality	Houses			Persons		Occupations			Total of Persons
	Inhabited	By how many Families occupied	Uninhabited	Males	Females	Persons chiefly employed in Agriculture	Persons chiefly employed in Trade Manufactures, or Handicraft	All other Persons not comprized in the Two preceding Classes	
St. Mary-le-bone	7,209	15,378	555	27,012	36,970	371	7,977	55,634	63,982
Paddington	324	417	33	870	1,011	158	160	1,563	1,881
St. Pancras	4,173	7,376	253	14,009	17,770	–	3,779	28,000	31,779
Kensington	1,314	2,214	119	3,487	5,069	44	1,165	7,347	8,556
St. Luke, Chelsea	1,637	2,746	128	4,651	6,953	183	1,069	10,352	11,604
	14,657	28,131	1,088	50,029	67,773	756	14,150	102,896	117,802

ABSTRACT OF THE POPULATION OF THE CITIES OF LONDON AND WESTMINSTER

	Inhabited	By how many Families occupied	Uninhabited	Males	Females	Agriculture	Trade	All other	Total
London within the Walls	10,224	16,229	325	37,020	38,151	14	23,659	50,837	75,171
London without the Walls	20,680	36,178	682	69,827	77,402	167	36,337	97,015	147,229
Out Parishes in Middlesex and Surrey .	56,207	93,886	2,244	163,899	100,627	5,011	69,632	287,941	364,526
City and Liberties of Westminster . .	18,231	40,833	784	71,301	86,909	278	35,031	122,891	158,210
Inns of Court, Extra Parochial . . .	1,230	816	62	1,293	614	–	46	1,682	1,907
Parishes not within the Bills of Mortality .	14,657	28,131	1,088	50,029	67,773	756	14,150	102,896	117,802
Total	121,229	216,073	5,185	393,369	471,476	6,226	178,855	663,262	864,845

Within the Bills of Mortality

Mortality of Within the Bills

Commons debate on the Cruelty to Animals Bill, 13 June 1809

Hansard, n.s., XIV, 1029-40; 1025*-32.*

The debate on this abortive measure is of interest since it pinpoints the conflict between those willing to use the power of the state to achieve reform and those concerned with preserving the culture of the poor.

Mr. *Windham* said, that his first and general objection to the Bill was, that the object of it, however commendable, was not such as to become a fit subject of legislation. For this opinion he had at least a pretty strong voucher, in the universal practice of mankind down to the present moment. In no country had it ever yet been attempted to regulate by law the conduct of men towards brute animals, except so far as such conduct operated to the prejudice of men. The province of criminal legislation had hitherto been confined to the injuries sustained by men. This fact, though affording a pretty strong presumption, (sufficient, one should think, to make us pause, and not hurry through the house, with hardly any discussion, a bill of so novel a character,) was yet, he would confess, not absolutely conclusive. It might be right, that "all this should be changed;" that what was not proposed, should be done, though it had never been done before. But the question was, at least, of some importance, and not to be decided without more discussion, than had hitherto taken place, or could now well be expected before the sessions would be at an end. The novelty of the subject, not in its details or particular application, but in its general character, was a topic not brought forward, as an objection, by the opposers of the bill, but claimed and insisted upon by its authors. In a pamphlet, circulated with great industry, (and of equal authority, as coming from the same source with the bill itself,) it was expressly stated, and with no small triumph, that the bill would form a new era of legislation! Two reflections arose upon this; first, that we ought to take care, to be cautious at least, how we began new eras of legislation; secondly, that we ought to have a reasonable distrust of the founders of such eras, lest they should be a little led away by an object of such splendid ambition, and be thinking more of themselves than of the credit of the laws or the interests of the community. To have done that which no one yet had ever thought of doing; to have introduced into legislation, at this period of the world, what had never yet been found in the laws of any country, and that too for a purpose of professed humanity, or rather of something more than humanity as commonly understood and practised; to be the first who had stood up as the champion of the rights of brutes, was as marked a distinction, even if it should not turn out, upon examination, to be as proud a one, as a man could well aspire to.

The legislature, however, must not be carried away with these impulses, of whatever nature they may be, but must consider soberly and coolly, whether it might not be something more than mere indifference or want of thought, that had kept men, for so many thousand years, from attempting to introduce this new principle, as it was now justly called, of legislation; and whether, in the attempt at present, they might not do far more harm than good.

Of the desirableness of the object speaking abstractedly, there could be no doubt. As far as wishes went, every man must wish, that the sufferings of all animated nature were less than they were. Why they were permitted at all, was a question, as had been observed by a great and pious writer, which must for ever continue to perplex mankind, as long as we were allowed to see only in part. But there was not only the wish that suffering universally should, if possible, be less than it was, but there was a duty, he was ready to admit, upon man, (the only animal, it was to be observed, that took cognizance of others pain,) to conform himself to that wish, in the little sphere to which his influence extended. Morality itself might perhaps be defined, "a desire rationally conducted to promote general happiness," and consequently to diminish general pain; and he was far from contending, that the operation of that principle (so glorious to man, the only animal that partook of it) should not be made to embrace in its effects the whole of animal life. Let the duty be as strongly enforced, as far as precept and persuasion could go, and the feeling as largely indulged, as its most eager advocates could wish. He had no objection to any sacrifices, which any one might be disposed to make in his own person, for sparing the pain or promoting the enjoyment of others of his fellow-creatures, whether men or inferior animals. The more lively the sympathy, within certain limits, and the greater the sacrifice, the more would be the amiableness and the merit. Within certain limits he had said, because theoretically, certainly, there were limits, which those feelings could not pass, without defeating instead of promoting the ends of Providence, which must be presumed to have intended them as the means of increasing the quantum of happiness. Sympathy was necessary to the production of virtue, and for the procuring mutual aid in case of distress. But were every one to feel with equal sensibility the pains of others as his own, the world must become one unvaried scene of suffering, in which the woes of all would be accumulated upon each, and every man be charged with a weight of calamity beyond what his individual powers of endurance were calculated to support. There was little danger, however, of this excess. One might safely lay down the rule, that the more any one should feel for the suffering of others, the more virtuous they should be accounted; and that they were at liberty, in this respect, to give a full loose to their feelings.

But the very same considerations would make it dangerous to allow of systems, in which men were to become virtuous at others' expence, and to enforce upon others what might be wanting in themselves. It was not sufficient to state of any thing that it was matter of obligation, to justify an attempt to enforce it by law. Laws were almost universally restrictive. They restrained acts which were injurious to the community, and were such moreover as should be clearly defined. There were whole classes of duties, known to writers on morals under the name of Imperfect Obligations, which no one ever thought of enforcing by law, not because they were, in point of moral duty, less obligatory than others, but because they were of a nature that, to exist at all, must be spontaneous, or such as that law could not be made to apply to them. What idea could any one have of a law, to enforce charity, gratitude, benevolence, or innumerable others of the Christian virtues? If a man with thousands in his coffers, of which he made no use, should suffer a fellow creature whose case was fully known to him, to perish in the next street for the want of a few shillings, you might inveigh against him for his want of humanity; but would you ever think, that there ought to be a law to punish him? The same might be said of cases that occurred, he feared, too frequently under the influence of the poor-laws, where paupers at the point of death, and women expecting at every moment to be seized with the pangs of labour, were turned out into the streets or roads, sooner than by the death in one case or the birth in the other, a burthen should be brought upon the parish. The poor-laws were an example of an attempt to force charity; and fine encouragement they gave to such attempts! But after all that they had done, unfortunately done, how much was left, which the law did not attempt to reach?

It would not be difficult to show, that the case was much the same in respect to the objects now meant to be provided for. The measure sets out with a preamble, containing a lofty maxim of morality or theology, too grand to be correct, too sublime to be seen distinctly, and most ludicrously disproportioned to the enactments that follow, wherein it is declared that God had *subdued* various classes of animals to the use and benefit of man: and from thence it seems to be inferred, not very consequentially, that we ought to treat them with humanity. That we ought to treat them with humanity, that is, that we ought, in all we did respecting them, to have a consideration of their pains and pleasures, was a maxim which he was not at all disposed to controvert; but it did not seem immediately inferable from the permission before recited. If humanity indeed were carried to its utmost extent, it would rather run counter to that permission, and lead us, like the Gentoos, at least to abstain from eating the animals thus consigned to us, if not from using them in any way that should not be productive to them of more gratification than suffering. The humanity, however, that is now recommended, is not meant, it seems, to go that length. We may destroy them for the purposes of food, that is of appetite and luxury, to whatever amount and in whatever ways those purposes require. Another class of us likewise, namely the rich, may destroy them, in any modes, however lingering and cruel, which are necessary for the purposes of sport and diversion. Even independently of the doubt which these striking exceptions create, we may ask reasonably, what humanity is? Is it any thing capable of being defined by precise limits? or is it a mere question of degree, and something consequently which is not capable of being set forth in words, but must be left to the decision of some living tribunal, giving its judgment upon each particular case?

Here we come back to the first and fundamental objection to legislating upon this, and various similar subjects. You inflict pains and penalties, upon conditions which no man is able previously to ascertain. You require men to live by an unknown rule. You make the condition of life uncertain, by exposing men to the operation of a law, which they cannot know till it visits them in the shape of punishment. What is humanity? It is generally the having a consideration for the sufferings of others, (men or other sentient beings) as compared with pains or gratifications of our own. But what the proportion was, necessary to be observed between our own and others pain, or, (as was oftener the case in the subject then under consideration,) what the proportion was between others pain and our pleasure or interest, no mortal attempted to ascertain: nor was it one and the same, but as various as there were various men, and various circumstances and subjects to which it was applied, and what was of not less consequence, varied as men were judging in their own case, or in that of their neighbours. It was not only not the same in any two men, but not the same in the same man for half an hour together, but changed, according as he applied it to one case or another, or was in one humour or another, or, above all, was judging in the case of others or of himself. This was no exaggerated representation. As a proof, let any man go through the instances where his humanity has been shocked, at one time, and where at others it has remained perfectly in repose. The instances of ill treatment of animals, which most frequently occurred, (and were most in the view of the advocates of this bill,) were those which arose from passion; a coach-man whipping his coach-horses, a carman beating his cart-horse. The undisturbed spectator, who knows nothing of the causes that have led to this, and who, as Swift says of men bearing others misfortunes, can bear the provocations, which have inflamed another, "perfectly like a Christian," is full of virtuous ire, and inveighs hotly against the man who can thus go into a senseless passion with his horse; but he does not consider that the irritability here shewn may have come upon a man wearied by long labour, and soured by some recent vexation, and have been excited withal by something in the horse, which he has been led, foolishly for the most part, to consider as perverseness; nor does the blamer recollect, how, he himself the day before, when he was riding comfortably to get an appetite for his dinner, spurred his horse most unmercifully, (as violently as his fears would let him), because the animal had been guilty of starting or stumbling. Here was an instance of that different standard of humanity, which men have in their breasts for themselves or others, for their cooler moments and for their passionate ones; and we might thence see what flagrant and scandalous injustice would be done, under a criterion subject to such variation. It was no answer to say, that the judgment was not unjust, because the judge might have been guilty of the same offence: and that as he punished others, others might punish him. The judge, we knew, would not be punished. Few would inform against his worship the squire because he had rode his hunter to death, or unmercifully whipped, or in a fit of anger shot, his pointer. The scandal therefore in the general administration of the law would remain, even though those who were convicted, were punished justly. But it was not true, that passion would not be mixed even in the judgment itself. Passion might be suspected to mix itself, and did in fact continually mix itself, in all judgments carried on by close and summary jurisdictions, and by persons who were little likely to be made responsible for their conduct. Such jurisdictions must of necessity exist in many cases; but they were not on that account the less to be deprecated. But there was one general passion applicable to the present case, and which would not fail to operate in every part of the process; in the judgment often, but still more frequently in the information; and which would form a complete answer to that childish plea in favour of the bill, viz. that as no reward was given, no temptation would be held out to informers. The passion here alluded to was one of great account in human nature, though not so often noted as it ought to be, namely, the love of tormenting. There was a book written some years ago, commonly ascribed to a sister of the author of Tom Jones, but really the work of a lady of the name of Collyer, which treated of this passion, under the title of "The Art of ingeniously Tormenting," and after illustrating, with great acuteness and much nice observation of character and manners, its operation in various relations of domestic life, as, how to torment an humble companion, how a wife should torment her husband, and a husband his wife, concluded with a chapter, entitled "General Rules how to torment all your Acquaintance." It would be found by any one who perused this book, how much there was of this principle continually in operation, of which he had often witnessed the effects, without at the time having understood or attended to the cause. But frequent as these instances were, as seen and described by the author referred to, they were nothing in extent and amount to those which were carried on, under a new and more enlarged head, which did not come within the scheme of her work, nor fall, possibly, within the scope of her contemplation, viz. the art of tormenting people in the name of the public good, an art which seemed to have been gaining ground considerably in our days, and to have had a larger share in the acts of the legislature, as well as to have produced more annoyance in society, than people were commonly aware. Here the trade of course was wholesale, and carried on upon a large scale. And it was not to be told how eager the passion was, when animated and sanctioned by the auxiliary motive of supposed zeal for the public service. It was childish for people to ask What pleasure can any one have in tormenting others? None in the mere pain inflicted, but the greatest possible in the various effects that may accompany it, in the parade of virtue and in the exercise of power. A man cannot torment another without a considerable exercise of power—in itself a pretty strong and general passion. But if he can at once exercise his power and make a parade of his virtue, (which will eminently be the case in the powers to be exercised under this law) the combination of the two forms a motive, which we might fairly say, flesh and blood could not withstand. Young's "universal passion" had not a wider range, nor a stronger influence, than the union of these two feelings.

In what a state then should we put the lower orders of people in this country (for it was they only who would be affected) when for the sake of punishing some rare, and hardly-heard-of enormities, (the narrow but only rational object of the measure) we should let loose upon them a principle of action like that above described, armed with such a weapon as this bill would put into its hands? All the fanatical views and feelings, all the little bustling spirit of regulation, all the private enmities and quarrels would be at work, in addition to those more general passions before stated, and men be daily punished by summary jurisdiction, or left to wait in gaol for the meeting of a more regular tribunal, for offences, which were incapable of being defined, and which must be left therefore to the arbitrary and fluctuating standard, which the judge in either case happened to carry in his breast. The bill, instead of being called A Bill for preventing Cruelty to Animals, should be entitled, A Bill for harrassing and oppressing certain classes among the lower orders of the people.

The manner in which it would be thrown upon them, and the scandalous injustice with which it would be attended, might be exemplified by one of the instances set forth by the authors of the bill themselves. The cruelties suffered by post-horses was a favourite topic. But on whom was the punishment to fall? on the post boy or on the traveller? On the post boy, who was the only person who would be seen inflicting these severities? or on the traveller, who sat snug in the chaise, having only hinted to the post boy, that he meant to dine at the next stage, and that if he should not bring him in in time he would never go to his master's house again, nor give him any thing for himself.

This case of post horses belonged also to another head, to which he would now proceed; namely, the objections to the bill on the score that it was doing that by law, which if people were sincere in their feeling, might be done by other methods. Laws never ought to be called in but where other powers fail. Upon whom was the whole force of this bill to be discharged? what were the instances which were uppermost in every one's mind, which had been first cited as proofs of the necessity of such a measure, and in which indeed the bill either would or was intended to act? Why, the cruelties inflicted on horses by grooms, coach-men, post-boys, carmen, servants in husbandry, or others, to whom such animals were entrusted. But whose property were these? Why, the property of persons, who had some, (generally great,) power respectively over the several classes of persons above enumerated? Why do not these masters and owners exert themselves in earnest, in punishing such offences whenever they come within their cognizance, or are even known to them in a way which, though sufficient for them to act, would not authorize a legal process? But, no; they are often the direct parties, the parties interested in, and the parties instigating, the very cruelties or severities which they affect to decry. One of the favourite instances in the fashionable female circles, as they are called, of this town, and who appear by the bye to have been very diligently canvassed, as the cases with which they have been continually shocked, of coachmen whipping their horses in public places: an instance by the way by no means of magnitude enough to call for the interference of the legislature. But be its magnitude what it will, why must the legislature be called in? are there not means (sufficient probably for punishing the offence adequately in each instance, but certainly for preventing the practice,) in the power possessed by masters and mistresses? But apply to any of these ladies, and satisfy them, after much difficulty, that their coachman was the most active and the most in the wrong, in the struggle, which caused so much disturbance at the last Opera, and the answer probably would be, "Oh! to be sure; it is very shocking; but then John is so clever in a crowd! the other night at Lady Such-a-one's, when all the world was perishing in the passage, waiting for their carriages, ours was up in an instant, and we were at Mrs. Such-a-one's half an hour before any one else. We should not know what to do, if we were to part with him." Was it the coachman here who most deserved punishment? or was it for the parties here described to call for a law, which was to lay the foundation of a new era of legislation, and to operate with great severity and most flagrant injustice upon whole classes of people? A similar instance would be found in the case just alluded to of the traveller and the post horses. Whose fault was it, in nineteen cases out of twenty, that these sufferings were incurred? the traveller drives up in haste, his servant having half killed one post-horse in riding forward to announce his approach; the horses are brought out; they are weak, spavined, galled, hardly dry from their last stage. What is the dialogue that ensues? does the traveller ever offer to stop on his journey, or even to wait till the horses can be refreshed? such a thought never enters his head; he swears at the landlord, and threatens never to come again to his house, because he expects to go only seven miles an hour, when he had hoped to go nine; but when the landlord has assured him, that the horses, however bad in their appearance, will carry his honour very well, and has directed the post boys to "make the best of their way," the traveller's humanity is satisfied, and he hears with perfect composure and complacency the cracking whips of the postillions, only intimating to them, by-the-bye, that if they do not bring him in in time, they shall not receive a farthing. What revolting and disgusting hypocrisy was it in persons daily witnessing without remonstrance, or acting in such scenes, who would not sacrifice the smallest particle of their convenience in consideration of any pain that was to result from it, to be inveighing with such exaggerated sensibility against the cruelties practised on the brute creation, and calling for a law to punish them; much of that cruelty being incurred in their service, and under their own immediate inspection and orders! Where was the justice of punishing the inn-keeper here? who, if he refused his horses, lost his customers, and his means of livelihood; or the post-boy, who when once employed must perform the task assigned him by such means as he had, and must ply his whip till the pain or threat overcome the pain of the effort, which the horses had to make in order to go through their stage?

Such were the proofs of the injustice of the law, and such the proofs that no law, just or unjust, was necessary, even in the cases to which it applied. But what should be said of the flagrant and horrid injustice, of withdrawing from its operation and cognizance, a whole class of cases, which, if such a bill was to pass, could not, one should think, be allowed to stand an instant, as being more than any others in the very line and point-blank aim of the statute, and having nothing to protect them, but that which ought in justice and decency to be the strongest reason against them, namely that they were the mere sports of the rich? Was it to be endured or believed, that a legislature setting about the great and original work of enacting laws to prevent the sufferings of the brute creation, should still reserve to themselves, and that too by a most invidious and oppressive code, the privilege of killing animals by a cruel and lingering death, in mere sport and wantonness? The reason assigned for this extraordinary omission, by the author of the bill, might be suspected as having been intended in mere mockery. It was said that being *ferae naturae* (a learned distinction, but never before, surely, applied to such a purpose) they were not entitled to the protection of man? But why, because they did not ask his protection, were they to be liable in consequence to be persecuted and tormented by him? On the contrary, if he did nothing for their good, he ought the rather to be required to do nothing for their harm. They would perish, it was said, if left to themselves, often by a cruel death. But what was the animal, man not excepted, that was not liable so to perish? If this argument was good for any thing, it might justify, in pure kindness, our killing one another. Another danger was, that they would become so numerous as to overrun the earth. But this danger, formidable as it might be in respect to other animals, certainly did not apply to one great class, with which notwithstanding we made pretty free, namely the fishes. After all, when humanity was the question, what connection was there between the necessity of destroying those animals and the right which we claimed of being ourselves the destroyers? It was very disinterested, no doubt, in all the higher orders of people to offer themselves gratuitiously as vermin killers to the rest of the community; but it was an odd choice for them, as men of humanity; particularly as it was found, that there vermin were encouraged and protected for the sake of being afterwards killed, and certainly by a mode of destruction in many instances, not capable of being exceeded in cruelty by any to which they could naturally be liable. Even in the case of sheep and oxen, which must, it is admitted, be killed, and might be killed possibly by a gentleman with as little pain as by the butcher, we should think it an odd taste in any one, to be desirous literally to kill his own mutton, and to beg of his butcher that he might be allowed on the next slaughter day to take his place. It was in vain therefore by such wretched evasions and subterfuges to attempt to disguise the fact, that if with such a preamble on our statutes, and with acts passed in consequence to punish the lower classes for any cruelty inflicted upon animals, we continued to practise and to reserve in great measure to ourselves the sports of hunting, shooting, and fishing, we must exhibit ourselves as the most hardened and unblushing hypocrites that ever shocked the feelings of mankind. He did not know any thing, that could so justly call for a measure, which he had always been among the first to resist, a parliamentary reform. Strongly as he had always declared against such a measure, as wholly uncalled for by any thing in the practice of parliament as now constituted, he must fairly confess, that if it should appear in any instance that so scandalous a distinction could be made between the interests of high and low, rich and poor, he should be not a little shaken in his opposition, and must be driven in a great measure from that argument, which, as long as it could be maintained, was conclusive against every such proposal, namely, that there was no class in the community whose interests, even as parliament was at present constituted, were not upon the whole fairly taken care of. What a pretty figure must we make in the world, if in one column of the newspapers we should read a string of instances of men committed under "the Cruelty Bill," some to the county gaol to wait for trial at the assizes, some by summary process to the house of correction; and in another part, an article of "Sporting Intelligence," setting forth the exploits of my lord Such-a-one's hounds, how the hounds threw off at such a cover; that bold Reynard went off in a gallant stile, etc., and was not killed till after a chace [sic] of ten hours; that of fifty horsemen who were out at the beginning not above five were in at the *death*, that three horses *died* in the field, and *several* it was thought would never *recover*; and that upon the whole it was the most glorious day's *sport*, ever remembered since the pack was first set up! Was it possible that men could stand the shame of such statements? that this house which tolerated such sports, nay, which claimed them, as the peculiar privilege of the class to which it belonged, a house of hunters and shooters, should, while they left these untouched, be affecting to take the brute creation under their protection; and be passing bills for the punishment of every carter or driver, whom an angry passenger should accuse of chastising his horse with over severity? He begged not to be understood, as condemning the sports, to which he had been alluding, and much less, as charging with cruelty all those who took delight in them, cruel as the acts themselves undoubtedly were. He would not dispute with his friend, the hon. mover (sir Ch. Bunbury) what the *quantum* of cruelty was in horse racing, whether the whip was always as much spared as he supposed, or whether when it was, the forbearance proceeded from humanity, or from an opinion that more would be lost, by the horse's swerving and the rider's seat being rendered unsteady than would be gained by the pain. Though no sportsman himself, he should lament the day, if ever it should happen in this country, that from false refinement and mistaken humanity they should be abolished or fall into disuse. So far from arraigning those who followed them, his doctrine had ever been, that, odd as it might seem, cruel sports did not make cruel people: and he would quote for this the great body of the English country gentlemen, now and in all former times. But as long as, upon that ground, and for wise and salutary purposes, such practices, cruel as they were, were permitted, and even upheld, he could not consent, that the house should go off into that wild career of humanity, that was proposed by the present bill. He denied, generally speaking, the existence of the abuses complained of. He denied at least the increase of them, and that the treatment of animals now was worse than in former times, or with us than in other countries. There was in general, no doubt, a very coarse and harsh treatment of them, such as might be expected from the coarseness of the people to whom the management of them was for the most part entrusted; but which was often founded more in ignorance and unskilfulness, than in malice or ferocity. Many of these instances were moreover falsely estimated, by those who allowed their sensibilities, (always ready in their application to others,) to outrun their judgment. He himself had had as many squabbles as others, with carmen and drivers of different descriptions for ill treating their horses: but he had more than once had reason afterwards to think himself in the wrong, and that his complaints had been ill-founded, or were at least exaggerated. Instances were however unquestionably to be met with, of shocking and attrocious cruelty, which every one must wish to have the means of punishing. A case of this sort known or related, instantly inflamed men's minds, and disposed them, without further consideration, to call out for a law. But a law was a serious thing, and ought not to be adopted, merely upon such impulses. There had grown up in the country, of late years, a habit of far too great facility in passing laws. The immediate object only was looked to; some marked cases were selected, in which its operation coincided with the general feeling: but no account was taken of the silent depredations which it would make in numerous instances, on the peace and happiness of individuals, of the manner in which it would embitter the general comfort and security of life, particularly among the lower classes. It was always a question, whether the good effects of a law were, in a few rare instances, a compensation for the general constraint imposed by it, and the instances in which it would operate unjustly. Nor was it true, that in the very cases that would be cited on behalf of the present bill, the crime would go, (or at least need go,) unpunished, even though there were no law specially provided for that purpose. What would be the number of instances for example, in which the animal ill-treated, was not the property of some one, who, if his zeal for humanity was what the calls of many for this bill would indicate, might surely, either by himself, or with the aid of others, inflict ample punishment on the offender, on the score of pecuniary injury? But even where means for that purpose could not be had, or an injury of that description could not be pleaded, the mere publication of the fact, which might be the work of any one, with the steps that might be taken to turn upon it the public attention and indignation, would produce in the end consequences as severe as any that the case required, or that could be hoped from a law. If there was not virtue or humanity enough in the country to make the commission of such outrages ruinous to the party even in point of fortune and circumstances, to hunt down such offenders by a general exclusion from all the benefits of intercourse, and by marking them out as objects of general detestation, it might well be doubted, what the effect of law would be, and whether among those who called for a law, there was not more of a fondness for persecution, and lust of power, than of real concern for the interests of humanity.

It must at all events be more by manners than by laws that any good could be done upon this subject. Animals used in the service of man were left unavoidably so entirely at his mercy, were exposed to much to clandestine mischief, and could so little make known their own injuries, that it would always be a question, whether an attempt to protect them with vindicative justice, would not subject them to more ill treatment than it was likely to guard them from. If manners could not protect them, miserable indeed must be their condition, in spite of all that law could do for them. It was not possible, in the nature of things, that law could with so much precision define the duty as to be able to ensure the performance of it. It was duty evidently of that sort which are called imperfect obligations; of which the definition is, that though equally binding in conscience with other duties, they are not capable of being inforced by law. They must in consequence be left to morals. Let them be inculcated upon that footing in every possible way, from the pulpit, from the press, by precept, by exhortation, by example. But let us not run counter to the nature of things, by attempting, what, as the authors themselves of the bill tell us, never yet was attempted; and above all things let us not bring in such a bill as the present, which, without contributing possibly in the smallest degree to the very object in view, will let loose the most dreadful scourge upon the lower orders of the people, will commit the most flagrant injustice in the manner in which the bill will be executed, and constitute a general charge of injustice against the house, such as it has never before been exposed to, and from which it will be impossible to vindicate it.

The objections to the bill were indeed so numerous, and of such a nature, that he was satisfied it would never have passed, so as to be now a subject of discussion in this house, if those who were really adverse to it would fairly have stood by their opinion, and had not been awed by the apprehension, that in opposing a bill, introduced with such a preamble, they should be considered as the abettors of cruelty. He had no doubt that such would be the charge made against him. But for that he should care very little, compared with the object of opposing a bill so objectionable, as he thought this to be, in every view in which it could be contemplated. He should have no fear in trusting his justification to the reasons he had already given (much as they fell short of what might be urged upon the subject, if he was not unwilling to trespass further on the attention of the house). But whatever had been wanting on his part would be amply supplied by an admirable paper in one of the late Volumes of the Edinburgh Review, the 26th he believed, in which would be found much masterly discussion upon this subject, considered in a point of view in which he had abstained from speaking of it, namely, in its connection with the Society for the Suppression of Vice. As well with a view to that Society as to the present subject, and to the connection between the two, he earnestly recommended to gentlemen the perusal of the paper.—He should now propose to negative the motion for the Speaker's leaving the Chair, with a view to moving afterwards that the Bill be committed to this day three months.

Mr. Stephen was ready to do justice to the ingenuity and talents of the right hon. gentleman, but begged, when he talked of the humanity claimed by others, to ask whether that right hon. gent, and those who thought with him, did not affect to be above vulgar prejudices? He denied, that this was a new era, as had been stated, in legislation, because humanity had ever been a characteristic of British jurisprudence. It was the duty of that house to protect useful animals from wanton and malicious cruelties; and he contended that if any of the cases alluded to by the right hon. gent. should come within that description, the persons concerned would be within the operation of the act. The bill was intended to prevent practices specifically mentioned, and all the objections of the right hon. gent. went only to the enactments of the bill, and might be removed in the Committee.

Mr. Davies Giddy had hoped that the able and convicting speech of the right hon. gent. opposite, would have produced an unanimous vote against the bill in that house. He was an enemy to the bill on the grounds stated by the right hon. gent. as well as because it did not draw any definite line to mark the offence, and would consequently lead to arbitrary decisions.

Mr. Wilberforce felt surprised at the rejection of a measure coming recommended as this did from so respectable a quarter, and expressed his regret that such distinguished talents should be employed in opposition to it. He possessed a letter, which, if he read, he was sure would create in the breast of the right hon. gent., sentiments congenial to his own. If the bill had been more general, it would be argued that it went too far, and now that it was confined to distinct offences it was said it did not go far enough. By raising the estimation of the animal creation in the minds of the ignorant, this bill would create a sum of sensitive happiness almost impossible to calculate.

Mr. Frankland thought that a bill so novel in its nature as the present required more time for its due consideration. He did not credit many of the facts which had been stated and called for evidence to be produced at the bar. He then mentioned that he himself saw a man once striking a horse on the head with the butt end of his whip, in a manner that appeared to him most cruel and brutal. He interfered; but the man, with a most good-humoured countenance, assured him that it was necessary to frighten the horse by striking him on the head, that if he had struck him with the small end of the whip, it would have put the animal to greater pain.

Mr. Jekyll professed himself a warm friend to the bill, which was founded on moral principle. He had many years since considered this subject of cruelty to animals, together with his noble frend (lord Erskine) the mover of it.

Sir Robert Williams mentioned a case, where he himself had met a man beating and spurring his horse most cruelly, and he threatened to take him before a magistrate. The man defied him, and said the horse was his own, and he would treat him as he pleased.

The Chancellor of the Exchequer was ready to give full credit to the intentions of the noble mover of this bill, but thought that it was a subject which required great consideration. If such cases as that stated by his hon. and learned friend (Mr. Jekyll) were intended to be included under the general words of wantonly and maliciously abusing those animals, he could not readily bring his mind to assent to it: for who was to judge exactly of the quantity of food which ought to be given, or of the quantity of punishment or of spurring which was necessary to oblige a horse to make the exertion that was necessary? Who was to judge of the exertion that was necessary? Suppose the man who had been met by the hon. baronet was riding to get a physician for a sick wife, was to be made liable to be stopped in his journey, and taken before a magistrate, if any person passing thought he beat or spurred his horse too severely? He thought that it would be much safer not to adopt a measure of this nature, at the very close of the session; and that if the noble lord who had been so long considering the subject, had not made his bill complete, they might well despair of their powers of mending it with so little time for consideration.

Sir Samuel Romilly could not allow that there was any thing in this bill so vague and indefinite as had been stated by the right hon. gent. The words of the bill were "wantonly and maliciously abusing." These were not words of vague and indefinite signification, but such as magistrates and juries on other occasions conceived sufficient for their direction. As to the quantity of punishment or severity, the crime was entirely in the degree of it. Thus, where a man had dominion over his fellow creatures, such as a master over his apprentice, or a father over his child, they could never be accountable for that ordinary severity, which may be necessary, or be conceived to be necessary with respect to those whom it was their duty to govern. There was no one, however, would say that there were not degrees of cruelty in the exercise of this power which our laws very properly punished, and which juries and magistrates did not find it difficult to determine. But in this bill the words "wantonly and maliciously" being introduced, it would be still harder for the juries to mistake the proper line. He did not see how there could be any doubt; and he thought it would be a strange thing, indeed, if the legislature were to forbear from making laws, merely on the statement that magistrates and juries would not understand them, and would determine in a manner that the law never intended. This was also supposing magistrates and juries to be absolutely void of common sense, and incapable of finding out what should be conceived wanton cruelty to an animal, although they are allowed to be perfectly capable of judging of what was unreasonable cruelty to a child, or an apprentice. He differed very much with the right hon. gent., (the Chancellor of the Exchequer) in his opinion of the case that had been stated. Could any body doubt, but that if a man were to bring a number of horses, or any other sensitive animals, and keep them in a confined place, famishing to such a degree as to prey upon each other, that this was a wanton and malicious abuse of his dominion over those animals? (Hear, hear! from many members.) An hon. gent. (Mr. Frankland) had expressed some doubts of the existence of this cruelty; he should therefore cite a case from Leach's Crown Law, which was a pretty recent one, in confirmation of the fact. A man of the name of John Shaw was indicted on the black act, in the year 1798, at the Old Bailey, for the following offence. His master had refused to lend him a particular horse, and he was seen shortly after beating that horse on the head with the butt-end of a whip which he held in one hand, while with the other he had hold of the horse's tongue. The horse was the same day found dead near the spot, with the tongue almost torn from its head. The man was acquitted, because hitherto no degree of cruelty to animals could be punished, unless it was proved to proceed from express malice to the master. There was no doubt at all but that the cruel act which he mentioned had been done, but hitherto the laws with respect to cruelty to animals only referred to the injury of the property of the owners of them. There was another point of view in which this bill might be of great political importance. It was a great public interest that the people of this country should not be depraved, and it was well known that cruelty to animals generally led the way to cruelty to our fellow-creatures. This was well described by our inimitable artist Hogarth, who traced the cruel murderer from the early tormentor of animals. He really believed this bill might be considered in a great degree as a bill for the prevention of cruel murders.

Mr. Morris defended the principle of the measure.

Lord Portchester declared himself friendly to the bill. The evil which it went to correct called for some interposition, and he could see no force in the objection that it came not within a legislative remedy.

The Solicitor General expressed an anxious desire that this measure, which exacted a new penal statute, and was avowed to be an aera in legislation, should be delayed until the house would be enabled to view the nature and extent of its provisions in their respective bearings.

After a few words from Mr. W. Smith and Mr. Windham, the house divided.

For going into the Committee 40.—Against it 27.

The house then went into the Committee.—A conversation of considerable length took place, on the point whether the offence should or should not be deemed a misdemeanor, triable before a jury. Mr. D. Giddy, the Chancellor of the Exchequer, and Mr. R. Dundas thought it ought not to be such a misdemeanor, but that at all events the Committee should not at that time proceed further. Mr. Windham and Mr. W. Smith thought the chairman should report progress. Mr. Stephen thought the clause might stand, by adding a few words. Mr. Jekyll and Mr. Morris were of opinion the offence should be a misdemeanor. Mr. Lockhart observed, that as so much diversity of opinion prevailed at that late hour, he thought it right to move that the Committee be counted. A cry from the opposition side of No; No. The Speaker said, that as an hon. member had moved that the house be counted—the rule of the house must be strictly complied with, and it was not in the power of the chairman of a Committee, or of the Speaker in the chair of the house, to put any other question after that motion was made. The house was accordingly counted, and there not being more than eighteen members present, the house adjourned.

Report of the Select Committee on Madhouses, with Minutes of Evidence, 11 July 1815

Parliamentary Papers, 1814-15, IV, Cmd. 296, 3-7, 10-14.

The parliamentary committee (1814-15) set up to investigate the problem of making provision for the insane issued four reports and published a mass of testimony demonstrating the need for reform in this area. These reports were ignored, in the main.

Your Committee, deeply sensible of the importance of the Matter referred to their consideration, have applied themselves with great earnestness, to the performance of the duty imposed on them by The House.

The Evidence presented herewith, will show how extensive their inquiries have been. It was their intention to make Observations in detail on the several Heads of the Examination taken before them, and on the several public and private Establishments, for the reception of Insane Persons; but on reconsidering the whole subject, they have thought it advisable, in the first instance, to make their Report more general, for the reasons which will be stated.

Your Committee cannot however hesitate to suggest, with the utmost confidence, from the Evidence they now offer to the House, that some new provision of law is indispensably necessary for insuring better care being taken of Insane Persons, both in *England* and *Ireland*, than they have hitherto experienced; the number of whom appear to be very considerable; as the inquiries of the Committee have convinced them, that there are not in the Country a set of Beings more immediately requiring the protection of the Legislature than the persons in this state; a very large proportion of whom are entirely neglected by their relations and friends. If the treatment of those in the middling or in the lower classes of life, shut up in hospitals, private madhouses, or parish workhouses, is looked at, Your Committee are persuaded that a case cannot be found where the necessity for a remedy is more urgent.

It will appear on reference to the Evidence (relying principally on the testimony of the persons keeping the houses,) that in a few of them, the arrangement is as good as the contracted size of the houses, and the small extent of the ground attached to them, will admit; and that the treatment of the inhabitants in them has been kind and proper;—but it is in proof, that there is just and great cause of complaint against by far the greater part of the houses of this description, which have hardly, in any instance, been built for the purpose, and are incapable of being conveniently adapted to it.

Your Committee have classed their Observations under the following Heads, that each may be referred to as the occasion may arise:—

    Ist.   Keepers of the Houses receiving a much greater number of persons in them than they are calculated for; and the consequent want of accommodation for the Patients, which greatly retards recovery; they are, indeed, represented by the President of the College of Physicians, and the Physician acting as Secretary to the visiting Commissioners, who must be considered as the most competent judges on the subject, to be better calculated for the imprisonment than the cure of patients.

IIdly. The insufficiency of the number of Keepers, in proportion to the number of persons intrusted to their care, which unavoidably leads to a proportionably greater degree of restraint than the Patients would otherwise be under.

IIIdly. The mixing Patients who are outrageous, with those who are quiet and inoffensive; and those who are insensible to the calls of nature, with others who are cleanly.

IVthly. The want of medical assistance, *as applied to the malady* for which the persons are confined; a point worthy of the most serious attention, as the practice very generally is to confine medical aid to corporeal complaints; which circumstance the Committee are the more desirous of inforcing on The House, as an opinion has been given, by a respectable Physician and another person of great experience, that where the mental faculties are only partially affected (stated by them to be so in seven eights of the cases,) medical assistance is of the highest importance.

Vthly. Restraint of persons much beyond what is necessary, certainly retarding recovery, even beyond what is occasioned by the crowded state of the house; of which many instances were stated to the Committee. In the course of the Evidence there will be found opinions unfavourable to the use of strait waistcoats, as more oppressive to the Patient even than irons; which induce Your Committee to observe, that a waistcoat has been invented, under the view of one of the Members of it, which appears likely to be quite as secure as the one now in use, and infinitely less distressing to the wearer.

VIthly. The situation of the parish paupers in some of the houses for Insane Persons; respecting the care of whom, when confined in parochial workhouses, the Committee also made some inquiries, as connected with the matter before them, although not expressly included in the reference to them.

VIIthly. Detentions of persons, the state of whose minds did not require confinement:—On this ground of complaint, Your Committee had very slender means of information.

VIIIthly. Insufficiency of certificates on which Patients are received into the madhouses.

IXthly. The defective visitation of private Madhouses, under the provisions of the 14 Geo. III, c. 49.

The references are made by Your Committee to the pages of the Evidence, to show, with as little trouble as possible to the reader, what has been said respecting each. On consideration of which, Your Committee are persuaded, that no doubt will be entertained of the insufficiency of the visitation which has taken place, even within the limits of the district assigned to the care of the College of Physicians, from the professional occupations of the visitors not allowing them sufficient time to perform the duties required; and still less doubt will probably remain, of the utter insufficiency or total neglect of those duties in other parts of England. It follows of course, that some amendment of the law is requisite for this part of the subject.

Your Committee cannot resist observing also, that the Commissioners have not the power of withholding a new licence to a person deprived of one for the most flagitious conduct.

In *Ireland*, the necessity of making some further provision for Insane Persons, appears to be more urgent even than in this part of the United Kingdom; as it will be seen in the Evidence, that, with the exception of two public establishments, and some private houses in Dublin, there are no places appropriated separately for the reception of persons in this state in Ireland. In a few hospitals for general relief of patients, there are wards for Insane Persons, but these are very ill calculated for the attainment of the objects that should be had in view; and as there are no poor houses in that part of the United Kingdom, the pauper lunatics are allowed to wander about the country, till those who are outrageous are sent up to Dublin, in a manner shocking to humanity; while the idiots are left to go about the villages, the sport of the common people.

As the Governors of the Asylum at York called the attention of the other House of Parliament, by petition, in the last session, to the management of the establishment, in order to show that it was unnecessary to subject it to the provisions of a Bill then depending, respecting madhouses; and the Governors of Bethlem succeeded on that occasion in obtaining a clause, while the Bill was in the House, for a partial exemption from the provisions of the Act in favour of that Hospital; Your Committee are desirous of directing the attention of the House, to the parts of the Evidence which relate to those two establishments.

Your Committee, impressed with the inadequacy of the Buildings for the reception of Insane Persons throughout England, obtained from an Architect, who has given great attention to this subject, and who has been employed to make designs for an Asylum for the West Riding of the county of York, Plans with Estimates, which they think may be useful to the public, especially in counties where there may be a disposition to erect houses for the reception of Insane Persons under the Act 48 Geo. III, c. 96; at it appears to Your Committee to be highly desirable to promote the operation of that wise and beneficent law, in order to prevent the intolerable evil of these unhappy persons being imprisoned in gaols or in parish workhouses, or permitted to wander about the country in a state of total helplessness and neglect; in the former case, to the great annoyance of the other prisoners or poor, as well as the unnecessary restraint and suffering to themselves; and in the latter, to the great danger of their doing mischief to others or to themselves.

Some suggestions for the improvement in the care and management of Houses for the reception of Insane Persons, will be found in the Evidence.

The length to which this Inquiry has been unavoidably drawn, must in any event have prevented, at this period of the Session, a Bill being passed in the remaining part of it, as perfect as the necessity of the case demands; Your Committee deeply lament the necessity for this delay, because the management in more than one of the places for the reception of the unhappy persons, has been so reprehensible, as, in their opinion, to subject the persons concerned, if it had been known, to criminal prosecutions; but that regret is somewhat abated by a conviction, that the state of those establishments has already been considerably meliorated by the Inquiries which have taken place.

Your Committee are persuaded also, that when the extent of the evil pointed out in this Report shall be generally known, the visiting Physicians in London and its neighbourhood will, as far as the professional calls upon them will permit, give additional attention to the duty they have been desirous of discharging; and that the Justices of the Peace in the several counties, will feel it to be their duty to watch as narrowly as circumstances will admit, over the conduct of the keepers of these houses, and the treatment of the Patients in them. The Committee trust also, that every Magistrate in the kingdom, who may think the condition of Insane Persons worthy of his attentions, will inform himself as well as he can, respecting abuses of the nature alluded to, that it may be submitted to His Majesty's Secretary of State for the Home Department, whether it may be fit in such case, that a prosecution should be instituted at the suit of His Majesty's Attorney General.

If in any instance a Magistrate (during the approaching recess) shall be refused admittance into one of these houses, Your Committee cannot doubt, but that such refusal will have due weight with the persons who may hereafter be authorized to grant licences for keeping Houses of this description, if they shall be invested with a discretion to refuse them to unfit persons.

After the patient Inquiry made by Your Committee on the matters referred to them, they thought it desirable to inspect the *New Bethlem Hospital*, erected in Saint George's Fields, but not yet inhabited; that they might consider, with the advantage they have acquired from this examination, how far the Building might appear to be well calculated for the accommodation of, and to afford the best chance of cure to, the patients intended to be soon removed into it; and having accordingly made a careful inspection of that Building, they submit the following Observations:—

On entering the Gallery on the principal Floor, they observed that the windows were so high as to prevent the Patients looking out; with the unfitness of which Your Committee were struck, as intelligent persons had stated in the course of the examination, that the greatest advantage might be derived from the Patients having opportunities of seeing objects that might amuse them. An alteration might be made in this respect, if it shall be deemed proper by the Governors, at little expense, and with no risk of injury to the building; as it was stated by Mr. Upton, the Deputy Architect, that these windows were at first so constructed, but were afterwards built up at the lower part, on a suggestion that it would be inconvenient to expose the

Patients to the view of passengers; which inconvenience it is conceived might be very easily obviated. The windows in the upper story appear to be properly constructed.

In the Sleeping Apartments the windows are not glazed, which Your Committee think deprives the Patients, generally, of a reasonable comfort, and may in many cases be really injurious; but what appears to be still more important, there are no flues constructed for the purpose of conducting warm air through the house, except in the lower galleries on the basement story, which are proposed to be warmed by steam. This appears to be deserving of serious consideration, because it is represented that the Patients suffer sensibly from cold; and Doctor Munro, the Physician to the Hospital stated, that it had not been thought advisable to administer medicines in the winter, on account of the cold of the house.

In this opinion, respecting the advantage to be derived from the Hospital being properly warmed, the Committee are strengthened by the testimony of the Reverend Mr. Becher, who has witnessed the good effect of it in the *Nottingham* Asylum, and in other places.

In the Infirmary for Female Patients, there are only three small windows at a great height, on the northern side of the room; it appears therefore, that something should be done for ventilation, which might easily be accomplished.

The construction of the Privies appears to be very objectionable; and there is only one in each of the upper galleries, one in the criminal part, and two on the basement story; nor are there any privies or urinals in the airing grounds. And it seems doubtful, whether the drain passing under the beds, is on such a construction as will answer the intended purpose.

There is no room set apart for the reception of the dead bodies, which should be provided for.

There are eight acres of ground occupied for the Hospital, including the site of the buildings, the airing grounds, and one acre and an half intended for a kitchen garden; and there are nearly four acres more adjoining, which it is the intention of the Governors to turn to profit, the Act of Parliament restraining them to the use of eight. The Committee however, think it may be expedient to submit to the consideration of Parliament, the propriety of enabling the Governors to devote this ground to the general purposes of the Hospital, from a conviction of the benefits the Patients derive from exercise, and in many cases from labour.

And that the Patients may not be entirely deprived of these benefits in wet weather, it appears to be desirable that penthouses should be erected against the cross walls of the airing grounds, or a sort of covering in the middle thereof, like those at St. Luke's Hospital.

In the Criminal Part of the building, the Committee find the same objection to the height of the windows, as before-mentioned; and that no provision whatever is made for warming this department, although the warming pipes from the basement story are continued to the door at which this part is entered; and it may be useful, if external doors of iron grating should be provided on the basement story.

The Committee have only further to remark, that in this part of the Building there is no Infirmary.

Resolved, That the Chairman be directed to move the House, That leave be given to bring in a Bill, to amend and enforce the Provisions of the Act of the 14th Geo. III, c. 49, intituled, "An Act for regulating Madhouses." . . .

Mr. Edward Wakefield, of Pall Mall, called in, and Examined

What is your profession?—A land agent.

Have you been led in any way to examine into the treatment of Insane persons?—I have for many years been in the habit of visiting all places where I have heard they have been confined.

Have you any, and if so, what interest, direct or collateral, in the subject?—None whatever, in any way.

You have no other interest, but motives of general humanity and benevolence?—None, whatever.

Are you of opinion, that a useful Act of Parliament may be introduced for the government of the houses in which Insane persons are kept?—I have no doubt, a very beneficial one indeed.

Have you considered the particular objects, which a Committee of Parliament appointed to investigate this subject, should have in view?--It strikes me, that the first and great object of an Act should be, that of holding in confinement persons under this malady, who may be dangerous, either to the public or to their relatives, and in that point of view, I rather consider it as a matter of police. The late Act, commonly called Mr. Wynn's Act, were it rendered imperative upon the different counties of England, instead of optional as it now is, would at once have a great effect upon all the labouring classes of society; and I know not a single step that would produce so great an effect, as the rendering that Act imperative, laying it down as the basis of an Act of Parliament, that it was to confine Insane persons. I think the next great object should be, if possible, securing to those persons in confinement every possible degree of comfort.

How does Mr. Wynn's Act operate, as affecting the labouring classes of the community, you meaning by that expression, pauper Lunatics?—As I understand it, in a county which has built an Asylum, in consequence of that Act, the overseers of the several parishes within that county can no longer retain their pauper Lunatics in their respective workhouses, but are compelled to send them to the County Asylum.

Have you any particular knowledge as to the treatment of pauper Lunatics in workhouses?—I have.

Why do you conceive those pauper Lunatics would be better off in county asylums than in workhouses?—Because in workhouses they are under the care of persons totally and entirely ignorant of the proper treatment of Lunatics in general; because in workhouses, the rooms in which they are kept are ill adapted to the confinement of such persons, and because in some cases which I have seen from those causes, those unfortunate persons have been constantly confined in strait-waistcoats, frequently kept in bed night and day; and because I should hope, that a county Lunatic asylum would be placed under the direction of a competent superintendent; and also, because Lunatics in workhouses are an extreme annoyance to the other inhabitants of those houses.

Do you believe that many Lunatic establishments have been raised under that Act?—I have heard, in twelve counties.

Have you visited the different public establishments for Insane persons, in and about the Metropolis?—Yes; frequently.

Have you visited Bethlem?—I have, frequently; I first visited Bethlem on the 25th of April 1814.

What observations did you make?—I was introduced, with others, by Mr. Alderman Cox, an official governor, whose feelings being overpowered before we had gone over the men's side, was under the necessity of retiring to the Steward's office, whither he was soon afterwards followed by us, in consequence of a message from the steward, who then informed us, that Mr. Cox was prevented from accompanying us farther. We solicited permission to continue our inspection whilst Mr. Cox remained in the Hospital, but this was declined, and we were compelled to close our visit on that day. On Monday, the 2d of May, we re-visited the Hospital, introduced by Robert Calvert, Esquire, a governor, and accompanied by Charles Callis Western, Esquire, Member of Parliament for Essex, and four other gentlemen. At this visit, attended by the steward of the Hospital and likewise by a female keeper, we first proceeded to visit the women's galleries: one of the side rooms contained about ten patients, each chained by one arm or leg to the wall; the chain allowing them merely to stand up by the bench or form fixed to the wall, or to sit down on it. The nakedness of each patient was covered by a blanket-gown only; the blanket-gown is a blanket formed something like a dressing-gown, with nothing to fasten it with in front; this constitutes the whole covering; the feet even were naked. One female in this side room, thus chained, was an object remarkably striking; she mentioned her maiden and married names, and stated that she had been a teacher of languages; the keepers described her as a very accomplished lady, mistress of many languages; and corroborated her account of herself. The Committee can hardly imagine a human being in a more degraded and brutalizing situation than that in which I found this female, who held a coherent conversation with us, and was of course fully sensible of the mental and bodily condition of those wretched beings, who, equally without clothing, were closely chained to the same wall with herself. Unaware of the necessities of nature, some of them, though they contained life, appeared totally inanimate and unconscious of existence. The few minutes which we passed with this lady did not permit us to form a judgment of the degree of restraint to which she ought to be subject; but I unhesitatingly affirm, that her confinement with patients in whom she was compelled to witness the most disgusting idiotcy, and the most terrifying distraction of the human intellect, was injudicious and improper. She intreated to be allowed pencil and paper, for the purpose of amusing herself with drawing, which were given to her by one of the gentlemen with me. Many of these unfortunate women were locked up in their cells, naked and chained on straw, with only one blanket for a covering. One who was in that state, by way of punishment, the keeper described as the most dissatisfied patient in the house, she talked coherently, complained of the want of tea and sugar, and lamented that her friends whom she stated to be respectable people, neither came to see her nor supplied her with little necessary comforts; the patients generally complained much of being deprived of tea and sugar. On leaving the gallery, we enquired of them, whether the visit had been inconvenient or unpleasant, they all joined in saying, No; but (which was sufficiently apparent) that the visit of a friend was always pleasant. In the men's wing in the side room, six patients were chained close to the wall, five handcuffed, and one locked to the wall by the right arm as well as by the right leg; he was very noisy; all were naked, except as to the blanket gown or a small rug on the shoulders, and without shoes; one complained much of the coldness of his feet; one of us felt them, they were very cold. The patients in this room, except the noisy one, and the poor lad with cold feet, who was lucid when we saw him, were dreadful idiots; their nakedness and their mode of confinement, gave this room the complete appearance of a dog-kennel. From the patients not being classed, some appear objects of resentment to the others; we saw a quiet civil man, a soldier, a native of Poland, brutally attacked by another soldier, who we were informed by the keepers always singled out the Pole as an object of resentment; they said, there were no means of separating these men, except by locking one up in solitary confinement. Whilst looking at some of the bed-lying patients, a man arose naked from his bed, and had deliberately and quietly walked a few paces from his cell door along the gallery; he was instantly seized by the keepers, thrown into his bed, and leg-locked, without enquiry or observation: chains are universally substituted for the strait-waistcoat. In the men's wing were about 75 or 76 patients, with two keepers and an assistant, and about the same number of patients on the women's side; the patients were in no way distinguished from each other as to disease, than as those who were not walking about or chained in the side rooms, were lying stark naked upon straw on their bedsteads, each in a separate cell, with a single blanket or run, in which the patient usually lay huddled up, as if impatient of cold, and generally chained to the bed-place in the shape of a trough; about one-fifth were in this state, or chained in the side rooms. It appeared that the wet patients, and all who were inclined to lie a-bed, were allowed to do so, from being less troublesome in that state than when up and dressed. The end window towards Fore-street was the chief source of entertainment to the patients; they seemed greatly to enjoy the sight of the people walking, and to derive great pleasure from our visit. In one of the cells on the lower gallery we saw William Norris; he stated himself to be 55 years of age, and that he had been confined about 14 years; that in consequence of attempting to defend himself from what he conceived the improper treatment of his keeper, he was fastened by a long chain, which passing through a partition, enabled the keeper by going into the next cell, to draw him close to the wall at pleasure; that to prevent this, Norris muffled the chain with straw, so as to hinder its passing through the wall; that he afterwards was confined in the manner we saw him, namely, a stout iron ring was rivetted round his neck, from which a short chain passed to a ring made to slide upwards or downwards on an upright massive iron bar, more than six feet high, inserted into the wall. Round his body a strong iron bar about two inches wide was rivetted; on each side the bar was a circular projection, which being fashioned to and inclosing each of his arms, pinioned them close to his sides. This waist bar was secured by two similar bars which, passing over his shoulders, were rivetted to the waist bar both before and behind. The iron ring round his neck was connected to the bars on his shoulders, by a double link. From each of these bars another short chain passed to the ring on the upright iron bar. We were informed he was enabled to raise himself, so as to stand against the wall, on the pillow of his bed in the trough bed in which he lay; but it is impossible for him to advance from the wall in which the iron bar is soldered, on account of the shortness of his chains, which were only twelve inches long. It was, I conceive, equally out of his power to repose in any other position than on his back, the projections which on each side of the waist bar inclosed his arms, rendering it impossible for him to lie on his side, even if the length of the chains from his neck and shoulders would permit it. His right leg was chained to the trough; in which he had remained thus encaged and chained more than twelve years. To prove the unnecessary restraint inflicted on this unfortunate man, he informed us that he had for some years been able to withdraw his arms from the manacles which encompassed them. He then withdrew one of them, and observing an expression of surprise, he said, that when his arms were withdrawn he was compelled to rest them on the edges of the circular projections, which was more painful than keeping them within. His position, we were informed, was mostly lying down, and that as it was inconvenient to raise himself and stand upright, he very seldom did so; that he read a great deal of books of all kinds, history, lives or any thing that the keepers could get him; the newspaper every day, and conversed perfectly coherent on the passing topics and the events of the war, in which he felt particular interest. On each day that we saw him he discoursed coolly, and gave rational and deliberate answers to the different questions put to him. The whole of this statement relative to William Norris was confirmed by the keepers. On Wednesday the 7th of June, when we again visited Bethlem, we discovered that all the male patients who were then naked and chained to their beds in their cells, were in that situation by way of punishment for misbehaviour, and not from disease. In consequence of the discovery made by the gentlemen who went with me and myself, of the situation of William Norris, and of a drawing which we procured to be made of him in his irons, he was visited by the following gentlemen:—George Holme Sumner, Esq. M. P. Lord Robert Seymour, M. P. William Smith, Esq. M. P. the Hon. Henry Grey Bennet, M. P. R. J. Lambton, Esq. M. P. Thomas Thompson, Esq. M. P. and other Members of the House of Commons; and I have not to state that, at this last visit, I observed that the whole of the irons had been removed from Norris's body, and that the length of chain from his neck, which was only twelve inches, had been doubled. [*The Witness delivered in the Drawing of William Norris, referred to in his Answer.*]

Do you know what has become of those chains?—I was informed by Mr. Wallet, the new steward to Bethlem Hospital, that the chains are now in the Hospital, and are to be seen. I was at Bethlem on Saturday week the 23d of April, and found that the old steward, Mr. Alavoine, no longer held the office; and that a new steward, Mr. Wallet, was filling his situation. Mr. Wallet sent for an official governor, Mr. Deputy Greenaway of Bishopsgate-street, to attend me; and although the number of patients was nearly the same as during the last year, I found but one single one chained to his bed, and not a single patient in any one of the side rooms chained to the wall. Mrs. Fenwick, the teacher of languages, to whom I have referred, was walking about the gallery, who, Mr. Wallet told me, was an entirely different creature since she had been treated like a human being.

How was she dressed?—She was dressed like a woman. She immediately came up to me, and asked me how Mr. William Fry, with whom she had lived as a governess, was, and all his family. Mr. Deputy Greenaway stated, that a great reformation had taken place in the Hospital lately, very much in consequence of a speech that Lord Robert Seymour had made in Parliament; and that so far from the inspection which took place last year having done any harm, he was satisfied that the Hospital had been essentially served. The patients, I understand, are to be removed to the new Bethlem next Midsummer, a great part of which is to be warmed with steam. Mr. Greenaway stated, that were that not the case he felt the necessity of glazing the cells of the present Hospital, they in point of fact having been without any glazing for many years.

Did the patients make as many complaints of the ill treatment they received, as they had done on your former visits?—I did not hear any complaints. Norris died on the 26th of February.

Do you happen to know, of your own knowledge, any thing concerning the death of Norris, that would leave you to believe it was occasioned by the long confinement which he had undergone, and the chains he had worn?—No person can doubt that his death in all probability was brought on by the state of confinement in which he was held.

What was his age?—I understand fifty-five.

Was his body examined?—I understand his body was dissected by Mr. Lawrence of St. Bartholomew's Hospital.

Had you any difficulty in obtaining an entrance into the Hospital?– I originally went to Bethlem Hospital with a written order from a governor. Mr. Alavoine the then steward said, he was extremely sorry that he could not shew me the Hospital, as he could have done the week before; but that a resolution of twenty years standing had been revived, to prevent any persons seeing that Hospital but in company with a governor; and that in consequence of something which had been publickly said at a meeting, which had been held at the City of London Tavern. I asked Mr. Alavoine, who were the Governors; he said it was more than his place was worth to tell. He held in his hand a printed list of the governors; I requested permission to look at it; he said he could not allow me to do so; that Mr. Poynder the secretary, who lived at Bridewell Hospital, would furnish me with a copy of the list of governors. In consequence of which I sent two persons on Friday the 22d of April 1814 to the office of Mr. Poynder, clerk of Bethlem Hospital, who asked his clerk for a list of the governors of Bethlem Hospital; the clerk said, "I cannot give a list; Mr. Poynder is below stairs. On furnishing a list, the fee charged by Mr. Poynder must be paid." "What is the fee?" "One guinea." Mr. Poydner now entered from below stairs, and finally refused to give the person, I sent, a list of the governors. He however forwarded me a list in the course of a few days.

Did he know for whom the application was made, and did he refuse it in consequence of knowing that fact?—He refused to let me have a list at any price whatever. Upon obtaining the list, finding that the Mr. Calverts were governors, Mr. Western applied to Mr. Robert Calvert, and, accompanied by him, Mr. Western and myself visited the Hospital. After having visited the Hospital, I received a letter from Mr. Poynder to say, that on a Saturday, fixing the day, the Hospital was open for my inspection.

Were you acquainted with a person of the name of Matthews, who was confined for many years as a Lunatic in Bethlem?—I found the late James Tilley Matthews at Mr. Fox's, who kept a private house, London House, Hackney. He was sent to this private Madhouse, half at the expense of Bethlem Hospital, and the other half at the expense of his own friends, in consequence of the representation of Mr. Crowther, the surgeon to Bethlem Hospital, who, from his having a bad abscess in his back, thought that his remaining within the air of the Hospital would shorten his life, and recommended his being placed somewhere in the country. I understand that he had been confined seventeen years in Bethlem Hospital, during the greater part of which time his relations or friends had been endeavouring to obtain his liberation, with a view to his being sent to Jamaica, where his wife and family were resident. An application, I believe, had been made to the Court of King's Bench, and his liberation refused, but upon what specific ground I cannot tell. During the last summer Mr. Western applied to the Home Secretary of State, presenting a petition from his relations for his discharge. In my opinion, Mr. Matthews was a very unfit person for confinement in Bethlem, without pen, ink, or paper, the use of knife or fork, any fire-place to which he could retire by himself, and shut up of a night from the time of locking up till the opening next morning; being a man of considerable accomplishments and great learning, and who evidently had never kept such society as that in which he was confined for so many years. The latter years of his being in Bethlem he was taken from the galleries, where the people generally were, and had a room to himself.

Do you know in what way he was confined prior to his removal to the room you have just mentioned?—I have heard from Mr. Stavely, his nephew, that he was confined in the common gallery, and frequently chained to his bed.

Is Mr. Matthews now alive?—He died some time in the last autumn.

Speech by Sir James Mackintosh on criminal law reform, House of Commons, 21 May 1823

Hansard, n.s., IX, 397-409.

A champion of penal reform, Sir James Mackintosh (1765-1832) advocated abolishing the death penalty for most offenses. Several measures for the reform of the legal system were carried through by the Liverpool government during this period, partly in response to Mackintosh's initiative.

Sir J. Mackintosh, after a few preliminary remarks regarding the difficulty of attracting the attention of the House to so hacknied a subject as that upon which he was about to address it, said, that the first public discussion at which he had been present after his return from India, was a discussion in another place, upon a measure of his late lamented friend, sir Samuel Romilly, tending to ameliorate the existing state of our Criminal Laws. In the course of that discussion, he had heard it stated, in an excellent speech made in favour of the principle for which he was now prepared to contend, that if a foreigner were to form his estimate of the people of England from a consideration of their penal code, he would undoubtedly conclude that they were a nation of barbarians. This expression, though strong, was unquestionably true; for what other opinion could a humane foreigner form of us, when he found, that in our criminal law there were two hundred offences against which the punishment of death was denounced, upon twenty of which only, that punishment was ever inflicted—that we were savage in our threats, and yet were feeble in our execution of punishments—that we cherished a system, which in theory was odious, but which was impotent in practice, from its excessive severity—that, in cases of high treason, we involved innocent children in all the consequences of their father's guilt—that in cases of corruption of blood, we were even still more cruel, punishing the offspring, when we could not reach the parent—and that, on some occasions, we even proceeded to wreak our vengeance upon the bodies of the inanimate dead? If the same person were told, that we were the same nation which had been the first to give full publicity to every part of our judicial system—that we were the same nation which had established the trial by jury, which, blameable as it might be in theory, was so invaluable in practice—that we were the same nation which had found out the greatest security which had ever been devised for individual liberty, the writ of *habeas corpus*, as settled by the act of Charles II.—that we were the same nation which had discovered the full blessings of a representative government, and which had endeavoured to diffuse them throughout every part of our free empire—he would wonder at the strange anomalies of human nature, which could unite things that were in themselves so totally incompatible. If the same foreigner were, in addition to this, told, that the abuses which struck so forcibly on his attention were abuses of the olden time, which were rather overlooked than tolerated, he might perhaps relent in his judgment, and confer upon us a milder denomination than that of barbarians; but if, on the contrary, he were told, that influence and authority, learning and ingenuity, had combined to resist all reformation of these abuses as dangerous innovations—if he were informed that individuals, who, from their rank and talents, enjoyed not an artificial but a real superiority, rose to vindicate the worst of these abuses, even the outrages on the dead, and to contend for them as bulwarks of the constitution and landmarks of legislation, he would revert to his first sentiments regarding us, though he might perhaps condemn the barbarism of the present, instead of the barbarism of the past generation. He would take the liberty of reading to the House a short description of the law of England, by a native of another country, in which its imperfections were ably and pointedly exposed to public view. The learned gentleman then read a passage, of which the following is the substance:

The criminal code of England in many respects was admirable and well adapted for the object which it had in view. Its judges were pure and placed beyond the reach of suspicion: they acted by the intervention of a jury, and were open to the censure of an acute bar, and to the control of a free press. The system, however, had its imperfections: it contained some relics of antiquated barbarism, and others of scarcely less barbarious modern misdirected legislation. There was no proportion observed by it in the punishments which it awarded to offences. Many small delinquencies were raised to the rank of capital crimes, and the same vengeance was denounced by the law against the offender who destroyed a tree, or cut down a twig, as was denounced against the wretch who committed a parricide. Laws of undue severity were also unduly executed; and the consequence was, that when a hundred individuals escaped, and one fell under the vengeance of the law, the fate of the individual who so fell was considered as an act of arbitrary rigour, instead of being considered as a sacrifice required by justice. He was regarded as a martyr, rather than as a victim to the offended majesty of the laws.

Such was the opinion of an individual who, by his professional occupations and abilities, was entitled to some respect upon this subject, and who enjoyed such a reputation with those who knew his merits, that all praise at his (Sir J. M.'s) hands was totally unnecessary. The individual to whom he alluded was his eloquent friend Mr. Cranstoun, and the mention of his name rendered all further eulogy on his character quite superfluous.

The learned gentleman then said, that to be perfectly in order with the House, he ought to have moved, before he commenced his observations on this subject, that the resolution of the House upon it, on the 4th of June, 1822, viz. "That this House will, at an early period of the next Session of Parliament, take into their most serious consideration the means of increasing the efficacy of the Criminal Laws, by abating their undue rigour," should be entered as read. He would now suppose that it had been so read, and would proceed to remind the House of what they had already done upon this subject. In the year 1819, the House, upon his motion, appointed a committee to examine into the state of the criminal law of the country, on the express allegation, that considerable defects existed therein, and appointed it in express defiance of an allegation that was then made, that such an inquiry as he proposed was calculated to paralyze the operation of the laws, and to hold them up to public scorn and indignation. In the year 1820, in consequence of the report of the committee appointed in the former session, some bills were brought into that House and passed, which little satisfied his views and wishes on the subject. Small and scanty as the reformation then effected was, it was the only reformation of the severity of the law that had been effected since the reign of Edward VI. For two hundred and fifty years, the House had proceeded, year after year, to heap one capital felony upon another; and in all that time, down to the year 1820, the first year of the reign of his present majesty, no repeal of any capital felony had ever been made, or attempted, with success. Amongst the felonies which, after the passing of those bills, were no longer to be considered capital, were comprised several crimes which were of a very heinous nature, and which could not be committed without grave forethought and deliberation on the part of the offender. Fraudulent bankruptcy, for instance, was a crime which excited as little compassion for the party who committed it as any that could be found in all the black catalogue of offences, and was one which could not be effected without due consideration on the part of the individual who meditated it. It was not, therefore, from any feelings of compassion towards the offender, that the capital punishment attached to this kind of felony had been repealed, but from a conviction, that the severity of the punishment gave impunity to the offence, and that the undue rigour of the law absolutely tended to defeat the object for which it was enacted—a principle which, as it had before been recognized by the House, he trusted it would not be reluctant to re-affirm on the present evening. In the year 1821, all that was effected was, to obtain the approbation of a majority of that House, to the principle of the necessity of altering the punishment inflicted upon certain cases of forgery. The bill, however, which was brought in upon that occasion, was subsequently thrown out by a strategem, of which he would say nothing more than this—that it was perfectly inconsistent with the usual practice of parliamentary proceedings, where no political interest was at stake. In 1822, the House adopted a general resolution— that it would, at an early period of the ensuing session, take into its serious consideration the means of increasing the efficacy of the criminal code, by abating its undue rigour; and that resolution it was his duty, perhaps at an earlier period in the present session, to have called upon the House to carry into execution. Circumstances, however, which he would not trouble the House by detailing, had prevented him from bringing the question under their consideration until the present moment; and he should not even now proceed to the discussion of it, until he had called their attention to another case, which was almost as bad as fraudulent bankruptcy. He had, by some accident or another, seen that a bill was now under consideration in another place, for a new regulation of the law of marriage. He approved of that bill, because it repealed the act of the 26th of Geo. II., which was a disgrace to the English law, as it established the principle of voiding marriages, and thereby enabled any heartless profligate to spread misery through families, and to rob them of their just inheritances. In 1820, he had attempted, but in vain, to obtain the repeal of five capital felonies created by that act. He was happy to see that they were abolished for ever by the bill to which he had just been alluding. When he ventured to propose their abolition, he was censured and abused, as a rash innovator who was anxious to destroy the principal provisions of an act which guarded the sacred institution of marriage. Not only had his bill been strongly reprobated in parliament, it had also been attacked by much eloquent declamation out of it. But still, in spite of the opposition which it had encountered in parliament, and the mingled powers of argument and ridicule that had been brought to play upon it elsewhere, they now found that those from whom such an admission was least to be expected, admitted the principle on which it rested, and agreed with them, that the best mode of giving efficacy to the laws was, to diminish their undue rigour. They had therefore obtained this advantage, that their very opponents recognized the justice of the principle on which they acted—"*Graiâ pandetur ab urbe.*" By the delay, of which he had unintentionally been the occasion, he had gained in his favour the authority of those who were the enemies of innovation in their own, and of reformation in his language. If, therefore, in the course of the debate, any hon. gentlemen should taunt him with being an innovator, and with entertaining desires to overthrow the constitution, he should reply to them by saying, "I appeal to your own patriarchs and elders; I appeal to the leaders of your own sect; and I say that their decision is full in your teeth and in my favour. On two distinct occasions—first, on the bill respecting fraudulent bankruptcy, and now on this, their new law of marriage, they have solemnly pronounced their opinion, that the best method of increasing the efficacy of the law is by abating its undue rigour. Why, then, taunt me as an innovator, when, if I do innovate, I innovate under the sanction of your patriarchs and teachers?"

The hon. and learned gentleman next proceeded to observe, that, in 1822, he had been told, that the abstract proposition which he then brought forward was calculated to paralyze the laws, and to suspend their operation. Now, nothing of that kind had occurred. Indeed, year after year had such a prediction been made, and year after year had it been falsified. Whenever the question was brought forward, this self-same objection was made to it, and the interval that elapsed between the time of discussing it always showed that there was not the slightest weight in it. Standing, therefore, upon the decisions to which the House had so repeatedly come of late years, he would contend, that if ever there was a case in which it was bound to preserve its own consistency, it was that on which he was at present speaking. They had before admitted, that there was undue rigour in the present state of the law, and that the best mode of relief was by abating it. What was it that he now felt called upon to propose to them? He would answer the question as shortly as possible. Adhering to the principles he had formerly laid down, he felt himself called upon to submit to the House, first of all, a proposition which would embrace a recognition of the propriety of all the particular measures which the House had formerly thought it right to adopt; and secondly, a proposition which would carry it somewhat further, and in which he should embody such small additions of detail, as would lead those who blamed him to blame him for lukewarmness rather than for rashness—for an error in deficiency, rather than for an error in excess. Though the propriety of abating the undue rigour of the law had in its favour the authority of all the wisest men who had either written or spoken on the subject, there was something startling in the proposition to those who only thought slightly upon it, which would, perhaps, render his illustration of it not unacceptable. There could not be a greater error in criminal legislation, than to suppose that the mischief of an action was to be the sole regulator of the amount of punishment to be attached to it. For a punishment to be wise, nay even to be just, it must be exemplary. Now, what was requisite to make it exemplary?—that it should be of such a nature as to excite fear in the breast of the public. But, if it excited any feeling that was capable of conquering fear—for instance, if it excited abhorrence—then it was not exemplary, but the reverse. The maximum of punishment depended on the sympathy of mankind; since every thing that went beyond it reflected discredit on the whole system of law, and tended to paralyze its proper operation. What was the cause of the inefficacy of religious persecution?—that it inflicted a punishment which was felt to be too severe for the offence which it was intended to check: that it had no support in the sympathies of the public; but on the contrary injured and outraged them all. That was the cause that "the blood of the martyr always proved the seed of the church." People felt that opinions, if correct, ought not to be met by force; and if incorrect, they would sink into oblivion if force were not employed to put them down—"*Opinionum commenta delet dies, naturae judicia confirmat.*" He thought that the total inefficacy of persecution to check the growth of opinions—a persecution which always made the martyr be considered as a hero, and the law as a code of oppression and tyranny—served also to prove, that laws of undue severity could in no instance effectually serve the purposes for which they were enacted. To ensure them full efficacy, they ought to be in accordance, not only with the general feelings of mankind, but with the particular feelings of the age;

for if they were not so supported, they were certain to meet with its contempt and indignation.

The hon. and learned gentleman then proceeded to show, that nothing was more false than the arguments usually urged in behalf of punishments: namely, that the crimes which rendered them necessary were the result of great deliberation. He thought that the contrary was the fact, and that in general offenders were hurried away by the strong passions that were implanted in their nature, and that "grew with their growth, and strengthened with their strength." The law was then most efficacious when it served as a school for morals—when it attracted to it the feelings of all good men, and when it called silently, but powerfully, upon all such to assist in its administration. Now, he would ask, what was the lesson to be derived from a consideration of the criminal law of England? Why, that the man who cut down a twig, or injured a cherry-tree, or stole a sheep, or he would even say forged a note, was as black a criminal as he who murdered his father, or betrayed the interests of his country to a foreign enemy. He acknowledged that this conspiracy of the law of England against the principles of nature was not successful. The feelings of nature in the people of England prevailed over the immoral lessons taught by its penal law. That law would be detestable in its success, and was now contemptible in its failure. He had always thought that there was an under-statement of the argument, on the part of those who contended that an alteration in the law was necessary. They had stated, that a mitigation of it was principally required by the reluctance of prosecutors and witnesses to come forward to prosecute, under the present severe statutes. They had forgotten, however, to state the effect produced on the feelings of the spectators. They had forgotten to state, that they rose in arms, not merely against the charge, but against the verdict of the jury, and the sentence of the judge. They had forgotten to state, that the law was thus made an object of that abhorrence, which ought only to be attached to crime; and that, instead of resting for its support on the aid of good men, it rested on the fear of the gibbet alone. The hon. and learned gentleman then complained, that under the present system of law, proportionate punishments were not assigned to different offences; and contended, that heavy punishments inflicted on crimes of a smaller degree of delinquency; lessened the effect of it when inflicted on crimes of great atrocity. It was curious to reflect, that lord Hale spoke of England—with reference, of course, to the time in which he wrote—as the country of all others in which the laws were most literally executed, and least committed as to their effect *arbitrio judicis*. Now, how matters were changed! From four capital felonies upon our Statute book, we had come to 200; and, instead of being the country of the world where the laws were most literally carried into effect, and least dependant upon the will of judges, we had become the country of all the world in which they were least literally executed, and in which the life and death of man was the most frequently intrusted to the feeling of an individual. These arrangements had no foundation in the principles of British jurisprudence: they were contradicted by the spirit of *Magna Charta*: they were hostile to the principles of the first writers on the subject of criminal law: they were but the mushroom growth of modern wantonness of legislation. As a test of the antiquity of the existing criminal code, he would take the result of his intended proceedings. He wished to abolish the punishment of death, as applied to a great variety of offences; and yet there were only two statutes with which he should meddle, which were older than the Revolution. Then, if these laws had no foundation in antiquity, what foundation had they in wisdom? Why, they had neither any foundation in policy nor in common sense. There had been, in the present age, an immense multiplication of capital punishments, just at the very time when society was growing more civilized and humane, and wanted old severities of the law repealed, rather than new ones enacted. He did not accuse parliament of cruelty or bad feeling; but he accused them of negligence—culpable negligence. He accused them of having overlooked that deep regard for the life and liberty of man, which, while it gave the strongest effect to occasional inflictions of the law, formed, at the same time, the best safeguard for the moral feeling of the community.

To look in another view, for a moment, at the progress of the present system. The oldest reports of criminal law were the tables of the home circuit, begun in the year of the Revolution, which were to be found in the appendix to the report of the criminal laws committee. Those tables began in the year of the Revolution. It appeared that, during the first forty years from that date, more than half the persons capitally convicted upon the home circuit had been executed; during the last forty years, the proportion of executions to convictions upon the home circuit had not been more than one in four; and, taken throughout the kingdom, not so much as one in ten. Indeed, as the number of capital convictions went on increasing, the number of executions kept diminishing; for the laws were so obviously barbarous, that it became absolutely necessary, by some expedient or other, to render them nugatory. It was absolutely a fact—deny it who could—that, as the severity of the penal laws increased, the impunity of crime increased along with them. He would not press this general portion of the subject much further, nor advert to ancient laws, or to the codes of foreign countries, any more than was necessary to explain something which had fallen from his last session. He should not be suspected of selecting the Hebrew law as a model for the law of other nations; but he liked the Hebrew law for the reverence which it paid to liberty and to human life. The felony of the Hebrew code was the shedding of blood; the only theft which that code punished with death was the stealing of men; all other thefts were to be commuted for twofold or for fourfold restitution. He looked upon the Hebrew law, in its aversion to the shedding of blood, as entitled to the highest veneration. He would not pause upon the ancient Roman law, so remarkably merciful on the same point; but upon that modern law— the law of France—which now prevailed half over the continent, it was impossible for him not to dwell for a moment. Six crimes, by the French law, were punishable with death—only one of them a theft; and that a burglary of such complicated circumstance as could seldom, if ever, take place. He had tables, from the year 1811, of the number of capital convictions which had taken place in France, and similar documents with respect to this country. In the year 1811, there had been 404 sentences of death in England, and 264 in France, the population of Great Britain being twelve millions, and that of France twenty seven millions: in the year 1820, the sentences of death in England had been 1,236, and in France 361 only; so that, in the course of nine years, the amount of capital conviction had trebled itself in England, while in France the increase had been something less than one-third. He did not attribute this variance entirely, but he certainly did trace it in a very great degree, to the difference between the French and English criminal codes. He denied that the fact warranted any inference of the superior morality of the French over the English character. With regard to the police, as far as related to the prevention of crime, it had been not at all improved in France during the last nine years; while in England it had been improved considerably. He traced the difference mainly to the ill effect of the English criminal code: he believed that if France had lived under the same code as England, she would have had as many convictions; and he thought that the example of France authorized him at least to use this argument. If the House would not believe that great good could be done by lessening the catalogue of capital offences, it must, at any rate, admit, that no evil was to be apprehended from such a course. The hon. and learned member said, he should next state to the House the resolutions which he intended to move. With the substance of those resolutions, the honourable gentlemen on the other side were acquainted. What those gentlemen themselves had to propose, he did not know. His first resolution would declare in general terms, that it was expedient to take away the punishment of death in a certain number of cases which would be specified; he should then move to substitute, in those cases, the punishment of transportation and imprisonment; and he should add two resolutions, of which he trusted the House would approve—the one recommending, that judges should not pronounce sentence of death in cases where they had no expectation of such sentence being carried into execution: and the other doing away the forfeiture of goods and chattels, and the indignities offered to the dead body in cases of suicide. The cases in which he proposed to take away the punishment of death were these. He should put his resolutions into such a shape, as to found a bill eventually upon each resolution. The cases as to which he proposed to take away the punishment of death were; first, those three classes of offences with respect to which bills had so often already passed the House; namely, larceny from shops, from dwelling houses, and on navigable rivers. Secondly, he should touch all the felonies contained in the Black act, except the wilfully setting fire to dwelling houses, and the maliciously shooting. His next resolution would embrace the five felonies created by the Marriage act. Afterwards, he should come to all these capital felonies proposed to be done away by the committee on criminal law; the measures which he was thus proposing, having in fact already received the assent of the House of Commons, although they had been lost in the upper House. And he should besides move resolutions with respect to the crimes of forgery, and of uttering forged instruments, and three other capital offences, viz.; horse-stealing, sheep-stealing, and cattle-stealing. Upon the subject of larcenies from shops, dwelling-houses, and on navigable canals, he had a few observations to address to the House. The executions under those laws for the last fourteen years had been, compared with the convictions, just one in sixty-six; and it had been very truly said, that they operated as a surprise upon the sixty-sixth man, who suffered, but not at all as a terror or warning to the sixty-five who escaped. In fact, a law under which one criminal out of sixty-six was executed, was a law to all practical intents and purposes given up; and the execution of the sixty-sixth man was nothing else than a wanton and criminal waste of human existence. He objected strongly also to the principle of making the amount of property stolen any criterion for the punishment inflicted upon an offender. There was no greater moral depravity in stealing a large sum than a small one; nor was it fit that the treasures of the rich should be more strongly guarded, than the comparatively small possessions of the poor. He was far from imputing to the legislature, or to the judges, any sentiment inconsistent with equal justice; but laws should not only be just, they should appear to be just; they should not only not be unequal, they should be above the suspicion of inequality. There was the less reason for inflicting a greater punishment in proportion to the amount of property stolen, as persons in possession of larger property had also better means of securing it. Another objection to making the amount of property the criterion of guilt and punishment was, that it opened a temptation to those pious frauds under which juries, from humane motives, so often violated their oaths, by verdicts of acquittal. The mind easily persuaded itself, that there was no great immorality in undervaluing a little the property stolen, and compassion would, in such cases, induce juries to violate their most sacred duty; whereas, if the punishment were dependent on substantial facts and circumstances instead of the amount of property, they could not hesitate to convict. And, while he was upon this subject, he would make one observation upon the statute of the 1st George 4th, which, as it had originally passed the House of Commons, took away the punishment of death for stealing privately in a shop, and in which the lords had made an alteration, changing the felony from an amount of 5s. to an amount of 15l. Now, the constant observation made, in justification of the old law was, that it was necessary to protect the small property of poor traders from general depredation. A noble and learned lord had said, in the other House of Parliament, that the statute, which made the offence of privately stealing in shops to the amount of 5s. capital, was the great safeguard of the retail trade of the country. The whole retail trade of the country, then, was abandoned by the 1st of George 4th; all the property of poor traders was given up to depredation by that act which raised the amount from 5s. to 15l. In shops, however, attached to dwelling-houses, which was so in 99 cases out of 100, although the offence could no longer be prosecuted under the statute of William, it might be prosecuted under the statute of Ann, if the sum stolen exceeded 40s.; so that the statute of George 4th raising the sum to 15l. was, in effect, reduced to a dead letter. He did not, in stating this fact, arraign the legislature, or the construction which had been adopted by the judges; but he stated it as an additional reason for repealing that statute. . . .

Act abolishing the death penalty for minor larceny offences, 8 July 1823

4 Geo. 4, c. 53   *Statutes of the United Kingdom*, 1823, 320-21.

Whereas by an Act passed in the Twenty second Year of the Reign of His late Majesty King *Charles*, the Second, intituled *An Act for taking away the Benefit of Clergy from such as steal Cloth from the Rack, and from such as shall steal or imbezil His Majesty's Ammunition and Stores*, the Benefit of Clergy is taken away from Persons convicted of cutting and taking, stealing or carrying away any Cloth or other Woollen Manufactures from the Rack or Tenter in the Night-time, or of stealing or imbezling any of His Majesty's Sails, Cordage or any other His Majesty's Naval Stores, to the Value of Twenty Shillings; provided that it shall be lawful for the Judges to grant a Reprieve for the staying of the Execution of such Offenders, and to cause them to be transported for the Space of Seven Years, and kept to hard Labour: And Whereas by an Act passed in the Tenth and Eleventh Years of the Reign of King *William* the Third, intituled *An Act for the better apprehending, prosecuting and punishing of Felons that commit Burglary, Housebreaking or Robbery, in Shops, Warehouses, Coachhouses or Stables, or that steal Horses*, as the same is altered by an Act passed in the First Year of His present Majesty's Reign, the Benefit of Clergy is taken away from Persons convicted of privately and feloniously stealing any Goods, Wares or Merchandize of the Value of Fifteen Pounds, in any Shop, Warehouse, Coachhouse or Stable, or of assisting, hiring or commanding any Person to commit any such Offence: And Whereas by an Act passed in the Twenty fourth Year of the Reign of King *George* the Second, intituled *An Act for the more effectual preventing of Robberies and Thefts upon any navigable Rivers, Ports of Entry or Discharge, Wharfs and Keys adjacent*, the Benefit of Clergy is taken away from Persons convicted of feloniously stealing any Goods, Wares or Merchandize of the Value of Forty Shillings in any Ship, Barge, Lighter, Boat or other Vessel or Craft, upon any navigable River, or in any Port of Entry or Discharge, or in any Creek belonging to any navigable River, Port of Entry or Discharge, within the Kingdom of *Great Britain*, or of feloniously stealing any Goods, Wares or Merchandize of the Value of Forty Shillings upon any Wharf or Key adjacent to any navigable River, Port of Entry or Discharge, or of being present, aiding and assisting in the committing any of the Offences aforesaid: And Whereas it is expedient that a lesser Degree of Punishment than that of Death should be provided for the Offences from which the Benefit of Clergy is so taken away as aforesaid, and that the same Punishment should be extended in Manner hereinafter mentioned: Be it therefore enacted by the King's most Excellent Majesty, by and with the Advice and Consent of the Lords Spiritual and Temporal, and Commons, in this present Parliament assembled, and by the Authority of the same, That so much of the said recited Acts as takes away the Benefit of Clergy from the Persons convicted of the Offences hereinbefore mentioned, shall be and the same are hereby repealed; and that from and after the passing of this Act, every Person who shall be lawfully convicted of cutting, taking, stealing or carrying away any Cloth or other Woollen Manufactures from the Rack or Tenters in the Night-time, or of stealing or embezzling His Majesty's Ammunition, Sails, Cordage or Naval or Military Stores, or of privately stealing any Goods or Chattels in any Shop, Warehouse, Coachhouse or Stable, or of stealing any Goods, Wares or Merchandize in any Ship, Barge, Lighter, Boat or other Vessel or Craft, upon any navigable River or Canal, or in any Port of Entry or Discharge, or in any Creek belonging to any such River, Canal or Port, or from any Dock, Wharf or Quay adjacent to any such River, Canal or Port, or of procuring, counselling, aiding or abetting any such Offender, shall be liable, at the Discretion of the Court, to be transported beyond the Seas for Life, or for any Term not less than Seven Years, or to be imprisoned only, or to be imprisoned and kept to hard Labour in the Common Gaol or House of Correction, for any Term not exceeding Seven Years.

Gaols Act, 10 July 1823

4 Geo. 4, c. 64   *Statutes of the United Kingdom*, 1823, 476-91, 501-02.

This act provided for the building, repairing, and regulating of jails and houses of correction.

Whereas the Laws now existing relative to the building, repairing and regulating of Gaols and Houses of Correction, in *England* and *Wales*, are complicated, and have in many Cases been found ineffective: And Whereas it is expedient that such Measures should be adopted, and such Arrangements made in Prisons, as shall not only provide for the safe Custody, but shall also tend more effectually to preserve the Health and to improve the Morals of the Prisoners confined therein, and shall insure the proper Measure of Punishment to convicted Offenders: And Whereas due Classification, Inspection, regular Labour and Employment, and Religious and Moral Instruction, are essential to the Discipline of a Prison, and to the Reformation of Offenders: And Whereas the present Laws directing the Separation, Superintendence, Employment and Instruction of Prisoners, require to be amended and enlarged, and to be more uniformly and strictly carried into Effect; and it is therefore expedient that the most useful Provisions contained in the several Statutes and Acts, and Parts of Statutes and Acts hereinafter mentioned, should be consolidated, and that some new Provisions should be added thereto: Be it therefore enacted by the King's most Excellent Majesty, by and with the Advice and Consent of the Lords Spiritual and Temporal, and Commons, in this present Parliament assembled, and by the Authority of the same, That from and after the Commencement of this Act, the several Statutes and Acts, and Parts of Statutes and Acts following, shall be repealed, so far as relates to such Gaols or Prisons, or Houses of Correction, as this Act shall extend to; (that is to say), so much of a Statute passed in the First Year of the Reign of King *Edward* the Third, as relates to Inquiry to be made of Gaolers, which by Duress compel Prisoners to appeal; and also, so much of a Statute passed in the Fourth Year of the Reign of the said King *Edward* the Third, as relates to Sheriffs and Gaolers receiving Offenders without taking any thing; and also, so much of a Statute passed in the Fourteenth Year of the Reign of the said King *Edward* the Third, as relates to the Punishment of a Gaoler compelling a Prisoner by Duress to become an Approver; and also, so much of an Act passed in the Seventh Year of the Reign of King *James* the First, intituled *An Act for the due Execution of divers Laws and Statutes heretofore made against Rogues, Vagabonds and sturdy Beggars, and other lewd and idle Persons*, as relates to the providing Houses of Correction, to the Appointment, Authority and Allowance of the Governor, and to his accounting to Justices for Persons committed to his Custody; and also, so much of an Act passed in the Nineteenth Year of the Reign of King *Charles* the Second, intituled *An Act for the Relief of poor Prisoners, and setting them to work*, as relates to the providing

Stocks for setting such Prisoners to work, and to the Removal of Prisoners on occasion of Sickness; and also, so much of an Act passed in the Twenty second and Twenty third Years of the Reign of the said King *Charles* the Second, intituled *An Act for the Relief and Release of poor distressed Prisoners for Debt*, as relates to Prisoners being allowed to send for Victuals and other Necessaries, and to Fees and Charities, and to the Separation of Felons and Debtors; and also, an Act passed in the Eleventh and Twelfth Years of the Reign of King *William* the Third, intituled *An Act to enable Justices of Peace to build and repair Gaols in their respective Counties*; any Thing in an Act made in the Sixth Year of the Reign of King *George* the First, for making perpetual any Act or Acts relating to the building and repairing of County Gaols, to the contrary in anywise notwithstanding; and also, so much of an Act passed in the Second Year of the Reign of King *George* the Second, intituled *An Act for the Relief of Debtors, with respect to the Imprisonment of their Persons*, as relates to Prisoners being allowed by Keepers of Prisons and Gaols to send for Victuals and other Necessaries, and to the taking of Fees, and the making and hanging up Tables thereof, and to Inquiries concerning the same, and to the hearing of Complaints of Extortion against Gaolers, and examining into Gifts and Legacies for the Benefit of poor Prisoners, and hanging up Tables thereof; and also, so much of an Act passed in the Fourteenth Year of the Reign of the said King *George* the Second, intituled *An Act to supply some Defects in the Laws for repairing and rebuilding County Bridges, for repairing, enlarging, erecting and providing Houses of Correction, and for passing Rogues and Vagabonds*, as relates to repairing, enlarging and building Houses of Correction, and to buying Houses and Lands for that Purpose; and also, so much of an Act passed in the Sixteenth Year of the Reign of the said King *George* the Second, intituled *An Act for the farther Punishment of Persons who shall aid or assist Prisoners to attempt to escape out of lawful Custody*, as relates to the Escape of Prisoners from any Gaol or Prison to which this Act shall extend; and also, so much of an Act passed in the Seventeenth Year of the Reign of the said King *George* the Second, intituled *An Act to amend and make more effectual the Laws relating to Rogues, Vagabonds and other idle and disorderly Persons, and to Houses of Correction*, as relates to the erecting, enlarging and managing the Houses of Correction, and the finding or turning out of Masters of them for Misbehavour; and also, so much of an Act passed in the Twenty fourth Year of the Reign of the said King *George* the Second, (made among other Things for granting an additional Duty upon Spirituous Liquors, and upon Licences for retailing the same, and for repealing an Act of the Twentieth Year of King *George* the First, made among other Things for more effectually restraining the retailing of distilled Spirituous Liquors), as relates to the retailing of Spirituous Liquors in Gaols, Prisons or Houses of Correction, to the carrying of Liquors into the same, to the Search for such Liquors, and to the hanging up of a Copy of certain Clauses of the said Act in such Gaols, Prisons or Houses; and also, so much of an Act passed in the Thirty second Year of the Reign of the said King *George* the Second, for Relief of Debtors, with respect to the Imprisonment of their Persons, as relates to Prisoners being allowed to send for Victuals and other Necessaries, and to the settling, signing, reviewing, enrolling and hanging up of Tables of Fees, Rates and Benefactions, and Rules for the

Government of Gaols and Prisons; and also, an Act passed in the Thirteenth Year of the Reign of His late Majesty King *George* the Third, intituled *An Act for providing Clergymen to officiate in Gaols within that Part of* Great Britain *called* England; and also, an Act passed in the Fourteenth Year of the Reign of His said late Majesty, intituled *An Act for preserving the Health of Prisoners in Gaol, and preventing the Gaol Distemper*; and also, an Act passed in the Twenty second Year of His said late Majesty's Reign, intituled *An Act for the amending and rendering more effectual the Laws in being relative to Houses of Correction*; and also, Two Acts passed in the Twenty fourth Year of His said late Majesty's Reign, the one made to explain and amend the hereinbefore recited Act, made in the Eleventh and Twelfth Years of the Reign of King *William* the Third, and the other made to explain and amend the hereinbefore recited Act of the Twenty second Year of the Reign of His said late Majesty King *George* the Third; and also, an Act passed in the Twenty ninth Year of His said late Majesty's Reign, intituled *An Act for the more effectual Execution of the Laws respecting Gaols*; and also, an Act passed in the Thirty first Year of His said late Majesty's Reign, intituled *An Act for the better regulating of Gaols and other Places of Confinement*, except only so much of the said Act as relates to the Imprisonment and Employment in Hard Labour in the Common Gaol of the County, of Prisoners sentenced to Transportation, or to whom the Royal Mercy shall be extended on Condition of Transportation; and also, an Act passed in the Fifty fifth Year of His said late Majesty's Reign, for enlarging the Powers of the hereinbefore recited Acts of the Thirteenth and Twenty second Years of His said late Majesty's Reign, for providing Clergymen to officiate in Gaols and Houses of Correction within *England* and *Wales*; and also, an Act passed in the Fifty eighth Year of His said late Majesty's Reign, to amend so much of the said Act of the Fifty fifth Year of His said late Majesty's Reign, as relates to the Salaries of the Clergymen officiating as Chaplains in Houses of Correction; and the said several Statutes and Acts, and Parts of Statutes and Acts, are hereby repealed accordingly, and from and after the Commencement of this Act shall cease and determine, so far as relates to Gaols and Houses of Correction to which this Act shall extend; save and except so far as the said Acts, or any of them, repeal any former Act or Acts, or any Clause, Matter or Thing therein; and also, save and except as to any Proceeding for the Punishment of any Person for any Offence which shall before the Commencement of this Act have been committed; and as to any Presentment before that Time made by any Justice of the Peace or Grand Jury; and as to any Appointment before that Time made by any Officer or other Person, to perform any Duties under the said recited Acts, or any of them; and as to any Rules and Regulations, Acts and Deeds, before that Time lawfully established, made or done, under or by virtue of any One or more of the said Acts; and as to the Fulfilment of any Contracts or Agreements before that Time lawfully made, under or by virtue of the said recited Acts, or any of them.

   II. And be it further enacted, That from and after the Commencement of this Act, there shall be maintained, at the Expence of every County in *England* and *Wales*, One Common Gaol, and at the Expence of every County not divided into Ridings or Divisions, and of every Riding or Division of a County, (having several and distinct Commissions of the Peace, or several or distinct Rates in the Nature of

County Rates, applicable by Law to the Maintenance of a Prison for such Division, in *England* and *Wales*, at least One House of Correction; and One Gaol and One House of Correction shall be maintained in the several Cities, Towns and Places mentioned in the Schedule marked (A.) annexed to this Act; and the Regulations and Provisions contained in this Act shall extend, in Manner hereinafter mentioned, to every such Gaol and House of Correction maintained at the Expence of such County, Riding, Division, City, Town or Place, and to the several Gaols and Houses of Correction in the Cities of *London* and *Westminster*.

III. Provided always, and be it enacted, That where there shall have been already established, and shall be existing at the Time of passing of this Act, in any County, Riding, Division, City, Town or Place, one or more House or Houses of Correction, not sufficient or capable of being made sufficient for the extended Classification required by this Act, it shall be lawful for the Justices assembled at their General or Quarter Sessions, or the major Part of them, if they shall so think fit, to order and direct that, in Addition to the House of Correction hereinbefore directed to be maintained for the Purposes of this Act, one or more of such Houses of Correction shall be so existing as aforesaid at the Time of the passing of this Act, shall be continued and maintained for the Reception of One or more particular Class or Classes or Description or Descriptions of Prisoners, as may be prescribed by the Justices assembled at their General or Quarter Sessions as directed by this Act.

IV. And be it further enacted, That at the *Michaelmas* General Quarter Sessions which shall be held in every County, Riding or Division of a County in *England* and *Wales*, and in the several Districts, Cities, Towns and Places to which this Act shall extend, next after the Commencement of this Act, and at any subsequent General or Quarter Sessions to be held from Time to Time, the Justices of the Peace there assembled shall proceed in carrying this Act into Effect; and such Justices shall, by Orders to be made for that Purpose, ascertain and declare to what Class or Classes of Prisoners every such Gaol, House or Houses of Correction, or any Part or Parts of any of them respectively, shall be applicable; and every such Order shall be signed by the Chairman of such Sessions, and shall be notified by the Clerks of the Peace to the several Justices of the Peace in every such County, Riding or Division, District, City, Town or Place respectively, and Notice thereof shall be inserted in Three of the Newspapers usually circulated in such County, Riding or Division, or District, City, Town or Place respectively, within Three Weeks after any such Order shall be made at any such Sessions; and a Copy thereof shall be served upon the Keeper of every Gaol or House of Correction within every such County, Riding, Division, City, District, Town or Place; and after the making of such Order, and Serve of such Copy thereof upon such Keeper as aforesaid, such Class or Classes of Prisoners as shall be specified in such Order, and no other, shall be committed to or detained in any such Gaol, House or Houses of Correction, or any Part of any of them respectively; and all Persons not coming within the Class or Description of Prisoners who may lawfully be committed to or detained in such Prison as shall be appointed by the Justices for the Confinement of One or more Class or Classes of Prisoners, may be removed to the Gaol or House of Correction of the County, Riding or Division; and every such Gaol or House of Correction shall be deemed the legal Gaol, Prison or Place of Confinement of every Person respectively committed to the same in pursuance of such Order as aforesaid; any thing in any Act or Acts, or any Law, Custom or Usage to the contrary notwithstanding; Provided always, that no Classification of Prisoners shall be made in any House of Correction appropriated to the Reception of any particular Class or Classes of Prisoners, which shall be in any way inconsistent with or contrary to the Classification directed by this Act.

V. Provided always, and be it further enacted, That where, in any County, Riding or Division of a County, or in any of the Cities, Towns and Places named in the said Schedule (A.), any House of Correction shall be Part of the same Building, or inclosed in the same Boundary Wall as or shall be contiguous to the Common Gaol, and shall be under the Superintendence of the same Keeper and the same Visiting Justices, it shall be lawful for the Justices of the Peace of the County, Division, City, Town or Place, assembled at any General or Quarter Sessions, from time to time, with the Consent of the Sheriff of the County for the Time being, signified in Writing under his Hand, to proceed to carry into Effect the Classification and Separation directed by this Act in the whole of such united or contiguous Building or Buildings, instead of in each such House of Correction and Gaol, and to divide the whole of such Building, or united or contiguous Buildings, into such Number of Compartments for the purpose of such Separation and Classification as would be required under the Regulations of this Act, if the same had been one distinct Gaol or House of Correction; and also at any General or Quarter Sessions from time to time, by their Order or Orders, and with such Consent of the Sheriff as aforesaid, to ascertain and declare what Part or Parts of the same Building, or united or contiguous Buildings, shall be considered as the Gaol, and what Part or Parts thereof respectively shall be considered as the House of Correction, and shall be appropriated to the Confinement of particular Classes and Descriptions of Prisoners, and to direct what Classes and Descriptions respectively shall be confined in each Part or Division of such Building, or united or contiguous Buildings; and all Persons to be committed to or detained in the respective Parts and Divisions so to be ascertained and appropriated of any such Building, or united or contiguous Buildings, to them respectively applicable, shall be deemed and held to be in legal Custody: Provided that Prisoners for Debt may be removed to and shall always be confined in the Part or Parts of such Building, or united or contiguous Buildings, which shall be so ascertained or be appropriated as and for the Gaol of the County, Division, City, Town or Place; and such Removal shall not be deemed or taken to be an Escape.

VI. Provided always, and be it further enacted, That all Persons who in pursuance of any such Orders shall be removed to, committed to or detained in the Part of such united or contiguous Buildings, which shall be so declared and ascertained aforesaid to be the Gaol, shall from thenceforth be deemed to be in the legal Custody of the Sheriff and of the Gaoler appointed by the Sheriff, in the same Manner as if such Person had been committed to the Common Gaol before the passing of this Act: Provided also, that the Sheriff shall not be answerable for the safe Custody of any Person who in pursuance of any such Order shall from time to time be removed to, committed to or detained in any Part of such united or contiguous Buildings other than the Part so ascertained and declared to be the Gaol.

VII. And Whereas the Practice of committing Vagrants to Common Gaols has been attended with much Inconvenience to the Classification of Prisoners, and has prevented a Uniformity of Practice in the Management of Prisons, Be it therefore enacted, That from and after the First Day of *September* One thousand eight hundred and twenty four, in every County, Riding or Division of a County in *England* and *Wales*, and in the several Districts, Cities, Towns or Places to which this Act shall extend, all idle and disorderly Persons, Rogues and Vagabonds, incorrigible Rogues and other Vagrants, shall be committed to some House of Correction belonging to such County, Riding or Division, District, City, Town or Place respectively; and that such House of Correction shall be deemed the only legal Place of Commitment of any such Person in pursuance of any Conviction by lawful Authority; any Thing in any Act contained to the contrary in any wise notwithstanding.

VIII. Provided also, and be it enacted, That in all Cases where any Person liable by Law to be committed to the House of Correction shall be apprehended within any District, City, Town or Place mentioned in the Schedule to this Act annexed, and the Inhabitants of any such District, City, Town or Place are or shall be contributory to the Support and Maintenance of the House or Houses of Correction of the County, Riding or Division in which such District, City, Town or Place is situate, it shall and may be lawful for the Justices of the Peace of such District, City, Town or Place, to commit such Person to the House of Correction of the County, Riding or Division in which such District, City, Town or Place is situate; and every Person so committed shall and may be received, detained, dealt with and ordered to be set and kept to Hard Labour or other Work, or conveyed and sent away or discharged, and be subject and liable to the same Correction and Punishment, to all Intents and Purposes, as if committed by any Justice or Justices of the Peace of such County, Riding or Division; and in such Case it shall not be necessary or required that any other House of Correction shall be built or maintained in or for such District, City, Town or Place, and the Inhabitants of such District, City, Town or Place shall not be compelled or compellable to the Payment of any Rate or Sum of Money whatever for the building or maintaining of any other House of Correction in or for such District, City, Town or Place; any Thing in this Act contained to the contrary in any wise notwithstanding.

IX. Provided also, and be it enacted, That nothing in this Act contained shall extend to take away, lessen, vary, alter or affect any Right, Privilege or Franchise, which before the passing of this Act any Mayor, Bailiff or Justice of the Peace for the Time being of any City, Town or Liberty, having a separate Jurisdiction, had by Means of any Grant, Charter or special or local Act of Parliament, to commit Prisoners to the Gaol or House of Correction of any County, Riding or Division.

X. And Whereas it is fit and proper to secure an Uniformity of Practice in the Management of the several Prisons to which this Act shall extend; Be it therefore further enacted, That the following Rules and Regulations shall be observed and carried into Effect in every such Prison in *England* and *Wales*, which shall be maintained by any County or Riding, or Division of a County as aforesaid, as a Gaol or House of Correction, and in the Gaol and House of Correction of every District, City, Town or Place mentioned in the Schedule marked (A.) annexed to this Act, and in every united and contiguous Gaol and House of Correction which shall be jointly used in Manner aforesaid for the Purposes of this Act, and in every Prison authorized to be continued under this Act as aforesaid, in any County or Riding or Division of a County, so far as such Rules may be applicable or can be applied to the particular Description or Class of Prisoners confined in such Prison:

First:—The Keeper of every such Prison shall reside therein; he shall not be an Under Sheriff or Bailiff, nor shall be concerned in any Occupation or Trade whatsoever; no Keeper or Officer of a Prison shall sell, nor shall any Person in Trust for him or employed by him sell or have any Benefit or Advantage from the Sale of any Article to any Prisoner, nor shall he, directly or indirectly, have any Interest in any Contract or Agreement for the Supply of the Prison.

Second:—A Matron shall be appointed in every Prison in which Female Prisoners shall be confined, who shall reside in the Prison; and it shall be the Duty of the Matron constantly to superintend the Female Prisoners.

Third:—The Keeper shall, as far as may be practicable, visit every Ward, and see every Prisoner and inspect every Cell Once at least in every Twenty four Hours; and when the Keeper or any other Officer shall visit the Female Prisoners, he shall be accompanied by the Matron, or in Case of her unavoidable Absence, by some Female Officer of the Prison.

Fourth:—The Keeper shall keep a Journal, in which he shall record all Punishments inflicted by his Authority or by that of the Visiting Justices, and the Day when such Punishments shall have taken place and all other Occurrences of Importance within the Prison, in such Manner as shall be directed by the Regulations to be made under this Act; which Journal shall be laid before the Justices at every General or Quarter Sessions, to be signed by the Chairman, in Proof of the same having been there produced.

Fifth:—Due Provision shall be made in every Prison for the Enforcement of Hard Labour in the Cases of such Prisoners as may be sentenced thereto and for the Employment of other Prisoners. The Means of Hard Labour shall be provided and the Materials requisite for the Employment of Prisoners shall be purchased, under such Regulations as may be made for that Purpose by the Justices in General or Quarter Sessions assembled. If the Work to be performed by the Prisoners be of such a Nature as to require previous Instruction, proper Persons shall be appointed to afford the same.

Sixth:—The Male and Female Prisoners shall be confined in separate Buildings or Parts of the Prison, so as to prevent them from seeing, conversing or holding any Intercourse with each other; and the Prisoners of each Sex shall be divided into distinct Classes, Care being taken that Prisoners of the following Classes do not intermix with each other: In Gaols—First, Debtors and Persons confined for Contempt of Court on Civil Process; Second, Prisoners convicted of Felony; Third, Prisoners convicted of Misdemeanors; Fourth, Prisoners committed on Charge or Suspicion of Felony; Fifth, Prisoners committed on Charge or Suspicion of Misdemeanors or for Want of Sureties: In House of Correction—First, Prisoners convicted of Felony; Second, Prisoners convicted of Misdemeanors; Third, Prisoners committed on Charge or Suspicion of Felony; Fourth, Prisoners committed on Charge or Suspicion of Misdemeanors; Fifth, Vagrants. Such Prisoners as are intended to be examined as Witnesses in behalf of the Crown in any Prosecution shall also be kept separate in all Gaols and Houses of Correction.

Provided always, that nothing herein contained shall be construed to extend to prevent the Justices from authorizing, at their Discretion, the Employment of any Prisoner in the Performance of any menial Office within the Prison, or for the Purpose of instructing others; and provided also, that if the Keeper shall at any Time deem it improper or inexpedient for a Prisoner to associate with the other Prisoners of the Class to which he or she may belong, it shall be lawful for him to confine such Prisoner with any other Class or Description of Prisoners, or in any other Part of the Prison, until he can receive the Directions of a Visiting Justice thereon, to whom he shall apply with as little Delay as possible, and who in every such Instance shall ascertain whether the Reasons assigned by the Keeper warrant such Deviation from the established Rules, and shall give such Orders in Writing as he shall think fit, under the Circumstances of the particular Case.

Seventh:—Female Prisoners shall in all Cases be attended by Female Officers.

Eighth:—Every Prisoner sentenced to Hard Labour shall, unless prevented by Sickness, be employed so many Hours in every Day, not exceeding Ten, exclusive of the Time allowed for Meals, as shall be directed by the Rules and Regulations to be made under this Act, except on *Sundays, Christmas Day*, and *Good Friday*, and on any Days appointed by public Authority for Fasting or Thanksgiving.

Ninth:—Prayers, to be selected from the Liturgy of the Church of *England* by the Chaplain, shall be read at least every Morning by the Chaplain, the Keeper, or by some other Person, as by the Rules and Regulations shall be directed; and Portions of the Scriptures shall be read to the Prisoners, when assembled for Instruction, by the Chaplain, or by such Person as he may appoint or authorize.

Tenth:—Provision shall be made in all Prisons for the Instruction of Prisoners of both Sexes in Reading and Writing, and that Instruction shall be afforded under such Rules and Regulations, and to such Extent, and to such Prisoners, as to the Visiting Justices may seem expedient.

Eleventh:—Prisoners under Charge or Conviction of any Crime shall attend Divine Service on *Sundays*, and on other Days when such Service is performed, unless prevented by Illness or by other reasonable Cause, to be allowed by the Keeper, or unless their Attendance shall be dispensed with by One of the Visiting Justices.

Twelfth:—No Prisoner shall be put in Irons by the Keeper of any Prison, except in case of urgent and absolute Necessity; and the Particulars of every such Case shall be forthwith entered in the Keeper's Journal, and Notice forthwith given thereof to One of the Visiting Justices; and the Keeper shall not continue the Use of Irons on any Prisoner longer than Four Days, without an Order in Writing from a Visiting Justice, specifying the Cause thereof; which Order shall be preserved by the Keeper, as his Warrant for the same.

Thirteenth:—Every Prisoner maintained at the Expence of any County, Riding, Division, City, Town or Place, shall be allowed a sufficient Quantity of plain and wholesome Food, to be regulated by the Justices in General or Quarter Sessions assembled, Regard being had (so far as may relate to convicted Prisoners) to the Nature of the Labour required from or performed by such Prisoners, so that the Allowance of Food may be duly apportioned thereto. And it shall be lawful for the Justices to order for such Prisoners of every Description, as are not able to work, or being able cannot procure Employment sufficient to sustain themselves by their Industry, or who may not be otherwise provided for, such Allowance of Food, as the said Justices shall from time to time think necessary for the Support of Health. Prisoners under the Care of the Surgeon shall be allowed such Diet as he may direct. Care shall be taken that all Provisions supplied to the Prisoners be of proper Quality and Weight. Scales and legal Weights and Measures shall be provided, open to the Use of any Prisoners, under such Restrictions as shall be made by the Regulations of each Prison.

Fourteenth:—Prisoners who shall not receive any Allowance from the County, whether confined for Debt or before Trial, for any supposed Crime or Offence, shall be allowed to procure for themselves, and to receive at proper Hours, any Food, Bedding, Clothing or other Necessaries, subject to a strict Examination, and under such Limitations and Restrictions, to be prescribed by the Regulations to be made in Manner directed by this Act, as may be reasonable and expedient, to prevent Extravagance and Luxury within the Walls of a Prison; all Articles of Clothing and Bedding shall be examined, in order that it may be ascertained that such Articles are not likely to communicate Infection or facilitate Escape.

Fifteenth:—No Prisoner who is confined under the Sentence of any Court, nor any Prisoners confined in pursuance of any Conviction before a Justice, shall receive any Food, Clothing or Necessaries, other than the Gaol Allowance, except under such Regulations and Restrictions as to the Justices in General or Quarter Sessions assembled may appear expedient, with reference to the several Classes of Prisoners, or under special Circumstances, to be judged of by One or more of the Visiting Justices.

Sixteenth:—Due Provision shall be made for the Admission, at proper Times and under proper Restrictions, of Persons with whom Prisoners committed for Trial may desire to communicate; and such Rules and Regulations shall be made, by the Justices in General Quarter Sessions assembled, for the Admission of the Friends of convicted Prisoners, as to such Justices may seem expedient; and the Justices shall also impose such Restrictions upon the Communication and Correspondence of all such Prisoners with their Friends, either within or without the Walls of the Prison, as they shall judge necessary for the Maintenance of good Order and Discipline in such Prison.

Seventeenth:—The Surgeon shall examine every Prisoner who shall be brought into the Prison, before he or she shall be passed into the proper Ward; and no Prisoner shall be discharged from Prison if labouring under any acute or dangerous Distemper, nor until, in the Opinion of the Surgeon, such Discharge is safe, unless such Prisoner shall require to be discharged. The Wearing Apparel of every Prisoner shall be fumigated and purified, if requisite, after which the same shall be returned to him or her, or in case of the Insufficiency of such Clothing, then other sufficient Clothing shall be furnished, according to the Rules and Regulations of the Prison; but no Prisoner before Trial shall be compelled to wear a Prison Dress, unless his or her own Clothes be deemed insufficient or improper, or necessary to be preserved for the Purposes of Justice; and no Prisoner who has not been convicted of Felony shall be liable to be clothed in a Party coloured Dress; but if it be deemed expedient to have a Prison Dress for Prisoners not convicted of Felony, the same shall be plain.

Eighteenth:—Every Prisoner shall be provided with suitable Bedding; and every Male Prisoner with a separate Bed, Hammock or Cot, either in a separate Cell, or in a Cell with not less than Two other Male Prisoners.

Nineteenth:—The Walls and Ceilings of the Wards, Cells, Rooms and Passages used by the Prisoners throughout every Prison, shall be scraped and Lime washed at least Once in the Year: the Day Rooms, Work Rooms, Passages and Sleeping Cells shall be washed or cleansed Once a Week, or oftener if requisite. Convenient Places for the Prisoners to wash themselves shall be provided, with an adequate Allowance of Soap, Towels and Combs.

Twentieth:—All Prisoners shall be allowed as much Air and Exercise as may be deemed proper for the Preservation of their Health.

Twenty first:—No Tap shall be kept in any Prison; nor shall Spirituous Liquors of any Kind be admitted for the Use of any of the Prisoners therein, under any Pretence whatever, unless by a written Order of the Surgeon, specifying the Quantity and for whose Use. No Wine, Beer, Cider or other fermented Liquors shall be admitted for the Use of any Prisoners, except in such Quantities, in such Manner and at such Times, as shall be allowed by the Rules hereafter to be made in pursuance of this Act.

Twenty second:—No Gaming shall be permitted in any Prison; and the Keeper shall seize and destroy all Dice, Cards or other Instruments of Gaming.

Twenty third:—No Money under the Name of Garnish shall be taken from any Prisoner on his or her Entrance into the Prison, under any Pretence whatever.

Twenty fourth:—Upon the Death of a Prisoner, Notice thereof shall be given by the Keeper forthwith to One of the Visiting Justices, as well as to the Coroner of the District, and to the nearest Relative of the Deceased, where practicable.

XI. And be it further enacted, That in case the Coroner shall hold an Inquest on the Body of any Prisoner who shall have died within the Prison, none of the Prisoners confined in that Prison shall be a Juror on such Inquest.

XII. And be it further enacted, That it shall be lawful for the Court of Mayor and Aldermen of the City of *London*, so far as respects the Prisons within the said City and Liberties thereof, and for Five Justices of the Peace in General or Quarter Sessions assembled, of each County, Riding or Division of a County, or of any District, City, Town or Place to which this Act shall extend, so far as respects the Prisons within their respective Jurisdictions, to make such further and additional Rules for the Government of such Prisons respectively, and for the Duties to be performed by the Officers of the same, as to them may seem expedient; provided, that no such further or additional Rules shall be enforced, until the same shall have been submitted, in *London* and *Middlesex*, to the Two Chief Justices, and elsewhere to the Justices of Gaol Delivery or of Great Sessions respectively, at some Gaol Delivery or Great Sessions to be held after the making such Rules, and until such Chief Justice or Justices of Gaol Delivery or of Great Sessions respectively, shall have subscribed a Certificate or Declaration that they do not see any Thing contrary to Law therein: Provided always, that all such Rules and Regulations shall be consistent with and conformable to the Rules and Regulations in this Act contained: And the Justices in General or Quarter Sessions assembled shall and they are hereby required from time to time to cause Copies of so much of the Rules of each Prison as relates to the Treatment and Conduct of Prisoners confined therein, to be printed in legible Characters, and to be fixed up in conspicuous Parts of every Prison, so that every Prisoner may be enabled to have Access thereto; and all Rules and Regulations made and approved pursuant to the Directions of this Act shall be binding upon the Sheriff and upon all other Persons; provided, that no such Rules shall be so construed as to interfere with the Right or Duty of the Sheriff to appoint or remove any Keeper of a County Gaol or other Prison subject to the Authority of such Sheriff.

XIII. Provided always, and be it enacted, That all the Powers and Authorities given by this Act to Justices of the Peace in General or Quarter Sessions assembled, in the several Counties, and all other Acts to be done and performed by Justices of the Peace at any Sessions in pursuance of this Act, shall be exercised and performed, so far as regards the Prisons in the City of *London* and Liberties thereof, by the Court of Mayor and Aldermen of the said City, as heretofore has been accustomed, and not by the said Mayor and Aldermen as Magistrates at the General or Quarter

Sessions of the Peace to be holden in and for the said City; any Thing in this Act contained to the contrary thereof in any wise notwithstanding.

XIV. And be it further enacted, That the Gaoler and Keeper of every Gaol and House of Correction, maintained at the Expence of any County, or of any such Riding or Division of a County as aforesaid, in *England* and *Wales*, or maintained by any District, City, Town or Place specified in the Schedule to this Act annexed marked (A.), shall make a Report in Writing, of the actual State and Condition of every such Gaol and House of Correction, and of the Number and Description of Prisoners confined therein, to the Justices at the several General or Quarter Sessions to be holden next after the Commencement of this Act, and at every ensuing General or Quarter Sessions in every such County, Riding, Division, District, City, Town or Place; and shall at every such General or Quarter Sessions attend and give Answer, upon Oath, to all such Inquiries as shall be made by the Justices at such Sessions, with respect to the State and Condition of every such Gaol and House of Correction, and of the Prisoners confined therein, and with respect to any other Matters and Things relating to the said Gaol and House of Correction, respecting which such Justices shall deem it necessary to make any Inquiry for the Purpose of proceeding and continuing to carry this Act into Execution, and of ascertaining how far every such Gaol and House of Correction is capable of affording the Means of the Classification required by this Act.

XV. And be it further enacted, That the Chairman of the *Michaelmas* Quarter Sessions of the Peace, which shall be held next after the Commencement of this Act, for every County, Riding, Division, District, City, Town or Place to which this Act shall extend, shall transmit, within Fourteen Days after the Termination of such Session, to One of His Majesty's Principal Secretaries of State, a true and correct Account of their Proceedings at such Sessions for carrying this Act into Effect, and also a Copy of all such Rules and Regulations as shall be then in force for the Government of every Prison within the Jurisdiction of the Justices assembled at such Sessions, and shall also transmit at the same Time, or within Three Months afterwards, to such Secretary of State, Plans of all such Prisons, drawn upon a Scale of One sixteenth of an Inch to a Foot; and the said Copies and Plans shall be carefully preserved in the Office of such Secretary of State; and the Chairman of every such succeeding *Michaelmas* Quarter Sessions shall transmit, within Fourteen Days after the Termination of such *Michaelmas* Quarter Sessions, a true and correct Copy of all such Additions to such Rules and Regulations, or Alterations made therein, as shall have been duly sanctioned since the preceding *Michaelmas* Quarter Sessions, together with Plans, on the Scale above mentioned, of any Additions to the Buildings of such Prison, or Alterations made in the Construction thereof, during the same Period.

XVI. And be it further enacted, That the Justices in every County, Riding, Division, District, City, Town or Place, to which this Act shall extend, at the General or Quarter Sessions next after the Commencement of this Act, and at every ensuing General or Quarter Sessions, shall and they are hereby required to nominate Two or more Justices who shall consent thereto, to be Visitors of each Gaol and House of Correction within their Jurisdiction, and to report the Names and Places of Abode of such Visiting Justices to One of His Majesty's Principal

Secretaries of State; and One or more of the Visiting Justices so appointed shall personally visit and inspect each Prison at least Three Times in each Quarter of a Year, and oftener if Occasion shall require, and shall examine into the State of the Buildings, so as to form a Judgment as to the Repairs, Additions or Alterations which may appear necessary, strict Regard being had to the Classification, Inspection, Instruction, Employment or Hard Labour, required by this Act, and shall further examine into the Behaviour and Conduct of the respective Officers, and the Treatment, Behaviour and Condition of the Prisoners, the Means of setting them to work, the Amount of their Earnings and the Expences attending the Prison, and of all Abuses within the same, and in Matters of pressing Necessity, and within the Powers of their Commission as Justices, shall take Cognizance thereof, and proceed to regulate and redress the same; and if the said Visitors shall at any Time observe, or be satisfactorily informed of any extraordinary Diligence or Merit in any Prisoners under their Inspection, they shall report the same to the Justices of Peace for the County, Riding, Division, District, City, Town or Place, at their next or any subsequent General or Quarter Session to be holden for the County or Place in which such Prison is situate, in order that such Justices may, if they shall think proper, recommend any such Offender to the Royal Mercy, in such Degree or upon such Terms as to them shall seem meet; and if His Majesty shall thereupon be graciously pleased to shorten the Duration of such Prisoner's Confinement, such Prisoner shall, upon his or her Discharge, together with necessary Clothing, receive such Sum of Money for his or her Subsistence, as the Visiting Justices for the Time being shall think proper; so as such Sum shall not exceed Twenty Shillings, nor be less than Five Shillings, in case such Offender shall have been confined for the Space of One Year, and so in Proportion for any shorter Term of Confinement: and such Sums of Money, as also the Expence of such Clothing, shall be paid out of the County Rate, or other Rate applicable to the Expences of Prisons.

XVII. Provided always, and be it enacted, That it shall be lawful for any Justice of the Peace for any County, Riding or Division, District, City, Town or Place, at his own free Will and Pleasure, and without being appointed a Visitor, to enter into and examine any Prison of such County, Riding, Division, District, City, Town or Place, at such Time or Times and so often as he shall see fit, and if he shall discover any Abuse or Abuses therein, he is hereby required to report them in Writing at the next General or Quarter Sessions of the Peace, or adjourned Sessions, which shall be holden for such County, Riding or Division, District, City, Town or Place; and then and so often as a Report of any Abuse or Abuses in any such Prison shall be made by the Visiting Justices, or either of them, or by any other Justice of the Peace for such County, Riding or Division, District, City, Town or Place, the Abuse or Abuses so reported shall be taken into immediate Consideration by the Justices of the Peace for such County, Riding or Division, District, City, Town or Place, at the General or Quarter Sessions at which such Report shall be made; and they are hereby required to adopt the most effectual Measures for inquiring into and rectifying such Abuse or Abuses as soon as the Nature of the Case will allow.

XVIII. Provided also, and be it enacted, That nothing herein contained shall extend or be construed to extend to authorize or empower any Visiting or other

Justice of the Peace to converse or hold any Intercourse or Communication, except as hereinafter mentioned, with any Person who may be committed by lawful Authority to any such Gaol or other Prison, there to be kept in safe and close Confinement; but that, nevertheless, it shall and may be lawful for any Visiting Justice, so appointed as aforesaid, to visit and inspect, at all Times when he shall think proper, the Apartment or Place in which such Person shall be kept or confined in any Prison, and also to see such Person, and to hear or receive any Representation from him or her as to his or her Treatment in such Prison, and to enquire and examine into the same; any Thing herein contained to the contrary thereof notwithstanding.

XIX. And be it further enacted, That the Keeper of every Gaol and House of Correction, to which this Act shall extend, shall, previously to the First Day of every Assizes, Great Sessions or Sessions of Gaol Delivery, make out a true and just Return in Writing of all Persons in his Custody who have been sentenced to Hard Labour by the Court at any previous Assizes, Great Sessions or Sessions of Gaol Delivery, specifying in such Return the Manner in which such Sentences have been carried into Execution, the particular Species of Labour in which such Prisoners have been employed, and the average Number of Hours in a Day for which such Persons so sentenced have been kept to work; which Return shall be signed by such Keeper, and also by one at least of the Visiting Justices, who shall add thereto such Observations as the Case and Circumstances may appear to him to require; and such Return shall be delivered to the Justice of Assize and Gaol Delivery, and of Great Sessions, and shall be kept and filed by the proper Officer amongst the Records of the Court

XX. And be it further enacted, That the Keeper of every Prison within *England* and *Wales*, having the Custody of Prisoners charged with Felony, shall, on the Second Day next after the Termination of every Session of the Peace, Session of Oyer and Terminer, or Session of Gaol Delivery, Great Session or other Session held for the Trial of Prisoners being in such Prison, whether such Session shall be held under any Commission, or by virtue of any Charter or Prescription, transmit by the Post of that Day to One of His Majesty's Principal Secretaries of State, a Calendar containing the Names, the Crimes and the Sentences of every Prisoner tried at such Session, and distinguishing, with respect to all Prisoners capitally convicted, such of them as may have been reprieved by the Court, and stating the Day on which Execution is to be done upon those who have not been reprieved; and that whenever the Court shall adjourn for any longer Time than One Week, the Day upon which the Adjournment shall be made shall be deemed the Termination of the Session within the Meaning of this Act; and every Keeper of any such Prison, who shall neglect or refuse to transmit such Calendar, or shall wilfully transmit a Calendar containing any false or imperfect Statement, shall for every such Offence forfeit the Sum of Twenty Pounds.

XXI. And, for the better ensuring the strict Observance of the Rules and Regulations to be made for the Government of the Prisons to which this Act shall extend, be it enacted, That at each Quarter Sessions of the Peace, the Keeper of every Prison within the Jurisdiction of the Court holding such Session shall and is hereby required to deliver or cause to be delivered to such Court, a Certificate, signed by himself, which Certificate shall contain a Declaration how far the Rules laid down for the Government of his Prison have been complied with, and shall point out any and every Deviation therefrom which may have taken place; and if any Keeper of a Prison shall neglect to deliver, or cause to be delivered, such Certificate as aforesaid, he shall forfeit for every such Offence the Sum of Ten Pounds.

XXII. And be it further enacted, That One Week before the *Michaelmas* Session in every Year, the Keeper of every Prison to which this Act shall extend shall make up a Return of the State of his Prison for the Year then ending, in the Form contained in the Schedule annexed to this Act, marked (B.), and shall deliver the same, or cause the same to be delivered, to the Clerk of the Peace or his Deputy, for the Use of the Justices assembled at such Quarter Session.

XXIII. And be it further enacted, That at every General or Quarter Sessions, the Visiting Justices shall make a Report in Writing of the State and Condition of each Prison within their Jurisdiction, of what Repairs, Additions or Alterations shall have been made or may be required, and of any Abuse or Abuses which they may have observed, or of which they may have received Information, in the Management of the Prison, as well as of the general State of the Prisoners, as to Morals, Discipline, Employment and Hard Labour, and Observance of Rules; and the Justices assembled at such Sessions shall proceed to consider every such Report, and to act forthwith as they may see Occasion.

XXIV. And be it further enacted, That a General Report, founded on the Report of the Visiting Justices, on the Report of the Chaplain or Chaplains, and on the Certificates of the Keepers of the several Prisons, shall be prepared by the Clerk of the Peace, and submitted to the Justices assembled at every *Michaelmas* Quarter Sessions; and when approved by the Justices at such Sessions, such Report shall be signed by the Chairman of such Sessions, and shall be by him transmitted (together with a Copy of the Schedule (B.) delivered by the Gaoler) to one of His Majesty's Principal Secretaries of State; a Copy of which Report, with the said Schedule attached to it, shall be laid before both Houses of Parliament, within One Month next ensuing, if Parliament shall be sitting, or within One Month after the Time when Parliament shall next sit. . . .

XLIX. And be it further enacted, That in the altering, enlarging, repairing, building or rebuilding of any Gaol or House of Correction under this Act, the Justices shall adopt such Plans as shall afford the most effectual Means for the Security, Classification, Health, Inspection, Employment and Religious and Moral Instruction of the Prisoners; the Building shall be so constructed or applied, and the Keepers' and Officers' Apartments so situated, as may best ensure the Safety of the Prison, and facilitate the Controul and Superintendence of those committed thereto; distinct Wards, and dry and airy Cells shall be provided, in which Prisoners of the several Descriptions and Classes hereinafter enumerated may be respectively confined; and it shall be considered as a primary and invariable Rule, that the Male Prisoners shall in all Cases be separated from the Female, so as to prevent any Communication between them: Provision shall be made for the Separation of Prisoners into the following Classes: If a Gaol; First, Debtors and Persons confined for Contempt of Court on Civil Process; Secondly, Prisoners convicted of Felony;

Thirdly, Those convicted upon Trial of Misdemeanors; Fourthly, Those committed on Charge or Suspicion of Felony; Fifthly, Those committed on Charge of Misdemeanors, or for Want of Sureties: If a House of Correction; First, Prisoners convicted of Felony; Secondly, Prisoners convicted upon Trial of Misdemeanors; Thirdly, Those committed on Charge or Suspicion of Felony; Fourthly, Those committed on Charge of Misdemeanors; Fifthly, Vagrants: Places of Confinement shall also be set apart in every Gaol and House of Correction for such Prisoners as are intended to be examined as Witnesses in Behalf of the Crown in any Prosecutions, and such further Means of Classification shall be adopted as the Justices shall deem conducive to good Order and Discipline; separate Rooms shall be provided as Infirmaries or Sick Wards for the Two Sexes, and as far as is practicable for the different Description of Prisoners; and warm and cold Baths, or Bathing Tubs, shall be introduced into such Parts of the Prison as may be best adapted for the Use of the Several Classes; proper Yards shall be allotted to the different Classes for Air and Exercise, and each Class shall have the Use of a Privy, and be furnished with a Supply of good Water; a separate sleeping Cell shall, if possible, be provided for every Prisoner; but as the Numbers may sometimes be greater than the Prison is calculated to contain, under the Arrangement required by this Act, and as it is expedient that Two Male Prisoners only should never be lodged together, a small Proportion of Cells or Rooms shall be provided for the Reception of Three or more Persons; every Prison shall contain Rooms and Places properly fitted up for the Exercise of Labour and Industry, and also a competent Number of Cells adapted to solitary Confinement, for the Punishment of refractory Prisoners, and for the Reception of such Persons as may by Law be confined therein; a Chapel shall be provided in every Prison, in such a convenient Situation as to be easy of Access to all the Prisoners, it shall be fitted up with separate Divisions for Males and Females, and also for the different Classes; it shall be strictly set apart for Religious Worship, or for the occasional Religious and Moral Instructions of the Prisoners, and shall never be appropriated to or employed for any other Purpose whatsoever; in Cases where the Justices shall deem it necessary that the Chaplain should reside, either occasionally or permanently, within the Prison or near to it, proper Apartments shall be provided therein, or in the Neighbourhood thereof, for his Accommodation. . . .

Jury Act, 22 June 1825

6 Geo. 4, c. 50   *Statutes of the United Kingdom*, 1825, 232-42.

This great consolidating statute expedited several legal processes, including the procedure for selecting juries.

Whereas the Laws relative to the Qualification and summoning of Jurors, and the Formation of Juries in *England* and *Wales*, are very numerous and complicated, and it is expedient to consolidate and simplify the same, and to increase the Number of Persons qualified to serve on Juries, and to alter the Mode of striking Special Juries, and in some other respects to amend the said Laws; Be it therefore enacted by the King's most Excellent Majesty, by and with the Advice and Consent of the Lords Spiritual and Temporal, and Commons, in this present Parliament assembled, and by the Authority of the same, That every Man, except as hereinafter excepted, between the Ages of Twenty one Years and Sixty Years, residing in any County in *England*, who shall have in his own Name or in Trust for him, within the same County, Ten Pounds by the Year above Reprizes in Lands or Tenements, whether of Freehold, Copyhold or Customary Tenure, or of Ancient Demesne, or in Rents issuing out of any such Lands or Tenements, or in such Lands, Tenements and Rents taken together, in Fee Simple, Fee Tail, or for the Life of himself or some other Person, or who shall have within the same County Twenty Pounds by the Year above Reprizes, in Lands or Tenements, held by Lease or Leases for the absolute Term of Twenty one Years, or some longer Term, or for any Term of Years determinable on any Life or Lives, or who being a Householder shall be rated or assessed to the Poor Rate, or to the Inhabited House Duty in the County of *Middlesex*, on a Value of not less than Thirty Pounds, or in any other County on a Value of not less than Twenty Pounds, or who shall occupy a House containing not less than Fifteen Windows, shall be qualified and shall be liable to serve on Juries for the Trial of all Issues joined in any of the King's Courts of Record at *Westminster*, and in the Superior Courts, both Civil and Criminal, of the Three Counties Palatine, and in all Courts of Assize, Nisi Prius, Oyer and Terminer and Gaol Delivery, such Issues being respectively triable in the County in which every Man so qualified respectively shall reside, and shall also be qualified and liable to serve on Grand Juries in Courts of Sessions of the Peace and on Petty Juries, for the Trial of all Issues joined in such Courts of Sessions of the Peace, and triable in the County, Riding or Division in which every Man so qualified respectively shall reside; and that every Man (except as hereinafter excepted) being between the aforesaid ages, residing in any County in *Wales*, and being there qualified to the Extent of Three fifths of any of the foregoing Qualifications, shall be qualified and shall be liable to serve on Juries for the Trial of all Issues joined in the Courts of Great Sessions, and on Grand Juries in Courts of Sessions of the Peace, and on Petty Juries for the Trial of all Issues joined in such Courts of Sessions of the Peace, in every County of *Wales*, in which every Man so qualified as last aforesaid respectively shall reside.

II.   Provided always, and be it further enacted, That all Peers; all Judges of the King's Courts of Record at *Westminster*, and of the Courts of Great Session in *Wales*; all Clergymen in Holy Orders; all Priests of the Roman Catholic Faith who shall have duly taken and subscribed the Oaths and Declarations required by Law; all Persons who shall teach or preach in any Congregation of Protestant Dissenters, whose Place of Meeting is duly registered, and who shall follow no secular Occupation except that of a Schoolmaster, producing a Certificate of some Justice of the Peace of their having taken the Oaths, and subscribed the Declaration required by Law; all Serjeants and Barristers at Law actually practising; all Members of the Society of Doctors of Law, and Advocates of the Civil Law, actually practising; all Attorneys, Solicitors and Proctors duly admitted in any Court of Law or Equity, or of Ecclesiastical or Admiral Jurisdiction, in which Attorneys, Solicitors and Proctors have usually been admitted actually practising, and having duly taken out their Annual Certificates; all Officers of any such Courts actually exercising the Duties of their respective Offices; all Coroners, Gaolers and Keepers of Houses of Correction; all Members and Licentiates of the Royal College of Physicians in *London* actually practising; all Surgeons being Members of One of the Royal Colleges of Surgeons in *London, Edinburgh* or *Dublin*, and actually practising; all Apothecaries certificated by the Court of Examiners of the Apothecaries Company, and actually practising; all Officers in His Majesty's Navy or Army on Full Pay; all Pilots licensed by the Trinity House of *Deptford Strond, Kingston upon Hull* or *Newcastle upon Tyne*, and all Masters of Vessels in the Buoy and Light Service employed by either of those Corporations, and all Pilots licensed by the Lord Warden of the Cinque Ports, or under any Act of Parliament or Charter for the Regulation of Pilots in any other Port; all the Household Servants of His Majesty, His Heirs and Successors; all Officers of Customs and Excise; all Sheriff's Officers, High Constables and Parish Clerks, shall be and are hereby absolutely freed and exempted from being returned, and from serving upon any Juries or Inquests whatsoever, and shall not be inserted in the Lists to be prepared by virtue of this Act as hereinafter mentioned: Provided also, that all Persons exempt from serving upon Juries in any of the Courts aforesaid, by virtue of any Prescription, Charter, Grant or Writ, shall continue to have and enjoy such Exemption in as ample a Manner as before the passing of this Act, and shall not be inserted in the Lists hereinafter mentioned.

   III. Provided also, and be it enacted and declared, That no Man, not being a natural born Subject of the King, is or shall be qualified to serve on Juries or Inquests, except only in the Cases hereinafter expressly provided for; and no Man who hath been or shall be attainted of any Treason or Felony, or convicted of any Crime that is infamous, unless he shall have obtained a free Pardon, nor any Man who is under Outlawry or Excommunication, is or shall be qualified to serve on Juries or Inquests in any Court, or on any Occasion whatsoever.

   IV. And be it further enacted, That the Clerk of the Peace in every County, Riding and Division in *England* and *Wales*, shall, within the First Week of *July* in every Year, issue and deliver his Warrant (in the Form set forth in the Schedule hereunto annexed, or as near thereto as may be) to the High Constables of each Hundred, Lathe, Wapentake or other like District, by which he shall command them to issue forth their Precepts to the Churchwardens and Overseers of the Poor of the several Parishes, and to the Overseers of the Poor of the several Townships within their respective Constablewicks, requiring them to prepare and make out, before the First Day of *September* then next ensuing, a true List of all Men residing within their respective Parishes and Townships, qualified and liable to serve on Juries according to this Act as aforesaid, and also to perform and comply with all other the Requisitions in the said Precepts contained.

   V. And be it further enacted, That every such Clerk of the Peace shall cause a sufficient Number of Warrants, Precepts and Returns to be printed, according to the several Forms set forth in the Schedule hereunto annexed, at the Expence of the

County, Riding or Division, and shall annex to every Warrant a competent Number of Precepts and Returns, for the Use of the respective Persons by whom such Precepts are to be issued and such Returns to be made.

VI.   And be it further enacted, That within Fourteen Days after the Receipt of such Warrant of the Clerk of the Peace, every High Constable shall issue and deliver his Precept (in the Form set forth in the Schedule hereunto annexed, or as near thereto as may be), together with a Competent Number of the printed Forms of Returns, to the Churchwardens and Overseers of the Poor of the several Parishes, and to the Overseers of the Poor of the several Townships within his Constablewick, requiring them by such Precept to prepare and make out a true List of all Men residing within their respective Parishes and Townships, qualified and liable to serve as Jurors as aforesaid, and to perform and comply with all the Requisitions in the said Precept contained: Provided always, that where in any Hundred, Lathe, Wapentake or other like District, there shall be more than One High Constable, in such Case the Clerk of the Peace shall issue and deliver his Warrant, together with a competent Number of the Precepts and Returns as aforesaid, to every One of such High Constables, each of whom shall be individually liable for the due Performance of the several Matters commanded in such Warrant throughout the whole of such Hundred, Lathe, Wapentake or other like District, and shall for the Nonperformance thereof be subject to all and every the Penalties by this Act imposed upon any High Constable: Provided also, that where in any Parish there shall be no Overseers of the Poor, other than the Churchwardens, such Churchwardens shall be deemed and taken to be the Churchwardens and Overseers of the Poor of such Parish within the Meaning of this Act, to all Intents and Purposes: Provided also, that where any Parish or Township shall extend into more than one Hundred, Lathe, Wapentake or other like District, either in the same or different Counties, such Parish or Township shall be deemed and taken, for all the Purposes of this Act, to be within that Hundred, Lathe, Wapentake or other like District, in which the principal Church of such Parish or Township shall be situate.

VII.   And be it further enacted, That it shall be lawful for the Justices of the Peace of any Division in *England* or *Wales*, at a Special Petty Sessions to be holden for that Purpose before the First Day of *July* in any Year, to make an Order for annexing any Extraparochial Place, whenever they shall think it expedient, to any Parish or Township adjoining thereto, for the Purposes of this Act, and a Copy of such Order shall, within Five Days from the making thereof, be served upon the Churchwardens and Overseers of such adjoining Parish, or upon the Overseers of such adjoining Township, and such Extraparochial Place shall from thence continually be deemed and taken, for all the Purposes of this Act, to be within and to form an integral Part of such Parish or Township; and the Churchwardens and Overseers of such Parish, and the Overseers of such Township, shall be, and they are hereby respectively authorized and required to make out, according to this Act, a true List of all Men qualified and liable to serve on Juries as aforesaid, residing as well in their own respective Parish or Township as in the Extraparochial Place thereto annexed, and shall from time to time perform and execute within such Extraparochial Place, for the Purposes of this Act, but for no other Purpose, all and every the same Acts, Duties, Powers and Authorities, as in their own respective

Parish or Township, and shall be as fully liable to the same Penalties for the Nonperformance thereof within such Extraparochial Place, as if they had in every Instance been mentioned in this Act with reference to such Extraparochial Place.

VIII. And be it further enacted, That the Churchwardens and Overseers of every Parish, and the Overseers of every Township, within the Meaning of this Act, shall forthwith, after the Receipt of such Precept from the High Constable, prepare and make out in Alphabetical Order a true List of every Man residing within their respective Parishes or Townships, who shall be qualified and liable to serve on Juries as aforesaid, with the Christian and Surname written at full Length, and with the true Place of Abode, the Title, Quality, Calling or Business, and the Nature of the Qualification of every such Man, in the proper Columns of the Form of Return set forth in the Schedule hereunto annexed.

IX. And be it further enacted, That the Churchwardens and Overseers of each Parish, and the Overseers of each Township, having made out according to this Act a List of every Man qualified and liable to serve on Juries as aforesaid, shall, on the Three First *Sundays* in the Month of *September*, fix a true Copy of such List upon the principal Door of every Church, Chapel and other public Place of Religious Worship within their respective Parishes or Townships, having first subjoined to every such Copy a Notice, stating that all Objections to the List will be heard by the Justices of the Peace at a Time and Place to be mentioned in such Notice, and having also signed their Names at the Foot of such Copy, and shall likewise keep the Original List, or a true Copy thereof, to be perused by any of the Inhabitants of their respective Parishes or Townships, at any reasonable Time during the Three first Weeks of the Month of *September*, without any Fee or Reward, to the End that Notice may be given of Men qualified who are omitted, or of Men inserted who ought to be omitted out of such List; and the Churchwardens and Overseers of each Parish, and the Overseers of each Township, are hereby authorized to cause a sufficient Number of Copies of such Lists, for the Purposes aforesaid, to be printed at the Expence of their respective Parishes or Townships.

X. And be it further enacted, That the Justices of the Peace in every Division in *England* and *Wales* shall hold a Special Petty Sessions for the Purposes herein mentioned, within the last Seven Days of *September* in every Year, on some Day and at some Place, of which Notice shall be given by their Clerk, before the Twentieth Day of *August* next preceding, to the High Constable and to the Churchwardens and Overseers of every Parish, and to the Overseers of every Township, within such Division; and the Churchwardens and Overseers of each Parish, and the Overseers of each Township, shall then and there produce the List of Men qualified and liable to serve on Juries as aforesaid within their respective Parishes or Townships, by them prepared and made out, as hereinbefore directed, and shall answer upon Oath such Questions touching the same as shall be put to them, or any of them, by the Justices then present; and if any Man, not qualified and liable to serve on Juries as aforesaid, is inserted in any such List, it shall be lawful for the said Justices, upon Satisfaction from the Oath of the Party complaining, or other Proof or upon their own Knowledge that he is not qualified and liable to serve on Juries, to strike his Name out of such List, and also to strike thereout the Names of Men disabled by Lunacy or Imbecility of Mind, or by Deafness, Blindness or other permanent Infirmity of Body, from serving on Juries; and it shall also be lawful for such Justices to insert in such List the Name of any Man omitted therein, and likewise to reform any Errors or Omissions which shall appear to them to have been committed in respect to the Name, Place of Abode, Title, Quality, Calling, Business or the Nature of the Qualification of any Man included in any such List: Provided always, that no Man's Name, if omitted, shall be inserted in such List, nor shall any Error or Omission in the Description of any Man in such List be reformed by the said Justices, unless upon the Application of such Men respectively, or unless such Men respectively shall have had Notice that an Application for such Purpose would be made to the Justices at such Petty Sessions, or unless the said Justices at such Sessions, or any Two of them, shall cause Notice to be given to such Men respectively, requiring them to show Cause, at some Adjournment of such Petty Sessions to be holden within Four Days thereafter, why their Names should not be inserted in such List, or why any Error or Omission in the Description of such Men in such List should not be reformed; and when every such List shall be duly corrected at such Sessions, or at such Adjournment thereof, it shall be allowed by the Justices present, or Two of them, at such Sessions or such Adjournment, who shall sign the same, with their Allowance thereof; and the High Constable shall receive every List so allowed, and deliver the same to the Court of Quarter Sessions next holden for the County, Riding or Division, on the First Day of its Sitting, at the same Time attesting on Oath his Receipt of every such List from the Petty Sessions, and that no Alteration hath been made therein since his Receipt thereof.

XI. And be it further enacted, That the respective Churchwardens and Overseers of every Parish, and the Overseers of every Township, shall for their Assistance in completing the Lists, pursuant to the Intent of this Act (upon Request made by them or any of them at any reasonable Time between the First Day of *July* and the First Day of *October* in every Year, to any Collector or Assessor of Taxes, or to any other Officer having the Custody of any Duplicate or Tax Assessment for such Parish or Township), have free Liberty to inspect any such Duplicate or Assessment, and take from thence the Names of such Men qualified to serve on Juries, dwelling within their respective Parishes or Townships, as may appear to them or any of them to be necessary or useful; and every Court of Petty Sessions and Justice of the Peace shall, upon the like Request to any Collector or Assessor of Taxes, or any other Officer having the Custody of any Duplicate or Tax Assessment, or to any Churchwarden or Churchwardens, or Overseer or Overseers, having the Custody of any Poor Rate within their respective Divisions, have the like free Liberty to inspect and make Extracts from any such Duplicate Tax Assessment or Poor Rate, for the Purpose of assisting them in the Reformation and Completion of the Jury Lists within their respective Divisions.

XII. And be it further enacted, That the Clerk of the Peace shall keep the Lists, so returned by the High Constable to the Court of Quarter Sessions, among the Records of the Sessions, arranged with every Hundred in Alphabetical Order, and every Parish or Township within such Hundred, likewise in Alphabetical Order, and shall cause the same to be fairly and truly copied in the same Order, in a Book to be by him provided for that Purpose, at the Expence of the County, Riding or Division, with proper Columns for making the Register hereinafter directed, and shall deliver the same Book to the Sheriff of the County or his Undersheriff, within Six Weeks next after the Close of such Sessions, which Book shall be called "The Jurors' Book for the Year   (inserting the Calendar Year for which such Book is to be in use); and that every Sheriff on quitting his Office shall deliver the same to the succeeding Sheriff; and that every Jurors' Book so prepared shall be brought into use on the First Day of *January* after it shall be so delivered by the Clerk of the Peace to the Sheriff or his Undersheriff, and shall be used for One Year then next following.

XIII. And be it further enacted, That every Writ of Venire Facias Juratores for the Trial of any Issue whatsoever, whether Civil or Criminal, or on any Penal Statute, in any of the Courts in *England* or *Wales* hereinbefore mentioned, shall direct the Sheriff to return Twelve good and lawful Men of the Body of his County, qualified according to Law, and the rest of the Writ shall proceed in the accustomed Form; and that every Precept to be issued for the Return of Jurors before Courts of Oyer and Terminer, Gaol Delivery, the Superior Criminal Courts of the Three Counties Palatine, and Courts of Sessions of the Peace in *England*, and before the Courts of Great Sessions and Sessions of the Peace in *Wales*, shall in like Manner direct the Sheriff to return a competent Number of good and lawful Men of the Body of his County, qualified according to Law, and shall not require the same to be returned from any Hundred or Hundreds, or from any particular Venue within the County, and that the Want of Hundredors shall be no Cause of Challenge; any Law, Custom or Usage to the contrary notwithstanding.

XIV. And be it further enacted, That every Sheriff, upon the Receipt of every such Writ of Venire Facias and Precept for the Return of Jurors, shall return the Names of Men contained in the Jurors' Book for the then current Year, and no others; and that where Process for returning a Jury for the Trial of any of the Issues aforesaid shall be directed to any Coroner, Elisor or other Minister, he shall have free Access to the Jurors' Book for the current Year, and shall in like Manner return the Names of Men contained therein, and no others: Provided always, that if there shall be no Jurors' Book in existence for the current Year, it shall be lawful to return Jurors from the Jurors' Book for the Year preceding.

XV. And be it further enacted, That every Sheriff or other Minister to whom the Return of Juries for the Trial of Issues before any Court of Assize or Nisi Prius in any County of *England*, except the Counties Palatine, may belong, shall, upon his Return of every Writ of Venire Facias (unless in Causes intended to be tried at Bar, or in Cases where a Special Jury shall be struck by Order or Rule of Court), annex a Panel to the said Writ, containing the Names alphabetically arranged, together with the Places of Abode and Additions, of a competent Number of Jurors names in the Jurors' Book, and that the Names of the same Jurors shall be inserted in the Panel annexed to every Venire Facias for the Trial of all Issues at the same Assizes or Sessions of Nisi Prius in each respective County, which Number of Jurors shall not in any County be less than Forty eight nor more than Seventy two, unless by the Direction of the Judges appointed to hold the Assizes or Sessions of Nisi Prius in the same County or One of them, who are and is hereby empowered, by Order under their or his Hands or Hand, to direct a greater or lesser Number, and then such Number as shall be so directed shall be the Number to be returned; and that in the Writ of Habeas Corpora Juratorum or Distringas, subsequent to such Writ of Venire Facias, it shall not be requisite to insert the Names of all the Jurors contained in such Panel, but it shall be sufficient to insert in the mandatory Part of such Writs respectively, "the Bodies of the several Persons in the Panel to this Writ annexed named," or Words of the like Import; and to annex to such Writs respectively Panels containing the same Names as were returned in the Panel to such Venire Facias, with their Places of Abode and Additions; and that for making the Returns and Panels aforesaid, and annexing the same to the respective Writs, the ancient legal Fee and no other, shall be taken; and that the Men named in such Panels, and no others, shall be summoned to serve on Juries at the then next Court of Assizes or Sessions of Nisi Prius for the respective Counties named in such Writs.

XVI. And be it further enacted, That if any Plaintiff or Demandant in any Cause which shall be at Issue in any of His Majesty's Courts of Record at *Westminster*, or any Defendant in any Action of Quare Impedit or Replevin which shall be so at issue, shall sue out any Writ of Venire Facias, upon which any Writ of Habeas Corpora or Distringas with the Nisi Prius shall issue, in order to the Trial of the said Issue at the Assizes or Sessions of Nisi Prius, and shall not proceed to Trial at the First Assizes or Sessions of Nisi Prius after the Teste of such Writ of Habeas Corpora or Distringas, then and in every such Case (except when a View by Jurors shall be directed as hereinafter mentioned), such Plaintiff, Demandant or Defendant, whensoever he shall think fit to try the said Issue at any other Assizes or Sessions of Nisi Prius, shall sue forth a new Writ of Venire Facias commanding the Sheriff to return anew Twelve good and lawful Men of the Body of his County, qualified according to Law, and the rest of the Writ shall proceed in the accustomed Manner; which Writ being duly returned, a Writ of Habeas Corpora or Distringas with a Nisi Prius shall issue thereupon (for which the same Fees shall be paid as in the Case of the Pluries Habeas Corpora or Distringas with a Nisi Prius), upon which such Plaintiff, Demandant or Defendant shall and may proceed to Trial as lawfully and effectually to all Intents and Purposes as if no former Writ of Venire Facias had been prosecuted in that Cause and so *toties quoties*, as the Case shall require; and if any Defendant or Tenant in any Action depending in any of the said Courts shall be minded to bring to Trial any Issue joined against him, where by the Practice of the Court he may do the same by Proviso, he shall or may, of the issuable Term next preceding such intended Trial to be had at the next Assizes or Sessions of Nisi Prius, sue out a new Venire Facias to the Sheriff in the Form aforesaid by Proviso, and prosecute the same by Writ of Habeas Corpora or Distringas with a Nisi Prius, as lawfully and effectually to all Intents and Purposes as if no former Writ of Venire Facias had been sued out or returned in that Cause, and so *toties quoties*, as the Matter shall require.

XVII. And be it further enacted, That every Sheriff or other Minister to whom the Return of Juries for the Trial of Causes in the Superior Courts of the said Counties Palatine may belong, shall, Ten Days at least before the said Courts shall respectively be held, summon a competent Number of Men, named in the Jurors Book, to serve on Juries in the said Courts, so as such Number be not less than Forty eight nor more than Seventy two, without the Direction of the Judge or Judges of the Courts for such Counties Palatine respectively; and the Sheriff or other Minister who shall summon such Jurors shall return a List containing the Names, alphabetically arranged, and the Places of Abode and Additions of the Jurors so summoned, on the First Day of the Court to be held for the said Counties Palatine respectively; and the Jurors so summoned, or a competent Number of them, as the Judge or Judges of such Courts respectively shall direct, and no others, (unless in Cases where a Special Jury shall be struck,) shall be named in every Panel to be annexed to every Writ of Venire Facias Juratores, Habeas Corpora Juratorum, and Distringas, which shall be issued out and returnable for the Trial of Causes in such Courts respectively.

XVIII. And be it further enacted, That every Sheriff or other Minister to whom the Return of Juries for the Trial of Causes in the Court of Great Sessions in any County of *Wales* may belong, shall, at least Ten Days before every Great Sessions, summon a competent Number of Men named in the Jurors' Book, so as such Number be not less than Forty eight or more than Seventy-two, without the Direction of the Judge or Judges of the Great Sessions for such County, who is and are hereby empowered, if he or they shall see cause, by Rule of Court, or by an Order of any Judge thereof, to be made in Vacation, if necessary, to direct a greater or lesser Number to be summoned; and that the Sheriff or other Minister who shall summon such Jurors shall return a List containing the Names alphabetically arranged, and the Places of Abode and Additions of the Jurors so summoned, at the First Court of the Second Day of every Great Sessions; and that the Jurors so summoned, or a competent Number of them, as the Judge or Judges of such Great Sessions shall direct, and no others (unless in Cases where a Special Jury shall be struck), shall be named in every Panel to be annexed to every Writ of Venire Facias Juratores, Habeas Corpora Juratorum and Distringas, which shall be issued out and returnable for the Trial of Causes at such Great Sessions.

XIX. And be it further enacted, That the Sheriff or other Minister to whom the Return of Jurors for the Trial of Causes in any County in *England* (except the Counties Palatine) may belong, shall cause to be made out an Alphabetical List of the Names of all the Jurors contained in the Panels to the several Writs of Venire Facias annexed as aforesaid, with their respective Places of Abode and Additions; and the Sheriff or other Minister to whom the Return of Jurors for the Trial of Causes in any County Palatine, or in any County in *Wales*, may belong, shall cause to be made out in like Manner a List of all the Jurors so summoned in such respective Counties as aforesaid; and every such Sheriff or other Minister shall keep such List in the Office of his Undersheriff or Deputy for Seven Days at least before the Sitting of the next Court of Assize or Nisi Prius, or the next Court to be holden for any County Palatine, or the next Court of Great Sessions in any County in *Wales*; and the Parties in all Causes to be tried at any such Court of Assize or Nisi Prius, or Court of any County Palatine or Great Sessions, and their respective Attornies, shall, on Demand, have full Liberty to inspect such List, without any Fee or Reward to be paid for Inspection.

XX. Provided always, and be it further declared and enacted, That the Court of King's Bench, and all Courts of Oyer and Terminer, Gaol Delivery, the Superior Criminal Courts of the Three Counties Palatine, and Courts of Sessions of the Peace in *England*, and all Courts of Great Sessions and Sessions of the Peace in

Wales, shall respectively have and exercise the same Power and Authority as they have heretofore had and exercised in issuing any Writ or Precept, or in making any Award or Order, orally or otherwise, for the Return of a Jury for the Trial of any Issue before any of such Courts respectively, or for the amending or enlarging the Panel of Jurors returned for the Trial of any such Issue; and the Return to every such Writ, Precept, Award or Order shall be made in the Manner heretofore used and accustomed in such Courts respectively, save and except, that the Jurors shall be returned from the Body of the County, and not from any Hundred or Hundreds, or from any particular Venue within the County, and shall be qualified according to this Act.

XXI. And be it further enacted, That when any Person is indicted for High Treason or Misprision of Treason, in any Court other than the Court of King's Bench, a List of the Petit Jury, mentioning the Names, Profession and Place of Abode of the Jurors, shall be given at the same Time that the Copy of the Indictment is delivered to the Party indicted, which shall be Ten Days before the Arraignment, and in the Presence of Two or more credible Witnesses; and when any Person is indicted for High Treason or Misprision of Treason in the Court of King's Bench, a Copy of the Indictment shall be delivered within the Time and in the Manner aforesaid; but the List of the Petit Jury made out as aforesaid, may be delivered to the Party indicted at any Time after the Arraignment, so as the same be delivered Ten Days before the Day of Trial: Provided always, that nothing herein contained shall any ways extend to any Indictment for High Treason in compassing and imagining the Death of the Kind, or for Misprision of such Treason where the Overt Act or Overt Acts of such Treason alleged in the Indictment shall be Assassination or killing of the King, or any direct Attempt against his Life, or any direct Attempt against his Person, whereby his Life may be endangered, or his Person may suffer bodily Harm; or to any Indictment of High Treason for counterfeiting His Majesty's Coin, the Great Seal or Privy Seal, his Sign Manuel or Privy Signet; or to any Indictment of High Treason, or to any Proceedings thereupon, against any Offender or Offenders who by any Act or Acts now in force is and are to be indicted, arraigned, tried and convicted by such like Evidence, and in such Manner as is used and allowed against Offenders for counterfeiting His Majesty's Coin. . . .

Metropolitan Police Act, 19 June 1829

10 Geo. 4, c. 44   *Statutes of the United Kingdom*, 1829, 225-30, 233-36.

This act established a police force for London and placed it under the jurisdiction of the home secretary. It is a landmark in the transition to an administrative system dependent upon professional expertise and a measure of centralization.

Whereas Offences against Property have of late increased in and near the Metropolis; and the local Establishments of Nightly Watch and Nightly Police have been found inadequate to the Prevention and Detection of Crime, by reason of the frequent Unfitness of the Individuals employed, the Insufficiency of their Number, the limited Sphere of their Authority, and their Want of Connection and Co-operation with each other: And Whereas it is expedient to substitute a new and more efficient System of Police in lieu of such Establishments of Nightly Watch and Nightly Police, within the Limits hereinafter mentioned, and to constitute an Office of Police, which, acting under the immediate Authority of One of His Majesty's Principal Secretaries of State, shall direct and controul the Whole of such new System of Police within those Limits: Be it therefore enacted by the King's most Excellent Majesty, by and with the Advice and Consent of the Lords Spiritual and Temporal, and Commons, in this present Parliament assembled, and by the Authority of the same, That it shall be lawful for His Majesty to cause a new Police Office to be established in the City of *Westminster*, and by Warrant under His Sign Manual to appoint Two fit Persons as Justices of the Peace of the Counties of *Middlesex, Surrey, Hertford, Essex*, and *Kent*, and of all Liberties therein, to execute the Duties of a Justice of the Peace at the said Office, and in all Parts of those several Counties, and the Liberties therein, together with such other Duties as shall be hereinafter specified, or as shall be from Time to Time directed by One of His Majesty's Principal Secretaries of State, for the more efficient Administration of the Police within the Limits hereinafter mentioned; and His Majesty may remove either of the said Justices, if he shall see Occasion so to do, and may, upon any Vacancy in the said Office by Death, Removal, or otherwise, appoint another fit Person as a Justice of the Peace of the Counties of *Middlesex, Surrey, Hertford, Essex*, and *Kent*, and of all Liberties therein, to execute the Duties aforesaid, in lieu of the Person making such Vacancy; and it shall be lawful for His Majesty to appoint any Person to be a Justice of the Peace by virtue of this Act, and for such Person, during the Continuance of his Appointment, to execute the Duties of a Justice of the Peace for the several Counties of *Middlesex, Surrey, Hertford, Essex*, and *Kent*, and for all Liberties therein, although he may not have any such Qualification by Estate as is required by Law in the Case of any other Person being a Justice of the Peace for any County: Provided always, that no such Person shall act as a Justice of the Peace at any Court of General or Quarter Sessions, nor in any Matter out of Sessions, except for the Preservation of the Peace, the Prevention of Crimes, the Detection and Committal of Offenders, and in carrying into Execution the Purposes of this Act.

II.   And be it enacted, That every Person to be appointed a Justice of the Peace by virtue of this Act shall, before he shall begin to execute the Duties of his Office, take the following Oath before some Justice or Baron of One of His Majesty's Courts of Record at *Westminster*; (that is to say,)

I A. B. do swear, That I will faithfully, impartially, and honestly, according to the best of my Skill and Knowledge, execute all the Powers and Duties of a Justice of the Peace, under and by virtue of an Act passed in the Tenth Year of the Reign of King *George* the Fourth, intituled *An Act for improving the Police in and near the Metropolis*.

III.   And be it enacted, That it shall be lawful for His Majesty to direct that an annual Salary, not exceeding the Sum of Eight hundred Pounds, shall be paid out of the Consolidated Fund of the United Kingdom of *Great Britain* and *Ireland*, to each of the Justices to be appointed under this Act, and that the same shall be payable quarterly.

IV. And be it enacted, That the Whole of the City and Liberties of *Westminster*, and such of the Parishes, Townships, Precincts, and Places in the Counties of *Middlesex, Surrey*, and *Kent*, as are enumerated in the Schedule to this Act, shall be constituted, for the Purposes of this Act, into One District, to be called "The Metropolitan Police District;" and a sufficient Number of fit and able Men shall from Time to Time, by the Directions of One of His Majesty's Principal Secretaries of State, be appointed as a Police Force for the Whole of such District, who shall be sworn in by One of the said Justices to act as Constables for preserving the Peace, and preventing Robberies and other Felonies, and apprehending Offenders against the Peace; and the Men so sworn shall, not only within the said District, but also within the Counties of *Middlesex, Surrey, Hertford, Essex*, and *Kent*, and within all Liberties therein, have all such Powers, Authorities, Privileges, and Advantages, and be liable to all such Duties and Responsibilities, as any Constable duly appointed now has or hereafter may have within his Constablewick by virtue of the Common Law of this Realm, or of any Statutes made or to be made, and shall obey all such lawful Commands as they may from Time to Time receive from any of the said Justices for conducting themselves in the Execution of their Office.

V. And be it enacted, That the said Justices may from Time to Time, subject to the Approbation of One of His Majesty's Principal Secretaries of State, frame such Orders and Regulations as they shall deem expedient, relative to the general Government of the Men to be appointed Members of the Police Force under this Act; the Places of their Residence; the Classification, Rank, and particular Service of the several Members; their Distribution and Inspection; the Description of Arms, Accoutrements, and other Necessaries to be furnished to them; and which of them shall be provided with Horses for the Performance of their Duty; and all such other Orders and Regulations, relative to the said Police Force, as the said Justices shall from Time to Time deem expedient for preventing Neglect or Abuse, and for rendering such Force efficient in the Discharge of all its Duties; and the said Justices may at any Time suspend or dismiss from his Employment any Man belonging to the said Police Force whom they shall think remiss or negligent in the Discharge of his Duty, or otherwise unfit for the same; and when any Man shall be so dismissed, or cease to belong to the said Police Force, all Powers vested in him as a Constable by virtue of this Act shall immediately cease and determine.

VI. And be it enacted, That if any Victualler or Keeper of any House, Shop, Room, or other Place for the Sale of any Liquors, whether spirituous or otherwise, shall knowingly harbour or entertain any Man belonging to the said Police Force, or permit such Man to abide or remain in his House, Shop, Room, or other Place during any Part of the Time appointed for his being on Duty, every such Victualler or Keeper as aforesaid, being convicted thereof before any Two Justices of the Peace, shall for every such Offence forfeit and pay such Sum, not exceeding Five Pounds, as they shall think meet.

VII. And be it enacted, That it shall be lawful for any Man belonging to the said Police Force, during the Time of his being on Duty, to apprehend all loose, idle, and disorderly Persons whom he shall find disturbing the Public Peace, or whom he shall have just Cause to suspect of any evil Designs, and all Persons whom he shall find between Sunset and the Hour of Eight in the Forenoon lying in any Highway, Yard, or other Place, or loitering therein, and not giving a satisfactory Account of themselves, and to deliver any Person so apprehended into the Custody of the Constable appointed under this Act, who shall be in Attendance at the nearest Watch-house in order that such Person may be secured until he can be brought before a Justice of the Peace, to be dealt with according to Law, or may give Bail for his Appearance before a Justice of the Peace, if the Constable shall deem it prudent to take Bail, in the Manner hereinafter mentioned.

VIII. And be it enacted, That if any Person shall assault or resist any Person belonging to the said Police Force in the Execution of his Duty, or shall aid or incite any Person so to assault or resist, every such Offender, being convicted thereof before Two Justices of the Peace, shall for every such Offence forfeit and pay such Sum, not exceeding Five Pounds, as the said Justices shall think meet.

IX. And be it enacted, That where any Person charged with any Petty Misdemeanor shall be brought, without the Warrant of a Justice of the Peace, into the Custody of any Constable appointed under this Act, during his Attendance in the Night-time at any Watch-house within the Metropolitan Police District, it shall be lawful for such Constable, if he shall deem it prudent, to take Bail by Recognizance, without any Fee or Reward, from such Person, conditioned that such Person shall appear for Examination before a Justice of the Peace, at some Place to be specified in the Recognizance, at the Hour of Ten in the Forenoon next after such Recognizance shall be taken, unless that Hour shall fall on a *Sunday* or on *Christmas Day* or *Good Friday*, and in that Case at the like Hour on the succeeding Day; and every Recognizance so taken shall be of equal obligation on the Parties entering into the same, and liable to the same Proceedings for the estreating thereof, as if the same had been taken before a Justice of the Peace; and the Constable shall enter, in a Book to be kept for that Purpose in every Watch-house, the Names, Residence, and Occupation of the Party and his Surety or Sureties, if any, entering into such Recognizance, together with the Condition thereof, and the Sums respectively acknowledged, and shall lay the same before such Justice as shall be present at the Time and Place when and where the Party is required to appear; and if the Party does not appear at the Time and Place required, or within One Hour after, the Justice shall cause a Record of the Recognizance to be drawn up, to be signed by the Constable, and shall return the same to the next General or Quarter Sessions of the Peace, with a Certificate at the Back thereof, signed by such Justice, that the Party has not complied with the Obligation therein contained; and the Clerk of the Peace shall make the like Estreats and Schedules of every such Recognizance as of Recognizances forfeited in the Sessions of the Peace; and if the Party not appearing shall apply, by any Person on his Behalf, to postpone the Hearing of the Charge against him, and the Justice shall think fit to consent thereto, the Justice shall be at liberty to enlarge the Recognizance to such further Time as he shall appoint; and when the Matter shall be heard and determined, either by the Dismissal of the Complaint, or by binding the Party over to answer the Matter thereof at the Sessions, or otherwise, the Recognizance for the Appearance of the Party before a Justice shall be discharged without Fee or Reward.

X. And be it enacted, That it shall be lawful for His Majesty to appoint a proper Person to receive all Sums of Money applicable to the Purposes of this Act, who shall be called "The Receiver for the Metropolitan Police District;" and His Majesty may remove any such Receiver, if he shall see Occasion so to do, and may upon any Vacancy in that Office, by Death, Removal, or otherwise, appoint another Person to be such Receiver; and the Receiver for the Time being shall give Security to His Majesty, in a Bond, with Two Sureties, in such Sum as the Commissioners of His Majesty's Treasury of the United Kingdom of *Great Britain* and *Ireland* shall direct, such Bond to be conditioned for the faithful Performance of his Duty by such Receiver, and for the due Application of all Monies paid to him under this Act; and the Receiver for the Time being shall receive all Sums of Money applicable to the Purposes of this Act, and shall keep an exact and particular Account thereof, and shall immediately pay all Monies, Bills, and Notes by him received under this Act into the Hands of the Governor and Company of the Bank of *England*; and the same shall be placed to an Account in the Books of the said Governor and Company, which shall be entitled "The Account of the Public Monies of the Receiver for the Metropolitan Police District," inserting the Name of the Receiver for the Time being; and the said Receiver shall draw out of the Bank from Time to Time such Sums of Money as may be necessary for the Payment of the Salaries, Wages, and Allowances to be paid as herein-after mentioned to the Persons belonging to the Police Force appointed under this Act, and also for the Payment of all other Charges and Expences in carrying this Act into Execution; and every Draft or Order for Money on the Bank of *England* drawn by the Receiver shall be countersigned by One of the Justices appointed under this Act; and all Drafts and Orders so drawn and countersigned, but not otherwise, shall be a sufficient Authority to the Bank to pay the Amount thereof to the Persons named in them, or to the Bearers of them.

XI. And be it enacted, That the Receiver shall account for the due Application of all Monies so to be drawn by him out of the Bank of *England*, and shall, once in every Six Months, and oftener, if required by One of His Majesty's Principal Secretaries of State, make out and sign a full and particular Account of all Monies which shall have been received by him under this Act, and how much thereof hath been paid by him, and for what Purposes, together with proper Vouchers for the Receipts and Payments; and such Account shall be delivered, for the Purpose of being examined and audited, either to the Commissioners for auditing the Public Accounts of this Kingdom, or to any other Person or Persons whom such Principal Secretary of State may from Time to Time direct; and the Receiver, if directed to account before the said Commissioners, shall be subject to the same Regulations and Penalties in that Respect as any Public Accountant.

XII. And be it enacted, That the Receiver, out of the Monies so received by him, shall be allowed a yearly Salary not exceeding Seven hundred Pounds, to be payable quarterly; and the Receiver, out of the same Monies, shall from Time to Time pay to the Persons belonging to the Police Force appointed under this Act, such Salaries, Wages, and Allowances, and at such Periods, as One of His Majesty's Principal Secretaries of State shall direct, and also any extraordinary Expences which they shall appear to have necessarily incurred in apprehending Offenders and executing the Orders of either of the Justices appointed under this Act, such Expences being first examined and approved of by One of the said Justices; and the Receiver shall likewise pay any further Sums which such Principal Secretary of State shall direct to be paid to any of the Persons belonging to the said Police Force, as a Reward for extraordinary Diligence or Exertion, or as a Compensation for Wounds or severe Injuries received in the Performance of their Duty, or as an Allowance to such of them as shall be disabled by bodily Injury received, or shall be worn out by Length of Service; and he shall also pay all other Charges and Expences which such Principal Secretary of State shall direct to be paid for carrying this Act into Execution. . . .

XIX. And Whereas some Time must elapse before a new Police Force can be appointed throughout the Whole of the Metropolitan Police District; Be it therefore enacted, That the Watchmen and others of the Night Police already appointed in any Parish, Township, Precinct, or Place within the Limits of the said District, may, notwithstanding the passing of this Act, continue to act in their respective Appointments, and shall be subject to the same Authorities as heretofore, until it shall be notified by the Justices appointed under this Act, that a new Police will be ready to undertake the Charge of any such Parish, Township, Precinct, or Place, on some Day to be specified in the Notice of the said Justices; which Notice shall be fixed on the Door of the Church or Chapel, or some other conspicuous Part of the Parish, Township, Precinct, or Place, on Two *Sundays* previous to the Day named for the same to take effect; and upon the Day so named the Night Watch and other Night Police appointed within any such Parish, Township, Precinct, or Place, previously to or independently of this Act, shall be discontinued; and all Powers and Authorities for assessing and levying any Rate in any such Parish, Township, Precinct, or Place, the Whole or any Part of which Rate shall be applicable to the Payment of the Night Watch or Night Police, or any Expences incident thereto, shall, so far as such Powers and Authorities relate to any whole Rate so applicable, or to that Part of any Rate which shall be so applicable, cease and determine; and all Watch-houses and Watch-boxes in any such Parish, Township, Precinct, or Place, and all Arms, Accoutrements, and other Necessaries provided at the Public Expence for the Night Watch and Night Police therein, shall be given up to such Persons as shall be named by the said Justices, for the Use and Accommodation of the Police to be appointed under this Act; and in case any Person having the Charge, Controul, or Possession of any Watch-house, Watch-box, Arms, Accoutrements, or Necessaries as aforesaid, shall neglect or refuse to give up the same as hereinbefore required, every such Offender, being convicted thereof before any Two Justices of the Peace, shall for every such Offence forfeit and pay, over and above the Value of the Property not given up, such Sum, not exceeding Five Pounds, as the said Justices shall think meet; and where there shall be any Building in any such Parish, Township, Precinct, or Place as aforesaid, a Part only of which Building shall have been heretofore used as a Watch-house, such Part shall be given up every Day from the Hour of Four in the Afternoon until the Hour of Nine in the Forenoon, for the Use and Accommodation of the Police Force to be appointed under this Act; and if any Person having the Charge, Controul, or Possession of any such Building shall neglect or refuse to give up such Part thereof for the Purposes aforesaid, or to permit free Access thereto or Egress therefrom, during any Portion of the Time above prescribed, every such Offender, being convicted thereof before any Two Justices of the Peace, shall for every such Offence forfeit and pay such Sum, not exceeding Five Pounds, as the said Justices shall think meet. . . .

XXIII. And be it enacted, That as soon as the Police to be appointed under this Act shall take charge of any Parish, Township, Precinct, or Place, whether Parochial or Extra-parochial, within the Metropolitan Police District, it shall be lawful for the Justices appointed under this Act, forthwith, and so from Time to Time, subject to the Approbation of One of His Majesty's Principal Secretaries of State, to issue a Warrant under their Hands to the Overseers of the Poor of every such Parish, Township, Precinct, or Place; by which Warrant they shall command the said Overseers, out of the Money collected for the Relief of the Poor in such Parish, Township, Precinct, or Place, to pay the Amount mentioned in the Warrant for the Purposes of the Police under this Act, or to levy such Amount as a Part of the Rate for the Relief of the Poor in such Parish, Township, Precinct, or Place, and that the Overseers shall pay over the Amount mentioned in the Warrant, to the Receiver to be appointed under this Act, within Forty Days from the Delivery of such Warrant to any One of the Overseers: Provided always, that the Sum to be paid for the Purposes of the Police under this Act shall not exceed in the Whole in any One Year the Rate of Eight-pence in the Pound on the full and fair annual Value of all Property rateable for the Relief of the Poor within such Parish, Township, Precinct, or Place, such full and fair annual Value to be computed according to the last Valuation for the Time being acted upon in assessing the County Rate; and that the Warrant shall specify the Rate in the Pound at which the Sum mentioned therein shall be computed.

XXIV. And be it enacted, That where any Persons other than the Overseers of the Poor shall, by virtue of any Office or Appointment, be authorized and required to make and collect or cause to be collected the Rate for the Relief of the Poor in any Parish, Township, Precinct, or Place within the Metropolitan Police District, such Persons, by whatsoever Title they may be called, shall be deemed to be Overseers of the Poor within the Meaning of this Act, and to be included under and denoted by the Words "Overseers of the Poor," for all the Purposes of this Act, as fully as if they were commonly called or known by the Title of Overseers of the Poor.

XXV. And be it enacted, That the Overseers of the Poor of every Parish, Township, Precinct, or Place within the Metropolitan Police District, to whom any such Warrant as aforesaid shall be issued, shall pay the Amount mentioned in the Warrant out of any Money in their Hands collected for the Relief of the Poor; and if there be no such Money in their Hands, or an insufficient Sum, they shall levy the Amount required as a Part of the Rate for the Relief of the Poor, and shall for that Purpose proceed in the same Manner, and have the same Powers, Remedies, and Privileges as for levying Money for the Relief of the Poor; and such Overseers shall pay to the Receiver the Amount mentioned in the Warrant within the Time specified for that Purpose, and at the Time of making any Payment to the Receiver shall deliver to him a Note in Writing signed by them, specifying the Amount so paid, which Note shall be kept by the Receiver as a Voucher for his Receipt of that particular Amount; and the Receipt of the Receiver, specifying the Amount paid to him by the Overseers, shall be a sufficient Discharge to the Overseers for such Amount, and shall be allowed as such in passing their Accounts with their respective Parishes, Townships, Precincts, or Places. . . .

GOVERNMENT AND THE ECONOMY

BULLION COMMITTEE REPORT

Cash payments by the Bank of England were suspended in 1797 due to the financial strains produced by the war with France. The effect of suspension was to depreciate the value of bank notes. In 1810, a select committee of the Commons (known as the Bullion Committee) recommended a resumption of specie payments; that is, the renewed convertibility of paper into gold. Its recommendations, embodied in the resolutions reprinted below, were not adopted in essence until the passage of Peel's Act in 1819.

Committee resolutions recommending a resumption of cash payments by the Bank of England, 13 May 1811

Select Speeches of the Right Honourable George Canning, ed. Robert Walsh (Philadelphia: Crissy & Markley, n.d.), 188-90.

Mr. Vansittart moved the following Resolutions:—

First.—Resolved, that it is the opinion of this Committee, that the right of establishing and regulating the legal money of this Kingdom, hath at all times been a royal prerogative, vested in the Sovereigns thereof, who have from time to time exercised the same, as they have seen fit, in changing such legal money, or altering and varying the value, and enforcing or restraining the circulation thereof, by proclamation, or in concurrence with the estates of the realm, by Act of Parliament: and that such legal money cannot lawfully be defaced, melted down, or exported.

Second.—That it is the opinion of the Committee, that the promissory notes of the Governor and Company of the Bank of England, are engagements to pay certain sums of money, in the legal coin of this kingdom; and that, for more than a century past, the said Governor and Company were at all times ready to discharge such promissory notes in legal coin of the realm, until restrained from so doing on the 25th February, 1797, by an order of council confirmed by Act of Parliament.

Third.—That it is the opinion of this Committee, that the promissory notes of the Company have hitherto been, and are at this time, held in public estimation to be equivalent to the legal coin of the realm, and generally accepted as such in all pecuniary transactions to which such coin is lawfully applicable.

Fourth.—That it is the opinion of this Committee, that, at various periods, as well as before as since the said restriction, the Exchange between Great Britain and

888

several other countries have been unfavourable to Great Britain; and that during such periods, the prices of gold and silver bullion, especially of such gold bullion as could be legally exported, have frequently risen above the mint price; and the coinage of money at the mint has been either wholly suspended or greatly diminished in amount: and that such circumstances have usually occurred when expensive naval and military operations have been carried on abroad, and in times of public danger and alarm, or when large importations of grain from foreign parts have taken place.

Fifth.—That it is the opinion of this Committee, that such unfavourable exchanges, and rise in the price of bullion, occurred to a greater or less degree, during the wars carried on by King William the Third and Queen Anne, and also during part of the Seven Years' war, and of the American war, and during the war and scarcity of grain in 1795 and 1796, when the difficulty of procuring cash or bullion increased to such a degree, that on the 25th of February, 1797, the Bank of England was restrained from making payments in cash, by an Order of Council, confirmed and continued to the present time by divers Acts of Parliament; and the exchanges became still more unfavourable, and the price of bullion higher, during the scarcity which prevailed for two years previous of the peace of Amiens.

Sixth.—That it is the opinion of this Committee, that the unfavourable state of the exchanges, and the high price of bullion, do not, in any of the instances above referred to, appear to have been produced by the restriction upon cash payments at the Bank of England, or by any excess in the issue of bank notes; inasmuch as all the said instances, except the last, occurred previously to any restriction on such cash payments; and because, as far as appears by such information as has been procured, the price of bullion has frequently been highest, and the exchanges most unfavourable, at periods when the issues of bank notes have been considerably diminished; and they have been afterwards restored to their ordinary rates, although those issues have been increased.

Seventh.—That it is the opinion of this Committee, that during the period of nearly seventy-eight years, ending with the 1st of January, 1796, and previous to the aforesaid restriction, of which period accounts are before the House, the price of standard gold in bars had been at or under the Mint price twenty-eight years and five months, and above the said Mint price forty-eight years and eleven months; and that the price of foreign gold coin has been at or under 3*l*. 18*s*. per ounce thirty-six years and seven months, and above the said price thirty-nine years and three months; and that during the remaining intervals, no prices are stated. And that, during the same period of seventy-eight years, the price of standard silver appears to have been at or under the Mint price three years and two months only.

Eighth.—That it is the opinion of this Committee, that during the latter part, and for some months after the close of the American War, during the years 1781, 1782, and 1783, the exchange with Hamburgh fell from 34. 1. to 31. 5. being about eight per cent.; and the price of foreign gold rose from 3*l*. 17*s*. 6*d*. to 4*l*. 2*s*. 3*d*. per ounce, and the price of dollars from 5*s*. 4½. per ounce to 5*s*. 11¼*d*.; and that the Bank notes in circulation were reduced between March 1782 and September 1782, from 9,160,000*l*. to 5,905,000*l*., being a diminution of above one-third, and continued (with occasional variations) at such reduced rate until December, 1784;

and that the exchange with Hamburgh rose to 34. 6., and the price of gold fell to 3*l*. 17*s*. 6*d*. and dollars to 5*s*. 1½*d*. per ounce before the 25th of February, 1787, the amount of Bank notes being then increased to 8,688,000*l*.

Ninth.—That it is the opinion of this Committee, that the amount of Bank notes in February, 1787, was 8,688,000*l*. and in February, 1791, 11,699,000*l*., and that during the same period, the sum of 10,704,000*l*. was coined in gold, and that the exchange with Hamburgh rose about 3 per cent.

Tenth.—That it is the opinion of this Committee, that the average amount of Bank notes in the year 1795 was about 11,497,000*l*., and on the 25th of February, 1797, was reduced to 8,640,000*l*. during which time the exchange with Hamburg fell from 36. to 35., being about 3 per cent.; and the said amount was increased to 11,855,000*l*. exclusive of 1,542,000*l*. in notes of 1*l*. and 2*l*. each, on the 1st February, 1798, during which time the exchange rose to 38. 2. being about 9 per cent.

Eleventh.—That it is the opinion of this Committee, that the average price of wheat per quarter in England in the year 1798, was 50*s*. 3*d*.; in 1799, 67*s*. 5*d*.; in 1800, 113*s*. 7*d*.; in 1801, 118*s*. 3*d*.; and in 1802, 67*s*. 5*d*. The amount of Bank notes of 5*l*. and upwards, was—

	£	£ £		£
In 1798, about 10,920,400, and under 5, 1,786,000				12,706,400
In 1799, about 12,048,790, and under 5, 1,626,110		making		13,674,900
In 1800, about 13,421,920, and under 5, 1,831,820		together		15,253,740
In 1801, about 13,454,370, and under 5, 2,715,180				16,169,550
In 1802, about 13,917,980, and under 5, 3,136,470				17,054,450

That the exchange with Hamburgh was, in January 1798, 38. 2.; January 1799, 37. 7.; January 1800, 32.; January 1801, 29. 8.; being in the whole a fall of above 22 per cent.; in January 1802, 32. 2.; and December 1802, 34., being in the whole a rise of about 13 per cent.

Twelfth.—That it is the opinion of this Committee, that during all the periods above referred to, previous to the commencement of the war with France in 1793, the principal states of Europe preserved their independence, and the trade and correspondence thereof were carried on conformably to the accustomed law of nations; and that, although from the time of the invasion of Holland by the French in 1795, the trade of Great Britain with the Continent was in part circumscribed and interrupted, it was carried on freely with several of the most considerable ports, and commercial correspondence was maintained at all times previous to the summer of 1807.

Thirteenth.—That it is the opinion of this Committee, that since the month of November 1806, and especially since the summer of 1807, a system of exclusion has been established against the British trade on the Continent of Europe under the influence and terror of the French power, and enforced with a degree of violence and rigour never before attempted; whereby all trade and correspondence between Great Britain and the Continent of Europe has (with some occasional exceptions, chiefly in Sweden and in certain parts of Spain and Portugal) been hazardous, precarious and expensive, the trade being loaded with excessive freights to foreign shipping, and other unusual charges; and that the trade of Great Britain with the United States of America, has also been uncertain and interrupted; and that in addition to these circumstances, which have greatly affected the course of payments between this country and other nations, the naval and military expenditure of the United Kingdom in foreign parts has, for three years past, been very great, and the price of grain, owing to a deficiency in the crops, higher than at any time whereof the accounts appear before Parliament, except during the scarcity of 1800 and 1801, and that large quantities thereof have been imported.

Fourteenth.—That it is the opinion of this Committee, that the amount of currency necessary for carrying on the transactions of the country must bear a proportion to the extent of its trade and its public revenue and expenditure; and that the annual amount of the exports and imports of Great Britain, on an average of three years, ending 5th January, 1797, was 48,732,651*l.* official value; the average amount of revenue paid into the Exchequer, including monies raised by lottery, 18,759,165*l.;* and of loans, 18,409,842*l.,* making together 37,169,007*l.;* and the average amount of the total expenditure of Great Britain 42,855,111*l.;* and that the average amount of Bank notes in circulation (all of which were for 5*l.* or upwards) was about 10,782,780*l.;* and that 57,274,617*l.* had been coined in gold during His Majesty's reign, of which a large sum was then in circulation.

That the annual amount of the exports and imports of Great Britain, on an average of three years, ending 5th January, 1811, supposing the imports from the East Indies and China to have been equal to their amount in the preceding year, was 77,971,318*l.,* the average amount of revenue paid into the Exchequer, 62,763,746*l.,* and of loans, 12,673,548*l.,* making together 75,437,294*l.;* and the average amount of the total expenditure of Great Britain 82,205,066*l.,* and that the average amount of Bank notes above 50*l.* was about 14,265,850*l.,* and of notes under 5*l.* about 5,283,320*l.,* and that the amount of gold coin in circulation was greatly diminished.

Fifteenth.—That it is the opinion of this Committee, that the situation of this kingdom, in respect of its political and commercial relations with foreign countries, as above stated, is sufficient, without any change in the internal value of its currency, to account for the unfavourable state of the foreign exchanges, and for the high price of bullion.

Sixteenth.—That it is the opinion of this Committee, that it is highly important that the restriction on the payments in cash of the Bank of England should be removed, whenever the political and commercial relations of the country shall render it compatible with the public interest.

Seventeenth.—That it is the opinion of this Committee, that under the circumstances affecting the political and commercial relations of this kingdom with foreign countries, it would be highly inexpedient and dangerous now to fix a definite period for the removal of the restriction of cash payments at the Bank of England prior to the term already fixed by the Act 44 Geo. III. c. 1, of six months after the conclusion of a definite treaty of peace.

Speech by George Canning on the Bullion Committee report, House of Commons, 13 May 1811

Select Speeches of the Right Honourable George Canning, ed. Robert Walsh (Philadelphia: Crissy & Markley, n.d.), 191-217.

Canning (1770-1827; prime minister and chancellor of the exchequer, 1827) accepted the general premises of the report, but rejected a return to full convertibility.

I should not have thought it necessary, Sir, to trouble the Committee with the expression of my sentiments in this night's debate, after the able and lucid speech of the honourable gentleman who spoke last (Mr. H. Thornton,) if I had not been desirous of addressing myself more particularly than he has done to the propositions now brought forward, in the shape of Resolutions, by the right honourable gentleman opposite to me (Mr. Vansittart,) which are the immediate subject of this night's deliberation.

I should, indeed, be unpardonable, if, after having already trespassed at so great length on the indulgence of the Committee, when the original Resolutions were under discussion, I should again expatiate upon the general subject which I conceive to have been disposed of by the vote of the former night. The present, however, is a very different question from that which was then decided. We decided by our former vote, not to adopt the practical recommendation of the Bullion Committee. In that vote I concurred. We decided farther, not to sanction and record the declaration of the principles of our money system, on which the recommendation of the Bullion Committee was founded. In that decision I did not concur, and it is one which I deeply regret; because those principles were, as I think, correctly defined in the original Resolutions; and because I think that a declaration of them, under the sanction of this House, would have been eminently useful at the present moment.

But the House having thought otherwise, and having rejected all the Resolutions of the honourable and learned gentleman; my next wish would have been, that with that rejection the whole discussion should have terminated. Why pursue it farther? The Bullion Committee is defeated; its doctrines are, at least for the present, set aside. Why could not its antagonists be contented with this negative victory? Why must they aim at the unnecessary and perilous triumph of substituting their own doctrines in the place of those which they have discomfited?

In the majority of the former night were numbered many persons who profess to disapprove of abstract propositions. Those persons must, in common consistency, oppose the propositions of the right honourable gentleman, which are to the full as abstract as the original Resolutions. In that majority were many who not only did not agree with the right honourable gentleman opposite to me, in denying the existence of a depreciation of the paper currency; but who distinctly declared their entire conviction of the existence of that depreciation, and only thought it too notorious and undeniable to require the formality of a parliamentary affirmation. Can those persons be expected by the right honourable gentleman to concur in the Resolutions which he is now bringing forward? Others again there were, who, neither admitting nor denying the depreciation, were desirous only of escaping from the necessity of a decision either way: contending that no result could be so satisfactory, as the discussion itself was mischievous. Will those persons thank the right honourable gentleman for reviving a discussion which, if it had finally closed on Friday night, would have left them in quiet possession of their doubts,— doubts which any man might very reasonably prefer to a decision in support of the right honourable gentleman's third Resolution?

Independently of this violence to the feelings and judgments of his supporters, has the right honourable gentleman no consideration for the reputation of the House of Commons itself, when he calls upon us, by voting that Resolution, to affirm a proposition, which, I will venture to say, there is no man who, without the doors of the House, could affirm with a grave countenance?

The third Resolution is the essential part, the soul and spirit, of the right honourable gentleman's system. Of the other Resolutions, the first and the fifteenth are the only two, which, in my view of the subject, appear to require particular observation. The remainder, from the fourth to the fourteenth, inclusive, contain a vast variety of statements, historical, political, commercial, financial and agricultural; some accurate, some inaccurate; but all valuable rather from their intrinsic erudition, than from any very near connexion with the subject before us. With none of these, therefore, shall I presume to meddle.

But, before I proceed to the three Resolutions in which the whole of the right honourable gentleman's argument lies, I must say a word or two in answer to a challenge of the right honourable gentleman as to his sixteenth and seventeenth Resolutions. He states, and states very truly, that I had declared myself ready to vote for those two Resolutions, provided they were prefaced and introduced, not by his own preceding Resolutions, but by the first ten of the original Resolutions moved by the honourable and learned Chairman of the Bullion Committee. The right honourable gentleman triumphs in this declaration of mine, as if it had been a concession to his argument, instead of an exposition of my own. He has caught me in a great inconsistency it seems. And what is this inconsistency? That I am ready to affirm two things irreconcilable with each other? That I would vote premises that did not bear out their conclusion, or a conclusion contradictory to its premises? No such thing; but, simply, that I am ready to adopt the premises suggested by one man, and the conclusion drawn by another. This is what he considers as an inconsistency; as if consistency had reference not to the compatibility of doctrines, but to the identity of persons holding them.

It is true that if the first ten of the original Resolutions had been carried, I should not have objected to adding to them the two concluding propositions of the right honourable gentleman. But I cannot consent to vote for them by themselves, nor if introduced by his own preceding propositions.

I am not, any more than the right honourable gentleman himself, for changing the period now fixed by law for the repeal of the Bank restriction. I could therefore have been contented to vote for the sixteenth and seventeenth of the right honourable gentleman's propositions, if those principles, respecting the standard of our money, which were luminously and accurately developed in the Resolutions moved by the Chairman of the Bullion Committee had been previously recognised and sanctioned. The truth of these principles once admitted, there might have been comparatively little danger in deciding either way the question, whether the period for returning to the strict practical application of them should be accelerated. But to decide that question in a way which should imply a denial of the truth of those principles, would be productive of a mischief than which none can be greater, except, indeed, that of adopting the right honourable gentleman's Resolutions, in which the truth of those principles is denied, not by implication, but directly.

To have abstained from adopting the original Resolutions, provided no others were agreed to in their room, would be to leave the true principles of our money system unvouched indeed, but not discredited, and to leave the Bank restriction precisely as it stands. To declare the continuance of the Bank restriction, by adopting the right honourable gentleman's sixteenth and seventeenth resolutions only, without adverting at the same time to the principles laid down by the Bullion Committee, would be to leave it matter of doubt whether the restriction was continued because those principles were false, or only because their force was overborne by considerations of expediency. This result would be unsatisfactory enough. To adopt and record the right honourable gentleman's premises as the foundation of his own conclusion, would be, in his view, no doubt, perfectly consistent; but it would be a consistency obtained at no less an expense than that of abrogating, so far as the Resolutions of this House can abrogate it, the whole system under which the currency of this country has been hitherto regulated and preserved in a state of purity and integrity, equally creditable to the character of the state, and to the increasing vigilance and anxiety of Parliament.

In matters which have been frequently the object of parliamentary revision, it is no light thing to come to Resolutions of a general and abstract nature without taking the former proceedings of Parliament for our guide.

If they who dissented from the doctrines of the Bullion Committee thought the errors of that Committee the more formidable on account of the authority by which they were inculcated, how much more cautious ought we to be in ascertaining, beyond possibility of doubt, the truth of those doctrines which we are now called upon to promulgate by the much higher authority of the House itself?

A declaration of the law by one of the branches of the Legislature ought not to be made at all but for a grave and adequate object; and, at least, ought to be unimpeachably correct.

Let us examine the right honourable gentleman's first Resolution, in this double view. First, let us see how far it is positively correct; and secondly, what is the object to which it is directed, and how far it attains that object.

That the right of establishing and regulating the legal money of this kingdom is a prerogative of the Sovereign, is most undoubtedly true: that the Sovereigns of this kingdom have at different times altered the value of such money, is also true—if by value be intended only the denomination of such money, that is, the rate at which any given quantity of gold or silver should be current within these realms. But "value," absolutely stated, is by no means a correct expression. To alter the positive intrinsic value of the precious metals, or make it other than it is by nature, and by the relation which those metals bear to other commodities, is a power, which neither kings nor parliaments have hitherto, so far as I know, arrogated; but the existence of which, to be sure, would at once put an end to all dispute, and give to the right honourable gentleman, and those who side with him, a complete triumph. If value were, indeed, the offspring of authority, there is no doubt but that paper or pasteboard, or any viler material, might be raised by that authority to a level with gold. But the only power which Sovereigns have ever yet exercised or claimed, has been to fix the rate or "current" value of coin within their own dominions.

Nor is it merely an inaccuracy of expression to omit this qualification of the word "value." It is an inaccuracy which may lead to serious misconception in a case where the whole controversy turns upon this single question, "whether there be or be not an inherent inextinguishable value in the precious metals estimated according to their relation to other commodities generally, throughout the world; and independent of any arbitrary valuation, which positive edicts or enactments can affix to them?" The right honourable gentleman's proposition, as it stands, without the addition to the word "value" of the epithets "current" or "denominative," would go to favour the notion that edicts and enactments have this power: a notion so wild that it might seem almost unnecessary to guard against it, if it, or something very like it, were not in fact the foundation of almost all the right honourable gentleman's arguments.

He cannot, however, intend to avow such a notion. He will, therefore, I presume, have no objection to qualify the word "value," by the addition of one or other of the epithets which I have suggested. So qualified, the proposition, that the Sovereign has at different times varied the "current" or "denominative" value of the coin, would be true, and perfectly harmless.

The Resolution proceeds to state, that this has been done by proclamation, "or" by Act of Parliament. This is also a true proposition; but upon this also I must observe, that it is not stated with sufficient qualification. The Resolution seems to imply that the option between the two modes of proceeding is perfectly arbitrary; that Parliament may be either admitted into, or excluded from, a share in the operation, exactly according to the will and pleasure of the Crown. But, I would take the liberty of suggesting to the right honourable gentleman, that it was not enough to state the abstract principles and theory of the constitution; it was incumbent on him to state them as they have been acted upon, as they are modified by practice, as they are to be found, not in the proclamations of Henry the VIIIth, but in the statute book; in statutes of the last century; in those of the present reign.

The Sovereign (says the right honourable gentleman) can alter the value of the coin—but can he do that at the present moment, without consent of Parliament? Can he do it against existing Acts of Parliament? Can he, except by the aid and concurrence of Parliament, repeal the Acts of the 14th of the present reign, which were passed on occasion of the last recoinage of the gold; and which must be repealed or amended, if any alteration should be made in the current value of the guinea? Unquestionably the King, according to the theory of the prerogative, can, by his proclamation, reduce or raise the denomination of the current coin. But, if by doing so, he would place his subjects in the dilemma of either disregarding his proclamation, or acting in contravention of an Act of Parliament, would it be in that case a sound or a safe statement of the law, to give a naked definition of the prerogative, without reference to the practical restrictions by which the exercise of it must necessarily be controlled?

Are the opinions of lawyers so settled and uniform upon this subject as to warrant the right honourable gentleman's sweeping and unqualified assertion? Do lawyers agree that there is no limit to the power of the Crown in this respect? that the Crown may give what current value it pleases to coin, which it may debase at its pleasure?

I do not mean to assert that all such authorities are uniformly the other way: it would, perhaps, be difficult to name that branch of the prerogative which has not been exalted to an excess in the speeches or writings of some one or other of the great Crown lawyers who have spoken or written upon the prerogative. But such opinions, even if they were more general than they will be found to be, surely could not avail against positive statute.

> The *denomination* [says Blackstone,] or the value for which the coin is to pass current, is likewise in the breast of the King; and if any unusual pieces are coined, that value must be ascertained by proclamation. In order to fix the value, the weight and the fineness of the metal are to be taken into consideration together. When a given weight of gold or silver is of a given fineness, it is then of the true *standard*, and is called sterling. Of this sterling metal all the coin of the kingdom must be made by the statute 25 Edw. III. cap. 15; so that the King's prerogative seemeth not to extend to the debasing or enhancing the value of the coin below or above the sterling value: though Sir Matthew Hale appears to be of another opinion.

The right honourable gentleman may perhaps tell me that his opinion agrees with that of Sir Matthew Hale; to which Judge Blackstone here refers as seemingly more favourable to the prerogative than his own. But if he will look into that elaborate and instructive treatise, which contains an abstract of all the learning and all the history relating to our coinage—I mean the Letter of the late Earl of Liverpool to the King—he will there find in what respects the Legislature has limited the exercise of that prerogative, since the death of Sir Matthew Hale. He will find it stated that, even in Sir Matthew Hale's opinion, "though this great prerogative is unquestionable, it is certainly advisable that in the exercise of it, whenever any great change is intended to be made, the King should avail himself of the wisdom and support of his Parliament." "Sir Matthew Hale observes," says Lord Liverpool, "that it is neither safe nor honourable for the King to imbase his coin below sterling; if it be at any time done, it is fit to be done by the assent of Parliament: and he concludes, that on such occasions '*fieri non debuit, factum valet.*' "

Even if such were still the state of the prerogative, would it justify a Resolution of the House of Commons, which describes that prerogative as absolute and indefinite, and describes "the assent of Parliament" not as that with which, according to Sir Matthew Hale, "it is fit" that such alteration should be made, if made at all; and without which, according to the same authority, *"fieri non debuit;"* but merely as that which it is optional with the Crown to ask or not to ask, according to its good pleasure? Would such a Resolution have befitted the House of Commons, even at the time when Sir Matthew Hale wrote? Is it possible to pass it now; when that prerogative, which by Sir Matthew Hale was considered as unfit to be exercised without consent of Parliament, stands actually limited by statute?

Let us now consider what is the object with a view to which this exposition of the law is made, and how far that object is attained by it.

The question in agitation is, whether our paper currency be or be not depreciated? The price of gold in that paper currency is adduced in proof of the depreciation. What answer is it to this question—what refutation is it of this proof—to say, "The King's prerogative can alter the value of the coin?"   Granted that it can. At least it has not done so in the present instance. The coin is not varied in value: the paper currency, it is contended, is. The King's prerogative has nothing to do with the paper of the Bank. The paper of the Bank is not (God forbid it ever should be!) the legal money of the realm. How, then, does the King's prerogative decide—how does it even affect—the question as to the depreciation of Bank paper? It can by no possibility affect it at all, unless the right honourable gentleman be prepared to address us in something like the following manner—"The King has a power to make whatever he pleases money; and to make that money of what value he pleases. If you murmur at this supposed depreciation of bank notes, beware that you do not provoke an exercise of the prerogative, which shall make those bank notes to all intents and purposes legal money; or which shall cure that pretended disparity between paper and gold about which you clamour so loudly, by raising the denomination of the coin."

Is this what the right honourable gentleman means to say? If so, though I do not think that there would be much wisdom in the measure, I admit that his Resolution is an apt and natural introduction to it. I can at least understand its application to the subject. I can see what is meant by it. But unless this be his meaning, I am at a loss to conceive how the assertion that the paper currency is actually depreciated, is disproved, or even touched, by the assertion of the King's prerogative to establish and alter at his pleasure the legal money of the realm.

The Resolutions on the subject of the coinage laws, which we rejected on a former night, and for which this of the right honourable gentleman is intended as a substitute, had a direct and sensible bearing upon the question in dispute. In affirming the depreciation of the paper currency, it was necessary to define the standard by which such currency was to be measured. The honourable and learned mover of the original Resolutions did define it, and, as I think, with perfect truth as well as precision. Can it be the right honourable gentleman's intention, by stating with such laxity the absolute and indefinite power of the Crown over the legal money of the realm, to imply that, where every thing is liable to such arbitrary fluctuation, there can be no fixed standard by which to measure the value of the currency? If his argument be good for any thing, it can only be so by being pushed to this extent: but even then it affords no answer to the Resolutions of the honourable and learned gentleman. Those resolutions asserted that the paper currency is in a state of depreciation, if measured by the existing standard of our legal currency. The right honourable gentleman does not contradict this assertion; he passes it by; he says nothing at all as to what the standard of our currency really is; but contents himself with disparaging its fitness as a measure of value, by insinuating that, whatever it may be at the present moment, the King has, by his prerogative, an unlimited power of changing it.

But, again, even if the King has this power, it is not pretended that he has in point of fact thought fit to exercise it. If any part of our currency has been varied in its value, either in respect to another part of it, or in respect to the standard, it is not pretended that this has been done by the interposition of the Crown. The complaint is, however, that such a variation has in fact taken place in the value of Bank paper. What answer is it to this complaint, to say, that though the King has not, yet he might, if he pleased, have made a like variation in the current value of the coin?

There is, however, another operation of the prerogative, which, to make his definition complete, the right honourable gentleman ought to have noticed: but which he has altogether omitted, perhaps because he saw that it would bear inconveniently upon his argument: I mean the King's power of giving currency to foreign coin within his own dominions. Now one of the plainest illustrations of the actual depreciation of our paper currency has been derived from the change which has been recently made in the current value of the dollar.

"The King," says Mr. Justice Blackstone in the same part of his work to which I have already referred, "may also, by his proclamation, legitimate foreign coin, and make it current here: declaring at what value it shall be taken in payments. But this, I apprehend, ought to be by comparison with the standard of our own coin; otherwise the consent of Parliament will be necessary."

"This great prerogative," says Lord Liverpool in his Letter to the King, "which the Kings of this realm have immemorially enjoyed and exercised, of giving currency to the coins made at their mint, and sometimes to foreign coins, at a determinate rate or value, and of enhancing and debasing them at their pleasure, is of so important and delicate a nature, and the justice and honour of the Sovereign, as well as the interests of the people, are so deeply concerned in it, that it ought to be exercised with the greatest judgment and discretion."

We here see the limitations in point of law, which, in the opinion of so able a lawyer as Blackstone,—and those in point of prudence and discretion which, in the opinion of so profound a practical statesman as the Earl of Liverpool, would have governed the exercise of the prerogative of the Crown in giving currency to the dollar. Have these limitations, has this caution, been observed in fixing the rate at which the dollar now circulates? The intrinsic value of the dollar "by comparison with the standard of our own coin,"—as compared, for example, with the British crown piece—is nearly in the proportion of nine to ten. The current rate at which the dollar circulates, as compared with the crown piece, is now in the proportion of eleven to ten.

By what authority has so strange an anomaly been introduced into our money system?—an anomaly which, according to Blackstone, the Crown, in the exercise of its prerogative, is bound to avoid. By an ordinance of the Bank. The prerogative of the Crown, we have seen, might have given currency to the dollar: but it could only have done so at a rate proportionate to its intrinsic value, as compared with the standard of the realm; or for any deviation from that standard it must have obtained the concurrence of Parliament. But the thing is done. It is one of the main features of our present system. It makes one of the grounds of the complaint which the right honourable gentleman proposes to answer by the authoritative language of his first Resolution. And how does he answer it? By referring to the prerogative of the Crown as the authority by which alone the currency can be regulated; and yet omitting altogether a part of that prerogative, so essential to the present subject, as the power of giving currency to foreign coin! He omits it—Why?—Evidently because he could not state it, without acknowledging, at the same time, that the rules by which the exercise of that part of the prerogative has always been governed, have been entirely neglected in the issue of the dollar at its present rate; and because he could not make that acknowledgment without avowing the depreciation of our currency.

Before the late ordinance of the Bank, nine crown pieces would have exchanged for ten dollars. Now, ten dollars cannot be had for less than eleven crowns. If this be not depreciation, what is it? Perhaps I shall be warned that this argument proves too much; for that the depreciation here established would be that of the lawful coin of the realm,—not of the paper currency, of which alone the depreciation is asserted.

I answer—the depreciation of the lawful coin in respect to the dollar is effected through the medium of the paper. If the crown piece and the dollar circulated together without the intervention of the paper, it would be impossible that they should bear to each other any other relation than that which arises naturally from their respective intrinsic values. It is by the intervention of the paper, which measures the one according to its nominal, the other according to its intrinsic value, that this relation is forcibly inverted, and the more valuable is degraded below the less valuable coin.

I shall probably be told, however, that the dollar is a mere token; it is no more than a promissory note in silver, which no man is bound to accept in payment. This is perfectly true: but it is a singular argument to be relied upon by the practical school, since it is no less true that the dollar, such as it is, constitutes in fact by far the greater part of the metallic currency now in circulation. In the same way it has been argued, that a bank note is not a legal tender—that no man is bound to take a bank note from his neighbour in satisfaction of a just debt. This also is true: but it is no less so that the public creditor is bound to receive bank notes, or at least can get nothing else, in payment of his demand upon the state; and it seems to be no great consolation to the public creditor to be assured that what he is compelled to take from the Government, nobody is compellable to take from him.

This being then practically the state of our currency, what satisfaction, I must again ask, does the first Resolution of the right honourable gentleman afford to those who complain of the depreciation of bank paper, by stating, and stating, as it appears, incorrectly, the money prerogatives of the Crown?—prerogatives, which, in respect to the bulk of our currency, the paper, have no operation at all; and which, in respect to the small portion of metallic currency which we possess, have been suffered to lie dormant and passive, while that currency has been regulated, by another authority, on principles directly contrary to those by which the Crown must have been guided in giving currency to a foreign coin.

This Resolution, therefore, the House of Commons cannot but reject: first, because it is defective as a definition of the prerogative which it affects to define; secondly, because it is not applicable to the only points about which there is any dispute,—namely, bank paper, which is out of the province of the prerogative; and the foreign silver currency, of which in fact it has taken no cognizance; and lastly, because it is calculated, by implication at least, to exclude Parliament from all share in the regulation of a subject, in which, in all good times, Parliament has claimed it as a right, and felt it a duty, to interfere, whenever the occasion has called for its interference.

It is impossible to pass over the second Resolution without observing, that it remains liable to the objection which I took the liberty of making to it in a former debate. The words "on demand" are still omitted: I trust, the right honourable gentleman intends to supply this omission. I must say, that the persisting in it would afford just ground of serious suspicion and alarm.

I now come to the main Resolution of all, the third. This it is that contains the sum and substance of all the right honourable gentleman's arguments and doctrines; and to which I cannot believe it possible, until the vote shall actually have passed, that any assembly of reasonable men can be persuaded to give their concurrence. The Resolution is as follows:

> III. That the Promissory Notes of the said Company have hitherto been, and are at this time, held in public estimation to be equivalent to the legal coin of the Realm, and generally accepted as such in all pecuniary transactions to which such coin is legally applicable.

The right honourable gentleman, in stating what he considered to be the effect of this Resolution, made use of an expression which does indeed most truly describe its character, and the character of that assent which he reckons upon obtaining to it. By this Resolution, said the right honourable gentleman, we "pledge ourselves to believe the equivalency of bank notes to coin." Pledge ourselves to believe! This is perhaps more than any man ever before avowed of himself; but certainly more than any man ever openly declared his intention to exact from others. Belief is not usually matter of volition; therefore, one should think, it cannot reasonably be made matter of undertaking and engagement. Of all martyrs of whatever faith, I have always conceived the just praise to be, that they adhered stedfastly to a belief founded on sincere conviction, not that they anticipated that conviction by pledging themselves beforehand what their belief should be. The right honourable gentleman's martyrdom is of a superior description: it not only professes its faith, but creates it: and to say the truth, it does require a faith, rather of the will than of the understanding, to believe the doctrine which the right honourable gentleman has promulgated in this third Resolution.

The right honourable gentleman, however, has not done full justice to his own Resolution. The pledge which it contains goes much farther than he describes. It is not we, the resolvers, that are pledged by it to the creed of the right honourable gentleman: it pledges all mankind, except ourselves. It is so contrived, that even I might consistently vote for it, denying as I do every syllable of the doctrine which it contains. Whatever other merit the Resolution may want, this is at least ingenious, and I think I may venture to say it is altogether new in parliamentary proceeding.

The object of the right honourable gentleman is to settle the public mind on a question on which there is a great division of opinion. There are various modes in which the public mind may be settled in matters depending on positive authority. The first is a proclamation by the King, where the subject matter is one to which the Royal prerogative is of itself competent; and such the right honourable gentleman contends this matter to be. A second mode is by Act of Parliament, in which the united wisdom of the two branches of the Legislature is sanctioned by the authority of the Crown. A third mode is by concurrent resolution of the two Houses of Parliament declaring their joint opinion. A fourth mode is, by resolution of one or other House of Parliament, declaring its opinion alone. But to these four recognized modes, it remained for the ingenuity of the right honourable gentleman to add a fifth—that of a resolution of the House of Commons, declaring, not its own opinion, but that of the litigants themselves.

Are bank notes equivalent to the legal standard coin of the realm? This is the question which divides and agitates the public opinion. I, says the right honourable gentleman, will devise a mode of settling this question to the satisfaction of the public. By advising a proclamation? No.—By bringing a bill into Parliament? No —By proposing to declare the joint opinion of both Houses, or the separate opinion of one? No.—By what process, then? Why, simply by telling the disputants that they are, and have been all along, however unconsciously, agreed upon the subject of their variance; and gravely resolving, for them, respectively, an unanimous opinion. This is the very judgment, I should imagine, which Milton ascribes to the venerable Anarch, whom he represents as adjusting the disputes of the conflicting element:

> Chaos umpire sits,
> And by decision more embroils the fray.

That the public would have bowed in reverence and submission to the pronounced opinion of the House of Commons, cannot be doubted: but when the House of Commons speaks, not as a judge but as an interpreter, it can hardly expect to be regarded as infallible by those whose sentiments it professes to interpret.

"In public estimation," says the right honourable gentleman's Resolution, "bank notes and coin are equivalent." Indeed? What then is become of all those persons who, for the last six months, have been by every outward and visible indication evincing, maintaining, and inculcating an opinion diametrically opposite? Who wrote that multitude of pamphlets, with the recollection of which one's head is still dizzy? What is become of the whole class of readers of those pamphlets, of whom to my cost I was one; and a great number of whom at least were convinced, like me, of the actual depreciation of our paper currency? Were these writers and readers no part of the public? or does the right honourable gentleman apprehend that his arguments must have wrought their conversion? Far be it from me to say that, whatever I may think of his arguments, the authority of his name would not have great weight with me and with the public. Therefore do I regret that, if he does not think fit to frame his Resolution in the name of the House of Commons, he should not at least resolve in his own name the equivalency which he is so bent upon establishing. A Resolution, importing that "in the estimation" of the right honourable gentleman individually, "bank notes are equivalent to the legal coin of the realm," though I do not pretend to say it would carry all the force of a decision of the legislature, would yet be a prodigious comfort even to those who are hardened in their disbelief of that equivalency; as it would show them in what quarter to apply when they wished to make an exchange on equal terms.

Nor would such a declaration of individual opinion, though unusual, be wholly without example. I saw the other day an address to the public from a patriotic lottery-office keeper, which in truth I should think had not escaped the right honourable gentleman's notice, since his third resolution is nearly a transcript of it. This worthy distributor of the favours of Fortune disclaims, in the most indignant terms, the intention to "make any distinction between bank notes and the current coin of the realm." He is "at all times ready," he says, "to serve the public with tickets or shares, on equal terms for either." Why should not the right honourable gentleman give a similar demonstration of the sincerity of his own opinion? It is obvious that if the lottery-office keeper, instead of speaking for himself, had only declared that "in the estimation of the public," bank notes and coin were equal, his assurance would have gone for but little: and I really cannot see why, in adopting, as he has done, the very words of the lottery advertisement, the right honourable gentleman should decline adopting the advertiser's test of his sincerity.

I must, however, observe, that the right honourable gentleman carries his doctrine somewhat farther than his prototype, the lottery office-keeper. The advertisement is much more cautiously worded than the Resolution. The advertisement only affirms the equivalency of bank notes to the "current" coin of the realm. The Resolution says that they are equivalent to the "legal" coin. Now the assertion of the advertisement may be perfectly safe from contradiction, forasmuch as "current" coin of the realm, there is at this moment none. But the "legal" coin of the realm, though driven out of circulation, is capable of strict definition. The right honourable gentleman's proposition therefore admits of a test, which the advertiser's does not. To make his proposition perfect, the right honourable gentleman ought to define both those things which he declares to be equivalent to each other. Bank notes he has defined in his second Resolution: they are "engagements to pay certain sums of money in the legal coin of this kingdom." But he has omitted to define the "legal coin."

With his leave, I will venture to remind him that one pound in sterling money of this realm, is either 20/21 of a guinea, weighing not less than 5dwts. 8grs. standard fineness; or it is 20/62 of a lb. of standard silver. Does the right honourable gentleman object to either of those definitions? If not, does he maintain his proposition of equivalency? Does he maintain that a one-pound note is equivalent to 20/21 of a lawful guinea, or to 20/62 of a lb. of standard silver? Does he not know that a guinea is intrinsically worth not a one-pound note, with one shilling in addition, but with the addition of four or five shillings, at the present moment?— and that so far from purchasing nearly the third part of a lb. of standard silver, a bank note of one pound would now purchase little more than the fourth part of it?

But the right honourable gentleman warns us, that we overlook the force and real meaning of the word "legal" as employed in his Resolution. He alludes not to the laws which have fixed the standard, and which ensure the weight and purity of our coin; but to those which provide by wholesome penalties against the influence of its real upon its denominative value. The gold of a guinea may be worth what we will; the Resolution applies only to the gold in a guinea. It does not say that a bank note is worth as much as a guinea. It says only that the guinea can pass for no more than the bank note. It ties the living to the dead, and then pronounces them equal to each other. The gold which is necessary to constitute a guinea, may be worth twenty-six or twenty-seven shillings. The right honourable gentleman's business with it commences only when it has received the stamp and sanction of the Sovereign. It is then that, degraded by this distinction, and restricted by this guarantee, it looses about a fifth of its value, and becomes worth only a one-pound note and one shilling.

Be it so. This then may be the state of the law: but how does this prove "public estimation?" If the Resolution had purported merely that by law the guinea could pass for no more than twenty-one shillings, perhaps the right honourable gentleman may have the law on his side. But this proposition he had the sagacity to see would not answer his purpose. It would do nothing for the bank note. It would settle the proportion between gold and silver coin; but not between either of those metals and bank paper. Bank paper, until it is made the paper of the state, and a legal tender (which as yet happily it is not,) must depend upon confidence for its value; and I am afraid that confidence may rather be imparied than restored by such a Resolution as the right honourable gentleman's.

There is, however, yet one addition, which qualifies the right honourable gentleman's proposition. Bank notes are not only "equivalent to legal coin," it seems, but are "generally accepted as such;" which to be sure it is natural to expect they should be, if equivalent. There are so accepted, however, not in all transactions. No—only in "transactions to which such coin is legally applicable." There are transactions, then, it seems, in which they are not accepted as equivalent? Yes; but those transactions are not legal ones. Is the purchase of gold bullion a legal transaction? I presume it is. A pound of gold bullion is at this moment worth about 58*l*. 16*s*. in bank notes: 58*l*. 16*s*. in guineas, according to their current value, makes fifty-six guineas. Now according to their current value, makes fifty-six guineas. Now forty-four and a half of these guineas, we know, weigh exactly one pound. The right honourable gentleman, therefore, means gravely to affirm that there exist persons who will with equal readiness give 58*l*. 16*s*. in bank notes, or fifty-six golden guineas, in payment for a commodity which is intrinsically worth exactly forty-four guineas and a-half. It warms one's heart to hear such heroic instances of more than Roman virtue: but I must be permitted to doubt whether they can be truly stated to be as "general," as the right honourable gentleman supposes. I doubt whether even the patriotic lottery-man, from whom the right honourable gentleman has borrowed his third Resolution, would make such a sacrifice as this to the laws of his country. I doubt whether the right honourable gentleman himself does not stand the single instance of such striking self-devotion: and would again submit to him, therefore, whether his third Resolution, instead of affirming any thing about the public, ought not to run singly in his own name.

But, after all, is the right honourable gentleman sure that he is prepared to define exactly, at this moment, the legality or illegality of interchanging guineas and bank notes, at any other than the nominal current value? What cognizance does the law take of the rate at which bank notes shall pass? Is there any law which touches this matter? If any body had such a fancy for bank notes, and differed so entirely from the Bullion Committee, and from the right honourable gentleman, as to think them not only not depreciated in respect to coin, but as worth being bought up in coin at a premium; is there any law which would prevent them from gratifying his taste in this particular? If for more, might he not also buy them for less, than their nominal value? Is there any law to prevent that? The man who has been convicted, and is now expecting judgment for buying guineas at a premium, might he not justly aver that he had only sold bank notes at a loss? Is there any law which forbids that? The right honourable gentleman may tell me, that this question is at this very moment before the judges of the land, by whose determination the conviction to which I have referred, will be either confirmed or reversed. And so I tell the right honourable gentleman; and from that very circumstance, from the law on that subject being in such a state of uncertainty as to require a reference to the judges, it is, in my opinion, unseemly, and must be most unsatisfactory, for the House of Commons to assume the law to be such as the right honourable gentleman's Resolution declares it.

But, supposing the declaration of the law by the right honourable gentleman's Resolution to be correct, how does it bear out his assertions as to "public estimation?"—Does he not know—is it not notorious—has it not been admitted in the course of this debate—that in one part of the United Kingdom, at least in Ireland, so far are bank notes from being "equivalent to the legal coin in the public estimation," that a premium is openly given for guineas? Does the right honourable gentleman forget, that the House of Commons to which he proposes his Resolution, is the House of Commons of Ireland as well as of Great Britain? And can he conceive a proceeding more likely to bring that House of Commons into contempt with the people of Ireland, than that, with the perfect knowledge which we have that they are every day exchanging bank notes against guineas at a discount, we should come to a Resolution that—not in our estimation, but in theirs—bank notes and guineas are equivalent?

When Buonaparte, not long ago, was desirous of reconciling the nations under his dominion to the privations resulting from the exclusion of all colonial produce, he published an edict, which commenced in something like the following manner:— "Whereas sugar made from beet-root or the maple-tree is infinitely preferable to that of the sugar-cane. . . ." and then proceeded to denounce penalties against those who should persist in the use of the inferior commodity. The denunciation might be more effectual than the right honourable gentleman's Resolution; but the preamble did not go near so far; for though it asserted the superiority of the maple and beet-root sugar, it rested that assertion merely on the authority of the state, and did not pretend to sanction it by "public estimation."

When Galileo first promulgated the doctrine that the earth turned round the sun, and that the sun remained stationary in the centre of the universe, the holy fathers of the Inquisition took alarm at so daring an innovation, and forthwith declared the first of these propositions to be false and heretical, and the other to be erroneous in point of faith. The Holy Office "pledged itself to believe" that the earth was stationary and the sun moveable. This pledge had little effect in changing the natural course of things: the sun and the earth continued, in spite of it, to preserve their accustomed relations to each other, just as the coin and the bank note will, in spite of the right honourable gentleman's Resolution.

The reverend fathers, indeed, had the advantage of being enabled to call in the aid of the secular arm, to enforce the acceptance of their doctrines. I confess, I am not wholly without apprehension that some of the zealous advocates for the right honourable gentleman's doctrine may have it in contemplation to employ similar means of proselytism. There is something ominous in that mixture of law and opinion, which pervades the right honourable gentleman's Resolution. The business of law is with conduct; but when it is put forward to influence opinion, pains and penalties are seldom far behind. I like but little the period of our history, to which my honourable and learned friend, the Attorney-General, was obliged to go back to find a penal statute for settling opinions upon the value of money   that statute upon which the late convictions have taken place, and upon the applicability of which to the present times the Judges are now deliberating. This statute was passed at a period when our coin had been debased, in the course of three years, considerably upwards of £200 per cent,—and when the total debasement, as compared with the original standard, was not less than £355 per cent. The consequence of this debasement, as stated by Lord Liverpool, was, that merchants and tradesmen increased the price of every article which they had to sell To counteract this effect, Government tried every method to keep up the value of the debased coin; prices were set on all the necessary articles of consumption; laws were passed for regulating the manner of buying and selling; the law against regraters, forestallers, and engrossers, since repealed, was passed on that occasion. Amongst those admirable and judicious efforts of wholesome and enlightened legislation, was enacted the law for inflicting penalties on those who should "exchange any coined gold or coined silver at a greater value than the same was or should be declared, by His Majesty's proclamation, to be current for within his dominions."

Such is the law which, according to the right honourable gentleman, secures the equivalency of the different sorts of our currency. Such is the shelf from which that law has been taken down and brought into use on the present auspicious occasion: a law passed at a time which the late Lord Liverpool forcibly describes as a "period of convulsion in our monetary system," and in company with laws which have since been repealed as a disgrace to the statute book. Faulty, however, as our legislation appears to have been at the period to which we are referring, it at least did not fall into the absurdity of declaring such laws to be the opinions of the people. If the right honourable gentleman is determined to force opinions to conform to his law, he must come down a few years later in our history. He must pass from the reign of Edward the VIth, to that of Queen Mary, to find the most approved method of applying the operation of law to the reformation of speculative opinions.

Even in times, however, of such ignorance, and such licentious theory, in respect to the value of money, there were not wanting in one part of this island shrewder spirits, who saw the errors into which the English Government were running, and determined to guard against their effects, at least upon themselves. In the year 1529, it is related in a note to Lord Liverpool's Treatise,

> Gavin Dunbar, Bishop of Aberdeen, in a contract with William Sutherland, of Duffus, stipulated, that "if it should happen that the money of Scotland, or of any other kingdom, which passes in Scotland, be raised to a higher price than it is now taken in payment for, whereby the reverend father, his heirs or assigns, be made poorer or in a worse condition, he the said William Sutherland should pay to the possessors (whoever they may be) of the annual rent reserved therein, for every mark of thirty-two pennies, one ounce of pure silver of certain fineness, or else its true value in the usual money of the kingdom of Scotland."

This contract took place about twenty years before the statute of Edward VI. If that statute shall be revived and acted upon, and if the doctrine of the right honourable gentleman's Resolutions shall be sanctioned by Parliament, it requires no great stretch of apprehension to foresee that men will, ere long, endeavour to guard themselves against the effects of such a system by resorting to contracts of a similar nature.

I have now done with the right honourable gentleman's third Resolution. I will only again say, that if any man had mentioned it to me out of this House as a proposition which the right honourable gentleman intended to offer for our acceptance, I should have utterly disbelieved him: I should have considered such a rumour as a mere device on the part of his opponents, to place in the strongest light imaginable the absurdity to which, if pushed to all their consequences, the right honourable gentleman's arguments were capable of going.

Passing over the statistical Resolutions, from the fourth to the fourteenth inclusive, I come now to the fifteenth, which contains the right honourable gentleman's doctrine of exchanges.

This Resolution partakes, in a very striking degree, of the faults which I had occasion to remark upon in the first of the series to which it belongs. From the vague and imperfect manner in which it is expressed, the proposition intended to be conveyed by it is rather insinuated than affirmed. The right honourable gentleman does not distinctly deny that the state of our currency has any influence on the foreign exchanges, or on the price of bullion; at the same time, he certainly does not admit that it has any such influence. He only asserts that there are other causes "sufficient to account for the unfavourable state of the exchange, and the high price of bullion, without any change in" (what he calls) "the internal value of our currency."

Now it cannot escape so accurate an understanding as that of the right honourable gentleman, that this mode of stating his argument, is not an answer to the main points in dispute, but an evasion of them. The Bullion Report asserts that our paper currency is depreciated, and that the depreciation of our currency has raised the price of gold, and turned and kept the foreign exchanges against us. The right honourable gentleman replies, not by denying both these assertions, but by affirming with respect to the latter, that the imputed consequences may have been produced by other causes, without the existence of the cause specifically assigned for them.

We know, indeed, from the preceding part of the right honourable gentleman's argument, that he does deny the depreciation of our currency. So far he is perfectly intelligible. But as to the second proposition, "that the depreciated currency has occasioned the rise in the price of bullion and the unfavourableness of the foreign exchanges," are we to understand him as saying, that a depreciated currency would not have those effects? or only, that as our currency is not depreciated, such effects cannot in this instance be attributable to that cause?

If he admits that such would be the natural effects of a depreciated currency, admitting at the same time (as he does) that such effects do exist, the whole of his argument is destroyed by his own admissions. The utmost advantage that he could then derive, even from the undisputed admission of all the facts enumerated in his statistical Resolutions—of his prices of stocks, and prices of corn, his exports and imports, and revenue and expenditure—would be to show that there are other causes which may enter for something into the degree of the rise in the price of bullion, and into the degree of the unfavourableness of the exchange, which nobody denies.

But to acknowledge the tendency of a depreciated currency to produce certain effects, to acknowledge these effects to have been produced to an extent, and to have continued for a length of time, unexampled in the history of the country,—and then to expect that upon the mere *dictum* of the right honourable gentleman, his adversaries in the argument shall consent to ascribe those effects wholly to other causes, of which they deny the sufficiency, altogether excluding the operation of that one, the efficacy of which he himself admits, is to reckon upon a degree of ductility in those with whom he argues, which even the right honourable gentleman's authority is not entitled to command.

On the other hand, does the right honourable gentleman content, that the depreciation of our currency, even if it existed, would not affect the exchange? To argue that it would not affect the price of bullion in that currency, is certainly more than he can venture. But it has been contended by others who take the same side with him, that depreciation "of internal value" in the currency of a country has no tendency to alter the foreign exchange. Is this the right honourable gentleman's meaning?

By "internal value," I now understand the right honourable gentleman to signify not "intrinsic value," as I was at first inclined to suppose, but value in internal or domestic currency, as opposed to value abroad. The proposition, then, of those who push the right honourable gentleman's argument to its extent is, that the currency of a country may be depreciated to an indefinite degree, and yet, if the inhabitants of that country continue, no matter whether voluntarily or by legal compulsion, to receive that depreciated currency at its full nominal value, the foreigner has no business with it, and the foreign exchange would not exhibit any symptom of being affected by it. The very definition of exchange, about which I apprehend there is no dispute, is of itself sufficient to confute this doctrine. The par of exchange between any two countries, being an equal quantity of precious metal in the respective currencies of those countries, how is it possible, that if, by any process, the currency of one of those countries shall cease to contain or to represent that quantity of precious metal which it did represent or contain when the par of exchange with the other country was assigned—the currency of that other country remaining precisely the same—there should not take place a proportionate variation in the rate of the exchange? To say that the rate of exchange will continue unaltered, when one of the currencies between which the comparison is made has lost part of its value, is to say, in other words, that an equation is not destroyed by a change in the value of one of its terms.

We should be sufficiently alive to the fallacy of such a doctrine, if applied to the currency of other countries. In the edict lately published in Austria, which has been referred to more than once in the course of these debates, while a gradual depreciation, amounting in the end to no less than £400 per cent. is acknowledged, and the paper directed to be current henceforth at £400 per cent. below its nominal value; sundry excellent reasons are given why, in Austria, in the particular circumstances of that country, this depreciation ought to occasion no manner of alarm; and especially why foreigners ought not to consider it as vitiating or confounding the transactions of exchange. The foreign creditors of Austria, however, probably entertain a very different opinion: and it is a curious fact, which has been vouched to me on what I believe to be unquestionable authority, that even before the Austrian paper money was depreciated to the present extravagant degree, the monied men on the continent, who were engaged in loans to the Emperor, were in the habit of stipulating that those loans, of repaid any where else than at Hamburgh or at Amsterdam, should be repaid, not in the currency of Austria, or of any other country, according to its denomination, but in specific quantities of gold or silver. And why this exception in favour of Hamburgh and Amsterdam? For a reason which at once explains the nature of exchange, and the true principles of value in money, namely, that at the Banks of Hamburgh and Amsterdam, all payments are made, not in reference to coins of any country or any denomination, but by the transfer from the debtor to the creditor of a specific quantity of bullion.

Can we really flatter ourselves, then, that the currency of this kingdom might be depreciated with impunity so far as relates to transactions with foreign countries? If a bill upon England for 46*l*. 14*s*. 6*d*. would heretofore have purchased, on the exchange of Hamburgh or Amsterdam, a credit on those Banks for a pound of gold bullion, and if a pound of gold bullion cannot now be purchased in England for less than 58*l*. in English currency, we can imagine that, nevertheless, the bill upon England for 46*l*. 14*s*. 6*d*. will still purchase a pound of gold at Hamburgh or Amsterdam? Yet this is, in fact, the proposition of those who contend that an alteration in the value of the internal currency of a country does not proportionably affect the foreign exchange.

But while this is the argument of many who have taken part in the debate— whilst it is covertly, though not avowedly, the argument of the right honourable gentleman's fifteenth Resolution—it is not the argument of my right honourable friend the Chancellor of the Exchequer, who has admitted the influence of the internal currency of a country upon its foreign exchanges, by admitting that a diminution in the quantity of our paper would tend to turn the exchanges in our favour. Does the right honourable gentleman agree in this admission, or differ from it? If he differs, I refer him for conviction to my right honourable friend: if he agrees, there is no escape from the conclusion to which this admission leads—that the unfavourableness of the exchange, which would be, in part at least, cured by the diminution in the amount, and consequent rise in the value of our paper currency, is, in part at least, occasioned by the excess and consequent depreciation of it.

What then becomes of the assertion of the right honourable gentleman's fifteenth Resolution, whichever sense we assign to it? If it is meant to deny the connexion of internal currency with foreign exchange, can the House consent to adopt a vote so directly at variance with the fact? If, admitting that connexion, it is meant only to deny its effect now, why, I should be glad to know, is the present time to afford an exception to an universal rule? What is there now to suspend the operation of principles, not dependent upon circumstances, but inherent in the nature of things? There is a great stagnation of commerce it is true, but that stagnation of commerce is not peculiar to this country. The continent shares largely in all the distress which the decrees of the tyrant of the continent produce; and yet it is in comparison with the continent that the exchanges are in our disfavour. True, we are carrying on an expensive and extended war; but the exchanges have been permanently against us in peace as well as in war, when the same cause, a depreciated currency, has operated to produce that effect. In 1696, a period of war, the deterioration of our silver, then our standard coin—in 1773, a time of peace, the deterioration of our gold coin, were indicated alike by the long continued unfavourableness of the foreign exchanges. In both instances the reformation of the coin remedied the evil. What the deterioration of coin occasioned in those instances, the depreciation of paper has occasioned now. The coin had then ceased to contain, as the paper has now ceased to represent, the quantity of precious metal implied by its denomination. Foreign countries estimated the coin then as they do the paper now, not by what it is called, but by what it would exchange for in those commodities—gold and silver—which are, by the consent and practice of mankind, the common measures of all marketable value.

However gentlemen may endeavour to disguise and perplex this simple view of the question, it is, after all, that by which it must be decided. If this be not the test, there is no other. If gold and silver have ceased to be the common measures of the value of other commodities, and weight and fineness combined have ceased to be the standard of value in gold and silver, there is no more to be said: but in that case, instead of these Resolutions, let the right honourable gentleman come forward boldly at once with an assertion, not merely that paper is equivalent to the precious metals, but that it has altogether superseded them.

If, on the other hand, the same standard of value remains, let not the right honourable gentleman attempt to draw a veil over it. In all our departures from it, let us fairly own that we are departing from it—by necessity, if you please, but with a resolution of returning to it again. Let us not, like men who, when hurried down a rapid stream, fancy that the shores are flying from them—"terraeque urbesque recedunt;" let us not conceive that, by some strange revolution in the physical world, the precious metals are retreating beyond our reach; when it is, in fact, only by a rapid depreciation that our currency is leaving them behind. Neither let us suppose that we have already gone down so far, that to reascend the stream is impossible— that,

> Should we wade no more,
> Returning were as tedious as go o'er.

A very little firmness, a very little sacrifice, might at present enable us to retrace our course. The half of the ingenuity which is employed in the right honourable gentleman's Resolutions to gloss over our situation, might suffice to find a remedy for it.

It is asked—shall we attempt this in time of war? Can we attempt it without abandoning our present military system, with all its hopes and all its glories? Undoubtedly, I think, we can. I never can believe of this mighty empire, that it has not sufficient energy in itself at once to right whatever may be amiss in its own internal situation, and to maintain its accustomed place and movement in the system of the world.

But, it is said, we are only going on in the course in which greater authorities have led the way; Mr. Pitt had made up his mind to this depreciation of our currency. "He contrived it," says one honourable gentleman. "He could not avoid foreseeing it," says my right honourable friend (the Chancellor of the Exchequer.)

First, the inconveniencies which now result from that depreciation, and which constitute the proof of it, were not felt in Mr. Pitt's time. Neither could they possibly be foreseen by Mr. Pitt, if they in fact arise only from the causes to which my right honourable friend and the right honourable gentleman's fifteenth Resolution ascribe them: Mr. Pitt certainly could not foresee the Berlin and Milan decrees. The war, indeed, raged in his life time with not less violence than since; but yet in the very hottest and most disastrous part of the war, at the moment of the greatest public alarm and calamity, the exchanges were in our favour, and the price of gold did not materially rise. He therefore did not witness any of those symptoms which have awakened anxiety, and led to investigation on the present occasion.

Further, we have the testimony of my honourable friend opposite to me, (Mr. Wilberforce,) that in the year 1802, when the probable tendency of unredeemable bank paper to excessive issue, and consequent depreciation, became a subject of alarm to some men of great ability in financial matters—we have, I say, that most satisfactory testimony, that Mr. Pitt at that time professed his entire agreement in the principles laid down in a very able publication of the honourable gentleman who preceded me in this night's debate (Mr. H. Thornton,) which I presume every man who has attended to this question, has read. And what are those principles?—Why, these—"It is the maintenance of our general exchanges" (says Mr. Thornton,) "or, in other words, it is the agreement of the mint price with the bullion price of gold, which seems to be the true proof that the circulating paper is not depreciated."

If these are the principles which Mr. Pitt sanctioned, what pretence is there for saying that he foresaw the present state of things? or that, if he had lived to see it, he would now have asserted our circulating paper to be in an undepreciated state? Are our "general exchanges" now "maintained?" "Does the bullion price of gold" now "agree with the mint price?" Are not, on the contrary, the unfavourable exchanges, and the high price of bullion, the very particulars which are cited as affording the most irrefragable proof of a depreciation? If the absence of these criteria at that time was conclusive one way, must not the presence of them be now admitted to be conclusive the other? If Mr. Pitt was then satisfied that all was right because these symptoms had not appeared, is it fair to infer, that he would have been equally satisfied now, when they are seen in so aggravated a degree? Is not the fair inference directly the contrary?

Nor is it an unimportant evidence of Mr. Pitt's general view of this subject, that the Letter of Lord Liverpool to the King was the result of an investigation commenced in Mr. Pitt's first administration in 1798, and concluded in the year 1805, when he was again minister of the country. In that letter, not only are all the principles of our money system distinctly and ably expounded, according to the authority and the practice of the best times; but, with respect to the system of our paper currency, the danger of its being carried to excess, and the necessity of a parliamentary revision of it, are stated in a manner which shows with how much attention, in the opinion of the Government of those days, that system required to be watched.

But if Mr. Pitt had happily been still alive, what remedy would he have applied to this evil? Far be it from me to presume on this or on any other occasion to usurp the authority of his name, or to employ it for any purpose, which is not warranted by his recorded opinions. But that he would have applied some remedy—that he would not have been contented to let the evil take its course, if there were in human wisdom the means of checking it—that he would not have sought to reconcile delusion with credit, and to palliate a departure from principles by a denial of the principles themselves; every man who remembers his characteristic firmness, who recollects the difficulties which he had to combat, and the manner in which he combated and overcame them, will, I think, be ready to acknowledge.

If I am asked what remedy I would myself apply, I again say, as I have said before, that it must rest with the Executive Government to propose, as they alone can advantageously carry into effect, any measure of practical benefit. But I have no difficulty in offering one suggestion, which has indeed been in some degree anticipated in the course of these debates. The Bank proprietors have made great and unusual gains under the operation of the Bank restriction. I say this without the smallest intention of laying blame upon the Bank, or of exciting any invidious feeling towards them. The Directors of that Institution, I again repeat, have, so far as I can judge, acted for the best in the discharge of a new and most difficult duty. But the fact I believe will not be disputed. Great gains have been made in consequence of the Bank restriction. The issues of bank paper, whether too large or not in another view, have undeniably been much larger than they could have been, had the obligation to pay in cash upon demand continued, or been renewed. These gains certainly formed no part of the inducement to lay on or to renew the Bank restriction. They form no ground to continue it. But it is obvious—it is in the principles of human nature—that they must form a temptation to the Bank proprietors to wish for its continuance. It is obvious also, that if the issues are inordinately extended, the difficulty of resuming cash payments must be proportionably augmented. And it is still more obvious, that whether those motives and those causes do in fact so operate or no, from the natural invidiousness attendant on great gains, the world in general will be apt to suspect and impute their operation.

Now the public has no right to complain that the Bank restriction, though not laid or continued in contemplation of advantage to the Bank proprietors, has incidentally been productive of such advantage; but they have a right to expect that no impediment shall on that ground be thrown in the way of the removal of the restriction. A continued increase of profit, and a continued raising of the dividends to the Bank proprietors, if it had not that effect, would have that appearance. The dividend is now, I believe, ten per cent. There surely it might stop. All surplus profit beyond that amount, during the continuance of the restriction, might be strictly appropriated as a fund for the purchase of bullion, at whatever price.

It is not in my contemplation that the public (as has been suggested in several quarters since this question has been in discussion) should enter into any share of the extraordinary profits, or meddle in any degree in the management, of the Bank. No such thing. Let those extraordinary profits remain, in full, undisputed, and unenvied property, to the Bank. But as they are created by the suspension of cash payments, let the public have the assurance that they are so employed by the Bank, as to ensure their ability to resume those payments, without convulsion or distress, at the period which the Legislature has fixed for the resumption of them.

This, I think, is a suggestion, the adoption of which would be no less creditable to the Bank than satisfactory to the public.

For this, or any other measure calculated to remedy the evils acknowledged to exist, we can, after the decision to which this House has already come, rely only on the effect which may be produced by our discussions upon the advised discretion of the Bank, and upon the awakened attention of the public.

But at least, if we will do no good, let us, in the name of common sense, not do any harm. If we will not set right the course of the vessel, let us at least not destroy the chart and compass by which it may steer.

Let us leave the evil, if it must be so, to the chance of a gradual and noiseless correction. But let us not resolve as law, what is an incorrect and imperfect exposition of the law. Let us not resolve as fact, what is contradictory to universal experience. Let us not expose ourselves to ridicule, by resolving, as the opinions of the people, opinions which the people do not, and which it is impossible they should, entertain. This is not the way to settle the public feeling, and to set the subject at rest. It is the way to ensure renewed and interminable discussions. That we may at least not incur this unnecessary mischief, by adopting the Resolutions now before us, I move, Sir, that you do now leave the Chair.

The House divided on Mr. Canning's Amendment, when there appeared—For Mr. Canning's Amendment, 42; Against it, 82; Majority against it, 40.

Mr. Vansittart's Resolutions were then agreed to *pro forma*, with an understanding that they should be discussed upon the Report. The discussion on Mr. Vansittart's Resolutions was resumed on the following day; and on the 15th, after some verbal amendments, they were agreed to.

Act to repeal the Statute of Artificers, 15 April 1813

53 Geo. 3, c. 40   *Statutes of the United Kingdom,* 1813, 191.

The Statute of Artificers (1563) enforced apprenticeship in the textile industry and empowered magistrates to set wage and price levels. Repeal of the act in 1813 reflected the growing movement towards freer trade.

Whereas an Act passed in the Fifth Year of the Reign of Her late Majesty Queen *Elizabeth,* intituled *An Act containing divers Orders for Artificers, Labourers, Servants of Husbandry or Apprentices*: And whereas another Act passed in the First Year of the Reign of His late Majesty King *James* the First, intituled *An Act made for the Explanation of the Statute made in the Fifth Year of the late Queen* Elizabeth's *Reign, concerning Labourers*: And whereas an Act passed in *Scotland,* in the Twenty second Parliament of His Majesty King *James* the First in *England* and the Sixth of *Scotland,* intituled *Anent the Justices for keeping His Majesty's Peace, and their Constables*: And whereas another Act passed in *Scotland,* in the First Parliament of His Majesty King *Charles* the Second, intituled *Commission and Instruction to the Justices of the Peace and Constables*: And whereas it is expedient, that the Powers given by the said Acts, and by various other Acts passed in the Parliaments of *Scotland,* to Justices of the Peace and Magistrates of Cities and Boroughs, to rate Wages or fix Prices for Work, for Artificers, Labourers and Craftsmen, should be repealed: May it therefore please Your Majesty that it may be enacted; and be it enacted by the King's Most Excellent Majesty, by and with the Advice and Consent of the Lords Spiritual and Temporal, and Commons, in this present Parliament assembled, and by the Authority of the same, That so much of the said recited Acts, and of each of them, or of any other Act of Parliament in force in *Scotland,* as authorizes and empowers any Justices of the Peace or Magistrates of Cities and Burghs to rate Wages or fix Prices of Work for Artificers, Labourers and Craftsmen, shall be and the same is hereby repealed; and all Orders heretofore made by any Justice or Justices of the Peace or Magistrates, in *England* or *Scotland* respectively, under the Authority of the said recited Acts, or any or either of them, for or in relation to the rating any Wages, or settling or fixing any Prices of Work to be done or performed by any Artificers, Labourers or Craftsmen, or Servants, shall be and the same are hereby declared to be void and of none Effect; any thing in the said Acts, or any or either of them, to the contrary notwithstanding.

Corn Law, 23 March 1815

55 Geo. 3, c. 26   *Statutes at Large*, V, 93-96.

Large-scale imports of foreign grain from 1813 onward depressed prices and reduced the prosperity of landowners. The latter demanded protection against overseas competition and secured passage of the Corn Bill (1815), a measure prohibiting the importation of foreign grain at certain price levels.

Whereas it is expedient to amend the Laws now in force, relating to the Importation of and Trade in Corn; May it therefore please Your Majesty that it may be enacted; and be it enacted by The King's Most Excellent Majesty, by and with the Advice and Consent of the Lords Spiritual and Temporal, and Commons, in this present Parliament assembled, and by the Authority of the same, That, from and after the passing of this Act, all Corn, Meal or Flour, the Growth, Produce or Manufacture of any Foreign Country, which may now by Law be imported into the United Kingdom, shall and may at all times be allowed to be brought to the said United Kingdom, and to be warehoused there, under the Regulations and Provisions of the Laws now in force relating to Corn, without Payment of any Duty whatever; and that such Corn, Meal and Flour, so warehoused, may at all times be taken out of Warehouse, under the Regulations and Provisions now by Law in force, and be exported according to such Laws, without Payment of any Duty whatever.

II. And be it further enacted, That such Corn, Meal or Flour, may be taken out of Warehouse, and be entered for Home Consumption, in the said United Kingdom, under and subject to the Regulations and Provisions now in force, without Payment of any Duty whatever, whenever Foreign Corn, Meal or Flour of the same Sort, shall or may by Law be admissible into the said United Kingdom, for Home Consumption.

III. And be it further enacted, That such Foreign Corn, Meal or Flour, shall and may be permitted to be imported into the said United Kingdom, for Home Consumption, under and subject to the Provisions and Regulations now in force, without Payment of any Duty whatever, whenever the Average Prices of the several Sorts of *British* Corn, made up and published in the manner now by Law required, shall be at or above the Prices hereafter mentioned; that is to say, whenever Wheat shall be at or above the Price of Eighty Shillings *Per* Quarter; whenever Rye, Pease and Beans, shall be at or above the Price of Fifty three Shillings *per* Quarter; whenever Barley, Beer or Bigg, shall be at or above the Price of Forty Shillings *per* Quarter; and whenever Oats shall be at or above the Price of Twenty seven Shillings *per* Quarter.

IV. And be it further enacted, That whenever the Average Prices of *British* Corn so made up and published, shall respectively be below the Prices hereinbefore stated, no Foreign Corn, or Meal, or Flour, made from any of the respective Sorts of Foreign Corn hereinbefore enumerated, shall be allowed to be imported into the United Kingdom, for the Purpose of Home Consumption, or taken out of Warehouse for that Purpose.

V. And be it further enacted, That the Average Price of the several Sorts of *British* Corn, by which the Importation of Foreign Corn, Meal or Flour, into the United Kingdom, shall be regulated and governed, shall continue to be made up and published in any manner now required by Law; but that if it shall hereafter at the time after the Importation of Foreign Corn, Meal or Flour shall be permitted, under the Provisions of this Act, appear that the Average Prices of the different Sorts of *British* Corn respectively, in the Six Weeks immediately succeeding the Fifteenth Day of *February*, the Fifteenth Day of *May*, the Fifteenth Day of *August* and the Fifteenth Day of *November* in each Year, shall have fallen below the Prices at which Foreign Corn, Meal or Flour, may be, under the Provisions of this Act, allowed to be imported for Home Consumption, no such Foreign Corn, Meal or Flour, shall be allowed to be imported into the United Kingdom for Home Consumption, from any Place between the Rivers *Eyder* and *Bidassoa*, both inclusive, until a new Average shall be made up, and published in the *London Gazette*, for regulating the Importation into the United Kingdom for the succeeding Quarter.

VI. And be it further enacted, That such Corn, Meal or Flour, being the Growth, Produce or Manufacture of any *British* Colony or Plantation in *North America*, as may now by Law be imported into the United Kingdom, may hereafter respectively be imported for Home Consumption, without Payment of any Duty, whenever the Average Prices of *British* Corn, made up and published as now by Law required, shall respectively be at or above the Prices hereafter specified; that is to say, whenever the Price of Wheat shall be at or above Sixty seven Shillings *per* Quarter; whenever the Price of Rye, Pease and Beans, shall be at or above Forty four Shillings *per* Quarter; whenever the Price of Barley, Beer or Bigg shall be at or above Thirty three Shillings *per* Quarter; and whenever the Price of Oats shall be at or above Twenty two Shillings *per* Quarter.

VII. Provided always, and be it further enacted, That whenever the Prices of *British* Corn respectively shall be below the Prices herein specified, Corn, or Meal, or Flour made from any of the respective Sorts of Corn herein enumerated, the Growth, Produce or Manufacture of any *British* Colony or Plantation in *North America*, shall no longer be allowed to be imported into the United Kingdom for Home Consumption.

VIII. And be it further enacted, That such Corn, Meal or Flour, and Growth, Produce or Manufacture of any *British* Colony or Plantation in *North America*, as may now by Law be imported into the United Kingdom, shall at all times be permitted to be imported into the United Kingdom, and warehoused according to the Laws now in force, without Payment of any Duty whatever; and be taken out of the Warehouse, and exported according to the Laws now in force, without Payment of any Duty whatever.

IX. And be it further enacted, That such Corn, Meal or Flour, so warehoused, may be taken out of Warehouse, and entered for Home Consumption in the United

Kingdom, whenever Corn, Meal or Flour, of the like Description, imported direct from any such Colony or Plantation, shall be admissible by Law for Home Consumption, but not otherwise.

X.   Provided always, That nothing in this Act contained shall extend or be construed to extend to repeal or any wise alter the Duties of Package, Scavage, Baillage or Portage, or any other Duties payable to the Mayor and Commonalty and Citizens of the City of *London*, or to the Lord Mayor of the said City for the time being, or to any other City or Town Corporate within *Great Britain*, or any other special Privilege or Exemption to which any Person or Persons, Bodies Politic or Corporate, is or are now entitled by Law; but the same shall be continued as heretofore: Provided always, that nothing in this Act shall extend or be construed to extend to repeal or alter the Payments to be made to the Inspector of Corn Returns, as directed by an Act made in the Forty third Year of the Reign of His present Majesty, respecting Corn brought into the Port of *London*.

XI.   And be it further enacted, That every Act of Parliament in force on and immediately before the passing of this Act, by which any Rules, Regulations or Conditions were made, established or directed, regulating the Importation and Exportation of Corn, Meal and Flour, or for ascertaining the Average Prices, except where any Alteration is expressly made by this Act, and all Provisions, Clauses, Matters and Things relating thereto, shall and are hereby declared to be and remain in full Force and Effect, and shall be applied to this Act, as fully and effectually as if they had been repeated and re-enacted in this present Act.

XII.   Provided always, and be it further enacted, That this Act may be varied, altered or repealed during this present Session of Parliament.

Peel's Act, 2 July 1819

59 Geo. 3, c. 49   *Statutes of the United Kingdom*, 1819, 725-27.

This act provided for the gradual resumption of cash payments by the Bank of England in line with the reports of the Bullion Committee (1810) and of a select committee of the House of Commons (1819). Provisions of the act scheduled to take effect in 1823 were actually brought into operation in May 1821.

Whereas an Act was passed in the Parliament of *Great Britain*, in the Thirty seventh Year of the Reign of His present Majesty, intituled *An Act for confirming and continuing for a limited time, the Restriction contained in the Minute of Council of the Twenty sixth of* February *One thousand seven hundred and ninety seven, on Payments of Cash by the Bank*; which Act was continued, under certain Regulations and Restrictions by another Act made in the said Parliament in the Thirty seventh Year aforesaid; and by an Act made in the Parliament of *Great Britain* in the Thirty eighth Year of His present Majesty's Reign, the Provisions contained in the said last recited Act of the Thirty seventh Year, were amended and continued; and by an Act made in the Forty second Year of His present Majesty's Reign, the several Provisions of the said Acts passed in the Thirty seventh Year aforesaid, so far as the same are amended and continued by the said Act passed in the Thirth eighth Year aforesaid, and also the recited Act of the Thirty eighth Year aforesaid, were further continued; and by an Act passed in the Forty third Year of His present Majesty's Reign, the several Provisions of the said Acts passed in the Thirty seventh Year aforesaid, so far as the same are amended by the said Act passed in the Thirty eighth Year aforesaid, and continued by the said Act of the Forty second Year, were further continued and amended; and by an Act made in the Forty fourth Year of His present Majesty's Reign, the several Provisions of the said Acts passed in the Thirty seventh Year aforesaid, so far as the same are amended by the said Act passed in the Thirty eighth Year aforesaid, and continued and amended by the said Act of the Forty third Year aforesaid, were further continued; and by several Acts passed in the Fifty fourth, Fifty fifth, Fifty sixth, and Fifty eighth Years of His present Majesty's Reign, the said recited Act of the Forty fourth Year has been continued, and is now in force, until the Fifth Day of *July* One thousand eight hundred and nineteen: And Whereas an Act was passed in the present Session of Parliament, intituled *An Act to restrain, until the End of the present Session of Parliament, the Governor and Company of the Bank of* England *from making Payments in Cash under certain Notices given by them for that Purpose*: And Whereas it is expedient that the Restrictions on Payments in Cash by the said Bank should be continued beyond the time to which such Restrictions are at present limited, and that a definite Period should be fixed for the Termination of such Restrictions, and that preparatory Measures should be taken with a view to facilitate and ensure, on the Arrival of that Period, the Payment of the Promissory Notes of the Bank of *England* in the Legal Coin of the Realm. Be it therefore enacted by The King's Most Excellent Majesty, by and with the Advice and Consent of the Lords Spiritual and Temporal, and Commons, in this present Parliament assembled, and by the Authority of the same, That the several Provisions of the said hereinbefore recited Acts passed in the Parliament of *Great Britain* in the Thirty seventh Year of His present Majesty's Reign, so far as the same are amended by the said Act passed in the Parliament of *Great Britain* in the Thirty eighth Year of His present Majesty's Reign, and by the said Act of the Forty third Year of His present Majesty's Reign, for continuing and amending the same, and also of the said hereinbefore recited Act of this present Session of Parliament, and each and every of the said Acts, shall be and the same and ever of them is and are hereby further continued, until the First Day of *May* One thousand eight hundred and twenty three; and that from and after the said First Day of *May* One thousand eight hundred and twenty three, the Restrictions on Payments in Cash under the said several Acts shall finally cease and determine.

II. Provided always, and be it further enacted, That at any time on or after the First Day of *February* One thousand eight hundred and twenty, and before the First Day of *October* One thousand eight hundred and twenty, whenever any Person shall tender to the Governor and Company of the Bank of *England* any Note or Notes of the said Governor and Company payable on demand, to an Amount not less than the Price or Value of Sixty Ounces of Gold, calculated after the Rate of

Four Pounds One Shilling for every Ounce of Gold, and shall require such Note or Notes to be paid in Standard Gold, the Governor and Company of the said Bank of *England* shall, upon demand, pay and deliver to the Person tendering such Notes, such Quantity of Gold of the Fineness declared by Law to be the Standard of and for the lawful Gold Coin of the Realm, the same having been first assayed and stamped at His Majesty's Mint in *London*, as shall, at the said Rate of Four Pounds One Shilling for every Ounce of such Gold, be equal to the Amount of the Notes so presented for Payment.

III. Provided also, and be it further enacted, That at any time on or after the First Day of *October* One thousand eight hundred and twenty, and before the First Day of *May* One thousand eight hundred and twenty one, whenever any Person shall tender to the Governor and Company of the Bank of *England* any Note or Notes of the said Governor and Company payable on demand, to an Amount not less than the Price or Value of Sixty Ounces of Gold, calculated after the Rate of Three Pounds Nineteen Shillings and Sixpence for every Ounce of Gold, and shall require such Note or Notes to be paid in Standard Gold, the Governor and Company of the said Bank of *England* shall, upon demand, pay and deliver to the Person tendering such Notes, such Quantity of Gold of the Fineness declared by Law to be the Standard of and for the lawful Gold Coin of the Realm, the same having been first assayed and stamped at His Majesty's Mint in *London*, as shall, at the said Rate of Three Pounds Nineteen Shillings and Sixpence for every Ounce of such Gold, be equal to the Amount of the Notes so presented for Payment.

IV. Provided also, and be it further enacted, That at any time on or after the First Day of *May* One thousand eight hundred and twenty one, and before the First Day of *May* One thousand eight hundred and twenty three, whenever any Person shall tender to the Governor and Company of the Bank of *England* any Note or Notes of the said Governor and Company payable on demand, to an Amount not less than the Price or Value of Sixty Ounces of Gold, calculated after the Rate of Three Pounds Seventeen Shillings and Ten pence Halfpenny for every Ounce of Gold, and shall require such Note or Notes to be paid in Standard Gold, the Governor and Company of the said Bank of *England* shall, upon demand, pay and deliver to the Person tendering such Notes, such Quantity of Gold of the Fineness declared by Law to be the Standard of and for the lawful Gold Coin of the Realm, the same having been first assayed and stamped at His Majesty's Mint in *London*, as shall, at the said Rate of Three Pounds Seventeen Shillings and Ten pence Halfpenny for every Ounce of such Gold, be equal to the Amount of the Notes so presented for Payment.

V. And be it further enacted, That it shall and may be lawful for the Governor and Company of the said Bank of *England*, at any time between the said First Day of *February* One thousand eight hundred and twenty, and the said First Day of *October* One thousand eight hundred and twenty, to pay and deliver to any Person who shall present Notes of the said Governor and Company of the said Bank, such Quantity of Gold of such Fineness as aforesaid, and assayed and stamped as aforesaid, as shall be equal to the Amount of the Notes so presented, at any Rate less than Four Pounds One Shilling and not less than Three Pounds Nineteen Shillings and Sixpence for every Ounce of such Gold; and in like manner at any time between the First Day of *October* One thousand eight hundred and twenty, and the First Day of *May* One thousand eight hundred and twenty one, to pay and deliver such Gold at any Rate less than Three Pounds Nineteen Shillings and Sixpence, and not less than Three Pounds Seventeen Shillings and Ten pence Halfpenny for every Ounce of such Gold: Provided always, that the Governor and Company of the said Bank of *England* shall give Three Days' Notice in *The London Gazette* of their Intention to make such Payments after such Rates, specifying the Rates at which such Payments shall be made; and provided also, that it shall not be lawful for the Governor and Company of the said Bank of *England*, at any time after making such Payments at the Rates mentioned in any such Notice, to pay or deliver any such Gold at a Rate higher than the Rate mentioned in any such Notice; any thing in this Act to the contrary notwithstanding.

VI. Provided also, and be it enacted, That the Governor and Company of the Bank of *England* shall not be required to compelled to pay or deliver any such Gold, except in Ingots or Bars of the Weight of Sixty Ounces each, assayed and stamped as aforesaid; any thing hereinbefore contained to the contrary notwithstanding.

VII. Provided also, and be it enacted, That it shall and may be lawful for the Governor and Company of the said Bank of *England* to pay any Fraction less than Forty Shillings of any Sum so demanded above the Value of Sixty Ounces, in the lawful Silver Coin of the Realm.

VIII. Provided also, and be it further enacted, That the Governor and Company of the Bank of *England*, if they shall see fit, may at any time on or after the First Day of *May* One thousand eight hundred and twenty two, pay or exchange the lawful Coin of the Realm for any Note or Notes of the said Governor and Company payable on demand; any Provisions in the said before recited Acts, or in this Act, to the contrary notwithstanding.

IX. And be it further enacted, That the Governor and Company of the Bank of *England* shall, from time to time after the passing of this Act, and until the First Day of *May* One thousand eight hundred and twenty three, cause a true and perfect Account in Writing, to be taken and attested by the proper Officer, of the average Amount of all Promissory Notes and Bills of the said Governor and Company which shall be in Circulation during every Week, from *Monday* until *Saturday* both inclusive, distinguishing the respective Denominations and Values of the several Notes and Bills, and the average Amount of the Notes and Bills of each Denomination and Value respectively so in Circulation, and to cause such Account to be transmitted and delivered to one of the Clerks of His Majesty's Privy Council, on the *Tuesday* in every Week next ensuing the *Saturday* to which such Account shall be made up; and the said Governor and Company shall also from time to time, in like manner, cause an Account to be taken and attested of the average Amount of all Promissory Notes and Bills of the said Governor and Company which shall be in Circulation during every Quarter of a Year ending on the Fifth Day of *July*, the Tenth Day of *October*, the Fifth Day of *January*, and the Fifth Day of *April* in every Year after the passing of this Act, and until the First Day of *May* One thousand eight hundred and twenty three, distinguishing the respective Denominations and Values of the several Notes and Bills, and the average Amount of the Notes and Bills of each Denomination and Value respectively, and to cause such Quarterly Account to be published in *The London Gazette* within One Week next after the End of each Quarter respectively. . . .

Act to repeal and simplify earlier Navigation Acts, 24 June 1822

3 Geo. 4, c. 43   *Statutes of the United Kingdom*, 1823, 186-90, 195-96.

Whereas an Act was passed in the Twelfth Year of the Reign of His Majesty King *Charles* the Second, for the encouraging and increasing of Shipping and Navigation, on which the Strength and Safety of this Kingdom do greatly depend: And Whereas by an Act passed in the Parliament of *Ireland*, in the Twenty seventh Year of the Reign of His Late Majesty King *George* the Third, intituled *An Act for the further Increase and Encouragement of Shipping and Navigation*, it was enacted, that the said recited Act passed in *England*, in the Twelfth Year of the Reign of King *Charles* the Second, and every Provision therein contained, (so far as the same are not altered or repealed by the said Act of Parliament of *Ireland*), should be of full Force and Effect within *Ireland*: And Whereas divers Acts have been from time to time passed for the further Regulation of Shipping, Navigation and Commerce; and it is expedient that such of the Provisions contained in the said several Acts as relate to the Countries or Places from whence, and the Ships in which Goods and Merchandize shall be imported into the United Kingdom of *Great Britain* and *Ireland*, should be revised and amended, and together with other Regulations, be declared and provided, so that the Law by which such Importation is to be regulated, may be simplified and rendered more certain, as well as more effectual, in promoting the Objects of the said several Acts, and in facilitating and extending the Commerce of the Realm: May it therefore please Your Majesty, that, for the establishing by Law the several Rules and Provisions under which the Importation of Goods and Merchandize into *Great Britain* shall be regulated, so far as relates to the Countries or Places from whence, and the Ships in which, such Importations shall be made, it may be enacted: And be it enacted by the King's most Excellent Majesty, by and with the Advice and Consent of the Lords Spiritual and Temporal and Commons, in this present Parliament assembled, and by the Authority of the same, That from and after the passing of this Act, Goods and Merchandize, being of the Growth, Production or Manufacture of *Asia, Africa* or *America*, shall be imported into the United Kingdom of *Great Britain* and *Ireland*, from any Place whatever, in *British* built Ships or Vessels only, or in Ships or Vessels which by Law are or may be entitled to the Privileges of *British* built Ships, registered and navigated according to Law, and not in any Ship or Vessel of any other Country or Place whatever, under Penalty of the Forfeiture of all such Goods and Merchandize, the Growth, Production or Manufacture of *Asia, Africa* or *America*, as shall be imported from any Place whatever, in any Ship or Vessel not being a *British* built Ship or Vessel, or not being entitled to the Privileges of a *British* built Ship or Vessel, registered and navigated according to Law; except only in Cases hereinafter specially excepted or provided for.

II. Provided always, and be it enacted, That all Goods and Merchandize, the Growth, Production or Manufacture of *Asia, Africa* or *America*, which shall be imported into the United Kingdom from any Port or Place in *Europe*, shall be so imported for Exportation only, except in Cases where it is by this Act otherwise specially provided.

III. Provided also, and be it enacted, That from and after the passing of this Act, any Goods or Merchandize being of the Growth, Production or Manufacture of any Country or Place in *America* or the *West Indies*, being or having been a Part of the Dominions of the King of *Spain*, and which Goods or Merchandize may at any time be lawfully imported into the United Kingdom in *British* built Ships, may be imported into the United Kingdom directly from the Place of their Growth, Production or Manufacture, or from those Ports in such Country or Place where such Goods or Merchandize can only be or have usually been first shipped for Transportation, in Ships or Vessels of the Built of the Country or Place of which such Goods or Merchandize may be the Growth, Production or Manufacture; or in Ships or Vessels of the Built of the Port in such Country or Place where such Goods or Merchandize can only be or have usually been first shipped for Transportation; and all which Ships or Vessels shall be wholly owned by the People of such Country, Place or Port, and navigated by the Master and Three fourths of the Mariners of such Country, Place or Port.

IV. Provided always, and be it enacted, That if it shall happen that any such Country or Place in *America* or the *West Indies* shall, before or at the Time of the Importation from thence into the United Kingdom of any Goods or Merchandize, be under the Dominion of the King of *Spain*, or if any Doubt shall exist thereon, then and in any such case the Goods and Merchandize of the Growth, Production or Manufacture of such Country or Place in *America* or the *West Indies*, may be imported directly from thence into the United Kingdom in Ships or Vessels of the Built of any Country or Place within the Dominion of the King of *Spain*, and wholly owned by the People of such Country or Place, and navigated by a Master and Three fourths of the Mariners thereof of such Country or Place.

V. Provided also, and be it enacted, That nothing contained in this Act shall extend, or be construed to extend, to admit the Importation into the United Kingdom of any such Goods or Merchandize in any Foreign Ship or Vessel from any such Country, Port or Place in *America* or the *West Indies*, except only from such Country, Port or Place where *British* Ships or Vessels shall be entitled to Privileges equal to those by this Act granted to the Ships and Vessels of such Country, Port or Place.

VI. And be it further enacted, That from and after the passing of this Act, the several Sorts of Goods and Merchandize hereinafter particularly enumerated, mentioned and described, being of the Growth or Production of any Place in *Europe*, that is to say, Masts, Timber, Boards, Salt, Pitch, Tar, Tallow, Rosin, Hemp, Flax, Currants, Raisins, Figs, Prunes, Olive Oil, Corn or Grain, Potashes, Wine, Sugar, Vinegar, Brandy or Tobacco, shall be imported into the United Kingdom, either in *British* built Ships or Vessels, or in Ships or Vessels which by Law are or may be entitled to the Privileges of *British* built Ships or Vessels, registered and navigated according to Law, or in Ships or Vessels of the Built of and belonging to the Country or Place in *Europe*, of which such Goods and Merchandize are the Growth, Produce or Manufacture respectively, or in Ships or Vessels of the Built of and belonging to any Port or Place in *Europe* into which such Goods and Merchandize shall have been brought or imported, and in which the same shall have been landed; and all which Foreign Ships shall be wholly owned by the People of such Country, Port or Place, and shall be navigated by a Master and Three fourths at least of the Mariners thereof of such Country, Port or Place, and not in any other Ship or Vessel whatsoever, under Penalty of the Forfeiture of all such Goods or Merchandize as shall be imported from any Place in *Europe*, in any Ship or Vessel not being such *British* built Ship or Vessel, or not being a Ship or Vessel entitled to the Privileges of a *British* built Ship or Vessel as aforesaid, or not being a Ship or Vessel of such Country, Port or Place in *Europe* as aforesaid, and navigated as aforesaid, and also of the Forfeiture of a Sum not exceeding One hundred Pounds by the Master or Person having the Charge or Command of such Ship or Vessel; except only in Cases hereinafter specially excepted or provided for.

VII. Provided always, and be it enacted, That nothing in this Act contained shall extend or be construed to extend to prohibit the Importation of any Goods or Merchandize, the Growth, Production or Manufacture of any Part of *Europe*, and not hereinbefore expressly specified, enumerated or described, in any Ship or Vessel whatsoever, and from any Place whatsoever, as such Goods or Merchandize might have been imported into *Great Britain* at any Time before the passing of this Act.

VIII. Provided also, and be it enacted, That from and after the passing of this Act, Goods or Merchandize the Growth, Production or Manufacture of any Places within the Dominions of the Grand Seignior, may be imported into the United Kingdom in *British* built Ships or Vessels, registered and navigated according to Law, or in Ships or Vessels of the Built of any Country or Place within the Dominions of the Grand Seignior, wholly owned by the People of such Country or Place, and navigated by a Master and Three fourths at least of the Mariners thereof of such Country or Place; and that such Goods and Merchandize may be imported for Consumption in the United Kingdom; any thing hereinbefore contained to the contrary in any wise notwithstanding.

IX. Provided also, and be it enacted, That from and after the passing of this Act, Raw Silk and Mohair Yarn, of the Growth, Production or Manufacture of *Asia*, exported to the United Kingdom of *Great Britain* and *Ireland*, from any Port or Places in the Streights or *Levant* Seas, within the Dominions of the Grand Seignior; and also Raw Silk or Mohair Yarn, being the Growth, Production or Manufacture of any Place within the Dominions of the Grand Seignior within the *Levant* Seas, exported to the United Kingdom of *Great Britain* and *Ireland*, from the Island of *Malta* or the Dependencies thereof, or from the Port of *Gibraltar*; and also all Goods and Merchandize the Growth, Production or Manufacture of the Dominions of the Emperor of *Morocco*, and which shall have been imported into *Gibraltar* directly from any Part of the Dominions of the said Emperor, not lying or being to the Southward of the Port of *Mogadore*, in *British* built Ships or Vessels, navigated and registered according to Law, or in Ships or Vessels belonging to the Subjects of the said Emperor of *Morocco*, and which shall be exported from *Gibraltar* to the United Kingdom of *Great Britain* and *Ireland*; and also all

Diamonds, Pearls, Rubies, Emeralds and all other Jewels and Precious Stones, from any Place whatever, may be imported into the United Kingdom in *British* built Ships or Vessels, registered and navigated according to Law, for Consumption in the United Kingdom; any thing in this Act contained to the contrary thereof in any wise notwithstanding; and that all such Diamonds shall pass inwards without Warrant or Fee.

X. And be it declared and enacted, That the Island of *Malta* and its Dependencies shall, for all Purposes whatever, be deemed and taken to be in *Europe*.

XI. And be it further enacted, That from and after the passing of this Act, it shall and may be lawful for the Commissioners of His Majesty's Treasury of the United Kingdom of *Great Britain* and *Ireland*, or any Three or more of them, and they are hereby authorized and empowered, by Warrant under their Hands, or the Hands of any Three or more of them, to order and direct that any *British* Ship or Vessel, which at any time before the First Day of *May* One thousand seven hundred and eighty six was duly registered as a *British* Ship, shall have and be entitled to all the Privileges and Advantages belonging to a *British* built Ship, and shall and may be registered as a *British* built Ship; provided it shall in all cases be made appear to the Satisfaction of the said Commissioners of the Treasury, or any Three or more of them, that every such Ship or Vessel for which such Privilege shall be claimed, was actually and identically registered as a *British* Ship before the said First Day of *May* One thousand seven hundred and eighty six, and that no Foreigner had at any time, while such Ship or Vessel was so registered, any Share, Property or Concern in such Ship or Vessel, and that such Ship or Vessel has not been repaired in any Foreign Port at any Expence beyond what is allowed by Law, and that such Ship or Vessel is in every other respect entitled to the Privilege of a *British* Ship; and in such case, every such Ship or Vessel, from and after the Date of the Registry made of such Ship or Vessel as a *British* Ship; and in such case, every such Ship or Vessel, from and after the Date of the Registry made of such Ship or Vessel as a *British* built Ship, by virtue of such Warrant, shall be deemed and taken to be a *British* built Ship, and shall be entitled to all the Privileges and Advantages to which a *British* built Ship is by Law entitled, and as if such Ship or Vessel had been originally *British* built, to all Intents and Purposes whatsoever.

XII. And be it further enacted, That from and after the passing of this Act, any *British* built Ship or Vessel which shall have been or shall be registered as such, and which after being so registered shall have been or shall be sold to or become wholly the Property of any Person or Persons, not being a Subject or Subjects of His Majesty, His Heirs or Successors, shall to all Intents and Purposes be deemed and taken to be a Ship or Vessel of the Built of the Foreign Country, Port or Place, if in *Europe*, of which the Person or Persons to whom such Ship or Vessel shall be sold shall be a Subject or Subjects, or to which such Person or Persons shall belong; and it shall and may be lawful to import in any such Ship or Vessel any Goods or Merchandize from any such Foreign Country, Port or Place in *Europe*, in like manner as if such Ship or Vessel were of the Built of such Foreign Country, Port or Place in *Europe*; any Law, Usage or Custom to the Contrary notwithstanding: Provided always, that in case any such *British* built Ship or Vessel, having once become the Property of any Person or Persons not being a *British* Subject or Subjects, shall again become the Property of any *British* Subject or Subjects, otherwise than by Capture and legal Condemnation, such Ship or Vessel shall not, on any Pretence whatsoever, be again deemed, taken, or considered to be a *British* built Ship or Vessel, nor entitled to be registered as such, nor to any other Privileges or Advantages as a *British* built Ship or Vessel, but shall be subject and liable to all the Penalties and Forfeitures to which Foreign Ships or Vessels are or may be subject or liable by Law. . . .

XXXI. And be it further enacted, That all Goods and Merchandize which shall be imported pursuant to this Act, and the Importers of such Goods and Merchandize, shall be subject and liable to the Payment of all such Duties of Customs and Excise, and also to all such Conditions, Rules, Regulations, Penalties and Forfeitures, as relate to the securing the Payment of the said Duties, and as relate to the due and regular Entry, Landing, Warehousing, Securing and Delivery of such Goods and Merchandize, and as relate to the Burthen of the Ships or Vessels in which, and the Ports into which such Goods and Merchandize shall be imported, and the Packages in which the same shall be contained; and all such Goods and Merchandize, and the Importers thereof, shall in all other respects, not especially provided for by this Act, be subject and liable to all such Rules, Regulations, Penalties and Forfeitures as any such Goods and Merchandize, or the Importers thereof, are subject or liable to under or by virtue of any Act or Acts in force on or immediately before the passing of this Act, or as shall be in force with respect to any such Goods or Merchandize, or the Importers thereof, at the Time of the Importation thereof; any thing in this Act contained to the contrary in any wise notwithstanding.

XXXII. And be it further enacted, That all Penalties and Forfeitures imposed by this Act, or which shall or may be incurred for any Offence against this Act, shall and may be sued for, recovered, levied or mitigated by such Ways, Means or Methods, as any Fine, Penalty or Forfeiture against the said several Acts of the Twelfth Year of the Reign of King *Charles* the Second, and of the Twenty seventh Year of the Reign of King *George* the Third, for the encouraging and increasing of Shipping and Navigation, may be sued for, recovered, levied or mitigated under the said recited Acts respectively, or as any Fine, Penalty or Forfeiture, may be sued for, recovered, levied or mitigated by any Law or Laws relating to the Importation of Goods or Merchandize into *Great Britain* and *Ireland* respectively, or by Action of Debt, Bill, Plaint or Information in any of His Majesty's Courts of Record at *Westminster* or *Dublin*, or in the Court of Exchequer in *Scotland*, respectively, and that One Moiety of every such Penalty or Forfeiture shall be to His Majesty, His Heirs and Successors, and the other Moiety to him or them who shall inform, discover or sue for the same.

XXXIII. And be it further enacted, That this Act may be amended, altered or repealed by any Act or Acts to be made in this present Session of Parliament.

Act to repeal the 1773 Spitalfields Act, 17 June 1824

5 Geo. 4, c. 66   *Statutes of the United Kingdom*, 1824, 306-09.

This act ended legislative interference in the fixing of wages in the silk industry.

Whereas by an Act made in the Thirteenth Year of the Reign of His late Majesty King *George* the Third, intituled *An Act to empower the Magistrates therein mentioned to settle and regulate the Wages of Persons employed in the Silk Manufacture within their respective Jurisdictions,* it was enacted, that the Wages and Prices for Work of the Journeymen Weavers within the City of *London* should be settled, regulated and declared by the Lord Mayor, Recorder and Aldermen of the said City, and in all Places in the County of *Middlesex* by the Justices of the Peace of the said County, and in all Places within the City and Liberty of *Westminster* at the General Quarter Sessions of the Peace holden in and for the said City and Liberty, and in all Places within the Liberty of the Tower of *London*, at the General Quarter Sessions of the Peace holden in and for the said Liberty, at their General Quarter Sessions of the Peace respectively; and certain Penalties are by the said Act inflicted on all Master Weavers within any of the said Districts who should give more or less Wages, or pay larger or less Prices, to any of the said Journeymen Weavers for their Work, than should be settled or allowed as aforesaid, and also upon all Journeymen Weavers within the Districts aforesaid who should ask, receive or take more or less Wages, or larger or less Prices for their Work, than should be settled by the respective Quarter Sessions as aforesaid; and by the said Act certain other Penalties are also inflicted on all Master Weavers within any of the Districts aforesaid, who should directly or indirectly in any Manner retain or employ any Journeyman Weaver out of or beyond the Limits therein mentioned, with Intent to evade that Act, or who should give, allow or pay to such Journeyman any more or less Wages than should be settled in Manner in the said Act provided; and by the said Acts certain other Penalties are also inflicted on any Person or Persons, being Silk Weavers residing within any of the Districts aforesaid, who should have in his or their Service at any one Time more than Two Apprentices: And Whereas by an Act made in the Thirty second Year of the Reign of His said late Majesty, intituled *An Act for extending the Provisions of an Act made in the Thirteenth Year of the Reign of His Present Majesty, intituled 'An Act to empower the Magistrates therein mentioned to settle and regulate the Wages of Persons employed in the Silk Manufacture within their respective Jurisdiction,' to Manufactories of Silk mixed with other Materials, and for the more effectual Punishment of Buyers and Receivers of Silk purloined and embezzled by Persons employed in the Manufacture thereof*; it is enacted and declared, that the Lord Mayor, Recorder and Aldermen of the City of *London*, and the Justices of the Peace within their respective Jurisdictions throughout the several and respective Districts in the said Act of the Thirteenth Year of His late Majesty mentioned, should from time to time settle, regulate, order and declare the Wages and Prices of Work of the Journeymen Weavers working within their respective Jurisdictions in any Manufacture of Silk mixed or wrought up with any other Materials, in the like Manner as they are respectively authorized and empowered by the said recited Act of the Thirteenth Year of His late Majesty to settle, regulate, order and declare the same in the Manufacture of Silk only; and that the said therein recited Act, and all and every the Clauses, Provisions, Regulations, Restrictions, Pains, Penalties, Forfeitures and other Matters and Things therein contained, should extend, and be deemed, adjudged and construed to extend, to all Persons employed in or about any of the Manufactures of Silk mixed or wrought up with any other Materials within the respective Districts in the said Act mentioned, in as full and ample Manner as they are by the said therein recited Act declared to extend to the several and respective Persons therein mentioned: And Whereas by an Act passed in the Fifty first Year of the Reign of His said late Majesty, intituled *An Act to amend Two Acts of the Thirteenth and Thirty second Years of His present Majesty, relating to the Wages of Persons employed in the Silk Manufacture*, the Provisions made by the said recited Acts of the Thirteenth and Thirty second Years of His late Majesty for settling and regulating the Wages and Prices of Work of the Journeymen Weavers in the Manufacture of Silk, and in the Manufacture of Silk mixed or wrought up with any other Materials, within the Cities of *London* and *Westminster* and the County of *Middlesex*, are declared to extend to Journeywomen Weavers employed in the said Manufactories: And Whereas by an Act passed in the Parliament of *Ireland*, in the Nineteenth and Twentieth Years of the Reign of His said late Majesty, intituled *An Act for the better Regulation of the Silk Manufacture*, it is enacted that the Wages of Journeymen Silk Weavers, within the City of *Dublin*, and the adjacent Liberties for the Distance of Two Miles and a Half round from the Castle of *Dublin*, should be regulated, settled and declared by the *Dublin* Society; and certain Penalties are by the said Act imposed on any Master Silk Weaver within the aforesaid District who shall give more or less Wages, or pay larger or smaller Prices, to any of the Journeymen Weavers aforesaid, for their Work, than shall be settled or allowed as aforesaid; and by the same Act certain Penalties are also imposed on any Journeyman Weaver or Weavers, within the District aforesaid, who should ask, receive or take more or less Wages, or larger or smaller Prices for their Work, than should be settled as aforesaid, or who should enter into any Combination to raise the Wages or Prices of said Work, or for that Purpose should decoy, solicit or intimidate any Journeyman or Journeymen Weavers within the District aforesaid; and it is by the same Act further enacted, that the *Dublin* Society should superintend the Silk Manufacture, and make such Orders, Bye Laws and Regulations touching all Matters pertaining thereto, as should appear to them useful and necessary, and that all Persons concerned in the said Manufacture should obey all such Orders of the *Dublin* Society: And Whereas an Act was passed in the Parliament of *Ireland* in the Thirty sixth Year of the Reign of His late Majesty, intituled *An Act to explain and amend an Act passed in the Nineteenth and Twentieth Years of His Majesty's Reign, intituled 'An Act for the better Regulation of the Silk Manufacture:'* And Whereas an Act passed in the Fortieth Year of the Reign of His said late Majesty, intituled *An Act to continue an Act passed in the Thirty sixth Year of His present Majesty's Reign, intituled 'An Act to explain and amend an Act passed in the Nineteenth and Twentieth Years of His Majesty's Reign,' intituled "An Act for the better Regulation of the Silk Manufacture;"* by which last mentioned Acts the said Act of the Nineteenth and Twentieth *George* Third was continued in Force: And Whereas an Act was passed in the Fiftieth Year of the Reign of His said late Majesty, intituled *An Act to continue, until the Twenty fifth Day of* March *One thousand eight hundred and thirty one, certain Acts made in the Parliament of* Ireland, *for the better Regulation of the Silk Manufacture:* And Whereas the Provisions of the said recited Acts have not been found beneficial to the Persons employed in the Silk Manufacture, but on the contrary the Regulations and Restrictions contained in the said Acts have been found in their Operation vexatious and injurious, and it is therefore expedient that the said Acts should be wholly repealed: May it therefore please Your Majesty that it may be enacted; and be it enacted by the King's most Excellent Majesty, by and with the Advice and Consent of the Lords Spiritual and Temporal, and Commons, in this present Parliament assembled, and by the Authority of the same, That from and after the passing of this Act, the said several recited Acts, and every Clause, Provision, Regulation, Restriction, Pain, Penalty, Forfeiture, Matter and Thing therein respectively contained, shall be, and the same is and are hereby severally and respectively repealed.

Combination Act, 21 June 1824

5 Geo. 4, c. 95   *Statutes at Large,* XLIV, 508 19.

This act virtually legalized trade unions by repealing earlier restrictions on their formation. Francis Place, the Westminster reformer, and Joseph Hume (1777-1855), the radical MP, were instrumental in its passage. Restrictions on trade unions were partially reimposed in 1825 after a series of strikes.

Whereas it is expedient that the Laws relative to the Combination of Workmen, and to fixing the Wages of Labour should be repealed; that certain Combinations of Masters and Workmen should be exempted from Punishment; and that the Attempt to deter Workmen from Work should be punished in a summary Manner; Be it therefore enacted by the King's most Excellent Majesty, by and with the Advice and Consent of the Lords Spiritual and Temporal, and Commons, in this present Parliament assembled, and by the Authority of the same, That from and after the passing of this Act, so much of a certain Act passed in the Thirty third Year of King *Edward* the First, intituled *Who be Conspirators and who be Champertors,* as relates to Combinations or Conspiracies of Workmen or other Persons to obtain an Advance or to fix the Rate of Wages, or to lessen or alter the Hours or Duration of the Time of working, or to decrease the Quantity of Work, or to regulate or controul the Mode of carrying on any Manufacture, Trade or

Business, or the Management thereof, and as relates to Combinations or Conspiracies of Masters, Manufacturers or other Persons, to lower or fix the Rate of Wages, or to increase or alter the Hours or Duration of the Time of working, or to increase the Quantity of Work, or to regulate or controul the Mode of carrying on any Manufacture, Trade or Business, or the Management thereof, or to oblige Workmen to enter into Work; and also a certain other Act passed in the Third Year of King *Henry* the Sixth, intituled *Masons shall not confederate themselves in Chapiters and Assemblies*; also a certain other Act passed in the Parliament of *Ireland*, in the Thirty third Year of King *Henry* the Eighth, intituled *An Act for Servants' Wages*; also a certain other Act passed in the Second and Third Years of King *Edward* the Sixth, intituled *The Bill of Conspiracies of Victuallers and Craftsmen*; also a certain other Act passed in the Parliament of *Scotland*, in the Fifth Parliament of King *James* the First of *Scotland*, intituled *Of the Fees of Craftsmen and the Price of their Worke*; also a certain other Act passed in the Parliament of *Scotland*, in the Fifth Parliament of King *James* the First of *Scotland*, intituled *Of the Fees of Workmen*; also a certain other Act passed in the Parliament of *Scotland*, in the Fifth Parliament of King *James* the First of *Scotland*, intituled *Of Writches and Masones*; also a certain other Act passed in the Parliament of *Scotland*, in the Seventh Parliament of King *James* the First of *Scotland*, intituled *The Price of Silk Workmanshippe;* also a certain other Act, passed in the Parliament of *Scotland*, in the Fifth Parliament of Queen *Mary* of *Scotland*, intituled *The Price of Craftesmenne's Wark, of Meate and Drinke in Tavernes*; also a certain other Act passed in the Parliament of *Scotland*, in the Seventh Parliament of King *James* the Sixth of *Scotland*, intituled *Anent the setting of Ordour and Price in all Stuffe*; also so much of a certain other Act passed in the Thirteenth and Fourteenth Years of King *Charles* the Second, intituled *An Act for regulating the Trade of Silk Throwing*, as provides and enacts, that the Corporation of Silk Throwers should not, by virtue of that Act, nor any Thing therein contained, make any Orders, Ordinances or Bye Laws, to set any Rates or Prices whatsoever upon the throwing of Silk, to bind or enforce their Members to work at; also a certain other Act passed in the Seventh Year of King *George* the First, intituled *An Act for regulating the Journeymen Tailors within the Weekly Bills of Mortality*, excepting so much thereof as relates to the Recovery of Wages, or to Journeymen Tailors or Servants department from their Service, or refusing to enter into Work or Employment, as therein mentioned; also so much of an Act passed in the Twelfth Year of King *George* the First, intituled *An Act to prevent unlawful Combinations of Workmen employed in the Woollen Manufactures, and for better Payment of their Wages*, as provides that Contracts, Covenants or Agreements, Bye Laws, Ordinances, Rules and Orders, made or entered into by or between Persons brought up in, or professing, using or exercising the Art and Mystery of a Woolcomber or Weaver, or Journeyman Woolcomber or Journeyman Weaver, as therein mentioned, shall be illegal, null and void, and as punishes Woolcombers, Weavers, Journeyman Woolcombers and Weavers, and other Persons concerned in the Woollen Manufactures, for keeping up, continuing, acting in, making, entering into, signing, sealing or being knowingly concerned in, presuming or attempting to put in Execution such Agreements, Bye Laws, Ordinances, Rules or Orders, as therein mentioned, and as provides that the Provisions of the said Act of the Twelfth of *George* the First, just recited, shall extend to the Persons therein mentioned; also so much of a certain other Act passed in the Parliament of *Ireland*, in the Third Year of King *George* the Second, intituled *An Act to prevent unlawful Combinations of Workmen, Artificers and Labourers, employed in the several Trades and Manufactures of this Kingdom, and for the better Payment of their Wages; as also to prevent Abuses in making of Bricks, and to ascertain their Dimensions*, as declares illegal, null and void the Contracts, Covenants, Agreements, Bye Laws, Ordinances, Rules and Orders therein mentioned, and makes it an Offence to keep up, continue, act in, make, enter into, sign, seal or to be knowingly concerned therein, and to presume or attempt to put the same into Execution, as therein mentioned; also so much of a certain other Act passed in the Parliament of *Ireland*, in the Seventeenth Year of King *George* the Second, intituled *An Act for continuing several Statutes now nearing expiring, and for amending other Statutes, and for other Purposes therein mentioned*, as declares the Assemblies therein mentioned to be unlawful Assemblies, the Houses where they meet common Nuisances, and punishes the Master and Mistress thereof, as likewise those who enter into the Contracts, Covenants or Articles therein mentioned, or collect or pay Money for the Support of Persons as therein mentioned; also so much of a certain other Act passed in the Twenty second Year of King *George* the Second, intituled *An Act for the more effectual preventing of Frauds and Abuses committed by Persons employed in the Manufacture of Hats, and in the Woollen, Linen, Fustian, Cotton, Iron, Leather, Fur, Hemp, Flax, Mohair and Silk Manufactures, and for preventing unlawful Combinations of Journeymen Dyers and Journeymen Hotpressers, and of all Persons employed in the said several Manufactures, and for the better Payment of their Wages*, as extends those Provisions of the said Act of the Twelfth of *George* the First herein mentioned to the Persons therein mentioned; also so much of a certain other Act passed in the Twenty ninth Year of King *George* the Second, intituled *An Act to render more effectual an Act passed in the Twelfth Year of the Reign of His late Majesty King George, to prevent unlawful Combinations of Workmen employed in the Woollen Manufactures, and for better Payment of their Wages; and also an Act passed in the Thirteenth Year of the Reign of His said late Majesty, for the better Regulations of the Woollen Manufacture, and for preventing Disputes among the Persons concerned therein, and for limiting a Time for Prosecution for the Forfeiture appointed by the aforesaid Act, in case of the Payment of the Workmen's Wages in any other Manner than in Money*, as relates to the making of Rates for the Payment of Wages, continuing and altering and notifying them as therein mentioned; also so much of a certain other Act passed in the Parliament of *Ireland*, in the Third Year of King *George* the Third, intituled *An Act for continuing and amending certain temporary Statutes heretofore made, for the better Regulation of the City of Cork, and for enlarging the Salary of the Treasurer, and for the better regulating the Sale of Coals in the said City, and for erecting and continuing Lamps in the same, and for the better preserving the Streets and Highways therein, and for confirming and establishing a Court of Conscience in the said City, and for regulating the Assize of Bread therein, and for securing the Quays by Parapet Walls*, as relates to the Assemblies and Combinations of

Artificers, Journeymen, Apprentices, Labourers and Manufacturers therein mentioned; also so much of a certain other Act passed in the Parliament of *Ireland*, in the Third Year of King *George* the Third, intituled *An Act for the better Regulation of the Linen and Hempen Manufactures*, as relates to meeting in order to consult upon or enter into Rules, Agreements or Combinations to ascertain or fix the Price of Labour or Workmanship, and as relates to administering Oaths or Declarations tending to fix the Price of Wages or Workmanship, and as relates to issuing and delivering Tickets, Certificates and Tokens of Parties being licensed to work, and as relates to Rules, Orders and Regulations relating to the Price or Wages of Labour or Workmanship, and as relates to Oaths to enter into Combinations or Agreements to ascertain or fix the Price of Wages or Workmanship, and to Oaths and Combinations not to work for a particular Employer, as therein mentioned; also a certain other Act, passed in the Eighth Year of King *George* the Third, intituled *An Act to amend an Act made in the Seventh Year of King* George *the First, intituled 'An Act for regulating the Journeymen Tailors within the Weekly Bills of Mortality;'* also so much of a certain other Act, passed in the Parliament of *Ireland* in the Eleventh and Twelfth Years of King *George* the Third, intituled *An Act for the Regulation of the City of* Cork*, and for other Purposes therein mentioned relative to the said City*, as relates to the Meetings and Assemblies therein mentioned, the administering and taking Oaths and Declarations, to the Tickets, Certificates, Advertisements and Writings, and to the Rules, Orders, Agreements and Regulations, and to the Combinations and Agreements to ascertain or fix the Price of Wages, Labour or Workmanship, or not to work, and as relates to the Refusal or Neglect, by Persons not in actual Service, to work on Application made, and as relates to the Detection and Discovery of Assemblies and Combinations for any of the above recited Purposes, and as relates to ascertaining Wages as therein mentioned; also so much of a certain Act, passed in the Parliament of *Ireland* in the Eleventh and Twelfth Years of King *George* the Third, intituled *An Act for regulating the Journeymen Tailors and Journeymen Shipwrights of the City of* Dublin *and the Liberties thereof, and of the County of* Dublin, as punishes those who permit the Clubs and Societies therein mentioned to be kept or held in their Houses or Apartments, and as makes the Contracts, Covenants and Agreements therein mentioned, and Oaths to enforce them, illegal, and as punishes Persons for keeping up, continuing, acting in, making, entering into, signing, sealing or being knowingly interested or concerned in such Contracts, Covenants or Agreements, and as punishes Persons not retained or employed for refusing to enter into Work or Employment on Request made, as therein mentioned, and as regulates the Hours of Work and the Rate of Wages as therein mentioned; also so much of a certain other Act, passed in the Thirteenth Year of King *George* the Third, intituled *An Act to empower the Magistrates therein mentioned to settle and regulate the Wages of Persons employed in the Silk Manufacture within their respective Jurisdictions,* as relates to settling, regulating, ordering and declaring the Wages and Prices of Work, and the Notification thereof, and makes it an Offence to deviate from such Settlement, Regulation, Order and Declaration, or to ask, receive or take more or less Wages or larger or less Prices than shall be so settled, or to enter into Combinations, or for that Purpose to decoy or solicit, or to assemble, as therein mentioned, and as relates to the Detection of such Offences, and as makes it an Offence to retain or employ Journeymen Weavers, or to give, allow or pay, or cause to be given, allowed or paid, more or less Wages than shall be settled, as therein mentioned; also so much of a certain other Act, passed in the Seventeenth Year of King *George* the Third, intituled *An Act for the better regulating the Hat Manufactory*, as relates to the keeping up, acting in, making, entering into, signing, sealing or being knowingly concerned in the Contracts, Covenants or Agreements, Bye Laws, Ordinances, Rules or Orders of the Clubs, Societies or Combinations therein mentioned, or the presuming or attempting to put the Agreements, Bye Laws, Ordinances, Rules or Orders in Execution, or to the attending Meetings, Clubs, Societies or Combinations, or to the Summoning, giving Notice to or calling upon, collecting, demanding or receiving, persuading, enticing or inveigling, or endeavouring to persuade, entice or inveigle, paying Money, making or entering into Subscriptions or Contributions, as therein mentioned; also so much of a certain other Act, passed in the Parliament of *Ireland* in the Nineteenth and Twentieth Years of King *George* the Third, intituled *An Act to prevent Combinations, and for the further Encouragement of Trade*, as declares that Combinations in Trade are public Nuisances, and that the Acts therein enumerated shall be considered as Evidences of unlawful Combinations, and sufficient for the Conviction of any Person who shall be guilty of the same, and as avoids Rules, Bye Laws and Regulations contrary to its Provisions and Oaths for obeying or executing the same, and as provides for the Case of an Act of Combination for which no specific Punishment is pointed out, as therein mentioned; also so much of a certain other Act, passed in the Parliament of *Ireland* in the Nineteenth and Twentieth Years of King *George* the Third, intituled *An Act for the better Regulation of the Silk Manufacture*, as relates to the Wages and Prices for Work, to Combinations to raise Wages, and the decoying or soliciting Journeymen Weavers, as therein mentioned; also so much of a certain other Act, passed in the Parliament of *Ireland* in the Nineteenth and Twentieth Years of King *George* the Third, intituled *An Act for regulating the curing and preparing Provisions, and for preventing Combinations among the several Tradesmen and other Persons employed in making up such Provisions, and for regulating the Butter Trade in the City of Dublin, and for other Purposes therein mentioned*, as relates to summoning Persons to appear at Meetings and Assemblies, and as relates to administering Oaths or Declarations, to the issuing and delivering of Messages, Tickets, Certificates and Tokens, Advertisements or Writings, to making or joining in making Rules, Orders, Agreements and Regulations as therein mentioned, and as relates to taking Oaths, or entering into Combinations or Agreements to ascertain or fix the Price of Wages or of Labour or Workmanship, or to make any Rule, Order, Agreement or Regulation, and to taking Oaths and entering into Combinations and Agreements not to work for a particular Person, as therein mentioned, and as relates to the fixing of Wages; also so much of a certain other Act, passed in the Parliament of *Ireland* in the Twenty fifth Year of King *George* the Third intituled *An Act for granting the Sums of Twenty thousand Pounds, Five thousand Pounds, and Four thousand Pounds, to certain Trustees, and for promoting the several Manufactures therein named*, as relates to ascertaining the Rates of Labour and Prices of

Workmanship, as therein mentioned, and as requires an Affidavit to be filed previous to the Commencement of a Suit, as therein mentioned; also so much of a certain other Act, passed in the Thirty second Year of King *George* the Third, intituled *An Act for extending the Provisions of an Act made in the Thirteenth Year of the Reign of His present Majesty, intituled 'An Act to empower the Magistrates therein mentioned to settle and regulate the Wages of Persons employed in the Silk Manufacture within their respective Jurisdictions,' to Manufactories of Silk mixed with other Materials, and for the more effectual Punishment of Buyers and Receivers of Silk purloined and embezzled by Persons employed in the Manufacture thereof* as extend the Provisions of the said Act of the Thirteenth of *George* the Third, hereby repealed, to the Persons therein mentioned; also a certain other Act, passed in the Thirty sixth Year of King *George* the Third, intituled *An Act to prevent unlawful Combinations of Workmen employed in the Paper Manufactory*; also so much of a certain other Act passed in the Thirty ninth Year of King *George* the Third, intituled *An Act to explain and amend the Laws relative to Colliers in that Part of* Great Britain *called* Scotland, as relates to the fixing and appointing of Hire and Wages; also an Act passed in the Thirty ninth and Fortieth Years of King *George* the Third, intituled *An Act to repeal an Act passed in the last Session of Parliament, intituled 'An Act to prevent unlawful Combinations of Workmen,' and to substitute other Provisions in lieu thereof,* excepting so much thereof as relates to the Adjustment of Disputes between Masters and Workmen, as therein mentioned; also so much of a certain other Act passed in the Forty third Year of King *George* the Third, intituled *An Act to prevent unlawful Combinations of Workmen, Artificers, Journeymen and Labourers, in* Ireland, *and for other Purposes relating thereto,* as makes illegal and void Contracts, Covenants and Agreements for obtaining an Advance of Wages, or for lessening or altering the Hours of Time of working, or for decreasing the Quantity of Work, or for controlling or affecting the Conduct or Management of any Manufacture, Trade or Business, and as prohibits the making or entering into or being concerned in the same, and as punishes Persons for so doing, and as relates to the Combinations therein mentioned, and as relates to endeavouring by Gift, Persuasion or Solicitation to prevent Persons hiring themselves, and as relates to attending the Meetings therein mentioned, or endeavouring to induce the Attendance of others, and collecting, demanding, asking or receiving Money for the Purposes therein mentioned, and as relates to persuading, enticing, soliciting or endeavouring to induce others to enter into or be concerned in the Combinations therein mentioned, and to paying Money, making or entering into Subscriptions or Contributions, and to Oaths and Declarations, and to Tickets, Certificates and Tokens, and to Contributions supporting and maintaining others, as therein mentioned, and as punishes Persons for permitting Assemblies in their Houses or Apartments, as therein mentioned; also a certain other Act passed in the Forty seventh Year of King *George* the Third, intituled *An Act to declare that the Provisions of an Act, made in the Parliament of* Ireland *in the Thirty third Year of King* Henry *the Eighth, relating to Servants Wages, shall extend to all Counties of Cities and Counties of Towns in* Ireland; also so much of a certain other Act passed in the Fifty seventh Year of King *George* the Third, intituled *An Act to extend the Provisions of an Act of the Twelfth*

Year of His late Majesty King George *the First, and an Act of the Twenty second Year of His late Majesty King* George *the Second, against Payment of Labourers in Goods or by Truck, and to secure their Payment in the lawful Money of this Realm, to Labourers employed in the Collieries, or in the working and getting of Coal, in the United Kingdom of* Great Britain *and* Ireland *and for extending the Provisions of the said Acts to* Scotland *and* Ireland, as extends such of the Provisions of the said Acts as are hereby repealed to *Scotland* and *Ireland*; together with all other Laws, Statutes and Enactments now in force throughout or in any Part of the United Kingdom of *Great Britain* and *Ireland*, relative to Combinations to obtain an Advance of Wages, or to lessen or alter the Hours or Duration of the Time of working, or to decrease the Quantity of Work, or to regulate or controul the Mode of carrying on any Manufacture, Trade or Business, or the Management thereof; relative also to Combinations to lower the Rate of Wages, or to increase or alter the Hours or Duration of the Time of working, or to increase the Quantity of Work, or to regulate or controul the Mode of carrying on any Manufacture, Trade or Business, or the Management thereof; relative also to fixing the Amount of the Wages of Labour; relative also to obliging Workmen not hired to enter into Work; together with every other Act and Enactment enforcing or extending the Application of any of the Acts or Enactments repealed by this Act, shall be and the same are hereby repealed, save and except in as far as the same may have repealed any prior Act or Enactment. [*See Section 6. post.*]

II.   And be it further enacted, That Journeymen, Workmen or other Persons who shall enter into any Combination to obtain an Advance, or to fix the Rate of Wages, or to lessen or alter the Hours or Duration of the Time of working, or to decrease the Quantity of Work, or to induce another to depart from his Service before the End of the Time or Term for which he is hired, or to quit or return his Work before the same shall be finished, or not being hired, to refuse to enter into Work or Employment, or to regulate the Mode of carrying on any Manufacture, Trade or Business, or the Management thereof, shall not therefore be subject or liable to any Indictment or Prosecution for Conspiracy, or to any other Criminal Information or Punishment whatever, under the Common or the Statute Law.

III.   And be it further enacted, That Masters, Employers or other Persons, who shall enter into any Combination to lower or to fix the Rate of Wages, or to increase or alter the Hours or Duration of the Time of working, or to increase the Quantity of Work, or to regulate the Mode of carrying on any Manufacture, Trade or Business, or the Management thereof, shall not therefore be subject or liable to any Indictment or Prosecution, or, for Conspiracy, or to any other Criminal Information or Punishment whatever, under the Common or the Statute Law.

IV.   And be it further enacted, That all penal Proceedings for any Act or Omission against any Enactment hereby repealed, and not made punishable by the Provisions of this Act or for any Act or Omission hereby exempted from Punishment, shall become null and void; and that no penal Proceedings for any Act or Omission against any Enactment hereby repealed, and not made punishable by the Provisions of this Act, or for any Act or Omission hereby exempted from Punishment, shall be instituted against any one in relation to any such Offence already incurred; provided that no Person shall be subjected to Loss or Liability for any Thing already done, touching any Act or Omission, the penal Proceedings against which are hereby made null and void, or shall lose any Privilege or Protection to which the Enactments hereby repealed entitle him.

V. And be it further enacted, That if any Person by Violence to the Person or Property, by Threats or by Intimidation, shall wilfully or maliciously force another to depart from his Hiring or Work before the End of the Time or Term for which he is hired, or return his Work before the same shall be finished, or damnify, spoil or destroy any Machinery, Tools, Goods, Wares or Work, or prevent any Person not being hired from accepting any Work or Employment; or if any Person shall wilfully or maliciously use or employ Violence to the Person or Property, Threats or Intimidation towards another on account of his not complying with or conforming to any Rules, Orders, Resolutions or Regulations made to obtain an Advance of Wages, or to lessen or alter the Hours of working, or to decrease the Quantity of Work, or to regulate the Mode of carrying on any Manufacture, Trade or Business, or the Management thereof; or if any Person, by Violence to the Person or Property, by Threats or by Intimidation, shall wilfully or maliciously force any Master or Mistress Manufacturer, his or her Foreman or Agent, to make any Alteration in their Mode of regulating, managing, conducting or carrying on their Manufacture, Trade or Business; every Person so offending, or causing, procuring, aiding, abetting or assisting in such Offence, being convicted thereof in Manner hereafter mentioned, shall be imprisoned only, or imprisoned and kept to hard Labour, for any Time not exceeding Two Calendar Months.

VI. And be it further enacted, That if any Persons shall combine, and by Violence to the Person or Property, or by Threats or Intimidation, wilfully and maliciously force another to depart from his Service before the End of the Time or Term for which he or she is hired, or return his or her Work before the same shall be finished, or damnify, spoil or destroy any Machinery, Tools, Goods, Wares or Work, or prevent any Person not being hired from accepting any Work or Employment; or if any Persons so combined shall wilfully or maliciously use or employ Violence to the Person or Property, or Threats or Intimidation towards another, on account of his or her not complying with or conforming to any Rules, Orders, Resolutions or Regulations made to obtain an Advance of Wages, or to lessen or alter the Hours of working, or to decrease the Quantity of Work, or to regulate the Mode of carrying on any Manufacture, Trade or Business, or the Management thereof; or if any Persons shall combine, and by Violence to the Person or Property, or by Threats or Intimidation, wilfully or maliciously force any Master or Mistress Manufacturer, his or her Foreman or Agent, to make any Alteration in their Mode of regulating, managing, conducting or carrying on their Manufacture, Trade or Business; each and every Person so offending, or causing, procuring, aiding, abetting or assisting in such Offence, being convicted thereof in Manner hereinafter mentioned, shall be imprisoned only, or imprisoned and kept to hard Labour, for any Time not exceeding Two Calendar Months: Provided always, that nothing herein contained shall alter or affect any Law now in force for the Prosecution and Punishment of the said several Offences; only that a Conviction under this Act for any of such Offence shall exempt the Offender from Prosecution under any other Law or Statute. [*See Section 1. ante.*]

VII. And for the more effectual Prosecution of Offenders against this Act, be it further enacted, That on Complaint and Information upon Oath before any One or more Justice or Justices of the Peace, of any Offence having been committed against this Act within his or their respective Jurisdictions, such Justice or Justices are hereby authorized and required to summon the Person or Persons charged with any such Offence against this Act to appear before any Two Justices at a certain Time and Place to be specified, such Place to be as near to the Place where Cause of such Complaint shall have arisen as may be; and if any Person or Persons so summoned shall not appear according to such Summons, then such Justices (Proof on Oath having been first made before them or him of the due Service of such Summons upon such Person or Persons, by delivering the same to him or her personally, or leaving the same at his or her usual Place of Abode, provided the same shall be so left Twenty four Hours at the least before the Time which shall be appointed to attend the said Justices upon such Summons) shall make and issue their or his Warrants or Warrant for apprehending the Person or Persons so summoned and not appearing as aforesaid, and bringing him or her before such Justices; or it shall be lawful for such Justices, if they shall think fit, without issuing any previous Summons, and instead of issuing the same, upon such Complaint and Information upon Oath as aforesaid, to make and issue their Warrant or Warrants for apprehending the Person or Persons by such Information charged to have offended against this Act, and bringing him or her before such Justices; such Justices shall and they are hereby authorized and required forthwith to make Enquiry touching the Matters complained of, and to examine into the same, and to hear and determine the Matter of every such Complaint; and upon Confession by the Party, or Proof by Two or more credible Witnesses upon Oath, (which Oath such Justice or Justices are hereby authorized to administer,) to convict or acquit the Party against whom Complaint shall have been made as aforesaid; such Conviction, and the Commitment thereon, to be in the Form or to the Effect of the Form in the Schedule to this Act annexed.

VIII. Provided always, and be it further enacted, That no Justice of the Peace, being also a Master, or the Father or Son of any Master, in any Trade or Manufacture, shall act as such Justice under this Act. . . .

Banking Act, 26 May 1826

7 Geo. 4, c. 46   *Statutes of the United Kingdom*, 1826, 129–34.

This act reorganized the banking system and permitted certain banks to be established on a joint stock basis.

Whereas an Act was passed in the Thirty ninth and Fortieth Years of the Reign of His late Majesty King *George* the Third, intituled *An Act for establishing an Agreement with the Governor and Company of the Bank of* England, *for advancing the Sum of Three Millions towards the Supply for the Service of the Year One thousand eight hundred*: And Whereas it was, to prevent Doubts as to the Privilege of the said Governor and Company, enacted and declared in the said recited Act, that no other Bank should be erected, established or allowed by Parliament; and that it should not be lawful for any Body Politic or Corporate whatsoever, erected or to be erected, or for any other Persons united or to be united in Covenants or Partnership, exceeding the Number of Six Persons, in that Part of *Great Britain* called *England*, to borrow, owe or take up any Sum or Sums of Money on their Bills or Notes payable on Demand, or at any less Time than Six Months from the borrowing thereof, during the Continuance of the said Privilege to the said Governor and Company, who were thereby declared to be and remain a Corporation, with the Privilege of Exclusive Banking, as before recited; but subject nevertheless to Redemption on the Terms and Conditions in the said Act specified: And Whereas the Governor and Company of the Bank of *England* have consented to relinquish so much of their exclusive Privilege as prohibits any Body Politic or Corporate, or any Number of Persons exceeding Six, in *England*, acting in Copartnership, from borrowing, owing or taking up any Sum or Sums of Money on their Bills or Notes payable on Demand, or at any less Time than Six Months from the borrowing thereof; provided that such Body Politic or Corporate, or Persons united in Covenants or Partnerships, exceeding the Number of Six Persons in each Copartnership, shall have the whole of their Banking Establishments and carry on their Business as Bankers at any Place or Places in *England* exceeding the Distance of Sixty five Miles from *London*, and that all the Individuals composing such Corporations or Copartnerships, carrying on such Business, shall be liable to and responsible for the due Payment of all Bills and Notes issued by such Corporations or Copartnerships respectively: Be it therefore enacted by the King's most Excellent Majesty, by and with the Advice and Consent of the Lord Spiritual and Temporal, and Commons, in this present Parliament assembled, and by the Authority of the same, That from and after the passing of this Act it shall and may be lawful for any Bodies Politic or Corporate erected for the Purposes of Banking, or for any Number of Persons united in Covenants or Copartnership, although such Persons so united or carrying on Business together shall consist of more than Six in Number, to carry on the Trade or Business of Bankers in *England*, in like Manner as Copartnerships of Bankers consisting of not more than Six Persons in Number may lawfully do; and for such Bodies Politic or Corporate, or such Persons so united as aforesaid, to make and issue their Bills or Notes at any Place or Places in *England* exceeding the Distance of Sixty five Miles from *London*, payable on Demand, or otherwise at some Place or Places specified upon such Bills or Notes, exceeding the Distance of Sixty five Miles from *London* and not elsewhere, and to borrow, owe or take up any Sum or Sums of Money on their Bills or Notes so made and issued at any such Place or Places as aforesaid: Provided always, that such Corporations or Persons carrying on such Trade or Business of Bankers in Copartnership shall not have any House of Business or Establishment as Bankers in *London*, or at any Place or Places not exceeding the Distance of Sixty five Miles from *London*; and that every Member of any such Corporation or Copartnership shall be liable to and responsible for the due Payment of all Bills and Notes which shall be issued, and for all Sums of Money which shall be borrowed, owed or taken up by the Corporation or Copartnership of which such Person shall be a Member, such Person being a Member at the Period of the Date of the Bills or Notes, or becoming or being a Member before or at the Time of the Bills or Notes being payable, or being such Member at the Time of the borrowing, owing or taking up of any Sum or Sums of Money upon any Bills or Notes by the Corporation or Copartnership, or while any Sum of Money on any Bills or Notes is owing or unpaid, or at the Time the same became due from the Corporation or Copartnership; any Agreement, Covenant or Contract to the contrary notwithstanding.

II. Provided always, and be it further enacted, That nothing in this Act contained shall extend or be construed to extend to enable or authorize any such Corporation, or Copartnership exceeding the Number of Six Persons, so carrying on the Trade or Business of Bankers as aforesaid, either by any Member of or Person belonging to any such Corporation or Copartnership, or by any Agent or Agents, or any other Person or Persons on behalf of any such Corporation or Copartnership, to issue or re-issue in *London*, or at any Place or Places not exceeding the Distance of Sixty five Miles from *London*, any Bill or Note of such Corporation or Copartnership, which shall be payable to Bearer on Demand, or any Bank Post Bill; nor to draw upon any Partner or Agent, or other Person or Persons who may be resident in *London*, or at any Place or Places not exceeding the Distance of Sixty five Miles from *London*, any Bill of Exchange which shall be payable on Demand, or which shall be for a less Amount than Fifty Pounds: Provided also, that it shall be lawful, notwithstanding any Thing herein or in the said recited Act contained, for any such Corporation or Copartnership to draw any Bill of Exchange for any Sum of Money amounting to the Sum of Fifty Pounds or upwards, payable either in *London* or elsewhere, at any Period after Date or after Sight.

III. Provided also, and be it further enacted, That nothing in this Act contained shall extend or be construed to extend to enable or authorize any such Corporation or Copartnership exceeding the Number of Six Persons, so carrying on the Trade or Business of Bankers in *England* as aforesaid, or any Member, Agent or Agents of any such Corporation or Copartnership, to borrow, owe or take up in *London* or at any Place or Places not exceeding the Distance of Sixty five Miles from *London* any Sum or Sums of Money on any Bill or Promissory Note of any such Corporation or Copartnership payable on Demand, or at any less Time than Six Months from the borrowing thereof, nor to make or issue any Bill or Bills of Exchange or Promissory Note or Notes of such Corporation or Copartnership contrary to the Provisions of the said recited Act of the Thirty ninth and Fortieth Years of King *George* the Third, save as provided by this Act in that Behalf: Provided also, that nothing contained shall extend or be construed to extend to prevent any such Corporation or Copartnership, by any Agent or Person authorized by them, from discounting in *London*, or elsewhere, any Bill or Bills of Exchange not drawn by or upon such Corporation or Copartnership, or by or upon any Person on their Behalf.

IV. And be it further enacted, That before any such Corporation or Copartnership exceeding the Number of Six Persons, in *England*, shall begin to issue any Bills or Notes, or borrow, owe or take up any Money on their Bills or Notes, an Account or Return shall be made out, according to the Form contained in the Schedule marked (A) to this Act annexed, wherein shall be set forth the true Names, Title or Firm of such intended or existing Corporation or Copartnership, and also the Names and Places of Abode of all the Members of such Corporation or of all the Partners concerned or engaged in such Copartnership, as the same respectively shall appear on the Books of such Corporation or Copartnership, and the Name or Firm of every Bank or Banks established or to be established by such Corporation or Copartnership, and also the Names and Places of Abode of Two or more Persons, being Members of such Corporation or Copartnership, and being resident in *England*, who shall have been appointed Public Officers of such Corporation or Copartnership, together with the Title of Office or other Description of every such Public Officer respectively, in the Name of any One of whom such Corporation shall sue and be sued as hereinafter provided, and also the Name of every Town and Place where any of the Bills or Notes of such Corporation or Copartnership shall be issued by any such Corporation or by their Agent or Agents; and every such Amount of Return shall be delivered to the Commissioners of Stamps, at the Stamp Office in *London*, who shall cause the same to be filed and kept in the said Stamp Office, and an Entry and Registry thereof to be made in a Book or Books to be there kept for that Purpose by some Person or Persons to be appointed by the said Commissioners in that Behalf, and which Book or Books any Person or Persons shall from time to time have liberty to search and inspect on Payment of the Sum of One Shilling for every Search.

V.   And be it further enacted, That such Account or Return shall be made out by the Secretary or other Person, being One of the Public Officers appointed as aforesaid, and shall be verified by the Oath of such Secretary or other Public Officer, taken before any Justice of the Peace, and which Oath any Justice of the Peace is hereby authorized and empowered to administer; and that such Account or Return shall, between the Twenty eighth Day of *February* and the Twenty fifth Day of *March* in every Year, after such Corporation or Copartnership shall be formed, be in like Manner delivered by such Secretary or other Public Officer as aforesaid, to the Commissioners of Stamps, to be filed and kept in the Manner and for the Purposes as hereinbefore mentioned.

VI.   And be it further enacted, That a Copy of any such Account or Return so filed or kept and registered at the Stamp Office, as by this Act is directed, and which Copy shall be certified to be a true Copy under the Hand or Hands of One or more of the Commissioners of Stamps for the Time being, upon Proof made that such Certificate has been signed with the Handwriting of the Person or Persons making the same, and whom it shall not be necessary to prove to be a Commissioner or Commissioners, shall in all Proceedings, Civil or Criminal, and in all Cases whatsoever, be received in Evidence as Proof of the Appointment and Authority of the Public Officers named in such Account or Return, and also of the Fact that all Persons named therein as Members of such Corporation or Copartnership were Members thereof at the Date of such Account or Return.

VII.   And be it further enacted, That the said Commissioners of Stamps for the Time being shall and they are hereby required, upon Application made to them by any Person or Persons requiring a Copy certified according to this Act, of any such Account or Return as aforesaid, in order that the same may be produced in Evidence or for any other Purpose, to deliver to the Person or Persons so applying for the same such certified Copy, he, she or they paying for the same the Sum of Ten Shillings and no more.

VIII. Provided also, and be it further enacted, That the Secretary or other Officer of every such Corporation or Copartnership shall and he is hereby required, from time to time, as often as Occasion shall render it necessary, make out upon Oath, in Manner hereinbefore directed, and cause to be delivered to the Commissioners of Stamps as aforesaid, a further Account or Return according to the Form contained in the Schedule marked (B) to this Act annexed, of the Name or Names of any Person or Persons who shall have been nominated or appointed a new or additional Public Officer or Public Officers of such Corporation or Copartnership, and also of the Name or Names of any Person or Persons who shall have ceased to be Members of such Corporation or Copartnership, and also of the Name or Names of any Person or Persons who shall have become a Member or Members of such Corporation or Copartnership, either in addition to or in the Place or Stead of any former Member or Members thereof, and of the Names or Names of any new or additional Town or Towns, Place or Places, where such Bills or Notes are or are intended to be issued, and where the same are to be made payable; and such further Accounts or Returns shall from time to time be filed and kept, and entered and registered at the Stamp Office in *London*, in like Manner as is hereinbefore required with respect to the original or annual Account or Return hereinbefore directed to be made.

IX. And be it further enacted, That all Actions and Suits, and also all Petitions to found any Commission of Bankruptcy against any Person or Persons, who may be at any Time indebted to any such Copartnership carrying on Business under the Provisions of this Act, and all Proceedings at Law or in Equity under any Commission of Bankruptcy, and all other Proceedings at Law or in Equity to be commenced or instituted for or on behalf of any such Copartnership against any Person or Persons, Bodies Politic or Corporate, or others, whether Members of such Copartnership or otherwise, for recovering any Debts or enforcing any Claims or Demands due to such Copartnership, or for any other Matter relating to the Concerns of such Copartnership, shall and lawfully may, from and after the passing of this Act, be commenced or instituted and prosecuted in the Name of any One of the Public Officers nominated as aforesaid for the Time being of such Copartnership, as the nominal Plaintiff or Petitioner for and on behalf of such Copartnership; and that all Actions or Suits, and Proceedings at Law or in Equity, to be commenced or instituted by any Person or Persons, Bodies Politic or Corporate, or others, whether Members of such Copartnership or otherwise, against such Copartnership, shall and lawfully may be commenced, instituted and prosecuted against any One or more of the Public Officers nominated as aforesaid for the Time being of such Copartnership, as the nominal Defendant for and on behalf of such Copartnership; and that all Indictments, Informations and Prosecutions by or on behalf of such Copartnership, for any Stealing or Embezzlement of any Money, Goods, Effects, Bills, Notes, Securities or other

Property of or belonging to such Copartnership, or for any Fraud, Forgery, Crime or Offence committed against or with Intent to injure or defraud such Copartnership, shall and lawfully may be had, preferred and carried on in the Name of any One of the Public Officers nominated as aforesaid for the Time being of such Copartnership; and that in all Indictments and Informations to be had or preferred by or on behalf of such Copartnership against any Person or Persons whomsoever, notwithstanding such Person or Persons may happen to be a Member or Members of such Copartnership, it shall be lawful and sufficient to state the Money, Goods, Effects, Bills, Notes, Securities or other Property of such Copartnership, to be the Money, Goods, Effects, Bills, Notes, Securities or other Property of any One of the Public Officers nominated as aforesaid for the Time being of such Copartnership; and that any Forgery, Fraud, Crime or other Offence committed against or with Intent to injure or defraud any such Copartnership, shall and lawfully may in such Indictment or Indictments, notwithstanding as aforesaid, be laid or stated to have been committed against or with Intent to injure or defraud any One of the Public Officers nominated as aforesaid for the Time being of such Copartnership; and any Offender or Offenders may thereupon be lawfully convicted for any such Forgery, Fraud, Crime or Offence; and that in all other Allegations, Indictments, Informations or other Proceedings of any Kind whatsoever, in which it otherwise might or would have been necessary to state the Names of the Persons composing such Copartnership, it shall and may be lawful and sufficient to state the Name of any One of the Public Officers nominated as aforesaid for the Time being of such Copartnership; and the Death, Resignation, Removal or any Act of such Public Officer, shall not abate or prejudice any such Action, Suit, Indictment, Information, Prosecution or other Proceeding commenced against or by or on behalf of such Copartnership, but the same may be continued, prosecuted and carried on in the Name of any other of the Public Officers of such Copartnership for the Time being. . . .

Corn Law, 15 July 1828

9 Geo. 4, c. 60   *Statutes of the United Kingdom*, LXVIII, 310-13, 327-30.

This statute reduced the stringency of the Corn Law (1815) by introducing a sliding scale of duties.

Whereas an Act was passed in the Fifty-fifth Year of the Reign of His late Majesty King *George* the Third, intituled *An Act to amend the laws now in force for regulating the Importation of Corn*: And Whereas an Act was passed in the Third Year of the Reign of His present Majesty, intituled *An Act to amend the Laws relating to the Importation of Corn*: And Whereas a certain Act was passed in the Seventh and Eighth Years of His Majesty's Reign, intituled *An Act to make Provision for ascertaining from time to time the Average Prices of British Corn*:

And Whereas it is expedient that the said Acts should be repealed, and that new Provisions should be made in lieu thereof; Be it therefore enacted, by the King's Most Excellent Majesty, by and with the Advice and Consent of the Lords Spiritual and Temporal, and Commons, in this present Parliament assembled, and by the Authority of the same, That the said Acts shall be and the same are hereby repealed: Provided nevertheless, that all Acts or Parts of Acts, which by virtue of the above-recited Acts, or either of them, were repealed, shall still be deemed and taken to be and remain repealed: Provided also, that all Actions, Suits, and Prosecutions, now depending or hereafter to be brought for or by reason of any Breach or Nonperformance of any of the Provisions of the said Acts, or for the Recovery of any Duties or Sums of Money payable under and by virtue of the same, shall and may be proceeded with, as fully and effectually, to all Intents and Purposes as if this present Act had not been made.

II. And Whereas an Act was passed in the Sixth Year of His Majesty's Reign, intituled *An Act for granting Duties of Customs*, whereby certain Duties were imposed on the Importation of Buck Wheat and Indian Corn; and it is expedient that the said Duties should be repealed; Be it therefore enacted, That so much of the said Act passed in the Sixth Year of His Majesty's Reign, as imposes Duties on the Importation of Buck Wheat and Indian Corn, shall be and the same is hereby repealed.

III. And Whereas it is expedient that Corn, Grain, Meal, and Flour, the Growth, Produce, and Manufacture of any Foreign Country, or of any *British* Possession out of *Europe*, should be allowed to be imported into the United Kingdom for Consumption, upon the Payment of Duties to be regulated from time to time according to the Average Price of *British* Corn made up and published in manner hereinafter required; Be it therefore enacted, That there shall be levied and paid to His Majesty, upon all Corn, Grain, Meal, or Flour entered for Home Consumption in the United Kingdom from Parts beyond the Seas, the several Duties specified and set forth in the Table annexed to this Act; and that the said Duties shall be raised, levied, collected, and paid in such and the same Manner in all respects as the several Duties of Customs mentioned and enumerated in the Table of Duties of Customs Inwards annexed to the said Act passed in the Sixty Year of the Reign of His Majesty, and by virtue and in pursuance of the several Powers and Provisions in that Act contained, and not otherwise.

IV. Provided always, and be it further enacted, That no Corn, Grain, Meal, or Flour shall be shipped from any Port in any *British* Possession out of *Europe*, as being the Produce of any such Possession, until the Owner or Proprietor or Shipper thereof shall have made and subscribed, before the Collector or other Chief Officer of Customs at the Port of Shipment, a Declaration in Writing, specifying the Quantity of each Sort of such Corn, Grain, Meal, or Flour, and that the same was the Produce of some *British* Possession out of *Europe* to be named in such Declaration, nor until such Owner or Proprietor or Shipper shall have obtained from the Collector or other Chief Officer of the Customs at the said Port a Certificate, under his Signature, of the Quantity of Corn, Grain, Meal, or Flour so declared to be shipped; and before any Corn, Grain, Meal, or Flour shall be entered at any Port or Place in the United Kingdom, as being the Produce of any *British*

Possession out of *Europe*, the Master of the Ship importing the same shall produce and deliver to the Collector or other Chief Officer of Customs of the Port or Place of Importation a Copy of such Declaration, certified to be a true and accurate Copy thereof under the Hand of the Collector and other Chief Officer of Customs at the Port of Shipment before whom the same was made, together with the Certificate, signed by the said Collector or other Chief Officer of Customs, of the Quantity of Corn so declared to be shipped; and such Master shall also make and subscribe, before the Collector or other Chief Officer of Customs at the Port or Place of Importation, a Declaration in Writing, that the several Quantities of Corn, Grain, Meal, or Flour on board such Ship, and proposed to be entered under the Authority of such Declaration, are the same that were mentioned and referred to in the Declaration and Certificate produced by him, without any Admixture or Addition; and if any Person shall, in any such Declaration, wilfully and corruptly make any false Statement respecting the Place of which any such Corn, Grain, Meal, or Flour was the Produce, or respecting the Identity of any such Corn, Grain, Meal, or Flour, such Persons shall forfeit and become liable to pay to His Majesty the Sum of One hundred Pounds, and the Corn, Grain, Meal, or Flour to such Person belonging, on board any such Ship, shall also be forfeited; and such Forfeitures shall and may be sued for, prosecuted, recovered, and applied in such and the same Manner in all respects as any Forfeiture incurred under and by virtue of the said Act so passed in the Sixth Year of His Majesty's Reign: Provided always, that the Declarations aforesaid shall not be required in respect of any Corn, Grain, Meal, or Flour which shall have been shipped within Three Months next after the passing of this Act.

V. Provided always, and be it further enacted, That it shall not be lawful to import, from Parts beyond the Seas into the United Kingdom, for Consumption there, any Malt, or to import, for Consumption, into *Great Britain*, any Corn ground, except Wheat Meal, Wheat Flour, and Oatmeal; or to import, for Consumption, any Corn ground into *Ireland*; and that if any such Article as aforesaid shall be imported contrary to the Provisions aforesaid, the same shall be forfeited.

VI. Provided always, and be it further enacted, That the Commissioners of His Majesty's Customs shall, once in each Calendar Month, cause to be published in the *London Gazette* an Account of the Total Quantity of each Sort of the Corn, Grain, Meal, and Flour respectively, which shall have been imported into the United Kingdom; and also an Account of the Total Quantity of each Sort of the Corn, Grain, Meal, and Flour respectively, upon which the Duties of Importation shall have been paid in the United Kingdom during the Calendar Month next preceding; together with an Account of the Total Quantity of each Sort of the said Corn, Grain, Meal, and Flour respectively remaining in Warehouse at the End of such next preceding Calendar Month.

VII. Provided always, and be it further enacted, That if it shall be made to appear to His Majesty in Council that any Foreign State or Power hath subjected *British* Vessels, at any Port within the Dominions of such State or Power, to any other or higher Duties or Charges whatever than are levied on National Vessels at any such Port, or hath subjected, at any such Port, Goods the Growth, Produce, or Manufacture of any of His Majesty's Dominions, when imported from any of such

Dominions in *British* Vessels, to any other or higher Duties or Charges whatever than are levied on such or the like Goods, of whatever Growth, Produce, or Manufacture, when so imported in National Vessels, or hath subjected, at any Port or Place within the Dominions of such Foreign State or Power, any Article of the Growth, Produce, or Manufacture of His Majesty's Dominions, when imported from any of such Dominions in *British* Vessels or in National Vessels, to any Duties or Charges which would not be payable on the like Article being of the Growth, Produce, or Manufacture of any other Country, and imported from such other Country in National Vessels; or that any such Foreign State or Power hath granted any Bounties, Drawbacks, or Allowances upon the Exportation from any Port or Place within the Dominions thereof of any Articles the Growth, Produce, or Manufacture of the Dominions of any other Foreign State or Power, which hath not also been granted upon the Exportation from such Port or Place of such or the like Articles, being the Growth, Produce, or Manufacture of His Majesty's Dominions; then and in any of the Cases aforesaid, it shall and may be lawful for His Majesty, by an Order or Orders to be by Him made, with the Advice of His Privy Council, to prohibit the Importation of all or of any Sort of Corn, Grain, Meal, or Flour from the Dominions of any such Foreign State or Power; and it shall also be lawful for His Majesty from time to time, with the Advice of His Privy Council, to revoke and to renew any such Orders or Order as aforesaid, as there shall be Occasion. . . .

TABLE OF DUTIES TO WHICH THIS ACT REFERS

If imported from any Foreign Country:	£	s.	d.
Wheat			
According to the average Price of Wheat, made up and published in manner required by Law: *videlicet,*			
Whenever such Price shall be Sixty-two Shillings and under Sixty-three Shillings the Quarter, the Duty shall be for every Quarter -	1	4	8
Whenever such Price shall be 63s. and under 64s. the Quarter, the Duty shall be for every Quarter - - - - - - - - - - - - - -	1	3	8
Whenever such Price shall be 64s. and under 65s. the Quarter, the Duty shall be for every Quarter - - - - - - - - - - - - - -	1	2	8
Whenever such Price shall be 65s. and under 66s. the Quarter, the Duty shall be for every Quarter - - - - - - - - - - - - - -	1	1	8
Whenever such Price shall be 66s. and under 67s. the Quarter, the Duty shall be for every Quarter - - - - - - - - - - - - - -	1	0	8
Whenever such Price shall be 67s. and under 68s. the Quarter, the Duty shall be for every Quarter - - - - - - - - - - - - - -	0	18	8
Whenever such Price shall be 68s. and under 69s. the Quarter, the Duty shall be for every Quarter - - - - - - - - - - - - - -	0	16	8
Whenever such Price shall be 69s. and under 70s. the Quarter, the Duty shall be for every Quarter - - - - - - - - - - - - - -	0	13	8

	£	s.	d.

Whenever such Price shall be 70s. and under 71s. the Quarter, the Duty shall be for every Quarter ---------------- · · · 0 10 8

Whenever such Price shall be 71s. and under 72s. the Quarter, the Duty shall be for every Quarter ---------------- · · · 0 6 8

Whenever such Price shall be 72s. and under 73s. the Quarter, the Duty shall be for every Quarter ---------------- · · · 0 2 8

Whenever such Price shall be at or above Seventy-three Shillings, the Duty shall be for every Quarter -------- · · · 0 1 0

Whenever such Price shall be under Sixty-two Shillings and not under Sixty-one Shillings, the Duty shall be for every Quarter ----------------------------------- · · · 1 5 8

And in respect of each integral Shilling, or any Part of each integral Shilling, by which such Price shall be under Sixty-one Shillings, such Duty shall be increased by One Shilling.

Barley

Whenever the Average Price of Barley, made up and published in manner required by Law, shall be Thirty-three Shillings and under Thirty-four Shillings the Quarter, the Duty shall be for every Quarter ------------------- · · · 0 12 4

And in respect of every integral Shilling by which such Price shall be above Thirty-three Shillings, such Duty shall be decreased by One Shilling and Sixpence, until such Price shall be Forty-one Shillings.

Whenever such Price shall be at or above Forty-one Shillings, the Duty shall be for every Quarter ---------------- · · · 0 1 0

Whenever such Price shall be under Thirty-three Shillings and not under Thirty-two Shillings, the Duty shall be for every Quarter ------------------------------- · · · 0 13 10

And in respect of each integral Shilling, or any Part of each integral Shilling, by which such Price shall be under Thirty-two Shillings, such Duty shall be increased by One Shilling and Sixpence.

Oats

Whenever the Average Price of Oats, made up and published in manner required by Law, shall be Twenty-five Shillings and under Twenty-six Shillings the Quarter, the Duty shall be for every Quarter ------------------------ · · · 0 9 3

And in respect of every integral Shilling by which such Price shall be above Twenty-five Shillings, such Duty shall be decreased by One Shilling and Sixpence, until such Price shall be Thirty-one Shillings.

Whenever such Price shall be at or above Thirty-one Shillings, the Duty shall be for every Quarter -------- · · · 0 1 0

Whenever such Price shall be under Twenty-five Shillings and not under Twenty-four Shillings, the Duty shall be for every Quarter ------------------------------- · · · 0 10 9

	£	s.	d.

And in respect of each integral Shilling, or any Part of each integral Shilling, by which such Price shall be under Twenty-four Shillings, such Duty shall be increased by One Shilling and Sixpence.

Rye, Pease, and Beans

Whenever the Average Price of Rye, or of Pease, or of Beans, made up and published in manner required by Law, shall be Thirty-six Shillings, and under Thirty-seven Shillings the Quarter, the Duty shall be for every Quarter - - - - -   0   15   6

And in respect of every integral Shilling by which such Price shall be above Thirty-six Shillings, such Duty shall be decreased by One Shilling and Sixpence, until such Price shall be Forty-six Shillings.

Whenever such Price shall be at or above Forty-six Shillings, the Duty shall be for every Quarter - - - - - - - - - - - - - -   0   1   0

Whenever such Price shall be under Thirty-six Shillings and not under Thirty-five Shillings, the Duty shall be for every Quarter -   0   16   9

And in respect of each integral Shilling, or any Part of each integral Shilling, by which such Price shall be under Thirty-five Shillings, such Duty shall be increased by One Shilling and Sixpence.

Wheat Meal and Flour

For every Barrel, being One hundred and ninety-six Pounds:—A Duty equal in Amount to the Duty payable on Thirty-eight and a Half Gallons of Wheat.

Oatmeal

For every Quantity of One hundred and eighty-one Pounds and a Half:—A Duty equal in Amount to the Duty payable on a Quarter of Oats.

Maize or Indian Corn, Buck Wheat, Beer or Bigg

For every Quarter:—A Duty equal in Amount to the Duty payable on a Quarter of Barley.

If the Produce of and imported from any British Possession in North America, or elsewhere out of Europe:

Wheat

For every Quarter -   0   5   0

Until the Price of British Wheat, made up and published in manner required by Law, shall be Sixty-seven Shillings per Quarter.

Whenever such Price shall be at or above Sixty-seven Shillings, the Duty shall be for every Quarter - - - - - - - -   0   0   6

Barley

For every Quarter -   0   2   6

Until the Price of British Barley, made up and published in manner required by Law, shall be Thirty-four Shillings per Quarter.

	£	s.	d.

Whenever such Price shall be at or above Thirty-four Shillings, the Duty shall be for every Quarter - - - - - - - -   0   0   6

Oats

For every Quarter -   0   2   0

  Until the Price of British Oats, made up and published in manner required by Law, shall be Twenty-five Shillings per Quarter.

Whenever such Price shall be at or above Twenty-five Shillings, the Duty shall be for every Quarter - - - - - - - -   0   0   6

Rye, Pease, and Beans

For every Quarter -   0   3   0

  Until the Price of British Rye, or of Pease, or of Beans, made up and published in manner required by Law, shall be Forty-one Shillings.

Whenever such Price shall be at or above Forty-one Shillings, the Duty shall be for every Quarter - - - - - - - - - - - - - - - -   0   0   6

Wheat Meal and Flour

For every Barrel, being One hundred and ninety-six Pounds:—A Duty equal in Amount to the Duty payable on Thirty-eight Gallons and a Half of Wheat.

Oatmeal

For every Quantity of One hundred and eighty-one Pounds and a Half:—A Duty equal in Amount to the Duty payable on a Quarter of Oats.

Maise or Indian Corn, Buck Wheat, Beer or Bigg

For every Quarter:—A Duty equal in Amount to the Duty payable on a Quarter of Barley.

CLAIMS OF CATHOLICS AND DISSENTERS

Speech by Edmund Burke supporting the Protestant Dissenters' Relief Bill, House of Commons, 7 March 1773

The Speeches of the Right Honourable Edmund Burke, in the House of Commons, and in Westminster Hall, 4 vols. (London: Longman, Hurst, Rees, Orme, and Brown, 1816), I, 151-64.

The bill, which proposed to exempt Dissenters from the provisions of several penal statutes, passed the Commons but was defeated in the House of Lords.

I assure you, Sir, that the honourable gentleman who spoke last but one, need not be in the least fear that I should make a war of particles upon his opinion, whether the church of England should, would, or ought to be alarmed. I am very clear that this House has no one reason in the world to think she is alarmed by the bill brought before you. It is something extraordinary that the only symptom of alarm in the church of England should appear in the petition of some dissenters; with whom I believe very few in this House are yet acquainted; and of whom you know no more than that you are assured by the honourable gentleman, that they are not Mahometans. Of the church we know they are not, by the name that they assume. They are then dissenters. The first symptom of an alarm comes from some dissenters assembled round the lines of Chatham: these lines become the security of the church of England! The honourable gentleman, in speaking of the lines of Chatham, tells us, that they serve not only for the security of the wooden walls of England, but for the defence of the church of England. I suspect the wooden walls of England secure the lines of Chatham, rather than the lines of Chatham secure the wooden walls of England.

Sir, the church of England, if only defended by this miserable petition upon your table, must, I am afraid, upon the principles of true fortification, be soon destroyed. But fortunately her walls, bulwarks, and bastions, are constructed of other materials than of stubble and straw; are built up with the strong and stable matter of the gospel of liberty, and founded on a true, constitutional, legal establishment. But, Sir, she has other securities; she has the security of her own doctrine; she has the security of the piety, the sanctity of her own professors; their learning is a bulwark to defend her; she has the security of the two universities, not shook in any single battlement, in any single pinnacle.

But the honourable gentleman has mentioned, indeed, principles, which astonish me rather more than ever. The honourable gentleman thinks that the dissenters enjoy a large share of liberty under a connivance; and he thinks that the establishing toleration by law is an attack upon christianity.

The first of these is a contradiction in terms. Liberty under a connivance! Connivance is a relaxation from slavery, not a definition of liberty. What is connivance, but a state under which all slaves live? If I was to describe slavery, I would say with those, who hate it, it is living under will, not under law: if, as it is stated by its advocates, I would say, that, like earthquakes, like thunder, or other wars the elements make upon mankind, it happens rarely, it occasionally comes now and then upon people, who upon ordinary occasions enjoy the same legal government of liberty. Take it under the description of those who would soften those features, the state of slavery and connivance is the same thing. If the liberty enjoyed be a liberty not of toleration, but of connivance, the only question is, whether establishing such by law is an attack upon christianity. Toleration an attack upon christianity? What, then, are we to come to this pass, to suppose that nothing can support christianity, but the principles of persecution? Is that, then, the idea of establishment? It is, then, the idea of christianity itself, that it ought to have establishments, that it ought to have laws against dissenters, but the breach of which laws is to be connived at? What a picture of toleration; what a picture of laws, of establishments; what a picture of religious and civil liberty! I am persuaded the honourable gentleman does not see it in this light. But these very terms become the strongest reasons for my support of the bill; for I am persuaded that toleration, so far from being an attack upon christianity, becomes the best and surest support, that possibly can be given to it. The christian religion itself arose without establishment, it arose even without toleration; and whilst its own principles were not tolerated, it conquered all the powers of darkness, it conquered all the powers of the world. The moment it began to depart from these principles, it converted the establishment into tyranny; it subverted its foundations from that very hour. Zealous as I am for the principle of an establishment, so just an abhorrence do I conceive against whatever may shake it.—I know nothing but the supposed necessity of persecution, that can make an establishment disgusting. I would have toleration a part of establishment, as a principle favourable to christianity, and as a part of christianity.

All seem agreed that the law, as it stands, inflicting penalties on all religious teachers and on schoolmasters, who do not sign the thirty-nine articles of religion, ought not to be executed. We are all agreed that the law is not good; for that, I presume, is undoubtedly the idea of a law that ought not to be executed. The question therefore is, whether in a well-constituted commonwealth, which we desire ours to be thought, and, I trust, intend that it should be, whether in such a commonwealth it is wise to retain those laws, which it is not proper to execute? A penal law, not ordinarily put in execution, seems to me to be a very absurd and a very dangerous thing. For if its principles be right, if the object of its prohibitions and penalties be a real evil, then you do in effect permit that very evil, which not only the reason of the thing, but your very law, declares ought not to be permitted; and thus it reflects exceedingly on the wisdom, and consequently derogates not a little from the authority, of a legislature, who can at once forbid and suffer, and in the same breath promulgate penalty and indemnity to the same persons, and for the very same actions. But if the object of the law be no moral or political evil, then you ought not to hold even a terror to those whom you ought certainly not to punish—

for if it is not right to hurt, it is neither right nor wise to menace. Such laws, therefore, as they must be defective either in justice or wisdom, or both, so they cannot exist without a considerable degree of danger. Take them which way you will, they are prest with ugly alternatives.

1st. All penal laws are either upon popular prosecution, or on the part of the crown. Now, if they may be roused from their sleep, whenever a minister thinks proper, as instruments of oppression, then they put vast bodies of men into a state of slavery and court dependence; since their liberty of conscience and their power of executing their functions depend entirely on his will. I would have no man derive his means of continuing any function, or his being restrained from it, but from the laws only; they should be his only superior and sovereign lords.

2d. They put statesmen and magistrates into a habit of playing fast and loose with the laws, straining or relaxing them as may best suit their political purposes; and in that light tend to corrupt the execution power through all its offices.

3d. If they are taken up on popular actions, their operation in that light also is exceedingly evil. They become the instruments of private malice, private avarice, and not of public regulation; they nourish the worst of men to the prejudice of the best, punishing tender consciences, and rewarding informers.

Shall we, as the honourable gentleman tell us we may with perfect security, trust to the manners of the age? I am well pleased with the general manners of the times; but the desultory execution of penal laws, the thing I condemn, does not depend on the manners of the times. I would however have the laws tuned in unison with the manners—very dissonant are a gentle country, and cruel laws; very dissonant, that your reason is furious, but your passions moderate, and that you are always equitable except in your courts of justice.

I will beg leave to state to the House one argument, which has been much relied upon—that the dissenters are not unanimous upon this business; that many persons are alarmed; that it will create a disunion among the dissenters.

When any dissenters, or any body of people, come here with a petition, it is not the number of people, but the reasonableness of the request, that should weigh with the House. A body of dissenters come to this House, and say, "Tolerate us—we desire neither the parochial advantage of tithes, nor dignities, nor the stalls of your cathedrals: no! let the venerable orders of the hierarchy exist with all their advantages." And shall I tell them, I reject your just and reasonable petition, not because it shakes the church, but because there are others, while you lie grovelling upon the earth, that will kick and bite you? Judge which of these descriptions of men comes with a fair request—that which says, Sir, I desire liberty for my own, because I trespass on no man's conscience;—or the other, which says, I desire that these men should not be suffered to act according to their consciences, though I am tolerated to act according to mine. But I sign a body of articles, which is my title to toleration; I sign no more, because more are against my conscience. But I desire that you will not tolerate these men, because they will not go so far as I, though I desire to be tolerated, who will not go as far as you. No, imprison them, if they come within five miles of a corporate town, because they do not believe what I do in point of doctrines.

Shall I not say to these men, "arrangez vous, canaille?" You, who are not the predominant power, will not give to others the relaxation under which you are yourself suffered to live. I have as high an opinion of the doctrines of the church as you. I receive them implicitly, or I put my own explanation on them, or take that which seems to me to come best recommended by authority. There are those of the dissenters, who think more rigidly of the doctrine of the articles relative to predestination, than others do. They sign the article relative to it *ex animo*, and literally. Others allow a latitude of construction. These two parties are in the church, as well as among the dissenters; yet in the church we live quietly under the same roof. I do not see why, as long as Providence gives us no further light into this great mystery, we should not leave things as the Divine Wisdom has left them. But suppose all these things to me to be clear, (which Providence however seems to have left obscure,) yet whilst dissenters claim a toleration in things, which, seeming clear to me, are obscure to them, without entering into the merit of the articles, with what face can these men say, Tolerate us, but do not tolerate them? Toleration is good for all, or it is good for none.

The discussion this day is not between establishment on one hand, and toleration on the other, but between those who, being tolerated themselves, refuse toleration to others. That power should be puffed up with pride, that authority should degenerate into rigour, if not laudable, is but too natural. But this proceeding of theirs is much beyond the usual allowance to human weakness; it not only is shocking to our reason, but it provokes our indignation. "*Quid domini facient, audent cum talia fures?*" It is not the proud prelate thundering in his commission court, but a pack of manumitted slaves with the lash of the beadle flagrant on their backs, and their legs still galled with their fetters, that would drive their brethren into that prisonhouse from whence they have just been permitted to escape. If, instead of puzzling themselves in the depths of the Divine counsels, they would turn to the mild morality of the gospel, they would read their own condemnation—"O thou wicked servant, I forgave thee all that debt because thou desiredst me: shouldest not thou also have compassion on thy fellow-servant, even as I had pity on thee?"

In my opinion, Sir, a magistrate, whenever he goes to put any restraint upon religious freedom, can only do it upon this ground, that the person dissenting does not dissent from the scruples of ill-informed conscience, but from a party ground of dissension, in order to raise a faction in the state. We give, with regard to rights and ceremonies, an indulgence to tender consciences. But if dissent is at all punished in any country, if at all it can be punished upon any pretence, it is upon a presumption, not that a man is supposed to differ conscientiously from the establishment, but that he resists truth for the sake of faction; that he abets diversity of opinions in religion to distract the state, and to destroy the peace of his country. This is the only plausible, for there is no true ground of persecution. As the laws stand, therefore, let us see how we have thought fit to act.

If there is any one thing within the competency of a magistrate with regard to religion, it is this, that he has a right to direct the exterior ceremonies of religion; that whilst interior religion is within the jurisdiction of God alone, the external part, bodily action, is within the province of the chief governor. Hooker, and all the great lights of the church, have constantly argued this to be a part within the province of the civil magistrate; but look at the Act of Toleration of William and Mary, there you will see the civil magistrate has not only dispensed with those things, which are more particularly within his province, with those things which faction might be supposed to take up for the sake of making visible and external divisions, and raising a standard of revolt, but has also from sound politic considerations relaxed on those points which are confessedly without his province.

The honourable gentleman, speaking of the heathens, certainly could not mean to recommend any thing that is derived from that impure source. But he has praised the tolerating spirit of the heathens. Well! but the honourable gentleman will recollect that heathens, that polytheists, must permit a number of divinities. It is the very essence of its constitution. But was it ever heard that polytheism tolerated a dissent from a polytheistic establishment? the belief of one God only? Never, never! Sir, they constantly carried on persecution against that doctrine. I will not give heathens the glory of a doctrine, which I consider the best part of christianity. The honourable gentleman must recollect the Roman law, that was clearly against the introduction of any foreign rites in matters of religion. You have it at large in Livy, how they persecuted in the first introduction the rites of Bacchus: and even before Christ, to say nothing of their subsequent persecutions, they persecuted the Druids and others. Heathenism, therefore, as in other respects erroneous, was erroneous in point of persecution. I do not say, every heathen, who persecuted, was therefore an impious man: I only say he was mistaken, as such a man is now. But, says the honourable gentleman, they did not persecute Epicureans. No; the Epicureans had no quarrel with their religious establishment, nor desired any religion for themselves. It would have been very extraordinary, if irreligious heathens had desired either a religious establishment or toleration. But, says the honourable gentleman, the Epicureans entered, as others, into the temples. They did so; they defied all subscription; they defied all sorts of conformity; there was no subscription, to which they were not ready to set their hands, no ceremonies they refused to practise; they made it a principle of their irreligion outwardly to conform to any religion. These atheists eluded all that you could do; so will all freethinkers for ever. Then you suffer, or the weakness of your law has suffered, those great dangerous animals to escape notice, whilst you have nets, that entangle the poor fluttering silken wings of a tender conscience.

The honourable gentleman insists much upon this circumstance of objection, namely, the division amongst the dissenters. Why, Sir, the dissenters by the nature of the term are open to have a division among themselves. They are dissenters, because they differ from the church of England; not that they agree among themselves. There are Presbyterians, there are Independents, some, that do not agree to infant baptism, others, that do not agree to the baptism of adults, or any baptism. All these are however tolerated under the acts of King William, and subsequent acts; and their diversity of sentiments with one another did not, and could not, furnish an argument against their toleration, when their difference with ourselves furnished none.

But, says the honourable gentleman, if you suffer them to go on, they will shake the fundamental principles of Christianity. Let it be considered that this argument goes as strongly against connivance, which you allow, as against toleration, which you reject. The gentleman sets out with a principle of perfect liberty, or, as he describes it, connivance. But for fear of dangerous opinions, you leave it in your power to vex a man, who has not held any one dangerous opinion whatsoever, If one man is a professed atheist, another man the best christian, but dissents from two of the 39 articles, I may let escape the atheist, because I know him to be an atheist, because I am, perhaps, so inclined myself, and because I may connive where I think proper; but the conscientious dissenter, on account of his attachment to that general religion, which perhaps I hate, I shall take care to punish, because I may punish when I think proper. Therefore, connivance being an engine of private malice or private favour, not of good government; an engine, which totally fails of suppressing atheism, but oppresses conscience; I say that principle becomes not serviceable, but dangerous to christianity: that it is not toleration, but contrary to it, even contrary to peace; that the penal system, to which it belongs, is a dangerous principle in the economy either of religion or government.

The honourable gentleman, and in him I comprehend all those who oppose the bill, bestowed in support of their side of the question as much argument as it could bear, and much more of learning and decoration than it deserved. He thinks connivance consistent, but legal toleration inconsistent, with the interests of christianity. Perhaps I would go as far as that honourable gentleman, if I thought toleration inconsistent with those interests. God forbid! I may be mistaken, but I take toleration to be a part of religion. I do not know which I would sacrifice; I would keep them both; it is not necessary I should sacrifice either. I do not like the idea of tolerating the doctrines of Epicurus: but nothing in the world propagates them so much as the oppression of the poor, of the honest, and candid disciples of the religion we profess in common, I mean revealed religion; nothing sooner makes them take a short cut out of the bondage of sectarian vexation into open and direct infidelity, than tormenting men for every difference. My opinion is, that in establishing the christian religion wherever you find it, curiosity or research is its best security; and in this way a man is a great deal better justified in saying, tolerate all kinds of conscience, than in imitating the heathens, whom the honourable gentleman quotes, in tolerating those who have none. I am not over fond of calling for the secular arm upon these misguided or misguiding men; but if ever it ought to be raised, it ought surely to be raised against these very men, not against others, whose liberty of religion you make a pretext for proceedings, which drive them into the bondage of impiety. What figure do I make in saying, I do not attack the works of these atheistical writers, but I will keep a rod hanging over the conscientious man, their bitterest enemy, because these atheists may take advantage of the liberty of their foes to introduce irreligion? The best book, that ever, perhaps has been written against these people, is that, in which the author has collected in a body the whole of the infidel code, and has brought the writers into one body to cut them all off together. This was done by a dissenter, who never did subscribe the 39 Articles—Dr. Leland. But if, after all, this danger is to be apprehended, if you are really fearful that christianity will indirectly suffer by this liberty, you have my free consent; go directly, and by the straight way, and not by a circuit, in which in your road you may destroy your friends, point your arms against these men, who do the mischief you fear promoting: point your arms against men, who, not contented with endeavouring to turn your eyes from the blaze and effulgence of light, by which life and immortality is so gloriously demonstrated by the gospel, would even extinguish that faint glimmering of nature, that only comfort supplied to ignorant man before this great illumination—them, who by attacking even the possibility of all revelation, arraign all the dispensations of Providence to man. These are the wicked dissenters you ought to fear; these are the people against whom you ought to aim the shaft of the law; these are the men to whom, arrayed in all the terrors of government, I would say, you shall not degrade us into brutes; these men, these factious men, as the honourable gentleman properly called them, are the just objects of vengeance, not the conscientious dissenter; these men, who would take away whatever ennobles the rank, or consoles the misfortunes of human nature, by breaking off that connexion of observances, of affections, of hopes and fears which bind us to the Divinity, and constitute the glorious and distinguishing prerogative of humanity, that of being a religious creature; against these I would have the laws rise in all their majesty of terror, to fulminate such vain and impious wretches, and to awe them into impotence by the only dread they can fear or believe, to learn that eternal lesson—*Discite justitian morali, et non temnere Divos.*

At the same time that I would cut up the very root of atheism, I would respect all conscience; all conscience that is really such, and which perhaps its very tenderness proves to be sincere. I wish to see the established church of England great and powerful; I wish to see her foundations laid low and deep, that she may crush the giant powers of rebellious darkness; I would have her head raised up to that heaven to which she conducts us. I would have her open wide her hospitable gates by a noble and liberal comprehension; but I would have no breaches in her wall; I would have her cherish all those who are within, and pity all those who are without; I would have her a common blessing to the world, an example, if not an instructor, to those who have not the happiness to belong to her; I would have her give a lesson of peace to mankind, that a vexed and wandering generation might be taught to seek for repose and toleration in the maternal bosom of christian charity, and not in the harlot of infidelity and indifference. Nothing has driven people more into that house of seduction than the mutual hatred of christian congregations. Long may we enjoy our church under a learned and edifying episcopacy. But episcopacy may fail, and religion exist. The most horrid and cruel blow that can be offered to civil society is through atheism. Do not promote diversity; when you have it, bear it; have as many sorts of religion as you find in your country; there is a reasonable worship in them all. The others, the infidels, are outlaws of the constitution; not of this country, but of the human race. They are never, never to be supported, never to be tolerated. Under the systematic attacks of these people, I see some of the props of good government already begin to fail; I see propagated principles, which will not leave to religion even a toleration. I see myself sinking every day under the attacks of these wretched people—How shall I arm myself against them? By uniting all those in affection who are united in the belief of the great principles of the Godhead, that made and sustains the world. They who hold revelation give double assurance to their country. Even the man who does not hold revelation, yet who wishes that it were proved to him, who observes a pious silence with regard to it, such a man, though not a christian, is governed by religious principles. Let him be tolerated in this country. Let it be but a serious religion, natural or revealed, take what you can get; cherish, blow up the slightest spark. One day it may be a pure and holy flame. By this proceeding you form an alliance offensive and defensive, against those great ministers of darkness in the world who are endeavouring to shake all the works of God established in order and beauty.

Perhaps I am carried too far, but it is in the road into which the honourable gentleman has led me. The honourable gentleman would have us fight this confederacy of the powers of darkness with the single arm of the church of England; would have us not only fight against infidelity, but fight at the same time with all the faith in the world except our own. In the moment we make a front against the common enemy, we have to combat with all those who are the natural friends of our cause. Strong as we are, we are not equal to this. The cause of the church of England is included in that of religion, not that of religion in the church of England. I will stand up at all times for the rights of conscience, as it is such, not for its particular modes against its general principles. One may be right, another mistaken; but if I have more strength than my brother, it shall be employed to support, not oppress his weakness; if I have more light, it shall be used to guide, not to dazzle him.

Catholic Relief Act, 1778

18 Geo. 3, c. 60   *Statutes at Large*, XXXII, pt. 1, 152-54.

This act relieved Roman Catholics from certain penalties and disabilities imposed upon them by previous statutes. The act increased anti-Catholic feeling and so contributed indirectly to the 1780 outbreak known as the Gordon Riots.

Whereas it is expedient to repeal certain provisions in an act of the eleventh and twelfth years of the Reign of King William the Third, intituled, *An act for the further preventing the growth of popery*, whereby certain penalties and disabilities are imposed on persons professing the popish religion; may it please your Majesty that it may be enacted; and be it enacted by the King's most excellent majesty, by and with the advice and consent of the lords spiritual and temporal, and commons, in this present parliament assembled, and by the authority of the same, That so much of the said act as relates to the apprehending, taking, or prosecuting, of popish bishops, priests, or jesuits; and also so much of the said act as subjects popish bishops, priests, or jesuits, and papists, or persons professing the popish religion, and keeping school, or taking upon themselves the education or government or boarding of youth, within this realm, or the dominions thereto belonging, to perpetual imprisonment; and also so much of the said act as disables persons educated in the popish religion, or professing the same, under the circumstances therein mentioned, to inherit or take by descent, devise, or limitation, in possession, reversion, or remainder, any lands, tenements, or hereditaments, within the kingdom of *England*, dominion of *Wales*, and town of *Berwick upon Tweed*, and gives to the next of kin, being a protestant, a right to have and enjoy such lands, tenements, and hereditaments; and also so much of the said act as disables papists, or persons professing the popish religion, to purchase any manors, lands, profits out of lands, tenements, rents, terms, or hereditaments within the kingdom of *England*, dominion of *Wales*, or town of *Berwick upon Tweed*, and makes void all and singular estates, terms, and other interests or profits whatsoever out of lands, to be made, suffered, or done, from and after the day therein mentioned, to or for the use or behoof of any such person or persons, or upon any trust or confidence, mediately or immediately, for the relief of any such person or persons; shall be, and the same, and every clause and matter and thing herein-before mentioned, is and are hereby repealed.

II. And be it enacted by the authority aforesaid, That every person and persons having or claiming any lands, tenements, or hereditaments, under titles not hitherto litigated, though derived from any descent, devise, limitation, or purchase, shall have, take, hold, and enjoy, the same, as if the said act, or any thing therein contained, had not been made, any thing in the said act contained to the contrary notwithstanding.

III. Provided always, and be it enacted, That nothing herein contained shall extend, or be construed to affect any action or suit now depending, which shall be prosecuted with effect, and without delay.

IV. Provided also, That nothing herein contained shall extend, or be construed to extend, to any person or persons but such who shall, within the space of six calendar months after the passing of this act, or of accruing of his, her, or their title, being of the age of twenty-one years, or who, being under the age of twenty-one years, shall, within six months after he or she shall attain the age of twenty-one years, or being of unsound mind, or in prison, or beyond the seas, then within six months after such disability removed, take and subscribe an oath in the words following:

> *I A. B.* do sincerely promise and swear, That I will be faithful and bear true allegiance to his majesty King *George* the Third, and him will defend, to the utmost of my power, against all conspiracies and attempts whatever that shall be made against his person, crown, or dignity; and I will do my utmost endeavour to disclose and make known to his Majesty, his heirs and successors, all treasons and traiterous conspiracies which may be formed against him or them; and I do faithfully promise to maintain, support, and defend, to the utmost of my power, the succession of the crown in his Majesty's family, against any person or persons whatsoever; hereby utterly renouncing and abjuring any obedience or allegiance unto the person taking up himself the stile and title of *Prince of Wales*, in the life time of his father, and who, since his death, is said to have assumed the stile and title of *King of Great Britain*, by the name of *Charles the Third*, and to any other person claiming or pretending a right to the crown of these realms; and I do swear, that I do reject and detest, as an unchristian and impious position, That it is lawful to murder or destroy any person or persons whatsoever, for or under pretence of their being hereticks; and

also that unchristian and impious principle, that no faith is to be kept with hereticks: I further declare, that it is no article of my faith, and that I do renounce, reject, and abjure, the opinion, that princes excommunicated by the pope and council, or by any authority of the see of *Rome*, or by any authority whatsoever, may be deposed or murdered by their subjects, or any person whatsoever: and I do declare, that I do not believe that the pope of *Rome*, or any other foreign prince, prelate, state, or potentate, hath, or ought to have, any temporal or civil jurisdiction, power, superiority, or pre-eminence, directly or indirectly, within this realm. And I do solemnly, in the presence of God, profess, testify, and declare, that I do make this declaration, and every part thereof, in the plain and ordinary sense of the words of this oath; without any evasion, equivocation, or mental reservation whatever, and without any dispensation already granted by the pope, or any authority of the see of *Rome*, or any person whatever; and without thinking that I am or can be acquitted before God or man, or absolved of this declaration, or any part thereof, although the pope, or any other persons or authority whatsoever, shall dispense with or annul the same, or declare that it was null or void.

Which oath it shall be competent to his Majesty's high court of chancery, or to any of his Majesty's courts of record at *Westminster*, the courts of great sessions within the principality of *Wales* and county palatine of *Chester*, the courts of chancery or common pleas within the counties palatine of *Lancaster* and *Durham*, or to any court of general or quarter sessions of the peace of any county, riding, liberty, city, borough, town, or place, in the kingdom of *England*, or in the principality of *Wales*, to administer, and they are hereby required to administer the same accordingly: of the taking and subscribing of which oaths a register shall be kept and preserved, in the manner prescribed by the laws now in being requiring oaths from persons taking offices or employments.

V. Provided always, and it is hereby enacted and declared, That nothing in this act contained shall extend, or be construed to extend, to any popish bishop, priest, jesuit, or schoolmaster, who shall not have taken and subscribed the above oath in the above words before he shall have been apprehended or any prosecution commenced against him.

Speech by the attorney general prosecuting Lord George Gordon for leading the "No-Popery" Riots of 1780 in London, 5 February 1781

The Proceedings at Large in the Trial of . . . Lord George Gordon, for High Treason, in the Court of King's Bench, Westminster . . . on Monday and Tuesday, February 5th & 6th 1781 (London: privately printed, 1781), 6-12.

The Gordon Riots of 2-8 June 1780 resulted in extensive destruction to Catholic property. Gordon (1751-93) was acquitted of treason after an eloquent speech on his behalf by Thomas Erskine.

May it please your Lordship, and you Gentlemen of the Jury, I am likewise of Counsel in support of this prosecution against the prisoner at the bar, upon this indictment, which imputes to him a crime of the highest class of offences known to the law of this country, that of High Treason. And the particular species of high treason you find from the indictment, is levying war against the King within this realm. Gentlemen, the offence of levying war, within the act of the 25th of Edw. III. is of two sorts; the one, directly and immediately against the person of the King; the other, which is called constructive levying war, is, where there is an insurrection of a great and numerous multitude, to carry and effect by force and numbers the alteration of the established law of the country; to redress or support national grievances, or to reform any evil, real, or imaginary, in which the insurgents have no particular or special interest. Gentlemen, it is the constructive war levying of which the prisoner at the bar stands accused by this indictment. You who reside in this county are not strangers to the occasion of this prosecution. In the latter end of the year 1778, an act was passed, repealing certain provisions of an act affecting Roman Catholics, made in the eleventh and twelfth years of the reign of King William III. By the statute of King William every Popish Priest exercising any part of his function in this country, was liable to perpetual imprisonment; and every person of the Popish Religion, keeping a school, or educating youth, was liable to the same punishment. And, by another part of the act, the estates coming to Roman Catholics, by descent, devise, or limitation, from their ancestors, parents, or others, could not be possessed by them immediately and directly, unless they took oaths, and subscribed a declaration, which, by their religion, they could not do; but the estates were to go immediately over to the next of kin, being Protestants, leaving them and their families to starve. There was another provision respecting estates too, which made them incapable of taking them by purchase from any person whatsoever. This act of Parliament, containing such severe penalties and punishments, could only be justified, as I conceive, by the necessity of the case, the salvation of the state, and of our religion; for it is the height of severity, indeed, to punish men who are serving God in their own way, or discharging one of the most important duties of society in the education of youth, should undergo a confinement in a loathsome prison for their lives, in the society of the worst and most profligate part of mankind. The other part of the act was extremely severe, which deprives man of his birthright and inheritance: one can scarce suppose acts of such severity to be justified by any thing but absolute necessity. The history of the times don't furnish any ground of necessity, or any apology for the act. We have an account of it by a very learned person of that time, a member of the Parliament, Bishop Burnet. It was the effect of party faction against the Court at that time. It was brought into the House, in order that the Court might reject the bill, and that they might fix an odium upon them for that measure. Those who brought in that bill did not wish, or mean it to pass; but they were disappointed in their views, for the Court gave no opposition to it. The party wished to drop it; and Bishop Burnet says, they added very severe and unreasonable clauses to the bill, and sent it up to the House of Lords, in hopes that House would reject it. In that they were disappointed, for it passed the House of Lords. The passing that bill with those severe penalties and punishments I was speaking of, was the mere operation of faction. It was too much, in my opinion, for any party or faction to stake upon their game, the liberties and fortunes of others.

Gentlemen, The Roman Catholics, of course, submitted to this very severe law; they expected, no doubt, Parliament would see the hardships in which they were involved by these provisions, and would, themselves give redress. They made no application, indeed; the penalties and punishments appeared to every body so extremely severe, that very few prosecutions were brought upon this act. In my own time, I only remember one: If I recollect right, it was a person for officiating in a house somewhere about Wapping, to some foreign sailors, for which he was doomed to perpetual imprisonment. But they were still liable to private extortionary demands, which they yielded to, to avoid many prosecutions, or that they might have the liberty of enjoying what long had been in their families, and descended to them. This law remained in the statute book, but scarcely put into execution; though sufficient to keep up perpetual alarm, till the year 1778, when an act of Parliament was brought into the House, to relieve the Roman Catholic subjects from these particular provisions. The propriety of the measure, and the justice of it, the circumstances of that repeal, pretty plainly evince. The bill was brought in by a member of the House of Commons, who is distinguished for his love of the civil rights of mankind, and for his firm and zealous attachment to the Protestant Religion; and who, besides, possesses every public and private virtue that can adorn a citizen and a man—I mean Sir George Saville. It passed through the House of Commons with almost an unanimity. The opposition made to it, was not to the principle of the bill, but that it did not go far enough in the redress; it was thought right they should be relieved from other penalties. Gentlemen, I must let you know, at the time of passing this act, the Roman Catholics stood by law excluded from any share of government, and from any office of trust, military or civil; and the persons performing any part of the functions of Priests, or teaching of schools, were liable to many pecuniary penalties, and, in some instances, to imprisonment for one year. The law stood so at the time of making the act of Parliament, when these additional punishments were inflicted.

Gentlemen, after passing the repeal, which did not extend to all persons affected by the statute of William, but was conditional and restrained to those who should take an oath established by that act, containing the strongest assurances of their loyalty and affection to the King and Government, and of their steady support of it, and a renunciation, in the most explicit terms, of every pretender to the crown and government of this kingdom; and besides, a positive renunciation of any authority of the See of Rome, in civil or temporal cases, in this kingdom. None could receive the benefit of this repeal, who did not give the public that pledge.

Upon passing this act, many Roman Catholics of the first families in this kingdom, and others of all descriptions, came in to give that pledge to Government which the act required; no person seemed dissatisfied; every body were contented. But in the winter following, it was supposed that a bill would be brought into

Parliament, to take off some penalties which were inflicted by the laws of Scotland upon the Roman Catholics of that country. In the beginning of February we received accounts from Edinburgh, published in every news paper, of a most violent insurrection in that country by a mob, to put an end to the attempt to carry such measures into a law. It appeared from those accounts, that upon the second of February, an insurrection happened in the city of Edinburgh. Two Roman Catholic Chapels, in distant parts of the town, were attacked, set on fire, and demolished. The utmost exertions of the Civil Magistrates, assisted with some Fencibles upon the spot, could not put an end to the insurrection; when they resorted to one place, they found an attack in a distant quarter. Houses of Roman Catholics were also demolished, and the furniture and effects destroyed; and no check could be given to the violence and outrage, until the Lord Provost gave assurance that the design of a bill was dropped; and, thus, a measure was defeated which, in the opinion of many, · was proper and just.

Gentlemen, I took notice of this insurrection in Scotland, because, when I come to state to you the conduct of the prisoner at the bar, it will appear to be a very material circumstance. Things remained for some time afterwards, and until an association was formed, called the Protestant Association, which every one of you have heard of, and where pains was taken to create a belief that the repeal was attended with evident danger to the State and the Protestant Religion. Upon that ground it seems a petition was determined upon, and if they thought it necessary, they did right to petition. It is the inherent birth-right of every subject to petition Parliament, and whenever they imagine a case proper for the consideration of Parliament, they do right to bring it before them. I believe this petition was intended to be presented in a legal, constitutional, and proper manner. Gentlemen, you will find, that upon the second of June, in consequence of public advertisements, posted up at the corners of the streets, and from hand-bills, there was collected together in St George's fields, a multitude of people, or more properly a very large army, of many thousands, (the particulars you will hear from the witnesses) twenty, thirty, or forty thousand, under the pretext of presenting a petition to Parliament. Though it is the birth-right of every subject to present a petition, yet the petitioners are not to take from Parliament their deliberation and judgment upon the subject. They are not to dictate what Parliament shall do, that directly tends to the subversion of government. This body of men were arranged, according to the direction of the advertisement, into three or four divisions. The London division was directed to the right; the Scotch to the left; and the Southwark and Westminster in other quarters. One division, consisting of many thousands, marched over London-bridge, through the city, down the Strand, and so to the Parliament House, with colours flying, distinguished by blue cockades, making a march as regular as an army. There were bagpipes attending the Scotch division. In this way they marched to the Parliament House; they arrived about one o'clock; they took possession of all the avenues to the House, and of the Lobby. With the utmost difficulty could the members get admittance into the House, and some of them in coming down were ill treated by the populace, as an example, I presume, to the rest, if things were not done according to the wishes of the mob. The petition was presented. They were desired to withdraw, when the legal constitutional purpose was answered. They would not stir, but with great riot and confusion, insisted upon a repeal of the act, and the cry was *a Repeal, a Repeal; no Popery!* The civil power was sent for to disperse them; their attempts were in vain, for they still kept possession. They besieged the House, and kept the members imprisoned; and thus they continued till between nine and ten at night, when the civil power, with the assistance of the military, were able to deliver the House of Commons from the disgraceful situation in which they were to that time, and must have been confined till they had granted the prayer of the petition. As soon as the House was delivered, they ordered the petition to be considered, and adjourned to the Tuesday following; but the mob not having succeeded there, they immediately went to and attacked the Ambassadors Chapels' which, in every civilized country, are protected and deemed sacred from insult. Some of the mob were apprehended, about thirteen that night and the next morning. On Saturday the mob paraded in different parts of the town, but I don't find much mischief was done. Upon Sunday they appeared in Moorfields, they attacked a chapel in that neighbourhood, and the houses of many Roman Catholics, situated thereabouts. They pulled down the houses, took the furniture out, and burned it; and completely demolished the houses and effects of those poor unfortunate people. Gentlemen, I only state the operations in general, because I am convinced, many of you were witnesses to what I am now mentioning. Upon the Monday, the men who were taken up, were examined at Sir John Fielding's, five of them were committed to Newgate; they were examined under the apprehension of a rescue, by violence, from the people that were assembled without the door, and it was with difficulty they were conducted by the guards. But as soon as they were lodged in Newgate, the mob made an attack upon the house of Mr Rainsforth, who had been active in apprehending the men committed, and had been a witness against them. They made an attack likewise upon the house of a Mr Maberly, another witness; and they did other mischief that night. Next day, being Tuesday, when Parliament was to meet again, all the parts of this army re-assembled about the House. They there continued with great riot, confusion, and great shouts, for a *Repeal* and *no Popery*. The House was obliged to adjourn. After this, the first attack was made upon the house of Mr Hyde. The offence given by Mr Hyde, was partly his attendance upon the Justices on the Monday; but, principally, for his activity as a magistrate, in saving the life of Lord Sandwich, who was going to attend his duty in the House of Peers. They ransacked the house, set on fire the furniture, and totally demolished every thing they could. They were accompanied with their flags. Immediately they went to Newgate, which they attacked. They burnt the keeper's house, they broke the prison, and in a very short time delivered all the prisoners confined in that place, which, for its strength, seemed to me to be equal to a prison in the center of the earth. They attacked many houses of the Roman Catholics, which they burnt and destroyed. Upon the Wednesday, they opened all the prisons in and about this metropolis, with an exception of the Compter, and let out all the prisoners. They continued their proceedings, without controul or check, till some time the next morning. During that night, the flames appeared in every quarter. In short, nothing was expected less than a general conflagration. The next day they meditated an attack upon the Bank, and, I believe, upon the Pay and Excise Offices; when his Majesty, by the most unremitting exertions, had been able to collect together a force which gave them a check. Gentlemen, every body, I believe, thinks if a check had not been given at that moment, the whole of this town would have been destroyed in a very little time. Though this was the case upon a pretence of relief against the Bill, and notwithstanding their cry of *No Popery*, yet distinctions would soon have vanished; the reputed Papists, or the friends of the Papists, and any one that had the least connection with them, if obnoxious to the mob, would have fallen in their turn. And it was a matter of astonishment to me, that the whole town was not burnt before that period; for, consider the number of Roman Catholics in the manufactures and the most laborious employments in this town; had they interposed in the relief of their innocent brethren who had been attacked, what must have been the consequence? A bloody war must have been the case; and if the attack upon the houses had been returned, one does not know what men would have done under such circumstances; the whole of this town, even before the military could have come in to have quelled this riot, would have been in a conflagration. Gentlemen, the execrable designs of our inveterate enemies appeared in the proceedings of this mob. What was intended by the opening of the prisons? What was the meaning of the attack upon the national credit, the Bank of England? Was that upon the ground of Popery, or for the repeal of this Bill? Other circumstances concurring, leave no doubt that greater and more destructive and horrid designs were formed than at first appeared, or were expected by the public. Gentlemen, having stated the general outlines of the violences committed during those few days, to the eternal disgrace of this country, which can never be wiped off, it remains for me to state to you what share the prisoner at the bar had in these detestable violences. There can be no doubt that every man who contributed in any degree is a criminal as the persons perpetrating them. Gentlemen, you have now before you, as will appear from the evidence, the author of all these tumults, and to whom the whole is to be ascribed; an offender of such a description as seldom has appeared in a court of justice. Gentlemen, I have already taken notice of the Protestant Association; but I have not mentioned to you before, that the prisoner at the bar was the President of that Association. I have great reason to believe it will come out before this day is over, that the Association meant to state their apprehensions to parliament, willing to leave them to their consideration and judgment, and to present their Petition in an orderly form and a constitutional way, attended by very few. This measure did not square with the views of their president. Their president had been in Parliament, he had observed the sentiments of men upon the subject of this Repeal; and knew it was impossible immediate relief could be given, for the subject required consideration, whether any circumstances had arose to shew the danger apprehended was a matter of enquiry, difficulties were thrown upon the business, the bill had invited the Roman Catholics to give a pledge of their fidelity, which they had done, as the condition of enjoying that degree of freedom from penalties imposed by the act upon them. But no delay could be admitted; the Session of Parliament was near expiring. The prisoner at the bar advertised for a general meeting, and proposed a numerous attendance on this petition, at the general meeting, all might come that pleased. The proposal was no sooner made than immediately assented to; there are people in this town who cannot exist without an opportunity of plunder. Gentlemen, The prisoners upon this declared, that he would not present the petition unless he was attended by twenty thousand people. Was there ever such an idea struck any man that meant well to the peace and tranquillity of the country? He would not present it without he was attended by twenty thousand people, and they were to be marked and distinguished by cockades, that they might know the friends to the petition, or friends to the Protestant Cause. Is a cockade to be a sole test of adherence to any good cause?— Every man that came there with a cockade, whatever his views were, was considered as a friend to the Protestant Cause. There was no other distinction of this body of petitioners but having the cockades in their hats. He then gave directions for the march to divisions; a General could not make a better disposition of his army; the London and Scotch over London-bridge, the Westminster and Southwark were to come another way. It struck many that the method of marching proposed, must be attended with tumult and breaches of the peace at least; the very collection of such a number of men was a very dangerous measure; but, to take off every apprehension of that kind from those who attended, he bid them recollect what the Scotch had done, that they had prevented the bill extending to them, by firm conduct. To recommend to this body of twenty thousand men the firm conduct of the Scotch, which consisted in a most violent insurrection and tumult ever known in the city of Edinburgh; where the Catholics had committed no fault, had applied for no redress. Is a multitude of men not capable of taking the hint? it would have been too much for the prisoner to have said, Gentlemen, go and pull down all the houses of the Catholics? That would have been too gross, the civil magistrate would have interposed; but he said, recollect what the Scotch did by their conduct, and he added, he did not desire them to run any danger which he was not ready to share with them; and that he would meet them there, and was ready to go to the gallows in their cause. Greater encouragement could not be given; they looked up to him as a man of education and of high birth; they might not suspect at that time he was drawing them into any snare, when he offered and pledged himself, that he would even go to the gallows, but he would do the business. Gentlemen, He published an advertisement for the meeting of these people, and though he mentioned only twenty thousand, he had an expectation of a much larger army. The advertisement I will read to you: "Protestant Association. Whereas no Hall in London can contain forty thousand men, Resolved, that this Association do meet on Friday next."

Court to the Jury. You should not take notes of this from the Attorney General's opening, till it is given in evidence.

Mr. Attorney General. Gentlemen, I only open according to my instructions; witnesses will be called to the different facts. I do not pledge myself for the proofs of them; God forbid any thing I should state should turn to the prejudice of the prisoner at the bar if not proved. Gentlemen, The first resolution is, "That this Association do meet on Friday next, in St George's Fields, at ten o'clock in the morning, to consider of the most prudent and respectful manner of attending their petition, which will be presented the same day to the House of Commons,." Twenty thousand men, to meet to consider the most prudent and respectful manner of presenting a petition! How were they to be consulted? How was their opinion to be asked? Gentlemen, This is a disguise to the business. Then the advertisement goes on:

> Resolved, For the sake of good order and regularity, that this Association, on coming to the ground, do separate themselves into four distinct divisions, *viz.* the London division, the Westminster division, the Southwark division, and the Scotch division. Resolved, That the London division do take place upon the right of the ground towards Southwark, the Westminster division second, the Southwark division third, and the Scotch division upon the left; all wearing blue cockades in their hats, to distinguish themselves from the Papists, and those who approve of the late act in favour of Popery.

So that every man that did not wear a blue cockade in his hat, was to be considered as a favourer of Popery and the late act of parliament. Every man that would put on a blue cockade, let him be of what religion he might, he was to be considered as a friend of this bill. Here is another resolution: "Resolved, That that the Magistrates of London, Westminster, and Southwark, are requested to attend, that their presence may overawe and controul any riotous or evil-minded persons, who may wish to disturb the legal and peaceable deportment of his Majesty's Protestant subjects." Gentlemen, this last paragraph adds to the mockery of the advertisement, for it is of a piece with the other which I observed upon before. In order to preserve the orderly deportment of these people, he calls for the protection of the civil magistrates. Against whom? Those who should disturb their legal and peaceable deportment? For God's sake, who dare look in the face of forty thousand men, or give any offence to them? This army wants the protection of the magistrates. What magistrates of London or Westminster could act? and in Southwark, not one magistrate resided. No magistrates could controul the real purpose of the meeting. In consequence of this advertisement, upon the second of June, this assembly met. The prisoner at the bar appeared there at the head of them with his cockade, they were drawn up under the order, I presume, of him, because upon a person carrying a message from him, the march began; that I have already stated to you; he received them at, or came along with them to, the House of Commons, and there presented the petition. This body of men attended, and appeared to be totally under his influence and management. Their behaviour in the Lobby, and about the House, I have already stated; no means could be used to deliver the House of Commons from the situation they were in, till very late at night; he had it in his power at any moment to have done it; nay, the mob called on him to know whether they should quit the Lobby; for it was impossible, upon a division which was ordered in the House, for the members to divide without the Lobby was cleared. Nothing was to be done without his advice. It was not safe for him, he thought, to say, Stay, and obstruct the proceedings of the House; but he did that which was equivalent, he told them to be steady, he said he had called for a division; that there was no doubt at all but it was against them, and therefore, if they were not in the Lobby, the House would divide against them. But, that he might not appear to give advice, he said, I leave it to you, gentlemen. It was enough to leave to them that the business was going to be put off, whereas they wanted it to be instantly urged on, and carried thro'. He was applied to over and over to desire them to go out of the Lobby, and save Parliament from the disgrace of passing an act without examining, or being able to form any judgment upon it. Gentlemen, You will find here, that he reminded them over and over of the conduct of the Scotch; he told them the civil magistrates were sent for; he would not say, but he believed the petition was signed by the magistrates; he said that the guards, when they came, would do them no hurt. In short, by his persuasions, and by his influence, he kept up this body of people at that door, imprisoning the House; he said to them, you know what the Scotch did by their steady conduct; to which they answered, Yes, Yes, Yes. He told them too, when the Scotch pulled down the mass-houses, they had redress. That Lord Weymouth sent an assurance that the bill should not be extended to Scotland, and should the Scotch be better than you? Gentlemen, no language can be plainer to these people, that, if they did not succeed there, they were to pursue another plan. The Scotch had redress when they pulled the mass-houses down. You know what the Scotch did. And they acted entirely by his motions; that was enough to them; they could not misunderstand him. He added, there was no doubt his Majesty, when he heard of the insurrections within ten miles of London, and people coming to London, would send instructions to his ministers to repeal this act; and he urged them by every argument he could to get the repeal. Gentlemen, as soon as the House was delivered, and they found they were not able to accomplish their purposes there, the Scotch plan he recommended was adopted instantly; they flew to the chapels of the foreign ambassadors, and destroyed them; they proceeded afterwards to the houses of the Catholics, and every body that had given any obstruction to them were doomed to suffer. After violent outrages had been committed, not only upon the ambassadors chapels, but in other places; they made an attack upon Sir George Saville's house; they attacked Mr Rainsforth's and Mr Maberly's, and other houses. The different parties of this army reassembled at the House of Commons on the Tuesday; the prisoner came there with the same symbol he had before of being their head and leader, that of the cockade. They had all their colours flying, about Palace-yard; his Lordship appeared without remorse, without exhorting them to depart peaceably, without mentioning the mischief which they had done, or remonstrating about it. He was drawn in triumph through the city of London to the Mansion-house, and other parts of the city, by a part of this mob. Upon the Wednesday, he sent an advertisement of a very singular nature to be put in the Thursday's paper. It is thus:

> Lord George Gordon went in person to the different places, when the tumults were subsisting, to harrangue the multitude, and exhort them to a legal and peaceable deportment; he stood a considerable time among the horse and foot, and with the Sheriffs spoke upon the same subject, but all was without effect, for Lord George Gordon not being able to give them any assurances the act would be repealed. They continued their violences without intermission.

This advertisement encouraged the mob to look for some assurances, they were to continue their depredations till they had some assurances the act would be repealed; and this was the only reason why the violences were not stopped. Did he flatter himself when this appeared, he would have some assurances that this bill would be repealed? And yet it is manifest that this was held out, not only as an encouragement to the mob, but to induce some assurances of the repeal. This advertisement tells you, that several merchants had applied to him for protections. He states himself, in his own hand-writing, that he was the person to be applied to for protection; and several merchants had applied. We shall give you in evidence one of the protections granted upon the Wednesday. Nothing carries a stronger evidence; it is under his own hand. All the world looked upon the mob to be under his influence. No man can doubt it; he does not say, I refused them, or granted them. But what was the meaning of this advertisement? That other persons should apply the same way for protections. He was looked up to by the merchants and people of all descriptions as the man who, by his name and signature, could protect them from the violence of this mob. His name did protect in one case, which we will give you in evidence, where he gave a protection to a person that applied who had a Catholic lodger in the house; he found his house was threatened, and he got a protection from him, under his own hand, which I shall prove. Can there be any doubt, after this evidence, that the prisoner at the bar was the author and beginner of all the disturbances? Perhaps he will tell us, they were carried to a greater extent than he foresaw, and that he had no other object than a repeal of this bill. I don't know whether he had or not. But if he had no other object than the repeal of this bill, surely his measure of guilt is of no ordinary size. Gentlemen, will it be enough for him to say, I would have stopped the outrage, but I could not. When he had tempted the mob to look for assurances of a repeal, nothing short of that could have any avail; and, if he did turn out this many-headed monster, is it an excuse to say, I wanted to check its rage and fury? None at all. You have given birth to the outrage, you must stand by the consequences; it is just you should. Gentlemen, if these facts are proved, lay your hands on your hearts, and ask yourselves, whether to him the whole is not to be imputed? It is not an accidental assistance or encouragement, but he is the contriver of the whole. Gentlemen, if you are satisfied of this, your verdict will carry to the present and future ages this lesson, That, however exalted in birth, situation, or connection, no man can violate the peace and order of government, and the laws of his country, with impunity! Gentlemen, I shall call to prove these facts, some witnesses; not so many, I hope, as are in a list which by some means has been published. It is not the object, in delivering lists of witnesses, that they should appear in the public papers; but you have seen a list of a great many witnesses published: the necessity of inserting many will be obvious to you. We put down several to the same fact, that in case any should be absent through sickness, or other cause, others may be called whose names must be in the list. When I come to the proofs, I shall not trouble you with more than will be sufficient to establish the facts.

Gentlemen, I beg pardon for having troubled you so long, but in a case of so much importance and expectation, I could not avoid stating as particularly as I could the facts which directly affect the prisoner.

A Letter to . . . William Pitt by **Joseph Priestley, 1787**

A Letter to the Right Hon. William Pitt, First Lord of the Treasury, and Chancellor of the Exchequer; on the subject of Toleration and Church Establishments; Occasioned by his speech against the repeal of the Test and Corporation Acts, on Wednesday, the 28th of March, 1787 (London: J. Johnson, 1787), 1-23.

In this famous letter, Priestley, a Unitarian reformer, attacked Pitt's opposition to repeal of the Test and Corporation Acts and his defense of the Church of England.

Sir, Having had the opportunity of hearing your speech against the repeal of the Test and Corporation Acts, and thinking I could perceive that you had not given sufficient attention to the subject, or seen it in a true point of light, I take the liberty which I conceive not to be unbecoming an Englishman, and which, being well intended, and respecting an object of great national importance, is not, I presume, without some title to gratitude, to suggest what appear to me to be clearer ideas than you seemed to be possessed of, and such as may be the foundation of a better policy than you have adopted.

Educated as you have been by clergymen, who are interested in the support of the present establishment, and whose minds may therefore be supposed to be biassed in favour of it, it is not much to be wondered at, that you should have adopted their idea of its inseparable connection with the political constitution of this country, and that you should have caught their fears on the subject. But that these notions, and others which you advanced in the course of the debate, are destitute of all foundation, I do not despair of being able to prove, even to your own satisfaction, and so as to influence your future conduct.

I shall previously observe, that besides being misled by your education and connections, there was the appearance of your being farther embarrassed, and misled, by your situation; and that your attention to the real merits of the question was distracted by a wish to recommend yourself to a majority of the people, without offending the minority; an object, Sir, which much older statesmen than yourself have seldom been able to accomplish. As far as I can perceive, you have failed with respect to both, and that even Lord North, who spoke the honest sentiments of his heart, has left an impression of much greater respect on the minds of those against whom he pleaded, than you have done on those for whom you exerted yourself so much. But it has been the common deception of statesmen, to think to gain their ends by *address*, over-rating their own talents, and undervaluing those of others, who are as quick-sighted as themselves.

Believe an older man than you are, that a common proverb, older than our grandfathers, viz. *honesty is the best policy*, applies to the case of statesmen as fully as to that of tradesmen, for whose use it might be more particularly intended. Keep this in view in all measures of policy, invariably pursue what shall appear to be *right*, and you will be respected in all your conduct, and all the changes of your conduct, produced by a real conviction; because it is not disgraceful to any man, and least of all to a young man, to change his opinion, on farther reflecting upon a subject. If any pretend to the extraordinary merit of deciding upon every thing intuitively, and without taking the pains that other men must do in order to misunderstand it, he affects to be more than man; and those who see him to be in other respects like themselves, will not give him credit for his pretentions. But they will forgive a *mistake*, because they know that they are subject to mistakes themselves.

In this letter, in which I mean to take a pretty large scope, and bring before your view objects, to which, if I may judge by the tenor of your speech, you have not given much attention (at least I hope to place them in lights in which you have not been used to consider them) I require no other apology for the liberty I take, than what is given me by the *postulatum*, that the greatest politicians are but *men*; and notwithstanding their profound knowledge of the things to which they have given attention, they may be profoundly ignorant of things to which they have not attended. And there are many things, and those in which great national interests are involved, to which, educated as you have been, and circumstanced as you are, I apprehend you have not sufficiently studied. Among these, I must take the liberty to rank that of the intimate connection of any particular mode of religion with the welfare of the state, by a regard to which alone, and by no means to religion, in itself considered, your conduct, as a *statesman*, ought to be governed. As an individual give as much attention to religion, and a future life, as you please; but as the ostensible prime minister of this country, you have nothing to do with any life besides *the present*, and the happiness of the inhabitants of this island in it. *This* is a province large enough for yourself, and all your colleagues in office. For other things we shall look to other persons, or provide for ourselves as well as we can.

When you say that the present establishment of the church of England is necessary to the civil establishment of the country, and that this is necessary to the peace and happiness of it, you may be misled by several fallacies, and the propositions you advance may be true or false, according as they are understood.

A change, and especially a great and sudden change in matters of religion would, no doubt, be dangerous, on the supposition that the people continued to think as they now do; because, in that case, they would certainly be dissatisfied, they would probably resist the innovation, and public calamity might ensue. But, Sir, this would not be the consequence of any change, how great soever, in matters civil or religious, which the people themselves should be persuaded to think well of. Nay, in this case, the same mischiefs which you now apprehend from a change, might arise from any attempts to prevent the change.

This island was, I presume, the seat of much happiness and temporal prosperity before either of the parts of our present boasted constitution had any existence. Our present form of government was not coeval with the nation; for our Saxon ancestors were heathens, and in a later period they were Catholics. As those, therefore, who approve of the present state of things must believe that past changes have been advantageous to us, and such changes as Englishmen in former times would certainly have opposed; why may not other changes be also advantageous, though, at the first proposal, the minds of the present generation may equally revolt at them. If the maxims on which you laid so much stress had always been rigorously adhered to, the established religion of this country must now have been Pagan, and our priests Druids. If they had been adopted at any period before the reformation, we must have been Catholics, and without a shadow of a toleration. Indeed, though you disclaimed persecution in words, you admitted, as Mr. Fox justly observed, the whole extent of its *principle*. But are there are men now authorized to say, that *wisdom shall die with them*; and is it for you, Sir, to say to reformation *Hitherto shalt thou go, and no farther?*

Surely then, Sir, there can be no danger in any alteration which the people can be brought to approve of; and any present attempts to infuse into them a dread of innovation, is of the same nature with all attempts in the preceding periods of our history to keep the people blind to their future interests, for the sake of the present interest of certain individuals.

I do not say, however, that nothing should be done by the governors of a nation but what the body of it shall have previously considered and approved, though in matters of great consequence the maxim ought to be adhered to; because many lesser changes may be made by way of *experiment*, or the better to excite attention and discussion; and things may easily revert to their former situation, if, after sufficient experience, the alterations should not be approved. The minds of the higher ranks in any community may well be presumed to be more enlightened than those of the lower. It is therefore their proper business to speculate, to devise plans for the public good, and to make trials of such as promise the best.

Now, Sir, if any change would be justifiable on these maxims, in the present state of things in this country, it would certainly be that which was proposed to the consideration of the House of Commons on the 28th of March last, and which you opposed on the principle of its being too *hazardous*. If the safety of the state depended upon there being no justices of peace among the more opulent Dissenters, and no excisemen, etc. among those of the lower ranks, and on all the members of corporations being true churchmen, I would agree with you that no such characters ought to be admitted into such stations. But, Sir, is not the apprehension of *danger to the state* from such a change as this perfectly chimerical and ridiculous? Can you say that any danger, or shadow of danger, has arisen from Dissenters being admitted into any other offices of trust or power, as from their being members of either House of Parliament? If the danger arise from the King being permitted to make Dissenters justices of peace or excisemen, would not the same, or greater danger, have arisen from the power which the crown unquestionably has of making Dissenters peers? Indeed, Sir, there is no more danger of the constitution suffering from this quarter, than of the river Thames rising so high as to overflow the whole city of London; and you might as well propose the immediate raising of banks high enough to prevent so great a mischief.

What has been the conduct of those Dissenters who can comply with the present requisitions so far as actually to get into those offices from which you think it so necessary to exclude them, for many do this? And though I disapprove of the practice, I am far from thinking that Dissenters, truly conscientious in other respects, may not think it right. Do they behave worse as justices of peace, mayors, aldermen, excisemen, etc. than members of the church of England in the same offices; or do Dissenters in parliament propose or second worse measures, measures more inimical to the peace and best interests of the country than other members?

You, Sir, strongly declared the contrary, when you allowed the Dissenters the greatest merit as good citizens. Why then should not the proposed trial be made? For every regulation of this kind can be nothing more than a trial, or experiment. If any danger should arise from it, it could not be so sudden, but that there might be time enough to prevent the mischief from being fatal to us. The consequence would not be the instantly filling of all the executive offices of government with Dissenters. And if one in an hundred was so filled, it would be far less than the number of Scotchmen who have promotion in this country; and yet nobody apprehends that, in consequence of this, any thing will be done hostile to England, or more favourable to the interests of Scotland. Why then excite the laughter, or indignation, of men of sense, by telling us of the alarms of the bishops, and holding out to our view the horrors of 1780.

Bishops are recorded in all histories, as the most jealous, the most timorous, and of course the most vindictive of all men, apprehensive of danger from quarters from which no eye but their own could have suspected any. They have always dreaded and opposed, as Mr. Fox observed, every change that, by any mode of construction, could be thought to have the least aspect towards themselves. Indeed, Sir, it would have become you, as an enlightened statesman, instead of confessing that you were influenced by the chimerical apprehensions of this unwarlike body of men, and caught their fears, to have endeavoured to give them some of your courage, and to have persuaded them that the thing which, to their disturbed imagination appeared to be a mountain, was, in reality, nothing more than a molehill.

You alluded to some Dissenters as of a more dangerous complexion than others, in consequence of their being enemies to all ecclesiastical establishments; and, in order, I suppose, to pay a compliment to the rest, you said it was against *these* only that it was so necessary to be upon your guard. I avow myself to be of this class of Dissenters, and I glory in it. I have even no doubt, but that, as Christianity was promulgated, and prevailed in the world, without any aid from civil power, it will, when it shall have recovered its pristine purity, and its pristine vigour, entirely disengage itself from such an unnatural *alliance* as it is at present fettered with, and that our posterity will even look back with astonishment at the infatuation of their ancestors, in imagining that things so wholly different from each other as *Christianity*, and *civil power*, had any natural connection. Let the corruptions of Christianity, such as in this country, and on the continent of Europe, pass for it, avail themselves of such aid. The Christianity that I profess does not require, but disdains it. It wants no support that you, Sir, as a statesman, can give it, and will prevail in spite of any obstruction that you can throw in its way.

If these principles render the Dissenters among whom I class myself unfit to be trusted in any office of power, take proper measures to prevent us; but make a discrimination, and do not confound our case with that of those Dissenters who think that there ought to be an establishment of Christianity in every country. But do you think that the sovereign, aided by the advice of his ministers, is ever likely to make choice of such persons as myself to fill any important executive office of the state, if there should be any apprehension of our acting upon these principles, to the hazard of the establishment? If there be no real danger from them, I must maintain that their mere *opinion* on the subject is no reasonable disqualification. Whatever mischief any person may intend to do me, I never think of using any precaution against him, if I know that it is not in his power to execute his intention.

Equally chimerical, Sir, are your apprehensions of danger to the *Articles of the Union* between England and Scotland, from any alterations in the ecclesiastical constitution of this country, which the members of it should be disposed to make. If, however, it be a thing of so very sacred and inviolable a nature, as that no alteration which the most enlightened among us can devise, can ever take place, we ought to rejoice that it was not made before the reign of Henry the eighth; for then it would have prevented the *Reformation*. However, as this union did take place before the last improvements of the *Toleration*, and it was not dissolved in consequence of them, I cannot think it to be of so very delicate a nature as is pretended; but that having borne so much, there can be no great risk in trying whether it may not bear a little more. There are objects, however, in which the welfare and glory of this country are concerned, to which, I am very confident, you would yourself not hesitate to sacrifice this favourite *Union*, or any thing else that might interfere with them. Let every greater good be pursued, and every lesser inconvenience be slighted; but above all let *justice* be done.

It has been said that, if the Dissenters gain this point, they will aim at something more. This I acknowledge. We should ask many things more, because there are many things more that we conceive ourselves to be entitled to, and which it will be no injury, but an advantage, to our country to grant us. We are a part of the community which, in return for great merit, have received great injuries. Part of them no doubt are removed; but it does not follow that the remainder are no burden. We feel them to be so, and shall take every fair opportunity of endeavouring to relieve ourselves. Let the bench of bishops be fully apprized of this, and take their measures accordingly. We have the frankness and magnanimity of which they are destitute, and shall not endeavour to take them by surprize. I shall therefore beg leave to tell you, Sir, and *them* through you, what it is that we do want, and what we shall certainly claim some time or other; and I shall afterwards speak to other things, which I conceive would be for the honour and advantage of this country, and which we, or our more enlightened posterity, will probably be aiming at, after all our claims as *Dissenters* are granted.

But to quiet their apprehensions from the dangerous attempts of such furious sectaries as myself and my friends, and the terror which they have conceived from our gunpowder plots, etc. I shall inform them that the means we propose to employ are not *force*, but *persuasion*. The *gunpowder* which we are so assiduously laying *grain by grain under the old building of error and superstition*, in the highest regions of which they inhabit, is not composed of saltpetre, charcoal, and sulphur, but consists of *arguments*; and if we lay mines with such materials as these, let them countermine us in the same way, or in any other way they please, and more congenial to their natures. What we are aiming at is to enlighten the minds of the people, and to show them that in the church-establishment of this country there is much of error and superstition; and if we can convince them that it is so (and of this I have no doubt) in proper time they will take it down of themselves, and either erect something better in its place, or dispose of the materials (if they should think them of any value) for some other purpose; and who will then be aggrieved or complain? After this there may be no *bishops*, as the term is now understood, but there may be christian ministers, the people may be as well instructed in their duty, they may live as happily here, and make as good provision for their happiness hereafter.

I was particularly happy in hearing from Lord North, who approved himself to be a sincere friend to the present establishment, that a *complete toleration* was proper, and that if any thing remained to make ours so, it ought to be brought forward. This was a sentiment which I heard from several quarters of the house, and from yourself. I therefore think myself encouraged, and *required*, to mention some things which are certainly wanting to a complete toleration in this country, and which do not at all affect the established church. They are complaints which, if redressed, would give Dissenters no civil power, but would only make them secure in the public profession and exercise of their religion. If, then, you were sincere in your declarations, redress these grievances, and do it generously, without any farther solicitation on our part. If the bishops have any magnanimity, let the motion come from themselves.

If you would make the toleration *complete*, you must give us a power of doing that by *law*, which we now do by *connivance*, that is, the power of declaring and defending our religious principles. This power the laws of this country do not now give us. Many of us hold our property, and even our liberty, on the mere good will of our neighbours, and the generous spirit of the times, when the law would deprive us of both. As Christians, we think it our duty to hazard this, rather than neglect to take any measures in our power to propagate important truth; but we should certainly prefer a situation in which we might do this without being obliged to any person.

To place us in this situation, you must, in the first place, repeal the act of King William, which makes it *blasphemy* to impugn the doctrine of the Trinity. I think it my duty to attempt the utter overthrow of this doctrine, which I conceive to be a fundamental corruption of the religion which I profess, the greatest of those that mark the church of Rome, and which was left untouched at the reformation. My reasons for this may be seen at large in my writings on the subject, and especially in my *History of Early Opinions concerning Jesus Christ*. But whether the doctrine be true or false, give us the power of a free and fearless discussion of it. This, as friends to *toleration* simply, you and the bishops ought to do, as it cannot be pretended to be any infringement of the established religion of the country.

Repeal then this statute of King William, and all other penal laws in matters of religion, as a measure evidently necessary to render the toleration complete. If you will not do this without solicitation, though you acknowledge the propriety of it, you cannot complain if we should solicit. This is what I should have applied for in the first place, being as it were one of the *necessaries* of life, whereas the business of civil offices is a mere *superfluity*. Men may live, and live comfortably, without being justices of peace, or excisemen; but the confiscation of goods, and imprisonment for life, which would be my fate if the laws now existing were executed, every man will say would be a serious hardship, and in my opinion more severe than any mode of present death.

You consider the celebration of marriage as belonging to *religion*, as appears by your confining it to the clergy of the church of England, though with the exception of granting it to the Quakers. If this was wanting to *their* complete toleration, it must be also wanting to *ours*. Allow us, then, to be married by our own ministers. It is true we do not say with the Quakers, that we cannot in conscience comply with your forms, but we extremely dislike them; and if we were not taken, as it were, at an advantage, when we are disposed to make light of small obstacles, we should certainly make loud remonstrances on the subject. The service itself is a very aukward and indelicate one; and though it does not enforce upon the parties the obnoxious doctrine of the Trinity, it obliges us to attend a religious service, into which that doctrine enters. Independently, however, of this consideration, it is certainly a very unreasonable thing, that the fees for marriage should all be given to the ministers of the church of England, and that those of the Dissenters themselves should not go to their own ministers.

You will certainly have an application to Parliament on this subject some time or other. The equity of the request you will hardly deny. If, therefore, you wish, as you pretend to do, that the toleration of this country should be *complete*, make this concession to us, without our asking for it; and let it not be said, as hitherto it may, that you have never had the generosity to do what is *right*, till you were in a manner compelled to it, and did it to avoid a greater evil. . . .

Methodist Conference minute, with an ..ddendum, 1795

Minutes of the Methodist Conferences (London: Methodist Conference Office, 1812), I, 322-26.

The "Articles of Agreement for General Pacification" issued by the conference authorized the separate administration of the Lord's Supper, signifying a break with the Church of England.

ARTICLES OF AGREEMENT FOR GENERAL PACIFICATION
[27 JULY 1795]

I. Concerning the Lord's Supper, Baptism, etc.

1. The Sacrament of the Lord's Supper shall not be administered in any chapel, except the majority of the Trustees of that chapel on the one hand, and the majority of the Stewards and Leaders belonging to that chapel (as the best qualified to give the sense of the people) on the other hand, allow of it. Nevertheless, in all cases, the consent of the Conference shall be obtained, before the Lord's Supper be administered.

2. Wherever there is a society, but no chapel, if the majority of the Stewards and Leaders of that society testify, that it is the wish of the people that the Lord's

Supper should be administered to them, their desire shall be gratified: provided, that the consent of the Conference be previously obtained.

3. Provided nevertheless, that in Mount Pleasant chapel in Liverpool, and in all other chapels where the Lord's Supper has been already peaceably administered, the administration of it shall be continued in future.

4. The administration of Baptism, the Burial of the Dead, and Service in Church-hours, shall be determined according to the regulations above-mentioned.

5. Wherever the Lord's Supper shall be administered according to the before-mentioned regulations, it shall always be continued, except the Conference order the contrary.

6. The Lord's Supper shall be administered by those *only* who are authorised by the Conference; and at such times, and in such manner *only*, as the Conference shall appoint.

7. The administration of Baptism, and the Lord's Supper, according to the above regulations, is intended only for the members of our own Society.

8. We agree, that the Lord's Supper be administered among us, on Sunday evenings only: except where the majority of the Stewards and Leaders desire it in church-hours; or where it has already been administered in those hours. Nevertheless, it shall never be administered on those Sundays, on which it is administered in the Parochial Church.

9. The Lord's Supper shall be always administered in England, according to the form of the Established Church: but the person who administers, shall have full liberty to give out hymns, and to use exhortation and extemporary prayer.

10. Wherever Divine Service is performed in England, on the Lord's day in Church-hours, the officiating Preacher shall read either the Service of the Established Church, our venerable father's Abridgement, or at least, the Lessons appointed by the Calendar. But we recommend either the full Service, or the Abridgement.

II. Concerning Discipline

1. The appointment of Preachers shall remain solely with the Conference; and no Trustee, or number of Trustees, shall expel or exclude from their chapel or chapels, any Preachers so appointed.

2. Nevertheless, if the majority of the Trustees, or the majority of the Stewards and Leaders of any Society, believe that any Preacher appointed for their Circuit, is immoral, erroneous in doctrines, deficient in abilities, or that he has broken any of the rules above-mentioned, they shall have authority to summon the Preachers of the District, and all the Trustees, Stewards, and Leaders of the Circuit, to meet in their chapel on a day and hour appointed, (sufficient time being given.) The Chairman of the District shall be President of the assembly: and every Preacher, Trustee, Steward, and Leader, shall have a single vote, the Chairman possessing also the casting voice. And if the majority of the meeting judge, that the accused Preacher is immoral, erroneous in doctrines, deficient in abilities, or has broken any of the rules above-mentioned, he shall be considered as removed from that Circuit:

and the District-Committee shall, as soon as possible, appoint another Preacher for that Circuit, instead of the Preacher so removed: and shall determine among themselves how the removed Preacher shall be disposed of till the Conference, and shall have authority to suspend the said Preacher from all public duties, till the Conference, if they judge proper. The District Committee shall also supply, as well as possible, the place of the removed Preacher, till another Preacher be appointed. And the Preacher thus appointed, and all other Preachers, shall be subject to the above mode of trial. And if the District-Committee do not appoint a Preacher for that Circuit, instead of the removed Preacher, within a month after the aforesaid removal, or do not fill up the place of the removed Preacher, till another Preacher be appointed, the majority of the said Trustees, Stewards, and Leaders, being again regularly summoned, shall appoint a Preacher for the said Circuit, provided he be a member of the Methodist Connexion, till the ensuing Conference.

3. If any Preacher refuse to submit to the above mode of trial, in any of the cases mentioned above, he shall be considered as suspended till the Conference. And if any Trustees expel from any chapel, a Preacher, by their own *separate* authority, the Preachers appointed for that Circuit, shall not preach in that chapel till the ensuing Conference, or till a trial take place, according to the mode mentioned above.

4. If any Trustees expel or exclude a Preacher, by their own *separate* authority from any chapel in any Circuit, the Chairman of the District shall summon the members of the District-Committee, the Trustees of that Circuit who have not offended, and the Stewards and Leaders of the Circuit. And the members of such assembly shall examine into the evidence on both sides; and if the majority of them determine, that the state of the Society in which the exclusion took place, requires that a new chapel should be built previous to the meeting of the Conference, every proper step shall be immediately taken for erecting such chapel. And no step shall on any account be taken, to erect a chapel for *such purpose*, before the meeting of the Conference, till such meeting be summoned, and such determination be made.

5. No Preacher shall be suspended or removed from his Circuit by any District-Committee, except he have the privilege of the trial before-mentioned.

6. The hundred Preachers mentioned in the enrolled Deed, and their successors, are the only *legal* persons, who constitute the Conference: and we think the junior brethren have no reason to object to this proposition, as they are regularly elected according to seniority.

7. Inasmuch as in drawing up the preceding regulations, we have laboured to restore and preserve the peace and unity of the Society, and, in order thereto, have endeavoured to keep the Preachers out of all disputes on the subjects therein specified: Be it understood, that any Preacher who shall disturb the peace of the Society, by speaking for or against the introduction of the Lord's Supper in our Societies, or concerning the old or new plan, so called, shall be subject to the trial and penalties before mentioned.

8. And in order that the utmost impartiality may be manifest in these regulations, for the peace of the whole body, we also resolve, that if any Local Preacher, Trustee, Steward, or Leader, shall disturb the peace of the Society, by speaking for or against the introduction of the Lord's Supper, or concerning the old

or new plan, so called, the Superintendant of the Circuit, or the majority of the Trustees, Stewards, and Leaders of the Society so disturbed, shall have authority to summon a meeting of the Travelling Preachers of the Circuit, and the Trustees, Stewards, and Leaders of that Society. Evidence shall be examined on both sides; and if the charge be proved, the Superintendant Preacher shall expel from the Society the person so offending.

[ADDENDUM, 6 AUGUST 1795]

1. The Conference, by no means, wishes to divide any Society, by the introduction of the Lord's Supper, and therefore expect that the majority of the Stewards and Leaders, who desire the Lord's Supper among themselves, testify in writing to the Conference, that they are persuaded no separation will be made thereby.

2. The Sacrament shall not be administered to a Society in any private house, within two miles of any Methodist chapel, in which it is regularly administered.

3. We all agree, that the pulpit shall not be a vehicle of abuse.

4. It has been our general custom, never to appoint or remove a Leader or Steward, without first consulting the Leaders and Stewards of the Society; and we are resolved to walk by the same rule.

5. To prevent, as much as possible, the progress of *strife* and *debate*, and consequent divisions in our connexion, no pamphlet or printed letter shall be circulated among us, without the author's name, *and the postage or carriage paid.*

6. Nothing contained in these rules, shall be construed to violate the rights of the Trustees, as expressed in their respective deeds.

Thus, beloved brethren, have we done our utmost to satisfy every party, and to unite the whole. You, by your Trustees on the one hand, and your proper representatives, the Leaders and Stewards, on the other, are to determine concerning the introduction of the Sacraments, or the Service in Church-hours, among yourselves. We have gone abundantly farther. We have, in some degree, deposited our characters and usefulness in your hands, or the hands of your representatives, by making them judges of our morals, doctrines, and gifts. We apprehend, that we could have made no further sacrifice, without sapping the foundations of Methodism, and particularly destroying the itinerant plan. O brethren, be as zealous for peace and unity in your respective Societies, as your Preachers have been in this blessed Conference. Let the majorities and minorities on both sides, exercise the utmost forbearance towards each other: let them mutually concede one to the other as far as possible; and, by thus bearing each other's burdens, fulfil the law of Christ. Let all resentment be buried in eternal oblivion; and let contention and strife be for ever banished from the borders of our Israel.

Surely our present complete and happy union, so contrary to the fears of many, is a signal of good times. God will, we believe, pour out his Spirit upon us more largely than ever; and, by the exercise of his most gracious prerogative, bring abundance of good out of all our past evils.

To his grace and holy keeping we commend you. May nothing ever separate you and us from the love of God, or from each other; but may you be our crown of rejoicing in the great day of the Lord.

Speech by William Pitt linking his resignation as prime minister to the question of Catholic emancipation, House of Commons, 25 March 1801

The Speeches of William Pitt, in the House of Commons, 3rd ed., 3 vols. (London: Longman, Hurst, Rees, Orme, and Brown, 1817), III, 251-60.

Pitt's resignation as prime minister was occasioned by George III's refusal to support Catholic emancipation, linked politically to the Act of Union with Ireland (1800). Pitt remained on friendly terms with the monarch and gave support to the Addington ministry. He returned to office in May 1804.

Having said this, he would now utter a word or two for his colleagues, and for himself. With regard to their quitting their offices, he did not see any mystery about that subject, and he thought he was entitled to rely on the candour of gentlemen on the other side for believing the sincerity of their declarations on the occasion. The honourable gentleman who spoke first, was pleased to say, he would allow that, in case of a public measure of importance which a minister found he could not propose with success, or that he was not able to propose as a measure which was assuredly to receive the assistance of those who compose the executive government, and that such a measure a minister could not conscientiously give up or abandon—that such a condition of things would be sufficient to excuse a minister for retiring, and would, indeed, give a minister a right to retire. Now, after that allowance of the honourable gentleman, it was matter of astonishment to him that any doubt could have been entertained by that honourable gentleman on that part of the subject, or that he did not at once admit, that the circumstance which had been sufficiently explained already, had amounted, in the opinion of that honourable gentleman, to a complete justification of himself and others who had retired. He admitted, however, to the honourable gentleman, that if a person who filled an office of important trust under government had formed the project of proposing some measure which did not appear to him to be of much public importance, although he had made up his mind upon it, but which he could not carry into effect, seeing clearly that the bent of the government of which he made a part was against him, then it was the duty of such a minister to forego that opinion, and to sacrifice rather than withdraw his assistance from government in the hour of peril.

Mr. Pitt said, it was extremely painful to him to be obliged to say so much, and so long to occupy the attention of the House; but he would observe, that he had lived to very little purpose for the last seventeen years of his life, if it was necessary for him to say, that he had not quitted his situation in order to shrink from its difficulties;

for, in the whole of that time, he had acted, whether well or ill, it was not for him to say, but certainly in a manner that had no resemblance to shrinking from difficulty. He might say this, if he were to strike the seventeen years out of the account, and refer only to what had taken place within the last two months; and he would venture to allege, that enough had happened within that time to wipe off the idea of his being disposed to shrink from difficulty, or wishing to get rid of any responsibility. What had happened within that period had afforded him an opportunity of shewing, in a particular manner, that he was willing to be responsible to any extent which his situation cast upon him: in that particular he had had the good fortune, however unfortunate the cause, to have shewn that he was not only a party, but that he was the deepest of all parties in responsibility, in the adoption of a measure the most critical with regard to himself and his colleagues. He was therefore led to say, as to the measure which had induced him to quit his situation, that he did believe the importance of it, and the circumstances by which it was attended, to be such, that while he remained in office he should have been unable to bring it forward in the way which was likely to be eventually successful; and therefore he judged that he should serve less beneficially the public, as well as the parties more immediately the objects of it, in making the attempt, than in desisting from the measure. His idea of the measure itself, was that it was one which upon the whole had been better adopted than refused under all the circumstances: such was also the idea of those who had acted with him, and they had therefore thought it better that they should quit their offices than continue under such circumstances in His Majesty's service. In doing this, they had acted purely from principle; they had acted in such a manner as had satisfied their own minds, which was to them important; and he hoped they had acted in such a manner as would, one day or other, be perfectly satisfactory to the public, so far as the public should ever think it worth their while to be concerned in his conduct.

The measure to which he alluded, had he proposed it, as at one time he wished, was not one which gentlemen on the other side of the House were likely to look on lightly, although he should have had the good fortune to have their support if he had brought it forward, that is, on one part: but he did not think that he should upon the whole of it, nor did he believe those gentlemen would have favoured the whole of the principle on which he should have proposed the measure. He was not anxious to have the question agitated at all at this moment. I do not think, said Mr. Pitt, that this is a period in which it can be agitated beneficially to the public, or even to those who are more immediately the objects of it, and who are supposed to be so interested in its success; but whenever it is agitated, I shall be ready and I shall be willing to go fully into it, and to give at large my opinion on it. I will say only at present, that as to any thing which I and my colleagues meditated to bring forward, I disclaim the very words in common use, "the emancipation of the catholics," or, "catholic emancipation." I have never understood that subject so—I never understood the situation of the catholics to be such as that any relief from it could be correctly so described; but I think the few remaining benefits, of which they have not yet participated, might have been added safely to the many benefits which have been so bounteously conferred on them in the course of the present reign. I was of opinion, and I am still of opinion, that these benefits, if they had gone before the union, would have been rash and destructive, I was of opinion then,—I am of opinion now, that the very measure I allude to, as a claim of right cannot be maintained; and it is on the ground of liberality alone, and political expedience, (and in that sense wisdom, as connected with other measures,) that I should have thought it desirable, advisable and important: but I would not have had it founded on a naked proposition, to repeal any one thing which former policy had deemed expedient for the safety of the church and state. No, Sir, it was a comprehensive and an extensive system which I intended to propose—to relinquish things certainly intended once as a security, which I thought in some respect ineffectual, and which were liable to additional objections, from the very circumstance of the object of the union having been accomplished, and getting other security for the same objects, to have a more consistent and rational security both in church and state, according to the principle, but varying the mode, which the wisdom of our ancestors had adopted to prevent danger. The measure I intended to propose, I think, would give more safety to the church and state, as well as more satisfaction to all classes and all descriptions of the King's subjects, to take away that which no man would wish to remain, provided there could be perfect security without it. The House will, I am sure, forgive me for this part of my address to it.

As to what might be the nature of the measure, I am sure the House will in a moment feel, that what I am going to allege will satisfy it, that nothing of this nature could ever be accomplished by having a committee of the whole House on the state of the nation; for, independent of the many things which would be necessary to be done, if such a measure were set on foot, there is one thing which will make it obvious how inefficient for such a purpose a committee on the state of the nation would be. In the first place, that committee would not have any power whatever to interrogate any one member of parliament; and therefore all that part of the speech of the honourable gentleman which tended to connect the committee on the state of the nation with the condition of the catholics in Ireland, although it might serve the purpose of engaging men's affections for a moment, had, in reality, nothing whatever to do with it; and gentlemen are not such novices in the affairs of parliament as not to know that they may, whenever they please, move this or any other subject, independent of any other consideration, and that there is no necessity for a committee to enquire into the state of the nation for that purpose. I think, however, that the question with regard to the condition of the catholics, according to my view of things, cannot be improved by a committee on the state of the nation being brought forward at this time. It will cast no light whatever on any one subject connected with the catholic question. I am absolutely certain, as little can it throw on the cause, or the propriety or impropriety of our resignation:—this is too obvious to require any argument. How can the committee proceed to the examination of the cause of the resignation of His Majesty's ministers, to which some gentlemen, for purposes, perhaps, not very doubtful, have been pleased to attach so much importance? I know of no right which the House of Commons itself, still less a committee, can have to require of any man to state his reasons for tendering his resignation to his sovereign; nor is it a common thing for the public to require it. A man very often, indeed, makes his appeal to the public on going out of office, and that sometimes as much with a wish to be reinstated as any thing; but I never heard of a man being called on to exculpate himself from the charge of resigning. But gentlemen say, that, by our being silent on the subject of the catholic question, we have brought the name of our sovereign into disrepute; and the honourable gentleman chooses to put a construction on our remaining silent, and then to ask a question, whether the catholics had or had not been deceived. And upon the obstacles to the measure, as they are stated in a paper, of which I shall take notice shortly, the honourable gentleman says, that *innumerable* obstacles are in the way of the measure. I do not know what paper he took up; I cannot be responsible for it; nor, indeed, for the verbal accuracy of any paper whatever. I believe the word which the honourable gentleman has alluded to was really *insuperable*, and not *innumerable*. Upon that subject, all I will say is this:—That although I wished to submit the question of the catholics to parliament, there were such objections stated as made me feel it impossible, with propriety, to bring the measure forward as a minister. These are the general words I choose to use upon the subject: the honourable gentleman shall draw from me no admissions, and no denials on this subject. He may argue as he pleases from the words I use. ["Hear! hear!" from the other side.] Gentlemen may draw what inference they please.

But I shall say a few words more upon this subject. Gentlemen say, that I left this case in a state in which the name of the sovereign is brought into question; and they appear to be angry, because I will not tell them whether they ought to be angry or not. They wonder why I do not make it a matter of question, and they put distantly some points in the way of question; but I will not answer interrogatories. I will tell those gentlemen, however, that upon this subject they deceive themselves grossly. Should they be able to establish that the opinion of the sovereign made it impossible to bring the subject forward, they would gain nothing by it; for, should the opinion of the sovereign be what it might, or the opinion of his servants what it might; of the sovereign to dispense with the services, or of the servant to tender his resignation, it would still remain the same. Let these gentlemen but once be able to shake this principle, and they will have done more than they will be willing to avow towards the destruction of the monarchy: they will have established the most extravagant part of an oligarchy that ever was erected in any state; for then neither the sovereign could dismiss, nor the subject resign, without an explanation being made to the public. So that the sovereign, the father of his people, could never part from his servants, unless he condescended to show that they gave him bad advice; nor his servants tender their resignation, unless they could prove that something was attempted to be imposed upon them which they could not, in their consciences, approve. Now, I would ask, is that the state, or is it desirable it should be the state, of the monarchy of this country? Certainly it is not. The use of the name of the sovereign for the purpose of influencing opinions in this House, or in any deliberate assembly, is justly deemed unconstitutional. The sovereign exercises his opinion on the sentiments, as well as capacity, of his ministers; and if, upon either, he judges them to be incompetent, or in any degree unfit, it is the prerogative, and, with perfect loyalty, let me add, aye the duty, of the crown to dismiss such ministers. Allow me also to say, that if a minister feels, that, from a sense he entertains of his duty, he ought to propose a measure, but is convinced that his endeavours must be ineffectual, so that his services must be limited to a narrower compass than he could desire, and that success, in some material point, is impossible, he ought to be permitted to retire: but, in proportion to the difficulty which the sovereign may have in accepting the resignation of such a minister, ought to be his love for such a sovereign. I hope I am not deficient in my duty to the best of sovereigns; and I hope the whole ground and motive of my actions will continue to be justified during the whole of his reign. This is all I shall say upon this subject, which may perhaps be saying more than I ought.

With respect, however, to the assurances said, or supposed, to have been held out to the catholics of Ireland, I would add a few words. The honourable gentleman has alluded to a paper circulated in that part of His Majesty's dominions. It was a memorandum sent in the name of a noble lord at the head of the executive government of Ireland—a character revered by all who know him, and whose name I am persuaded will not be profaned, nor mentioned in this country with any disrespect. I know it to be true that the noble lord did feel it right, as a matter of public duty, to make a communication to persons most immediately among the catholics, and to state the motives which led to the late change that took place in His Majesty's councils, in order to prevent any misrepresentation of that subject than adding to the danger of the public tranquillity. I beg to state that matter clearly and distinctly; it was my express desire, not conveyed by myself, but through a noble friend of mine sitting near me, that the noble lord should take the opportunity of doing this. I do not arrogate any merit for it; but I think it is an answer to any charge against us upon this subject for remissness, that we lost no time in making that representation and explanation of our motives; and the principle of it was this, that the attempt to realise our wishes at this time would only be productive of public embarrassment. The representation was therefore made; but with respect to the particular paper delivered, it was not previously consulted with me how it should be perused, and therefore, for the particular phrases of it I do not hold myself responsible. All the knowledge I derived or conveyed was founded on verbal interpretation. As to the tenour of the paper that I have alluded to, the sentiments in it are conformable to those which I have already expressed in this House, and shall again express whenever I have occasion to deliver my sentiments on that subject; and it is fit, not only that this House should know them, but also that the community at large should know them.—I mean this: that a measure of that sort appeared to me to be of much importance under all the circumstances; and that being unable to bring it forward as a measure of government, I thought I could not therefore in honour remain in the situation in which I then stood; and that I was desirous of letting it also be understood, that whenever the objection I alluded to did not exist, the same obstacle did not interpose, every thing depending on me, as well as those who thought with me, I should do, for that I was desirous of carrying that measure, thinking it of great importance to the empire at large; but that, in the mean time, if any attempt to press it, so as to endanger the public tranquillity, should be made, or to pervert the affection of any part of His Majesty's subjects, we should take our full share in resisting such attempts, and that we should do so with firmness and resolution. These are the sentiments which I expressed, and I did hope that the day would come when, on the part of the catholics, should such a measure be revived, it would be carried in the only way in which I wished to see it carried, which was certainly conformable to the general tranquillity of the empire. As to any other pledge, I beg leave to give none—I am engaged myself to give none—I will give none—either now or at any time. I have contributed, as far as peaceable endeavours could go, according to my judgment, in the best manner I could at the moment, for the general interests of the country.

This is all I shall say on this part of the subject, and I am ashamed to have been obliged to trouble the House so much as I have done, especially as another branch of it remains, and on which I must still say a few words—it relates to a question, Whether any of those who have retired from office, had so pledged themselves to the catholics as to be under the necessity of resigning their offices because they could not perform their pledge? I beg leave to deny that; and, what is more satisfactory, I believe I am authorised in denying that the catholics conceived themselves to have received any such pledge. I know that the noble lord to whom I have alluded, and my noble friend near me, who must have been a party to such transaction, if any such had passed, did not so convey to me, I do not now, nor ever did, so conceive it. That the catholics might have conceived such an expectation, is most natural.—Why? Because the more attentively I have reflected on it, especially after the union, the measure has appeared to me to be salutary and expedient; and I can have no reason to think that they were less sanguine in their expectations on that subject than I was. That they thought there was a very probable chance for the measure, is most certain; for I believe there was no one in this House, nor, I believe, in the other House of parliament, who, in argument, has attempted to deny that the difficulties would be considerably diminished on this subject, after the measure of the union was accomplished: I was of that opinion when this subject was debated—I am of that opinion still—and the reasons in favour of it do very much preponderate; this, however, was afterwards given up, on motives of expediency. An expectation in favour of this measure there was; but a pledge, I do distinctly state, there was none. . . .

Sir Francis Burdett's motion on behalf of Catholic emancipation, House of Commons, 28 February 1825

Hansard, n.s., XII, 764-84.

Burdett's Catholic Relief Bill embodied certain qualifying clauses, or "wings," which would have diluted the full impact of Catholic emancipation. The bill passed the Commons, but was rejected by the House of Lords.

Sir;—Filled as my mind always is with anxiety and apprehension, whenever I am called upon to address this House, never did I feel that anxiety and that apprehension in so strong a degree as at the present moment, when a duty is imposed upon me, which I cannot help feeling I am unable adequately to perform, and which I should unquestionably have been anxious to decline, could I have done so, without the appearance of a desertion of my duty and principles—without the appearance of my not having that warm and zealous feeling in the cause of the Catholics, which I will venture to say, no gentleman in this House—no gentleman in any part of the united kingdom—entertains with more heartfelt earnestness and sincerity, than I do. When, however, I call to mind, Sir, the phalanx of splendid talent which, in times past, has been exercised in support of the present question— when I call to mind those great and eminent men, those venerable names now no more, whose eloquence and genius and intellects have been marshalled in support of it—when I call to mind, that the brightest talents of the present day have been, and will be, within a few hours, again drawn forth in the same cause—when, Sir, I consider all these things, it becomes impossible for me not to feel, in the midst of all my anxiety and apprehension, considerable consolation in the reflection, that every defect on my part will be more than compensated by the abilities of those who surround, and will support me; and that my cause—the cause of the Catholics of Ireland—of itself alone strong enough to bear up the weakest advocate—will be brought, and on the night on which I am speaking, to a favourable issue. It is, still further, a source of great consolation to me, in casting my eyes on every part of the House, to see men the most enlightened, and in possession of the best information, as anxious to promote the great cause, as I myself can possibly be; and, perhaps still more so, to know, that the brilliant talents of many right hon. and hon. gentlemen on the opposite side of the House, which have so often been exerted against the feeble efforts that I may have been led to make, will, upon this occasion, be zealously exerted, to give strength to my arguments, and to repair any defects of which I may be guilty.

Sir, the petition which I have just had the honour of presenting to the House— large and bulky as it is in appearance, and numerously and respectably as it is signed—is but a "trifle light as air," an atom of the smallest magnitude, when considered with reference to the immense body of the people of the united empire, whose interests it represents; and of which the full figure, if signed by all those whose interests are deeply involved in its success, would have been so tall and so gigantic, that even the roof of the English House of Commons would scarcely have been lofty enough to contain it. The case, Sir, is one of the greatest magnitude. We shall form nothing like a just estimate of the importance of this question, if we merely consider it as one exclusively involving the interests of the Catholics—as one exclusively involving the interests of the whole population of Ireland. The question to which it applies is one which affects no partial interests, but the immediate welfare, and, I may say, the safety of the British community at large. Of such vast and momentous importance did I feel it to be, that I should almost have shrunk from undertaking the duty which now devolves upon me—and should still be inclined to do so—if I did not feel myself supported by the encouraging reflection to which I have just alluded.

Sir, the grounds upon which the petitioners come before the House, appear to me so strong and so irresistible, that I can scarcely frame to myself the nature of the objections that are to be raised up against them. Upon every principle of justice— upon every motive of sound policy—upon every ground of strict right, good faith, and honour—upon all these grounds, Sir, it appears to me, that the Catholics of Ireland stand before the House in a way which renders it utterly impossible that the prayer of their petition should be rejected.

I am extremely anxious, Sir, at the present moment, not to weary the House by a recurrence to any of those painful topics which have recently been under its consideration. And, above all things, I shall endeavour to touch upon no topic— upon no point—which can, by possibility, excite, in the mind of any person, the least angry feeling. On the contrary, it shall be my endeavour, so to advocate the claims of the petitioners, as to conciliate the minds of all men; and, earnestly do I implore those around me, of whatever side and party they may be, to merge for a moment every private and particular feeling, in their anxiety for the public interest, and to consider only by what course the great interests of the empire at large are most likely to be served, and consolidated. With this object constantly before me, I shall cautiously avoid every thing in the shape of a retrospective view. I will not, with unhallowed hand, tear open the wounds of Ireland. I shall do all that in me lies to conciliate the people on the one hand, and the persons who are opposed to them on the other, and I shall endeavour to show, that it is equally the interest of both, to put an end, at once and for ever, to a state of things, which is calculated only to perpetuate dissention.

Sir, partly from the conciliatory conduct of the existing government, by liberalizing (as was well observed the other night, by the Attorney-general for Ireland) the old policy which was pursued in that country; and partly, perhaps, from other causes, Ireland may have attained an unusual state of tranquillity. Still, Sir, it is quite irrational to suppose, that this calm can be, for any length of time, maintained, until justice be done to those who now come with their petition before you—until full and ample justice be done to those, whose claims are alike founded in policy and in reason.

Now, Sir, with respect to this claim of justice: it should be recollected, that, at the period of the Revolution, when there really was danger to be apprehended from the Catholics—when a king had recently been expelled from the throne, because he was endeavouring to subvert the constitution, and introduce principles of arbitrary power—when the government of king William was but newly-established—it should be recollected, I say, that, even at that period, the hostility entertained in this country to the members of the Catholic persuasion, was not a religious hostility. It was the connection of that religion with principles of arbitrary power, which made the Catholics obnoxious; and a distinction was then, as at all times, taken, between the state Catholic, and the religious Catholic. The latter was always safe: whilst the former was an object of great suspicion and hostility; because he was believed to be in constant correspondence with the See of Rome, the Family which had been exiled, and the Catholic powers of Europe. Under a government newly established, with a Popish pretender supported by foreign princes abroad, it is not at all wonderful, that the hostility of our forefathers should have been roused and excited against the Catholic religion: but that hostility was excited, and naturally excited, because they were led to believe, that the religion of the Catholics was inseparably connected with arbitrary principles, with slavery, and the utter subversion of a free constitution.

Sir, in those times of difficulty and danger, after king William had made good his footing in this country, and James 2nd, expelled from the throne, had fled to Ireland—to the protection of his subjects there—those subjects did not think themselves at liberty to renounce their allegiance to him; and, being honestly of that opinion, they considered themselves bound, as loyal and faithful subjects, to defend him. They were any thing but rebels. If rebels there were, we, Sir, were the rebels—we, in England: but, I own, justified rebels—justified in defence of our rights, our religion, and our constitution. Neither were the people of Ireland rebels; as they have been unjustly designated; but loyal men, who, in defending their legitimate sovereign, were, at the same time, maintaining their own individual rights. The people of Ireland fought many battles; and shewed great courage, and invincible bravery, in his cause. The army was intrenched in a strong hold, from which it would have been difficult to dislodge them: but, at length, they lost their esteem for king James, in consequence of that monarch's desertion of them, and of himself; while, perhaps, they acquired, at the same time, some respect for the character of king William, who had distinguished himself by qualifications of a very different description. The country was, at that time, in a divided state. Louis 14th was at the head of the powers who supported the pretensions of James 2nd; and, at this critical juncture it was, that king William, in order to pacify Ireland, sent over commissioners, with full and unqualified instructions to grant her any terms, in order to put an end to so dangerous a war, and secure the peace and tranquillity of that country.

Under these circumstances of difficulty and of danger to the newly-constituted government, what, Sir, was the conduct of the Catholics of Ireland? They entered into an agreement, treaty, and covenant, that, provided liberty of conscience—that is to say, the free and unconstrained exercise of their religion; together with all the other advantages possessed by the rest of the king's subjects—were secured to them, they were ready to submit. And, upon this being solemnly guaranteed to them, in the name of king William—though it was notorious at the time, that a French fleet was advancing to their aid, and though that fleet had actually entered the Shannon before the treaty was ratified—they preserved their good faith, surrendered their arms, and put it out of their power to become ever again formidable to England. It is, too, a curious fact, that one of the conditions of this memorable treaty was, that they were not to be compelled to take the oath of supremacy. They were to be admitted to all the rights enjoyed by English subjects; and were not to be subjected to any disabilities, for adhering to the religion of their forefathers. Indeed, Sir, there were not wanting many adherents of the new establishment, who thought the terms conceded to the Catholics of Ireland too good, and who endeavoured to raise objections to them: but they could never persuade parliament to reconsider them, and the treaty of Limerick was, in consequence, fully ratified and confirmed. By this treaty king William, relieved from his embarrassments at home, was enabled to consolidate the whole force of the empire, and successfully to resist the ambition of Louis 14th.

Now, Sir, of all the infringements upon the treaty of Limerick which have since been made, experience has proved, that not one of them can be held to have been taken as a security; seeing that, in the moment of danger, the people of Ireland have never been found wanting. It was in the hour of triumph and security, that the angry passions of an interested faction were triumphant. Infractions of the treaty then followed, by degrees, one after the other: each infraction constituting an attack upon all honour and good faith; and the whole ending by imposing upon the

Catholic population of Ireland, a set of laws the most sanguinary and cruel—
breathing a spirit of tyranny the most detestable, and imposing a yoke the most
heavy, that ever weighed down the necks of any people of any country on the face of
the globe. But, Sir, unjust and cruel and unwarrantable as these laws were, they were
not so unwise as they were wicked. The effect of them had been to bend the people of
Ireland to the earth; and if they had been persevered in, doubtless they would soon
have left England without any thing to dread, in the way of disturbance, from the
Catholics; for, if followed up, they would inevitably have succeeded in extirpating
the whole body; and, however wicked, and tyrannical, and murderous, such a
course would have been, there would have been something like common sense and
meaning in it. But, in better times, the establishments of later days had deemed such
a course too revolting to be persevered in. By degrees, those severities were relaxed;
and I could wish the Catholics never to forget, that year after year, they have been
receiving benefits from this country—benefits to which, no doubt, they were
entitled; but which, nevertheless, they would do better to bear in mind, than the
remembrance of the grievous injuries which have been inflicted on them. I could
wish them to carry their views a little further, and see how certainly—how
necessarily—that system of conciliation, which only commenced in the last reign,
will, sooner or later, be accomplished in the present. I could wish to talk to the
Catholics of Ireland, of the good done to them by their friends, and of the very
mitigated rancour of those who, in former times, were their most determined
enemies. I could desire to impress upon them, the absolute certainty of the final
success of their claims—firmly resting, as those claims unquestionably do, on
reason, sound policy, justice, and good faith. If, Sir, the Catholics of Ireland will but
so far keep a restraint upon themselves, as to make the best use of all the advantages
held out to them—if they will but exert themselves to forget old injuries—injuries
which now bid fair to cease for ever—If they will only use common forbearance, and
prudence, and discretion—I think it quite impossible, Sir, that their claims should
not be successful. With only a reasonable portion of care—I repeat it—their cause,
both out of doors, and in parliament, must triumph: for they may feel the most
perfect assurance, that, unless the peace of the country should be disturbed, the
enlightened mind of the people of England is making a rapid progress in their
favour.

Therefore, Sir, in bringing forward the present question, I do not consider
myself, at the present moment, as the advocate peculiarly of the people of Ireland:
still less do I consider myself the advocate of the Catholic religion: but, though I am
not the advocate, neither am I the adversary of that religion, nor the adversary of the
various descriptions of religion, which different men according to the different
notions and inclinations of the human mind have embraced. My own opinion, Sir,
is, that all forms of religion are right—equally right—provided the persons
professing them follow them with sincerity of heart; and provided they inculcate
sound morality, and produce visible fruits, in the virtuous life and conversation of
those who adhere to them. Now, that the Catholic religion can furnish as abundant
proofs of good faith as any other system with which we are acquainted, I am fully
persuaded. At the same time, for myself, I have no hesitation in saying, that, bred
up, as I have been, in the religion of the Church of England,—(and that I consider as

ample reason as any man can be called upon to give for his adherence to any particular faith)—I am attached to that Church, because I was born in it. And further, upon reflection I do think, that if I had to choose my religion again, the Church of England, of all others, is that which I should adopt. But, Sir, when I state this, I by no means mean to assert, that the Church of England is not open to objections, or that many things embraced by it, might not be altered and modified with great propriety. My opinion applies to the system, as a whole. And with respect, Sir, to the clergy of the church of England—(I may be partial, though I believe I am not)—I have no hesitation in declaring, that the conviction of my mind is, that a more enlightened, liberal, virtuous, and useful body of men does not exist, in this, or in any other country in the world [hear, hear!]. I wish, however, to be understood, as not embracing in this class the ecclesiastical corporations—which, like all other corporations, invariably exhibit, at all times and under all circumstances, the same uncharitable, narrow-minded, monopolizing spirit. If, however, I am a member of the church of England, it behoves me, Sir, to remember that my first care should be, not to forget one of her first precepts—to "do unto others, as I would that others should do unto me." And, moreover, I have further to remember what the constitution of my country teaches me; namely, that all men bearing an equality of burthens are, in a free state of society, entitled to the enjoyment of an equality of rights [hear, hear!]. Upon these two grand axioms do I fortify myself. On their authority I contend, that, so far from this being a Catholic question, the Catholics themselves stand upon a Protestant principle; and that I am now maintaining their claims, upon the very principles which assured the security of England.

And, upon this subject, Sir, it is singular enough to remark the sort of change which has taken place in the views and situations of the parties. For we find, that those same men who formerly rejected Catholicism, on account of the alleged illiberality of its doctrines, are now acting upon the very principles they opposed, and refusing to proceed in conformity with their own; while the Catholics are asking for nothing more than what the Protestants first desired—namely, that we should deal out to them the principles of constitutional and religious freedom [hear, hear!].

We have heard much, Sir, of the danger to be apprehended from granting to the Catholics that which they desire. I cannot, however, but imagine, that there is some incongruity in the existence of such a feeling. What the apprehended perils are, I confess I have never been able to find out. But this, perhaps, is not very extraordinary; seeing that people are not unfrequently alarmed, without knowing very distinctly what at. The very mention of his holiness, the Pope of Rome, seems to raise, in the minds of some men, images of horror—half historical, half romantic—which have nothing to do with the world as it now exists. Their terrors have been extracted out of books, which, in early life, prejudiced their minds so deeply, as to impede their progress; and they foolishly think, because their own minds have stood still at a particular point, that the Catholics of the present day are the same persons as the Catholics of whom they read in history. Whereas, in point of fact, all those absurd notions have no more to do with the present state of the Roman Catholic religion, or the state of this world at all, than it has to do with that of the next [hear, hear!].

Sir, in discussing this question, the great difficulty we have to contend with, is that of having to encounter perverted understandings. It has been said by a favourite poet—

> where Ignorance is bliss,
> 'Tis folly to be wise.

And most certainly, Sir, in this instance, the grossest ignorance must be bliss, compared to the misfortune of having the mind imbued with a mass of antiquated tales and prejudices—greatly exaggerated, perhaps, at the times at which the statements were made, and which have no longer any existence, or chance of future existence, whatever.

Now, Sir, a curious example of this failing, is to be found in the fears entertained of the power of the Pope—concerning whom, a gentleman, coming up to me the other day, expressed his great alarm. It seems to me not a little extraordinary, that his majesty's government, or at least that portion of it who are hostile to the claims of the Catholics, on the ground of this apprehension of the power of the Pope—it seems to me, I say, Sir, not a little extraordinary, that they should be the very persons, who, not many years ago, expended in profusion the blood and the treasure of this country, in order to reinstate that potentate in the very place in which they now think fit to be afraid of him. He was found in a state of the lowest subjection: and, at the moment when his power was literally overturned, he was replaced in his authority, by those very servants of his majesty, who now profess to be so mighty alarmed at his shadow. Surely, Sir, it is not a little unreasonable in the right hon. gentlemen, first to raise up this phantom, and then to go out of their wits with terror at it! If, indeed, there existed now, as was the case at a former day, a league of Foreign Catholic princes abroad, caballing with a Catholic king of England at home, to subvert the liberties, through the religion, of the country—if Sir, there existed any danger of this description at the present day—then, perhaps, there might be some ground for apprehension. But, if any danger has been re-created by the re-establishment of the Pope, why then, I say, Sir, that that portion of his majesty's cabinet ministers deserve to be impeached for having created the danger, by contributing to the consolidation of the papal power. They themselves are the authors of the existing continental system. They it was, who caused English soldiers to mount guard at the Vatican, to protect and do honour to the dignitary, who is now the object of their alarm; and allowed those soldiers to receive medals from him, in token of the service they had performed. What a mass of monstrous inconsistencies is all this! What a premunire have these right hon. gentlemen drawn themselves into—if, at this time of day we are to be told, that there is so much danger in the papal authority, that to avoid that peril, we have no other choice but to keep six millions of people in a state of hostility against us, discontented—and justly discontented—with their condition, when we might, by a wise and liberal and generous policy, permanently secure the tranquillity and safety of the kingdom at large! The peril, forsooth, from the Pope, is so imminent, that it is better, in the eyes of these right hon. gentlemen, to meet the hostility of the six millions of the people of Ireland, than to face it! Why, Sir, this certainly is a pleasant situation to be in! And that, too, at a time, when, we had assisted in the destruction of all the secondary powers of Europe—when we had given up all those minor States which England formerly was wisely accustomed to support, and, up to a certain point, always to rely on—when every thing like the balance of power had been destroyed—and when we had distributed out Europe among two or three great powers, who may, at any moment, take offence at our conduct; and who are not unlikely to do so, as often as we refuse to keep pace with the measures of their unholy alliance. It has been avowed, Sir, by the right hon. the Secretary of State for Foreign Affairs, that one of those potentates feels already galled, that England should have consulted her own interests, by recognizing the independence of the South American States. And we have so far obliged and cringed to another, as to allow him silently to lay violent hands upon Spain—to effect the military occupation of that country—a thing which England, at no former period of our history, would have suffered, for a moment. We are surrounded, Sir, by these holy allies, whose strength we have either created or upheld, by the loss of our best blood and treasure, and at the expense of the liberties of Europe. Those powers, Sir, every one of them, are objects of alarm to us, rather than security. And, yet, in such a situation it is, that England continues to reject, and cast from her, that best of all alliances, the firm adherence of her own subjects, by keeping six millions of men, close to her own shores, in a state of constant hostility to her government. Sir, this very neglect of Ireland—or rather this contempt of Ireland—for it is worse than neglect—affords a ready opening for the first of those holy allies, who shall find it convenient to do so, to invade her. Instead of finding Ireland—as they would find her, if England did her justice—an insurmountable barrier which our enemies would be unable to pass, she will become the readiest point of all others, through which they will be enabled to wound us. Why, then, expose her to be tampered with by those states, who would appeal to her through the medium of a common religion! Why not affix a barrier round that country which would exclude all foreign influence? If England be destined to sink, Ireland is the sea in which she will be swamped. "Holy Allies," Sir! Ireland is indeed worthy of English alliance. Our "Holy Friends!" In the hour of danger we should call on them in vain. And yet we refuse—obstinately refuse—to make the best of leagues with the brave inhabitants of the sister kingdom—desirous of the alliance—anxious to be attached to this country, by an equality of rights and of benefits.

Can any man, Sir, repress his astonishment—can he account, on any principle short of miracle, for the fact—when he reflects on the hair-breadth 'scapes which England, during the late war, got out of with regard to Ireland? Had, Sir, the French fleet which anchored in Bantry Bay been successful to a certain extent—had it not so happened that the commander-in-chief was separated from his forces—had it so happened that the second in command had possessed enterprise enough to land—Ireland was gone; and the Sun of England would have set, I fear, in eternal night. The failure of that attempt upon Ireland can only be attributed to the extraordinary ignorance of the enemy, with regard to the temper and the spirit of the people of Ireland. They did not know how to take advantage of the opportunity which was offered to them. But, Sir, we must not presume upon our good fortune. The ignorance which then saved us exists no longer. Since that period, the powers of the continent have had an extensive intercourse with us. They have been too much upon our territories to continue ignorant. I say distinctly, that they are casting many an anxious eye at Ireland. From time to time, they are reproaching us with our conduct towards that unhappy country. Several of their Court journals appear to take a most tender interest—a most sensitive interest—in her concerns. A variety of parties, with whom we may not always be on the same friendly footing that we are at present, have, on a sudden, become most seriously desirous to promote the welfare of Ireland. They dwell on her calamities and injuries: they reproach England with hypocrisy: they laugh at her sympathy for the negroes, and her desire to get rid of the Slave Trade; and protest, that there is not, in all the world, a tyranny so odious, as that which we exercise over our Irish Catholic subjects; nor any spot on the face of the globe, where men are subjected to such intolerable injustice and oppression.

Now, Sir, these benevolent intimations, with regard to Ireland, which we are constantly seeing in the French papers, are well calculated in themselves to excite suspicion in the breasts of Englishmen; and it becomes the first duty of the government to inquire how the impending evil can best be counteracted—to see what measures can be adopted to promote that consolidation of our resources, and that conciliation of all parties in the united empire, without which no man can answer for what may be the consequences, if this country should again be involved in a war with the powers of the continent. I would therefore, Sir, address myself to the feelings of men of all parties; and, founding the question upon policy and justice, I would appeal to their good passions as well as to their bad—to their feelings of patriotism as well as to their self-interest—and, whether worshippers of God, or worshippers of Mammon, I would tell them, that it was their interest, in this case, to do justice—immediate justice to the unfortunate people of Ireland [hear, hear!]. The claims of that people rest on the broad basis of justice—on a covenant—on all which ought to be held sacred between country and country—between man and man. If, indeed, there were any danger to be apprehended from fulfilling that contract, which, upon every principle of good faith we are bound to fulfil—still, even then, I would say, it was the height of irrationality not to complete the work we have already begun, and, by refusing to give something further, to lose the benefit of all that we have already given.

And what, Sir, after all, is it that the Roman Catholics of Ireland ask at our hands? What is the mighty increase of power which, if every thing they ask were granted to them, they would obtain? Why, Sir, a few most respectable Catholic gentlemen, would, probably, have seats in the House of Lords—and the king would have his prerogatives so far enlarged, as to be empowered, provided he thought fit, to nominate Roman Catholic gentlemen to certain offices in the state. And, in point of fact, what substantial power would this right of eligibility confer? Does any gentleman now entertain any apprehension, that we should have a popish king using the power of popish election to overturn the liberties of the country? What, Sir, is the danger? I should like to hear it stated. For, until I hear what the danger is, I really cannot conceive what the views and the sentiments are, of those who set themselves up against the claims of the petitioners.

The present time, Sir, appears to me most peculiarly auspicious for taking the step, which the Roman Catholics of Ireland implore us to take. The public mind of this country is decidedly in favour of granting their claims. The larger as well as the better part of the Protestant population of Ireland, anxious for the prosperity and happiness of their country, have petitioned to have their Catholic fellow subjects admitted to the privileges of the constitution. There is only one small faction in Ireland which opposes itself to this wise and liberal policy; and that opposition arises from an unwillingness, on their part, to be deprived of the power which they have, for so long a series of years, been accustomed to exercise over their unfortunate Catholic countrymen.

And here, Sir, I must be allowed to do justice to those who, in Ireland, are called Orangemen. It was my good fortune, when in Ireland, to have had frequent opportunities of witnessing the conduct of Orangemen as well as Catholics. Both of them I have always found equally disposed to be kind and bounteous to their inferiors; and fulfilling alike the duties of good citizens. And it is a great mistake to suppose, that the gentlemen of Ireland are worse landlords or worse neighbours, than those of any other country. There may, certainly, be a low, pettifogging, ignorant class hanging about the system; but, Sir, the result of my observation is, that, with this single exception, a more liberal, a more kind, and a more excellent set of men does not exist than the Orangemen of Ireland. I speak of them, of course, subject to the exception of that unfortunate error in their education, and the right which they fancy they have, even by birth, to trample upon their Catholic fellow subjects: but, with this exception, I found them as kind in manner, if not more so; and at least as kind in the essential, as the gentlemen of England, or of any other country. But, it is high time for them to get rid of this exclusive spirit, which they have too much cherished—it is high time for them to consider only of the means by which the prosperity and the happiness of their native country can be best promoted—a prosperity in which they cannot fail largely to share. They should consider, that, by shaking hands with their Catholic brethren, instead of living in a society constantly tumultuous and distressed, they would behold wealth and tranquillity rising up around them, and superseding those measures of severity and coercion, which are at once the shame and the misery of every state in which they are called into operation [hear, hear!].

I beg also to address myself to the people of England, and to remind them how much and how deeply they are interested in the adjustment of this question,—Independently of the security of the country against foreign danger, and taking the question as a matter of economy, I would ask them to consider what it costs them to support this system in Ireland. I would ask those who pay the taxes to examine the expense attendant upon the present state of things. They talk of the necessity of taking off taxes: and the right hon. the chancellor of the Exchequer, in his statement last night, took credit for removing a portion of the taxes—a small portion, I admit, but still an important portion—because the collection of them was a source of vexation to the people. But here, Sir, you have an opportunity of effecting a much larger measure of economy. In Ireland—instead of thousands—millions may at once be saved by a change of system; to say nothing of the wealth which would necessarily flow into this country from Ireland, if the present mischievous, mistaken, narrow-minded, bigotted system, were exchanged for a more liberal and more enlightened policy [hear, hear!]. If tyranny, Sir, be a luxury, it certainly is a most expensive one. Of all the forms of government under Heaven, the most grinding and oppressive is that which is founded upon religions exclusive—and I will add, too, the most burthensome and costly. And all this expense, be it recollected by the House, comes out of the pockets of the people of England; who pay for the luxury of keeping Ireland enchained and miserable. How much more wisely, then, would the people of this country act—though, perhaps, they may not think so—in crowding the table of this House with petitions in favour of Catholic emancipation, than in praying for the repeal of a few hundreds of thousands of pounds, in the shape of Assessed taxes!

On the ground, therefore, of justice—on the ground of good faith and sound policy—and on the ground of the pledge given by solemn treaty—for I never will abandon the treaty of Limerick—we are imperatively called on to grant the claims of the Roman Catholics of Ireland. The title to a free exercise of their religion, conveyed to them by that memorable treaty, has, moreover, Sir, been strengthened and confirmed, by the engagements entered into at the period of the Union. Those engagements, it is true, were not formally reduced to the shape of a treaty—they were not signed, and are not productible, like the former—but, at the period of the Union, the people of Ireland were induced to acquiesce in that measure; and all they have got in return is a mere parchment Union, one which, in point of fact, has left the disunion between the two countries even more wide and more open than ever. At the period of the Union the understanding was complete and distinct, that the Catholics of Ireland might expect from an Imperial parliament that justice, which they were sensible they could never look for from the narrow and corporate spirit of their own. Without this understanding, the measure of an incorporate Union would never have been carried. The people of Ireland were led to hope, that tranquillity, wealth, and prosperity, would follow in the train of that measure; and such, I am persuaded would have been the case, if good faith had been kept with the people of that country. The Catholics of Ireland, much to their honour, placed confidence in the promises then held out. Although constantly deceived, and, I am ashamed to say it, basely and treacherously dealt with, they still confided. Their hopes, however, have hitherto been blasted: but, until the promises then held out shall be fulfilled, by a yielding up to the Catholics of that which has been so long and so unjustly withheld from them, it will be idle to look for the benefits which were expected to flow from the Union of the two countries.

Sir; the right hon. the Attorney-general for Ireland has told us—and the assertion is quite in conformity with my own opinion—that the liberalized policy of the government of the marquis Wellesley, as far as it has gone, has produced the happiest effects in that country. Sir, when that noble lord was first appointed to the government of Ireland, I ventured to anticipate, that such would be the result of the appointment; and I am quite prepared to give the noble marquis full credit for the best intention to carry his measures of conciliation into effect; and that with his true, warm-hearted, Irish feelings, and his enlightened mind, he has endeavoured to change the policy of the government of Ireland, and directed his best efforts to amalgamate the dispositions, and unite the sentiments of the two nations, so as to make the people of Ireland feel, that the interests of an Irish province are regarded in the same light as those of Yorkshire or Lancashire; and which, in fact, is the only sound and true light in which the interests of that part of the United empire can and ought to be, considered: seeing that that which, heretofore, has been looked upon as the greatest obstacle to such a state of things, has, by the recent improvements of modern science, been almost, if not altogether removed.

Having, therefore, Sir, given the noble marquis credit for all those large and generous views and feelings of policy at the period to which I have alluded, I am, of course, now ready to give him credit for those acts of his government which the right hon. the Attorney-general for Ireland has referred to, and am disposed to believe, that his endeavours to liberalize the system hitherto acted upon have, in many instances, been crowned with success. The right hon. and learned gentleman has told us, that when the noble marquis undertook the government of Ireland, he found the vessel of the state a wreck upon the breakers, and that he enabled her to float upon the tide of prosperity that has since flowed in upon her. Let me then hope, Sir, that the government will not stop there—but that they will trim the rigging, set every thing to rights, and, above all, see that she be well manned, for any future contingency [hear, hear!]. I can readily believe, Sir, that great advantages have already resulted to Ireland from the government of the noble marquis—and that, whatever inconveniences the right hon. and learned gentleman may have been exposed to, in consequence of his accepting office—whatever sarcasms may have been directed against him on that account—though the inconvenience may have been his, the benefit has belonged to the people of Ireland. I trust the right hon. and learned gentleman will persevere; and I hope he will be able to make a convert of a right hon. gentleman, who continues, unfortunately, opposed to the claims of the Catholics of Ireland. I trust, I say, Sir, that he will be able to make a convert of the only cabinet minister in this House, who has not been converted to my side of the question. For, in looking at the array of right hon. gentlemen opposite, I see, by the expression of their countenances, that four out of five of the cabinet ministers in this House are friendly to the principle of my motion. And, Sir, when I see this, and recollect that one of those right hon. gentlemen—the Chancellor of the Exchequer—who is one of the heartiest friends of the measure, was originally hostile to the claims of the Catholics—when I recollect this, Sir, I cannot despair of seeing the right hon. the Secretary of State for the Home Department the advocate of this great measure of conciliation. As the right hon. the Chancellor of the Exchequer is himself a convert, I hope he will endeavour to work the conversion of his only remaining colleague in this House in opposition to those claims; and that, by their united efforts, they will be able to give to Ireland the benefits of this all-important measure, and thereby establish the security of this country, restore tranquillity to Ireland, and consolidate the strength of the United empire [hear, hear!].

Sir, when we look back and see, that since the system of the relaxation of the penal code has commenced in Ireland, the benefits which that relaxation has conferred upon them have been received by the people of that country with the most ardent expressions of gratitude, we have every encouragement to proceed, and to anticipate the best fruits from a concession to them of the remainder of their just claims. Yet, Sir, though the Catholics of Ireland are grateful to you for the enactments which have been already carried in their favour, it is, at the same time, impossible for them to shut their eyes to the injustice of withholding the rights which so clearly and justly belong to them. Those rights, Sir, they claim as their due: but, while they are anxious to obtain them, I hope that the gratitude of the Catholics of Ireland for the benefits they have already received, will be made manifest by their continuing to pursue that line of conduct, which shall enable the friends of their cause in this House—where only it can be advocated with effect—to bring it to a successful issue. That the question in which they are so deeply interested—founded, as it is, in common reason and sound sense—will triumph, I can have no doubt; and, earnestly do I trust that that triumph may not be impeded by any indiscretion on the part of the Catholics themselves. The tranquillity in Ireland—a state of things so unusual in that country as to be almost deemed a phenomenon—is at this moment universally admitted. To what cause, more immediately, that tranquillity is to be attributed, it is not necessary for me to stop to inquire. But, so it is. Ireland, by the admission of all parties, is peaceful. That state of tranquillity I consider to be the result of the expectation of what will be done in their favour, combined with the recollection of what has already been done for them. If, then, so much has been produced from so small a beginning, what encouragement does it not afford to proceed to the consummation of the work of justice! If the field has been so grateful to the husbandman as to yield so large a crop with such little labour, what a plentiful harvest may we not expect, when greater attention shall be paid to the soil, and greater pains shall be bestowed on its cultivation! [hear, hear!].

Sir; it has been my good fortune to have spent some time in Ireland. My knowledge of the character and habits of her people has been drawn, in a considerable degree, from my own personal observation. I visited her, not so much for the purpose of seeing the natural beauties of the county of Antrim, or the splendid scenery of the lakes of Killarney, or even of enjoying that kind hospitality which is scarcely to be equalled in any other part of the world—I had a far greater gratification in seeing the Irish character—in beholding the kind and benevolent feeling which pervades all classes of her people. And, so much, Sir, am I impressed with this feeling, that if I had now a country to choose—and if I had no ties to connect me with the other—I have no hesitation in saying, that I would select Ireland, in preference to all other countries in the world [hear, hear!]. The people of Ireland, Sir, are undoubtedly, the most docile people that ever existed. Nothing proves the fact more striking, than the state of that country at the present moment. Hold out to the population the hope of impartial justice, and their feelings are at once enlisted in your cause. The Roman Catholic priests are said to have great influence with the people of that country. They have, Sir. And a very great misfortune should I consider it to see that influence diminished. The effects of their example on the conduct of the people are most beneficial. I form my judgment of them, not from what I have seen in Dublin alone, but in those remote districts, which have so often been represented as barbarous. And I declare, Sir, before this House, that they appeared to me to be the most honest and the most innocent set of people I ever met with [hear, hear!]. The influence they possess over their flocks is certainly great: but that influence is always exerted to secure the peace and tranquillity of the country. In one of the wildest counties, and which, at that time, was declared out of the king's peace, the Protestant gentry had no idea of bolting their doors and windows—a state of things which was mainly to be attributed to the exhortations of the Roman Catholic clergy. It is true of the people of Ireland now, as it was in the time of Sir John Davies, who said, two centuries ago, that "they were the most orderly, the most ready to submit to the law, provided the law would protect them, and, he would add, the most contented with the least portion of it, of any other people in the world."

Why, then, Sir, should such a people be debarred of their just right? Why should such a soil—rich in the beneficence of nature—having a population possessing virtues such as I have described them to possess—having the advantages of such ports and harbours and rivers—and possessing the most promising views of successful intercourse with all the nations of the globe—why, I say, should such a country be stinted in its natural growth? What is it that Ireland requires to become prosperous, and powerful, and happy? She wants only that, of which, for centuries, she has been deprived—a good government. That want it is—and that alone—which has, hitherto, crippled all her energies, and rendered her population discontented, disunited, and unhappy [hear, hear!].

I do not mean to say, Sir, that the particular measure of which I am now the advocate, ought to be looked upon as a panacea for all the evils which afflict Ireland. It would be absurd to view the question in that light. I rather wish it to be considered on its own grounds. I would rather wish it to be considered as the first step, the sine quâ non, of all the other measures which it may be necessary to adopt for the relief of Ireland. I wish that the great question of Catholic emancipation should be considered, unmixed with baser metal. I sincerely believe that the granting of that measure would not only be the means of preserving the present tranquillity in Ireland, but of opening a brighter and more cheerful prospect for the future. I trust, Sir, that the House will no longer delay putting the final hand to this great work; confident as I am, that the effect of so doing will be to unite both countries in the bond of mutual affection—in the bond of mutual interest—in the bond of the constitution. The people who now seek the full benefits of that constitution are of minds not inferior to those of our own country: and, if there be any difference in the habit, arising out of difference of legal enactments, that difference would be speedily removed, by a removal of the disabilities which have produced it.

Sir, I will not trouble the House by entering into any disquisition on supposed objections to this measure, on the score of religion. I will not presume that there can be any gentleman in this House, at this time of day, whose mind is so warped by prejudice, as to assert, that religious opinion ought to be made the ground of political disability. I presume, therefore, that the only ground of objection is to be founded on some contingent danger. Until, Sir, I hear such an objection urged—until I hear that danger stated—until it shall be presented to me in a tangible shape—it is impossible for me to grapple with it. It will be enough for me to meet the objection, when it shall be presented to me. For the present, therefore, I shall say nothing upon the subject, but shall conclude, Sir, with moving, "That this House do resolve itself into a Committee of the whole House, to consider the State of the Laws by which Oaths and Declarations are required to be taken, or made, as qualifications to the enjoyment of offices, or for the exercise of civil functions, so far as the same affect his majesty's Roman Catholics subjects; and whether it would be expedient, in any and what manner, to alter or modify the same, and subject to what provisions of regulations."

Speech by George Canning, the prime minister, explaining his government's attitude towards Catholic emancipation, House of Commons, 1 May 1827

The Speeches of the Right Honourable George Canning, ed. R. Therry, 6 vols. (London: James Ridgway, 1836), VI, 204-31.

Though committed personally to Catholic emancipation, Canning agreed upon taking office in April not to make it a Cabinet question. In the following speech Canning defended his controversial position.

It would be uncourteous to the House, and to my right honourable friend (Mr. Peel), were I to allow this debate to close without expressing the sentiments which his speech has excited, or rather confirmed, in my mind; and at the same time that I rise for the express purpose of doing so;– as there have been calls made on me to answer questions on different subjects, I am prepared, in the discharge of my duty, to answer those questions. To begin with the more agreeable part of my task, the speech of my right honourable friend (Mr. Peel) who has, in one or two instances, appealed to my testimony for the confirmation of some parts of his narrative of his own conduct. I confirm them in the fullest degree. I can bear testimony that, throughout the whole of the discussions that have taken place since Parliament adjourned, I have kept up with my right honourable friend the most constant intercourse—that throughout I have found in him the same candour and sincerity— the expression of the same just feelings, and the uniform exhibition of the same high principle, to which he has laid claim in the speech which he has this night delivered.

I assure the House that they much mistake the position in which I have the honour to stand, who believe that position to be one of gratified ambition, or of unalloyed satisfaction. From the beginning of these discussions, I foresaw—both of us foresaw—that they must terminate in our mutual separation. Would to God— that separation may be but for a time! Had the question been merely between my right honourable friend and myself, and had it been to be decided by his retirement or by mine, I do most solemnly declare it should have been decided by the latter. Sir, my right honourable friend had the courtesy to state to me yesterday his intention of making some observations to the House on the present occasion. I had, therefore, the opportunity of doing that without which I should never have been able to address the House with satisfaction to myself—of asking the gracious permission of the King to state such circumstances concerning His Majesty in the late discussions, as might be necessary to explain my conduct. I know not whether the House will be surprised to hear—my right honourable friend will not, for I have already stated it to him—that when I was first called upon by His Majesty for advice, in the critical situation in which the Government was placed, aware—for why should I disguise the fact?—of His Majesty's individual opinions, I counselled him to make the Government conformable to those opinions. To carry that counsel into effect, would of course have involved the necessity of my retirement from office; and I can declare most conscientiously that I would have laid at the feet of my Sovereign the situation I had the honour to hold, with a more cheerful heart, and with much more confidence, with respect to my future position apart from the Government, than with respect to what it could be with the question differently settled.

But, Sir, it was not for me to offer advice to my Sovereign as to the mode by which he was to accomplish the formation of a Cabinet opposed to my own opinions; all, therefore, that remained for me to do was to ask leave to retire, and make way, as far as I was concerned, for its formation. Now, why did I do this? Why did I, who have hitherto differed from many of my late colleagues upon this question, and who, as has been truly observed, thus differing, still continued to act with them—why did I thus stake the existence of an Administration, even though divided on the subject of the Catholic Claims, and advise His Majesty to form an Administration wholly hostile to those claims?

I will state my reasons briefly for that course.

Not many months ago His Majesty received a letter, from a source which I will not name, most strenuously advising His Majesty to place the Government of the country in a state of uniformity, and that that uniformity should be one of a decided opposition to the Catholic claims. Lord Liverpool, to whom this advice was communicated, at the same time that it was addressed to His Majesty, in a letter to His Majesty, stated first, that having been one of the authors of a Government divided in opinion upon that question, he, for one, never would belong to an Administration which should be formed on the principle of the exclusion of its advocates. Lord Liverpool added his opinion of the great difficulty there would be in the forming of such a Government. Such was Lord Liverpool's opinion; but when I advised His Majesty to form such a Government, it was not for me to estimate the difficulties which would impede it. It was, had His Majesty thought fit to adopt the advice, for those of his counsellors who were to form part of an Administration so constituted, to counsel such a course as they might have thought would attain their end. I did not disguise from my Sovereign that I thought it would be a work of difficulty, but I was far from thinking it a work of impracticability. What became of that advice is manifest by the result. It was not acted upon; but for what reason it was not acted upon, I am not aware; and more than I know I cannot state. But from the time when I first saw the King, and gave the advice I have described, down to the period when His Majesty came to town, I had no knowledge to any certainty that the advice which I gave had not been adopted. So far, therefore, from seeking or soliciting, as the honourable gentleman (Mr. Dawson) charges me, the post which I have now the honour to hold, I withdrew myself altogether from any participation in the arrangements, in order that the experiment which was said to be so loudly called for by the country might be fairly tried—an experiment which was sought to be enforced, by the abortive motion of the honourable member for Somersetshire (Sir T. Lethbridge).

I withdrew, Sir, in order to have that experiment fully and fairly tried; and I solemnly declare, that there was nothing at that moment for which I was more anxious than that my stepping out of the way might remove every obstacle to that trial. But when it was distinctly stated to me that such an Administration could not be formed, and when I received His Majesty's commands to model a Government on the same principle as that of Lord Liverpool's, of which I had been a member, nothing remained but to construct a Government of the divided character to which I have alluded, upon the subject of Catholic emancipation, with the necessary consequence that the question of the removal of Catholic disabilities should not be made a Cabinet measure.

But then, with the proposal to form a Government upon that principle—upon the very principle of my predecessor—came a new question: a question which at once involved the point of—whether I was to remain in the situation which I then filled, disgraced in my own opinion, and discredited in the eyes of my country, or whether I was to receive from the hands of my Sovereign, undiminished and unencumbered, that inheritance which a dreadful misfortune (for dreadful I may indeed call it) had placed at his disposal. Now, what was it I proposed? What was it I had it in command to do in the reconstruction of the Government? To form a ministry upon the principle of Lord Liverpool's Administration. That the Government should even consist of the very same individuals, I am sure I had every wish. But what was proposed to me? That I, having His Majesty's commands to form a Government upon the very same principles as those of my lamented predecessor, should place at the head of that Government some peer who was known to entertain anti-catholic sentiments. Now what principle was it I was desired to sanction by the adoption of that course? Why, I was desired to acknowledge in the face of the country, that *I*, forming a Government upon the principle of Lord Liverpool's, that is, composed of persons divided in their opinions on the Catholic claims, was, from the very holding of opinions favourable to those claims, disqualified from being placed at the head of that Government. I will retire altogether, and for ever, from public life—I will betake myself to the farthest boundary of the earth, and into perpetual banishment—I will resign any and every hope of office—for I care nothing for office—but I will not disgrace myself by consenting to sanction a principle which must bring degradation as well upon myself as upon those who would become subject to such exclusion, on account of holding these opinions. That principle, Sir, I repeat, I will not at any time, as I would not then, sanction. I would a thousand times rather quit office—I would rather be proscribed and persecuted by all who are disposed to proscribe and persecute for opinions, than live to be execrated to all futurity, for having, in my person, fixed such a blot upon the cause of those who think that every man is free to hold opinions, although he might not be able to persuade others to adopt them. I hope, Sir, I have now vindicated myself, to the satisfaction of the House, from the charge of overweening ambition. I throw myself upon this House and the country for a candid construction of my conduct.

My first object was to quit office—my next to remain in it with all my old colleagues, exactly upon the same terms as we had hitherto acted towards each other upon this very Catholic Question. It was for this that I have been arraigned, not, indeed, by my right honourable friend (Mr. Peel), who fairly stated his opinions to me, but by another honourable gentleman (Mr. Dawson), who, in the coarsest language, preferred against me as a charge—"That the new Government which has been formed, consists chiefly of Catholics," (that is, of members friendly to the question of emancipation)—as if there had been a breach of faith on my part in dealing with the late Cabinet, for not having proposed to my Sovereign a plan for a new Cabinet, that should have embraced an equal portion of the supporters of both sides of that question. I did suggest, as the honourable gentleman (Mr. Dawson) who makes the charge himself well knows, and did endeavour and intend to execute, such a plan of a new Administration. But, Sir, that honourable gentleman equally well knows that when, upon the 12th of April last, I intended to propose to my Sovereign a plan of arrangement which should comprise all the members of Lord Liverpool's Government, and embrace, therefore, an equality of Protestant and Catholic votes, circumstances occurred which prevented that intention from taking effect. And was it my fault, Sir, that (by a sort of concert, I will not venture to say, but by a singular coincidence, undoubtedly,) I either carried with me, or received in the closest of my Sovereign, *exclusive* of the resignation of my right honourable friend, of which I knew beforehand, six Protestant resignations. (I call them Protestant only in the parlance of this House.) Observe, Sir, the charge against me is, that I have organized a Government all Catholic, as to its views upon that question, having promised to form one that should be half and half; and my honourable accuser sinks the indisputable fact, that the Protestant half of the Administration themselves withdrew. I think that it is rather too hard to charge that withdrawal upon their parts, as a breach of faith upon mine.

Mr. Peel here observed, in a low tone, that the right honourable gentleman did not state the matter quite correctly. There were not, he was understood to say, so many resignations.

Mr. Canning.—My right honourable friend is, I believe, right; *exclusive* of his resignation, I think I had not received six Protestant resignations, when I was with the King. One came after I had left His Majesty.

Mr. Peel here observed, that one of them was not an opponent to Catholic emancipation.

Mr. Canning.—I beg pardon of the House; there was one Catholic lord (Lord Melville) among the number of those who thus resigned; and yet we are now told these resignations grew out of the question of Catholic emancipation. However, these six resignations came within twenty-four hours; and I would now ask the House whether it is fair, after such abandonment of place by these Protestant peers, to impeach me of a wilful nonexecution of the orders of my Sovereign? But, Sir, the matter did not end here. It was about the middle of Thursday—the day on which the House adjourned—about two hours before the meeting of the House, and after I had given directions to move a new writ for my return, that I received four of these resignations. Upon receiving them, I said to my Sovereign, "Here, Sire, is that which disables me from executing the orders I have received from you, respecting the formation of a new Administration. It is now open to your Majesty to adopt a new course, for no step has yet been taken, in the execution of those orders, that is irrevocable; but I must fairly state to your Majesty, that if I am to go on in the position where you have been pleased to place me, my writ must be moved for to-day; for if we wait until the holidays, without adopting any definitive steps, I see that it is quite hopeless for me to attempt to persevere in the objects I have undertaken." I need not repeat to the House the words in which my Sovereign graciously replied to this representation; but I may state that he gave me his hand to kiss, and confirmed me in the office to which I had been named.

These, then, Sir, are the steps which I really have taken; these are the means by which I have been placed in the station I at present fill. I have meddled not with the conduct or the opinions of any other man. I have already expressed my unequivocal approbation of the course pursued by my right honourable friend (Mr. Peel). What have been the principles of conduct of others among my late colleagues, for the best of reasons and the wisest, I do not present to say, for really I do not know them. That conduct I can only view by its results, results which have been assuredly most painful; and I may truly say, to me as painful as, in most every instance—(every instance I do not say, for I sedulously except my right honourable friend)—they were unexpected. Sir, I really knew not in what way I had sinned in the eyes of my late colleagues—those other of my late colleagues, I should rather say—that they should decline acting with me. I had never offended them intentionally, nor did I know that I had ever excited among them unwittingly any feeling so hostile or personal to me, as to be at all likely to lead to this result. Between my right honourable friend and myself, it is almost unnecessary for me to observe, that upon every subject, in every discussion I can call to mind, upon all great questions of foreign or domestic policy and legislation- -this one unhappy question of Catholic emancipation excepted —there has been that sort of general agreement, that I do not believe there exists the individual with whom my opinions are in more complete accordance; and I do not think any greater calamity could have befallen the country than my right honourable friend's secession from the Cabinet, not only as respects, his administration of his office, the duties of which he had discharged with so much ability, and such signal advantages to the public, but in the general councils of the Government. We shall nevertheless, I hope, though deprived at this moment of his aid in the Administration, have the benefit of it in his place, in the general share of the legislative business of the kingdom as a member of Parliament. But as to others of my late colleagues, I am not prepared to express an opinion on the proceeding they have adopted, because of its motives I am not aware. So far, indeed, as I had reason to know any thing of their dispositions in relation to myself—I speak now more particularly in reference to the line of foreign policy I have pursued, as being that department of the Government with which I was more immediately connected—I understood that my official conduct had received their approbation. Both in the Cabinet, and in the two Houses of Parliament, they expressed such favourable opinions; nor can I charge myself with having, by any measures of my own, produced intentionally any such change in those opinions as should have led to this unwillingness on their parts to continue to act with me. I am determined, however, to say nothing of the conduct of any body, with whose motives I am unacquainted, and to abstain from animadversions, where I do not know them to have been really provoked. I have resolved, Sir, therefore, to make no further observations at this time, than might be necessary to accompany the facts which I conceived requisite to bring before the House, with the view of explaining how I came into this situation, and how it is that my late colleagues are no longer around me.

There were two topics growing out of the speech of my right honourable friend, upon which he will allow me to make one or two observations, not, as I can most cordially assure him, in any hostile or unpleasant feeling; but that I may set myself right upon points, touching which, he has laboured, I think, under some degree of misunderstanding. My right honourable friend says, how should it be possible that when I—(and I trust, Sir, that the House will excuse me for the painful necessity which compels me to use this monosyllable so often)—that when I have been advanced to the high situation in which I now stand, how should it be possible that, without saying or doing any thing actively and expressly to promote the success of the Catholic Question, my existence, nevertheless, in that situation, and other contingent results, arising out of it, but for which I am not responsible, should not be a great moral advancement of that cause? Sir, I cannot deny the truth of this proposition of my right honourable friend.

I cannot, I frankly avow, deny the general truth of my right honourable friend's observation, and in the admission of that identical fact, will be found the obvious answer to the taunts of the honourable baronet opposite (Sir. T. Lethbridge) at the support which the present Government are now receiving from the gentlemen of the opposition. Why have these gentlemen supported me? Because they saw, in the aspect of the present state of things, exactly the same tendency which my right honourable friend has seen towards the moral advancement of that great question; namely, that without my official interference, indeed, with my present inaction, they behold a considerable prospect of improvement in a question for which they feel with me a common interest. If so, it is a good reason why I should have their support, and equally so for my right honourable friend to oppose me; but it is a little too much for an honourable member to say that the reason is good at one side and bad at the other; whilst both parties concur in anticipating the same result. If my right honourable friend is justified in resigning, because with my passive existence in office the Catholic Question must thrive, surely the same reason holds good for my receiving the support of other gentlemen who contemplate, in the success of such a question, the tranquillity and consolidation of the empire. My right honourable friend's defence of his own retreat must, therefore, be taken as a complete and conclusive answer to all the taunts which are levelled at the support held out to me from other quarters of the House; that support, I feel confident, will be continued to me as long they respect and approve the measures which I shall introduce; and, in the same relative feeling, and no other, I am persuaded I shall have to receive the support, and encounter the opposition of my right honourable friend.

But, Sir, I am asked—"Is the Roman Catholic Question, in point of fact, with the new Government, a Cabinet question?" I answer, No. It stands exactly, Sir, as it did in the year 1812, but in a part of the year 1812, which my right honourable friend has not exactly distinguished from another part of that year to which his speech referred. It is very tiresome to refer to books in discussions of this kind, and not being prepared to anticipate the necessity of consulting them on this occasion, I did not bring them down with me; but in consequence of my right honourable friend's speech, I have sent for them, and I can now recur to them. My right honourable friend says, that in a debate which took place on the 21st of May, 1812, in assigning my reasons for not joining Lord Liverpool's Government at that time, I stated, that my belief was, that, were I so to do, I should be coming into a Cabinet that would nullify my own opinions, or that I used expressions to that effect. He further supposes, that *as*, in 1812, notwithstanding the failure of Mr. Grattan's motion, I immediately after introduced and carried by a large majority a motion to the same effect, so now, in 1827, notwithstanding the failure of the motion of the honourable member for Westminster (Sir F. Burdett), the situation of this question being "pretty nearly the same," he sees no reason for my not again pursuing the same course in this very session. But, Sir, the circumstances which existed in 1812 are not "pretty nearly the same" as those which exist at present.

Did nothing, I will ask my right honourable friend, intervene between the period of the failure of Mr. Grattan's motion and the 22nd of June, to cause the change to which he alludes? Was there no alteration in the condition of the Government, and *consequently* in the feeling of Parliament upon that subject during this interval? Yes: for on the 17th of May, which was shortly after the death of Mr. Perceval, Lord Liverpool came to me, to propose to me to become a member of the Administration. What passed on this subject, Gentlemen will be pleased to remember, was published, together with all the negociations entered into on that occasion, and having been so recorded, cannot have been since altered, to answer any temporary purpose. After one or two questions—I believe, indeed, after one preliminary question—I asked (the right honourable gentleman here read from the Annual Register of that year, apologising for the want of any better reference, by stating he was taken wholly by surprise)—"Whether I was to consider the opinion and policy of the Government as remaining altogether unchanged, upon the question relating to the laws affecting the Roman Catholics?" Lord Liverpool answered, "that his own opinions upon this subject remained unchanged: and that he was not aware that those of his colleagues had undergone any alteration."

Now, here, Sir, I pause to ask what was the condition in which the Catholic Question stood then? At the period of the unrestricted Regency, Mr. Perceval invited into his Government Lord Sidmouth and Lord Castlereagh; and in the very first debate upon this question which took place in this House, after that junction, Mr. Perceval and Lord Castlereagh both declared themselves, in the course of the discussion, inimical to the agitation of the question at that opportunity. Lord Castlereagh said, (the House will observe, that it was upon Mr. Grattan's motion, in April, 1812) "with respect to the vote I shall give to-night, my right honourable friend has clearly stated, that the Cabinet intimates an opinion, that the propriety of further concessions to the Catholics could not now be agitated, nor any inquiry be gone into at present, on the subject of the disabilities affecting His Majesty's Roman Catholic subjects in Ireland, with advantage to the empire, or a due regard to the welfare of the community at large." Why, then, Sir, the footing upon which the Cabinet *then* stood, in respect of the Catholic Question, was one of general resistance to it, and in the Government itself, there was a joint determination to act upon that principle. It was in this state of things, that on the 18th of May, 1812, I refused to join in Lord Liverpool's arrangements, and I gave him my reasons for not doing so, which were involved in that determination on the part of the Administration. But what happened in the mean time, between May the 18th, and June the 22nd? Why, that on June the 10th, Lord Castlereagh came down to this House, when I find that Mr. Spencer Stanhope rose to put a question to the noble lord:—"He wished to know if it was intended, on the part of the present Ministers, that the same policy, in every respect, should be observed by them, in reference to the Catholic Question, which had been observed by the Administration, under a late right honourable gentleman (Mr. Perceval)?" Lord Castlereagh said,

> that he felt some difficulty in answering the question of the honourable gentleman literally, the arrangements for the new Ministry not having been yet fully completed. But as to the spirit of the question, he thought he could be more satisfactory. He could say this, from his knowledge of those employed in forming that Administration, that, generally, their sentiments remained the same. Upon a former occasion, they had thought, inclusive even of those who were favourable to the measure, that the present was not the time for discussing that question, and in still thinking so, that recent decisions of Parliament formed a leading consideration in influencing the adoption of that opinion. The sense of Parliament having been, at least for the present, definitively pronounced, they thought that any immediate revived discussion would only create irritation, without being productive of any thing useful. He was aware, however, of the growing change in favour of those claims; and, in submission to that change, and the real sentiments of certain members of the Government, it had been resolved on, as a principle, that the discussion of this question should be left free from all interference, on the part of the Government, and that every member of that Government should be left to the free and unbiassed suggestions of his own conscientious discretion.

Here, then, it is evident that a complete change had occurred between the 18th of May and the 22d of June 1812, in the opinions of the Government. At the former period, the Cabinet were all united in resistance to the Catholic Question; at the latter, it was to be left open and free to the unbiassed discussion of all or any of the members of that Cabinet.

Then, I contend, Sir, that between these two periods, of which my right honourable friend has spoken, the Cabinet itself was changed in its character, as regarded this question. It was changed, by this question being put upon that independent footing, on which it has remained during the many years that my right honourable friend and myself have acted together. Did this altered condition of circumstances effect no change in the condition of the Catholic Question? Assuredly it did; and I well recollect its being hailed by Mr. Grattan, and many others who voted with him, as a most important accession to that cause: and the proof of the fact is, that my motion was carried by a triumphant majority.

Now, I think, I have sufficiently explained the difference which had arisen between the two periods in question, as to this important subject, and as to my views upon it. I have not the vanity to believe (and I am sure I beg pardon of the House for troubling it with these passages from the debates) that the speech to which my right honourable friend refers procured that result of which I have spoken.

But to come to the present condition of that Question, I say again, it remains in this Government, in the state it was truly described to be in by Lord Castlereagh in 1812; and precisely as it has been since repeatedly described by myself; in short, as it was described to be in 1825, in a debate which took place in the month of March upon the state of Ireland; and in the very last debate in the last session of Parliament, in the same year, upon Catholic emancipation. On that occasion I used these words: "I hold myself as perfectly free as any other member of this House, to pronounce an opinion upon this as a great national question, and as such, to give it my support, reserving only to myself the right of selecting the time when I am to give that support, and the manner in which it is to be afforded, according to my judgment of the degree of success which is likely to attend such an exertion." These were the words I used then, and my opinions are not in the slightest degree varied at the present moment. Such was the footing upon which this question stood when I was the colleague of my right honourable friend; and such *is* the footing on which it stands now. Let it be observed, therefore, by those with whom I have formerly acted, and from whose objections on this occasion I do not shrink, however the acknowledgment I have made may be attempted to be converted into matter of opposition, that, with those who form the present Cabinet, and some of whom formed part of the last, the Catholic Question now stands on the same ground as it stood on under Lord Liverpool's Government;—that is, it is a question which each member of the Government is at liberty, if he pleases, to bring forward in the Cabinet, or to propound to Parliament; but if any member of the Government shall so bring it forward in either House of Parliament, he is bound distinctly to state that he does so in his individual capacity only, and not as pledging his colleagues to his own opinions on the subject. This, Sir, is the position of the Catholic Question now; it is the same in which it was placed in the year 1812; it is the same in which it has now stood for fifteen years successively. That it should remain in this state is a fact which I know has been much objected to by many; but, if I consider the state of the country at large—the inclination of men's minds upon this matter in England as well as in Ireland—and the infinite difficulties which surround the attempt at present to alter that state   in my judgment, and in my conscience I believe it to be the only footing upon which it can be at present left; unless the views of partizans are to be consulted, the accomplishment of whose wishes on the one hand, or whose attempt to stifle free and growing opinions on the other, would, in the result, lead to a convulsion, in one part or other, of the United Kingdom. Now, Sir, I am not prepared for convulsion, in either. I would not raise hopes which I do not see any immediate means of realising. In making this observation, I am not speaking of the moral accomplishment of those hopes, but of exciting expectations without having good grounds to anticipate their immediate or speedy fulfilment. I remember too well, and but a short memory indeed is required for that purpose, how much has been uttered in the way of complaint in debates of this House upon the Catholic Question, about things being said and done that had raised expectations in Ireland which ought not, it has been observed, to have been excited, unless the authorities from whom those acts and declarations emanated were prepared to follow them up.

Now, Sir, it is precisely because of my not being at present prepared to follow them up, that I will not raise such expectations. Much and cordially as I agree with those who view the measure itself of emancipation, as calculated to tranquillize

Ireland, I yet estimate very highly the degree of passive resistance to it, which exists in this country. I would not act against the feelings any more than I would against the interests of England. But if, looking to the character and extent of that resistance, I am asked whether I despair of the ultimate success of the question, I answer, that I do not despair that the good sense of the English people, by candid discussion, and repeated consideration of it, will ultimately concede the question. I say, I think, Sir, the time will come, when well-meaning and conscientious, and even intelligent people, now among the most strenuous and most honest opponents of the great measure, will look back with a degree of surprise, and almost incredulity, at the opposition which they have, up to this time, manifested to it. But, though I think this, I am not prepared to run counter, in the mean time, to English feeling. A single week of peace in England, is worth a much larger portion of time devoted to the accomplishment of a great, but yet, partly, a theoretical, good, in another portion of the empire. Though I thus confidently expect the dawn, I am by no means prepared to hasten it; though I know the present darkness upon this subject—for darkness I must consider it—will be succeeded by a great illumination in the minds of men, I am disposed to watch patiently the progress of that enlightenment. This result, I heartily hope, but I will not endeavour to anticipate it by any attempt to force the judgments of the community.

I hope I have now, Sir, given to honourable gentlemen every satisfactory explanation upon the topics which have been this night referred to.

So far as I am aware, I have kept nothing back; but when I am taunted by questions such as that which some honourable gentlemen have put to me, whether I do not know that in the very *penetralia* of the royal breast there exist feelings repugnant to the Catholic claims, I reply, that I would venerate in that most illustrious individual, as I did in his royal father, the repugnant feelings which actuate him on this question. I would hurt no feelings, as I have already said, of that nature. But if I am asked by that honourable gentleman, whether I think the Coronation Oath is any obstacle in the way of concession on the part of the Crown, I answer, No. No more did Lord Liverpool—no more did my right honourable friend himself (Mr. Peel); and if the time shall ever come when it may be necessary to argue this question, I shall derive my best argument, for the view I take of that point, from the opinions which have already been addressed to Parliament upon the subject by those great authorities. Let not, then, the people of England take up the notion, that, by the carrying of the Catholic Question, the peace of their country would be endangered. The time has passed when those pernicious influences, which have been so much adverted to, could be any longer exercised by the Catholic Church, with any effect upon its peace or its welfare. But do the honourable gentlemen, who so much deprecate all discussion of this question, imagine that discussion can be avoided? Do they suppose that if we will not consider it, it is a question which will sleep? Or do they believe, that if it should sleep, it will be awakened by any other than a dreadful and deplorable emergency? No, Sir, we must look it in the face: We must not turn from it. But, though I believe that it is a question which has gained strength from the change which has taken place in the Government—(a change, God knows! not of my seeking, but arising out of the King's determination)— though I concur with those who imagine that it is a cause which has acquired additional power—I would not force it by pressing it upon Parliament now, any more than I did when I formed, with my right honourable friend near me, one of the Government of Lord Liverpool.

I am not conscious that I have omitted to reply to any of the matters which have been suggested to me; but if I have, I shall be sincerely obliged to any querist who will remind me, but he who he may, of any such omissions.

I trust I have succeeded in showing that I am, where I have the honour to be, not by my own solicitation, but by the pleasure of my Sovereign. I had previously recommended the formation of an Administration, from which I should have been excluded. That plan was rejected by those whom it embraced, and another proposed in its stead, to which I could not have acceded, without, at the same time, recording my acknowledgment that the opinions of my past political life, upon one of the most important of all the questions which I have ever been called on to consider, furnished a justifiable ground of exclusion from the highest office in the Government. I will conclude, by repeating one or two remarks which I remember to have made to the House in 1822. I was then appointed to a post, which I owed not to the favour of His Majesty's Government, but to the commands of His Majesty himself: a post, fraught with wealth, distinction, and honour. From this post I was recalled immediately after my nomination to it, contrary to my own feelings and wishes, to hold office in this country. I made the sacrifice—(to a poor man, be it permitted me to say, no indifferent or trivial one),—without hesitation, and—so help me God—without any stipulations. But if, Sir, when that proposal to take office was made to him, it had been accompanied—(as in fairness it should have been, if I was to be ousted on account of the opinions that have since been excepted against me)—with this sort of intimation from the Ministers who recalled me—"Though we call you into the Government, because your services are necessary to us, yet remember, that if, by any unfortunate chance, the highest situation in that Government should become vacant, and should in all other respects be eligible for a person holding your situation in Parliament and in the councils of the country—remember, that because you support the Catholic claims you are to waive all pretentions to it." If their proposal, I say, had been accompanied with such an intimation, I would, with the same disdain and indignation with which I have more recently rejected their offer to serve under a Protestant Premier (using the term Protestant in the familiar sense only in which we are accustomed to use it in discussions of this kind), have rejected that proposal, containing, as it would have done, a condition which I should have regarded as the badge of my helotism, and as the indelible disgrace of my political existence.

Act to repeal the Test and Corporation Acts, 9 May 1828

9 Geo. 4, c. 17   *Statutes at Large*, LXVIII, 22-25.

The Test and Corporation Acts, which dated from the late seventeenth century, had prohibited non-Anglicans from holding certain offices and employments.

Whereas an Act was passed in the Thirteenth Year of the Reign of King *Charles* the Second, intituled *An Act for the well governing and regulating of Corporations:* And Whereas another Act was passed in the Twenty-fifth Year of the Reign of King *Charles* the Second, intituled *An Act for preventing Dangers which may happen from Popish Recusants:* And Whereas another Act was passed in the Sixteenth Year of the Reign of King *George* the Second, intituled *An Act to indemnify Persons who have omitted to qualify themselves for Offices and Employments within the Time limited by Law, and for allowing further Time for that Purpose; and also for amending so much of an Act made in the Twenty-fifth Year of the Reign of King* Charles *the Second, intituled 'An Act for preventing Dangers which may happen from Popish Recusants,' as relates to the Time for receiving the Sacrament of the Lord's Supper now limited by the said Act:* And Whereas it is expedient that so much of the said several Acts of Parliament as imposes the Necessity of taking the Sacrament of the Lord's Supper according to the Rites or Usage of the Church of *England*, for the Purposes therein respectively mentioned, should be repealed; Be it therefore enacted by the King's most Excellent Majesty, by and with the Advice and Consent of the Lords Spiritual and Temporal, and Commons, in this present Parliament assembled, and by the Authority of the same, That so much and such Parts of the said several Acts passed in the Thirteenth and Twenty-fifth Years of the Reign of King *Charles* the Second, and of the said Act passed in the Sixteenth Year of the Reign of King *George* the Second, as require the Person or Persons in the said Acts respectively described to take or receive the Sacrament of the Lord's Supper according to the Rites or Usage of the Church of *England*, for the several Purposes therein expressed, or to deliver a Certificate or make Proof of the Truth of such his or their receiving the said Sacrament in manner aforesaid, or as impose upon any such Person or Persons any Penalty, Forfeiture, Incapacity, or Disability whatsoever for or by reason of any Neglect or Omission to take or receive the said Sacrament, within the respective Periods and in the Manner in the said Acts respectively provided in that Behalf, shall, from and immediately after the passing of this Act, be and the same are hereby repealed.

II. And Whereas the Protestant Episcopal Church of *England* and *Ireland*, and the Doctrine, Discipline, and Government thereof, and the Protestant Presbyterian Church of *Scotland*, and the Doctrine, Discipline, and Government thereof, are by the Laws of this Realm severally established, permanently and inviolably: And Whereas it is just and fitting, that on the Repeal of such Parts of the said Acts as impose the Necessity of taking the Sacrament of the Lord's Supper according to the Rites or Usage of the Church of *England*, as a Qualification for Office, a Declaration to the following Effect should be substituted in lieu thereof; Be it therefore enacted, That every Person who shall hereafter be placed, elected, or chosen in or to the Office of Mayor, Alderman, Recorder, Bailiff, Town Clerk or Common Councilman, or in or to any Office of Magistracy, or Place, Trust, or Employment relating to the Government of any City, Corporation, Borough, or Cinque Port within *England* and *Wales* or the Town of *Berwick-upon-Tweed*, shall, within One Calendar Month next before or upon his Admission into any of the aforesaid Offices or Trusts, make and subscribe the Declaration following:

I *A. B.* do solemnly and sincerely, in the Presence of God, profess, testify, and declare, upon the true Faith of a Christian, That I will never exercise any Power, Authority, or Influence which I may possess by virtue of the Office of   to injure or weaken the Protestant Church as it is by Law established in *England*, or to disturb the said Church, or the Bishops and Clergy of the said Church, in the Possession of any Rights or Privileges to which such Church, or the said Bishops and Clergy, are or may be by Law entitled.

III.   And be it enacted, That the said Declaration shall be made and subscribed as aforesaid, in the Presence of such Person or Persons respectively, who, by the Charters or Usages of the said respective Cities, Corporations, Boroughs, and Cinque Ports, ought to administer the Oath for due Execution of the said Offices or Places respectively, and in default of such, in the Presence of Two Justices of the Peace of the said Cities, Corporations, Boroughs, and Cinque Ports, if such there be, or otherwise in the Presence of Two Justices of the Peace of the respective Counties, Ridings, Divisions, or Franchises wherein the said Cities, Corporations, Boroughs, and Cinque Ports are; which said Declaration shall either be entered in a Book, Roll, or other Record, to be kept for that Purpose, or shall be filed amongst the Records of the City, Corporation, Borough, or Cinque Port.

IV.   And be it enacted, That if any Person placed, elected, or chosen into any of the aforesaid Offices or Places, shall omit or neglect to make and subscribe the said Declaration in manner above mentioned, such Placing, Election, or Choice shall be void; and that it shall not be lawful for such Person to do any Act in the Execution of the Office or Place into which he shall be so chosen, elected, or placed.

V.   And be it further enacted, That every Person who shall hereafter be admitted into any Office or Employment, or who shall accept from His Majesty, His Heirs and Successors, any Patent, Grant, or Commission, and who by his Admittance into such Office or Employment or Place of Trust, or by his Acceptance of such Patent, Grant, or Commission, or by the Receipt of any Pay, Salary, Fee, or Wages by reason thereof, would, by the Laws in force immediately before the passing of this Act, have been required to take the Sacrament of the Lord's Supper according to the Rites or Usage of the Church of *England*, shall, within Six Calendar Months after his Admission to such Office, Employment, or Place of Trust, or his Acceptance of such Patent, Grant, or Commission, make and subscribe the aforesaid Declaration, or in Default thereof his Appointment to such Office, Employment, or Place of Trust, and such Patent, Grant, or Commission, shall be wholly void.

VI.   And be it further enacted, That the aforesaid Declaration shall be made and subscribed in His Majesty's High Court of Chancery, or in the Court of King's Bench, or at the Quarter Sessions of the County or Place where the Person so required to make the same shall reside; and the Court in which such Declaration shall be so made and subscribed shall cause the same to be preserved among the Records of the said Court.

VII.   Provided always, That no Naval Officer below the Rank of Rear Admiral, and no Military Officer below the Rank of Major General in the Army or

Colonel in the Militia, shall be required to make or subscribe the said Declaration, in respect of his Naval or Military Commission; and that no Commissioner of Customs, Excise, Stamps, or Taxes, or any Person holding any of the Offices concerned in the Collection, Management, or Receipt of the Revenues which are subject to the said Commissioners, or any of the Officers concerned in the Collection, Management, or Receipt of the Revenues subject to the Authority of the Postmaster General, shall be required to make or subscribe the said Declaration, in respect of their said Offices or Appointments: Provided also, that nothing herein contained shall extend to require any Naval or Military Officer, or other Person as aforesaid, upon whom any Office, Place, Commission, Appointment, or Promotion shall be conferred during his Absence from *England*, or within Three Months previous to his Departure from thence, to make and subscribe the said Declaration until after his Return to *England*, or within Six Months thereafter.

VIII. And be it further enacted, That all Persons now in the actual Possession of any Office, Command, Place, Trust, Service, or Employment, or in the Receipt of any Pay, Salary, Fee, or Wages, in respect of or as a Qualification for which, by virtue of or under any of the before-mentioned Acts or any other Act or Acts, they respectively ought to have heretofore taken or ought hereafter to receive the said Sacrament of the Lord's Supper, shall be and are hereby confirmed in the Possession and Enjoyment of their said several Offices, Commands, Places, Trusts, Services, Employments, Pay, Salaries, Fees, and Wages respectively, notwithstanding their Omission or Neglect to take or receive the Sacrament of the Lord's Supper in manner aforesaid, and shall be and are hereby indemnified, freed, and discharged from all Incapacities, Disabilities, Forfeitures, and Penalties whatsoever, already incurred or which might hereafter be incurred in consequence of any such Omission or Neglect; and that no Election of or Act done or to be done by any such Person or under his Authority, and not yet avoided, shall be hereafter questioned or avoided by reason of any such Omission or Neglect, but that every such Election and Act shall be as good, valid, and effectual as if such Person had duly received the said Sacrament of the Lord's Supper in manner aforesaid.

IX. Provided nevertheless, That no Act done in the Execution of any of the Corporate or other Offices, Places, Trusts, or Commissions aforesaid, by any such Person omitting or neglecting as aforesaid, shall by reason thereof be void or voidable as to the Rights of any other Person not privy to such Omission or Neglect, or render such last-mentioned Person liable to any Action or Indictment.

CATHOLIC EMANCIPATION

Under pressure from the Catholic Association movement launched by Daniel O'Connell (1775-1847) in Ireland, the Wellington government pushed through a Catholic Emancipation Act in 1829. This landmark measure allowed Catholics to sit in Parliament and to hold civil, military, and corporate offices.

Speech by the archbishop of Armagh opposing the Catholic Emancipation Bill, House of Lords, 2 April 1829

Hansard, n.s. XXI, 67-75.

My lords, in rising to give my decided and uncompromising opposition to the measure under your lordships' consideration, I do not expect that your lordships will be so far influenced by any words of mine, as to reject a bill which has already passed the other House of parliament, which has been introduced into this House, at the recommendation of his majesty, under the auspices of the noble duke, and with the approbation of many noble lords, who, until this session, have been hostile to its principle. But I feel that, however fruitless my opposition may be, I have a sacred duty to discharge to the Irish branch of the United Church, and to the country, in laying before your lordships my views of the proposed measure.

My lords, I stop not to throw blame on any man for the change which may have taken place in his opinions; nor shall I say a word calculated to inflame the animosities, or to widen the breach of contending parties; but as amongst those who were once opposers of this measure, but who are now its supporters, there are men with whom I am connected in the strictest ties of friendship, and who have been accustomed on former occasions to pay a partial deference to my suggestions, I trust I may be permitted to express the deep concern I feel at their having committed themselves upon this important question, without even imparting to me the course they intended to pursue. Still, my lords, I am forward to believe that they have been actuated by a desire for the public good, not less intense than my own; and what I now solicit from your lordships is, that while their arguments are received with favour, you will vouchsafe a patient and candid hearing to those reasons with which I would vindicate my own consistency. My lords, I believe that, in yielding to this measure, the persons to whom I have alluded, entertain a hope, either of at length satisfying the claims of Roman Catholic ambition, or, if that be impossible, of uniting the now divided Protestant parties in the resolute defense of their common interests. If I mistake not, the arguments of the advocates of the measure, who are at the same time the friends of the church, may be reduced to one or other of these heads.

In the first place, then, I would ask, will the passing of this bill give tranquillity, as they suppose, to Ireland? Is the removal of the disabilities specified in the bill, all that the Roman Catholics seek, or with which they will rest contented? Have they so much as condescended to assure you, that they confine their views to this measure? So far from it, their leaders have explicitly told you, that their ambition is limited to no such objects. What then, is the emancipation which they seek? I verily believe, that they themselves could not, at the present moment, define it, so progressive are their encroachments—and durst not if they could. It so happens, that in the very paper which announced his majesty's recommendation to parliament to revise the laws affecting Roman Catholics, with a view to the removal of civil disabilities—in that very paper, was contained a list of some of the grievances which are hereafter to be used as a means of again disturbing the peace of Ireland. The great mover of agitation is there reported to have declared, that he will accept seven shillings and sixpence in the pound this sessions, with the full purpose of demanding, with renewed energy, in the ensuing one, the twelve and sixpence remaining due—that the regeneration of the country will not be complete, until the odious Act of Union shall have been repealed, and Ireland, from the state of a pitiful province, to which she is reduced, restored to her just independence amongst kingdoms—that Mr. Pitt's pledge at the Union was to embody the Roman Catholic religion with the state, as the Presbyterian religion was embodied at the Scottish Union, abolishing tithes, however, and making the clergy dependent on the charitable contributions of those who are to be benefited by their ministry. After the announcement of the measure, and even before the bill was introduced into the other House, such was the formal declaration of the conciliatory effects likely to be produced by it. It may be said, that these are the wild and visionary schemes of a public agitator. Wild and visionary as they may appear to those noble lords, who are prepared to go only certain lengths with Roman Catholics in their encroachments, they are approved and adopted as legitimate claims, by the most influential leaders of the party, and constitute the principal part of those alleged grievances which we have been asked to remedy.

It may be thought the Roman Catholic aristocracy and gentry are far more moderate in their views, and the fact I believe to be so; but it is evident that the aristocracy and gentry possess little or no influence over the great body of Irish Roman Catholics; their voice is seldom heard, and when heard, it is disregarded. The priesthood are in fact every thing; and the people, and even the agitators themselves, are but instruments in their hands. It is, then, the absolute power of the Romish priesthood over a population like that of Ireland, and the projects of ambition founded on that power, which make the still-existing barriers necessary to Protestant establishments under a free and mixed constitution like our own; and, by the present bill, you take away these the only effectual securities that can be devised, without making friends of the persons against whom they are your defence; you increase the power of doing mischief, without lessening the inclination to do it. Could you by these concessions hope to appease the hostility of the Roman Catholic priesthood to what is Protestant; could you disarm them of their unbounded influence over the people; could you dissolve their blind allegiance to the see of Rome; could you free them from its jurisdiction, and make them citizens of their own country, quietly taking their stand, with other classes of Dissenters, where the wisdom of the legislature shall place them—then much good might be anticipated from this measure: but, does any one believe that by these concessions the Church of Rome will be suddenly rendered tolerant, that the Romish priesthood will be content to hold an inferior rank to a clergy, the validity of whose orders they deny, and leave in possession of its privileges a church which they revile as intrusive and heretical—that they will become indifferent to domination the nearer they approach to it, and the greater their means for obtaining it—that they will quit their hold upon the wills and affections, the passions and prejudices, of the people, at the very moment that their spiritual despotism may be turned to most account, in forwarding their temporal aggrandizement? It is because I am persuaded that the proposed concessions will not produce these effects—that they are not desired for their own value, but as the means of attaining those ulterior objects which a legislature, essentially Protestant, can never voluntarily surrender—it is because I am persuaded that the increase of power will tend only to exasperate, if not successful in effecting the purposes for which it is coveted—it is, my lords, with this conviction on my mind, that, regardless of the obloquy and disquietude I bring upon myself, I take my stand on that ground which affords me the only firm footing for defence, and am unwilling to abandon the position, until at least I have warned the country of its importance to the security of the Protestant institutions of Ireland.

But, my lords, necessity is, in the second place, pleaded in justification of the measure. It is described as the only means, if not of satisfying the Roman Catholics, at least of uniting the Protestants, particularly the members of the administration, in firm resistance to further encroachments. On the one hand, it is said, that with the cabinet and the two Houses of parliament divided on this great subject, a wavering and undecided policy must necessarily follow—that in such a state of things no useful measure can be adopted for the improvement of the country, or for the efficient administration of the laws, much less for extending to the church that share of protection and support which is her due. On the other hand, we are assured, if, after this last boon be granted, new demands shall be preferred and old discontents continued, and the Roman Catholics shall strive to raise themselves, by your concessions, to a degree of power, subversive of our establishments, that the eyes of all men will be at length opened, that the incorrigible restlessness of this sect will deprive it of every Protestant supporter, and unite the friends of the establishment in a phalanx, which will at once overwhelm the efforts of those who are leagued together for its destruction.

All this, my lords, sounds well, and may seem to promise much security in perspective. I am bound to give the persons who use this language full credit for the sincerity of their intentions; and I trust we shall not call upon them in vain to redeem their pledges of attachment to the church, whenever her hour of need shall come. But as to the united stand that is to be made against future encroachments, after the most effectual securities have been wrested from us, in consequence of our divisions, I confess myself to be most incredulous. If difference of views in the administration, and in the Houses of parliament, be now assigned as a reason for the surrender of our safeguards, is it to be supposed that ministers and parliament will not be again divided upon a subject so fruitful of contention—that when new demands are made, and the physical force of the five millions is once more arrayed in debate against us, as it will no doubt be after the recent experience of the efficacy of such a topic of persuasion, variance of opinion will not again exist, and that our divisions will not be again brought forward as a resistless argument for the necessity of larger sacrifices, in order to obtain that peace, which is continually receding from us, the more eager we shew ourselves by compromise to secure it.

But the advocates of the bill deny that our dangers will be increased by concession. It might be enough to answer, "the Roman Catholics themselves do not think so." My lords, upon this point I am content to rest my cause. If it can be made appear that Roman Catholics can be admitted into both Houses of parliament, without increased danger to the Irish church, I shall not vote for their exclusion. It will not be thought unnatural or indecorous in your eyes, that the welfare of that church should be my first and principal object. I regard it as one of the great providential instruments of doing good; as the great barrier against superstition on the one hand, and fanaticism on the other—as the incorrupt witness of truth in a land abounding with error and delusion. Now, my lords, on this point I would entreat your lordships, and every man who is acquainted with the state of political parties, and the manner in which business is conducted in parliament, to consider how great would be the influence exercised over public measures, by a body so large as that which we have reason to think the Roman Catholic representation will eventually form in the popular branch of the legislature;—a body firmly compacted for carrying Roman Catholic measures, modelling its votes solely with a view to that end, ready to throw itself into the scale of the party which shall bid the highest for its accession, embarrassing the measures of any administration that shall honestly and boldly set it at defiance; sent into the House by the influence of the Romish priesthood, who, as they have made, so they can unmake their representatives—that priesthood, governed by a foreign state, and armed with the terrors of a superstition all-powerful in Ireland. Will it be said, that such a number of representatives, so constituted and so bound together by unity of purpose, so governed and so directed, would not have a preponderating weight in all deliberations—would not possess that kind of influence, which would expose the Protestant church in Ireland to the greatest danger, under the most upright and vigorous administration—would not accomplish its downfall under a weak or corrupt ministry? Of this, at least, I am confident,—that to raise up such a force against the established church in the popular branch of the legislature, under the notion of strengthening her defences, and in expectation of controlling her adversaries, is the most unwise and hazardous policy—a policy which has already served the purposes of the Roman Catholics, by disuniting the church's friends. If it be said, that I am alarming myself with a phantom of my own imagination, I would beg noble lords to consider, that the party proposed to be formed in parliament against the church, is one of no ordinary description. The Roman Catholic representatives, about to be admitted from Ireland into the other House, will not be the representatives of property, or of the people; they will not even express public feeling, or well-directed public opinion: they will, in effect, be the agents and commissioners of the Roman priesthood, sent thither to give utterance to the sentiments, and to manage the interests of that body; a body, it should be recollected, which has objects to gain and views to promote, irreconcileable with the general good of the empire. The priesthood of the Church of Rome, must ever stand alone in a Protestant country; Protestant sects run into each other, and finally unite with the Established Church. But the Romish priesthood have set the mark of separation upon their own foreheads, by their unnatural though politic restrictions; by their exclusive and arrogant pretensions; by their dangerous, and, as it was until of late supposed, unconstitutional connection with a foreign power. With other sects, ascendancy is hopeless; their opposition is confined to matters of inferior moment; it ceases when the common cause of Protestantism is endangered. With the Roman Catholics of Ireland ascendancy will be placed within their reach by this measure; and with the Roman Catholic priesthood, the promotion of the interests of their church is their point of honour: it ranks, in their estimation, above country, kindred, and friends. It is, then, the confederacy of the Romish priesthood, actuated by a never-dying hostility to what is Protestant, that we have to dread; and not merely that of Roman Catholic representatives, who, it may be thought, will be acted upon and divided into parties like other men.

If we are told, indeed, that Romish counsellors and Romish legislators are found to be in foreign states as honest and patriotic as men of other creeds, I would answer that, without minutely sifting the truth of the assertion, the cases are, in my opinion, quite dissimilar. In the instances alluded to, the Roman Catholic religion is either already the established one—and, in that case the point is carried, and there is nothing further to be gained by agitation—or else the government is absolute, there is no voice heard but its own; and should a disposition to encroachment on the part of the Romish church be manifested, a single rescript from a minister would suffice for the correction of the evil. With us the Romanists constitute an active party in the commonwealth,—dangerous to our establishments, in proportion to the power with which it is invested; ever restless, because it has still an object to attain, and constantly excited to fresh machinations, by the increasing hope of accomplishing its purpose. I do not, however, mean to say, that the subversion of the Irish Church establishment will be immediate on the passing of this bill, nor do I think that it will be far removed from it. It is probable that, at first, the approaches will be cautious, and concealed under various pretences; until at length the assailants shall become emboldened by success, and favoured by political occurrences.

I ask, then—for this appears to me to be the only fair and intelligible way of discussing the question—are you prepared, my lords, to go the length to which you will be urged, after you have conceded all that is now demanded? Are you prepared to sacrifice the Irish Church establishment and the Protestant institutions connected with it—to efface the Protestant character of the Irish portion of the empire—to transfer from Protestants to Roman Catholics the ascendancy in Ireland?—for to one or other of these opposed parties, it is admitted on all hands, ascendancy must be granted. I would fain hope, my lords, that those who view with indifference the establishment of popery in Ireland, know not what that religion is in its practical effects upon the human mind. It has been represented to your lordships, within the last few years, in the form most capable of bearing the light of day—the line of defence taken up by its champions has been that of extenuation and apology, and some have described it in harsher terms. I shall not, however, trouble your lordships with a theological discussion: suffice it to say, that those doctrines and practices of the Romish Church—which, however modified or disguised, form the distinguishing features of her creed—are in irreconcileable variance with purity of faith and morals—the firmest basis of national prosperity and individual happiness. I do not think that England, with her intelligence and her independent spirit of inquiry, will ever become a vassal of the pope of Rome, but I do think that, with a considerable number of the representative Roman Catholics, and with a large proportion of the remainder, either indifferent to, or dissenting from the established religion, her church will share the fate of our own—her ascendancy and incorporation with the state will be no longer maintained—the equal right to national support and national favour will be asserted for sects the most erroneous and the most discordant; a neglect of religious truths will ensue, and the pure light of the Reformation be extinguished here also.

I thank you, my lords, for the courteous attention with which you have listened to me; and, whatever impression my observations may have made upon your minds, I feel that, in delivering them, I have discharged a duty which I owe to the Church of Ireland, and to that of England also,—if those establishments are to be spoken of as distinct, which the legislature has indissolubly united. In conclusion, my lords, I would only add, that if I am asked what is to be done for Ireland, I explicitly answer—tolerate, but do not encourage, still less do any thing to establish, religious error;—cherish, with equal care, all classes of his majesty's subjects; withhold nothing in the spirit of monopoly, which can be safely granted;—but, for the sake of all—yes, for the sake of Roman Catholics themselves, let the constitution be ever Protestant in its essential members,—in its monarch, and in his responsible advisers;—in its legislature,—in its public institutions for education;—but, above all, in its religious establishment.

Catholic Emancipation Act, 13 April 1829

10 Geo. 4, c. 7   *Statutes at Large*, XXIX, 693-96.

Whereas by various Acts of Parliament certain Restraints and Disabilities are imposed on the Roman Catholic Subjects of His Majesty, to which other Subjects of His Majesty are not liable: And Whereas it is expedient that such Restraints and Disabilities shall be from henceforth discontinued: And Whereas by various Acts certain Oaths and certain Declarations, commonly called the Declaration against Transubstantiation, and the Declaration against Transubstantiation and the Invocation of Saints and the Sacrifice of the Mass, as practised in the Church of *Rome*, are or may be required to be taken, made, and subscribed by the Subjects of His Majesty, as Qualifications for sitting and voting in Parliament, and for the Enjoyment of certain Offices, Franchises, and Civil Rights: Be it enacted by the King's most Excellent Majesty, by and with the Advice and Consent of the Lords Spiritual and Temporal, and Commons, in this present Parliament assembled, and by the Authority of the same, That from and after the Commencement of this Act all such Parts of the said Acts as require the said Declarations, or either of them, to be made or subscribed by any of His Majesty's Subjects, as a Qualification for sitting and voting in Parliament, or for the Exercise or Enjoyment of any Office,

Franchise, or Civil Right, be and the same are (save as hereinafter provided and excepted) hereby repealed.

II. And be it enacted, That from and after the Commencement of this Act it shall be lawful for any Person professing the Roman Catholic Religion, being a Peer, or who shall after the Commencement of this Act be returned as a Member of the House of Commons, to sit and vote in either House of Parliament respectively, being in all other respects duly qualified to sit and vote therein, upon taking and subscribing the following Oath, instead of the Oaths of Allegiance, Supremacy, and Abjuration:

I *A. B.* do sincerely, promise and swear, That I will be faithful and bear true Allegiance to His Majesty King *George* the Fourth, and will defend him to the utmost of my Power against all Conspiracies and Attempts whatever, which shall be made against his Person, Crown, or Dignity; and I will do my utmost Endeavour to disclose and make known to His Majesty, His Heirs and Successors, all Treasons and traitorous Conspiracies which may be formed against Him or Them: And I do faithfully promise to maintain, support, and defend, to the utmost of my Power, the Succession of the Crown, which Succession, by an Act, intituled *An Act for the further Limitation of the Crown, and better securing the Rights and Liberties of the Subject*, is and stands limited to the Princess *Sophia*, Electress of *Hanover*, and the Heirs of her Body, being Protestants; hereby utterly renouncing and abjuring any Obedience or Allegiance unto any other Person claiming or pretending a Right to the Crown of this Realm: And I do further declare, That it is not an Article of my Faith, and that I do renounce, reject, and abjure the Opinion, that Princes excommunicated or deprived by the Pope, or any other Authority of the See of *Rome*, may be deposed or murdered by their Subjects, or by any Person whatsoever: And I do declare, That I do not believe that the Pope of *Rome*, or any other Foreign Prince, Prelate, Person, State, or Potentate, hath or ought to have any Temporal or Civil Jurisdiction, Power, Superiority, or Pre-eminence, directly or indirectly, within this Realm. I do swear, That I will defend to the utmost of my Power the Settlement of Property within this Realm, as established by the Laws: And I do hereby disclaim, disavow, and solemnly abjure any Intention to subvert the present Church Establishment, as settled by Law within this Realm: And I do solemnly swear, That I never will exercise any Privilege to which I am or may become entitled, to disturb or weaken the Protestant Religion or Protestant Government in the United Kingdom: And I do solemnly, in the presence of God, profess, testify, and declare, That I do make this Declaration, and every Part thereof, in the plain and ordinary Sense of the Words of this Oath, without any Evasion, Equivocation, or mental Reservation whatsoever. So help me God.

III. And be it further enacted, That wherever, in the Oath hereby appointed and set forth, the Name of His present Majesty is expressed or referred to, the Name of the Soveriegn of this Kingdom for the Time being, by virtue of the Act for the further Limitation of the Crown and better securing the Rights and Liberties of the Subject, shall be substituted from Time to Time, with proper Words of Reference thereto.

IV. Provided always, and be it further enacted, That no Peer professing the Roman Catholic Religion, and no Person professing the Roman Catholic Religion, who shall be returned a Member of the House of Commons after the Commencement of this Act, shall be capable of sitting or voting in either House of Parliament respectively, unless he shall first take and subscribe the Oath hereinbefore appointed and set forth, before the same Persons, at the same Times and Places, and in the same Manner as the Oaths and the Declaration now required by Law are respectively directed to be taken, made, and subscribed; and that any such Person professing the Roman Catholic Religion, who shall sit or vote in either House of Parliament, without having first taken and subscribed, in the Manner aforesaid, the Oath in this Act appointed and set forth, shall be subject to the same Penalties, Forfeitures, and Disabilities, and the Offence of so sitting or voting shall be followed and attended by and with the same Consequences, as are by Law enacted and provided in the Case of Persons sitting or voting in either House of Parliament respectively, without the taking, making, and subscribing the Oaths and the Declaration now required by Law.

V. And be it further enacted, That it shall be lawful for Persons professing the Roman Catholic Religion to vote at Elections of Members to serve in Parliament for *England* and for *Ireland*, and also to vote at the Elections of Representative Peers of *Scotland* and of *Ireland*, and to be elected such Representative Peers, being in all other respect duly qualified, upon taking and subscribing the Oath hereinbefore appointed and set forth, instead of the Oaths of Allegiance, Supremacy, and Abjuration, and instead of the Declaration now by Law required, and instead also of such other Oath or Oaths as are now by Law required to be taken by any of His Majesty's Subjects professing the Roman Catholic Religion, and upon taking also such other Oath or Oaths as may now be lawfully tendered to any Persons offering to vote at such Elections.

VI. And be it further enacted, That the Oath hereinbefore appointed and set forth shall be administered to His Majesty's Subjects professing the Roman Catholic Religion, for the Purpose of enabling them to vote in any of the Cases aforesaid, in the same Manner, at the same Time, and by the same Officers or other Persons as the Oaths for which it is hereby substituted are or may be now by Law administered; and that in all Cases in which a Certificate of the taking, making, or subscribing of any of the Oaths or of the Declaration now required by Law is directed to be given, a like Certificate of the taking or subscribing of the Oath hereby appointed and set forth shall be given by the same Officer or other Person, and in the same Manner as the Certificate now required by Law is directed to be given, and shall be of the like Force and Effect.

VII. And be it further enacted, That in all Cases where the Persons now authorized by Law to administer the Oaths of Allegiance, Supremacy, and Abjuration to Persons voting at Elections, are themselves required to take an Oath previous to their administering such Oaths, they shall, in addition to the Oath now by them taken, take an Oath for the duly administering the Oath hereby appointed and set forth, and for the duly granting Certificates of the same.

VIII. And Whereas in an Act of the Parliament of *Scotland* made in the Eighth and Ninth Session of the First Parliament of King *William* the Third, intituled *An Act for the preventing the Growth of Popery*, a certain Declaration or Formula is therein contained, which it is expedient should no longer be required to be taken and subscribed: Be it therefore enacted, That such Parts of any Acts as authorize the said Declaration or Formula to be tendered, or require the same to be taken, sworn, and subscribed, shall be and the same are hereby repealed, except as to such Offices, Places and Rights as are hereinafter excepted; and that from and after the Commencement of this Act it shall be lawful for Persons professing the Roman Catholic Religion to elect and be elected Members to serve in Parliament for *Scotland*, and to be enrolled as Freeholders in any Shire or Stewartry of *Scotland*, and to be chosen Commissioners or Delegates for choosing Burgesses to serve in Parliament for any Districts or Burghs in *Scotland*, being in all other respects duly qualified, such Persons always taking and subscribing the Oath hereinbefore appointed and set forth, instead of Oaths of Allegiance and Abjuration as now required by Law, at such Time as the said last-mentioned Oaths, or either of them, are now required by Law to be taken.

IX. And be it further enacted, That no Person in Holy Orders in the Church of *Rome* shall be capable of being elected to serve in Parliament as a Member of the House of Commons; and if any such Person shall be elected to serve in Parliament as aforesaid, such Election shall be void; and if any Person, being elected to serve in Parliament as a Member of the House of Commons, shall, after his Election, take or receive Holy Orders in the Church of *Rome*, the Seat of such Person shall immediately become void; and if any such Person shall, in any of the Cases aforesaid, presume to sit or vote as a Member of the House of Commons, he shall be subject to the same Penalties, Forfeitures, and Disabilities as are of the House of Commons, he shall be subject to the same Penalties, Forfeitures, and Disabilities as are enacted by an Act passed in the Forty-first Year of the Reign of King *George* the Third, intituled *An Act to remove Doubts respecting the Eligibility of Persons in Holy Orders to sit in the House of Commons;* and Proof of the Celebration of any Religious Service by such Person, according to the Rites of the Church of *Rome*, shall be deemed and taken to be *prima facie* Evidence of the Fact of such Person being in Holy Orders, within the Intent and Meaning of this Act.

X. And be it enacted, That it shall be lawful for any of His Majesty's Subjects professing the Roman Catholic Religion to hold, exercise, and enjoy all Civil and Military Offices and Places of Trust or Profit under His Majesty, His Heirs or Successors, and to exercise any other Francise or Civil Right, except as hereinafter excepted, upon taking and subscribing, at the Times and in the Manner hereinafter mentioned, the Oath hereinbefore appointed and set forth, instead of the Oaths of Allegiance, Supremacy, and Abjuration, and instead of such other Oath or Oaths as are or may be now by Law required to be taken for the Purpose aforesaid by any of His Majesty's Subjects professing the Roman Catholic Religion.

XI. Provided always, and be it enacted, That nothing herein contained shall be construed to exempt any Person professing the Roman Catholic Religion from the Necessity of taking any Oath or Oaths, or making any Declaration, not hereinbefore mentioned, which are or may be by Law required to be taken or subscribed by any Person on his Admission into any such Office or Place of Trust or Profit as aforesaid.

XII. Provided also, and be it further enacted, That nothing herein contained shall extend or be construed to extend to enable any Person or Persons professing the Roman Catholic Religion to hold or exercise the Office of Guardians and Justices of the United Kingdom, or of Regent of the United Kingdom, under whatever Name, Style, or Title such Office may be constituted; nor to enable any Person, otherwise than as he is now by Law enabled, to hold or enjoy the Office of Lord High Chancellor, Lord Keeper or Lord Commissioner of the Great Seal of *Great Britain* or *Ireland*; or the Office of Lord Lieutenant, or Lord Deputy, or other Chief Governor or Governors of *Ireland*; or His Majesty's High Commissioner to the General Assembly of the Church of *Scotland*.

XIII. Provided also, and be it further enacted, That nothing herein contained shall be construed to affect or alter any of the Provisions of an Act passed in the Seventh Year of His present Majesty's Reign, intituled *An Act to consolidate and amend the Laws which regulate the Levy and Application of Church Rates and Parish Cesses, and the Election of Churchwardens, and the Maintenance of Parish Clerks, in* Ireland.

XIV. And be it enacted, That it shall be lawful for any of His Majesty's Subjects professing the Roman Catholic Religion to be a Member of any Lay Body Corporate, and to hold any Civil Office or Place of Trust or Profit therein, and to do any Corporate Act, or vote in any Corporate Election or other Proceeding, upon taking and subscribing the Oath hereby appointed and set forth, instead of the Oaths of Allegiance, Supremacy, and Abjuration; and upon taking also such other Oath or Oaths as may now by Law be required to be taken by any Persons becoming Members of such Lay Body Corporate, or being admitted to hold any Office or Place of Trust or Profit within the same.

XV. Provided nevertheless, and be it further enacted, That nothing herein contained shall extend to authorize or empower any of His Majesty's Subjects professing the Roman Catholic Religion, and being a Member of any Lay Body Corporate, to give any Vote at, or in any Manner to join in the Election, Presentation, or Appointment of any Person to any Ecclesiastical Benefice whatsoever, or any Office or Place belonging to or connected with the United Church of *England* and *Ireland*, or the Church of *Scotland*, being in the Gift, Patronage, or Disposal of such Lay Corporate Body.

XVI. Provided also, and be it enacted, That nothing in this Act contained shall be construed to enable any Persons, otherwise than as they are now by Law enabled, to hold, enjoy, or exercise any Office, Place, or Dignity of, in, or belonging to the United Church of *England* and *Ireland*, or the Church of *Scotland*, or any Place or Office whatever of, in, or belonging to any of the Ecclesiastical Courts of Judicature of *England* and *Ireland* respectively, or any Court of Appeal from or Review of the Sentences of such Courts, or of, in, or belonging to the Commissary Court of *Edinburgh*, or of, in, or belonging to any Cathedral or Collegiate or

Ecclesiastical Establishment or Foundation; or any Office or Place whatever of, in, or belonging to any of the Universities of this Realm; or any Office or Place whatever, and by whatever Name the same may be called, of, in or belonging to any of the Colleges or Halls of the said Universities, or the Colleges of *Eton, Westminster,* or *Winchester,* or any College or School within this Realm; or to repeal, abrogate, or in any Manner to interfere with any local Statute, Ordinance, or Rule, which is or shall be established by competent Authority within any University, College, Hall, or School, by which Roman Catholics shall be prevented from being admitted thereto, or from residing or taking Degrees therein: Provided also, that nothing herein contained shall extend or be construed to extend to enable any Person, otherwise than as he is now by Law enabled, to exercise any Right of Presentation to any Ecclesiastical Benefice whatsoever; or to repeal, vary, or alter in any Manner the Laws now in Force in respect to the Right of Presentation to any Ecclesiastical Benefice.

XVII. Provided always, and be it enacted, That where any Right of Presentation to any Ecclesiastical Benefice shall belong to any Office in the Gift or Appointment of His Majesty, His Heirs or Successors, and such Office shall be held by a Person professing the Roman Catholic Religion, the Right of Presentation shall devolve upon and be exercised by the Archbishop of *Canterbury* for the Time being.

XVIII. And be it enacted, That it shall not be lawful for any Person professing the Roman Catholic Religion, directly or indirectly, to advise His Majesty, His Heirs or Successors, or any Person or Persons holding or exercising the Office of Guardians of the United Kingdom, or of Regent of the United Kingdom, under whatever Name, Style, or Title such Office may be constituted, or the Lord Lieutenant, or Lord Deputy, or other Chief Governor or Governors of *Ireland,* touching or concerning the Appointment to or Disposal of any Office or Preferment in the United Church of *England* and *Ireland,* or in the Church of *Scotland;* and if any such Person shall offend in the Premises, he shall, being thereof convicted by due Course of Law, be deemed guilty of a high Misdemeanor, and disabled for ever from holding any Office, Civil or Military, under the Crown.

XIX. And be it enacted, That every Person professing the Roman Catholic Religion, who shall after the Commencement of this Act be placed, elected, or chosen in or to the Office of Mayor, Provost, Alderman, Recorder, Bailiff, Town Clerk, Magistrate, Councillor, or Common Councilman, or in or to any Office of Magistracy or Place of Trust or Employment relating to the Government of any City, shall, within One Calendar Month next before or upon his Admission into any of the same respectively, take and subscribe the Oath herein-before appointed and set forth, in the Presence of such Person or Persons respectively as by the Charters or Usages of the said respective Cities, Corporations, Burghs, Boroughs, or Districts ought to administer the Oath for due Execution of the said Offices or Places respectively; and in Default of such, in the Presence of Two Justices of the Peace, Councillors or Magistrates of the said Cities, Corporations, Burghs, Boroughs, or Districts, if such there be; or otherwise, in the Presence of Two Justices of the Peace of the respective Counties, Ridings, Divisions, or Franchises wherein the said Cities, Corporations, Burghs, Boroughs, or Districts are; which said Oath shall either be entered in a Book, Roll, or other Record to be kept for that Purpose, or shall be filed amongst the Records of the City, Corporation, Burgh, Borough, or District.

XX. And be it enacted, That every Person professing the Roman Catholic Religion, who shall after the Commencement of this Act be appointed to any Office or Place of Trust or Profit under His Majesty, His Heirs or Successors, shall within Three Calendar Months next before such Appointment, or otherwise shall, before he presumes to exercise or enjoy or in any Manner to act in such Office or Place, take and subscribe the Oath herein-before appointed and set forth, either in His Majesty's High Court of Chancery, or in any of His Majesty's Courts of King's Bench, Common Pleas, or Exchequer, at *Westminster* or *Dublin*; or before any Judge of Assize, or in any Court of General or Quarter Sessions of the Peace in *Great Britain* or *Ireland*, for the County or Place where the Person so taking and subscribing the Oath shall reside; or in any of His Majesty's Courts of Session, Justiciary, Exchequer, or Jury Court, or in any Sheriff or Stewart Court, or in any Burgh Court, or before the Magistrates and Councillors of any Royal Burgh in *Scotland*, between the Hours of Nine in the Morning and Four in the Afternoon; and the proper Officer of the Court in which such Oath shall be so taken and subscribed shall cause the same to be preserved amongst the Records of the Court; and such Officer shall make, sign, and deliver a Certificate of such Oath having been duly taken and subscribed, as often as the same shall be demanded of him, upon Payment of Two Shillings and Sixpence for the same; and such Certificate shall be sufficient Evidence of the Person therein named having duly taken and subscribed such Oath.

XXI. And be it enacted, That if any Person professing the Roman Catholic Religion shall enter upon the Exercise or Enjoyment of any Office or Place of Trust or Profit under His Majesty, or of any other Office or Franchise, not having in the Manner and at the Times aforesaid taken and subscribed the Oath herein-before appointed and set forth, then and in every such Case such Person shall forfeit to His Majesty the Sum of Two hundred Pounds; and the Appointment of such Person to the Office, Place, or Franchise so by him held shall become altogether void, and the Office, Place, or Franchise shall be deemed and taken to be vacant to all Intents and Purposes whatsoever.

XXII. Provided always, That for and notwithstanding any thing in this Act contained, the Oath herein-before appointed and set forth shall be taken by the Officers in His Majesty's Land and Sea Service, professing the Roman Catholic Religion, at the same Times and in the same Manner as the Oaths and Declarations now required by Law are directed to be taken, and not otherwise.

XXIII. And be it further enacted, That from and after the passing of this Act, no Oath or Oaths shall be tendered to or required to be taken by His Majesty's Subjects professing the Roman Catholic Religion, for enabling them to hold or enjoy any Real or Personal Property, other than such as may by Law be tendered to and required to be taken by His Majesty's other Subjects; and that the Oath herein appointed and set forth, being taken and subscribed in any of the Courts, or before any of the Persons above mentioned, shall be of the same Force and Effect, to all Intents and Purposes, as, and shall stand in the Place of, all Oaths and Declarations required or prescribed by any Law now in force for the Relief of His Majesty's Roman Catholic Subjects from any Disabilities, Incapacities, or Penalties; and the proper Officer of any of the Courts above mentioned, in which any Person professing the Roman Catholic Religion shall demand to take and subscribe the Oath herein appointed and set forth, is hereby authorized and required to administer the said Oath to such Person; and such Officer shall make, sign, and deliver a Certificate of such Oath having been duly taken and subscribed, as often as the same shall be demanded of him, upon Payment of One Shilling; and such Certificate shall be sufficient Evidence of the Person therein named having duly taken and subscribed such Oath. . . .

Victorian Britain at Its Apogee
1830-1870

Victorian Britain at Its Apogee
1830-1870

The prosperity and greatness of modern Britain reached its peak during the mid-nineteenth century. At the outset of the period, however, enormous social tensions threatened to rend the fabric of society. The parliamentary reform crisis, Chartism, the agitation for corn law repeal, and a host of related grievances, muted and overt, had to be absorbed and subordinated to a broader social consciousness. This process of social sublimation was superficially achieved by mid-century. The pace of economic expansion then quickened immeasurably, and material wealth was more generously distributed. Likewise, on the fundament of a perceived stability important administrative and constitutional changes were carried out.

The process of defining a more modern nation took about twenty years to complete. It made Britain the acknowledged "workshop of the world," *the* successful exemplar of her own work ethic. Yet at the very moment when her products and capital were penetrating the outermost regions of the globe, the core of British economic supremacy was being undermined. Although this decline did not become irreversible until the twentieth century, it was visible from about 1875 onward. British "greatness"—the maturation of a consciousness of superiority and of effortless advantage—was to be permanently tarnished.

The pace of economic advance between 1830 and 1870 was relentless. Trade, productivity, investment, and related indices of economic growth surpassed all previous levels. For those fortunate enough to secure a share of the inequitably distributed new wealth, the material rewards were exceedingly handsome. More importantly, a psychological sense of progress gripped and held the nation until the latter part of the century. The most spectacular aspect of this period of expansion was railway construction. The "railway age" dates from the opening of the Manchester-Liverpool Railway in 1830. Railroads speeded up the distribution of goods, reduced the cost of developing resources, and opened up cultural and social vistas. To fuel the speculative expansion partly unleashed by railway investment, new credit and banking institutions were devised. Profit and entrepreneurial initiative became the mainsprings of a continuing economic momentum. The transition from hand labor to a steam economy accelerated; engineering, metallurgy, and related heavy industries gained in significance; woolen joined cotton cloth in the front rank of exports; and mineral resources were exploited with a fury that brooked no ecological caution. The great northern cities towered above all: Manchester, Bradford, Birmingham, Leeds, and Sheffield defaced their landscapes and did so with a material dynamism which was the essence of the national mood. The 1851 Great Exhibition of the Works of Industry of all Nations, housed in Paxton's splendidly translucent iron and glass Crystal Palace in the center of Hyde Park, symbolized the age. Redolent of mechanical grandeur, it was the Victorian industrialist's equivalent of a Turkish seraglio, stocked with all the hard necessities of a wondrous age. This was Britain's economic peak.

The period 1830-70 opened and closed with great suffrage reforms. The first struggle for parliamentary reform (1831-32) was among the most decisive events of the nineteenth century, not only because the provisions of the Reform Act (1832) permanently altered the relationship between the landed and urban classes, but also because of the manner in which the bill passed through Parliament. A formidable coalition of middle- and working-class reformers successfully agitated for an impressive measure of political change and, by doing so, opened the floodgates of legal and social transformation. Barricades of resistance that had held back innovation for centuries were knocked down. The ensuing reforms of municipal corporations, of the poor laws, and of the Church were seminal in reshaping the political system and its social and administrative underpinnings. Sir Robert Peel's Tamworth address of 1834, in which the Conservative leader accepted the ramifications of some of these changes notwithstanding personal convictions to the contrary, pointed to the future.

By reducing property qualifications, the Reform Act enfranchised the middle class and eliminated the most glaring anomalies in the system; ironically, however, it increased rather than lessened tensions. The political aspirations of the factory owner were satisfied; those of the factory worker were not. Many of those who remained unenfranchised were bitterly disappointed by the outcome of the reform agitation and turned to more effective levers of pressure. Working-class activism intensified. Trade union experimentation, Owenite agitation, the development of an illegal but vocal cheap press, and, most strikingly, the creation of the Chartist movement were all expressions of this disillusionment. None of these movements secured immediate success, but they articulated a social consciousness based upon an emergent democracy. The pot was kept boiling; the intensity of commitment assured that long-term social equilibrium could be secured only on the basis of a better distribution of wealth.

Corn law repeal, supported by influential reformers and members of Parliament and carried by the Peel government in 1845-46, was another, more "respectable" aspect of this phenomenon of class tension and divisiveness. The landed and mercantile interests clashed over the corn laws, and debates on the subject ran as deep as those comprehending any other issue of the century. (Benjamin Disraeli's successful rise within the Conservative party, at the cost of Peel's political emasculation, was a by-product of this struggle.) Commerce, property, and middle-class "respectability" successfully challenged landed monopoly, and simultaneously fought a triumphant rearguard action against Chartists and working-class "revolutionaries." Thus when Victorian values stabilized during the 1850s and 1860s, following upon the resolution of these interrelated crises, they were framed along middle-class lines and dominated by middle-class "respectability." The scope of change was kept within the framework of a conservatizing consensus. The landed class gave way (although much more slowly than oversimplified analyses suggest), but the middle-class groups which replaced them wished to retain a property system that stressed integration of fluid social elements rather than a reevaluation of fundamental relationships. The necessity for reform of established institutions was acknowledged. Those who questioned the basic tenets of the system, however, were almost always compelled to compromise with it.

Mid-Victorian administrative changes were of the greatest importance. The spectacular pace of economic advance and the eruption of political and cultural tensions necessitated a more professional administrative mechanism. The dictates of efficiency and pragmatic centralization came increasingly into play. Early factory legislation pointed the way. But it was the controversial Poor Law Amendment Act (1834)—devised by the Benthamite reformer, Edwin Chadwick—that set the pace for subsequent administrative modifications. The precise alterations introduced into the poor law in 1834, comprehending the abolition of outdoor relief and other "efficient" eleemosynary principles, were less important than the spark that the measure gave to centralization. The device of a central commission to oversee local governmental activities, for example, was imitated throughout the century. Subsequent prison reforms, public health regulations, and factory legislation all followed the poor law model. The range of activity by the central government was extended dramatically. Female and adolescent mineworkers, chimney sweeps, merchant sailors, cholera victims, and others slowly came under the overall protection of a diminutive welfare state. Although it was the merest foreshadowing of extended central power, such a process could not even have been anticipated in the gentle rural Britain of the eighteenth century.

This miniature apparatus of governmental machinery brought with it men and women trained to a particular task of government or fitted to a specialist activity. "Respectability" was the watchword of these careerists. Doctors, nurses, solicitors, civil servants, army officers: all shaped their careers according to the principle of merit. It was the task of political leaders, notably William E. Gladstone, to institutionalize this crucial social development.

All this state intervention in the social sphere was accompanied, paradoxically, by the strengthening of economic laissez-faire. After the repeal of the corn laws, Lord John Russell and Gladstone tore down the remaining tariff barriers. The long-standing navigation acts were entirely annulled. Excise duties, including the explosive "taxes on knowledge," were removed. Economic freedom was seen as the desirable and logical complement of intellectual and political libertarianism. So pervasive did the ethos of free trade become that all attempts to revert to protectionism were doomed until the mid-twentieth century.

But the government's simultaneous abandonment of laissez-faire in social affairs and strengthening of it in economic affairs is only one of the seeming paradoxes of this period. There were equally inconsistent political and cultural configurations. Numerous changes of ministries occurred, for example, in the 1850s and 1860s. These reflected the fact that expediency had become a more impelling stimulus to political ambition than avowed commitment to principle. Frequent reversals of position over corn law repeal and other major issues, especially by Peel, blurred much of the surface of political life. In the absence of a party machine that could exact sanctions against recusant members, unpredictability and instability became endemic to politics. Yet—and this is the nub of the difficulty—the great political and constitutional truths were not open to debate. It was an unstated political consensus that British values were superior to all others and that the *game* (a word redolent of meaning) must be played according to autarchic rules. An element of constitutional shadow-boxing followed from these assumptions, but considerable scope for change remained, as in the continuing decline of monarch and Lords. Parliamentary debates, too, were indulged in with panache and elegance.

There were similar cultural incongruities. Confronted by widespread intellectual uncertainties, the Church of England sought to confound its critics with administrative tamperings and an inspired social evangelism. It failed, and continued to weaken in the face of Nonconformity and outright scepticism. But the common culture which bound the Church of England to the center of the nation assured for it a continuing formal predominance. In the nonreligious sphere, literary thinkers declaimed against the pervasiveness of a materialism that threatened to corrode British society. Yet they, too, operated on agreed assumptions which proved too attractive to allow more than a few—Thomas Carlyle and William Morris among them—to probe towards the outer limits of social criticism.

Viscount Palmerston was a unifying symbol during the 1850s. Though his political appeal was dependent upon an aggressive diplomacy, he was a conservative domestic presence who typified the more arrogant and complacent elements in mid-Victorian Britain. His death in 1865 unleashed renewed demands for reform. The aggregate of forces which had produced economic growth and social coherence began to fracture. Gladstone and Disraeli, the great political gladiators, commenced their domination of the national scene.

The second great struggle for parliamentary reform, which began in the 1850s and peaked after the death of Palmerston, culminated in the passage of the Representation of the People Act (1867) enfranchising the working class. Renewed agitation once again ruffled public self-assurance. Lord John Russell's notion of "finality," articulated so unconvincingly in November 1837, was now permanently interred. Dormant discontents revived. The act of 1867, which demonstrated the failure of mid-Victorian middle-class rule, pushed Britain several irreversible steps in the direction of democracy. An awakened and aggressive mass populace, demanding concessions and prepared to exert more radical pressures to satisfy its aspirations, started to sweep aside the "respectable" culture of mid-century.

CRISIS OVER PARLIAMENTARY REFORM

Address and aims of the Birmingham Political Union, 25 January 1830

Authorized copy of the Resolutions passed at the meeting in Birmingham, held on the 25th January, 1830, together with the Declaration, Rules and Regulations, of the Political Union, for the Protection of Public Rights (Birmingham: William Hodgetts, 1830), 6-15.

A combination of factors—widespread economic distress, Catholic emancipation, the revival of Whig fortunes, the impact of the second French Revolution— produced a major political crisis during 1830-32 which centered upon the question of franchise reform. The events of these years culminated in the passage of the Reform Act (1832), one of the most important measures ever enacted by the British Parliament. The Birmingham Political Union, founded by the currency reformer Thomas Attwood (1783-1856) in 1830, was the first of many extraparliamentary associations formed to agitate for extension of the suffrage.

The experience of the last 15 years, must certainly have convinced the most incredulous that the rights and interests of the middle and lower classes of the people are not efficiently represented in the Commons House of Parliament. A very few observations will be sufficient to place this important subject beyond the possibility of doubt.

In the year 1819, a bill was passed into a law, under the assumption that it would add only *four per cent.* to the national taxes and burthens. It is now very generally acknowledged that the bill thus passed into a law, has literally added *cent. per cent.* to the national burthens; instead of *four percent.*, that it has literally *doubled*, or is in the undeniable process of *doubling*, the real weight, and the real value of every tax, rent, and monied obligation, in the kingdom. Ten years have since elapsed; and yet, to this day, no adequate effort has been made by the representatives of the people to reduce the taxes in a degree corresponding with the increase which has thus been *surreptitiously* effected in their weight and pressure! What further proof is required of the absolute necessity of reform?

Nor has any attempt been made by the legislature to retrace their steps, and to rectify the grievous oppression which has thus been occasioned. On the contrary, the fatal error is now coolly acknowledged, and the country is gravely assured, by the very men who benefit by the measure, that it is *now too late to retreat*!!

At three different periods, during the operation of this fatal measure, and now a fourth time, the industrious classes of the community generally, have been reduced to a state of distress which has heretofore been unexampled in its general extent and severity. At each of these periods, the profits of productive capital and industry have been destroyed, or so much reduced, as no longer to afford the just and necessary inducements to the employment of labour. The working classes of the country have thus been thrown generally out of employment, or they have been compelled to endure more labour than nature can support, or their fair and reasonable earnings have been sacrificed, in order to prevent the ruin of their employers.

Strange and unnatural as this state of things evidently is, it has, more than once, been attended with anomalies which have rendered it ten times more unnatural still. The markets have been glutted with food and clothing on the one hand, and with a hungry and naked population on the other. The most eminent parliamentary authorities have declared that the *loaves* have been too many for the *mouths*, and that the *mouths* have been too many for the *loaves, at the very same time!*

It is most certain, that if the rights and interests of the industrious classes of the community had been properly represented in Parliament, a general state of distress, attended with anomalies like these, would have commanded the instant attention of the House of Commons. The *cause* of the distress would have been ascertained, and the proper remedy would have been applied without delay. But, what has been the conduct of the House of Commons? To this very day, the *cause* of these strange and unnatural, and distressful anomalies has never once been enquired into! At 3 different periods, when this vital subject has been brought before the House of Commons, *they have literally refused to allow its investigation!* In the year 1822, Mr. Western gave notice of a motion to enquire into the *cause* of the *national* distress. *The House of Commons refused to grant the enquiry!* In 1827, Mr. Edward Davenport gave notice of a similar motion! *The House of Commons refused to grant the enquiry!* In the last year, Sir Richard Vyvyan gave notice of a similar motion. *And again the House of Commons refused to grant the enquiry!* Upon three different occasions, the House of Commons has thus exposed itself to the suspicion of either a total *unwillingness*, or a total *inability* to protect the most vital interests of the country.

Here then, we have *proof* that the rights and interests of the great mass of the community are not properly represented in Parliament. A triple proof has been added to every argument which has previously been drawn from reason and experience, that an effectual representation of the industrious classes in the Commons House of Parliament is alike necessary to the welfare of the people, and the safety of the throne.

Nor is this state of things much to be wondered at, when the present state and composition of the Commons' House of Parliament are considered. That honourable House, in its present state, is evidently too far removed in habits, wealth, and station, from the wants and interests of the lower and middle classes of the people, to have any just views respecting them, or any close identity of feeling with them. The great aristocratical interests of all kinds are well represented there. The landed interest, the church, the law, the monied interest,—all these have *engrossed*, as it were, the House of Commons into their own hands, the members of that honourable House being all immediately and closely connected with those great interests. *But the interests of industry and of trade have scarcely any representatives at all!* These, the most vital interests of the nation, the sources of all its wealth and of all its strength, are comparatively *unrepresented*; whilst every interest connected in any way with the *national burthens* is represented in the fullest degree! If any few individual members of the House of Commons should happen to be concerned in trade, it may be truly said that such members are in general far more concerned in interests hostile to trade, than in trade itself. They are, too often, rich and retired capitalists, who have, perhaps, left *one tenth* of their wealth in trade, and have withdrawn the other *nine tenths* from active occupation. It is, therefore, of but little consequence to *them* whether trade flourishes or not. It is possible, indeed, that upon some occasions, these rich and retired capitalists may look with indifference on the sufferings of their competitors in trade; and after having availed *themselves* of the facilities of *credit*, to accumulate their own fortunes, they may possibly contemplate without pain the removal of those facilities from others, and their hopeless and unavailing struggles to follow in the same career.

Undoubtedly, it is essential to the national welfare that this state of things should be changed. The *"Citizens and Burgesses"* of the House of Commons should, in general, be real "Citizens and Burgesses;" men engaged in trade, and actively concerned in it; and having their fortunes and their prospects in life committed in it. The present members of the House of Commons, although *called* "Knights, Citizens, and Burgesses," are *practically* all *"Knights of the Shire;"* inasmuch as they are generally possessed of the same fortunes, and living under the same habits, influencies, and impressions as *"Knights of the Shire."* It is not, therefore, to be wondered at that the members of the House of Commons should exhibit, generally, a total ignorance of trade, and of the wants and interests of the industrious classes of the community; and too frequently an indisposition to enquire into the distresses of trade, or to give themselves any great trouble in relieving them.

It is idle to blame this kind of conduct in them. It is in the nature of man to look principally to his own interest. *It is the public themselves who are to blame for having allowed a state of things to grow up, in which the public interests are frequently entrusted into inefficient hands.* If the public had kept a proper guard over their own concerns—if they had sent to Parliament *real "Citizens and Burgesses,"* selected from among *themselves*, and having the same interests as *themselves*, acquainted with the same *wants, and modes' and means, and living under* the same habits, influences and impressions as themselves; *then* the rights and interests of the industrious classes would have been properly guarded and secured. *This was* the practice in the better days of the constitution; and unless it become the practice *again*, there can be no prosperity, no liberty, no security for this injured and degraded nation.

But it is not merely of the want of a community of interest, of feeling, and of knowledge in the House of Commons, that the industrious classes have a right to complain. A majority of that honourable House is generally believed to be elected by a few hundred rich individuals only; and near one hundred of its members are exposed to the suspicion of having their judgments biassed by the influence of emoluments drawn from the public purse. The interests of the mass of the people are thus exposed to dangers on all sides and protected on none. Every thing, in short, combines to render the cause of the industrious classes hopeless in England unless some measures can be devised for restoring to those important classes that legal influence in the legislative functions, which the constitution has originally placed in their hands. Without this, it is probable that the reward of industry will be permanently destroyed; and that the merchants, manufacturers, farmers, and traders of the United Kingdom will be reduced to a state of general poverty and degradation; whilst the working classes will be driven down in their wages, and deprived of employment generally, until they have no other resource but the overcrowded workhouse for their support.

From all these considerations, it follows, therefore, that an effectual reform in the Commons House of Parliament is absolutely necessary for the welfare and security of the country.

But how is reform to be obtained? Is it reasonable to expect that the system which has caused the national injuries and distresses, should rectify itself? The thing is not possible. What then must we do? Shall we have recourse to a vigour trenching upon the law? God forbid. Fortunately for us and for our country, the constitution has yet preserved to us some conservatory principles, to which we may have recourse, and by means of which we may hope that this great and vital object may be accomplished in a just, legal, and peaceful way.

The exercise of those principles, however, is surrounded with many legal difficulties and dangers, which can only be counteracted by a general union and organization of the industrious classes, and which render council, caution, and discretion, necessary at every step. The soundest legal advice, the most inflexible integrity, the most generous, upright, and honourable motives, and the most dutiful submission to the laws, are all required to ensure ultimate success.

Under these circumstances, therefore, it is necessary to form a general political union and organization of the industrious classes, and to appoint a political council, to inquire, consult, consider, and determine, and report from time to time, upon the legal rights, which yet remain to us, and upon the political measures which it may be legal and adviseable to have recourse to. It is necessary also, to provide permanent funds for the defrayment of the necessary legal expenses, which may be incurred, under the direction of the Political Council; for *money* is the *sinew of law*, and without great expense, no great object can be secured.

But it is not alone in the cause of *reform*, that union, and council, and organization, and co-operation, are necessary on the part of the industrious classes. The benefits which even the present state of the representation is capable of administering, are not properly secured to the public, from the want of some organized and efficient means of bringing the interests and opinions, and the wants and modes and means of the community to the knowledge of the legislative bodies. It is an old proverb, that "*what is every one's* business is *no one's* business," and, therefore, the common business of "*every one,*" is generally attended to by *none.* What more important business can "*every one*" have, than that of bringing the interests and the wants of the community to the knowledge of the legislative councils? However desirous both houses of parliament may be of promoting the happiness and welfare of the community, they have not sufficient means of obtaining a knowledge of their wants and interests, nor of the measures necessary for their gratification and protection. Bred up in the lap of luxury, and surrounded by bands of flatterers and parasites, and of interested and designing men, whose business it is to deceive and misrepresent, the members of the legislature have no sufficient means of coming to a knowledge of the widespread havoc which their own measures produce throughout the country. A casual town's meeting now and then, without system, consistency, or permanency of object, or operation, and, perhaps, a county meeting at distant intervals, still more precarious and irregular, combined with dubious and generally delusive representations from the public press; these furnish, at present, almost the only means of bringing the constituent and the legislative bodies into contact with each other. *Hence* the pernicious legislation under which the country now suffers. *Hence*, the innumerable acts of parliament, which have a constant and encreasing tendency to trench upon the rights and interests of the industrious classes of the community. If those important classes of men had been properly protected by political unions among themselves, if they had possessed political councils in all the great towns and districts, with ample funds at their command, and with such intellect and integrity as their own ranks abundantly afford; under *these* circumstances, it would not have been possible for those innumerable acts to have been passed, which now *hem in*, as it were, the rights and liberties of the subject on every side, and render it almost impossible for the *poor man* to *move*, without *trenching upon a law*. Societies of this kind, would have watched closely the proceedings of the legislature, they would have sounded the alarm on the approach of danger, they would have pointed out every rash, unjust, destructive or oppressive measure, the very moment it was first agitated; and there is no reason to believe that parliament would not have listened to remonstrances thus timely, constitutionally, and efficiently supplied. The *tax receivers*, would have been reduced in their capital and income, in the same degree as the *tax payers*; or they would, at any rate, never have been permitted to build up their own aggrandisement out of the plunder and degradation of the *tax payers*! The *taxes* of the country, instead of pressing almost exclusively upon the *poor*, would have been made to press justly and equally upon the *rich*; instead of *throttling* as it were, the industry of the country, and consigning the struggling tradesman to the gaol, they would have been collected out of the accumulations and superfluities of the nation, and not out of its difficulties, embarrassments, and distresses. The prosperity *of all* would have been preserved; and *all* would have been brought to contribute *equally* to the national emergencies, according to their respective means.

Undoubtedly, it is just and necessary that the taxes of the country should be reduced in the same degree, as the price of labour is reduced, and as the value of the money in which they are collected, is increased. We estimate this reduction of taxes at full *one half* their present amount. By a measure of this kind, much distress and injury must certainly be experienced among the *tax receivers* and dependents of the government. But this distress and injury have already been experienced in a *sevenfold degree* by the *tax payers*. The same justice *ought* to exist for one as for the other. We could have wished that all distress and injury might have been prevented, among either of these great divisions of society, by a just and proper adaptation of the money of the country, to the existing state of the taxes, rents, debts, contracts, and obligations of the country. By this great measure, all the distress which the country has endured, *might have been prevented*. By this great measure, all the distress which the country now suffers, *may yet be relieved*. By this great measure, the general state of prosperity which existed in the years 1824 and 1825, *may yet be restored, and rendered permanent throughout the country.*

All this was and is in the power of the Government, *unless indeed the devastation of agriculture, combined with the exclusion of Foreign grain from our markets, have already destroyed the stocks of provisions necessary for the support of the Population.*

But the Government have refused this just, wholesome, and necessary measure. Instead of *adjusting the measure of value*, they have decreed that the country shall be forced through the rugged path *of adjusting the innumerable things which it measures!!* Instead of accommodating their money to the existing habits and associations of men's minds, and to the state of prices, Taxes, Contracts, Wages, Rents, Debts, and obligations existing among the present generation of men, they have thought proper to *force back* all those great interests into conformity with an ancient obsolete and unsuitable Standard of value! It is through this *rugged road*, that the Government *compels the nation to travel*. Be it so then. The government have chosen their *own path*. It is but just that it should lead them to the same reckoning as it brings the country. It is but just that the *Taxes of the Government* should be reduced in the same degree as the *wages of labour*. The government will give *to us* the *ancient prices* and the *ancient wages*. We will give to *them* the *ancient Taxes* and the *ancient Salaries*. All their salaries, payments, and expences were doubled in *depreciated money*. But they were not doubled in the *ancient coins*. Nor shall they so be doubled *with our consent*. We will give them *one-half* the present *monied amount of the Taxes*. We will give them the *full amount* of the *property and labour* which we contracted to give them when the present taxes were imposed. But we will not willingly give them one shilling more. This is the line of conduct which the government *forces* upon us. The taxes of the country are now *doubled in real value*, by the increase which is effected in the value of the money in which they are collected. And when the present monetary measures of the government shall have produced their full effect in *forcing down* the prices of British property and labour to the continental level, there can then be no doubt that the pressure of the taxes upon the industrious classes will be *double what it now is.*

Unless the taxes, therefore, are reduced in the same degree as the value of money is raised, all the property and all the labour of the country will be laid prostrate at the feet of the government! *Therefore the taxes must be reduced.*

One other subject requires the most serious investigation. No one can have read the Bank Reports of the two houses of parliament, upon which, the Act which has had the effect of confiscating the property and labour of the industrious classes was founded in 1819, without being struck with the remarkable discrepancy which exists between the *evidence given*, and the *decision come to*. Almost every witness that was examined, gave *warning* of the general *distress* which such a tremendous measure must produce; but when the distress came, it was strangely and perversely attributed to every possible *cause* that could be imagined, *excepting only the one which the witnesses had pointed out and foretold!!* Nor can any one have attended to the proceedings of Parliament for the last ten years, without being still more forcibly struck with the oblique and pertinaceous determination which has been constantly exhibited, to refuse all further enquiry into this most important subject. The subject indeed has been *shunned* as a very pestilence, as if it were not possible to allude to it without some great and undefined danger, which it was of the last importance to avoid. In the mean while it is undoubted that this very measure has occasioned hundreds of millions sterling of *profit* to some parties, whilst much greater losses have been occasioned to others. Now, if any part of this enormous and unjust *profit* should have found its way *corruptly* into the pockets of individuals who may possibly have made both the Parliament and the country their *dupes*, the national justice most certainly requires that such individuals, in whatever station, should be brought to trial, and to condign punishment.

When the notorious *South Sea Scheme* was exposed and brought to light about a hundred years ago, the whole country resounded with petitions from all quarters, calling for justice on the heads of the guilty. In this nefarious conspiracy, members of Parliament, Lords of the Treasury, Chancellors of the Exchequer, and Secretaries of State, were found implicated; *and all were brought to justice.* An Act of Parliament was passed, to prevent the parties implicated from leaving the kingdom; and also from alienating their estates and effects. Another Act of Parliament was passed for the purpose of enquiring into the *private fortunes* of the directors and promoters of the scheme; and of compelling them to give up the plunder which they had made. Under this act of parliament, the directors were compelled to give up from their *private fortunes*, the sum of £1,700,000. an immense sum in those days, which was afterwards distributed among their victims as some small compensation, for the losses which they had sustained. Upon the present occasion, there can be no doubt that the losses and injuries which have already been inflicted by the Act of 1819, have been a hundred times greater than any which attended the South Sea Scheme. It is, therefore, of the highest importance, that an effectual Parliamentary enquiry should be instituted into this mysterious subject, and that any individuals, who may *corruptly* have derived profit from the national injuries, should be compelled to give up such profit for the purpose of distributing it among the victims of their policy, or of otherwise appropriating it as circumstances may require.

Thousands of respectable families have been ruined. Tens of thousands have been more or less impoverished and deprived of the hard-earned fruits of their honest industry. Hundreds of thousands of valuable workmen have been deprived of employment and reduced to a state of indigence and degradation. The whole country has been covered with difficulties, discords and anxieties, with losses, injuries and privations, with broken fortunes, with broken hearts. Who has done these things? *A national investigation must be instituted.*

On whatsoever side we turn our eyes, we thus find subjects of the highest public importance every where demanding the public attention, and every where requiring the legal interference of the industrious classes. The vindication of the National Justice, the equalization and reduction of the National Taxes, the protection of public rights, The Redress of Public Wrongs, the necessity of Reform in Parliament, and the relief of the National Distress, *all require that the* National Mind *should slumber no more.*

Under these views and impressions, it is therefore that we propose to form in Birmingham, a General Political Union of the Industrious Classes, for the Protection of Public Rights. We are forbidden to exercise the constitutional privilege of electing Members of Parliament. But we are not forbidden to appoint *Councils of our own*, under whose guidance we may act, and through whose means we may bring the moral force of the public opinion, to act legally upon the legislative functions. By means of these *councils* dependent on the breath of the People, and representing the true interests of the People, we may yet hope to have the Rights, Liberties, and Interests of All peacefully and legally restored and secured. We shall, at any rate, succeed in collecting and organizing the public opinion, and in bringing the public wrongs and grievances to the knowledge of the legislative bodies, and more particularly of the Crown itself, the natural refuge of the people under all complaints against the House of Commons. Our Gracious King still possesses high and extensive prerogatives regarding the elections of members of Parliament, and those prerogatives we cannot doubt that he will put in force for the protection of his faithful people, whenever their wants and interests shall have been fully and efficiently made known to him.

The following then are

THE OBJECTS OF THE POLITICAL UNION

1st.—To obtain by every just and legal means, such a Reform in the Commons' House of Parliament, as may ensure a *real* and *effectual* Representation of the Lower and Middle Classes of the People in that House.

2nd.—To enquire, consult, consider, and determine respecting the rights and liberties of the industrious classes, and respecting the legal means of securing those which remain and recovering those which are lost.

3rd.—To prepare Petitions, addresses, and Remonstrances to the Crown and the Legislative Bodies, respecting the *preservation* and *restoration* of Public Rights, and respecting the repeal of *bad laws*, and the enactment of *good laws*.

4th.—To prevent and redress as far as practicable, all *local public wrongs and oppressions*, and all *local encroachments* upon the rights, interests, and privileges of the community.

5th.—To obtain the repeal of the Malt and the Bear Taxes; and, in general, to obtain an alteration in the system of taxation, so as to cause it to press less severely upon the industrious classes of the community, and more equally upon the wealthy classes.

6th.—To obtain the *reduction of each separate Tax and expence* of the Government in the same degree as the *legislative increase* in the *value of money*, has increased their *respective values*, and *has reduced and is reducing the general prices of labour* throughout the country.

7th.—To promote *peace*, union, and concord, among all classes of His Majesty's subjects, and to guide and direct the public mind into uniform, peaceful, and legitimate operations; instead of leaving it to waste its strength in loose, desultory, and unconnected exertions, or to carve to its own objects, unguided, unassisted, and uncontrouled.

8th.—To collect and organize the peaceful expression of the Public Opinion, so as to bring it to act upon the legislative functions in a just, legal, and effectual way.

9th.—To influence by every legal means, the elections of members of Parliament, so as to promote the return of upright and capable representatives of the People.

10th.—To adopt such measures as may be legal and necessary for the purpose of obtaining an effectual Parliamentary investigation into the situation of the country, and into the cause of its embarrassments and difficulties; with the view of relieving the National Distress, or rendering justice to the injured as far as practicable, and of bringing to trial, any individuals in whatever station, who may be found to have acted from criminal or corrupt motives.

Statement by the duke of Wellington, the prime minister, opposing parliamentary reform, House of Lords, 2 November 1830

Hansard, 3.s., 1, 52-53.

Sir Arthur Wellesley (1769-1852), first duke of Wellington (1814), was prime minister from January 1828 to November 1830 and again for a brief period in November 1834. In this speech Wellington eulogised the existing political system, contending that it possessed the country's confidence. He resigned on 16 November, and the Whigs, pledged to parliamentary reform, took office under Lord Grey.

. . . The noble Earl [Lord Grey] had alluded to the propriety of effecting Parliamentary Reform. The noble Earl had, however, been candid enough to acknowledge that he was not prepared with any measure of reform, and he could have no scruple in saying that his Majesty's Government was as totally unprepared with any plan as the noble Lord. Nay, he, on his own part, would go further, and say, that he had never read or heard of any measure up to the present moment which could in any degree satisfy his mind that the state of the representation could be improved, or be rendered more satisfactory to the country at large than at the present moment. He would not, however, at such an unseasonable time, enter upon the subject, or excite discussion, but he should not hesitate to declare unequivocally what were his sentiments upon it. He was fully convinced that the country possessed at the present moment a Legislature which answered all the good purposes of legislation, and this to a greater degree than any Legislature ever had answered in any country whatever. He would go further and say, that the Legislature and the system of representation possessed the full and entire confidence of the country— deservedly possessed that confidence—and the discussions in the Legislature had a very great influence over the opinions of the country. He would go still further and say, that if at the present moment he had imposed upon him the duty of forming a Legislature for any country, and particularly for a country like this, in possession of great property of various descriptions, he did not mean to assert that he could form such a Legislature as they possessed now, for the nature of man was incapable of reaching such excellence at once; but his great endeavour would be, to form some description of legislature which would produce the same results. The representation of the people at present contained a large body of the property of the country, and in which the landed interests had a preponderating influence. Under these circumstances, he was not prepared to bring forward any measure of the description alluded to by the noble Lord. He was not only not prepared to bring forward any measure of this nature, but he would at once declare that as far as he was concerned, as long as he held any station in the government of the country, he should always feel it his duty to resist such measures when proposed by others.

Speech by Thomas Babington Macaulay supporting the first Reform Bill, House of Commons, 2 March 1831

Hansard, 3.s., II, 1190-1205.

In March 1831 Lord John Russell introduced the first Reform Bill. In an eloquent speech, Thomas Babington Macaulay (1800-59; first Baron Macaulay, 1857), the Whig reformer and future historian, endorsed the measure. The bill passed the Commons on its second reading by one vote, but was rejected by the House of Lords. A slightly modified Reform Bill passed through Parliament and received the royal assent in June 1832. Russell (1792-1878; cr. first Earl Russell of Kingston Russell, 1861) later served as leader of the Whigs in the House of Commons (1834), home secretary (1835-39), colonial secretary (1838-41), prime minister (1846-52, 1865-66), foreign secretary (1852-53, 1859-65), and president of the council (1854-55).

It is a circumstance, Sir, of happy augury for the measure before the House, that almost all those who have opposed it have declared themselves altogether hostile to the principle of Reform. Two Members, I think, have professed, that though they disapprove of the plan now submitted to us, they yet conceive some alteration of the Representative system to be advisable. Yet even those Gentlemen have used, as far as I have observed, no arguments which would not apply as strongly to the most moderate change, as to that which has been proposed by his Majesty's Government. I say, Sir, that I consider this as a circumstance of happy augury. For what I feared was, not the opposition of those who shrink from all Reform,—but the disunion of reformers. I knew, that during three months every reformer had been employed in conjecturing what the plan of the Government would be. I knew, that every reformer had imagined in his own mind a scheme differing doubtless in some points from that which my noble friend, the Paymaster of the Forces, has developed. I felt therefore great apprehension that one person would be dissatisfied with one part of the Bill, that another person would be dissatisfied with another part, and that thus our whole strength would be wasted in internal dissensions. That apprehension is not at an end. I have seen with delight the perfect concord which prevails among all who deserve the name of reformers in this House, and I trust that I may consider it as an omen of the concord which will prevail among reformers throughout the country. I will not, Sir, at present express any opinion as to the details of the Bill; but having during the last twenty-four hours, given the most diligent consideration to its general principles, I have no hesitation in pronouncing it a wise, noble, and comprehensive measure, skilfully framed for the healing of great distempers, for the securing at once of the public liberties and of the public repose, and for the reconciling and knitting together of all the orders of the State. The hon. Baronet (Sir John Walsh) who has just sat down has told us, that the Ministers have attempted to unite two inconsistent principles in one abortive measure. He thinks, if I understand him rightly, that they ought either to leave the representative system such as it is, or to make it symmetrical. I think, Sir, that they would have acted unwisely if they had taken either of these courses. Their principle is plain, rational, and consistent. It is this,—to admit the middle class to a large and direct share in the Representation, without any violent shock to the institutions of our country [hear!] I understand those cheers—but surely the Gentlemen who utter them will allow, that the change made in our institutions by this measure is far less violent than that which, according to the hon. Baronet, ought to be made if we make any Reform at all. I praise the Ministers for not attempting, under existing circumstances, to make the Representation uniform—I praise them for not effacing the old distinction between the towns and the counties,—for not assigning Members to districts, according to the American practice, by the Rule of Three. They have done all that was necessary for the removing of a great practical evil, and no more than was necessary. I consider this, Sir, as a practical question. I rest my opinion on no general theories of government. I will not positively say, that there is any form of polity which may not, under some conceivable circumstances, be the best possible. I believe that there are societies in which every man may safely be admitted to vote [hear!]. Gentlemen may cheer, but such in my opinion. I say, Sir, that there are countries in which the condition of the labouring classes is such that they may safely be intrusted with the right of electing Members of the Legislature. If the labourers of England were in that state in which I, from my soul, wish to see them,—if employment were always plentiful, wages always high, food always cheap,—if a large family were considered not as an encumbrance, but as a blessing—the principal objections to Universal Suffrage would, I think, be removed. Universal Suffrage exists in the United States without producing any very frightful consequences; and I do not believe; that the people of those States, or of any part of the world, are in any good quality naturally superior to our own countrymen. But, unhappily, the lower orders in England, and in all old countries, are occasionally in a state of great distress. Some of the causes of this distress are, I fear, beyond the control of the Government. We know what effect distress produces, even on people more intelligent than the great body of the labouring classes can possibly be. We know that it makes even wise men irritable, unreasonable, and credulous—eager for immediate relief—heedless of remote consequences. There is no quackery in medicine, religion, or politics, which may not impose even on a powerful mind when that mind has been disordered by pain or fear. It is therefore no reflection on the lower orders of Englishmen, who are not, and who cannot in the nature of things be highly educated, to say that distress produces on them its natural effects, those effects which it would produce on the Americans, or on any other people,—that it blunts their judgment, that it inflames their passions, that it makes them prone to believe those who flatter them, and to distrust those who would serve them. For the sake, therefore, of the whole society, for the sake of the labouring classes themselves, I hold it to be clearly expedient, that in a country like this, the right of suffrage should depend on a pecuniary qualification. Every argument, Sir, which would induce me to oppose Universal Suffrage, induces me to support the measure which is now before us. I oppose Universal Suffrage, because I think that it would produce a destructive revolution. I support this measure, because I am sure that it is our best security against a revolution. The noble Paymaster of the Forces hinted, delicately indeed and remotely, at this subject. He spoke of the danger of disappointing the expectations of the nation; and for this he was charged with threatening the House. Sir, in the year 1817, the late Lord Londonderry proposed a suspension of the Habeas Corpus Act. On that occasion he told the House, that, unless the measures which he recommended were adopted, the public peace could not be preserved. Was he accused of threatening the House? Again, in the year 1819, he brought in the bills known by the name of the Six Acts. He then told the House, that, unless the executive power were reinforced, all the institutions of the country would be overturned by popular violence. Was he then accused of threatening the House? Will any Gentleman say, that it is parliamentary and decorous to urge the danger arising from popular discontent as an argument for severity; but that it is unparliamentary and indecorous to urge that same danger as an argument for conciliatory measures? I, Sir, do entertain great apprehension for the fate of my country. I do in my conscience believe, that unless this measure, or some similar measure, be speedily adopted, great and terrible calamities will befal us. Entertaining this opinion, I think myself bound to state it, not as a threat, but as a reason. I support this measure as a measure of Reform: but I support it still more as a measure of conservation. That we may exclude those whom it is necessary to exclude, we must admit those whom it may be safe to admit. At present we oppose the schemes of revolutionists with only one half, with only one quarter of our proper force. We say, and we say justly, that it is not by mere numbers, but by property and intelligence, that the nation ought to be governed. Yet, saying this, we exclude from all share in the government vast masses of property and intelligence,—vast numbers of those who are most interested in preserving tranquillity, and who know best how to preserve it. We do more. We drive over to the side of revolution those whom we shut out from power. Is this a time when the cause of law and order can spare one of its natural allies? My noble friend, the Paymaster of the Forces, happily described the effect which some parts of our representative system would produce on the mind of a foreigner, who had heard much of our freedom and greatness. If, Sir, I wished to make such a foreigner clearly understand what I consider as the great defects of our system, I would conduct him through that great city which lies to the north of Great Russell-street and Oxford-street,—a city superior in size and in population to the capitals of many mighty kingdoms; and probably superior in opulence, intelligence, and general respectability; to any city in the world. I would conduct him through that interminable succession of streets and squares, all consisting of well-built and well-furnished houses. I would make him observe the brilliancy of the shops, and the crowd of well-appointed equipages. I would lead him round that magnificent circle of palaces which surrounds the Regent's-park. I would tell him, that the rental of this district was far greater than that of the whole kingdom of Scotland, at the time of the Union. And then I would tell him, that this was an unrepresented district! It is needless to give any more instances. It is needless to speak of Manchester, Birmingham, Leeds, Sheffield, with no representation; or of Edinburgh and Glasgow with a mock representation. If a property-tax were now imposed on the old principle, that no person who had less than 150l. a year should contribute, I should not be surprised to find, that one-half in number and value of the contributors had no votes at all; and it would, beyond all doubt, be found, that one-fiftieth part in number and value of the contributors had a larger share of the representation than the other forty-nine-fiftieths. This is not government by property. It is government by certain detached portions and fragments of property, selected from the rest, and preferred to the rest, on no rational principle whatever. To say that such a system is ancient is no defence. My hon. friend, the member for the University of Oxford (Sir. R. Inglis) challenges us to show, that the Constitution was ever better than it is. Sir, we are legislators, not antiquaries. The question for us is, not whether the Constitution was better formerly, but whether we can make it better now. In fact, however, the system was not in ancient times by any means so absurd as it is in our age. One noble Lord (Lord Stormont) has to-night told us, that the town of Aldborough, which he represents, was not larger in the time of Edward 1st than it is at present. The line of its walls, he assures us, may still be traced. It is now built up to that line. He argues, therefore, that, as the founders of our representative institutions gave Members to Aldborough when it was as small as it now is, those who would disfranchise it on account of its smallness have no right to say, that they are recurring to the original principle of our representative institutions. But does the noble Lord remember the change which has taken place in the country during the last five centuries? Does he remember how much England has grown in population, while Aldborough has been standing still? Does he consider, that in the time of Edward 1st this part of the island did not contain two millions of inhabitants? It now contains nearly fourteen millions. A hamlet of the present day would have been a place of some importance in the time of our early Parliaments. Aldborough may be absolutely as considerable a place as ever. But compared with the kingdom, it is much less considerable, by the noble Lord's own showing, than when it first elected burgesses. My hon. friend, the member for the University of Oxford, has collected numerous instances of the tyranny which the kings and nobles anciently exercised, both over this House, and over the electors. It is not strange, that, in times when nothing was held sacred, the rights of the people, and of the Representatives of the people, should not have been held sacred. The proceedings which my hon. friend has mentioned, no more prove, that, by the ancient constitution of the realm, this House ought to be a tool of the king and of the aristocracy, than the Benevolences and the Ship-money prove their own legality; or than those unjustifiable arrests, which took place long after the ratification of the great Charter, and even after the Petition of Right, prove that the subject was not anciently entitled to his personal liberty. We talk of the wisdom of our ancestors—and in one respect at least they were wiser than we. They legislated for their own times. They looked at the England which was before them. They did not think it necessary to give twice as many Members to York as they gave to London, because York had been the capital of Britain in the time of Constantious Chlorus; and they would have been amazed indeed if they had foreseen, that a city of more than a hundred thousand inhabitants would be left without Representatives in the nineteenth century, merely because it stood on ground which, in the thirteenth century, had been occupied by a few huts. They formed a representative system, which was not indeed without defects and irregularities, but which was well adapted to the state of England in their time. But a great revolution took place. The character of the old corporations changed. New forms of property came into existence. New portions of society rose into importance. There were in our rural districts rich cultivators, who were not freeholders. There were in our capital rich traders, who were not liverymen. Towns shrank into villages. Villages swelled into cities larger than the London of the Plantagenets. Unhappily, while the natural growth of society went on, the artificial polity continued unchanged. The ancient form of the representation remained; and precisely because the form remained, the spirit departed. Then came that pressure almost to bursting—the new wine in the old bottles—the new people under the old institutions. It is now time for us to pay a decent, a rational, a manly reverence to our ancestors—not by superstitiously adhering to what they, under other circumstances, did, but by doing what they, in our circumstances, would have done. All history is full of revolutions, produced by causes similar to those which are now operating in England. A portion of the community which had been of no account, expands and becomes strong. It demands a place in the system, suited, not to its former weakness, but to its present power. If this is granted, all is well. If this is refused, then comes the struggle between the young energy of one class, and the ancient privileges of another. Such was the struggle between the Plebeians and the Patricians of Rome. Such was the struggle of the Italian allies for admission to the full rights of Roman citizens. Such was the struggle of our North American colonies against the mother country. Such was the struggle which the *Tiers Etat* of France maintained against the aristocracy of birth. Such was the struggle which the Catholics of Ireland maintained against the aristocracy of creed. Such is the struggle which the free people of colour in Jamaica are now maintaining against the aristocracy of skin. Such, finally, is the struggle which the middle classes in England are maintaining against an aristocracy of mere locality—against an aristocracy, the principle of which is to invest 100 drunken pot-wallopers in one place, or the owner of a ruined hovel in another, with powers which are withheld from cities renowned to the furthest ends of the earth, for the marvels of their wealth and of their industry. But these great cities, says my hon. friend, the member for Oxford, are virtually, though not directly represented. Are not the wishes of Manchester, he asks, as much consulted as those of any town which sends Members to Parliament? Now, Sir, I do not understand how a power which is salutary when exercised virtually, can be noxious when exercised directly. If the wishes of Manchester have as much weight with us, as they would have under a system which should give Representatives to Manchester, how can there be any danger in giving Representatives to Manchester? A virtual Representative is, I presume, a man who acts as a direct Representative would act: for surely it would be absurd to say, that a man virtually represents the people of property in Manchester, who is in the habit of saying No, when a man directly representing the people of property in Manchester would say Aye. The utmost that can be expected from virtual Representation is, that it may be as good as direct Representation. If so, why not grant direct Representation to places which, as every body allows, ought, by some process or other, to be represented? If it be said, that there is an evil in change as change, I answer, that there is also an evil in discontent as discontent. This, indeed, is the strongest part of our case. It is said that the system works well. I deny it. I deny that a system works well, which the people regard with aversion. We may say here, that it is a good system and a perfect system. But if any man were to say so to any 658 respectable farmers or shopkeepers, chosen by lot in any part of England, he would be hooted down, and laughed to scorn. Are these the feelings with which any part of the Government ought to be regarded? Above all, are these the feelings with which the popular branch of the Legislature ought to be regarded? It is almost as essential to the utility of a House of Commons, that it should possess the confidence of the people, as that it should deserve that confidence. Unfortunately, that which is in theory the popular part of our Government, is in practice the unpopular part. Who wishes to dethrone the King? Who wishes to turn the Lords out of their House? Here and there a crazy radical, whom the boys in the street point at as he walks along. Who wishes to alter the constitution of this House? The whole people. It is natural that it should be so. The House of Commons is, in the language of Mr. Burke, a check for the people—not on the people, but for the people. While that check is efficient, there is no reason to fear that the King or the nobles will oppress the people. But if that check requires checking, how is it to be checked? If the salt shall lose its savour, wherewith shall we season it? The distrust with which the nation regards this House may be unjust. But what then? Can you remove that distrust? That it exists cannot be denied. That it is an evil cannot be denied. That it is an increasing evil cannot be denied. One Gentleman tells us that it has been produced by the late events in France and Belgium; another, that it is the effect of seditious works which have lately been published. If this feeling be of origin so recent, I have read history to little purpose. Sir, this alarming discontent is not the growth of a day or of a year. If there be any symptoms by which it is possible to distinguish the chronic diseases of the body politic from its passing inflammations, all these symptoms exist in the present case. The taint has been gradually becoming more extensive and more malignant, through the whole life-time of two generations. We have tried anodynes. We have tried cruel operations. What are we to try now? Who flatters himself that he can turn this feeling back? Does there remain any argument which escaped the comprehensive intellect of Mr. Burke, or the subtlety of Mr. Wyndham? Does there remain any species of coercion which was not tried by Mr. Pitt and by Lord Londonderry? We have had laws. We have had blood. New treasons have been created. The Press has been shackled. The Habeas Corpus Act has been suspended. Public meetings have been prohibited. The event has proved that these expedients were mere palliatives. You are at the end of your palliatives. The evil remains. It is more formidable than ever. What is to be done? Under such circumstances, a great measure of reconciliation, prepared by the Ministers of the Crown, has been brought before us in a manner which gives additional lustre to a noble name, inseparably associated during two centuries with the dearest liberties of the English people. I will not say, that the measure is in all its details precisely such as I might wish it to be; but it is founded on a great and a sound principle. It takes away a vast power from a few. It distributes that power through the great mass of the middle order. Every man, therefore, who thinks as I think, is bound to stand firmly by Ministers, who are resolved to stand or fall with this measure. Were I one of them, I would sooner—infinitely sooner—fall with such a measure than stand by any other means that ever supported a Cabinet. My hon. friend, the member for the University of Oxford tells us, that if we pass this law, England will soon be a republic. The reformed House of Commons will, according to him, before it has sat ten years, depose the King, and expel the Lords from their House. Sir, if my hon. friend could prove this, he would have succeeded in bringing an argument for democracy, infinitely stronger than any that is to be found in the works of Paine. His proposition is in fact this—that our monarchical and aristocratical institutions have no hold on the public mind of England; that those institutions are regarded with aversion by a decided majority of the middle class. This, Sir, I say, is plainly deducible from his proposition; for he tells us, that the Representatives of the middle class will inevitably abolish royalty and nobility within ten years: and there is surely no reason to think that the Representatives of the middle class will be more inclined to a democratic revolution than their constituents. Now, Sir, if I were convinced that the great body of the middle class in England look with aversion on monarchy and aristocracy, I should be forced, much against my will, to come to this conclusion, that monarchical and aristocratical institutions are unsuited to this country. Monarchy and aristocracy, valuable and useful as I think them, are still valuable and useful as means, and not as ends. The end of government is the happiness of the people: and I do not conceive that, in a country like this, the happiness of the people can be promoted by a form of government, in which the middle classes place no confidence, and which exists only because the middle classes have no organ by which to make their sentiments known. But, Sir, I am fully convinced that the middle classes sincerely wish to uphold the Royal prerogatives, and the constitutional rights of the Peers. What facts does my hon. friend produce in support of his opinion? One fact only—and that a fact which has absolutely nothing to do with the question. The effect of this Reform, he tells us, would be, to make the House of Commons all-powerful. It was all-powerful once before, in the beginning of 1649. Then it cut off the head of the King, and abolished the House of Peers. Therefore, if this Reform should take place, it will act in the same manner. Now, Sir, it was not the House of Commons that cut off the head of Charles the 1st; nor was the House of Commons then all-powerful. It had been greatly reduced in numbers by successive expulsions. It was under the absolute dominion of the army. A majority of the House was willing to take the terms offered by the King. The soldiers turned out the majority; and the minority—not a sixth part of the whole House—passed those votes of which my hon. friend speaks—votes of which the middle classes disapproved then, and of which they disapprove still.

My hon. friend, and almost all the Gentlemen who have taken the same side with him in this Debate, have dwelt much on the utility of close and rotten boroughs. It is by means of such boroughs, they tell us, that the ablest men have been introduced into Parliament. It is true that many distinguished persons have represented places of this description. But, Sir, we must judge of a form of government by its general tendency, not by happy accidents. Every form of government has its happy accidents. Despotism has its happy accidents. Yet we are not disposed to abolish all constitutional checks, to place an absolute master over us, and to take our chance whether he may be a Caligula or a Marcus Aurelius. In whatever way the House of Commons may be chosen, some able men will be chosen in that way who would not be chosen in any other way. If there were a law that the hundred tallest men in England should be Members in Parliament, there would probably be some able men among those who would come into the House by virtue of this law. If the hundred persons whose names stand first in the alphabetical list of the Court Guide were made Members of Parliament, there would probably be able men among them. We read in ancient history, that a very able king was elected by the neighing of his horse. But we shall scarcely, I think, adopt this mode of election. In one of the most celebrated republics of antiquity—Athens—the Senators and Magistrates were chosen by lot; and sometimes the lot fell fortunately. Once, for example, Socrates was in office. A cruel and unjust measure was brought forward. Socrates resisted it at the hazard of his own life. There is no event in Grecian history more interesting than that memorable resistance. Yet who would have offices assigned by lot, because the accident of the lot may have given to a great and good man a power which he would probably never have attained in any other way? We must judge, as I said, by the general tendency of a system. No person can doubt that a House of Commons chosen freely by the middle classes will contain many very able men. I do not say, that precisely the same able men who would find their way into the present House of Commons, will find their way into the reformed House—but that is not the question. No particular man is necessary to the State. We may depend on it, that if we provide the country with free institutions, those institutions will provide it with great men. There is another objection, which, I think, was first raised by the hon. and learned member for Newport (Mr. H. Twiss). He tells us that the elective franchise is property—that to take it away from a man who has not been judicially convicted of any malpractices is robbery—that no crime is proved against the voters in the close boroughs—that no crime is even imputed to them in the preamble of the Bill—and that to disfranchise them without compensation, would therefore be an act of revolutionary tyranny. The hon. and learned Gentleman has compared the conduct of the present Ministers to that of those odious tools of power, who, towards the close of the reign of Charles the 2nd, seized the charters of the Whig Corporations. Now there was another precedent, which I wonder that he did not recollect, both because it was much more nearly in point than that to which he referred, and because my noble friend, the Paymaster of the Forces, had previously alluded to it. If the elective franchise is property—if to disfranchise voters without a crime proved, or a compensation given, be robbery—was there ever such an act of robbery as the disfranchising of the Irish forty-shilling freeholders? Was any pecuniary compensation given to them? Is it declared in the preamble of the bill which took away their votes, that they had been convicted of any offence? Was any judicial inquiry instituted into their conduct? Were they even accused of any crime? Or say, that it was a crime in the electors of Clare to vote for the hon. and learned Gentleman who now represents the county of Waterford—was a Protestant forty-shilling freeholder in Louth, to be punished for the crime of a Catholic forty-shilling freeholder in Clare? If the principle of the hon. and learned member for Newport be sound, the franchise of the Irish peasant was property. That franchise, the Ministry under which the hon. and learned Member held office, did not scruple to take away. Will he accuse the late Ministers of robbery? If not, how can he bring such an accusation against their successors? Every gentleman, I think, who has spoken from the other side of the House has alluded to the opinions which some of his Majesty's Ministers formerly entertained on the subject of Reform. It would be officious in me, Sir, to undertake the defence of Gentlemen who are so well able to defend themselves. I will only say, that, in my opinion, the country will not think worse either of their talents or of their patriotism, because they have shown that they can profit by experience, because they have learned to see the folly of delaying inevitable changes. There are others who ought to have learned the same lesson. I say, Sir, that there are those who, I should have thought, must have had enough to last them all their lives of that humiliation which follows obstinate and boastful resistance to measures rendered necessary by the progress of society, and by the development of the human mind. Is it possible that those persons can wish again to occupy a position, which can neither be defended, nor surrendered with honour? I well remember, Sir, a certain evening in the month of May, 1827. I had not then the honour of a seat in this House; but I was an attentive observer of its proceedings. The right hon. Baronet opposite, (Sir R. Peel) of whom personally I desire to speak with that high respect which I feel for his talents and his character, but of whose public conduct I must speak with the sincerity required by my public duty, was then, as he is now, out of office. He had just resigned the Seals of the Home Department, because he conceived that the Administration of Mr. Canning was favourable to the Catholic claims. He rose to ask whether it was the intention of the new Cabinet to repeal the Test and Corporation Acts, and to reform the Parliament. He bound up, I well remember, those two questions together; and he declared, that if the Ministers should either attempt to repeal the Test and Corporation Acts, or bring forward a measure of Parliamentary Reform, he should think it his duty to oppose them to the utmost. Since that declaration was made nearly four years have elapsed; and what is now the state of the three questions which then chiefly agitated the minds of men? What is become of the Test and Corporation Acts? They are repealed. By whom? By the late Administration. What has become of the Catholic disabilities? They are removed. By whom? By the late Administration. The question of Parliamentary Reform is still behind. But signs, of which it is impossible to misconceive the import, do most clearly indicate, that, unless that question also be speedily settled, property and order, and all the institutions of this great monarchy, will be exposed to fearful peril. Is it possible, that Gentlemen long versed in high political affairs cannot read these signs? Is it possible that they can really believe that the Representative system of England, such as it now is, will last till the year 1860? If not, for what would they have us wait? Would they have us wait merely that we may show to all the world how little we have profited by our own recent experience? Would they have us wait, that we may once again hit the exact point where we can neither refuse with authority, nor concede with grace? Would they have us wait, that the numbers of the discontented party may become larger, its demands higher, its feeling more acrimonious, its organization more complete? Would they have us wait till the whole tragi-comedy of 1827 has been acted over again; till they have been brought into office by a cry of "No Reform!" to be reformers, as they were once before brought into office by a cry of "No Popery!" to be emancipators? Have they obliterated from their minds—gladly perhaps would some among them obliterate from their minds—the transactions of that year? And have they forgotten all the transactions of the succeeding year? Have they forgotten how the spirit of liberty in Ireland, debarred from its natural outlet, found a vent by forbidden passages? Have they forgotten how we were forced to indulge the Catholics in all the license of rebels, merely because we chose to withhold from them the liberties of subjects? Do they wait for associations more formidable than that of the Corn Exchange,—for contributions larger than the Rent,—for agitators more violent than those who, three years ago, divided with the King and the Parliament, the sovereignty of Ireland? Do they wait for that last and most dreadful paroxysm of popular rage,—for that last and most cruel test to military fidelity? Let them wait, if their past experience shall induce them to think that any high honour or any exquisite pleasure is to be obtained by a policy like this. Let them wait, if this strange and fearful infatuation be indeed upon them,—that they should not see with their eyes, or hear with their ears, or understand with their heart. But let us know our interest and our duty better. Turn where we may,   within,—around,—the voice of great events is proclaiming to us, Reform, that you may preserve. Now, therefore, while every thing at home and abroad forebodes ruin to those who persist in a hopeless struggle against the spirit of the age,—now, while the crash of the proudest throne of the continent is still resounding in our ears,—now, while the roof of a British palace affords an ignominious shelter to the exiled heir of forty kings,—now, while we see on every side ancient institutions subverted, and great societies dissolved,—now, while the heart of England is still sound,—now, while the old feelings and the old associations retain a power and a charm which may too soon pass away,—now, in this your accepted time,—now in this your day of salvation,—take counsel, not of prejudice,—not of party spirit,—not of the ignominious pride of a fatal consistency,—but of history,—of reason,—of the ages which are past,—of the signs of this most portentous time. Pronounce in a manner worthy of the expectation with which this great Debate has been anticipated, and of the long remembrance which it will leave behind. Renew the youth of the State. Save property divided against itself. Save the multitude, endangered by their own ungovernable passions. Save the aristocracy, endangered by its own unpopular power. Save the greatest, and fairest, and most highly civilized community that ever existed, from calamities which may in a few days sweep away all the rich heritage of so many ages of wisdom and glory. The danger is terrible. The time is short. If this Bill should be rejected, I pray to God that none of those who concur in rejecting it may ever remember their votes with unavailing regret, amidst the wreck of laws, the confusion of ranks, the spoliation of property, and the dissolution of social order.

Reform Act, 7 June 1832

2 Will. 4, c. 45   *Statutes at Large*, LXXII, 154-66.

The act in its most important provisions created a uniform £10 household suffrage in boroughs and brought about a significant redistribution of seats.

Whereas it is expedient to take effectual Measures for correcting divers Abuses that have long prevailed in the Choice of Members to serve in the Commons House of Parliament, to deprive many inconsiderable Places of the Right of returning Members, to grant such Privilege to large, populous, and wealthy Towns, to increase the Number of Knights of the Shire, to extend the Elective Franchise to many of His Majesty's Subjects who have not heretofore enjoyed the same, and to diminish the Expence of Elections; be it therefore enacted by the King's most Excellent Majesty, by and with the Advice and Consent of the Lords Spiritual and Temporal, and Commons, in this present Parliament assembled, and by the Authority of the same, That each of the Boroughs enumerated in the Schedule marked (A.) to this Act annexed, (that is to say,) *Old Sarum, Newtown, St. Michael's* or *Midshall, Gatton, Bramber, Bossiney, Dunwich, Ludgershall, St. Mawe's, Beeralston, West Looe, St. Germain's, Newport, Blechingley, Aldborough, Camelford, Hindon, East Looe, Corfe Castle, Great Bedwin, Yarmouth, Queenborough, Castle Rising, East Grinstead, Higham Ferrers, Wendover, Weobly, Winchelsea, Tregony, Haslemere, Saltash, Orford, Callington, Newton, Ilchester, Boroughbridge, Stockbridge, New Romney, Hedon, Plympton, Seaford, Heytesbury, Steyning, Whitchurch, Wootton Bassett, Downton, Fowey, Milborne Port, Aldeburgh, Minehead, Bishop's Castle, Okehampton, Appleby, Lostwithiel, Brackley,* and *Amersham,* shall from and after the End of this present Parliament cease to return any Member or Members to serve in Parliament.

II.   And be it enacted, That each of the Boroughs enumerated in the Schedule marked (B.) to this Act annexed, (that is to say,) *Petersfield, Ashburton, Eye, Westbury, Wareham, Midhurst, Woodstock, Wilton, Malmesbury, Liskeard, Reigate, Hythe, Droitwich, Lyme Regis, Launceston, Shaftesbury, Thirsk, Christchurch, Horsham, Great Grimsby, Calne, Arundel, St. Ives, Rye, Clitheroe, Morpeth, Helston, North Allerton, Wallingford,* and *Dartmouth,* shall from and after the End of this present Parliament return One Member and no more to serve in Parliament.

III.   And be it enacted, That each of the Places named in the Schedule marked (C.) to this Act annexed, (that is to say,) *Manchester, Birmingham, Leeds, Greenwich, Sheffield, Sunderland, Devonport, Wolverhampton, Tower Hamlets, Finsbury, Mary-le-bone, Lambeth, Bolton, Bradford, Blackburn, Brighton, Halifax, Macclesfield, Oldham, Stockport, Stoke-upon-Trent,* and *Stroud,* shall for the Purposes of this Act be a Borough, and shall as such Borough include the Place or Places respectively which shall be comprehended within the Boundaries of such Borough, as such Boundaries shall be settled and described by an Act to be passed for that Purpose in this present Parliament, which Act, when passed, shall be deemed and taken to be Part of this Act as fully and effectually as if the same were incorporated herewith; and that each of the said Boroughs named in the said Schedule (C.) shall from and after the End of this present Parliament return Two Members to serve in Parliament.

IV.   And be it enacted, That each of the Places named in the Schedule marked (D.) to this Act annexed, (that is to say,) *Ashton-under-Lyne, Bury, Chatham, Cheltenham, Dudley, Frome, Gateshead, Huddersfield, Kidderminster, Kendal, Rochdale, Salford, South Shields, Tynemouth, Wakefield, Walsall, Warrington, Whitby, Whitehaven,* and *Merthyr Tydvil,* shall for the Purposes of this Act be a Borough, and shall as such Borough include the Place or Places respectively which shall be comprehended within the Boundaries of such Borough, as such Boundaries shall be settled and described by an Act to be passed for that Purpose in this present Parliament, which Act, when passed, shall be deemed and taken to be Part of this Act as fully and effectually as if the same were incorporated herewith; and that each of the said Boroughs named in the said Schedule (D.) shall from and after the End of this present Parliament return One Member to serve in Parliament.

V.   And be it enacted, That the Borough of *New Shoreham* shall for the Purposes of this Act include the whole of the Rape of *Bramber* in the County of *Sussex,* save and except such Parts of the said Rape as shall be included in the Borough of *Horsham* by an Act to be passed for that Purpose in this present Parliament; and that the Borough of *Cricklade* shall for the Purposes of this Act include the Hundreds and Divisions of *Highworth, Cricklade, Staple, Kingsbridge,* and *Malmsbury* in the County of *Wilts,* save and except such Parts of the said Hundred of *Malmsbury* as shall be included in the Borough of *Malmsbury* by an Act to be passed for that Purpose in this present Parliament; and that the Borough of *Aylesbury* shall for the Purposes of this Act include the Three Hundreds of *Aylesbury* in the County of *Buckingham*; and that the Borough of *East Retford* shall for the Purposes of this Act include the Hundred of *Bassetlaw* in the County of *Nottingham,* and all Places locally situate within the outside Boundary or Limit of the Hundred of *Bassetlaw,* or surrounded by such Boundary and by any Part of the County of *Lincoln* or County of *York.*

VI.   And be it enacted, That the Borough of *Weymouth* and *Melcombe Regis* shall from and after the End of this present Parliament return Two Members, and no more, to serve in Parliament; and that the Borough of *Penryn* shall for the Purposes of this Act include the Town of *Falmouth*; and that the Borough of *Sandwich* shall for the Purposes of this Act include the Parishes of *Deal* and *Walmer.*

VII.   And be it enacted, That every City and Borough in *England* which now returns a Member or Members to serve in Parliament, and every Place sharing in the Election therewith, (except the several Boroughs enumerated in the said Schedule (A.), and except the several Boroughs of *New Shoreham, Cricklade, Aylesbury,* and *East Retford,*) shall, and each of the said Boroughs of *Penryn* and *Sandwich* also shall, for the Purposes of this Act, include the Place or Places respectively which shall be comprehended within the Boundaries of every such City,

Borough, or Place, as such Boundaries shall be settled and described by an Act to be passed for that Purpose in this present Parliament, which Act, when passed, shall be deemed and taken to be Part of this Act as fully and effectually as if the same were incorporated herewith.

VIII.   And be it enacted, That each of the Places named in the First Column of the Schedule (E.) to this Act annexed shall have a Share in the Election of a Member to serve in all future Parliaments for the Shire-Town or Borough which is mentioned in conjunction therewith and named in the Second Column of the said Schedule (E.)

IX.   And be it enacted, That each of the Places named in the First Column of the said Schedule (E.), and each of the Shire-Towns or Boroughs named in the Second Column of the said Schedule (E.), and the Borough of *Brecon*, shall for the Purposes of this Act include the Place or Places respectively which shall be comprehended within the Boundaries of each of the said Places, Shire-Towns, and Boroughs respectively, as such Boundaries shall be settled and described by an Act to be passed for that Purpose in this present Parliament, which Act, when passed, shall be deemed and taken to be Part of this Act as fully and effectually as if the same were incorporated herewith.

X.   And be it enacted, That each of the Towns of *Swansea, Loughor, Neath, Aberavon*, and *Ken-fig* shall for the Purposes of this Act include the Place or Places respectively which shall be comprehended within the Boundaries of each of the said Towns, as such Boundaries shall be settled and described by an Act to be passed for that Purpose in this present Parliament, which Act, when passed, shall be deemed and taken to be Part of this Act as fully and effectually as if the same were incorporated herewith; and that the said Five Towns, so including as aforesaid, shall for the Purposes of this Act be One Borough, and shall as such Borough, from and after the End of this present Parliament, return One Member to serve in Parliament; and that the Portreeve of *Swansea* shall be the Returning Officer for the said Borough; and that no Person, by reason of any Right accruing in any of the said Five Towns, shall have any Vote in the Election of a Member to serve in any future Parliament for the Borough of *Cardiff.*

XI.   And be it enacted, That the Persons respectively described in the said Schedule (C.) and (D.) shall be the Returning Officers at all Elections of a Member or Members to serve in Parliament for the Boroughs in conjunction with which such Persons are respectively mentioned in the said Schedules (C.) and (D.); and that for those Boroughs in the said Schedules for which no Persons are mentioned in such Schedules as Returning Officers the Sheriff for the Time being of the County in which such Boroughs are respectively situate shall, within Two Months after the passing of this Act, and in every succeeding respective Year in the Month of *March*, by Writing under his Hand, to be delivered to the Clerk of the Peace of the County within One Week, and to be by such Clerk of the Peace filed and preserved with the Records of his Office, nominate and appoint for each of such Boroughs a fit Person, being resident therein, to be, and such Person so nominated and appointed shall accordingly be, the Returning Officer for each of such Boroughs respectively until the Nomination to be made in the succeeding *March*; and in the Event of the Death of any such Person, or of his becoming incapable to act by reason of Sickness or other sufficient Impediment, the Sheriff for the Time being shall on Notice thereof forthwith nominate and appoint in his Stead a fit Person, being so resident as aforesaid, to be, and such Person so nominated and appointed shall accordingly be, the Returning Officer for such Borough for the Remainder of the then current Year; and no Person, having been so nominated and appointed as Returning Officer for any Borough, shall after the Expiration of his Office be compellable at any Time thereafter to serve again in the said Office for the same Borough: Provided always, that no Person being in Holy Orders, nor any Churchwarden or Overseer of the Poor within any such Borough, shall be nominated or appointed as such Returning Officer for the same; and that no Person nominated and appointed as Returning Officer for any Borough now sending or hereafter to send Members to Parliament shall be appointed a Churchwarden or Overseer of the Poor therein during the Time for which he shall be such Returning Officer: Provided also, that no Person qualified to be elected to serve as a Member in Parliament shall be compellable to serve as Returning Officer for any Borough for which he shall have been nominated and appointed by the Sheriff as aforesaid if within One Week after he shall have received Notice of his Nomination and Appointment as Returning Officer he shall make Oath of such Qualification before any Justice of the Peace, and shall forthwith notify the same to the Sheriff: Provided also, that in case His Majesty shall be pleased to grant His Royal Charter of Incorporation to any of the Boroughs named in the said Schedules (C.) and (D.) which are not now incorporated, and shall by such Charter give Power to elect a Mayor or other Chief Municipal Officer for any such Borough, then and in every such Case such Mayor or other Chief Municipal Officer for the Time being shall be the only Returning Officer for such Borough; and the Provisions herein-before contained with regard to the Nomination and Appointment of a Returning Officer for such Borough shall thenceforth cease and determine.

XII. And be it enacted, That in all future Parliaments there shall be Six Knights of the Shire, instead of Four, to serve for the County of *York*, (that is to say,) Two Knights for each of the Three Ridings of the said County, to be elected in the same Manner, and by the same Classes and Descriptions of Voters, and in respect of the same several Rights of voting, as if each of the Three Ridings were a separate County; and that the Court for the Election of Knights of the Shire for the North Riding of the said County shall be holden at the City of *York*, and the Court for the Election of Knights of the Shire for the West Riding of the said County shall be holden at *Wakefield*, and the Court for the Election of Knights of the Shire for the East Riding of the said County shall be holden at *Beverly*.

XIII. And be it enacted, That in all future Parliaments there shall be Four Knights of the Shire, instead of Two, to serve for the County of *Lincoln*, (that is to say,) Two for the Parts of *Lindsey* in the said County, and Two for the Parts of *Kesteven* and *Holland* in the same County; and that such Four Knights shall be chosen in the same Manner, and by the same Classes and Descriptions of Voters, and in respect of the same several Rights of voting, as if the said Parts of *Lindsey* were a separate County, and the said Parts of *Kesteven* and *Holland* together were also a separate County; and that the Court for the Election of Knights of the Shire for the Parts of *Lindsey* in the said County shall be holden at the City of *Lincoln*, and the Court for the Election of Knights of the Shire for the Parts of *Kesteven* and *Holland* in the said County shall be holden at *Sleaford.*

XIV. And be it enacted, That each of the Counties enumerated in the Schedule marked (F.) to this Act annexed shall be divided into Two Divisions, which Divisions shall be settled and described by an Act to be passed for that Purpose in this present Parliament, which Act, when passed, shall be deemed and taken to be Part of this Act as fully and effectually as if the same were incorporated herewith; and that in all future Parliaments there shall be Four Knights of the Shire, instead of Two, to serve for each of the said Counties, (that is to say,) Two Knights of the Shire for each Division of the said Counties; and that such Knights shall be chosen in the same Manner, and by the same Classes and Descriptions of Voters, and in respect of the same several Rights of voting, as if each of the said Divisions were a separate County; and that the Court for the Election of Knights of the Shire for each Division of the said Counties shall be holden at the Place to be named for that Purpose in the Act so to be passed as aforesaid, for settling and describing the Divisions of the said Counties.

XV. And be it enacted, That in all future Parliaments there shall be Three Knights of the Shire, instead of Two, to serve for each of the Counties enumerated in the Schedule marked (F.2.) to this Act annexed, and Two Knights of the Shire, instead of One, to serve for each of the Counties of *Carmarthen, Denbigh,* and *Glamorgan.*

XVI. And be it enacted, That the *Isle of Wight* in the County of *Southampton* shall for the Purposes of this Act be a County of itself, separate and apart from the County of *Southampton*, and shall return One Knight of the Shire to serve in every future Parliament; and that such Knight shall be chosen by the same Classes and Descriptions of Voters, and in respect of the same several Rights of voting, as any Knight of the Shire shall be chosen in any County in *England*; and that all Elections for the said County of the *Isle of Wight* shall be holden at the Town of *Newport* in the *Isle of Wight*, and the Sheriff of the *Isle of Wight*, or his Deputy, shall be the Returning Officer at such Elections.

XVII. And be it enacted, That for the Purposes of electing a Knight or Knights of the Shire to serve in any future Parliament, the East Riding of the County of *York*, the North Riding of the County of *York*, the Parts of *Lindsey* in the County of *Lincoln*, and the several Counties at large enumerated in the Second Column of the Schedule marked (G.) to this Act annexed, shall respectively include the several Cities and Towns, and Counties of the same, which are respectively mentioned in conjunction with such Ridings, Parts, and Counties at large, and named in the First Column of the said Schedule (G.)

XVIII. And be it enacted, That no Person shall be entitled to vote in the Election of a Knight or Knights of the Shire to serve in any future Parliament, or in the Election of a Member or Members to serve in any future Parliament for any City or Town being a County of itself, in respect of any Freehold Lands or Tenements whereof such Person may be seised for his own Life, of for the Life of another, or for any Lives whatsoever, except such Person shall be in the actual and *bona fide* Occupation of such Lands or Tenements, or except the same shall have come to such Person by Marriage, Marriage Settlement, Devise, or Promotion to any

Benefice or to any Office, or except the same shall be of the clear yearly Value of not less than Ten Pounds above all Rents and Charges payable out of or in respect of the same; any Statute or Usage to the contrary notwithstanding: Provided always, that nothing in this Act contained shall prevent any Person now seised for his own Life, or for the Life of another, or for any Lives whatsoever, of any Freehold Lands or Tenements in respect of which he now has, or but for the passing of this Act might acquire, the Right of voting in such respective Elections, from retaining or acquiring, so long as he shall be so seised of the same Lands or Tenements, such Right of voting in respect thereof, if duly registered according to the respective Provisions herein-after contained.

XIX. And be it enacted, That every Male Person of full Age, and not subject to any legal Incapacity, who shall be seised at Law or in Equity of any Lands or Tenements of Copyhold or any other Tenure whatever except Freehold, for his own Life, or for the Life of another, or for any Lives whatsoever, or for any larger Estate, of the clear yearly Value of not less than Ten Pounds over and above all Rents and Charges payable out of or in respect of the same, shall be entitled to vote in the Election of a Knight or Knights of the Shire to serve in any future Parliament for the County, or for the Riding, Parts, or Division of the County, in which such Lands or Tenements shall be respectively situate.

XX. And be it enacted, That every Male Person of full Age, and not subject to any legal Incapacity, who shall be entitled, either as Lessee or Assignee, to any Lands or Tenements, whether of Freehold or of any other Tenure whatever, for the unexpired Residue, whatever it may be, of any Term originally created for a Period of not less than Sixty Years, (whether determinable on a Life or Lives, or not,) of the clear yearly Value of not less than Ten Pounds over and above all Rents and Charges payable out of or in respect of the same, or for the unexpired Residue, whatever it may be, of any Term originally created for a Period of not less than Twenty Years, (whether determinable on a Life or Lives, or not,) of the clear yearly Value of not less than Fifty Pounds over and above all Rents and Charges payable out of or in respect of the same, or who shall occupy as Tenant any Lands or Tenements for which he shall be *bona fide* liable to a yearly Rent of not less than Fifty Pounds, shall be entitled to vote in the Election of a Knight or Knights of the Shire to serve in any future Parliament for the County, or for the Riding, Parts, or Division of the County, in which such Lands or Tenements shall be respectively situate: Provided always, that no Person, being only a Sub-Lessee, or the Assignee of any Underlease, shall have a Right to vote in such Election in respect of any such Term of Sixty Years or Twenty Years as aforesaid, unless he shall be in the actual Occupation of the Premises. . . .

XXVI. And be it enacted, That notwithstanding any thing herein-before contained no Person shall be entitled to vote in the Election of a Knight or Knights of the Shire to serve in any future Parliament unless he shall have been duly registered according to the Provisions herein-after contained; and that no Person shall be so registered in any Year in respect of his Estate or Interest in any Lands or Tenements, as a Freeholder, Copyholder, Customary Tenant, or Tenant in Ancient Demesne, unless he shall have been in the actual Possession thereof, or in the Receipt of the Rents and Profits thereof for his own Use, for Six Calendar Months at least next previous to the last Day of *July* in such Year, which said Period of Six Calendar Months shall be sufficient, any Statute to the contrary notwithstanding; and that no Person shall be so registered in any Year, in respect of any Lands or Tenements held by him as such Lessee or Assignee, or as such Occupier and Tenant as aforesaid, unless he shall have been in the actual Possession thereof, or in the Receipt of the Rents and Profits thereof for his own Use, as the Case may require, for Twelve Calendar Months next previous to the last Day of *July* in such Year: Provided always, that where any Lands or Tenements, which would otherwise entitle the Owner, Holder, or Occupier thereof to vote in any such Election, shall come to any Person, at any Time within such respective Periods of Six or Twelve Calendar Months, by Descent, Succession, Marriage, Marriage Settlement, Devise, or Promotion to any Benefice in a Church, or by Promotion to any Office, such Person shall be entitled in respect thereof to have his Name inserted as a Voter in the Election of a Knight or Knights of the Shire in the Lists then next to be made by virtue of this Act as herein-after mentioned, and, upon his being duly registered according to the Provisions herein-after contained, to vote in such Election.

XXVII. And be it enacted, That in every City or Borough which shall return a Member or Members to serve in any future Parliament, every Male Person of full Age, and not subject to any legal Incapacity, who shall occupy, within such City or Borough, or within any Place sharing in the Election for such City or Borough, as Owner or Tenant, any House, Warehouse, Counting-house, Shop, or other Building, being, either separately, or jointly with any Land within such City, Borough, or Place occupied therewith by him as Owner, or occupied therewith by him as Tenant under the same Landlord, of the clear yearly Value of not less than Ten Pounds, shall, if duly registered according to the Provisions herein-after contained, be entitled to vote in the Election of a Member or Members to serve in any future Parliament for such City or Borough: Provided always, that no such Person shall be so registered in any Year unless unless he shall have occupied such Premises as aforesaid for Twelve Calendar Months next previous to the last Day of *July* in such Year, nor unless such Person, where such Premises are situate in any Parish or Township in which there shall be a Rate for the Relief of the Poor, shall have been rated in respect of such Premises to all Rates for the Relief of the Poor in such Parish or Township made during the Time of such his Occupation so required as aforesaid, nor unless such Person shall have paid, on or before the Twentieth Day of *July* in such Year, all the Poor's Rates and assessed Taxes which shall have become payable from him in respect of such Premises previously to the Sixth Day of *April* then next preceding: Provided also, that no such Person shall be so registered in any Year unless he shall have resided for Six Calendar Months next previous to the last Day of *July* in such Year within the City or Borough, or within the Place sharing in the Election for the City or Borough, in respect of which City, Borough, or Place respectively he shall be entitled to vote, or within Seven Statute Miles thereof or of any Part thereof.

XXVIII. And be it enacted, That the Premises in respect of the Occupation of which any Person shall be entitled to be registered in any Year, and to vote in the Election for any City or Borough as aforesaid, shall not be required to be the same Premises, but may be different Premises occupied in immediate Succession by such

Person during the Twelve Calendar Months next previous to the last Day of *July* in such Year, such Person having paid, on or before the Twentieth Day of *July* in such Year, all the Poor's Rates and Assessed Taxes which shall previously to the Sixth Day of *April* then next preceding have become payable from him in respect of all such Premises so occupied by him in succession.

XXIX. And be it enacted, That where any Premises as aforesaid, in any such City or Borough, or in any Place sharing in the Election therewith, shall be jointly occupied by more Persons than One as Owners or Tenants, each of such joint Occupiers shall, subject to the Conditions herein-before contained as to Persons occupying Premises in any such City, Borough, or Place, be entitled to vote in the Election for such City or Borough, in respect of the Premises so jointly occupied, in case the clear yearly Value of such Premises shall be of an Amount which, when divided by the Number of such Occupiers, shall give a Sum of not less than Ten Pounds for each and every such Occupier, but not otherwise.

XXX. And be it enacted, That in every City or Borough which shall return a Member or Members to serve in any future Parliament, and in every Place sharing in the Election for such City or Borough, it shall be lawful for any Person occupying any House, Warehouse, Counting-house, Shop, or other Building, either separately, or jointly with any Land occupied therewith by him as Owner, or occupied therewith by him as Tenant under the same Landlord, in any Parish or Township in which there shall be a Rate for the Relief of the Poor, to claim to be rated to the Relief of the Poor in respect of such Premises, whether the Landlord shall or shall not be liable to be rated to the Relief of the Poor in respect thereof; and upon such Occupier so claiming, and actually paying or tendering the full Amount of the Rate or Rates, if any, then due in respect of such Premises, the Overseers of the Parish or Township in which such Premises are situate are hereby required to put the Name of such Occupier upon the Rate for the Time being; and in case such Overseers shall neglect or refuse so to do, such Occupier shall nevertheless for the Purposes of this Act be deemed to have been rated to the Relief of the Poor in respect of such Premises from the Period at which the Rate shall have been made in respect of which he shall have so claimed to be rated as aforesaid: Provided always, that where by virtue of any Act of Parliament the Landlord shall be liable to the Payment of the Rate for the Relief of the Poor in respect of any Premises occupied by his Tenant, nothing herein contained shall be deemed to vary or discharge the Liability of such Landlord; but that in case the Tenant who shall have been rated for such Premises in consequence of any such Claim as aforesaid shall make Default in the Payment of the Poor's Rate due in respect thereof, such Landlord shall be and remain liable for the Payment thereof in the same Manner as if he alone had been rated in respect of the Premises so occupied by his Tenant.

XXXI. And be it enacted, That in every City or Town being a County of itself, in the Election for which Freeholders or Burgage Tenants, either with or without any superadded Qualification, now have a Right to vote, every such Freeholder or Burgage Tenant shall be entitled to vote in the Election of a Member or Members to serve in all future Parliaments for such City or Town, provided he shall be duly registered according to the Provisions herein-after contained; but that no such Person shall be so registered in any Year in respect of any Freehold or Burgage

Tenement, unless he shall have been in the actual Possession thereof, or in the Receipt of the Rents and Profits thereof for his own Use, for Twelve Calendar Months next previous to the last Day of *July* in such Year, (except where the same shall have come to him, at any Time within such Twelve Months, by Descent, Succession, Marriage, Marriage Settlement, Devise, or Promotion to any Benefice in a Church, or to any Office,) nor unless he shall have resided for Six Calendar Months next previous to the last Day of *July* in such Year within such City or Town, or within Seven Statute Miles thereof or of any Part thereof: Provided always, that nothing in this Enactment contained shall be deemed to vary or abridge the Provisions herein-before made relative to the Right of voting for any City or Town being a County of itself, in respect of any Freehold for Life or Lives: Provided also, that every Freehold or Burgage Tenement which may be situate without the present Limits of any such City or Town being a County of itself, but within the Limits of such City or Town, as the same shall be settled and described by the Act to be passed for that Purpose as herein-before mentioned, shall confer the Right of voting in the Election of a Member or Members to serve in any future Parliament for such City or Town in the same Manner as if such Freehold or Burgage Tenement were situate within the present Limits thereof.

XXXII. And be it enacted, That every Person who would have been entitled to vote in the Election of a Member or Members to serve in any future Parliament for any City or Borough not included in the Schedule marked (A.) to this Act annexed, either as a Burgess or Freeman, or in the City of *London* as a Freeman and Liveryman, if this Act had not been passed, shall be entitled to vote in such Election, provided such Person shall be duly registered according to the Provisions herein-after contained; but that no such Person shall be so registered in any Year, unless he shall, on the last Day of *July* in such Year, be qualified in such Manner as would entitle him then to vote if such Day were the Day of Election, and this Act had not been passed, nor unless, where he shall be a Burgess or Freeman or Freeman and Liveryman of any City or Borough, he shall have resided for Six Calendar Months next previous to the last Day of *July* in such Year within such City or Borough, or within Seven Statute Miles from the Place where the Poll for such City or Borough shall heretofore have been taken, nor unless, where he shall be a Burgess or Freeman of any Place sharing in the Election for any City or Borough, he shall have resided for Six Calendar Months next previous to the last Day of *July* in such Year within such respective Place so sharing as aforesaid, or within Seven Statute Miles of the Place mentioned in conjunction with such respective Place so sharing as aforesaid and named in the Second Column of the Schedule marked (E. 2.) to this Act annexed: Provided always, that no Person shall have been elected, made, or admitted a Burgess or Freeman since the First Day of *March* One thousand eight hundred and thirty-one, otherwise than in respect of Birth or Servitude, or who shall hereafter be elected, made, or admitted a Burgess or Freeman, otherwise than in respect of Birth or Servitude, shall be entitled to vote as such in any such Election for any City or Borough as aforesaid, or to be so registered as aforesaid: Provided also, that no Person shall be so entitled as a Burgess or Freeman in respect of Birth unless his Right be originally derived from or through some Person who was a Burgess or Freeman, or entitled to be admitted a Burgess or Freeman, previously to the First Day of *March* in the Year One thousand eight hundred and thirty-one, or from or through some Person who since that Time shall have become or shall hereafter become a Burgess or Freeman in respect of Servitude: Provided also, that every Person who would have been entitled, if this Act had not been passed, to vote as a Burgess or Freeman of *Swansea, Loughor, Neath, Aberavon,* or *Ken-fig,* in the Election of a Member to serve in any future Parliament for the Borough of *Cardiff,* shall cease to vote in such Election, and shall instead thereof be entitled to vote as such Burgess or Freeman in the Election of a Member to serve in all future Parliaments for the Borough composed of the Towns of *Swansea, Loughor, Neath, Aberavon,* and *Ken-fig,* subject always to the Provisions herein-before contained with regard to a Burgess or Freeman of any Place sharing in the Election for any City or Borough.

XXXIII. And be it enacted, That no Person shall be entitled to vote in the Election of a Member or Members to serve in any future Parliament for any City or Borough, save and except in respect of some Right conferred by this Act, or as a Burgess or Freeman, or as a Freeman and Liveryman, or, in the Case of a City or Town being a County of itself, as a Freeholder or Burgage Tenant, as herein-before mentioned: Provided always, that every Person now having a Right to vote in the Election for any City or Borough (except those enumerated in the said Schedule (A.) in virtue of any other Qualification than as a Burgess or Freeman, or as a Freeman and Liveryman, or, in the Case of a City or Town being a County of itself, as a Freeholder or Burgage Tenant, as herein-before mentioned, shall retain such Right of voting so long as he shall be qualified as an Elector according to the Usages and Customs of such City or Borough or any Law now in force, and such Person shall be entitled to vote in the Election of a Member or Members to serve in any future Parliament for such City or Borough, if duly registered according to the Provisions herein-after contained; but that no such Person shall be so registered in any Year unless he shall, on the last Day of *July* in such Year, be qualified as such Elector in such Manner as would entitle him then to vote if such Day were the Day of Election and this Act had not been passed, nor unless such Person, where his Qualification shall be in any City or Borough, shall have resided for Six Calendar Months next previous to the last Day of *July* in such Year within such City or Borough, or within Seven Statute Miles from the Place where the Poll for such City or Borough shall heretofore have been taken, nor unless such Person, where his Qualification shall be within any Place sharing in the Election for any City or Borough, shall have resided for Six Calendar Months next previous to the last Day of *July* in such Year within such respective Place so sharing as aforesaid, or within Seven Statute Miles of the Place so sharing as aforesaid, and named in the Second Column of the Schedule marked (E.2.) to this Act annexed: Provided nevertheless, that every such Person shall for ever cease to enjoy such Right of voting for any such City or Borough as aforesaid if his Name shall have been omitted for Two successive Years from the Register of such Voters for such City or Borough herein-after directed to be made, unless he shall have been so omitted in consequence of his having received Parochial Relief within Twelve Calendar Months next previous to the last Day of *July* in any Year, or in consequence of his Absence on the Naval or Military Service of His Majesty.

XXXIV. And be it enacted, That every Person now having a Right to vote for the Borough of *New Shoreham*, or of *Cricklade, Aylesbury*, or *East Retford* respectively, in respect of any Freehold, wheresoever the same may be situate, shall retain such Right of voting, subject always to the same Provisions as are herein-before mentioned with regard to Persons whose Right of voting for any Borough is saved and reserved by this Act, save and except that such Persons now having a Right to vote for the Borough of *New Shoreham*, or of *Cricklade, Aylesbury*, or *East Retford* respectively, shall not be registered in any Year unless they shall have resided for Six Calendar Months next previous to the last Day of *July* in such Year within the Borough of *New Shoreham*, or of *Cricklade, Aylesbury*, or *East Retford* respectively, as defined by this Act, or within Seven Statute Miles of such respective Borough or of any Part thereof; and that for the Purpose of the Registration herein-after required all Persons now having a Right to vote for the Borough of *New Shoreham* in respect of any Freeholds which may be situate in the Borough of *Horsham*, or for the Borough of *Cricklade* in respect of any Freeholds which may be situate in the Borough of *Malmsbury*, as such Boroughs of *Horsham* or *Malmsbury* may respectively be defined by the Act to be passed for that Purpose as herein-before mentioned, shall be inserted in the List of Voters herein-after directed to be made by the Overseers of that Parish or Township within the Borough of *New Shoreham* or the Borough of *Cricklade* respectively, as defined by this Act, which shall be next adjoining to the Parish or Township in which such Freeholds shall respectively be situate; and if the Parish or Township in which any such Freeholds shall be situate shall adjoin Two or more Parishes or Townships within either of the said Boroughs of *New Shoreham* or *Cricklade*, the Persons so having a Right to vote in respect of such Freeholds shall be inserted in the List of Voters to be made by the Overseers of the least populous of such adjoining Parishes or Townships, according to the last Census for the Time being.

XXXV. Provided nevertheless, and be it enacted, That notwithstanding any thing herein-before contained no Person shall be entitled to vote in the Election of a Member or Members to serve in any future Parliament for any City or Borough (other than a City or Town being a County of itself, in the Election for which Freeholders or Burgage Tenants have a Right to vote as herein-before mentioned,) in respect of any Estate or Interest in any Burgage Tenement or Freehold which shall have been acquired by such Person since the First Day of *March* One thousand eight hundred and thirty-one, unless the same shall have come to or been acquired by such Person, since that Day, and previously to the passing of this Act, by Descent, Succession, Marriage, Marriage Settlement, Devise, or Promotion to any Benefice in a Church, or by Promotion to any Office.

XXXVI. And be it enacted, That no Person shall be entitled to be registered in any Year as a Voter in the Election of a Member or Members to serve in any future Parliament for any City or Borough who shall within Twelve Calendar Months next previous to the last Day of *July* in such Year have received Parochial Relief or other Alms which by the Law of Parliament now disqualify from voting in the Election of Members to serve in Parliament. . . .

Scottish Reform Act, 17 July 1832

2 Will. 4, c. 65   *Statutes of the United Kingdom,* LXXII, 383-89.

Whereas the Laws which regulate the Election of Members to serve in the Common House of Parliament for *Scotland* are defective, whereby great Inconveniences and Abuses have been occasioned: And whereas it is expedient, and would be for the evident Utility of the Subjects within *Scotland*, that those Defects should be remedied, and especially that Members should be provided for Places hitherto unrepresented, and the Right of Election extended to Persons of Property and Intelligence, and that the Mode of conducting Elections should be better regulated and ordered: Be it therefore enacted by the King's most Excellent Majesty, by and with the Advice and Consent of the Lords Spiritual and Temporal, and Commons, in this present Parliament assembled, and by the Authority of the same, That from and after the End of this present Parliament, and in all future Parliaments to be assembled, there shall be Fifty-three Representatives returned for *Scotland* to the Commons House of Parliament, of whom Thirty shall be for the several or conjoined Shires or Stewartries herein-after enumerated, and Twenty-three for the several Cities, Burghs, and Towns, or Districts of Cities, Burghs, and Towns, herein-after enumerated or described.

II.   And be it enacted, That after the End of this present Parliament the Burghs of *Peebles* and *Selkirk* shall no longer form Parts of the District to which they now belong, or be entitled to contribute with any other Burghs in the Election of any Member of Parliament, but shall, in the Matter of Elections, be held to be Parts of the Counties of *Peebles* and *Selkirk* respectively; and in like Manner that the Burgh of *Rothsay* in the County of *Bute* shall no longer form Part of the District to which it now belongs, but be held, in the Matter of Elections, to be Part of the County of *Bute.*

III.   And be it enacted, That of the Thirty Members hereafter to be returned to Parliament by the separate or combined Shires of *Scotland*, One shall always be returned by each of the separate Shires or Parts of Shires enumerated in the Schedule (A.) hereunto annexed, and One by each Two of the combined Shires or Parts of Shires enumerated and described in Schedule (B.) hereunto annexed: Provided always, that all Properties lying locally within the Limits of any County or Shire, though hitherto constituting Part of some other County, shall, for the Purposes of this Act, be held to be Part of the County within which they are locally included.

IV.   And be it enacted, That of the Twenty-three Members to be returned for the several or combined Cities, Burghs, and Towns of *Scotland*, Two shall always be returned by each of the separate Cities, Burghs, and Towns enumerated and described in Schedule (C.) hereunto annexed, One by each of the separate Cities, Burghs, and Towns enumerated and described in Schedule (D.) hereunto annexed, and One by each of the Districts or Sets of Cities, Burghs, and Towns enumerated and described in Schedule (E.) hereunto annexed.

V. And be it enacted, That the Limits and Boundaries of all the Cities, Burghs, and Towns enumerated in any of the above-mentioned Schedules shall, for the Purposes of this Act, be taken and held to be according to the Description and Specification of such Limits and Boundaries set forth and contained in Schedule (M.) to this Act annexed; and all the Properties within the Boundaries therein specified shall hereafter, for the Purposes of this Act, be Parts of the said Cities, Burghs, and Towns, and not of the Adjoining of any other County: . . .

VI. . . . No person shall acquire, by succession, purchase, gift or otherwise, the Right of voting for a Member of Parliament, either in Shires, or in Cities, Burghs, or Towns, except by one or other of the Qualifications herein-after prescribed and directed: Provided always, that all Persons who at the passing of this Act shall be lawfully on the Roll of Freeholders of any Shire in *Scotland*, or who shall then be entitled to be put on such Roll, or who shall previous to the First Day of *March* One thousand eight hundred and thirty-one have become the Owners or Superiors of Lands affording the Qualification for being so enrolled, shall, so long as they retain the necessary Qualification on which they are now enrolled or are entitled to be enrolled as aforesaid, be entitled to be registered and to vote as herein-after directed in the Election of a Member for such Shire.

VII. And be it enacted, That from and after the passing of this Act every Person, not subject to any legal Incapacity, shall be entitled to be registered as herein-after directed, and thereafter to vote at any Election for a Shire in *Scotland*, who, when the Sheriff proceeds to consider his Claim for Registration in the present or in any future Year, shall have been, for a Period of not less than Six Calendar Months next previous to the last Day of *August* in the present or the last Day of *July* in any future Year, the Owner (whether he has made up his Titles, or is infeft, or not,) of any Lands, Houses, Feu Duties, or other Heritable Subjects (except Debts heritably secured) within the said Shire, provided the Subject or Subjects on which he so claims shall be of the yearly Value of Ten Pounds, and shall actually yield or be capable of yielding that Value to the Claimant, after deducting any Feu Duty, Ground Annual, or other Consideration which he may be bound to pay or to give or account for as a Condition of his Right, provided he be, by himself, his Tenants, Vassals, or others, in possession of the said Subjects, and be either himself in the actual Occupation or in receipt of the Profits and Issues thereof to the Extent above mentioned: Provided always, that where the whole Profits and Issues of any such Subject do not arise annually, but a longer Intervals, the Worth and Amount of such occasional Profits shall be taken into Computation in estimating the annual Value: Provided also, that where any Property which would entitle the Owner to be registered and to vote as above shall come to any Person, within the said Period of Six Months, by Inheritance, Marriage, Marriage Settlement, or *mortis causa* Disposition, or by Appointment to any Place or Office, such Person shall be entitled to be registered on the first Occasion of making up the Lists of Voters, as herein-after provided, next following such Succession or Acquisition.

VIII. And be it enacted, That in Elections for Shires, where Two or more Persons are interested in any Subject to which a Right of voting is for the first Time attached by this Act, as Life-renter and as Fiar, the Right of voting shall be in the Life-renter, and not in the Fiar; and all Co-proprietors or joint Owners shall be entitled each to vote in respect of their joint Property within the Shire, provided the Share or Interest of each joint Owner so claiming on such Property is of the yearly Value of Ten Pounds, as above specified, but not otherwise: Provided also, that Husbands shall be entitled to vote in respect of Property belonging to their Wives, or owned or possessed by such Husbands after the Death of their Wives by the Courtesy of *Scotland.*

IX. And be it enacted, That Tenants in Lands, Houses, or other Heritable Subjects shall also be entitled to be registered, and to vote at Elections for the Shires in which the said Heritable Subjects are situated, provided each Tenant (whether joint or several) when the Sheriff proceeds to consider his Claim for Registration, shall, for a Period of not less than Twelve Months next previous to the last Day of *August* in the present or the last Day of *July* in any future Year, have held such Subjects or Tenements, whether in his personal Possession or not, under a Lease or Leases, Missive of Lease, or other written Title, for a Period of not less than Fifty-seven Years (exclusive of Breaks), at the Option of the Landlord, or the the Life-time of the said Tenant, where the clear yearly Value of such Tenant's Interest, after paying the Rent and any other Consideration due by him for his said Right, is not less than Ten Pounds, or for a Period of not less than Nineteen Years where the clear yearly Value of such Tenant's Interest is not less than Fifty Pounds, or where such Tenant shall, for the foresaid Period of Twelve Months, have been in the actual personal Occupancy of any such Subject, where the yearly Rent is not less than Fifty Pounds, or where the Tenant, whatever the Rent may be, has truly paid for his Interest in such Subject a Price, Grassum, or Consideration of not less than Three hundred Pounds: Provided always, that where, in any of these Cases, the Rent is payable in whole or in part in Grain, the Value shall be estimated according to the average Fiars of the Counties in which the Heritable Subjects are situated for the Three preceding Years, and where payable in any other Species of Produce, according to the average Market Prices of the Neighbourhood for the said Period; and the said Values being once so fixed at the Time of registering or refusing to register shall be held as settled for the whole Period of the Lease: Provided also, that where the Right to any such Lease as would entitle the Tenant to be registered and to vote as herein-before provided shall come to any Person, within the preceding Twelve Calendar Months above specified, by Interitance, Marriage, Marriage Settlement, or *mortis causa* Disposition, such Person shall be entitled to be registered on the first Occasion of making up the Lists of Voters, as herein-after provided, next following such Succession or Acquisition: Provided also, that no Sub-tenant or Assignee to any Sub-lease for Fifty-seven or Nineteen Years shall be entitled to be registered or to vote in respect of his Interest under such Lease unless he shall be in the actual Occupation of the Premises thereby set.

X. And be it enacted, That from and after the End of this present Parliament the Members who are to be returned to serve in any future Parliament for any single City, Town, or Burgh on which the Right of returning a Member or Members is by this Act conferred, shall no longer be elected by the Town Councils of such Cities, Burghs, or Towns, but directly by the several Individuals on whom the Right of electing such Members to serve in Parliament is by this Act conferred; and where the Election is by Districts or Sets of Cities, Burghs, or Towns conjoined, the Right of electing shall no longer be in the Town Councils or Corporations of the said Cities, Burghs, or Towns, or in Delegates appointed by them, but in the Individual Voters on whom the Right of Election is by this Act conferred; and the Member to serve in Parliament for any such District shall be returned according to the Majority of individual Votes given in the whole District.

XI. And be it enacted, That every Person, not subject to any legal Incapacity, shall be entitled to be registered as herein-after directed, and to vote at Elections for any of the Cities, Burghs, or Towns, or Districts of Cities, Burghs, or Towns, herein-before mentioned, who, when the Sheriff proceeds to consider his Claim for Registration, shall have been, for a Period of not less than Twelve Calendar Months next previous to the last Day of *August* in the present or the last Day of *July* in any future Year, in the Occupancy, either as Proprietor, Tenant, or Life-renter, of any House, Warehouse, Counting-house, Shop, or other Building within the Limits of such City, Burgh, or Town, which either separately or jointly with any other House, Warehouse, Counting-house, Shop, or other Building within the same Limits, or with any Land owned and occupied by him, or occupied under the same Landlord, and also situate within the same Limits, shall be of the yearly Value of Ten Pounds: Provided always, that the Claimant shall have paid, on or before the Twentieth Day of *August* in the present or the Twentieth Day of *July* in any future Year, all Assessed Taxes which shall have become payable by him in respect of such Premises previously to the Sixth Day of *April* then next preceding: Provided also, that no such Person shall be entitled to be registered or to vote in the present or any future Year unless he shall have resided for Six Calendar Months next previous to the last Day of *August* in the present or the last Day of *July* in any future Year within such City, Burgh, or Town, or within Seven Statute Miles of some Part thereof: Provided also, that Persons so resident shall be entitled to be registered and to vote if they are the true Owners or such Premises as are herein-before mentioned, within such City, Burgh, or Town, of the yearly Value of Ten Pounds or upwards, although they should not occupy any Premises within its Limits, or although the Premises actually occupied by them should be of less yearly Value than Ten Pounds; and that the Husbands of such Owners shall be entitled to vote, either in the Lifetime of their Wives, or after their Death, if then holding such Property by the Courtesy of *Scotland*: Provided also, that no Person shall be entitled to be registered or to vote for any City, Burgh, or Town, who shall have been in the Receipt of Parochial Relief within Twelve Calendar Months next previous to the last Day of *August* in the Year One thousand eight hundred and thirty-two, or next previous to the last Day of *July* in any succeeding Year.

XII. And be it enacted, That the Premises in respect of which any Person shall be deemed entitled to be registered, and to vote in the Election for any City, Burgh, or Town, or District, shall not be required to have been the same Premises for the whole Twelve Months of his Occupancy, but may be different Premises (but always of the requisite Value) occupied in succession by such Person; provided always, that such Person shall have paid all the Assessed Taxes legally exigible from him in respect of all such Premises; and that where such Premises shall be of the yearly Value of Twenty Pounds or upwards, and shall be jointly occupied by more than One Person, each of such joint Occupiers shall be entitled to be registered and to vote, provided his Share and Interest in the same shall be of the yearly Value of Ten Pounds or upwards. . . .

National Political Union report detailing its activities during the Reform Bill crisis, 4 February 1833

Proceedings at the Second Annual Meeting of the National Political Union, held at the Crown and Anchor Tavern, Strand, on Monday, February 4, 1833 (London: National Political Union, 1833), 4-17.

The National Political Union was formed in London in 1831 under the leadership of Francis Place (1771-1854). It agitated effectively for passage of the Reform Bill, including a famous "Go for Gold" campaign against the duke of Wellington when the latter tried to form an anti-reform government in May 1832.

At the time your Council was elected, The English Reform Bill was in committee in the House of Commons, and the Council, following the mode adopted by their predecessors, diligently employed every means in their power to carry into effect the wishes of the great body by whom they had been appointed to office. Nothing within their power which the law permitted to be done, was neglected; every legal means was carefully used to induce the people to support ministers in their endeavours to procure the passing of the Bills, and, at the same time, to convince the aristocracy that the people were determined, at all events, to have the small measure of justice meted to them which the Reform Bills contained, not as "*final measures*," not as the conclusion of reform, but as measures of the utmost importance in the circumstances in which the country was then placed, and consequently worth any exertion, and almost any sacrifice, as first steps towards the attainment of cheap, and good government.

Much that was done, as well by the Union as by the Council, notwithstanding its utility at the moment, can only be alluded to, much must necessarily be passed over without notice. Those proceedings which appear to be of general importance, can alone be noticed in a report, the extent of which must be limited to what may be considered a reasonable extent.

At the time the Council was appointed, a petition to the House of Commons had been prepared and placed in the hands of Mr. Warburton;—it prayed the House not to permit the *non-payment* of either rate or tax, to disqualify any man who would otherwise be entitled to vote for a member of Parliament;—it pointed out the inconvenience, the bribery, the corruption, and the perjury, which even in much more modified forms had been produced by the demand for rates; and it predicted, as inevitable consequences, the extension of these evils to almost every borough in England, if any words enacting the payment of other tax or rate as a qualification, was permitted to remain in the Bill.

Plainly as these consequences were stated, and great as were the pains taken by the Council to make the petition known to the people, it did not meet with the support they expected, and the importance of the subject demanded; the clause which, had it been properly objected to, would have been omitted, was retained, and the result has corresponded to the predictions contained in the petition. Great, however, as the mischiefs have been, they are as nothing to what they will be, if the clause should remain as it is at the next election; it will then, as was remarked in the petition, "be destructive of the freedom of election, will make the return of members to your Honourable House a mere contention of the purse, and will cause the perpetration of many enormities in almost every one of the boroughs in the kingdom." The Reform Bill destroyed 56 rotten boroughs, but this clause, if retained, will at no distant period make the right of suffrage of no use to the honest elector in any but a very few of the largest boroughs; in all other places, the elections will be decided by a small number of bribed and perjured voters, who will be previously prepared to sell their country to the highest bidder for their mercenary voices. Your Council hope that the reformed Parliament will cause so much of the 27th clause of the English Reform Bill, as relates to the payment of rates and taxes, to be repealed.

This petition was the first which the National Political Union sent to the unreformed House of Commons, and, as your Council anticipated, an effort was made to prevent its being received by the Honourable House. The objection taken was to the wording of the description given by the petitioners of themselves; but the intention of the objectors was, to cause the petition to be rejected in a way that might serve as a precedent for rejecting all future petitions from Political Unions: as, however, the objection had been made to words only, Mr. Warburton wisely withdrew it, and thereby prevented a decision which might have been injurious to this and other Unions; and the words objected to having been changed for others of like import, the petition was again presented, and being received, established a precedent for all future petitions from Political Unions.

Towards the end of the month of February, considerable sensation was produced from apprehension that the Irish Reform Bill was inadequate, when compared with the English Reform Bill, and the Council being desirous that their Irish brethren should participate equally with the English in whatever benefits might result from the Reform Bills, caused petitions for that purpose to be presented to both Houses of Parliament, praying that the Irish Reform Bill might be made as efficient as that of England.

On the 14th March, the Council caused an address to the people of England to be printed, and extensively circulated; it is a short but powerful appeal to the people, on the English Reform Bill being sent up to the House of Lords, and an energetic call on them to come forward and do their duty. It states the reasons for the apprehension entertained by the Council that the Lords would reject the Bill, and declares, that unless the "public energy be powerfully and significantly expressed, the cause of *peaceful* reform will be lost for ever;" it entreats the people "distinctly to signify their desires, to speak in so plain a manner that their wishes cannot be misunderstood, and so forcibly that they cannot be denied."

That good must have resulted from this address, will be acknowledged by every real reformer capable of appreciating the circumstances under which it was issued.

On the 26th March, your Council resolved to petition the House of Lords to pass the English Reform Bill unmutilated. The petition which was presented by Lord King, was printed, and extensively circulated.

The matters treated of in this petition, the facts it contains, and the statements relative to the former and present relative state of the aristocratic body to the people, are still so applicable, and so likely to continue to be applicable and useful, that your Council have appended it to this report (App. No. 1), and they beg to call the particular attention of the members of the Union thereto.

Fears were entertained lest the Lords should again reject the Bill; and your Council, ever watchful of this great measure, feeling the importance to the public cause of the proceedings of the Union, came to the following resolution, 11th April, 1832:—

> That in the event of the English Reform Bill being again rejected by the Lords, this Council will hold a special meeting on the following evening, at eight o'clock, to consider of the proper course to be adopted in so unfortunate an emergency.

The apprehensions of the Council was partaken of by intelligent reformers in many places, and became more and more general every day; the conduct of the Lords was well calculated to produce this effect, and to excite even the most languid to a contemplation of impending evils. Considerable agitation prevailed, public meetings were held in many places, and other demonstrations, which could not be misunderstood, were made. During the discussion of the first English Reform Bill, a proposition had been made that, in the event of the Bill being rejected, the people should refrain from paying taxes. The legality of the proposition being doubtful, it was not adopted; but an impression was made, and symptoms of a disposition to act on the proposition, were manifested in several places.

Much discussion on the subject had taken place; the probable refusal of any considerable portion of the people to pay taxes, was understood; and men became every day more and more reconciled to the inevitable consequences of a refusal to pay taxes, should the necessity be forced on them.

The attention of the people in all parts of the kingdom was now fixed on the House of Lords, a kind of pause in their usual occupations took place, and produced an intense desire that the Bill should be speedily passed, that their apprehensions might thereby be allayed, and their several concerns restored to their usual course. Your Council strongly participated in the general feeling, and, on the 18th April, resolved—

> That the business committee do forthwith prepare resolutions for the consideration of a general meeting of the Union, and that they convene the same as soon as they shall deem it necessary; to take into consideration the best means of resisting any attempt to abridge the proposed £10. franchise, as well as any other mutilation of the Bill.

The apprehensions of the people increased continually, and the Council resolved to call a general meeting of the members of the Union, which was accordingly held on the 3d of May, when *Joseph Hume, Esq., M.P.* presided

At this meeting, resolutions were passed expressing the apprehension the members entertained:—

1. That the Reform Bill will not be passed by the Lords, unless the opinion of the public be generally and energetically expressed.

2. That they will resist the infringement of any of the rights proposed to be created by the Bill, by every legal means in their power.

3. That they will support their Scotch and Irish brethren in obtaining a measure of reform equal to that proposed for England.

The English Reform Bill having been read a second time in the Lords, a new expedient to defeat it was adopted; and on the 7th of May, Lord Lyndhurst moved "that the consideration of the first and second clauses of the Reform Bill be postponed;" on a division of the House, there appeared—

For Lord Lyndhurst's motion	151
Against it	116
Majority for the motion	35

Thus were the apprehensions of the Council, and of the members generally, realized. The country was at once thrown into a state of agitation more general and more intense than at any period since that which immediately preceded the revolution in 1688.

Your Council will neither attempt to describe the state of men's minds, nor to depict the consequences which seemed all but inevitable during the eleven following days. Highly important and generally useful at such an account would be, and desirable too as it is that it should be given at once by men properly qualified and sufficiently informed for the task, it could not properly be placed in this report; all the Council can do, and all which in this report it seems to them they are warranted in doing, is to state the leading facts, and to make a few short observations on such of them as more particularly relate to the proceedings of the Union.

The desire entertained by a majority of the Peers to embarrass the proceedings respecting the Reform Bill, to oust the administration of Lord Grey and restore the Duke of Wellington to power, had been openly declared. The reluctance to create Peers, and the countenance which it was concluded the King gave to the proceedings of the conservative Peers, had induced the people to mistreat both the King and the Lords. Meetings were therefore held in various parts of the country, the most important of which—one indeed by far the most important of any—was held at Birmingham; it was admirably arranged, well conducted, and consisted of a larger number of persons than had ever before assembled for political discussion. This magnificant display of the understanding and temper of the people was of the utmost importance; it was held at noon of the day on which ministers were defeated by Lord Lyndhurst's motion, and, operating with it on the public, produced very desirable effects,—not only on the people generally, but probably on the ministers also,—who two days afterwards tendered their resignations of office to the King, who was *graciously pleased* to accept them. That they were accepted without reluctance, was not then, nor has it since been doubted.

The aristocracy, essentially selfish, having long had its own way, never having at any time but for a moment, and then only at long intervals, been at all controled by the people, were the only body of men in the kingdom who remained in ignorance of the feelings, the knowledge, the courage, and the resources of the people. Hitherto the government had been conducted by and for the aristocracy, almost solely with a view to their separate advantage; the people being nothing—their order being every thing. Never was any thing done for the people, if its real or supposed tendency was not to advance some purpose either immediately or remotely for the interest of the aristocracy; even in matters favourable to the people, which seemed entirely indifferent to them, nothing could be accomplished until some advantage to their order was coupled with it. So long as the people could be kept in ignorance, so long as they could be made to believe that the aristocracy ought to be looked up to with absurd reverence, and bowed down to with mean submission, their power was secure; they had only to talk of the good of the people now and then, and pretend to reverence the cabalistical *word* constitution—*the British constitution,* to excite the awe of those whom they degraded and plundered.

The changes which have for some years past been going on among the people, the intelligence they have been gradually acquiring, and the uses which on some emergency they might make of it, was unknown to, and consequently unappreciated by the aristocracy. They who thought they were, and wished others to believe they were, the most intelligent, and in all respects the best qualified to lead the people, were the most ignorant of the path which ought to be taken. The proceedings during the nine days from the resignation of Lord Grey to his restoration, showed how miserably they had been mistaken, and read a lesson to them which they should have learned by heart, and never more have forgotten.

Proud and tyrannical aristocracies have scarcely ever been teachable; never until now has any such body learned any thing from the people; ours is perhaps the only powerful aristocracy that ever was instructed by them; and further, good teaching, if rigorously continued, may not perhaps be wholly thrown away on this self-sufficient body.

On the day on which ministers resigned, the National Political Union held a special general meeting, *H. B. Churchill, Esq.,* in the Chair.

On this occasion, the public feeling was strongly manifested; short as was the notice, many hundreds of persons became members of the Union; and not only was the very large room in which the meeting was held, filled to the utmost, but the passages were also filled with members, whilst many who could gain no admittance remained at the doors.

At the preceding general meeting, it had been resolved that a respectful address to the King should be prepared, and also a petition to the Lords, praying that means might be taken to secure the passing of the Reform Bill unmutilated, and this meeting was intended to give effect to these resolutions; but, in the interval, short as it was between the calling and holding of the meeting, the King had accepted the resignation of his ministers, and a general persuasion was entertained that the Duke of Wellington, the avowed enemy of all reform, and, as it was also understood, in other respects the enemy of the people, would be called to office, the meeting unanimously resolved—

1. That the address to the King, which was ordered to be prepared, and the petition to the House of Lords, voted at the last general meeting, be rescinded, and the resolutions for their adoption be erased from the minute book of the Union.

2. That the betrayal of the cause of the people is not attributable to Earl Grey's administration, but to the base and foul treachery of others.

3. That the refusal of the King to create Peers, and thereby to secure the passing of the Bill, has thrown the people on their own resources; and that they, and they alone, can prevent the most horrible mischief by immediately meeting in counties, cities, towns, and parishes, and by their resolves insuring compliance with their wishes.

A respectful vote of thanks was given to Mr. Attwood, the people of Birmingham and the surrounding districts, for their support of the cause of reform at their late and former meetings. It was also resolved that the Council should meet in the great room on the next evening.

As the meetings of the Council had been usually held in the presence of as many of the members as accommodation could be made for, this resolution was equivalent to calling a general meeting; and accordingly a general meeting of the members was again held. *Henry Revell, Esq.*, in the Chair, when the following business was transacted. Resolved—

1. That the following petition be adopted; and that Mr. Hume be requested to present it to the House of Commons to-morrow evening:

"To the Honourable the Commons of the United Kingdom of Great Britain and Ireland, in Parliament assembled.

"The petition of the undersigned persons, who are members of a society calling itself the National Political Union,—Sheweth,

"That your petitioners, believing there is yet time to save the country from a frightful convulsion, and that the means are in your hands, urgently implore your Honourable House to take such measures as may be necessary to induce the return of Earl Grey to the post he has quitted, with sufficient power to carry the Reform Bill unmutilated; and, as one means of arresting the impending mischief, to put the supplies into the hands of Parliamentary commissioners—to be applied on the certainty only that the Reform Bill will become law."

2. That if the majority of the House of Commons do their duty to the country and to themselves, the success of the Reform Bill, and the tranquillity of the country, will be assured.

3. That, if the House of Commons should timidly or dishonestly neglect their duty, the success of reform is still certain from the energy and determination of the people.

4. That the Council of this Union be requested to meet at eight o'clock to-morrow evening, for the purpose of taking into their consideration the propriety of holding a meeting, at a distance from the metropolis, on the

earliest possible day, and of inviting thereto all the London districts and other reform unions and committees, to concur in resolutions, and to enter into arrangements for assembling in procession.

This meeting, like that held on the preceding evening, was numerously attended; many hundreds of persons had become members of the Union in the course of the day; and it was easy to foresee, that, excited as they now were, and resolved as they now were, not to be trifled with, no place under cover would much longer be adequate to the desire of more than a very small portion of those who wished to assemble. Numbers, who on this occasion could not obtain admission, were addressed in the square, in front of Saville House.

News of the resignation of Lord Grey and his colleagues in office, reached Birmingham early on the morning of the 10th, the Council of the Union, there, assembled spontaneously and promptly called a public meeting, to be held at 3 o'clock in the afternoon of the same day. The town and its neighbourhood was greatly excited, and a meeting of many thousands took place; the number was immense, the feeling and the determination of the assembled multitudes was admirable. A large meeting had been held at Manchester. The city of London, and a great many other places, either had met, or were preparing to meet, and a scene of astonishing activity was exhibited all over the country.

It now became necessary for your Council to meet daily, or rather continually, so great was the eagerness of the people for active co-operation; and so great was the number of persons who became members of the Union, that it was thought advisable to call another general meeting of the members immediately.

Every thing seemed to forebode a commotion; the first unquestionable and certain step to which would have been a dissolution of Parliament—yet this was expected. It seemed to many, as quite certain, that, should the Parliament be dissolved, and the Duke of Wellington be restored to office, the government must be carried on by such means as the Duke and his adherents might think most likely to maintain their mode of governing the people. This caused many to fear for the consequences of a dissolution of Parliament—some to dread these consequences; but these latter were comparatively few in number, or were persons not likely either to be useful or dangerous to the public in the event which was expected to take place. The energy of the people was generally roused, and preparations appeared to be rapidly making for the worst that could happen. The determination of the people increased continually; and no one was now so besotted as to believe, that they would quietly, or at all, submit to the domination of any set of men whatever. In discharge of their duty then, your Council called another general meeting of the members of the Union, which was held on the evening of the 12th. *Charles Buller, Esq.,* in the Chair.

This meeting was the largest which had been held; the number of persons assembled in the square, outside the house, amounted to several thousands; and it therefore became necessary, that they should be addressed by some members of the Council: this was done; and the resolutions which had been passed within doors, being read to those without doors, they were acknowledged by shouts of applause. The resolutions were as follows:

1. That, in the present awful crisis, any person who may advise his Majesty to dissolve the Parliament will be an enemy to the country.

2. That the members of the House of Commons who have composed the several majorities since the decision in the House of Lords on the 7th instant, and especially on Lord Ebrington's motion, deserve the thanks of the country.

Public affairs had now assumed so serious an aspect, as to make it evident to the Council that a general meeting of the inhabitants of the metropolis and places adjacent could not be safely held. The number of persons likely to attend such a meeting would, it was expected, consist of hundreds of thousands, very few of whom would be able to hear those who addressed them; and, consequently, the persons appointed to conduct the meeting would be unable to control the multitude; it appeared, therefore, probable, that they might proceed tumultuously to demand the restoration of ministers, and thus, perhaps, bring on prematurely a civil commotion. The Council, which now met daily, having carefully examined all the circumstances likely to influence the meeting, and having contrasted the result, as well for good as for evil, resolved, not at the present moment to convene the meeting. This they made known by a declaration on council.

Men of property and character had been appointed in many places, and sent to London, to confer with one another, with the Council of the Union, with the late ministers and others, and to take such measures as should appear to them most likely to cause the restoration of Earl Grey and his coadjutors to office, and to impede as much as possible the advancement of the Duke of Wellington and his adherents. They were expected to act promptly and boldly, and could rely for efficient support on those at whose instance they had been appointed. The determination and courage of every man rose with the appearance of increased danger to the public; all were prepared to do their duty, legally, as long as they and others were dealt with legally; to resist by every possible means any illegal attempt against the public, come from whom it might, or in whatever form it might; under no circumstances to submit to the conservative tories, but to resist their domination at all hazards.

The number of public meetings which were held in various places was very great; and though, from want of time, there was no consultation, nor any communication between distant parts of the country, the opinions of the people coincided in all material points; all appeared resolved not to acquiesce in the appointment of any administration at the head of which the Duke of Wellington should be placed; all expressed an earnest desire that Lord Grey should be restored to office. Tracts, pamphlets, and addresses out of number were written, printed, and distributed with unexampled celerity; hand-bills were given away, and placards were posted, in numbers so great as to seem incredible; nor were the newspapers deficient in aiding the good cause. With very few exceptions, they supported the claims of justice, which the people demanded: greater unanimity, and more determination to hold to their purpose, were never perhaps exhibited at any period of our history.

Among the placards was one (*it did not emanate from the Union*), which seems to have contributed materially to the settlement of affairs. It was in these words,

To stop the Duke, go for gold.

The newspapers copied it; some assenting to the words, some condemning them, many fearing them. The cue was given; a large number of persons drew their balances from their bankers in cash; persons who had money in savings' banks, gave notice to withdraw it; and an operation had commenced all over the nation, which, had the country remained but a few days longer without an administration, or had the Duke of Wellington been able to form one with himself at the head of it, would have closed all the banks, and brought the matter to a speedy issue.

On the evening of Tuesday the 15th, after, as it is believed, a private communication had been made by the bank of England, Lord Grey moved "the adjournment of the House of Lords till Thursday, in consequence of a communication he had received from his Majesty." The news of this communication was carried to all parts of the country with the utmost speed, and produced most remarkable consequences. The course taken by the people was as prompt, as decisive, and as uniformly the same, as it could have been had they acted by concert. No one appeared to relax in his endeavours to procure the re-appointment of Earl Grey: but every one seemed willing to suspend every other means which had been adopted for their own defence until the issue should be known. The demand for gold ceased almost instantly, and cheerfulness took place of the most serious, but not gloomy, determination of the people to accomplish the great object they had at heart. So extraordinary a proceeding never before occurred; none which so decidedly and perfectly proved the intelligence and good sense of the people.

The next day, the 16th, a meeting of the Council was held, previous to a general meeting of the members of the Union, and resolutions suitable to the occasion were proposed. *Daniel Wakefield, Jun., Esq,* in the Chair.

The meeting, like those which preceded it, was numerously attended, and an immense assemblage of people were addressed from the outside of the house. The following resolutions were unanimously agreed:—

1. That this meeting hails with pleasure the prospect of the re-appointment of Earl Grey's administration, in the confident expectation that he will make no compromise with the enemies of the people.

2. That it is absolutely necessary, for the peace and tranquillity of the nation, that Earl Grey should be empowered to carry the Reform Bill, unmutilated, and to secure to our Scotch and Irish brethren their full and fair share in the national representation.

3. That this Union firmly pledges itself to support Earl Grey against every effort that may be directed against him, either by open attack from a desperate faction, or by private intrigues, disgraceful to the king and insulting to the people.

On the 17th, the Council again assembled; Lord Grey had not been recalled; disappointment was very generally expressed, and fears were entertained that he would not be reinstated in office. It was believed that the Duke of Wellington had failed in his endeavours to form such an administration as he and other ultra-tories wished. It was also believed, that the Duke and his immediate adherents were desirous to undertake the government of the country; apprehensions were entertained that he would be permitted to make the attempt, and matters were rapidly approaching to the state they were in on the 15th, before Lord Grey's communication was made to the Lords. Resolved to be prepared for the worst, the Council ordered a general meeting of the Union to be held on the following Monday, at the City of London Tavern. It was expected, that if things remained as they were, and no commotion took place, which there were reasonable grounds for expecting, the number of persons likely to become members of the Union would make arrangements for meetings to be held in various parts of the metropolis necessary.

There was no responsible minister; and it was rumoured that the Duke would be permitted to undertake the management of public affairs, and to conduct them in his own way. To such an extent had this rumour spread, and so generally was it believed by men in every rank of life, as to create an awful pause, which foreboded the great events now evidently at hand. This was a truly fearful moment, and was felt by all to be so. The delegates who were in London prepared to return home, and other demonstrations were made, all evidencing a marked determination not to submit to any illegal conservative measure. Men who had been active in supporting Earl Grey, and had exerted themselves in behalf of the people, scarcely thought their persons safe, but none were intimidated; the courage of all rose as the time approached, when, as they expected they might be called upon to exercise it, various were the demonstrations, numerous the proofs, individually and collectively, of the determination of the people to support one another; all looked anxiously, yet yearlessly, for the moment when the King's determination should be made known, as on this depended the part the people *must* take. In the evening all apprehension and all fear of evil consequences were happily ended by the declaration of Lord Grey, that he and his colleagues, having acquired power to pass the bills, had resumed their places.

The news of Lord Grey's reappointment to office, and his declaration that he had ample powers to carry the bills, spread with amazing rapidity; its effects cannot be described: men felt as if relieved from an oppressive load; each congratulated his fellow on the prospect before him, and the persuasion he entertained, that the liberties of the people would be achieved by *peaceable* means, which, only an hour before, was considered as all but impossible.

The Council met again on the next day, Saturday, the 19th, and prepared the business for the general meeting of the Union on Monday the 21st, at the City of London Tavern. The resolutions to be proposed at the meeting were drawn up conformably with the change which had taken place since the meeting was first announced.—At this meeting the chair was taken by the Patriarch of Reform, *John Towill Rutt, Esq.,* and the following resolutions were unanimously voted.

   1. That the following address to Earl Grey be adopted:
   "To the Right Honourable Earl Grey, etc. etc. etc.
   "The address of the persons composing the society calling itself the National Political Union, in public meeting assembled, this 21st day of May, 1832, at the London Tavern:

"The members of the National Political Union most respectfully address themselves to your Lordship,

"To congratulate your Lordship on your re-appointment to office, with power to secure the passing of bills to reform the representation of the people in the Commons House of Parliament.

"To thank your Lordship and your colleagues, but more especially your Lordship, for the endurance and courage with which the solicitations of friends, and the open and concealed attacks and machinations of enemies, have been borne and resisted during the time you were endeavouring to destroy the dominant power of the boroughmongers,—a power which has long been exercised to the injury of the nation, and which, if continued, would have accomplished its ruin.

"To assure your Lordship of our unanimous determination to support to the utmost of our power those measures which it may be necessary for your Lordship and your colleagues to take for the purpose of promoting Reform of Parliament, and all such other reforms, ecclesiastical, civil, legal, criminal, and military, as may be requisite to promote the well-being of the people.

"We are fully convinced that the transactions of the last fortnight have exhibited to the world a state of things unparalleled in any nation; and have demonstrated the advantages of civilisation beyond all former examples: have shewn that an intelligent people, led by their enlightened and honest fellow-citizens, are equal to any circumstances in which they can be placed; and that when thus led, they can, by their calmness and courage, defeat the machinations of their enemies, and triumph over all attempts to establish arbitrary power.

"We beg to notice to your Lordship the fact, that when an enlightened people are directed to great and important objects, none can be found to commit even the most trifling outrage; that during the late very extraordinary excitement, not a window has been broken, nor has there been an unusually large assemblage of people at the houses of parliament.

"We beg your Lordship's acceptance of our sincere wishes for your health and happiness, and that the honour and fame of your Lordship may endure as long as mankind shall continue to exist."

2. That, precluded as we are by the forms of the House of Commons from presenting an address to the members who have composed majorities or minorities in that house, we thus present our best thanks to those members who composed the majority on Lord Ebrington's motion on the 10th instant, to address the King in favour of the Reform Bill and Lord Grey's administration.

3. That the conduct of the people of this country throughout their long-continued struggle for the attainment of their rights, by a Reform in the representation in Parliament, including those whose just claims are not recognised in the bills now in progress—the political information they have acquired, notwithstanding the taxes by which the diffusion of knowledge is obstructed, and the other arts which have been employed to

keep them in ignorance—the energy with which they have acted, and the patience with which they have endured; their having allowed neither insults, injuries, nor treachery, to mislead them to their ruin, nor to goad them to commit acts of violence, during the late extraordinary and critical state of public affairs—the prompt and universal determination they evinced—the sacrifices they were prepared to make—and the course of peaceful, but irresistible, opposition they had commenced against the renewed efforts to subject them to tory misrule, have ennobled the national character, established the best title to the political freedom they claim, and have excited the most exhilirating hopes of the future safety, prosperity, and happiness of the country.

4. That the public press, generally, by its able and energetic advocacy of Parliamentary Reform—by its watchfulness over the enemies of the people, and exposure of their machinations—by the exertions which its conductors have made—the talent and principles they have displayed—and the salutary influence they have exercised during the recent eventful proceedings in Parliament, and especially at the late crisis, has merited the lasting gratitude of all friends of their country, not only for the eminent services already accomplished, but also for its tendency to promote the civilisation and improvement, and to secure the liberty, of all mankind.

On Wednesday, the 23d, the Council again assembled, and a deputation of four members were appointed to present to Lord Grey the address, which had been agreed to at the general meeting: but, as the address was to be presented as the act of the Union, Lord Grey, as matter of *etiquette*, declined receiving your deputation.

It soon became apparent that the Reform Bill would be carried in the House of Lords; the great excitement which had generally prevailed rapidly subsided, and the meetings of the Council were held as formerly, once only in each week.

A bill having been brought into the House of Commons "for preserving the Independence and Dignity of the House," by excluding from it persons who were insolvent, or bankrupt, or against whom execution for debt had been issued, and apprehensions being entertained that it was a step towards excluding proper persons from obtaining seats in that House, the Council, after much deliberation, on the 13th of June, resolved to petition the House of Commons not to pass the proposed bill, and prayed the House to leave that bill, and all additional regulations to increase the disqualification of persons to sit in the House, to the consideration of a Reformed Parliament.

The English and Scotch Reform Bills having passed the House of Commons, and the Irish Reform Bill having been represented as inadequate and unequal in efficacy to the English and Scotch Bills, a special general meeting of the Union was held on the 19th of June, *Mr. George Rogers* in the Chair.

Daniel O'Connell, Esq. M. P. explained to the meeting the particulars in which the Irish bill was inadequate, and the meeting unanimously came to the following resolutions:—

1. That, in the opinion of this Union, England is greatly indebted to the people of Ireland and their popular representatives, especially Daniel

O'Connell, Esq. for the assistance he gave to the passing of the Reform Bill for England and Wales; and that therefore, independently of all other considerations, we tell ourselves bound to promote, as much as we can, a measure of Reform for Ireland proportionally equal, in all respects, to that which has been secured for England.

2. That this meeting reflects, with deep regret, on the long series of partial, unjust, and oppressive measures, to which Ireland has been subjected: that this regret has been changed into indignation, by the fresh and galling insults offered to that enduring and generous people in the provisions of the Irish Reform Bill, devised by the present Administration, and urged forwards against the repeated remonstrances of the people of Ireland, and by the whole of their popular representatives in Parliament.

A bill having been brought into the House of Lords to make it unnecessary for members of the House of Commons to vacate their seats on the acceptance of certain offices under the Crown, your Council, on the 27th of June, appointed a committee to draw up a petition to the Lords, praying them not to carry forward the bill, "inasmuch as it is not only pregnant with evils of great magnitude to the country, but is a direct violation of the Act of Settlement, and consequently of the compact made between the present dynasty and the people of this country."

The English Reform Bill received the royal assent on the 7th of June, and all apprehension for the fate of the Scotch and Irish bills having subsided, discussions took place in many parts of the country respecting the mode of demonstrating the satisfaction the people felt at the victory they had gained. Great and valid objections were made to the old mode of generally illuminating houses, and the tumults it occasioned. The Council therefore resolved to discountenance illumination, and to promote a dinner of the members of the Union; a committee was accordingly appointed to make the necessary arrangements.

On the 1st of August, after a discussion on the absurd custom of drinking the King's health at public dinners, the Council resolved to "omit naming the King in any toast to be given at the dinner." It was argued that drinking the King's health without any regard to the acts of the King for good or for evil, and without regard to any moral consideration, and this, too, with the same acclamations to all kings indiscriminately, was no mark of respect to any one; no mark of sense in those who did so, but a mere common-place exhibition of a slavish disposition; that, as it had been avoided by other associations, so it was becoming on the present occasion to avoid it altogether. The resolution having been communicated to Mr. Hume, he objected to take the chair at the dinner, unless he was permitted to give the King's health.

Mr. Hume's letter, containing his reasons for refusing to take the chair unless the King's health was made one of the toasts, was laid before the Council at its next meeting, when the subject was very fully discussed, but the Council did not rescind the resolutions they had before unanimously agreed to. The members who acted as stewards authorised the toast, and inserted it amongst the others.

Mr. Hume presided at the dinner, and gave the King's health, in the usual way; and, on this having been reported to the Council, it was resolved, unanimously, "That the proposal of the King's health as a toast at the dinner of the members of the

National Political Union was without the consent and in violation of the unanimous vote of this Council."

The objects which next claimed the attention of your Council, and without which their proceedings respecting the Reform of Parliament would have been incomplete, were, the pledges which ought to be taken from candidates, and *voting by* Ballot.

Your Council were fully acquainted with the vile practices which had been resorted to under the rotten borough system. They knew, that by these practices numbers of persons had been returned to Parliament, ready and willing to sell their country; to deprave the people; to shut them out from all interference in matters relating to the government; to keep them in ignorance; to assist in plundering and coercing them to the last point of endurance;—men, in fact, utterly unqualified for the office of legislators, and fit only for mischief;—men, who, whilst living on the plunder of the people, treated them with the contempt they almost merited for submitting to be thus treated. Your Council were fully satisfied that many such persons would again present themselves as candidates; and as the right of suffrage had been given to electors in places where it had never before been exercised, they feared lest the old tricks might be successfully put in practice. Knowing, also, that many who would offer themselves as Reformers were only sham Reformers, your Council concluded, that the best way they could proceed, to prevent, at least to some extent, the evils they foresaw as likely to take place, was, to advise electors to demand pledges. An essay was therefore prepared entitled, "On Pledges to be given by Candidates." This essay contained reasons why pledges should be demanded, and named the most general and most important of them: 10,000 copies were printed, and carefully distributed in all parts of the country. The good consequences of this publication have been manifested in numerous instances. It has been the means of preventing bad men from offering themselves; it has driven others away; it has, in a great many cases, caused candidates to put forth addresses containing numerous pledges, by which their future conduct can be tested. A howl, which showed the value of the publication, and the effect it was producing, was set up against pledges, in the hope that electors would be made to believe they were useless. In some very few instances, of which Westminster is the most prominent and disgraceful example, these assertions have been believed; and they who used them, have succeeded in obtaining the suffrages of the deluded people. Many candidates have declared that they would give no pledges; and yet their addresses have nearly, or entirely consisted of pledges; the objections in these cases must be considered as made solely to a word they disliked. No doubt can be entertained of the great usefulness of the trace; or that it will be still more extensively useful at the next election, when the people will have had the experience which the present Parliament will not fail to furnish.

The other important publication, of which also 10,000 copies were printed and distributed, "On the Ballot," is a careful abridgment of a most masterly article, which appeared in the Westminster Review. In that paper, the subject has been exhausted; and though much has been lately written against the Ballot, not an argument has been advanced for which an answer cannot be found in the essay referred to. There was a tacit assent at the time the English Reform Bill was first introduced, to refrain from embarrassing ministers, by demanding the Ballot; but when the Bills had been passed, it was the opinion of your Council, that the publication of the tract "On Ballot" would tend greatly to encourage the people to demand the Ballot from the reformed Parliament; and the proceedings now in progress, show how well founded was the opinion, and how correctly they anticipated the good consequences which have resulted, and are likely to result, from the large distribution they caused to be made.

Your Council have now gone through all that relates to the political conduct of the Union; and they feel assured, that you will approve of the account they have given of the circumstances which attended the several important measures they have noticed; and that, notwithstanding it occupies much space, it is a condensed account of the proceedings, a brief narrative only, of some of the occurrences of one of the most important periods of British History. . . .

WORKING-CLASS ACTIVISM

Address, rules, and objects of the London Working Men's Association, July 1836

Address and Rules of the Working Men's Association, for Benefitting Politically, Socially, and Morally, the Working Classes (London: John Cleave, 1837?), 2-6.

The London Working Men's Association was established in 1836 by William Lovett (1800-77) and other radical artisans. It issued numerous tracts and played an influential role in the moderate wing of the Chartist movement.

ADDRESS

Fellow Labourers in the Pursuit of Knowledge and Liberty.—We are anxious to express our grateful acknowledgments thus publicly, to those associations who have addressed us in the spirit of fraternity, and especially to those individuals who have so kindly assisted our missionaries in their exertions to form other associations.

It is a pleasing evidence of the progressive knowledge of those great principles of democracy which we are contending for, to find kindred minds prepared to appreciate, and noble hearts seeking their practical development in the remotest parts of the kingdom.

But we would respectfully caution our brethren in other societies, strictly to adhere to a judicious selection of their members; on this, more than on any other of their exertions, harmony and success will depend. Let us, friends, seek to make the principles of democracy as respectable in practice as they are just in theory, by excluding the drunken and immoral from our ranks; and in uniting in close compact with the honest, sober, moral, and thinking portion of our brethren.

Doubtless, by such selections, our numbers, in many instances, will be few compared with the vicious many; but these few will be more efficient for the political and social emancipation of mankind than an indiscriminate union of thousands, where the veteran drunkard contaminates by his example, and the profligate railer at abuses saps, by his private conduct, the cause he has espoused.

In forming Working Men's Associations, we seek not a mere exhibition of numbers; unless, indeed, they possess the attributes and character of *men*; and little worthy of the name are those who have no aspirations beyond mere sensual enjoyments—who, forgetful of their duties as fathers, husbands, and brothers, muddle their understandings and drown their intellect amid the drunken revelry of the pot-house—whose profligacy makes them the ready tools and victims of corruption, or slaves of unprincipled governors, who connive at their folly, and smile while they forge for themselves the fetters of liberty by their love of drink.

We doubt not, that the excessive toil and misery to which the sons of labour are subject, in the absence of that knowledge and mental recreation which all just governments should seek to diffuse, are mainly instrumental in generating that intemperance, the debasing influence of which we perceive and deplore. But, friends, though we possess not the political power to begin our reformation at the source of the evil, we cannot doubt the efficacy of our exertions to check by precept and example this politically-debasing, soul-subduing vice.

Fellow-countrymen, *when we contend for an equality of political rights*, it is not in order to lop off an unjust tax or useless pension, or to get a transfer of wealth, power, or influence for a party; but to be *able to probe our social evils to their source, and to apply effective remedies to prevent, instead of unjust laws to punish.* We shall meet with obstacles, disappointments, and it may be with persecutions, in our pursuit; but, with your united exertions and perseverance, we must and will succeed.

And if the teachers of temperance and preachers of morality would unite like us, and direct their attention to the source of the evil, instead of nibbling at the effects and seldom speaking of the cause; then, indeed, instead of splendid palaces of intemperance daily erected, as if in mockery of their exertions—built on the ruins of happy homes, despairing minds, and sickened hearts—we should soon have a sober, honest, and reflecting people.

In the pursuit, therefore, of our righteous object, it will be necessary to be prudent in our choice of members; we should also avoid by every possible means holding our meetings at public houses; habits and associations are too often formed at those places which mar the domestic happiness, and destroy the political usefulness of millions. Let us, then, in the absence of means to hire a better place of meeting, meet at each other's houses. Let us be punctual in our attendance, as best contributing to our union and improvement; and, as an essential requisite, seek to obtain a select library of books, choosing those at first which will best inform us of our political and social rights. Let us blend, as far as our means will enable us, study with recreation, and share in any rational amusement (unassociated with the means of intoxication) calculated to sooth our anxieties and alleviate our toils.

And, as our object is universal, so (consistent with justice) ought to be our means to compass it; and we know not of any means more efficient, than to enlist the sympathies and quicken the intellects of our wives and children to a knowledge of their rights and duties;—for, as, in the absence of knowledge, they are the most formidable obstacles to a man's patriotic exertions, so when imbued with it will they prove his greatest auxiliaries. Read, therefore; talk, and politically and morally instruct your wives and children; let them, as far as possible, share in your pleasures, as they must in your cares; and they will soon learn to appreciate your exertions, and be inspired with your own feelings against the enemies of their country. Thus instructed, your wives will spurn, instead of prompting you to accept, the base election bribe—your sons will scorn to wear the livery of tyrants—and your daughters be doubly fortified against the thousand ills to which the children of poverty are exposed.

Who can foretell the great political and social advantages that must accrue from the wide extension of societies of this description acting up to their principles? Imagine the honest, sober, and reflecting portion of every town and village in the kingdom linked together as a band of brothers,—honestly resolved to investigate all subjects connected with their interests, and to prepare their minds to combat with the errors and enemies of society—setting an example of propriety to their neighbours, and enjoying even in poverty a happy home. And, in proportion as home is made pleasant, by a cheerful and intelligent partner, by dutiful children, and by means of comfort their knowledge has enabled them to snatch from the alehouse, so are the bitters of life sweetened with happiness.

Think you a corrupt Government could perpetuate its exclusive and demoralizing influencing influence amid a people thus united and instructed? Could a vicious aristocracy find its servile slaves to render homage to idleness and idolatry to the wealth too often fraudently exacted from industry? Could the present gambling influences of money perpetuate the slavery of the millions, for the gains or dissipation of the few? Could corruption sit in the judgment seat—empty-headed importance in the senate-house—money-getting hypocrisy in the pulpit—and debauchery, fanaticism, poverty, and crime stalk triumphantly through the land,— if the millions were educated in a knowledge of their rights?

No, no, friends; and hence the efforts of the exclusive few to keep the people ignorant and divided. Be ours the task then to unite and instruct them; for, be assured, the good that is to be must be begun by ourselves. And is it not a task worthy of every generous mind, to endeavour to ameliorate the condition of humanity?

It has been said by some that our objects are exclusive, seeing we wish to confine our associations to working men. We reply, that judging from experience and appearances, the political and social regeneration of the working classes must be begun by themselves; and, therefore, they should not admit any preponderating influence of wealth or title to swerve them from their duty. By the laws of our Association all classes and conditions of men, whose character will stand the test of investigation, may be admitted to render us all the possible good they can desire— we only seek to prevent them from doing us evil. If they desire to impart to us their superior knowledge and advice, our laws permit them to do so on terms of perfect equality; but if they desire to rule and govern for their selfish interests, our rules oppose their domination. Let not however the men of wealth imagine that we have any ulterior designs inimical to their rights, or views opposed to the peace and harmony of society.—On the contrary, we seek to render property more secure; life more sacred; and to preserve inviolate every institution that can be made to contribute to the happiness of man. We only seek that share in the institutions and government of our country which our industry and usefulness justly merit. That the working millions may be induced to perceive their just interests and form themselves into Working Men's Associations,—and that those already enrolled may be urged by a sense of duty to their families and their country to persevere in their progress—is the ardent wish of the members of the London Working Men's Association.

Signed by the Committee, on behalf of the Association—

> *H. Hetherington*
> Printer, Treasurer, . . .
> *William Lovett*
> Cabinet-maker, Secretary, . . .

RULES, ETC.

Among the causes that most contribute to the perpetuation of abuses and corruptions in every department of the state, and the indifference manifested toward the interests of the millions, none have been more pregnant with evil than the divisions and dissensions among the working classes themselves.

The great variety and clashing of opinions on all important subjects, political and social—the contradictory and deficient evidence relating to the true condition of the labourer—the conflicting means suggested to remedy what each conceives to be the paramount evil—together with the bickerings and trifling of the most honest and influential amongst them—have long been subjects of regret and causes of vexatious disappointment.

Being convinced, then, that no reflecting and philanthropic mind can *witness* those scenes of misery that everywhere press upon his notice,—can *read* of the thousand wretched forms under which the demon of poverty tortures the millions, and at the same time *reflect* on the ample means wasted on folly and lavished on idleness—means sufficient to impart happiness to all, if wisely directed, without resolving to inquire into the causes of those evils, and to devise, if possible, some means of remedying or alleviating them.

And if the working classes themselves do not sympathise with each other, so many of whom have felt the bitterness of extreme poverty, how can they expect those, who, from their situations in life can scarcely form a conception of it, to feel or care respecting them? If they, whose interests are so identified, do not investigate the causes of the evils that oppress them, how can they expect others to do it for them?

A few persons, therefore, belonging to and associated with the working classes, having seen much of their state and condition, and knowing much more of their wants and necessities, sincerely lamenting their apathy to their *own affairs*, and their still more reprehensible dependence on wealth and power for their political and social rights, have resolved to use every exertion to form an Association, with the following objects in view:—

Objects

1. To draw into one bond of Unity the *intelligent* and *influential* portion of the working classes in town and country;

2.   To seek by every legal means to place all classes of society in possession of their equal, political, and social rights;

3.   To devise every possible means, and to use every exertion, to remove those cruel laws that prevent the free circulation of thought through the medium of a *cheap and honest press*;

4.   To promote, by all available means, the education of the rising generation, and the extirpation of those systems which tend to future slavery;

5.   To collect every kind of information appertaining to the interests of the working classes in particular, and society in general, especially statistics regarding the wages of labour, the habits and condition of the labourer, and all those causes that mainly contribute to the present state of things;

6.   To meet and communicate with each other for the purpose of digesting the information acquired, and to mature such plans as they believe will conduce in practice to the well-being of the working classes;

7.   To publish their views and sentiments in such form and manner as shall best serve to create a moral, reflecting, yet energetic public opinion, so as eventually to lead to a gradual improvement in the condition of the working classes, without violence or commotion;

8.   To form a library of reference and useful information; to maintain a place where they can associate for mental improvement, and where their brethren from the country can meet with kindred minds actuated by one great motive—that of benefitting politically, socially, and morally, the useful classes.

Though the persons forming this Association will be at all times disposed to co-operate with all those who seek to promote the happiness of the multitude, yet being convinced, from experience, that the division of interests in the various classes, in the present state of things, is too often destructive of that union of sentiment which is essential to the prosecution of any great object, that they have resolved to confine their members, as far as practicable, to the working classes. But as there are great differences of opinion as to where the line should be drawn which separates the working classes from the other portions of society, they leave to the members themselves to determine whether the candidate proposed is eligible to become a member. . . .

Pamphlet by George Loveless, one of the "Tolpuddle martyrs" convicted of trade union activities, 1837

The Victims of Whiggery; Being a Statement of the Persecutions Experienced by the Dorchester Labourers; Their trial, banishment, etc., also reflections upon the present system of transportation . . . (London: Effingham Wilson, 1837), 5-20.

Early in 1834 the Grand National Consolidated Trades Union was organized to give effect to Robert Owen's cooperative principles. This experiment in large-scale trade unionism had only a brief existence, but it touched off unrest and led to the prosecution of six farm laborers at Tolpuddle in Dorset. These six workers had formed a branch of the Friendly Society of Agricultural Labourers, affiliated to the GNCTU. They adopted an initiation oath and ceremony; for this they were arrested under one of Pitt's repressive acts—the Unlawful Oaths Act (1797)—and sentenced to seven years' transportation to Tasmania. Although this savage sentence provoked widespread agitation, it was four years before the remainder of the sentence was remitted.

In drawing up a brief statement concerning those persecutions which have subjected us to all the punishments, afflictions, and miseries connected with the present system of Transportation (which is far worse than death), I shall not attempt to give the subject an unfair colouring, but simply narrate the facts, just as they took place; mentioning sometimes the reflections of my own mind at the time those facts occurred. But it will first be necessary to mention what led me to become a member of that society which, by the idle and wealthy, has been branded with infamy; but which then, as now, appeared to me to be established on just and upright principles, and to have for its rule the universal law of equity, "as ye would that men should do unto you, do ye even so to them."

About the years 1831-2, when there was a general movement of the working classes for an increase of wages, the labouring men in the parish where I lived (Tolpuddle) gathered together, and met their employers, to ask them for an advance of wages, and they came to a mutual agreement, the masters in Tolpuddle promising to give the men as much for their labour as the other masters in the district. The whole of the men then went to their work, and the time that was spent in this affair did not exceed two hours. No language of intimidation or threatening was used on the occasion. Shortly after we learnt that, in almost every place around us, the masters were giving their men money, or money's worth, to the amount of ten shillings per week—we expected to be entitled to as much—but no—nine shillings must be our portion. After some months we were reduced to eight shillings per week. This caused great dissatisfaction, and all the labouring men in the village, with the exception of two or three invalids, made application to a neighbouring magistrate, namely, William Morden Pitt, Esq. of Kingston House, and asked his advice; he told us that if the labourers would appoint two or three, and come to the County-hall the following Saturday, he would apprize the chief magistrate, James Frampton, Esq. (whose name I shall not soon forget,) and at the same time our employers should be sent for to settle the subject. I was one nominated to appear, and when there we were told that we must work for what our employers thought fit to give us, as there was no law to compel masters to give any fixed sum of money to their servants. In vain we remonstrated that an agreement was made, and that the minister of the parish (Dr. Warren) was witness between the masters and the men; for this hireling parson, who at that time said, of his own accord, "I am witness between you men and your masters, that if you will go quietly to your work, you shall receive for your labour as much as any men in the district; and if your masters should attempt to run from their word, I will undertake to see you righted, so help me God!"—so soon as reference was made to him, denied having a knowledge of any such thing.

From this time we were reduced to seven shillings per week, and shortly after our employers told us they must lower us to six shillings per week. The labouring men consulted together what had better be done, as they knew it was impossible to live honestly on such scanty means. I had seen at different times accounts of Trade Societies; I told them of this, and they willingly consented to form a friendly society among the labourers, having sufficiently learnt that it would be vain to seek redress either of employers, magistrates, or parsons. I inquired of a brother to get information how to proceed, and shortly after, two delegates from a Trade Society paid us a visit, formed a Friendly Society among the labourers, and gave us directions how to proceed. This was about the latter end of October, 1833. On the 9th of December, 1833, in the evening. Edward Legg (a labourer), who was witness against us on our trial, came and desired to be admitted into the Society; by what means he was introduced there I cannot say; but well do I know that James Hammett, one of the six that he swore to, was not there.

Nothing particular occurred from this time to the 21st of February, 1834, when placards were posted up at the most conspicuous places, purporting to be cautions from the magistrates, threatening to punish with seven years' transportation any man who should join the Union. This was the first time that I heard of any law being in existence to forbid such societies. I met with a copy, read it, and put it into my pocket. February the 24th, at daybreak, I arose to go to my usual labour, and had just left my house, when Mr. James Brine, constable of the parish, met me and said, "I have a warrant for you, from the magistrates." "What is its contents, Sir?" "Take it yourself," said he, "you can read it as well as I can." I did so. He asked, "Are you willing to go to the magistrates with me?" I answered, "To any place wherever you wish me." Accordingly I an my companions walked in company with the constable to Dorchester, about seven miles distant, and was taken into the house of a Mr. Woolaston, magistrate, who, with his half brothers, James Frampton, and Edward Legg, were ready to receive us. After asking us several questions, to which I answered, by saying, "We are not aware that we have violated any law, if so, we must be amenable, I suppose, to that law," Legg was called upon to swear to us, and we were instantly sent to prison. As soon as we got within the prison doors, our clothes were stripped off and searched, and in my pocket was found a copy of the above placard, a note from a friend, and a small key. After our heads were shorn, we were locked up together in a room, where we remained, day and night, till the following Saturday, when we were called before a bench of magistrates in another part of the prison. Legg again swore to us, differing considerably from the first statement. We were then fully committed to take our trial at the next assizes.

Directly after we were put back, a Mr. Young, an attorney employed on our behalf, called me into the conversation room, and, among other things, inquired if I would promise the magistrates to have no more to do with the Union if they would let me go home to my wife and family? I said, "I do not understand you."—"Why," said he, "give them information concerning the Union, who else belongs to it, and promise you will have no more to do with it."—"Do you mean to say I am to betray my companions, and promise I will have nothing more to do with them?"—"That is just it," said he. "No; I would rather undergo any punishment."

The same day we were sent to the high jail, where we continued until the assizes. I had never seen the inside of a jail before, but now I began to feel it—disagreeable company, close confinement, bad bread, and, what was worse, hard and cold lodging—a small straw bed on the flags, or else an iron bedstead—"and this," said I to my companions, "is our fare for striving to live honest." In this situation the chaplain of the prison paid us a visit, to pour a volley of instruction into our ears; but, as it was mixed up in a cup of abuse, it did not exactly relish with me. After upbraiding and taunting us with being discontented and idle, and wishing to ruin our masters, he proceeded to tell us that we were better off than our masters, and that government had made use of every possible means for economy and retrenchment to make all comfortable. He inquired if I could point out any thing more that might be done to increase the comfort of the labourer. I told him I thought I could, and began to assure him our object was not to ruin the master, but that, for a long time, we had been looking for the head to begin, and relieve the various members down to the feet; but finding it was of no avail, we were thinking of making application to our masters, and for them to make application to their masters, and so up to the head; and as to their being worse off than ourselves, I could not believe it, while I saw them keep such a number of horses for no other purpose than to chase the hare and the fox. I had been thinking, that if a number of those useless animals were got rid of there would be a two-fold advantage; first, the owner would possess some ready money; and secondly, the expence of keeping them would be saved, to enable him to give a little more for labour: and, besides, I thought gentlemen wearing the clerical livery, like himself, might do with a little less salary, and that also would assist with the rest. "Is that how you mean to do it?" said he. "That is one way I have been thinking of, Sir."—"I hope the Court will favour you, but I think they will not; for I believe they mean to make an example of you." And saying this he left us.

On the 15th of March, we were taken to the County-hall to await our trial; and as soon as we arrived there we were ushered down some steps into a miserable dungeon, opened but twice a year, with only a glimmering light; and to make it more disagreeable, some wet and green brush-wood was served for firing. The smoke of this place, together with its natural dampness, amounted to nearly suffocation; and in this most dreadful situation we passed three whole days. As to the trial, I need not mention but little; the cowardice and dastardly conduct throughout are better known by all that were present than could be by any description that I can give of it: suffice it to say, the most unfair and unjust means were resorted to in order to frame an indictment against us; the grand jury appeared to ransack heaven and earth to get some clue against us, but in vain; our characters were investigated from our infancy to the then present moment; our masters were inquired of to know if we were not idle, or attended public houses, or some other fault in us; and much as they were opposed to us, they had common honesty enough to declare that we were good labouring servants, and that they never heard of any complaint against us; and when nothing whatever could be raked together, the unjust and cruel judge, Williams, ordered us to be tried for mutiny and conspiracy, under an act 37 Geo. III., cap. 123, for the suppression of mutiny amongst the marines and seamen, a number of years ago, at the Nore. The greater part of the evidence against us, on our trial, was put into the mouths of the witnesses by the judge; and when he evidently wished them to say any particular thing, and the witness would say, "I cannot remember," he would say, "Now think; I will give you another minute to consider;" and he would then repeat over the words, and ask, "Cannot you remember?" Sometimes, by charging them to be careful what they said, by way of intimidation, they would merely answer, "yes;" the judge would set it down as the witness's words. I shall not soon forget the address of the judge to the jury, in summing up the evidence: among other things, he told them, that if such Societies were allowed to exist, it would ruin masters, cause a stagnation in trade, destroy property,—and if *they should not find us guilty, he was certain they would forfeit the opinion of the grand jury*. I thought to myself, there is no danger but we shall be found guilty, as we have a special jury for the purpose, selected from among those who are most unfriendly towards us— the grand jury, landowners, the petty jury, land-renters. Under such a charge, from such a quarter, self-interest alone would induce them to say, "Guilty." The judge then inquired if we had anything to say. I instantly forwarded the following short defence, in writing, to him:

> My Lord, if we have violated any law, it was not done intentionally: we have injured no man's reputation, character, person, or property: we were uniting together to preserve ourselves, our wives, and our children, from utter degradation and starvation. We challenge any man, or number of men, to prove that we have acted, or intend to act, different from the above statement.

The judge asked if I wished it to be read in Court. I answered, "Yes." It was then mumbled over to a part of the jury, in such an inaudible manner, that although I knew what was there, I could not comprehend it. And here one of the counsel prevented sentence being passed, by declaring that not one charge brought against any of the prisoners at the bar was proved, and that if we were found guilty a great number of persons would be dissatisfied; "and I shall for one," said he.

Two days after this we were again placed at the bar to receive sentence, when the judge told us, "that not for any thing that we had done, or, as he could prove, we intended to do, but for an example to others, he considered it his duty to pass the sentence of seven years' transportation across his Majesty's high seas upon each and every one of us." Five of us were at the lodge at the time that Legg and Lock swore to our being present; but one, namely, James Hammett, was not there. As soon as the sentence was passed, I got a pencil and a scrap of paper, and wrote the following lines:—

> God is our guide! from field, from wave,
> From plough, from anvil, and from loom;
> We come, our country's rights to save,
> And speak a tyrant faction's doom:
> We raise the watch-word liberty;
> We will, we will, we will be free!
>
> God is our guide! no swords we draw,
> We kindle not war's battle fires;
> By reason, union, justice, law,

We claim the birth-right of our sires:
We raise the watch-word, liberty,
We will, we will, we will be free!!!

While we were being guarded back to prison, our hands locked together, I tossed the above lines to some people that we passed; the guard, however, seizing hold of them, they were instantly carried back to the judge; and by some this was considered a crime of no less magnitude than high treason.

Almost instantly after this I was taken ill, occasioned by being kept in the dungeon already spoken of, and two days after getting worse, I requested to be allowed to see the doctor, and consequently was taken to the hospital. As soon as I entered I had to cope with a new antagonist, Dr. Arden, surgeon of the hospital. I told him I was too ill for conversation, and requested him to allow me to go to bed; but he appeared so angry as not to regard what I said. At length, I threw myself on a bed and answered his questions, until he was very mild, and ever after this he manifested the greatest possible kindness and attention towards me until I left Dorchester Castle. I told him they could hang me with as much justice as transport me for what I had done.

On Wednesday, April the 2nd., Mr. Woolaston, magistrate, paid me a visit, and inquiring how I did, I thanked him, and told him I was much better. He said, "I am sorry, Loveless, to see a man like you in such a situation, but it is your own fault, you are now suffering for your own stubbornness and obstinacy; you have such a proud spirit, you would not pay attention to the cautions of the magistrates, but would rather hearken to idle fellows that were going about the country, who now have deceived you."—I told him I had not been deceived by any, for I knew of no such persons as he had been describing.—"Yes, you do, for you have hearkened to them rather than pay attention to the magistrate's cautions; for I am certain you saw them, one of them being found on your person when you went to prison."—"Is Mr. Woolaston in his right mind?" said I.—"What do you mean?"—"Why, you tell me that I would not listen to the advice and cautions put out by the magistrates, but a copy of those cautions being found in my pocket when taken to gaol, does it not prove that I did pay attention to them, or should I have taken so much care to preserve it in my pocket; and, besides, the circumstance concerning which the witnesses swore against us, took place on the 9th of December, and the magistrate's cautions did not appear till the 21st of February, following; so that we have been tried for what took place at least nine weeks before the cautions had existence; and yet you say I paid no attention to the magistrates, but listened to idle fellows going about the country; within three days after the cautions appeared I was in the body of the gaol."—"Ah," said he, "it is of no use talking to you."—"No, Sir, unless you talk more reasonable."

I intreated the doctor to allow me to be sent away, as I had just heard that my companions were gone. I did this with a view to overtake them; and on Saturday, April the 5th, early in the morning, I was called, to prepare for a journey to Portsmouth; and after getting irons on my legs, and locked on the coach, we proceeded to Salisbury, and at the entrance of the town, a Mr. Glinister, clerk of the prison, who accompanied me, offered to take the irons off my legs. I inquired if he meant to put them on again on leaving Salisbury, he said "Yes," but, as I should have to walk through some part of the town, I had better have them taken off, as the rattling of the chain would cause people to be looking after us. I told him I did not wish for any such thing, as I was not ashamed to wear the chain, conscious of my innocence.

We arrived at Portsmouth about nine o'clock at night, and I was given up in charge to the officers of the York Hulk. When I went on board I was struck with astonishment at the sight of the place, the clinking of the chains, and of so many men being stripped. When ordered to put on the hulk livery, and called upon to attend on the smith to have the fetters rivetted on my legs, for a moment I began to sink down, until the first mate, a Mr. Nicholson, told me I was to go into No. 9 ward, middle deck, one of the best and quietest wards in the ship, and that I was to go there by the captain's order, in consequence of a good character he had received with me from the prison. And yet, after all the striving and struggling by my adversaries, to discover some foul blot against my reputation, without effect, so cruel and reckless for revenge was some party, as to say that I and my brother were rioters; now, to prove the fallacy of such an assertion, I would just refer to the period already alluded to, when we asked our employers to advance our wages, no threats or intimidation were made use of by any of the labourers; and, at the time when so much incendiarism was prevailing in many parts of the kingdom, a watch was set in our parish for the protection of property in the night, and I and my brother, among others, was chosen to watch such property. Will any reasonable man believe, if we had been rioters, that we should have been so chosen? Again, I and my brother were reported to have been regular smugglers and poachers. But all this reporting, stabbing, and slandering men was in the dark, behind the back, out of sight; and well did the party know that there was no foundation for such foul and black assertions, and if there ever was an instance known in the space of thirty-seven years, which was my age when these vile slanders went abroad; I say, if ever, in any one instance, I stand chargeable for any misdemeanor or crime, I call upon James Frampton, Esq., or his satellites, or any one else, to stand out and declare it. Again, I challenge them to come forth and do it in a public manner, that the world may judge the case, and acquit me if innocent, or not let me escape with impunity if guilty. But the secret is this; I am from principle, a Dissenter, and by some, in Tolpuddle, it is considered as the sin of witchcraft; nay, there is no forgiveness for it in this world nor that which is to come; the years 1824-5 are not forgotten, and many a curious tale might be told of men that were persecuted, banished, and not allowed to have employ if they entered the Wesleyan Chapel at Tolpuddle. But enough of this subject, it is still on record.

Monday, April the 7th, I was called upon to go to work with the gun wharf party, and in this employment I continued the whole of the time I was at Portsmouth, being just six weeks. On the 17th of May, in the morning, I was called upon to prepare for a voyage to Botany Bay. One hundred and twenty were draughted from Portsmouth, to join one hundred and twenty that the ship brought down from Woolwich, and after having stripped off every thing, and putting a new suit on for sea, irons as well, we went on board the "William Metcalfe," lying at Spithead, where we remained till the 25th of May. In the afternoon we weighed anchor, and the next evening bid farewell to England, having passed the Land's

End. I now began to think I had seen and heard but very little. Two hundred and forty men, shut down together and locked in a prison, the greater part of them such monsters as I never expected to see, and whose conduct I am not capable of describing. A small bed, pillow, and blanket was allowed for each man, which would have contributed greatly to our comfort, had there been room sufficient to have laid on them, but we could not. A birth about five feet six inches square, was all that was allowed for six men to occupy day and night, with the exception of four hours we were allowed daily on deck, two hours in the forenoon, and two hours in the afternoon for air. For nearly ten weeks out of fourteen I was not able to lie down at length to take rest. But what then? I was a prisoner, and there is none to pity. "You have no business here, so you must take it as it comes, for better for worse," is the consolation you get when you complain.

On the 4th of September we cast anchor before Hobart Town, Van Dieman's Land, and as we had sailed nearly thirty miles already up the river Derwent, between the land, several came to me and asked if I did not think it a delightful country, I spoke the real sentiments of my mind when I gave them the following answer: "I think we are come to the wrong end of the world." Tuesday, September 9th, the magistrates came on board, as is usual to take dimensions, etc., of the prisoners, and one by one was called into the cabin as their names stood arranged on the alphabetical list, or rather as the towns stood from whence they were convicted. When I was called in, after asking me a number of questions about my father, mother, brothers, sisters, wife, children, etc., the following conversation took place between a Mr. Thomas Mason, and myself:

"What is all this about these Unions? you think of doing great things I suppose; now tell me what you meant."

"We meant nothing more, Sir, than uniting together to keep up the price of labour, and to support each other in time of need."

"Now, I know this is false; there is some secret design of conspiracy at the bottom, is there not?"

"No, Sir, quite the reverse of that, for every man that is a member of the Union is under an obligation not to violate the laws."

"Yes; surely, I know you mean they are bound not to break any of their laws."

"I mean they are under an obligation not to violate the laws of their country."

"I do not believe any thing you say about it, for there is so much secrecy belonging to it. Now what is that secret sign or signal by which the Unions knew when to meet all over England at the same time."

"I do not know of what you are talking, Sir."

"You daring fellow, will you tell me so again; do not you know that they did meet all over the kingdom at once?"

"I know of no such thing as their having secret signs or signals to know when to meet; I never heard of such a thing before."

"Where were you when they made such a noise then? will you be so false as to tell me you know nothing about it, now I am certain you know all about it. Be careful in what you say."

"I understand the Union had public meetings at different places, but I was at the York hulk, Portsmouth, at the time."

"It is no matter where you were, you are one of them, and you know all about it, and if you do not tell me here and now all and every thing about them, I will report you to the governor, you shall be taken on shore, and we will give you a second trial, and you shall be severely punished; now, what are those secrets you are so backward in revealing."

"I have none to tell, Sir."

"Now, you pretend from a scrupulous conscience you cannot reveal the secret to me; let me tell you that you ought to tell all that you know about them; and if you have taken an oath not to reveal, *you are sinning against God and man, until you break that oath,* and if you still refuse to tell me you shall be severely punished."

"I am in your hands, and am ready and willing to undergo any suffering you shall think proper to inflict upon me, rather than say I know any thing, when in reality I do not."

"That will do, I will report you to the governor, and you shall be punished."

Friday, September 12, at day-break, we were landed, and conducted to the prisoner's barracks. The same day we were marshalled in the yard for the inspection of the governor, who examines every man, and when he came to me, I was pointed out by the abovenamed magistrate, as being one of the Trades' Union, and very backward to say any thing about them, he therefore (that is Mason), thought it advisable to give me a second examination. What the governor replied I could not then comprehend; however, he began to talk to me on the subject; the following is a part of what passed:

"What a fool you must have been for having any thing to do with such things; what object had you in view for doing so?"

"The motives by which we were influenced were to prevent our wives and families from being utterly degraded and starved."

"Poh, poh, no such thing; what? cannot labouring men live by their labour?"

"Not always now, Sir."

"I mean good labouring men. Surely then can live comfortable?"

"No, Sir, times have been in England when labour was well rewarded, but it is not so now—there is many a good and willing workman that cannot get employed at all, and others get so little for their labour, that it is impossible for them to live if they have families."

"But you know that you did very wrong, do you not?"

"I had no idea whatever that I was violating any law."

"But you must know that you have broken the laws, or how came you here?"

"By some means or other I was sent here; but I cannot see how a man can break a law before he knows that such law is in existence."

"You might as well say I have done very wrong, I acknowledge it, and am sorry for it."

"I cannot do this until I see it."

September 13th, a constable came for me to go to the police-office; and when there I was introduced to Mr. Mason, in a private room, who calling a young man that acted as clerk for him, he asked if I could remember the conversation we had the other day. I answered in the affirmative, he bid me repeat it; I did, the young man looking at a paper he held in his hand, to see if I deviated or not; he again urged me to reveal the secret to him; I told him that I had told him already as far as I knew. "But," said he, "think, now, is there not something you have not told yet?"

"I have told you, Sir, all I can; it appears that you know more about it than I do."

"Well, I have to tell you that you was ordered for severer punishment; *you were to work in irons on the roads;* but in consequence of the conversation you had with the governor yesterday, his mind is disposed in your favour; he won't allow you to go where you was assigned to; he intends to take you to work on his farm."

I now began to feel the effects of transportation. I worked on the roads with the chain-gang in the day, and slept in the barracks at night, without a bed, or covering; whether any was allowed for me I cannot say, I had none. On the 22d September I was sent to the government domain farm, New Town, and here for a long time I found it very little better than at the barracks. Eight men, with only five beds, so of course the new comer must go without, and this was my portion, until some of the older hands unfortunately got into trouble, and I was entitled to a bed, having been longer on the farm than others. Our hut was none of the best: in fine weather we could lie in bed and view the stars, in foul weather feel the wind and rain; and this added more than a little to increase those rheumatic pains which were first brought on by cold irons round the legs and hard laying; and which, in all probability, will be my companions until I reach the tomb.

The weekly allowance of provisions I will now mention, and this I do to answer some objections to a letter I sent home to my wife, dated December, 1834, wherein I stated "our weekly allowance is eight pounds of flour and seven pounds of meat, short allowance for men that work as convicts are obliged to do." I said nothing about the quality, it may not be improper to do so now, recollect it is not of the first-rate quality—we have four pounds of wheat, and four pounds of maize, or Indian corn, or something worse, ground together. Twelve per cent. I believe, is allowed to be taken out as "sharps," by the storekeeper. The beef, or mutton, is of inferior quality also. What would be thought of sheep being killed if they would only weigh sixty pounds, and yet very few that I saw killed for prisoners exceeded twenty-five pounds, and many not twenty pounds; hold it up to the light, and it is no great trouble to see through it. But it has been asked cannot you offer complaints and seek recompense? I answer yes; you can complain to the commissary, and he will inquire of the storekeeper, and in all probability, the storekeeper receives "an allowance" from the contractor and declares that the provisions are storable, and that there is no room at all for complaining. What, then, is the recompense you get for complaining? Why, to use a colonial phrase, you "get married to the three sisters," or, in other words, you are tied to the triangles, and your flesh flogged from the bones for being discontented. Since I sent home the above statement, the scale of provisions has been altered, but not till some of the men at the road parties died through actual want; and others at the barracks were found cooking and eating of cats, etc. Each man had when I left the country, ten and a half pounds of flour, five and a quarter pounds of meat, and three and a half pounds of vegetables weekly, and yet I say it is short allowance for men that work as convicts, and for those who think differently I only wish they had a twelve months trial at it, and I am certain, after that, they would join in the general cry.

At the government farm I continued until I was exempted from government labour: once during that time, I wrote to the governor, hoping I might be allowed to be assigned off to a master, but received no answer. Sometime in the month of November, 1835, my character was inquired after by the governor, and this was repeated at different times for two months, as the overseer on the farm told me, and the last time his Excellency made the following inquiry, "Is there no fault whatever to be found with Loveless? does he never reply when you bid him do a thing? does he never neglect any part of his work?" etc., etc., which was answered in the negative. In the beginning of December, 1835, I was taken to the police office, charged with neglect of duty. W. Gun, Esq. was the sitting magistrate at the time. "Well," said the magistrate, "what have you brought this man here for?"

"For neglect of duty, Sir," said the overseer.

"In what manner has he neglected his duty; what is the man?"

"The man is shepherd and stock-keeper to the governor on the domain farm, and all the cattle, tame and wild, are put into his care: he is expected to see them all every day; nine of the wild cattle were taken to the public pound yesterday, and he did not miss them until this morning."

"I have not heard a clearer charge of neglect of duty for a long time; what have you to say, my man, in answer to this charge?"

"It is true," I said, "I have the charge of all the cattle, and I am expected to see the wild cattle in the bush once every twenty-four hours. I rise in the morning at sunrise, or before, and take the sheep to the bush to feed; I then return to the farm and milk nine cows and suckle as many calves; I am requested to follow the sheep and not lose sight of them for fear of dogs which often get among and worry them; I am ordered to search for the wild cattle to see that none of them are missing; I had just been weaning the lambs, and the ewes being very restless, I was afraid of leaving them; and this, Sir, was the reason the cattle were taken to the pound and I did not miss them."

"Is all this the truth that the man has been telling me?" said the magistrate.

"Yes, Sir,"

"How long have you known this man?"

"Nine months."

"Did you ever know him neglect his duty before?"

"No, Sir; never."

"Then you do not think that he went away from his duty now, but that, as he says, he was with the sheep in consequence of having weaned the lambs?"

"Yes, Sir, I think what he has told you is true; but then he has neglected his duty in losing the cattle."

"But do not you think that the man has more duty than he can perform? I really think it is a great pity you should have brought the man here. I shall return you to your duty, go to your duty my man."

"I thank you, Sir," said I, for I went in full expectation of getting fifty lashes.

December 29th—I went to the police office to answer a note my overseer received from the magistrate to know if my wife should be sent out to join me in the colony, and when I entered his presence the following conversation took place:

"I have sent for you, Loveless," said Mr. Spode, the magistrate, "to know if you wish your wife and family to be sent over to join you in this colony, if government will grant them the facility."

"I hope you will allow me to ask a question before I say any thing about my wife and children," said I.

"What is that?"

"Am I about to obtain my liberty?"

"Liberty! what do you mean?"

"Is there a prospect of my obtaining my free pardon?"

"Not that I know; that depends upon the ministry at home."

"Then, Sir, I can have nothing at all to say on the subject while I am a prisoner."

"You audacious rascal, will you come to insult me thus, after I have been at the pains of writing and sending for you, and all for your own advantage."

"I beg your pardon, Sir, I did not mean to insult you."

"You lie, you rascal, you did; and do you mean to continue that, obstinate fellow?" Here I was silent, knowing what the cruel system would have exposed me to; if I had simply answered "yes," I should have been charged with insolence, and punished accordingly. "But," continued he, "go to your work."

"I will go, Sir."

"Go instantly, or I will give you a d——d good flogging."

January 7th., 1836.—I was again sent for by Mr. Spode, and when I got to the police office he began, "Well, Loveless, I have sent for you once more."

"Yes, sir, and here I am."

"I want to know if you have any objection that your wife and family should be sent over to you, and let me tell you, before you answer me, it is intended for your advantage."

"Nothing could give me so much satisfaction as to join my wife and children had I my liberty, but I do not want them here while I am a prisoner."

"You want to be above the government, and tell them what they must do."

"No, Sir, I do not want to be above the government, nor tell them what they must do, but I tell you, rather than be the instrument of bringing my wife and children into the distress and misery of this colony, such as I feel it, I will remain as I am as long as I live." He then ordered me back.

January the 24th, 1836, his Excellency the governor, came out to the farm where I was living, and, walking with me into the field, he asked me if I had any objection that government should send over my wife and family to me, as they had offered to do it free of expense. I told him I had objections. "I should like to know your objections," said he.

"I should be sorry to send for my wife and children to come into misery."

"Misery! what do you mean?"

"Why, Sir, I have seen nothing but misery ever since I came into this country."

"How long have you been in the country?"

"Above seventeen months."

"And how is it that you have seen nothing but misery?"

"Because the food and clothing allowed to government men only renders them miserable. It is no better than slavery."

"Oh, no, there are no slaves under the British dominions; you are only prisoners."

"You may call it by what name you please, Sir, I call it slavery, and that of the worst description."

"But are you willing that your wife should come over? don't you think that you could do very well together here?"

"I do not know that I could."

"How is it you don't know? you are a good farming man, and you are a good shepherd, are you not?"

"As to that, other people are the best judges. I know nothing of what the colony can afford."

"How is it that you know nothing of what the colony can afford? you say that you have been seventeen months here, and yet you know nothing about it."

"Why, Sir, I have, as it were, been shut up in a cloister; since I came to this farm I have scarce ever put my feet from it; I know no person, and, comparatively speaking, no person knows me."

"Well, I think you could do well with your wife in this country; she would do very well here."

"Sir, I should be a monster to send for my wife to come over here, and see no way of supporting her; what could I do with my wife while I am a prisoner?"

"I have no doubt but you will have your liberty as soon as your wife arrives; I would gladly give you indulgence myself, but that I dare not, in consequence of an act of parliament passed that no seven years' man is to obtain a ticket of leave till he has been four years in the colony. Government has sent out to know how you have conducted yourself since you have been here, and I have sent home an excellent character of you to them. How would you support your wife and family in England?"

"By my labour, Sir."

"And why cannot you support them by your labour here?"

"I consider, while they are in England they are surrounded with friends; if they were here it might be otherwise."

"Ah, talk about friends, every one has enough to do to mind themselves now. Well, consider of it, and let me know in the course of two or three days."

I did so; and I considered what I had often been told, and what I had good authority to believe, that if a man opposes the authorities, he soon becomes a marked man, and parties are looking out to get a case against him to entangle him. Van Dieman's Land will long bear witness to the numbers that have thus fallen victims to revenge, to the utter deprivation of their reputation, property, and liberties. See Hobart Town newspapers, for 1835 and 1836.

January the 27th, I wrote a letter to my wife, requesting her to come to Van Dieman's Land; and sent it, unsealed, to the governor. February the 5th, my superintendant sent to me, saying, "George Loveless, I am requested, by a note from the magistrate, to send you to the police office without delay; you had better, therefore, repair thither as soon as possible." I went, and when there, Mr. Spode gave me a ticket; the following is a copy:

I am directed by his Excellency the governor, in accordance with the wish of his Majesty's government, to give George Loveless (848, per William Metcalfe) a ticket, exempting him from government labour, to employ himself to his own advantage, until further orders. Principal Superintendant's Office, Josiah Spode, February the 5th, 1836.

I was not allowed to receive the above ticket until I gave them some place I called my home, which was registered in their books, that no inconvenience might arise in finding me if required.

I now had my liberty to prove what the colony could afford; and I soon found, to my sorrow, the force of the observation I made to the governor a few days before, that I knew no one, and no one knew me. I was a stranger in the colony, without money, without clothes, without friends, and without a home. In this situation I travelled the country, seeking employment; and I have walked fifty miles without breaking my fast. I returned to Hobart Town, more strongly confirmed in my opinion that I had come to the wrong end of the world. After a week or two I got employment; and as soon as possible I advertised for a situation, and found a master, in whose service I remained until I left the country. This gentleman gave me the privilege of reading his newspapers in regular succession. Early in the month of September, he brought me the *London Dispatch*, dated, I believe, April the 2nd. It contained a speech of Sir W. Molesworth, in reference to Orange Lodges, the conduct of the Duke of Cumberland, Lord Kenyon, and the Bishop of Salisbury. It stated, that shortly after the above speech was delivered, Lord J. Russell gave notice, "that orders were forwarded that the Dorchester Unionists were not only to be set at liberty, but also to be sent back to England, free of expense, and with every necessary comfort." I instantly copied the paragraph. September the 16th, the Hobart Town *Tasmanian* mentioned the above statement, as from the London newspapers, the editor remarking at the time (for it was when the whole colony, with a few exceptions, was raising the cry against Governor Arthur's mal-administration, and the editor of the *Tasmanian* was one of those exceptions), in vindication of Governor Arthur's humane conduct, "He had no doubt, the gentlemanly spirit and humanity of Colonel Arthur had sent the whole of the men back before that time." And, as a proof that Governor Arthur was a man of the above description, he observed, "*that orders were sent from the home government to work the Dorchester Unionists in irons on the roads!* but that order had not been put into execution by the governor, thereby relieving the Secretary of State the trouble of retracting from what he had declared in the House of Commons, that the men had not been subjected to any extraordinary punishment."

I waited three weeks, and supposing that sufficient time had elapsed, I resolved to address the governor to inquire if he knew any thing about it. But, fearing that a private letter might be lost, I addressed the following to R. L. Murray, Esq., editor of the *Tasmanian*:

Sir, Of late frequent mention has been made in the *Tasmanian* of the men known as the Dorchester Unionists, and of the home government in reference to them. Last week you mentioned the subject again, and observed, "no doubt that Colonel Arthur has sent the whole of the men home before this time." I do not know whether Governor Arthur has received orders from home; I should like to know. If his Excellency has received intelligence to that effect, I hope he will have the goodness to communicate that knowledge to me before he leaves these shores. I hereby offer you my sincere thanks for the sympathy you manifest towards the fate of some half-dozen humble individuals, who, in 1834, were transported to these colonies for unwillingly and ignorantly giving offence. Few can imagine—experience alone teach—what it is to be bereaved of, and torn from, those who are dear to us; and who are still dearer to me than could possibly be all the treasures of the world—wife and children. A Dorchester Unionist.

Shortly after the above was published in the *Tasmanian* my master received a letter from the governor, to inquire if George Loveless was living with him, and if so, to tell him that the governor wished to see him at Hobart Town. My master told me that the governor wished to know if I was living with him, but did not tell me that my presence was wanted at Hobart Town. So I replied, by assuring the governor that I was living in the service of Major de Gillern, at Glenayr, near Richmond. I received the following in answer.

October the 6th, 1836, Principal Superintendant's Office. With reference to the letter from me to Major de Gillern, a few days since, requesting you would call upon me at this office, I have now to inform you that the reason of his Excellency wishing to see you, is in consequence of the Secretary of State, when he sent the order for your free pardon, having authorized his Excellency to give you a free passage to England, and he therefore wishes to be informed whether you are willing to go back; in that case his Excellency will give you a passage by the Elphinstone. Return me an answer by the bearer. Josiah Spode.

I wrote the following answer.

I highly appreciate the kind offer of his Excellency the governor, in giving me a passage to England by the Elphinstone. I would most gladly embark, as I have a strong wish to go back; but consider that I have placed myself in a very awkward situation. His Excellency knows that I have been persuaded to send for my wife, and for aught I know she now may be on the water, it being nine months since the invitation left this colony. It would be a dreadful thing for me to leave before I have heard from my wife, to know if she intends coming or not—for her to find, when she arrives at Hobart Town, I had gone to London. I hope I may be allowed to remain until I hear from her, and if she is not coming, to claim a free passage to England.

In answer to the above I received the following:—

George Loveless, in answer to your note, wishing to know if you could be allowed a passage to England in a few months, I have to inform you, that unless you go by the present opportunity, the government will not be able to give you a free passage. Josiah Spode, the 8th of October, 1836.

About eight or ten days after I went to Hobart Town, and called at the Colonial Secretary's Office, to speak with him on the subject, when the following conversation passed.

"I have called, Sir, to know if I can be allowed to stop in the colony until I shall receive a communication from my wife."

"You have been told what can be done; you was sent for to see the governor some time ago, but you seem to pay no attention to the authorities; nothing more can be done for you."

"I think, Sir, mine is a hard case; I was urged by the governor to send for my wife and family, and I know not but they are coming, and yet I must be forced to leave before sufficient time has been allowed me to ascertain whether they will come or not."

"Well, why did not you obey the governor when he sent for you; it appears you altogether treat the authorities with disrespect."

"I have no wish to disobey those in authority, but the reason I did not proceed to Hobart Town, in compliance with the first request, I was not told that I was wanted, my master only told me the governor wanted to know if I was living in his service; and lately I could not come in consequence of my master's illness, he having been for sometime at Hobart Town, under the doctor's care."

"Well, but the governor has an order to send you back by the first ship."

"I think, Sir, *you have had a free pardon for me in your office, some considerable time longer before I knew any thing about it, than I have delayed in coming since I have known it.*"

"Yes, my good fellow, but the reason of that was *we did not know where to send to you.*"

"I beg your pardon, Sir, that could not be the reason, *as the place I called my home was registered in the police office, by order of the governor.*"

"The order is you are to be sent home immediately."

"You say, Sir, the king's pardon for me is in your office, and yet I am to be sent home as a prisoner. I was sent out a prisoner, contrary to my wishes, and with a free pardon I am to be sent back a prisoner, contrary to my wishes. I hope Mr. Montague will place himself in my situation a few minutes; I know he is a husband and a father."

"Well, Loveless, what do you want?"

"I want a promise from the governor, that I shall be indulged with the privilege of stopping a few months until I shall receive a letter from my wife, and if she is not coming to Van Dieman's Land, to have something to show that I may claim a free passage to England."

"I will draw up a memorandum myself, and see what can be done for you, and you shall know the result in a few days."

The following letter was afterwards sent to me:

Principle Superintendant's Office, 24th October, 1836. Memorandum with reference to a former notification addressed to you from this office, relative to a free pardon having been ordered for you from England, I am now to inform you that his Excellency, the lieutenant-governor, is pleased to approve of that indulgence being issued to you immediately; and I am further to acquaint you, in consequence of your having expressed your disinclination to embark for England, by the Elphinstone, from having written some months ago to your wife, to join you with your three children in this colony, and that you are therefore anxious to await the result of that communication, that, in the event of your expectation not being fulfilled, as it regards the arrival of your family, and which an interval of three or four months may determine; his Excellency has been pleased to direct that a free passage is to be then offered you by the government that you may return to England.—Josiah Spode.

December 23rd, I received a letter from my wife, sent through the Secretary of State's Office, assuring me she did not intend coming to Van Dieman's Land, and wishing me to return as soon as possible. I instantly wrote the following to the Colonial Secretary:—

Honourable J. Montague, this will inform you that George Loveless, (848, per William Metcalfe) has received a letter from his wife, through the Home Office, refusing the offer to join him in this colony, and as through your kind interference a promise was made him by the government, of granting him a free passage to England, on receiving information that his wife was not coming, he therefore earnestly entreats and humbly demands of his Majesty's government in this colony, to provide for him a free passage to England; relying on your goodness, he offers you his warmest gratitude and acknowledgment, and subscribes himself your humble and obliged servant, George Loveless.

On the 20th of January, 1837, I resolved to go to Hobart Town, as I had received no answer, and when I got to the police office I was informed that a letter had that morning been sent to me at Major de Gillern's. I give it as follows:—

In reference to your request, that a passage may be provided for you to England, agreeably to the promise made you by the government, I am to inform you, that you can be allowed one by the ship Eveline, Captain Jameison, in the forecastle, with steerage passenger's allowance, provided you are satisfied with the accommodation; as this vessel will sail in the course of the month, you had better proceed to Hobart Town immediately, and satisfy yourself respecting it, and inform me of your decision.—Josiah Spode.

I instantly went on board and agreed with the captain, who told me that the ship would sail on Sunday, January the 29th. I returned and told the superintendant, Mr. Spode, that I had seen the captain, and was satisfied with the promised accommodations, and the same night returned to my master's. Saturday, the 28th, I proceeded to Hobart Town, and went on board the ship, and Monday, the 30th, at nine o'clock at night, we drew anchor and embarked for London, where I arrived June 13, 1837. . . .